Bond's Franchise Guide

2001 Edition

13ᵗʰ Annual Edition

Robert E. Bond, Publisher

Nicole Thompson, Editor

Source Book Publications
Serving the Franchising Industry
P.O. Box 12488, Oakland, CA 94604
510.839.5471

ISBN 1-887137-27-0

DISCLAIMER

BOND'S FRANCHISE GUIDE is based on data submitted by the franchisors themselves. Every effort has been made to obtain up-to-date, reliable information. As the information returned has not been independently verified, we assume no responsibility for errors or omissions and reserve the right to include or eliminate listings and otherwise edit and present the data based on our discretion and judgment as to what is useful to the readers of this directory. Inclusion in the publication does not imply endorsement by the editors or the publisher. Errors brought to the attention of the publisher and verified to the satisfaction of the publisher will be corrected in future editions. The publisher specifically disclaims all warranties, including the implied warranties of merchantability and fitness for a specific purpose.

BOND'S FRANCHISE GUIDE was previously published as *The Source Book of Franchise Opportunities*. *The Source Book of Franchise Opportunities* went through 7 Editions before the name was changed in 1995 to *Bond's Franchise Guide*.

This publication is designed to provide its readers with accurate and authoritative information with regard to the subject matter covered. It is sold with the understanding that neither the author nor the publisher is engaged in rendering legal, accounting or other professional services. If legal advice or other expert assistance is required, the services of a competent professional person should be sought.

From a Declaration of Principles jointly adopted by a Committee of the American Bar Association and a Committee of Publishers.

Cover Design by Joyce Coffland, Artistic Concepts, Oakland, CA.

ISBN 1-887137-27-0

Printed in the United States of America.
10 9 8 7 6 5 4 3 2 1

BOND'S FRANCHISE GUIDE is available at special discounts for bulk purchase. Special editions or book excerpts can also be created to specifications. For details, contact **Source Book Publications**, P.O. Box 12488, Oakland, CA 94604. Phone: (510) 839-5471; FAX: (510) 839-2104.

Preface

At its best, purchasing a franchise is a time-tested, paint-by-the-numbers method of starting a new business. It avoids many of the myriad pitfalls normally encountered by someone starting anew and vastly improves the odds of success. It represents an exceptional blend of operating independence with a proven system that includes a detailed blueprint on starting and managing the business, as well as the all-important on-going support.

But purchasing a franchise is clearly not a fool-proof investment that somehow guarantees the investor financial independence.

At its worst, if the evaluation and investment decision is sloppy or haphazard, franchising can be a nightmare. You can lose your original investment plus any assets used to personally secure your debt, not to mention your marriage and your self-confidence.

Your ultimate success as a franchisee will be determined by two factors:

1. The homework you do at the front-end to ensure that you are selecting the optimal franchise for your particular needs, experience and financial resources.

2. Your commitment to work hard and play by the rules once you have signed a binding, long-term franchise agreement. A franchise system is only as good as you make it. In most cases, this involves working 60+ hours per week until you can justify delegating some of the day-to-day responsibilities. It also requires being a team player within the system — not acting as an entrepreneur who does his or her own thing without regard for the system as a whole.

The motivation for writing this annual directory has always been to assist in the evaluation phase of the equation: to provide accurate, in-depth data on the many legitimate companies actively selling franchises. The book is written for the sophisticated businessperson seriously interested in the process of selecting an optimal franchise opportunity: someone willing to commit the time and resources necessary to find the best franchise for his or her particular needs; someone with the wisdom to know that the franchise selection process is exceedingly difficult and filled with potholes; someone keenly aware of the risks — including missed opportunities — of going through the process in a half-hearted way.

We hope we can facilitate the evaluation process by ensuring that the potential franchisee is exposed to the full range of options open to him or her and that he or she goes about the selection process in a logical and systematic manner.

☙

Over 2,150 franchising opportunities are listed on the following pages. An in-depth profile is available on over 1,000 of these. This franchisor profile is the result of the detailed three-page questionnaire noted in Appendix A. The names, addresses, telephone and fax numbers, contact and industry categories are provided on over 1,150 additional active North American franchisors.

No doubt you will be familiar with a large number of the listings. Many are household names. That, incidentally, is one of the primary benefits of franchising. Most people would agree that AAMCO Transmissions has a better ring to it than Bill's Transmission Shop. Apart from the proven systems and procedures, you are buying a recognized name and the reputation that the name enjoys in the marketplace.

☙

After you have decided which of the 45 industry groups hold the most interest, contact **all** of the companies listed and request a marketing brochure. Thoroughly read their literature and pick out the companies that interest you and that represent a natural fit with your talents and financial resources. You should be able to narrow your choices down to a manageable list of six or eight franchises that fit these criteria. Initiate an in-depth analysis of and dialogue with each of these franchisors. Concurrently, develop a thorough knowledge of the business and/or services that you are considering. Seek the advice of professionals, even if you are experienced in various elements of the evaluation process. Don't leave any stone unturned.

☙

Remember, this is not a game! You are quite literally betting the ranch on your ability to pick a well-managed, market-oriented franchise. You want one that will take advantage of your unique talents and experience and not take advantage of you in the process! Don't take short-cuts. Listen to what the franchisor and your advisors tell you. Don't think you are so clever or independent that you can't benefit from the advice of outside professionals. Don't assume that the franchisor's guidelines regarding the amount of investment, experience, temperament, etc., somehow don't apply to you. Don't accept any promises or "understandings" from the franchisor that are not committed in writing to the franchise agreement. Spend the extra money to talk to and/or meet with other franchisees in the system. The additional front-end investment you make, both in time and money, will pay off handsomely if it saves you from making a marginal, or poor, investment decision. This is one of the few times in business when second chances are rare. Make the extra effort to do it right the first time.

☙

Good luck and Godspeed.

Table of Contents

Table of Contents

Section Three — Appendix

Section Four — Index

Definitive Franchisor Database
Available for Rent

SAMPLE FRANCHISOR PROFILE

Name of Franchise:	AARON'S SALES & LEASE OWNERSHIP
Address:	309 East Paces Ferry Rd., N. E.
City/State/Zip/Postal Code:	Atlanta, GA 30305-2377
Country:	U. S. A.
800 Telephone #:	(800) 551-6015
Local Telephone #:	(404) 237-4016
Alternate Telephone #:	
Fax #:	(404) 240-6540
E-Mail:	jim.steger@aaronsfranchise.com
Internet Address:	www.aaronsfranchise.com
# Franchised Units:	186
# Company-Owned Units:	238
# Total Units:	424
Company Contact:	Mr. Jim Steger
Contact Title/Position:	Director of Franchise Development
Contact Salutation:	Mr. Steger
President:	Mr. R. Charles Loudermilk, Sr.
President Title:	Chairman/Chief Executive Officer
President Salutation:	Mr. Loudermilk
Industry Category (of 45):	37 / Rental Services
IFA Member:	International Franchise Association
CFA Member:	

KEY FEATURES

- Number of Active North American Franchisors   ~ 2,300
  - % US   ~85%
  - % Canadian   ~15%
- Data Fields (See Above)   24
- Industry Categories   45
- % With Toll-Free Telephone Numbers   67%
- % With Fax Numbers   97%
- % With Name of Preferred Contact   99%
- % With Name of President   97%
- % With Number of Total Operating Units   95%
- Guaranteed Accuracy — $.50 Rebate/Returned Bad Address
- Converted to Any Popular Database or Contact Management Program
- Initial Front-End Cost $600
- Quarterly Up-Dates $75
- Mailing Labels Only — One-Time Use $400

For More Information, Please Contact
Source Book Publications
1814 Franklin Street, Suite 820, Oakland, California 94612
(800) 841-0873 ❖ (510) 839-5471 ❖ FAX (510) 839-2104

In presenting this data, we have made some unilateral assumptions about our readers. The first is that you purchased the book because of the depth and accuracy of the data provided — not as a how-to manual. Chapter 3, Recommended Reading, lists several resources for anyone requiring additional background information on the franchising industry and on the process of evaluating a company. Clearly, dedication to hard work, adequate financing, commitment, good business sense and access to trusted professional counsel will determine your ultimate success as a franchisee. A strong working knowledge of the industry, however, will help ensure that you have made the best choice of franchise opportunities. I advise you to acquaint yourself with the dynamics of the industry before you initiate the evaluation and negotiation phases of selecting a franchise.

The second assumption is that you have already devoted the time necessary to conduct a detailed personal inventory. This self-assessment should result in a clear understanding of your skills, aptitudes, weaknesses, long-term personal goals,

commitment to succeed and financial capabilities. Most of the books in the Recommended Reading Chapter provide worksheets to accomplish this important step.

෫

There are three primary stages to the franchise selection process: 1) the investigation stage, 2) the evaluation stage and 3) and the negotiation stage. This book is intended primarily to assist the reader in the investigation stage by providing a thorough list of the options available. Chapters 1 and 2 include various observations based on my 15 or so years of involvement with the franchising industry. Hopefully, they will provide some insights that you will find of value.

Understand at the outset that the entire process will take many months and involve a great deal of frustration. I suggest that you set up a realistic timeline for signing a franchise agreement and that you stick with that schedule. There will be a lot of pressure on you to prematurely complete the selection and negotiation phases. Resist the temptation. The penalties are too severe for a seat-of-the-pants attitude. A decision of this magnitude clearly deserves your full attention. Do your homework!

Before starting the selection process, you would be well advised to briefly review the areas that follow.

Franchise Industry Structure

The franchising industry is made up of two distinct types of franchises. The first, and by far the larger, encompasses product and trade name franchising. Automotive and truck dealers, soft drink bottlers and gasoline service stations are included in this group. For the most part, these are essentially distributorships.

The second group encompasses business format franchisors. This book only includes information on this latter category.

Layman's Definition of Franchising

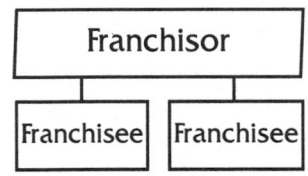

Classic Business Format Model

Business format franchising is a method of market expansion by which one business entity expands the distribution of its products and/or services through independent, third-party operators. Franchising occurs when the operator of a concept or system (the **franchisor**) grants an independent businessperson (the **franchisee**) the right to duplicate its entire business format at a particular location and for a specified period, under terms and conditions set forth in the contract (**franchise agreement**). The franchisee has full access to all of the trademarks, logos, marketing techniques, controls and systems that have made the

franchisor successful. In effect, the franchisee acts as a surrogate for a company-owned store in the distribution of the franchisor's goods and/or services. It is important to keep in mind that the franchisor and the franchisee are separate legal entities.

In return for a front-end **franchise fee** — which usually ranges from $15,000–35,000 — the franchisor is obligated to "set up" the franchisee in business. This generally includes assistance in selecting a location, negotiating a lease, obtaining financing, building and equipping a site and providing the necessary training, operating manuals, etc. Once the training is completed and the store is open, the new franchisee should have a carbon copy of other units in the system and enjoy the same benefits they do, whether they are company-owned or not.

Business format franchising is unique because it is a long-term relationship characterized by an on-going, mutually beneficial partnership. On-going services include research and development, marketing strategies, advertising campaigns, group buying, periodic field visits, training updates, and whatever else is required to make the franchisee competitive and profitable. In effect, the franchisor acts as the franchisee's "back office" support organization. To reimburse the franchisor for this support, the franchisee pays the franchisor an on-going **royalty fee**, generally four to eight percent of gross sales or income. In many cases, franchisees also contribute an **advertising fee** to reimburse the franchisor for expenses incurred in maintaining a national or regional advertising campaign.

For the maximum advantage, both the franchisor and the franchisees should share common objectives and goals. Both parties must accept the premise that their fortunes are mutually intertwined and that they are each better off working in a co-operative effort, rather than toward any self-serving goals. Unlike the parent/child relationship that has dominated franchising over the past 30 years, franchising is now becoming a true and productive relationship of partners.

Legal Definition of Franchising

The Federal Trade Commission (FTC) has its own definition of franchising. So do each of the 16 states that have separate franchise registration statutes. The State of California's definition, which is the model for the FTC's definition, follows:

Franchise means a contract or agreement, express or implied, whether oral or written, between two or more persons by which:

> *A franchisee is granted the right to engage in the business of offering, selling or distributing goods or services under a marketing plan or system prescribed in substantial part by a franchisor;*

> *The operation of the franchisee's business pursuant to that plan or system as substantially associated with the franchisor's trademark, service mark, trade name, logotype, advertising or other commercial symbol designating the franchisor or its affiliates; and*

> *The franchisee is required to pay, directly or indirectly, a franchise fee.*

Multi-Level Franchising

With franchisors continually exploring new ways to expand their distribution, the classic business format model shown above has evolved over the years. Modifications have allowed franchisors to grow more rapidly and at less cost than might have otherwise been possible.

If a franchisor wishes to expand at a faster rate than its financial resources or staff levels allow, it might choose to sell development rights in an area (state, national or international) and let the new entity do the development work. No matter which development method is chosen, the fran-

chisee should still receive the same benefits and support provided under the standard model. The major difference is the entity providing the training and on-going support and receiving the franchise and royalty fees changes.

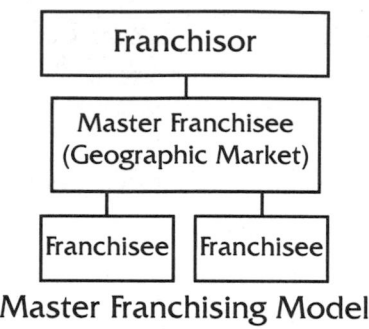

Master Franchising Model

Three variations of the master franchising model include: 1) master (or regional) franchising, 2) sub-franchising and 3) area development franchising.

In **master (or regional) franchising**, the franchisor sells the development rights in a particular market to a master franchisee who, in turn, sells individual franchises within the territory. In return for a front-end master franchise fee, the master franchisee has sole responsibility for developing that area under a mutually agreed upon schedule. This includes attracting, screening, signing and training all new franchisees within the territory. Once established, on-going support is generally provided by the parent franchisor.

The master franchisee is rewarded by sharing in the franchise fees and the on-going royalties paid to the parent franchisor by the franchisees within the territory.

Sub-franchising is similar to master franchising in that the franchisor grants development rights in a specified territory to a sub-franchisor. After the agreement is signed, however, the parent franchisor has no on-going involvement with the individual franchisees in the territory. Instead, the sub-franchisor becomes the focal point. All fees and royalties are paid directly to the sub-franchisor. It is solely responsible for all recruiting, training and on-going support, and passes on an agreed upon percentage of all incoming fees and royalties to the parent franchisor.

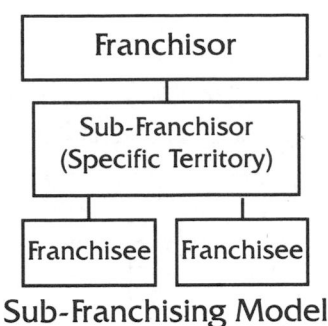

Sub-Franchising Model

In a sub-franchising relationship, the potential franchisee has to be doubly careful in his or her investigation. He or she must first make sure that the sub-franchisor has the necessary financial, managerial and marketing skills to make the program work. Secondarily, the potential franchisee has to feel comfortable that the parent franchisor can be relied upon to come to his or her rescue if the sub-franchisor should fail.

The third variation is an **area development agreement**. Here again, the franchisor grants exclusive development rights for a particular geographic area to an area development investment group. Within its territory, the area developer may either develop individual franchise units for its own account or find independent franchisees to develop units. In the latter case, the area developer has a residual equity position in the profits of its "area franchisees."

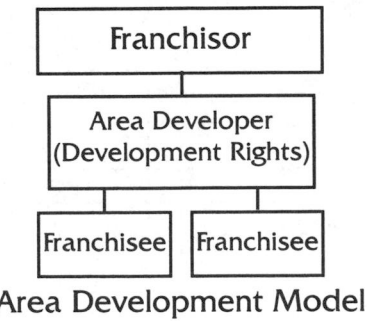

Area Development Model

In return for the rights to an exclusive territory, the area developer pays the franchisor a front-end development fee and commits to develop a certain number of units within a specified time period. (The front-end fee is generally significantly less than the sum of the individual unit fees.) Individual franchisees within the territory pay all contractual franchise, royalty and advertising fees directly to the parent franchisor. The area developer shares in neither the franchise fee nor in on-going royalty or advertising fees. Instead, the area developer shares only in the profitability of the individual franchises that it "owns." In essence, the area developer is buying multiple locations over time at a discount, since the franchise fee and (frequently) the royalty fee are less than the per unit rate.

Franchise Industry Statistics

The International Franchise Association (IFA) estimated that product and trade name franchising accounted for $554 billion in sales in 1992. This represents roughly 28% of all retail sales.

Business format franchising produced total sales of $249 billion in 1992, roughly 13% of all retail sales. In layman's language, this means that for every $1.00 spent at the retail level, more than $0.13 went to franchised establishments. There is no question that franchising has had a profound impact on the way business is conducted in the U.S. Most analysts anticipate that the overall numbers and market share of retail business will continue to grow well into the foreseeable future and at a faster rate than the economy in general.

Exhibits 1–5, noted on the following pages, and the other charts at the beginning of each chapter, are the result of querying our proprietary franchisor database (which has some 30 fields of information on 2,500 franchisors) and the database of some 1,050 detailed questionnaires that were returned as a result of our 2001 industry survey. You should spend some time reviewing the various Exhibits to get a better idea of the relative

BOND'S FRANCHISE GUIDE
ANNUAL FRANCHISING INDUSTRY OVERVIEW
(As of 1/1/2001)

Exhibit 1

CATEGORY	# of Fran-chisors	Fran-chised Units	Company-Owned Units	Total Operating Units	See Chapter
Automotive Products & Services	151	22,264	2,257	24,521	4
Auto / Truck / Trailer Rental	25	7,558	1,027	8,585	5
Building & Remodeling/Furniture/Appliance Repair	96	6,808	171	6,979	6
Business: Financial Services	34	11,182	5,952	17,134	7
Business: Advertising & Promotion	27	2,166	50	2,216	8
Business: Internet/Telecommunications/Misc.	63	5,273	953	6,226	9
Child Development / Education / Products	59	4,712	212	4,924	10
Education / Personal Development / Training	49	27,846	716	28,562	11
Employment & Personnel	67	4,576	2,276	6,852	12
Food: Donuts / Cookies / Bagels	70	12,090	1,566	13,656	13
Food: Coffee	27	1,560	179	1,739	14
Food: Ice Cream / Yogurt	43	16,543	1,168	17,711	15
Food: Quick Service / Take-out	329	103,278	24,836	128,114	16
Food: Restaurant / Family-Style	163	16,571	11,154	27,725	17
Food: Specialty Foods	92	7,100	915	8,015	18
Hairstyling Salons	29	5,700	876	6,576	19
Health / Fitness / Beauty	53	9,413	1,701	11,114	20
Laundry & Dry Cleaning	21	1,978	937	2,915	21
Lawn and Garden	20	1,185	150	1,335	22
Lodging	69	23,700	2,825	26,525	23
Maid Service & Home Cleaning	26	3,697	132	3,829	24
Maintenance / Cleaning / Sanitation	118	34,605	567	35,172	25
Medical / Optical / Dental Products & Services	21	2,248	354	2,602	26
Packaging & Mailing	18	8,560	26	8,586	27
Printing & Graphics	26	4,841	55	4,896	28
Publications	23	927	32	959	29
Real Estate Inspection Services	23	2,058	386	2,444	30
Real Estate Services	50	21,854	206	22,060	31
Recreation & Entertainment	36	2,247	132	2,379	32
Rental Services	11	2,478	378	2,856	33
Retail: Art, Art Supplies & Framing	11	737	34	771	34
Retail: Athletic Wear / Sporting Goods	21	2,157	443	2,600	35
Retail: Clothing / Shoes / Accessories	10	122	389	511	36
Retail: Convenience Stores / Supermarkets / Drugs	31	31,257	6,094	37,351	37
Retail: Home Furnishings	44	2,612	150	2,762	38
Retail: Home Improvement & Hardware	14	10,449	412	10,861	39
Retail: Pet Products & Services	18	1,023	153	1,176	40

CATEGORY	# of Fran- chisors	Fran- chised Units	Company- Owned Units	Total Operating Units	See Chapter
Retail: Photographic Products & Services	15	911	84	995	41
Retail: Specialty	116	6,698	3,716	10,414	42
Retail: Video / Audio / Electronics	19	4,940	11,034	15,974	43
Retail: Miscellaneous	16	1,538	133	1,671	44
Security & Safety Systems	17	859	101	960	45
Signs	16	1,820	7	1,827	46
Travel	20	4,823	575	5,398	47
Miscellaneous	87	4,953	565	5,518	48
Industry Total	**2,294**	**449,917**	**86,079**	**535,996**	
% of Total		**83.9%**	**16.1%**	**100.0%**	

Exhibit 2

Relative Size - By Number of Total Operating Units:	#	%	Cum. %
> 5,000 Total Operating Units	15	0.7%	0.7%
1,000 - 4,999 Total Operating Units	57	2.5%	3.1%
500 - 999 Total Operating Units	73	3.2%	6.3%
250 - 499 Total Operating Units	132	5.8%	12.1%
100 - 249 Total Operating Units	281	12.2%	24.3%
50 - 99 Total Operating Units	299	13.0%	37.4%
25 - 49 Total Operating Units	308	13.4%	50.8%
15 - 24 Total Operating Units	222	9.7%	60.5%
Less Than 15 Total Operating Units	907	39.5%	100.0%
Total	**2,294**	**100.0%**	

Exhibit 3

Country of Origin:	#	%
United States	1,954	85.2%
Canada	340	14.8%
Total	**2,294**	**100.0%**

All of the data in Exhibits 1 - 3 are proprietary and should not be used or quoted without specifically acknowledging Bond's Franchise Guide as the source.

BOND'S FRANCHISE GUIDE
ANNUAL FRANCHISING INDUSTRY OVERVIEW
(As of 1/1/2001)

Exhibit 4

CATEGORY	Average Franchise Fee	Average Total Investment	Average Royalty Fee	# Survey Partici-pants	% of Industry Represent.
Automotive Products & Services	$22.7K	$207.5K	5.7%	74	49.0%
Auto / Truck / Trailer Rental	36.2K	249.7K	5.8%	13	52.0%
Building & Remodeling/Furniture/Appliance Repair	22.3K	132.1K	5.5%	37	38.5%
Business: Financial Services	21.8K	75.3K	7.3%	12	35.3%
Business: Advertising & Promotion	20.0K	37.0K	5.7%	11	40.7%
Business: Internet/Telecommunications/Misc.	21.9K	70.0K	6.2%	21	33.3%
Child Development / Education / Products	21.6K	146.0K	6.6%	30	50.8%
Education / Personal Development / Training	28.8K	110.5K	7.9%	24	49.0%
Employment & Personnel	23.6K	106.0K	9.1%	33	49.3%
Food: Donuts / Cookies / Bagels	26.1K	279.6K	5.2%	35	50.0%
Food: Coffee	21.7K	202.3K	5.9%	12	44.4%
Food: Ice Cream / Yogurt	21.7K	200.8K	5.4%	22	51.2%
Food: Quick Service / Take-out	20.2K	335.4K	4.9%	140	42.6%
Food: Restaurant / Family-Style	35.5K	888.8K	4.4%	70	42.9%
Food: Specialty Foods	23.4K	236.9K	5.3%	38	41.3%
Hairstyling Salons	17.8K	105.0K	5.6%	11	37.9%
Health / Fitness / Beauty	18.5K	155.7K	6.6%	23	43.4%
Laundry & Dry Cleaning	19.6K	152.3K	6.8%	10	47.6%
Lawn and Garden	23.8K	65.6K	7.5%	12	60.0%
Lodging	37.3K	8,226.6K	4.3%	24	34.8%
Maid Service & Home Cleaning	14.4K	49.3K	5.4%	16	61.5%
Maintenance / Cleaning / Sanitation	17.2K	60.9K	7.8%	66	55.9%
Medical / Optical / Dental A52Products & Services	28.9K	189.0K	5.0%	7	33.3%
Packaging & Mailing	26.0K	95.9K	6.2%	11	61.1%
Printing & Graphics	25.4K	254.1K	5.6%	16	61.5%
Publications	13.1K	28.8K	7.0%	7	30.4%
Real Estate Inspection Services	20.1K	34.3K	7.5%	10	43.5%
Real Estate Services	14.4K	69.3K	5.9%	23	46.0%
Recreation & Entertainment	17.3K	366.7K	8.5%	12	33.3%
Rental Services	16.7K	199.6K	5.0%	8	72.7%
Retail: Art, Art Supplies & Framing	26.7K	142.0K	5.8%	6	54.5%
Retail: Athletic Wear / Sporting Goods	27.7K	277.4K	4.2%	14	66.7%
Retail: Clothing / Shoes / Accessories	20.0K	46.2K	6.0%	3	30.0%
Retail: Convenience Stores / Supermarkets / Drugs	17.7K	731.9K	4.4%	11	35.5%
Retail: Home Furnishings	18.6K	123.2K	4.1%	15	34.1%
Retail: Home Improvement & Hardware	30.6K	157.3K	6.0%	5	35.7%
Retail: Pet Products & Services	17.4K	90.4K	6.2%	9	50.0%

CATEGORY	Average Franchise Fee	Average Total Investment	Average Royalty Fee	# Survey Partici-pants	% of Industry Represent.
Retail: Photographic Products & Services	$21.4K	$153.3K	6.0%	4	26.7%
Retail: Specialty	23.3K	176.4K	5.5%	49	42.2%
Retail: Video / Audio / Electronics	21.3K	120.8K	4.7%	6	31.6%
Retail: Miscellaneous	28.3K	153.8K	4.4%	8	50.0%
Security & Safety Systems	20.7K	154.9K	5.9%	6	35.3%
Signs	20.1K	111.5K	5.3%	8	50.0%
Travel	13.7K	45.5K	2.5%	5	25.0%
Miscellaneous	38.3K	206.0K	8.2%	24	27.6%
Overall Industry Average	$23.4K	$433.2K	5.0%	1,001	100.0%

Exhibit 5

CATEGORY	Average Franchise Fee	Average Total Investment	Average Royalty Fee	# Survey Partici-pants	% of Industry Represent.
Categories with Lowest Franchise Fee:					
Publications	$13.1K	$28.8K	7.0%	7	30.4%
Travel	13.7K	45.5K	2.5%	5	25.0%
Maid Service & Home Cleaning	14.4K	49.3K	5.4%	16	61.5%
Categories with Lowest Total Investment:					
Publications	$13.1K	$28.8K	7.0%	7	30.4%
Real Estate Inspection Services	20.1K	34.3K	7.5%	10	43.5%
Business: Advertising & Promotion	20.0K	37.0K	5.7%	11	40.7%
Categories with Lowest Royalty Fee:					
Travel	$13.7K	$45.5K	2.5%	5	25.0%
Retail: Home Furnishings	18.6K	123.2K	4.1%	15	34.1%
Retail: Athletic Wear / Sporting Goods	27.7K	277.4K	4.2%	14	66.7%

All of the data in Exhibits 4 - 5 are proprietary and should not be used or quoted without specifically acknowledging Bond's Franchise Guide as the source.

size, fees and investment levels required in various industry categories. The industry specific statistics in each chapter provide an excellent overview of the various firms in that category. If the size of the franchise fee, total investment or royalty fee fall far outside the averages noted, the franchisor should have a ready explanation as to why.

The Players

Franchisors

Roughly 2,150 U.S. and Canadian franchisors are shown on the following pages.

In past publications, we have always included the names, addresses and contacts of all active franchisors. We felt there was value in touting the coverage of as many franchisors as possible. In retrospect, we did our readers a disservice. We have subsequently changed our listing criteria. We now include supplemental franchisors only under the following circumstances: 1) a company representative was reached directly by phone, 2) they gave us at least some cursory information about the franchise and 3) they confirmed they were still actively franchising. Firms that answered our call with an answering machine, used an uninformed answering service or had children screaming in the background are not listed in the 2001 Edition's Supplemental Listing of Franchisors. Similarly, we excluded those franchisors who had no operating units or had no active franchised units. Some 300 companies listed in our database fall into one of these categories.

By unilaterally restricting the franchising universe, we are effectively acting as a screen. The objective is to save the prospective franchisee the unnecessary time and aggravation associated with trying to get in touch with a franchisor that isn't substantial enough to answer its phones professionally. After you become a franchisee, occasions will undoubtedly arise in which you will have a major problem that has to be resolved immediately. That is clearly not the time to be con-

nected to an answering machine or an uninformed answering service. You want a substantial organization behind you — not a one- or two-man shop that may have priorities other than supporting its franchisees.

The Regulatory Agencies

The offer and sale of franchises are regulated at both the federal and state levels. Federal requirements cover all 50 states. In addition, certain states have adopted their own requirements.

In 1979, after many years of debate, the Federal Trade Commission (FTC) implemented Rule 436. This Rule requires that franchisors provide prospective franchisees with a disclosure statement (called an offering circular) containing specific information about a company's franchise offering. The Rule has two objectives: to ensure that the potential franchisee has sufficient background information to make an educated investment decision and to provide him or her with adequate time to do so.

Certain "registration states" require additional safeguards to protect potential franchisees. Their requirements are generally more stringent than the FTC's requirements. These states include California, Florida, Hawaii, Illinois, Indiana, Maryland, Michigan, Minnesota, New York, North Dakota, Oregon, Rhode Island, South Dakota, Virginia, Washington and Wisconsin. Separate registration is also required in the province of Alberta, Canada.

For the most part, registration states require a disclosure format know as the Uniform Franchise Offering Circular (UFOC). As a matter of convenience and because the state requirements are more demanding, most franchisors have adopted the UFOC format. This format requires that the franchisor provides a prospective franchisee with the required information at their first face-to-face meeting or at least 10 business days prior to the signing of the franchise agreement, whichever is earlier. Required information includes:

1. The Franchisor and Any Predecessors.
2. Identity and Business Experience of Persons Affiliated with the Franchisor.
3. Litigation.
4. Bankruptcy.
5. Franchisee's Initial Fee/Other Initial Payments.
6. Other Fees.
7. Franchisee's Initial Investment.
8. Obligations of Franchisee to Purchase or Lease from Designated Sources.
9. Obligations of Franchisee to Purchase or Lease in Accordance with Specifications or from Approved Suppliers.
10. Financing Arrangements.
11. Obligations of the Franchisor; Other Supervision, Assistance or Services.
12. Exclusive Area of Territory.
13. Trademarks, Service Marks, Trade Names, Logotypes and Commercial Symbols.
14. Patents and Copyrights.
15. Obligations of the Franchisee to Participate in the Actual Operation of the Franchise Business.
16. Restrictions on Goods and Services Offered by Franchisee.
17. Renewal, Termination, Repurchase, Modification and Assignment of the Franchise Agreement and Related Information.
18. Arrangements with Public Figures.
19. Actual, Average, Projected or Forecasted Franchise Sales, Profits or Earnings.
20. Information Regarding Franchises of the Franchisor.
21. Financial Statements.
22. Contracts.
23. Acknowledgment of Receipt by Respective Franchisee.

If you live in a registration state, make sure that the franchisor you are evaluating is, in fact, registered to sell franchises there. If not, and the franchisor has no near-term plans to register in your state, you should consider other options.

Keep in mind that neither the FTC nor any of the states has reviewed the offering circular to determine whether the information submitted is true or not. They merely require that the franchisor make representations based upon a prescribed format. If the information provided is false, franchisors are subject to civil penalties. That may not help a franchisee, however, who cannot undo a very expensive mistake.

It is up to you to read and thoroughly understand all elements of the offering circular. There is no question that it is tedious reading. Know exactly what you can expect from the franchisor and what your own obligations are. Under what circumstances can the relationship be unilaterally terminated by the franchisor? What is your protected territory? Specifically, what front-end assistance will the franchisor provide? You should have a professional review the UFOC. Shame on you if you don't take full advantage of the documentation that is available to you. The penalties are severe, and you will have no one to blame but yourself.

The Trade Associations

The **International Franchise Association** (IFA) was established as a non-profit trade association to promote franchising as a responsible method of doing business. The IFA currently represents over 650 franchisors in the U.S. and around the world. It is recognized as the leading spokesperson for responsible franchising. For most of its 30+ years, the IFA has represented the interests of franchisors only. In recent years, however, it has initiated an aggressive campaign to recruit franchisees into its membership and represent their interests as well. The IFA's address is 1350 New York Ave., NW, # 900, Washington, DC

20005. (202) 628-8000; FAX (202) 628-0812; www.franchise.org.

The **Canadian Franchise Association** (CFA), which has some 250+ members, is the Canadian equivalent of the IFA. Information on the CFA can be obtained from its offices at 2585 Skymark Ave., # 300, Mississauga, ON L4W 4L5, Canada. (905) 625-2896; FAX (905) 625-9076; www.cfa.ca.

The **American Association of Franchisees & Dealers** (AAFD) represents the rights and interests of franchisees and independent dealers. Formed in 1992 with the mission of "Bringing Fairness to Franchising," the AAFD represents thousands of franchised businesses, representing over 250 different franchise systems. It provides a broad range of services designed to help franchisees build market power, create legislative support, provide legal and financial support and provide a wide range of general member benefits. P.O. Box 81887, San Diego, CA 92138. (800) 733-9858, (619) 209-3775; FAX: (619) 209-3777.

Franchise Survival/Failure Rate

In order to promote the industry's attractiveness, most literature on the subject of franchising includes the same often-quoted, but very misleading, statistics that leave the impression that franchising is a near risk-free investment.

In the 1970s, the Small Business Administration produced a poorly documented report that 38% of all small businesses fail within their first year of operation and 77% fail within their first five years. With franchising, however, comparative failure rates miraculously drop to only three percent after the first year and eight percent after five years. No effort was made to define failure. Instead, "success" was defined as an operating unit still in business under the same name at the same location.

While most people would agree that the failure rates for franchised businesses are substantially lower than the failure rates for independent businesses, that assumption is not substantiated by reliable statistics. Part of the problem is definitional. Part is the fact that the industry has a vested interest in perpetuating the myth rather than debunking it.

FRANDATA, a Washington, DC-based franchise research firm, recently conducted a review of franchise terminations and renewals. It found that 4.4% of all franchisees left their franchise system each year for a variety of reasons. This figure does not include sales to third parties, however. To be fully meaningful, the data should include sales to third parties and the underlying reasons behind a sale.

The critical issue is to properly define failure and success, and then require franchisors to report changes in ownership based on these universally accepted definitions. A logical starting point in defining success should be whether the franchisee can "make an honest living" as a franchisee. A "success" would occur when the franchisee prefers to continue as a franchisee rather than sell the business. A "failure" would occur when the franchisee is forced to sell his or her business at a loss.

A reasonable measure of franchise success would be to ask franchisees "would you do it again?" If a legitimate survey were conducted of all franchisees of all systems, my guess is that the answer to this question would indicate a "success rate" well under 70% after a five-year period. Alternatively, one could ask the question "has the franchise investment met your expectations?" I estimate that fewer than 50% would say "yes" after a five-year period. These are just educated guesses. Like the franchising industry, I have no basis in fact for these estimates.

The failure rate is unquestionably lower for larger, more mature companies in the industry that have proven their systems and carefully chosen their franchisees. It is higher for smaller, newer companies that have unproven products and are less demanding in whom they accept as a franchisee.

As it now stands, the Uniform Franchise Offering Circular (UFOC) only requires the franchisor to provide the potential franchisee with the names of owners who have left the system within the past 12 months. In my opinion, this is a severe shortcoming of the regulatory process. Unless required, franchisors will not willingly provide information about failures to prospective franchisees. There is no question in my mind, however, that franchisors are fully aware of when and why past failures have occurred.

It is patently unfair that a potential investor should not have access to this critical information. To ensure its availability, I propose that the UFOC be amended to require that franchisors provide franchisee turn-over information for the most recent five-year period. Underlying reasons for a change in ownership would be provided by a departing franchisee on a universal, industry-approved questionnaire filled out during an "exit" interview. The questionnaire would then be returned to some central clearing house.

The only way to make up for this lack of information is to aggressively seek out as many previous and current franchisees as possible. Request past UFOCs to get the names of previous owners, and then contact them. Whether successful or not, these owners are an invaluable resource. Try to determine the reason for their failure and/or disenchantment. Most failures are the result of poor management or inadequate finances on the part of the departing franchisee. But people give up franchises for other reasons.

Current franchisees are even better sources of meaningful information. For systems with under 25 units, I strongly encourage you to talk to all franchisees. For those having between 25 and 100 units, I recommend talking to at least half. And for all others, interview a minimum of 50.

What Makes a Winning Franchise

Virtually every writer on the subject of franchising has his or her own idea of what determines a winning franchise. I maintain that there are five primary factors.

1. A product or service with a clear advantage over the competition. The advantage may be in brand recognition, a unique, proprietary product or 30 years of proven experience.

2. A standardized franchise system that has been time-tested. Look for a company in which most of the bugs in the system have been worked out through the cumulative experience of both company-owned and franchised units. By the time a system has 30 or more operating units, it should be thoroughly tested.

3. Exceptional franchisor support. This includes not only the initial training program, but the on-going support (R&D, refresher training, [800] help-lines, field representatives and on-site training, annual meetings, advertising and promotion, central purchasing, etc.).

4. The financial wherewithal and management experience to carry out any announced growth plans without short-changing its franchisees. Sufficient depth of management is often lacking in high-growth franchises.

5. A strong mutuality of interest between franchisor and franchisees. Unless both parties realize that their relationship is one of long-term partners, it is unlikely that the system will ever achieve its full potential. Whether they have the necessary rapport is easily determined by a few telephone calls.

19

Financial Projections

The single most important factor in buying a franchise — or any business for that matter — is having a realistic projection of sales, expenses and profits. Specifically, how much can you expect to make after working 65 hours a week for 52 weeks a year? No one is in a better position to supply accurate information (subject to caveats) about a franchise opportunity than the franchisor itself. A potential franchisee often does not have the experience to sit down and project what his or her sales and profits will be over the next five years. This is especially true if he or she has no applied experience in that particular business.

Earnings claim statements (Item 19 of the UFOC) present franchisor-supplied sales, expense and/or profit summaries based on actual operating results for company-owned and/or franchised units. Since no format is prescribed, however, the data may be cursory or detailed. The only constraint is that the franchisor must be able to substantiate the data presented. Further complicating the process is the fact that providing an earnings claim statement is strictly optional. Accordingly, less than 15% of franchisors provide one.

Virtually everyone agrees that the information included in an earnings claim statement can be exceedingly helpful to a potential franchisee. Unfortunately, there are many reasons why franchisors might not willingly choose to make their actual results available to the public. Many franchisors feel that a prospective investor would be turned off if he or she had access to actual operating results. Others may not want to go to the trouble and expense of collecting the data.

Other franchisors are legitimately afraid of being sued for "misrepresentation." There is considerable risk to a franchisor if a published earnings claim statement is interpreted in any way as a "guarantee" of sales or income for new units. Given today's highly litigious society, and the propensity of courts to award large settlements to the "little guy," it's not surprising that so few franchisors provide the information.

As an assist to prospective franchisees, Source Book Publications has recently published a book entitled *"How Much Can I Make?"* It includes over 143 earnings claim statements covering a diverse group of industries. It is the only publication that contains current earnings claim statements submitted by the franchisors. Given the scarcity of industry projections, this is an invaluable resource for potential franchisees or investors in determining what he or she might make by investing in a franchise or similar business. The book is $29.95, plus $4.00 for shipping. See the inside rear cover of this book for additional detail on the book and the companies that have submitted earnings claim statements. The book can be obtained from Source Book Publications, P.O. Box 12488, Oakland, CA 94604, or by calling (510) 839-5471, or by faxing a request to (510) 839-2104.

New vs. Used

As a potential franchisee, you have the option of becoming a franchisee in a new facility at a new location or purchasing an existing franchise. It is not an easy decision. Your success in making that choice will depend upon your business acumen and your insight into people

Purchasing a new franchise unit will mean that everything is current, clean and under warranty. Purchasing an existing franchise will probably involve a smaller investment and allow greater financial leverage. However, you will have to assess the seller's reason for selling. Is the business not performing to expectations because of poor management, poor location, poor support from the franchisor, an indifferent staff, obsolete equipment and/or facilities, etc.? The decision is further clouded because you may be working through a business broker who may or may not be giving you good information. Regardless of the obstacles, considering a "used" franchise merits your consideration. Apply the same analytical tools you would to a new franchise. Do your homework. Be thorough. Be unrelenting.

The Negotiation Process

Once you have narrowed your options down to your top two or three choices, you must negotiate the best deal you can with the franchisor. In most cases, the franchisor will tell you that the franchise agreement cannot be changed. If you accept this explanation, shame on you. Notwithstanding the legal requirement that all of a franchisor's agreements be **substantially** the same at any point in time, there are usually a number of variables in the equation. If the franchisor truly wants you as a franchisee, it may be willing to make concessions not available to the next applicant. Will the franchisor take a short-term note for all or part of the franchise fee? Can you expand from your initial unit after you have proven yourself? If so, can the franchise fee be eliminated or reduced on a second unit? Can you get a right of first refusal on adjacent territories? Can the term of the agreement be extended from 10 to 15 years? Can you include a franchise cancellation right if the training and/or initial support don't meet your expectations or the franchisor's promises? The list goes on ad infinitum.

To successfully negotiate, you must have a thorough knowledge of the industry, the franchise agreement you are negotiating (and agreements of competitive franchise opportunities) and access to experienced professional advice. This can be a lawyer, an accountant or a franchise consultant. Above all else, they should have proven experience in negotiating franchise agreements. Franchising is a unique method of doing business. Don't pay someone $100+ per hour to learn the industry. Make them demonstrate that they have been through the process several times before. Negotiating a long-term agreement of this type is extremely tricky and fraught with pitfalls. The

risks are extremely high. Don't be so smug as to think that you can handle the negotiations yourself. Don't be so frugal as to think you can't afford outside counsel. In point of fact, you can't afford not to employ an experienced professional.

The Four Rs of Franchising

We are told as children that the three Rs of reading, 'riting and 'rithmetic are critical to our scholastic success. Success in franchising depends on four Rs — realism, research, reserves and resolve.

Realism

At the outset of your investigation, it is important that you be realistic about your strengths and weaknesses, your goals and your capabilities. I strongly recommend that you take the time necessary to do a personal audit — possibly with the help of outside professionals — before investing your life's savings in a franchise.

Franchising is not a money machine. It involves hard work, dedication, set-backs and long hours. Be realistic about the nature of the business you are buying. What traits will ultimately determine your success? Do you have them? If it is a service-oriented business, will you be able to keep smiling when you know the client/customer is a fool? If it is a fast-food business, will you be able to properly manage a minimum-wage staff? How well will you handle the uncertainties that will invariably arise? Can you make day-to-day decisions based on imperfect information? Can you count on your spouse's support after you have gone through all of your working capital reserves, and the future looks cloudy and uncertain?

Be equally realistic about your franchise selection process. Have you thoroughly evaluated all of the alternatives? Have you talked with everyone you can to ensure that you have left no stone unturned? Have you carefully and realistically assessed the advantages and disadvantages of the system offered, the unique demographics of your territory, near-term market trends, the financial projections, etc.? The selection process is tiring. It is easy to convince yourself that the franchise opportunity in your hand is really the best one for you. The penalties for doing so, however, are extreme.

Research

There is no substitute for exhaustive research!

Bond's Franchise Guide contains over 2,150 franchise listings, broken into 45 distinct business categories. This represents a substantial number of options from which to choose. It is up to you to spend the time required to come up with an optimal selection. At a minimum, you will probably be in that business for five years. More likely, you will be in it 10 years or more. Given the long-term commitment, allow yourself the necessary time to ensure you won't regret having made a hasty decision. Research is a tedious, boring process. But doing it carefully and thoroughly can greatly reduce your risk and exposure. The benefits are measurable.

I suggest you first determine which industry groups hold your interest. Don't arbitrarily limit yourself to a particular industry in which you have first-hand experience. Next, request information from all of the companies that are listed in those industries. The incremental cost of mailing (or calling) requests to an additional 15 or 20 companies is insignificant in the larger picture. Based on personal experience, you may feel you already know the best franchise. Step back. Assume there is a competing franchise out there with a comparable product or service, comparable management, etc., that charges a royalty fee 2% of sales less than your intuitive choice. Over a 10-year period, that could add up to a great deal of money. It certainly justifies your requesting initial information.

A thorough analysis of the literature you receive should allow you to reduce the list of prime candidates down to six to eight companies. Aggressively evaluate each firm. Talking with current and former franchisees is the single best source of information you can get. Where possible, site visits are invaluable. My experience is that franchisees tend to be candid in their level of satisfaction with the franchisor. However, since they don't know you, they may be less candid about their sales, expenses and income. Go to the library and get studies that forecast industry growth, market saturation, industry problems, technical breakthroughs, etc. Don't find out a year after becoming a franchisee of a coffee company that earlier reports suggested that the coffee market was oversaturated or that coffee was linked to some form of colon cancer.

Reserves

As a new business, franchising is replete with uncertainty, uneven cash flows and unforeseen problems. It is an imperfect world that might not bear any relation to the clean pro formas you prepared to justify getting into the business. Any one of these unforeseen contingencies could cause a severe drain on your cash reserves. At the same time, you will have fixed and/or contractual payments that must be met on a current basis regardless of sales: rent, employee salaries, insurance, etc. Adequate back-up reserves may be in the form of savings, commitments from relatives, bank loans, etc. Just make certain that the funds are available when, and if, you need them. To be absolutely safe, I suggest you double the level of reserves recommended by the franchisor.

Keep in mind that the most common cause of business failure is inadequate working capital. Plan properly so you don't become a statistic.

Resolve

Let's assume for the time being that you have demonstrated exceptional levels of realism, research and reserves. You have picked an optimal franchise that takes full advantage of your strengths. You are in business and bringing in enough money to achieve a positive cash flow. The future looks bright. Now the fourth R — resolve — comes into play. Remember why you chose franchising in the first place: to take full advantage of a system that has been time-tested in the marketplace. Remember also what makes franchising work so well: the franchisor and franchisees maximize their respective success by working within the system for the common good. Invariably, two obstacles arise.

The first is the physical pain associated with writing that monthly royalty check. Annual sales of $250,000 and a 6% royalty fee result in a monthly royalty check of $1,250 that must be sent to the franchisor. Every month. As a franchisee, you may look for any justification to reduce this sizable monthly outflow. Resist the temptation. Accept the fact that royalty fees are simply another cost of doing business. They are also a legal obligation that you willingly agreed to pay when you signed the franchise agreement. They are the dues you agreed to pay when you joined the club.

Although there may be an incentive, don't look for loopholes in the contract that might allow you to sue the franchisor or get out of the relationship. Don't report lower sales than actual in an effort to reduce royalties. If you have received the support that you were promised, continue to play by the rules. Honor your commitment. Let the franchisor enjoy the rewards it has earned from your success.

The second obstacle is the desire to change the system. You need to honor your commitment to be a "franchisee" and to live within the franchise system. What makes franchising successful as far as your customers are concerned is uniformity and consistency of appearance, product/service quality and corporate image. The most damaging thing an individual franchisee can do is to suddenly and unilaterally introduce changes to a proven system. While these modifications may work in one market, they only serve to diminish the value of the system as a whole. Imagine what would happen to the national perception of your franchise if every franchisee had the latitude to make unilateral changes in his or her operations. Accordingly, any ideas you have on improving the system should be submitted directly to the franchisor for its evaluation. Accept the franchisor's decision on whether or not to pursue an idea.

If you suspect that you may be a closet entrepreneur who needs unrestrained experimenting and tinkering, you are probably not cut out to be a franchisee. Seriously consider this question before you get into a relationship, instead of waiting until you are locked into an untenable situation.

Summary

I hope that I have been clear in suggesting that the selection of an optimal franchise is both time- and energy-consuming. Done properly, the process may take six to nine months and involve the expenditure of several thousand dollars. The difference between a hasty, gut-feel investigation and an exhaustive, well-thought out investigation may mean the difference between finding a poorly-conceived, or even fraudulent, franchise and an exceptional one.

My sense is that there is a strong correlation between the efforts you put into the investigative process and the ultimate degree of success you enjoy as a franchisee. The process is to investigate, evaluate and negotiate. Don't try to bypass any one of these critical elements.

The appendix includes the original questionnaire sent to some 2,300 U.S. and Canadian franchisors. Franchisors who did not respond to the original mailing received a follow-up package roughly one month later. The end result was that roughly 50% of the contacted franchisors returned a completed questionnaire. Those franchisors who did not respond to either mailing, but who still actively franchise (subject to the restrictions noted in Chapter 1), are noted in the Supplemental Listing of Franchisors at the end of each chapter.

The data returned has been condensed into the profiles shown on the following pages. In some cases, an answer has been abbreviated to conserve room and to make the profiles more directly comparable. All of the data is displayed with the objective of providing as much background data as possible. In those cases where no answer was provided to a particular question within the questionnaire, an "NR" is used to signify "No Response."

Please take a few minutes to acquaint yourself with the composition of the sample profile. Supplementary comments have been added where some interpretation of the franchisor's response is required.

Keep in mind that all of the profile data is based on questionnaires returned by the franchisors themselves, with no effort to independently verify its accuracy. There is no doubt that franchisors had some latitude to exaggerate their responses in order to make themselves appear bigger, more mature and/or more franchisee-oriented than they really are. I am confident some small percentage did just that. The vast majority, however, would see any such deception as dishonest, counter-productive and a general waste of everyone's time.

∞

MAUI TACOS, a new fast-casual food concept, has been selected to illustrate how this book uses the collected data.

MAUI TACOS

1775 The Exchange, # 540
Atlanta, GA 30339
Tel: (888) 628-4822 (770) 226-8226
Fax: (770) 541-2300
E-Mail: normanw@mauitacos.com
Web Site: www.mauitacos.com

Mr. Norman D. Willden, VP Franchise Development

Fast-casual "Maui-Mex" restaurant featuring Mexican foods created by internationally recognized chef Mark Ellmao, using pineapple and lime juice marinade with island spices. Char-grilled chicken, steak and lean beef burritos topped with unique salsas is our mainstay. This food experience is like a vacation in Maui.

BACKGROUND: IFA MEMBER

Established: 1993;   1st Franchised: 1998
Franchised Units: 13
Company-Owned Units   <u>1</u>
Total Units: 14
Dist.:   US-14; CAN-0; O'seas-0
  North America: 2 States
  Density: 8 in HI, 3 in GA
Projected New Units (12 Months):   20
Qualifications: 4,4,3,3,4,4
Registered: CA, FL, HI, IN, MD, MI, MN, NY, ND, OR, RI, VA, WA, WI, DC

FINANCIAL/TERMS:

Cash Investment: $60-125K
Total Investment: $180-375K
Minimum Net Worth: $300K
Fees: Franchise — $20K
  Royalty — 6%;   Ad. — 4%
Earnings Claim Statement: Yes
Term of Contract (Years):   20/20
Avg. # Of Employees: 4 FT, 10 PT

Passive Ownership: Discouraged
Encourage Conversions: Yes
Area Develop. Agreements: Yes/50
Sub-Franchising Contracts: Yes
Expand In Territory: Yes
Space Needs: 2,000 SF; FS, SF, SC, RM, HB, open air

SUPPORT & TRAINING PROVIDED:

Financial Assistance Provided: Yes(I)
Site Selection Assistance: Yes
Lease Negotiation Assistance: Yes
Co-Operative Advertising: Yes
Franchisee Assoc./Member: Yes/Yes
Size Of Corporate Staff: 6
On-Going Support: A,B,C,D,E,F,G,h,I
Training: 160 Hours in Atlanta, GA.

SPECIFIC EXPANSION PLANS:

US: All United States
Canada: All Canada
Overseas: All Countries

Address/Contact:

1. **Company name, address, telephone and fax numbers**.

Comment: All of the data published in the book was current at the time the completed questionnaire was received or upon subsequent verification by phone. Over a 12-month period between annual publications, 10–15% of the addresses and/or telephone numbers become obsolete for various reasons. If you are unable to contact a franchisor at the address/telephone number listed, please give us a call at (510) 839-5471 (or fax [510] 839-2104) and we will provide you with the current address and telephone number.

2. **(888) 628-4822 (770) 226-8226.** In many cases, you may find that you cannot access the (800) number from your area. Do not conclude that the company has gone out of business. Simply call the local number.

Comment: An (800) number serves two important functions. The first is to provide an efficient, no-cost way for potential franchisees to contact the franchisor. Making the prospective franchisee foot the bill artificially limits the number of people who might otherwise make the initial contact. The second function is to demonstrate to existing franchisees that the franchisor is doing everything it can to efficiently respond to problems in the field as they occur. Many companies have a restricted (800) line for their franchisees that the general public cannot access. Since you will undoubtedly be talking with the franchisor's staff on a periodic basis, determine whether an (800) line is available to franchisees.

Over two-thirds of the companies listed in the book have (800) numbers. Extreme competition among telephone companies today makes the incremental cost of an (800) number relatively minor. My feeling is that it is an expense a franchisor should incur if it wants to stay competitive.

3. **Contact.** You should honor the wishes of the franchisor and address all initial correspondence to the contact listed. It would be counter-productive to try to reach the president directly if the designated contact is the director of franchising.

Comment: The president is the designated contact in approximately half of the profiles noted below. The reason for this varies among franchisors. The president is the best spokesperson for his or her operation. It flatters the franchisee to talk directly with the president. There is no one else around. Regardless of the justification, it is important to determine if the operation is a one-man show in which the president does everything or if the president merely feels that having an open line to potential franchisees is the best way for him or her to sense the "pulse" of the company and the market. Convinced that the president can only do so many things well, I would want assurances that, by taking all incoming calls,

he or she is not neglecting the day-to-day responsibilities of managing the business.

Description of Business:

4. **Description of Business:** The questionnaire provides franchisors with adequate room to differentiate their franchise from the competition. In a minor number of cases, some editing was required.

Comment: In instances where franchisors show no initiative or imagination in describing their operations, you must decide whether this is symptomatic of the company or simply a reflection on the individual who responded to the questionnaire.

Background:

5. **IFA MEMBER.** There are two primary affinity groups associated with the franchising industry — the International Franchise Association (IFA) and the Canadian Franchise Association (CFA). Both the IFA and the CFA are described in Chapter 1.

6. **Established: 1993.** MAUI TACOS was founded in 1993, and, accordingly, has only seven years of experience in its primary business. It should be intuitively obvious that a firm that has been in existence for over 20 years has a greater likelihood of being around five years from now than a firm that was founded only last year.

7. **1st Franchised: 1998.** 1998 was also the year that MAUI TACOS's first franchised unit(s) were established.

Comment: 10+ years of continuous operation, both as an operator and as a franchisor, is compelling evidence that a firm has staying power. The number of years a franchisor has been in business is one of the key variables to consider in choosing a franchise. This is not to say that a new franchise should not receive your full attention. Every company has to start from scratch. Ultimately, a prospective franchisee has to be convinced that the franchise has 1) been in operation long enough, or 2) its key management personnel have adequate industry experience to have worked out the bugs normally associated with a new business. In most cases, this experience can only be gained through on-the-job training. Don't be the guinea pig that provides the franchisor with the experience it needs to develop a smoothly running operation.

8. **Franchised Units: 13.** As of 1/1/2001, MAUI TACOS had 13 franchisee-owned and operated units.

9. **Company-Owned Units: 1.** As of 1/1/2001, MAUI TACOS had one Company-owned and operated units.

Comment: A younger franchise should prove that its concept has worked successfully in several company-owned units before it markets its "system" to an inexperienced franchisee. Without company-owned prototype stores, the new franchisee may well end up being the "testing kitchen" for the franchise concept itself.

If a franchise concept is truly exceptional, why doesn't the franchisor commit some of its resources to take advantage of the investment opportunity? Clearly, a financial decision on the part of the franchisor, the absence of company-owned units should not be a negative in and of itself. This is especially true of proven franchises, which may have previously sold their company-owned operations to franchisees.

Try to determine if there is a noticeable trend in the percentage of company-owned units. If the franchisor is buying back units from franchisees, it may be doing so to preclude litigation. Some firms also "churn" their operating units with some regularity. If the sales pitch is compelling, but the follow-through is not competitive, a franchisor may

sell a unit to a new franchisee, wait for him or her to fail, buy it back for $0.60 cents on the dollar, and then sell that same unit to the next unsuspecting franchisee. Each time the unit is resold, the franchisor collects a franchise fee, plus the negotiated discount from the previous franchisee.

Alternatively, an increasing or high percentage of company-owned units may well mean the company is convinced of the long-term profitability of such an approach. The key is to determine whether a franchisor is building new units from scratch or buying them from failing and/or unhappy franchisees.

10. **Total Units: 14.** As of 1/1/2001, MAUI TACOS had a total of 14 franchisee-owned and company-owned units.

Comment: Like a franchisor's longevity, its experience in operating multiple units offers considerable comfort. Those franchisors with over 15–25 operating units have proven that their system works and have probably encountered and overcome most of the problems that plague a new operation. Alternatively, the management of franchises with less than 15 operating units may have gained considerable industry experience before joining the current franchise. It is up to the franchisor to convince you that it is providing you with as risk-free an operation as possible. You don't want to be providing a company with its basic experience in the business.

11. **Distribution: US-14; CAN-0; O'seas-0.** As of 1/1/2001, MAUI TACOS had 14 operating units in the U.S., none in Canada and none Overseas.

12. **Distribution: North America: 2 States, 0 Provinces.** As of 1/1/2001, MAUI TACOS had operations in two states in the U.S. and zero provinces in Canada.

Comment: It should go without saying that the wider the geographic distribution, the greater the franchisor's level of success. For the most part, such distribution can only come from a large number of operating units. If, however, the franchisor has operations in 15 states but only 18 total operating units, it is unlikely that it can efficiently service these accounts because of geographic constraints. Other things being equal, a prospective franchisee would vastly prefer a franchisor with 15 units in New York to one with 15 units scattered throughout the U.S., Canada and overseas.

13. **Distribution: Density: 8 in HI, 3 in GA.** The franchisor was asked "what three states/provinces have the largest number of operating units." (No distinction was made between company-owned and franchisee-owned units.) As of 5/31/2000, MAUI TACOS had eight units in Hawaii and three units in Georgia.

Comment: For smaller, regional franchises, geographic distribution could be a key variable in deciding whether to buy. If the franchisor has a concentration of units in your immediate geographic area, it is likely you will be well-served. For those far removed geographically from the franchisor's current areas of operation, however, there can be problems. It is both time consuming and expensive to support a franchisee 2,000 miles away from company headquarters. To the extent that a franchisor can visit four franchisees in one area on one trip, there is no problem. If, however, your operation is the only one west of the Mississippi, you may not receive the on-site assistance you would like. Don't be a missionary who has to rely on his or her own devices to survive. Don't accept a franchisor's idle promises of support. If on-site assistance is important to your ultimate success, get assurances in writing that the necessary support will be forthcoming. Remember, you are buying into a system, and the availability of day-to-day support is one of the key ingredients of any successful franchise system.

14. **Projected New Units (12 Months): 20.** MAUI TACOS plans to open 20 new units within the following 12 months. Again, there was no distinction between franchised and company-owned units.

Comment: In business, growth has become a highly visible symbol of success. Rapid growth is generally perceived as preferable to slower, more controlled growth. I maintain, however, that the opposite is frequently the case. It is highly unlikely that a new franchise with only five operating units can successfully attract, screen, train and bring multiple new units on-stream in a 12-month period. If it suggests that it can, or even wants to, be properly wary. You must be confident a company has the financial and management resources necessary to pull off such a Herculean feat. If management is already thin, concentrating on attracting new units will clearly diminish the time it can and should spend supporting you. It takes many months, if not years, to develop and train a second level of management. You don't want to depend upon new hires teaching you systems and procedures they themselves know little or nothing about.

15. **Qualifications: 4,4,3,3,4,4.** Question 34 of the questionnaire in Appendix A was posed to determine which specific evaluation criteria were important to the franchisor. The franchisor was asked the following: "In qualifying a potential franchisee, please rank the following criteria from Unimportant (1) to Very Important (5)." The responses should be self-explanatory.

Financial Net Worth (Rank from 1–5)

General Business Experience (Rank from 1–5)

Specific Industry Experience (Rank from 1–5)

Formal Education (Rank from 1–5)

Psychological Profile (Rank from 1–5)

Personal Interview(s) (Rank from 1–5)

16. **Registered** refers to the 16 states that require specific formal registration at the state level before the franchisor may offer franchises in that state. State registration and disclosure to the Federal Trade Commission are separate issues that are discussed in Chapter 1.

Capital Requirements/Rights:

17. **Cash Investment: $60–125K.** On average, a MAUI TACOS franchisee will have made a cash investment of $60,000–125,000 by the time he or she finally opens the initial operating unit.

Comment: It is important that you be realistic about the amount of cash you can comfortably invest in a business. Stretching beyond your means can have grave and far-reaching consequences. Assume that you will encounter periodic set-backs and that you will have to draw on your reserves. The demands of starting a new business are harsh enough without adding the uncertainties associated with inadequate working capital. Trust the franchisor's recommendations regarding the suggested minimum cash investment. If anything, there is an incentive for setting the recommended level of investment too low, rather than too high. The franchisor will want to qualify you to the extent that you have adequate financing. No legitimate franchisor wants you to invest if there is a chance that you might fail because of a shortage of funds.

Keep in mind that you will probably not achieve a positive cash flow from the business before six months or more. In your discussions with the franchisor, be absolutely certain that its calculations include an adequate working capital reserve.

18. **Total Investment: $180–375K.** On average, MAUI TACOS franchisees will invest a total of $180,000–375,000, including both cash and debt, by the time the franchise opens its doors.

Comment: The total investment should be the cash investment noted above plus any debt that you will incur in starting up the new business. Debt could be a note to the franchisor for all or part of the franchise fee, an equipment lease, building and facilities leases, etc. Make sure that the total includes all of the obligations that you assume, especially any long-term lease obligations.

Be conservative in assessing what your real exposure is. If you are leasing highly specialized equipment or if you are leasing a single-purpose building, it is naive to think that you will recoup your investment if you have to sell or sub-lease those assets in a buyer's market. If there is any specialized equipment that may have been manufactured to the franchisor's specifications, determine if the franchisor has any form of buy-back provision.

19. **Minimum Net Worth: $300K.** In this case, MAUI TACOS feels that a potential franchisee should have a minimum net worth of $300,000. Although net worth can be defined in vastly different ways, the franchisor's response should suggest a minimum level of equity that the prospective franchisee should possess. Net worth is the combination of both liquid and illiquid assets. Again, don't think that franchisor-determined guidelines somehow don't apply to you.

20. **Fees (Franchise): $20K.** MAUI TACOS requires a front-end, one-time-only payment of $20,000 to grant a franchise for a single location. As noted in Chapter 1, the franchise fee is a payment to reimburse the franchisor for the incurred costs of setting the franchisee up in business — from recruiting through training and manuals.

The fee usually ranges from $15,000–30,000. It is a function of competitive franchise fees and the actual out-of-pocket costs incurred by the franchisor.

Depending upon the franchisee's particular circumstances and how well the franchisor thinks he or she might fit into the system, the franchisor may finance all or part of the franchise fee. (See below to see if a franchisor provides any direct or indirect financial assistance.)

The franchise fee is one area in which the franchisor frequently provides either direct or indirect financial support.

Comment: Ideally, the franchisor should do no more than recover its costs on the initial franchise fee. Profits come later in the form of royalty fees, which are a function of the franchisee's sales. Whether the franchise fee is $5,000 or $35,000, the total should be carefully evaluated. What are competitive fees and are they financed? How much training will you actually receive? Are the fees reflective of the franchisor's expenses? If the fees appear to be non-competitive, address your concerns with the franchisor.

Realize that a $5,000 differential in the one-time franchise fee is a secondary consideration in the overall scheme of things. You are in the relationship for the long-term.

By the same token, don't get suckered in by an extremely low fee if there is any doubt about the franchisor's ability to follow through. Franchisors need to collect reasonable fees to cover their actual costs. If they don't recoup these costs, they cannot recruit and train new franchisees on whom your own future success partially depends.

21. **Fees (Royalty): 6%** means that 6% of gross sales (or other measure, as defined in the franchise agreement) must be periodically paid directly to the franchisor in the form of royalties. This ongoing expense is your cost for being part of the larger franchise system and for all of the "back-office" support you receive. In a few cases, the amount of the royalty fee is fixed rather than variable. In others, the fee decreases as the volume of sales (or other measure) increases (i.e., 6% on the first $200,000 of sales, 5% on the next $100,000 and so on). In others, the fee is held at artificially low levels during the start-up phase of the franchisee's business, then increases once the franchisee is better able to afford it.

Comment: Royalty fees represent the mechanism by which the franchisor finally recoups the costs it has incurred in developing its business. It may take many years and many operating units before the franchisor is able to make a true operating profit.

Consider a typical franchisor who might have been in business for three years. With a staff of five, rent, travel, operating expenses, etc., assume it has annual operating costs of $300,000 (including reasonable owner's salaries). Assume also that there are 25 franchised units with average annual sales of $250,000. Each franchise is required to pay a 6% royalty fee. Total annual royalties under this scenario would total only $375,000. The franchisor is making a $75,000 profit. Then consider the personal risk the franchisor took in developing a new business and the initial years of negative cash flows. Alternatively, evaluate what it would cost you, as a sole proprietor, to provide the myriad services included in the royalty payment.

In assessing various alternative investments, the amount of the royalty percentage is a major ongoing expense. Assuming average annual sales of $250,000 per annum over a 15-year period, the total royalties at 5% would be $187,500. At 6%, the cumulative fees would be $225,000. You have to be fully convinced that the $37,500 differential is justified. While this is clearly a meaningful number, what you are really evaluating is the quality of management and the unique competitive advantages of the goods and/or services offered by the franchisor.

22. Fees (Advertising): 4%. Most national or regional franchisors require their franchisees to contribute a certain percentage of their sales (or other measure, as determined in the franchise agreement) into a corporate advertising fund. These individual advertising fees are pooled to develop a corporate advertising/marketing effort that produces great economies of scale. The end result is a national or regional advertising program that promotes the franchisor's products and services. Depending upon the nature of the business, this percentage usually ranges from two to six percent and is in addition to the royalty fee.

Comment: One of the greatest advantages of a franchised system is its ability to promote, on a national or regional basis, its products and services. The promotions may be through television, radio, print medias or direct mail. The objective is name recognition and, over time, the assumption that the product and/or service has been "time-tested." An individual business owner could never justify the expense of mounting a major advertising program at the local level. For a smaller franchise that may not yet have an advertising program or fee, it is important to know when an advertising program will start, how it will be monitored and its expected cost.

23. Earnings Claim Statement: Yes means MAUI TACOS does provide an Earnings Claim statement to potential franchisees. Unfortunately, only 12–15% of franchisors provide an earnings claim statement in their Uniform Franchise Offering Circular (UFOC). The franchising industry's failure to require earnings claim statements does a serious disservice to the potential franchisee. See

Chapter 1 for comments on this important document.

24. Term of Contract (Years): 20/20. MAUI TACOS's initial franchise period runs for 20 years. The first renewal period runs for an additional 20 years. Assuming that the franchisee operates within the terms of the franchise agreement, he or she has 40 years within which to develop and, ultimately, sell the business.

Comment: The potential value of any business (or investment) is the discounted sum of the operating income that is generated each year plus its value upon liquidation. Given this truth, the length of the franchise agreement and any renewals are extremely important to the franchisee. It is essential that he or she has adequate time to develop the business to its full potential. At that time, he or she will have maximized the value of the business as an on-going concern. The value of the business to a potential buyer, however, is largely a function of how long the franchise agreement runs. If there are only two years remaining before the agreement expires, or if the terms of an extension(s) are vague, the business will be worth only a fraction of the value assigned to a business with 15 years to go. For the most part, the longer the agreement and the subsequent extension, the better. (The same logic applies to a lease. If your sales are largely a function of your location and traffic count, then it is important that you have options to extend the lease under known terms. Your lease should never be longer than the remaining term of your franchise agreement, however.)

Assuming the length of the agreement is acceptable, be clear under what circumstances renewals might not be granted. Similarly, know the circumstances under which a franchise agreement might be prematurely and unilaterally canceled by the franchisor. I strongly recommend you have an experienced lawyer review this section of the franchise agreement. It would be devastating if, after spending years developing your business, there were a loophole in the contract that allowed the franchisor to arbitrarily cancel the relationship.

25. **Avg. # of Employees: 4 FT, 10 PT**. The question was asked "Including the owner/operator, how many employees are recommended to properly staff the average franchised unit?" In MAUI TACOS's case, four full-time employees and ten part-time employees are required.

Comment: Most entrepreneurs start a new business based on their intuitive feel that it will be "fun" and that their talents and experience will be put to good use. They will be doing what they enjoy and what they are good at. Times change. Your business prospers. The number of employees increases. You are spending an increasing percentage of your time taking care of personnel problems and less and less on the fun parts of the business. In Chapter 1, the importance of conducting a realistic self-appraisal was stressed. If you found that you really are not good at managing people, or you don't have the patience to manage a large minimum wage staff, cut your losses before you are locked into doing just that.

26. **Passive Ownership: Discouraged.** Depending on the nature of the business, many franchisors are indifferent as to whether you manage the business directly or hire a full-time manager to run it. Others are insistent that, at least for the initial franchise, the franchisee be a full-time owner/operator. MAUI TACOS allows franchisees to hire full-time managers to run their retail outlets, but does not encourage it.

Comment: Unless you have a great deal of experience in the business you have chosen or in managing similar businesses, I feel strongly that you should initially commit your personal time and energies to make the system work. After you have

developed a full understanding of the business and have competent, trusted staff members who can assume day-to-day operations, then consider delegating these responsibilities. Running the business through a manager can be fraught with peril unless you have mastered all aspects of the business and there are strong economic incentives and sufficient safeguards to ensure the manager will perform as desired.

27. **Conversions Encouraged: Yes.** This section pertains primarily to sole proprietorships or "mom and pop" operations. To the extent that there truly are centralized operating savings associated with the franchise, the most logical people to join a franchise system are those sole practitioners who are working hard but only eking out a living. The implementation of proven systems and marketing clout could significantly reduce operating costs and increase profits.

Comment: The franchisor has the option of 1) actively encouraging such independent operators to become members of the franchise team, 2) seeking out franchisees with limited or no applied experience or 3) going after both groups. Concerned that it will be very difficult to break independent operators of the bad habits they have picked up over the years, many only choose course two. "They will continue to do things their way. They won't, or can't, accept corporate direction," they might say to themselves. Others are simply selective in the conversions they allow. In many cases, the franchise fee is reduced or eliminated for conversions.

28. **Area Development Agreements: Yes/50.** Area development agreements are more fully described in Chapter 1. Essentially, they allow an investor or investment group to develop an entire area or region. The schedule for development is clearly spelled out in the area development agreement. (Note: "Var." means varies and "Neg." means negotiable.)

Comment: Area development agreements represent an opportunity for the franchisor to choose a single franchisee or investment group to develop an entire area. The franchisee's qualifications should be strong and include proven business experience and the financial depth to pull it off. An area development agreement represents a great opportunity for an investor to tie up a large geographical area and develop a concept that may not have proven itself on a national basis. Keep in mind that this is a quantum leap from making an investment in a single franchise and is relevant only to those with development experience and deep pockets.

29. **Sub-Franchising Agreements: Yes.** MAUI TACOS does grant sub-franchising agreements. (See Chapter 1 for a more thorough explanation.) Like area development agreements, sub-franchising also allows an investor or investment group to develop an entire area or region. The difference is that the sub-franchisor becomes a self-contained business, responsible for all relations with franchisees within its area, from initial training to ongoing support. Franchisees pay their royalties to the sub-franchisor, who in turn pays a portion to the master franchisor.

Comment: Sub-franchising is used primarily by smaller franchisors who have a relatively easy concept and who are prepared to sell a portion of the future growth of their business to someone for some front-end cash and a percentage of the future royalties they receive from their franchisees.

30. **Expand in Territory: Yes.** Under conditions spelled out in the franchise agreement, MAUI TACOS will allow its franchisees to expand within their exclusive territory.

Comment: Some franchisors define the franchisee's exclusive territory so tightly that there would never be room to open additional outlets within

an area. Others provide a larger area in the hopes that the franchisee will do well and have the incentive to open additional units.

There are clearly economic benefits to both parties from having franchisees with multiple units. There is no question that it is in your best interest to have the option to expand once you have proven to both yourself and the franchisor that you can manage the business successfully. Many would concur that the real profits in franchising come from managing multiple units rather than being locked into a single franchise in a single location. Additional fees may or may not be required with these additional units.

31. **Space Needs: 2,000 SF; FS, SF, SC, RM, HB, open air.** The average MAUI TACOS retail outlet will require 2,000 square feet in a Free-Standing (FS) building, Storefront (SF) location, Strip Center (SC), Regional Mall (RM), Home Based (HB) or open air location. Other types of leased space might be Executive Suite (ES), Industrial Park (IP), Kiosk (KI), Office Building (OB), Power Center (PC) or Warehouse (WH).

Comment: Armed with the rough space requirements, you can better project your annual occupancy costs. It should be relatively easy to get comparable rental rates for the type of space required. As annual rent and related expenses can be as high as 15% of your annual sales, be as accurate as possible in your projections.

Franchisor Support and Training Provided:

32. **Financial Assistance: Yes (I)** notes that MAUI TACOS is indirectly (I) involved in providing financial assistance. Indirect assistance might include making introductions to the franchisor's financial contacts, providing financial templates for preparing a business plan or actually assisting in the loan application process. In some cases, the franchisor becomes a co-signer on a financial obligation (equipment lease, space lease, etc.). Other

franchisors are (D) directly involved in the process. In this case, the assistance may include a lease or loan made directly by the franchisor. Any loan would generally be secured by some form of collateral. A very common form of assistance is a note for all or part of the initial franchise fee. Yes (B) indicates that the franchisor provides both direct and indirect financial assistance. The level of assistance will generally depend upon the relative strengths of the franchisee.

Comment: The best of all possible worlds is one in which the franchisor has enough confidence in the business and in you to co-sign notes on the building and equipment leases and allow you to pay off the franchise fee over a specified period of time. Depending upon your qualifications, this could happen. Most likely, however, the franchisor will only give you some assistance in raising the necessary capital to start the business. Increasingly, franchisors are testing a franchisee's business acumen by letting him or her assume an increasing level of personal responsibility in securing financing. The objective is to find out early in the process how competent a franchisee really is.

33. **Assistance with Site Selection: Yes** means that MAUI TACOS will assist the franchisee in selecting a site location. While the phrase "location, location, location" may be hackneyed, its importance should not be discounted, especially when a business depends upon retail traffic counts and accessibility. If a business is home- or warehouse-based, assistance in this area is of negligible or minor importance.

Comment: Since you will be locked into a lease for a minimum of three, and probably five, years, optimal site selection is absolutely essential. Even if you were somehow able to sub-lease and extricate yourself from a bad lease or bad location, the franchise agreement may not allow you to move to another location. Accordingly, it is imperative that you get it right the first time.

If a franchisor is truly interested in your success, it should treat your choice of a site with the same care it would use in choosing a company-owned site. Keep in mind that many firms provide excellent demographic data on existing locations at a very reasonable cost.

34. **Assistance with Lease Negotiations: Yes.** Once a site is selected, MAUI TACOS will be actively involved in negotiating the terms of the lease.

Comment: Given the complexity of negotiating a lease, an increasing number of franchisors are taking an active role in lease negotiations. There are far too many trade-offs that must be considered — terms, percentage rents, tenant improvements, pass-throughs, kick-out clauses, etc. This responsibility is best left to the professionals. If the franchisor doesn't have the capacity to support you directly, enlist the help of a well-recommended broker. The penalties for signing a bad long-term lease are very severe.

35. **Co-operative Advertising: Yes** refers to the existence of a joint advertising program in which the franchisor and franchisees each contribute to promote the company's products and/or services (usually within the franchisee's specific territory).

Comment: Co-op advertising is a common and mutually-beneficial effort. By agreeing to split part of the advertising costs, whether for television, radio or direct mail, the franchisor is not only supporting the franchisee, but guaranteeing itself royalties from the incremental sales. A franchisor that is not intimately involved with the advertising campaign — particularly when it is an important part of the business — may not be fully committed to your overall success.

36. **Franchisee Assoc./Member: Yes/Yes.** This response notes that the MAUI TACOS system does include an active association made up of MAUI TACOS franchisees. A Yes/Yes response indicates that MAUI TACOS has both an associa-

tion and is also a member of the franchisee association.

Comment: The empowerment of franchisees has become a major rallying cry within the industry over the past four years. Various states have recently passed laws favoring franchisee rights, and the subject has been widely discussed in congressional staff hearings. Political groups even represent franchisee rights on a national basis. Similarly, the IFA is now actively courting franchisees to become active members. Whether they are equal members remains to be seen.

Franchisees have also significantly increased their clout with respect to the franchisor. If a franchise is to grow and be successful in the long term, it is critical that the franchisor and its franchisees mutually agree they are partners rather than adversaries.

37. **Size of Corporate Staff: 6.** MAUI TACOS has six full-time employees on its staff to support its six operating units.

Comment: There are no magic ratios that tell you whether the franchisor has enough staff to provide the proper level of support. It would appear, however, that MAUI TACOS's staff of six is more than adequate to support 14 operating units. Less clear is whether a staff of three, including the company president and his wife, can adequately support 15 fledgling franchisees in the field.

Many younger franchises may be managed by a skeleton staff, assisted by outside consultants who are performing various management functions during the start-up phase. From the perspective of the franchisee, it is essential that the franchisor have actual in-house franchising experience, and that the franchisee not be forced to rely on outside consultants to make the system work. Whereas a full-time, salaried employee will probably have the franchisee's objectives in mind, an outside con-

sultant may easily not have the same priorities. Franchising is a unique form of business that requires specific skills and experience — skills and experience that are markedly different from those required to manage a non-franchised business. If you are thinking about establishing a long-term relationship with a firm just starting out in franchising, you should insist that the franchisor prove that it has an experienced, professional team on board and in place to provide the necessary levels of support to all concerned.

38. **On-Going Support: A,B,C,D,E,F,G,h,I**

Like initial training, the on-going support services provided by the franchisor are of paramount importance. Having a solid and responsive team behind you can certainly make your life much easier and allow you to concentrate your energies on other areas. As is noted below, the franchisors were asked to indicate their support for 9 separate on-going services:

Service Provided	Included in Fees	At Add'l. Cost	NA
Central Data Processing	A	a	NA
Central Purchasing	B	b	NA
Field Operations Evaluation	C	c	NA
Field Training	D	d	NA
Initial Store Opening	E	e	NA
Inventory Control	F	f	NA
Franchisee Newsletter	G	g	NA
Regional or National Meetings	H	h	NA
800 Telephone Hotline	I	i	NA

If the franchisor provides the service at no additional cost to the franchisee (as indicated by letters A–I), a capital letter was used to indicate this. If the service is provided, but only at an additional cost, a lower case letter was used. If the franchisor responded with a NA, or failed to note an answer for a particular service, the corresponding letter was omitted from the data sheet.

39. **Training: 160 Hours in Atlanta, GA.**

Comment: Assuming that the underlying business concept is sound and competitive, adequate

35

training and on-going support are among the most important determinants of your success as a franchisee. The initial training should be as lengthy and as "hands-on" as necessary to allow the franchisee to operate alone and with confidence. Obviously, every potential situation cannot be covered in any training program. But the franchisee should come away with a basic understanding of how the business operates and where to go to resolve problems when they come up. Depending on the business, there should be operating manuals, procedures manuals, company policies, training videos, (800) help-lines, etc. It may be helpful at the outset to establish how satisfied recent franchisees are with a company's training. I would also have a clear understanding about how often the company updates its manuals and training programs, the cost of sending additional employees through training, etc.

Remember, you are part of an organization that you are paying (in the form of a franchise fee and on-going royalties) to support you. Training is the first step. On-going support is the second step.

Specific Expansion Plans:

40. **U.S.: All United States.** MAUI TACOS is currently focusing its growth on the entire United States. Alternatively, the franchisor could have listed particular states or regions into which it wished to expand.

41. **Canada: All Canada.** MAUI TACOS is currently seeking additional franchisees in Canada.

Specific markets or provinces could have also been indicated.

42. **Overseas: All Countries.** MAUI TACOS is currently expanding overseas.

Comment: You will note that many smaller companies suggest that they will concurrently expand throughout the U.S., Canada and internationally. In many cases, these are the same companies that foresee a 50+% growth rate in operating units over the next 12 months. Generally, the chances of this happening are negligible. Although MAUI TACOS lacks a critical mass in terms of operating units, it can draw upon the operating experience of its parent company, BLIMPIE, which clearly does have sufficient expansion experience. As a prospective franchisee, you should be wary of any company that thinks it can expand throughout the world without a solid base of experience, staff and financial resources. Even if adequate financing is available, the demands on existing management will be extreme. New management cannot adequately fill the void until they are able to fully understand the system and absorb the corporate culture. If management's end objective is expansion for its own sake rather than by design, the existing franchisees will suffer.

If you have not already done so, I would strongly encourage you to invest the modest time required to read Chapter 1 — 30 Minute Overview.

My strong sense is that every potential franchisee should be well-versed in the underlying fundamentals of the franchising industry before he or she commits to the way of life it involves. The better you understand the industry, the better prepared you will be to take maximum advantage of the relationship with your franchisor. There is no doubt that it will also place you in a better position to negotiate the franchise agreement — the conditions of which will dictate every facet of your life as a franchisee for the term of the agreement. The few extra dollars spent on educating yourself could well translate into tens of thousand of dollars to the bottom line in the years ahead.

In addition to general franchising publications, we have included several special interest books that relate to specific, but critical, parts of the start-up and on-going management process — site selection, hiring and managing minimum wage employees, preparing accurate cash flow projections, developing comprehensive business and/or marketing plans, etc. Also included are several

audio tapes and software packages that we feel represent good values.

We have also attempted to make the purchasing process easier by allowing readers to purchase the books directly from Source Book Publications, either via our 800-line or our website. All of the books are currently available in inventory and are generally sent the same day an order is received. A 15% discount is available on all orders over $100.00. See page 46 for an order form. Your complete satisfaction is 100% guaranteed on all books.

Background/Evaluation

Franchise Bible: A Comprehensive Guide, 3rd Edit., Keup, Oasis Press. 1996. 314 pp. $24.95.

This recently updated classic is equally useful for prospective franchisees and franchisors alike. The comprehensive guide and workbook explain in detail what the franchise system entails and the precise benefits it offers. The book features the new franchise laws that became effective January, 1995. To assist the prospective franchisee in rating a potential franchisor, Keup provides necessary checklists and forms. Also noted are the franchisor's contractual obligations to the franchisee and what the franchisee should expect from the franchisor in the way of services and support.

How to Buy and Manage a Franchise, Mancuso and Boroian, Simon & Schuster. 1993. 287 pp. $11.00.

If your objective is to either be your own boss or to expand a business you already own, you should seriously consider franchising. The authors share their expert advice on purchasing, owning and operating a franchise. Keen insights into the mechanics and advantages of franchising. Good starter book.

Tips & Traps When Buying a Franchise, Revised 2nd Edition, Tomzack, Source Book Publications. 1999. 236 pp. $19.95.

Many a green franchisee is shocked to discover that the road to success in franchising is full of hidden costs, inflated revenue promises, reneged marketing support and worse. In this candid, hard-hitting book, Tomzack steers potential franchisees around the pitfalls and guides them in making a smart, lucrative purchase. Topics include: matching a franchise with personal finances and lifestyle, avoiding the five most common pitfalls, choosing a prime location, asking the right questions, etc.

Franchising 101, Dugan, Upstart Publishing Company. 1998. 267 pp. $22.95.

A thoughtful, thorough guide that offers indispensable advice on everything you need to know about evaluating, buying and growing a franchise — from choosing the right franchise to handling taxes and banks to keep records. It will help you evaluate your needs and your personality in order to determine the type of franchise that will make you happy — and prosperous — for the long term. You'll also learn how to scout for a franchise company that is a leader within the strong, vibrant and growing franchise industry. This book offers valuable guidance and support from respected professionals in the franchising industry.

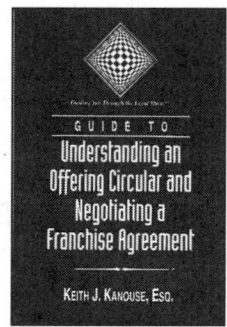

Understanding an Offering Circular and Negotiating a Franchise Agreement, Kanouse, Professional Press. 1995. 159 pp. $21.95.

Allows you to better understand and evaluate the information in the franchisor's Uniform Franchise Offering Circular (UFOC). Discusses 62 legal and business issues which should be "negotiated" in a franchise agreement to make it fairer from a franchisee's standpoint. With an understanding of the key underlying issues, you will be better able to communicate with your own franchise attorney.

Databases

Franchisor Database, Source Book Publications. (800) 841-0873/(510) 839-5471.

Listing of over 2,300 active North American franchisors. 23 fields of information per company:

full address, telephone/800/fax numbers, Internet address, contact/title/salutation, president/title/salutation, # of franchised units, # of company-owned units, # total units, IFA/CFA Member, etc. 54 industry categories. Unlimited use. Guaranteed deliverability — $0.50 rebate for any returned mail. $550 for initial database, $75 per quarter for updates. See page 186 for details.

Directories

Bond's Franchise Guide — 2001 Edition, Bond, Source Book Publications, 2001. 496 pp. $29.95.

The definitive and most comprehensive franchising directory available. Over 2,150 listings, including over 1,050 detailed franchisor profiles resulting from an exhaustive 40-point questionnaire. 45 distinct business categories. Excellent industry overview.

Bond's Minority Franchise Guide — 2000 Edition, Bond, Source Book Publications, 2000. 272 pp. $19.95.

The only minority franchising directory! Contains detailed profiles and company logos of over 400 forward-looking franchisors that encourage and actively support the inclusion of minority franchisees. It also includes a listing of resources available to prospective minority franchisees.

Earnings Claims

"How Much Can I Make?", Bond, Source Book Publications. 2000. 476 pp. $29.95.

The single most important task for a prospective investor is to prepare a realistic cash flow statement that accurately reflects the economic poten-

tial of that business. *"How Much Can I Make?"* is an invaluable "insider's guide" that details historical sales, expense and/or profit data on actual franchise operations, **as provide by the franchisors themselves**. Whether you plan to buy a franchise or start your own business, these actual performance statistics will ensure that you have a realistic starting point in determining how much you can expect to make in a similar business. 140 current Earnings Claims Statements, in their entirety, are included for 33 major industry categories. Unfortunately, less than 15% of franchisors provide such projections/guidelines to prospective franchisees. *"How Much Can I Make?"* includes roughly half of the total universe of earnings claim statements available. The list of companies included runs from the McDonald's and Subways of the world to newer, smaller franchises with only a few operating units. Any serious investor would be short-sighted not to take full advantage of this extra-ordinary resource.

General

Guide to Negotiating a Business Lease, Kanouse, Professional Press. 1995. 167 pp. $15.95.

This book clearly defines words and phrases unique to leases that will enable you to communicate with your landlord, leasing agent and attorney in an educated manner. It also includes 77 lease provisions that might need to be renegotiated in your best interest and "tenant-oriented" business lease forms. In addition, the book addresses the special issues involved in sub-leasing from a franchisor.

Guide to Selecting the Best Entity to Own and Operate Your Business, Kanouse, Professional Press. 1995. 139 pp. $15.95.

Clearly explains the differences between joint ventures, sole proprietorships, general partnerships, "C" corps, "S" corps, etc. Learn the advantages and disadvantages of these and many more organizational forms from a formation, tax, liability and management perspective. Understand complex financial, business and legal words and phrases. Extremely valuable in forming your business.

How to Really Create a Successful Marketing Plan, Gumpert, Inc., Business Resources. 319 pp. $19.95.

By examining the actual marketing plans of many "hot" companies, you'll learn practical steps for developing a winning plan, including the wisdom of: targeting the right market, staying current with your competition, communicating with your market, developing and executing your budget, linking your marketing plan to your business plan and maximizing your marketing efforts. Real experience-based advice.

How to Really Start Your Own Business, Gumpert, Inc., Business Resources. 278 pp. $19.95.

Takes you step-by-step through the launch process, exploring questions like: where do the best, most viable launch ideas come from; what kind of legal protection do entrepreneurs need; how to attract the best employees on start-up budgets; and how to create cash flow projections that are on target. Packed with eye-opening detailed worksheets that allow you to assess launch ideas, evaluate market potential, determine needs, projections, financing. Includes worksheets/forms.

International Franchising

International Herald Tribune International Franchise Guide, Bond/Thompson, Source Book Publications. 1999. 192 pp. $34.95.

This annual publication, sponsored by the International Herald Tribune, is the definitive guide to international franchising. It lists comprehensive, in-depth profiles of major franchisors who are committed (not just the usual lip service) to promote and support overseas expansion. Details specific geographic areas of desired expansion for each company, country by country — as well as the number of units in each foreign country as of the date of publication. Geared specifically to the needs and requirements of prospective international area developers, master franchisees and investors. Investors must be prepared to assume responsibility for the development of large geographic areas. Also listed are international franchise consultants, attorneys and service providers. Covers 32 distinct business categories.

Ranking of Franchises

Bond's Top 50 Food-Service Franchises, Bond/Schiller, Source Book Publications, 2000. 288 pp. $19.95

In response to the constantly asked question, *"What are the best franchises?"*, Bond's new book focuses on the top 50 franchises. Over 500 food-service systems were evaluated for inclusion. Companies were analyzed on the basis of historical performance, brand identification, market dynamics, franchisee satisfaction, the level of training and on-going support, financial stability, etc. Detailed four to five page profiles on each company, as well as key statistics and industry overview. All companies are proven performers and most have a national presence. Excellent starting point for someone focusing on the food-service industry.

Bond's Top 50 Service-Based Franchises, Bond/Schiller, Source Book Publications, 2000. 300 pp. $19.95

In response to the constantly asked question, *"What are the best franchises?"*, Bond's new book focuses on the top 50 franchises. Over 400 service-based systems were evaluated for inclusion. Companies were analyzed on the basis of historical performance, brand identification, market dynamics, franchisee satisfaction, the level of training and on-going support, financial stability, etc. Detailed four to five page profiles on each company, as well as key statistics and industry overview. All companies are proven performers and most have a national presence. Excellent starting point for someone focusing on the service-based industry.

Site Selection

Location, Location, Location: How to Select the Best Site for Your Business, Salvaneschi, Oasis Press. 1996. 280 pp. $19.95.

Whether you are searching for a new business site or relocating an existing business, you have the power to dramatically increase your profits

by choosing the right location. For any business that depends on a customer's ability to find it, location is the most important ingredient for success. Learn how to: spot the essential characteristics of the best location; understand why and how people move from one point to another; analyze and learn from your competitor's business; and learn about the retail trading zone and how to use it to capture the most customers.

Other Franchise Publications

Franchise Times, Restaurant Finance Corp., 2500 Cleveland Ave., North, # D-South, Roseville, MN 55113; (651) 631-4995; FAX (651) 633-8749.

Published 10 times per year, *Franchise Times* magazine focuses on the issues multi-unit franchisees and franchisors need to take their businesses to the next level. Issues such as financing (where is it; who's doing it), real estate (tips for site selection, leases, etc.) and legal issues are tackled. The magazine also highlights successful franchisees and franchisors. In these profiles, the reveal how they have grown their companies to be large franchise businesses and discuss the problems they have conquered along the way. Along with those profiles, *Franchise Times* covers the constantly changing relationship between franchisors and franchisees; how they offer support to each other and conversely the never-ending legal battles that sometimes ensue. The franchise owner survey and the top 200 franchise businesses are eagerly anticipated issues.

The Franchise Bookstore
Order Form

Call (800) 841-0873 or (510) 839-5471; or FAX (510) 839-2104

Item #	Title	Price	Qty.	Total

Basic postage (1 Book)	$5.00
Each additional book add $4.00	
California tax @ 8.25% (if CA resident)	
Total due in U.S. dollars	
Deduct 15% if total due is over $100.00	
Net amount due in U.S. dollars	

Please include credit card number and expiration date for all charge card orders! Checks should be made payable to Source Book Publications. All prices are in U.S. dollars.

Mailing Information: All books shipped by USPS Priority Mail (2nd Day Air). Please print clearly and include your phone number in case we need to contact you. Postage and handling rates are for shipping within the U.S. Please call for international rates.

Name: _____

Company: _____

Address: _____

City: _____

❑ Check enclosed or

Charge my:

❑ MasterCard   ❑ VISA

Card #: _____

Expiration Date: _____

Signature: _____

Title: _____

Telephone No.: (____)_____

State/Prov.: _____ Zip:_____

Special Offer — Save 15%

If your total order above exceeds $100.00, deduct 15% from your bill.

Please send order to:
Source Book Publications
P.O. Box 12488, Oakland, CA 94604
Satisfaction Guaranteed. If not fully satisfied, return for a prompt, 100% refund.

AUTOMOTIVE PRODUCTS & SERVICES INDUSTRY PROFILE

Total # Franchisors in Industry Group	151
Total # Franchised Units in Industry Group	22,262
Total # Company-Owned Units in Industry Group	2,257
Total # Operating Units in Industry Group	24,521
Average # Franchised Units/Franchisor	147.4
Average # Company-Owned Units/Franchisor	14.9
Average # Total Units/Franchisor	162.3
Ratio of Total # Franchised Units/Total # Company-Owned Units	9.9:1
Industry Survey Participants	74
Representing % of Industry	49.0%
Average Franchise Fee*:	$22.7K
Average Total Investment*:	$207.5K
Average On-Going Royalty Fee*:	5.7%

If a range was provided, the mid-point of the range was used. See detailed profiles for actual ranges.

FIVE LARGEST PARTICIPANTS IN SURVEY

Company	# Fran-chised Units	# Co-Owned Units	# Total Units	Franchise Fee	On-Going Royalty	Total Investment
1. Midas Auto Service Experts	2,712	1	2,713	20K	10%	298-428K
2. Novus	2,510	2	2,512	8.4-20K	5-6%	25-142K
3. Custom Auto Restoration	841	257	1,098	N/A	0%	1-10K
4. Meineke Discount Mufflers	859	8	867	25K	2.5-7%	140-250K
5. AAMCO Transmissions	712	2	714	30K	7%	200K

All of the data provided are proprietary and should not be quoted without acknowledging *Bond's Franchise Guide.*

AAMCO TRANSMISSIONS
One Presidential Blvd.
Bala Cynwyd, PA 19004
Tel: (800) 523-0402 (610) 668-2900
Fax: (610) 617-9532
E-Mail: franchise@aamco.com
Web Site: www.aamco.com
Mr. Bob Castellani, Director Franchise Development

AAMCO is the world's largest chain of transmission specialists with 37 years' experience as the undisputed industry leader. An American icon, AAMCO's trademark is recognized by 94% of the driving public.

BACKGROUND: IFA MEMBER
Established: 1963; 1st Franchised: 1963
Franchised Units: 712
Company-Owned Units: 2
Total Units: 714
Dist.: US-685; CAN-29; O'seas-0
North America: 48 States, 4 Provinces
Density: 101 in CA, 61 in FL, 44 NY
Projected New Units (12 Months): 40
Qualifications: 4, 4, 3, 3, 4, 4
Registered: All States
FINANCIAL/TERMS:
Cash Investment: $75K
Total Investment: $200K
Minimum Net Worth: $250K
Fees: Franchise - $30K
Royalty - 7%; Ad. - Varies
Earnings Claim Statement: Yes
Term of Contract (Years): 15/15
Avg. # Of Employees: 4 FT, 1 PT
Passive Ownership: Not Allowed
Encourage Conversions: Yes
Area Develop. Agreements: No
Sub-Franchising Contracts: No
Expand In Territory: Yes
Space Needs: 4,000 SF; FS, SF, Auto Mall
SUPPORT & TRAINING PROVIDED:
Financial Assistance Provided: Yes(I)
Site Selection Assistance: Yes
Lease Negotiation Assistance: Yes
Co-Operative Advertising: No
Franchisee Assoc./Member: Yes/No

Size Of Corporate Staff: 180
On-Going Support: A,B,C,D,E,G,H,I
Training: 5 Weeks Home Office, Philadelphia, PA.
SPECIFIC EXPANSION PLANS:
US: NE, Great Lakes Region
Canada: All Canada
Overseas: No

≺≺ ≻≻

ABRA AUTO BODY & GLASS
6601 Shingle Creek Pkwy., # 200
Brooklyn Center, MN 55430
Tel: (800) 536-2334 (612) 585-6289
Fax: (612) 561-7433
E-Mail: earl@abraauto.com
Web Site: www.abraauto.com
Mr. Earl W. Farr, VP Corporate Development

One of the first automobile collision and glass franchises. Operating company and franchised auto body collision and auto glass replacement shops. We offer support with marketing, business management, equipment and material purchases. Investment opportunities for qualifying owners and managers.

BACKGROUND:
Established: 1984; 1st Franchised: 1987
Franchised Units: 36
Company-Owned Units: 18
Total Units: 54
Dist.: US-54; CAN-0; O'seas-0
North America: 12 States
Density: 28 in MN, 7 in TN, 6 in WI
Projected New Units (12 Months): 12
Qualifications: 5, 5, 5, 3, 3, 5
Registered: IL,IN,MI,MN,ND,SD,WI
FINANCIAL/TERMS:
Cash Investment: $60-100K
Total Investment: $229.6-422.6K
Minimum Net Worth: $500K
Fees: Franchise - $22.5K
Royalty - 5%; Ad. - 3%
Earnings Claim Statement: Yes
Term of Contract (Years): 10/10
Avg. # Of Employees: NR
Passive Ownership: Allowed
Encourage Conversions: Yes
Area Develop. Agreements: Yes/Varies
Sub-Franchising Contracts: No
Expand In Territory: Yes
Space Needs: 8,000-15,000 SF; FS, SF
SUPPORT & TRAINING PROVIDED:
Financial Assistance Provided: No
Site Selection Assistance: Yes

Lease Negotiation Assistance: Yes
Co-Operative Advertising: N/A
Franchisee Assoc./Member: NR
Size Of Corporate Staff: 53
On-Going Support: a,B,C,D,E,F,g,h,I
Training: 2-4 Weeks ABRA Training Center, Minneapolis, MN; 6 Weeks On-Site.
SPECIFIC EXPANSION PLANS:
US: Central, South, Southeast
Canada: No
Overseas: No

≺≺ ≻≻

ACTIVE GREEN + ROSS TIRE & AUTOMOTIVE CENTRE
580 Evans Ave.
Toronto, ON M8W 2W1 CANADA
Tel: (416) 255-5581
Fax: (416) 255-4793
E-Mail: acttire@idirect.com
Web Site: www.activegreenross.com
Mr. Ralph Chiodo, President

Tire and automotive sales and service. The company currently has locations in Toronto and surrounding area and is one of the largest independent groups of tire and automotive service centres in Canada. Company operations began in 1982. Franchised first outlet in 1983; Training provided for up to 2 months; Dealers elect representatives on Dealer Advisory Committee.

BACKGROUND:
Established: 1982; 1st Franchised: 1983
Franchised Units: 25
Company-Owned Units: 5
Total Units: 30
Dist.: US-0; CAN-29; O'seas-0
North America: 1 Province
Density: 29 in ON
Projected New Units (12 Months): NR
Qualifications: 4, 4, 4, 4, 4, 4
Registered: None
FINANCIAL/TERMS:
Cash Investment: $NR
Total Investment: $115-200K
Minimum Net Worth: $250K
Fees: Franchise - $25K
Royalty - 5%; Ad. - 2.5%
Earnings Claim Statement: No
Term of Contract (Years): 5/5
Avg. # Of Employees: 4+ FT
Passive Ownership: Not Allowed
Encourage Conversions: Yes
Area Develop. Agreements: No

Sub-Franchising Contracts: Yes
Expand In Territory: Yes
Space Needs: 3,000-5,000 SF; NR
SUPPORT & TRAINING PROVIDED:
Financial Assistance Provided: Yes(I)
Site Selection Assistance: Yes
Lease Negotiation Assistance: N/A
Co-Operative Advertising: Yes
Franchisee Assoc./Member: Yes
Size Of Corporate Staff: 9
On-Going Support: NR
Training: Head Office and On-Site.
SPECIFIC EXPANSION PLANS:
US: N/A
Canada: ON
Overseas: No

≪ ≫

AERO-COLOURS
6971 Washington Ave. S., # 102
Minneapolis, MN 55439-1508
Tel: (800) 696-2376 (612) 277-0309
Fax: (612) 942-0628
E-Mail: jspellmire@aerocolours.com
Web Site: www.aerocolours.com
Mr. James F. Spellmire, President

AERO-COLOURS is an exclusive mobile automotive paint repair process, providing service to dealerships, fleet operations and individual vehicle owners. Our solid support system, complemented by our industry-leading training, allows our franchisees to provide unmatched service. We will show you how to operate, market and grow your own business.

BACKGROUND: IFA MEMBER
Established: 1985; 1st Franchised: 1993
Franchised Units: 181
Company-Owned Units 51
Total Units: 232
Dist.: US-229; CAN-0; O'seas-3
North America: 28 States
Density: 60 in CA, 15 in TX
Projected New Units (12 Months): 50
Qualifications: 5, 3, 5, 3, 5, 5
Registered: CA,FL,IL,IN,MD,MI,MN, ND,NY,OR,VA,WI
FINANCIAL/TERMS:
Cash Investment: $5-30K
Total Investment: $5-60K
Minimum Net Worth: $100K
Fees: Franchise - $25K
Royalty - 7%; Ad. - 0%

Earnings Claim Statement: No
Term of Contract (Years): 10/10
Avg. # Of Employees: 4-5 FT
Passive Ownership: Allowed
Encourage Conversions: No
Area Develop. Agreements: No
Sub-Franchising Contracts: Yes
Expand In Territory: Yes
Space Needs: 2,000 SF; Warehouse
SUPPORT & TRAINING PROVIDED:
Financial Assistance Provided: Yes(I)
Site Selection Assistance: Yes
Lease Negotiation Assistance: Yes
Co-Operative Advertising: No
Franchisee Assoc./Member: Yes/Yes
Size Of Corporate Staff: 14
On-Going Support: A,B,C,D,E,G,H,I
Training: 2 Weeks Tampa, FL; 2 Weeks Territory.
SPECIFIC EXPANSION PLANS:
US: All United States
Canada: No
Overseas: All Countries

≪ ≫

AIRBAG SERVICE
9675 SE 36th St., # 100
Mercer Island, WA 98040
Tel: (800) 224-7224 (206) 275-4105
Fax: (206) 275-4112
E-Mail: pjsmith@airbagservice.com
Web Site: www.airbagservice.com
Mr. Peter Smith, Nat'l. Marketing Mgr.

Automotive service company, specializing in airbag system repair. Our mobile service supplies a needed expertise to the automotive collision repair industry. Specialized software and tools allow us to work on any system right on site for increased efficiency.

BACKGROUND:
Established: 1992; 1st Franchised: 1995
Franchised Units: 39
Company-Owned Units 1
Total Units: 40
Dist.: US-37; CAN-2; O'seas-0
North America: 20 States, 2 Province
Density: 7 in TX, 4 in CA, 3 in WA
Projected New Units (12 Months): 18
Qualifications: 3, 5, 4, 1, 1, 4
Registered: CA,FL,HI,IL,IN,MD,MI, NY,VA
FINANCIAL/TERMS:
Cash Investment: $50-100K

Total Investment: $50-125K
Minimum Net Worth: $75K
Fees: Franchise - $25-30K
Royalty - 8.5% Net; Ad. - 2% Net
Earnings Claim Statement: No
Term of Contract (Years): 10/5+5
Avg. # Of Employees: 2 FT
Passive Ownership: Discouraged
Encourage Conversions: N/A
Area Develop. Agreements: Yes/10
Sub-Franchising Contracts: No
Expand In Territory: Yes
Space Needs: 1,000 SF; Commercial Office
SUPPORT & TRAINING PROVIDED:
Financial Assistance Provided: Yes(I)
Site Selection Assistance: No
Lease Negotiation Assistance: No
Co-Operative Advertising: Yes
Franchisee Assoc./Member: No
Size Of Corporate Staff: 10
On-Going Support: C,D,G,H,I
Training: 3 Weeks Seattle, WA.
SPECIFIC EXPANSION PLANS:
US: All United States
Canada: No
Overseas: No

≪ ≫

ALTA MERE COMPLETE AUTO IMAGING
4444 W. 147th St.
Midlothian, IL 60445
Tel: (800) 377-9247 (708) 389-5922
Fax: (708) 389-9882
E-Mail: vsmithson@moranindustries.com
Web Site: www.moranindustries.com
Ms. Virginia Smithson, Qualification Specialist

ALTA MERE offers complete auto imaging; window tinting, auto security, cellular phones, beepers and auto accessories. This specialty division of Moran Industries franchises complete auto imaging service centers throughout the US. We offer our franchisees a superior business system, strong brand name, customized marketing and a service that is in strong demand. Our exclusive business system, along with the skills of our franchisees, create customer experiences that result in satisfaction and loyalty.

BACKGROUND: IFA MEMBER
Established: 1993; 1st Franchised: 1993
Franchised Units: 36
Company-Owned Units 1
Total Units: 37

Dist.: US-37; CAN-0; O'seas-0
North America: 9 States
Density: 15 in TX, 7 in OK, 4 in AK
Projected New Units (12 Months): 12
Qualifications: 4, 3, 1, 2, 4, 5
Registered: IL

FINANCIAL/TERMS:
Cash Investment: $35-40K
Total Investment: $93K
Minimum Net Worth: $90K
Fees: Franchise - $27.5K
Royalty - 7%; Ad. - $100/Mo.
Earnings Claim Statement: Yes
Term of Contract (Years): 20/20
Avg. # Of Employees: 3 FT
Passive Ownership: Discouraged
Encourage Conversions: Yes
Area Develop. Agreements: Yes
Sub-Franchising Contracts: No
Expand In Territory: Yes
Space Needs: 2,500 SF; FS, SF, SC, RM

SUPPORT & TRAINING PROVIDED:
Financial Assistance Provided: Yes(I)
Site Selection Assistance: Yes
Lease Negotiation Assistance: Yes
Co-Operative Advertising: Yes
Franchisee Assoc./Member: Yes/Yes
Size Of Corporate Staff: 55
On-Going Support: A,C,D,E,G,H,I
Training: Training is provided.

SPECIFIC EXPANSION PLANS:
US: All United States
Canada: No
Overseas: No

◁◁ ▷▷

ALTRACOLOR SYSTEMS
P.O. Box 2124
Kenner, LA 70063
Tel: (800) 678-5220
Fax: (504) 454-7233
E-Mail: altra@home.com
Web Site: www.altracolor.com
Mr. Jeff Richards, President

ALTRACOLOR SYSTEMS is the state-of-the-art mobile, on-site touch-up and spot repair system for automotive paint repair.

BACKGROUND: IFA MEMBER
Established: 1988; 1st Franchised: 1991
Franchised Units: 82
Company-Owned Units 92

Total Units: 174
Dist.: US-174; CAN-0; O'seas-0
North America: 27 States
Density: 14 in NC, 13 in VA, 13 in SC
Projected New Units (12 Months): 23
Qualifications: 3, 3, 1, 1, 2, 4
Registered: CA,FL,IN,MI,MN,NY,OR, VA,WA,WI,DC

FINANCIAL/TERMS:
Cash Investment: $5-11.7K
Total Investment: $16.9-25.2K
Minimum Net Worth: $N/A
Fees: Franchise - $9.95K
Royalty - $95/Wk.; Ad. - 0%
Earnings Claim Statement: Yes
Term of Contract (Years): 15/5
Avg. # Of Employees: 1 FT
Passive Ownership: Not Allowed
Encourage Conversions: Yes
Area Develop. Agreements: Yes/15
Sub-Franchising Contracts: Yes
Expand In Territory: Yes
Space Needs: N/A SF; Mobile Bus

SUPPORT & TRAINING PROVIDED:
Financial Assistance Provided: Yes(D)
Site Selection Assistance: N/A
Lease Negotiation Assistance: N/A
Co-Operative Advertising: N/A
Franchisee Assoc./Member: No
Size Of Corporate Staff: 5
On-Going Support: C,D,G,H,I
Training: 1 Week in Metairie, LA.

SPECIFIC EXPANSION PLANS:
US: All United States
Canada: No
Overseas: No

◁◁ ▷▷

AMERICAN BRAKE SERVICE
1325 Franklin Ave., # 165
Garden City, NY 11530
Tel: (800) TILDENS (516) 746-7911
Fax: (516) 746-1288
E-Mail: info@tildencarcare.com
Web Site: www.tildencarcare.com
Mr. Jason Basking, Director Franchise Development

We're not just brakes. The total care concept allows you to offer a full menu of automotive services for maximum customer procurement - rather than a limited niche market. You benefit from a management team whose concept system and training were proven and perfected before we even considered offering franchises.

BACKGROUND:
Established: 1923; 1st Franchised: 1996
Franchised Units: 60
Company-Owned Units 0
Total Units: 60
Dist.: US-60; CAN-0; O'seas-0
North America: 13 States
Density: 24 in FL, 15 in NY, 6 in GA
Projected New Units (12 Months): 10
Qualifications: 3, 4, 3, 3, 3, 4
Registered: CA,FL,IL,IN,MN,NY,VA,WA

FINANCIAL/TERMS:
Cash Investment: $50-60K
Total Investment: $131-171K
Minimum Net Worth: $150K
Fees: Franchise - $25K
Royalty - 6%/$350/Wk.; Ad. - 3%/$175/Wk.
Earnings Claim Statement: No
Term of Contract (Years): 10/5/5
Avg. # Of Employees: 4 FT, 2 PT
Passive Ownership: Discouraged
Encourage Conversions: Yes
Area Develop. Agreements: Yes/10
Sub-Franchising Contracts: No
Expand In Territory: Yes
Space Needs: 3,500 SF; FS, Auto Mall

SUPPORT & TRAINING PROVIDED:
Financial Assistance Provided: Yes(I)
Site Selection Assistance: Yes
Lease Negotiation Assistance: Yes
Co-Operative Advertising: Yes
Franchisee Assoc./Member: Yes/Yes
Size Of Corporate Staff: 4
On-Going Support: C,d,E,F,G,H,I
Training: 2 Weeks Home Office.

SPECIFIC EXPANSION PLANS:
US: All United States
Canada: All Canada
Overseas: No

◁◁ ▷▷

AMERICAN TRANSMISSIONS
340 N. Main, # 207
Plymouth, MI 48170-1237
Tel: (734) 459-3104
Fax: (734) 459-1836
Mr. John F. Folino, President

We offer specialty transmission repair facilities for autos and trucks. We also provide complete training for new franchisees, as well as full home office support.

BACKGROUND:
Established: 1981; 1st Franchised: 1985

Franchised Units: 6
Company-Owned Units: 0
Total Units: 6
Dist.: US-6; CAN-0; O'seas-0
 North America: 1 State
 Density: 6 in MI
Projected New Units (12 Months): 4
Qualifications: 4, 4, 3, 3, 3, 5
Registered: FL,MI

FINANCIAL/TERMS:

Cash Investment: $40K
Total Investment: $80-120K
Minimum Net Worth: $200K
Fees: Franchise - $25K
 Royalty - 7%; Ad. - 3%/$400/Wk.
Earnings Claim Statement: No
Term of Contract (Years): 15/15
Avg. # Of Employees: 5 FT, 1 PT
Passive Ownership: Not Allowed
Encourage Conversions: Yes
Area Develop. Agreements: No
Sub-Franchising Contracts: No
Expand In Territory: Yes
Space Needs: 3,200 SF; FS

SUPPORT & TRAINING PROVIDED:

Financial Assistance Provided: Yes(I)
Site Selection Assistance: Yes
Lease Negotiation Assistance: Yes
Co-Operative Advertising: Yes
Franchisee Assoc./Member: Yes/Yes
Size Of Corporate Staff: 5
On-Going Support: A,C,D,E,F,G,H,I
Training: 14 Days Home Office, Plymouth, MI.

SPECIFIC EXPANSION PLANS:

US: MI,FL
Canada: No
Overseas: No

≪ ≫

APPLE AUTO GLASS

360 Applewood Crescent
Concord, ON L4K 4V2 CANADA
Tel: (905) 669-7800
Fax: (905) 669-7821
Web Site: www.tcgi.com/apple
Mr. Calvin Hughes, President

APPLE AUTO GLASS is a Canadian franchise network specializing in automotive glass replacement and stone chip repair, the repair of automotive upholstery, and the sale and installation of vehicle accessories. Franchisees benefit by joining an established network with national name recognition, national and local marketing programs, purchasing strength and the ability to increase sales through new products and services.

BACKGROUND:

Established: 1983; 1st Franchised: 1983
Franchised Units: 126
Company-Owned Units: 2
Total Units: 128
Dist.: US-0; CAN-128; O'seas-0
 North America: 8 Provinces
 Density: 86 in ON, 12 in NS, 11 in NB
Projected New Units (12 Months): 5
Qualifications: 4, 4, 5, 3, 3, 4
Registered: AB

FINANCIAL/TERMS:

Cash Investment: $40-60K
Total Investment: $65-95K
Minimum Net Worth: $75K
Fees: Franchise - $5K
 Royalty - 5%; Ad. - 2.5%
Earnings Claim Statement: No
Term of Contract (Years): 10/10
Avg. # Of Employees: 3 FT
Passive Ownership: Discouraged
Encourage Conversions: Yes
Area Develop. Agreements: No
Sub-Franchising Contracts: No
Expand In Territory: Yes
Space Needs: 2,500 SF; SC

SUPPORT & TRAINING PROVIDED:

Financial Assistance Provided: Yes(I)
Site Selection Assistance: Yes
Lease Negotiation Assistance: Yes
Co-Operative Advertising: Yes
Franchisee Assoc./Member: Yes/No
Size Of Corporate Staff: 23
On-Going Support: a,B,d,e,G,h,I
Training: Head Office for Varied Duration.

SPECIFIC EXPANSION PLANS:

US: No
Canada: Western Canada
Overseas: No

≪ ≫

AUTO ACCENT CENTERS

6550 Pearl Rd.
Parma Heights, OH 44130
Tel: (800) 567-3120 (440) 888-8886
Fax: (440) 888-4333
Mr. Walter E. Poston, VP Franchising

AUTO ACCENTS specializes in the sales and installation of the most in-demand automotive after-market products, such as cellular phones, pagers, alarms, stereos, sunroofs, auto and truck accessories (including auto dealership on-site installation).

BACKGROUND:

Established: 1985; 1st Franchised: 1992

Franchised Units: 5
Company-Owned Units: 7
Total Units: 12
Dist.: US-12; CAN-0; O'seas-0
 North America: 1 State
 Density: 10 in OH
Projected New Units (12 Months): 15
Qualifications: 4, 4, 3, 3, 1, 5
Registered: NR

FINANCIAL/TERMS:

Cash Investment: $50K
Total Investment: $70-120K
Minimum Net Worth: $250K
Fees: Franchise - $14.9K
 Royalty - 5%; Ad. - 1%
Earnings Claim Statement: No
Term of Contract (Years): 10/10
Avg. # Of Employees: 3 FT, 1 PT
Passive Ownership: Discouraged
Encourage Conversions: Yes
Area Develop. Agreements: Yes/Negot.
Sub-Franchising Contracts: No
Expand In Territory: No
Space Needs: 2,000-2,500 SF; FS, SC

SUPPORT & TRAINING PROVIDED:

Financial Assistance Provided: Yes
Site Selection Assistance: Yes
Lease Negotiation Assistance: Yes
Co-Operative Advertising: Yes
Franchisee Assoc./Member: No
Size Of Corporate Staff: 25
On-Going Support: A,B,C,D,E,F,G,H,I
Training: 2 Weeks Corporate Headquarters; 1 Week On-Site.

SPECIFIC EXPANSION PLANS:

US: All U.S. (OH and Bordering)
Canada: No
Overseas: No

≪ ≫

AUTO-LAB DIAGNOSTIC & TUNE-UP CENTERS

1050 W. Columbia Ave.
Battle Creek, MI 49015
Tel: (877) 349-4968 (616) 966-0500
Fax: (616) 966-0520
Web Site: www.AutoLabusa.com
Mr. Daniel J. Kiefer, President

Full service automotive repair facility, performing all aspects of auto service and repair. Our specialty is in the diagnostics and repair of computerized and electrical systems. Our goal is to be a professional alternative to auto dealer repair shops.

BACKGROUND:

Established: 1984; 1st Franchised: 1989
Franchised Units: 25

Company-Owned Units   1
Total Units: 26
Dist.:   US-40; CAN-0; O'seas-0
  North America: 2 States
  Density: 25 in MI, 1 in OH
Projected New Units (12 Months):   18
Qualifications: 3, 2, 3, 3, 2, 5
Registered: IN,MI
FINANCIAL/TERMS:
Cash Investment: $35-75K
Total Investment: $110-175K
Minimum Net Worth: $250K
Fees: Franchise - $19.5K
  Royalty - 6%;   Ad. - 3%
Earnings Claim Statement: No
Term of Contract (Years):   15/15
Avg. # Of Employees: 5 FT, 1 PT
Passive Ownership: Discouraged
Encourage Conversions: Yes
Area Develop. Agreements: Yes/15
Sub-Franchising Contracts: No
Expand In Territory: Yes
Space Needs: 3,000+ SF; FS
SUPPORT & TRAINING PROVIDED:
Financial Assistance Provided: No
Site Selection Assistance: Yes
Lease Negotiation Assistance: Yes
Co-Operative Advertising: Yes
Franchisee Assoc./Member: No
Size Of Corporate Staff: 10
On-Going Support: a,b,C,D,E,G,H,I
Training: 2 Weeks Grand Rapids, MI; 2-4
  Weeks Battle Creek, MI.
SPECIFIC EXPANSION PLANS:
US: MW & E to Gulf of Mexico
Canada: All Canada
Overseas: All Countries

≪ ≫

BATTERIES PLUS
925 Walnut Ridge Dr., # 100
Hartland, WI 53029
Tel: (800) 274-9155 (262) 369-0690
Fax: (262) 369-0680
E-Mail: batplus@batteriesplus.com
Web Site: www.batteriesplus.com
Mr.   Richard   Zimmerman,   Director
  Franchise Marketing

BATTERIES PLUS is America's Battery
Store, providing 1,000's of batteries for
1,000's of items, serving both retail and
commercial customers. The $17 billion
battery market, growing 6% annually,
is driven by technology and lifestyles.
BATTERIES   PLUS   is   a   unique
opportunity in this growth industry not yet
saturated with competitors. Our turn-key
program includes a unique store design,
graphics, signage and product brands and
proven operating methods.

BACKGROUND: IFA MEMBER
Established: 1988;   1st Franchised: 1992
Franchised Units: 218
Company-Owned Units   20
Total Units: 238
Dist.:   US-238; CAN-0; O'seas-0
  North America: 33 States
  Density: 17 in WI, 16 in MN, 15 in MI
Projected New Units (12 Months):   36
Qualifications: 5, 5, 2, 3, 2, 3
Registered: All Except HI
FINANCIAL/TERMS:
Cash Investment: $100-150K
Total Investment: $185-225K
Minimum Net Worth: $300K
Fees: Franchise - $25K
  Royalty - 4%;   Ad. - 1%
Earnings Claim Statement: No
Term of Contract (Years):   15
Avg. # Of Employees: 3-4 FT
Passive Ownership: Not Allowed
Encourage Conversions: No
Area Develop. Agreements: Yes
Sub-Franchising Contracts: No
Expand In Territory: No
Space Needs: 1,800-2,000 SF; FS, SC
SUPPORT & TRAINING PROVIDED:
Financial Assistance Provided: Yes(I)
Site Selection Assistance: Yes
Lease Negotiation Assistance: Yes
Co-Operative Advertising: No
Franchisee Assoc./Member: No
Size Of Corporate Staff: 39
On-Going Support: C,D,E,F,G,h,I
Training: 3 Weeks Corporate Training
  Center; 2 Weeks On-Site Franchisee's
  Store.
SPECIFIC EXPANSION PLANS:
US: SW,SC,W,NE,SE
Canada: No
Overseas: No

≪ ≫

BIG BOYZ TOYS
13180 N. Cleveland Ave.
North Fort Myers, FL 33903
Tel: (800) 347-9482 (941) 945-0101
Fax: (941) 540-9770

Web Site: www.autotoysonline.com
Ms. Debbie Olievera, Vice President

BIG BOYZ TOYS is the only full-service
franchise auto accessories store nationwide
with over 9 years experience as one of the
undisputed auto accessories leaders. They
have full one-stop shopping for all your
custom auto accessory needs and parts in
the U.S. This is a 32 billion dollar industry.

BACKGROUND:
Established: 1990;   1st Franchised: 1994
Franchised Units: 14
Company-Owned Units   1
Total Units: 15
Dist.:   US-15; CAN-0; O'seas-0
  North America: 14 States
  Density: 2 in FL, 1 in NY, 1 in NJ
Projected New Units (12 Months):   12
Qualifications: 5, 2, 1, 4, 4, 3
Registered: CA,FL,IL,IN,MD,MI,MN,NY,
  ND,OR,RI,SD,VA,WA,WI,DC
FINANCIAL/TERMS:
Cash Investment: $12K
Total Investment: $60-80K
Minimum Net Worth: $100K
Fees: Franchise - $17K
  Royalty - 5%;   Ad. - 2%
Earnings Claim Statement: Yes
Term of Contract (Years):   5/5/5
Avg. # Of Employees: 2 FT, 1 PT
Passive Ownership: Not Allowed
Encourage Conversions: Yes
Area Develop. Agreements: No
Sub-Franchising Contracts: Yes
Expand In Territory: Yes
Space Needs: 1,300-2,000 SF; SC
SUPPORT & TRAINING PROVIDED:
Financial Assistance Provided: Yes(I)
Site Selection Assistance: Yes
Lease Negotiation Assistance: Yes
Co-Operative Advertising: Yes
Franchisee Assoc./Member: Yes/Yes
Size Of Corporate Staff: 11
On-Going Support: A,B,D,E,F,I
Training: 2   Weeks   at   Corporate
  Headquarters in Ft. Meyers, FL
SPECIFIC EXPANSION PLANS:
US: All United States
Canada: All Canada
Overseas: No

≪ ≫

BIG O TIRES
12650 E. Briarwood Ave. # 2D
Englewood, CO 80112
Tel: (800) 622-2446 (303) 728-5500
Fax: (303) 728-5700

Web Site: www.bigotires.com
Mr. Troy Benson, Franchise Qual. Specialist

BIG O TIRES

BIG O TIRES is the fastest-growing retail tire and under-car service center franchisor in North America. We offer over 30 years' experience and proven success, site selection assistance, comprehensive training and on-going field support, protected territory, exclusive product lines, consistent product supply, unique marketing programs, contemporary building designs, effective advertising support, and proven business systems.

BACKGROUND: IFA MEMBER
Established: 1962; 1st Franchised: 1967	
Franchised Units:	438
Company-Owned Units	16
Total Units:	454
Dist.: US-415; CAN-39; O'seas-0	
North America: 19 States, 1 Province	
Density: 153 in CA, 52 in AZ, 42 CO	
Projected New Units (12 Months):	30
Qualifications:	5, 5, 1, 2, 1, 5
Registered: NR	

FINANCIAL/TERMS:
Cash Investment:	$100K
Total Investment:	$300K
Minimum Net Worth:	$300K
Fees: Franchise -	$25K
Royalty - 2%;	Ad. - 2-4%
Earnings Claim Statement:	No
Term of Contract (Years):	10
Avg. # Of Employees:	6 FT
Passive Ownership:	Discouraged
Encourage Conversions:	Yes
Area Develop. Agreements:	Yes/Varies
Sub-Franchising Contracts:	Yes
Expand In Territory:	Yes
Space Needs: NR SF; FS	

SUPPORT & TRAINING PROVIDED:
Financial Assistance Provided:	Yes(I)
Site Selection Assistance:	Yes
Lease Negotiation Assistance:	Yes
Co-Operative Advertising:	Yes
Franchisee Assoc./Member:	NR
Size Of Corporate Staff:	100
On-Going Support:	A,B,C,d,E,F,G,h,I
Training: 5 Weeks Denver, CO.	

SPECIFIC EXPANSION PLANS:
US:	All United States
Canada:	BC
Overseas:	No

<< >>

BRAKE CENTERS OF AMERICA
35 Old Battery Rd.
Bridgeport, CT 06605
Tel: (203) 336-1995
Fax: (203) 336-1995
E-Mail: brakesusa@aol.com
Web Site: www.infonews.com/franchise/bcoa
Mr. Bill Pelletier, President

True brakes only brake specialist. Eliminate the headaches of operating a "we do everything shop." Do one thing right. This is a great opportunity for the right person cooking for a business in the Northeast.

BACKGROUND:
Established: 1989; 1st Franchised: 1992	
Franchised Units:	0
Company-Owned Units	8
Total Units:	8
Dist.: US-8; CAN-0; O'seas-0	
North America:	1 State
Density:	8 in CT
Projected New Units (12 Months):	6
Qualifications:	3, 3, 2, 2, 3, 3
Registered: NY	

FINANCIAL/TERMS:
Cash Investment:	$50-90K
Total Investment:	$50-100K
Minimum Net Worth:	$Open
Fees: Franchise -	$12K
Royalty - 6%;	Ad. - 4%
Earnings Claim Statement:	No
Term of Contract (Years):	17/10
Avg. # Of Employees:	3 FT, 1 PT
Passive Ownership:	Not Allowed
Encourage Conversions:	Yes
Area Develop. Agreements:	No
Sub-Franchising Contracts:	No
Expand In Territory:	Yes
Space Needs: 2,500 SF; FS, SC	

SUPPORT & TRAINING PROVIDED:
Financial Assistance Provided:	Yes(I)
Site Selection Assistance:	Yes
Lease Negotiation Assistance:	Yes
Co-Operative Advertising:	Yes
Franchisee Assoc./Member:	No
Size Of Corporate Staff:	3
On-Going Support:	a,B,c,d,e,F
Training: 80 Hours in Norwalk, CT.	

SPECIFIC EXPANSION PLANS:
US:	Northeast
Canada:	No
Overseas:	No

<< >>

CAR WASH GUYS/GALS, THE
74478 Highway 111, PMB 378
Palm Desert, CA 92260
Tel: (800) 879-TRUE (818) 519-9344
Fax: (888) WASH-GAL
E-Mail: lance@carwashguys.com
Web Site: www.carwashguys.com
Mr. Lance Winslow, III, President/CEO

Mobile car wash - biggest on the planet - with most experience in the world and looking to dominate and conquer markets. We only take winners. You may not qualify - you must prove you are good enough.

BACKGROUND:
Established: 1979; 1st Franchised: 1997	
Franchised Units:	90
Company-Owned Units	60
Total Units:	150
Dist.: US-146; CAN-2; O'seas-2	
North America:	NR
Density: 60 in CA, 8 in CO, 7 in FL	
Projected New Units (12 Months):	200
Qualifications:	1, 1, 1, 1, 1, 5
Registered: All States	

FINANCIAL/TERMS:
Cash Investment:	$0-22K
Total Investment:	$50-79K
Minimum Net Worth:	$N/A
Fees: Franchise -	$20K
Royalty - $600;	Ad. - $0-100
Earnings Claim Statement:	Yes
Term of Contract (Years):	5/20
Avg. # Of Employees:	1-5 FT, 2-3 PT
Passive Ownership:	Allowed
Encourage Conversions:	No
Area Develop. Agreements:	No
Sub-Franchising Contracts:	Yes
Expand In Territory:	Yes
Space Needs: N/A SF; N/A	

SUPPORT & TRAINING PROVIDED:
Financial Assistance Provided:	Yes(D)
Site Selection Assistance:	Yes
Lease Negotiation Assistance:	N/A
Co-Operative Advertising:	Yes
Franchisee Assoc./Member:	No
Size Of Corporate Staff:	NR

On-Going Support: A,B,C,D,E,G,h,I
Training: 7-10 Days in Denver, CO; 7-10
   Days in Phoenix, AZ; 7-10 Days GA.
SPECIFIC EXPANSION PLANS:
US: West, South, Midwest
Canada: BC,AB,ON
Overseas: Europe, North America,
   Phillipines, Africa, Australia

≪ ≫

CAR-X AUTO SERVICE
8750 Bryn Mawr Ave., # 410 E
Chicago, IL 60631
Tel: (800) 359-2359 (773) 693-1000
Fax: (773) 693-0309
E-Mail: dmaltzman@carx.com
Web Site: www.carx.com
Mr. David Maltzman, Director Franchise
   Sales

Retail automotive specialists providing
service in brakes, exhaust, road handling,
tune-ups, steering systems, air conditioning,
and oil changes for all makes of cars and
light trucks.

BACKGROUND:
Established: 1971;   1st Franchised: 1973
Franchised Units: 133
Company-Owned Units   53
Total Units: 186
Dist.:   US-186; CAN-0; O'seas-0
   North America: 10 States
   Density: 59 in IL, 27 in MN, 23 in MO
Projected New Units (12 Months):   8
Qualifications: 5, 3, 2, 2, 2, 5
Registered: FL,IL,IN,MI,MN,SD,WI
FINANCIAL/TERMS:
Cash Investment: $75-100K
Total Investment: $250-310K
Minimum Net Worth: $250K
Fees: Franchise - $20K
   Royalty - 5%;   Ad. - 5-7%
Earnings Claim Statement: Yes
Term of Contract (Years):   15/5
Avg. # Of Employees: 4 FT
Passive Ownership: Discouraged
Encourage Conversions: Yes
Area Develop. Agreements: No
Sub-Franchising Contracts: No
Expand In Territory: Yes

Space Needs: 5,000 SF; FS
SUPPORT & TRAINING PROVIDED:
Financial Assistance Provided: Yes(I)
Site Selection Assistance: Yes
Lease Negotiation Assistance: Yes
Co-Operative Advertising: No
Franchisee Assoc./Member: Yes/No
Size Of Corporate Staff: 24
On-Going Support: C,D,E,F,G,H,I
Training: 5 Weeks Headquarters; 2 Weeks
   at Franchisee's Shop.
SPECIFIC EXPANSION PLANS:
US: MW,SW,SE
Canada: No
Overseas: No

≪ ≫

CARTEX LIMITED
42816 Mound Rd.
Sterling Heights, MI 48314-3256
Tel: (800) 421-7328 (810) 739-4339
Fax: (810) 739-4331
E-Mail: crismar@aol.com
Ms. Diana Klukowski, Secretary

CARTEX LIMITED, better known as
Fabrion, is a mobile service business,
specializing in automotive interior repair.
The Fabrion repair process electrostatically
repairs auto cloth, velour and carpet. Due to
our specialization, we have revolutionized
auto upholstery repair. Updating on current
(OEM) original equipment materials and
providing the tools to match all current
patterns being used in auto interiors are
our strong points.

BACKGROUND:
Established: 1980;   1st Franchised: 1988
Franchised Units: 85
Company-Owned Units   1
Total Units: 86
Dist.:   US-86; CAN-0; O'seas-0
   North America: 32 States
   Density: 15 in CA, 14 in FL, 8 in OH
Projected New Units (12 Months):   10
Qualifications: 3, 3, 3, 3, 3, 3
Registered: CA,FL,HI,IL,MD,MI,MN,NY,
   OR,VA,WA,DC,AB
FINANCIAL/TERMS:
Cash Investment: $23.5K
Total Investment: $25K
Minimum Net Worth: $N/A
Fees: Franchise - $15-23.5K
   Royalty - $160-300/Mo.;   Ad. - 0%
Earnings Claim Statement: No
Term of Contract (Years):   5/5
Avg. # Of Employees: 6 FT, 1 PT

Passive Ownership: Discouraged
Encourage Conversions: Yes
Area Develop. Agreements: No
Sub-Franchising Contracts: No
Expand In Territory: Yes
Space Needs: N/A SF; N/A
SUPPORT & TRAINING PROVIDED:
Financial Assistance Provided: Yes
Site Selection Assistance: N/A
Lease Negotiation Assistance: N/A
Co-Operative Advertising: N/A
Franchisee Assoc./Member: No
Size Of Corporate Staff: 6
On-Going Support: B,C,D,G,H,I
Training: 3 Weeks On-Site under
   Development.
SPECIFIC EXPANSION PLANS:
US: All United States
Canada: All Canada
Overseas: All Countries

≪ ≫

CERTIGARD (PETRO-CANADA)
2489 North Sheridan Way
Mississauga, ON L5K 1A8 CANADA
Tel: (800) 668-0220 (905) 804-4555
Fax: (905) 804-4595
E-Mail: Bridger@petro-canada.ca
Web Site: www.certigard.com
Mr. Peter Bridger, Category Manager -
   Certigard

Petro-Canada is a major integrated oil
and gasoline company in Canada.
CERTIGARD is Petro-Canada's franchise
organization of automotive repair/service
outlets across Canada. In operation since
1987, the CERTIGARD franchisee
network is supported by a team of
dedicated, corporate specialists. The top
sales performers now measure annual
sales/bay in excess of $260,000.
Competitive pricing; convenient locations;
national warranties on repairs, lifetime on
certain products.

BACKGROUND:
Established: 1975;   1st Franchised: 1987
Franchised Units: 156
Company-Owned Units   0
Total Units: 156
Dist.:   US-0; CAN-155; O'seas-0
   North America: 9 Provinces
   Density: 53 in ON, 30 in BC, 24 in AB
Projected New Units (12 Months):   6

Qualifications: 4, 5, 4, 3, 3, 4
Registered: AB
FINANCIAL/TERMS:
Cash Investment: $40-60K
Total Investment: $100-150K
Minimum Net Worth: $30K
Fees: Franchise - $20K
 Royalty - 5%; Ad. - 2%
Earnings Claim Statement: No
Term of Contract (Years): 5/5
Avg. # Of Employees: 6 FT
Passive Ownership: Not Allowed
Encourage Conversions: Yes
Area Develop. Agreements: No
Sub-Franchising Contracts: No
Expand In Territory: Yes
Space Needs: 4,000 SF; FS
SUPPORT & TRAINING PROVIDED:
Financial Assistance Provided: No
Site Selection Assistance: Yes
Lease Negotiation Assistance: No
Co-Operative Advertising: Yes
Franchisee Assoc./Member: Yes/Yes
Size Of Corporate Staff: 25
On-Going Support: C,D,E,F,G,H,I
Training: 3 Days System Training -- Local
 Classroom; 3 Days Automation Training
 (Class & On-Site).
SPECIFIC EXPANSION PLANS:
US: No
Canada: All Canada
Overseas: No

◄◄ ►►

CLUTCH DOCTORS
2701 NW Vaughn St., #438
Portland, OR 98721
Tel: (888) 258-8248 (503) 525-5808
Fax: (503) 525-5812
E-Mail: bill@clutchdoctor.com
Web Site: www.clutchdoctor.com
Mr. Bill Nootenboom, Chief Executive
 Officer

CLUTCH DOCTORS is the leading, innovative automotive clutch and brake repair franchise, offering our exclusive QuoteBase clutch pricing software, state-of-the-art POS system, in-house bookkeeping and nationally and internationally award-winning advertising

program. We offer complete training for the franchisee and employees, site selection assistance and a proven profitable automotive repair facility.

BACKGROUND:
Established: 1995; 1st Franchised: 2000
Franchised Units: 2
Company-Owned Units: 6
Total Units: 8
Dist.: US-8; CAN-0; O'seas-0
 North America: 2 States
 Density: 5 in OR, 1 in WA
Projected New Units (12 Months): 6
Qualifications: 3, 2, 1, 2, 3, 5
Registered: WA
FINANCIAL/TERMS:
Cash Investment: $10K
Total Investment: $60-130K
Minimum Net Worth: $100K
Fees: Franchise - $10K
 Royalty - 8%; Ad. - 7%
Earnings Claim Statement: NR
Term of Contract (Years): 5/5
Avg. # Of Employees: 3 FT
Passive Ownership: Not Allowed
Encourage Conversions: Yes
Area Develop. Agreements: No
Sub-Franchising Contracts: No
Expand In Territory: Yes
Space Needs: 2,000 SF; RM
SUPPORT & TRAINING PROVIDED:
Financial Assistance Provided: No
Site Selection Assistance: Yes
Lease Negotiation Assistance: Yes
Co-Operative Advertising: Yes
Franchisee Assoc./Member: No
Size Of Corporate Staff: 20
On-Going Support: a,C,D,E,F,G,H,I
Training: 3 Weeks in Portland, OR; 2
 Weeks On-Site.
SPECIFIC EXPANSION PLANS:
US: Pacific NW
Canada: No
Overseas: No

◄◄ ►►

COLLISION SHOP, THE
15965 Jeanette St.
Southfield, MI 48075
Tel: (248) 559-1415
Fax: (248) 557-7931
E-Mail: wfcnet@cris.com
Web Site: www.wfcnet.com
Dr. Geoffrey Stebbins, Franchise Sales

THE COLLISION SHOP has developed a time-proven system for repairing today's

vehicles. THE COLLISION SHOP focuses on body and paint repairs, including unibody repair, metal finishing, two-stage painting system and detailing. THE COLLISION SHOP has body and paint specialists, and retail auto collision service.

BACKGROUND:
Established: 1991; 1st Franchised: 1998
Franchised Units: 21
Company-Owned Units: 2
Total Units: 23
Dist.: US-21; CAN-0; O'seas-0
 North America: 2 States
 Density: 19 in MI, 2 in FL
Projected New Units (12 Months): 8
Qualifications: 3, 3, 2, 3, 1, 5
Registered: FL,MI
FINANCIAL/TERMS:
Cash Investment: $65K
Total Investment: $150K
Minimum Net Worth: $100K
Fees: Franchise - $35K
 Royalty - 6%; Ad. - $250
Earnings Claim Statement: Yes
Term of Contract (Years): 10/5
Avg. # Of Employees: 5 FT
Passive Ownership: Discouraged
Encourage Conversions: Yes
Area Develop. Agreements: Yes
Sub-Franchising Contracts: Yes
Expand In Territory: Yes
Space Needs: 6,000-8,000 SF; FS
SUPPORT & TRAINING PROVIDED:
Financial Assistance Provided: Yes(I)
Site Selection Assistance: Yes
Lease Negotiation Assistance: Yes
Co-Operative Advertising: Yes
Franchisee Assoc./Member: NR
Size Of Corporate Staff: NR
On-Going Support: D,E
Training: 10 Days Headquarters; 10 Days
 On-Site.
SPECIFIC EXPANSION PLANS:
US: All United States
Canada: Regional
Overseas: Regional

◄◄ ►►

COLORS ON PARADE
642 Century Circle
Conway, SC 29526
Tel: (800) 929-3363 (843) 347-8818
Fax: (843) 347-0349
E-Mail: stephens/@colorsfranchise.com
Web Site: www.colorsfranchise.com

Ms. Linda Stevens, Director, Franchise Sales

We use our patented and proprietary techniques to make minor auto body damage disappear. We perform our quick and economical services on-site for dealers and fleet operators. COLORS ON PARADE franchisees ranked number one in financial satisfactionin the Success Magazine Gold 100 Survey. Extensive training and support provided. Major metropolitan markets available.

BACKGROUND: IFA MEMBER

Established: 1988;	1st Franchised: 1991
Franchised Units:	358
Company-Owned Units	2
Total Units:	360
Dist.:	US-360; CAN-0; O'seas-0
North America:	26 States
Density:	35 in CA, 34 in FL, 18 in TX
Projected New Units (12 Months):	50
Qualifications:	3, 3, 2, 3, 5, 5
Registered: All States	

FINANCIAL/TERMS:

Cash Investment:	$7.5-75K
Total Investment:	$50K+
Minimum Net Worth:	$50-250K
Fees: Franchise -	$5K
Royalty - Varies;	Ad. - 0%
Earnings Claim Statement:	No
Term of Contract (Years):	10/5
Avg. # Of Employees:	4 FT
Passive Ownership:	Discouraged
Encourage Conversions:	Yes
Area Develop. Agreements:	Yes/10
Sub-Franchising Contracts:	No
Expand In Territory:	Yes
Space Needs: N/A SF; N/A	

SUPPORT & TRAINING PROVIDED:

Financial Assistance Provided:	Yes(I)
Site Selection Assistance:	N/A
Lease Negotiation Assistance:	N/A
Co-Operative Advertising:	Yes
Franchisee Assoc./Member:	Yes/No
Size Of Corporate Staff:	21
On-Going Support:	A,B,C,D,F,G,H,I
Training: 2 Weeks Conway, SC.	

SPECIFIC EXPANSION PLANS:

US:	All United States
Canada:	All Canada
Overseas:	Mexico

◄◄ ►►

COTTMAN TRANSMISSION SYSTEMS

240 New York Dr.
Fort Washington, PA 19034

Tel: (888) 4COTTMAN (215) 643-5885
Fax: (215) 643-2519
E-Mail: cottman@cottman.com
Web Site: www.cottman.com
Mr. Barry Auchenbach, Franchise Dir.

Automotive transmission service franchise with centers nationwide. A market leader with new opportunities available in major markets as a result of our expansion plans. A highly-supportive company that offers intensive training, outstanding advertising and on-site support.

BACKGROUND: IFA MEMBER

Established: 1962;	1st Franchised: 1964
Franchised Units:	300
Company-Owned Units	0
Total Units:	300
Dist.:	US-295; CAN-4; O'seas-1
North America:	35 States, 3 Province
Density:	45 in PA, 23 in NJ, 19 in CA
Projected New Units (12 Months):	50
Qualifications:	3, 4, 3, 2, 1, 5
Registered: CA,FL,IL,IN,MD,MI,MN,NY, OR,RI,VA,WA,WI,DC,AB	

FINANCIAL/TERMS:

Cash Investment:	$45K
Total Investment:	$140K
Minimum Net Worth:	$100K
Fees: Franchise -	$27.5K
Royalty - 7.5%;	Ad. - $635/Wk.
Earnings Claim Statement:	Yes
Term of Contract (Years):	15/15
Avg. # Of Employees:	3 FT
Passive Ownership:	Not Allowed
Encourage Conversions:	Yes
Area Develop. Agreements:	Yes/6
Sub-Franchising Contracts:	No
Expand In Territory:	Yes
Space Needs: 3,000-4,000 SF; FS, SC, Auto Mall	

SUPPORT & TRAINING PROVIDED:

Financial Assistance Provided:	Yes(I)
Site Selection Assistance:	Yes
Lease Negotiation Assistance:	Yes
Co-Operative Advertising:	No
Franchisee Assoc./Member:	No
Size Of Corporate Staff:	58
On-Going Support:	B,C,D,E,F,G,H,I
Training: 3 Weeks Ft. Washington, PA; 1 Week Franchise Location.	

SPECIFIC EXPANSION PLANS:

US:	All United States
Canada:	All Canada
Overseas:	Open

◄◄ ►►

CUSTOM AUTO RESTORATION SYSTEMS

479 Interstate Ct.
Sarasota, FL 34240
Tel: (800) 736-1307 (941) 378-1193
Fax: (941) 378-3472
Web Site: www.autorestoration.com/cars/
Mr. Robert Wyatt, President

C.A.R.S. Inc. offers a wide variety of automobile reconditioning systems for people wishing to service dealerships and the retail market as well. These services include paint repair, paintless dent repair, interior repair, odor removal and windshields.

BACKGROUND:

Established: 1984;	1st Franchised: 1986
Franchised Units:	841
Company-Owned Units	257
Total Units:	1,098
Dist.:	US-584; CAN-131; O'seas-126
North America:	NR
Density:	PA, AL, TX
Projected New Units (12 Months):	60
Qualifications:	3, 3, 3, 3, 3, 3
Registered: FL	

FINANCIAL/TERMS:

Cash Investment:	$1-10K
Total Investment:	$1-10K
Minimum Net Worth:	$N/A
Fees: Franchise -	$N/A
Royalty - 0%;	Ad. - 0%
Earnings Claim Statement:	No
Term of Contract (Years):	N/A
Avg. # Of Employees:	1 FT
Passive Ownership:	NR
Encourage Conversions:	NR
Area Develop. Agreements:	No
Sub-Franchising Contracts:	No
Expand In Territory:	Yes
Space Needs: NR SF; N/A	

SUPPORT & TRAINING PROVIDED:

Financial Assistance Provided:	No
Site Selection Assistance:	No
Lease Negotiation Assistance:	No
Co-Operative Advertising:	No
Franchisee Assoc./Member:	No
Size Of Corporate Staff:	6
On-Going Support:	G,I
Training: 1-2 Weeks Sarasota, FL.	

SPECIFIC EXPANSION PLANS:

US:	All United States
Canada:	All Canada
Overseas:	All Countries

≪ ≫

DENT DOCTOR

11301 W. Markham St.
Little Rock, AR 72211
Tel: (800) 946-3368 (501) 224-0500
Fax: (501) 224-0507
E-Mail: info@dentdoctor.com
Web Site: www.dentdoctor.com
Mr. Tom Harris, President

DENT DOCTOR gives you a strategy to succeed. Earn extrodinary rewards removing minor dents, door dings and hail damage from vehicles without painting. Customers receive same day service. No automotive experience is required. You can operate from a retail shop along with providing mobile service.

BACKGROUND: IFA MEMBER

Established: 1988;	1st Franchised: 1990
Franchised Units:	34
Company-Owned Units	4
Total Units:	38
Dist.:	US-37; CAN-1; O'seas-0
North America:	24 States, 1 Province
Density:	5 in CO, 4 in TN, 3 in TX
Projected New Units (12 Months):	20
Qualifications:	4, 4, 2, 3, 4, 5
Registered: CA,FL,IL,IN,MI,NY,WA,WI	

FINANCIAL/TERMS:

Cash Investment:	$9.9-49.9K
Total Investment:	$22.9-79.9K
Minimum Net Worth:	$25K
Fees: Franchise -	$9.9-22.8K
Royalty - 6%;	Ad. - 0%
Earnings Claim Statement:	No
Term of Contract (Years):	10/20
Avg. # Of Employees:	4 FT
Passive Ownership:	Allowed
Encourage Conversions:	Yes
Area Develop. Agreements:	Yes/10
Sub-Franchising Contracts:	No
Expand In Territory:	Yes
Space Needs: 1,200 SF; FS, SF	

SUPPORT & TRAINING PROVIDED:

Financial Assistance Provided:	No
Site Selection Assistance:	Yes
Lease Negotiation Assistance:	Yes
Co-Operative Advertising:	Yes
Franchisee Assoc./Member:	No
Size Of Corporate Staff:	6
On-Going Support:	B,C,E,G,H,I

Training: 4 Weeks Little Rock, AR; 1 Week Franchisee's Home Area (Optional).

SPECIFIC EXPANSION PLANS:

US:	All United States
Canada:	All Canada
Overseas:	All Countries

≪ ≫

DENTPRO

4075 Nelson Ave., # A
Concord, CA 94520
Tel: (800) 868-3368 (925) 288-8900
Fax: (925) 288-8905
E-Mail: bhiggins@dentpro.com
Web Site: www.dentpro.com
Mr. Mitch Buich, President

Paintless, body filler-free minor dent and ding removal from automobiles and other vehicles using the DENTPRO methods, service marks and trade secrets. Franchisees operate their business on a mobile basis, within agreed geographic areas from vehicles, traveling to agreed locations where customers' vehicles are located.

BACKGROUND:

Established: 1991;	1st Franchised: 1993
Franchised Units:	42
Company-Owned Units	4
Total Units:	46
Dist.:	US-45; CAN-0; O'seas-1
North America:	7 States
Density:	14 in CA, 4 in ID, 2 in NV
Projected New Units (12 Months):	6
Qualifications:	3, 5, 2, 2, 4, 5
Registered: CA,HI,OR	

FINANCIAL/TERMS:

Cash Investment:	$25K
Total Investment:	$51-65K
Minimum Net Worth:	$250K
Fees: Franchise -	$25K+
Royalty - 7%;	Ad. - 2% Opt.
Earnings Claim Statement:	No
Term of Contract (Years):	10/5/5
Avg. # Of Employees:	1 FT, 1 PT
Passive Ownership:	Discouraged
Encourage Conversions:	N/A
Area Develop. Agreements:	No
Sub-Franchising Contracts:	No
Expand In Territory:	Yes
Space Needs: N/A SF; HB	

SUPPORT & TRAINING PROVIDED:

Financial Assistance Provided:	Yes(D)
Site Selection Assistance:	N/A
Lease Negotiation Assistance:	N/A
Co-Operative Advertising:	Yes
Franchisee Assoc./Member:	No

Size Of Corporate Staff:	2
On-Going Support:	B,C,D,E,G,H,i
Training: 6 Weeks Walnut Creek, CA.	

SPECIFIC EXPANSION PLANS:

US:	Southwest,Northwest,E. Coast
Canada:	All Canada
Overseas:	Caribbean

≪ ≫

DETAIL GUYS, THE

74478 Highway 111, PMB 378
Palm Desert, CA 92260
Tel: (888) 879-8783 (818) 519-9344
Fax: (888) 927-4425
E-Mail: lance@carwashguys.com
Web Site: www.detailguys.com
Mr. Lance Winslow, III, President/CEO

Successful mobile detailing franchise with 4-bay shops and 8-bay super-shops.

BACKGROUND:

Established: 1997;	1st Franchised: 1998
Franchised Units:	39
Company-Owned Units	10
Total Units:	49
Dist.:	US-49; CAN-0; O'seas-0
North America:	NR
Density:	NR
Projected New Units (12 Months):	100+
Qualifications:	1, 1, 1, 1, 1, 5
Registered: CA,FL,WA	

FINANCIAL/TERMS:

Cash Investment:	$NR
Total Investment:	$15-40K
Minimum Net Worth:	$N/A
Fees: Franchise -	$7.5K
Royalty - $280/Mo.;	Ad. - 0%
Earnings Claim Statement:	Yes
Term of Contract (Years):	5/20
Avg. # Of Employees:	1 FT, 1 PT
Passive Ownership:	Allowed
Encourage Conversions:	No
Area Develop. Agreements:	No
Sub-Franchising Contracts:	No
Expand In Territory:	Yes
Space Needs: NR SF; FS, HB	

SUPPORT & TRAINING PROVIDED:

Financial Assistance Provided:	Yes(I)
Site Selection Assistance:	Yes
Lease Negotiation Assistance:	Yes

Co-Operative Advertising:	Yes
Franchisee Assoc./Member:	No
Size Of Corporate Staff:	0
On-Going Support:	A,B,C,D,E,F,G,h,I
Training: 1 Week in Reno, NV.	

SPECIFIC EXPANSION PLANS:

US:	All United States
Canada:	All Canada
Overseas:	No

◁◁ ▷▷

ESTRELLA INSURANCE

7480 NW 186th St.
Miami, Fl 33015
Tel: (888) 511-7722 (305) 828-2444
Fax: (305) 556-7788
E-Mail: estrella@sunnyweb.com
Web Site: www.estrellainsurance.net
Mr. Jose E. Merille, President

ESTRELLA INSURANCE is the leader in the state of Florida in the auto insurance agency field and currently insures close to 100,000 autos in Dade and Broward county alone. Future expansion plans are to West Palm, Tampa, Orlando and other large cities. We offer outstanding support and advertising (TV, radio, outdoor, direct mail, etc.).

BACKGROUND: IFA MEMBER

Established: 1980;	1st Franchised: 1997
Franchised Units:	5
Company-Owned Units	35
Total Units:	40
Dist.:	US-40; CAN-0; O'seas-0
North America:	1 State
Density:	40 in FL
Projected New Units (12 Months):	8
Qualifications:	5, 3, 1, 4, 3, 5
Registered: FL	

FINANCIAL/TERMS:

Cash Investment:	$20-30K
Total Investment:	$79.5-99.5K
Minimum Net Worth:	$75-100K
Fees: Franchise -	$39.5K
Royalty - 2-4%;	Ad. - 1%
Earnings Claim Statement:	Yes
Term of Contract (Years):	7/7
Avg. # Of Employees:	3 FT, 1 PT
Passive Ownership:	Discouraged
Encourage Conversions:	Yes
Area Develop. Agreements:	Yes/10
Sub-Franchising Contracts:	No
Expand In Territory:	No
Space Needs: 800 SF; FS, SF, SC, RM	

SUPPORT & TRAINING PROVIDED:

Financial Assistance Provided:	Yes

Site Selection Assistance:	Yes
Lease Negotiation Assistance:	Yes
Co-Operative Advertising:	Yes
Franchisee Assoc./Member:	Yes/Yes
Size Of Corporate Staff:	30
On-Going Support:	A,B,C,D,E,H
Training: 8 Weeks Miami, FL.	

SPECIFIC EXPANSION PLANS:

US:	FL
Canada:	No
Overseas:	No

◁◁ ▷▷

EXPRESS OIL CHANGE

190 W. Valley Ave.
Birmingham, AL 35209
Tel: (888) 945-1771 (205) 945-1771
Fax: (205) 940-6026
Web Site: www.expressoil.com
Mr. R. Kent Feazell, Vice President Development

We are among the top ten fast oil change chains in the world. Per unit, sales out-pace our competitors by over 40%. Attractive, state-of-the-art facilities offer expanded, highly profitable services in addition to our ten minute oil change. We also provide transmission service, air conditioning service, brake repair, tire rotation and balancing and miscellaneous light repairs... Most extensive training and franchise support in the industry.

BACKGROUND: IFA MEMBER

Established: 1979;	1st Franchised: 1986
Franchised Units:	111
Company-Owned Units	12
Total Units:	123
Dist.:	US-123; CAN-0; O'seas-0
North America:	5 States
Density:	62 in AL, 35 in GA, 6 in TN
Projected New Units (12 Months):	20
Qualifications:	5, 5, 1, 3, 4, 4
Registered: NR	

FINANCIAL/TERMS:

Cash Investment:	$92-207K
Total Investment:	$700-915K
Minimum Net Worth:	$450K
Fees: Franchise -	$17.5K
Royalty - 5%;	Ad. - 3%

Earnings Claim Statement:	Yes
Term of Contract (Years):	10/10
Avg. # Of Employees:	7 FT
Passive Ownership:	Allowed
Encourage Conversions:	Yes
Area Develop. Agreements:	Yes
Sub-Franchising Contracts:	No
Expand In Territory:	Yes
Space Needs: 22,000 SF; FS	

SUPPORT & TRAINING PROVIDED:

Financial Assistance Provided:	Yes(I)
Site Selection Assistance:	Yes
Lease Negotiation Assistance:	Yes
Co-Operative Advertising:	Yes
Franchisee Assoc./Member:	No
Size Of Corporate Staff:	37
On-Going Support:	A,B,C,D,E,G,H,I
Training: 8 Weeks Closest Training Center; 1 Yr. On-Site, Post-OpeningTraining; Continuous Training.	

SPECIFIC EXPANSION PLANS:

US:	Southeast
Canada:	No
Overseas:	No

◁◁ ▷▷

GLASS DOCTOR

1010 N. University Parks Dr.
Waco, TX 76707
Tel: (800) 638-9858 (254) 745-2400
Fax: (254) 848-5907
Web Site: www.dwyer.com
Mr. Mike Hawkins, Vice President Franchising

GLASS DOCTOR is an exclusive, worldwide glass replacement franchise organization. The bulk of our business is replacing auto windshields and tempered glass.

BACKGROUND: IFA MEMBER

Established: 1962;	1st Franchised: 1977
Franchised Units:	46
Company-Owned Units	0
Total Units:	46
Dist.:	US-46; CAN-0; O'seas-0
North America:	27 States
Density:	NR
Projected New Units (12 Months):	36
Qualifications:	3, 4, 2, 3, 3, 5
Registered: All States	

FINANCIAL/TERMS:

Cash Investment:	$25-50K
Total Investment:	$109.9-252.5K
Minimum Net Worth:	$Open
Fees: Franchise -	$18.9K
Royalty - 6% or $200/Wk.;	Ad. - 2%

Earnings Claim Statement:	Yes
Term of Contract (Years):	10/10
Avg. # Of Employees:	4 FT
Passive Ownership:	NR
Encourage Conversions:	Yes
Area Develop. Agreements:	NR
Sub-Franchising Contracts:	No
Expand In Territory:	Yes
Space Needs: 1,500 SF; NR	

SUPPORT & TRAINING PROVIDED:

Financial Assistance Provided:	Yes
Site Selection Assistance:	No
Lease Negotiation Assistance:	No
Co-Operative Advertising:	NR
Franchisee Assoc./Member:	No
Size Of Corporate Staff:	20
On-Going Support:	C,D,E,F,G,H,I

Training: 1 Week in Headquarters in Waco, TX.

SPECIFIC EXPANSION PLANS:

US:	All United States
Canada:	All Canada
Overseas:	No

◄◄ ►►

10 Minute Lube & Oil Pros

GREASE MONKEY INTERNATIONAL

633 17th St., # 400
Denver, CO 80202
Tel: (800) 364-0352 (303) 308-1660
Fax: (303) 308-5908
E-Mail: gmonkey@rmi.net
Web Site: www.greasemonkeyintl.com
Mr. Michael Brunetti, VP Franchise Sales/
   Development

GREASE MONKEY Centers provide convenient vehicle preventive maintenance services. We provide comprehensive technical training for all franchisees, including instruction performing all GREASE MONKEY approved services thoroughly and safely. You will also learn basic accounting, computer marketing and customer satisfaction techniques to help you operate your business.

BACKGROUND:

Established: 1978;	1st Franchised: 1979
Franchised Units:	177
Company-Owned Units	36
Total Units:	213
Dist.:	US-190; CAN-0; O'seas-23

North America:	28 States
Density: 57 in CO, 14 in CA, 13 in WA	
Projected New Units (12 Months):	20
Qualifications:	5, 4, 2, 2, 3, 5
Registered: All States Except HI,SD	

FINANCIAL/TERMS:

Cash Investment:	$120-170K
Total Investment:	$222.5-999K
Minimum Net Worth:	$300K
Fees: Franchise -	$28K
Royalty - 5%;	Ad. - 6%
Earnings Claim Statement:	Yes
Term of Contract (Years):	15/15
Avg. # Of Employees:	3 FT, 3 PT
Passive Ownership:	Discouraged
Encourage Conversions:	Yes
Area Develop. Agreements:	Yes/Negot.
Sub-Franchising Contracts:	No
Expand In Territory:	Yes
Space Needs: 1,800 SF; FS, SC	

SUPPORT & TRAINING PROVIDED:

Financial Assistance Provided:	Yes(I)
Site Selection Assistance:	Yes
Lease Negotiation Assistance:	Yes
Co-Operative Advertising:	Yes
Franchisee Assoc./Member:	Yes
Size Of Corporate Staff:	45
On-Going Support:	A,B,C,D,E,F,G,H,I

Training: 1 Week Corporate Headquarters, Denver, CO; 1 Week Market Center.

SPECIFIC EXPANSION PLANS:

US:	All United States
Canada:	No
Overseas:	Mexico

◄◄ ►►

INDY LUBE

6515 E. 82nd St., # 209
Indianapolis, IN 46250
Tel: (800) 326-5823 (317) 845-9444
Fax: (317) 577-3169
E-Mail: rance@1quest.net
Web Site: www.indylube.com
Mr. James C. Yates, President

INDY LUBE oil change centers specialize in fluid maintenance of both passenger and light industrial vehicles. Each INDY LUBE facility is up-scale with a spacious reception room with television, wallpaper and courtesy phone. The INDY LUBE full-service oil change includes a 20-point safety and fluid check. Each center also has a point-of-sale computer system.

BACKGROUND:

Established: 1986;	1st Franchised: 1989
Franchised Units:	8
Company-Owned Units	20

Total Units:	28
Dist.:	US-28; CAN-0; O'seas-0
North America:	2 States
Density:	22 in IN, 6 in MN
Projected New Units (12 Months):	5
Qualifications:	4, 5, 4, 3, 1, 4
Registered: IN	

FINANCIAL/TERMS:

Cash Investment:	$50-90K
Total Investment:	$250-450K
Minimum Net Worth:	$100K
Fees: Franchise -	$7.5K
Royalty - 5%;	Ad. - 5%
Earnings Claim Statement:	No
Term of Contract (Years):	20/5-10
Avg. # Of Employees:	4 FT, 2 PT
Passive Ownership:	Discouraged
Encourage Conversions:	No
Area Develop. Agreements:	Yes/20
Sub-Franchising Contracts:	No
Expand In Territory:	Yes
Space Needs: 2,100 SF; FS	

SUPPORT & TRAINING PROVIDED:

Financial Assistance Provided:	Yes(I)
Site Selection Assistance:	Yes
Lease Negotiation Assistance:	Yes
Co-Operative Advertising:	Yes
Franchisee Assoc./Member:	No
Size Of Corporate Staff:	10
On-Going Support:	a,b,C,D,E,F,G,H,I

Training: 2-3 Weeks Headquarters.

SPECIFIC EXPANSION PLANS:

US:	Midwest
Canada:	No
Overseas:	No

◄◄ ►►

J. D. BYRIDER SYSTEMS

12802 Hamilton Crossing Blvd.
Carmel, IN 46032
Tel: (800) 947-4532 (317) 249-3000
Fax: (317) 249-3001
E-Mail: info@jdbyrider.com
Web Site: www.jdbyrider.com
Mr. Greg Delks, Vice President

J. D. BYRIDER is the largest used car sales/auto finance franchise in North America, with over 151 locations in 36 states and Canada. We provide proven operating systems, brand name advertising and world class on-going support. With over 10 years of franchise growth, we can deliver our franchise partners with a clear path to financial success.

BACKGROUND:

Established: 1980; 1st Franchised: 1989
Franchised Units: 139
Company-Owned Units   12
Total Units: 151
Dist.:   US-148; CAN-3; O'seas-0
  North America: 36 States, 1Province
  Density: 26 in OH, 24 in IN, 8 in FL
Projected New Units (12 Months):   30
Qualifications: 3, 4, 2, 3, 1, 3
Registered: All States

FINANCIAL/TERMS:

Cash Investment: $150-300K
Total Investment: $268K-1.9MM
Minimum Net Worth: $250K
Fees: Franchise - $39K
  Royalty - 3%;   Ad. - $1.8K/Mo.
Earnings Claim Statement: Yes
Term of Contract (Years):   10/10
Avg. # Of Employees: 10 FT
Passive Ownership: Allowed
Encourage Conversions: Yes
Area Develop. Agreements: Yes/5
Sub-Franchising Contracts: No
Expand In Territory: Yes
Space Needs: 6,000 SF; FS

SUPPORT & TRAINING PROVIDED:

Financial Assistance Provided: Yes(I)
Site Selection Assistance: Yes
Lease Negotiation Assistance: Yes
Co-Operative Advertising: N/A
Franchisee Assoc./Member: Yes/Yes
Size Of Corporate Staff: 86
On-Going Support: C,D,E,G,h
Training: 3 Days System Orientation; 1 Day Credit/Collections; 1 Day Sales Man. -- all Carmel, IN.

SPECIFIC EXPANSION PLANS:

US: All United States
Canada: All Canada
Overseas: No

<< >>

KING BEAR AUTO SERVICE CENTERS

130 - 29 Merrick Blvd.
Springfield Gardens, NY 11434
Tel: (800) 311-KING (718) 527-1252
Fax: (718) 527-4985
E-Mail: kingbear32@aol.com
Web Site:
www.KingBearAutoFranchise.com

Mr. Melvin D. Messinger, Director of Franchising

KING BEAR AUTO SERVICE CENTER was the first organized automotive franchise in the state of New York. Founded in 1973, it has been a household name known for quality auto service at a reasonable cost. KING BEAR has retained its status as a complete one-stop auto service center.

BACKGROUND: IFA MEMBER

Established: 1973; 1st Franchised: 1973
Franchised Units: 33
Company-Owned Units   0
Total Units: 33
Dist.:   US-28; CAN-0; O'seas-0
  North America: 1 State
  Density: 33 in NY
Projected New Units (12 Months):   12
Qualifications: 2, 3, 1, 1, 1, 5
Registered: NY

FINANCIAL/TERMS:

Cash Investment: $65-90K
Total Investment: $159-294K
Minimum Net Worth: $50K
Fees: Franchise - $29.5K
  Royalty - 5% or Fee;   Ad. - 7% or Fee
Earnings Claim Statement: No
Term of Contract (Years):   25/25
Avg. # Of Employees: 3 FT
Passive Ownership: Allowed
Encourage Conversions: Yes
Area Develop. Agreements: Yes/25
Sub-Franchising Contracts: No
Expand In Territory: Yes
Space Needs: 2,000-6,000 SF; FS, SC

SUPPORT & TRAINING PROVIDED:

Financial Assistance Provided: Yes(I)
Site Selection Assistance: Yes
Lease Negotiation Assistance: Yes
Co-Operative Advertising: Yes
Franchisee Assoc./Member: No
Size Of Corporate Staff: 6
On-Going Support: B,C,D,E,F,H,I
Training: 2 Weeks at Corporate Office; On-Site as Needed.

SPECIFIC EXPANSION PLANS:

US: All United States
Canada: No
Overseas: No

<< >>

LEE MYLES TRANSMISSIONS

140 Route 17 N.
Paramus, NJ 07652
Tel: (800) 533-6953 (201) 262-0555
Fax: (201) 262-5177

Web Site: www.leemyles.com
Mr. Sal Gargone, Director Franchise Development

Service, repair and replace automatic and standard transmissions for the car and light truck market. Turn-key and existing locations are available. On-going operational support, business and technical assistance. Major expansion into new markets. Area developers are welcome.

BACKGROUND: IFA MEMBER

Established: 1947; 1st Franchised: 1964
Franchised Units: 86
Company-Owned Units   0
Total Units: 86
Dist.:   US-86; CAN-0; O'seas-0
  North America: 10 States
  Density: 30 in NY, 15 in NJ, 13 in AZ
Projected New Units (12 Months):   10
Qualifications: 4, 4, 4, 5, 5, 5
Registered: CA,FL,MD,NY,OR,RI, VA,WA,DC

FINANCIAL/TERMS:

Cash Investment: $40-60K
Total Investment: $98-127K
Minimum Net Worth: $60K
Fees: Franchise - $25K
  Royalty - 7%;   Ad. - 4.5%
Earnings Claim Statement: No
Term of Contract (Years):   25/15/5/5
Avg. # Of Employees: 4 FT
Passive Ownership: Not Allowed
Encourage Conversions: Yes
Area Develop. Agreements: Yes/15
Sub-Franchising Contracts: No
Expand In Territory: Yes
Space Needs: 3,000 SF; FS, SC, HB, Auto Mall

SUPPORT & TRAINING PROVIDED:

Financial Assistance Provided: N/A
Site Selection Assistance: Yes
Lease Negotiation Assistance: Yes
Co-Operative Advertising: Yes
Franchisee Assoc./Member: Yes/Yes
Size Of Corporate Staff: 15
On-Going Support: C,D,E,F,G,I
Training: 1-2 Weeks Corporate Office.

SPECIFIC EXPANSION PLANS:

US: All United States
Canada: All Canada
Overseas: No

LENTZ USA SERVICE CENTERS

1001 Riverview Dr.
Kalamazoo, MI 49048
Tel: (800) 354-2131 (616) 342-2200
Fax: (616) 342-9461
E-Mail: quietcar@lentzusa.com
Web Site: www.lentzusa.com
Mr. Gary R. Thomas, Franchise Liaison

Specialty automotive repairs -- features direct to you product purchases from manufacturers at the best cost, allowing for greater profit opportunities. Great expansion areas available for multiple location ownership.

BACKGROUND: IFA MEMBER
Established: 1972; 1st Franchised: 1989
Franchised Units: 25
Company-Owned Units: 11
Total Units: 36
Dist.: US-36; CAN-0; O'seas-0
North America: 5 States
Density: 28 in MI, 6 in IN, 2 in NC
Projected New Units (12 Months): 6
Qualifications: 4, 3, 1, 3, 4, 5
Registered: FL,IL,IN,MD,MI
FINANCIAL/TERMS:
Cash Investment: $35-70K
Total Investment: $90-112K
Minimum Net Worth: $100K
Fees: Franchise - $20K
 Royalty - 0-7%; Ad. - 0%
Earnings Claim Statement: No
Term of Contract (Years): 10/10
Avg. # Of Employees: 3-5 FT
Passive Ownership: Not Allowed
Encourage Conversions: Yes
Area Develop. Agreements: Yes/10
Sub-Franchising Contracts: No
Expand In Territory: Yes
Space Needs: 3,600 SF; FS, SC
SUPPORT & TRAINING PROVIDED:
Financial Assistance Provided: Yes(I)
Site Selection Assistance: Yes
Lease Negotiation Assistance: Yes
Co-Operative Advertising: No
Franchisee Assoc./Member: No
Size Of Corporate Staff: 10
On-Going Support: B,C,D,E,F,G,H,I

Training: 2 Weeks Kalamazoo, MI; 1 Week
 Franchise Site; On-Going Visits.
SPECIFIC EXPANSION PLANS:
US: Midwest
Canada: All Canada
Overseas: Middle East, India, Europe

LINE-X SPRAY-ON TRUCK BEDLINERS

2525-A S. Birch St.
Santa Ana, CA 92707
Tel: (800) 831-3232 (714) 850-1662
Fax: (714) 850-8759
E-Mail: linexcor@pacbell.net
Web Site: www.linexcorp.com
Mr. Scott Jewett, General Manager

A LINE-X franchisee operates a retail/ industrial location that applies sprayed on coatings. LINE-X has a number of applications from flooring to industrial applications. LINE-X is in a growing, new and unsaturated market with extraordinary opportunities for minority entrepreneurs.

BACKGROUND:
Established: 1993; 1st Franchised: 1998
Franchised Units: 360
Company-Owned Units: 1
Total Units: 361
Dist.: US-334; CAN-0; O'seas-27
North America: 50 States
Density: 20 in CA, 15 in WA, 10 in GA
Projected New Units (12 Months): NR
Registered: All States
FINANCIAL/TERMS:
Cash Investment: $25K
Total Investment: $68-147K
Minimum Net Worth: $20K
Fees: Franchise - $20K
 Royalty - 0%; Ad. - 1.5%
Earnings Claim Statement: No
Term of Contract (Years): 5/15
Avg. # Of Employees: 2 FT
Passive Ownership: Discouraged
Encourage Conversions: NR
Area Develop. Agreements: Yes
Sub-Franchising Contracts: Yes
Expand In Territory: Yes
Space Needs: 2,500 SF; Industrial/ Commercial
SUPPORT & TRAINING PROVIDED:
Financial Assistance Provided: NR

Site Selection Assistance: Yes
Lease Negotiation Assistance: Yes
Co-Operative Advertising: No
Franchisee Assoc./Member: No
Size Of Corporate Staff: 14
On-Going Support: C,D,E,G,H,I
Training: Up to 5 Days at Our Location;
 up to 7 Days at Franchisee's Location.
SPECIFIC EXPANSION PLANS:
US: All United States
Canada: All Canada
Overseas: All Countries

LUBEPRO'S INTERNATIONAL, INC.

1630 Colonial Pkwy.
Inverness, IL 60067
Tel: (800) 654-5823 (847) 776-2500
Fax: (847) 776-2542
Mr. Robert Cesario, President/CEO

Our building design, our training program and our unique approach to marketing truly set us ahead of our competitors.

BACKGROUND:
Established: 1978; 1st Franchised: 1985
Franchised Units: 26
Company-Owned Units: 14
Total Units: 40
Dist.: US-36; CAN-0; O'seas-0
North America: 4 States
Density: 28 in IL, 6 in WI
Projected New Units (12 Months): 4
Qualifications: 4, 3, 1, 2, 2, 4
Registered: IL,IN,MN,WI
FINANCIAL/TERMS:
Cash Investment: $100K
Total Investment: $170-200K
Minimum Net Worth: $300K
Fees: Franchise - $25K
 Royalty - 5%; Ad. - 5%
Earnings Claim Statement: No
Term of Contract (Years): 20/10/10
Avg. # Of Employees: 6 FT
Passive Ownership: Allowed
Encourage Conversions: N/A
Area Develop. Agreements: No
Sub-Franchising Contracts: No
Expand In Territory: Yes
Space Needs: 1,800 SF; FS
SUPPORT & TRAINING PROVIDED:
Financial Assistance Provided: No
Site Selection Assistance: Yes
Lease Negotiation Assistance: No
Co-Operative Advertising: Yes
Franchisee Assoc./Member: No
Size Of Corporate Staff: 7

On-Going Support: C,D,E,G,H,I
Training: 10 Days Rockford, IL.
SPECIFIC EXPANSION PLANS:
US: Central, North Central
Canada: No
Overseas: No

‹‹ ››

MAACO AUTO PAINTING & BODYWORKS
381 Brooks Rd.
King of Prussia, PA 19406
Tel: (800) 296-2226 (610) 265-6606
Fax: (610) 337-6176
E-Mail: franchise@maaco.com
Web Site: www.maaco.com
Mr. Bill Chaffee, VP Franchise Development

MAACO has developed a system relating to the establishment and operation of centers specializing in auto painting and body repair. The system includes market analysis, research and development, sales and merchandising methods, training, record keeping, advertising and business management, all of which are constantly being improved, up-dated and further developed by a fully-staffed and knowledgeable corporate structure to service its owners.

BACKGROUND: IFA MEMBER
Established: 1972; 1st Franchised: 1972
Franchised Units: 556
Company-Owned Units 0
Total Units: 556
Dist.: US-510; CAN-42; O'seas-4
North America: 47 States, 7 Provinces
Density: 42 in CA, 26 in NJ, 21 in PA
Projected New Units (12 Months): 50
Qualifications: 3, 3, 1, 1, 3, 5
Registered: All States
FINANCIAL/TERMS:
Cash Investment: $60K
Total Investment: $224.5K
Minimum Net Worth: $250K
Fees: Franchise - $30K
Royalty - 8%; Ad. - $850/Wk.

Earnings Claim Statement: No
Term of Contract (Years): 15/5
Avg. # Of Employees: 10 FT
Passive Ownership: Not Allowed
Encourage Conversions: No
Area Develop. Agreements: No
Sub-Franchising Contracts: No
Expand In Territory: Yes
Space Needs: 7,500-10,000 SF; FS
SUPPORT & TRAINING PROVIDED:
Financial Assistance Provided: Yes(I)
Site Selection Assistance: Yes
Lease Negotiation Assistance: Yes
Co-Operative Advertising: Yes
Franchisee Assoc./Member: No
Size Of Corporate Staff: 125
On-Going Support: A,B,C,D,E,F,G,H,I
Training: 4 Weeks King of Prussia, PA; 3 Weeks On-Site.
SPECIFIC EXPANSION PLANS:
US: All United States
Canada: All Canada
Overseas: No

‹‹ ››

MAACO AUTO PAINTING & BODYWORKS (CANADA)
10 Kingsbridge Garden Cir., # 501
Mississauga, ON L5R 3K6 CANADA
Tel: (800) 387-6780 (905) 501-1212
Fax: (905) 501-1218
E-Mail: hdelisle@maaco.com
Web Site: www.maaco.com
Mr. Hermann Delisle, Manager Franchise Development

Production car painting and bodyworks center.

BACKGROUND:
Established: 1972; 1st Franchised: 1972
Franchised Units: 560
Company-Owned Units 0
Total Units: 560
Dist.: US-515; CAN-45; O'seas-0
North America: 47 States, 7 Provinces
Density: 18 in ON, 7 in AB, 6 in BC
Projected New Units (12 Months): 6-8
Qualifications: 4, 4, 1, 3, 3, 3
Registered: All States and AB
FINANCIAL/TERMS:
Cash Investment: $80K
Total Investment: $240K
Minimum Net Worth: $NR
Fees: Franchise - $25K
Royalty - 8%; Ad. - $700/Wk.
Earnings Claim Statement: No
Term of Contract (Years): 15/5

Avg. # Of Employees: 8 FT
Passive Ownership: Not Allowed
Encourage Conversions: Yes
Area Develop. Agreements: NR
Sub-Franchising Contracts: Yes
Expand In Territory: Yes
Space Needs: 8,000 SF; FS, SF, SC
SUPPORT & TRAINING PROVIDED:
Financial Assistance Provided: N/A
Site Selection Assistance: Yes
Lease Negotiation Assistance: Yes
Co-Operative Advertising: Yes
Franchisee Assoc./Member: No
Size Of Corporate Staff: 10
On-Going Support: A,B,C,D,E,F,G,H,I
Training: 3 Weeks in King of Prussia, PA; 2 Weeks On-Site.
SPECIFIC EXPANSION PLANS:
US: No
Canada: All Canada
Overseas: No

‹‹ ››

MASTER MECHANIC, THE
1989 Dundas St. E.
Mississauga, ON L4X 1M1 CANADA
Tel: (800) 383-8523 (905) 629-3773
Fax: (905) 629-3864
Mr. Andrew Wanie, President

General auto repair and emission testing center, with a reputation in high-tech automotive excellence that provides to its customers the convenience of one-stop shopping for all of their automotive maintenance and repair needs.

BACKGROUND:
Established: 1979; 1st Franchised: 1983
Franchised Units: 31
Company-Owned Units 1
Total Units: 32
Dist.: US-0; CAN-31; O'seas-0
North America: 1 Province
Density: 31 in ON
Projected New Units (12 Months): 4
Qualifications: 4, 3, 4, 3, 4, 5
Registered: NR
FINANCIAL/TERMS:
Cash Investment: $60-80K
Total Investment: $125-175K
Minimum Net Worth: $200K
Fees: Franchise - $25K
Royalty - 6%; Ad. - 3% (Varies)

Earnings Claim Statement: Yes
Term of Contract (Years): 20/Open
Avg. # Of Employees: 3-5 FT, 1-2 PT
Passive Ownership: Discouraged
Encourage Conversions: Yes
Area Develop. Agreements: Yes/20
Sub-Franchising Contracts: Yes
Expand In Territory: Yes
Space Needs: 4,000 SF; FS, SF, SC, RM
SUPPORT & TRAINING PROVIDED:
Financial Assistance Provided: Yes(I)
Site Selection Assistance: Yes
Lease Negotiation Assistance: Yes
Co-Operative Advertising: Yes
Franchisee Assoc./Member: Yes/Yes
Size Of Corporate Staff: 6
On-Going Support: a,B,C,D,E,F,G,H,I
Training: 1 Week Classroom; 4 Weeks Training Shop; On-Going -- 2 Weeks/Yr. On-Site.
SPECIFIC EXPANSION PLANS:
US: No
Canada: ON
Overseas: No

MEINEKE DISCOUNT MUFFLERS
128 S. Tryon St., # 900
Charlotte, NC 28202
Tel: (800) 275-5200 (704) 377-8855
Fax: (704) 358-4706
E-Mail: Alice_Griffin@meineke.com
Web Site: www.meineke.com
Ms. Cynthia Weiss, Franchise Develop. Coord.

MEINEKE DISCOUNT MUFFLERS is the nation's largest discount muffler and brake repair specialist with more than 860 shops across the nation. They have been offering great service at discount prices for more than 25 years. Their franchisees come from all walks of life and represent many nationalities.

BACKGROUND: IFA MEMBER
Established: 1972; 1st Franchised: 1973
Franchised Units: 859
Company-Owned Units: 8
Total Units: 867
Dist.: US-861; CAN-8; O'seas-1
North America: 46 States
Density: 77 in NY, 64 in PA, 58 in NJ

Projected New Units (12 Months): 20
Qualifications: 5, 2, 1, 2, 1, 5
Registered: All States
FINANCIAL/TERMS:
Cash Investment: $40-50K
Total Investment: $140-250K
Minimum Net Worth: $100K
Fees: Franchise - $25K
Royalty - 2.5-7%; Ad. - 1.5-10%
Earnings Claim Statement: Yes
Term of Contract (Years): 15/15
Avg. # Of Employees: 3 FT
Passive Ownership: Not Allowed
Encourage Conversions: Yes
Area Develop. Agreements: Yes/Varies
Sub-Franchising Contracts: No
Expand In Territory: Yes
Space Needs: 2,880 SF; FS, SC
SUPPORT & TRAINING PROVIDED:
Financial Assistance Provided: Yes(I)
Site Selection Assistance: No
Lease Negotiation Assistance: Yes
Co-Operative Advertising: No
Franchisee Assoc./Member: Yes/No
Size Of Corporate Staff: 134
On-Going Support: C,D,E,G,H,I
Training: 4 Weeks Charlotte, NC.
SPECIFIC EXPANSION PLANS:
US: All United States
Canada: All Except PQ
Overseas: Caribbean, Central America

MERLIN'S MUFFLER & BRAKE
1 N. River Ln., # 206
Geneva, IL 60134
Tel: (800) 652-9900 (630) 208-9900
Fax: (630) 208-8601
E-Mail: Merlins-undercar@worldnet.att.net
Web Site: www.merlins.com
Mr. Mark M. Hameister, Director Franchise Development

MERLIN'S is an up-scale automotive service business, specializing in brakes, exhaust, suspension, oil/lubrication and related services. Automotive experience is not always necessary, but candidates must have significant experience in managing employees and serving customers honestly. MERLIN'S is expanding in Illinois, Michigan, Georgia, Texas and Wisconsin.

BACKGROUND: IFA MEMBER
Established: 1975; 1st Franchised: 1975
Franchised Units: 59
Company-Owned Units: 3
Total Units: 62
Dist.: US-62; CAN-0; O'seas-0
North America: 5 States
Density: 47 in IL, 5 in TX, 5 in GA
Projected New Units (12 Months): 6
Qualifications: 3, 5, 4, 3, 4, 5
Registered: IL,MI,WI
FINANCIAL/TERMS:
Cash Investment: $45-60K
Total Investment: $190-210K
Minimum Net Worth: $75K
Fees: Franchise - $26-30K
Royalty - 6.9%; Ad. - 5%
Earnings Claim Statement: Yes
Term of Contract (Years): 20/20
Avg. # Of Employees: 3-4 FT, 1 PT
Passive Ownership: Not Allowed
Encourage Conversions: Yes
Area Develop. Agreements: No
Sub-Franchising Contracts: No
Expand In Territory: Yes
Space Needs: 3,850 SF; FS, SC, RM, Other Center
SUPPORT & TRAINING PROVIDED:
Financial Assistance Provided: Yes(I)
Site Selection Assistance: Yes
Lease Negotiation Assistance: Yes
Co-Operative Advertising: Yes
Franchisee Assoc./Member: Yes/Yes
Size Of Corporate Staff: 20
On-Going Support: B,C,D,E,F,G,H,I
Training: 6 Weeks Corporate Headquarters; in Shop as Needed.
SPECIFIC EXPANSION PLANS:
US: IL,MI,GA,TX,WI
Canada: No
Overseas: No

MERMAID CAR WASH
526 Grand Canyon Dr.
Madison, WI 53719
Tel: (608) 833-9273
Fax: (608) 833-9272
Mr. Peter H. Aspinwall, President

Own a MERMAID franchise. MERMAID CAR WASH was designed with the feeling that our customers have a love affair with their vehicle. It is our desire to have customers visit an enjoyable, attractive business run by friendly, helpful, well-groomed, well-trained employees and leave MERMAID with a pleasant experience and a professionally-cleaned vehicle.

BACKGROUND:

Established: 1984; 1st Franchised: 1986	
Franchised Units:	6
Company-Owned Units	2
Total Units:	8
Dist.: US-8; CAN-0; O'seas-0	
North America:	3 States
Density: 5 in MN, 2 in WI, 1 in IL	
Projected New Units (12 Months):	1
Qualifications:	5, 3, 1, 1, 2, 2
Registered: IL,MN,WI	

FINANCIAL/TERMS:

Cash Investment:	$NR
Total Investment:	$1.75-2.0MM
Minimum Net Worth:	$NR
Fees: Franchise -	$50K
Royalty - 2%;	Ad. - 0%
Earnings Claim Statement:	No
Term of Contract (Years):	20/20
Avg. # Of Employees:	30 FT
Passive Ownership:	Allowed
Encourage Conversions:	Yes
Area Develop. Agreements:	No
Sub-Franchising Contracts:	No
Expand In Territory:	Yes
Space Needs: 16,000-68,000 SF; FS	

SUPPORT & TRAINING PROVIDED:

Financial Assistance Provided:	Yes(I)
Site Selection Assistance:	Yes
Lease Negotiation Assistance:	Yes
Co-Operative Advertising:	No
Franchisee Assoc./Member:	No
Size Of Corporate Staff:	3
On-Going Support:	b,C,D,E,F,H
Training: 3 Weeks Madison, WI.	

SPECIFIC EXPANSION PLANS:

US:	All United States
Canada:	Not Actively
Overseas:	No

<< >>

MIDAS AUTO SERVICE EXPERTS
1300 Arlington Heights Rd.
Itasca, IL 60143
Tel: (800) 621-0144 (630) 438-3000
Fax: (630) 438-3700
E-Mail: bkorus@midas.com
Web Site: www.midasfran.com
Ms. Barbara Korus, Fran. Recruitment Coor.

MIDAS is one of the world's largest providers of automotive service, providing exhaust, brake, steering and suspension services, as well as batteries and maintenance services at 2,700 franchised and licensed MIDAS shops in 19 countries, including over 2,000 in the United States and Canada.

BACKGROUND: IFA MEMBER

Established: 1956; 1st Franchised: 1956	
Franchised Units:	2,712
Company-Owned Units	1
Total Units:	2,713
Dist.: US-1,836; CAN-241; O'seas-636	
North America:	NR
Density:	NR
Projected New Units (12 Months):	40
Qualifications:	4, 4, 2, 2, 3, 5
Registered: All States	

FINANCIAL/TERMS:

Cash Investment:	$75-150K
Total Investment:	$298-428K
Minimum Net Worth:	$300K
Fees: Franchise -	$20K
Royalty - 10%;	Ad. - Incl. Roy.
Earnings Claim Statement:	No
Term of Contract (Years):	20/20
Avg. # Of Employees:	6 FT, 4 PT
Passive Ownership:	Discouraged
Encourage Conversions:	Yes
Area Develop. Agreements:	Varies
Sub-Franchising Contracts:	No
Expand In Territory:	Yes
Space Needs: 4,000-5,000 SF; FS	

SUPPORT & TRAINING PROVIDED:

Financial Assistance Provided:	Yes(I)
Site Selection Assistance:	Yes
Lease Negotiation Assistance:	Yes
Co-Operative Advertising:	Yes
Franchisee Assoc./Member:	Yes/Yes
Size Of Corporate Staff:	NR
On-Going Support:	B,C,D,e,f,G,H,I
Training: 1-2 Weeks of Self Study; 1-2 Weeks In-Shop Assignment; 3 Weeks in Palatine, IL.	

SPECIFIC EXPANSION PLANS:

US:	All United States
Canada:	All Canada
Overseas:	No

<< >>

MIGHTY DISTRIBUTING SYSTEM OF AMERICA
650 Engineering Dr.
Norcross, GA 30092
Tel: (800) 829-3900 (770) 448-3900
Fax: (770) 446-8627

E-Mail:
tracy.brown@mightyautoparts.com
Web Site: www.mightyautoparts.com
Ms. Tracy Brown, Franchise Marketing Manager

Wholesale distribution of original equipment-quality, MIGHTY-branded auto parts. Franchisees operate in exclusive territories, supplying automotive maintenance and repair facilities with undercar and underhood products, such as filters, belts, tune-up and brake parts.

BACKGROUND: IFA MEMBER

Established: 1963; 1st Franchised: 1970	
Franchised Units:	142
Company-Owned Units	5
Total Units:	147
Dist.: US-147; CAN-0; O'seas-0	
North America:	45 States
Density: 12 in PA, 10 in FL, 9 in CA	
Projected New Units (12 Months):	12
Qualifications:	5, 4, 3, 3, 3, 4
Registered: CA,FL,HI,IL,IN,MD,MI,MN, NY,ND,OR,RI,SD,VA,WA,WI	

FINANCIAL/TERMS:

Cash Investment:	$42-95K
Total Investment:	$84-190K
Minimum Net Worth:	$200K
Fees: Franchise -	$5K+ $.035/Vcl
Royalty - 5%;	Ad. - 0.5%
Earnings Claim Statement:	Yes
Term of Contract (Years):	10
Avg. # Of Employees:	4 FT
Passive Ownership:	Not Allowed
Encourage Conversions:	Yes
Area Develop. Agreements:	No
Sub-Franchising Contracts:	No
Expand In Territory:	N/A
Space Needs: 2,500 SF; Warehouse	

SUPPORT & TRAINING PROVIDED:

Financial Assistance Provided:	Yes(I)
Site Selection Assistance:	No
Lease Negotiation Assistance:	No
Co-Operative Advertising:	Yes
Franchisee Assoc./Member:	Yes/No
Size Of Corporate Staff:	50
On-Going Support:	C,D,F,G,h
Training: 1 Week Home Office; 1 Week On-the-Job Training.	

SPECIFIC EXPANSION PLANS:

US:	All United States
Canada:	All Canada
Overseas:	No

≪ ≫

MILEX

4444 W. 147th St.
Midlothian, IL 60445
Tel: (800) 377-9247 (708) 389-5922
Fax: (708) 389-9882
E-Mail: vsmithson@moranindustries.com
Web Site: www.moranindustries.com
Ms. Virginia Smithson, Qualification Specialist

MILEX TUNE-UPS, BRAKES AND AIR CONDITIONING is a division of Moran Industries that franchises service centers throughout the US. We offer our franchisees a superior business system, strong brand name, customized marketing and a service that is in strong demand. Comprehensive training and continuous support ensure our franchisee's potential. Our exclusive business system, along with the skills of our franchisees, create customer experiences that result in satisfaction and loyalty.

BACKGROUND: IFA MEMBER

Established: 1967;	1st Franchised: 1967
Franchised Units:	9
Company-Owned Units	0
Total Units:	9
Dist.:	US-9; CAN-0; O'seas-0
North America:	2 States
Density:	8 in IL, 1 in CT
Projected New Units (12 Months):	5
Qualifications:	4, 3, 2, 2, 4, 5
Registered: IL	

FINANCIAL/TERMS:

Cash Investment:	$60K
Total Investment:	$144K
Minimum Net Worth:	$120K
Fees: Franchise -	$27.5K
Royalty - 7%;	Ad. - $100/Mo.
Earnings Claim Statement:	Yes
Term of Contract (Years):	20/20
Avg. # Of Employees:	4-6 FT
Passive Ownership:	Discouraged
Encourage Conversions:	Yes
Area Develop. Agreements:	Yes/Varies
Sub-Franchising Contracts:	No
Expand In Territory:	Yes
Space Needs: 3,500 SF; FS	

SUPPORT & TRAINING PROVIDED:

Financial Assistance Provided:	Yes(I)
Site Selection Assistance:	Yes
Lease Negotiation Assistance:	Yes
Co-Operative Advertising:	Yes
Franchisee Assoc./Member:	Yes/Yes
Size Of Corporate Staff:	55
On-Going Support:	C,D,E,G,H,I
Training: 3 Weeks at Various Locations.	

SPECIFIC EXPANSION PLANS:

US:	Midwest
Canada:	No
Overseas:	No

≪ ≫

MINUTE MUFFLER AND BRAKE

1600 - 3rd Ave. S.
Lethbridge, AB T1J 0L2 CANADA
Tel: (888) 646-6833 (403) 329-1020
Fax: (403) 328-9030
E-Mail: minmuff@agt.net
Web Site: www.minutemuffler.com
Mr. Robb Sloan, VP Sales/Marketing

Retail exhaust, brake, suspension outlets with 0% royalty, 0% advertising fee. Your 65-70% average gross profit goes in your pocket, not ours. Unsurpassed support systems by actual store owner/operators. Service is our business!!

BACKGROUND:

Established: 1969;	1st Franchised: 1977
Franchised Units:	120
Company-Owned Units	1
Total Units:	121
Dist.:	US-0; CAN-119; O'seas-2
North America:	NR
Density:	25 in BC, 24 in AB, 18 in ON
Projected New Units (12 Months):	12
Qualifications:	4, 3, 2, 3, 3, 5
Registered: AB	

FINANCIAL/TERMS:

Cash Investment:	$50-100K
Total Investment:	$150-250K
Minimum Net Worth:	$75-100K
Fees: Franchise -	$0-25K
Royalty - 0%;	Ad. - 0%
Earnings Claim Statement:	No
Term of Contract (Years):	On-going
Avg. # Of Employees:	3-5 FT, 1 PT
Passive Ownership:	Discouraged
Encourage Conversions:	Yes
Area Develop. Agreements:	No
Sub-Franchising Contracts:	Yes
Expand In Territory:	Yes
Space Needs: 3,200-3,500 SF; FS	

SUPPORT & TRAINING PROVIDED:

Financial Assistance Provided:	No
Site Selection Assistance:	Yes
Lease Negotiation Assistance:	Yes
Co-Operative Advertising:	N/A
Franchisee Assoc./Member:	No
Size Of Corporate Staff:	13
On-Going Support:	B,C,D,e,F,G,h,I
Training: 1-10 Weeks Head Office; 1-2 Weeks On-Site.	

SPECIFIC EXPANSION PLANS:

US:	No
Canada:	All Canada
Overseas:	Carribean, South/Central America, Europe

≪ ≫

MIRACLE AUTO PAINTING & BODY REPAIR

3157 Corporate Place
Hayward, CA 94545
Tel: (877) MIR-ACLE (510) 887-2211
Fax: (510) 887-3092
E-Mail: jim@miracleautopainting.com
Web Site: www.miracleautopainting.com
Mr. Jim Jordan, Marketing Director

MIRACLE is a production collision repair and refinishing company that specializes in complete paint jobs. MIRACLE caters to individual vehicle owners, insurance carriers, other body shop facilities and new and used automobile dealers.

BACKGROUND: IFA MEMBER

Established: 1953;	1st Franchised: 1964
Franchised Units:	29
Company-Owned Units	5
Total Units:	34
Dist.:	US-34; CAN-0; O'seas-0
North America:	3 States
Density:	28 in CA, 5 in TX, 1 in AZ
Projected New Units (12 Months):	2
Qualifications:	3, 3, 3, 1, 2, 5
Registered: CA,OR,WA	

FINANCIAL/TERMS:

Cash Investment:	$75-100K
Total Investment:	$215-275K
Minimum Net Worth:	$NR

Fees: Franchise - $35K
   Royalty - 5%;   Ad. - 5%
Earnings Claim Statement: No
Term of Contract (Years):   10/10
Avg. # Of Employees: 10 FT, 2 PT
Passive Ownership: Discouraged
Encourage Conversions: Yes
Area Develop. Agreements: Yes/5
Sub-Franchising Contracts: Yes
Expand In Territory: Yes
Space Needs: 9,000-11,000 SF; FS, SF

SUPPORT & TRAINING PROVIDED:
Financial Assistance Provided: Yes(I)
Site Selection Assistance: Yes
Lease Negotiation Assistance: Yes
Co-Operative Advertising: No
Franchisee Assoc./Member: Yes/No
Size Of Corporate Staff: 20
On-Going Support: B,C,D,E,G,H
Training: 10 Days Headquarters; 10 Days On-Site.

SPECIFIC EXPANSION PLANS:
US: West, Southwest
Canada: No
Overseas: No

<< >>

MISTER TRANSMISSION (INTERNATIONAL) LIMITED

9675 Yonge St.
Richmond Hill, ON L4C 1V7 CANADA
Tel: (800) 886-3399 (905) 886-1511
Fax: (905) 886-1545
E-Mail: mrt@idirect.com
Web Site: www.MisterTransmission.com
Mr. Kevin Brillinger, VP Corporate Development

With over 30 years' experience, MISTER TRANSMISSION is the established name for transmission repair service in Canada. We make sales, training, advertising, a computer program, national fleet accounts, site selection and a warranty program available to all franchisees. MISTER TRANSMISSION is Canadian-owned.

BACKGROUND:
Established: 1963;   1st Franchised: 1969
Franchised Units: 89
Company-Owned Units   0
Total Units: 89
Dist.:   US-0; CAN-89; O'seas-0
   North America: 7 Provinces
   Density: 63 in ON, 14 in BC, 4 in MB
Projected New Units (12 Months):   3
Qualifications: 3, 3, 3, 2, 3, 4
Registered: NR

FINANCIAL/TERMS:
Cash Investment: $60-80K
Total Investment: $125-150K
Minimum Net Worth: $300K
Fees: Franchise - $25K
   Royalty - 7%;   Ad. - Varies
Earnings Claim Statement: Yes
Term of Contract (Years):   10/10
Avg. # Of Employees: 5 FT
Passive Ownership: Discouraged
Encourage Conversions: Yes
Area Develop. Agreements: No
Sub-Franchising Contracts: No
Expand In Territory: NR
Space Needs: 2,800 SF; FS, SC

SUPPORT & TRAINING PROVIDED:
Financial Assistance Provided: No
Site Selection Assistance: Yes
Lease Negotiation Assistance: Yes
Co-Operative Advertising: No
Franchisee Assoc./Member: Yes/Yes
Size Of Corporate Staff: 12
On-Going Support: C,D,E,G,H,I
Training: 1 Week Head Office.

SPECIFIC EXPANSION PLANS:
US: No
Canada: All Canada
Overseas: No

<< >>

MOTORWORKS

4210 Salem St.
Philadelphia, PA 19124
Tel: (800) 327-9905 (215) 533-4456
Fax: (215) 533-7801
E-Mail: motorworks@motorworksinc.com
Web Site: www.motorworksinc.com
Mr. Dennis J. Prendergast, Director Franchise Sales

The nation's leading chain of remanufactured engine installation centers franchise.

BACKGROUND:
Established: 1969;   1st Franchised: 1987
Franchised Units: 68
Company-Owned Units   2
Total Units: 70
Dist.:   US-70; CAN-0; O'seas-0
   North America: 25 States
   Density: 15 in PA, 10 uin VA, 6 in NJ
Projected New Units (12 Months):   NR
Registered:

FINANCIAL/TERMS:
Cash Investment: $52K
Total Investment: $73-97K

Minimum Net Worth: $250K
Fees: Franchise - $23.5K
   Royalty - 5%;   Ad. - 1
Earnings Claim Statement: Yes
Term of Contract (Years):   10/5
Avg. # Of Employees: 3 FT, 1 PT
Passive Ownership: Discouraged
Encourage Conversions: NR
Area Develop. Agreements: Yes/10
Sub-Franchising Contracts: No
Expand In Territory: No
Space Needs: NR SF; FS, SF, SC, 2-Bay Garage

SUPPORT & TRAINING PROVIDED:
Financial Assistance Provided: NR
Site Selection Assistance: Yes
Lease Negotiation Assistance: Yes
Co-Operative Advertising: Yes
Franchisee Assoc./Member: No
Size Of Corporate Staff: 17
On-Going Support: C,D,E,F,G,I
Training: 1 Week Philadelphia, PA; 1 Week On-Site.

SPECIFIC EXPANSION PLANS:
US: All United States
Canada: NR
Overseas: NR

<< >>

MR. TRANSMISSION

4444 W. 147th St.
Midlothian, IL 60445
Tel: (800) 377-9247 (708) 389-5922
Fax: (708) 389-9882
E-Mail: vsmithson@moranindustries.com
Web Site: www.moranindustries.com
Ms. Virginia Smithson, Qualifications Specialist

MR. TRANSMISSION, a division of Moran Industries, franchises transmission service centers throughout the US. We offer our franchisees a superior business system, strong brand name, customized marketing and a service that is in strong demand. In addition, comprehensive training and continuous support help to ensure our franchisees maximize their potential. Our exclusive business system, along with the skills of our franchisees, create customer experiences that result in satisfaction and loyalty.

BACKGROUND: IFA MEMBER
Established: 1956;   1st Franchised: 1990

Franchised Units: 86
Company-Owned Units 1
Total Units: 87
Dist.: US-87; CAN-0; O'seas-0
North America: 14 States
Density: 21 in GA, 12 in IN, 12 in FL
Projected New Units (12 Months): 24
Qualifications: 4, 5, 1, 3, 4, 5
Registered: IL,IN,VA

FINANCIAL/TERMS:
Cash Investment: $50K
Total Investment: $149K
Minimum Net Worth: $100K
Fees: Franchise - $27.5K
Royalty - 7%; Ad. - $100/Mo.
Earnings Claim Statement: Yes
Term of Contract (Years): 20/20
Avg. # Of Employees: 3-5 FT
Passive Ownership: Discouraged
Encourage Conversions: No
Area Develop. Agreements: Yes/Varies
Sub-Franchising Contracts: No
Expand In Territory: Yes
Space Needs: 4,000 SF; FS, SC, Automotive Use

SUPPORT & TRAINING PROVIDED:
Financial Assistance Provided: Yes(I)
Site Selection Assistance: Yes
Lease Negotiation Assistance: Yes
Co-Operative Advertising: No
Franchisee Assoc./Member: Yes
Size Of Corporate Staff: 55
On-Going Support: A,C,D,E,F,G,H,I
Training: Yes.

SPECIFIC EXPANSION PLANS:
US: All United States
Canada: No
Overseas: Limited

<< >>

NOVUS
10425 Hampshire Ave., S.
Minneapolis, MN 55438
Tel: (800) 328-1117 (612) 944-8000
Fax: (612) 946-0481
E-Mail: dougs@novuswsr.com
Web Site: www.novuswsr.com
Mr. Terry Smith, Vice President Franchising

NOVUS invented windshield repair. Factory-trained NOVUS franchisees have successfully repaired over 18 million windshields in the US, Canada and over 40 other countries. Today, many NOVUS franchisees are also trained and equipped to replace windshields too badly damaged to be repaired. In 1999, NOVUS added automotive paint restoration to their list of services.

BACKGROUND: IFA MEMBER
Established: 1972; 1st Franchised: 1985
Franchised Units: 2,510
Company-Owned Units 2
Total Units: 2,512
Dist.: US-453; CAN-58; O'seas-2,000
North America: 50 States,10 Provinces
Density: 31 in WA, 22 in IL, 18 in WI
Projected New Units (12 Months): 20
Qualifications: 5, 3, 1, 3, 3, 5
Registered: All States and AB

FINANCIAL/TERMS:
Cash Investment: $8.4-36K
Total Investment: $25-142K
Minimum Net Worth: $100K
Fees: Franchise - $8.4-20K
Royalty - 5-6%; Ad. - 2-4%
Earnings Claim Statement: No
Term of Contract (Years): 10/10
Avg. # Of Employees: 2-4 FT
Passive Ownership: Discouraged
Encourage Conversions: Yes
Area Develop. Agreements: Yes
Sub-Franchising Contracts: No
Expand In Territory: Yes
Space Needs: 3,000 SF; FS, SF, SC, RM, HB

SUPPORT & TRAINING PROVIDED:
Financial Assistance Provided: Yes(D)
Site Selection Assistance: No
Lease Negotiation Assistance: No
Co-Operative Advertising: No
Franchisee Assoc./Member: Yes
Size Of Corporate Staff: 39
On-Going Support: C,D,G,H,I
Training: 7.5 Days Windshield Repair Minneapolis; 10 Days Replacement in 1 of 4 Locations.

SPECIFIC EXPANSION PLANS:
US: All United States
Canada: All Canada
Overseas: All Countries

<< >>

OIL BUTLER INTERNATIONAL
1599 Route 22 W.
Union, NJ 07083
Tel: (908) 687-3283
Fax: (908) 687-7617
Web Site: www.oilbutlerinternational.com
Mr. John Dicocco, Vice President of Marketing

OIL BUTLER INTERNATIONAL is a mobile oil-change service and windshield repair franchise combining two money-making opportunities in one. Our uniquely designed vehicle provides the corporate image and service your customers will expect from the leader in the field of on-site service. Low-investment, low-overhead, complete training and on-going support.

BACKGROUND:
Established: 1987; 1st Franchised: 1991
Franchised Units: 104
Company-Owned Units 1
Total Units: 105
Dist.: US-89; CAN-4; O'seas-12
North America: 22 States
Density: 21 in TX, 13 in CA, 8 in CO
Projected New Units (12 Months): 100
Qualifications: 3, 3, 2, 2, 5, 5
Registered: CA,IL,IN,MD,MI,NY, VA,WA,WI

FINANCIAL/TERMS:
Cash Investment: $8-15K
Total Investment: $9-18K
Minimum Net Worth: $NR
Fees: Franchise - $4-7K
Royalty - 7%; Ad. - 2%
Earnings Claim Statement: No
Term of Contract (Years): 10/5
Avg. # Of Employees: 1 FT
Passive Ownership: Discouraged
Encourage Conversions: N/A
Area Develop. Agreements: Yes
Sub-Franchising Contracts: No
Expand In Territory: Yes
Space Needs: NR SF; Mobile Unit

SUPPORT & TRAINING PROVIDED:
Financial Assistance Provided: Yes(I)
Site Selection Assistance: Yes
Lease Negotiation Assistance: N/A
Co-Operative Advertising: Yes
Franchisee Assoc./Member: No
Size Of Corporate Staff: 9
On-Going Support: B,C,D,F,G,H
Training: 4 Days to 2 Weeks Union, NJ.

SPECIFIC EXPANSION PLANS:
US: All United States
Canada: All Canada
Overseas: All Countries

<< >>

ONE STOP UNDERCAR
2938 S. Daimler St.
Santa Ana, CA 92705
Tel: (714) 505-2600
Fax: (714) 505-1817
Mr. Clive Goldberg, Secretary

ONE STOP UNDERCAR outlets distribute automobile parts, accessories and equipment to automotive-repair and maintenance shops.

BACKGROUND:

Established: 1993; 1st Franchised: 1993	
Franchised Units:	10
Company-Owned Units	4
Total Units:	14
Dist.:	US-14; CAN-0; O'seas-0
North America:	1 State
Density:	13 in CA
Projected New Units (12 Months):	2
Qualifications:	5, 3, 2, 3, 2, 5
Registered: CA	

FINANCIAL/TERMS:

Cash Investment:	$200K
Total Investment:	$292-460K
Minimum Net Worth:	$350K
Fees: Franchise -	$40-80K
Royalty - 5%;	Ad. - 3%
Earnings Claim Statement:	No
Term of Contract (Years):	20/20
Avg. # Of Employees:	8 FT
Passive Ownership:	Discouraged
Encourage Conversions:	NR
Area Develop. Agreements:	Yes/5
Sub-Franchising Contracts:	No
Expand In Territory:	Yes
Space Needs: 3,500 SF; Warehouse	

SUPPORT & TRAINING PROVIDED:

Financial Assistance Provided:	No
Site Selection Assistance:	No
Lease Negotiation Assistance:	No
Co-Operative Advertising:	Yes
Franchisee Assoc./Member:	NR
Size Of Corporate Staff:	7
On-Going Support:	D,E,F,g,h
Training: 4 Weeks Orange County, CA.	

SPECIFIC EXPANSION PLANS:

US:	Southwest
Canada:	No
Overseas:	No

≪ ≫

PETRO STOPPING CENTERS
6080 Surety Dr.
El Paso, TX 79905
Tel: (800) 331-8809 (915) 779-4711
Fax: (915) 774-7373
E-Mail: lglines@petrotruckstops.com
Web Site: www.petrotruckstops.com
Mr. Larry Glines, Exec, Dir. Fran. Business

PETRO SHOPPING CENTERS is a nationwide network of premier, full-service, interstate Travel Plazas. PETRO offers the Iron Skillet Restaurant, Petro Lube Truck Service, featuring Mobil Oil products and Volvo and Cummings light warranty service, Mercantile Travel Stores and quality Mobil fuels. PETRO provides the expertise and systems to help develop successful businesses.

BACKGROUND:

Established: 1975; 1st Franchised: 1985	
Franchised Units:	22
Company-Owned Units	35
Total Units:	57
Dist.:	US-57; CAN-0; O'seas-0
North America:	33 States
Density:	6 in TX, 6 in PA, 4 in OH
Projected New Units (12 Months):	4
Qualifications:	5, 4, 4, 3, 3, 4
Registered: CA,FL,IL,IN,MD,MI,NY,ND, SD,VA,WA,WI	

FINANCIAL/TERMS:

Cash Investment:	$NR
Total Investment:	$NR
Minimum Net Worth:	$NR
Fees: Franchise -	$NR
Royalty - NR;	Ad. - NR
Earnings Claim Statement:	No
Term of Contract (Years):	10/5/5
Avg. # Of Employees:	125 FT, 40 PT
Passive Ownership:	Discouraged
Encourage Conversions:	No
Area Develop. Agreements:	No
Sub-Franchising Contracts:	No
Expand In Territory:	Yes
Space Needs: 20 Acres SF; Other	

SUPPORT & TRAINING PROVIDED:

Financial Assistance Provided:	No
Site Selection Assistance:	No
Lease Negotiation Assistance:	No
Co-Operative Advertising:	Yes
Franchisee Assoc./Member:	Yes/No
Size Of Corporate Staff:	NR
On-Going Support:	B,C,D,E,G,H,I
Training: 8 Weeks at Various US Locations.	

SPECIFIC EXPANSION PLANS:

US:	All U.S. Exc. TX,AZ,NM
Canada:	All Canada
Overseas:	No

≪ ≫

PRECISION TUNE AUTO CARE CENTER
748 Miller Dr. SE
Leesburg, VA 20175
Tel: (800) 438-8863 (703) 777-9095
Fax: (703) 777-9190
E-Mail: Kevin.Rooney@precisionac.com
Web Site: www.precisionAC.com
Mr. Kevin B. Rooney, VP Franchise Development

PRECISION TUNE AUTO CARE is America's largest engine performance car care company, specializing in tune-up, quick oil and lube and brake services. Also offered are complete diagnostics, engine performance, fluid and maintenance services, with 20 years' experience. We provide quality support in site selection, training, marketing, operations, management, business profitability and much more. Comprehensive training program for everyone.

BACKGROUND: IFA MEMBER

Established: 1975; 1st Franchised: 1978	
Franchised Units:	556
Company-Owned Units	1
Total Units:	557
Dist.:	US-478; CAN-1; O'seas-90
North America:	36 States
Density:	40 in MI, 38 in FL, 32 in GA
Projected New Units (12 Months):	55
Qualifications:	4, 5, 2, 2, 3, 5
Registered: CA,HI,IL,IN,MD,MN,NY, ND,RI,SD,VA,WA,WI	

FINANCIAL/TERMS:

Cash Investment:	$75-100K
Total Investment:	$142-203K
Minimum Net Worth:	$NR
Fees: Franchise -	$25K
Royalty - 7.5%;	Ad. - 9.0%
Earnings Claim Statement:	No
Term of Contract (Years):	10/5
Avg. # Of Employees:	6 FT, 1-2 PT
Passive Ownership:	Discouraged
Encourage Conversions:	Yes
Area Develop. Agreements:	Yes/5
Sub-Franchising Contracts:	Yes
Expand In Territory:	Yes
Space Needs: 3,000 SF; FS, SF, SC	

SUPPORT & TRAINING PROVIDED:

Financial Assistance Provided:	Yes
Site Selection Assistance:	Yes
Lease Negotiation Assistance:	Yes
Co-Operative Advertising:	Yes
Franchisee Assoc./Member:	Yes
Size Of Corporate Staff:	52
On-Going Support:	B,C,D,E,F,G,H,I
Training: 2 Weeks Leesburg, VA.	

SPECIFIC EXPANSION PLANS:

US:	All United States
Canada:	All Canada
Overseas:	All Countries

RYAN ENGINE EXCHANGE

9301 W. Colfax
Lakewood, CO 80215
Tel: (800) 466-1664 (303) 232-0023
Fax: (303) 205-0172
Mr. Johnny M. Wilson, Marketing Dir.

RYAN ENGINE EXCHANGE installs and exchanges remanufactured engines. The old engine is exchanged for a new engine and the new engine is installed on the premises. Using the system developed by Ryan, the turn around time is 3 days and a factory warranty of 5 years - 50,000 miles is given.

BACKGROUND:

Established: 1987;	1st Franchised: 1999
Franchised Units:	0
Company-Owned Units	1
Total Units:	1
Dist.:	US-1; CAN-0; O'seas-0
North America:	1 State
Density:	1 in CO
Projected New Units (12 Months):	4
Qualifications:	3, 4, 2, 1, 2, 5
Registered:	

FINANCIAL/TERMS:

Cash Investment:	$40K
Total Investment:	$78-112.8K
Minimum Net Worth:	$50K
Fees: Franchise -	$20K
Royalty - 3% or $30/engine;	Ad. - 5% Local
Earnings Claim Statement:	No
Term of Contract (Years):	15/5
Avg. # Of Employees:	4 FT, 1 PT
Passive Ownership:	Discouraged
Encourage Conversions:	Yes
Area Develop. Agreements:	No
Sub-Franchising Contracts:	No
Expand In Territory:	Yes
Space Needs: 2,500 SF; Warehouse	

SUPPORT & TRAINING PROVIDED:

Financial Assistance Provided:	Yes(I)
Site Selection Assistance:	Yes
Lease Negotiation Assistance:	Yes
Co-Operative Advertising:	No
Franchisee Assoc./Member:	No
Size Of Corporate Staff:	3
On-Going Support:	B,C,D,E,F,G,H,I
Training: 1 Week in Denver; 3 Days at Factory in Nebraska	

SPECIFIC EXPANSION PLANS:

US:	All United States
Canada:	No
Overseas:	No

SAF-T AUTO CENTERS

121 N. Plains Industrial Rd., Unit H
Wallingford, CT 06492
Tel: (800) 382-7238 (203) 294-1094
Fax: (203) 269-2532
E-Mail: saft@snet.net
Web Site: www.saftauto.com
Mr. Richard Biladeau, President

SAF-T AUTO CENTERS is an owner-operated, auto repair shop offering steering, suspension, brakes, muffler, lubrication and minor repair. Our main effort is to put good mechanics in a business opportunity, where they can capitalize on their trade.

BACKGROUND:

Established: 1978;	1st Franchised: 1985
Franchised Units:	8
Company-Owned Units	1
Total Units:	9
Dist.:	US-9; CAN-0; O'seas-0
North America:	1 State
Density:	9 in CT
Projected New Units (12 Months):	1
Qualifications:	1, 1, 4, 2, 4, 5
Registered: FL	

FINANCIAL/TERMS:

Cash Investment:	$25K
Total Investment:	$32-65K
Minimum Net Worth:	$50K
Fees: Franchise -	$15K
Royalty - $500/Mo.;	Ad. - 1%
Earnings Claim Statement:	No
Term of Contract (Years):	10/10
Avg. # Of Employees:	2 FT
Passive Ownership:	Discouraged
Encourage Conversions:	No
Area Develop. Agreements:	Yes
Sub-Franchising Contracts:	No
Expand In Territory:	Yes
Space Needs: 2,000 SF; FS, SC	

SUPPORT & TRAINING PROVIDED:

Financial Assistance Provided:	Yes(D)
Site Selection Assistance:	Yes
Lease Negotiation Assistance:	Yes
Co-Operative Advertising:	Yes
Franchisee Assoc./Member:	No
Size Of Corporate Staff:	3
On-Going Support:	A,B,C,E,F,G,H,I
Training: 1 Month On-Site.	

SPECIFIC EXPANSION PLANS:

US:	CT
Canada:	No
Overseas:	No

SHINE FACTORY

320 Monument Pl., SE
Calgary, AB T2A 1X3 CANADA
Tel: (403) 243-3030
Fax: (403) 243-3031
Mr. Bruce H. Cousens, President

A solid, proven program to put entrepreneurs into the automotive protection and detail business. Car wash combinations are available.

BACKGROUND:

Established: 1979;	1st Franchised: 1979
Franchised Units:	31
Company-Owned Units	0
Total Units:	31
Dist.:	US-0; CAN-31; O'seas-0
North America:	6 Provinces
Density:	12 in NS, 12 in AB, 4 in BC
Projected New Units (12 Months):	3-4
Qualifications:	4, 4, 3, 3, 3, 5
Registered: AB	

FINANCIAL/TERMS:

Cash Investment:	$100K
Total Investment:	$125K
Minimum Net Worth:	$60K
Fees: Franchise -	$10-50K
Royalty - 8%;	Ad. - 5%
Earnings Claim Statement:	No
Term of Contract (Years):	5/5
Avg. # Of Employees:	3 FT, 2 PT
Passive Ownership:	Discouraged
Encourage Conversions:	Yes
Area Develop. Agreements:	Yes/5
Sub-Franchising Contracts:	Yes
Expand In Territory:	Yes
Space Needs: 4,000 SF; FS, SC	

SUPPORT & TRAINING PROVIDED:

Financial Assistance Provided:	No
Site Selection Assistance:	Yes
Lease Negotiation Assistance:	Yes
Co-Operative Advertising:	Yes
Franchisee Assoc./Member:	No
Size Of Corporate Staff:	4
On-Going Support:	C,D,E,F,H,I
Training: 2 Weeks Training Center; 2 Weeks On-Site.	

SPECIFIC EXPANSION PLANS:

US:	No
Canada:	All Canada
Overseas:	No

SPEEDEE OIL CHANGE & TUNE-UP

159 Hwy. 22 East
Madisonville, LA 70447-1035
Tel: (800) 451-7461 (504) 845-1969
Fax: (504) 845-1936
E-Mail: bruce@speedcore.com
Web Site: www.speedee.com
Mr. Bruce A. McNeal, Director of Franchising

SPEEDEE offers preventive auto maintenance services, specializing in a 17-point quick oil change, diagnostic tune-up and brake services. Also offered: fuel system cleanings, radiator flushes, emission/smog checks and transmission/differential services. No appointment necessary. Performed while you wait. Successful franchisees are enthusiastic, have a strong commitment to customer service and people management skills. Retail experience preferred.

BACKGROUND:

Established: 1980;	1st Franchised: 1982
Franchised Units:	141
Company-Owned Units	2
Total Units:	143
Dist.:	US-121; CAN-0; O'seas-13
North America:	15 States
Density:	50 in CA, 22 in LA, 10 in MA
Projected New Units (12 Months):	14
Qualifications:	5, 5, 3, 3, 3, 4
Registered: CA,VA,FL,HI	

FINANCIAL/TERMS:

Cash Investment:	$100-150K
Total Investment:	$186-765.5K
Minimum Net Worth:	$250K
Fees: Franchise -	$30K
Royalty - 6%;	Ad. - 8%
Earnings Claim Statement:	No
Term of Contract (Years):	15/5/5
Avg. # Of Employees:	6 FT, 2 PT
Passive Ownership:	Discouraged
Encourage Conversions:	Yes
Area Develop. Agreements:	Yes/15
Sub-Franchising Contracts:	No
Expand In Territory:	Yes
Space Needs: 2,700 SF; FS	

SUPPORT & TRAINING PROVIDED:

Financial Assistance Provided:	No
Site Selection Assistance:	Yes
Lease Negotiation Assistance:	Yes
Co-Operative Advertising:	Yes
Franchisee Assoc./Member:	No
Size Of Corporate Staff:	16
On-Going Support:	C,D,E,G,H
Training: 3-Day Orientation Headquarters;	
2-4 Weeks Local Office; 1-2 Weeks Shop.	

SPECIFIC EXPANSION PLANS:

US:	All United States
Canada:	All Canada
Overseas:	All Countries

≪ ≫

SPEEDY TRANSMISSION CENTERS

902 Clint Moore Rd., #216
Boca Raton, FL 33487
Tel: (800) 336-0310 (561) 995-8282
Fax: (561) 995-8005
E-Mail: speedytrans@mindspring.com
Web Site: www.speedytransmission.com
Mr. Scott Jobin, Operations Manager

Centers repair, rebuild and recondition automatic and standard transmissions. Other drive train repair services also available. Training, marketing and operational assistance. Warranties are honored throughout the U.S. and Canada.

BACKGROUND: IFA MEMBER

Established: 1974;	1st Franchised: 1974
Franchised Units:	28
Company-Owned Units	0
Total Units:	28
Dist.:	US-28; CAN-0; O'seas-0
North America:	6 States
Density:	18 in FL, 7 in GA, 2 in CA
Projected New Units (12 Months):	8
Qualifications:	3, 3, 2, 4, 4, 3
Registered: FL	

FINANCIAL/TERMS:

Cash Investment:	$40K
Total Investment:	$80-100K
Minimum Net Worth:	$NR
Fees: Franchise -	$19.5K
Royalty - 7%;	Ad. - $100/Mo.
Earnings Claim Statement:	No
Term of Contract (Years):	20/10
Avg. # Of Employees:	4 FT, 1 PT
Passive Ownership:	Discouraged
Encourage Conversions:	Yes
Area Develop. Agreements:	Yes/10
Sub-Franchising Contracts:	Yes
Expand In Territory:	Yes
Space Needs: 2,400 SF; FS, SC	

SUPPORT & TRAINING PROVIDED:

Financial Assistance Provided:	Yes(I)
Site Selection Assistance:	Yes
Lease Negotiation Assistance:	Yes
Co-Operative Advertising:	No
Franchisee Assoc./Member:	Yes/Yes
Size Of Corporate Staff:	4
On-Going Support:	C,D,E,F,G,H,I
Training: 2 Weeks Home Office; 1 Week On-Site.	

SPECIFIC EXPANSION PLANS:

US:	Southeast, Northeast
Canada:	No
Overseas:	Latin America

≪ ≫

SPOT-NOT CAR WASHES

2011 W. 4th St.
Joplin, MO 64801-3297
Tel: (800) 682-7629
Fax: (417) 781-3906
Web Site: www.spot-not.com
Mr. Doug Myers, Executive Vice President

High-pressure spray brushless automatic car wash, complemented by full-featured, self-service wash bays. Each facility offers canopied, lighted vacuum areas. An all cash business with few employees.

BACKGROUND: IFA MEMBER

Established: 1968;	1st Franchised: 1985
Franchised Units:	36
Company-Owned Units	0
Total Units:	36
Dist.:	US-36; CAN-0; O'seas-0
North America:	6 States
Density:	10 in AR, 10 in IL, 8 in IN
Projected New Units (12 Months):	3
Registered: IL,IN,MI,WI	

FINANCIAL/TERMS:

Cash Investment:	$300K
Total Investment:	$622K-1.1MM
Minimum Net Worth:	$NR
Fees: Franchise -	$25K
Royalty - 5%;	Ad. - 1%
Earnings Claim Statement:	No
Term of Contract (Years):	10/5/5
Avg. # Of Employees:	2 FT, 3 PT
Passive Ownership:	Discouraged
Encourage Conversions:	Yes
Area Develop. Agreements:	Yes/Varies
Sub-Franchising Contracts:	No
Expand In Territory:	Yes
Space Needs: 40,000 SF; FS	

SUPPORT & TRAINING PROVIDED:

Financial Assistance Provided:	Yes(I)
Site Selection Assistance:	Yes
Lease Negotiation Assistance:	Yes

Co-Operative Advertising: Yes
Franchisee Assoc./Member: No
Size Of Corporate Staff: 18
On-Going Support: B,C,D,E,F,G,H,I
Training: 3 Sessions -- 17 Days Total Joplin, MO and OJT Site.

SPECIFIC EXPANSION PLANS:
US: Midwest, South and Southwest
Canada: No
Overseas: No

◄◄ ►►

SUPERGLASS WINDSHIELD REPAIR

6101 Chancellor Dr., # 200
Orlando, FL 32809
Tel: (888) 771-2700 (407) 240-1920
Fax: (407) 240-3266
E-Mail: sgwr@aol.com
Web Site: www.sgwr.com
Mr. David A. Casey, President

SUPERGLASS WINDSHIELD REPAIR is the largest repair-only franchisor in the United States, with locations in 43 states. Two weeks of training, including one week in Orlando and one week in the franchisee's exclusive territory, are provided along with all equipment, uniforms, manuals, printing and bookkeeping systems.

BACKGROUND:
Established: 1992; 1st Franchised: 1993
Franchised Units: 196
Company-Owned Units 0
Total Units: 196
Dist.: US-182; CAN-1; O'seas-13
North America: 43 States, 1 Province
Density: 14 in GA, 13 in FL, 11 in CO
Projected New Units (12 Months): 25
Qualifications: 2, 4, 1, 2, 3, 4
Registered: CA,FL,MI,SD
FINANCIAL/TERMS:
Cash Investment: $9.5-11.5K
Total Investment: $9.5-28.5K
Minimum Net Worth: $15K
Fees: Franchise - $5.4K
 Royalty - 3%; Ad. - 1%/$20 Min.
Earnings Claim Statement: No
Term of Contract (Years): 10/10
Avg. # Of Employees: 2 FT
Passive Ownership: Discouraged
Encourage Conversions: Yes
Area Develop. Agreements: Yes/10/10

Sub-Franchising Contracts: No
Expand In Territory: Yes
Space Needs: N/A SF; N/A
SUPPORT & TRAINING PROVIDED:
Financial Assistance Provided: Yes(D)
Site Selection Assistance: N/A
Lease Negotiation Assistance: Yes
Co-Operative Advertising: Yes
Franchisee Assoc./Member: No
Size Of Corporate Staff: 6
On-Going Support: a,B,C,D,E,F,G,H,I
Training: 5 Days Orlando, FL; 5 Days Exclusive Franchisee Territory.

SPECIFIC EXPANSION PLANS:
US: All United States
Canada: All Canada
Overseas: Portugal, Mexico, Brazil

◄◄ ►►

TILDEN CAR CARE CENTERS

1325 Franklin Ave., # 165
Garden City, NY 11530
Tel: (800) TILDENS (516) 746-7911
Fax: (516) 746-1288
E-Mail: info@tildencarcare.com
Web Site: www.tildencarcare.com
Mr. Jason Baskind, Dir. of Franchise Development

We're not just brakes. The total care concept allows you to offer a full menu of automotive services for maximum customer procurement - rather than a limited niche market. You benefit from a management team whose concept system and training were proven and perfected before we even considered offering franchises.

BACKGROUND: IFA MEMBER
Established: 1923; 1st Franchised: 1996
Franchised Units: 60
Company-Owned Units 0
Total Units: 60
Dist.: US-60; CAN-0; O'seas-0
North America: 13 States
Density: 24 in FL, 15 in NY, 5 in GA
Projected New Units (12 Months): 10
Qualifications: 3, 4, 3, 3, 3, 4
Registered: CA,FL,IL,IN,NY,VA,WA
FINANCIAL/TERMS:
Cash Investment: $50-60K
Total Investment: $131-171.5K

Minimum Net Worth: $150K
Fees: Franchise - $25K
 Royalty - 6%/$350/Wk.; Ad. -
3%/$175/Wk.
Earnings Claim Statement: No
Term of Contract (Years): 10/5/5
Avg. # Of Employees: 4 FT, 2 PT
Passive Ownership: Discouraged
Encourage Conversions: Yes
Area Develop. Agreements: Yes/10
Sub-Franchising Contracts: No
Expand In Territory: Yes
Space Needs: 3,500+ SF; FS, Auto Mall
SUPPORT & TRAINING PROVIDED:
Financial Assistance Provided: Yes(I)
Site Selection Assistance: Yes
Lease Negotiation Assistance: Yes
Co-Operative Advertising: Yes
Franchisee Assoc./Member: Yes/Yes
Size Of Corporate Staff: 6
On-Going Support: A,B,C,D,E,F,G,H,I
Training: 2 Weeks Home Office.
SPECIFIC EXPANSION PLANS:
US: All United States
Canada: All Canada
Overseas: No

◄◄ ►►

TIRES PLUS AUTO SERVICE CENTERS

600 W. Travelers Tr.
Burnsville, MN 55311
Tel: (800) 754-6519 (612) 882-4820
Fax: (612) 808-2573
E-Mail: franchise@tiresplus.com
Web Site: www.tiresplus.com
Mr. Alan Storry, Franchise Dev. Dir.

TIRES PLUS is one of the fastest growing retail tire store franchisors in the U.S. We are taking a new and innovative approach to tire retailing. Our franchisees enjoy thorough education programs, in-field support, marketing and advertising assistance, name brand product lines, exclusive territories and a proven operational system.

BACKGROUND: IFA MEMBER
Established: 1976; 1st Franchised: 1981

Franchised Units: 62
Company-Owned Units 480
Total Units: 542
Dist.: US-542; CAN-0; O'seas-0
 North America: 24 States
 Density: 173 in FL, 55 in MN, 47 GA
Projected New Units (12 Months): 50
Qualifications: 5, 4, 1, 3, 1, 5
Registered: IL,FL,MI,MN,ND,SD,WI
FINANCIAL/TERMS:
Cash Investment: $100-125K
Total Investment: $325-510K
Minimum Net Worth: $250K
Fees: Franchise - $20-30K
 Royalty - 4%; Ad. - 1%
Earnings Claim Statement: No
Term of Contract (Years): 20/20
Avg. # Of Employees: 10 FT, 5 PT
Passive Ownership: Discouraged
Encourage Conversions: Yes
Area Develop. Agreements: Yes
Sub-Franchising Contracts: No
Expand In Territory: NR
Space Needs: 6,000 SF; FS
SUPPORT & TRAINING PROVIDED:
Financial Assistance Provided: No
Site Selection Assistance: Yes
Lease Negotiation Assistance: Yes
Co-Operative Advertising: NR
Franchisee Assoc./Member: No
Size Of Corporate Staff: 130
On-Going Support: B,C,D,E,F,I
Training: 1 Week in Classroom; 15 Weeks
 at various store locations.
SPECIFIC EXPANSION PLANS:
US: All United States
Canada: No
Overseas: No

TOP VALUE MUFFLER AND BRAKE SHOPS

36887 Schoolcraft
Livonia, MI 48150
Tel: (800) 860-8258 (734) 462-3633 x.16
Fax: (734) 462-1088
E-Mail: franchiseinfo@top-value.com
Web Site: www.top-value.com

Mr. Richard E. Zimmer, Dir. of Franchise
 Development

We fix cars. People are holding onto and maintaining their vehicles longer than ever. Our menu of repair specialization includes: brakes, exhaust, suspension, shocks, struts, air conditioning, general maintenance and general repair. We focus on customer service and franchisee satisfaction, with on-going training, strong purchasing power and field support that you can count on!

BACKGROUND:
Established: 1977; 1st Franchised: 1980
Franchised Units: 32
Company-Owned Units 8
Total Units: 40
Dist.: US-40; CAN-0; O'seas-0
 North America: 3 States
 Density: 27 in MI, 3 in OH, 1 in IN
Projected New Units (12 Months): 8
Qualifications: 3, 3, 3, 3, 3, 4
Registered: MI,IN,IL
FINANCIAL/TERMS:
Cash Investment: $25K
Total Investment: $125K
Minimum Net Worth: $Not Required
Fees: Franchise - $15K
 Royalty - 2-5%; Ad. - 3%
Earnings Claim Statement: Yes
Term of Contract (Years): 10/5
Avg. # Of Employees: 2-3 FT
Passive Ownership: Discouraged
Encourage Conversions: Yes
Area Develop. Agreements: Yes
Sub-Franchising Contracts: Yes
Expand In Territory: Yes
Space Needs: 2,500-3,500 SF; FS
SUPPORT & TRAINING PROVIDED:
Financial Assistance Provided: Yes(I)
Site Selection Assistance: Yes
Lease Negotiation Assistance: Yes
Co-Operative Advertising: Yes
Franchisee Assoc./Member: No
Size Of Corporate Staff: 12
On-Going Support: B,C,D,E,F,G,H,I
Training: 3 Weeks in Livonia, MI; 1 Week
 On-Site.
SPECIFIC EXPANSION PLANS:
US: MI,OH,IN,IL,N. KY
Canada: No
Overseas: No

TUFFY AUTO SERVICE CENTERS

1414 Baronial Plaza Dr.
Toledo, OH 43615

Tel: (800) 228-8339 (419) 865-6900
Fax: (419) 865-7343
E-Mail: jacobs@tuffy.com
Web Site: www.tuffy.com
Mr. Jim Jacobs, Director of Franchising

Tuffy Does It Right!

TUFFY AUTO SERVICE CENTERS have been ranked by Success and Entrepreneur Magazines as one of the top franchises in the country. We are an upscale automotive repair franchise specializing in brakes, exhaust, shocks, alignments, air conditioning, batteries, starting and charging, lube-oil-filter, and more. We provide initial and on-going operations, technical and marketing support. Excellent sites being developed in IN, IA, WI, VA, FL, OH, MN, ND, SD, NE and IL

BACKGROUND:
Established: 1970; 1st Franchised: 1971
Franchised Units: 240
Company-Owned Units 7
Total Units: 247
Dist.: US-247; CAN-0; O'seas-0
 North America: 16 States
 Density: 67 in MI, 63 in OH, 32 in FL
Projected New Units (12 Months): 25
Qualifications: 4, 4, 2, 2, 2, 4
Registered: FL,IL,IN,MD,MI,MN,
 NY,ND,VA,WI
FINANCIAL/TERMS:
Cash Investment: $75K
Total Investment: $127.5-273K
Minimum Net Worth: $250K
Fees: Franchise - $25K
 Royalty - 5%; Ad. - 5%
Earnings Claim Statement: No
Term of Contract (Years): 15/10
Avg. # Of Employees: 4 FT, 1 PT
Passive Ownership: Discouraged
Encourage Conversions: Yes
Area Develop. Agreements: Yes/Negot.
Sub-Franchising Contracts: Yes
Expand In Territory: Yes
Space Needs: 3,800 SF; FS
SUPPORT & TRAINING PROVIDED:
Financial Assistance Provided: Yes(I)
Site Selection Assistance: Yes
Lease Negotiation Assistance: Yes
Co-Operative Advertising: Yes
Franchisee Assoc./Member: Yes/Yes

Size Of Corporate Staff: 36
On-Going Support: C,D,E,G,H,I
Training: 3-4 Weeks in Toledo, OH; 3
  Weeks On-Site at Franchise.
SPECIFIC EXPANSION PLANS:
US: North Central U.S., FL
Canada: No
Overseas: No

≪ ≫

TUNEX INTERNATIONAL

556 East 2100 S.
Salt Lake City, UT 84106
Tel: (800) 448-8639 (801) 486-8133
Fax: (801) 484-4740
E-Mail: info@tunex.com
Web Site: www.tunex.com
Mr. Frank Hauber, Franchise Sales

We offer diagnostic, engine performance, tune-up services and repairs of engine related systems, i.e. ignition, carburetion, fuel injection, emission controls, computer controls, cooling, air conditioning, emission inspections, used-car evaluations, and lubrication services. For maximum customer satisfaction, we always analyze systems for the problem and maintenance requirements, so the customer can make service and repair decisions.

BACKGROUND: IFA MEMBER
Established: 1974; 1st Franchised: 1975
Franchised Units: 23
Company-Owned Units 2
Total Units: 25
Dist.: US-24; CAN-0; O'seas-1
  North America: 6 States
  Density: 16 in UT, 4 in CO, 1 in AZ
Projected New Units (12 Months): 5
Qualifications: 4, 3, 2, 3, 2, 5
Registered: NR
FINANCIAL/TERMS:
Cash Investment: $50-60K
Total Investment: $122.5-163.1K
Minimum Net Worth: $200K
Fees: Franchise - $19K
  Royalty - 5%; Ad. - $600/Mo.
Earnings Claim Statement: No
Term of Contract (Years): 10/10
Avg. # Of Employees: 4 FT
Passive Ownership: Discouraged
Encourage Conversions: N/A

Area Develop. Agreements: Yes/10
Sub-Franchising Contracts: Yes
Expand In Territory: No
Space Needs: 2,750 SF; FS, SF, SC
SUPPORT & TRAINING PROVIDED:
Financial Assistance Provided: Yes(I)
Site Selection Assistance: Yes
Lease Negotiation Assistance: Yes
Co-Operative Advertising: Yes
Franchisee Assoc./Member: No
Size Of Corporate Staff: 7
On-Going Support: C,D,E,G,H,I
Training: 1 Week Corporate Headquarters;
  1 Week On-Site.
SPECIFIC EXPANSION PLANS:
US: Inter-Mountain, Southwest
Canada: Master Franchise
Overseas: Mexico

≪ ≫

CARS. WE KNOW 'EM. WE LOVE 'EM.

VALVOLINE INSTANT OIL CHANGE

3499 Blazer Pkwy.
Lexington, KY 40509
Tel: (800) 622-6846 (606) 357-7070
Fax: (606) 357-7049
Web Site: www.vioc.com
Mr. Les Fry, Manager Franchise Sales

Offers licenses for the establishment and operation of a business which provides a quick oil change, chassis lubrication and routine maintenance checks on automobiles. The licensor and/or its affiliates will offer (to qualified prospects) leasing programs for equipment, signage, POS systems and mortgage based financing for land, building.

BACKGROUND:
Established: 1988; 1st Franchised: 1988
Franchised Units: 275
Company-Owned Units 358
Total Units: 633
Dist.: US-633; CAN-0; O'seas-0
  North America: 35 States
  Density: 73 in OH, 62 in MI, 53 in MN

Projected New Units (12 Months): 65
Qualifications: 5, 4, 2, 3, 5, 5
Registered: All States
FINANCIAL/TERMS:
Cash Investment: $150K
Total Investment: $96-201.8K
Minimum Net Worth: $200K
Fees: Franchise - $30K
  Royalty - 6%; Ad. - 2%
Earnings Claim Statement: Yes
Term of Contract (Years): 15/5/5
Avg. # Of Employees: 4 FT, 2 PT
Passive Ownership: Allowed
Encourage Conversions: Yes
Area Develop. Agreements: No
Sub-Franchising Contracts: No
Expand In Territory: Yes
Space Needs: 15,000 SF; FS
SUPPORT & TRAINING PROVIDED:
Financial Assistance Provided: Yes(I)
Site Selection Assistance: Yes
Lease Negotiation Assistance: Yes
Co-Operative Advertising: Yes
Franchisee Assoc./Member: No
Size Of Corporate Staff: 84
On-Going Support: A,B,C,D,E,F,G,h,I
Training: 3+ Weeks Classroom/OJT/On-
  Site Training.
SPECIFIC EXPANSION PLANS:
US: All United States
Canada: No
Overseas: No

≪ ≫

VICTORY LANE QUICK OIL CHANGE

405 Little Lake Dr.
Ann Arbor, MI 48103
Tel: (734) 996-1196
Fax: (734) 996-4912
E-Mail: victorylane@aol.com
Web Site: www.victorylaneqdc.com
Mr. Derrick B. Oxender, President/CEO

VICTORY LANE QUICK OIL CHANGE is a low-overhead, high-profit, drive-thru, quick oil change operation. We also perform transmission flush, fuel injection cleaning, serpentine belts, radiator flush and other high-profit services. Most franchisees are multi-shop owners.

BACKGROUND:
Established: 1980; 1st Franchised: 1986

Franchised Units:	24
Company-Owned Units	8
Total Units:	32
Dist.: US-32; CAN-0; O'seas-0	
North America:	3 States
Density:	21 in MI, OH, IN
Projected New Units (12 Months):	10
Qualifications:	3, 2, 1, 1, 1, 5
Registered: MI	

FINANCIAL/TERMS:

Cash Investment:	$40-80K
Total Investment:	$80K
Minimum Net Worth:	$80K
Fees: Franchise -	$20K
Royalty - 6%;	Ad. - 1%
Earnings Claim Statement:	No
Term of Contract (Years):	10/10
Avg. # Of Employees:	5 FT
Passive Ownership:	Discouraged
Encourage Conversions:	Yes
Area Develop. Agreements:	Yes/5
Sub-Franchising Contracts:	Yes
Expand In Territory:	Yes
Space Needs: 1,500 SF; FS, SC	

SUPPORT & TRAINING PROVIDED:

Financial Assistance Provided:	Yes(I)
Site Selection Assistance:	Yes
Lease Negotiation Assistance:	Yes
Co-Operative Advertising:	Yes
Franchisee Assoc./Member:	No
Size Of Corporate Staff:	8
On-Going Support:	B,C,D,E,F,G,H
Training: 1 Week Corporate Office.	

SPECIFIC EXPANSION PLANS:

US:	Midwest
Canada:	No
Overseas:	No

YIPES STRIPES

520 Court St., P.O. Box 775
Dover, DE 19903-0775
Tel: (800) 947-3755 (302) 736-1735
Fax: (302) 736-2693
Ms. Diane M. Scinto, President

YIPES STRIPES offers custom striping, graphics and lettering. Exclusive Insta-dry paint formula, on-site servicing of new and used automobile dealerships, total products/inventory package, comprehensive training program and protected territories.

BACKGROUND:

Established: 1972;	1st Franchised: 1988
Franchised Units:	25
Company-Owned Units	1
Total Units:	26

Dist.:	US-26; CAN-0; O'seas-0
North America:	16 States
Density:	7 in OH, 3 in MO, 3 in PA
Projected New Units (12 Months):	12
Qualifications:	3, 4, 2, 2, 2, 4
Registered: NR	

FINANCIAL/TERMS:

Cash Investment:	$40K
Total Investment:	$40-75K
Minimum Net Worth:	$N/A
Fees: Franchise -	$32K
Royalty - 5%/$500;	Ad. - 0%
Earnings Claim Statement:	No
Term of Contract (Years):	5/5
Avg. # Of Employees:	1 FT
Passive Ownership:	Discouraged
Encourage Conversions:	NR
Area Develop. Agreements:	Yes/10
Sub-Franchising Contracts:	No
Expand In Territory:	Yes
Space Needs: NR SF; HB	

SUPPORT & TRAINING PROVIDED:

Financial Assistance Provided:	Yes(I)
Site Selection Assistance:	Yes
Lease Negotiation Assistance:	N/A
Co-Operative Advertising:	No
Franchisee Assoc./Member:	No
Size Of Corporate Staff:	2
On-Going Support:	B,c,d,e,G,H,I
Training: 2 Weeks Dover, DE.	

SPECIFIC EXPANSION PLANS:

US:	All United States
Canada:	No
Overseas:	No

◄◄ ►►

ZIEBART

1290 E. Maple Rd., P. O. Box 1290
Troy, MI 48007-1290
Tel: (800) 877-1312 (248) 588-4100
Fax: (248) 588-0718
E-Mail: rbass@ziebart.com
Web Site: www.ziebart.com
Mr. Dick Bass, Director Franchise Development

Business format consists of automobile detailing, accessories and protection services. Ultra-modern showrooms maximize the exposure for the services offered by the franchisee. The customer base consists of retail, wholesale and fleet - making ZIEBART #1 in the world.

BACKGROUND:

Established: 1954;	1st Franchised: 1962
Franchised Units:	427
Company-Owned Units	22
Total Units:	449

Dist.:	US-265; CAN-50; O'seas-253
North America:	39 States, 7 Provinces
Density:	NR
Projected New Units (12 Months):	50
Qualifications:	5, 4, 2, 3, 4, 5
Registered: All States	

FINANCIAL/TERMS:

Cash Investment:	$60K
Total Investment:	$100-161K
Minimum Net Worth:	$250K
Fees: Franchise -	$24K
Royalty - 8%;	Ad. - 5%
Earnings Claim Statement:	No
Term of Contract (Years):	10/10
Avg. # Of Employees:	2 FT, 3 PT
Passive Ownership:	Discouraged
Encourage Conversions:	Yes
Area Develop. Agreements:	Yes
Sub-Franchising Contracts:	No
Expand In Territory:	Yes
Space Needs: 500 SF; FS	

SUPPORT & TRAINING PROVIDED:

Financial Assistance Provided:	Yes(I)
Site Selection Assistance:	Yes
Lease Negotiation Assistance:	Yes
Co-Operative Advertising:	Yes
Franchisee Assoc./Member:	Yes/Yes
Size Of Corporate Staff:	100
On-Going Support:	a,B,C,D,E,F,G,h,I
Training: 3-6 Weeks Sales, Management and Technical Training at Home Office.	

SPECIFIC EXPANSION PLANS:

US:	All United States
Canada:	All Canada
Overseas:	All Countries

SUPPLEMENTAL LISTING OF FRANCHISORS

Airchek, 5001 A. N. Fwy., Fort Worth, TX 76106 ; (817) 624-9259; Mr. Michael J. Childs (800) 288-6247; (817) 624-8867

All Night Auto, 15965 Jeanette St., Southfield, MI 48075 ; (248) 557-7931; Mr. Dennis Spencer ; (248) 559-1415

AltraTouch Systems, 111 Phlox Ave., Metairie, LA 70001 ; (504) 454-7233; Mr. James A. Richards (800) 678-5220; (504) 454-7233

ATL International, 8334 Veterans Hwy., Millersville, MD 21108 ; (410) 987-9080; Mr. Louis L. Kibler, Jr. (800) 935-8863; (410) 987-1011

Auto Purchase Consulting, 9841 Airport Blvd., # 1517, Los Angeles, CA 90045-5631 ; (310) 670-5603; Mr. David Breslow (800) 756-4CAR; (310) 670-2886

Automated Rustproof of Quebec, 2005 Du Centre, Ste-Rosalie, QC J0H 1X0 CANADA; (450) 799-4846; Ms. Lynda Dube ; (450) 799- 5336

Automotive Technologies, 1807 Berlin Turnpike, Wethersfield, CT 06109 ; (860) 257-7109; Mr. Ed Rose ; (860) 571-7600

Autopro, 7025 Ontario St. E., Montreal, PQ H1N 2B3 CANADA; (514) 256-5497; Mr. Dennis Bellemore ; (514) 899-0044

Autoqual U.S.A., 4 West Dry Creek Cir. #245, Littleton, CO 80120 ; (303) 789-7695; Mr. James T. Orr ; (303) 798-7695

Avis Lube Fast Oil Change, 900 Old Country Rd., Garden City, NY 11530 ; (516) 222-4339; Mr. Jay Sanderson ; (516) 222-3400

Ax Racks, 2285 Austell Rd., Marietta, GA 30060 ; (770) 436-8139; Mr. Wayne Nix (800) 851-8567; (770) 434-2277

Bandag, 2905 N. Highway 61, Muscatine, IA 52761-5886 ; (319) 262-1218; Ms. Twyla Hartman ; (319) 262-1400

Battery Patrol, 1901 E. University Ave., Des Moines, IA 50316 ; (800) 246-1024; Mr. John Williamson (800) 203-6549;

Boomer McCloud, 14 Industrial Park Pl., # 12V, Middletown, CT 06457 ; (860) 632-4877; Mr. Bob Zinno ; (860) 632-4874

Budget Brake & Muffler, 4940 Canada Way, #422, Burnaby, BC V5G 4K6 CANADA; (604) 294-1648; Mr. Warren Swanson (800) 746-9659; (604) 294-6114

Bullhide Liner Corporation, 525 N. Fancher Way, Spokane, WA 99212 ; (509) 532-9028; Mr. Kyle Freeman (800) 789-2855; (509) 532-9007

Canadian Tire Associate Store, Sta. K, 2180 Yonge, P.O. Box 770, Toronto, ON M4P 2V8 CANADA; (416) 480-8165; Ms. Marilyn Rubin ; (416) 480-3000

Cap-It International, 4428 Juneau Street, Burnably, BC V5C 4C8 CANADA; (403) 473-7999; Mr. Hank Funk ; (604) 473-7979

Carstar Automotive, 1124 Rymal Rd. E., Hamilton, ON L8W 3N7 CANADA; (905) 388- 1124; Mr. Larry Jefferies ; (905) 388-4720

Carstar Automotive, 8400 W. 110th St., # 200, Overland Park, KS 66210 ; (913) 451-4436; Mr. Tom Hyland (800) 999-1949; (913) 451-1294

Champion Auto Stores, 2565 Kasota Ave., St. Paul, MN 55108 ; (651) 644-7204; Mr. Jerry R. Hoover (800) 899-6528; (651) 644-6448

Chem-Glass Windshield Repair, 7111-7115 Ohms Ln., Minneapolis, MN 55439 ; (612) 835-1395; Mr. Scott L. Smith (800) 333-8523; (612) 835-1338

Color Tech Systems, 479 Interstate Court, Sarasota, FL 34240 ; (941) 378-3472; Mr. Jerry Wyatt (800) 736-1307; (941) 378-1193

CV Pros, 2301 Advance Rd., Madison, WI 53718 ; (608) 222-0759; Mr. Joe Kielbasa (888) 287-7671; (608) 222-0728

Dealer Specialties International, 60 S. American Way, #A, Monroe, OH 45050 ; (513) 539-2202; Mr. George Nenni (800) 647-8425; (513) 539-2200

Dent Zone, 1919 S. 40th St., # 202, Lincoln, NE 68506-5248 ; (402) 434-5624; Mr. Jack L. Rediger (800) 865-2378; (402) 434-5620

Dents Plus, 2960 Hartley Rd. W., Jacksonville, FL 32257 ; (904) 268-8666; Mr. Jeffrey L. Block ; (904) 268-9916

Ding King, 1280 Bison Ave., # B-9, Newport Beach, CA 92660 ; (949) 442-7611; Mr. Todd Sudeck (800) 304-3464; (949) 979-0966

Doan & Company Auto Appraising, 5090 Hwy. 212, Covington, GA 30016 ; (770) 788-0135; Mr. Peter Sciandra (800) 647-DOAN; (770) 788-8328

Econo Lube N' Tune, 4911 Birch St., Newport Beach, CA 92660 ; (800) 748-5183; Mr. David Schaefers (800) 478-3795; (949) 851-2259

End-A-Flat Tire Safety Sealant, 1155 Green Brian Dr., Bethel Park, PA 15102 ; (412) 833-3409; Mr. Gary B. Griser ; (412) 831-1255

Endrust Auto Appearance Centers, 1155 Greenbriar Dr.,, Bethel Park, PA 15102 ; (412) 833-3409; Mr. William Griser ; (412) 831-1255

Fas-Break Franchise Corporation, 4014 E. Broadway Rd., #408, Phoenix, AZ 85040 ; (602) 437-8848; Mr. Kerry Soat (800) 777-5169; (602) 437-8282

Firestone Tire & Automotive Centres, 5770 Hurontario St., # 400, Mississauga, ON L5R 3G5 CANADA; (905) 890-1991; Mr. Jim West (800) 267-1318; (905) 890-1990

Fixx-A-Dent, P.O. Box 942, Norcross, GA 30017 ; (770) 448-8131; Mr. Greg Huntsman (888) 432-3499; (770) 449-4878

Fleetbay, 500 W. 7th St., # 1720, Fort Worth, TX 76102 ; (817) 348-8905; Mr. Lee Shahwan (888) 24-FLEET;

Gas Tank Renu-USA, 12727 Greenfield St., Detroit, MI 48227 ; (313) 273-4759; Mr. Jim Dupuie (800) 932-2766; (313) 837-6122

Goodeal Discount Transmissions, P.O. Box 50, National Park, NJ 08063 ; (609) 273-6913; Mr. John Mikulski (800) 626-8695; (609) 665-5225

Hamilton Radiator, 624 Parkdale Ave. N., P.O. Box 3760 Station C, Hamilton, ON L8H 7N1 CANADA; (905) 549-4254; Mr. Larry Hammond (800) 263-9950; (905) 549-4181

Hawkinson Tread Service, 1325 Winter St., NE, Minneapolis, MN 55413 ; (612) 331-6569; Ms. Judith Paurus ; (612) 331-1397

It's Dents Or Us, 7801 W. 63rd St., Overland Park, KS 66202 ; (913) 384-6923; Mr. Rick Carrell (800) 279-6787; (913) 384-6787

J.D. Byrider Franchising Inc., 5780 W. 71 St., Indianapolis, IN 46278 ; (317) 387-2373; Mr. Steele Gudal (800) 947-4532;

Kennedy Transmission, 2225 Daniels St., Longlake, MN 55356 ; (612) 476-1983; Mr. Steve Hendrickson ; (612) 894-7020

Leaverton Auto, 827 S. Ninth, St. Joseph, MO 64501 ; (816) 279-8840; Mr. Ronald J. Martin ; (816) 279-7483

Ming Auto Beauty Centers, 346 E. 100 South, Salt Lake City, UT 84111 ; (801) 521-4723; Mr. Irvin D. Bird, Jr. (800) 443-3213; (801) 521-8799

Mitey Muffler Shops/Miteyfast Centers, 3530 Jefferson Hwy., Jefferson, LA 70121 ; (504) 832-4931; Ms. Terry Eckert ; (504) 832-7925

Mobile Wheel Refinishing, 31337 Walker Rd., Bay Village, OH 44140 ; ; Mr. Daniel Koorey (800) 283-2755; (216) 835-0337

Moran Industries, 4444 W. 147th St., Midlothian, IL 60445 ; (708) 389-9882; Mr. Fred Haas (800) 377-9247; (708) 389-5922

Motorcade Industries Ltd., 90 Kincart St., Toronto, ON M6M 5G1 CANADA; (604) 532- 8841; Ms. Linda Lowenthal ; (604) 532- 8896

Mr. Front-End, 192 Northqueen St., Etobicoke, ON M9C 1A8 CANADA; (416) 622-9999; Mr. Gerry Jones ; (416) 622-9998

Mr. Lube, 111 Brunel Rd., # 210, Mississauga, ON L4Z 1X3 CANADA; (905) 890-6977; Mr. Dave Blundell (800) 667-7809; (905) 890-5503

Multi Tune & Tire, 2457 Covington Pike, Memphis, TN 38128 ; ; Mr. Glen Whiteman ; (901) 386-9600

Oil Can Henry's International, 1200 NW Naito Pkwy., # 690, Portland, OR 97209 ; (503) 228-5227; Ms. Kaye Branche (800) 765-6244; (503) 243-6311

Owners Auto Mart, 3100 W. 12th St., # 108, Sioux Falls, SD 57104 ; (605) 336-7375; Mr. Mike Wosje (800) 437-7228; (605) 333-0199

Pacific Pride, P.O. Box 2099, Salem, OR 97308 ; (503) 371-6708; Mr. Paul Sarrell (800) 367-5066; (503) 588-0455

Pick-Ups Plus, 3532 Irwin Simpson Rd., # 85, Mason, OH 45040 ; (513) 398-4271; Mr. John J. Fitzgerald ; (513) 398-4344

Precision Auto Wash, 748 Miller Dr. SE, Leesburg, VA 20177 ; (703) 779-9190; Mr. Lisa Anderson (800) 438-8863; (703) 777-9095

Precision Lube Express, 748 Miller Dr. SE, Leesburg, VA 20175 ; (703) 779-0136; Mr. Kevin Bates (800) 438-8863; (703) 777-9095

Quick Lube & Oil, 4505 Spicewood Springs Rd., # 106, Austin, TX 78759 ; (512) 418-0971; Mr. Art Graf (800) 282-0292; (512) 418-0061

Rent A Tire, Inc., 501 Jones St., Fort Worth, TX 76102 ; (817) 810-9595; Mr. James H. Kauffman ; (817) 810 9600

Rip n' Tear Vinyl Repair Systems Inc., 6832 King George Highway, #316, Surrey, BC V3W 4Z9 CANADA; (604) 536-1870; Mr. Lloyd Orr ; (604) 880-5094

SprayGlo Auto Refinishing & Body Repair, 807 Tillman St., Hahira, GA 31632 ; (912) 794-3502; Mr. Stuart Damron ; (912) 794-3446

Tint King Auto World Supermarkets, 136 Castle Rock Dr., Richmond Hill, ON L4C 5K5 CANADA; ; Mr. Allan Starkman ; (416) 464-TINT

Tint Master and Auto Glass, 6033 Shawson Dr., Unit 9, Mississauga, ON L5T 1H8 CANADA; (905) 670-8468; Mr. James Formosa ; (905) 670-TINT

Tire Warehouse, 492 Main St., P.O. Box 486, Keene, NH 03431-0486 ; (603) 357-5108; Ms. Pam LaFleur (800) 756-9876; (603) 352-4478

TravelCenters of America, 24601 Center Ridge Rd., # 200, Westlake, OH 44145-5634 ; (440) 808-4458; Mr. Pete P. Ward (800) 872-7496; (440) 808-3298

Truck Options, 5865 University Blvd. W., Jacksonville, FL 32216 ; (904) 731-3558;

Mr. Michael Balanky (800) 463-7978; (904) 731-7548

Truckin' America, 2120 Veasley St. #A, Greensboro, NC 27407-4736 ; (336) 854-5858; Mr. Les Standefer ; (336) 852-5799

Vehicare, 701 E. Franklin St., # 1501, Richmond, VA 23219 ; (804) 225-0946; Mr. Bill Killpack (800) 836-2468; (804) 225-0982

Winzer Corporation, 10560 Markison Rd., Dallas, TX 75238 ; (800) 867-7714; Ms. Diane Vanderbilt (800) 527-4126; (214) 341-2122

Xpress Auto, 1200 Spears Rd., Unit 16, Oakville, ON L6L 2X4 CANADA; (905) 815-1196; Mr. Hugh Tulk ; (905) 815-1121

For a full explanation of the data provided in the Franchisor Profiles, please refer to **Chapter 2, "How to Use the Data."**

AUTO/TRUCK/TRAILER RENTAL INDUSTRY PROFILE

Total # Franchisors in Industry Group	25
Total # Franchised Units in Industry Group	7,558
Total # Company-Owned Units in Industry Group	1,027
Total # Operating Units in Industry Group	8,585
Average # Franchised Units/Franchisor	302.3
Average # Company-Owned Units/Franchisor	41.0
Average # Total Units/Franchisor	343.3
Ratio of Total # Franchised Units/Total # Company-Owned Units	7.4:1
Industry Survey Participants	13
Representing % of Industry	52.0%
Average Franchise Fee*:	$36.2K
Average Total Investment*:	$249.7K
Average On-Going Royalty Fee*:	5.8%

If a range was provided, the mid-point of the range was used. See detailed profiles for actual ranges.

FIVE LARGEST PARTICIPANTS IN SURVEY

Company	# Franchised Units	# Co-Owned Units	# Total Units	Franchise Fee	On-Going Royalty	Total Investment
1. Budget Car & Truck Rental	2,490	640	3,130	20K	5%	Varies
2. Thrifty Car Rental	1,226	7	1,233	Varies	3%	200-250K
3. Dollar Rent A Car	827	69	896	12.5K+	8%	100K-2MM
4. Rent-A-Wreck of America	684	0	684	2.5K+	$30/Car	32.8-209K
5. U-Save Auto Rental	462	0	462	20K	$26/Car	56.5-103.5K

All of the data provided are proprietary and should not be quoted without acknowledging *Bond's Franchise Guide.*

AFFORDABLE CAR RENTAL
96 Freneau Ave., # 2
Matawan, NJ 07747
Tel: (800) 631-2290 (732) 290-8300
Fax: (732) 290-8305
Mr. Charles A. Vitale, Vice President

We offer a rental car program which provides training, insurance and management support.

BACKGROUND:
Established: 1981;   1st Franchised: 1981
Franchised Units: 85
Company-Owned Units   0
Total Units: 85
Dist.:   US-85; CAN-0; O'seas-0
  North America: 15 States
  Density: NR
Projected New Units (12 Months):   20
Qualifications: 2, 3, 4, 2, 2, 5
Registered: All States Except CA,WI,LA.
FINANCIAL/TERMS:
Cash Investment: $30K-50K
Total Investment: $Varies
Minimum Net Worth: $Varies
Fees: Franchise - $3.5K Min.
  Royalty - $10-15/Car;   Ad. - 0%
Earnings Claim Statement: No
Term of Contract (Years):   Perpetual
Avg. # Of Employees: 1 FT, 2 PT
Passive Ownership: Not Allowed
Encourage Conversions: N/A
Area Develop. Agreements: No
Sub-Franchising Contracts: No
Expand In Territory: Yes
Space Needs: NR SF; FS
SUPPORT & TRAINING PROVIDED:
Financial Assistance Provided: No
Site Selection Assistance: N/A
Lease Negotiation Assistance: N/A
Co-Operative Advertising: N/A
Franchisee Assoc./Member: Yes/Yes
Size Of Corporate Staff: 9
On-Going Support: C,D,F,G,H,I
Training: 2 Days Corporate in NJ.
SPECIFIC EXPANSION PLANS:
US: All United States
Canada: No
Overseas: No

◄◄ ►►

BUDGET CAR & TRUCK RENTAL
4225 Naperville Rd.
Lisle, IL 60532
Tel: (630) 955-7039
Fax: (630) 955-7811
Web Site: www.budget.com

Mr. Bill Weckstein, Dir. Fran.Operations

Car and truck rental, both in airports and local markets.

BACKGROUND:
Established: 1958;   1st Franchised: 1960
Franchised Units: 2,490
Company-Owned Units   640
Total Units: 3,130
Dist.:   US-960; CAN-375; O'seas-1,458
  North America: 50 States, 9 Provinces
  Density: 108 in CA, 107 in FL, 57 AZ
Projected New Units (12 Months):   25
Qualifications: 4, 5, 5, 3, 3, 5
Registered: All States
FINANCIAL/TERMS:
Cash Investment: $55K
Total Investment: $Varies
Minimum Net Worth: $NR
Fees: Franchise - $20K
  Royalty - 5%;   Ad. - 2.5%
Earnings Claim Statement: No
Term of Contract (Years):   5/5
Avg. # Of Employees: Varies
Passive Ownership: Discouraged
Encourage Conversions: Yes
Area Develop. Agreements: No
Sub-Franchising Contracts: Yes
Expand In Territory: Yes
Space Needs: 15,000 SF; FS
SUPPORT & TRAINING PROVIDED:
Financial Assistance Provided: Yes(D)
Site Selection Assistance: Yes
Lease Negotiation Assistance: Yes
Co-Operative Advertising: Yes
Franchisee Assoc./Member: Yes/Yes
Size Of Corporate Staff: 300
On-Going Support: b,C,D,E,G,H,I
Training: 1 Week Corporate Office; On-Site
  as Necessary.
SPECIFIC EXPANSION PLANS:
US: All United States
Canada: All Canada
Overseas: All Countries

◄◄ ►►

BUDGET RENT A CAR OF CANADA
3080 Yonge St., #4000
Toronto, ON M4N 3N1 CANADA
Tel: (800) 268-8941 (416) 622-3366
Fax: (416) 622-5555
Mr. Ron Groves, Mgr. Franchising/Bus. Dev.

Car and truck rental, both in airports and local markets.

BACKGROUND:
Established: 1963;   1st Franchised: 1963
Franchised Units: 380
Company-Owned Units   8
Total Units: 388
Dist.:   US-0; CAN-388; O'seas-0
  North America: NR
  Density: NR
Projected New Units (12 Months):   5
Qualifications: 4, 4, 5, 3, 3, 3
Registered: AB
FINANCIAL/TERMS:
Cash Investment: $100K
Total Investment: $100K+
Minimum Net Worth: $1MM
Fees: Franchise - $20K
  Royalty - 7.5%;   Ad. - 0%
Earnings Claim Statement: No
Term of Contract (Years):   5/5
Avg. # Of Employees: 2 FT, 2 PT
Passive Ownership: Discouraged
Encourage Conversions: No
Area Develop. Agreements: No
Sub-Franchising Contracts: Yes
Expand In Territory: Yes
Space Needs: NR SF; FS, SF, Dealership
SUPPORT & TRAINING PROVIDED:
Financial Assistance Provided: No
Site Selection Assistance: Yes
Lease Negotiation Assistance: Yes
Co-Operative Advertising: No
Franchisee Assoc./Member: Yes/Yes
Size Of Corporate Staff: 40
On-Going Support: A,B,C,D,E,f,G,H,I
Training: 3 Days in Chicago, IL.
SPECIFIC EXPANSION PLANS:
US: No
Canada: AB,SK,MB,ON,PQ
Overseas: No

◄◄ ►►

DOLLAR RENT A CAR
5330 E. 31st St.
Tulsa, OK 74135
Tel: (800) 555-9893 (918) 669-3103
Fax: (918) 669-3006
E-Mail: pfritz@dollar.com
Web Site: www.dollar.com
Mr. Peter Fritz, Dir. Franchise Dev.

DOLLAR RENT A CAR operates and licenses others to operate daily car rental operations. Established over 30 years ago, DOLLAR RENT A CAR now serves the worldwide car rental market.

BACKGROUND:
Established: 1965;   1st Franchised: 1966

Franchised Units: 827
Company-Owned Units: <u>69</u>
Total Units: 896
Dist.: US-266; CAN-76; O'seas-554
North America: NR
Density: CA, TX, FL
Projected New Units (12 Months): 24
Qualifications: 5, 5, 4, 4, 4, 5
Registered: All States

FINANCIAL/TERMS:
Cash Investment: $100K-2MM
Total Investment: $100K-2MM
Minimum Net Worth: $250K
Fees: Franchise - $12.5K+
Royalty - 8%; Ad. - Included
Earnings Claim Statement: No
Term of Contract (Years): 10/10
Avg. # Of Employees: Varies
Passive Ownership: Not Allowed
Encourage Conversions: Yes
Area Develop. Agreements: No
Sub-Franchising Contracts: No
Expand In Territory: Yes
Space Needs: 2,000+ SF; FS, SF, SC

SUPPORT & TRAINING PROVIDED:
Financial Assistance Provided: Yes(I)
Site Selection Assistance: No
Lease Negotiation Assistance: No
Co-Operative Advertising: Yes
Franchisee Assoc./Member: Yes/No
Size Of Corporate Staff: 400
On-Going Support: a,B,C,D,E,G,H,I
Training: 3 Days Headquarters Orientation;
2 Weeks On-Site Field Training; 1 Week
Automation.

SPECIFIC EXPANSION PLANS:
US: Not FL,MA,VT,NH,NV,AR,UT,MT
Canada: 2 Master Fran.
Overseas: Australia, China, Southeast Asia

⋘ ⋙

DOLLAR RENT A CAR (CANADA)
1027 Yonge St., 3rd Fl.
Toronto, ON M4W 2K9 CANADA
Tel: (800) 254-7561 (416) 969-1190
Fax: (416) 969-9582
E-Mail: rmohammed@dollarcanada.com
Mr. Ray Mohammed, Franchise
Operations

Daily, weekly, monthly car and truck rental.

BACKGROUND:
Established: 1966; 1st Franchised: 1990
Franchised Units: 40
Company-Owned Units: <u>0</u>
Total Units: 40

Dist.: US-0; CAN-42; O'seas-0
North America: 9 Provinces
Density: ON, BC, PQ
Projected New Units (12 Months): 20
Qualifications: 5, 5, 5, 3, 3, 3
Registered: AB

FINANCIAL/TERMS:
Cash Investment: $100-160K
Total Investment: $150-300K
Minimum Net Worth: $250K
Fees: Franchise - $10-50K
Royalty - 7%; Ad. - 2%
Earnings Claim Statement: Yes
Term of Contract (Years): 5/5
Avg. # Of Employees: 3 FT, 1 PT
Passive Ownership: Discouraged
Encourage Conversions: Yes
Area Develop. Agreements: Yes/3
Sub-Franchising Contracts: Yes
Expand In Territory: Yes
Space Needs: 1,200 SF; FS

SUPPORT & TRAINING PROVIDED:
Financial Assistance Provided: Yes(I)
Site Selection Assistance: Yes
Lease Negotiation Assistance: Yes
Co-Operative Advertising: Yes
Franchisee Assoc./Member: No
Size Of Corporate Staff: 10
On-Going Support: B,C,D,E,F,H,I
Training: 5 Days Toronto, ON.

SPECIFIC EXPANSION PLANS:
US: No
Canada: All Canada
Overseas: No

⋘ ⋙

PAYLESS CAR RENTAL SYSTEM
2350 34th St. N.
St. Petersburg, FL 33713
Tel: (800) 729-5255 (727) 321-6352
Fax: (727) 323-6856
E-Mail: fran@paylesscarrental.com
Web Site: www.paylesscarrental.com
Mr. Marty Juarez, Director of Franchise Sales

PAYLESS CAR RENTAL SYSTEM, Inc., has been a recognized name in the car rental industry for almost 30 years. Car rental expertise and an experienced corporate office staff give each franchisee individual assistance and the competitive edge. We offer the tools to become successful in the vehicle rental and sales business. The

franchise fee includes an innovative rental industry computer system and image items worth $10K-25K.

BACKGROUND:
Established: 1971; 1st Franchised: 1971
Franchised Units: 132
Company-Owned Units: <u>0</u>
Total Units: 132
Dist.: US-76; CAN-0; O'seas-56
North America: 20 States
Density: 14 in FL, 7 in CA, 5 in AK
Projected New Units (12 Months): 75
Qualifications: 5, 4, 3, 1, 3, 5
Registered: All States

FINANCIAL/TERMS:
Cash Investment: $100K (Varies)
Total Investment: $Varies
Minimum Net Worth: $Varies
Fees: Franchise - $35-500K
Royalty - 5%; Ad. - 3%
Earnings Claim Statement: No
Term of Contract (Years): 5/5
Avg. # Of Employees: Varies
Passive Ownership: Discouraged
Encourage Conversions: Yes
Area Develop. Agreements: Yes/5
Sub-Franchising Contracts: Int
Expand In Territory: Yes
Space Needs: Varies SF; FS

SUPPORT & TRAINING PROVIDED:
Financial Assistance Provided: Yes(I)
Site Selection Assistance: Yes
Lease Negotiation Assistance: No
Co-Operative Advertising: Yes
Franchisee Assoc./Member: Yes/Yes
Size Of Corporate Staff: 55
On-Going Support: A,B,C,D,E,G,h,I
Training: 3-5 Days Corporate Office; 3-5
Days Franchisee's Location

SPECIFIC EXPANSION PLANS:
US: All United States
Canada: All Canada
Overseas: All Countries

⋘ ⋙

RENT-A-WRECK OF AMERICA
10324 S. Dolfield Rd.
Owings Mills, MD 21117
Tel: (800) 421-7253 (410) 581-5755
Fax: (410) 581-1566
E-Mail: raw@rent-a-wreck.com
Web Site: www.rent-a-wreck.com
Mr. Alan Wagner, Director of Sales

America's # 1 neighborhood car rental company, RENT-A-WRECK has attained the highest ratings in the franchising industry. For 5 successive years, Entrepreneur Magazine rated RENT-A-WRECK # 1 in its category for the prestigious Franchise 500 awards. The annual Success Magazine named RENT-A-WRECK 'one of the best-managed franchises in America.' Success surveyed over 2,800 franchise companies in all industries and ranked RENT-A-WRECK 4th.

BACKGROUND: IFA MEMBER
Established: 1973; 1st Franchised: 1978
Franchised Units: 684
Company-Owned Units 0
Total Units: 684
Dist.: US-663; CAN-0; O'seas-21
  North America: 49 States
  Density: 53 in CA, 33 in NY, 24 in NJ
Projected New Units (12 Months): 75
Qualifications: 3, 5, 2, 3, 3, 3
Registered: All States
FINANCIAL/TERMS:
Cash Investment: $32.8K
Total Investment: $32.8-209K
Minimum Net Worth: $50K
Fees: Franchise - $2.5K+
  Royalty - $30/Car; Ad. - $7/Car
Earnings Claim Statement: Yes
Term of Contract (Years): 10/5
Avg. # Of Employees: 1 FT
Passive Ownership: Discouraged
Encourage Conversions: No
Area Develop. Agreements: No
Sub-Franchising Contracts: No
Expand In Territory: Yes
Space Needs: 1,500 SF; FS, SF, SC
SUPPORT & TRAINING PROVIDED:
Financial Assistance Provided: Yes(D)
Site Selection Assistance: No
Lease Negotiation Assistance: Yes
Co-Operative Advertising: Yes
Franchisee Assoc./Member: Yes/Yes
Size Of Corporate Staff: 25
On-Going Support: C,D,e,G,h,I
Training: 1 Week Baltimore, MD.
SPECIFIC EXPANSION PLANS:
US: All United States
Canada: No
Overseas: All Countries

≪ ≫

RENT-A-WRECK OF CANADA
7710 5th St., SE, # 204
Calgary, AB T2H 2L9 CANADA
Tel: (800) 668-8591 (403) 259-6666
Fax: (403) 259-6776
E-Mail: susanh@rentawreck.ca
Web Site: www.rentawreck.ca
Ms. Susan Hunt, Dir. Franchise
  Development

Our success is based upon teaching our franchisees how to achieve their professional goals. Our reputation is based upon providing the lowest car and truck rental rates across Canada.

BACKGROUND:
Established: 1976; 1st Franchised: 1976
Franchised Units: 82
Company-Owned Units 0
Total Units: 82
Dist.: US-0; CAN-82; O'seas-0
  North America: 9 Provinces
  Density: 21 in BC, 15 in AB, 12 in NF
Projected New Units (12 Months): 21
Qualifications: 5, 4, 2, 3, 4, 5
Registered: AB
FINANCIAL/TERMS:
Cash Investment: $Varies
Total Investment: $Varies
Minimum Net Worth: $75K
Fees: Franchise - $10-30K
  Royalty - 6%; Ad. - 4%
Earnings Claim Statement: No
Term of Contract (Years): 5/5
Avg. # Of Employees: 3 FT, 2 PT
Passive Ownership: Discouraged
Encourage Conversions: Yes
Area Develop. Agreements: No
Sub-Franchising Contracts: No
Expand In Territory: Yes
Space Needs: 1,000 SF; SF
SUPPORT & TRAINING PROVIDED:
Financial Assistance Provided: Yes(I)
Site Selection Assistance: Yes
Lease Negotiation Assistance: Yes
Co-Operative Advertising: Yes
Franchisee Assoc./Member: Yes/Yes
Size Of Corporate Staff: 8
On-Going Support: C,d.E,f,G,H,I
Training: 2 Weeks Calgary, AB.
SPECIFIC EXPANSION PLANS:
US: N/A
Canada: All Canada
Overseas: No

≪ ≫

SENSIBLE CAR RENTAL
96 Freneau Ave., # 2
Matawan, NJ 07747
Tel: (800) 367-5159 (732) 583-8500
Fax: (732) 290-8305
E-Mail: sensible96@aol.com
Mr. Charles A. Vitale, Vice President
  General Manager

We offer a rental car program which provides training, insurance and support. Majority of franchisee are used car dealers and other automotive related businesspersons.

BACKGROUND:
Established: 1986; 1st Franchised: 1986
Franchised Units: 110
Company-Owned Units 0
Total Units: 110
Dist.: US-110; CAN-0; O'seas-0
  North America: 22 States
  Density: 25 in NY, 24 in NJ, 10 in MA
Projected New Units (12 Months): 25
Qualifications: 2, 3, 4, 2, 2, 5
Registered: All States Except CA,WI,LA
FINANCIAL/TERMS:
Cash Investment: $20-25K
Total Investment: $25-30K
Minimum Net Worth: $Varies
Fees: Franchise - $4-7K
  Royalty - $10-15/Car; Ad. - 0%
Earnings Claim Statement: No
Term of Contract (Years): Perpetual
Avg. # Of Employees: 1 FT, 1 PT
Passive Ownership: Not Allowed
Encourage Conversions: N/A
Area Develop. Agreements: No
Sub-Franchising Contracts: No
Expand In Territory: Yes
Space Needs: NR SF; FS
SUPPORT & TRAINING PROVIDED:
Financial Assistance Provided: Yes
Site Selection Assistance: No
Lease Negotiation Assistance: No
Co-Operative Advertising: Yes
Franchisee Assoc./Member: Yes/Yes
Size Of Corporate Staff: 10
On-Going Support: C,d,F,G,H,I
Training: 2 Days in Matawan, NJ.
SPECIFIC EXPANSION PLANS:
US: All United States
Canada: No
Overseas: No

≪ ≫

THRIFTY CAR RENTAL
5310 E. 31st St.
Tulsa, OK 74135
Tel: (800) 532-3401 (918) 669-2219
Fax: (918) 669-2061
E-Mail: franchisesales@thrifty.com

Web Site: www.thrifty.com
Mr. Monty Merrill, Executive Director

Thrifty *Car Rental*

THRIFTY operates in over 65 countries and territories, with over 1,200 locations throughout North and South America, Europe, the Middle East, Caribbean, Asia and the Pacific, and is the fastest-growing car rental company in Canada and Australia. THRIFTY has a significant presence both in the airport and local car rental markets. Approximately 51% of its business is in the airport market, 49% in the local market.

BACKGROUND:

Established: 1950; 1st Franchised: 1970
Franchised Units: 1,226
Company-Owned Units   7
Total Units: 1,233
Dist.:   US-519; CAN-132; O'seas-475
North America: 48 States
Density: 54 in CA, 28 in TX, 28 in FL
Projected New Units (12 Months): 50-100
Qualifications: 5, 5, 5, 3, 3, 5
Registered: All States
FINANCIAL/TERMS:
Cash Investment: $150K+
Total Investment: $200-250K
Minimum Net Worth: $600K
Fees: Franchise - $Varies
Royalty - 3%;   Ad. - 2.5-5%
Earnings Claim Statement: No
Term of Contract (Years):   10/5
Avg. # Of Employees: 4-6 FT Min.
Passive Ownership: Not Allowed
Encourage Conversions: Yes
Area Develop. Agreements: No
Sub-Franchising Contracts: No
Expand In Territory: Yes
Space Needs: Varies SF; FS, SF, SC, RM
SUPPORT & TRAINING PROVIDED:
Financial Assistance Provided: Yes(B)
Site Selection Assistance: No
Lease Negotiation Assistance: Yes
Co-Operative Advertising: Yes
Franchisee Assoc./Member: No
Size Of Corporate Staff: 650
On-Going Support: A,B,C,D,E,F,G,h,I
Training: 8 Days + Mentor Program at
Headquarters in Tulsa, OK.
SPECIFIC EXPANSION PLANS:
US: Selected Markets Remaining
Canada: All Canada
Overseas: All Countries

◁◁ ▷▷

Thrifty *Car Rental*

THRIFTY CAR RENTAL
(CANADA)
6050 Indian Line
Mississauga, ON L4V 1G5 CANADA
Tel: (800) 667-5925 (905) 612-1881
Fax: (905) 612-1893
E-Mail: jforrester@thrifty.com
Mr. Jack Forrester, Manager Franchise Sales

THRIFTY CAR RENTAL's high name awareness and consistent image of quality and reliable service have resulted in THRIFTY becoming one of North America's fastest-growing car rental companies. THRIFTY has over 1,200 locations in 60 countries worldwide, with approximately 145 locations in Canada. Represented at all major Canadian airport locations, also the largest off-airport car rental in the U. S. and the 5th largest in # of locations throughout North America. Full range of innovative support services.

BACKGROUND:

Established: 1958; 1st Franchised: 1984
Franchised Units: 125
Company-Owned Units   20
Total Units: 145
Dist.:   US-560; CAN-145; O'seas-500
North America: NR
Density: NR
Projected New Units (12 Months):   10
Qualifications: 5, 4, 3, 4, 3, 3
Registered: All States
FINANCIAL/TERMS:
Cash Investment: $50-300K
Total Investment: $200-500K
Minimum Net Worth: $250K
Fees: Franchise - $15K+
Royalty - 5%;   Ad. - 3%
Earnings Claim Statement: No
Term of Contract (Years):   10/5
Avg. # Of Employees: 3 FT, 2 PT
Passive Ownership: Not Allowed
Encourage Conversions: Yes
Area Develop. Agreements: No
Sub-Franchising Contracts: No
Expand In Territory: Yes
Space Needs: Varies SF; FS, SF, SC, RM,
Dealership
SUPPORT & TRAINING PROVIDED:
Financial Assistance Provided: Yes(I)
Site Selection Assistance: Yes
Lease Negotiation Assistance: Yes
Co-Operative Advertising: Yes

Franchisee Assoc./Member: Yes/Yes
Size Of Corporate Staff: 465
On-Going Support: B,C,D,e,F,G,h,I
Training: 1 Week On-Site; 1 Week at
Headquarters.
SPECIFIC EXPANSION PLANS:
US: All United States
Canada: All Canada
Overseas: All Countries

◁◁ ▷▷

U-SAVE AUTO RENTAL
4780 I-55 North, # 300
Jackson, MS 39211
Tel: (800) 438-2300 (601) 713-4333
Fax: (601) 713-4330
E-Mail: info@usave.net
Web Site: www.usave.net
Mr. Jay Mitchell, Vice President of Sales

U-SAVE is strategically positioned as the #2 operator in the local neighborhood rental car market, providing superior customer service and affordable rental cars to consumers who need a rental car to temporarily augment their personal use vehicle, or who need a car to replace a vehicle being repaired, and to local businesses that rent vehicles on an an-needed basis.

BACKGROUND: IFA MEMBER
Established: 1979; 1st Franchised: 1979
Franchised Units: 462
Company-Owned Units   0
Total Units: 462
Dist.:   US-456; CAN-0; O'seas-6
North America: 47 States
Density: 35 in GA, 34 in OH, 25 in TN
Projected New Units (12 Months):   80
Qualifications: 5, 4, 3, 2, 1, 4
Registered: All States
FINANCIAL/TERMS:
Cash Investment: $60K Liquid
Total Investment: $56.5-103.5K
Minimum Net Worth: $250K
Fees: Franchise - $20K
Royalty - $26/Vehicle; Ad. - $0.50/Car
Earnings Claim Statement: No
Term of Contract (Years):   10/10
Avg. # Of Employees: 2 FT, 2 PT
Passive Ownership: Discouraged
Encourage Conversions: Yes
Area Develop. Agreements: No

Sub-Franchising Contracts:	No
Expand In Territory:	Yes

Space Needs: 1,500-2,000 SF; FS, SF, SC, Other Businesses

SUPPORT & TRAINING PROVIDED:

Financial Assistance Provided:	Yes(D)
Site Selection Assistance:	No
Lease Negotiation Assistance:	No
Co-Operative Advertising:	Yes
Franchisee Assoc./Member:	Yes/Yes
Size Of Corporate Staff:	50
On-Going Support:	b,C,D,E,F,G,H,I

Training: 5 Days Jackson, MS.

SPECIFIC EXPANSION PLANS:

US:	All United States
Canada:	No
Overseas:	No

◅◅ ▻▻

WHEELCHAIR GETAWAYS

P.O. Box 605
Versailles, KY 40383-0605
Tel: (800) 536-5518 (606) 873-4973
Fax: (606) 873-8039
E-Mail: sgatewood@aol.com
Web Site: www.wheelchair-getaways.com
Mr. Richard Gatewood, President

WHEELCHAIR GETAWAYS rents wheelchair-accessible vans to wheelchair users by the day, week, month or year. We receive referrals from the major car rental companies and travel agencies. We are the leader in our field and encourage any and all applicants. We will train and continue to support you in every aspect of ownership and management. Affordable, accessible transportation is becoming a necessity as a result of the Americans With Disabilities Act.

BACKGROUND:

Established: 1988;	1st Franchised: 1989
Franchised Units:	39
Company-Owned Units	0
Total Units:	39
Dist.:	US-39; CAN-0; O'seas-0
North America:	43 States, Puerto Rico
Density:	5 in FL, 3 in NY, 2 in CA
Projected New Units (12 Months):	5
Qualifications:	3, 5, 3, 3, 4, 4
Registered:	CA,FL,IL,IN,MD,MI,NY, VA,WA,DC

FINANCIAL/TERMS:

Cash Investment:	$38-100K
Total Investment:	$38-100K
Minimum Net Worth:	$75K
Fees: Franchise -	$17.5K
Royalty - $550/Van/Yr.;	Ad. -

$550/Van/Yr

Earnings Claim Statement:	No
Term of Contract (Years):	10/10
Avg. # Of Employees:	2 FT
Passive Ownership:	Discouraged
Encourage Conversions:	No
Area Develop. Agreements:	No
Sub-Franchising Contracts:	No
Expand In Territory:	Yes

Space Needs: 500 SF; FS, SF, RM, HB

SUPPORT & TRAINING PROVIDED:

Financial Assistance Provided:	Yes(I)
Site Selection Assistance:	Yes
Lease Negotiation Assistance:	No
Co-Operative Advertising:	N/A
Franchisee Assoc./Member:	No
Size Of Corporate Staff:	3
On-Going Support:	E,G,h,I

Training: 1 Day Corporate Headquarters or at Franchisee Site.

SPECIFIC EXPANSION PLANS:

US:	IL,WI,SC,TX,AL,OR,Northwest
Canada:	All Canada
Overseas:	All Countries

◅◅ ▻▻

SUPPLEMENTAL LISTING OF FRANCHISORS

AvisCar Inc. Avis Car & Truck Rental, 1 Convair Dr.E., Etobicoke, ON M9W 6Z9 CANADA; (416) 213-8511; Mr. David McWilliams ; (416) 213-4274

Discount Car & Truck Rentals, 720 Arrow Rd., North York, ON M9M 2M1 CANADA; (416) 744-0624; Mr. John Stanaitis (800) 263-2355; (416) 744-0123

Driver's Delight Auto Rentals, 414 Autobahn Dr., Mississauga, ON L38 2L9 CANADA; (905) 625-9076; Ms. Rachel Hudson ; (905) 625-9076

National Car Rental Licensing, 208 St. James Ave., Goose Creek, SC 29445 ; (843) 818-6053; Mr. William F. Cahill (888) 659-3046; (843) 553-6229

Practical Rent A Car, 4780 I-55 N., # 300, Jackson, MS 39211 ; (601) 713-4330; Mr. Robert Hoeffner (800) 424-7722; (601) 713-4333

Price King Rent A Car, 203 W. Mulberry, Ft. Collins, CO 80521 ; (970) 490-1514; Mr. Jerry King (800) 985-4647; (970) 490-2000

Rent 'N Drive, 1919 S. 40th St., # 202, Lincoln, NE 68506-5248 ; (402) 434-5624; Mr. Jack L. Rediger (800) 865-2378; (402) 434-5620

Rent A Vette, 1025 W. Laurel, # 102, San Diego, CA 92101 ; (619) 238-4279; Mr. John Pounds (800) 627-0808; (619) 238-3883

Select Leasing, 2942 N. 16th St., Phoenix, AZ 85016 ; (602) 279-6188; Mr. Gerd D. Linke (800) 782-2522; (602) 279-3430

Wheels 4 Rent Used Car Rentals, 77 Nassau St., Toronto, ON M5T 1M6 CANADA; (416) 585-4797; Mr. Ernest Weintraub (877) 707-2500; (416) 585-7782

BUILDING & REMODELING/FURNITURE & APPLIANCE REPAIR INDUSTRY PROFILE

Total # Franchisors in Industry Group	96
Total # Franchised Units in Industry Group	6,808
Total # Company-Owned Units in Industry Group	<u>171</u>
Total # Operating Units in Industry Group	56,979
Average # Franchised Units/Franchisor	70.9
Average # Company-Owned Units/Franchisor	<u>1.8</u>
Average # Total Units/Franchisor	72.7
Ratio of Total # Franchised Units/Total # Company-Owned Units	39.8:1
Industry Survey Participants	37
Representing % of Industry	38.5%
Average Franchise Fee*:	$22.3K
Average Total Investment*:	$132.1K
Average On-Going Royalty Fee*:	5.5%

If a range was provided, the mid-point of the range was used. See detailed profiles for actual ranges.

FIVE LARGEST PARTICIPANTS IN SURVEY

Company	# Fran-chised Units	# Co-Owned Units	# Total Units	Franchise Fee	On-Going Royalty	Total Investment
1. Furniture Medic	595	0	595	14.9-18K	7%/$200 Min.	25-35K
2. Dreammaker Bath & Kitchen	357	0	357	27K	3-6%	25-50K
3. Kitchen Tune-Up	290	1	291	15K	4.5-7%	28-35K
4. Four Seasons Sunrooms	234	2	236	7.5-15K	0%	13.3-82.5K
5. Perma-Glaze	177	1	178	21.5K+	6/5/4%	22-25K+

All of the data provided are proprietary and should not be quoted without acknowledging *Bond's Franchise Guide.*

ABC SEAMLESS
3001 Fiechtner Dr.
Fargo, ND 58103
Tel: (800) 732-6577 (701) 293-5952
Fax: (701) 293-3107
E-Mail: theduck@abcseamless.com
Web Site: www.abcseamless.com
Mr. Veryl Vick, Franchise Director

Franchisor of seamless steel siding, gutters, soffit and fascia. A portable machine embosses and creates seamless siding profiles of any length on the job site.

BACKGROUND:
Established: 1978;   1st Franchised: 1978
Franchised Units: 126
Company-Owned Units   6
Total Units: 132
Dist.:   US-132; CAN-0; O'seas-0
 North America: 38 States
 Density: 22 in MN, 16 in WI, 12 in IL
Projected New Units (12 Months):   10
Qualifications: 5, 4, 5, 4, 4, 4
Registered: CA,FL,HI,IL,IN,MD,MI,MN,
 NY,ND,OR,RI,SD,VA,WA,WI,DC
FINANCIAL/TERMS:
Cash Investment: $20-40K
Total Investment: $73.8-212K
Minimum Net Worth: $150K
Fees: Franchise - $12K
 Royalty - 2-5%;   Ad. - 0.05%
Earnings Claim Statement: No
Term of Contract (Years):   10/10
Avg. # Of Employees: 4 FT
Passive Ownership: Discouraged
Encourage Conversions: No
Area Develop. Agreements: Yes/Varies
Sub-Franchising Contracts: No
Expand In Territory: Yes
Space Needs: NR SF; NR
SUPPORT & TRAINING PROVIDED:
Financial Assistance Provided: Yes(I)
Site Selection Assistance: N/A
Lease Negotiation Assistance: Yes
Co-Operative Advertising: N/A
Franchisee Assoc./Member: No
Size Of Corporate Staff: 15
On-Going Support: C,D,E,G,H,I
Training: 2 Weeks at Franchisee's Site;
 On-Going at Corporate Location.
SPECIFIC EXPANSION PLANS:
US: All United States
Canada: No
Overseas: No

<< >>

AIRE SERV HEATING & AIR CONDITIONING
1020 N. University Parks Dr.
Waco, TX 76707
Tel: (800) 583-2662 (254) 745-2440
Fax: (254) 745-2546
E-Mail: aireserv@dwyergroup.com
Web Site: www.aireserv.com
Mr. Mike Hawkins, VP Franchising

Serving the heating, cooling and air balancing needs of all residential and light commercial buildings, including the repair and installation of systems and "whole house" analysis involving infiltrometer testing, duct cleaning, etc.

BACKGROUND: IFA MEMBER
Established: 1992;   1st Franchised: 1994
Franchised Units: 57
Company-Owned Units   0
Total Units: 57
Dist.:   US-53; CAN-2; O'seas-2
 North America: 31 States, 2 Provinces
 Density: 5 in GA, 4 in TX, 3 in NJ
Projected New Units (12 Months):   24
Qualifications: 4, 3, 5, 3, 2, 4
Registered: All States
FINANCIAL/TERMS:
Cash Investment: $15-71K
Total Investment: $52-91K
Minimum Net Worth: $100K
Fees: Franchise - $25K
 Royalty - 2.5-4.5%;   Ad. - 2%
Earnings Claim Statement: No
Term of Contract (Years):   10/5
Avg. # Of Employees: Varies
Passive Ownership: Discouraged
Encourage Conversions: Yes
Area Develop. Agreements: No
Sub-Franchising Contracts: No
Expand In Territory: No
Space Needs: NR SF; N/A
SUPPORT & TRAINING PROVIDED:
Financial Assistance Provided: Yes(B)
Site Selection Assistance: N/A
Lease Negotiation Assistance: N/A
Co-Operative Advertising: No
Franchisee Assoc./Member: Yes
Size Of Corporate Staff: 7
On-Going Support: C,D,E,G,h,I
Training: 6 Days Corporate Office; 3 Days
 On-Site.

SPECIFIC EXPANSION PLANS:
US: All United States
Canada: All Canada
Overseas: U.K., Latin America

<< >>

AMERICAN ASPHALT SEALCOATING
8735 Palomino Trail, # 700
Kirtland, OH 44090
Tel: (888) 603-7325 (440) 256-0333
Fax: (440) 256-6325
E-Mail: asphaltusa@aol.com
Mr. Todd W. Tornstrom, Chief Executive
 Officer

Get your share at the billion dollar pavement maintenance industry with our franchise. Residential, commercial and industrial sealcoating and pavement services. 94% of all pavement is asphalt that needs our service. (50 million driveways, 7+ million parking lots, 4 million miles of road.) Our expert training staff and low start-up investment of $20K will get you up and running within 60 days. Your trained crew will perform the work while you manage the business from your home-based office.

BACKGROUND: IFA MEMBER
Established: 1988;   1st Franchised: 1998
Franchised Units: 6
Company-Owned Units   1
Total Units: 7
Dist.:   US-7; CAN-0; O'seas-0
 North America: 4 States
 Density: 4 in OH, 1 in MI, 1 in VA
Projected New Units (12 Months):   10
Qualifications: 4, 3, 1, 1, 1, 3
Registered: NR
FINANCIAL/TERMS:
Cash Investment: $10-30K
Total Investment: $25-40K
Minimum Net Worth: $50K
Fees: Franchise - $9.5-12.5K
 Royalty - 7%;   Ad. - 1%
Earnings Claim Statement: No
Term of Contract (Years):   15/15
Avg. # Of Employees: 1-2 FT, 1-2 PT
Passive Ownership: Not Allowed
Encourage Conversions: Yes
Area Develop. Agreements: Yes/5
Sub-Franchising Contracts: No
Expand In Territory: Yes
Space Needs: N/A SF; N/A
SUPPORT & TRAINING PROVIDED:
Financial Assistance Provided: Yes(I)

Site Selection Assistance: Yes
Lease Negotiation Assistance: Yes
Co-Operative Advertising: No
Franchisee Assoc./Member: No
Size Of Corporate Staff: 6
On-Going Support: B,C,d,H,I
Training: 1-3 Days.

SPECIFIC EXPANSION PLANS:
US: All United States
Canada: No
Overseas: No

≪ ≫

ARCHADECK
2112 W. Laburnam Ave., # 100
Richmond, VA 23227
Tel: (800) 789-3325 (804) 353-6999
Fax: (804) 358-1878
E-Mail: franchising@ussi.net
Web Site: www.archadeck.com
Mr. Pete Wiggins, Vice President

The leading resources for franchise information all list ARCHADECK as one of the top franchise opportunities available today. Without any construction experience, our franchisees are at the forefront of a $122 billion market, enhancing the home environment with custom decks, gazebos, porches and more! If you have sales and/or management experience and the drive to succeed, ARCHADECK will provide the rest with on-going support.

BACKGROUND:
Established: 1980; 1st Franchised: 1984
Franchised Units: 58
Company-Owned Units 0
Total Units: 58
Dist.: US-57; CAN-0; O'seas-1
North America: 24 States
Density: 6 in GA, 4 in IL, 4 in NC
Projected New Units (12 Months): 8
Qualifications: 4, 3, 2, 2, 3, 4
Registered: CA,FL,HI,IL,IN,MD,MI,MN, NY,OR,RI,VA,WA,WI

FINANCIAL/TERMS:
Cash Investment: $20-40K
Total Investment: $45-65K
Minimum Net Worth: $100K
Fees: Franchise - $25K
Royalty - 6.5%; Ad. - 1%
Earnings Claim Statement: No
Term of Contract (Years): 10/10

Avg. # Of Employees: 2 PT
Passive Ownership: Discouraged
Encourage Conversions: Yes
Area Develop. Agreements: No
Sub-Franchising Contracts: No
Expand In Territory: Yes
Space Needs: NR SF; N/A

SUPPORT & TRAINING PROVIDED:
Financial Assistance Provided: Yes(D)
Site Selection Assistance: N/A
Lease Negotiation Assistance: No
Co-Operative Advertising: No
Franchisee Assoc./Member: Yes/Yes
Size Of Corporate Staff: 20
On-Going Support: D,G,H,I
Training: 20 Days in Richmond, VA.

SPECIFIC EXPANSION PLANS:
US: All United States
Canada: All Canada
Overseas: No

≪ ≫

B-DRY SYSTEM
1341 Copley Rd.
Akron, OH 44320
Tel: (800) 321-0985 (330) 867-2576
Fax: (330) 867-7693
Mr. Carl A. Rakich, Vice President

Basement waterproofing system. Low cash investment - high return on investment. Intensive and continuous training. No high-cost site expenditure. No previous experience necessary. Unique patented system. Full customer warranty for the life of the structure.

BACKGROUND: IFA MEMBER
Established: 1958; 1st Franchised: 1978
Franchised Units: 63
Company-Owned Units 5
Total Units: 68
Dist.: US-68; CAN-0; O'seas-0
North America: NR
Density: 10 in OH, 8 in PA, 7 in NY
Projected New Units (12 Months): 3
Qualifications: 2, 3, 2, 2, 3, 5
Registered: NR

FINANCIAL/TERMS:
Cash Investment: $25-50K
Total Investment: $40-74K
Minimum Net Worth: $NR
Fees: Franchise - $15-60K
Royalty - 6%; Ad. - 0%
Earnings Claim Statement: No
Term of Contract (Years): 5/5
Avg. # Of Employees: 6 FT, 1 PT
Passive Ownership: Discouraged
Encourage Conversions: No

Area Develop. Agreements: No
Sub-Franchising Contracts: No
Expand In Territory: Yes
Space Needs: 4,000 SF; FS, HB

SUPPORT & TRAINING PROVIDED:
Financial Assistance Provided: Yes(D)
Site Selection Assistance: No
Lease Negotiation Assistance: No
Co-Operative Advertising: No
Franchisee Assoc./Member: Yes/No
Size Of Corporate Staff: 10
On-Going Support: B,C,D,F,G,h,I
Training: 2 Wks. National Office in Akron, OH; 2 Wks. On-Site; 1-2 Days On-Going Regional Seminars.

SPECIFIC EXPANSION PLANS:
US: Northeast, Northwest
Canada: No
Overseas: No

≪ ≫

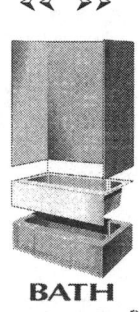

BATH FITTER

BATH FITTER
27 Berard Dr., # 2701
South Burlington, VT 05403-5810
Tel: (800) 892-2847 (802) 860-2919
Fax: (802) 862-7976
E-Mail: bathfitter@together.net
Web Site: www.bathfitter.com
Ms. Linda F. Brakel, VP Franchise Operations

Since 1984, BATH FITTER has been installing custom-molded acrylic bathtub liners, shower bases and one-piece, seamless wall surrounds over existing fixtures in just a few hours in countless residential and commercial properties. We provide full training, specialized tools, marketing and technical manuals and on-going support through regular visits to your location. We award exclusive territories with enormous residential and commercial market potential to qualified franchise owners.

BACKGROUND:
Established: 1984; 1st Franchised: 1992
Franchised Units: 88

Company-Owned Units	15
Total Units:	103
Dist.:	US-76; CAN-27; O'seas-0
North America:	24 States, 8 Provinces
Density:	9 in PA, 8 in NY, 8 in ON
Projected New Units (12 Months):	14
Qualifications:	3, 3, 2, 1, 4, 5
Registered: CA,FL,IL,IN,MD,MN,MI,MN, NY,OR,RI,VA,WA,WI,DC,AB	

FINANCIAL/TERMS:

Cash Investment:	$N/A
Total Investment:	$60-100K
Minimum Net Worth:	$N/A
Fees: Franchise -	$24.5K
Royalty - N/A;	Ad. - N/A
Earnings Claim Statement:	Yes
Term of Contract (Years):	5/5
Avg. # Of Employees:	3 FT
Passive Ownership:	Not Allowed
Encourage Conversions:	No
Area Develop. Agreements:	Yes/Varies
Sub-Franchising Contracts:	No
Expand In Territory:	Yes
Space Needs: 2,000-2,500 SF; Industrial Park	

SUPPORT & TRAINING PROVIDED:

Financial Assistance Provided:	No
Site Selection Assistance:	Yes
Lease Negotiation Assistance:	N/A
Co-Operative Advertising:	N/A
Franchisee Assoc./Member:	No
Size Of Corporate Staff:	13
On-Going Support:	B,C,D,E,G,h,I
Training: 10 Days Headquarters; 10 Days Franchisee Site.	

SPECIFIC EXPANSION PLANS:

US:	All United States
Canada:	All Canada
Overseas:	No

◢◣ ◥◤

BMR BATH MASTER REGLAZING
4498 Trepanier Rd.
Peachland, BC V0H 1X3 CANADA
Tel: (877) 767-2336 (250) 767-2336
Fax: (250) 767-2718
E-Mail: sales@bathmaster.com
Web Site: www.bathmaster.com
Mr. Trevor Dixon, President

Quality bathtub, tile reglazing, acrylic bathtub liners, tub walls, porcelain restoration and countertop resurfacing with superior materials. Transform dull, worn, unsightly fixtures to a brilliant new finish in just a few hours. This system leaves no mess or odor behind and offers same day use. This franchise includes equipment, training and on-going support. Our goal is to be the best, not the biggest.

BACKGROUND:

Established: 1989;	1st Franchised: 1992
Franchised Units:	15
Company-Owned Units	1
Total Units:	16
Dist.:	US-0; CAN-16; O'seas-0
North America:	5 Provinces
Density:	6 in BC, 5 in ON, 2 in SK
Projected New Units (12 Months):	6
Qualifications:	3, 2, 4, 3, 4, 3
Registered: NR	

FINANCIAL/TERMS:

Cash Investment:	$25-28K Can.
Total Investment:	$25-28K Can.
Minimum Net Worth:	$N/A
Fees: Franchise -	$3.9K
Royalty - 5%/$200/Mo.;	Ad. - 2%
Earnings Claim Statement:	No
Term of Contract (Years):	5/5
Avg. # Of Employees:	1 FT
Passive Ownership:	Discouraged
Encourage Conversions:	Yes
Area Develop. Agreements:	No
Sub-Franchising Contracts:	No
Expand In Territory:	Yes
Space Needs: 300 SF; HB	

SUPPORT & TRAINING PROVIDED:

Financial Assistance Provided:	No
Site Selection Assistance:	N/A
Lease Negotiation Assistance:	No
Co-Operative Advertising:	N/A
Franchisee Assoc./Member:	Yes/Yes
Size Of Corporate Staff:	1
On-Going Support:	B,C,D,F,G,H,I
Training: 15 Days Minimum Peachland, BC.	

SPECIFIC EXPANSION PLANS:

US:	All United States
Canada:	All Canada
Overseas:	No

◢◣ ◥◤

CALIFORNIA CLOSET COMPANY
1000 Fourth St., # 800
San Rafael, CA 94901
Tel: (800) 241-3222 (415) 256-8500
Fax: (415) 256-8501
E-Mail: sales@calclosets.com
Web Site: www.calclosets.com
Mr. David Lamb, Franchise Development Manager

The CALIFORNIA CLOSET brand is the leader in customized closet, garage and storage space design and installation services. As part of this exciting franchise system, you will receive specialized training, management and marketing support. Newsletters, seminars, conventions and a top notch corporate staff keep you current. A formula for success!

BACKGROUND: IFA MEMBER

Established: 1979;	1st Franchised: 1982
Franchised Units:	157
Company-Owned Units	0
Total Units:	157
Dist.:	US-130; CAN-9; O'seas-18
North America:	35 States, 5 Provinces
Density:	14 in CA, 10 in NY, 10 in FL
Projected New Units (12 Months):	4
Registered:	CA,IL,IN,MD,MI,MN, NY,RI,VA,WA,WI

FINANCIAL/TERMS:

Cash Investment:	$75-225K
Total Investment:	$75-225K
Minimum Net Worth:	$NR
Fees: Franchise -	$39.5K
Royalty - 6%;	Ad. - 3%
Earnings Claim Statement:	No
Term of Contract (Years):	10/10
Avg. # Of Employees:	3-25 FT
Passive Ownership:	Discouraged
Encourage Conversions:	N/A
Area Develop. Agreements:	No
Sub-Franchising Contracts:	No
Expand In Territory:	Yes
Space Needs: 2,000-6,000 SF; Light Industrial	

SUPPORT & TRAINING PROVIDED:

Financial Assistance Provided:	Yes(I)
Site Selection Assistance:	Yes
Lease Negotiation Assistance:	Yes
Co-Operative Advertising:	Yes
Franchisee Assoc./Member:	NR
Size Of Corporate Staff:	28
On-Going Support:	A,B,C,D,E,F,G,H,I
Training: 1 Week Headquarters; 2 Weeks On-Site.	

SPECIFIC EXPANSION PLANS:

US:	Various U.S. Locations
Canada:	PQ
Overseas: Europe, Asia, Mexico, South America	

◢◣ ◥◤

CLOSET & STORAGE CONCEPTS
424 Commerce Ln., # 1&2
West Berlin, NJ 08091
Tel: (888) 843-2567 (856) 767-5700
Fax: (856) 768-8698
Web Site: www.closetandstorageconcepts.com
Mr. Bob Lewis, President

Closet & Storage Concepts designs, manufacturers and installs a wide variety of custom closet, garage, laundry room, home office and storage units. All franchisees receive complete training in all aspects of the operation of the business, both prior to opening and on an on-going basis. Call 1-888-THE-CLOSET.

BACKGROUND: IFA MEMBER

Established: 1987; 1st Franchised: 2000	
Franchised Units:	1
Company-Owned Units	1
Total Units:	2
Dist.:	US-2; CAN-0; O'seas-0
North America:	NR
Density:	NR
Projected New Units (12 Months):	5
Qualifications:	3, 4, 1, 3, 4, 5
Registered: All States	

FINANCIAL/TERMS:

Cash Investment:	$20-40K
Total Investment:	$85-125K
Minimum Net Worth:	$100K
Fees: Franchise -	$40K
Royalty - 5%;	Ad. - 0%
Earnings Claim Statement:	No
Term of Contract (Years):	10/10
Avg. # Of Employees:	8 FT
Passive Ownership:	Discouraged
Encourage Conversions:	N/A
Area Develop. Agreements:	No
Sub-Franchising Contracts:	No
Expand In Territory:	Yes
Space Needs: 4,000 SF; FS	

SUPPORT & TRAINING PROVIDED:

Financial Assistance Provided:	No
Site Selection Assistance:	Yes
Lease Negotiation Assistance:	Yes
Co-Operative Advertising:	N/A
Franchisee Assoc./Member:	Yes
Size Of Corporate Staff:	4
On-Going Support:	C,D,E,G,H,I
Training: 2 Weeks in NJ.	

SPECIFIC EXPANSION PLANS:

US:	All United States
Canada:	All Canada
Overseas:	No

<< >>

CLOSET FACTORY, THE

12800 S. Broadway
Los Angeles, CA 90061-1116
Tel: (800) 318-8800 (310) 715-1000
Fax: (310) 576-8065
Web Site: www.closet-factory.com
Mr. David J. Louy, VP/Franchise Director

Join the industry leader, ranked #1 in custom closets by Entrepreneur Magazine worldwide. Franchisees design, sell, manufacture and install custom closet systems, garage organizers, kitchen pantries, entertainment centers and custom office systems. Operate a large, vertically integrated cash business during normal business hours in an exclusive territory. A complete turn-key business through training and on-going support. No technical experience is necessary.

BACKGROUND: IFA MEMBER

Established: 1983; 1st Franchised: 1985	
Franchised Units:	86
Company-Owned Units	26
Total Units:	112
Dist.:	US-97; CAN-5; O'seas-10
North America:	39 States, 2 Provinces
Density:	14 in CA, 8 in NY, 7 in FL
Projected New Units (12 Months):	15
Qualifications:	5, 5, 2, 4, 3, 3
Registered: CA,FL,IL,IN,MD,MI,MN,NY, OR,VA,WA,WI,DC,AB	

FINANCIAL/TERMS:

Cash Investment:	$40-50K
Total Investment:	$99.5-185K
Minimum Net Worth:	$150-350K
Fees: Franchise -	$28.5-39.5K
Royalty - 5.8%;	Ad. - 1%
Earnings Claim Statement:	No
Term of Contract (Years):	5/5
Avg. # Of Employees:	5-6 FT
Passive Ownership:	Allowed
Encourage Conversions:	Yes
Area Develop. Agreements:	No
Sub-Franchising Contracts:	No
Expand In Territory:	No
Space Needs: 3,500-4,000 SF; Warehouse or Industrial Park	

SUPPORT & TRAINING PROVIDED:

Financial Assistance Provided:	Yes(I)
Site Selection Assistance:	Yes
Lease Negotiation Assistance:	Yes
Co-Operative Advertising:	No
Franchisee Assoc./Member:	No
Size Of Corporate Staff:	NR
On-Going Support:	B,C,D,E,G,h
Training: 2 Weeks Corporate Headquarters; 4 Weeks On-Site.	

SPECIFIC EXPANSION PLANS:

US:	All United States
Canada:	All Canada
Overseas:	All Countries

<< >>

CLOSETTEC

55 Carnegie Row
Norwood, MA 02062
Tel: (800) 365-2021 (781) 769-9997
Fax: (781) 769-9996
E-Mail: closettec@closettec.com
Web Site: www.closettec.com
Mr. David Rogers, President

CLOSETTEC sells, manufactures and installs residential and commercial storage systems, using the finest melamine laminates and exclusive European hardware. We offer comprehensive training, field support, site selection, sales/ marketing programs and on-going design assistance to every franchisee. Exclusive CAD and database programs.

BACKGROUND:

Established: 1985; 1st Franchised: 1986	
Franchised Units:	35
Company-Owned Units	0
Total Units:	35
Dist.:	US-35; CAN-0; O'seas-0
North America:	NR
Density:	4 in MA, 2 in NY, 2 in OH
Projected New Units (12 Months):	2
Qualifications:	4, 4, 2, 3, 3, 5
Registered: NR	

FINANCIAL/TERMS:

Cash Investment:	$NR
Total Investment:	$128-240K
Minimum Net Worth:	$NR
Fees: Franchise -	$30K
Royalty - 4.5%;	Ad. - NR
Earnings Claim Statement:	No
Term of Contract (Years):	15/15

Avg. # Of Employees:	3-5 FT
Passive Ownership:	Discouraged
Encourage Conversions:	Yes
Area Develop. Agreements:	No
Sub-Franchising Contracts:	No
Expand In Territory:	Yes
Space Needs: 2,500-3,000 SF; Light Industrial	

SUPPORT & TRAINING PROVIDED:

Financial Assistance Provided:	No
Site Selection Assistance:	Yes
Lease Negotiation Assistance:	Yes
Co-Operative Advertising:	No
Franchisee Assoc./Member:	No
Size Of Corporate Staff:	9
On-Going Support:	C,D,E,H,I
Training: 2 Weeks Norwood, MA.	

SPECIFIC EXPANSION PLANS:

US:	All United States
Canada:	No
Overseas:	No

<< >>

CREATIVE COLORS INTERNATIONAL
5550 W. 175th St.
Tinley Park, IL 60477
Tel: (800) 933-2656 (708) 614-7786
Fax: (708) 614-9685
E-Mail: mark@creativecolorsintl.com
Web Site: www.creativecolorsintl.com
Mr. Mark Bollman, President

Mobile units providing repair and restoration in all markets that have leather, vinyl, fabric, velour, plastics and fiberglass. These markets include car dealerships (new and used), furniture retailers and manufactures, hotels, airports, car rental agencies and company fleet cars.

BACKGROUND:

Established: 1980;	1st Franchised: 1991
Franchised Units:	38
Company-Owned Units	2
Total Units:	40
Dist.:	US-39; CAN-1; O'seas-0
North America:	20 States, 1 Province

Density:	IL, FL, OH
Projected New Units (12 Months):	10+
Qualifications:	4, 4, 3, 4, 4, 5
Registered:	CA,FL,IL,IN,MI, NY,OR,WI,AB

FINANCIAL/TERMS:

Cash Investment:	$19.5K+
Total Investment:	$19.5K+
Minimum Net Worth:	$50K+
Fees: Franchise -	$27.5K
Royalty - 6%/$173.33/Mo.;	Ad. - 0%
Earnings Claim Statement:	Yes
Term of Contract (Years):	10
Avg. # Of Employees:	5 FT
Passive Ownership:	Discouraged
Encourage Conversions:	Yes
Area Develop. Agreements:	Yes/10
Sub-Franchising Contracts:	No
Expand In Territory:	Yes
Space Needs: N/A SF; HB	

SUPPORT & TRAINING PROVIDED:

Financial Assistance Provided:	Yes(D)
Site Selection Assistance:	Yes
Lease Negotiation Assistance:	N/A
Co-Operative Advertising:	Yes
Franchisee Assoc./Member:	Yes/Yes
Size Of Corporate Staff:	8
On-Going Support:	A,B,C,D,E,F,G,H,I
Training: 3 Weeks Headquarters, Tinley Park, IL; 1 Week in Franchisee's Territory.	

SPECIFIC EXPANSION PLANS:

US:	All United States
Canada:	All Canada
Overseas:	All Countries

<< >>

DECKARE SERVICES
1501 Raff Rd., SW
Canton, OH 44710
Tel: (800) 711-3325 (330) 478-3665
Fax: (330) 478-0311
E-Mail: deckcare1@aol.com
Web Site: www.deckcare.com
Mr. Joe McClellan, Vice President

Rejuvenating exterior wood surfaces such as decks, fences, docks, gazebos and bridges with a total commitment to being the first nationally-recognized franchise based on image and quality. Franchisees will receive complete business and field training with on-going support services.

BACKGROUND: IFA MEMBER

Established: 1995;	1st Franchised: 1997
Franchised Units:	35
Company-Owned Units	0
Total Units:	35

Dist.:	US-25; CAN-0; O'seas-0
North America:	16 States
Density:	4 in OH, 3 in MO, 3 in TN
Projected New Units (12 Months):	40
Qualifications:	5, 4, 3, 3, 2, 5
Registered: CA,IL,IN,MD,MI,MN,NY,VA	

FINANCIAL/TERMS:

Cash Investment:	$25K
Total Investment:	$45K
Minimum Net Worth:	$50K
Fees: Franchise -	$14.5K
Royalty - 5%;	Ad. - N/A
Earnings Claim Statement:	No
Term of Contract (Years):	5/5
Avg. # Of Employees:	1 FT, 1 PT
Passive Ownership:	Allowed
Encourage Conversions:	No
Area Develop. Agreements:	No
Sub-Franchising Contracts:	No
Expand In Territory:	Yes
Space Needs: NR SF; HB	

SUPPORT & TRAINING PROVIDED:

Financial Assistance Provided:	No
Site Selection Assistance:	N/A
Lease Negotiation Assistance:	N/A
Co-Operative Advertising:	N/A
Franchisee Assoc./Member:	No
Size Of Corporate Staff:	5
On-Going Support:	C,D,G,H,I
Training: 5 Days at Corporate Office; 4 Days Franchisee's Location.	

SPECIFIC EXPANSION PLANS:

US:	All United States
Canada:	No
Overseas:	No

<< >>

DELBE HOME SERVICES
5185 MacArthur Blvd. NW, # 115
Washington, DC 20016
Tel: (800) 753-3523 (202) 237-0187
Fax: (202) 237-0348
E-Mail: hjm@delbefranchise.com
Web Site: www.delbefranchise.com
Mr. Howard J. Margolis, Dir. of Business Development

DHS is a membership-based service company that assists homeowners (members) in solving their home's maintenance, repair and improvement problems and needs. DHS provides its members with licensed and insured contractors, handles scheduling and assigns a personal service representative to manage every member's job. As a full-service company, DHS is able to meet all of the homeowner's needs.

BACKGROUND:
Established: 2000;   1st Franchised: 2000
Franchised Units: 1
Company-Owned Units   0
Total Units: 1
Dist.:   US-1; CAN-0; O'seas-0
  North America: DC
  Density: 1 in DC
Projected New Units (12 Months):   13
Qualifications: 5, 4, 3, 3, 2, 5
Registered: FL,MD,VA,DC
FINANCIAL/TERMS:
Cash Investment: $5.9-15.6K
Total Investment: $17.8-46.9K
Minimum Net Worth: $53K
Fees: Franchise - $11-25K
  Royalty - 3%;   Ad. - N/A
Earnings Claim Statement: No
Term of Contract (Years):   10/10
Avg. # Of Employees: 1 FT, 1PT
Passive Ownership: Not Allowed
Encourage Conversions: N/A
Area Develop. Agreements: No
Sub-Franchising Contracts: No
Expand In Territory: No
Space Needs: 100 SF; HB
SUPPORT & TRAINING PROVIDED:
Financial Assistance Provided: Yes(I)
Site Selection Assistance: N/A
Lease Negotiation Assistance: N/A
Co-Operative Advertising: Yes
Franchisee Assoc./Member: Yes/Yes
Size Of Corporate Staff: 3
On-Going Support: C,D,I
Training: 7 Days, Washington, DC.
SPECIFIC EXPANSION PLANS:
US: PA,NJ,DE,MD,VA,NC,SC,GA,FL
Canada: No
Overseas: No

≪ ≫

DR. VINYL & ASSOC.
821 NW Commerce St.
Lee's Summit, MO 64086
Tel: (800) 531-6600 (816) 525-6060
Fax: (816) 525-6333
E-Mail: tbuckley@drvinylcom
Web Site: www.drvinyl.com
Mr. Tom Buckley, Jr., President

We offer vinyl, leather and velour fabric repair and coloring, auto windshield repair, dashboard and hard plastic repair, vinyl striping and protective molding to new and used car dealers.

BACKGROUND: IFA MEMBER
Established: 1972;   1st Franchised: 1980
Franchised Units: 149
Company-Owned Units   1
Total Units: 150
Dist.:   US-146; CAN-1; O'seas-3
  North America: NR
  Density: 18 in MO, 10 in IL, 7 in OH
Projected New Units (12 Months):   30
Qualifications: 3, 2, 2, 2, 2, 4
Registered: CA,FL,IL,IN,MD,MI,OR,
  VA,WI
FINANCIAL/TERMS:
Cash Investment: $23.5K
Total Investment: $35-40K
Minimum Net Worth: $23.5K
Fees: Franchise - $23.5K
  Royalty - 7%;   Ad. - 1%
Earnings Claim Statement: Yes
Term of Contract (Years):   10/10
Avg. # Of Employees: 1 FT
Passive Ownership: Discouraged
Encourage Conversions: N/A
Area Develop. Agreements: Yes/10
Sub-Franchising Contracts: Yes
Expand In Territory: Yes
Space Needs: N/A SF; N/A
SUPPORT & TRAINING PROVIDED:
Financial Assistance Provided: Yes(B)
Site Selection Assistance: N/A
Lease Negotiation Assistance: N/A
Co-Operative Advertising: No
Franchisee Assoc./Member: Yes
Size Of Corporate Staff: 15
On-Going Support: b,C,D,F,G,h,I
Training: 2 Weeks Corporate Office; 2
  Weeks Field Training.
SPECIFIC EXPANSION PLANS:
US: All United States
Canada: All Canada
Overseas: All Countries

≪ ≫

**DREAMMAKER BATH &
KITCHEN BY WORLDWIDE**
1020 N. University Parks Dr.
Waco, TX 76707
Tel: (800) 583-9099 (254) 745-2477
Fax: (254) 745-2588
E-Mail: dreammaker@dwyergroup.com
Web Site: www.dreammaker-remodel.com
Ms. Brenda Payne, Exec. Assistant to
  President

Unique combination of bath and kitchen remodeling options, consisting of: cabinet refacing, tubliners, traditional remodeling and more. Delivering the style and value that today's consumer demands.

BACKGROUND: IFA MEMBER
Established: 1970;   1st Franchised: 1971
Franchised Units: 357
Company-Owned Units   0
Total Units: 357
Dist.:   US-153; CAN-9; O'seas-195
  North America: 50 States, 3 Provinces
  Density: 48 in NY, TX, and IL
Projected New Units (12 Months):   32
Qualifications: 3, 3, 1, 2, 4, 5
Registered: All States
FINANCIAL/TERMS:
Cash Investment: $6K
Total Investment: $25-50K
Minimum Net Worth: $50K
Fees: Franchise - $27K
  Royalty - 3-6%;   Ad. - 2%
Earnings Claim Statement: No
Term of Contract (Years):   10/5
Avg. # Of Employees: Varies
Passive Ownership: Discouraged
Encourage Conversions: Yes
Area Develop. Agreements: Yes
Sub-Franchising Contracts: No
Expand In Territory: Yes
Space Needs: NR SF; Case by Case
SUPPORT & TRAINING PROVIDED:
Financial Assistance Provided: Yes(B)
Site Selection Assistance: Yes
Lease Negotiation Assistance: Yes
Co-Operative Advertising: Yes
Franchisee Assoc./Member: Yes/Yes
Size Of Corporate Staff: 25

On-Going Support: B,C,D,G,H,I
Training: 3 Weeks Headquarters, Waco, TX.
SPECIFIC EXPANSION PLANS:
US: All United States
Canada: All Canada
Overseas: All Countries

<< >>

ELDORADO STONE
P.O. Box 489
Carnation, WA 98014
Tel: (800) 925-1491 (425) 333-6722
Fax: (425) 333-4755
Web Site: www.eldoradostone.com
Mr. Phil Pearlman, Director of Franchising

Franchisor of manufacturing plants that manufacture and distribute lightweight concrete stone veneers and landscape stepstones and pavers. Manufacturers market and distribute through masonry and building supply. World's largest family of manufacturers of this product type.

BACKGROUND:
Established: 1969; 1st Franchised: 1969
Franchised Units: 26
Company-Owned Units: 0
Total Units: 26
Dist.: US-14; CAN-1; O'seas-11
North America: 13 States, 1 Province
Density: 2 in PA, 1 in OH, 1 in CA
Projected New Units (12 Months): 2
Qualifications: 5, 4, 2, 2, 3, 3
Registered: CA,FL,IL,MN,WA,WI,DC
FINANCIAL/TERMS:
Cash Investment: $80-149K
Total Investment: $80-149K
Minimum Net Worth: $80-149K
Fees: Franchise - $50K
 Royalty - 5%/10c/SF; Ad. - $0
Earnings Claim Statement: No
Term of Contract (Years): 10/10
Avg. # Of Employees: 6 FT+
Passive Ownership: Discouraged
Encourage Conversions: N/A
Area Develop. Agreements: Yes/10
Sub-Franchising Contracts: No
Expand In Territory: Yes
Space Needs: 5,000-8,000 SF; FS
SUPPORT & TRAINING PROVIDED:
Financial Assistance Provided: No
Site Selection Assistance: Yes
Lease Negotiation Assistance: No
Co-Operative Advertising: No
Franchisee Assoc./Member: No
Size Of Corporate Staff: 8

On-Going Support: B,C,D,G,H,I
Training: 4-5 Days Training Facility at Washington; 4-5 Days Franchisee's Facility.
SPECIFIC EXPANSION PLANS:
US: All United States
Canada: Eastern
Overseas: South America, Europe, China

<< >>

FOUR SEASONS SUNROOMS
5005 Veterans Memorial Hwy.
Holbrook, NY 11741
Tel: (800) 521-0179 (516) 563-4000
Fax: (516) 563-4010
Web Site: www.four-seasons-sunrooms.com
Mr. Tony Russo, VP Business Development

FOUR SEASONS SUNROOMS is the largest manufacturer of sunrooms, conservatories and solariums in the Unites States. The FOUR SEASONS franchise opportunity is targeted to the $121 billion remodeling industry. We offer comprehensive training and exclusive products.

BACKGROUND: IFA MEMBER
Established: 1974; 1st Franchised: 1985
Franchised Units: 234
Company-Owned Units: 2
Total Units: 236
Dist.: US-188; CAN-12; O'seas-47
North America: 48 States, 5 Provinces
Density: 17 in CA, 21 in NY, 16 in PA
Projected New Units (12 Months): 24
Qualifications: 2, 5, 4, 3, 3, 4
Registered: All States
FINANCIAL/TERMS:
Cash Investment: $10-25K
Total Investment: $13.3-82.5K
Minimum Net Worth: $100K
Fees: Franchise - $7.5-15K
 Royalty - 0%; Ad. - 0%
Earnings Claim Statement: No
Term of Contract (Years): 10/10
Avg. # Of Employees: 2 FT, 1 PT
Passive Ownership: Not Allowed
Encourage Conversions: Yes
Area Develop. Agreements: No
Sub-Franchising Contracts: No
Expand In Territory: Yes
Space Needs: 750 SF; FS, SF
SUPPORT & TRAINING PROVIDED:
Financial Assistance Provided: No
Site Selection Assistance: Yes
Lease Negotiation Assistance: Yes

Co-Operative Advertising: Yes
Franchisee Assoc./Member: Yes
Size Of Corporate Staff: 250
On-Going Support: C,D,E,F,G,H,I
Training: 5 Days Holbrook, NY; 5 Days Hayward, CA; 5 Days Regionally.
SPECIFIC EXPANSION PLANS:
US: All United States
Canada: All Canada
Overseas: U.K., Spain, France, Germany, Italy

<< >>

FURNITURE MEDIC
860 Ridge Lake Blvd.
Memphis, TN 38120
Tel: (800) 877-9933 (901) 820-8600
Fax: (901) 820-8660
E-Mail: furnmedic@worldnet.att.net
Web Site: www.furnituremedicfranchise.com
Mr. David Messenger, VP Market Expansion

FURNITURE MEDIC is a division of ServiceMaster Consumer Services. It has grown into an international franchise operation providing complete on-site precision repair as well as furniture stripping and refinishing. Targeting the residential, commercial and insurance markets, their patented Restoration-Refinishing process yields efficiency plus cost saving to customers. A solid training program and strong business support has effectively positioned FURNITURE MEDIC as the premier furniture repair company.

BACKGROUND: IFA MEMBER
Established: 1992; 1st Franchised: 1992
Franchised Units: 595
Company-Owned Units: 0
Total Units: 595
Dist.: US-466; CAN-53; O'seas-76
North America: 47 States,10 Province
Density: 36 in CA, 35 in FL, 28 in VA
Projected New Units (12 Months): 70
Qualifications: 4, 4, 2, 3, 3, 5
Registered: All States
FINANCIAL/TERMS:
Cash Investment: $15-25K
Total Investment: $25-35K
Minimum Net Worth: $75-100K
Fees: Franchise - $14.9-18.4K
 Royalty - 7%/$200 Min.;Ad. - 1%/$30 Min.

Earnings Claim Statement:	No
Term of Contract (Years):	5/5
Avg. # Of Employees:	1 FT, 1 PT
Passive Ownership:	Not Allowed
Encourage Conversions:	N/A
Area Develop. Agreements:	No
Sub-Franchising Contracts:	No
Expand In Territory:	Yes
Space Needs: NR SF; N/A	

SUPPORT & TRAINING PROVIDED:

Financial Assistance Provided:	Yes(D)
Site Selection Assistance:	N/A
Lease Negotiation Assistance:	No
Co-Operative Advertising:	No
Franchisee Assoc./Member:	Yes/Yes
Size Of Corporate Staff:	21
On-Going Support:	A,B,G,h,I
Training: 2 Weeks Memphis, TN.	

SPECIFIC EXPANSION PLANS:

US:	All United States
Canada:	All Canada
Overseas:	All Countries

≪ ≫

FURNITURE MEDIC OF CANADA
6540 Tomken Rd.
Mississauga, ON L5T 2E9 CANADA
Tel: (800) 263-5928 (905) 670-0000
Fax: (905) 670-0077
E-Mail: mgreenwood@svm.com
Web Site: www.furnituremedic.com
Mr. Murray Greenwood, Market Expansion
   Manager

The first franchise network of mobile furniture touch-up and restoration. Exclusive patented, environmentally conscious restoration techniques allow FURNITURE MEDIC to restore wood and furniture damage on-site for a fraction of replacement costs.

BACKGROUND:

Established: 1992;	1st Franchised: 1993
Franchised Units:	55
Company-Owned Units:	0
Total Units:	55
Dist.:	US-0; CAN-28; O'seas-0
North America:	8 Provinces
Density:	15 in ON, 5 in AB, 3 in PQ
Projected New Units (12 Months):	20
Qualifications:	2, 3, 1, 3, 3, 4
Registered: AB	

FINANCIAL/TERMS:

Cash Investment:	$20K (Can)
Total Investment:	$28-40K
Minimum Net Worth:	$50K
Fees: Franchise -	$19.9K
Royalty - 7%;	Ad. - 1%

Earnings Claim Statement:	No
Term of Contract (Years):	5/5
Avg. # Of Employees:	1 FT
Passive Ownership:	Not Allowed
Encourage Conversions:	Yes
Area Develop. Agreements:	No
Sub-Franchising Contracts:	No
Expand In Territory:	Yes
Space Needs: NR SF; HB	

SUPPORT & TRAINING PROVIDED:

Financial Assistance Provided:	Yes(D)
Site Selection Assistance:	N/A
Lease Negotiation Assistance:	N/A
Co-Operative Advertising:	N/A
Franchisee Assoc./Member:	Yes
Size Of Corporate Staff:	18
On-Going Support:	B,C,D,G,h,I
Training: 2 Weeks Memphis, TN; 1 Week at Home Study Program.	

SPECIFIC EXPANSION PLANS:

US:	All United States
Canada:	All Canada
Overseas:	All Countries

≪ ≫

GUARDSMAN WOODPRO
4999 36th St. SE
Grand Rapids, MI 49512
Tel: (800) 496-6377 (616) 285-7877
Fax: (616) 285-7882
E-Mail: woodpro@lillyindustries.com
Web Site: www.guardsmanwoodpro.com
Franchise Development,

Partner and profit with a world leader. As a business unit of Lilly Industries, the largest manufacturer of furniture finishes in N. America, GUARDSMAN WOODPRO is the premier choice of residential and commercial customers alike for furniture repair and refinishing services. Lilly has been involved in the furniture industry for 130 years, supplying finishes, furniture care products and now furniture repair services. If you want to be in the furniture business, you want to be with us.

BACKGROUND:

Established: 1865;	1st Franchised: 1994

Franchised Units:	124
Company-Owned Units:	0
Total Units:	124
Dist.:	US-110; CAN-14; O'seas-0
North America:	36 States, 2 Provinces
Density:	9 in MI, 6 in OH, 6 in TX
Projected New Units (12 Months):	36
Qualifications:	4, 4, 4, 3, 5, 5
Registered: All States	

FINANCIAL/TERMS:

Cash Investment:	$10-25K
Total Investment:	$7-25K
Minimum Net Worth:	$50K
Fees: Franchise -	$7K
Royalty - Fixed;	Ad. - Fixed
Earnings Claim Statement:	No
Term of Contract (Years):	5/5
Avg. # Of Employees:	1-3 FT, 1-2 PT
Passive Ownership:	Discouraged
Encourage Conversions:	Yes
Area Develop. Agreements:	Yes/2-5 Yrs.
Sub-Franchising Contracts:	Yes
Expand In Territory:	Yes
Space Needs: NR SF; HB	

SUPPORT & TRAINING PROVIDED:

Financial Assistance Provided:	Yes(D)
Site Selection Assistance:	N/A
Lease Negotiation Assistance:	N/A
Co-Operative Advertising:	Yes
Franchisee Assoc./Member:	Yes/Yes
Size Of Corporate Staff:	80
On-Going Support:	A,C,D,G,H,I
Training: 2 Weeks Grand Rapids, MI.	

SPECIFIC EXPANSION PLANS:

US:	All United States
Canada:	All Canada
Overseas:	All Countries

≪ ≫

HANDYMAN CONNECTION
227 Northland Blvd.
Cincinnati, OH 45246
Tel: (800) 466-5530 (513) 771-3003
Fax: (513) 771-6439
E-Mail:
tom.gyuro@handymanconnection.com
Web Site: www.handymanconnection.com
Mr. Tom Gyuro, Vice President

HANDYMAN CONNECTION special-izes in the small to medium size home repair and remodeling industry. We offer a turnkey package that includes marketing, advertising and a complete training program. 90%of our franchise partners had NO handyman experience.

BACKGROUND: IFA MEMBER
Established: 1990;   1st Franchised: 1993
Franchised Units: 101
Company-Owned Units   4
Total Units: 105
Dist.:   US-48; CAN-15; O'seas-0
  North America: 35+ States
  Density: 24 in CA, 7 in OH, 4 in TN
Projected New Units (12 Months):   20
Qualifications: 4, 3, 1, 2, 2, 4
Registered: NR
FINANCIAL/TERMS:
Cash Investment: $50-150K
Total Investment: $50-250K
Minimum Net Worth: $50K+
Fees: Franchise - $Varies
  Royalty - 5%;   Ad. - 2%
Earnings Claim Statement: No
Term of Contract (Years):   10/10
Avg. # Of Employees: Varies
Passive Ownership: Allowed
Encourage Conversions: N/A
Area Develop. Agreements: Yes/10
Sub-Franchising Contracts: No
Expand In Territory: Yes
Space Needs: 500-600 SF; FS, Industrial
  Warehouse
SUPPORT & TRAINING PROVIDED:
Financial Assistance Provided: Yes
Site Selection Assistance: No
Lease Negotiation Assistance: Yes
Co-Operative Advertising: No
Franchisee Assoc./Member: Yes/Yes
Size Of Corporate Staff: 10
On-Going Support: B,C,D,E,G,h,I
Training: 2 Weeks Flagship (Cincinnati,
  OH); 1 Week Franchisee Location.
SPECIFIC EXPANSION PLANS:
US: All United States
Canada: All Canada
Overseas: All Countries

KITCHEN SOLVERS
401 Jay St.
La Crosse, WI 54601
Tel: (800) 845-6779 (608) 791-5516
Fax: (608) 784-2917
E-Mail: dave@kitchensolvers.com
Web Site: www.kitchensolvers.com
Mr. David Woggon, Dir. of Franchise
  Operations

Specialize or diversify... It's your option. '10 in 1' business concept offered by the most experienced kitchen remodeling franchise system in the United States. Home-based business with no inventory required. Complete start-up and on-going marketing program, experienced technical support. Call for a FREE introductory video.

BACKGROUND:
Established: 1982;   1st Franchised: 1984
Franchised Units: 104
Company-Owned Units   3
Total Units: 107
Dist.:   US-104; CAN-3; O'seas-0
  North America: 31 States, 3 Provinces
  Density: 17 in WI, 12 in IA, 11 in IL
Projected New Units (12 Months):   15
Qualifications: 2, 2, 2, 2, , 5
Registered: CA,FL,IL,IN,MD,MI,MN,ND,
  OR,SD,VA,WA,WI,AB
FINANCIAL/TERMS:
Cash Investment: $25K
Total Investment: $27.6-41.5K
Minimum Net Worth: $NR
Fees: Franchise - $14-16K
  Royalty - 4-8%;   Ad. - 1%
Earnings Claim Statement: No
Term of Contract (Years):   10/10
Avg. # Of Employees: 1 FT
Passive Ownership: Not Allowed
Encourage Conversions: Yes
Area Develop. Agreements: No
Sub-Franchising Contracts: No
Expand In Territory: Yes
Space Needs: N/A SF; HB
SUPPORT & TRAINING PROVIDED:
Financial Assistance Provided: Yes(D)
Site Selection Assistance: N/A
Lease Negotiation Assistance: No
Co-Operative Advertising: No
Franchisee Assoc./Member: Yes
Size Of Corporate Staff: 8
On-Going Support: a,B,C,D,G,h,I
Training: 6 Days La Crosse, WI (Refacing);
  3 Days Houston, TX (Recoloring); Pre-
  Training Program.
SPECIFIC EXPANSION PLANS:
US: All United States
Canada: All Canada
Overseas: No

KITCHEN TUNE-UP
813 Circle Dr.
Aberdeen, SD 57401-3349
Tel: (800) 333-6385 (605) 225-4049
Fax: (605) 225-1371
E-Mail: kituneup@midco.net
Web Site: www.kitchentuneup.com
Mr. Craig Green, Franchise Acquisitions
  Dir.

America's #1 home improvement franchise. We offer 'Kitchen Solutions For Any Budget.' Cabinet and wood restoration, cabinet refacing and custom cabinetry, along with shelf lining, replacement hardware and cabinet organization systems. Excellent initial and on-going training and support. High residential and commercial potential. Home-based and retail locations available.

BACKGROUND: IFA MEMBER
Established: 1975;   1st Franchised: 1988
Franchised Units: 290
Company-Owned Units   1
Total Units: 291
Dist.:   US-290; CAN-1; O'seas-291
  North America: 34 States, 1 Province
  Density: 13 in CA, 10 in IL, 7 in CO
Projected New Units (12 Months):   20
Qualifications: 3, 4, 2, 2, 4, 4
Registered: All States Except HI,RI
FINANCIAL/TERMS:
Cash Investment: $18-25K
Total Investment: $28-35K
Minimum Net Worth: $N/A
Fees: Franchise - $15K
  Royalty - 4.5-7%;   Ad. - 0%
Earnings Claim Statement: Yes
Term of Contract (Years):   10/10
Avg. # Of Employees: 1-2 FT, As
Needed PT
Passive Ownership: Discouraged
Encourage Conversions: Yes
Area Develop. Agreements: Yes/10
Sub-Franchising Contracts: No
Expand In Territory: Yes
Space Needs: 500-2,500 SF; FS, SF, SC,
  HB
SUPPORT & TRAINING PROVIDED:
Financial Assistance Provided: Yes(D)

88

Site Selection Assistance:	Yes
Lease Negotiation Assistance:	Yes
Co-Operative Advertising:	No
Franchisee Assoc./Member:	No
Size Of Corporate Staff:	8
On-Going Support:	A,B,C,D,E,G,H,I

Training: 2 Weeks Pre-Training Home Study; 6-10 Days Corporate Office; 12 Wks. Home Study; On-Going.

SPECIFIC EXPANSION PLANS:

US:	All United States
Canada:	All Canada
Overseas:	No

<< >>

MARBLE RENEWAL

P.O. Box 56349
Little Rock, AR 72215
Tel: (888) 664-7866 (501) 663-2080
Fax: (501) 663-2401
E-Mail: marble@marblerenewal.com
Web Site: www.marblerenewal.com
Ms. Kimberly Colclasure, Director Sales & Marketing

International franchise company specializing in the care and treatment of natural stones and hardwood. Advanced and innovative techniques to give back the value and beauty of marble, granite, terrazzo, slate, limestone, time and other natural stones, as well as hardwood.

BACKGROUND:

Established: 1988;	1st Franchised: 1989
Franchised Units:	24
Company-Owned Units	1
Total Units:	25
Dist.:	US-13; CAN-3; O'seas-8
North America:	12 States, 2 Provinces
Density:	1 in GA, 1 in NJ, 1 in NC
Projected New Units (12 Months):	8
Qualifications:	5, 5, 2, 3, 4, 5
Registered: NR	

FINANCIAL/TERMS:

Cash Investment:	$10-35K
Total Investment:	$49-162K
Minimum Net Worth:	$Varies
Fees: Franchise -	$15-50K
Royalty - 5-8%;	Ad. - 0%
Earnings Claim Statement:	No
Term of Contract (Years):	10/10
Avg. # Of Employees:	2 FT
Passive Ownership:	Discouraged
Encourage Conversions:	N/A
Area Develop. Agreements:	No
Sub-Franchising Contracts:	Yes
Expand In Territory:	Yes
Space Needs: NR SF; HB	

SUPPORT & TRAINING PROVIDED:

Financial Assistance Provided:	Yes
Site Selection Assistance:	N/A
Lease Negotiation Assistance:	N/A
Co-Operative Advertising:	No
Franchisee Assoc./Member:	Yes
Size Of Corporate Staff:	13
On-Going Support:	C,D,E,F,G,H,I

Training: 2 Weeks in Little Rock, AR.

SPECIFIC EXPANSION PLANS:

US:	All United States
Canada:	All Canada
Overseas:	All Countries

<< >>

MARBLELIFE

805 W. North Carrier Pkwy., # 220
Grand Prairie, TX 75050
Tel: (800) 627-4569 (972) 623-0500
Fax: (972) 623-0220
E-Mail: marblelife@marblelife.com
Web Site: www.marblelife.com
Ms. Kimberly K. Colclasure, Marketing Director

Specializes in the restoration, preservation and maintenance services for natural stones and other surfaces.

BACKGROUND:

Established: 1987;	1st Franchised: 1993
Franchised Units:	48
Company-Owned Units	1
Total Units:	49
Dist.:	US-39; CAN-1; O'seas-9
North America:	38 States, 1 Province
Density:	3 in TX, 3 in CA, 2 in FL
Projected New Units (12 Months):	24
Qualifications:	4, 4, 2, 2, 2, 4
Registered: CA,FL,IL,NY,VA,WI	

FINANCIAL/TERMS:

Cash Investment:	$50K+
Total Investment:	$15-100K
Minimum Net Worth:	$Varies/terr.
Fees: Franchise -	$5K/100K pop.
Royalty - 6%;	Ad. - 2%
Earnings Claim Statement:	No
Term of Contract (Years):	10/10
Avg. # Of Employees:	3+ FT
Passive Ownership:	Discouraged
Encourage Conversions:	Yes
Area Develop. Agreements:	Yes
Sub-Franchising Contracts:	No
Expand In Territory:	No
Space Needs: N/A SF; N/A	

SUPPORT & TRAINING PROVIDED:

Financial Assistance Provided:	Yes(I)
Site Selection Assistance:	N/A
Lease Negotiation Assistance:	No

Co-Operative Advertising:	No
Franchisee Assoc./Member:	Yes/Yes
Size Of Corporate Staff:	12
On-Going Support:	C,D,E,G,H,I

Training: 2 Weeks at Grand Prairie, TX.

SPECIFIC EXPANSION PLANS:

US:	All United States
Canada:	All Canada
Overseas:	All Europe and Middle East

<< >>

MIRACLE METHOD

4239 N. Nevada, # 115
Colorado Springs, CO 80907
Tel: (800) 444-8827 (719) 594-9196
Fax: (719) 594-9282
E-Mail: pleonard@miraclemethod.com
Web Site: www.miraclemethod.com
Mr. Paul Leonard, Vice President

Make money in the growing remodeling industry by running your own bath and kitchen refinishing business. Save customers money by refinishing instead of replacing. Bathtubs, tile, showers, counter tops and more. Excellent income potential!

BACKGROUND:	IFA MEMBER
Established: 1979;	1st Franchised: 1980
Franchised Units:	150
Company-Owned Units	0
Total Units:	150
Dist.:	US-100; CAN-0; O'seas-50
North America:	30 States
Density:	20 in CA, 5 in TX, 3 in CT
Projected New Units (12 Months):	20+
Qualifications:	3, 5, 4, 3, 3, 5
Registered: CA,FL,RI,WA	

FINANCIAL/TERMS:

Cash Investment:	$5-10K
Total Investment:	$20K
Minimum Net Worth:	$N/A
Fees: Franchise -	$15K
Royalty - 5-7.5%;	Ad. - 1%
Earnings Claim Statement:	Yes
Term of Contract (Years):	5
Avg. # Of Employees:	1-5 FT & PT
Passive Ownership:	Discouraged
Encourage Conversions:	Yes
Area Develop. Agreements:	No
Sub-Franchising Contracts:	Yes
Expand In Territory:	No
Space Needs: N/A SF; HB	

SUPPORT & TRAINING PROVIDED:

Financial Assistance Provided:	Yes(D)
Site Selection Assistance:	No
Lease Negotiation Assistance:	No
Co-Operative Advertising:	Yes
Franchisee Assoc./Member:	Yes
Size Of Corporate Staff:	4
On-Going Support:	C,D,G,H,I

Training: 1 Week at Headquarters Location.

SPECIFIC EXPANSION PLANS:

US:	All United States
Canada:	All Canada
Overseas:	All Countries

≪ ≫

MR. APPLIANCE CORPORATION

1020 N. University Parks Dr.
Waco, TX 76707
Tel: (800) 207-8515 (254) 745-2500
Fax: (254) 745-5098
E-Mail: mowens@dwyergroup.com
Web Site: www.mrapplaince.com
Mr. Mike Hawkins, VP Franchising

Full-service appliance repair service for all brands; residential and commercial business.

BACKGROUND: IFA MEMBER
Established: 1996; 1st Franchised: 1997

Franchised Units:	40
Company-Owned Units	0
Total Units:	40
Dist.:	US-40; CAN-0; O'seas-0
North America:	15 States
Density:	9 in TX, 4 in FL, 2 in CA
Projected New Units (12 Months):	48
Qualifications:	4, 4, 4, 2, 3, 4
Registered: All States	

FINANCIAL/TERMS:

Cash Investment:	$NR
Total Investment:	$NR
Minimum Net Worth:	$Varies
Fees: Franchise -	$14.5K
Royalty - 3-6%;	Ad. - 2%
Earnings Claim Statement:	No
Term of Contract (Years):	10/10
Avg. # Of Employees: Depends on Sales	
Passive Ownership:	Discouraged
Encourage Conversions:	Yes
Area Develop. Agreements:	No
Sub-Franchising Contracts:	Yes
Expand In Territory:	Yes
Space Needs: NR SF; N/A	

SUPPORT & TRAINING PROVIDED:

Financial Assistance Provided:	Yes(I)
Site Selection Assistance:	N/A
Lease Negotiation Assistance:	N/A
Co-Operative Advertising:	N/A
Franchisee Assoc./Member:	No
Size Of Corporate Staff:	4
On-Going Support:	A,C,D,E,F,G,H,I

Training: 1 Week Waco, TX.

SPECIFIC EXPANSION PLANS:

US:	All United States
Canada:	Master Franchise
Overseas:	Master Franchise Only

≪ ≫

MR. ELECTRIC CORP.

1020 N. University Parks Dr.
Waco, TX 76707
Tel: (800) 805-0575 (254) 745-2466
Fax: (254) 745-5098
E-Mail: mrelectric@dwyergroup.com
Web Site: www.mrelectric.com
Mr. Mike Hawkins, Vice President Franchising

Serving the electrical repair needs of residential and light commercial establishments, in addition to offering other electrical products to the 'same user,' including such items as surcharge protectors, communication and data cabling, ceiling fans, decorative light fixtures, security and landscape lighting, etc.

BACKGROUND: IFA MEMBER
Established: 1994; 1st Franchised: 1994

Franchised Units:	84
Company-Owned Units	0
Total Units:	84
Dist.:	US-80; CAN-4; O'seas-0
North America:	37 States, 1 Province
Density:	11 in CA, 5 in IL, 4 in TX
Projected New Units (12 Months):	18
Qualifications:	3, 2, 5, 3, 2, 4
Registered: All States	

FINANCIAL/TERMS:

Cash Investment:	$30.2-68K
Total Investment:	$50-88K
Minimum Net Worth:	$75K
Fees: Franchise -	$17.5K
Royalty - 3-6%;	Ad. - 2%
Earnings Claim Statement:	No

Term of Contract (Years):	10/5
Avg. # Of Employees:	3 FT, 1 PT
Passive Ownership:	Discouraged
Encourage Conversions:	Yes
Area Develop. Agreements:	No
Sub-Franchising Contracts:	Yes
Expand In Territory:	No
Space Needs: 500-1,000 SF; FS, HB	

SUPPORT & TRAINING PROVIDED:

Financial Assistance Provided:	Yes(B)
Site Selection Assistance:	N/A
Lease Negotiation Assistance:	N/A
Co-Operative Advertising:	No
Franchisee Assoc./Member:	No
Size Of Corporate Staff:	4
On-Going Support:	C,D,E,G,h,I

Training: 5 Business Days at Corporate Offices; 3 Business Days On-Site in Business.

SPECIFIC EXPANSION PLANS:

US:	All United States
Canada:	Not This Year
Overseas: Most Latin American and Asian Countries	

≪ ≫

MR. HANDYMAN

3948 Ranchero Dr.
Ann Arbor, MI 48108
Tel: (800) 289-4600 (734) 822-6800
Fax: (734) 822-6888
E-Mail: info@mrhandyman.com
Web Site: www.mrhandyman.com
Mr. Marc A. Kiekenapp, Vice President

Seeking a business with tremendous consumer demand? Stop right here. MR. HANDYMAN is the solution to today's fix-it problems for millions of time-starved families. An affordable investment gives you a franchise catering to 100 million homeowners and commercial customers needing property maintenance and repair. Technicians do the work. You manage the business.

BACKGROUND:
Established: 2000; 1st Franchised: 2000

Franchised Units:	10
Company-Owned Units	0
Total Units:	10
Dist.:	US-10; CAN-0; O'seas-0
North America:	10 States

Density:	NR
Projected New Units (12 Months):	25
Qualifications:	3, 3, 1, 3, 4, 5
Registered: CA,FL,IL,IN,MD,MI,MN,NY,	
OR,RI,VA,WA,WI,DC	

FINANCIAL/TERMS:

Cash Investment:	$10-20K
Total Investment:	$47-76K
Minimum Net Worth:	$150K
Fees: Franchise -	$6.9K
Royalty - 7%;	Ad. - 0%
Earnings Claim Statement:	No
Term of Contract (Years):	10/10
Avg. # Of Employees:	6 FT
Passive Ownership:	Discouraged
Encourage Conversions:	Yes
Area Develop. Agreements:	No
Sub-Franchising Contracts:	No
Expand In Territory:	Yes
Space Needs: 200 SF; HB	

SUPPORT & TRAINING PROVIDED:

Financial Assistance Provided:	Yes(I)
Site Selection Assistance:	N/A
Lease Negotiation Assistance:	N/A
Co-Operative Advertising:	N/A
Franchisee Assoc./Member:	No
Size Of Corporate Staff:	15
On-Going Support:	C,D,E,G,h,I
Training: 4 Days Home Office; 1 Day Field; 6 Months Right Start Program; 2 Days Franchise Location.	

SPECIFIC EXPANSION PLANS:

US:	All United States
Canada:	All Canada
Overseas:	All Countries

≪ ≫

PERMA-GLAZE

1638 S. Research Loop Rd., # 160
Tucson, AZ 85710
Tel: (800) 332-7397 (520) 722-9718
Fax: (520) 296-4393
E-Mail: permaglaze@permaglaze.com
Web Site: www.permaglaze.com
Mr. Dale R. Young, President

PERMA GLAZE specializes in multi-surface restoration of bathtubs, sinks, countertops, appliances, porcelain, metal, acrylics, cultured marble and more. PERMA GLAZE licensed representatives provide valued services to hotels/motels, private residences, apartments, schools, hospitals, contractors, property managers and many others.

BACKGROUND: IFA MEMBER

Established: 1978; 1st Franchised: 1981	
Franchised Units:	177
Company-Owned Units	1
Total Units:	178
Dist.: US-124; CAN-3; O'seas-51	
North America: 36 States, 1 Province	
Density: 15 in CA, 7 in AZ, 6 in PA	
Projected New Units (12 Months):	20
Qualifications:	4, 2, 1, 3, 4, 3
Registered: CA,IL,IN,MD,MI,MN,NY,	
ND,OR,SD,VA,WA,WI	

FINANCIAL/TERMS:

Cash Investment:	$2.5-3K
Total Investment:	$22-25K+
Minimum Net Worth:	$21.5K
Fees: Franchise -	$21.5K+
Royalty - 6/5/4%/$200 Min.; Ad. - NR	
Earnings Claim Statement:	Yes
Term of Contract (Years):	10/10
Avg. # Of Employees:	1 FT
Passive Ownership:	Not Allowed
Encourage Conversions:	N/A
Area Develop. Agreements:	Yes/10
Sub-Franchising Contracts:	No
Expand In Territory:	No
Space Needs: N/A SF; HB	

SUPPORT & TRAINING PROVIDED:

Financial Assistance Provided:	No
Site Selection Assistance:	Yes
Lease Negotiation Assistance:	N/A
Co-Operative Advertising:	N/A
Franchisee Assoc./Member:	No
Size Of Corporate Staff:	6
On-Going Support:	C,D,G,H,I
Training: 5 Days Tucson, AZ.	

SPECIFIC EXPANSION PLANS:

US:	All United States
Canada:	All Canada
Overseas:	All Countries

≪ ≫

RE-BATH

1055 S. Country Club Dr., Bldg. # 2
Mesa, AZ 85210-4613
Tel: (800) 426-4573 (480) 844-1575
Fax: (480) 833-7199
E-Mail: newfranchise@re-bath.com
Web Site: www.re-bath.com
Mr. David W. Andow, General Manager

The franchise sells and installs custom-molded, acrylic bathtub liners, shower base liners and wall surrounds for homes, apartments, condos and commercial

establishments. RE-BATH has proven products and installation technology, plus over 750,000 installations during the past 20 years. Go with the leader in the bathtub liner industry.

BACKGROUND:

Established: 1978; 1st Franchised: 1991	
Franchised Units:	100
Company-Owned Units	2
Total Units:	102
Dist.: US-99; CAN-1; O'seas-2	
North America: 34 States, 1 Province	
Density: 8 in NY, 7 in PA, 6 in CA,	
Projected New Units (12 Months):	20
Qualifications:	4, 5, 4, 2, 3, 4
Registered: All Except ND,SD,DC	

FINANCIAL/TERMS:

Cash Investment:	$15-30K
Total Investment:	$35-80K
Minimum Net Worth:	$100K
Fees: Franchise -	$15-30K
Royalty - $25/Unit;	Ad. - 0%
Earnings Claim Statement:	No
Term of Contract (Years):	7/7
Avg. # Of Employees:	3 FT, 1 PT
Passive Ownership:	Not Allowed
Encourage Conversions:	N/A
Area Develop. Agreements:	No
Sub-Franchising Contracts:	No
Expand In Territory:	Yes
Space Needs: 200 SF; FS, SF	

SUPPORT & TRAINING PROVIDED:

Financial Assistance Provided:	No
Site Selection Assistance:	Yes
Lease Negotiation Assistance:	Yes
Co-Operative Advertising:	Yes
Franchisee Assoc./Member:	Yes/No
Size Of Corporate Staff:	12
On-Going Support:	B,d,G,h,I
Training: 9 Days Corporate Training Facility.	

SPECIFIC EXPANSION PLANS:

US:	All United States
Canada:	All Canada
Overseas:	No

≪ ≫

REFACE IT KITCHEN SYSTEMS

P.O. Box 874
Ferndale, WA 98248
Tel: (360) 384-3546
Fax: (360) 384-0246
Web Site: www.refaceit.com
Mr. H. Ronald Good, President

REFACE IT KITCHEN SYSTEMS renovates kitchens and baths. We have home-based sales franchises and manufacturing franchises available. Each manufacturing franchisee is surrounded by sales franchisees. This is a fabulous two-way relationship that is unique to our industry.

BACKGROUND:

Established: 1989; 1st Franchised: 1990	
Franchised Units:	13
Company-Owned Units	0
Total Units:	13
Dist.:	US-13; CAN-0; O'seas-0
North America:	3 States
Density:	5 in WA, 5 in CO, 3 in OR
Projected New Units (12 Months):	6
Qualifications:	4, 4, 2, 2, 3, 5
Registered: CA,HI,OR,WA	

FINANCIAL/TERMS:

Cash Investment:	$24-100K
Total Investment:	$75-140K
Minimum Net Worth:	$50-250K
Fees: Franchise -	$15-27.5K
Royalty - 4%;	Ad. - 1%
Earnings Claim Statement:	No
Term of Contract (Years):	5/5/5
Avg. # Of Employees:	1-10 FT
Passive Ownership:	Not Allowed
Encourage Conversions:	Yes
Area Develop. Agreements:	No
Sub-Franchising Contracts:	No
Expand In Territory:	Yes
Space Needs: 3,500 SF; Warehouse, HB	

SUPPORT & TRAINING PROVIDED:

Financial Assistance Provided:	No
Site Selection Assistance:	Yes
Lease Negotiation Assistance:	No
Co-Operative Advertising:	Yes
Franchisee Assoc./Member:	No
Size Of Corporate Staff:	4
On-Going Support:	D,G,H
Training: 1-2 Weeks in Ferndale, WA.	

SPECIFIC EXPANSION PLANS:

US:	NW,SW, Mountain States, TX
Canada:	No
Overseas:	No

◄◄ ►►

SCREEN MACHINE, THE
19636 8th St. e.
Sonoma, CA 95476
Tel: (707) 996-5551
Fax: (707) 996-0139
E-Mail: screens@screen-machine.com
Web Site: www.screen-machine.com
Mr. Wayne T. Wirick, Sr., President

A mobile service unit, specializing in new window and door screens, and the re-screening of same. Security and pet doors, and a full line of Hunter Douglas window coverings.

BACKGROUND:

Established: 1986; 1st Franchised: 1988	
Franchised Units:	23
Company-Owned Units	1
Total Units:	24
Dist.:	US-24; CAN-0; O'seas-0
North America:	1 State
Density:	24 in CA
Projected New Units (12 Months):	4
Qualifications:	3, 3, 2, 3, 4, 4
Registered: CA	

FINANCIAL/TERMS:

Cash Investment:	$25K
Total Investment:	$53-72.1K
Minimum Net Worth:	$53K
Fees: Franchise -	$25K
Royalty - 5%;	Ad. - 3%
Earnings Claim Statement:	No
Term of Contract (Years):	10/10
Avg. # Of Employees:	1 FT
Passive Ownership:	Discouraged
Encourage Conversions:	N/A
Area Develop. Agreements:	No
Sub-Franchising Contracts:	No
Expand In Territory:	Yes
Space Needs: N/A SF; HB	

SUPPORT & TRAINING PROVIDED:

Financial Assistance Provided:	Yes(I)
Site Selection Assistance:	N/A
Lease Negotiation Assistance:	N/A
Co-Operative Advertising:	N/A
Franchisee Assoc./Member:	Yes/No
Size Of Corporate Staff:	2
On-Going Support:	A,C,D,G,H
Training: 6 Days Sonoma, CA.	

SPECIFIC EXPANSION PLANS:

US:	West
Canada:	No
Overseas:	No

◄◄ ►►

SUPERIOR WALLS OF AMERICA
937 E. Earl Rd.
New Holland, PA 17557
Tel: (800) 452-9255 (717) 351-9255
Fax: (717) 351-9263
E-Mail: shuman@superiorwalls.com
Web Site: www.superiorwalls.com
Mr. Scott Shuman, Director of Sales

We provide license agreements to manufacturer, sell and install the patented SUPERIOR WALLS SYSTEM, a pre-cast,

insulated, studded, waterproof concrete foundation wall for new residential and light commercial construction.

BACKGROUND:

Established: 1981; 1st Franchised: 1985	
Franchised Units:	20
Company-Owned Units	0
Total Units:	20
Dist.:	US-19; CAN-0; O'seas-1
North America:	10 States
Density:	6 in PA, 2 in MI, 2 in WI
Projected New Units (12 Months):	3
Qualifications:	5, 4, 5, 3, 2, 3
Registered: IN,NY	

FINANCIAL/TERMS:

Cash Investment:	$500K
Total Investment:	$2-3MM
Minimum Net Worth:	$500K
Fees: Franchise -	$30K
Royalty - 4%;	Ad. - 0%
Earnings Claim Statement:	No
Term of Contract (Years):	10/10/10
Avg. # Of Employees:	8 FT, 2 PT
Passive Ownership:	Discouraged
Encourage Conversions:	No
Area Develop. Agreements:	No
Sub-Franchising Contracts:	No
Expand In Territory:	Yes
Space Needs: ~30,000 SF; 28' Ceilings, O/H Crane	

SUPPORT & TRAINING PROVIDED:

Financial Assistance Provided:	Yes(I)
Site Selection Assistance:	Yes
Lease Negotiation Assistance:	N/A
Co-Operative Advertising:	Yes
Franchisee Assoc./Member:	No
Size Of Corporate Staff:	20+
On-Going Support:	B,c,D,G,H,I
Training: 2 Weeks Corporate Office; 3 Weeks Field Location.	

SPECIFIC EXPANSION PLANS:

US:	All United States
Canada:	All Canada
Overseas:	England, Philippines

◄◄ ►►

SURFACE SPECIALISTS SYSTEMS
5168 Country Club Dr.
High Ridge, MO 63049
Tel: (888) 376-4468 (636) 378-4468
Fax: (636) 376-8889
Web Site: www.surfacespecialists.com
Ms. Amy Irali, Marketing/Sales Director

SURFACE SPECIALISTS franchisees specialize in repairing and refinishing kitchen and bathroom surfaces. These surfaces include acrylic spas, fiberglass tubs and showers, porcelain tubs, cultured marble, Formica countertops, and PVC/ABS (plastic). Become a factory authorized warranty service provider for more than 34 manufacturers nationwide. We are the only franchisor in the industry providing full service to the new construction market. Excellent opportunity of high profit potential at low investment.

BACKGROUND: IFA MEMBER
Established: 1981; 1st Franchised: 1982
Franchised Units: 26
Company-Owned Units 0
Total Units: 26
Dist.: US-26; CAN-0; O'seas-0
North America: 16 States
Density: 5 in MI, 4 in WI, 2 in FL
Projected New Units (12 Months): 4
Qualifications: 4, 3, 2, 3, 3, 5
Registered: FL,IL,MI,DC
FINANCIAL/TERMS:
Cash Investment: $10-15K
Total Investment: $13.9-42K
Minimum Net Worth: $90K
Fees: Franchise - $9.5-30K
Royalty - 5%; Ad. - N/A
Earnings Claim Statement: No
Term of Contract (Years): 10/10
Avg. # Of Employees: 2 FT, 2 PT
Passive Ownership: Discouraged
Encourage Conversions: Yes
Area Develop. Agreements: Yes
Sub-Franchising Contracts: No
Expand In Territory: Yes
Space Needs: 300 SF; HB
SUPPORT & TRAINING PROVIDED:
Financial Assistance Provided: Yes(D)
Site Selection Assistance: N/A
Lease Negotiation Assistance: N/A
Co-Operative Advertising: No
Franchisee Assoc./Member: No
Size Of Corporate Staff: 4
On-Going Support: B,c,D,G,h,I
Training: 3 Weeks High Ridge, MO.
SPECIFIC EXPANSION PLANS:
US: All United States
Canada: No
Overseas: No

≪ ≫

U BUILD IT
12006 98th Ave., # 200
Kirkland, WA 98034
Tel: (800) 992-4357 (425) 821-6200
Fax: (425) 821-6876
E-Mail: franchiseinfo@ubuildit.com
Web Site: www.ubuildit.com
Mr. Mark Kruschwitz, VP Franchise Sales

For 10 years, the U BUILD IT system has been assisting homeowners to act as their own general contractor for both remodeling and new home construction. By teaming a homeowner with a construction professional, the project is efficiently completed while avoiding the common pitfalls and saving thousands. Providing subcontractors, bank financing, site visits, etc., U BUILD IT is a perfect complementary service for the building professional or entrepreneur looking for a huge untapped niche.

BACKGROUND:
Established: 1997; 1st Franchised: 1998
Franchised Units: 43
Company-Owned Units 0
Total Units: 43
Dist.: US-43; CAN-0; O'seas-0
North America: 16 States
Density: 13 in WA
Projected New Units (12 Months): 50
Qualifications: 4, 5, 4, 3, 4, 5
Registered: CA,IN,MD,MN,VA,WA
FINANCIAL/TERMS:
Cash Investment: $30.5-100K
Total Investment: $30.5-100K
Minimum Net Worth: $100K
Fees: Franchise - $25K
Royalty - 8-12%/$300; Ad. - 2%/$50/Mo.
Earnings Claim Statement: No
Term of Contract (Years): 10/10
Avg. # Of Employees: 1 FT, 1 PT
Passive Ownership: Not Allowed
Encourage Conversions: Yes
Area Develop. Agreements: No
Sub-Franchising Contracts: No
Expand In Territory: No
Space Needs: 400 SF; Class B Office
SUPPORT & TRAINING PROVIDED:
Financial Assistance Provided: No
Site Selection Assistance: No
Lease Negotiation Assistance: No
Co-Operative Advertising: Yes
Franchisee Assoc./Member: No
Size Of Corporate Staff: 13
On-Going Support: C,D,E,H,I
Training: 2 Weeks Seattle, WA.

SPECIFIC EXPANSION PLANS:
US: All United States
Canada: All Canada
Overseas: No

≪ ≫

SUPPLEMENTAL LISTING OF FRANCHISORS

A-1 Concrete Leveling, 2417 Manchester Rd., Akron, OH 44314 ; ; Mr. Jim Creed (800) 848-1808; (330) 848-1804

American Concrete Raising, 916 Westwood Ave., Addison, IL 60101 ; (630) 543-5930; Mr. John G. Meyers ; (630) 543-5775

American Restoration Services, 2061 Monongahela Ave., Pittsburgh, PA 15218 ; (412) 351-2544; Mr. Russell K. Case (800) 245-1617; (412) 351-7100

AmerLink, P.O. Box 669, Battleboro, NC 27809 ; (252) 442-6900; Mr. Thomas Slocum (800) 872-4254; (252) 977-2545

Arthur Rutenberg Homes, 13922 58th St., N., Clearwater, FL 33760 ; (727) 538-9089; Mr. Raja Jaghab (800) 274-6637; (727) 536-5900

Artistic Stone Products, 9290 Matt Hwy., Ballground, GA 30107 ; (770) 888-8658; Mr. Todd Hamby ; (770) 888-8278

Bath Genie, 20 River St., Marlboro, MA 01752 ; (508) 624-6444; Mr. John Foley (800) 255-8827; (508) 481-8338

Bathcrest, 2425 S. Progress Dr., Salt Lake City, UT 84119 ; (801) 977-0328; Mr. Lloyd Peterson (800) 826-6790; (801) 972-1110

C. G. I., 7111-7115 Ohms Ln., Minneapolis, MN 55439 ; (612) 835-1395; Mr. Scott L. Smith (800) 328-6347; (612) 835-1338

Canadian Residential Inspection Services, P.O. Box 2121 D. E. P. S., Dartmouth, NS B2W 3Y2 CANADA; (902) 827-3404; Mr. Russell Cook (888) 499-0999; (902) 499-0999

Castart, 1041 E. Miles, Tucson, AZ 85719 ; (520) 670-0062; Mr. Dave Wienert (800) 871-8838; (520) 623-8858

Certa ProPainters, 1140 Valley Forge Rd., Valley Forge, PA 19482 ; (770) 455-4422;

Mr. Tom Wood (800) 452-3782; (770) 455-4300

Certa ProPainters of Canada, 5397 Eglinton Ave., W., # 109, Etobicoke, ON M9C 5K6 CANADA; (800) 446-6840; Mr. Scott Mossip (888) 295-3555; (416) 620-4600

Closets By Design, 13151 S. Western Ave., Gardena, CA 90249 ; (310) 515-1028; Mr. Jerry Egner (800) 293-3744; (310) 365-2041

College Pro Painters, 341 Broadway, Cambridge, MA 02139 ; (617) 576-6827; Ms. Kimberly Blackmore (888) 427-7672; (617) 576-6822

Color-Glo International, 7111-7115 Ohms Ln., Minneapolis, MN 55439-2158 ; (612) 835-1395; Mr. Scott L. Smith (800) 333-8523; (612) 835-1338

Concrete Grinding Company, 188 Civil Circle, # 109, Lewisville, TX 75067 ; (800) 474-6332; Mr. Joel Kilian (800) 922-2488; (972) 353-9220

Doors Unlimited, 301 W. Hunting Park Ave., # B, Philadelphia, PA 19140-2697 ; (215) 843-4066; Mr. Dale Glenney (800) 338-5330; (215) 455-2100

Elevators Etc., 6802 Ringgold Rd., Chattanooga, TN 37412 ; (423) 265-7477; Mr. Gordon D. Hulgan III (800) 451-8336; (423) 267-5438

Enviro-Shield Energy Systems, 6033 Shawson Dr., Unit 9, Mississauga, ON L5T 1H8 CANADA; (905) 670-8468; Mr. James Formosa (800) 670-8468; (905) 670-5181

Epmark, 6277 Riverside Dr., Dublin, OH 43017 ; (614) 761-1155; Mr. Don Smiley (800) 783-3838; (614) 761-1010

Everdry Waterproofing, 365 Highland Rd., E., Macedonia, OH 44056 ; (216) 468-3231; Mr. Jack M. Jones (800) 365-7295; (216) 467-1055

Floorguard, 1130 Carolina Dr., # C, West Chicago, IL 60185 ; (630) 231-3836; Ms. Pamela Schuberth (800) 701-6364; (630) 231-9070

IDRS, 152 SE Fifth Ave., Hillsboro, OR 97123 ; (503) 693-1993; Mr. John Powell (800) 779-1357; (503) 693-1619

Insulated Dry Roof Systems, 152 SE 5th Ave., Hillsboro, OR 97123 ; (503) 693-1993; Mr. John Powell (800) 779-1357; (503) 693-1619

Jet-Black Sealcoating & Repair, 25 West Cliff Rd., # 103, Burnsville, MN 55337 ; (612) 890-7022; Mr. Doug Hoiland (888) 538-2525; (612) 890-8343

K.T.U. Worldwide, 813 Circle Dr., Aberdeen, SD 57401-2670 ; (605)225-1305; Mr. Dave Haglund (800) 333-6385; (605) 225-4049

Kitchen Saver, 94 Bessemer Rd., London, ON N6E 1K7 CANADA; (519) 685-7283; Mr. Craig Jones (800) 265-0933; (519) 686-8820

Kott Koatings, 27161 Burbank St., Foothill Ranch, CA 92610 ; (949) 770-5101; Mr. John M. Kott (800) 452-6161; (949) 770-5055

Liberty Seamless Gutters, 102 E. Railroad Ave., Knoxville, PA 16928 ; (814) 326-4123; Mr. Kurt Heisey (800) 806-7109; (814) 326-4121

LINC Corporation, The, 4 Northshore Center, 106 Isabella, Pittsburgh, PA 15212 ; (412) 321-3809; Mr. Brad Petvold ; (412) 359-2197

Magnum Piering, 13230 Ferguson Ln., Bridgeton, MO 63044 ; (314) 291-1115; Mr. Kevin Kaufman (800) 822-7437; (314) 291-7437

Outdoor Lighting Perspectives, 6930 Ancient Oak Ln., Charlotte, NC 28277 ; (704) 841-1822; Mr. Tom Fenning ; (704) 849-8808

PaintNet, 681 Pullman Ave., Rochester, NY 14615 ; (716) 458-1803; Mr. Donald Youst, Jr. (800) 505-6210; (716) 458-5320

Perma Ceram Enterprises, 65 Smithtown Blvd., Smithtown, NY 11788 ; (516) 724-9626; Mr. Joseph A. Tumolo (800) 645-5039; (516) 724-1205

Perma-Jack Company, 9066 Watson Rd., St. Louis, MO 63126-2234 ; (314) 843-7898; Ms. Joan L. Robinson (800) 843-1888; (314) 843-1957

Permacrete Systems, 21 Williams Ave., Dartmouth, NS B3B 1X3 CANADA; (902) 468-7474; Ms. Colleen Cole (800) 565-5325; (902) 468-1700

Rich's Chimney Fix-It, 15965 Jeanette St., Southfield, MI 48075 ; (248) 557-7931; Mr. Richard Zawack ; (248) 559-1415

Roof Champion, 1676 W. Village Round, Park City, UT 84098 ; (435) 655-8425; Mr. William Cowie (888) 655-8850; (435) 655-8850

Screenmobile, The, 457 W. Allen Ave., # 107, San Dimas, CA 91773 ; (909) 394-0273; Mr. Monty M. Walker ; (909) 394-4581

Solid / Flue Chimney Systems, 4937 Starr St., SE, Grand Rapids, MI 49546 ; (616) 940-0921; Mr. Doug La Fleur (800) 444-FLUE; (616) 940-8809

Super Seamless, 560 Henderson Dr., Regina, SK S4N 5X2 CANADA; (306) 721-2532; Mr. Nestor Mryglod (800) 565-4334; (306) 721-8000

Surface Doctor, 6849 Fairview Rd., Charlotte, NC 28210 ; (704) 364-1202; Mr. Bruce Mullan (800) 444-4138; (704) 364-7707

Trades Guild.com, The, 308 Pendelton Way, Oakland, CA 94621 ; (510) 639-1870; Mr. Seth Wiles ; (510) 639-1871

United Energy Partners, 905 Bolger Ct., Fenton, MO 63026-2030 ; (314) 230-3020; Mr. Jeffrey Wilkinson (800) 467-8887; (314) 230-9900

Wise Cracks Restorations, # 2 Lakeside Place, Unit 9, Halifax, NS B3T 1L7 CANADA; (902) 876-8863; Ms. Andrea Mackey (800) 587-7325; (902) 876-8400

BUSINESS: FINANCIAL SERVICES INDUSTRY PROFILE

Total # Franchisors in Industry Group	34
Total # Franchised Units in Industry Group	11,182
Total # Company-Owned Units in Industry Group	5,952
Total # Operating Units in Industry Group	17,134
Average # Franchised Units/Franchisor	328.9
Average # Company-Owned Units/Franchisor	175.1
Average # Total Units/Franchisor	504.0
Ratio of Total # Franchised Units/Total # Company-Owned Units	1.9:1
Industry Survey Participants	12
Representing % of Industry	35.3%
Average Franchise Fee*:	$21.8
Average Total Investment*:	$75.3
Average On-Going Royalty Fee*:	7.3%

If a range was provided, the mid-point of the range was used. See detailed profiles for actual ranges.

FIVE LARGEST PARTICIPANTS IN SURVEY

Company	# Fran- chised Units	# Co- Owned Units	# Total Units	Franchise Fee	On-Going Royalty	Total Investment
1. Jackson Hewitt Tax Service	3,250	0	3,250	25K	15%	47.4-75K
2. Ace- America's Cash Express	120	791	911	15-30K	5%/$850 Min.	77.5-186K
3. Peyron Tax Service	700	2	702	25K.	5%	25K
4. Padgett Business Services	423	1	424	34.5K	9-4.5%	40-60K
5. Triple Check Income Tax Service	279	2	281	0	Varies	5-8K

All of the data provided are proprietary and should not be quoted without acknowledging *Bond's Franchise Guide*.

ACE - AMERICA'S CASH EXPRESS

1231 Greenway Dr., # 800
Irving, TX 75038
Tel: (800) 713-3338 (972) 550-5000
Fax: (972) 582-1406
E-Mail: rpryor@acecashexpress.com
Web Site: www.acecashexpress.com
Mr. Richard Pryor, Mgr. of Fran. Dev.

Cash in with the leader in retail financial services! ACE is a 30-year-old publicly-traded company operating and franchising over 900+ locations across 29 states. ACE offers customers a number of financial services, including check cashing, bill payments, money orders, wire transfers, short-term loans or cash advances, prepaid telecommunication products and other related services.

BACKGROUND:

Established: 1968; 1st Franchised: 1996	
Franchised Units:	120
Company-Owned Units	791
Total Units:	911
Dist.:	US-911; CAN-0; O'seas-0
North America:	29 States
Density: 237 in TX, 53 in AZ, 44 MD	
Projected New Units (12 Months): 120+	
Qualifications:	5, 4, 2, 2, 4, 5
Registered: All States and AB	

FINANCIAL/TERMS:

Cash Investment:	$50K
Total Investment:	$77.5-186.1K
Minimum Net Worth:	$150K
Fees: Franchise -	$15-30K
Royalty - 5%/$850 Min.;	Ad. - 3%
Earnings Claim Statement:	Yes
Term of Contract (Years):	10/5
Avg. # Of Employees:	2 FT
Passive Ownership:	Discouraged
Encourage Conversions:	Yes
Area Develop. Agreements:	Yes
Sub-Franchising Contracts:	No
Expand In Territory:	Varies
Space Needs: 250-1,500 SF; FS, SC, Kiosk	

SUPPORT & TRAINING PROVIDED:

Financial Assistance Provided:	Yes(I)
Site Selection Assistance:	Yes
Lease Negotiation Assistance:	N/A
Co-Operative Advertising:	Yes
Franchisee Assoc./Member:	Yes/Yes
Size Of Corporate Staff:	151
On-Going Support:	A,C,G,I
Training: 10 Days Corporate Office (excludes travel and lodging expenses).	

SPECIFIC EXPANSION PLANS:

US:	All United States
Canada:	No
Overseas:	No

CASH PLUS

3002 Dow Ave., # 12010
Tustin, CA 92780
Tel: (888) 707-2274 (714) 731-2274
Fax: (714) 731-2099
E-Mail: cpcorp@cashplusinc.com
Web Site: www.cashplusinc.com
Mr. Bruce Corzine, Frnachise Development Director

We are meeting America's changing financial needs with tasteful, attractive, retail stores that have proven to be appealing to customers across the socio-economic spectrum. Our unique style shows genuine care for our customers - this is good for business. A powerful marketing program is designed to be cost-effective and offers support from major retailers. Shorter hours, fewer employees, computer management systems and training - it's all here for you.

BACKGROUND: IFA MEMBER

Established: 1985; 1st Franchised: 1988	
Franchised Units:	60
Company-Owned Units	3
Total Units:	63
Dist.:	US-62; CAN-1; O'seas-0
North America:	8 States, 1 Province
Density: 46 in CA, 3 in NV, 3 in FL	
Projected New Units (12 Months):	30
Qualifications:	4, 5, 1, 3, 4, 5
Registered: CA,MD,WA	

FINANCIAL/TERMS:

Cash Investment:	$50-100K
Total Investment:	$108-179K
Minimum Net Worth:	$200K
Fees: Franchise -	$22.5K
Royalty - 6%;	Ad. - 3%
Earnings Claim Statement:	Yes
Term of Contract (Years):	10/10
Avg. # Of Employees:	2 FT, 2 PT
Passive Ownership:	Allowed
Encourage Conversions:	Yes
Area Develop. Agreements:	Yes/5
Sub-Franchising Contracts:	No
Expand In Territory:	Yes
Space Needs: 1,200 SF; FS, SF, SC	

SUPPORT & TRAINING PROVIDED:

Financial Assistance Provided:	Yes(I)
Site Selection Assistance:	Yes
Lease Negotiation Assistance:	Yes
Co-Operative Advertising:	Yes
Franchisee Assoc./Member:	Yes/Yes
Size Of Corporate Staff:	9
On-Going Support:	a,b,C,D,E,F,G,h,I
Training: 1 Week Tustin, CA; 3 Days at	

Franchisee Store.

SPECIFIC EXPANSION PLANS:

US:	West, SW, NW, Midwest, SE
Canada:	No
Overseas:	No

CHECKCARE SYSTEMS

P.O. Box 9636
Columbus, GA 31908
Tel: (706) 596-1306
Fax: (706) 596-0337
Web Site: www.checkcare.com
Mr. William Brandon, SVP Finance

CHECKCARE SYSTEMS is the fastest-growing check guarantee and verification company in the U.S. Proprietary software and hardware configuration included in total investment. Our national account base makes this opportunity a 'must investigate.'

BACKGROUND:

Established: 1982; 1st Franchised: 1984	
Franchised Units:	71
Company-Owned Units	0
Total Units:	71
Dist.:	US-71; CAN-0; O'seas-0
North America:	22 States
Density: 7 in GA, 6 in FL, 5 in TX	
Projected New Units (12 Months):	3
Qualifications:	4, 3, 2, 3, 3, 3
Registered: CA,FL,IL,IN,MD,MI,MN,VA, DC	

FINANCIAL/TERMS:

Cash Investment:	$65-85K
Total Investment:	$110-169K
Minimum Net Worth:	$100K
Fees: Franchise -	$12.5-45K
Royalty - 5%;	Ad. - 0.5%
Earnings Claim Statement:	Yes
Term of Contract (Years):	7/7
Avg. # Of Employees:	13 FT, 2 PT
Passive Ownership:	Discouraged
Encourage Conversions:	Yes
Area Develop. Agreements:	Yes/1
Sub-Franchising Contracts:	No
Expand In Territory:	No
Space Needs: 2,000 SF; Office Park	

SUPPORT & TRAINING PROVIDED:

Financial Assistance Provided:	Yes
Site Selection Assistance:	Yes
Lease Negotiation Assistance:	No
Co-Operative Advertising:	Yes
Franchisee Assoc./Member:	Yes/Yes
Size Of Corporate Staff:	20
On-Going Support:	b,c,d,e,f,G,h
Training: 2 Weeks Columbus, GA.	

SPECIFIC EXPANSION PLANS:

US:	West Coast, Northeast
Canada:	All Canada
Overseas:	No

◄◄ ►►

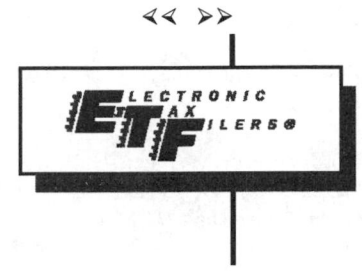

ELECTRONIC TAX FILERS

P.O. Box 2077
Cary, NC 27512-2077
Tel: (800) 945-9277 (919) 469-0651
Fax: (919) 460-5935
Ms. Rachel Wishon, President

We do no tax preparation! Instead, we provide a local, reasonably-priced, walk-in retail location where the 51% of the taxpayers who prepare their own returns can obtain electronic filing without being pressured into tax preparation they do not need. We transmit the data from self-prepared returns to the IRS and states in order that the taxpayer may receive his refunds in days, not months, via direct deposit into his bank, mail or refund loan.

BACKGROUND:

Established: 1990;	1st Franchised: 1990
Franchised Units:	39
Company-Owned Units	3
Total Units:	42
Dist.:	US-42; CAN-0; O'seas-0
North America:	15 States
Density:	11 in NC, 4 in GA, 3 in MI
Projected New Units (12 Months):	6
Qualifications:	3, 4, 1, 3, , 4
Registered: All States	

FINANCIAL/TERMS:

Cash Investment:	$22.5K
Total Investment:	$22.5K
Minimum Net Worth:	$25K
Fees: Franchise -	$7.5K
Royalty - 8%;	Ad. - 4%
Earnings Claim Statement:	No
Term of Contract (Years):	3/17
Avg. # Of Employees:	2 FT, 4 PT
Passive Ownership:	Discouraged
Encourage Conversions:	No
Area Develop. Agreements:	No
Sub-Franchising Contracts:	No
Expand In Territory:	Yes

Space Needs: 1,000 SF; FS, SF, SC, RM

SUPPORT & TRAINING PROVIDED:

Financial Assistance Provided:	Yes(D)
Site Selection Assistance:	Yes
Lease Negotiation Assistance:	Yes
Co-Operative Advertising:	Yes
Franchisee Assoc./Member:	No
Size Of Corporate Staff:	Varies
On-Going Support:	A,C,D,h,I
Training: 1 Week in Cary, NC; 2-3 Days On-Site.	

SPECIFIC EXPANSION PLANS:

US:	Eastern United States
Canada:	No
Overseas:	No

◄◄ ►►

FAST BUCKS CHECK CASHING SERVICE

3615 N. 44th St., #1
Lincoln, NE 68504
Tel: (402) 464-3949
Fax: (402) 464-3181
Mr. Mike Fox, Pres., Franchise Developers

Invest in your future: today's fast-paced society has created an increasing demand for a variety of quick, convenient and reliable services. Consumer financial needs are no exception. In fact, FAST BUCKS CHECK CASHING has proven to be a highly attractive alternative to traditional banking. When you add all the other valuable services for your customer, FAST BUCKS CHECK CASHING is your road to success.

BACKGROUND:

Established: 1994;	1st Franchised: 1995
Franchised Units:	7
Company-Owned Units	2
Total Units:	9
Dist.:	US-9; CAN-0; O'seas-0
North America:	2 States
Density:	7 in NE, 2 in IA
Projected New Units (12 Months):	10
Qualifications:	4, 3, 2, 1, 4, 4
Registered: IN,SD,WA	

FINANCIAL/TERMS:

Cash Investment:	$20-95K
Total Investment:	$48.3-95K
Minimum Net Worth:	$75K
Fees: Franchise -	$20K
Royalty - 5%;	Ad. - 2%
Earnings Claim Statement:	No
Term of Contract (Years):	10/5/5
Avg. # Of Employees:	2 FT, 1-2 PT

Passive Ownership:	Discouraged
Encourage Conversions:	Yes
Area Develop. Agreements:	No
Sub-Franchising Contracts:	No
Expand In Territory:	Yes
Space Needs: 1,000 SF; FS, SF, SC, RM	

SUPPORT & TRAINING PROVIDED:

Financial Assistance Provided:	Yes(I)
Site Selection Assistance:	Yes
Lease Negotiation Assistance:	Yes
Co-Operative Advertising:	No
Franchisee Assoc./Member:	No
Size Of Corporate Staff:	7
On-Going Support:	a,b,C,D,e,f,I
Training: 1-2 Weeks -- Location to be Determined.	

SPECIFIC EXPANSION PLANS:

US:	All United States
Canada:	No
Overseas:	No

◄◄ ►►

JACKSON HEWITT TAX SERVICE

339 Jefferson Rd.
Parsippany, NJ 07054
Tel: (800) 475-2904 (973) 496-1040
Fax: (973) 496-2760
E-Mail: william.scavone@jtax.com
Web Site: www.jacksonhewitt.com
Mr. William Scavone, SVP Franchise Sales

JACKSON HEWITT is the fastest-growing national tax preparation service and is currently the nation's second largest company in this category. Through more than 3,000 locations in 48 states, the company provides full service, individual Federal and state income tax preparation and bank products. A leader and pioneer in electronic filing, the company has always provided the service to its tax preparation customers at no cost.

BACKGROUND:	IFA MEMBER
Established: 1960;	1st Franchised: 1986
Franchised Units:	3,250

Company-Owned Units   0
Total Units: 3,250
Dist.:   US-3,250; CAN-0; O'seas-0
  North America: 48 States
  Density: 310 in TX, 306 in FL, 256 IL
Projected New Units (12 Months):   350
Qualifications: 5, 5, 3, 4, 4, 5
Registered: All States

FINANCIAL/TERMS:
Cash Investment: $25-50K
Total Investment: $47.4-75.2K
Minimum Net Worth: $100K
Fees: Franchise - $25K
  Royalty - 15%;   Ad. - 6%
Earnings Claim Statement: No
Term of Contract (Years):   10/10
Avg. # Of Employees: 1 FT, 6 PT
Passive Ownership: Allowed
Encourage Conversions: Yes
Area Develop. Agreements: No
Sub-Franchising Contracts: No
Expand In Territory: Yes
Space Needs: 400-1,000 SF; SF, SC, RM

SUPPORT & TRAINING PROVIDED:
Financial Assistance Provided: Yes(I)
Site Selection Assistance: Yes
Lease Negotiation Assistance: No
Co-Operative Advertising: Yes
Franchisee Assoc./Member: Yes/Yes
Size Of Corporate Staff: 205
On-Going Support: A,B,C,D,G,H,I
Training: 5 Days in Parsippany, NJ.

SPECIFIC EXPANSION PLANS:
US: All United States
Canada: No
Overseas: No

≪≪ ≫≫

*Helping Small Businesses
Succeed Financially.*

LEDGERPLUS

401 St. Francis St.
Tallahassee, FL 32301
Tel: (888) 643-1348 (850) 681-1941
Fax: (850) 561-1374
E-Mail: lpp@vistech.net
Web Site: www.ledgerplus.com
Mr. Ron Baker, Marketing Director

Accounting and tax franchise, offering services to America's small business clients. Reports they can understand and use, professional services at affordable prices.

BACKGROUND:
Established: 1989;   1st Franchised: 1990

Franchised Units: 205
Company-Owned Units   2
Total Units: 207
Dist.:   US-206; CAN-0; O'seas-1
  North America: NR
  Density: Fl, NC, CA
Projected New Units (12 Months):   200
Qualifications: 3, 5, 5, 3, 2, 4
Registered: All States Except ND,SD

FINANCIAL/TERMS:
Cash Investment: $16.4-29.4K
Total Investment: $16.4-29.4K
Minimum Net Worth: $NR
Fees: Franchise - $16K
  Royalty - 8%;   Ad. - 2%
Earnings Claim Statement: No
Term of Contract (Years):   10/10
Avg. # Of Employees: 1 FT
Passive Ownership: Allowed
Encourage Conversions: Yes
Area Develop. Agreements: No
Sub-Franchising Contracts: No
Expand In Territory: Yes
Space Needs: 400 SF; OB

SUPPORT & TRAINING PROVIDED:
Financial Assistance Provided: Yes
Site Selection Assistance: N/A
Lease Negotiation Assistance: No
Co-Operative Advertising: Yes
Franchisee Assoc./Member: No
Size Of Corporate Staff: 7
On-Going Support: b,C,D,G,H
Training: 3 Days Tallahassee, FL.

SPECIFIC EXPANSION PLANS:
US: All United States
Canada: All Canada
Overseas: No

≪≪ ≫≫

PADGETT BUSINESS SERVICES

160 Hawthorne Park
Athens, GA 30606
Tel: (800) 323-7292 (706) 548-1040
Fax: (706) 543-8537
E-Mail: bgrimes@smallbizpros.com
Web Site: www.smallbizpros.com
Mr. Bob Grimes, Dir. Franchise Dev.

America's top-rated and fastest-growing tax and accounting franchise - serving the fastest-growing segment of the economy

- America's small business owners. Initial training. Specialized software. On-going support.

BACKGROUND: IFA MEMBER
Established: 1966;   1st Franchised: 1975
Franchised Units: 423
Company-Owned Units   1
Total Units: 424
Dist.:   US-304; CAN-120; O'seas-0
  North America: 45 States, 8 Provinces
  Density: 67 in ON, 38 in QC, 26 in GA
Projected New Units (12 Months):   25
Qualifications: 3, 3, 4, 4, 2, 4
Registered: All States

FINANCIAL/TERMS:
Cash Investment: $15-35K
Total Investment: $40-60K
Minimum Net Worth: $60K
Fees: Franchise - $34.5K
  Royalty - 9-4.5%;   Ad. - 0%
Earnings Claim Statement: No
Term of Contract (Years):   20/20
Avg. # Of Employees: 1 FT, 2 PT
Passive Ownership: Discouraged
Encourage Conversions: Yes
Area Develop. Agreements: No
Sub-Franchising Contracts: No
Expand In Territory: Yes
Space Needs: 200-400 SF; HB, OB, ES

SUPPORT & TRAINING PROVIDED:
Financial Assistance Provided: Yes(I)
Site Selection Assistance: N/A
Lease Negotiation Assistance: N/A
Co-Operative Advertising: N/A
Franchisee Assoc./Member: Yes/No
Size Of Corporate Staff: 20
On-Going Support: C,D,G,H,I
Training: 2.5 Weeks Athens, GA; 3 (2.5 Day) Site Visits

SPECIFIC EXPANSION PLANS:
US: All United States
Canada: All Canada
Overseas: No

≪≪ ≫≫

PEOPLES INCOME TAX

4915 Radford Ave., #100A
Richmond, VA 23230
Tel: (800) 984-1040 (804) 204-1040
Fax: (804) 213-4248
E-Mail: peoplesinc@aol.com
Web Site: www.peoplestax.com
Mr. Charles E. McCabe, President/CEO

Professional income tax preparation service specializing in middle-income and upwardly-mobile individual and small business taxpayers. Proven marketing and operating methods. Income tax school. Business training and support provided. Minimal start-up cost.

BACKGROUND:

Established: 1987; 1st Franchised: 1998	
Franchised Units:	0
Company-Owned Units	13
Total Units:	13
Dist.: US-0; CAN-0; O'seas-0	
North America:	1 State
Density:	13 in VA
Projected New Units (12 Months):	NR
Registered:	

FINANCIAL/TERMS:

Cash Investment:	$40-60K
Total Investment:	$51-86K
Minimum Net Worth:	$100K
Fees: Franchise -	$16K
Royalty - 9%;	Ad. - 6%
Earnings Claim Statement:	No
Term of Contract (Years):	5
Avg. # Of Employees:	1 Ft, 9
PT (seasonal)	
Passive Ownership:	Not Allowed
Encourage Conversions:	NR
Area Develop. Agreements:	No
Sub-Franchising Contracts:	No
Expand In Territory:	Yes
Space Needs: 600-1,000 SF; SF, SC, RM	

SUPPORT & TRAINING PROVIDED:

Financial Assistance Provided:	NR
Site Selection Assistance:	Yes
Lease Negotiation Assistance:	Yes
Co-Operative Advertising:	No
Franchisee Assoc./Member:	No
Size Of Corporate Staff:	10
On-Going Support:	C,d,E,G,H,I
Training: 25 Hours Richmond, VA.	

SPECIFIC EXPANSION PLANS:

US:	VA Only
Canada:	NR
Overseas:	NR

<< >>

PEYRON TAX SERVICE
3212 Preston St.
Louisville, KY 40213
Tel: (888) 314-2023 (502) 637-7483

Fax: (888) 314-2024
E-Mail: dpeyron@earthlink.net
Mr. Ken Irek, Vice President

License franchisees to prepare tax returns using the PEYRON system for electronic filing, fax in returns for car dealers which PEYRON secures fro franchisees, tax newsletter publisher for tax practitioners and taxpayers, etc.

BACKGROUND:

Established: 1960; 1st Franchised: 1965	
Franchised Units:	700
Company-Owned Units	2
Total Units:	702
Dist.: US-702; CAN-0; O'seas-0	
North America:	50 States
Density:	CA, TX, FL
Projected New Units (12 Months):	1,000
Qualifications:	4, 5, 4, 4, 4, 4
Registered: All States	

FINANCIAL/TERMS:

Cash Investment:	$7.5K
Total Investment:	$25K
Minimum Net Worth:	$No Minimum
Fees: Franchise -	$25K
Royalty - 5%;	Ad. - 0%
Earnings Claim Statement:	No
Term of Contract (Years):	1/1
Avg. # Of Employees:	2 FT, 3 PT
Passive Ownership:	Allowed
Encourage Conversions:	Yes
Area Develop. Agreements:	Yes/1
Sub-Franchising Contracts:	Yes
Expand In Territory:	Yes
Space Needs: 50-100 SF; FS, SF, SC, RM, HB	

SUPPORT & TRAINING PROVIDED:

Financial Assistance Provided:	Yes(I)
Site Selection Assistance:	Yes
Lease Negotiation Assistance:	Yes
Co-Operative Advertising:	N/A
Franchisee Assoc./Member:	Yes/No
Size Of Corporate Staff:	5
On-Going Support:	a,D,G,I
Training: 2 Weeks Franchisee's Home Area; On-Going Phone/Fax/E-Mail; Approx. 2 Hrs/Wk for 10 Weeks.	

SPECIFIC EXPANSION PLANS:

US:	All United States
Canada:	No
Overseas:	No

<< >>

TRIPLE CHECK INCOME TAX SERVICE
2441 Honolulu Ave.
Montrose, CA 91020

Tel: (800) 283-1040 (818) 236-2944
Fax: (818) 249-5344
E-Mail: tripck@aol.com
Web Site: www.triplecheck.com
Mr. David W. Lieberman, President

TRIPLE CHECK offers a full range of support services to build a quality tax and small business consulting/accounting practice. Through TRIPLE CHECK Financial Services, franchisees are able to add a separate profit center providing their clients with need- oriented, conservative financial planning.

BACKGROUND:

Established: 1941; 1st Franchised: 1979	
Franchised Units:	279
Company-Owned Units	2
Total Units:	281
Dist.: US-281; CAN-0; O'seas-1	
North America:	43 States
Density:	92 in CA, 24 in FL, 9 in NY
Projected New Units (12 Months):	30
Registered: CA,FL,HI,IL,IN,MD,MI,MN, NY,OR,RI,VA,WA,WI,DC	

FINANCIAL/TERMS:

Cash Investment:	$5-8K
Total Investment:	$5-8K
Minimum Net Worth:	$NR
Fees: Franchise -	$0
Royalty - Varies;	Ad. - Varies
Earnings Claim Statement:	No
Term of Contract (Years):	5/5
Avg. # Of Employees:	NR
Passive Ownership:	Discouraged
Encourage Conversions:	Yes
Area Develop. Agreements:	No
Sub-Franchising Contracts:	No
Expand In Territory:	Yes
Space Needs: Varies SF; SF, SC, HB	

SUPPORT & TRAINING PROVIDED:

Financial Assistance Provided:	Yes(I)
Site Selection Assistance:	Yes
Lease Negotiation Assistance:	No
Co-Operative Advertising:	No
Franchisee Assoc./Member:	Yes
Size Of Corporate Staff:	35
On-Going Support:	a,b,C,G,h,I
Training: 80 Hours on Tape.	

SPECIFIC EXPANSION PLANS:

US:	All United States
Canada:	No
Overseas:	No

<< >>

UNITED CHECK CASHING
325 Chestnut St., # 1005
Philadelphia, PA 19106

Tel: (800) 626-0787 (215) 238-0300
Fax: (215) 238-9056
E-Mail: UnitedCC12@aol.com
Web Site: www.unitedcheckcashing.com
Mr. Seth N. Schonberg, Vice President of
Development

UNITED CHECK CASHING provides financial & convenience services to today's busy individual. Our friendly centers offer more than just check cashing. We are a one-stop center for money orders, Western Union, e-bill payments, ATM/MAC, tax preparation, faxes, copies, notary and much more! The convenience store of banking, United centers are emerging all over the U.S. as people are discovering our high standards of service.

BACKGROUND: IFA MEMBER
Established: 1977;   1st Franchised: 1992
Franchised Units: 79
Company-Owned Units   3
Total Units: 82
Dist.:   US-82; CAN-0; O'seas-0
  North America: 11 States
  Density: 38 in PA, 28 in NJ, 5 in DE
Projected New Units (12 Months):   20
Qualifications: 5, 3, 2, 2, 4, 5
Registered: All States
FINANCIAL/TERMS:
Cash Investment: $50K
Total Investment: $155-165K
Minimum Net Worth: $200K
Fees: Franchise - $21.5K
  Royalty - 0.002% of Volume; Ad. - 10%
Royal.
Earnings Claim Statement: Yes
Term of Contract (Years):   15/15
Avg. # Of Employees: 2 FT
Passive Ownership: Allowed
Encourage Conversions: Yes
Area Develop. Agreements: No
Sub-Franchising Contracts: Yes
Expand In Territory: Yes
Space Needs: 12,000 SF; FS, SC
SUPPORT & TRAINING PROVIDED:
Financial Assistance Provided: Yes(I)
Site Selection Assistance: Yes
Lease Negotiation Assistance: Yes
Co-Operative Advertising: Yes
Franchisee Assoc./Member: No
Size Of Corporate Staff: 12
On-Going Support: A,B,C,D,E,G,h,I
Training: 1 Week Corporate Headquarters;
  1 Week in Open Store; 1 Week
  Opening.

SPECIFIC EXPANSION PLANS:
US: All United States
Canada: No
Overseas: No

≪ ≫

SUPPLEMENTAL LISTING OF FRANCHISORS

ABS Systems, 1260 Palmetto Ave., Winter Park, FL 32789 ; ; Franchise Development Director (800) ABS-7504; (407) 644-5400

Accountax Services, 499 Ray Lawson Blvd., Unit 32, Brampton, ON L6Y 4E6 CANADA; (905) 453-9562; Mr. Vijay Kapur ; (905) 453-3220

Accounting Business Systems, 1260 Palmetto Ave., # C, Winter Park, FL 32789 ; (407) 869-0077; Mr. Mark B. Silverberg (800) ABS-7504; (407) 644-5400

Acctcorp International, Inc., 7414 NE Hazel Dell Ave., # 209, Vancouver, WA 98665 ; (800) 844-2369; Mr. Michael Roskam (800) 844-4024;

Advantage Payroll Services, 126 Merrow Rd., P.O. Box 1330, Auburn, ME 04211-1330 ; (207) 786-0490; Mr. David M. Meagher (800) 876-0178; (207) 784-0178

Comprehensive Business Services (Canada), 8500 Leslie St., # 520, Thornhill, ON L3T 7M8 CANADA; (905) 771-9060; Mr. Leo G. Lauzen, Sr. (800) 561-1200; (905) 771-1200

Done Right Accounting, 410 Registration Dr., Kelowna, BC V48 4T5 CANADA; (204) 957-0265; Ms. Susan Harrison (888) 573-1136;

EconoTax, P.O. Box 13829, Jackson, MS 39236 ; (601) 956-0583; Mr. James T. Marsh (800) 748-9106; (601) 956-0500

H & R Block, 4400 Main St., Kansas City, MO 64111 ; (816) 932-8489; Mr. Ken Treat ; (816) 753-6900

H & R Block Canada, 340 Midpark Way, SE, # 200, Calgary, AB T2X 1P1 CANADA; (403) 254-9949; Mr. Arthur Arnott ; (403) 254-8689

Ledgers Professional Bookkeeping, Bedford Tower, # 222, Bedford, NS B4A 1E5 CANADA; (902) 835-0612; Ms. Nadine Morrison (888) 822-8884;

Liberty Tax Service, 2610 Potters Rd., Virginia Beach, VA 23452 ; (757) 340-7612; Mr. Chuck Lovelace (800) 790-3863; (757) 340-7610

Liberty Tax Service (Canada), 1245 Pembina Highway, Winnipeg, MB R3T 2B6 CANADA; (204) 284-8954; Mr. Steve Cardo (800) 665-5144;

Mr. Payroll, 1600 W. 7th St., # 800, Fort Worth, TX 76102-2599 ; (817) 335-8200; Mr. Mike Stinson (800) 322-3250; (817) 335-7200

Padgett Business Services, 6700 Cote-de Liesse, #105, Montreal, QC H4T 1E3 CANADA; (800) 428-5297; Ms. Lisa Goulet (888) PADGETT;

Paid Inc., 1600 Lake Air Dr., Waco, TX 76710 ; (254) 772-4642; Mr. David Byrd (877) 674-7543; (254) 772-8131

Precise Accounting Professionals, Logan Ln., 1820 Lexington Dr. #200, Winnipeg, MB R1K 37A CANADA; ; Mr. Shane Ross ; (905) 625-2896

Professor Tax of N. C., 34 Maxwell St., Asheville, NC 28801 ; (828) 255-0990; Mr. Henry C. Burley, III (800) 220-8775; (828) 254-0999

TaxPro Electronic Filing, P.O. Box 13829, Jackson, MS 39236 ; (601) 956-0583; Mr. James T. Marsh (800) 748-9106; (601) 956-0500

TeleCheck Services, P.O. Box 4514, Houston, TX 77210 ; (713) 331-7326; Ms. Keela Wicker (800) 733-3400; (713) 599-7600

U & R Tax Services, 1345 Pembina Hwy., # 201, Winnipeg, MB R3T 2B6 CANADA; (204) 284-8954; Mr. John Hewitt (800) 665-5144; (204) 949-3636

X-Bankers Check Cashing, 809 Chapel St., New Haven, CT 06510 ; (203) 773-0418; Mr. Robert A. Swift, Jr. (800) 873-9226; (203) 374-1377

BUSINESS: ADVERTISING & PROMOTION INDUSTRY PROFILE

Total # Franchisors in Industry Group	27
Total # Franchised Units in Industry Group	2,166
Total # Company-Owned Units in Industry Group	<u>50</u>
Total # Operating Units in Industry Group	2,216
Average # Franchised Units/Franchisor	80.2
Average # Company-Owned Units/Franchisor	<u>1.9</u>
Average # Total Units/Franchisor	82.1
Ratio of Total # Franchised Units/Total # Company-Owned Units	43.3:1
Industry Survey Participants	11
Representing % of Industry	40.7%
Average Franchise Fee*:	$20.0K
Average Total Investment*:	$37.0K
Average On-Going Royalty Fee*:	5.7%

If a range was provided, the mid-point of the range was used. See detailed profiles for actual ranges.

FIVE LARGEST PARTICIPANTS IN SURVEY

Company	# Fran-chised Units	# Co-Owned Units	# Total Units	Franchise Fee	On-Going Royalty	Total Investment
1. Worldsites	550	0	550	34.7K	10%	35K+
2. Super Coups	434	4	438	32K	$148/Mailing	41K
3. Money Mailer	319	0	319	25-35K	Varies	37-71.5K
4. Val-Pak Direct Marketing	240	6	246	7K	0%	25-85K
5. Adventure in Advertising	130	0	130	27.5K	4%	35-45K

ADVENTURES IN ADVERTISING

400 Crown Colony Dr.
Quincy, MA 02169
Tel: (800) 432-6332 (617) 472-9901
Fax: (617) 472-9979
E-Mail: opportunity@adinadv.com
Web Site: www.advinadv.com
Mr. Tim Quinn,

The man who launched Boston Chicken acknowledges the ADVENTURES IN ADVERTISING franchise as the hottest new business service and sales business in America. $290,076 gross revenue = first year, $85,498 gross profit. Call us and get our detailed information.

BACKGROUND: IFA MEMBER
Established: 1979;   1st Franchised: 1994
Franchised Units: 130
Company-Owned Units   <u>0</u>
Total Units: 130
Dist.:   US-76; CAN-4; O'seas-0
  North America: 27 States, 2 Provinces
  Density: 12 in WA, 9 in MA, 9 in CA
Projected New Units (12 Months):   60
Qualifications: 3, 3, 3, 2, 5, 5
Registered: All States and AB

FINANCIAL/TERMS:
Cash Investment: $7.5-15K
Total Investment: $35-45K
Minimum Net Worth: $40K
Fees: Franchise - $27.5K
  Royalty - 4%;   Ad. - 1%
Earnings Claim Statement: Yes
Term of Contract (Years):   10/10
Avg. # Of Employees: 1 FT, 0 PT
Passive Ownership: Discouraged
Encourage Conversions: Yes
Area Develop. Agreements: Yes/Varies
Sub-Franchising Contracts: No
Expand In Territory: Yes
Space Needs: N/A SF; HB

SUPPORT & TRAINING PROVIDED:
Financial Assistance Provided: Yes(D)
Site Selection Assistance: N/A
Lease Negotiation Assistance: N/A
Co-Operative Advertising: N/A
Franchisee Assoc./Member: Yes/Yes
Size Of Corporate Staff: 19
On-Going Support: a,C,D,G,h,I
Training: 2 Weeks Headquarters in Quincy, MA.

SPECIFIC EXPANSION PLANS:
US: All United States
Canada: All Canada
Overseas: No

<< >>

COUPON TABLOID INTERNATIONAL, THE

5775 SW Jean Rd., # 101
Lake Oswego, OR 97035
Tel: (800) 888-8575 (503) 697-1968
Fax: (503) 697-1978
E-Mail: jon@coupontabloid.com
Web Site: www.coupontabloid.com
Mr. Jonathan D. Crane, President

COUPON TABLOID INTERNA-TIONAL is a publisher of a direct mail coupon newspaper that has a price point attractive to smaller retailers. Clean look, affordable advertising at 80% plus renewal rate. Bankers hours, no inventory, plenty of freedom and unlimited earning potential. Ideal home-based business. Franchise fee is a low $4,500.

BACKGROUND:
Established: 1986;   1st Franchised: 1994
Franchised Units: 23
Company-Owned Units   <u>1</u>
Total Units: 24
Dist.:   US-24; CAN-0; O'seas-0
  North America: 23 States
  Density: 11 in AZ, 11 in OR, 2 in ID
Projected New Units (12 Months): 5-10
Qualifications: 2, 3, 3, 2, 3, 4
Registered: CA,WA

FINANCIAL/TERMS:
Cash Investment: $10K
Total Investment: $7-12K
Minimum Net Worth: $10K
Fees: Franchise - $4.5K
  Royalty - Graphic fee;   Ad. - 0%
Earnings Claim Statement: Yes
Term of Contract (Years):   5/5
Avg. # Of Employees: 1 FT
Passive Ownership: Discouraged
Encourage Conversions: N/A
Area Develop. Agreements: No
Sub-Franchising Contracts: No
Expand In Territory: Yes
Space Needs: N/A SF; HB

SUPPORT & TRAINING PROVIDED:
Financial Assistance Provided: Yes(D)
Site Selection Assistance: Yes
Lease Negotiation Assistance: N/A
Co-Operative Advertising: N/A
Franchisee Assoc./Member: No
Size Of Corporate Staff: 5
On-Going Support: E,G,H,I
Training: 4 Days at Your Franchise Location.

SPECIFIC EXPANSION PLANS:
US: Northwest, Southwest
Canada: No
Overseas: No

<< >>

COUPON-CASH SAVER

1020 Milwaukee Ave., # 240
Deerfield, IL 60015-3513
Tel: (847) 537-6420
Fax: (847) 537-6499
E-Mail: coupon@poweruser.com
Web Site: www.couponcashsaver.com
Ms. Myrna O'Reilly, President

Co-operative direct mail coupon company and internet coupons. We specialize in designing ads for our customers that increase their sales. We have about 70% repeat customers in our publications. Our system teaches franchisees how to get and keep customers.

BACKGROUND:
Established: 1984;   1st Franchised: 1990
Franchised Units: 2
Company-Owned Units   <u>10</u>
Total Units: 12
Dist.:   US-12; CAN-0; O'seas-0
  North America: 1 State
  Density: 12 in IL
Projected New Units (12 Months):   1
Qualifications: 2, 3, 3, 1, 4, 4
Registered: FL,IL

FINANCIAL/TERMS:
Cash Investment: $10K
Total Investment: $24.4-52.8K
Minimum Net Worth: $150K
Fees: Franchise - $9.5K
  Royalty - 6% or $400/Zone;   Ad. - 0%
Earnings Claim Statement: No
Term of Contract (Years):   20
Avg. # Of Employees: 1 FT
Passive Ownership: Discouraged
Encourage Conversions: NR
Area Develop. Agreements: No
Sub-Franchising Contracts: No
Expand In Territory: Yes
Space Needs: NR SF; HB, OB

SUPPORT & TRAINING PROVIDED:
Financial Assistance Provided: No
Site Selection Assistance: Yes
Lease Negotiation Assistance: N/A
Co-Operative Advertising: Yes
Franchisee Assoc./Member: No
Size Of Corporate Staff: 1
On-Going Support: A,b,C,D,E,H
Training: 1 Week in Deerfield, IL; 3 Days at Franchisee's Store.

SPECIFIC EXPANSION PLANS:

US:	NW,SW
Canada:	No
Overseas:	No

DIAL-A-STORK USA

15 N. Quaker Ln.
West Hartford, CT 06119
Tel: (800) 51-STORK (860) 519-2602
Fax: (860) 519-2603
E-Mail: franchises@dialastork.com
Web Site: www.dialastork.com
Ms. Cynthia Burke, President

DIAL-A-STORK (sm) USA is a celebratory yard sign rental service. We specialize in the delivery of 7 ft. stork birth announcement signs, signs for all occasions and accompanying products. We grow with the customer -- every occasion sign from birth to retirement! We handle our franchisee customers' calls through our 1-800-51-STORK # to ensure quality, uniformity and A-1 customer service. Our franchisees receive corporate support that is second to none!

BACKGROUND:

Established: 1995; 1st Franchised: 1998	
Franchised Units:	9
Company-Owned Units	0
Total Units:	9
Dist.:	US-9; CAN-0; O'seas-0
North America:	4 States
Density:	3 in CT, 2 in GA, 1 in NM
Projected New Units (12 Months):	36
Qualifications:	2, 3, 2, 3, 5, 5
Registered: FL,DC,MD	

FINANCIAL/TERMS:

Cash Investment:	$6.3-35.3K
Total Investment:	$6.3-35.3K
Minimum Net Worth:	$None
Fees: Franchise -	$By Population
Royalty - 1-6% of Rental;	Ad. - N/A
Earnings Claim Statement:	No
Term of Contract (Years):	3/3
Avg. # Of Employees:	1 FT
Passive Ownership:	NR
Encourage Conversions:	N/A
Area Develop. Agreements:	No
Sub-Franchising Contracts:	No
Expand In Territory:	Yes
Space Needs: N/A SF; HB	

SUPPORT & TRAINING PROVIDED:

Financial Assistance Provided:	No
Site Selection Assistance:	Yes
Lease Negotiation Assistance:	N/A
Co-Operative Advertising:	No
Franchisee Assoc./Member:	No
Size Of Corporate Staff:	5
On-Going Support:	A,B,C,D,F,G,h,I

Training: Telephone Training, Initial and On-Going; On-Site, as Needed; Operations Manual Included.

SPECIFIC EXPANSION PLANS:

US:	All U.S., Still Registering
Canada:	Eventually
Overseas:	Eventually

GREETINGS

P.O. Box 25623
Lexington, KY 40524
Tel: (606) 272-5624
Fax:
Mr. Larry Kargel, President

Every ad has two hurdles it must clear before it has any value. Hurdle #1 - it must be read, seen or heard. Hurdle #2 - it must be placed with someone who has a need. GREETINGS clears both hurdles with room to spare. We are a target market advertising company with an unique method of addressing new homeowners and apartment residents, offering the most timely cost effective method of reaching new customers possible. We produce a coupon magazine for colleges and universities each semester.

BACKGROUND:

Established: 1984; 1st Franchised: 1990	
Franchised Units:	5
Company-Owned Units	3
Total Units:	8
Dist.:	US-8; CAN-0; O'seas-0
North America:	3 States
Density:	5 in KY, 2 in TN, 1 in IL
Projected New Units (12 Months):	2
Qualifications:	2, 5, 1, 2, 2, 4
Registered: None	

FINANCIAL/TERMS:

Cash Investment:	$15-30K
Total Investment:	$15-30K
Minimum Net Worth:	$N/A
Fees: Franchise -	$15K
Royalty - 5%;	Ad. - 0%
Earnings Claim Statement:	No
Term of Contract (Years):	10/5
Avg. # Of Employees:	1 FT, 1 PT
Passive Ownership:	Discouraged
Encourage Conversions:	N/A
Area Develop. Agreements:	No
Sub-Franchising Contracts:	No

Expand In Territory:	Yes
Space Needs: 250 SF; HB	

SUPPORT & TRAINING PROVIDED:

Financial Assistance Provided:	No
Site Selection Assistance:	Yes
Lease Negotiation Assistance:	N/A
Co-Operative Advertising:	N/A
Franchisee Assoc./Member:	No
Size Of Corporate Staff:	2
On-Going Support:	b,C,D,G,H

Training: 5 Days Lexington, KY; 5 Days Franchisee Location.

SPECIFIC EXPANSION PLANS:

US:	Southeast, Northeast, MW
Canada:	No
Overseas:	No

MERCHANT ADVERTISING SYSTEMS

4115 Tiverton Rd.
Randallstown, MD 21133-2019
Tel: (410) 655-3201
Fax: (410) 655-0262
Mr. Don Goldvarg, President

Local merchant display centers for supermarkets and malls. Utilize as customer information centers. Co-op advertising with local merchants. Large custom-made sign and literature dispensers sold to merchants for 1-year term. Unique, high visibility, cost- effective and professional advertising display. High profitability and cash flow.

BACKGROUND:

Established: 1985; 1st Franchised: 1987	
Franchised Units:	2
Company-Owned Units	9
Total Units:	11
Dist.:	US-11; CAN-0; O'seas-0
North America:	4 States
Density:	5 in MD, 3 in PA, 2 in VA
Projected New Units (12 Months):	12
Qualifications:	2, 4, 3, 4, 5, 5
Registered: FL,MI,OR,VA,DC	

FINANCIAL/TERMS:

Cash Investment:	$13.5-25.5K
Total Investment:	$17-29K
Minimum Net Worth:	$50K
Fees: Franchise -	$13.5-25.5K
Royalty - 0%;	Ad. - 0%
Earnings Claim Statement:	Yes
Term of Contract (Years):	10/10
Avg. # Of Employees:	3 FT, 1 PT
Passive Ownership:	Discouraged
Encourage Conversions:	N/A

Area Develop. Agreements: Yes/10
Sub-Franchising Contracts: Yes
Expand In Territory: Yes
Space Needs: 5 SF; Supermarket, RM

SUPPORT & TRAINING PROVIDED:
Financial Assistance Provided: No
Site Selection Assistance: Yes
Lease Negotiation Assistance: Yes
Co-Operative Advertising: N/A
Franchisee Assoc./Member: No
Size Of Corporate Staff: 4
On-Going Support: B,C,D,E,F,G,H,I
Training: 1 Week Headquarters; 1 Week
    Franchisee's Territory.

SPECIFIC EXPANSION PLANS:
US: All United States
Canada: All Canada
Overseas: No

◄◄ ►►

"Helping Businesses Get & Keep More Customers".

MONEY MAILER
14271 Corporate Dr.
Garden Grove, CA 92843
Tel: (800) 624-5371 (714) 265-4100
Fax: (714) 265-4130
Web Site: www.moneymailer.com
Mr. Godfred P. Otuteye, President

MONEY MAILER is one of America's leading direct mail advertising companies with over 300 franchises in the U.S. and Canada. Over its 20 year history, MONEY MAILER has been at the forefront of introducing innovative direct mail advertising products and programs to the marketplace - helping businesses get and keep more customers and helping consumers save money everyday.

BACKGROUND: IFA MEMBER
Established: 1978; 1st Franchised: 1980
Franchised Units: 319
Company-Owned Units 0
Total Units: 319
Dist.: US-312; CAN-6; O'seas-1
    North America: NR
    Density: 31 in CA, 23 in NJ, 20 in NC
Projected New Units (12 Months): 40
Qualifications: 4, 3, 4, 3, 4, 5
Registered: CA,FL,IL,IN,NY,VA,WA,WI
FINANCIAL/TERMS:
Cash Investment: $37-71.5K
Total Investment: $37-71.5K

Minimum Net Worth: $Varies
Fees: Franchise - $25-35K
    Royalty - Varies; Ad. - N/A
Earnings Claim Statement: No
Term of Contract (Years): 10/10
Avg. # Of Employees: 1 FT, 1 PT
Passive Ownership: Not Allowed
Encourage Conversions: N/A
Area Develop. Agreements: No
Sub-Franchising Contracts: Yes
Expand In Territory: Yes
Space Needs: NR SF; HB

SUPPORT & TRAINING PROVIDED:
Financial Assistance Provided: No
Site Selection Assistance: N/A
Lease Negotiation Assistance: N/A
Co-Operative Advertising: No
Franchisee Assoc./Member: Yes/Yes
Size Of Corporate Staff: 300
On-Going Support: C,D,H,I
Training: 1 Week Regional Office; 2
    Weeks Corporate Headquarters; 1 Week
    Regional Office.

SPECIFIC EXPANSION PLANS:
US: All United States
Canada: No
Overseas: No

◄◄ ►►

SUPER COUPS
180 Bodwell St.
Avon, MA 02322
Tel: (800) 626-2620 (508) 580-4340
Fax: (508) 588-3347
E-Mail: gliset@supercoups.com
Web Site: www.supercoups.com
Mr. Glen R. Liset, VP Sales & Marketing

SUPER COUPS is one of the top co-op direct mail companies in America. We specialize in developing an integrated marketing solution for local and regional businesses, featuring co-op coupon mailings, co-op TV and internet advertising. We are known for our personalized training, outstanding field support and state-of-the-art production facilities.

BACKGROUND: IFA MEMBER
Established: 1984; 1st Franchised: 1983
Franchised Units: 434
Company-Owned Units 4
Total Units: 438
Dist.: US-438; CAN-0; O'seas-0
    North America: 29 States
    Density: 47 in MA, 38 in NY, 38 in NJ
Projected New Units (12 Months): 50
Qualifications: 5, 5, 4, 3, 1, 5

Registered: CA,DC,FL,IL,IN,MD,MI,MN,
    NY,ND,OR,SD,VA,WA,WI
FINANCIAL/TERMS:
Cash Investment: $5-10K
Total Investment: $41K
Minimum Net Worth: $50K
Fees: Franchise - $32K
    Royalty - $148/Mailing; Ad. - $500/Yr.
Earnings Claim Statement: Yes
Term of Contract (Years): 10/10
Avg. # Of Employees: 1 FT
Passive Ownership: Not Allowed
Encourage Conversions: Yes
Area Develop. Agreements: No
Sub-Franchising Contracts: Yes
Expand In Territory: Yes
Space Needs: N/A SF; HB

SUPPORT & TRAINING PROVIDED:
Financial Assistance Provided: Yes(I)
Site Selection Assistance: No
Lease Negotiation Assistance: No
Co-Operative Advertising: Yes
Franchisee Assoc./Member: Yes/Yes
Size Of Corporate Staff: 180
On-Going Support: C,D,F,G,H,I
Training: 1 Week Headquarters, Avon, MA;
    1 Week in Field.

SPECIFIC EXPANSION PLANS:
US: All United States
Canada: All Canada
Overseas: No

◄◄ ►►

TRIMARK
621 Delaware St., # 200
Newcastle, DE 19720
Tel: (888) 321-MARK (302) 322-2143
Fax: (302) 322-9910
E-Mail: trimark@universal.dca.net
Web Site: www.trimarkinc.com
Mr. John E. Kinch, President

Multiple-unit TRIMARK master franchises offer excellent opportunities for former corporate executives and entrepreneurs with the desire to build a big and profitable business in the growing, dynamic direct-mail advertising industry. No store-front real estate or inventory. Low start-up costs, low overhead and full corporate support. An outstanding franchise business. Single unit franchises also available.

BACKGROUND:

Established: 1969;   1st Franchised: 1978
Franchised Units: 34
Company-Owned Units   0
Total Units: 34
Dist.:   US-34; CAN-0; O'seas-0
 North America: 18 States
 Density: 4 in PA, 3 in NY, 3 in FL
Projected New Units (12 Months):   12
Qualifications: 4, 5, 3, 3, 3, 5
Registered: FL,HI,MI,NY

FINANCIAL/TERMS:

Cash Investment: $25-100K
Total Investment: $31-122K
Minimum Net Worth: $50-150K
Fees: Franchise - $Included
 Royalty - 0%;   Ad. - N/A
Earnings Claim Statement: No
Term of Contract (Years):   10/10
Avg. # Of Employees: 1 FT, 1 PT
Passive Ownership: Allowed
Encourage Conversions: No
Area Develop. Agreements: Yes/2
Sub-Franchising Contracts: Yes
Expand In Territory: Yes
Space Needs: NR SF; HB

SUPPORT & TRAINING PROVIDED:

Financial Assistance Provided: No
Site Selection Assistance: N/A
Lease Negotiation Assistance: N/A
Co-Operative Advertising: N/A
Franchisee Assoc./Member: No
Size Of Corporate Staff: 15
On-Going Support: b,c,D,G,h
Training: 40-80   Hours   Corporate
 Headquarters; 80 Hours On-Site.

SPECIFIC EXPANSION PLANS:

US: All United States
Canada: All Except AB
Overseas: U.K.

<< >>

VAL-PAK DIRECT MARKETING

8605 Largo Lakes Dr.
Largo, FL 33773
Tel: (800) 237-6266 (727) 393-1270
Fax: (727) 392-0049
E-Mail: david_elmer@valpak.com
Web Site: www.valpak.com
Mr. David Elmer, Director of Franchise
 Sales

North America's oldest and largest local
co-operative direct mail advertising
franchisor, with distribution of over 490
million coupon envelopes annually to
over 53 million unduplicated homes and

businesses. Subsidiary of Cox Enterprises,
Inc. VAL-PAK OF CANADA is the
Canadian franchisor.

BACKGROUND: IFA MEMBER

Established: 1968;   1st Franchised: 1989
Franchised Units: 240
Company-Owned Units   6
Total Units: 246
Dist.:   US-209; CAN-36; O'seas-1
 North America: 49 States, 10 Provinces
 Density: 19 in ON, 15 in CA, 14 in NY
Projected New Units (12 Months):   10
Qualifications: 4, 3, 3, 2, 1, 4
Registered: All States

FINANCIAL/TERMS:

Cash Investment: $25K+
Total Investment: $25-85K
Minimum Net Worth: $Varies
Fees: Franchise - $7K
 Royalty - 0%;   Ad. - 0%
Earnings Claim Statement: No
Term of Contract (Years):   10/5
Avg. # Of Employees: Varies
Passive Ownership: Discouraged
Encourage Conversions: Yes
Area Develop. Agreements: No
Sub-Franchising Contracts: No
Expand In Territory: No
Space Needs: N/A SF; HB

SUPPORT & TRAINING PROVIDED:

Financial Assistance Provided: Yes(I)
Site Selection Assistance: N/A
Lease Negotiation Assistance: N/A
Co-Operative Advertising: Yes
Franchisee Assoc./Member: Yes/Yes
Size Of Corporate Staff: 1,100
On-Going Support: C,D,G,h,I
Training: 5 Days Home Study with Trainer;
 2   Weeks   Corporate   Headquarters;
 On-Going, On- and Off-Site

SPECIFIC EXPANSION PLANS:

US: All US, Limited Areas Remain
Canada: All Canada
Overseas: No

<< >>

WORLDSITES

5915 Airport Rd., # 300
Mississauga, ON L4V 1T1 CANADA
Tel: (888) 678-7588 (905) 678-7588

Fax: (416) 213-8025
E-Mail: franchise@worldsites.net
Web Site: www.worldsites.net
Mr. Mario Lui, Dir. Franchise Dev.

WORLDSITES has been ranked the #
1 Internet franchise by Entrepreneur
Magazine, providing specialized Internet
marketing solutions in over 30 countries
around the globe. The WORLDSITES
network provides: results-oriented Website
development,   E-commerce   solutions,
Internet telephone solutions, advanced
promotional   programs,   high-speed
corporate   hosting   and   full-service
consulting and education.

BACKGROUND:

Established: 1995;   1st Franchised: 1996
Franchised Units: 550
Company-Owned Units   0
Total Units: 550
Dist.:   US-151; CAN-54; O'seas-345
 North America: 9 States
 Density: 4 in TX, FL Mast. Fran, WA
Projected New Units (12 Months):   400
Qualifications: 2, 2, 1, 1, 4, 5
Registered: FL,AB

FINANCIAL/TERMS:

Cash Investment: $35K+
Total Investment: $35K+
Minimum Net Worth: $NR
Fees: Franchise - $34.7K
 Royalty - 10%;   Ad. - NR
Earnings Claim Statement: No
Term of Contract (Years):   5/5
Avg. # Of Employees: 1-2 FT
Passive Ownership: Allowed
Encourage Conversions: N/A
Area Develop. Agreements: Yes/5
Sub-Franchising Contracts: No
Expand In Territory: Yes
Space Needs: N/A SF; HB

SUPPORT & TRAINING PROVIDED:

Financial Assistance Provided: No
Site Selection Assistance: N/A
Lease Negotiation Assistance: N/A
Co-Operative Advertising: Yes
Franchisee Assoc./Member: Yes/Yes
Size Of Corporate Staff: 42
On-Going Support: b,c,G,H,I
Training: 1 Week Mississauga, ON.

SPECIFIC EXPANSION PLANS:

US: All United States
Canada: All Canada
Overseas: All Countries

◁◁ ▷▷

SUPPLEMENTAL LISTING
OF FRANCHISORS

Advertising On The Move, 1900 NW 32nd St., Pompano Beach, FL 33064 ; (954) 969-8171; Mr. Jacki Jacquot (800) 566-2450; (954) 969-8558

Americorp Realty Network, 185 Hillside Ave., Williston, NY 11596 ; (516) 248-4091; Mr. Anthony Biancaniello (877) 248-4080; (516) 248-4080

Creativworks, 4818 Washington Blvd., St. Louis, MO 63108 ; (314) 367-5510; Mr. Steven Leek (888) 304-IDEA; (314) 367-8500

Effective Mailers, 28510 Hayes Rd., Roseville, MI 48066-2314 ; (810) 777-4141; Mr. Jai Gupta ; (810) 777-3223

Focus On Sales, 5689 S. Ouray St., Aurora, CO 80015 ; (303) 617-9431; Mr. Dave Shaw (888) 373-6287; (303) 617-9526

Gifts Remembered, 5678 C.T.H., #R, Denmark, WI 54208-9107 ; (920) 863-5241; Mr. Daniel Pantzlaff (888) 685-9484; (920) 863-8326

Mobil' Ambition USA, 1900 NW 32nd St., Pompano Beach, FL 33064 ; (954) 969-8171; Mr. Dale Easton (800) 566-2450; (954) 969-8558

Profit-On-Hold, 3401 Ridgelake Dr., # 108, Metairie, LA 70002 ; (504) 828-2141; Mr. Otto Mehrgut (800) 569-4653; (504) 832-8000

Scorecard Plus, 1101 Portage St., NW, North Canton, OH 44720-2353 ; (330) 493-9274; Mr. Ed Kalail (800) 767-9273; (330) 493-9900

Specialty Promotions & Advertising, 80 Garden Center, # 30, Broomfield, CO 80020 ; (303) 460-9723; Mr. Tom Bauder (800) 450-1054; (303) 460-7600

Super Saver Coupons, 80 Eighth Ave., New York, NY 10011 ; ; Mr. Allan Horwitz ; (212) 243-6800

United Coupon Corporation, 8380 Alban Rd., Springfield, VA 22150 ; (703) 569-1465; Mr. Frank Curran (800) 368-3501; (703) 644-0200

Val-Pak of Canada, 40 Wynford Dr., # 301, Don Mills, ON M3C 1J5 CANADA; (416) 510-5002; Mr. David Elmer (800) 237-6266; (727) 392-0049

Welcome Host of America, 13953 Perkins Rd., Baton Rouge, LA 70810-3438 ; (504) 751-9039; Ms. Sing VanCleave (800) 962-5431; (504) 769-3000

Yellow Jacket Direct Mail Advertising, 23101 Moulton Pkwy., # 110, Laguna Hills, CA 92653 ; (949) 859-0899; Mr. Bob Philpott (800) 893-5569; (949) 951-9500

Business: Internet/Telecommunications/Miscellaneous

Chapter

9

BUSINESS: INTERNET/TELECOMMUNICATIONS/MISCELLANEOUS INDUSTRY PROFILE

Total # Franchisors in Industry Group	63
Total # Franchised Units in Industry Group	5,273
Total # Company-Owned Units in Industry Group	953
Total # Operating Units in Industry Group	6,226
Average # Franchised Units/Franchisor	83.7
Average # Company-Owned Units/Franchisor	151.0
Average # Total Units/Franchisor	98.8
Ratio of Total # Franchised Units/Total # Company-Owned Units	5.5:1
Industry Survey Participants	21
Representing % of Industry	33.3%
Average Franchise Fee*:	$21.9K
Average Total Investment*:	$70.0K
Average On-Going Royalty Fee*:	6.2%

If a range was provided, the mid-point of the range was used. See detailed profiles for actual ranges.

FIVE LARGEST PARTICIPANTS IN SURVEY

Company	# Fran-chised Units	# Co-Owned Units	# Total Units	Franchise Fee	On-Going Royalty	Total Investment
1. Century Small Business Solutions	642	8	650	35K	8.2%	50-75K
2. Sunbelt Business Brokers	204	1	205	5-10K	$3-6K/Yr.	5-50K
3. Quik Internet	200	0	200	35K	10%	65-75K
4. Money Concepts (Canada)	94	0	94	49.5K	Varies	80K
5. VR Business Brokers	85	0	85	12K	6%	40-75K

All of the data provided are proprietary and should not be quoted without acknowledging *Bond's Franchise Guide*.

AMERICAN INSTITUTE OF SMALL BUSINESS

7515 Wayzata Blvd., # 129
Minneapolis, MN 55426
Tel: (800) 328-2906 (612) 545-7001
Fax: (612) 545-7020
E-Mail: aisbofmn@aol.com
Web Site: www.aisbofmn.com
Mr. Max Fallek, President

THE AMERICAN INSTITUTE OF SMALL BUSINESS provides educational materials, including books, on small business and entrepreneurship. It also provides a seminar for training people on how to set up and operate their own small business. THE INSTITUTE also supplies business software sold by franchisees.

BACKGROUND:

Established: 1985;   1st Franchised: 1988
Franchised Units: 5
Company-Owned Units   1
Total Units: 6
Dist.:   US-4; CAN-0; O'seas-2
North America: 7 States
Density: 1 in MN, 1 in CO, 1 in IL
Projected New Units (12 Months):   NR
Qualifications: 3, 4, 3, 2, 1, 1
Registered: MN

FINANCIAL/TERMS:

Cash Investment: $5K
Total Investment: $10K
Minimum Net Worth: $NR
Fees: Franchise - $5K
  Royalty - 0%;   Ad. - 0%
Earnings Claim Statement: NR
Term of Contract (Years):   2/Varies
Avg. # Of Employees: 1 PT
Passive Ownership: Allowed
Encourage Conversions: N/A
Area Develop. Agreements: No
Sub-Franchising Contracts: No
Expand In Territory: Yes
Space Needs: 600 SF; NR

SUPPORT & TRAINING PROVIDED:

Financial Assistance Provided: Yes
Site Selection Assistance: Yes
Lease Negotiation Assistance: N/A
Co-Operative Advertising: N/A
Franchisee Assoc./Member: NR
Size Of Corporate Staff: 8

On-Going Support: B,D,E,h,I
Training: 1 Day Headquarters.

SPECIFIC EXPANSION PLANS:

US: All United States
Canada: All Canada
Overseas: All Countries

CENTURY SMALL BUSINESS SOLUTIONS

26722 Plaza Dr.
Mission Viejo, CA 92691
Tel: (800) 323-9000 (949) 348-5100
Fax: (949) 348-5126
E-Mail: franchise@centurysmallbiz.com
Web Site: www.centurysmallbiz.com
Ms. Karen Cagle, Director Franchise Development

CENTURY SMALL BUSINESS SOLUTIONS is a business services franchise specializing in accounting, tax, payroll and business counseling to the small business owner. Package includes all software and materials to start a professional practice. If you have a business and accounting background, we can show you how to develop a CENTURY business. Full training and support.

BACKGROUND: IFA MEMBER

Established: 1935;   1st Franchised: 1999
Franchised Units: 642
Company-Owned Units   8
Total Units: 650
Dist.:   US-550; CAN-50; O'seas-50
North America: 48 States, 1 Province
Density: 60 in CA, 37 in TX, 34 FL
Projected New Units (12 Months):   31
Qualifications: 3, 4, 4, 4, 3, 4
Registered: All States

FINANCIAL/TERMS:

Cash Investment: $35K
Total Investment: $50-75K
Minimum Net Worth: $150K
Fees: Franchise - $35K
  Royalty - 8-2%;   Ad. - 0%
Earnings Claim Statement: No
Term of Contract (Years):   10/10
Avg. # Of Employees: 2 FT, 1 PT
Passive Ownership: Not Allowed
Encourage Conversions: Yes
Area Develop. Agreements: No

Sub-Franchising Contracts: No
Expand In Territory: No
Space Needs: 600 SF; OB

SUPPORT & TRAINING PROVIDED:

Financial Assistance Provided: Yes(I)
Site Selection Assistance: Yes
Lease Negotiation Assistance: No
Co-Operative Advertising: No
Franchisee Assoc./Member: Yes/Yes
Size Of Corporate Staff: 60
On-Going Support: a,b,C,D,G,H,I
Training: 2 Weeks Training Center; 4 Days Post Grad, Various; 4 Days Tax Training, Baltimore, MD.

SPECIFIC EXPANSION PLANS:

US: All United States
Canada: All Canada
Overseas: All Countries

COMM PLUS

317 NE Killingsworth St., #A
Portland, OR 97211
Tel: (800) 735-1422 (503) 735-1422
Fax: (503) 735-0482
Web Site: www.wirelessshopping.com/commplus
Mr. Mike Harrison, President

Total communication paging cellular local dial tone internet access web design discount computer systems repair and service.

BACKGROUND:

Established: 1993;   1st Franchised: 1998
Franchised Units: 12
Company-Owned Units   6
Total Units: 18
Dist.:   US-18; CAN-0; O'seas-0
North America: 3 States
Density: OR, WA, SC
Projected New Units (12 Months):   4
Qualifications: 3, 4, 3, 2, 3, 3
Registered: CA,OR,WA

FINANCIAL/TERMS:

Cash Investment: $15K
Total Investment: $15-30K
Minimum Net Worth: $85K
Fees: Franchise - $5K
  Royalty - None;   Ad. - 2%
Earnings Claim Statement: Yes
Term of Contract (Years):   5/5
Avg. # Of Employees: 1 FT, 2 PT
Passive Ownership: Discouraged
Encourage Conversions: Yes
Area Develop. Agreements: No
Sub-Franchising Contracts: No

Expand In Territory: Yes
Space Needs: 800 SF; FS, SF, SC, RM, HB
SUPPORT & TRAINING PROVIDED:
Financial Assistance Provided: Yes
Site Selection Assistance: No
Lease Negotiation Assistance: Yes
Co-Operative Advertising: Yes
Franchisee Assoc./Member: NR
Size Of Corporate Staff: 10
On-Going Support: A,B,c,D,e,f,G,H,I
Training: 3 Weeks at Corporate Headquarters in Portland, OR.
SPECIFIC EXPANSION PLANS:
US: NR
Canada: NR
Overseas: NR

≪ ≫

CONFIDENTIAL BUSINESS CONNECTION

4155 E. Jewell Ave., # 1010
Denver, CO 80222
Tel: (888) 446-1414 (303) 759-2334
Fax: (303) 584-0793
E-Mail: rwbert@ix.netcom.com
Mr. Chris W. Sales, President

Reorganized in 1997, CBC offers a unique alternative to the traditional business brokerage market by providing a non-exclusive clearinghouse for business/franchise buyers and sellers. Services range from 'List & Match' to full valuation and total structuring. CBC relies on confidential profiles, matching capabilities and heavy advertising/telemarketing on a national level to ensure the right connection is made.

BACKGROUND:
Established: 1997;   1st Franchised: 1997
Franchised Units: 1
Company-Owned Units   <u>0</u>
Total Units: 1
Dist.:   US-1; CAN-0; O'seas-0
   North America: 1 State
   Density: 1 in CO
Projected New Units (12 Months):   8
Qualifications: 4, 3, 3, 4, 2, 5
Registered: NR
FINANCIAL/TERMS:
Cash Investment: $50-100K
Total Investment: $50-100K

Minimum Net Worth: $70K
Fees: Franchise - $15.5-31K
   Royalty - 6%;   Ad. - 2%
Earnings Claim Statement: No
Term of Contract (Years):   10/10
Avg. # Of Employees: 3 FT, 1 PT
Passive Ownership: Discouraged
Encourage Conversions: No
Area Develop. Agreements: No
Sub-Franchising Contracts: No
Expand In Territory: Yes
Space Needs: 700 SF; Class A Office
SUPPORT & TRAINING PROVIDED:
Financial Assistance Provided: No
Site Selection Assistance: Yes
Lease Negotiation Assistance: Yes
Co-Operative Advertising: Yes
Franchisee Assoc./Member: No
Size Of Corporate Staff: 2
On-Going Support: c,d,E,G,h,I
Training: 1 Week Denver, CO; 3 Days On-Site.
SPECIFIC EXPANSION PLANS:
US: All United States
Canada: All Canada
Overseas: No

≪ ≫

EMPIRE BUSINESS BROKERS

336 Harris Hill Rd.
Buffalo, NY 14221
Tel: (716) 677-5229
Fax: (716) 677-0955
Web Site:
www.empirebusinessbrokers.com
Mr. Nicholas R. Gugliuzza, President

We sell existing businesses and business opportunities throughout the U. S. and the world. Other profit centers relating to this are: franchise sales and development, financial brokering, equipment leasing, business valuation, business plans and business consulting. A complete training program is held, and therefore previous experience is not required. Success Magazine has ranked us the #1 business brokerage in the U.S. for two consecutive years.

BACKGROUND:
Established: 1981;   1st Franchised: 1989
Franchised Units: 49
Company-Owned Units   <u>2</u>
Total Units: 51
Dist.:   US-45; CAN-1; O'seas-5
   North America: 22 States, 1 Province
   Density: 6 in GA, 4 in OH, 3 in NY

Projected New Units (12 Months):   15
Qualifications: 2, 5, 2, 2, 2, 5
Registered: All States
FINANCIAL/TERMS:
Cash Investment: $10K
Total Investment: $10K
Minimum Net Worth: $NR
Fees: Franchise - $8.9K
   Royalty - $150/Mo.;   Ad. - 0%
Earnings Claim Statement: No
Term of Contract (Years):   20/10
Avg. # Of Employees: 1 FT
Passive Ownership: Allowed
Encourage Conversions: Yes
Area Develop. Agreements: Yes/5
Sub-Franchising Contracts: Yes
Expand In Territory: Yes
Space Needs: 500 SF; HB, OB
SUPPORT & TRAINING PROVIDED:
Financial Assistance Provided: Yes(D)
Site Selection Assistance: Yes
Lease Negotiation Assistance: Yes
Co-Operative Advertising: Yes
Franchisee Assoc./Member: Yes/Yes
Size Of Corporate Staff: 5
On-Going Support: a,b,C,D,E,G,H,I
Training: 1 Week at Home Office.
SPECIFIC EXPANSION PLANS:
US: All United States
Canada: All Canada
Overseas: All Countries

≪ ≫

ENTREPRENEUR'S SOURCE, THE

900 Main St. S., Bldg. # 2
Southbury, CT 06488
Tel: (800) 289-0086 (203) 264-2006
Fax: (203) 264-3516
E-Mail: bill@thesource.com
Web Site: www.FranchiseMatch.com
Mr. Bill Chemero, National Franchise Director

We provide consulting, education and guidance to people exploring self-employment as an additional career option. Using a unique profiling system, ENTREPRENEUR'S SOURCE consultants help people discover the best options for them.

BACKGROUND: IFA MEMBER
Established: 1984; 1st Franchised: 1998
Franchised Units: 44
Company-Owned Units 0
Total Units: 44
Dist.: US-43; CAN-1; O'seas-0
North America: 27 States
Density: 5 in GA, 5 in FL, 3 in SC
Projected New Units (12 Months): 40
Qualifications: 4, 4, 1, 1, 2, 5
Registered: CA,FL,MD,MI,MN,
NY,VA,WA,WI
FINANCIAL/TERMS:
Cash Investment: $50K
Total Investment: $45-50K
Minimum Net Worth: $100K
Fees: Franchise - $35K
Royalty - 0%; Ad. - $350/Mo.
Earnings Claim Statement: No
Term of Contract (Years): 10/10
Avg. # Of Employees: 1 FT
Passive Ownership: Not Allowed
Encourage Conversions: Yes
Area Develop. Agreements: No
Sub-Franchising Contracts: Yes
Expand In Territory: Yes
Space Needs: NR SF; N/A
SUPPORT & TRAINING PROVIDED:
Financial Assistance Provided: Yes(I)
Site Selection Assistance: N/A
Lease Negotiation Assistance: N/A
Co-Operative Advertising: Yes
Franchisee Assoc./Member: No
Size Of Corporate Staff: 6
On-Going Support: D,H,I
Training: 8 Days in CT.
SPECIFIC EXPANSION PLANS:
US: All United States
Canada: All Canada
Overseas: Most Countries

◄◄ ►►

**FORTUNE PRACTICE
MANAGEMENT**
9191 Towne Centre Dr., # 600
San Diego, CA 92122
Tel: (800) 628-1052 (858) 535-6287
Fax: (858) 535-6387
E-Mail: Bradfpm@aol.com
Web Site: www.fortunemgmt.com
Mr. Brad Hunsaker, General Manager

FORTUNE PRACTICE MANAGE-
MENT is a comprehensive health care
coaching/management company. We offer
franchisees a set program to help health
care professional run successful practices.

BACKGROUND:
Established: 1990; 1st Franchised: 1991
Franchised Units: 38
Company-Owned Units 0
Total Units: 38
Dist.: US-37; CAN-1; O'seas-0
North America: 23 States
Density: 7 in CA, 3 in FL, 3 in WA
Projected New Units (12 Months): 4
Qualifications: 2, 5, 2, 3, 4, 5
Registered: CA,FL,IL,IN,MD,MI,NY
FINANCIAL/TERMS:
Cash Investment: $20-60K
Total Investment: $43.9-114.7K
Minimum Net Worth: $100K
Fees: Franchise - $42K
Royalty - 10%; Ad. - 5%
Earnings Claim Statement: No
Term of Contract (Years): 5/5
Avg. # Of Employees: 1 FT
Passive Ownership: Discouraged
Encourage Conversions: N/A
Area Develop. Agreements: No
Sub-Franchising Contracts: No
Expand In Territory: Yes
Space Needs: N/A SF; HB
SUPPORT & TRAINING PROVIDED:
Financial Assistance Provided: Yes(I)
Site Selection Assistance: N/A
Lease Negotiation Assistance: N/A
Co-Operative Advertising: Yes
Franchisee Assoc./Member: Yes/No
Size Of Corporate Staff: 3
On-Going Support: B,C,D,G,H,I
Training: 1 Week in Memphis, TN.
SPECIFIC EXPANSION PLANS:
US: Midwest, Northeast
Canada: AB, ON
Overseas: No

◄◄ ►►

full circle image
FULL CIRCLE IMAGE
6256 34th Ave., NW
Rochester, MN 55901
Tel: (800) 584-7244 (507) 280-0136
Fax: (800) 280-2076
E-Mail: fullinfo@fullcircleimage.com
Web Site: www.fullcircleimage.com

Mr. Charles Benson, President

FULL CIRCLE IMAGE is a direct sales
franchise specializing in remanufactured
laser toner, ink jet and printer ribbon
cartridges. Tap into the $15 billion industry
of imaging products used in every business
every day. Help reduce waste through
recycling while presenting your customers
with guaranteed product with guaranteed
savings.

BACKGROUND: IFA MEMBER
Established: 1991; 1st Franchised: 1997
Franchised Units: 26
Company-Owned Units 0
Total Units: 26
Dist.: US-23; CAN-0; O'seas-3
North America: NR
Density: 11 in MN, 2 in WI
Projected New Units (12 Months): 20
Qualifications: 2, 2, 1, 1, 1, 3
Registered: CA,FL,IL,IN,MD,MI,MN,
NY,ND,OR,SD,WI
FINANCIAL/TERMS:
Cash Investment: $3K
Total Investment: $20-25K
Minimum Net Worth: $20K
Fees: Franchise - $20K
Royalty - 5%; Ad. - 3%
Earnings Claim Statement: No
Term of Contract (Years): 10/10
Avg. # Of Employees: 1 FT
Passive Ownership: Not Allowed
Encourage Conversions: N/A
Area Develop. Agreements: No
Sub-Franchising Contracts: No
Expand In Territory: Yes
Space Needs: NR SF; N/A
SUPPORT & TRAINING PROVIDED:
Financial Assistance Provided: Yes(I)
Site Selection Assistance: N/A
Lease Negotiation Assistance: N/A
Co-Operative Advertising: Yes
Franchisee Assoc./Member: No
Size Of Corporate Staff: 30
On-Going Support: a,B,C,D,F,G,h,I
Training: 1 Week at Home Office; 1 Week
at Your Center Location.
SPECIFIC EXPANSION PLANS:
US: All United States
Canada: All Canada
Overseas: Panama, Costa
Rica, Mexico, Guatemala, El Slavador,
Venezuela, Columbia

◄◄ ►►

IMPRESSIONS ON HOLD

4880 S. Lewis Ave #200
Tulsa, OK 74105-5100
Tel: (800) 580-4653 (918) 744-0988
Fax: (918) 744-0989
E-Mail: sales@impressionsonhold.com
Web Site: www.impressionsonhold.com
Mr. John Bersin, President

We are an advertising company tied to the tele-communications industry. We enable businesses to use the "on-hold" time of their phone system as a marketing tool. Our franchisees market and sell the "on-hold" service to businesses on a local level, and corporate offices then custom-produce the work that is sold on behalf of the franchise owner.

BACKGROUND: IFA MEMBER
Established: 1991;   1st Franchised: 1994
Franchised Units: 70
Company-Owned Units   5
Total Units: 75
Dist.:   US-75; CAN-0; O'seas-0
  North America: NR
  Density: NR
Projected New Units (12 Months):   18
Qualifications: 3, 4, 3, 3, 3, 5
Registered: CA,FL,HI,MD,MI,NY,VA,WA
FINANCIAL/TERMS:
Cash Investment: $47K
Total Investment: $50K
Minimum Net Worth: $150K
Fees: Franchise - $47K
  Royalty - 4%;   Ad. - 1%
Earnings Claim Statement: No
Term of Contract (Years):   10/10
Avg. # Of Employees: NR
Passive Ownership: Discouraged
Encourage Conversions: N/A
Area Develop. Agreements: No
Sub-Franchising Contracts: No
Expand In Territory: Yes
Space Needs: NR SF; HB
SUPPORT & TRAINING PROVIDED:
Financial Assistance Provided: Yes(I)
Site Selection Assistance: N/A
Lease Negotiation Assistance: N/A
Co-Operative Advertising: N/A
Franchisee Assoc./Member: Yes
Size Of Corporate Staff: 50
On-Going Support: A,B,C,D,G,h,I
Training: 5 Days at Corporate Office; 2
  Days On-Site.
SPECIFIC EXPANSION PLANS:
US: All United States
Canada: All Canada
Overseas: No

⧏⧏ ⧐⧐

INTELLIGENT OFFICE, THE
4450 Arapahoe Ave.
Boulder, CO 80303
Tel: (800) 800-1956 (303) 447-9000
Fax: (303) 415-2500
E-Mail: dballen@mfvexpo.com
Web Site: www.intelligentoffice.com
Mr. Dennis A. Ballen, Exclusive Agent

This highly-evolved alternative to the traditional office provides a prestigious address, anywhere communications and a live receptionist for businesses, corporate executives and professionals, releasing them from the limitations and expense of a residential office. THE INTELLIGENT OFFICE offers private offices, conference rooms and professional office services on an as-needed basis and at only a fraction of the cost of a traditional office.

BACKGROUND: IFA MEMBER
Established: 1999;   1st Franchised: 1999
Franchised Units: 19
Company-Owned Units   3
Total Units: 22
Dist.:   US-2; CAN-0; O'seas-0
  North America: 3 States
  Density: 9 in FL, 2 in CO
Projected New Units (12 Months):   18
Qualifications: 1, 5, 1, 3, 1, 1
Registered: NR
FINANCIAL/TERMS:
Cash Investment: $120K+
Total Investment: $262.5-469.5K
Minimum Net Worth: $N/A
Fees: Franchise - $38K
  Royalty - 5%;   Ad. - $250/Mo.
Earnings Claim Statement: No
Term of Contract (Years):   20/20
Avg. # Of Employees: 5 FT
Passive Ownership: Allowed
Encourage Conversions: No
Area Develop. Agreements: Yes
Sub-Franchising Contracts: Yes
Expand In Territory: Yes
Space Needs: 4,500-5,500 SF; OB
SUPPORT & TRAINING PROVIDED:
Financial Assistance Provided: Yes(I)
Site Selection Assistance: Yes
Lease Negotiation Assistance: Yes
Co-Operative Advertising: Yes
Franchisee Assoc./Member: Yes/IFA
Size Of Corporate Staff: 6

On-Going Support: C,D,E,H,G
Training: 1 Week Boulder, CO; 1 Week
  On-Site.
SPECIFIC EXPANSION PLANS:
US: All United States
Canada: All Canada
Overseas: All Countries

⧏⧏ ⧐⧐

THE INTERFACE FINANCIAL GROUP

INTERFACE FINANCIAL GROUP, THE
4521 PGA Blvd., # 211
Palm Beach Gardens, FL 33418
Tel: (800) 387-0860 (905) 475-5701
Fax: (905) 475-8688
E-Mail: ifg@interfacefinancial.com
Web Site: www.interfacefinancial.com
Mr. David T. Banfield, President

Franchise buys quality accounts receivables from client companies at a discount to provide short-term working capital to expanding businesses.

BACKGROUND:
Established: 1971;   1st Franchised: 1991
Franchised Units: 50
Company-Owned Units   0
Total Units: 50
Dist.:   US-17; CAN-33; O'seas-0
  North America: 8 States, 5 Provinces
  Density: 7 in ON, 6 in CA
Projected New Units (12 Months):   12
Qualifications: 3, 3, 4, 2, 2, 3
Registered: CA,FL,IL,MI,MN,NY,VA,WA
  & FTC Disclosure States
FINANCIAL/TERMS:
Cash Investment: $50K
Total Investment: $50-100K
Minimum Net Worth: $50K
Fees: Franchise - $25K
  Royalty - 8%;   Ad. - 1%
Earnings Claim Statement: No
Term of Contract (Years):   10/10
Avg. # Of Employees: 1 PT
Passive Ownership: Discouraged
Encourage Conversions: N/A
Area Develop. Agreements: Yes
Sub-Franchising Contracts: NR
Expand In Territory: Yes
Space Needs: N/A SF; HB

SUPPORT & TRAINING PROVIDED:

Financial Assistance Provided:	Yes
Site Selection Assistance:	N/A
Lease Negotiation Assistance:	N/A
Co-Operative Advertising:	No
Franchisee Assoc./Member:	No
Size Of Corporate Staff:	NR
On-Going Support:	D,E,I
Training: 2 Days + Minimum 3 Days On-Site.	

SPECIFIC EXPANSION PLANS:

US:	All United States
Canada:	All Canada
Overseas:	All Countries

◄◄ ►►

INTERNATIONAL MERGERS & ACQUISITIONS

4300 N. Miller Rd., # 230
Scottsdale, AZ 85251
Tel: (480) 990-3899
Fax: (480) 990-7480
E-Mail: imahq@aol.com
Web Site: www.ima-world.com
Mr. Neil D. Lewis, President/CEO

An international affiliation of members engaged in the profession of serving merger and acquisitions-minded companies, offering consulting services, financing services, M & A services and other services of a distinctive nature. A one-stop service for corporate needs.

BACKGROUND:

Established: 1969;	1st Franchised: 1979
Franchised Units:	65
Company-Owned Units	0
Total Units:	65
Dist.:	US-60; CAN-0; O'seas-8
North America:	24 States
Density:	7 in AZ, 4 in CA, 3 in NY
Projected New Units (12 Months):	6-12
Qualifications:	3, 5, 5, 4, 1, 5
Registered: All States	

FINANCIAL/TERMS:

Cash Investment:	$10-50K
Total Investment:	$10-50K
Minimum Net Worth:	$N/A
Fees: Franchise -	$10K
Royalty - $375/Qtr.;	Ad. - N/A
Earnings Claim Statement:	No
Term of Contract (Years):	10/10
Avg. # Of Employees:	2 FT
Passive Ownership:	Not Allowed
Encourage Conversions:	N/A
Area Develop. Agreements:	No
Sub-Franchising Contracts:	Yes

Expand In Territory:	No
Space Needs: N/A SF; N/A	

SUPPORT & TRAINING PROVIDED:

Financial Assistance Provided:	No
Site Selection Assistance:	N/A
Lease Negotiation Assistance:	N/A
Co-Operative Advertising:	N/A
Franchisee Assoc./Member:	No
Size Of Corporate Staff:	3
On-Going Support:	A,G,H
Training: 3 Days World Headquarters; 2 Days Creative Work Sessions; As Needed World Headquarters.	

SPECIFIC EXPANSION PLANS:

US:	All United States
Canada:	All Canada
Overseas:	All Countries

◄◄ ►►

JAY ROBERTS & ASSOCIATES

81 N. Chicago St., # 200
Joliet, IL 60431-1362
Tel: (815) 722-0683
Fax: (815) 722-4750
Mr. John S. Meers, President

JAY ROBERTS & ASSOCIATES is a management/financial consultant firm started in 1965. It specializes in start-up, general and turn-around consulting to small and medium-sized businesses. An emphasis is put on loan brokerage, particularly government loans.

BACKGROUND:

Established: 1965;	1st Franchised: 1981
Franchised Units:	30
Company-Owned Units	2
Total Units:	32
Dist.:	US-32; CAN-0; O'seas-0
North America:	16 States
Density:	2 in IL, 2 in NY, 2 in CA
Projected New Units (12 Months):	12
Qualifications:	3, 4, 2, 3, 4, 3
Registered: NR	

FINANCIAL/TERMS:

Cash Investment:	$25-50K
Total Investment:	$Varies
Minimum Net Worth:	$NR
Fees: Franchise -	$2K
Royalty - Varies;	Ad. - N/A
Earnings Claim Statement:	No
Term of Contract (Years):	Open/Open
Avg. # Of Employees:	2 FT
Passive Ownership:	Not Allowed
Encourage Conversions:	N/A
Area Develop. Agreements:	Yes
Sub-Franchising Contracts:	No

Expand In Territory:	Yes
Space Needs: Varies SF; HB	

SUPPORT & TRAINING PROVIDED:

Financial Assistance Provided:	Yes(D)
Site Selection Assistance:	No
Lease Negotiation Assistance:	No
Co-Operative Advertising:	No
Franchisee Assoc./Member:	No
Size Of Corporate Staff:	5
On-Going Support:	A,C,D,G,h
Training: 1 Week Joliet, IL.	

SPECIFIC EXPANSION PLANS:

US:	All United States
Canada:	No
Overseas:	No

◄◄ ►►

MANUFACTURING MANAGEMENT ASSOCIATES

1301 W. 22nd St., # 500
Oak Brook, IL 60523
Tel: (800) 574-0308 (630) 575-8700
Fax: (630) 574-0309
E-Mail: licensing@consult-mma.com
Web Site: www.consult-mma.com
Mr. Roger Dykstra, President

Manufacturing consulting: for the small- and medium-size company. Teaching you the market development and sales techniques that made the 'big guys' big. We use your experience and knowledge with our proven methodologies to deliver a quality service.

BACKGROUND:

Established: 1982;	1st Franchised: 1992
Franchised Units:	7
Company-Owned Units	0
Total Units:	7
Dist.:	US-6; CAN-1; O'seas-0
North America:	5 States
Density:	2 in IN, 2 in IL
Projected New Units (12 Months):	2
Qualifications:	4, 5, 4, 4, 3, 5
Registered: IL,MI,KS	

FINANCIAL/TERMS:

Cash Investment:	$10-15K
Total Investment:	$15-25K

Minimum Net Worth:	$25-50K
Fees: Franchise -	$6-8K
Royalty - 5%;	Ad. - 1%/$500
Earnings Claim Statement:	No
Term of Contract (Years):	10/10
Avg. # Of Employees:	1 FT
Passive Ownership:	Not Allowed
Encourage Conversions:	Yes
Area Develop. Agreements:	No
Sub-Franchising Contracts:	No
Expand In Territory:	Yes
Space Needs: NR SF; N/A	

SUPPORT & TRAINING PROVIDED:

Financial Assistance Provided:	N/A
Site Selection Assistance:	Yes
Lease Negotiation Assistance:	Yes
Co-Operative Advertising:	Yes
Franchisee Assoc./Member:	No
Size Of Corporate Staff:	20
On-Going Support:	a,E,G,H,I
Training: 8-10 Days Chicago, IL.	

SPECIFIC EXPANSION PLANS:

US:	All United States
Canada:	All Canada
Overseas:	No

⋖⋖ ⋗⋗

MISTER MONEY - USA

238 Walnut St.
Ft. Collins, CO 80524
Tel: (800) 827-7296 (970) 493-0574
Fax: (970) 490-2099
E-Mail: tim@mistermoney.com
Web Site: www.mistermoney.com
Mr. Don Ettinger, Franchise Sales
  Director

MISTER MONEY - USA franchises offer pawn loans, payday loans, check cashing, money orders, and other financial services. Franchisees operate full-service retail stores or loan only outlets. MISTER MONEY - USA stores are modern, customer friendly and located in solid blue collar areas.

BACKGROUND:

Established: 1976; 1st Franchised: 1996	
Franchised Units:	36
Company-Owned Units	14
Total Units:	50
Dist.:	US-48; CAN-0; O'seas-2
North America:	11 States
Density:	13 in IA, 9 in CO, 4 in WI
Projected New Units (12 Months):	12
Qualifications:	5, 4, 3, 3, 5, 5
Registered: FL,IL,IN,MN,ND,WI	

FINANCIAL/TERMS:

Cash Investment:	$65-150K

Total Investment:	$65-200K
Minimum Net Worth:	$65K
Fees: Franchise -	$21.5-24.5K
Royalty - 3-5%;	Ad. - 3%
Earnings Claim Statement:	Yes
Term of Contract (Years):	5/5
Avg. # Of Employees:	3 FT, 1 PT
Passive Ownership:	Discouraged
Encourage Conversions:	Yes
Area Develop. Agreements:	No
Sub-Franchising Contracts:	Yes
Expand In Territory:	Yes
Space Needs: 4,000-10,000 SF; FS, SF, SC	

SUPPORT & TRAINING PROVIDED:

Financial Assistance Provided:	Yes(D)
Site Selection Assistance:	Yes
Lease Negotiation Assistance:	Yes
Co-Operative Advertising:	Yes
Franchisee Assoc./Member:	Yes/Yes
Size Of Corporate Staff:	25
On-Going Support:	a,B,C,D,E,F,G,I
Training: 10-14 Days Fort Collins, CO.	

SPECIFIC EXPANSION PLANS:

US:	All United States
Canada:	No
Overseas:	Mexico

⋖⋖ ⋗⋗

MONEY CONCEPTS (CANADA)

180 Attwell Dr., # 501
Etobicoke, ON M9W 6A9 CANADA
Tel: (800) 661-7296 (416) 674-0450
Fax: (416) 674-4785
Mr. Rob Sylvester, President

MONEY CONCEPTS offers financial planning control. We are the fastest-growing independent franchise in financial services in Canada, specializing in complete financial planning and searching the market for financial products to implement our plan.

BACKGROUND:

Established: 1984; 1st Franchised: 1985	
Franchised Units:	94
Company-Owned Units	0
Total Units:	94
Dist.:	US-0; CAN-94; O'seas-0
North America:	8 Provinces
Density:	53 in ON, 21 in BC, 5 in NB
Projected New Units (12 Months):	25
Qualifications:	3, 4, 1, 2, 4, 5
Registered: AB	

FINANCIAL/TERMS:

Cash Investment:	$50K
Total Investment:	$80K
Minimum Net Worth:	$200K+

Fees: Franchise -	$49.5K
Royalty - Varies;	Ad. - 2%/$5K Max.
Earnings Claim Statement:	No
Term of Contract (Years):	5/1
Avg. # Of Employees:	4 FT
Passive Ownership:	Discouraged
Encourage Conversions:	N/A
Area Develop. Agreements:	Yes/5
Sub-Franchising Contracts:	No
Expand In Territory:	Yes
Space Needs: 750-1,000 SF; N/A	

SUPPORT & TRAINING PROVIDED:

Financial Assistance Provided:	No
Site Selection Assistance:	Yes
Lease Negotiation Assistance:	No
Co-Operative Advertising:	Yes
Franchisee Assoc./Member:	Yes/Yes
Size Of Corporate Staff:	25
On-Going Support:	A,b,C,D,G,H,I
Training: 2 Weeks Head Office.	

SPECIFIC EXPANSION PLANS:

US:	No
Canada:	All Canada
Overseas:	No

⋖⋖ ⋗⋗

QUIK INTERNET

170 E. 17th St., # 101
Costa Mesa, CA 92627
Tel: (888) 784-5266 (949) 548-2171
Fax: (949) 548-0569
E-Mail: murray@quik.com
Web Site: www.quik.com
Mr. Murray Mead, Director of Marketing

QUIK INTERNET is the world's first and largest Internet services franchise, with over 200 franchises worldwide. Provide highly-demanded Internet services in your local community, including Internet access, Web design, on-line marketing and more. Prime territories, low fees - apply today!

BACKGROUND: IFA MEMBER

Established: 1996; 1st Franchised: 1996	
Franchised Units:	200
Company-Owned Units	0
Total Units:	200
Dist.:	US-200; CAN-0; O'seas-0
North America:	NR
Density:	CA, TX, FL
Projected New Units (12 Months):	250
Qualifications:	5, 5, 1, 4, 4, 4
Registered: All States and AB	

FINANCIAL/TERMS:

Cash Investment:	$65-75K
Total Investment:	$65-75K
Minimum Net Worth:	$N/A

113

Fees: Franchise - $35K
  Royalty - 10%; Ad. - 3%
Earnings Claim Statement: No
Term of Contract (Years): 10/10
Avg. # Of Employees: 1 FT
Passive Ownership: NR
Encourage Conversions: N/A
Area Develop. Agreements: NR
Sub-Franchising Contracts: No
Expand In Territory: N/A
Space Needs: N/A SF; N/A

SUPPORT & TRAINING PROVIDED:
Financial Assistance Provided: No
Site Selection Assistance: N/A
Lease Negotiation Assistance: N/A
Co-Operative Advertising: No
Franchisee Assoc./Member: No
Size Of Corporate Staff: 30
On-Going Support: A,B,C,D,F
Training: 1 Week Costa Mesa, CA.

SPECIFIC EXPANSION PLANS:
US: All United States
Canada: All Canada
Overseas: All Countries

≪ ≫

SERVICE CENTER
5202 E. Mt. View Rd.
Scottsdale, AZ 85253
Tel: (800) 729-7424 (480) 998-1616
Fax: (480) 998-4091
E-Mail: gerald@primenet.com
Mr. Gerald Zukerman, President

SERVICE CENTER is a business based on the fact that sooner or later, everything breaks. Through the use of the tested Ad Program, customers will call. Just send your technician to do the repair. Cash business, no inventory, low cost. Home-based.

BACKGROUND:
Established: 1991; 1st Franchised: 1992
Franchised Units: 8
Company-Owned Units: 1
Total Units: 9
Dist.: US-9; CAN-0; O'seas-0
  North America: 10 States
  Density: 2 in TX, 2 in AZ, 2 in CA
Projected New Units (12 Months): 4
Qualifications: 1, 3, 1, 3, 4, 4
Registered: All States
FINANCIAL/TERMS:
Cash Investment: $1K
Total Investment: $1-50K
Minimum Net Worth: $1K
Fees: Franchise - $1-35K

Royalty - 5.3%; Ad. - 0%
Earnings Claim Statement: No
Term of Contract (Years): 10/10
Avg. # Of Employees: 1 FT
Passive Ownership: Allowed
Encourage Conversions: N/A
Area Develop. Agreements: No
Sub-Franchising Contracts: No
Expand In Territory: Yes
Space Needs: 300 SF; SC, OB

SUPPORT & TRAINING PROVIDED:
Financial Assistance Provided: Yes(D)
Site Selection Assistance: Yes
Lease Negotiation Assistance: N/A
Co-Operative Advertising: No
Franchisee Assoc./Member: Yes/Yes
Size Of Corporate Staff: 2
On-Going Support: E,I
Training: 1 Week at Las Vegas, NV.

SPECIFIC EXPANSION PLANS:
US: All United States
Canada: No
Overseas: No

≪ ≫

SUNBELT BUSINESS BROKERS
2 Amherst St.
Charleston, SC 29403
Tel: (800) 771-7866 (843) 853-4781
Fax: (843) 853-4135
E-Mail: sales@sunbeltnetwork.com
Web Site: www.sunbeltnetwork.com
Mr. Edward T. Pendarvis, President

We offer business brokerage/merger and acquisition franchises. SUNBELT is the largest and fastest-growing business brokerage firm in the world. Our success comes from our name recognition, quality training programs and hands-on assistance. We are the leaders in computerized office management, networking and Internet technology. We take no percentage fees. All of our services are covered in our low semi-annual fee.

BACKGROUND: IFA MEMBER
Established: 1978; 1st Franchised: 1993
Franchised Units: 204

Company-Owned Units: 1
Total Units: 205
Dist.: US-199; CAN-0; O'seas-6
  North America: 38 States
  Density: 16 in FL, 10 in NC, 10 in VA
Projected New Units (12 Months): 50
Registered: CA,FL,HI,IL,IN,MD,MI,MN, NY,OR,RI,SD,VA,WA,WI
FINANCIAL/TERMS:
Cash Investment: $5-15K
Total Investment: $5-50K
Minimum Net Worth: $N/A
Fees: Franchise - $5-10K
  Royalty - $3-6K/Yr.; Ad. - 0%
Earnings Claim Statement: No
Term of Contract (Years): On-going
Avg. # Of Employees: Independent Contrac.
Passive Ownership: Not Allowed
Encourage Conversions: Yes
Area Develop. Agreements: No
Sub-Franchising Contracts: No
Expand In Territory: Yes
Space Needs: 1,000 SF; FS

SUPPORT & TRAINING PROVIDED:
Financial Assistance Provided: Yes(D)
Site Selection Assistance: N/A
Lease Negotiation Assistance: N/A
Co-Operative Advertising: N/A
Franchisee Assoc./Member: Yes/Yes
Size Of Corporate Staff: 9
On-Going Support: C,D,G,H,I
Training: 4 Days Various Regional Centers.

SPECIFIC EXPANSION PLANS:
US: All United States
Canada: All Canada
Overseas: All Countries

≪ ≫

VR BUSINESS BROKERS
2601 E. Oakland Park Blvd., # 205
Ft. Lauderdale, FL 33306
Tel: (800) 377-8722 (954) 565-1555
Fax: (954) 565-6855
E-Mail: pking@vrbusinessbrokers.com
Web Site: www.vrbusinessbrokers.com
Mr. Peter King, Principal

Oldest established chain of franchised business brokers in the nation. We also publish 'Today's Business Owner Magazine' for exclusive use of franchisees at no additional cost.

BACKGROUND:
Established: 1978; 1st Franchised: 1979
Franchised Units: 85

Company-Owned Units	0
Total Units:	85
Dist.:	US-85; CAN-0; O'seas-0
North America:	37 States
Density:	12 in FL, 10 in CA, 5 in NC
Projected New Units (12 Months):	NR
Qualifications:	3, 3, 3, 3, 2, 5
Registered: CA,FL,IL,MD,MI, OR,WA	

FINANCIAL/TERMS:

Cash Investment:	$40-75K
Total Investment:	$40-75K
Minimum Net Worth:	$150K
Fees: Franchise -	$12K
Royalty - 6%;	Ad. - $150/Mo.
Earnings Claim Statement:	No
Term of Contract (Years):	10/10
Avg. # Of Employees:	2 FT, 1 PT
Passive Ownership:	Not Allowed
Encourage Conversions:	Yes
Area Develop. Agreements:	No
Sub-Franchising Contracts:	No
Expand In Territory:	No
Space Needs: Varies SF; OB	

SUPPORT & TRAINING PROVIDED:

Financial Assistance Provided:	No
Site Selection Assistance:	Yes
Lease Negotiation Assistance:	Yes
Co-Operative Advertising:	Yes
Franchisee Assoc./Member:	Yes/Yes
Size Of Corporate Staff:	10
On-Going Support:	A,B,C,d,G,H,I
Training: 2.5 Weeks Greensboro, NC; 2.5 Weeks Ft. Lauderdale, FL.	

SPECIFIC EXPANSION PLANS:

US:	All United States
Canada:	Soon
Overseas:	Soon

WORLD TRADE NETWORK

580 Lincoln Park Blvd., # 255
Dayton, OH 45429
Tel: (800) 227-3772 (937) 298-3383
Fax: (937) 298-2550
E-Mail: wtnet@infinet.com
Web Site: www.wnetwork.com
Mr. Michael J. Wenzler, President/CEO

WORLD TRADE NETWORK has created a structure and system for the import/export business and combined it with the franchise/licensing industry to create an international trading company with self-motivated entrepreneurs and existing import/export companies. The WTN structure was created over a 9-year period. In 4 years, it has trained over 40 offices in over 30 countries. The international trading business is booming!

BACKGROUND:

Established: 1993;	1st Franchised: 1993
Franchised Units:	40
Company-Owned Units	1
Total Units:	41
Dist.:	US-5; CAN-1; O'seas-35
North America:	NR
Density:	2 in CA, 1 in WI, 1 in OH
Projected New Units (12 Months):	5
Qualifications:	4, 4, 3, 2, 3, 2
Registered: FL	

FINANCIAL/TERMS:

Cash Investment:	$85K
Total Investment:	$135K
Minimum Net Worth:	$Varies
Fees: Franchise -	$12K
Royalty - 7%;	Ad. - 3%
Earnings Claim Statement:	No
Term of Contract (Years):	10/15
Avg. # Of Employees:	1 FT, 1 PT
Passive Ownership:	Discouraged
Encourage Conversions:	Yes
Area Develop. Agreements:	No
Sub-Franchising Contracts:	No
Expand In Territory:	No
Space Needs: 400 SF; OB	

SUPPORT & TRAINING PROVIDED:

Financial Assistance Provided:	Yes(D)
Site Selection Assistance:	No
Lease Negotiation Assistance:	No
Co-Operative Advertising:	No
Franchisee Assoc./Member:	No
Size Of Corporate Staff:	3
On-Going Support:	d,G,h
Training: 5 Days in Dayton, OH.	

SPECIFIC EXPANSION PLANS:

US:	All United States
Canada:	All Canada
Overseas:	All Countries

SUPPLEMENTAL LISTING OF FRANCHISORS

Ad Com Express, 7424 W. 78th St., P. O. Box 390048, Edina, MN 55439 ; (612) 829-7995; Mr. Robert F. Friedman (800) 829-7991; (612) 829-7990

Alternative Board, The (TAB), 225 E. 16th Ave.,#1200, Denver, CO 80203-1622 ; (800) 420-7055; Ms. Tamyra A. Wallace (800) 219-7718; (303) 839-1200

American Lenders Service Co., P.O. Box 7238, Odessa, TX 79760 ; (915) 335-3412; Mr. Jim Golden ; (915) 332-0361

Cash America Pawn, 1600 W. Seventh St., Fort Worth, TX 76102 ; (817) 390-9209; Mr. Mike Gaston (800) 645-3811; (817) 390-9232

Commworld International, 7315 S. Revere Pkwy., # 602, Englewood, CO 80112 ; (303) 721-8299; Ms. Patti Hildebrand (800) 525-3200; (303) 721-8200

Connect.Ad, 1000 W. McNab Rd., # 236, Pompano Beach, FL 33069 ; (954) 942-0701; Mr. Jerry G. Nestos ; (954) 942-5070

Corporate Minutes Made, 15010 Tanglewood Court, Fountain Hills, AZ 85268 ; (480) 837-4989; Mr. Dale Smith ; (480) 837-8797

Direct Opinions, 23600 Mercantile Rd., Beachwood, OH 44122 ; (216) 464-0621; Mr. Simon Cohen (800) 229-7978; (216) 831-7979

Enrollment Center, The, 7924 Ivanhoe Ave., # 2, La Jolla, CA 92037 ; (619) 459-7086; Mr. Joseph G. Smollen (800) 336-9222; (619) 459-7020

Executive Business Centers / EBC, 11465 John's Creek Pkwy., # 300, Duluth, GA 30097 ; (770) 814-4301; Mr. Thomas Dye ; (770) 814-4300

Fiducial Triple Check, 2441 Honolulu Ave., Montrose, CA 91020 ; (818) 249-5344; Mr. David Lieberman (800) 283-1040; (818) 236-2944

Franchise Company, The, 5397 Eglinton Ave. W., # 108, Etobicoke, ON M9C 5K6 CANADA; (416) 620-9955; Ms. Sandra Benaglia ; (416) 620-4700

Franchise Consortium International, 245 S. 84th St., # 200, Lincoln, NE 68510 ; (402) 484-7811; Mr. Joseph J. Field (800) 301-9504; (402) 484-7100

Franklin Traffic Service, P.O. Box 100, Ransomville, NY 14131 ; (716) 731-2705; Mr. James R. Golding ; (716) 731-3131

Freefone, 1001 W. Loop South, # 603, Houston, TX 77027 ; (713) 355-1855; Mr. Jim McCune (888) 373-3971; (713) 355-1886

GroupAdvantage, 100 Cummings Center, # 206C, Beverly, MA 01915 ; (978) 927-6688; Mr. John F. McCarthy, Jr. (888) 772-2472; (978) 927-6633

Int'l. Center for Entrepreneurial Development, One Entrepreneur Way, Cypress, TX 77429 ; (281) 256-4178; Mr. Bob Dolan (888) 280-2053; (281) 256-4100

ISU International, 100 Pine St., # 1700, San Francisco, CA 94111 ; (415) 397-5530; Ms. Nyla Starr (800) 782-9400; (415) 788-9810

Medical Management Inc., 11815 NE Glen Widing Dr., Portland, OR 97220 ; (503) 256-7636; Mr. Sunil Dewan (800) 838-6929; (503) 345-5200

Money Mart, 1640 Oak Bay Ave., 3rd Fl., Victoria, BC V8R 1B2 CANADA; (250) 595-0410; Mr. Bruce Marshall ; (250) 595-5211

NetSavings, 2630 Sand Lake Rd., Longwood, FL 32779 ; (877) 649-5125; Ms. Ashley Nault ; (407) 287-0840

Paytrak Payroll Services, 541 High St., Westwood, MA 02090 ; (781) 251-9520; Mr. Greg Williams (877) 729-8725; (781) 251-9410

Power Broker Systems, 7924 Ivanhoe Ave., # 2, La Jolla, CA 92037 ; (619) 459-7086; Mr. Joseph G. Smollen (800) 336-9222; (619) 459-7020

Prime Business Communications, 3900 Skyhawk Dr., Chantilly, VA 20151 ; ; Mr. Ron Beer (888) 767-4PBC;

ProVenture Business Group, P.O. Box 338, Needham Heights, MA 02494 ; (781) 444-0565; Mr. William J. Tedoldi ; (781) 444-8278

Sterling Kennedy USA, 2980 Watt St., #6, Ste-Foy, PQ G1X-4A6 CANADA; (418) 650-9967; Mr. Jean-Francois Montreuil (800) 883-9979; (418) 650-9979

Strategic Living International, 10409 Stevenson Village, Stevenson, MD 21153 ; (301) 358-7858; Mr. Bruce Seidman (800) 727-4754; (410) 653-1993

Stratis Business Centers, 1293 Professional Dr., #D, Myrtle Beach, SC 29577 ; (843) 497-9848; Mr. John Arenas ; (843) 692-3000

CHILD DEVELOPMENT/EDUCATION/PRODUCTS INDUSTRY PROFILE

Total # Franchisors in Industry Group	59
Total # Franchised Units in Industry Group	4,712
Total # Company-Owned Units in Industry Group	<u>212</u>
Total # Operating Units in Industry Group	4,924
Average # Franchised Units/Franchisor	79.9
Average # Company-Owned Units/Franchisor	<u>3.6</u>
Average # Total Units/Franchisor	83.5
Ratio of Total # Franchised Units/Total # Company-Owned Units	22.2:1
Industry Survey Participants	30
Representing % of Industry	50.8%
Average Franchise Fee*:	$21.6K
Average Total Investment*:	$146.0K
Average On-Going Royalty Fee*:	6.6%

If a range was provided, the mid-point of the range was used. See detailed profiles for actual ranges.

FIVE LARGEST PARTICIPANTS IN SURVEY

Company	# Fran- chised Units	# Co- Owned Units	# Total Units	Franchise Fee	On-Going Royalty	Total Investment
1. Future Kids (Canada)	596	0	596	50K	10% + $360	100-142K
2. Gymboree	408	27	435	35K	6%	80-150K
3. Once Upon A Child	244	4	248	20K	5%	85-145K
4. Fourth R, The	228	0	228	16K	$240/Mo.+5%	26K+
5. Tutor Time Learning Centers	136	70	206	50K	6%	250K

All of the data provided are proprietary and should not be quoted without acknowledging *Bond's Franchise Guide.*

BABY NEWS CHILDRENS STORES

23521 Foley St.
Hayward, CA 94545
Tel: (510) 786-3460
Fax: (510) 785-1580
Web Site: www.babynewsonline.com
Mr. Roger O'Callaghan, President

BABY NEWS is the oldest established association of individually-owned baby stores.

BACKGROUND:

Established: 1950; 1st Franchised: 1961	
Franchised Units:	44
Company-Owned Units	1
Total Units:	45
Dist.:	US-35; CAN-0; O'seas-10
North America	35 States
Density:	20 in CA
Projected New Units (12 Months):	2
Qualifications:	5, 3, 3, 3, 3, 5
Registered: CA	

FINANCIAL/TERMS:

Cash Investment:	$100K
Total Investment:	$150-250K
Minimum Net Worth:	$NR
Fees: Franchise -	$15K
Royalty - 1%;	Ad. - 0%
Earnings Claim Statement:	Yes
Term of Contract (Years):	5/5
Avg. # Of Employees:	3 FT, 4 PT
Passive Ownership:	Not Allowed
Encourage Conversions:	Yes
Area Develop. Agreements:	No
Sub-Franchising Contracts:	No
Expand In Territory:	Yes
Space Needs: 5,000 SF; FS, SC, RM	

SUPPORT & TRAINING PROVIDED:

Financial Assistance Provided:	No
Site Selection Assistance:	Yes
Lease Negotiation Assistance:	Yes
Co-Operative Advertising:	No
Franchisee Assoc./Member:	No
Size Of Corporate Staff:	14
On-Going Support:	A,B,C,d,E,F,G,H
Training: 1-2 Weeks at Various Locations.	

SPECIFIC EXPANSION PLANS:

US:	All United States
Canada:	All Canada
Overseas:	All Countries

◄◄ ►►

BABY USA

857 N. Larch Ave.
Elmhurst, IL 60126
Tel: (800) 323-4108 (630) 832-9880
Fax: (630) 832-0139
E-Mail: franchise@usababy.com
Web Site: www.usababy.com
Mr. Ronald A. Eriksen, VP Market Development

USA BABY is America's leading specialty retailer of infant and juvenile furniture and accessories. Franchisees receive market evaluation, site selection, store design, financing, opening, advertising, merchandising and on-going operational support. Exclusive territories and substantial single, multi-unit and area development opportunities exist for candidates with a passion for serving customers, developing employee teams and participating in a proven retail environment.

BACKGROUND: IFA MEMBER

Established: 1975; 1st Franchised: 1986	
Franchised Units:	52
Company-Owned Units	0
Total Units:	52
Dist.:	US-48; CAN-0; O'seas-4
North America	16 States
Density:	9 in IL, 8 in NY, 5 in MI
Projected New Units (12 Months):	6
Qualifications:	3, 4, 2, 2, 2, 5
Registered:	CA,FL,IL,IN,MD,MI,MN, NY,OR,VA,WA,WI,DC

FINANCIAL/TERMS:

Cash Investment:	$60-80K
Total Investment:	$250-350K
Minimum Net Worth:	$100K
Fees: Franchise -	$16.5-33K
Royalty - 3%;	Ad. - 5%
Earnings Claim Statement:	No

Term of Contract (Years):	10/10
Avg. # Of Employees:	3-4 FT, 3-5 PT
Passive Ownership:	Discouraged
Encourage Conversions:	Yes
Area Develop. Agreements:	Yes/Varies
Sub-Franchising Contracts:	No
Expand In Territory:	Yes
Space Needs: 7,000-9,000 SF; FS, SF, SC	

SUPPORT & TRAINING PROVIDED:

Financial Assistance Provided:	Yes(I)
Site Selection Assistance:	Yes
Lease Negotiation Assistance:	Yes
Co-Operative Advertising:	Yes
Franchisee Assoc./Member:	Yes
Size Of Corporate Staff:	8
On-Going Support:	B,C,D,E,G,H,I
Training: 7-8 Days Corporate Office; 2-3 Days Existing Store; 4-5 Days Franchisee's Store.	

SPECIFIC EXPANSION PLANS:

US:	All United States
Canada:	All Canada
Overseas:	Mexico

◄◄ ►►

CHILDREN'S ORCHARD

2100 S. Main St., # B
Ann Arbor, MI 48103
Tel: (800) 999-KIDS (734) 994-9199
Fax: (734) 994-9323
E-Mail: Whamilton@childorch.com
Web Site: www.childorch.com
Ms. Josephine Gonzalez, Franchise Development Director

CHILDREN'S ORCHARD is a children's retailer of upscale resale franchise stores featuring 'gently used' clothing, toys and equipment for kids under the age 7 at 50-80% less than retail. New items also sold. Franchise support ranked highly in Income Opportunities, Platinum 100 and Success Magazine's Gold 100. Also ranked in the Entrepreneur 500 since 1992.

BACKGROUND: IFA MEMBER

Established: 1980; 1st Franchised: 1985	
Franchised Units:	90
Company-Owned Units	2
Total Units:	92
Dist.:	US-92; CAN-0; O'seas-0
North America	25 States
Density:	19 in CA, 16 in MA, 8 in MI

Projected New Units (12 Months): 20
Qualifications: 5, 5, 3, 2, 2, 5
Registered: CA,FL,IL,IN,MD,MI,NY,VA
FINANCIAL/TERMS:
Cash Investment: $30-48K
Total Investment: $69.5-155K
Minimum Net Worth: $100K
Fees: Franchise - $19.5K
  Royalty - 4.5-6%; Ad. - 1.5%
Earnings Claim Statement: No
Term of Contract (Years): 10/5
Avg. # Of Employees: 1 FT, 1-4 PT
Passive Ownership: Not Allowed
Encourage Conversions: Yes
Area Develop. Agreements: Yes/10
Sub-Franchising Contracts: Yes
Expand In Territory: No
Space Needs: 1,700-1,800 SF; SC
SUPPORT & TRAINING PROVIDED:
Financial Assistance Provided: Yes(I)
Site Selection Assistance: Yes
Lease Negotiation Assistance: Yes
Co-Operative Advertising: Yes
Franchisee Assoc./Member: No
Size Of Corporate Staff: 8
On-Going Support: A,B,C,D,E,F,G,H,I
Training: 2 Weeks in Ann Arbor, MI; 5
  Days On-Site.
SPECIFIC EXPANSION PLANS:
US: All United States
Canada: All Except AB
Overseas: All Countries

<< >>

Computer fun . . . for little ones

**COMPUTERTOTS/COMPUTER
EXPLORERS**
10132 Colvin Run Rd.
Great Falls, VA 22066
Tel: (800) 531-5053 (703) 759-2556
Fax: (703) 759-1938
E-Mail: sgould@computertots.com
Web Site: www.computertots.com
Ms. Sandy Gould, Director Fran. Dev./
  Training

A network of computer education services
for children 3 - 12. The program was
established in 1984 and offers programs
through outreach programs at private and
public educational sites.

BACKGROUND: IFA MEMBER
Established: 1984; 1st Franchised: 1988
Franchised Units: 190
Company-Owned Units: 2
Total Units: 192
Dist.: US-110; CAN-0; O'seas-82
  North America: 38 States
  Density: 12 in CA, 8 in TX, 7 in OH
Projected New Units (12 Months): 6
Qualifications: 3, 4, 4, 3, 3, 5
Registered: All States
FINANCIAL/TERMS:
Cash Investment: $45K
Total Investment: $45K
Minimum Net Worth: $100K
Fees: Franchise - $10-29.9K
  Royalty - 8%/$350; Ad. - 1%
Earnings Claim Statement: Yes
Term of Contract (Years): 10/10
Avg. # Of Employees: 1 FT, 5 PT
Passive Ownership: Discouraged
Encourage Conversions: N/A
Area Develop. Agreements: No
Sub-Franchising Contracts: No
Expand In Territory: No
Space Needs: N/A SF; HB
SUPPORT & TRAINING PROVIDED:
Financial Assistance Provided: No
Site Selection Assistance: N/A
Lease Negotiation Assistance: N/A
Co-Operative Advertising: N/A
Franchisee Assoc./Member: Yes/Yes
Size Of Corporate Staff: 10
On-Going Support: b,c,d,g,h,I
Training: 7 Days Great Falls, VA.
SPECIFIC EXPANSION PLANS:
US: All United States
Canada: No
Overseas: No

<< >>

DANCERCISE KIDS
P.O. Box 219
Anoka, MN 55303-0219
Tel: (800) 613-8231 (952) 920-9880
Fax: (952) 925-1141
E-Mail: franchiseinfo@dancercise.com
Web Site: www.dancercise.com
Ms. Jennifer Gordon, Franchise Operations
  Director

DANCERCISE KIDS is a comprehensive
dance program designed for young children
at child care facilities. Our unique
educational curriculum and lesson plans are
provided along with marketing materials,
computer software, ongoing training and
corporate support. DANCERCISE KIDS
offers an exciting opportunity to impact
children's lives and enjoy a rewarding
career. Call us today!

BACKGROUND:
Established: 1988; 1st Franchised: 1999
Franchised Units: 3
Company-Owned Units: 9
Total Units: 12
Dist.: US-12; CAN-0; O'seas-0
  North America: 7 States
  Density: 3 in MN, 3 in IL, 2 in VA
Projected New Units (12 Months): 5
Qualifications: 3, 4, 3, 3, 5, 5
Registered: CA,FL,MD,MI,MN,WI
FINANCIAL/TERMS:
Cash Investment: $3-9.5K
Total Investment: $16.8-23.3K
Minimum Net Worth: $25K
Fees: Franchise - $9.5K
  Royalty - 10%; Ad. - 0%
Earnings Claim Statement: Yes
Term of Contract (Years): 10/15
Avg. # Of Employees: 1 FT
Passive Ownership: Discouraged
Encourage Conversions: Yes
Area Develop. Agreements: No
Sub-Franchising Contracts: No
Expand In Territory: Yes
Space Needs: N/A SF; HB
SUPPORT & TRAINING PROVIDED:
Financial Assistance Provided: Yes(I)
Site Selection Assistance: Yes
Lease Negotiation Assistance: N/A
Co-Operative Advertising: N/A
Franchisee Assoc./Member: No
Size Of Corporate Staff: 5
On-Going Support: B,C,D,E,G,H,I
Training: 1 Week at Corporate Office in
  Minneapolis.
SPECIFIC EXPANSION PLANS:
US: All United States
Canada: All Canada
Overseas: No

<< >>

**FASTRACKIDS INTERNATIONAL
LTD.**
6900 E. Belleview Ave.
Englewood, CO 80111
Tel: (888) 576-6888 (303) 224-0200
Fax: (303) 224-0222

119

E-Mail: info@fastrackids
Web Site: www.fastrackids.com
Mr. Kevin Krause, Director Franchise Development

"Enrichment Education for Tomorrow's Leaders"

FASTRACKIDS® is a remarkable new, technologically-advanced educational system designed to enrich the knowledge of young children. FASTRACKIDS® enrichment education encourages the development of a child's creativity, leadership, speaking and communication skills in a stimulating, participatory learning environment.

BACKGROUND: IFA MEMBER
Established: 1998; 1st Franchised: 1998
Franchised Units: 87
Company-Owned Units 0
Total Units: 87
Dist.: US-11; CAN-1; O'seas-75
 North America: 3 States
 Density: NR
Projected New Units (12 Months): 25
Qualifications: 4, 4, 4, 4, 5, 5
Registered: All Except SD,VA
FINANCIAL/TERMS:
Cash Investment: $10.2-35.9K
Total Investment: $10.2-35.9K
Minimum Net Worth: $NR
Fees: Franchise - $5-15K
 Royalty - 1.5%; Ad. - 5%
Earnings Claim Statement: Yes
Term of Contract (Years): 5/5
Avg. # Of Employees: 1-5 FT
Passive Ownership: Discouraged
Encourage Conversions: N/A
Area Develop. Agreements: Yes/5
Sub-Franchising Contracts: No
Expand In Territory: Yes
Space Needs: 500 SF; N/A
SUPPORT & TRAINING PROVIDED:
Financial Assistance Provided: Yes(B)
Site Selection Assistance: Yes
Lease Negotiation Assistance: No
Co-Operative Advertising: Yes
Franchisee Assoc./Member: No
Size Of Corporate Staff: 12

On-Going Support: C,G,h,I
Training: 3-4 Days in Denver, CO.
SPECIFIC EXPANSION PLANS:
US: All United States
Canada: All Canada
Overseas: All Countries

‹‹ ››

THE FOURTH R®
Computer Training Solutions

FOURTH R, THE
1715 Market St., # 103
Kirkland, WA 98033
Tel: (800) 821-8653 (425) 828-0336
Fax: (425) 828-0192
E-Mail: fourthR@fourthR.com
Web Site: www.FourthR.com
Mr. Robert L. McCauley, President

Computers have changed virtually all aspects of our lives. As we move into the information age, many experts agree that computer literacy has become THE FOURTH R in education today. As an international leader in computer training, THE FOURTH R is one of the fastest-growing companies in the computer training sector and has been highlighted in prominent national publications as one of the top franchisors both in the U. S. and abroad.

BACKGROUND: IFA MEMBER
Established: 1991; 1st Franchised: 1992
Franchised Units: 228
Company-Owned Units 0
Total Units: 228
Dist.: US-45; CAN-8; O'seas-172
 North America: 21 States, 2 Provinces
 Density: 6 in CA, 6 in PA, 5 in WA
Projected New Units (12 Months): 54
Qualifications: 2, 4, 3, 4, 2, 3
Registered: CA,HI,IL,IN,MD,MI,MN,NY, OR,VA,WA,WI,DC,AB
FINANCIAL/TERMS:
Cash Investment: $N/A
Total Investment: $26K+
Minimum Net Worth: $None
Fees: Franchise - $16K
 Royalty - ~$240/Mo+5%; Ad. - 0%
Earnings Claim Statement: No
Term of Contract (Years): 5/5
Avg. # Of Employees: Varies
Passive Ownership: Allowed
Encourage Conversions: Yes

Area Develop. Agreements: Yes/5
Sub-Franchising Contracts: No
Expand In Territory: Yes
Space Needs: 800-3,000 SF; SF, SC, HB, Commercial
SUPPORT & TRAINING PROVIDED:
Financial Assistance Provided: Yes(I)
Site Selection Assistance: Yes
Lease Negotiation Assistance: Yes
Co-Operative Advertising: Yes
Franchisee Assoc./Member: Yes/Yes
Size Of Corporate Staff: 7
On-Going Support: B,C,G,H,I
Training: 5 Days Seattle, WA.
SPECIFIC EXPANSION PLANS:
US: All United States
Canada: All Canada
Overseas: All Countries

‹‹ ››

FUTUREKIDS (CANADA)
18 Crimson Millway
Willowdale, ON M2L 1T6 CANADA
Tel: (416) 445-6488
Fax: (416) 445-5750
Mr. Elliot Sachar, President

Computer-training centers. We train children and adults how to use the computer as a tool. Teach out of learning centers through regular classes, camps and special interest groups. We also go out on-location to work with schools, daycares, etc., and provide teacher training for public and private schools.

BACKGROUND:
Established: 1983; 1st Franchised: 1989
Franchised Units: 596
Company-Owned Units 0
Total Units: 596
Dist.: US-243; CAN-31; O'seas-322
 North America: 38 States, 7 Provinces
 Density: 58 in CA, 26 in NY, 14 in ON
Projected New Units (12 Months): 20
Qualifications: 5, 5, 4, 3, 3, 5
Registered: AB
FINANCIAL/TERMS:
Cash Investment: $48K
Total Investment: $100-142.9K
Minimum Net Worth: $100K
Fees: Franchise - $50K
 Royalty - 10% + $360; Ad. - 2%/$250
Earnings Claim Statement: No
Term of Contract (Years): 10/10
Avg. # Of Employees: Varies
Passive Ownership: Discouraged
Encourage Conversions: No
Area Develop. Agreements: Yes/1.5

Sub-Franchising Contracts: Yes
Expand In Territory: Yes
Space Needs: 1,000 SF; SF, SC
SUPPORT & TRAINING PROVIDED:
Financial Assistance Provided: No
Site Selection Assistance: Yes
Lease Negotiation Assistance: Yes
Co-Operative Advertising: Yes
Franchisee Assoc./Member: NR
Size Of Corporate Staff: 1
On-Going Support: B,C,D,e,G,H,I
Training: 2 Weeks Los Angeles, CA
SPECIFIC EXPANSION PLANS:
US: No
Canada: All Canada
Overseas: All Countries

<< >>

GYMBOREE
700 Airport Blvd., # 200
Burlingame, CA 94010-1912
Tel: (800) 520-PLAY
Fax: (650) 696-7452
E-Mail: karol_caballero@gymboree.com
Web Site: www.gymboree.com
Ms. Karol Caballero, Franchise
  Development Asst.

GYMBOREE, the world's largest development play and music program, offers weekly classes to parents and their children, ages newborn through 4 years, on custom-designed equipment. The program is based on sensory integration theory, positive parenting, child development principles and the importance of play. GYMBOREE has recently rolled out a new Music Program designed to support your child's development through an array of enriching experiences and Fun!

BACKGROUND: IFA MEMBER
Established: 1976; 1st Franchised: 1978
Franchised Units: 408
Company-Owned Units 27
Total Units: 435
Dist.: US-280; CAN-22; O'seas-100
  North America: 40 States, 3 Provinces
  Density: 52 in CA, 30 in NY, 28 in NJ
Projected New Units (12 Months): 25
Qualifications: 4, 4, 3, 3, 2, 4
Registered: CA,FL,HI,IL,IN,MD,MI,MN,
  NY,OR,RI,SD,VA,WA,WI,DC,AB
FINANCIAL/TERMS:
Cash Investment: $35-60K

Total Investment: $80-150K
Minimum Net Worth: $150K
Fees: Franchise - $35K
  Royalty - 6%; Ad. - 2.25%
Earnings Claim Statement: No
Term of Contract (Years): 10/10
Avg. # Of Employees: 1 FT, 3 PT
Passive Ownership: Not Allowed
Encourage Conversions: No
Area Develop. Agreements: No
Sub-Franchising Contracts: No
Expand In Territory: Yes
Space Needs: 1,800 SF; SF, SC, RM
SUPPORT & TRAINING PROVIDED:
Financial Assistance Provided: No
Site Selection Assistance: Yes
Lease Negotiation Assistance: Yes
Co-Operative Advertising: Yes
Franchisee Assoc./Member: Yes
Size Of Corporate Staff: 19
On-Going Support: B,D,G,h,I
Training: 6 Days Headquarters.
SPECIFIC EXPANSION PLANS:
US: All United States
Canada: All Canada
Overseas: Asia, Europe

<< >>

The Fitness Program that comes to Children

GYMSTERS
6135 E. Danbury Rd.
Scottsdale, AZ 85254-6447
Tel: (480) 315-0351
Fax: (480) 315-0311
E-Mail: gymsters.inc@home.com
Ms. Lonnie Coppock, President

The GYMSTERS® system brings physical education to children from two to twelve by providing the equipment, the staff and the program. Experts in education and health agree that learning through physical movement is the primary way that children develop. The children's fitness industry offers a vast and huge market place whose potential has become even greater, due to budget cuts, and GYMSTERS® is the answer.

BACKGROUND:
Established: 1980; 1st Franchised: 1988
Franchised Units: 7
Company-Owned Units 1
Total Units: 8
Dist.: US-8; CAN-0; O'seas-0
  North America: 3 States

Density: 6 in CA, 1 in OH, 1 in AZ
Projected New Units (12 Months): 6
Qualifications: 4, 3, 5, 5, 5, 5
Registered: All States
FINANCIAL/TERMS:
Cash Investment: $19.8-24.5K
Total Investment: $19.8-24.5K
Minimum Net Worth: $NR
Fees: Franchise - $12K
  Royalty - 7%; Ad. - 3%
Earnings Claim Statement: Yes
Term of Contract (Years): 5/5
Avg. # Of Employees: 1 PT
Passive Ownership: Discouraged
Encourage Conversions: N/A
Area Develop. Agreements: No
Sub-Franchising Contracts: No
Expand In Territory: NR
Space Needs: NR SF; N/A
SUPPORT & TRAINING PROVIDED:
Financial Assistance Provided: No
Site Selection Assistance: Yes
Lease Negotiation Assistance: N/A
Co-Operative Advertising: N/A
Franchisee Assoc./Member: No
Size Of Corporate Staff: 1
On-Going Support: b,C,D,f,G,h,I
Training: Initially 5 Days in Scottsdale,
  AZ.
SPECIFIC EXPANSION PLANS:
US: All United States
Canada: No
Overseas: No

<< >>

HEAD OVER HEELS
2106 Cahaba Rd.
Birmingham, AL 35223
Tel: (800) 850-3547 (205) 879-6305
Fax: (205) 877-8377
Ms. Renee O'Neal, President

Gymnastics/motor skill development for children. HEAD OVER HEELS provides mobile gymnastics instruction to children in public/private schools, daycares, health clubs, community centers and anywhere there are children! We also provide fun gymnastics birthday parties and sell clothing and gymnastics equipment too!

BACKGROUND:
Established: 1990; 1st Franchised: 1993
Franchised Units: 7
Company-Owned Units 2
Total Units: 9
Dist.: US-9; CAN-0; O'seas-0
  North America: 5 States
  Density: 2 in AL, 2 in TN

Projected New Units (12 Months):   0
Qualifications: 2, 5, 3, 5, 2, 5
Registered: NR

FINANCIAL/TERMS:
Cash Investment: $17.5K
Total Investment: $20-30K
Minimum Net Worth: $20K Min.
Fees: Franchise - $12.5K
  Royalty - 8%;   Ad. - 0%
Earnings Claim Statement: No
Term of Contract (Years):   20/10
Avg. # Of Employees: 1 FT, 5 PT
Passive Ownership: Allowed
Encourage Conversions: No
Area Develop. Agreements: Yes
Sub-Franchising Contracts: Yes
Expand In Territory: Yes
Space Needs: NR SF; HB

SUPPORT & TRAINING PROVIDED:
Financial Assistance Provided: Yes(D)
Site Selection Assistance: N/A
Lease Negotiation Assistance: N/A
Co-Operative Advertising: No
Franchisee Assoc./Member: No
Size Of Corporate Staff: 5
On-Going Support: a,B,C,D,E,f,G,h,I
Training: 1 Week Birmingham, AL; 1 Week
  On-Site.

SPECIFIC EXPANSION PLANS:
US: All United States
Canada: BC
Overseas: All Countries

◂◂ ▸▸

HIGH TOUCH-HIGH TECH
12352 Wiles Rd.
Coral Springs, FL 33076
Tel: (800) 444-4968 (954) 755-2900
Fax: (954) 755-1242
E-Mail: info@hightouch-hightech.com
Web Site: www.hightouch-hightech.com
Mr. Daniel Shaw, President/CEO

Provides hands-on science experiences that
go right into the classroom. We provide
in-school field trips. We also provide fun,
science-oriented birthday parties.

BACKGROUND:
Established: 1992;   1st Franchised: 1994
Franchised Units: 26
Company-Owned Units   2
Total Units: 28
Dist.:   US-21; CAN-0; O'seas-1
  North America: 12 States
  Density: 5 in FL, 2 in NJ, 2 in IL
Projected New Units (12 Months): 8-10
Qualifications: 5, 5, 3, 5, 3, 3
Registered: CA,FL,IL,NY,VA,WI

FINANCIAL/TERMS:
Cash Investment: $5-8K
Total Investment: $28-42K
Minimum Net Worth: $NR
Fees: Franchise - $20-35K
  Royalty - 7%;   Ad. - 0%
Earnings Claim Statement: Yes
Term of Contract (Years):   10/10
Avg. # Of Employees: 2-3 PT
Passive Ownership: NR
Encourage Conversions: N/A
Area Develop. Agreements: No
Sub-Franchising Contracts: Yes
Expand In Territory: Yes
Space Needs: NR SF; HB

SUPPORT & TRAINING PROVIDED:
Financial Assistance Provided: Yes(D)
Site Selection Assistance: Yes
Lease Negotiation Assistance: N/A
Co-Operative Advertising: N/A
Franchisee Assoc./Member: No
Size Of Corporate Staff: 6
On-Going Support: D,G,H,I
Training: 5   Full   Days   National
  Programming Offices.

SPECIFIC EXPANSION PLANS:
US: All United States, Global
Canada: All Canada
Overseas: Europe, Asia, Pacific Region

◂◂ ▸▸

J. W. TUMBLES, A CHILDREN'S GYM
12750 Carmel Country Rd., # 102
San Diego, CA 92130
Tel: (800) 886-2532 (858) 481-5576
Fax: (858) 756-7719
Web Site: www.jwtumbles.com
Mr. Jeff Woods, President

A gym just for children, ages 4 months to 9
years, with a 2,000 sq. ft. space of colorful
equipment. We have instructional class
formats designed to teach young children
basic physical education fundamentals, all
in a non-competitive environment where
building self-esteem and having fun are
#1! Birthday parties, summer and winter
camps, and mobile programs available.

BACKGROUND:
Established: 1985;   1st Franchised: 1993
Franchised Units: 4
Company-Owned Units   2
Total Units: 6
Dist.:   US-5; CAN-0; O'seas-1
  North America: NR
  Density: NR
Projected New Units (12 Months):   4
Qualifications: 5, 3, 2, 3, 5, 5
Registered: CA,OR

FINANCIAL/TERMS:
Cash Investment: $85-110K
Total Investment: $85-110K
Minimum Net Worth: $200K
Fees: Franchise - $25K
  Royalty - $2.4K/Yr.;   Ad. - 0%
Earnings Claim Statement: No
Term of Contract (Years):   5/5
Avg. # Of Employees: 1 FT, 2 PT
Passive Ownership: Discouraged
Encourage Conversions: N/A
Area Develop. Agreements: No
Sub-Franchising Contracts: No
Expand In Territory: Yes
Space Needs: 2,000 SF; SC

SUPPORT & TRAINING PROVIDED:
Financial Assistance Provided: No
Site Selection Assistance: Yes
Lease Negotiation Assistance: Yes
Co-Operative Advertising: Yes
Franchisee Assoc./Member: No
Size Of Corporate Staff: 8
On-Going Support: E,G,H,I
Training: 2-4 Weeks San Diego, CA.

SPECIFIC EXPANSION PLANS:
US: All United States
Canada: All Canada
Overseas: All Countries

◂◂ ▸▸

JACADI
72 Parkway E.
Mount Vernon, NY 10552
Tel: (914) 667-2183
Fax: (914) 665-0416
E-Mail: jacadi@juno.com
Web Site: www.jacadiusa.com

Mr. Bruce Pettibone, Chief Operations Officer

JACADI is a childrenswear retail company whose collections include clothing, shoes, accessories, furniture and nursery items in newborn through size 12 for both boys and girls. The merchandise is a European-style which adapts the latest trends to classic design and allows the customer to mix and match the various styles and color groups. JACADI also strives to give excellent customer service and the highest price/quality ratio.

BACKGROUND: IFA MEMBER
Established: 1988; 1st Franchised: 1992
Franchised Units: 21
Company-Owned Units 3
Total Units: 24
Dist.: US-22; CAN-2; O'seas-0
 North America: 10 States, 1 Province
 Density: 8 in CA, 4 in NY, 3 in FL
Projected New Units (12 Months): 8
Qualifications: 5, 3, 1, 2, 4, 5
Registered: CA,FL,IL,NY
FINANCIAL/TERMS:
Cash Investment: $120-250K
Total Investment: $183-313K
Minimum Net Worth: $750K Liquid
Fees: Franchise - $20K
 Royalty - 4%; Ad. - 1%
Earnings Claim Statement: No
Term of Contract (Years): 7/7
Avg. # Of Employees: 2-3 FT, 2-3 PT
Passive Ownership: Not Allowed
Encourage Conversions: N/A
Area Develop. Agreements: Yes/7
Sub-Franchising Contracts: No
Expand In Territory: Yes
Space Needs: 1,100 SF; FS, SF, RM
SUPPORT & TRAINING PROVIDED:
Financial Assistance Provided: Yes(I)
Site Selection Assistance: Yes
Lease Negotiation Assistance: Yes
Co-Operative Advertising: No
Franchisee Assoc./Member: No
Size Of Corporate Staff: 4
On-Going Support: B,C,d,E,f,G,h
Training: 3-5 Days in Subsidiary Shop; 3 Days Franchisee's Shop before Opening; On-Going Corporate.
SPECIFIC EXPANSION PLANS:
US: All United States
Canada: All Canada
Overseas: All Countries

≪ ≫

KID to KID
RECYCLED CHILDREN'S GOODS

KID TO KID
406 W. South Jordan Pkwy., # 160
South Jordan, UT 84095
Tel: (888) KID-2-KID (801) 553-8799
Fax: (801) 553-8793
E-Mail: k2kcorp@aol.com
Web Site: www.kidtokid.com
Mr. Brent Sloan, President

KID TO KID is an up-scale children's resale store based on the premise that 'kids grow faster than paychecks.' Parents buy and sell better-quality used children's clothing, toys, equipment and accessories. If you enjoy working with people and want to increase your financial security as you grow your own business, call KID TO KID today!

BACKGROUND: IFA MEMBER
Established: 1992; 1st Franchised: 1994
Franchised Units: 35
Company-Owned Units 0
Total Units: 35
Dist.: US-35; CAN-0; O'seas-0
 North America: 13 States, Puerto Rico
 Density: 13 in UT, 5 in TX, 3 in PA
Projected New Units (12 Months): 10
Qualifications: 4, 3, 1, 2, 4, 5
Registered: All States
FINANCIAL/TERMS:
Cash Investment: $25-35K
Total Investment: $88-116K
Minimum Net Worth: $150K
Fees: Franchise - $20K
 Royalty - 4.75%; Ad. - 0.5%
Earnings Claim Statement: Yes
Term of Contract (Years): 10/5
Avg. # Of Employees: 3 FT, 2 PT
Passive Ownership: Discouraged
Encourage Conversions: Yes
Area Develop. Agreements: Yes/Varies
Sub-Franchising Contracts: No
Expand In Territory: No
Space Needs: 2,400 SF; FS, SF, SC
SUPPORT & TRAINING PROVIDED:
Financial Assistance Provided: No
Site Selection Assistance: Yes
Lease Negotiation Assistance: Yes
Co-Operative Advertising: Yes
Franchisee Assoc./Member: No
Size Of Corporate Staff: 4
On-Going Support: B,C,d,E,f,G,H
Training: 10 Days Salt Lake City, UT.
SPECIFIC EXPANSION PLANS:
US: All United States

Canada: All Canada
Overseas: No

≪ ≫

KIDDIE ACADEMY INTERNATIONAL
108 Wheel Rd.
Bel Air, MD 21015
Tel: (800) 5-KIDDIE (410) 515-0788
Fax: (410) 569-2729
Web Site: www.kiddieacademy.com
Ms. Kathy Barry, Franchise Development

We offer comprehensive training and support without additional cost. KIDDIE ACADEMY's step-by-step program assists with staff recruitment, training, accounting support, site selection, marketing, advertising and curriculum. A true turn-key opportunity that provides on-going support so you can focus on running a successful business.

BACKGROUND: IFA MEMBER
Established: 1981; 1st Franchised: 1992
Franchised Units: 40
Company-Owned Units 11
Total Units: 51
Dist.: US-51; CAN-0; O'seas-0
 North America: 10 States
 Density: 15 in MD, 5 in NJ, 4 in IL
Projected New Units (12 Months): 100
Qualifications: 4, 4, 2, 3, 2, 4
Registered: CA,FL,IL,IN,MD,MI,MN, NY,OR,RI,VA,WI,DC
FINANCIAL/TERMS:
Cash Investment: $60K
Total Investment: $180-260K
Minimum Net Worth: $250K
Fees: Franchise - $40K
 Royalty - 7%; Ad. - 0%
Earnings Claim Statement: No
Term of Contract (Years): 10/5
Avg. # Of Employees: 10-20 FT, 2 PT
Passive Ownership: Discouraged
Encourage Conversions: No
Area Develop. Agreements: Yes/10
Sub-Franchising Contracts: No
Expand In Territory: Yes
Space Needs: 6,500-12,000 SF; FS, SF, SC
SUPPORT & TRAINING PROVIDED:
Financial Assistance Provided: Yes(I)
Site Selection Assistance: Yes
Lease Negotiation Assistance: Yes
Co-Operative Advertising: Yes
Franchisee Assoc./Member: No
Size Of Corporate Staff: 30
On-Going Support: a,B,C,D,E,G,I

Training: 2 Weeks Owner Train., Corp. HQ; 1 Wk. Director Train., Corp. HQ; 3-5 Day Staff Training.
SPECIFIC EXPANSION PLANS:
US: All United States
Canada: No
Overseas: No

≪ ≫

KIDDIE KOBBLER

68 Robertson Rd., # 106
Nepean, ON K2H 8P5 CANADA
Tel: (800) 561-9762 (613) 820-0505
Fax: (613) 820-8250
E-Mail: kiddiekobblerltd@sprint.ca
Web Site: www.kiddiekobbler.com
Mr. Fred Norman, President

Children's shoe stores, located in major shopping malls and strip centers. The extensive marketing program is designed to develop new and repeat business through intensive customer service, selection and value.

BACKGROUND:
Established: 1951;   1st Franchised: 1968
Franchised Units: 29
Company-Owned Units   0
Total Units: 29
Dist.:   US-0; CAN-31; O'seas-0
  North America: 6 Provinces
  Density: 25 in ON, 2 in NS, 2 in PQ
Projected New Units (12 Months):   2
Qualifications: 5, 3, 3, 3, 5, 5
Registered: NR
FINANCIAL/TERMS:
Cash Investment: $50K
Total Investment: $100K
Minimum Net Worth: $150K
Fees: Franchise - $25K
  Royalty - 4%;   Ad. - 1%
Earnings Claim Statement: No
Term of Contract (Years):   10/5/5
Avg. # Of Employees: 2 FT, 2 PT
Passive Ownership: Not Allowed
Encourage Conversions: Yes
Area Develop. Agreements: Yes
Sub-Franchising Contracts: Yes
Expand In Territory: Yes
Space Needs: 1,000-1,200 SF; SC, RM, SF
SUPPORT & TRAINING PROVIDED:
Financial Assistance Provided: N/A
Site Selection Assistance: Yes
Lease Negotiation Assistance: Yes
Co-Operative Advertising: Yes
Franchisee Assoc./Member: Yes
Size Of Corporate Staff: 6
On-Going Support: b,C,D,E,f,G,H,I

Training: 4 Weeks On-Site; 6 Weeks Supervised Home Study.
SPECIFIC EXPANSION PLANS:
US: Area & Master Franchise Terr
Canada: All Canada
Overseas: No

≪ ≫

KINDERDANCE INTERNATIONAL

268 N. Babcock St.
Melbourne, FL 32935
Tel: (800) 554-2334 (321) 242-0590
Fax: (321) 254-3388
E-Mail: kindercorp@kinderdance.net
Web Site: www.kinderdance.net
Mr. Jerry M. Perch, VP Sales & Marketing

KINDERDANCE franchisees are trained to teach 4 developmentally-unique dance and motor development programs: KINDERDANCE, KINDERGYM, KINDERTOTS and KINDERCOMBO, which are designed for boys and girls ages 2-8. They learn the basics of ballet, tap, gymnastics and creative dance, as well as learning numbers, colors, shapes and words. No studio or dance experience required. Franchisee teaches at child care center sites. Area development agreements available.

BACKGROUND: IFA MEMBER
Established: 1979;   1st Franchised: 1985
Franchised Units: 65
Company-Owned Units   1
Total Units: 66
Dist.:   US-62; CAN-3; O'seas-1
  North America: 29 States, 3 Provinces
  Density: 6 in CA, 6 in FL, 5 in TX
Projected New Units (12 Months):   12
Qualifications: 2, 2, 1, 2, 2, 5
Registered: CA,FL,HI,IL,MD,MI,MN,
  NY,OR,VA,WA,DC,AB
FINANCIAL/TERMS:
Cash Investment: $6.4-25.6K
Total Investment: $9-25.6K
Minimum Net Worth: $N/A
Fees: Franchise - $6.5-20K
  Royalty - 6-15%;   Ad. - 3%
Earnings Claim Statement: No
Term of Contract (Years):   10/10

Avg. # Of Employees: 3 FT, 1 PT
Passive Ownership: Discouraged
Encourage Conversions: Yes
Area Develop. Agreements: Yes/10
Sub-Franchising Contracts: Yes
Expand In Territory: Yes
Space Needs: NR SF; NR
SUPPORT & TRAINING PROVIDED:
Financial Assistance Provided: Yes(D)
Site Selection Assistance: N/A
Lease Negotiation Assistance: N/A
Co-Operative Advertising: Yes
Franchisee Assoc./Member: Yes/Yes
Size Of Corporate Staff: 7
On-Going Support: A,B,C,D,E,F,G,H,I
Training: 6 Days in Melbourne, FL; 1 Day On-Site.
SPECIFIC EXPANSION PLANS:
US: All United States
Canada: All Canada
Overseas: All Countries

≪ ≫

LITTLE GYM, THE

8160 N. Hayden Rd., # J-112
Scottsdale, AZ 85258
Tel: (888) 228-2878 (480) 948-2878
Fax: (480) 948-2765
E-Mail: sales@thelittlegymintl.com
Web Site: www.thelittlegymintl.com
Mr. Ron Cordova, Dir. Franchise Dev.

THE LITTLE GYM child development centers are for children 4 months to 12 years, and offer a unique, integrated approach to child development. THE LITTLE GYM'S highly-motivational and individualized programs are curriculum-based and provide physical, social and intellectual development. Classes develop basic motor skills, build self-esteem and encourage risk-taking through gymnastics, karate and sports skills development.

BACKGROUND:
Established: 1992;   1st Franchised: 1992
Franchised Units: 95
Company-Owned Units   5
Total Units: 100
Dist.:   US-95; CAN-0; O'seas-5
  North America: 27 States
  Density: 11 in TX, 9 in NY, 6 in NC
Projected New Units (12 Months):   24
Qualifications: 5, 5, 2, 3, 5, 5
Registered: CA,FL,IL,IN,MD,MI,
  MN,NY,OR,WA
FINANCIAL/TERMS:
Cash Investment: $51.2K
Total Investment: $125-160K

Minimum Net Worth:	$160K
Fees: Franchise -	$37.5K
Royalty - 8%;	Ad. - 1%
Earnings Claim Statement:	No
Term of Contract (Years):	10/10
Avg. # Of Employees:	2 FT, 2-3 PT
Passive Ownership:	Discouraged
Encourage Conversions:	Yes
Area Develop. Agreements:	Yes/10
Sub-Franchising Contracts:	No
Expand In Territory:	No
Space Needs: 3,500 SF; SC, Destination	

SUPPORT & TRAINING PROVIDED:

Financial Assistance Provided:	Yes(I)
Site Selection Assistance:	Yes
Lease Negotiation Assistance:	Yes
Co-Operative Advertising:	No
Franchisee Assoc./Member:	No
Size Of Corporate Staff:	18
On-Going Support:	C,D,G,H,I
Training: 1 Week Raynham, MA; 1 Week Bellevue, WA.	

SPECIFIC EXPANSION PLANS:

US:	All United States
Canada:	All Canada
Overseas:	All Countries

≪ ≫

MY GYM CHILDREN'S FITNESS CENTER
15300 Ventura Blvd., # 307A
Sherman Oaks, CA 91403
Tel: (800) 469-4967 (818) 907-6966
Fax: (818) 907-0735
E-Mail: mygym@aol.com
Web Site: www.my-gym.com
Mr. Gene Barr, Dir. of Franchise Dev.

MY GYM CHILDREN'S FITNESS CENTER's structured, age-appropriate weekly classes incorporates music, dance, relays, games, special rides, gymnastics, sports and other original activities. MY GYM kids have so much fun as they gain strength, balance, gross motor skills, agility, flexibility and social skills. Our programs' biggest benefit is the building of confidence and self esteem. We help design our state-of-the-art facility and assist in every aspect of getting you started.

BACKGROUND:

Established: 1983; 1st Franchised: 1994	
Franchised Units:	32
Company-Owned Units	8
Total Units:	40
Dist.:	US-40; CAN-0; O'seas-0
North America:	6 States
Density:	15 in CA, 14 in FL, 2 in GA

Projected New Units (12 Months):	40
Qualifications:	2, 3, 3, 3, 4, 5
Registered: CA,FL,IL,IN,MD,MI,MN,NY, OR,VA,WA,WI,DC	

FINANCIAL/TERMS:

Cash Investment:	$10-42K
Total Investment:	$110-150K
Minimum Net Worth:	$N/A
Fees: Franchise -	$32.5K
Royalty - 6%;	Ad. - 1%
Earnings Claim Statement:	No
Term of Contract (Years):	12/12
Avg. # Of Employees:	3 FT, 4 PT
Passive Ownership:	Discouraged
Encourage Conversions:	N/A
Area Develop. Agreements:	Yes/12
Sub-Franchising Contracts:	No
Expand In Territory:	Yes
Space Needs: 2,800 SF; SF, SC	

SUPPORT & TRAINING PROVIDED:

Financial Assistance Provided:	Yes(I)
Site Selection Assistance:	Yes
Lease Negotiation Assistance:	Yes
Co-Operative Advertising:	Yes
Franchisee Assoc./Member:	No
Size Of Corporate Staff:	15
On-Going Support:	B,C,D,E,F,I
Training: 19 Days Corporate Headquarters in Los Angeles, CA; Regional Pre-and Post-training	

SPECIFIC EXPANSION PLANS:

US:	All United States
Canada:	All Canada
Overseas:	No

≪ ≫

ONCE UPON A CHILD
4200 Dahlberg Dr.
Minneapolis, MN 55422-4837
Tel: (800) 453-7750 (612) 520-8500
Fax: (612) 520-8501
Web Site: www.ouac.com
Mr. John Lessler, Franchising Department

ONCE UPON A CHILD is an ultra high-value retail store that buys and sells new and used brand-name children's apparel, furniture, equipment and toys.

BACKGROUND: IFA MEMBER

Established: 1985; 1st Franchised: 1993	
Franchised Units:	244
Company-Owned Units	4
Total Units:	248
Dist.:	US-204; CAN-0; O'seas-0
North America:	NR
Density:	15 in OH
Projected New Units (12 Months):	140
Registered: All States	

FINANCIAL/TERMS:

Cash Investment:	$30-50K
Total Investment:	$85-145K
Minimum Net Worth:	$NR
Fees: Franchise -	$20K
Royalty - 5%;	Ad. - $500/Yr.
Earnings Claim Statement:	Yes
Term of Contract (Years):	10/10
Avg. # Of Employees:	3 FT, 2 PT
Passive Ownership:	Discouraged
Encourage Conversions:	Yes
Area Develop. Agreements:	No
Sub-Franchising Contracts:	No
Expand In Territory:	Yes
Space Needs: 2,000-3,000 SF; FS, SC	

SUPPORT & TRAINING PROVIDED:

Financial Assistance Provided:	Yes(I)
Site Selection Assistance:	Yes
Lease Negotiation Assistance:	Yes
Co-Operative Advertising:	Yes
Franchisee Assoc./Member:	NR
Size Of Corporate Staff:	200
On-Going Support:	B,C,D,E,F,G,H,I
Training: 12 Days Minneapolis, MN.	

SPECIFIC EXPANSION PLANS:

US:	All United States
Canada:	All Canada
Overseas:	No

≪ ≫

PEE WEE WORKOUT
34976 Aspenwood Ln.
Willoughby, OH 44094
Tel: (440) 946-7888
Fax: (440) 946-7888
E-Mail: PeeWeeWork@aol.com
Web Site: www.peeweeworkout.com
Ms. Margaret J. Carr, President

Mission Statement: to reach and educate children about the benefits of healthy living. Program teaches healthy living to preschoolers and grade school children. Classes consist of movement to original music that covers components of fitness and concludes with educational lessons. Trained instructors have weekly visits to day schools and recreation departments.

BACKGROUND:

Established: 1986; 1st Franchised: 1987	
Franchised Units:	38
Company-Owned Units	1
Total Units:	39
Dist.:	US-37; CAN-1; O'seas-1

North America:	18 States
Density:	NR
Projected New Units (12 Months):	5
Qualifications:	2, 4, 5, 3, 5, 5
Registered: NR	

FINANCIAL/TERMS:

Cash Investment:	$NR
Total Investment:	$2-2.3K
Minimum Net Worth:	$N/A
Fees: Franchise -	$1.5K
Royalty - 10%;	Ad. - 0%
Earnings Claim Statement:	Yes
Term of Contract (Years):	5/5
Avg. # Of Employees:	1 PT
Passive Ownership:	Discouraged
Encourage Conversions:	N/A
Area Develop. Agreements:	No
Sub-Franchising Contracts:	Yes
Expand In Territory:	Yes
Space Needs: NR SF; HB	

SUPPORT & TRAINING PROVIDED:

Financial Assistance Provided:	No
Site Selection Assistance:	No
Lease Negotiation Assistance:	N/A
Co-Operative Advertising:	No
Franchisee Assoc./Member:	No
Size Of Corporate Staff:	NR
On-Going Support:	B,G,I
Training: Video Based.	

SPECIFIC EXPANSION PLANS:

US:	All United States
Canada:	All Canada
Overseas:	All Countries

<< >>

PRE-FIT

10926 S. Western Ave.
Chicago, IL 60643
Tel: (773) 233-7771
Fax: (773) 233-7121
E-Mail: prefit@ameritech.net
Web Site: www.pre-fit.com
Ms. Latrice Lee, Franchise Director

PRE-FIT, INC offers America's premier sports, exercise and health systems for children. These systems include: PRE-FIT, a mobile preschool fitness program; FITNESS IS ELEMENTARY, our mobile elementary physical education program; and CHEC, the Children's Health and Executive Club. All of these programs are offered through our success-oriented franchise system that provides marketing, administrative and instructional training, an exclusive territory, and continuous support.

BACKGROUND:

Established: 1987;	1st Franchised: 1992
Franchised Units:	40
Company-Owned Units	1
Total Units:	41
Dist.:	US-40; CAN-1; O'seas-0
North America:	13 States
Density:	19 in IL, 6 in PA, 2 in MI
Projected New Units (12 Months):	10
Qualifications:	4, 4, 4, 3, 3, 5
Registered:	CA,FL,IL,MD,MI,MN, VA,WA

FINANCIAL/TERMS:

Cash Investment:	$10-41K
Total Investment:	$10-118.2K
Minimum Net Worth:	$25K
Fees: Franchise -	$8.5-24.5K
Royalty - 8-10%;	Ad. - 2%
Earnings Claim Statement:	No
Term of Contract (Years):	10/10
Avg. # Of Employees:	1-2 FT, 2-5 PT
Passive Ownership:	Discouraged
Encourage Conversions:	N/A
Area Develop. Agreements:	No
Sub-Franchising Contracts:	No
Expand In Territory:	Yes
Space Needs: 2,000-4,000 SF; SC, RM, HB	

SUPPORT & TRAINING PROVIDED:

Financial Assistance Provided:	Yes(I)
Site Selection Assistance:	Yes
Lease Negotiation Assistance:	Yes
Co-Operative Advertising:	No
Franchisee Assoc./Member:	No
Size Of Corporate Staff:	6
On-Going Support:	D,E,G,h,I
Training: Chicago, IL.	

SPECIFIC EXPANSION PLANS:

US:	All United States
Canada:	All Canada
Overseas:	All Countries

<< >>

PRIMROSE SCHOOLS

199 S. Erwin St.
Cartersville, GA 30120
Tel: (800) 745-0677 (770) 606-9600
Fax: (770) 606-0020
E-Mail: psfcfranchise@mindspring.com
Web Site:
www.primroseschoolsfranchise.com
Mr. Ray Orgera, VP Franchise Development

Educational child-care franchise, offering a traditional pre-school curriculum and programs while also providing quality childcare services. Site selection assistance, extensive training, operations manuals, building plans, marketing plans and on-going support.

BACKGROUND: IFA MEMBER

Established: 1982;	1st Franchised: 1989
Franchised Units:	117
Company-Owned Units	1
Total Units:	118
Dist.:	US-118; CAN-0; O'seas-0
North America:	14 States
Density: 37 in GA, 37 in TX, 10 in NC	
Projected New Units (12 Months):	22
Qualifications:	5, 5, 1, 4, 5, 5
Registered: FL,MN,WA	

FINANCIAL/TERMS:

Cash Investment:	$150-200K
Total Investment:	$1.3-2MM
Minimum Net Worth:	$250K
Fees: Franchise -	$50K
Royalty - 7%;	Ad. - 1%
Earnings Claim Statement:	Yes
Term of Contract (Years):	11/10/10
Avg. # Of Employees:	25 FT, 5 PT
Passive Ownership:	Not Allowed
Encourage Conversions:	N/A
Area Develop. Agreements:	No
Sub-Franchising Contracts:	No
Expand In Territory:	No
Space Needs: 8,500 SF; FS	

SUPPORT & TRAINING PROVIDED:

Financial Assistance Provided:	Yes(I)
Site Selection Assistance:	Yes
Lease Negotiation Assistance:	Yes
Co-Operative Advertising:	Yes
Franchisee Assoc./Member:	Yes/Yes
Size Of Corporate Staff:	23
On-Going Support:	A,C,D,E,f,G,h,I

Training: 1 Week Home Office; 1 Week at Existing School; 1 Week at Franchisee's New School.

SPECIFIC EXPANSION PLANS:

US:	SW,SE,TX,OH,CO
Canada:	No
Overseas:	No

SAFE-T-CHILD

203 Barsana Ave.
Austin, TX 78737
Tel: (512) 288-2882
Fax: (512) 288-2898
E-Mail: dennis@yellodyno.com
Web Site: www.safe-t-child.com
Mr. Dennis Wagner, Vice President

Experience the joy of empowering children to stay safe in today's exciting but dangerous world. You'll offer an important array of I. D. and entertainment-driven educational safety products that has families and experts raving. Personal security is booming. Home-based, proven, part-time/full-time, training and support. From $12,500.

BACKGROUND:

Established: 1986;	1st Franchised: 1992
Franchised Units:	71
Company-Owned Units	1
Total Units:	72
Dist.:	US-67; CAN-4; O'seas-1
North America:	NR
Density:	8 in CA, 6 in TX, 4 in NY
Projected New Units (12 Months):	36
Qualifications:	2, 3, 2, 2, 3, 5
Registered: CA,FL,HI,MI,MN,NY,OR	

FINANCIAL/TERMS:

Cash Investment:	$5-10K
Total Investment:	$15-30K
Minimum Net Worth:	$N/A
Fees: Franchise -	$12.5K
Royalty - 6%;	Ad. - 0%
Earnings Claim Statement:	No
Term of Contract (Years):	10/20
Avg. # Of Employees:	2 FT, 2 PT
Passive Ownership:	Allowed
Encourage Conversions:	N/A
Area Develop. Agreements:	Yes
Sub-Franchising Contracts:	No
Expand In Territory:	No
Space Needs: NR SF; N/A	

SUPPORT & TRAINING PROVIDED:

Financial Assistance Provided:	No
Site Selection Assistance:	N/A
Lease Negotiation Assistance:	N/A
Co-Operative Advertising:	N/A

Franchisee Assoc./Member:	Pending
Size Of Corporate Staff:	9
On-Going Support:	C,d,g,h
Training: NR	

SPECIFIC EXPANSION PLANS:

US:	All United States
Canada:	All Canada
Overseas:	New Zealand, England, Europe, Latin America, Australia

STORK NEWS OF AMERICA

1305 Hope Mills Rd., # A
Fayetteville, NC 28304
Tel: (800) 633-6395 (910) 426-1357
Fax: (910) 426-2473
E-Mail: no2stork@netquick.net
Web Site: www.storknewsusa.com
Mr. John M. Young, VP Franchise Development

The number one and the original newborn yard display business. New mothers, fathers, grandmothers and grandfathers, or any family relations want to tell the world about their new arrival. Rated in many publications as the best buy in home-operated businesses. Almost all operators are Mom's and some Mr. Mom's that don't want to have to ship their kids to day care and then go to work. With a STORK NEWS franchise, kids can go along to work, too.

BACKGROUND:

Established: 1983;	1st Franchised: 1986
Franchised Units:	128
Company-Owned Units	1
Total Units:	129
Dist.:	US-124; CAN-2; O'seas-3
North America:	23 States, 1 Province
Density:	14 in VA, 12 in FL, 11 in CA
Projected New Units (12 Months):	12
Qualifications:	1, 4, 1, 1, 3, 5
Registered:	CA,FL,HI,IL,MD,MI, MN,NY,VA,WA

FINANCIAL/TERMS:

Cash Investment:	$8-20K
Total Investment:	$7-12K
Minimum Net Worth:	$N/A
Fees: Franchise -	$7-10K
Royalty - $0.50-1K;	Ad. - N/A
Earnings Claim Statement:	No
Term of Contract (Years):	Perpetual
Avg. # Of Employees:	1 FT
Passive Ownership:	Allowed
Encourage Conversions:	N/A
Area Develop. Agreements:	No

Sub-Franchising Contracts:	No
Expand In Territory:	Yes
Space Needs: N/A SF; HB	

SUPPORT & TRAINING PROVIDED:

Financial Assistance Provided:	Yes(D)
Site Selection Assistance:	No
Lease Negotiation Assistance:	No
Co-Operative Advertising:	No
Franchisee Assoc./Member:	No
Size Of Corporate Staff:	0
On-Going Support:	D,F,G,I
Training: Manual.	

SPECIFIC EXPANSION PLANS:

US:	All United States
Canada:	All Canada
Overseas:	No

STRETCH-N-GROW INTERNATIONAL

3912 Tumbil Ln., P.O. Box 261397
Plano, TX 75023
Tel: (800) 348-0166 (972) 519-1635
Fax: (972) 612-5819
Web Site: www.Stretch-N-Grow.com
Mr. Robert E. Manly, Chief Executive Officer

STRETCH-N-GROW is a comprehensive mobile fitness program for children ages 2 1/2 to 8. It is taught primarily in child care facilities. We provide a corporate marketing system and a curriculum package which covers health-related issues and exercise that is age-appropriate, but adaptable to the age ranges above. The investment and time demands are minimal, the rewards, both financial and personal, immense.

BACKGROUND:

Established: 1992;	1st Franchised: 1994
Franchised Units:	88
Company-Owned Units	0
Total Units:	88
Dist.:	US-67; CAN-1; O'seas-0
North America:	24 States, 1 Province
Density:	10 in TX, 5 in NY, 5 in PA
Projected New Units (12 Months):	12
Qualifications:	3, 3, 4, 4, , 5
Registered: CA,FL,NY	

FINANCIAL/TERMS:

Cash Investment:	$7.6-12.6K
Total Investment:	$8.3-13.3K
Minimum Net Worth:	$N/A
Fees: Franchise -	$7.6-12.6K
Royalty - $100/Mo.;	Ad. - $100/Yr.
Earnings Claim Statement:	No
Term of Contract (Years):	N/A

Avg. # Of Employees:	1 FT, 1-2 PT
Passive Ownership:	Discouraged
Encourage Conversions:	N/A
Area Develop. Agreements:	No
Sub-Franchising Contracts:	No
Expand In Territory:	No
Space Needs: N/A SF; HB	

SUPPORT & TRAINING PROVIDED:

Financial Assistance Provided:	No
Site Selection Assistance:	N/A
Lease Negotiation Assistance:	N/A
Co-Operative Advertising:	Yes
Franchisee Assoc./Member:	No
Size Of Corporate Staff:	2
On-Going Support:	b,D,G,h,I
Training: 3 Days in Dallas, TX.	

SPECIFIC EXPANSION PLANS:

US:	All United States
Canada:	No
Overseas:	Australia

TENNISKIDS

417 20th Pl.
Manhattan Beach, CA 90266
Tel: (310) 796-1322
Fax: (310) 796-1362
E-Mail: tenniskids@aol.com
Web Site: www.tenniskids.net
Ms. Nancy Stevenson, VP Business Dev.

TENNISKIDS is a unique program designed to teach children ages 2 to 9 the sport of tennis. It was designed by world class professional tennis pro, Janet Craig Grossman, who also facilitates the training of each TENNISKIDS franchisee. TENNISKIDS gives the franchisee the opportunity to have fun, promote a positive learning environment and have the flexibility of scheduling.

BACKGROUND:	IFA MEMBER
Established: 1991;	1st Franchised: 1994
Franchised Units:	12
Company-Owned Units	8
Total Units:	20
Dist.:	US-20; CAN-0; O'seas-0
North America:	2 States
Density:	9 in CA, 2 in NJ
Projected New Units (12 Months):	10
Qualifications:	3, 3, 3, 3, 5, 5
Registered: CA	

FINANCIAL/TERMS:

Cash Investment:	$10-15K
Total Investment:	$10-25K
Minimum Net Worth:	$10K
Fees: Franchise -	$10K Min.
Royalty - 6%;	Ad. - 2%

Earnings Claim Statement:	No
Term of Contract (Years):	10/5
Avg. # Of Employees:	1 FT, 1 PT
Passive Ownership:	Allowed
Encourage Conversions:	No
Area Develop. Agreements:	Yes
Sub-Franchising Contracts:	No
Expand In Territory:	Yes
Space Needs: NR SF; Portable 20'x 20' Space	

SUPPORT & TRAINING PROVIDED:

Financial Assistance Provided:	Yes(I)
Site Selection Assistance:	Yes
Lease Negotiation Assistance:	N/A
Co-Operative Advertising:	Yes
Franchisee Assoc./Member:	No
Size Of Corporate Staff:	2
On-Going Support:	a,B,C,D,F,G,h
Training: 2 Weeks in Manhattan Beach, CA.	

SPECIFIC EXPANSION PLANS:

US:	All United States
Canada:	No
Overseas:	Not Yet

TUTOR TIME LEARNING CENTERS

621 N W 53rd St., # 450
Boca Raton, FL 33487
Tel: (800) 275-1235 (561) 237-2266
Fax: (561) 237-3466
E-Mail: franchisesales@tutortime.com
Web Site: www.tutortime.com
Mr. Glenn Geoghegan, VP Franchise Development

Our child care learning centers are serving children from the ages of 6 weeks to 5 years old. Our colorful state-of-the-art 10,000 square foot centers feature TUTOR TOWNE, a miniature play village, as well as computer labs, learning centers, innovative curriculum, high tech security systems, playgrounds and information management systems. No experience in child care or education is required. We are seeking franchisees domestically and internationally.

BACKGROUND:	IFA MEMBER
Established: 1980;	1st Franchised: 1990
Franchised Units:	136
Company-Owned Units	70

Total Units:	206
Dist.:	US-201; CAN-1; O'seas-5
North America:	28 States, 1 Province
Density:	23 in FL, 21 in CA, 19 in NY
Projected New Units (12 Months):	50-60
Qualifications:	5, 5, 2, 2, 3, 5
Registered: CA,FL,MI,MN,OR,RI,WI	

FINANCIAL/TERMS:

Cash Investment:	$75K
Total Investment:	$250K
Minimum Net Worth:	$500K+
Fees: Franchise -	$50K
Royalty - 6%;	Ad. - 1.25%
Earnings Claim Statement:	No
Term of Contract (Years):	15/15
Avg. # Of Employees:	12 FT, 10 PT
Passive Ownership:	Allowed
Encourage Conversions:	Yes
Area Develop. Agreements:	No
Sub-Franchising Contracts:	No
Expand In Territory:	Yes
Space Needs: 10,000 SF; FS, SC	

SUPPORT & TRAINING PROVIDED:

Financial Assistance Provided:	Yes(I)
Site Selection Assistance:	Yes
Lease Negotiation Assistance:	Yes
Co-Operative Advertising:	Yes
Franchisee Assoc./Member:	Yes/Yes
Size Of Corporate Staff:	102
On-Going Support:	A,B,C,D,E,G,h,I
Training: 1 Week Headquarters; 2 Weeks On-Site.	

SPECIFIC EXPANSION PLANS:

US:	All United States
Canada:	All Canada
Overseas:	All Countries

WEE WATCH

3948 Ranchero Dr.
Ann Arbor, MI 48108
Tel: (888) 822-6888
Fax: (734) 822-6888
E-Mail: info@weewatch.com
Web Site: www.weewatch.com
Mr. Marc A. Kiekenapp, Vice President

WEE WATCH - a private home day care franchise company, offering 13 years of experience. Total investment under $30,000. Our sysetm trains you to manage day care providers, expand your customer base and provide safe, educational child care environments. WEE WATCH - an exceptional day care system for today's families.

BACKGROUND:

Established: 1987; 1st Franchised:	1987
Franchised Units:	54
Company-Owned Units	0
Total Units:	54
Dist.:	US-0; CAN-54; O'seas-0
North America:	NR
Density:	NR
Projected New Units (12 Months):	25
Qualifications:	3, 3, 1, 3, 4, 5
Registered:	CA,FL,IL,IN,MD,MI,MN,N0,
	OR,RI,VA,WA,WI,DC

FINANCIAL/TERMS:

Cash Investment:	$10-20K
Total Investment:	$27-47K
Minimum Net Worth:	$100K
Fees: Franchise -	$6.9K
Royalty - 8%;	Ad. - N/A
Earnings Claim Statement:	No
Term of Contract (Years):	10/10
Avg. # Of Employees:	3 FT
Passive Ownership:	Discouraged
Encourage Conversions:	Yes
Area Develop. Agreements:	No
Sub-Franchising Contracts:	No
Expand In Territory:	Yes
Space Needs: 200 SF; HB	

SUPPORT & TRAINING PROVIDED:

Financial Assistance Provided:	Yes(I)
Site Selection Assistance:	Yes
Lease Negotiation Assistance:	N/A
Co-Operative Advertising:	N/A
Franchisee Assoc./Member:	No
Size Of Corporate Staff:	15
On-Going Support:	C,D,E,G,h,I
Training: 5 Days Home Office; 1 Week	
Right Start Program; 2 Days Franchise	
Location.	

SPECIFIC EXPANSION PLANS:

US:	All United States
Canada:	All Canada
Overseas:	All Countries

<< >>

SUPPLEMENTAL LISTING OF FRANCHISORS

A Choice Nanny, 5110 Ridgefield Rd., # 403 B, Bethesda, MD 20816 ; (301) 596-9939; Ms. Jacqueline F. Clark (800) 73-NANNY; (301) 652-2229

Baby Town, 1662 Clarkson Rd., Chesterfield, MO 63017 ; (314) 530-0068;

Mr. Mark Widdicombe (800) 822-2969; (314) 530-5995

Bellini Juvenile Designer Furniture, 301 N. Main St., New City, NY 10956 ; (914) 638-3878; Mr. Ronald Sommers (800) 332-2229; (914) 638-4111

Carousel Systems, 381 Brooks Rd., King of Prussia, PA 19406 ; (610) 265-7194; Mr. Bob Vearling (800) 272-4901; (610) 265-8510

Educate 'R' Kids, 3388 14th St., Detroit, MI 48208-2624 ; (313) 964-1106; Ms. Irma Givens (888) 598-KIDS; (313) 963-8555

Fit By Five Pre-School, 29520 Center Ridge Rd., Westlake, OH 44145 ; (440) 835-8838; Ms. Michelle DeMarsh ; (440) 835-8558

Futurekids, 1000 N. Studebaker Rd., #1, Long Beach, CA 90815 ; (562) 296-1110; Mr. Thomas L. Motter (800) 876-5444; (562) 296-1111

Genius Kid Academy, 398 Steeles Ave. W., # 214, Thornhill, ON L4J 6X3 CANADA; (905) 886-4919; Mr. Nathan Aryev ; (905) 886-1920

Goddard School, The, 381 Brooks Rd., King of Prussia, PA 19406 ; (610) 265-8867; Mr. Jeff Travitz (800) 272-4901; (610) 265-8510

Hoohobbers, 2847 W. 47th Place, Chicago, IL 60632 ; (773) 890-1467; Mr. Bill Sommerscheild (800) 533-1505; (773) 890-1466

Imagine That Discovery Museums, P.O. Box 493, New Vernon, NJ 07976 ; (973) 445-1917; Ms. Deborah Bodnar (800) 820-1145; (973) 267-2907

Kids "R" Kids Quality Learning Centers, 1625 Executive Drive S., Duluth, GA 30096 ; (770) 279-9699; Mr. George Anderson (800) 279-0033; (770) 279-8500

Kidsports International, 240 Penn Ave., Sinking Spring, PA 19608 ; (610) 372-8045; Mr. Jim Reese ; (610) 372-6830

Kumon Math & Reading Centres, 344 Consumer Rd., North York, ON M2J 1P8 CANADA; (416) 490-1694; Mr. Tim Bateman ; (416) 490-1722

Learning Express, 29 Buena Vista St., Devons, MA 01433 ; (978) 889-1010; Mr. Steven P. Manfredi (888) 725-8697; (978) 889-1000

Little People's Learning Center, 8305 S. Wadsworth Blvd., Littleton, CO 80128 ; (303) 972-9582; Mr. Barry Oman ; (303) 972-0787

Little Princess, P.O. Box 411, Gainsville, VA 20156 ; (703) 754-1334; Mrs. Dawn Yates (800) 489-0TEA; (703) 724-1284

Little Scientists, 200 Main St., 3rd Fl., Ansonia, CT 06401 ; (203) 736-2165; Ms. Ronda Margolis (800) FACT-FUN; (203) 732-3522

Mad Science Group, The, 3400 Jean Talon W. # 101, Montreal, PQ H3R 2E8 CANADA; (514) 344-6695; Mr. Joel Lazarovitz (800) 586-5231; (514) 344-4181

Peanut Club, The, 1212 Kingston Rd., Toronto, ON M1N 1P3 CANADA; (416) 751-5608; Mr. Brian Shedden ; (416) 693-1048

Romp Around, 215 Route 22 E., Greenbrook, NJ 08812 ; (732) 424-9229; Ms. Shelley Davimos ; (732) 752-1818

Safe & Sound, 530 S. Henderson Rd., # D, King of Prussia, PA 19406 ; (610) 265-5149; Mr. Ron Sommers (800) 384-SAFE; (610) 265-5155

Technokids, 2232Sheridan Garden Dr., Oakville, ON L6J 7T1 CANADA; (905) 829-4172; Mr. Scott Gerard (800) 221-7921; (905) 829-4171

Wee Watch Private Home Day Care, 105 Main St., Unionville, ON L3R 2G1 CANADA; (905) 479-9047; Mr. Terry Fullerton ; (905) 479-4274

Wonders of Wisdom Children's Centers, 3114 Golansky Blvd., # 201, Prince William, VA 22192-4200 ; (703) 670-2851; Ms. Domini Anderson (800) 424-0550; (703) 670-9344

EDUCATION/PERSONAL DEVELOPMENT/TRAINING INDUSTRY PROFILE

Total # Franchisors in Industry Group	49
Total # Franchised Units in Industry Group	27,846
Total # Company-Owned Units in Industry Group	<u>716</u>
Total # Operating Units in Industry Group	28,562
Average # Franchised Units/Franchisor	568.3
Average # Company-Owned Units/Franchisor	<u>14.6</u>
Average # Total Units/Franchisor	582.9
Ratio of Total # Franchised Units/Total # Company-Owned Units	38.9:1
Industry Survey Participants	24
Representing % of Industry	49.0%
Average Franchise Fee*:	$28.8K
Average Total Investment*:	$110.5K
Average On-Going Royalty Fee*:	7.9%

If a range was provided, the mid-point of the range was used. See detailed profiles for actual ranges.

FIVE LARGEST PARTICIPANTS IN SURVEY

Company	# Fran-chised Units	# Co-Owned Units	# Total Units	Franchise Fee	On-Going Royalty	Total Investment
1. Sylvan Learning Centers	756	81	837	38-46K	8-9%	121-219K
2. Berlitz International	65	336	401	30-50K	10%	150-300K
3. Leadership Management	365	0	365	NR	0%	N/A
4. Huntington Learning Centers	154	72	226	34K	8%/1.2K/M	139-192K
5. New Horizons	199	25	224	25-75K	6%	249-435K

ACADEMY FOR MATHEMATICS & SCIENCE

30 Glen Cameron Rd., # 200
Thornhill, ON L3T 1N7 CANADA
Tel: (800) 809-5555 (905) 709-3233
Fax: (905) 709-3045
E-Mail: info@acadfor.comc
Web Site: www.acadfor.com
Mr. Ron Ansett, Dir. Franchise Sales

Licensees provide math, science, English and computer tutoring to school age children from kindergarten to the end of high school. Individualized, self-paced learning is provided in learning centers located in major malls, using a unique photo-visual learning program.

BACKGROUND:
Established: 1992; 1st Franchised: 1993
Franchised Units: 36
Company-Owned Units   4
Total Units: 40
Dist.:   US-0; CAN-40; O'seas-0
  North America: 4 Provinces
  Density: 35 in ON, 4 in BC, 1 in AB
Projected New Units (12 Months):   18
Qualifications: 2, 3, 1, 4, 1, 5
Registered: AB
FINANCIAL/TERMS:
Cash Investment: $50-70K
Total Investment: $50-70K
Minimum Net Worth: $N/A
Fees: Franchise - $29.5K
  Royalty - 5-8%;   Ad. - 2%
Earnings Claim Statement: No
Term of Contract (Years):   5/5
Avg. # Of Employees: 2 FT, 6 PT
Passive Ownership: Not Allowed
Encourage Conversions: N/A
Area Develop. Agreements: Yes/10
Sub-Franchising Contracts: Yes
Expand In Territory: Yes
Space Needs: 1,000 SF; SC, RM
SUPPORT & TRAINING PROVIDED:
Financial Assistance Provided: Yes(I)
Site Selection Assistance: Yes
Lease Negotiation Assistance: Yes
Co-Operative Advertising: No
Franchisee Assoc./Member: Yes/No
Size Of Corporate Staff: 13
On-Going Support: C,D,E,G,H,I
Training: 1 Week Corporate Office; 1 Week
  Training Center.
SPECIFIC EXPANSION PLANS:
US: Not Yet
Canada: All Canada
Overseas: No

◄◄   ►►

AMRON SCHOOL OF THE FINE ARTS

1315 Medlin Rd.
Monroe, NC 28112
Tel: (704) 283-4290
Fax: (704) 283-7290
E-Mail: normawilliams@verizon.net
Ms. Norma W. Williams, President/CEO

(Educational) Teach modeling, acting, cosmetics and photography for portfolios. Agency to get clients jobs in acting and modeling.

BACKGROUND:
Established: 1979;   1st Franchised: 1986
Franchised Units: 0
Company-Owned Units   1
Total Units: 1
Dist.:   US-0; CAN-0; O'seas-0
  North America: 1 State
  Density: 1 in NC
Projected New Units (12 Months):   NR
Registered:
FINANCIAL/TERMS:
Cash Investment: $15K
Total Investment: $20K
Minimum Net Worth: $20K
Fees: Franchise - $10K
  Royalty - Sliding Scale;   Ad. - 1%
Earnings Claim Statement: Yes
Term of Contract (Years):   5/5
Avg. # Of Employees: 2 PT
Passive Ownership: Allowed
Encourage Conversions: NR
Area Develop. Agreements: No
Sub-Franchising Contracts: No
Expand In Territory: Yes
Space Needs: NR SF; FS, SF, SC, RM, HB
SUPPORT & TRAINING PROVIDED:
Financial Assistance Provided: NR
Site Selection Assistance: N/A
Lease Negotiation Assistance: N/A
Co-Operative Advertising: N/A
Franchisee Assoc./Member: No
Size Of Corporate Staff: 2
On-Going Support: A,B,D,d,E,F,G,H,h
Training: 1 Week at Home Office in
  Monroe, NC.
SPECIFIC EXPANSION PLANS:
US: All United States
Canada: NR
Overseas: NR

◄◄   ►►

Barbizon

BARBIZON SCHOOLS OF MODELING

2240 Woolbright Rd., # 300
Boynton Beach, FL 33426
Tel: (888) 999-9404 (561) 369-8600
Fax: (561) 369-1299
Web Site: www.barbizonmodeling.com
Mr.   Tom   Blangiardo,   Senior   Vice
  President

Proprietary, private schools of modeling and related creative arts.

BACKGROUND: IFA MEMBER
Established: 1939;   1st Franchised: 1968
Franchised Units: 60
Company-Owned Units   0
Total Units: 60
Dist.:   US-56; CAN-1; O'seas-3
  North America: 27 States
  Density: 7 in CA, 5 in NY, 5 in NJ
Projected New Units (12 Months):   7
Qualifications: 4, 3, 1, 4, 2, 5
Registered: CA,HI,IL,MD,MN,NY,VA,
  WA
FINANCIAL/TERMS:
Cash Investment: $30-50K
Total Investment: $47-67.5K
Minimum Net Worth: $NR
Fees: Franchise - $35K
  Royalty - 7.5%;   Ad. - 2.5%
Earnings Claim Statement: No
Term of Contract (Years):   10/10
Avg. # Of Employees: NR
Passive Ownership: Discouraged
Encourage Conversions: Yes
Area Develop. Agreements: No
Sub-Franchising Contracts: No
Expand In Territory: Yes
Space Needs: NR SF; NR
SUPPORT & TRAINING PROVIDED:
Financial Assistance Provided: Yes(D)
Site Selection Assistance: Yes
Lease Negotiation Assistance: Yes
Co-Operative Advertising: N/A
Franchisee Assoc./Member: Yes/Yes
Size Of Corporate Staff: NR
On-Going Support: C,D,E,G,H
Training: Varies Home Office; Varies
  On-Site.
SPECIFIC EXPANSION PLANS:
US: All United States

Canada: All Canada
Overseas: All Countries

≪ ≫

BERLITZ INTERNATIONAL
400 Alexander Park Dr.
Princeton, NJ 08540-6306
Tel: (800) 626-6419 (609) 514-3046
Fax: (609) 514-9675
E-Mail: frank.garton@berlitz.com
Web Site: www.berlitz.com
Mr. Frank Garton, VP Worldwide Franchising

Language instruction, publishing and translation services

BACKGROUND: IFA MEMBER
Established: 1900;   1st Franchised: 1996
Franchised Units: 65
Company-Owned Units   336
Total Units: 401
Dist.:   US-61; CAN-11; O'seas-328
  North America: NR
  Density: 18 in NY, 18 in CA, 18 in FL
Projected New Units (12 Months):   50
Qualifications: 4, 5, 2, 3, 4, 5
Registered: CA,FL,IL,MD,MI,NY,
  OR,VA,WA
FINANCIAL/TERMS:
Cash Investment: $150-300K
Total Investment: $150-300K
Minimum Net Worth: $300K
Fees: Franchise - $30-50K
  Royalty - 10%;   Ad. - 2%
Earnings Claim Statement: No
Term of Contract (Years):   10/10
Avg. # Of Employees: 1 FT, 1 PT
Passive Ownership: Discouraged
Encourage Conversions: Yes
Area Develop. Agreements: Yes/10
Sub-Franchising Contracts: No
Expand In Territory: No
Space Needs: 1,500-3,000 SF; N/A
SUPPORT & TRAINING PROVIDED:
Financial Assistance Provided: No
Site Selection Assistance: Yes
Lease Negotiation Assistance: Yes
Co-Operative Advertising: No
Franchisee Assoc./Member: No
Size Of Corporate Staff: 7000
On-Going Support: B,C,D,E,F,G,H
Training: 2 Weeks Home Office; 2 Weeks
  Division Training; 2 Weeks On-Site.
SPECIFIC EXPANSION PLANS:
US: Southeast, West
Canada: NB
Overseas: Africa, Central Asia, Asia

≪ ≫

BOSTON BARTENDERS SCHOOL ASSOCIATES
P.O. Box 176
Wilbraham, MA 01095
Tel: (800) 357-3210 (413) 596-4600
Fax: (413) 596-4631
Mr. William Green, COO

BBS offers a 35-hour course in Mixology and alcohol awareness to men and women ages 18 and up. College students, people in-between or changing jobs or those moving to a new area will be interested in a job bartending. It's easy, fun, quick and affordable. The program takes one or two weeks of evenings to complete. The program costs $400-600, paid up front.

BACKGROUND:
Established: 1968;   1st Franchised: 1995
Franchised Units: 3
Company-Owned Units   6
Total Units: 9
Dist.:   US-9; CAN-0; O'seas-0
  North America: NR
  Density: 4 in MA, 2 in CT, 2 in RI
Projected New Units (12 Months):   3
Qualifications: 1, 1, 1, 1, 1, 4
Registered: RI
FINANCIAL/TERMS:
Cash Investment: $30K
Total Investment: $30K
Minimum Net Worth: $50K
Fees: Franchise - $6.9K
  Royalty - 10%;   Ad. - NR
Earnings Claim Statement: No
Term of Contract (Years):   10/10
Avg. # Of Employees: 2 FT, 1 PT
Passive Ownership: Discouraged
Encourage Conversions: N/A
Area Develop. Agreements: No
Sub-Franchising Contracts: No
Expand In Territory: Yes
Space Needs: 1,000 SF; N/A
SUPPORT & TRAINING PROVIDED:
Financial Assistance Provided: No
Site Selection Assistance: Yes
Lease Negotiation Assistance: Yes
Co-Operative Advertising: N/A
Franchisee Assoc./Member: No
Size Of Corporate Staff: 2
On-Going Support: A,E,F,H,I
Training: 2 Weeks in Springfield, MA.
SPECIFIC EXPANSION PLANS:
US: All United States
Canada: All Canada
Overseas: No

≪ ≫

Career blazers
EXCELLENCE AT WORK

CAREER BLAZERS LEARNING CENTERS
Two Concourse Pkwy., # 100
Atlanta, GA 30328
Tel: (888) 478-8809 (305) 270-2200
Fax: (305) 270-0290
E-Mail: hkane@cblazers.com
Web Site: www.cblazers.com
Mr. Howard Kane, Vice President

State-of-the-art computer and information technology training centers, which are state licensed business schools, serving corporations, governmentally funded/ entitled groups and the public. The need for technology training increases exponentially every day and theses skills are essential to the individual, at the workplace and at home.

BACKGROUND: IFA MEMBER
Established: 1948;   1st Franchised: 1993
Franchised Units: 46
Company-Owned Units   11
Total Units: 57
Dist.:   US-54; CAN-3; O'seas-0
  North America: 20 States, 1 Province
  Density: 9 in PA, 4 in MA, 4 in OH
Projected New Units (12 Months):   10
Qualifications: 4, 4, 3, 3, 3, 4
Registered: CA,FL,IL,MI
FINANCIAL/TERMS:
Cash Investment: $150K
Total Investment: $350K
Minimum Net Worth: $300K
Fees: Franchise - $25K
  Royalty - 8-10%;   Ad. - 2%
Earnings Claim Statement: No
Term of Contract (Years):   10/10
Avg. # Of Employees: 4 FT, 2 PT
Passive Ownership: Allowed
Encourage Conversions: Yes
Area Develop. Agreements: No
Sub-Franchising Contracts: No
Expand In Territory: Yes
Space Needs: 3,000 SF; SF, SC, OB
SUPPORT & TRAINING PROVIDED:
Financial Assistance Provided: No
Site Selection Assistance: Yes
Lease Negotiation Assistance: Yes
Co-Operative Advertising: Yes
Franchisee Assoc./Member: No
Size Of Corporate Staff: 25
On-Going Support: b,C,D,E,G,H,I

Training: At Least 1 Week in Either New
  York City, NY or Atlanta, GA.
SPECIFIC EXPANSION PLANS:
US: All United States
Canada: No
Overseas: No

<< >>

CITIZENS AGAINST CRIME
2001 N. Collins, # 107
Richardson, TX 75080
Tel: (800) 466-1010 (972) 578-2287
Fax: (972) 509-0054
E-Mail: jerry@trainingexperience.com
Web Site: www.trainingexperience.com
Mr. Jerry Aris, Chief Executive Officer

CITIZENS AGAINST CRIME, INC. has
reached over 6 million people with its
premier safety education seminars and
safety products. Their international safety
education and products franchise has been
in business since 1980. CAC has taught
people how to avoid becoming victims of
crime. Their dynamic educational programs
have received acclaim from businesses,
schools, hospitals and other organizations
across the country.

BACKGROUND:
Established: 1980;   1st Franchised: 1986
Franchised Units: 25
Company-Owned Units   1
Total Units: 26
Dist.:   US-24; CAN-1; O'seas-1
  North America: 16 States
  Density: TX, FL, VA
Projected New Units (12 Months):   8
Qualifications: 5, 3, 3, 3, 5, 5
Registered: CA,DC
FINANCIAL/TERMS:
Cash Investment: $6K
Total Investment: $12.5-25K
Minimum Net Worth: $20K
Fees: Franchise - $6-12.5K
  Royalty - 0%;   Ad. - 3-6%
Earnings Claim Statement: Yes
Term of Contract (Years):   10/10
Avg. # Of Employees: 1-5 FT
Passive Ownership: Allowed
Encourage Conversions: Yes
Area Develop. Agreements: No

Sub-Franchising Contracts: No
Expand In Territory: No
Space Needs: N/A SF; HB, OB
SUPPORT & TRAINING PROVIDED:
Financial Assistance Provided: Yes(D)
Site Selection Assistance: Yes
Lease Negotiation Assistance: Yes
Co-Operative Advertising: No
Franchisee Assoc./Member: No
Size Of Corporate Staff: 4
On-Going Support: A,C,D,E,F,G,H,I
Training: 1 Week in Dallas, TX; 1 Week in
  Franchise.
SPECIFIC EXPANSION PLANS:
US: All United States
Canada: All Canada
Overseas: All Countries

<< >>

**COMPUTER U LEARNING
CENTERS**
75850 Osage Trl.
Indian Wells, CA 92210
Tel: (888) 708-7877 (760) 340-2453
Fax: (760) 340-0306
E-Mail: info@computeru.com
Web Site: www.computeru.com
Mr. Russ Beckner, Vice President

COMPUTER U LEARNING CENTERS
provides computer training to mature
adults through classroom instruction and
private tutoring. We teach in the context
of mid-life and retirement, with tested
programs developed especially for adults
ago 50 and over. We make it simple to
learn computers. We keep it simple for
our franchise partners with comprehensive
training and continuing on-line support.
Come GROW with us!

BACKGROUND: IFA MEMBER
Established: 1992;   1st Franchised: 1997
Franchised Units: 10
Company-Owned Units   5
Total Units: 15
Dist.:   US-15; CAN-0; O'seas-0
  North America: 4 States
  Density: CA, NV, FL

Projected New Units (12 Months):   10
Qualifications: 3, 3, 1, 4, 5, 5
Registered: CA,FL,MI,OR,WI,DC
FINANCIAL/TERMS:
Cash Investment: $30-40K
Total Investment: $30-40K
Minimum Net Worth: $N/A
Fees: Franchise - $20K
  Royalty - 6%;   Ad. - 1%
Earnings Claim Statement: Yes
Term of Contract (Years):   10/5
Avg. # Of Employees: 1 FT, 2 PT
Passive Ownership: Allowed
Encourage Conversions: N/A
Area Develop. Agreements: Yes
Sub-Franchising Contracts: No
Expand In Territory: Yes
Space Needs: 400 SF; N/A
SUPPORT & TRAINING PROVIDED:
Financial Assistance Provided: No
Site Selection Assistance: Yes
Lease Negotiation Assistance: Yes
Co-Operative Advertising: No
Franchisee Assoc./Member: No
Size Of Corporate Staff: 4
On-Going Support: NR
Training: 2 Days On-Site; 6 Days
  Headquarters, Palm Springs, CA.
SPECIFIC EXPANSION PLANS:
US: Where Registered
Canada: No
Overseas: No

<< >>

CPR SERVICES
22 Stoneybrook Dr.
Ashland, MA 01721
Tel: (800) 357-0091 (508) 881-8010
Fax: (508) 881-4718
E-Mail: info@cpr-services.com
Web Site: www.cpr-services.com
Mr. Steven H. Greenberg, Sales Manager

Health education and training the
community and allied health professionals
CPR and first aid.

BACKGROUND:
Established: 1984;   1st Franchised: 1998
Franchised Units: 0
Company-Owned Units   1
Total Units: 1
Dist.:   US-1; CAN-0; O'seas-0
  North America: 1 State
  Density: 1 in MA

Projected New Units (12 Months): 10
Qualifications: 3, 2, 4, 4, 4, 4
Registered: All States
FINANCIAL/TERMS:
Cash Investment: $13-16K
Total Investment: $13-16K
Minimum Net Worth: $N/A
Fees: Franchise - $7.5K
  Royalty - $3/Student; Ad. - N/A
Earnings Claim Statement: No
Term of Contract (Years): 10/10
Avg. # Of Employees: 1 FT
Passive Ownership: Allowed
Encourage Conversions: N/A
Area Develop. Agreements: No
Sub-Franchising Contracts: No
Expand In Territory: Yes
Space Needs: N/A SF; N/A
SUPPORT & TRAINING PROVIDED:
Financial Assistance Provided: No
Site Selection Assistance: N/A
Lease Negotiation Assistance: N/A
Co-Operative Advertising: Yes
Franchisee Assoc./Member: No
Size Of Corporate Staff: 2
On-Going Support: C,d,G,h,I
Training: 5 Days in Ashland, MA.
SPECIFIC EXPANSION PLANS:
US: All United States
Canada: No
Overseas: No

CRESTCOM INTERNATIONAL, LTD.

6900 E. Belleview Ave.
Englewood, CO 80111
Tel: (888) CRESTCOM (303) 267-8200
Fax: (303) 267-8207
E-Mail: franchiseinfo@crestcom.com
Web Site: www.crestcom.com
Mr. Kelly Krause, Dir. Int'l. Marketing

CRESTCOM is rated the #1 management training company of 2000 by Entrepreneur and other magazines. CRESTCOM uses a unique combination of video instruction and live facilitation to teach management, sales and office personnel. Internationally-renowned business/management training personalities appear on CRESTCOM videos. The company is active in 50 countries and CRESTCOM's materials are translated into 20+ languages.

BACKGROUND: IFA MEMBER
Established: 1987; 1st Franchised: 1992
Franchised Units: 122
Company-Owned Units 0
Total Units: 122
Dist.: US-39; CAN-6; O'seas-77
  North America: 22 States, 3 Provinces
  Density: NR
Projected New Units (12 Months): 30
Qualifications: 4, 5, 2, 4, 1, 5
Registered: All States
FINANCIAL/TERMS:
Cash Investment: $35-52.5K
Total Investment: $44.4-72K
Minimum Net Worth: $NR
Fees: Franchise - $35-52.5K
  Royalty - 1.5%; Ad. - N/A
Earnings Claim Statement: Yes
Term of Contract (Years): 7/7/7
Avg. # Of Employees: 2-5 FT
Passive Ownership: Discouraged
Encourage Conversions: N/A
Area Develop. Agreements: No
Sub-Franchising Contracts: No
Expand In Territory: Yes
Space Needs: NR SF; SF, HB
SUPPORT & TRAINING PROVIDED:
Financial Assistance Provided: Yes
Site Selection Assistance: N/A
Lease Negotiation Assistance: N/A
Co-Operative Advertising: Yes
Franchisee Assoc./Member: No
Size Of Corporate Staff: 15
On-Going Support: D,G,H
Training: 7-10 Days Denver, CO, Phoenix, AZ or Sacramento, CA.
SPECIFIC EXPANSION PLANS:
US: All United States
Canada: All Canada
Overseas: All Countries

⬻ ⭆

ELS LANGUAGE CENTERS

400 Alexander Park
Princeton, NJ 08540
Tel: (800) 468-8978 (609) 750-3508
Fax: (609) 750-3596
E-Mail: cgilbert@els.com
Web Site: www.els.com
Mr. Charles Gilbert, VP of Franchising

Leader in teaching English to the world. Franchises English-language schools overseas, students learn business English, conversational English, TOEFL and other programs. Franchisees also offer study-abroad programs and university placement assistance.

BACKGROUND: IFA MEMBER
Established: 1956; 1st Franchised: 1978
Franchised Units: 51
Company-Owned Units 33
Total Units: 84
Dist.: US-33; CAN-1; O'seas-50
  North America: 21 States, 1 Province
  Density: 5 in CA, 2 in NY, 2 in FL
Projected New Units (12 Months):
  Unsure
Qualifications: 4, 4, 4, 3, 4, 5
Registered: None
FINANCIAL/TERMS:
Cash Investment: $100-300K
Total Investment: $100-300K
Minimum Net Worth: $250K
Fees: Franchise - $30K
  Royalty - 5%; Ad. - 0%
Earnings Claim Statement: No
Term of Contract (Years): 10/10
Avg. # Of Employees: 6-20 FT
Passive Ownership: Discouraged
Encourage Conversions: Yes
Area Develop. Agreements: Yes/10-20
Sub-Franchising Contracts: No
Expand In Territory: Yes
Space Needs: Feasible SF; N/A
SUPPORT & TRAINING PROVIDED:
Financial Assistance Provided: No
Site Selection Assistance: Yes
Lease Negotiation Assistance: No
Co-Operative Advertising: Yes
Franchisee Assoc./Member: No
Size Of Corporate Staff: 65
On-Going Support: C,D,G,H
Training: 2 Weeks Princeton, NJ.
SPECIFIC EXPANSION PLANS:
US: No
Canada: No
Overseas: Case by Case Basis

⬻ ⭆

EXECUTRAIN

4800 Northpoint Pkwy.
Alpharetta, GA 30022
Tel: (800) 437-2034 (770) 667-7700
Fax: (770) 521-6283
Web Site: www.execut rain.com
Mr. Scott Smith, VP US Franchising

EXECUTRAIN is the world's leading computer-training franchise. EXECU-TRAIN offers over 800+ courses in the most popular business-applications software in order to increase the productivity of business people from all levels. This is achieved through instructor-led, hands-on training in a classroom setting.

BACKGROUND:

Established: 1984;   1st Franchised: 1986
Franchised Units: 183
Company-Owned Units   35
Total Units: 218
Dist.:   US-173; CAN-4; O'seas-41
 North America: NR
 Density: NR
Projected New Units (12 Months):   18
Qualifications: 5, 5, 3, 3, 1, 5
Registered: All States

FINANCIAL/TERMS:

Cash Investment: $200K
Total Investment: $200-250K
Minimum Net Worth: $250K
Fees: Franchise - $30K
 Royalty - 6-9%;   Ad. - 1.5%
Earnings Claim Statement: No
Term of Contract (Years):   7/7
Avg. # Of Employees: 15-20 FT/PT
Passive Ownership: Discouraged
Encourage Conversions: No
Area Develop. Agreements: No
Sub-Franchising Contracts: No
Expand In Territory: Yes
Space Needs: 3,500 SF; FS

SUPPORT & TRAINING PROVIDED:

Financial Assistance Provided: Yes(D)
Site Selection Assistance: Yes
Lease Negotiation Assistance: Yes
Co-Operative Advertising: No
Franchisee Assoc./Member: NR
Size Of Corporate Staff: 110
On-Going Support: NR
Training: 5 Days GM Training; 5 Days Instructor Training; 5 Days Sale Training -- all Atlanta, GA.

SPECIFIC EXPANSION PLANS:

US: No
Canada: All Canada
Overseas: All Countries

◄◄   ►►

GAME FILM CONSULTANTS

6300 Richmond Ave., # 208
Houston, TX 77057
Tel: (800) 461-4465 (713) 339-1204
Fax: (713) 339-1802
E-Mail: msinc@swbell.net
Web Site: www.gamefilm.com
Mr. Ken Silverman, Dir. of Franchising

GAME FILM CONSULTANTS provides video mystery shopping for its clients as a training tool that mirrors professional

sporganizations' use of coaching and scoring techniques - like taping your golf swing. This virtual reality training tapes your sales swing. With over 10 industries, from department stores to home builders, using some sort of written shopper, GAME FILM SHOPPERS' use of 'video reality shopping' brings a whole new dimension to the industry.

BACKGROUND:
Established: 1992;   1st Franchised: 2001
Franchised Units: 0
Company-Owned Units   1
Total Units: 1
Dist.:   US-1; CAN-0; O'seas-0
 North America: 1 State
 Density: 1 in TX
Projected New Units (12 Months):   12
Qualifications: 4, 2, 2, 2, 1, 4
Registered: All States
FINANCIAL/TERMS:
Cash Investment: $75K
Total Investment: $50K
Minimum Net Worth: $250K
Fees: Franchise - $25K
 Royalty - 10%;   Ad. - 0%
Earnings Claim Statement: No
Term of Contract (Years):   15/15
Avg. # Of Employees: 3 FT
Passive Ownership: Discouraged
Encourage Conversions: Yes
Area Develop. Agreements: No
Sub-Franchising Contracts: No
Expand In Territory: Yes
Space Needs: 800 SF; General Off. Space
SUPPORT & TRAINING PROVIDED:
Financial Assistance Provided: NR
Site Selection Assistance: Yes
Lease Negotiation Assistance: Yes
Co-Operative Advertising: N/A
Franchisee Assoc./Member: No
Size Of Corporate Staff: 10
On-Going Support: A,B,C,E,F,G,H,I
Training: 3 Weeks Houston, TX.
SPECIFIC EXPANSION PLANS:
US: All United States
Canada: No
Overseas: No

◄◄   ►►

GWYNNE LEARNING ACADEMY

1432 W. Emerald, # 735
Mesa, AZ 85202
Tel: (480) 644-1434
Fax: (480) 644-1434
Ms. Penny Gwynne, Treasurer

Video-based interactive training, based on the latest scientific training technology for individuals, blue chip groups in the business, government and education sectors.

BACKGROUND:

Established: 1991;   1st Franchised: 1991
Franchised Units: 14
Company-Owned Units   1
Total Units: 15
Dist.:   US-2; CAN-0; O'seas-12
 North America: 1 State
 Density: 2 in AZ
Projected New Units (12 Months):   6
Registered: NR

FINANCIAL/TERMS:

Cash Investment: $45K
Total Investment: $45-65K
Minimum Net Worth: $NR
Fees: Franchise - $25K
 Royalty - 7%;   Ad. - 2%
Earnings Claim Statement: No
Term of Contract (Years):   10/10
Avg. # Of Employees: 2 FT
Passive Ownership: Allowed
Encourage Conversions: N/A
Area Develop. Agreements: No
Sub-Franchising Contracts: No
Expand In Territory: Yes
Space Needs: 600 SF; FS, SF, SC, RM

SUPPORT & TRAINING PROVIDED:

Financial Assistance Provided: Yes(I)
Site Selection Assistance: Yes
Lease Negotiation Assistance: Yes
Co-Operative Advertising: Yes
Franchisee Assoc./Member: No
Size Of Corporate Staff: 2
On-Going Support: b,D,e,I
Training: 7 Days Phoenix, AZ.

SPECIFIC EXPANSION PLANS:

US: All United States
Canada: All Canada
Overseas: Australia, Malaysia

◄◄   ►►

HUNTINGTON LEARNING CENTER

496 Kinderkamack Rd.
Oradell, NJ 07649
Tel: (800) 653-8400 (201) 261-8400
Fax: (201) 261-3233
E-Mail: hlcorp@aol.com
Web Site: www.huntingtonlearning.com
Mr. Richard C. Pittius, VP Franchise

Offers services to 5-19 year-olds, and occasionally to adults, in reading, spelling, phonics, language development study skills and mathematics, as well as programs to prepare for standardized entrance exams. Instruction is offered in a tutorial setting and is predominately remedial in nature, although some enrichment is offered.

BACKGROUND: IFA MEMBER
Established: 1977; 1st Franchised: 1985
Franchised Units: 154
Company-Owned Units: <u>72</u>
Total Units: 226
Dist.: US-226; CAN-0; O'seas-0
  North America: 29 States
  Density: 26 in NY, 19 in NJ, 18 in FL
Projected New Units (12 Months): 25
Qualifications: 5, 3, 1, 3, 1, 5
Registered: CA,FL,IL,IN,MD,MI,NY,
  RI,VA,WA,WI
FINANCIAL/TERMS:
Cash Investment: $100K
Total Investment: $139.3-191.6K
Minimum Net Worth: $300K
Fees: Franchise - $34K
  Royalty - 8%/$1.2K Min.; Ad. -
2%/$300 Min
Earnings Claim Statement: Yes
Term of Contract (Years): 10/10
Avg. # Of Employees: 2-4 FT
Passive Ownership: Not Allowed
Encourage Conversions: No
Area Develop. Agreements: Yes
Sub-Franchising Contracts: No
Expand In Territory: No
Space Needs: 2,800 SF; SF, SC, RM
SUPPORT & TRAINING PROVIDED:
Financial Assistance Provided: Yes(D)
Site Selection Assistance: Yes
Lease Negotiation Assistance: Yes
Co-Operative Advertising: Yes
Franchisee Assoc./Member: Yes/Yes
Size Of Corporate Staff: 70
On-Going Support: B,C,D,E,F,G,h,I
Training: 2 1/2 Weeks at Oradell, NJ.
SPECIFIC EXPANSION PLANS:
US: NW,SW,MW, South
Canada: All Canada
Overseas: No

◄◄ ►►

John Casablancas
MODELING & CAREER CENTER

**JOHN CASABLANCAS
MODELING/CAREER CENTERS**
111 E. 22nd St., 4th Fl.
New York, NY 10010

Tel: (212) 420-0655
Fax: (212) 473-2725
E-Mail: cku2mmi@aol.com
Web Site: www.jc-centers.com
Ms. Charyn Parker Urban, Director
  Franchise Development

Our franchised schools and in-house modeling agencies provide cutting-edge professional modeling, personal image development and film and TV acting programs and workshops. Created by John Casablancas, former Chairman of Elite Model Management.

BACKGROUND: IFA MEMBER
Established: 1979; 1st Franchised: 1979
Franchised Units: 47
Company-Owned Units: <u>0</u>
Total Units: 47
Dist.: US-38; CAN-1; O'seas-8
  North America: 25 States, 1 Province
  Density: 5 in FL, 2 in OH, 3 in PA
Projected New Units (12 Months): 2
Qualifications: 5, 5, 5, 4, 5, 5
Registered: All States Except OR,DC
FINANCIAL/TERMS:
Cash Investment: $50-100K
Total Investment: $100-200K
Minimum Net Worth: $NR
Fees: Franchise - $40K
  Royalty - 7%; Ad. - 3%
Earnings Claim Statement: No
Term of Contract (Years): 10/10
Avg. # Of Employees: 4 FT, 6-8 PT
Passive Ownership: Not Allowed
Encourage Conversions: Yes
Area Develop. Agreements: No
Sub-Franchising Contracts: No
Expand In Territory: Yes
Space Needs: 1,800-2,500 SF; SC, RM
SUPPORT & TRAINING PROVIDED:
Financial Assistance Provided: No
Site Selection Assistance: Yes
Lease Negotiation Assistance: N/A
Co-Operative Advertising: Yes
Franchisee Assoc./Member: Yes
Size Of Corporate Staff: 8
On-Going Support: b,C,D,E,g,h
Training: 2-3 Days NY.
SPECIFIC EXPANSION PLANS:
US: Northwest, Southwest
Canada: All Canada
Overseas: Far East, Europe, South
  America

◄◄ ►►

**LEADERSHIP MANAGEMENT,
INC.**
4567 Lake Shore Dr.
Waco, TX 76710
Tel: (800) 365-7437 (254) 776-2060
Fax: (254) 757-4600
Web Site: www.lmi-inc.com
Mr. Tony Stigliano, Dir. Development
  Opportunities

Own a professional training dealership that helps companies achieve success. Producing measurable results for clients since 1966; interface with business executives; programs and a process to develop leaders, managers and executives; proven success system; long-term client relationships; national network. Call (800) 365-7437 or send resume.

BACKGROUND:
Established: 1965; 1st Franchised: 1965
Franchised Units: 365
Company-Owned Units: <u>0</u>
Total Units: 365
Dist.: US-365; CAN-0; O'seas-0
  North America: NR
  Density: NR
Projected New Units (12 Months): 60
Registered: All States
FINANCIAL/TERMS:
Cash Investment: $NR
Total Investment: $N/A
Minimum Net Worth: $NR
Fees: Franchise - $NR
  Royalty - 0%; Ad. - 0%
Earnings Claim Statement: No
Term of Contract (Years): 1
Avg. # Of Employees: Varies
Passive Ownership: Discouraged
Encourage Conversions: N/A
Area Develop. Agreements: No
Sub-Franchising Contracts: No
Expand In Territory: No
Space Needs: NR SF; NR
SUPPORT & TRAINING PROVIDED:
Financial Assistance Provided: Yes(D)
Site Selection Assistance: N/A
Lease Negotiation Assistance: N/A
Co-Operative Advertising: N/A
Franchisee Assoc./Member: NR
Size Of Corporate Staff: 25
On-Going Support: D,C,H,I
Training: 1-3 Weeks.
SPECIFIC EXPANSION PLANS:
US: All United States
Canada: All Canada
Overseas: No

NEW HORIZONS COMPUTER LEARNING CENTER

1231 E. Dyer Rd., # 110
Santa Ana, CA 92705-5643
Tel: (714) 438-9491
Fax: (714) 436-2362
E-Mail: na.franchising@newhorizons.com
Web Site: www.newhorizons.com
Mr. Ralph Loberger, Dir. N. Amer. Franchise Devel.

NEW HORIZONS COMPUTER LEARNING CENTERS, Inc. is the world's largest independent IT training company, meeting the needs of more than 2.4 million students each year. NEW HORIZONS offers a variety of flexible training choices: instructor-led classes, Web-based training, computer-based training via CD-ROM, computer labs, certification exam preparation tools and 24-hour, 7-day-a-week help-desk support.

BACKGROUND: IFA MEMBER
Established: 1982; 1st Franchised: 1992
Franchised Units: 199
Company-Owned Units: 25
Total Units: 224
Dist.: US-142; CAN-4; O'seas-69
North America: 36 States, 3 Provinces
Density: 18 in CA, 6 in NY, 6 in TX
Projected New Units (12 Months): 67
Qualifications: 5, 4, 2, 3, 3, 5
Registered: All States Except HI
FINANCIAL/TERMS:
Cash Investment: $100-150K
Total Investment: $249-435K
Minimum Net Worth: $300K
Fees: Franchise - $25-75K
Royalty - 6%; Ad. - 1%
Earnings Claim Statement: No
Term of Contract (Years): 10/5
Avg. # Of Employees: 15 FT
Passive Ownership: Discouraged
Encourage Conversions: Yes
Area Develop. Agreements: Yes/10
Sub-Franchising Contracts: Yes
Expand In Territory: Yes
Space Needs: 4,000-5,000 SF; FS, OB, Business Park
SUPPORT & TRAINING PROVIDED:
Financial Assistance Provided: Yes(D)

Site Selection Assistance: Yes
Lease Negotiation Assistance: Yes
Co-Operative Advertising: Yes
Franchisee Assoc./Member: Yes/Yes
Size Of Corporate Staff: 200+
On-Going Support: B,C,D,G,H,I
Training: 2 Weeks Headquarters; 1 Week Franchise Location; 2 Days Regional.
SPECIFIC EXPANSION PLANS:
US: All United States
Canada: All Canada
Overseas: All Countries

OXFORD LEARNING CENTRES

312 Commissioners Rd. W.
London, ON N6J 1Y3 CANADA
Tel: (888) 559-2212 (519) 473-1207
Fax: (519) 473-6086
E-Mail: lenkaw@oxfordlearning.com
Web Site: www.oxfordlearning.com
Ms. Lenka Whitehead, Dir. Of Fran. Dev.

Join the leaders in supplemental education. Our proprietary curriculum developed over the past 10 years, ensures that your students will make impressive academic gains while developing higher self-esteem. Successful, confident students and happy parents mean referrals and a growing business. We will assist you every step of the way, providing the proven training, marketing, and business expertise you will need. Excellent territories available.

BACKGROUND:
Established: 1984; 1st Franchised: 1990
Franchised Units: 44
Company-Owned Units: 3
Total Units: 47
Dist.: US-5; CAN-51; O'seas-0
North America: 2 States, 5 Provinces
Density: 38 in ON, 4 in MI
Projected New Units (12 Months): 18
Qualifications: 4, 4, 1, 3, 4, 5
Registered: MI,AB
FINANCIAL/TERMS:
Cash Investment: $35K
Total Investment: $85K
Minimum Net Worth: $300-500K
Fees: Franchise - $30K
Royalty - 9%; Ad. - 2%
Earnings Claim Statement: No
Term of Contract (Years): 10/10
Avg. # Of Employees: Varies
Passive Ownership: Allowed
Encourage Conversions: No
Area Develop. Agreements: No
Sub-Franchising Contracts: No

Expand In Territory: Yes
Space Needs: 2,000 SF; FS, SC
SUPPORT & TRAINING PROVIDED:
Financial Assistance Provided: Yes(I)
Site Selection Assistance: Yes
Lease Negotiation Assistance: Yes
Co-Operative Advertising: Yes
Franchisee Assoc./Member: Yes/Yes
Size Of Corporate Staff: 12
On-Going Support: B,C,D,E,F,G,H,I
Training: 2 Weeks London, ON; 1 Week + On-Site.
SPECIFIC EXPANSION PLANS:
US: NR
Canada: All Canada
Overseas: India, Hong Kong, Japan, Germany, Korea

PROFESSIONAL DYNAMETRIC PROGRAMS/PDP

750 E. Hwy. 24, Bldg. I
Woodland Park, CO 80863
Tel: (719) 687-6074
Fax: (719) 687-8587
E-Mail: jimf@pdpnet.com
Web Site: www.pdpnet.com
Mr. Jim Farmer, Executive Vice President

PDP is a business-to-business franchise and offers independence with lucrative opportunity in the executive management market. Sell, train, consult and service large and small businesses in highly-successful and proven programs for hiring, motivating, stress managing and evaluating. There is automatic, repeat business, low overhead, no inventory and no leases.

BACKGROUND:
Established: 1978; 1st Franchised: 1980
Franchised Units: 24
Company-Owned Units: 0
Total Units: 24
Dist.: US-17; CAN-4; O'seas-3
North America: 28 States, 3 Provinces
Density: 4 in TX, 3 in CO, 2 in CA.
Projected New Units (12 Months): 5
Qualifications: 4, 4, 4, 4, 5, 4
Registered: CA
FINANCIAL/TERMS:
Cash Investment: $5-19.5K
Total Investment: $31.5-49.5K
Minimum Net Worth: $250K
Fees: Franchise - $29.5K
Royalty - 0%; Ad. - 0%
Earnings Claim Statement: No
Term of Contract (Years): 7
Avg. # Of Employees: 1 FT

Passive Ownership:	Discouraged
Encourage Conversions:	N/A
Area Develop. Agreements:	No
Sub-Franchising Contracts:	Yes
Expand In Territory:	Yes
Space Needs: N/A SF; HB, ES, OB	

SUPPORT & TRAINING PROVIDED:

Financial Assistance Provided:	No
Site Selection Assistance:	N/A
Lease Negotiation Assistance:	N/A
Co-Operative Advertising:	N/A
Franchisee Assoc./Member:	No
Size Of Corporate Staff:	5
On-Going Support:	c,d,F,G,h,i,
Training: 1 Week Corporate; 2 Days Field; 3 Days Corporate.	

SPECIFIC EXPANSION PLANS:

US:	All United States
Canada:	All Canada
Overseas:	All Countries

<< >>

RENAISSANCE EXECUTIVE FORUMS

7855 Ivanhoe Ave., # 300
La Jolla, CA 92037
Tel: (858) 551-6600
Fax: (858) 551-8777
E-Mail: moreinfo@executiveforums.com
Web Site: www.executiveforums.com
Ms. Cyndi Sudberry, Coor. Franchise Dev.

RENAISSANCE EXECUTIVE FOR-UMS bring together top executives from similarly-sized, non-competing companies into an advisory board process in which thousands of chief executives throughout the world participate. These CEOs, presidents and owners meet once a month in small groups of approximately 8 -12 individuals. The meetings provide an environment designed to address the opportunities and challenges they face as individuals and leaders of their respective organizations.

BACKGROUND: IFA MEMBER

Established: 1994; 1st Franchised: 1994	
Franchised Units:	29
Company-Owned Units:	0
Total Units:	29
Dist.:	US-27; CAN-1; O'seas-1
North America:	13 States

Density:	10 in CA, 3 in AZ
Projected New Units (12 Months):	5
Qualifications:	4, 5, 4, 4, 4, 5
Registered: All States	

FINANCIAL/TERMS:

Cash Investment:	$60-100K
Total Investment:	$60-100K
Minimum Net Worth:	$500K
Fees: Franchise -	$49.5K
Royalty - 20%;	Ad. - 0%
Earnings Claim Statement:	No
Term of Contract (Years):	10/10
Avg. # Of Employees:	1 FT
Passive Ownership:	Not Allowed
Encourage Conversions:	N/A
Area Develop. Agreements:	Yes/5
Sub-Franchising Contracts:	No
Expand In Territory:	Yes
Space Needs: NR SF; Executive Suite	

SUPPORT & TRAINING PROVIDED:

Financial Assistance Provided:	No
Site Selection Assistance:	No
Lease Negotiation Assistance:	No
Co-Operative Advertising:	No
Franchisee Assoc./Member:	Yes/Yes
Size Of Corporate Staff:	13
On-Going Support:	A,b,c,d,G,H,h
Training: 5 Days La Jolla, CA.	

SPECIFIC EXPANSION PLANS:

US:	All United States
Canada:	All Canada
Overseas:	All Countries

<< >>

SANDLER SALES INSTITUTE

10411 Stevenson Rd.
Stevenson, MD 21153
Tel: (800) 669-3537 (410) 653-1993
Fax: (410) 358-7858
E-Mail: rtaylor@sandler.com
Web Site: www.sandler.com
Mr. Ron Taylor, Director of Franchising

SANDLER SALES INSTITUTE offers a distinctive style of training to companies and individuals in the fields of sales, management consulting and leadership development through on-going seminars and workshops. SANDLER SALES INSTITUTE provides intensive training, a unique lead generation program, on-going day-to-day support and protected territories to help you succeed in business.

BACKGROUND: IFA MEMBER

Established: 1967; 1st Franchised: 1983	
Franchised Units:	162
Company-Owned Units:	0
Total Units:	162
Dist.:	US-151; CAN-11; O'seas-0
North America:	NR
Density: 15 in PA, 14 in OH, 12 in TX	
Projected New Units (12 Months):	20
Qualifications:	3, 5, 5, 3, 1, 5
Registered: All States Except HI,AB	

FINANCIAL/TERMS:

Cash Investment:	$45K
Total Investment:	$51.5-68.5K
Minimum Net Worth:	$N/A
Fees: Franchise -	$39.5K
Royalty - $908/Mo.;	Ad. - N/A
Earnings Claim Statement:	No
Term of Contract (Years):	5/5/5/5
Avg. # Of Employees:	1 FT, 1 PT
Passive Ownership:	Discouraged
Encourage Conversions:	N/A
Area Develop. Agreements:	No
Sub-Franchising Contracts:	No
Expand In Territory:	Yes
Space Needs: N/A SF; N/A	

SUPPORT & TRAINING PROVIDED:

Financial Assistance Provided:	No
Site Selection Assistance:	Yes
Lease Negotiation Assistance:	N/A
Co-Operative Advertising:	No
Franchisee Assoc./Member:	Yes/Yes
Size Of Corporate Staff:	26
On-Going Support:	g,H,I
Training: 5 Days Home Office/Other; 1 Day Home Office/Other.	

SPECIFIC EXPANSION PLANS:

US:	All United States
Canada:	All Canada
Overseas:	All Countries

<< >>

SYLVAN LEARNING CENTERS

1000 Lancaster St.
Baltimore, MD 21202
Tel: (800) 284-8214 (410) 843-8000
Fax: (410) 843-6265
E-Mail: irene.vavas@educate.com

Web Site: www.educate.com
Mr. Greg Helwin, VP Franchise Dev.

SYLVAN is the leading provider of educational services to families, schools and industry. SYLVAN services kindergarten through adult-levels from more than 800 SYLVAN LEARNING CENTERS worldwide.

BACKGROUND: IFA MEMBER
Established: 1979; 1st Franchised: 1980
Franchised Units: 756
Company-Owned Units 81
Total Units: 837
Dist.: US-762; CAN-72; O'seas-3
North America: 50 States
Density: CA, TX, NY
Projected New Units (12 Months): 70
Qualifications: 4, 4, 2, 3, 2, 5
Registered: All States
FINANCIAL/TERMS:
Cash Investment: $101.1-171.3K
Total Investment: $121.1-219.3K
Minimum Net Worth: $N/A
Fees: Franchise - $38-46K
Royalty - 8-9%; Ad. - 1.5%
Earnings Claim Statement: Yes
Term of Contract (Years): 10/10
Avg. # Of Employees: 2 FT, 5 PT
Passive Ownership: Not Allowed
Encourage Conversions: No
Area Develop. Agreements: Yes/Varies
Sub-Franchising Contracts: No
Expand In Territory: Yes
Space Needs: 1,600-2,500 SF; FS, SF, SC
SUPPORT & TRAINING PROVIDED:
Financial Assistance Provided: Yes(B)
Site Selection Assistance: Yes
Lease Negotiation Assistance: No
Co-Operative Advertising: Yes
Franchisee Assoc./Member: Yes
Size Of Corporate Staff: 500
On-Going Support: B,C,D,E,G,H,I
Training: 6 Days Baltimore, MD; 5 Days in Various Other Locations.
SPECIFIC EXPANSION PLANS:
US: All United States
Canada: All Canada
Overseas: Asia, Europe, South America

SUPPLEMENTAL LISTING OF FRANCHISORS

Academy of Learning, Five Bank St., # 202, Attleboro, MA 02703 ; (508) 222-0005; Mr. Jeffrey A. Goldwasser ; (508) 222-0000

Alamo Learning Systems, 3160 Crow Canyon Rd., # 280, San Ramon, CA 94583 ; (925) 277-1919; Mr. Guy A. Hale (800) 829-8081; (925) 277-1818

Alphabetland/Child Enrichment Center, 139 Bergen Ave., Kearny, NJ 07032 ; (201) 991-2566; Mr. Ricardo Alvarez ; (201) 991-5684

Arthur Murray International, 1077 Ponce De Leon Blvd., Coral Gables, FL 33134 ; (305) 445-0451; Mr. George B. Theiss ; (305) 445-9645

Broadbelt & Fonte Model Centre, 696 Dufferin St., Toronto, ON M6K 2B5 CANADA; (416) 588-4984; Mr. Manuel Fonte ; (416) 588-8806

C. B. S. Interactive Multimedia, 80 Bloor St. W., 10th Floor, Toronto, ON M5S 2V1 CANADA; (416) 925-9220; Mr. Jeff Jaffery (888) 925-9929; (416) 925-9929

Club Z! In-Home Tutoring Services, 12000 N. Dale Mabry Hwy., # 262, Tampa, FL 33618 ; (813) 908-9001; Mr. James Murphy (800) 434-2582; (813) 264-0197

CompuCollege School of Business, 5650 Yonge St., # 1400, North York, ON M2M 4G3 CANADA; (416) 733-4627; Mr. Jerry Stessel (800) 465-2700; (416) 733-4452

Dale Carnegie & Assoc., 1475 Franklin Ave., Garden City, NY 11530 ; (516) 248-5817; Mr. Bob DelVecchio ; (516) 248-5100

DreamCatcher Learning Centers, 427 Main St., Windsor, CO 80550 ; (970) 686-7045; Dr. Margo W. Barnhart (888) 937-3121; (970) 686-9282

Edge Learning Franchise, 1501 Fountainhead Parkway, # 330, Tempe, AZ 85282 ; (602) 968-1419; Mr. William L. Cole (800) 858-1484; (602) 968-7273

Honors Learning Center, The, 5959 Shallowford Rd., # 517, Chattanooga, TN 37421 ; (423) 892-1800; Mr. Gary Miller ; (423) 892-1800

Interactive Training Institute, 5915 Airport Rd., # 700, Mississauga, ON L4V 1T1 CANADA; (416) 410-4634; Mr. David Kunkel (888) 679-2201; (416) 679-2201

JEI - Jaeneung Educational Institute, 4221 Wilshire Blvd., # 224, Los Angeles, CA 90010 ; (323) 936-0300; Mr. Sean Choe (800) 954-0777; (323) 936-0300

John Robert Powers, 9220 Sunset Blvd., #100, West Hollywood, CA 90069 ; (310) 858-3310; Mr. Tod Otte (888) 41-MODEL; (310) 858-3300

Knowledge Development Centers, 445 Hutchinson Ave., # 120, Columbus, OH 43235 ; (614) 888-0411; Ms. Dana Wells (800) 717-6708; (614) 888-2444

Kumon USA, 300 Frank Burr Blvd., 2nd Floor, Teaneck, NJ 07666 ; (201) 928-0044; Mr. Kodama (800) 222-6284; (201) 928-0444

Magna Dry, 14633 E. Atlantic Dr., P.O. Box 440848, Aurora, CO 80014 ; (303) 338-0803; Mr. Johnny M. Wilson (800) 275-9000; (303) 338-0822

Priority Management Systems, 13200 Delf Pl., # 180, Richmond, BC V6V 2A2 CANADA; (604) 214-7773; Ms. Karen Stanley (800) 221-9031; (604) 214-7772

Promentum, 22 E. Lahon, Park Ridge, IL 60068 ; (847) 825-1701; Mr. Gerry Waller (888) 552-7761; (847) 384-1900

Sandler Sales Institute of Canada, 745 Clark Dr., Vancouver, BC V5L 3J3 CANADA; (604) 251-8060; Mr. Hugh Corke (800) 670-1400; (604) 254-4363

Sears Driver Training, 247 N. Service Rd. W., # 301, Oakville, ON L6M 3E6 CANADA; (905) 842-4251; Ms. Luba Castracane ; (416) 363-7483

Success Motivation Institute, 5000 Lakewood Dr., Waco, TX 76702 ; (254) 741-0001; Mr. Steve Rose (800) 678-6103; (254) 776-1230

TrainAmerica Computer Learning Center, 4083 Main St., Bridgeport, CT 06606-2347 ; (203) 372-4853; Mr. R. A. Swift ; (203) 372-4836

Turbo Management Systems, 36280 NE Wilsonville Rd., Newberg, OR 97132 ; (503) 625-2699; Ms. Chris Tipp (800) 574-4373; (503) 625-1867

EMPLOYMENT & PERSONNEL INDUSTRY PROFILE

Total # Franchisors in Industry Group	67
Total # Franchised Units in Industry Group	4,576
Total # Company-Owned Units in Industry Group	<u>2,276</u>
Total # Operating Units in Industry Group	6,852
Average # Franchised Units/Franchisor	68.3
Average # Company-Owned Units/Franchisor	<u>34.0</u>
Average # Total Units/Franchisor	102.3
Ratio of Total # Franchised Units/Total # Company-Owned Units	2.0:1
Industry Survey Participants	33
Representing % of Industry	49.3%
Average Franchise Fee*:	$23.6K
Average Total Investment*:	$106.0K
Average On-Going Royalty Fee*:	9.1%

If a range was provided, the mid-point of the range was used. See detailed profiles for actual ranges.

FIVE LARGEST PARTICIPANTS IN SURVEY

Company	# Franchised Units	# Co-Owned Units	# Total Units	Franchise Fee	On-Going Royalty	Total Investment
1. Management Recruiters/Sales Con.	791	39	830	72.5K	7%	110-145K
2. Express Personnel Services	409	1	410	14.5-17.5K	8-9%	90-135K
3. Interim Healthcare	277	117	394	10K	7%	150-200K
4. Snelling Personnel Services	280	28	308	9K	4.5-7%	97-142K
5. Remedy Intelligent Staffing	172	105	277	18K	Varies	95-150K

All of the data provided are proprietary and should not be quoted without acknowledging *Bond's Franchise Guide.*

ATC HEALTH CARE SERVICES

1983 Marcus Ave.
Lake Success, NY 11042
Tel: (800) 444-4633 (516) 327-3379
Fax: (516) 358-3678
Web Site: www.staffbuildersintl.com
Mr. Robert Laufer, Business Dev.

ATC HEALTH CARE SERVICES provide temporary staffing and T. L. C.

BACKGROUND: IFA MEMBER
Established: 1984;   1st Franchised: 1995
Franchised Units: 38
Company-Owned Units   2
Total Units: 40
Dist.:   US-40; CAN-0; O'seas-0
  North America: NR
  Density: 5 in Ga, 5 in TN, 3 in PA
Projected New Units (12 Months):   15
Qualifications: 4, 4, 4, 5, 2, 5
Registered: All States
FINANCIAL/TERMS:
Cash Investment: $30-50K
Total Investment: $110K
Minimum Net Worth: $150K
Fees: Franchise - $19.5K
  Royalty - Varies;   Ad. - 0%
Earnings Claim Statement: No
Term of Contract (Years):   10/5/5
Avg. # Of Employees: 3 FT, 2 PT
Passive Ownership: Allowed
Encourage Conversions: Yes
Area Develop. Agreements: Yes/20
Sub-Franchising Contracts: No
Expand In Territory: Yes
Space Needs: 1,000 SF; FS, SF, SC
SUPPORT & TRAINING PROVIDED:
Financial Assistance Provided: Yes(D)
Site Selection Assistance: Yes
Lease Negotiation Assistance: No
Co-Operative Advertising: No
Franchisee Assoc./Member: No
Size Of Corporate Staff: 35
On-Going Support: A,B,C,D,E,G,H
Training: 1   Week   Corporate
  Headquarters.
SPECIFIC EXPANSION PLANS:
US: All United States
Canada: All Canada
Overseas: No

≪ ≫

ATS PERSONNEL

9700 Philips Hwy., #101
Jacksonville, FL 32256
Tel: (800) 346-5574 (904) 645-9505
Fax: (904) 645-0390

E-Mail: curt@ats-services.com
Web Site: www.ats-services.com
Mr. Curt A. Cavins, Director of Operations

ATS offers a unique franchise opportunity with three niche businesses in the temporary staffing industry. With over 19 years' experience, we've perfected systems for the temporary and permanent placement of office clerical, light industrial, professional and health-related positions. The three niche areas are: ATS PERSONNEL for clerical and light industrial staffing, ATS PROFESSIONAL SERVICES for accounting and technical staffing and ATS HEALTH.

BACKGROUND:
Established: 1978;   1st Franchised: 1991
Franchised Units: 5
Company-Owned Units   9
Total Units: 14
Dist.:   US-14; CAN-0; O'seas-0
  North America: 6 States
  Density: 7 in GA, 2 in SC, 2 in LA
Projected New Units (12 Months):   4
Qualifications: 4, 5, 3, 3, 4, 5
Registered: FL,NY
FINANCIAL/TERMS:
Cash Investment: $35-50K
Total Investment: $75-110K
Minimum Net Worth: $100K
Fees: Franchise - $12.5K
  Royalty - 6.9%;   Ad. - 0.5%
Earnings Claim Statement: No
Term of Contract (Years):   10/5
Avg. # Of Employees: 2 FT, 1 PT
Passive Ownership: Not Allowed
Encourage Conversions: No
Area Develop. Agreements: No
Sub-Franchising Contracts: No
Expand In Territory: Yes
Space Needs: 1,000 SF; SC
SUPPORT & TRAINING PROVIDED:
Financial Assistance Provided: Yes(I)
Site Selection Assistance: Yes
Lease Negotiation Assistance: Yes
Co-Operative Advertising: No
Franchisee Assoc./Member: No
Size Of Corporate Staff: 17
On-Going Support: A,B,C,D,E,F,G,h,I
Training: 2 Weeks at Corporate Office; 2 Weeks On-Site.
SPECIFIC EXPANSION PLANS:
US: FL,NC
Canada: No
Overseas: No

≪ ≫

ATWORK PERSONNEL SERVICES

7855 E. Evans, Suite C
Scottsdale, AZ 85260
Tel: (800) 233-6846 (480) 922-7283
Fax: (480) 922-9959
E-Mail: atwork1740@aol.com
Web Site: www.atworkpersonnel.com
Mr. John D. Hall, Senior VP of Marketing

ATWORK PERSONNEL SERVICES announces its new 3-for-1 Franchise Program. For the cost of one franchise, ATWORK offers temporary help, staff leasing and permanent placement programs for its franchisees. Here are some benefits of becoming a member of ATWORK's network: franchise fee - $11,500; training fee - $2,500; sliding volume discount sale for royalty and service fees. Call our franchise sales department today to receive our information package.

BACKGROUND: IFA MEMBER
Established: 1990;   1st Franchised: 1992
Franchised Units: 60
Company-Owned Units   0
Total Units: 60
Dist.:   US-40; CAN-0; O'seas-0
  North America: 12 States
  Density: 15 in TN, 3 in NC, 2 in ME
Projected New Units (12 Months):   24
Qualifications: 3, 2, 3, 2, 3, 3
Registered: All States
FINANCIAL/TERMS:
Cash Investment: $15K
Total Investment: $35-75K
Minimum Net Worth: $75K
Fees: Franchise - $1K
  Royalty - 8%;   Ad. - 0%
Earnings Claim Statement: No
Term of Contract (Years):   10/5
Avg. # Of Employees: 3 FT, 1 PT
Passive Ownership: Discouraged
Encourage Conversions: Yes
Area Develop. Agreements: No
Sub-Franchising Contracts: No
Expand In Territory: Yes
Space Needs: 800 SF; FS, SF, SC, RM
SUPPORT & TRAINING PROVIDED:
Financial Assistance Provided: Yes
Site Selection Assistance: Yes
Lease Negotiation Assistance: No
Co-Operative Advertising: No
Franchisee Assoc./Member: No
Size Of Corporate Staff: 15
On-Going Support: A,C,D,H,I
Training: 4-5 Days in Corporate Office.

SPECIFIC EXPANSION PLANS:

US:	All United States
Canada:	No
Overseas:	No

CAREERS USA

6501 Congress Ave., # 200
Boca Raton, Fl 33487
Tel: (888) CAREERS (561) 995-7000
Fax: (561) 995-7001
E-Mail: ghielsberg@careersusa.com
Web Site: www.careersusa.com
Mr. Greg Hielsberg, Dir. Franchise
    Development

CAREERS USA provides temporary, temp to hire, and permanent personnel to businesses and corporations in your market area. CAREERS USA's proprietary computer software program computes the franchisee's temporary payroll, taxes and insurance. You, the franchisee, can download and analyze your sales, margins, rates, cash flow, etc. CAREERS USA finances 100% of your temporary payroll and 100% of your accounts receivable, helping you eliminate cash flow problems. Territories available nationally.

BACKGROUND: IFA MEMBER

Established: 1981;	1st Franchised: 1987
Franchised Units:	5
Company-Owned Units	18
Total Units:	23
Dist.:	US-23; CAN-0; O'seas-0
North America:	8 States
Density:	5 in PA, 5 in FL, 3 in IL
Projected New Units (12 Months):	12
Qualifications:	3, 4, 2, 3, 3, 4
Registered: All States	

FINANCIAL/TERMS:

Cash Investment:	$40-50K
Total Investment:	$84-130K
Minimum Net Worth:	$150K
Fees: Franchise -	$14.5K
Royalty - 7%/Varies;	Ad. - N/A
Earnings Claim Statement:	No
Term of Contract (Years):	10/5
Avg. # Of Employees:	3 FT

Passive Ownership:	Discouraged
Encourage Conversions:	Yes
Area Develop. Agreements:	N/A
Sub-Franchising Contracts:	No
Expand In Territory:	Yes
Space Needs: 1,000-1,500 SF; OB	

SUPPORT & TRAINING PROVIDED:

Financial Assistance Provided:	No
Site Selection Assistance:	Yes
Lease Negotiation Assistance:	Yes
Co-Operative Advertising:	Yes
Franchisee Assoc./Member:	No
Size Of Corporate Staff:	38
On-Going Support:	A,b,C,D,E,G,H,I

Training: 2 Weeks Boca Raton, FL Headquarters; 1 Week Your Center Location.

SPECIFIC EXPANSION PLANS:

US:	All United States
Canada:	All Canada
Overseas:	All Countries

CHECKMATE SYSTEMS

661 St. Andrews Blvd.
Charleston, SC 29407
Tel: (800) 964-6298 (843) 763-9393
Fax: (843) 571-1851
E-Mail: checkmate@checkmatepeo.com
Web Site: www.checkmatepeo.com
Mr. Ed Arrington, Vice President of
    Marketing

Employee leasing companies, also known as professional employers, are growing at over 33% per year. This new and largely untapped market has little competition and CHECKMATE is the only franchise in this new field which allows you to operate independently.

BACKGROUND:

Established: 1992;	1st Franchised: 1993
Franchised Units:	19
Company-Owned Units	0
Total Units:	19
Dist.:	US-19; CAN-0; O'seas-0
North America:	11 States
Density:	4 in LA, 2 in SC, 2 in AZ
Projected New Units (12 Months):	8
Qualifications:	3, 5, 1, 3, 4, 4
Registered: NR	

FINANCIAL/TERMS:

Cash Investment:	$35-85K
Total Investment:	$30-75K

Minimum Net Worth:	$100K
Fees: Franchise -	$27.5K
Royalty - 7.5%;	Ad. - 0%
Earnings Claim Statement:	No
Term of Contract (Years):	10/5
Avg. # Of Employees:	3 FT, 1-2 PT
Passive Ownership:	Not Allowed
Encourage Conversions:	Yes
Area Develop. Agreements:	No
Sub-Franchising Contracts:	No
Expand In Territory:	Yes
Space Needs: N/A SF; HB, Rented Office	

SUPPORT & TRAINING PROVIDED:

Financial Assistance Provided:	No
Site Selection Assistance:	N/A
Lease Negotiation Assistance:	N/A
Co-Operative Advertising:	N/A
Franchisee Assoc./Member:	No
Size Of Corporate Staff:	7
On-Going Support:	G,h,I

Training: 1 Week New Orleans, LA.

SPECIFIC EXPANSION PLANS:

US:	All United States
Canada:	No
Overseas:	No

DUNHILL STAFFING SYSTEMS

150 Motor Pkwy.
Hauppauge, NY 11788
Tel: (800) 386-7823 (631) 952-3000
Fax: (631) 952-3500
E-Mail: jn@Dunhillstaff.com
Web Site: www.dunhillstaff.com
Ms. Joanne Naccarato, Director, New
    Business Devel.

DUNHILL offers Professional Search and Temporary Staffing franchises. Our franchisees provide permanent executives, mid-level management, professionals, technical staffing and temporaries. Professional Search franchisees benefit from the industry's best interview-to-placement ratio and leading edge computerized placement matching system. All DUNHILL executives have 'front line' industry experience. Our temporary offices are supported with back-office accounting, including payroll and accounts receivable.

BACKGROUND: IFA MEMBER

Established: 1952;	1st Franchised: 1961
Franchised Units:	125
Company-Owned Units	30

142

Total Units: 155
Dist.: US-151; CAN-4; O'seas-0
  North America: 50 States
  Density: 21 in TX, 19 in IN, 12 in CT
Projected New Units (12 Months): 12
Qualifications: 4, 3, 1, 3, 3, 5
Registered: All States

FINANCIAL/TERMS:

Cash Investment: $15-38K
Total Investment: $70-140K
Minimum Net Worth: $250K
Fees: Franchise - $15-38K
  Royalty - 7% Perm./Varies; Ad. - 1% Perm.
Earnings Claim Statement: No
Term of Contract (Years): 10/10/5
Avg. # Of Employees: 2-3 FT
Passive Ownership: Discouraged
Encourage Conversions: Yes
Area Develop. Agreements: No
Sub-Franchising Contracts: No
Expand In Territory: Yes
Space Needs: 700-1,500 SF; FS, SF, SC, RM, Suites

SUPPORT & TRAINING PROVIDED:

Financial Assistance Provided: Yes(D)
Site Selection Assistance: Yes
Lease Negotiation Assistance: Yes
Co-Operative Advertising: Yes
Franchisee Assoc./Member: Yes
Size Of Corporate Staff: 45
On-Going Support: A,B,C,D,E,G,H,I
Training: 1-2 Weeks Corporate; 1-2 Weeks Field.

SPECIFIC EXPANSION PLANS:

US: All United States
Canada: All Canada
Overseas: No

◄◄ ►►

EXPRESS PERSONNEL SERVICES
6300 Northwest Expy.
Oklahoma City, OK 73132
Tel: (877) 652-6400 (405) 840-5000
Fax: (405) 773-6442
E-Mail: djcarter@expresspersonnel.com
Web Site: www.expresspersonnel.com
Mr. Jeffrey C. Bevis, VP Franchising

Three divisions - permanent placement, temporary placement and executive search - offering full and complete coverage of the employment field.

BACKGROUND: IFA MEMBER
Established: 1983; 1st Franchised: 1985

Franchised Units: 409
Company-Owned Units 1
Total Units: 410
Dist.: US-385; CAN-8; O'seas-17
  North America: 45 States
  Density: 48 in TX, 32 in OK, 24 in WA
Projected New Units (12 Months): 50
Qualifications: 4, 4, 3, 4, 4, 4
Registered: All States

FINANCIAL/TERMS:

Cash Investment: $90-135K
Total Investment: $90-135K
Minimum Net Worth: $150K
Fees: Franchise - $14.5-17.5K
  Royalty - 8-9%; Ad. - 0.6-2%
Earnings Claim Statement: No
Term of Contract (Years): 5/5
Avg. # Of Employees: 2 FT, 1 PT
Passive Ownership: Not Allowed
Encourage Conversions: Yes
Area Develop. Agreements: Yes
Sub-Franchising Contracts: No
Expand In Territory: Yes
Space Needs: 1,200 SF; SC, RM, SF

SUPPORT & TRAINING PROVIDED:

Financial Assistance Provided: Yes(D)
Site Selection Assistance: Yes
Lease Negotiation Assistance: Yes
Co-Operative Advertising: Yes
Franchisee Assoc./Member: No
Size Of Corporate Staff: 186
On-Going Support: A,C,D,E,G,H,I
Training: 3 Weeks Oklahoma City, OK; 1 Week On-Site.

SPECIFIC EXPANSION PLANS:

US: All United States
Canada: ON Only
Overseas: W. Europe, South Africa, Australia, New Zealand or reviewed by request.

◄◄ ►►

F-O-R-T-U-N-E PERSONNEL CONSULTANTS
1155 Avenue of the Americas, 15th Floor
New York, NY 10036
Tel: (800) 886-7839 (212) 302-1141
Fax: (212) 302-2422
E-Mail: rich@pfcfind.com
Web Site: www.fpcweb.com
Mr. Richard A. Simeone, Dir. Fran. Dev.

As one of the largest and most successful executive recruiting firms in the world, F-O-R-T-U-N-E PERSONNEL CONSU-LTANTS has set a distinguished standard of leadership and integrity in the executive placement industry. Franchisees enjoy all of today's technologies, along with good old-fashioned service. Intensive training and unparalleled support by industry experienced professionals securely places qualified candidates in their own professional business. Extensive on-going training.

BACKGROUND: IFA MEMBER
Established: 1959; 1st Franchised: 1973
Franchised Units: 99
Company-Owned Units 1
Total Units: 100
Dist.: US-100; CAN-0; O'seas-0
  North America: 28 States
  Density: 7 in FL, 7 in MA, 7 in NJ
Projected New Units (12 Months): 12-15
Qualifications: 4, 3, 3, 4, 2, 4
Registered: All Except AB

FINANCIAL/TERMS:

Cash Investment: $31.4-63.9K
Total Investment: $71.4-103.9K
Minimum Net Worth: $250K
Fees: Franchise - $40K
  Royalty - 7%; Ad. - 1%
Earnings Claim Statement: Yes
Term of Contract (Years): 20/10
Avg. # Of Employees: 3-5 FT, 1-2 PT
Passive Ownership: Discouraged
Encourage Conversions: N/A
Area Develop. Agreements: No
Sub-Franchising Contracts: No
Expand In Territory: Yes
Space Needs: 1,000 SF; Commercial Office

SUPPORT & TRAINING PROVIDED:

Financial Assistance Provided: Yes(D)
Site Selection Assistance: Yes
Lease Negotiation Assistance: Yes
Co-Operative Advertising: Yes
Franchisee Assoc./Member: Yes
Size Of Corporate Staff: 15
On-Going Support: A,B,C,D,E,F,G,H,I
Training: 2 Weeks Home Office, New York, NY: 5 Days Franchise Location.

SPECIFIC EXPANSION PLANS:

US: All United States
Canada: All Canada
Overseas: No

◄◄ ►►

FIRSTAT NURSING SERVICES
801 Village Blvd., # 303
West Palm Beach, FL 33409
Tel: (800) 845-7828 (561) 689-7100
Fax: (561) 689-4057
Web Site: www.firstatnursingservices.com

Ms. Kerry Torres, Vice President

We are the provider of nurses and aides to patients in their homes and institutions. The niche is high-tech and continuous homecare. Additionally, we provide staff to hospitals in critical care areas.

BACKGROUND:

Established: 1989; 1st Franchised: 1990	
Franchised Units:	33
Company-Owned Units	2
Total Units:	35
Dist.:	US-34; CAN-1; O'seas-0
North America:	18 States, 1 Province
Density:	4 in FL, 4 in MN, 4 in OH
Projected New Units (12 Months):	20
Qualifications:	5, 5, 1, 3, 1, 5
Registered: All States	

FINANCIAL/TERMS:

Cash Investment:	$200K
Total Investment:	$200K
Minimum Net Worth:	$N/A
Fees: Franchise -	$25K
Royalty - 0.3-0.5%;	Ad. - N/A
Earnings Claim Statement:	No
Term of Contract (Years):	5/10
Avg. # Of Employees:	5 FT, 1 PT
Passive Ownership:	Not Allowed
Encourage Conversions:	Yes
Area Develop. Agreements:	No
Sub-Franchising Contracts:	No
Expand In Territory:	Yes
Space Needs: 1,500 SF; SF, SC, OB	

SUPPORT & TRAINING PROVIDED:

Financial Assistance Provided:	Yes(I)
Site Selection Assistance:	Yes
Lease Negotiation Assistance:	Yes
Co-Operative Advertising:	No
Franchisee Assoc./Member:	No
Size Of Corporate Staff:	15
On-Going Support:	C,D,E,G,H,I
Training: 5 Days Home Office; 5 Days Franchisee Location.	

SPECIFIC EXPANSION PLANS:

US:	All United States
Canada:	All Canada
Overseas:	No

HOME HELPERS
4338 Glendale Milford Rd.
Cincinnati, OH 45242
Tel: (800) 216-4196 (513) 563-8339
Fax: (513) 563-2691
E-Mail: jbuckles@fuse.net
Web Site: www.homehelpers.cc
Franchise Sales Department,

As America's population continues to age, there is a huge demand for non-medical, in-home companion care. There are over 33 million people in the US over 65 years old. Our franchise system is unique. At HOME HELPERS we provide non-medical, in-home companion care for the elderly, new mothers and those recuperating from illness. Our franchisees succeed due to our marketing expertise, market penetration and proven system. No experience or medical background needed.

BACKGROUND:

Established: 1997; 1st Franchised: 1997	
Franchised Units:	110
Company-Owned Units	0
Total Units:	110
Dist.:	US-110; CAN-0; O'seas-0
North America:	28 States
Density:	NR
Projected New Units (12 Months):	75
Qualifications:	, , 1, , 3, 5
Registered: All States	

FINANCIAL/TERMS:

Cash Investment:	$7.5-11.5K
Total Investment:	$19-39K
Minimum Net Worth:	$N/A
Fees: Franchise -	$13.9-23.9K
Royalty - 4-6% Varies;	Ad. - 3% Local
Earnings Claim Statement:	No
Term of Contract (Years):	10/10/10
Avg. # Of Employees:	N/A
Passive Ownership:	Discouraged
Encourage Conversions:	N/A
Area Develop. Agreements:	No
Sub-Franchising Contracts:	No
Expand In Territory:	N/A
Space Needs: N/A SF; HB	

SUPPORT & TRAINING PROVIDED:

Financial Assistance Provided:	Yes(D)
Site Selection Assistance:	N/A
Lease Negotiation Assistance:	N/A
Co-Operative Advertising:	N/A
Franchisee Assoc./Member:	No
Size Of Corporate Staff:	9
On-Going Support:	B,C,D,G,H,I

Training: 5 Days Cincinnati, OH.
SPECIFIC EXPANSION PLANS:

US:	All United States
Canada:	All Canada
Overseas:	All Countries

‹‹ ››

HOME INSTEAD SENIOR CARE
604 N. 109th Ct.
Omaha, NE 68154
Tel: (888) 484-5759 (402) 498-4466
Fax: (402) 498-5757
E-Mail: homeinsted@aol.com
Web Site: www.homeinstead.com
Mr. Jeff Huber, Franchise Development Manager

HOME INSTEAD SENIOR CARE is America's largest, most successful, non-medical companionship and home care franchise. Entrepreneur and other leading business publications have ranked us one of the top opportunities in all of franchising. The elderly market we serve is the fastest-growing segment of the population. Services such as companionship, light housework, errands and meal preparation assist the elderly in remaining in their homes rather than being institutionalized.

BACKGROUND: IFA MEMBER

Established: 1994; 1st Franchised: 1995	
Franchised Units:	230
Company-Owned Units	1
Total Units:	231
Dist.:	US-231; CAN-0; O'seas-0
North America:	34 States
Density:	24 in CA, 16 in FL, 9 in GA
Projected New Units (12 Months):	60
Qualifications:	5, 3, 1, 3, 1, 5
Registered: All States and AB	

FINANCIAL/TERMS:

Cash Investment:	$5.5-12.3K
Total Investment:	$23.1-29.8K
Minimum Net Worth:	$Varies
Fees: Franchise -	$17.5K
Royalty - 5%;	Ad. - 0%
Earnings Claim Statement:	Yes
Term of Contract (Years):	10/10
Avg. # Of Employees:	2 FT, 40 PT
Passive Ownership:	Discouraged
Encourage Conversions:	Yes
Area Develop. Agreements:	NR
Sub-Franchising Contracts:	No

Expand In Territory: Yes
Space Needs: 300-500 SF; Industrial/ Office

SUPPORT & TRAINING PROVIDED:
Financial Assistance Provided: No
Site Selection Assistance: Yes
Lease Negotiation Assistance: No
Co-Operative Advertising: No
Franchisee Assoc./Member: No
Size Of Corporate Staff: 28
On-Going Support: B,C,D,E,F,G,H,I
Training: 1 Week Corporate Headquarters; 2 Days Visit Franchise Office.

SPECIFIC EXPANSION PLANS:
US: All United States
Canada: All Canada
Overseas: All Countries

≪ ≫

HOMEWATCH CAREGIVERS
2865 S. Colorado Blvd.
Denver, CO 80222
Tel: (800) 916-9593 (303) 758-7290
Fax: (303) 758-1724
E-Mail: hwcorp@aol.com
Web Site: www.homewatch-intl.com
Mr. Paul A. Sauer, President/CEO

The mission of Homewatch Caregivers is to be the best provider of non-medical personal care services to seniors and others who are recovering, rehabilitating and convalescing within the communities we serve. The elderly make up 25% of the population. This unique franchise opportunity is not only financially rewarding, but offers the chance to make a difference in rendering a variety of basic need and personal care assistance to the elderly.

BACKGROUND: IFA MEMBER
Established: 1973; 1st Franchised: 1986
Franchised Units: 13
Company-Owned Units: 1
Total Units: 14
Dist.: US-14; CAN-0; O'seas-0
North America: 6 States
Density: 3 in CO, 2 in MN
Projected New Units (12 Months): 15
Qualifications: 4, 4, 3, 3, 3, 4
Registered: CA,FL,MN,WA,VA

FINANCIAL/TERMS:
Cash Investment: $15-30K
Total Investment: $35-40K
Minimum Net Worth: $150K
Fees: Franchise - $17.5K
Royalty - 5% on Gross; Ad. - 0%
Earnings Claim Statement: Yes
Term of Contract (Years): 10/10
Avg. # Of Employees: 3 FT, 45 PT
Passive Ownership: Allowed
Encourage Conversions: Yes
Area Develop. Agreements: Yes/10
Sub-Franchising Contracts: No
Expand In Territory: No
Space Needs: 800 SF; HB, OB

SUPPORT & TRAINING PROVIDED:
Financial Assistance Provided: Some
Site Selection Assistance: N/A
Lease Negotiation Assistance: N/A
Co-Operative Advertising: No
Franchisee Assoc./Member: No
Size Of Corporate Staff: 4
On-Going Support: D,E,G,H,I
Training: 5 Days Denver, CO; Grand Opening at Franchisee Location.

SPECIFIC EXPANSION PLANS:
US: All United States
Canada: All Canada
Overseas: All Countries

≪ ≫

HUNT PERSONNEL/ TEMPORARILY YOURS
P.O. Box 1564
Niagara On The Lake, ON L05 1J0
CANADA
Tel: (416) 920-4141
Fax: (905) 468-8174
E-Mail: info@hunt.ca
Web Site: www.hunt.ca
Mr. Ted Turner, President

Established in 1967, we have an unequalled reputation for quality service. Prefer local industry experience or conversion. Specialization encouraged.

BACKGROUND:
Established: 1967; 1st Franchised: 1974
Franchised Units: 12
Company-Owned Units: 0
Total Units: 12

Dist.: US-0; CAN-12; O'seas-0
North America: 4 Provinces
Density: 7 in ON, 3 in PQ, 1 in BC
Projected New Units (12 Months): 3
Qualifications: 5, 5, 5, 3, 4, 4
Registered: NR

FINANCIAL/TERMS:
Cash Investment: $100K
Total Investment: $150K
Minimum Net Worth: $200K
Fees: Franchise - $Varies
Royalty - Varies; Ad. - ~0.25%
Earnings Claim Statement: No
Term of Contract (Years): 5/5
Avg. # Of Employees: 3+ FT
Passive Ownership: Not Allowed
Encourage Conversions: Yes
Area Develop. Agreements: No
Sub-Franchising Contracts: Yes
Expand In Territory: Yes
Space Needs: 1,200 SF; OB

SUPPORT & TRAINING PROVIDED:
Financial Assistance Provided: No
Site Selection Assistance: Yes
Lease Negotiation Assistance: Yes
Co-Operative Advertising: No
Franchisee Assoc./Member: No
Size Of Corporate Staff: 4
On-Going Support: a,B,C,D,G,H
Training: 2-3 Weeks Local.

SPECIFIC EXPANSION PLANS:
US: No
Canada: ON,PQ,AB,MB,SKMR
Overseas: No

≪ ≫

INTERIM HEALTHCARE
1601 Sawgrass Corporate Pkwy.
Sunrise, FL 33323
Tel: (800) 338-7786 (954) 858-6000
Fax: (954) 858-2720
E-Mail: gigigarcia@interim.com
Web Site: www.interim.com
Ms. Aliza Deray, Franchise Support Coord.

INTERIM HEALTHCARE is one of the nation's largest proprietary home health care and staffing services. Since 1966, INTERIM has provided a wide variety of health care personnel to people in need at home as well as in traditional facilities, such as hospitals, physicians groups, convalescent centers and HMO's. From highly-skilled nursing to home companions, INTERIM HEALTHCARE offers its services 24 hours a day, 7 days a week.

BACKGROUND:
Established: 1946;   1st Franchised: 1966
Franchised Units: 277
Company-Owned Units   117
Total Units: 394
Dist.:   US-378; CAN-13; O'seas-3
 North America: 46 States, 4 Provinces
 Density: 36 in FL, 32 in NC, 29 in CA
Projected New Units (12 Months):   5
Qualifications: 5, 5, 2, 3, 3, 5
Registered: All States
FINANCIAL/TERMS:
Cash Investment: $50-75K
Total Investment: $150-200K
Minimum Net Worth: $NR
Fees: Franchise - $10K
 Royalty - 7%;   Ad. - 0.0025%
Earnings Claim Statement: No
Term of Contract (Years):   5/5
Avg. # Of Employees: 3 FT
Passive Ownership: Discouraged
Encourage Conversions: Yes
Area Develop. Agreements: No
Sub-Franchising Contracts: No
Expand In Territory: Yes
Space Needs: 1,000-1,200 SF; SC, OB
SUPPORT & TRAINING PROVIDED:
Financial Assistance Provided: Yes(I)
Site Selection Assistance: Yes
Lease Negotiation Assistance: Yes
Co-Operative Advertising: Yes
Franchisee Assoc./Member: Yes
Size Of Corporate Staff: 500
On-Going Support: A,C,D,E,G,H,I
Training: 2 Weeks Headquarters; 1 Week
 On-Site.
SPECIFIC EXPANSION PLANS:
US: ID,IN,MI,ND Only
Canada: No
Overseas: Latin America, Mexico, Europe

LABOR FINDERS
INTERNATIONAL
3910 RCA Blvd., # 1001
Palm Beach Gardens, FL 33410
Tel: (800) 864-7749 (561) 627-6507
Fax: (561) 627-6556
E-Mail: lfi@laborfinders.com
Web Site: www.laborfinders.com
Mr. Robert R. Gallagher, Vice President
 Marketing

LABOR FINDERS is a specialized labor staffing service that supplies highly productive skilled, semi-skilled and unskilled workers to companies in construction, industrial and commercial business segments.

BACKGROUND: IFA MEMBER
Established: 1975;   1st Franchised: 1975
Franchised Units: 152
Company-Owned Units   5
Total Units: 157
Dist.:   US-157; CAN-0; O'seas-0
 North America: 24 States
 Density: 41 in FL, 8 in AL, 7 in NC
Projected New Units (12 Months):   20
Qualifications: 4, 4, 3, 3, 4, 4
Registered: CA,FL,IL,IN,MD,MN,VA,
 WA,WI
FINANCIAL/TERMS:
Cash Investment: $45-75K
Total Investment: $66.8-110.5K
Minimum Net Worth: $500K
Fees: Franchise - $10K
 Royalty - % Billable Wages;   Ad. - 0%
Earnings Claim Statement: No
Term of Contract (Years):   10/5/5
Avg. # Of Employees: 2 FT, 1 PT
Passive Ownership: Discouraged
Encourage Conversions: Yes
Area Develop. Agreements: No
Sub-Franchising Contracts: No
Expand In Territory: Yes
Space Needs: 800-1,000 SF; FS, SF, SC
SUPPORT & TRAINING PROVIDED:
Financial Assistance Provided: Yes(D)
Site Selection Assistance: Yes
Lease Negotiation Assistance: No
Co-Operative Advertising: Yes
Franchisee Assoc./Member: Yes/Yes
Size Of Corporate Staff: 15
On-Going Support: C,D,E,G,h,I
Training: 2 Weeks Operating Unit; 2 Weeks
 On-Site; 1 Week Classroom.
SPECIFIC EXPANSION PLANS:
US: All United States
Canada: No
Overseas: No

LABOR FORCE
5225 Katy Fwy., # 600
Houston, TX 77007
Tel: (800) 299-4312 (713) 802-1284
Fax: (713) 802-1288
Web Site: www.laborforce.com
Ms. Carol Nagel, Franchising Department

We have small to large light industrial offices and finance 90% of weekly sales

for 49 days to give instant cash flow. Enjoy instant recognition with national companies.

BACKGROUND:
Established: 1970;   1st Franchised: 1992
Franchised Units: 23
Company-Owned Units   16
Total Units: 39
Dist.:   US-39; CAN-0; O'seas-0
 North America: 15 States
 Density: 17 in TX, 5 in GA, 3 in AZ
Projected New Units (12 Months):   10
Qualifications: 5, 5, 3, 3, 4, 4
Registered: NR
FINANCIAL/TERMS:
Cash Investment: $25-50K
Total Investment: $111-127K
Minimum Net Worth: $50K
Fees: Franchise - $15-25K
 Royalty - 6%;   Ad. - 0%
Earnings Claim Statement: No
Term of Contract (Years):   10/10
Avg. # Of Employees: 3 FT
Passive Ownership: Discouraged
Encourage Conversions: Yes
Area Develop. Agreements: No
Sub-Franchising Contracts: No
Expand In Territory: Yes
Space Needs: 800-1,200 SF; SC
SUPPORT & TRAINING PROVIDED:
Financial Assistance Provided: No
Site Selection Assistance: Yes
Lease Negotiation Assistance: Yes
Co-Operative Advertising: Yes
Franchisee Assoc./Member: No
Size Of Corporate Staff: 20
On-Going Support: B,C,D,E,G,H,I
Training: 2 Weeks at National Training
 Center; 1 Week On-Site.
SPECIFIC EXPANSION PLANS:
US: All Non-Registration States
Canada: All Canada
Overseas: Mexico

LAWCORPS LEGAL STAFFING
1819 L St., NW, 9th Fl.
Washington, DC 20036
Tel: (800) 437-8809 (202) 785-5996
Fax: (202) 785-1118
Web Site: www.lawcorps.com
Mr. Bryce A. Arrowood, President

Temporary legal staffing: attorneys, law clerks, paralegals and support staff. LAWCORPS Franchise Corporation is the first and only exclusively legal temporary service to franchise. Join the fastest-growing segment of the fastest-growing industry.

BACKGROUND: IFA MEMBER
Established: 1988; 1st Franchised: 1995
Franchised Units: 3
Company-Owned Units 4
Total Units: 7
Dist.: US-7; CAN-0; O'seas-0
North America: NR
Density: DC, NY, IL
Projected New Units (12 Months): 4-6
Qualifications: 5, 5, 5, 5, 5, 5
Registered: HI,IL,MI,MN,NY
FINANCIAL/TERMS:
Cash Investment: $88-110K
Total Investment: $88-110K
Minimum Net Worth: $N/A
Fees: Franchise - $25K
Royalty - 8%; Ad. - N/A
Earnings Claim Statement: No
Term of Contract (Years): 7/7
Avg. # Of Employees: 2 FT, 1 PT
Passive Ownership: Discouraged
Encourage Conversions: Yes
Area Develop. Agreements: No
Sub-Franchising Contracts: No
Expand In Territory: No
Space Needs: 200-500 SF; Executive Suite
SUPPORT & TRAINING PROVIDED:
Financial Assistance Provided: N/A
Site Selection Assistance: Yes
Lease Negotiation Assistance: No
Co-Operative Advertising: Yes
Franchisee Assoc./Member: No
Size Of Corporate Staff: 5
On-Going Support: a,b,C,D,E,g,H,I
Training: 2 Weeks Headquarters; 1 Week On-Site.
SPECIFIC EXPANSION PLANS:
US: All United States
Canada: All Canada
Overseas: No

<< >>

LINK STAFFING SERVICES
1800 Bering Dr., # 800
Houston, TX 77057-3129
Tel: (800) 848-5465 (713) 784-4400

Fax: (713) 784-4454
E-Mail: fran_dev@linkstaffing.com
Web Site: www.linkstaffing.com
Ms. Lana Peralta, Franchise Development Manager

LINK STAFFING SERVICES provides a variety of flexible staffing/productivity solutions. We allow our clients to build their own business while providing them the staff they need; they tell us one thing that sets us apart from other staffing services is our comprehensive screening process, which consistently delivers high-quality workers. Many fieldstaff have accepted full-time positions with our clients. Join a team with top-notch employees and the experience to support you all the way to success!

BACKGROUND: IFA MEMBER
Established: 1980; 1st Franchised: 1993
Franchised Units: 28
Company-Owned Units 17
Total Units: 45
Dist.: US-45; CAN-0; O'seas-0
North America: 13 States
Density: 17 in TX, 10 in FL, 6 in CA
Projected New Units (12 Months): 10
Qualifications: 3, 3, 2, 4, 4, 5
Registered: All Except HI,AB
FINANCIAL/TERMS:
Cash Investment: $25-35K
Total Investment: $95-159K
Minimum Net Worth: $N/A
Fees: Franchise - $15K
Royalty - Varies; Ad. - 0.05%
Earnings Claim Statement: No
Term of Contract (Years): 10/5/5/5
Avg. # Of Employees: 2 FT
Passive Ownership: Discouraged
Encourage Conversions: Yes
Area Develop. Agreements: No
Sub-Franchising Contracts: No
Expand In Territory: Yes
Space Needs: 1,200-1,800 SF; SF, SC, Industrial Office Park
SUPPORT & TRAINING PROVIDED:
Financial Assistance Provided: Yes(I)

Site Selection Assistance: Yes
Lease Negotiation Assistance: Yes
Co-Operative Advertising: Yes
Franchisee Assoc./Member: Yes/Yes
Size Of Corporate Staff: 42
On-Going Support: A,B,C,D,E,G,H,I
Training: 3-5 Days Existing Franchise; 5 Days (Sales), 5 Days (Operations) Support Center, TX.
SPECIFIC EXPANSION PLANS:
US: All United States
Canada: No
Overseas: No

<< >>

LLOYD STAFFING
445 Broadhollow Rd., #119
Melville, NY 11747
Tel: (888) 292-6678 (631) 777-7600
Fax: (631) 777-7626
E-Mail: cliff@lloydstaffing.com
Web Site: www.lloydstaffing.com
Mr. Cliff Alberti, Director of Franchising

Since 1971, we have successfully served thousands of employers, job seekers and temporary employees. Our blended service concept truly embodies the entire spectrum of staffing, including temporary personnel, consultant referrals, contingency placement and executive search. And because we recognize that the field of human resources has significantly changed its structure and focus over the years, we've added several complimentary and compatible staffing components to enhance the support we provide.

BACKGROUND: IFA MEMBER
Established: 1971; 1st Franchised: 1986
Franchised Units: 5
Company-Owned Units 7
Total Units: 13
Dist.: US-11; CAN-0; O'seas-0
North America: NR
Density: 5 in NY, 2 in NJ, 2 in CT
Projected New Units (12 Months): 3
Qualifications: 4, 5, 4, 3, 3, 5
Registered: FL,MD
FINANCIAL/TERMS:
Cash Investment: $75-100K
Total Investment: $85-150K
Minimum Net Worth: $100-150K
Fees: Franchise - $15-22K
Royalty - 60/40-7%; Ad. - N/A
Earnings Claim Statement: No
Term of Contract (Years): 10/10
Avg. # Of Employees: 4 FT
Passive Ownership: Not Allowed

Encourage Conversions: No
Area Develop. Agreements: No
Sub-Franchising Contracts: No
Expand In Territory: Yes
Space Needs: 1,500 SF; FS, SF, SC

SUPPORT & TRAINING PROVIDED:
Financial Assistance Provided: Yes(I)
Site Selection Assistance: Yes
Lease Negotiation Assistance: Yes
Co-Operative Advertising: No
Franchisee Assoc./Member: No
Size Of Corporate Staff: 123
On-Going Support: A,C,D,E,g,h,I
Training: 2 Weeks in Melville, NY; 1 Week
    at Your Location.

SPECIFIC EXPANSION PLANS:
US: Southeast, Northeast
Canada: No
Overseas: No

MANAGEMENT RECRUITERS/
SALES CONSULTANTS
200 Public Sq., 31st Fl.
Cleveland, OH 44114-2301
Tel: (800) 875-4000 (216) 696-1122
Fax: (216) 696-6612
E-Mail: webmaster@brilliantpeople.com
Web Site: www.brilliantpeople.com
Mr. Robert A. Angell, VP Franchise
    Marketing

Complete range of recruitment and human
resource services, including: permanent
executive, mid-management, professional,
marketing, sales management and sales
placement; temporary professional and
sales staffing; video-conferencing; permanent and temporary office support personnel; with coverage on all continents.
Franchises available outside of North
America through our wholly-owned subsidiary, the Humana Group International.

BACKGROUND: IFA MEMBER
Established: 1957;   1st Franchised: 1965
Franchised Units: 791
Company-Owned Units   39
Total Units: 830
Dist.:   US-829; CAN-0; O'seas-1
    North America: 48 States
    Density: 64 in FL, 62 in CA,60 in NC
Projected New Units (12 Months):   50
Qualifications: 3, 4, 1, 4, 3, 3
Registered: All States
FINANCIAL/TERMS:
Cash Investment: $110-145K
Total Investment: $110-145K
Minimum Net Worth: $N/A

Fees: Franchise - $72.5K
    Royalty - 7%;   Ad. - 0.5%
Earnings Claim Statement: Yes
Term of Contract (Years):   5-20/10
Avg. # Of Employees: 3-4 FT
Passive Ownership: Discouraged
Encourage Conversions: Yes
Area Develop. Agreements: No
Sub-Franchising Contracts: No
Expand In Territory: Yes
Space Needs: 600-1,000 SF; FS

SUPPORT & TRAINING PROVIDED:
Financial Assistance Provided: Yes(I)
Site Selection Assistance: Yes
Lease Negotiation Assistance: Yes
Co-Operative Advertising: N/A
Franchisee Assoc./Member: Yes
Size Of Corporate Staff: 91
On-Going Support: C,D,E,G,H,I
Training: 3 Weeks Headquarters, Cleveland,
    OH; 10 Days Franchisee's Location.

SPECIFIC EXPANSION PLANS:
US: All United States
Canada: No
Overseas: No

NURSEFINDERS
1701 E. Lamar Blvd., # 200
Arlington, TX 76006
Tel: (800) 445-0459 (817) 460-1181
Fax: (817) 460-1969
Web Site: www.nursefinders.com
Mr. Ed McGuinness, VP Franchising

Largest provider in United States of
temporary medical staffing to hospitals and
other health care facilities. Ranked Number
1 in category by Entrepreneur Magazine.
We also provide the full spectrum of home
health care.

BACKGROUND: IFA MEMBER
Established: 1974;   1st Franchised: 1978
Franchised Units: 55
Company-Owned Units   58
Total Units: 113
Dist.:   US-113; CAN-0; O'seas-0
    North America: 31 States
    Density: 14 in FL, 8 in IL, 7 in CA
Projected New Units (12 Months):   10
Registered: All States
FINANCIAL/TERMS:
Cash Investment: $50-100K
Total Investment: $110-200K
Minimum Net Worth: $250K
Fees: Franchise - $19.6K
    Royalty - 7%;   Ad. - 0%
Earnings Claim Statement: No

Term of Contract (Years):   10/5/5
Avg. # Of Employees: 5 FT, 100 PT
Passive Ownership: Discouraged
Encourage Conversions: Yes
Area Develop. Agreements: Yes/5/5
Sub-Franchising Contracts: No
Expand In Territory: Yes
Space Needs: 1,500-2,000 SF; Profess.
    Office. Bldg.

SUPPORT & TRAINING PROVIDED:
Financial Assistance Provided: Yes(D)
Site Selection Assistance: Yes
Lease Negotiation Assistance: Yes
Co-Operative Advertising: N/A
Franchisee Assoc./Member: No
Size Of Corporate Staff: 62
On-Going Support: A,B,C,D,E,G,h,I
Training: 2 Weeks Arlington, TX; 1 Week
    Company Office; 2 Weeks On-Site.

SPECIFIC EXPANSION PLANS:
US: All United States
Canada: No
Overseas: No

PMA FRANCHISE SYSTEMS
1950 Spectrum Circle, #B-310
Marietta, GA 30067
Tel: (800) 466-7822 (770) 916-1668
Fax: (770) 916-1429
E-Mail: jobs@pmasearch.com
Web Site: www.pmasearch.com/
franchise_opps.htm
Mr. Bill Lins, CPC Dir. of Operations

National employment firm specializing in
retail, restaurant and service management.

BACKGROUND: IFA MEMBER
Established: 1985;   1st Franchised: 1997
Franchised Units: 5
Company-Owned Units   1
Total Units: 6
Dist.:   US-6; CAN-0; O'seas-0
    North America: 5 States
    Density: 2 in TN, 1 in OR, 1 in OK
Projected New Units (12 Months):   NR
Registered:

FINANCIAL/TERMS:

Cash Investment:	$20K
Total Investment:	$25-35K
Minimum Net Worth:	$N/A
Fees: Franchise -	$20K
Royalty - 10%;	Ad. - 0%
Earnings Claim Statement:	NR
Term of Contract (Years):	5/5
Avg. # Of Employees:	NR
Passive Ownership:	Not Allowed
Encourage Conversions:	NR
Area Develop. Agreements:	Yes/Varies
Sub-Franchising Contracts:	NR
Expand In Territory:	Yes
Space Needs: 150+ SF; NR	

SUPPORT & TRAINING PROVIDED:

Financial Assistance Provided:	NR
Site Selection Assistance:	Yes
Lease Negotiation Assistance:	No
Co-Operative Advertising:	Yes
Franchisee Assoc./Member:	Yes/Yes
Size Of Corporate Staff:	12
On-Going Support:	A,C,E,G,h,I
Training: 4 Weeks Atlanta, GA.	

SPECIFIC EXPANSION PLANS:

US:	All United States
Canada:	NR
Overseas:	NR

◄◄ ►►

PRIDESTAFF

6780 N. West Ave., # 103
Fresno, CA 93711-1393
Tel: (800) 774-3316 (559) 432-7780
Fax: (559) 432-4371
E-Mail: rbladek@pridestaff.com
Web Site: www.pridestaff.com
Mr. Robert Bladek, Executive VPresident

We specialize in supplemental staffing (temporary help), outsourcing and full-time placement. PRIDESTAFF fills administrative, clerical, customer service, data entry, word processing and light industrial positions. The staffing industry is one of the fastest-growing industries in the United States.

BACKGROUND:

Established: 1974;	1st Franchised: 1994
Franchised Units:	26
Company-Owned Units	8
Total Units:	34
Dist.:	US-34; CAN-0; O'seas-0
North America:	13 States
Density:	12 in CA, 4 in AZ, 4 in IL
Projected New Units (12 Months):	NR
Registered:	

FINANCIAL/TERMS:

Cash Investment:	$75-100K
Total Investment:	$80.4-126.9K
Minimum Net Worth:	$N/A
Fees: Franchise -	$12.5K
Royalty - 65%Gross Margin;	Ad. - N/A
Earnings Claim Statement:	No
Term of Contract (Years):	10/5/5/5
Avg. # Of Employees:	2 FT
Passive Ownership:	Not Allowed
Encourage Conversions:	NR
Area Develop. Agreements:	No
Sub-Franchising Contracts:	No
Expand In Territory:	Yes
Space Needs: 1,200 SF; Single Story Office Building	

SUPPORT & TRAINING PROVIDED:

Financial Assistance Provided:	NR
Site Selection Assistance:	Yes
Lease Negotiation Assistance:	Yes
Co-Operative Advertising:	N/A
Franchisee Assoc./Member:	No
Size Of Corporate Staff:	16
On-Going Support:	A,C,D,E,G,H,I
Training: 1 Week in Fresno, CA; 1 Week at Branch Office.	

SPECIFIC EXPANSION PLANS:

US:	All United States
Canada:	NR
Overseas:	NR

◄◄ ►►

REMEDY INTELLIGENT STAFFING

101 Enterprise
Aliso Viejo, CA 92656
Tel: (800) 828-3726 (949) 425-7700
Fax: (800) 291-2060
E-Mail: gerryr@remedystaff.com
Web Site: www.remedystaff.com
Mr. Gerry Rhydderch, VP Franchise Dev.

A national full-service staffing company, providing contingent workers in the disciplines of law, accounting, professional office auditing, clerical and light industrial. Fully-automated office, with exclusive, validated behavioral testing. Entire back-office support and exclusive territories.

BACKGROUND: IFA MEMBER

Established: 1965;	1st Franchised: 1988
Franchised Units:	172
Company-Owned Units	105
Total Units:	277
Dist.:	US-277; CAN-0; O'seas-0
North America:	40 States
Density:	88 in CA, 24 in FL, 18 in TX
Projected New Units (12 Months):	30
Qualifications:	4, 4, 4, 3, 4, 5
Registered: CA,FL,HI,IL,IN,MD,MI,MN, NY,OR,RI,VA,WA,WI,DC,AB	

FINANCIAL/TERMS:

Cash Investment:	$30-60K
Total Investment:	$95-150K
Minimum Net Worth:	$250K
Fees: Franchise -	$18K
Royalty - Varies;	Ad. - 0%
Earnings Claim Statement:	No
Term of Contract (Years):	10/5
Avg. # Of Employees:	5 FT, 1 PT
Passive Ownership:	Discouraged
Encourage Conversions:	Yes
Area Develop. Agreements:	Yes/10
Sub-Franchising Contracts:	No
Expand In Territory:	Yes
Space Needs: 1,400 SF; OB	

SUPPORT & TRAINING PROVIDED:

Financial Assistance Provided:	Yes(I)
Site Selection Assistance:	Yes
Lease Negotiation Assistance:	Yes
Co-Operative Advertising:	Yes
Franchisee Assoc./Member:	Yes/Yes
Size Of Corporate Staff:	160
On-Going Support:	A,C,D,E,G,H,I
Training: 2 Weeks Home Office; 1 Week On-Site.	

SPECIFIC EXPANSION PLANS:

US:	All Except CA,WA,OR,NM,CO
Canada:	All Canada
Overseas:	No

◄◄ ►►

SALES CONSULTANTS

200 Public Square, 31st Fl.
Cleveland, OH 44114-2301
Tel: (800) 875-4000 (216) 696-1122
Fax: (216) 696-6612
E-Mail: Bob.Angell@BrilliantPeople.com
Web Site: www.BrilliantPeople.com
Mr. John D. Seager, Dir. Franchise Marketing

Complete range of recruitment and human resource services for sales, sales management and marketing professionals, including permanent placement, interim staffing; video-conferencing; with coverage on all continents through strategic alliances with leading search firms.

BACKGROUND: IFA MEMBER
Established: 1957; 1st Franchised: 1966
Franchised Units: 212
Company-Owned Units <u>14</u>
Total Units: 226
Dist.: US-226; CAN-0; O'seas-0
 North America: 39 States
 Density: 20 in CA, 15 in FL, 14 in MI
Projected New Units (12 Months): 20
Qualifications: 3, 4, 1, 4, 3, 3
Registered: All States
FINANCIAL/TERMS:
Cash Investment: $107-142K
Total Investment: $107-142K
Minimum Net Worth: $N/A
Fees: Franchise - $75K
 Royalty - 7%; Ad. - 1%
Earnings Claim Statement: Yes
Term of Contract (Years): 10-20/5
Avg. # Of Employees: 3-4
Passive Ownership: Discouraged
Encourage Conversions: Yes
Area Develop. Agreements: No
Sub-Franchising Contracts: No
Expand In Territory: Yes
Space Needs: 600-1,000 SF; FS
SUPPORT & TRAINING PROVIDED:
Financial Assistance Provided: Yes(I)
Site Selection Assistance: Yes
Lease Negotiation Assistance: Yes
Co-Operative Advertising: N/A
Franchisee Assoc./Member: Yes
Size Of Corporate Staff: 128
On-Going Support: C,D,E,G,H,I
Training: 3 Weeks Headquarters, Cleveland, OH; 2 Weeks Franchisee's Location.
SPECIFIC EXPANSION PLANS:
US: All United States
Canada: No
Overseas: No

◄◄ ►►

SANFORD ROSE ASSOCIATES
3737 Embassy Dr., # 200
Akron, OH 44333-8369
Tel: (800) 731-7724 (330) 670-9797
Fax: (330) 670-9798
E-Mail: massrai@aol.com
Web Site: www.franchiseSRA.com
Mr. Mark A. Sweeterman, Director Franchise Development

Executive search is distinct within the SRA organization. We provide a highly-reliable service to fill critical openings with our corporate clients. Only the most qualified candidates are presented. Our adaptability allows us to work at virtually all professional levels, developing repeat business.

BACKGROUND: IFA MEMBER
Established: 1959; 1st Franchised: 1970
Franchised Units: 53
Company-Owned Units <u>0</u>
Total Units: 53
Dist.: US-51; CAN-0; O'seas-2
 North America: 23 States
 Density: 7 in OH, 7 in IL, 5 in CA
Projected New Units (12 Months): 15
Qualifications: 3, 5, 3, 5, 5, 5
Registered: CA,IL,MD,NY,VA,WA
FINANCIAL/TERMS:
Cash Investment: $70-95K
Total Investment: $70-95K
Minimum Net Worth: $80K
Fees: Franchise - $40K
 Royalty - 3-7%; Ad. - 0%
Earnings Claim Statement: Yes
Term of Contract (Years): 7/1
Avg. # Of Employees: 10 FT, 1 PT
Passive Ownership: NR
Encourage Conversions: Yes
Area Develop. Agreements: No
Sub-Franchising Contracts: No
Expand In Territory: No
Space Needs: 600-1,000 SF; OB
SUPPORT & TRAINING PROVIDED:
Financial Assistance Provided: Yes(D)
Site Selection Assistance: Yes
Lease Negotiation Assistance: Yes
Co-Operative Advertising: No
Franchisee Assoc./Member: Yes/Yes
Size Of Corporate Staff: 6
On-Going Support: C,G,H,I
Training: 10 Days National Headquarters; 5 Days On-Site.
SPECIFIC EXPANSION PLANS:
US: All United States
Canada: All Canada
Overseas: All Developed Countries

◄◄ ►►

SNELLING PERSONNEL SERVICES
12801 N. Central Expy., # 700
Dallas, TX 75243

Tel: (800) 766-5556 (972) 239-7575
Fax: (972) 239-6881
Web Site: www.snelling.com
Mr. Joseph DeMarco, VP Franchise Development

SNELLING helps America work! Our full-service career placement, temp-to-hire, contract and temporary help franchises benefit from more than 45 years of experience and name recognition. We offer: a proven operating system; comprehensive training and on- going support; fully-computerized payroll financing; and award-winning advertising and PR programs. Locations are available nationally. Call today. (800) 766-5556.

BACKGROUND: IFA MEMBER
Established: 1951; 1st Franchised: 1955
Franchised Units: 280
Company-Owned Units <u>28</u>
Total Units: 308
Dist.: US-302; CAN-0; O'seas-6
 North America: 45 States
 Density: 31 in TX, 20 in MI, 18 in IL
Projected New Units (12 Months): 40
Qualifications: 5, 5, 1, 3, 1, 5
Registered: All States
FINANCIAL/TERMS:
Cash Investment: $97K
Total Investment: $97-142K
Minimum Net Worth: $NR
Fees: Franchise - $9K
 Royalty - 4.5-7%; Ad. - 0.5-1%
Earnings Claim Statement: No
Term of Contract (Years): Lifetime
Avg. # Of Employees: 4-6 FT
Passive Ownership: Discouraged
Encourage Conversions: Yes
Area Develop. Agreements: Yes
Sub-Franchising Contracts: No
Expand In Territory: No
Space Needs: 600-800 SF; FS, SF, SC
SUPPORT & TRAINING PROVIDED:
Financial Assistance Provided: Yes
Site Selection Assistance: Yes
Lease Negotiation Assistance: Yes
Co-Operative Advertising: NR
Franchisee Assoc./Member: Yes/Yes
Size Of Corporate Staff: 100
On-Going Support: A,b,C,D,E,G,H,I
Training: 2 Weeks Snelling University.
SPECIFIC EXPANSION PLANS:
US: All United States
Canada: No
Overseas: No

◄◄ ►►

STAFF BUILDERS HOME HEALTH CARE

1983 Marcus Ave.
Lake Success, NY 11042-7011
Tel: (800) 444-4633 (516) 358-1000
Fax: (516) 358-3678
Web Site: www.staffbuildersintl.com
Mr. Ed Teixeira, SVP Fran. Operations

STAFF BUILDERS provides home health care services to patients in their home ranging from hi-tech nursing to para-professional services.

BACKGROUND:	IFA MEMBER
Established: 1967;	1st Franchised: 1967
Franchised Units:	202
Company-Owned Units	48
Total Units:	250
Dist.:	US-248; CAN-0; O'seas-2
North America:	38 States
Density: 20 in PA, 19 in NY, 18 in OH	
Projected New Units (12 Months):	30
Qualifications:	4, 4, 5, 5, 1, 5
Registered: All States	

FINANCIAL/TERMS:

Cash Investment:	$50K
Total Investment:	$110-150K
Minimum Net Worth:	$200-250K
Fees: Franchise -	$29.5K
Royalty - Varies;	Ad. - N/A
Earnings Claim Statement:	No
Term of Contract (Years):	10/5
Avg. # Of Employees:	4 FT, 2 PT
Passive Ownership:	Allowed
Encourage Conversions:	Yes
Area Develop. Agreements:	No
Sub-Franchising Contracts:	No
Expand In Territory:	Yes
Space Needs: 1,000 SF; FS, SF, SC	

SUPPORT & TRAINING PROVIDED:

Financial Assistance Provided:	Yes(D)
Site Selection Assistance:	Yes
Lease Negotiation Assistance:	No
Co-Operative Advertising:	No
Franchisee Assoc./Member:	Yes/Yes
Size Of Corporate Staff:	350
On-Going Support:	A,B,C,D,E,G,H
Training: 5 Days at Corporate Office in NY; 5 Days Regional Location.	

SPECIFIC EXPANSION PLANS:

US:	All United States
Canada:	All Canada
Overseas:	Asia, Europe, Latin America

TALENT TREE

9703 Richmond Ave., # 216
Houston, TX 77042

Tel: (800) 999-1515 (713) 361-7531
Fax: (713) 974-6507
E-Mail: franchise@talenttree.com
Web Site: www.talenttree.com
Ms. Shelly Oldner, Franchise Business Development

Initial

Talent Tree Staffing

TALENT TREE offers full-service staffing franchise opportunities with the placement of clerical, administrative, technical support and light industrial staff. Franchisees are offered intensive on-going training and hands-on support by industry experts. Our franchisees have the advantage of our proven system and innovative, proprietary programs.

BACKGROUND:	
Established: 1976;	1st Franchised: 1990
Franchised Units:	24
Company-Owned Units	210
Total Units:	234
Dist.:	US-234; CAN-0; O'seas-0
North America:	30 States
Density: 32 in CA, 14 in TX, 14 in GA	
Projected New Units (12 Months):	3-5
Qualifications:	4, 4, 5, 1, 2, 4
Registered: All States	

FINANCIAL/TERMS:

Cash Investment:	$100-150K
Total Investment:	$120-170K
Minimum Net Worth:	$150-250K
Fees: Franchise -	$20K
Royalty - Varies;	Ad. - 0%
Earnings Claim Statement:	No
Term of Contract (Years):	10/5
Avg. # Of Employees:	2 FT
Passive Ownership:	Allowed
Encourage Conversions:	Yes
Area Develop. Agreements:	Yes
Sub-Franchising Contracts:	No
Expand In Territory:	Yes
Space Needs: 1,000 SF; FS, SF, SC	

SUPPORT & TRAINING PROVIDED:

Financial Assistance Provided:	Yes(I)
Site Selection Assistance:	Yes
Lease Negotiation Assistance:	Yes
Co-Operative Advertising:	Yes
Franchisee Assoc./Member:	No
Size Of Corporate Staff:	180
On-Going Support:	A,B,C,D,E,H,I
Training: 3-4 Weeks at Corporate Office &	

On-Going; 1st 120 Days and as Needed at Franchise.

SPECIFIC EXPANSION PLANS:

US:	All United States
Canada:	No
Overseas:	No

TECHSTAFF

11270 W. Park Pl., # 460
Milwaukee, WI 53224
Tel: (800) 515-4440 (414) 359-4444
Fax: (414) 359-4949
E-Mail: tom@techstaff.com
Web Site: www.techstaff.com
Mr. Thomas Montgomery, Franchise Director

Full-service employment firm, servicing the engineering and information technology niches. Long-term contract, contract to perm and permanent search. Computerized search and retrieval system. Funding of contract payroll. Marketing assistance, payroll, billing, funding, accounts receivable and all financial statements are provided. Large geographic availability, excellent franchise relations.

BACKGROUND:	IFA MEMBER
Established: 1985;	1st Franchised: 1987
Franchised Units:	9
Company-Owned Units	3
Total Units:	12
Dist.:	US-12; CAN-0; O'seas-0
North America:	NR
Density: 3 in CA, 2 in WI, 2 in MI	
Projected New Units (12 Months):	3
Qualifications:	5, 3, 2, 1, 2, 5
Registered: CA,FL,IL,IN,MD,MI,WI,DC	

FINANCIAL/TERMS:

Cash Investment:	$75K
Total Investment:	$100-125K
Minimum Net Worth:	$100K
Fees: Franchise -	$25K
Royalty - 3.9-6.9%;	Ad. - N/A
Earnings Claim Statement:	No
Term of Contract (Years):	20/20
Avg. # Of Employees:	6 FT
Passive Ownership:	Discouraged
Encourage Conversions:	N/A
Area Develop. Agreements:	Yes/2-3
Sub-Franchising Contracts:	Yes
Expand In Territory:	Yes
Space Needs: 1,000 SF; SF, OB	

SUPPORT & TRAINING PROVIDED:

Financial Assistance Provided:	Yes(I)
Site Selection Assistance:	Yes
Lease Negotiation Assistance:	Yes

Co-Operative Advertising:	N/A
Franchisee Assoc./Member:	No
Size Of Corporate Staff:	7
On-Going Support:	A,B,C,D,E,G,H

Training: 1 Week per Employee at Corporate Office; 10 Weeks in 1st Year Franchise Office.

SPECIFIC EXPANSION PLANS:

US:	All United States
Canada:	No
Overseas:	No

≪ ≫

TODAYS STAFFING

18111 Preston Rd., # 700
Dallas, TX 75252-4383
Tel: (800) 822-7868 (972) 380-9380
Fax: (972) 713-4198
Ms. Luann Boggs, VP Franchising

TODAYS STAFFING is a full-service, high-quality, office clerical temporary employment service, utilizing a distinctive sales, service, promotional, quality control and accounting procedure known as the TODAYS WAY method of operating a temporary employment service business. TODAYS is a national company, awarding franchisees an exclusive major market territory. TODAYS finances 100% of employees' payroll and accounts receivable.

BACKGROUND:

Established: 1982; 1st Franchised: 1983	
Franchised Units:	22
Company-Owned Units	<u>97</u>
Total Units:	119
Dist.:	US-108; CAN-11; O'seas-0
North America:	28 States, 2 Provinces
Density:	28 in TX, 11 in MO, 9 in FL
Projected New Units (12 Months):	6
Qualifications:	5, 5, 4, 4, 5, 5
Registered: CA,IN,MI,NY	

FINANCIAL/TERMS:

Cash Investment:	$90-145K
Total Investment:	$90-145K
Minimum Net Worth:	$150K
Fees: Franchise -	$20K
Royalty - Varies;	Ad. - 0%
Earnings Claim Statement:	Yes
Term of Contract (Years):	5/5/5
Avg. # Of Employees:	3 FT
Passive Ownership:	Not Allowed
Encourage Conversions:	Yes
Area Develop. Agreements:	Yes
Sub-Franchising Contracts:	No
Expand In Territory:	Yes

Space Needs: 1,200 SF; Class A Office

SUPPORT & TRAINING PROVIDED:

Financial Assistance Provided:	No
Site Selection Assistance:	Yes
Lease Negotiation Assistance:	No
Co-Operative Advertising:	No
Franchisee Assoc./Member:	Yes/Yes
Size Of Corporate Staff:	85
On-Going Support:	A,C,D,E,G,H,I

Training: 2 Weeks at Dallas, TX; 2 Weeks Field.

SPECIFIC EXPANSION PLANS:

US:	All United States
Canada:	No
Overseas:	No

≪ ≫

TRC STAFFING SERVICES

100 Ashford Center N., # 500
Atlanta, GA 30338
Tel: (800) 488-8008 (770) 392-1411
Fax: (770) 698-7885
E-Mail: sasanders@trcstaff.com
Web Site: www.trcstaff.com
Mr. Steve Sanders, VP of Franchise Operations

TRC offers a unique freedom franchise that provides special financing for experienced, temporary industry professionals. Start-up capital, computer equipment, payroll, workers' compensation, taxes and field and classroom support are all provided for an approved candidate.

BACKGROUND:

Established: 1980; 1st Franchised: 1984	
Franchised Units:	48
Company-Owned Units	<u>27</u>
Total Units:	75
Dist.:	US-69; CAN-0; O'seas-0
North America:	17 States
Density:	21 in GA, 10 in TX, 7 in CA
Projected New Units (12 Months):	12
Qualifications:	2, 2, 5, 2, 3, 5
Registered: CA,FL,HI,IL,IN,MD,MN,NY, OR,RI,VA,WA,WI,DC	

FINANCIAL/TERMS:

Cash Investment:	$25K
Total Investment:	$25K
Minimum Net Worth:	$150K
Fees: Franchise -	$0
Royalty - 9.5%;	Ad. - 0%
Earnings Claim Statement:	No
Term of Contract (Years):	5/5
Avg. # Of Employees:	2 FT
Passive Ownership:	Not Allowed
Encourage Conversions:	Yes
Area Develop. Agreements:	No
Sub-Franchising Contracts:	No

Expand In Territory:	Yes

Space Needs: 800 SF; Class A Office

SUPPORT & TRAINING PROVIDED:

Financial Assistance Provided:	Yes(D)
Site Selection Assistance:	Yes
Lease Negotiation Assistance:	Yes
Co-Operative Advertising:	No
Franchisee Assoc./Member:	No
Size Of Corporate Staff:	117
On-Going Support:	A,b,C,D,E,G,h,I

Training: 1 Week Atlanta, GA; 1 Week On-Site.

SPECIFIC EXPANSION PLANS:

US:	All United States
Canada:	No
Overseas:	No

≪ ≫

WESTERN MEDICAL SERVICES

220 N. Wiget Ln.
Walnut Creek, CA 94598
Tel: (800) 872-8367 (925) 256-1561
Fax: (925) 952-2591
E-Mail: franchise@westaff.com
Web Site: www.westaff.com
Ms. Bobbi George, VP Business Development

Full-service home health agency (staffing, home care). WESTERN offers exclusive territories, comprehensive training, Medicare certification, JCAHO accreditation, Medicare and non-Medicare billing, integrated payroll, billing, accounting and cost reporting services, complete caregiver payroll and accounts receivable financing, managed care contracts, professional risk management, credit and legal expertise, advertising/ promotional support and more.

BACKGROUND:

Established: 1967; 1st Franchised: 1975	
Franchised Units:	16
Company-Owned Units	<u>38</u>
Total Units:	54
Dist.:	US-54; CAN-0; O'seas-0
North America:	20 States
Density:	10 in IN, 8 in CA, 5 in OH
Projected New Units (12 Months):	20
Qualifications:	5, 2, 5, 4, 2, 5
Registered: CA,FL,IL,IN,MD,MI,MN,NY, OR,SD,VA,WA,WI	

FINANCIAL/TERMS:

Cash Investment:	$100-200K
Total Investment:	$200-250K
Minimum Net Worth:	$100K
Fees: Franchise -	$30-40K
Royalty - 8%;	Ad. - Included

Earnings Claim Statement: No
Term of Contract (Years):   Indefin.
Avg. # Of Employees: 3 FT
Passive Ownership: Not Allowed
Encourage Conversions: Yes
Area Develop. Agreements: No
Sub-Franchising Contracts: No
Expand In Territory: Yes
Space Needs: 500-750 SF; FS, SF, SC

SUPPORT & TRAINING PROVIDED:
Financial Assistance Provided: No
Site Selection Assistance: Yes
Lease Negotiation Assistance: No
Co-Operative Advertising: Yes
Franchisee Assoc./Member: Yes/Yes
Size Of Corporate Staff: 250
On-Going Support: A,B,C,D,E,G,H,I
Training: 5 Days Corporate Headquarters;
    5 Days On-Site.

SPECIFIC EXPANSION PLANS:
US: All United States
Canada: No
Overseas: No

<< >>

SUPPLEMENTAL LISTING OF FRANCHISORS

AAA Employment, 4914-A Creekside Dr., Clearwater, FL 33760 ; (727) 572-8709; Mr. David M. George (800) 237-2853; (727) 573-0202

Accountants Inc., 111 Anza Blvd., # 400, Burlingame, CA 94010 ; (650) 579-1927; Mr. Quentin Burt (800) 491-9411; (650) 373-3103

Accountants On Call, Park 80 West, Plaza II, 9th Fl., Saddle Brook, NJ 07663 ; (201) 712-1033; Ms. Linda E. Krutzsch ; (201) 843-0006

AccuStaff, 177 Crossways Park Dr., Woodbury, NY 11797 ; (516) 496-2492; Ms. Pat Hiller (800) 967-1001; (516) 682-1400

Ace Personnel, 6400 Glenwood, # 309, Overland Park, KS 66202 ; (913) 362-9076; Ms. Trish Oswald ; (913) 362-0090

Agency Nursing Network, 353 Cabot St., Beverly, MA 01915 ; (978) 922-8958; Ms. JoAnne Rainville (800) 729-8353; (978) 922-8353

Belcan Techservices, 3333 Earhart, # 120, Carrollton, TX 75006 ; (972) 239-4143; Mr. Steven Roth (800) 288-8418; (972) 239-0405

Business & Professional Consultants, 3255 Wilshire Blvd., 17th Fl., Los Angeles, CA 90010 ; (213) 387-2884; Mr. William A. LaPerch ; (213) 380-8200

Consultis, 1615 S. Federal Hwy., # 300, Boca Raton, FL 33432-7434 ; (561) 367-9802; Ms. Barbara Dettman Fleming (800) 275-2667; (561) 362-9104

Corestaff Staffing Service, 3040 Saturn St., # 200, Brea, CA 92621 ; (714) 572-4222; Mr. Gary Petsuch (800) 669-4887; (714) 572-4200

Drake International, P.O. Box 800, Toronto, ON M4Y 2N8 CANADA; (416) 216-1109; Mr. R. W. Pollock (800) GO DRAKE; (416) 967-7700

Firstaff, 3800 W. 80th St., # 1155, Bloomington, MN 55431 ; (612) 893-7550; Mr. Jim Ginther ; (612) 897-5222

Flex-Staff/Pro-Tem, 214 N. Main St., #202, Natick, MA 01760 ; (508) 650-0035; Mr. Giles Powers (800) 525-5527; (508) 650-0026

Health Force, 185 Crossways Park Dr., Woodbury, NY 11797-2047 ; (516) 496-3283; Mr. Harvey Kasden (800) 967-1001; (516) 490-1200

Hostess Helper, 20 Whittlesey Rd., Newton Centre, MA 02159 ; (617) 630-1744; Ms. Ellen Hochberger ; (617) 244-7465

Interim Personnel Services, 2050 Spectrum Blvd., Ft. Lauderdale, FL 33309 ; (954) 938-7770; Ms. Lisa McCarthy (888) 881-7751; (954) 938-7600

National Career Search Jobline, 4775 Walnut St., Boulder, CO 80301 ; (303) 440-3386; Mr. Gary Resnikoff ; (303) 440-5110

National Search & Discovery, 9864 W. Girton Dr., P. O. Box 36063, Denver, CO 80236 ; (800) 565-3082; Mr. Walt Queen (800) 639-7651; (800) 565-3082

OutSource International, 1144 E. Newport Center Dr., Deerfield Beach, FL 33442 ; (954) 418-4405; Mr. Bill Annonio (800) 275-5000; (954) 418-6400

Personet - The Personnel Network, P.O. Box 3436, Holiday, FL 34690 ; (813)

372-3608; Mr. Robert V. Riley (800) 628-3777; (813) 372-2996

Pharmacists: prn, P.O. Box 161, Walpole, MA 02081 ; (508) 668-5663; Ms. Beth J. Leney (800) 832-5560; (508) 660-1469

Professional Employee Management (PEM), 1819 Main St., 8th Fl., Sarasota, FL 34236 ; (941) 364-5799; Mr. Robin Barber (800) 329-7823; (941) 957-1444

Resume Hut, The, 743 View St., Victoria, BC V8W 1J9 CANADA; (250) 383-1580; Mr. Charles Dalgarno (800) 441-6488; (250) 383-3983

Roth Young Personnel Service, 535 5th Ave., 33rd Fl., New York, NY 10017 ; (212) 972-5367; Mr. William S. Beck (800) 343-8518; (212) 557-4900

Seniors for Seniors/ Seniors for Business, 55 Eglinton Ave. E., # 311, Toronto, ON M4P 1G8 CANADA; (416) 481-6752; Mr. Peter Cook ; (416) 481-4579

Sitters Unlimited, 25381-G Alicia Pkwy., # 215, Laguna Hills, CA 92653 ; (714) 448-5946; Ms. Sharon Gastel (800) 328-1191; (949) 643-8148

Tandem, 1144 E. Newport Center Dr., Deerfield Beach, FL 33442 ; (954) 418-4405; Mr. Bill Annonio (800) 275-5000; (954) 418-6400

TempForce, 177 Crossways Park Dr., Woodbury, NY 11797 ; (516) 677-6023; Mr. Tom Townsend (888) 536-1200; (516) 682-1432

Time Services, 6422 Lima Rd., Fort Wayne, IN 46818 ; (219) 489-1466; Mr. Thomas C. Ward (800) 837-8463; (219) 489-2020

USA Employment, 5533 Central Ave., St. Petersburg, FL 33710 ; (727) 343-2953; Ms. Colleen Rounds (800) 801-5627; (727) 343-3044

We Care Home Health Services, 201 City Centre Dr., # 606, Mississauga, ON L5B 2T4 CANADA; (905) 949-9717; Mr. Kim Berry (800) 316-2212; (416) 922-7601

Westaff, 301 Lennon Lane, Walnut Creek, CA 94598 ; (925) 952-2555; Ms. Florence Weiss (800) USA-TEMP; (925) 930-5000

FOOD: DONUTS/COOKIES/BAGELS INDUSTRY PROFILE

Total # Franchisors in Industry Group	70
Total # Franchised Units in Industry Group	12,090
Total # Company-Owned Units in Industry Group	1,566
Total # Operating Units in Industry Group	13,656
Average # Franchised Units/Franchisor	172.7
Average # Company-Owned Units/Franchisor	22.4
Average # Total Units/Franchisor	195.1
Ratio of Total # Franchised Units/Total # Company-Owned Units	7.7:1
Industry Survey Participants	35
Representing % of Industry	50.0%
Average Franchise Fee*:	$26.1K
Average Total Investment*:	$179.6K
Average On-Going Royalty Fee*:	5.2%

If a range was provided, the mid-point of the range was used. See detailed profiles for actual ranges.

FIVE LARGEST PARTICIPANTS IN SURVEY

Company	# Franchised Units	# Co-Owned Units	# Total Units	Franchise Fee	On-Going Royalty	Total Investment
1. Dunkin' Donuts	5,001	0	5,001	40-60K	4.9%	350K-3MM
2. Tim Hortons	1,760	120	1,880	35-50K	3-4.5%	300-360K
3. Mrs. Fields Cookies	186	390	576	25K	6%	146-245K
4. Cinnabon	254	188	442	25K	5%	178-253K
5. Coffee Time Donuts	304	20	324	NR	4.5%	160-250K

All of the data provided are proprietary and should not be quoted without acknowledging *Bond's Franchise Guide.*

BAGELSMITH RESTAURANTS & FOOD STORES

37 Van Syckel Rd.
Hampton, NJ 08827
Tel: (908) 730-8600
Fax: (908) 730-8165
Mr. Stephen Fiala, President

What makes us special is, of course, our BAGELSMITH Bagel. But we are also famous for our delicatessen, featuring only high-quality products. Whether in our restaurants or in our convenience food stores, we provide our customers with high-quality products, friendly, knowledgeable service, in a clean, pleasant family-oriented environment.

BACKGROUND:

Established: 1979; 1st Franchised: 1983	
Franchised Units:	21
Company-Owned Units	1
Total Units:	22
Dist.:	US-23; CAN-0; O'seas-0
North America:	2 States
Density:	20 in NJ, 3 in PA
Projected New Units (12 Months):	3
Qualifications:	3, 2, 1, 1, 4, 5
Registered: NR	

FINANCIAL/TERMS:

Cash Investment:	$NR
Total Investment:	$213-303K
Minimum Net Worth:	$NR
Fees: Franchise -	$25K
Royalty - 1-4%;	Ad. - 3%
Earnings Claim Statement:	No
Term of Contract (Years):	10
Avg. # Of Employees:	8 FT, 4 PT
Passive Ownership:	Discouraged
Encourage Conversions:	N/A
Area Develop. Agreements:	No
Sub-Franchising Contracts:	No
Expand In Territory:	Yes
Space Needs: 2,000 SF; FS, SC	

SUPPORT & TRAINING PROVIDED:

Financial Assistance Provided:	N/A
Site Selection Assistance:	Yes
Lease Negotiation Assistance:	Yes
Co-Operative Advertising:	Yes
Franchisee Assoc./Member:	No
Size Of Corporate Staff:	5
On-Going Support:	C,d,G
Training: 120-180 Hours Hampton, NJ.	

SPECIFIC EXPANSION PLANS:

US:	Northeast
Canada:	No
Overseas:	No

◁◁ ▷▷

BAKER'S DOZEN DONUTS

918 Dundas St., E. #500
Mississauga, ON L4Y 2B7 CANADA
Tel: (800) 265-6298 (905) 272-1825
Fax: (905) 272-0140
E-Mail: franchising@bakers-dozen-donuts.com
Web Site: www.bakers-dozen-donuts.com
Mr. Robert Gordon, Director of Franchising

Coffee, donuts, muffins, croissants, soups and sandwich combos, desserts.

BACKGROUND:

Established: 1977; 1st Franchised: 1984	
Franchised Units:	80
Company-Owned Units	1
Total Units:	81
Dist.:	US-0; CAN-75; O'seas-6
North America:	1 Province
Density:	75 in ON
Projected New Units (12 Months):	15
Qualifications:	3, 4, 4, 3, 3, 4
Registered:	

FINANCIAL/TERMS:

Cash Investment:	$30K
Total Investment:	$65-350K
Minimum Net Worth:	$60K+
Fees: Franchise -	$Included
Royalty - 5%;	Ad. - 2%
Earnings Claim Statement:	No
Term of Contract (Years):	10/5
Avg. # Of Employees:	3-4 FT, 6 PT
Passive Ownership:	Allowed
Encourage Conversions:	N/A
Area Develop. Agreements:	Yes
Sub-Franchising Contracts:	No
Expand In Territory:	Yes
Space Needs: 1,800-2,500 SF; FS, SC, RM, Kiosks	

SUPPORT & TRAINING PROVIDED:

Financial Assistance Provided:	Yes(I)
Site Selection Assistance:	Yes
Lease Negotiation Assistance:	Yes
Co-Operative Advertising:	Yes
Franchisee Assoc./Member:	Yes/Yes
Size Of Corporate Staff:	30
On-Going Support:	A,B,C,D,E,F,H,I
Training: 3 Weeks Toronto, ON	

SPECIFIC EXPANSION PLANS:

US:	All United States
Canada:	All Canada
Overseas:	China, Europe, Middle East

◁◁ ▷▷

BETWEEN ROUNDS BAGEL DELI & BAKERY

19A John Fitch Blvd.
South Windsor, CT 06074
Tel: (860) 291-0323
Fax: (860) 289-2732
Mr. Jerry Puiia, President

Providing customers with more choices than just bagels, cream cheese and gourmet coffee, BETWEEN ROUNDS sells a wide variety of bakery and deli items, as well as offers extensive catering. BETWEEN ROUNDS BAGEL DELI & BAKERY is your competitive edge in the explosive bagel franchise field because, soon, selling bagels won't be enough!

BACKGROUND: IFA MEMBER

Established: 1990; 1st Franchised: 1993	
Franchised Units:	5
Company-Owned Units	2
Total Units:	7
Dist.:	US-7; CAN-0; O'seas-0
North America:	3 States
Density:	4 in CT, 2 in MA, 1 in WV
Projected New Units (12 Months):	5
Qualifications:	4, 3, 3, 1, 3, 3
Registered: N/A	

FINANCIAL/TERMS:

Cash Investment:	$50-80K
Total Investment:	$160-210K
Minimum Net Worth:	$100K
Fees: Franchise -	$18K
Royalty - 4%;	Ad. - 2%
Earnings Claim Statement:	Yes
Term of Contract (Years):	10/15
Avg. # Of Employees:	3 FT, 5 PT
Passive Ownership:	Discouraged
Encourage Conversions:	Yes
Area Develop. Agreements:	Yes
Sub-Franchising Contracts:	No
Expand In Territory:	Yes
Space Needs: 1,600 SF; SC	

SUPPORT & TRAINING PROVIDED:

Financial Assistance Provided:	Yes(I)
Site Selection Assistance:	Yes
Lease Negotiation Assistance:	Yes
Co-Operative Advertising:	Yes
Franchisee Assoc./Member:	No

Size Of Corporate Staff: 3
On-Going Support: a,C,D,E,F,G
Training: 2 Weeks Company Stores in CT;
1-2 Weeks Own Unit.
SPECIFIC EXPANSION PLANS:
US: Mid-Atlantic, Northeast
Canada: No
Overseas: No

BIG APPLE BAGELS

8501 W. Higgins Rd., # 320
Chicago, IL 60631
Tel: (800) 251-6101 (773) 380-6100
Fax: (773) 380-6183
E-Mail: hmarks@babholdings.com
Web Site: www.babholdings.com
Mr. Howard B. Marks, Dir. Franchise
Development

Specialty bagel café, featuring fresh-from-scratch, proprietary recipes for bagels, cream cheeses, muffins and gourmet coffees. Our franchisees enjoy offering three of the hottest selling consumer concepts all under one roof. In addition, our franchise owners enjoy the right to develop "outside" wholesale business within their market.

BACKGROUND: IFA MEMBER
Established: 1992; 1st Franchised: 1993
Franchised Units: 268
Company-Owned Units: 22
Total Units: 290
Dist.: US-281; CAN-6; O'seas-7
North America: 32 States, 2 Provinces
Density: 48 in IL, 28 in NJ, 27 in WI
Projected New Units (12 Months): 40
Qualifications: 5, 4, 3, 3, 3, 5
Registered: All States
FINANCIAL/TERMS:
Cash Investment: $50K Min.
Total Investment: $250-300K
Minimum Net Worth: $300K
Fees: Franchise - $25K
Royalty - 5%; Ad. - 1%
Earnings Claim Statement: No
Term of Contract (Years): 10/Varies

Avg. # Of Employees: 2 FT, 10 PT
Passive Ownership: Discouraged
Encourage Conversions: Yes
Area Develop. Agreements: Yes/Varies
Sub-Franchising Contracts: No
Expand In Territory: Yes
Space Needs: 500-2,000 SF; FS, SF, SC, RM
SUPPORT & TRAINING PROVIDED:
Financial Assistance Provided: Yes(I)
Site Selection Assistance: Yes
Lease Negotiation Assistance: Yes
Co-Operative Advertising: No
Franchisee Assoc./Member: Yes/No
Size Of Corporate Staff: 34
On-Going Support: B,C,D,E,F,G,H,I
Training: 2 Weeks Milwaukee, WI; Store
Location 5 Days Prior to Opening
SPECIFIC EXPANSION PLANS:
US: All United States
Canada: All Canada
Overseas: All Countries

BLUE CHIP COOKIES

157 Barnwood Dr.
Edgewood, KY 41017
Tel: (800) 888-9866 (859) 331-7600
Fax: (859) 331-7604
E-Mail: bluechip@fuse.net
Web Site: www.bluechipcookies.com
Mr. Mark D. Hannahan, President/CEO

BLUE CHIP COOKIES brings pleasure to our customers by making the world's best gourmet cookies and brownies, fresh from scratch, everyday, at every one of our retail locations. We have won numerous awards, and our wonderful cookies and brownies continue to bring joy to young and old alike!

BACKGROUND:
Established: 1983; 1st Franchised: 1986
Franchised Units: 15
Company-Owned Units: 20
Total Units: 35

Dist.: US-35; CAN-0; O'seas-0
North America: 11 States
Density: 10 in OH, 10 in CA, 2 in KY
Projected New Units (12 Months): 4
Qualifications: 5, 4, 4, 3, 1, 5
Registered: N/A
FINANCIAL/TERMS:
Cash Investment: $50-100K
Total Investment: $120-200K
Minimum Net Worth: $200K
Fees: Franchise - $19.5K
Royalty - 6%; Ad. - 0%
Earnings Claim Statement: No
Term of Contract (Years): 10/10
Avg. # Of Employees: 2-3 FT, 4-8 PT
Passive Ownership: Allowed
Encourage Conversions: Yes
Area Develop. Agreements: No
Sub-Franchising Contracts: No
Expand In Territory: Yes
Space Needs: 600+ SF; SC, RM, Airport, Tourist Site
SUPPORT & TRAINING PROVIDED:
Financial Assistance Provided: No
Site Selection Assistance: Yes
Lease Negotiation Assistance: Yes
Co-Operative Advertising: No
Franchisee Assoc./Member: No
Size Of Corporate Staff: 6
On-Going Support: C,D,E,G,H,I
Training: 1-2 Weeks Cincinnati, OH.
SPECIFIC EXPANSION PLANS:
US: All United States
Canada: Would Consider
Overseas: Would Consider

BREADSMITH

409 E. Silver Spring Dr.
Whitefish Bay, WI 53217
Tel: (414) 962-1965
Fax: (414) 962-5888
E-Mail: jock@breadsmith.com
Web Site: www.breadsmith.com
Mr. Jock Mutschler, Dir. of Communications

Award-winning, European, hearth-bread bakery, featuring fresh-from-scratch crusty breads, gourmet jams and coffee. Open kitchen concept reveals an eight-ton, stone hearth oven imported from France used to bake the hand-crafted loaves each morning. BREADSMITH has been ranked by Bon Appetit, Best in 8 cities across the country.

BACKGROUND:
Established: 1993; 1st Franchised: 1994
Franchised Units: 41
Company-Owned Units 1
Total Units: 42
Dist.: US-42; CAN-0; O'seas-0
North America: 12 States
Density: 9 in IL, 9 in MI
Projected New Units (12 Months): 10
Qualifications: 5, 4, 2, 3, 5, 5
Registered: CA,FL,IL,IN,MI,MN,NY,OR, SD,VA,WA,WI
FINANCIAL/TERMS:
Cash Investment: $200-260K
Total Investment: $227-416K
Minimum Net Worth: $400K
Fees: Franchise - $30K
Royalty - 7%; Ad. - 0%
Earnings Claim Statement: Yes
Term of Contract (Years): 15/15
Avg. # Of Employees: 2 FT, 12 PT
Passive Ownership: Not Allowed
Encourage Conversions: N/A
Area Develop. Agreements: No
Sub-Franchising Contracts: No
Expand In Territory: Yes
Space Needs: 2,000 SF; FS, SF, SC
SUPPORT & TRAINING PROVIDED:
Financial Assistance Provided: Yes(I)
Site Selection Assistance: Yes
Lease Negotiation Assistance: Yes
Co-Operative Advertising: No
Franchisee Assoc./Member: Yes
Size Of Corporate Staff: 10
On-Going Support: C,D,E,F,G,I
Training: 3 Weeks Corporate Store; 2 Weeks Franchisee Store.
SPECIFIC EXPANSION PLANS:
US: All United States
Canada: All Canada
Overseas: No

<< >>

BRUEGGER'S BAGELS
159 Bank Street, 3rd Floor, P. O. Box 374
Burlington, VT 05402
Tel: (802) 660-4020
Fax: (802) 660-4032
E-Mail: franchising@brueggers.com
Web Site: www.brueggers.com
Ms. Joan Giard, Franchise Coordinator

Our mission is to be the dominant, first choice, neighborhood bagel bakery in all markets where we operate.

BACKGROUND: IFA MEMBER
Established: 1983; 1st Franchised: 1983
Franchised Units: 285
Company-Owned Units 0
Total Units: 285
Dist.: US-285; CAN-0; O'seas-0
North America: 16 States
Density: 35 in MN, 33 in OH, 32 in MA
Projected New Units (12 Months): 25
Qualifications: 4, 3, 5, 1, 4, 5
Registered: CA,FL,IN,MD,MI,MN,NY, RI,VA,WA,WI
FINANCIAL/TERMS:
Cash Investment: $NR
Total Investment: $250-706K
Minimum Net Worth: $400K
Fees: Franchise - $20K
Royalty - 2-5%; Ad. - 2-4%
Earnings Claim Statement: Yes
Term of Contract (Years): 10/5
Avg. # Of Employees: NR
Passive Ownership: Discouraged
Encourage Conversions: Yes
Area Develop. Agreements: No
Sub-Franchising Contracts: No
Expand In Territory: Yes
Space Needs: 1,500-2,200 SF; SF, SC, RM
SUPPORT & TRAINING PROVIDED:
Financial Assistance Provided: No
Site Selection Assistance: Yes
Lease Negotiation Assistance: No
Co-Operative Advertising: Yes
Franchisee Assoc./Member: NR
Size Of Corporate Staff: 25
On-Going Support: a,b,C,D,E,f,G,H
Training: NR
SPECIFIC EXPANSION PLANS:
US: All United States
Canada: No
Overseas: No

<< >>

BUNS MASTER BAKERY SYSTEMS
2 E. Beaver Creek Rd., Bldg. #1
Richmond Hill, ON L4B 2N3 CANADA
Tel: (905) 764-7066
Fax: (905) 764-7634
Mr. Peter A. Mertens, General Manager

Retail and commercial bakery, with a wide variety of self-serve products made and baked fresh on-site.

BACKGROUND:
Established: 1970; 1st Franchised: 1977
Franchised Units: 106
Company-Owned Units 0

Total Units: 106
Dist.: US-1; CAN-105; O'seas-0
North America: 1 State, 9 Provinces
Density: 50 in ON, 30 in BC, 9 in SK
Projected New Units (12 Months): 10
Qualifications: 4, 4, 1, 2, , 5
Registered: AB
FINANCIAL/TERMS:
Cash Investment: $95K
Total Investment: $275K
Minimum Net Worth: $NR
Fees: Franchise - $25K
Royalty - 5%; Ad. - 1%
Earnings Claim Statement: No
Term of Contract (Years): 20
Avg. # Of Employees: 6 FT, 12 PT
Passive Ownership: Not Allowed
Encourage Conversions: Yes
Area Develop. Agreements: No
Sub-Franchising Contracts: No
Expand In Territory: Yes
Space Needs: NR SF; SC
SUPPORT & TRAINING PROVIDED:
Financial Assistance Provided: Yes(I)
Site Selection Assistance: Yes
Lease Negotiation Assistance: Yes
Co-Operative Advertising: Yes
Franchisee Assoc./Member: No
Size Of Corporate Staff: 44
On-Going Support: A,B,C,D,E,F,G,h,I
Training: 7 Days Head Office; 14 Days On-Site.
SPECIFIC EXPANSION PLANS:
US: All United States
Canada: All Canada
Overseas: No

<< >>

CHESAPEAKE BAGEL BAKERY
Six Concourse Pkwy., # 1700
Atlanta, GA 30328
Tel: (800) 848-8248 (770) 321-6827
Fax: (770) 350-3652
Web Site: www.chesbagel.com
Mr. Gregg Kaplan, President

The nation's oldest, largest and fastest-growing national chain of "full scratch" bagel bakery restaurants. An exhibition kitchen displays fresh, hot bagels made from bags of flour in each unit. A popular combination of sandwiches, salads, gourmet coffee, cappuccino and espresso make this cafe a winning combination.

BACKGROUND:
Established: 1981; 1st Franchised: 1983
Franchised Units: 165
Company-Owned Units 0

Total Units: 165
Dist.: US-164; CAN-1; O'seas-0
North America: 46 States, 1 Province
Density: 31 in VA, 10 in MD, 9 in DC
Projected New Units (12 Months): 104
Qualifications: 5, 5, 3, 4, 3, 4
Registered: All States

FINANCIAL/TERMS:

Cash Investment: $150K
Total Investment: $400-500K
Minimum Net Worth: $500K
Fees: Franchise - $25K
Royalty - 5%; Ad. - 4%
Earnings Claim Statement: No
Term of Contract (Years): 20/10
Avg. # Of Employees: 3 FT, 21 PT
Passive Ownership: Allowed
Encourage Conversions: Yes
Area Develop. Agreements: No
Sub-Franchising Contracts: No
Expand In Territory: Yes
Space Needs: 1,800-2,400 SF; SF, SC

SUPPORT & TRAINING PROVIDED:

Financial Assistance Provided: Yes(I)
Site Selection Assistance: Yes
Lease Negotiation Assistance: Yes
Co-Operative Advertising: N/A
Franchisee Assoc./Member: Yes/Yes
Size Of Corporate Staff: 35
On-Going Support: B,C,D,E,F,G,H,I
Training: 4 Weeks Headquarters, Atlanta, GA.

SPECIFIC EXPANSION PLANS:

US: All United States
Canada: All Canada
Overseas: All Countries

≪ ≫

CINDY'S CINNAMON ROLLS
P.O. Box 1480
Fallbrook, CA 92028
Tel: (800) HOT-ROLL (760) 723-1121
Fax: (760) 723-4143
E-Mail: cindysin@aol.com
Mr. Thomas Harris, President

Fresh-baked cinnamon rolls and muffins. All shops in major shopping malls. Great family business. All products made in the shop and baked fresh all day.

BACKGROUND:
Established: 1985; 1st Franchised: 1986
Franchised Units: 35

Company-Owned Units 0
Total Units: 35
Dist.: US-29; CAN-0; O'seas-3
North America: 14 States
Density: 8 in NY, 3 in CA, 2 in NJ
Projected New Units (12 Months): 5
Qualifications: 3, 3, 3, 3, 3, 3
Registered: NY,CA

FINANCIAL/TERMS:

Cash Investment: $130K
Total Investment: $130K
Minimum Net Worth: $100K
Fees: Franchise - $25K
Royalty - 5%; Ad. - 0%
Earnings Claim Statement: No
Term of Contract (Years): 10/10
Avg. # Of Employees: 8 FT
Passive Ownership: Allowed
Encourage Conversions: Yes
Area Develop. Agreements: No
Sub-Franchising Contracts: No
Expand In Territory: Yes
Space Needs: 800 SF; RM

SUPPORT & TRAINING PROVIDED:

Financial Assistance Provided: No
Site Selection Assistance: Yes
Lease Negotiation Assistance: Yes
Co-Operative Advertising: No
Franchisee Assoc./Member: No
Size Of Corporate Staff: 3
On-Going Support: B,C,D,E,F,G,H,I
Training: 1 Week New York, NY; 4 Days in Store.

SPECIFIC EXPANSION PLANS:

US: All United States
Canada: All Canada
Overseas: All Countries

≪ ≫

CINNABON
Six Concourse Pkwy., # 1700
Atlanta, GA 30328
Tel: (800) 639-3826 (770) 353-3271
Fax: (770) 353-3093
E-Mail: whoas@afce.com
Web Site: www.cinnabon.com
Mr. D'Wayne Tanner, VP New Business Development

Since 1985, CINNABON has created a winning formula for leadership and growth in the industry. As the category leader in the U.S., CINNABON currently enjoys an 80% brand awareness. Millions throughout the world who have had the CINNABON experience will confirm that CINNABON has the perfect recipe for baking delicious, classic sweet rewards. Multi-unit development, limited exclusivity

and world-class franchisor support services are key tenets to our goal of becoming the world's franchisor of choice.

BACKGROUND: IFA MEMBER
Established: 1985; 1st Franchised: 1986
Franchised Units: 254
Company-Owned Units 188
Total Units: 442
Dist.: US-385; CAN-17; O'seas-40
North America: NR
Density: NR
Projected New Units (12 Months): 135
Qualifications: 5, 5, 4, 3, 4, 5
Registered: All States

FINANCIAL/TERMS:

Cash Investment: $NR
Total Investment: $178-253K
Minimum Net Worth: $600K
Fees: Franchise - $35K
Royalty - 5%; Ad. - 1.5-3%
Earnings Claim Statement: Yes
Term of Contract (Years): 10/5/5
Avg. # Of Employees: NR
Passive Ownership: Not Allowed
Encourage Conversions: N/A
Area Develop. Agreements: Yes
Sub-Franchising Contracts: No
Expand In Territory: Yes
Space Needs: 850 SF; RM

SUPPORT & TRAINING PROVIDED:

Financial Assistance Provided: Yes(I)
Site Selection Assistance: Yes
Lease Negotiation Assistance: Yes
Co-Operative Advertising: No
Franchisee Assoc./Member: Yes/Yes
Size Of Corporate Staff: 50
On-Going Support: A,B,C,D,E,f,G,H,I
Training: 3 Weeks Atlanta, GA.

SPECIFIC EXPANSION PLANS:

US: LA,OK,MA,TN,FL,OH
Canada: All Canada
Overseas: Taiwan, South America, Far East

≪ ≫

COFFEE TIME DONUTS
477 Ellesmere Rd.
Toronto, ON M1R 4E5 CANADA
Tel: (416) 288-8515
Fax: (416) 288-8895
Mr. Chris Ioannou, Dir. of Franchising

A quick-service restaurant-type donut chain, with great-tasting coffee, muffins, donuts, salads and sandwiches. Fresh, quality products are what set us apart from the competition.

BACKGROUND:

Established: 1982; 1st Franchised: 1987	
Franchised Units:	304
Company-Owned Units	20
Total Units:	324
Dist.:	US-0; CAN-324; O'seas-0
North America:	3 Provinces
Density: 319 in ON, 3 in MB, 1 in AB	
Projected New Units (12 Months):	65
Qualifications:	3, 3, 2, 2, 3, 5
Registered: NR	

FINANCIAL/TERMS:

Cash Investment:	$NR
Total Investment:	$160-250K
Minimum Net Worth:	$150K
Fees: Franchise -	$NR
Royalty - 4.5%;	Ad. - 2%
Earnings Claim Statement:	No
Term of Contract (Years):	NR
Avg. # Of Employees:	6 FT, 4 PT
Passive Ownership:	Not Allowed
Encourage Conversions:	Yes
Area Develop. Agreements:	NR
Sub-Franchising Contracts:	No
Expand In Territory:	Yes
Space Needs: NR SF; FS, SF, RM	

SUPPORT & TRAINING PROVIDED:

Financial Assistance Provided:	NR
Site Selection Assistance:	NR
Lease Negotiation Assistance:	N/A
Co-Operative Advertising:	NR
Franchisee Assoc./Member:	No
Size Of Corporate Staff:	50
On-Going Support:	b,C,D,E,F,G,H
Training: 3-6 Weeks Scarborough, ON.	

SPECIFIC EXPANSION PLANS:

US:	All United States
Canada:	All Canada
Overseas:	All Countries

≪ ≫

**COOKIE BOUQUET / COOKIES
BY DESIGN**

1865 Summit Ave., # 605
Plano, TX 75074
Tel: (800) 945-2665 (972) 398-9536
Fax: (972) 398-9542
E-Mail: frandevopment@mymail.com
Web Site: www.cookiebouquet.com
Mr. David Patterson, VP Franchise Dev.

Unique retail opportunity! Gift bakery, specializing in hand-decorated cookie arrangements and gourmet cookies, decorated for special events, holidays, centerpieces, etc. Clientele include both individual and corporate customers. A wonderfully delicious alternative to flowers or balloons.

BACKGROUND: IFA MEMBER

Established: 1983; 1st Franchised: 1987	
Franchised Units:	222
Company-Owned Units	1
Total Units:	223
Dist.:	US-223; CAN-0; O'seas-0
North America:	43 States
Density: 31 in TX, 18 in FL, 17 in CA	
Projected New Units (12 Months):	30
Qualifications:	3, 5, 4, 4, 4, 5
Registered: CA,FL,HI,IL,IN,MD,MI,NY,	
OR,RI,SD,VA,WA,WI	

FINANCIAL/TERMS:

Cash Investment:	$80-145K
Total Investment:	$80-145K
Minimum Net Worth:	$NR
Fees: Franchise -	$22.5K
Royalty - 6%;	Ad. - 1%
Earnings Claim Statement:	No
Term of Contract (Years):	5/5
Avg. # Of Employees:	3 FT, 2 PT
Passive Ownership:	Discouraged
Encourage Conversions:	No
Area Develop. Agreements:	Yes
Sub-Franchising Contracts:	No
Expand In Territory:	Yes
Space Needs: 1,200-1,500 SF; SC	

SUPPORT & TRAINING PROVIDED:

Financial Assistance Provided:	No
Site Selection Assistance:	Yes
Lease Negotiation Assistance:	Yes
Co-Operative Advertising:	Yes
Franchisee Assoc./Member:	No
Size Of Corporate Staff:	17
On-Going Support:	C,d,e,G,h,I
Training: 2 Weeks Dallas, TX.	

SPECIFIC EXPANSION PLANS:

US:	All United States
Canada:	No
Overseas:	No

≪ ≫

**COOKIES IN BLOOM/COOKIE
CADABRA**

5437 MacArthur Blvd.
Irving, TX 75038
Tel: (800) 222-3104 (972) 518-1749
Fax: (972) 580-1831
E-Mail: re-pinac@gte.net
Web Site: www.cookiesinbollom.com
Mr. Robert E. Pinac, Vice President

COOKIES IN BLOOM

Operation of retail cookie gift baking shops that produce and sell decorated cookies, gourmet cookies and whimsical cookie arrangements packaged as floral bouquets and related products for retail sale to the public.

BACKGROUND:

Established: 1988; 1st Franchised: 1992	
Franchised Units:	38
Company-Owned Units	2
Total Units:	40
Dist.:	US-14; CAN-0; O'seas-0
North America:	14 States
Density:	6 in TX, 2 in LA
Projected New Units (12 Months):	5
Qualifications:	4, 5, 1, 2, 3, 4
Registered:	CA,FL,IL,MD,MI,NY,
OR,VA,WA,WI	

FINANCIAL/TERMS:

Cash Investment:	$53-107K
Total Investment:	$53-107K
Minimum Net Worth:	$100K
Fees: Franchise -	$12.5K
Royalty - 5%;	Ad. - 2%
Earnings Claim Statement:	No
Term of Contract (Years):	5/5
Avg. # Of Employees:	3 FT, 2 PT
Passive Ownership:	Discouraged
Encourage Conversions:	N/A
Area Develop. Agreements:	Yes/5
Sub-Franchising Contracts:	No
Expand In Territory:	Yes
Space Needs: 1,200-1,500 SF; SC	

SUPPORT & TRAINING PROVIDED:

Financial Assistance Provided:	No
Site Selection Assistance:	Yes
Lease Negotiation Assistance:	Yes
Co-Operative Advertising:	Yes
Franchisee Assoc./Member:	No
Size Of Corporate Staff:	2
On-Going Support:	b,C,D,E,G,H,I
Training: 2 Weeks in Irving, TX.	

SPECIFIC EXPANSION PLANS:

US:	All United States
Canada:	No
Overseas:	No

≪ ≫

CREATIVE CAKERY

636 Redondo Blvd.
Long Beach, CA 90814
Tel: (800) 224-4261 (562) 438-2301

Fax: (562) 433-2423
E-Mail: cake@thegrid.net
Web Site: www.creative-cakery.com
Mr. Douglas Matheson, VP Marketing Director

CREATIVE CAKERY ® is a unique retail gift-giving concept that combines a simple cake making process with commercial and retail sales. Our stores present a fun, festive experience for our customers. We ship our cakes and other bakery products throughout the United States. Fine bundt shaped cakes are decorated for any occasion or event. From birthdays to corporate recognition, for over fifteen years Creative Cakery had been surpassing the expectations of its customers.

BACKGROUND:

Established: 1983;	1st Franchised: 1997
Franchised Units:	6
Company-Owned Units	1
Total Units:	7
Dist.:	US-14; CAN-0; O'seas-0
North America:	2 States
Density:	12 in CA, 1 in OR
Projected New Units (12 Months):	5
Qualifications:	4, 4, 1, 2, 5, 5
Registered: CA,WA	

FINANCIAL/TERMS:

Cash Investment:	$22.5-70K
Total Investment:	$150-350K
Minimum Net Worth:	$200K
Fees: Franchise -	$22.5K
Royalty - 5%;	Ad. - 0%
Earnings Claim Statement:	No
Term of Contract (Years):	15/15
Avg. # Of Employees:	8 FT
Passive Ownership:	Allowed
Encourage Conversions:	Yes
Area Develop. Agreements:	Yes/15
Sub-Franchising Contracts:	No
Expand In Territory:	Yes
Space Needs: 1,400 SF; SF, SC	

SUPPORT & TRAINING PROVIDED:

Financial Assistance Provided:	Yes(I)
Site Selection Assistance:	Yes
Lease Negotiation Assistance:	Yes
Co-Operative Advertising:	Yes
Franchisee Assoc./Member:	Yes/Yes
Size Of Corporate Staff:	4
On-Going Support:	b,C,D,E,F,G,H,I

Training: 3 Days at Long Beach, CA; 15 Days at Long Beach, CA; 8 Days at Franchisee's Location.

SPECIFIC EXPANSION PLANS:

US:	All United States
Canada:	All Canada
Overseas:	All Countries

◄◄ ►►

DUNKIN' DONUTS

DUNKIN' DONUTS
14 Pacella Park Dr. P.O. Box 317
Randolph, MA 02368
Tel: (800) 777-9983 (781) 961-4000
Fax: (781) 961-4207
Web Site: www.dunkin-baskin-togos.com
Mr. Lee Sanders, Director of Franchising

DUNKIN' DONUTS is the world's largest coffee and doughnut chain. We offer a full array of quick-service menu items, including muffins, bagels and donuts.

BACKGROUND: IFA MEMBER

Established: 1950;	1st Franchised: 1955
Franchised Units:	5,001
Company-Owned Units	0
Total Units:	5,001
Dist.: US-3,384; CAN-242; O'seas-1,110	
North America:	46 States
Density: 490 in MA, 359 in NY, 237 IL	
Projected New Units (12 Months):	350
Qualifications:	5, 4, 2, 2, 5, 4
Registered: CA,FL,IL,IN,MD,MI,MN,NY,	
OR,RI,VA,WA,WI,DC	

FINANCIAL/TERMS:

Cash Investment:	$200K
Total Investment:	$350K-3MM
Minimum Net Worth:	$400K
Fees: Franchise -	$40-60K
Royalty - 4.9%;	Ad. - 5.9%
Earnings Claim Statement:	No
Term of Contract (Years):	20
Avg. # Of Employees:	NR
Passive Ownership:	Discouraged
Encourage Conversions:	Yes
Area Develop. Agreements:	Yes/3
Sub-Franchising Contracts:	No
Expand In Territory:	Yes
Space Needs: 800-2,000 SF; FS, SF, SC, RM	

SUPPORT & TRAINING PROVIDED:

Financial Assistance Provided:	Yes(I)
Site Selection Assistance:	Yes
Lease Negotiation Assistance:	No
Co-Operative Advertising:	Yes
Franchisee Assoc./Member:	Yes/Yes
Size Of Corporate Staff:	700
On-Going Support:	B,C,D,E,F,G,H

Training: 5 Weeks Dunkin' Donuts University, Braintree, MA.

SPECIFIC EXPANSION PLANS:

US:	NY,MD,DC,GA,PA,FL,MI,IN,IL

Canada:	PQ,ON
Overseas:	All Countries

◄◄ ►►

GREAT AMERICAN BAGEL, THE

519 N. Cass Ave., #1W
Westmont, IL 60559
Tel: (888) BAGEL-ME (630) 963-3393
Fax: (630) 963-7799
Ms. Linda Rog, Director of Franchising

Bagel bakery and restaurant, specializing in freshly-made bagels - made daily from scratch on the store premises. Stores feature monthly specials along with 28 varieties of bagels daily. In addition, each store also prepares it's own fresh cream cheeses!

BACKGROUND:

Established: 1987;	1st Franchised: 1994
Franchised Units:	35
Company-Owned Units	5
Total Units:	40
Dist.:	US-40; CAN-0; O'seas-0
North America:	10 States
Density:	25 in IL, 3 in WA, 2 in IN
Projected New Units (12 Months):	20
Qualifications:	5, 3, 2, 3, 4, 5
Registered: FL,IL,IN,MI,MN,ND,WA,WI	

FINANCIAL/TERMS:

Cash Investment:	$60-80K
Total Investment:	$230-280K
Minimum Net Worth:	$250K
Fees: Franchise -	$20K
Royalty - 4%;	Ad. - 2%
Earnings Claim Statement:	No
Term of Contract (Years):	20/5
Avg. # Of Employees:	3 FT, 9 PT
Passive Ownership:	Not Allowed
Encourage Conversions:	N/A
Area Develop. Agreements:	No
Sub-Franchising Contracts:	No
Expand In Territory:	Yes
Space Needs: 2,000 SF; FS, SF, SC, RM	

SUPPORT & TRAINING PROVIDED:

Financial Assistance Provided:	No
Site Selection Assistance:	Yes
Lease Negotiation Assistance:	Yes
Co-Operative Advertising:	N/A
Franchisee Assoc./Member:	Yes
Size Of Corporate Staff:	NR
On-Going Support:	B,C,D,E,g,h

Training: 4 Weeks Western Springs, IL.

SPECIFIC EXPANSION PLANS:

US:	All United States
Canada:	No
Overseas:	No

≺≺ ≻≻

GREAT AMERICAN COOKIES
2855 E. Cottonwood Pkwy., # 400
Salt Lake City, UT 84121
Tel: (800) 346-6311
Fax: (888) 867-7343
E-Mail: squireji@greatamcookie.com
Web Site: www.greatamericancookies.com
Franchise Development, Franchise
    Development Manager

'Share the Fun of Cookies.' Established cookie concept with a great old family recipe, attractive retail price point, unique cookie cake program, available in combination store formats for traditional and non-traditional venues.

BACKGROUND: IFA MEMBER
Established: 1977;   1st Franchised: 1977
Franchised Units: 206
Company-Owned Units   <u>101</u>
Total Units: 307
Dist.:   US-327; CAN-0; O'seas-2
  North America: 39 States
  Density: 47 in TX, 24 in GA, 24 in FL
Projected New Units (12 Months):   23
Qualifications: 5, 3, 1, 1, 3, 5
Registered: All States
FINANCIAL/TERMS:
Cash Investment: $122-493K
Total Investment: $119.5-501K
Minimum Net Worth: $250K
Fees: Franchise - $25K
  Royalty - 7%;   Ad. - N/A
Earnings Claim Statement: No
Term of Contract (Years):   NR
Avg. # Of Employees: Varies
Passive Ownership: Allowed
Encourage Conversions: Yes
Area Develop. Agreements: No
Sub-Franchising Contracts: No
Expand In Territory: Yes
Space Needs: 625 SF; RM
SUPPORT & TRAINING PROVIDED:
Financial Assistance Provided: No
Site Selection Assistance: Yes
Lease Negotiation Assistance: Yes
Co-Operative Advertising: N/A
Franchisee Assoc./Member: Yes
Size Of Corporate Staff: 65
On-Going Support: B,C,D,E,G,H,I
Training: 6 Days Atlanta, GA.
SPECIFIC EXPANSION PLANS:
US: All United States
Canada: No
Overseas: No

≺≺ ≻≻

GREAT CANADIAN BAGEL, THE
270 Central Pkwy. W., # 301
Mississauga, ON L5C 4P4 CANADA
Tel: (905) 803-7796
Fax: (905) 566-1402
E-Mail: greatcanadianbagel.com
Web Site: www.greatcanadianbagel.com
Mr. Glen Tucker, Director of Franchising

Canada's largest chain devoted to bagels has elevated the bagel to a new culinary experience. The chain offers a healthy way to enjoy a sandwich, snack or meal, while providing an alternative to higher fat, fast-food establishments. The bagel has become the ideal convenience food of the 90's - low in fat, high in taste, nutritious and now, convenient, thanks to the expansion of THE GREAT CANADIAN BAGEL.

BACKGROUND:
Established: 1993;   1st Franchised: 1994
Franchised Units: 151
Company-Owned Units   <u>7</u>
Total Units: 158
Dist.:   US-0; CAN-152; O'seas-4
  North America: 9 Provinces
  Density: 90 in ON, 24 in BC, 13 Marit
Projected New Units (12 Months):   20
Qualifications: 5, 4, 3, 3, 2, 5
Registered: AB
FINANCIAL/TERMS:
Cash Investment: $100K
Total Investment: $260-300K
Minimum Net Worth: $10K
Fees: Franchise - $30K
  Royalty - 6%;   Ad. - 1.5%
Earnings Claim Statement: Yes
Term of Contract (Years):   10/5
Avg. # Of Employees: 7 FT, 5 PT
Passive Ownership: Discouraged
Encourage Conversions: No
Area Develop. Agreements: No
Sub-Franchising Contracts: Yes
Expand In Territory: Yes
Space Needs: 2,000 SF; N/A
SUPPORT & TRAINING PROVIDED:
Financial Assistance Provided: Yes
Site Selection Assistance: Yes
Lease Negotiation Assistance: N/A
Co-Operative Advertising: Yes
Franchisee Assoc./Member: Yes/Yes
Size Of Corporate Staff: NR
On-Going Support: A,B,C,D,E,F,G,h
Training: 4-6 Weeks Toronto, ON.
SPECIFIC EXPANSION PLANS:
US: See The Great American Bagel
Canada: All Canada
Overseas: All Countries

≺≺ ≻≻

GREAT HARVEST BREAD CO.
28 S. Montana St.
Dillon, MT 59725-2434
Tel: (800) 442-0424 (406) 683-6842
Fax: (406) 683-5537
E-Mail: inquiry@greatharvest.com
Web Site: www.greatharvest.com
Ms. Lisa Wagner, Director of Franchise
    Growth

Neighborhood bread bakery, specializing in whole wheat breads from scratch.

BACKGROUND: IFA MEMBER
Established: 1976;   1st Franchised: 1978
Franchised Units: 138
Company-Owned Units   <u>1</u>
Total Units: 139
Dist.:   US-139; CAN-0; O'seas-0
  North America: 35 States
  Density: 10 in UT, 8 in OR, 8 in IL
Projected New Units (12 Months):   20
Qualifications: 3, 4, 3, 5, 3, 5
Registered: All States
FINANCIAL/TERMS:
Cash Investment: $80K
Total Investment: $89-234K
Minimum Net Worth: $N/A
Fees: Franchise - $24K
  Royalty - 5-7%;   Ad. - 0%
Earnings Claim Statement: Yes
Term of Contract (Years):   10
Avg. # Of Employees: 6 FT, 2 PT
Passive Ownership: Not Allowed
Encourage Conversions: N/A
Area Develop. Agreements: Yes
Sub-Franchising Contracts: No
Expand In Territory: Yes
Space Needs: 1,800 SF; FS, SC
SUPPORT & TRAINING PROVIDED:
Financial Assistance Provided: Yes
Site Selection Assistance: Yes
Lease Negotiation Assistance: Yes
Co-Operative Advertising: Yes
Franchisee Assoc./Member: Yes
Size Of Corporate Staff: 34
On-Going Support: B,C,D,E,G,H,I
Training: 2 Weeks Host Bakeries; 1 Week at
    Headquarters; 3 Trainers for Opening.

SPECIFIC EXPANSION PLANS:

US:	All United States
Canada:	All Canada
Overseas:	No

≪ ≫

HOUSE OF BREAD

858 Higuera St.
San Luis Obispo, CA 93401
Tel: (800) 545-5146 (805) 542-0255
Fax: (805) 542-0255
E-Mail: houseofbread@mail.com
Web Site: www.houseofbread.com
Ms. Sheila McCann, CEO

Healthy, premium bread bakery, with over 20 varieties of delicious breads - from traditional honey whole wheat to irresistible sourdough pesto artichoke or the decadent triple chocolate bread. HOUSE OF BREAD's unique recipes use no dairy, refined sugar or fat, yet taste incredible.

BACKGROUND:

Established: 1996;	1st Franchised: 1998
Franchised Units:	6
Company-Owned Units	3
Total Units:	9
Dist.:	US-9; CAN-0; O'seas-0
North America:	2 States
Density:	7 in CA
Projected New Units (12 Months):	6
Qualifications:	3, 3, 1, 3, 3, 5
Registered: CA	

FINANCIAL/TERMS:

Cash Investment:	$24-65K
Total Investment:	$75-204K
Minimum Net Worth:	$50K
Fees: Franchise -	$24K
Royalty - 6%;	Ad. - 2%
Earnings Claim Statement:	No
Term of Contract (Years):	10/10
Avg. # Of Employees:	2 FT, 8 PT
Passive Ownership:	Discouraged
Encourage Conversions:	NR
Area Develop. Agreements:	Yes
Sub-Franchising Contracts:	NR
Expand In Territory:	Yes
Space Needs: 1,500 SF; SC, RM	

SUPPORT & TRAINING PROVIDED:

Financial Assistance Provided:	Yes(B)
Site Selection Assistance:	Yes
Lease Negotiation Assistance:	Yes
Co-Operative Advertising:	Yes

Franchisee Assoc./Member:	No
Size Of Corporate Staff:	2
On-Going Support:	C,D,E,F,G,H,I
Training: Minimum 9 Days San Luis Obispo, CA; Minimum 7 Days Franchisee Location.	

SPECIFIC EXPANSION PLANS:

US:	All United States
Canada:	All Canada
Overseas:	All Countries

≪ ≫

LAMAR'S DONUTS

245 S. 84th St., # 210
Lincoln, NE 68510
Tel: (800) 533-7489 (402) 484-5900
Fax: (402) 484-7811
E-Mail: lamars@binary.net
Web Site: www.lamars.com
Mr. Joseph J. Field, President/CEO

LAMAR'S DONUTS is a rapidly growing chain of retail donut shops, founded in Kansas City, specializing in 53 varieties of handmade donuts and specialties since 1933, served in an atmosphere rich in hospitality and authenticity. A K.C. institution and Chamber of Commerce tourist attraction, LAMAR's has received acclaim nationwide, creating what critics call "the perfect donut."

BACKGROUND: IFA MEMBER

Established: 1933;	1st Franchised: 1993
Franchised Units:	22
Company-Owned Units	5
Total Units:	27
Dist.:	US-27; CAN-0; O'seas-0
North America:	8 States
Density:	11 in MO, 6 in KS, 2 in VA
Projected New Units (12 Months):	10-20
Qualifications:	4, 5, 3, 2, 5, 5
Registered: FL,VA	

FINANCIAL/TERMS:

Cash Investment:	$Varies
Total Investment:	$200-240K
Minimum Net Worth:	$Varies
Fees: Franchise -	$26.5K
Royalty - 5%;	Ad. - 2%
Earnings Claim Statement:	No

Term of Contract (Years):	10/10
Avg. # Of Employees:	4-6 FT, 5-10 PT
Passive Ownership:	Allowed
Encourage Conversions:	Yes
Area Develop. Agreements:	Yes/Negot.
Sub-Franchising Contracts:	Yes
Expand In Territory:	Yes
Space Needs: 2,000 SF; SF, SC	

SUPPORT & TRAINING PROVIDED:

Financial Assistance Provided:	Yes(I)
Site Selection Assistance:	Yes
Lease Negotiation Assistance:	Yes
Co-Operative Advertising:	Yes
Franchisee Assoc./Member:	No
Size Of Corporate Staff:	10
On-Going Support:	a,b,C,D,E,F,G,H,I
Training: 2-4 Weeks Training Store, Kansas City; 3-5 On-Site in Franchise Store.	

SPECIFIC EXPANSION PLANS:

US:	All U.S., Midwest, Southeast
Canada:	No
Overseas:	No

≪ ≫

LOX OF BAGELS

3028 Palos Verdes Dr. W.
Palos Verdes, CA 90274
Tel: (800) 879-6927 (310) 373-6550
Fax: (310) 539-7494
E-Mail: mail@bagelfranchise.com
Web Site: www.bagelfranchise.com
Mr. Ted Taylor, Manager

Retail bagel bakery with gourmet coffees, espresso, juices and specialty breads.

BACKGROUND:

Established: 1986;	1st Franchised: 1995
Franchised Units:	13
Company-Owned Units	0
Total Units:	13
Dist.:	US-13; CAN-0; O'seas-0
North America:	NR
Density:	NR
Projected New Units (12 Months):	25
Qualifications:	4, 2, 1, 1, 5, 4
Registered: All States	

FINANCIAL/TERMS:

Cash Investment:	$80K
Total Investment:	$168-200K
Minimum Net Worth:	$NR
Fees: Franchise -	$24.5K
Royalty - 0%;	Ad. - 0%
Earnings Claim Statement:	No
Term of Contract (Years):	5/5
Avg. # Of Employees:	3 FT, 3 PT
Passive Ownership:	Allowed
Encourage Conversions:	Yes
Area Develop. Agreements:	Yes/20
Sub-Franchising Contracts:	No
Expand In Territory:	Yes
Space Needs: 900-1,200 SF; FS, SF, SC	

SUPPORT & TRAINING PROVIDED:

Financial Assistance Provided:	No
Site Selection Assistance:	Yes
Lease Negotiation Assistance:	Yes
Co-Operative Advertising:	No
Franchisee Assoc./Member:	No
Size Of Corporate Staff:	4
On-Going Support:	C,D,E,F,I
Training: 4 Days On-Site.	

SPECIFIC EXPANSION PLANS:

US:	All United States
Canada:	All Canada
Overseas:	Europe

◄◄ ►►

MANHATTAN BAGEL COMPANY
246 Industrial Way W.
Eatontown, NJ 07724-9886
Tel: (800) 308-2457 (732) 544-0155
Fax: (732) 544-1315
E-Mail: roccof@bgls.com
Web Site: www.manhattanbagel.com
Mr. Rocco Fiorentino, Dir. of Real Estate

MANHATTAN BAGEL CO. offers up-scale, efficient, bagel eateries, offering authentic New York bagels in 21 varieties, as well as gourmet spreads and deli items, plus full breakfast fare. Stores are configured 100% turn-key, including site selection and negotiation. We have comprehensive training with a detailed operations manual and continuing assistance in marketing, merchandising and food preparation. No baking experience is required.

BACKGROUND: IFA MEMBER

Established: 1987; 1st Franchised: 1988	
Franchised Units:	300
Company-Owned Units	11
Total Units:	311
Dist.:	US-311; CAN-0; O'seas-0
North America:	21 States
Density: 33 in NJ, 18 in PA, 17 in CA	
Projected New Units (12 Months):	35
Qualifications:	3, 3, 1, 1, 3, 5
Registered: All States	

FINANCIAL/TERMS:

Cash Investment:	$80-100K
Total Investment:	$150-337K
Minimum Net Worth:	$150K
Fees: Franchise -	$20K
Royalty - 5%;	Ad. - 2.5-4%
Earnings Claim Statement:	No
Term of Contract (Years):	10/10
Avg. # Of Employees:	3 FT, 9 PT
Passive Ownership:	Discouraged
Encourage Conversions:	Yes
Area Develop. Agreements:	Yes
Sub-Franchising Contracts:	Yes
Expand In Territory:	Yes
Space Needs: 1,200-1,600 SF; FS, SC	

SUPPORT & TRAINING PROVIDED:

Financial Assistance Provided:	No
Site Selection Assistance:	Yes
Lease Negotiation Assistance:	Yes
Co-Operative Advertising:	Yes
Franchisee Assoc./Member:	Yes
Size Of Corporate Staff:	313
On-Going Support:	B,C,D,E,F,G,h
Training: 2 Weeks in Corporate Office; 1 Week in Store.	

SPECIFIC EXPANSION PLANS:

US:	All United States
Canada:	No
Overseas:	Middle East, Iceland

◄◄ ►►

MMMARVELLOUS MMMUFFINS
16251 Dallas Pkwy.
Dallas, TX 75248
Tel: (972) 687-4091
Fax: (972) 687-4062
E-Mail: lboyd@richmont.com
Web Site: www.mmmuffins.com
Franchising Department,

Fresh, high-quality specialty baked goods including over 100 varieties of muffins as well as scones, cinnamon swirls, cookies and streusel cakes. In addition, we offer a selection of gourmet coffee, teas, and fruit juices.

BACKGROUND:

Established: 1979; 1st Franchised: 1980	
Franchised Units:	93
Company-Owned Units	9
Total Units:	102
Dist.:	US-0; CAN-116; O'seas-6
North America:	8 Provinces
Density: 43 in ON, 26 in PQ, 13 in BC	
Projected New Units (12 Months):	10
Qualifications:	5, 4, 3, 3, 4, 5
Registered: AB	

FINANCIAL/TERMS:

Cash Investment:	$40-60K+
Total Investment:	$160K
Minimum Net Worth:	$200K
Fees: Franchise -	$25K
Royalty - 7%;	Ad. - 1%
Earnings Claim Statement:	No
Term of Contract (Years):	10/10
Avg. # Of Employees:	2-3 FT, 4-7 PT
Passive Ownership:	Not Allowed
Encourage Conversions:	Yes
Area Develop. Agreements:	Yes (I'ntl.)
Sub-Franchising Contracts:	Yes
Expand In Territory:	Yes
Space Needs: 300 SF; SF, SC, RM	

SUPPORT & TRAINING PROVIDED:

Financial Assistance Provided:	Yes(I)
Site Selection Assistance:	Yes
Lease Negotiation Assistance:	Yes
Co-Operative Advertising:	Yes
Franchisee Assoc./Member:	No
Size Of Corporate Staff:	35
On-Going Support:	A,B,C,D,E,F,G,h
Training: 4 Weeks Toronto, ON.	

SPECIFIC EXPANSION PLANS:

US:	N/A
Canada:	All Canada
Overseas: Asia, Eastern Europe, Middle East, South America	

◄◄ ►►

MRS. FIELDS COOKIES
2855 E. Cottonwood Pkwy., # 400
Salt Lake City, UT 84121-7050
Tel: (800) 348-6311 (801) 736-5600
Fax: (888) 867-7343
E-Mail: timp@mrsfields.com
Web Site: www.mrsfields.com
Franchise Dev., Franchise Dev. Manager

Premier retail cookie business with 'uncompromising quality,' 94% brand recognition, easy to operate, flexible designs and combination store options that operate in traditional and non-traditional venues.

BACKGROUND: IFA MEMBER

Established: 1977; 1st Franchised: 1990	
Franchised Units:	186

Company-Owned Units   390
Total Units: 576
Dist.:   US-528; CAN-11; O'seas-34
  North America: 35 States, 1 Province
  Density: 86 in CA, 27 in IL, 19 in NY
Projected New Units (12 Months):   14
Qualifications: 4, 4, 2, 2, 2, 5
Registered: All States
FINANCIAL/TERMS:
Cash Investment: $10-73.5K
Total Investment: $146-245K
Minimum Net Worth: $75K
Fees: Franchise - $25K
  Royalty - 6%;   Ad. - 0-2%
Earnings Claim Statement: No
Term of Contract (Years):   7/5/5
Avg. # Of Employees: 3 FT, 4 PT
Passive Ownership: Not Allowed
Encourage Conversions: Yes
Area Develop. Agreements: Yes
Sub-Franchising Contracts: No
Expand In Territory: Yes
Space Needs: 650-800 SF; RM, SC, SF, Stadium
SUPPORT & TRAINING PROVIDED:
Financial Assistance Provided: Yes(I)
Site Selection Assistance: Yes
Lease Negotiation Assistance: Yes
Co-Operative Advertising: No
Franchisee Assoc./Member: Yes/Yes
Size Of Corporate Staff: 60
On-Going Support: A,B,C,D,E,F,G,H,I
Training: 10 Days Park City, UT; 5-10 Days
  Field Training.
SPECIFIC EXPANSION PLANS:
US: All United States
Canada: All Canada
Overseas: All Countries

≪ ≫

MRS. POWELL'S BAKERY EATERY
3380 S. Service Rd.
Burlington, ON L7N 3J5 CANADA
Tel: (905) 681-8448
Fax: (905) 637-7745
E-Mail: franchisedept@aftonfood.com
Web Site: www.aftonfood.com
Mr. Andrew Diveky, Dir. of Franchising

Production and baking of fresh cinnamon
rolls, custom sandwiches, European-style
sandwiches, soup, desserts and assorted
beverages.

BACKGROUND:
Established: 1984;   1st Franchised: 1986
Franchised Units: 25
Company-Owned Units   0
Total Units: 25
Dist.:   US-23; CAN-0; O'seas-2

North America: 14 States
Density: 6 in ID, 3 in WA, 3 in CA
Projected New Units (12 Months):   8
Qualifications: 3, 4, 2, 3, 3, 4
Registered: IN,WA,AB
FINANCIAL/TERMS:
Cash Investment: $50K
Total Investment: $125-160K
Minimum Net Worth: $100K
Fees: Franchise - $25K
  Royalty - 5%;   Ad. - 3%
Earnings Claim Statement: No
Term of Contract (Years):   10/10
Avg. # Of Employees: 2 FT, 4 PT
Passive Ownership: Discouraged
Encourage Conversions: Yes
Area Develop. Agreements: Yes/20
Sub-Franchising Contracts: Yes
Expand In Territory: Yes
Space Needs: 500-2,000 SF; SF, SC, RM
SUPPORT & TRAINING PROVIDED:
Financial Assistance Provided: No
Site Selection Assistance: Yes
Lease Negotiation Assistance: Yes
Co-Operative Advertising: No
Franchisee Assoc./Member: No
Size Of Corporate Staff: 10
On-Going Support: C,D,E,F,G,h
Training: 1 Week Head Office; 1 Week
  Franchised Store; 1 Week Own Store.
SPECIFIC EXPANSION PLANS:
US: All United States
Canada: All Canada
Overseas: Europe, Far East

≪ ≫

MUFFIN BREAK
3300 Bloor St., W., # 2900
Etobicoke, ON M8X 2X3 CANADA
Tel: (416) 236-0055
Fax: (416) 236-0054
Web Site: www.muffinbreak.com
Mr. Tim Grech, Franchise Administration

Muffins and pastries baked on premises
complement our gourmet coffees, teas and
refreshing fruit juices. Eat-in or take-out.

BACKGROUND: IFA MEMBER
Established: 1980;   1st Franchised: 1981
Franchised Units: 30
Company-Owned Units   0
Total Units: 30
Dist.:   US-0; CAN-30; O'seas-0
  North America: 4 Provinces
  Density: 25 in BC, 2 in AB, 2 in ON
Projected New Units (12 Months):   0
Qualifications: 5, 3, 2, 3, 4, 5
Registered: AB

FINANCIAL/TERMS:
Cash Investment: $60-80K
Total Investment: $160-200K
Minimum Net Worth: $80K
Fees: Franchise - $25K
  Royalty - 6%;   Ad. - 2%
Earnings Claim Statement: Yes
Term of Contract (Years):   10/10
Avg. # Of Employees: 4 FT, 5-7 PT
Passive Ownership: Not Allowed
Encourage Conversions: No
Area Develop. Agreements: No
Sub-Franchising Contracts: Yes
Expand In Territory: No
Space Needs: 1,500 SF; FS, SF, SC, RM
SUPPORT & TRAINING PROVIDED:
Financial Assistance Provided: Yes(I)
Site Selection Assistance: Yes
Lease Negotiation Assistance: Yes
Co-Operative Advertising: Yes
Franchisee Assoc./Member: Yes/Yes
Size Of Corporate Staff: 30
On-Going Support: A,B,C,D,E,G
Training: 10-14 Days Vancouver, BC.
SPECIFIC EXPANSION PLANS:
US: No
Canada: All Canada
Overseas: No

≪ ≫

MY FAVORITE MUFFIN
8501 W. Higgins Rd., # 320
Chicago, IL 60631
Tel: (800) 251-6101 (773) 380-6100
Fax: (773) 380-6183
E-Mail: hmarks@babholdings.com
Web Site: www.babholdings.com
Mr. Howard Marks, Director Franchise
  Development

As a MY FAVORITE MUFFIN franchisee,
you get to create and sell over 300 varieties
of our special muffins in both regular
and fat-free varieties. Where applicable,
you can add BIG APPLE BAGELS and
BREWSTER'S COFFEE to complement
your wonderful muffins.

BACKGROUND: IFA MEMBER
Established: 1987;   1st Franchised: 1988
Franchised Units: 63
Company-Owned Units   8
Total Units: 71
Dist.:   US-71; CAN-0; O'seas-0
  North America: 19 States
  Density: 18 in NJ, 10 in PA, 8 in FL
Projected New Units (12 Months):   15
Qualifications: 3, 3, 5, 2, 2, 5
Registered: All States

FINANCIAL/TERMS:

Cash Investment:	$NR
Total Investment:	$234-382.3K
Minimum Net Worth:	$50K Min.
Fees: Franchise -	$25K
Royalty - 5%;	Ad. - 2%
Earnings Claim Statement:	No
Term of Contract (Years):	10/10
Avg. # Of Employees:	3 FT, 15 PT
Passive Ownership:	Discouraged
Encourage Conversions:	N/A
Area Develop. Agreements:	Yes
Sub-Franchising Contracts:	No
Expand In Territory:	Yes
Space Needs: 1,800-2,200 SF; FS, SC, RM	

SUPPORT & TRAINING PROVIDED:

Financial Assistance Provided:	Yes(I)
Site Selection Assistance:	Yes
Lease Negotiation Assistance:	Yes
Co-Operative Advertising:	No
Franchisee Assoc./Member:	NR
Size Of Corporate Staff:	34
On-Going Support:	B,C,D,E,F,G,H,I
Training: 2 Weeks Milwaukee, WI; 5 Days Store Location Prior to Opening.	

SPECIFIC EXPANSION PLANS:

US:	All United States
Canada:	All Canada
Overseas:	All Countries

<< >>

PANERA BREAD COMPANY

7930 Big Bend Blvd.
Webster Groves, MO 63119
Tel: (800) 301-5566 (314) 918-7779
Fax: (314) 918-7773
E-Mail: slbfrandev@aol.com
Web Site: www.panerabread.com
Mr. P.J. Evans, VP Franchise Dev.

Founded in Saint Louis in 1987, SAINT LOUIS BREAD has expanded into new markets over the past few years, with strong consumer acceptance for its unique concept. Each SAINT LOUIS BREAD bakery-cafe features a comfortable neighborhood setting where residents can relax and enjoy a wide range of fresh-baked sourdough breads, along with other fresh-baked goods, bagels and hearty made-to-order sandwiches, salads and soups.

BACKGROUND: IFA MEMBER

Established: 1987; 1st Franchised: 1993	
Franchised Units:	37
Company-Owned Units	67
Total Units:	104
Dist.:	US-104; CAN-0; O'seas-0
North America:	14 States

Density:	36 in MO, 25 in IL, 8 in GA
Projected New Units (12 Months):	108
Qualifications:	5, 5, 5, 3, 3, 4
Registered: All States	

FINANCIAL/TERMS:

Cash Investment:	$135-165K
Total Investment:	$550-650K
Minimum Net Worth:	$3MM
Fees: Franchise -	$35K
Royalty - 5%;	Ad. - Up to 5%
Earnings Claim Statement:	Yes
Term of Contract (Years):	20/Agrmt.
Avg. # Of Employees:	17 FT, 17 PT
Passive Ownership:	Not Allowed
Encourage Conversions:	No
Area Develop. Agreements:	Yes/3-13
Sub-Franchising Contracts:	No
Expand In Territory:	No
Space Needs: 3,500 SF; FS, SF, SC, RM	

SUPPORT & TRAINING PROVIDED:

Financial Assistance Provided:	No
Site Selection Assistance:	Yes
Lease Negotiation Assistance:	No
Co-Operative Advertising:	Yes
Franchisee Assoc./Member:	No
Size Of Corporate Staff:	54
On-Going Support:	B,C,D,E,F,H,I
Training: 10 Weeks St. Louis, MO.	

SPECIFIC EXPANSION PLANS:

US:	All United States
Canada:	No
Overseas:	No

<< >>

PARADISE BAKERY & CAFE

5150 Fair Oaks Blvd., # 101-185
Carmichael, CA 95608-5758
Tel: (800) 951-9582 (916) 335-5166
Fax: (916) 568-1240
Mr. Karl Thompson, VP Franchise Dev.

Over 20 years of bakery and cafe experience, offering our signature fresh-baked goods, made from scratch and baked right on the premises all day long. Made-to-order sandwiches, soups, salads and gourmet coffee and a large selection of beverages.

BACKGROUND:

Established: 1976; 1st Franchised: 1987	
Franchised Units:	36
Company-Owned Units	16
Total Units:	52
Dist.:	US-52; CAN-0; O'seas-0
North America:	8 States
Density:	20 in CA, 8 in TX, 7 in AZ
Projected New Units (12 Months):	30
Registered: CA,HI	

FINANCIAL/TERMS:

Cash Investment:	$75-150K
Total Investment:	$222-439K
Minimum Net Worth:	$150K
Fees: Franchise -	$35K
Royalty - 6%;	Ad. - 2%
Earnings Claim Statement:	No
Term of Contract (Years):	10/5
Avg. # Of Employees:	5 FT, 11 PT
Passive Ownership:	Allowed
Encourage Conversions:	No
Area Develop. Agreements:	Yes/10
Sub-Franchising Contracts:	No
Expand In Territory:	Yes
Space Needs: 1,000-2,000 SF; NR	

SUPPORT & TRAINING PROVIDED:

Financial Assistance Provided:	Yes(I)
Site Selection Assistance:	Yes
Lease Negotiation Assistance:	Yes
Co-Operative Advertising:	Yes
Franchisee Assoc./Member:	No
Size Of Corporate Staff:	17
On-Going Support:	B,C,D,E,F,G,I
Training: 5 Weeks.	

SPECIFIC EXPANSION PLANS:

US:	All United States
Canada:	All Canada
Overseas:	No

<< >>

ROBIN'S DONUTS

2001 - 715 Hewitson St.
Thunder Bay, ON P7B 6B5 CANADA
Tel: (807) 623-4453
Fax: (807) 623-4682
E-Mail: robins@robinsdonuts.com
Web Site: www.robinsdonuts.com
Mr. Ian Sharp, Vice President

Since 1975, ROBIN'S DONUTS has grown to be the largest chain in Western Canada and the second largest in Canada, due to its proven system of providing consistent, high-quality donuts, coffee, deli-products, soups, sandwiches and salads in a contemporary, family-oriented environment.

BACKGROUND:

Established: 1975; 1st Franchised: 1977

Franchised Units:	212
Company-Owned Units	30
Total Units:	242
Dist.:	US-0; CAN-242; O'seas-0
North America:	9 Provinces
Density:	65 in ON, 49 in MB, 37 in AB
Projected New Units (12 Months):	10
Qualifications:	5, 5, 1, 3, 3, 5
Registered: MN,WA,AB	

FINANCIAL/TERMS:

Cash Investment:	$120K
Total Investment:	$240-260K
Minimum Net Worth:	$150K
Fees: Franchise -	$25K
Royalty - 4%;	Ad. - 3%
Earnings Claim Statement:	Yes
Term of Contract (Years):	10/10
Avg. # Of Employees:	12 FT, 6 PT
Passive Ownership:	Not Allowed
Encourage Conversions:	Yes
Area Develop. Agreements:	No
Sub-Franchising Contracts:	No
Expand In Territory:	Yes
Space Needs: 2,250 SF; FS, SC	

SUPPORT & TRAINING PROVIDED:

Financial Assistance Provided:	Yes(I)
Site Selection Assistance:	Yes
Lease Negotiation Assistance:	Yes
Co-Operative Advertising:	Yes
Franchisee Assoc./Member:	No
Size Of Corporate Staff:	65
On-Going Support:	B,C,D,E,F,G,H
Training: 4 Weeks Thunder Bay, ON; 2 Weeks Store Opening.	

SPECIFIC EXPANSION PLANS:

US:	No
Canada:	All Canada
Overseas:	No

◀◀ ▶▶

SAINT CINNAMON BAKE SHOPPE
7181 Woodbine Ave., # 222
Markham, ON L3R 1A3 CANADA
Tel: (905) 470-1517
Fax: (905) 470-8112
E-Mail: info@saintcinnamon.com
Web Site: www.saintcinnamon.com
Mr. Mark Halpern, Executive Vice President

Largest cinnamon-roll franchise in Canada. The rolls are made and baked daily at each location. The franchisee is given two weeks of intensive training in all aspects of the business.

BACKGROUND:
Established: 1986;   1st Franchised: 1986

Franchised Units:	127
Company-Owned Units	3
Total Units:	130
Dist.:	US-1; CAN-70; O'seas-57
North America:	1 State, 4 Provinces
Density:	44 in ON, 17 in PQ, 4 in MB
Projected New Units (12 Months):	15
Qualifications:	4, 4, 4, 4, 4, 5
Registered: NR	

FINANCIAL/TERMS:

Cash Investment:	$40-75K
Total Investment:	$80-150K
Minimum Net Worth:	$NR
Fees: Franchise -	$25K
Royalty - 6%;	Ad. - 3%
Earnings Claim Statement:	No
Term of Contract (Years):	10/5
Avg. # Of Employees:	2 FT, 5 PT
Passive Ownership:	Not Allowed
Encourage Conversions:	N/A
Area Develop. Agreements:	Yes/10
Sub-Franchising Contracts:	Yes
Expand In Territory:	Yes
Space Needs: 300-600 SF; RM	

SUPPORT & TRAINING PROVIDED:

Financial Assistance Provided:	N/A
Site Selection Assistance:	Yes
Lease Negotiation Assistance:	Yes
Co-Operative Advertising:	No
Franchisee Assoc./Member:	No
Size Of Corporate Staff:	7
On-Going Support:	A,B,C,D,e,F,G,h
Training: 2 Weeks in ON.	

SPECIFIC EXPANSION PLANS:

US:	All United States
Canada:	All Canada
Overseas:	Middle East, Europe, South America

◀◀ ▶▶

TIM HORTONS
874 Sinclair Rd.
Oakville, ON L6K 2Y1 CANADA
Tel: (905) 845-6511
Fax: (905) 845-0265
Web Site: www.timhortons.com
Ms. Lilian Longdo, Mgr. of Franchising

TIM HORTONS is Canada's largest franchised retail coffee, donuts and specialty baked goods chain, with over 1,300 stores in Canada and the U. S. The franchisee purchases a turn-key operation, the right to use TIM HORTONS trademarks and tradenames, as well as a comprehensive 8-week training program and on-going operational and marketing support.

BACKGROUND: IFA MEMBER
Established: 1964;   1st Franchised: 1965

Franchised Units:	1,760
Company-Owned Units	120
Total Units:	1,880
Dist.:	US-108; CAN-1,772; O'seas-0
North America:	4 States, 12 Provinces
Density:	ON, PQ, NS
Projected New Units (12 Months):	200
Qualifications:	5, 4, 3, 3, 3, 5
Registered: IN,MI,MN,NY,RI,WI,AB	

FINANCIAL/TERMS:

Cash Investment:	$100-110K
Total Investment:	$300-360K
Minimum Net Worth:	$NR
Fees: Franchise -	$35-50K
Royalty - 3-4.5%;	Ad. - 4%
Earnings Claim Statement:	No
Term of Contract (Years):	20/10/10
Avg. # Of Employees:	22-25 FT or PT
Passive Ownership:	Not Allowed
Encourage Conversions:	Yes
Area Develop. Agreements:	No
Sub-Franchising Contracts:	No
Expand In Territory:	Yes
Space Needs: 2,650-3,000 SF; FS, SF, SC, RM	

SUPPORT & TRAINING PROVIDED:

Financial Assistance Provided:	No
Site Selection Assistance:	Yes
Lease Negotiation Assistance:	Yes
Co-Operative Advertising:	Yes
Franchisee Assoc./Member:	No
Size Of Corporate Staff:	580
On-Going Support:	B,C,D,E,G,H
Training: 8 Weeks Oakville, ON.	

SPECIFIC EXPANSION PLANS:

US:	NY,MI,OH, North Central U.S.
Canada:	All Canada
Overseas:	No

◀◀ ▶▶

TREATS
418 Preston St.
Ottawa, ON K1S 4N2 CANADA
Tel: (800) 461-4003 (613) 563-4073
Fax: (613) 563-1982
Web Site: www.treats.com
Ms. Shirley Adams, Franchise Relations

Micro-bakery concept, featuring gourmet and specialty coffees and fresh-baked, on-site baked goods, including muffins, cookies and bagels. Three concept varia-tions are available: TREATS BAKERY (~400 SF) serves the base menu offering; TREATS CAFE (~1,200 SF) also serves sandwiches (baguettes), soups and salads; TREATS COFFEE EMPORIUM (~1,200 SF) also offers coffee beans, coffee-related merchandise and sandwiches.

BACKGROUND:

Established: 1977; 1st Franchised: 1979	
Franchised Units:	142
Company-Owned Units	3
Total Units:	145
Dist.:	US-5; CAN-140; O'seas-0
North America:	3 States, 9 Provinces
Density: 75 in ON, 25 in PQ, 10 in AB	
Projected New Units (12 Months):	12
Qualifications:	3, 3, 3, 2, 3, 5
Registered: CA,FL,IL,IN,MD,MI,MN,NY, OR,RI,VA,WA,WI,DC,AB	

FINANCIAL/TERMS:

Cash Investment:	$40-50K
Total Investment:	$100-150K
Minimum Net Worth:	$200K
Fees: Franchise -	$25K
Royalty - 7%;	Ad. - 1%
Earnings Claim Statement:	No
Term of Contract (Years):	Lease
Avg. # Of Employees:	3 FT, 2 PT
Passive Ownership:	Discouraged
Encourage Conversions:	Yes
Area Develop. Agreements:	Yes/15
Sub-Franchising Contracts:	Yes
Expand In Territory:	Yes
Space Needs: 500-1,500 SF; SF, SC, RM	

SUPPORT & TRAINING PROVIDED:

Financial Assistance Provided:	No
Site Selection Assistance:	Yes
Lease Negotiation Assistance:	Yes
Co-Operative Advertising:	Yes
Franchisee Assoc./Member:	No
Size Of Corporate Staff:	15
On-Going Support:	B,C,D,E,G,H,I
Training: 2 Weeks Training Center; 1 Week On-Site.	

SPECIFIC EXPANSION PLANS:

US:	East Coast
Canada:	All Canada
Overseas:	Chile, Brazil, Middle East

≪ ≫

SUPPLEMENTAL LISTING OF FRANCHISORS

Au Bon Pain, 19 Fid Kennedy Ave., Boston, MA 02210 ; (617) 423-7879; Mr. Peter Harwood ; (617) 423-2100

Bagelz, 95 Oak St., Glastonbury, CT 06033; Mr. Wesley Becher (800) 270-7900; (860) 657-4400

Benny's Bagels, 2636 Walnut Hill Ln., # 110, Dallas, TX 75229 ; (214) 351-2604; Mr. Don Wilson ; (214) 351-2600

Best Bagels, # 5 North Windham Shopping Plaza, North Windham, CT 06256 ; (860) 456-3817; Mr. David Shenker ; (860) 456-9505

Best Bagels In Town, 480-19 Patchogue Holbrook Rd., Holbrook, NY 11741 ; (516) 472-4105; Mr. Jay Squatriglia ; (516) 472-4104

Big City Bagels, 3101 West Coast Highway, # 311, Newport Beach, CA 92663-4034 ; (714) 515-7743; Mr. Michael S. Reynolds (800) 88-BAGEL; (714) 515-9300

Bun King Bakeries, 1173 N. Service Rd., E., Oakville, ON L6H 1A7 CANADA; (905) 842-8772; Mr. Angelo Rizzuti ; (905) 842-8770

Cinnamonster, 7346 S. Alton Way, # 10-A, Englewood, CO 80112 ; (303) 770-5083; Mr. Rick Doeksen ; (303) 770-5075

Company's Coming Bakery Cafe, 1121 Centre St. N.#, 440, Calgary, AB T2E 7K6 CANADA; (403) 230-2182; Mr. Sheldon Jones (800) 361-1151; (403) 230-1151

Cookie Factory Bakery, 13685 W. Bayshore Dr., # 101, Traverse City, MI 49684 ; (616) 922-0921; Mr. Robert Tischler (800) 968-2902; (616) 922-0920

Cookies By George, 650 Bath Rd., Kingston, ON K7M 4X6 CANADA; (613) 634-1556; Mr. Don Landon ; (613) 634-1069

Country Style Donuts, 2 E. Beaver Creek Rd., Bldg. 1, Richmond Hill, ON L4B 2N3 CANADA; (905) 764-8426; Mr. Gert Steinhards ; (905) 764-7066

Creative Croissants, 6335 Ferris Sq., # G, San Diego, CA 92121 ; (619) 587-7309; Mr. Ralph Boden (800) 735-3182; (619) 587-7300

Donut Delite Cafe, 3380 S. Service Rd., Burlington, ON L7N 3J5 CANADA; (905) 637-7745; Mr. Andrew Diveky ; (905) 681-8448

Donut Inn, 17525 Ventura Blvd., #200, Encino, CA 91316-5107; (818) 888-2893; Mr. Stan Teetle (800) 4 BAKERY; (818) 888-2220

Dunkin' Donuts (Canada), 50 Ronson Dr., # 131, Toronto, ON M9W 1B3 CANADA; (416) 245-3040; Franchise Development (800) 248-4923; (416) 245-3131

Honey Dew Donuts, 35 Braintree Hill Office Park, Suite 203, Braintree, MA 02184 ; (781) 849-3111; Mr. Mike Van Buren ; (781) 849-3000

Incredible Chocolate Chip Cookie Co., 640 Lower Poplar St., Macon, GA 31201 ; (618) 281-6888; Mr. Ted Senters ; (912) 742-8455

Jolly Pirate Donuts, 3923 E. Broad St., Columbus, OH 43213 ; (614) 235-4533; Mr. Nick Soulas ; (614) 235-4501

Krispy Kreme Doughnuts, P.O. Box 83, Winston-Salem, NC 27102 ; (910) 733-3791; Mr. Philip R. S. Waugh (800) 242-8880; (910) 725-2981

Michel's Baguette (Canada), 16521 Dallas Pkwy., Addison, TX 75001 ; (972) 687-4062; Director of Franchising (877) 7-BAKERY; (972) 687-4091

MMMarvellous MMMuffins Canada, 16521 Dallas Pkwy., Addison, TX 75001 ; (972) 687-4062; Director of Franchising (877) 3-MUFFIN; (972) 687-4091

Muffin Tin, The, P.O. Box 202, Alden, MI 49612 ; ; Ms. Jane Van Etten ; (616) 331-6808

Southern Maid Donuts, 3615 Cavalier Dr., Garland, TX 75042-7599 ; (972) 276-3549; Ms. Doris Franklin (800) 936-6887; (972) 272-6425

Stone Hearth Breads U. S. A., 12301 Coller Hwy., Tipton, MI 49287 ; (517) 431-3408; Mr. Vincent D. Cassone ; (517) 431-2593

Sweet Rosie's Cafe, 362 Sumach St., Toronto, ON M4X 1V4 CANADA; (416) 532-9576; Ms. Rosie Gumieniak (800) 923-9113; (416) 923-9113

T. J. Cinnamon's, 1000 Corporate Dr., Ft. Lauderdale, FL 33334 ; (954) 351-5190; Mr. Mike Hoglund (800) 592-6245; (954) 351-5305

Whole Donut, The, 894 New Britain Ave., Hartford, CT 06106 ; (860) 953-1692; Mr. Frank S. Gencarelli ; (860) 953-3569

Winchell's Donut House, 1800 E. 16th St., Santa Ana, CA 92701-3112 ; (714) 565-1801; Mr. Tom Stoerck (800) 347-9347; (714) 565-1800

FOOD: COFFEE INDUSTRY PROFILE

Total # Franchisors in Industry Group	27
Total # Franchised Units in Industry Group	1,560
Total # Company-Owned Units in Industry Group	<u>179</u>
Total # Operating Units in Industry Group	1,739
Average # Franchised Units/Franchisor	57.8
Average # Company-Owned Units/Franchisor	<u>6.6</u>
Average # Total Units/Franchisor	64.4
Ratio of Total # Franchised Units/Total # Company-Owned Units	8.7:1
Industry Survey Participants	12
Representing % of Industry	44.4%
Average Franchise Fee*:	$21.7K
Average Total Investment*:	$202.3K
Average On-Going Royalty Fee*:	5.9%

If a range was provided, the mid-point of the range was used. See detailed profiles for actual ranges.

FIVE LARGEST PARTICIPANTS IN SURVEY

Company	# Fran-chised Units	# Co-Owned Units	# Total Units	Franchise Fee	On-Going Royalty	Total Investment
1. Second Cup, The	391	8	399	25K	9%	~335K
2. New World Coffee	380	5	385	20K	5%	150-350K
3. Coffee Beanery, The	159	27	186	5-25K	6%	140-250K
4. Moxie Java	84	0	84	10K	0%	35-175K
5. Grabbajabba	59	0	59	25K	8%	150-225K

All of the data provided are proprietary and should not be quoted without acknowledging *Bond's Franchise Guide*.

ARABICA COFFEEHOUSE

5755 Granger Rd., # 200
Independence, OH 44131-1410
Tel: (800) 837-9599 (216) 398-1101
Fax: (216) 398-0707
E-Mail: jalmrhero@aol.com
Ms. Terri Sozio, Franchise Sales Admin.

Built to reflect the personality of the community, an ARABICA COFFEE-HOUSE is more than a place to enjoy 50 flavors of coffee, specialty drinks, unique teas, health-conscious sandwiches, decadent pastries and desserts. Superior food and beverages in well-appointed, comfortable surroundings is a perfect venue for any purpose.

BACKGROUND:

Established: 1994; 1st Franchised: 1994	
Franchised Units:	12
Company-Owned Units	0
Total Units:	12
Dist.:	US-12; CAN-0; O'seas-0
North America:	1 State
Density:	12 in OH
Projected New Units (12 Months):	35
Qualifications:	5, 3, 3, 2, 3, 5
Registered: NR	

FINANCIAL/TERMS:

Cash Investment:	$75K
Total Investment:	$126-363K
Minimum Net Worth:	$300K
Fees: Franchise -	$22.5K
Royalty - 5.5%;	Ad. - 1.5%
Earnings Claim Statement:	No
Term of Contract (Years):	10/10
Avg. # Of Employees:	4 FT, 6 PT
Passive Ownership:	Discouraged
Encourage Conversions:	Yes
Area Develop. Agreements:	Yes/3-5
Sub-Franchising Contracts:	Yes
Expand In Territory:	Yes
Space Needs: 2,500 SF; FS, SF, SC, RM, Co-Brand	

SUPPORT & TRAINING PROVIDED:

Financial Assistance Provided:	Yes(I)
Site Selection Assistance:	Yes
Lease Negotiation Assistance:	Yes
Co-Operative Advertising:	Yes
Franchisee Assoc./Member:	No
Size Of Corporate Staff:	40
On-Going Support:	B,C,D,E,F,G,H,I
Training: 3 Weeks Cleveland, OH.	

SPECIFIC EXPANSION PLANS:

US:	MI,OH,PA,KY,IN
Canada:	No
Overseas:	No

◄◄ ►►

BREWSTER'S COFFEE

8501 W. Higgins Rd., # 320
Chicago, IL 60631
Tel: (800) 251-6101 (773) 380-6100
Fax: (773) 380-6183
E-Mail: hmarks@babholdings.com
Web Site: www.babholdings.com
Mr. Howard Marks, Franchise Director

Our BREWSTER'S COFFEE franchisees expertly prepare coffee and espresso beverages from the freshest coffee, roasted to the peak of flavor for each varietal and unique blend we offer. They also offer the same fresh coffee on a bulk basis for customers to enjoy at home. BREWSTER'S franchisees learn to consult with their customers and suggest the appropriate coffee to match any food or occasion.

BACKGROUND: IFA MEMBER

Established: 1996; 1st Franchised: 1996	
Franchised Units:	7
Company-Owned Units	2
Total Units:	9
Dist.:	US-9; CAN-0; O'seas-0
North America:	3 States
Density:	7 in IL, 1 in OH
Projected New Units (12 Months):	5
Qualifications:	3, 3, 5, 2, 2, 5
Registered: All States	

FINANCIAL/TERMS:

Cash Investment:	$50K Min.
Total Investment:	$125.1-282.4K
Minimum Net Worth:	$Not Required
Fees: Franchise -	$25K
Royalty - 5%;	Ad. - 2%
Earnings Claim Statement:	No
Term of Contract (Years):	10/10
Avg. # Of Employees:	5 FT, 10PT
Passive Ownership:	Discouraged
Encourage Conversions:	Yes
Area Develop. Agreements:	Yes/Varies
Sub-Franchising Contracts:	No
Expand In Territory:	Yes
Space Needs: 1,200-1,400 SF; FS, SF, SC	

SUPPORT & TRAINING PROVIDED:

Financial Assistance Provided:	Yes(I)
Site Selection Assistance:	Yes
Lease Negotiation Assistance:	Yes
Co-Operative Advertising:	Yes
Franchisee Assoc./Member:	No
Size Of Corporate Staff:	34
On-Going Support:	B,C,D,E,F,G,H,I
Training: 2 Weeks Milwaukee, WI; 5 Days Store Location Prior to Opening.	

SPECIFIC EXPANSION PLANS:

US:	All United States
Canada:	All Canada
Overseas:	All Countries

◄◄ ►►

CAFFE APPASSIONATO

4001 21st Ave. W.
Seattle, WA 98199
Tel: (888) 502-2333 (206) 281-8040
Fax: (206) 282-5218
E-Mail: appassionato@halcyon.com
Mr. Tony del Fierro, Dir. of Operations

CAFFE APPASSIONATO is an up-scale, European-style specialty coffeehouse, featuring retail sales of our own special hand-roasted coffee, whole beans, iced specialty coffee drinks, panini sandwiches, light pasta salads, pastries, juices, ice cream, retail merchandise and specialty teas. CAFFE APPASSIONATO has recently launched its full-service, turn-key franchise expansion program, with exciting locations available nationally and internationally.

BACKGROUND:

Established: 1991; 1st Franchised: 1993	
Franchised Units:	5
Company-Owned Units	12
Total Units:	17
Dist.:	US-17; CAN-0; O'seas-0
North America:	3 States
Density:	13 in WA, 3 in MA, 1 in MD
Projected New Units (12 Months):	6
Qualifications:	5, 3, 1, 3, 1, 5
Registered: All States Except IN,NY	

FINANCIAL/TERMS:

Cash Investment:	$75-100K
Total Investment:	$230-275K
Minimum Net Worth:	$275-300K
Fees: Franchise -	$25K
Royalty - 4.5%;	Ad. - 1%
Earnings Claim Statement:	No
Term of Contract (Years):	10/5/5
Avg. # Of Employees:	5 FT, 7 PT
Passive Ownership:	Discouraged
Encourage Conversions:	Yes
Area Develop. Agreements:	Yes/5/5
Sub-Franchising Contracts:	No
Expand In Territory:	Yes
Space Needs: 1,200 SF; FS, SF, Corner Site	

SUPPORT & TRAINING PROVIDED:
Financial Assistance Provided: Yes(I)
Site Selection Assistance: Yes
Lease Negotiation Assistance: Yes
Co-Operative Advertising: Yes
Franchisee Assoc./Member: No
Size Of Corporate Staff: 4
On-Going Support: B,C,D,E,F,G,h,I
Training: 2-3 Weeks Corporate Headquarter in Seattle; 7-10 Days at Franchisee Site.

SPECIFIC EXPANSION PLANS:
US: All United States
Canada: BC,ON
Overseas: U.K., Asia

◄◄ ►►

COFFEE BEANERY, THE
3429 Pierson Place Rd.
Flushing, MI 48433
Tel: (800) 728-2326 (810) 728-2326
Fax: (810) 244-8151
E-Mail:
franchiseinfo@CoffeeBeanery.com
Web Site: www.CoffeeBeanery.com
Mr. Kevin Shaw, VP Franchise Development

THE COFFEE BEANERY, LTD. offers a variety of investment levels with storefront cafes being the main growth vehicle in the future. The cornerstone and foundation of the business is the exceptional quality of its own hand-roasted coffee. Our customers enjoy the best coffee and assorted products available from a network of over 180 opened franchised and corporate locations. Our operations department and training are superb.

BACKGROUND: IFA MEMBER
Established: 1976; 1st Franchised: 1985
Franchised Units: 159
Company-Owned Units 27
Total Units: 186
Dist.: US-186; CAN-0; O'seas-0
North America: 31 States
Density: 48 in MI, 19 in FL, 17 in NY
Projected New Units (12 Months): 25
Qualifications: 5, 5, 1, 1, 1, 5
Registered: CA,FL,IL,IN,MD,MI,MN, NY,VA
FINANCIAL/TERMS:
Cash Investment: $50-80K
Total Investment: $140-250K
Minimum Net Worth: $250K
Fees: Franchise - $5-25K
Royalty - 6%; Ad. - 2%

Earnings Claim Statement: Yes
Term of Contract (Years): 5,10,15+
Avg. # Of Employees: 1 FT, 8-10 PT
Passive Ownership: Allowed
Encourage Conversions: Yes
Area Develop. Agreements: Yes
Sub-Franchising Contracts: No
Expand In Territory: Yes
Space Needs: 2,000 SF; FS, SF, SC
SUPPORT & TRAINING PROVIDED:
Financial Assistance Provided: Yes(I)
Site Selection Assistance: Yes
Lease Negotiation Assistance: Yes
Co-Operative Advertising: Yes
Franchisee Assoc./Member: Yes/Yes
Size Of Corporate Staff: 100
On-Going Support: B,C,D,E,F,G,H,I
Training: 3.5 Days Corporate Office, Flushing, MI; 21 Days Flint, MI.

SPECIFIC EXPANSION PLANS:
US: All United States
Canada: No
Overseas: Yes, Guam (2)

◄◄ ►►

SINCE 1985

GOURMET CUP, THE
P.O. Box 490
Abbotsford, BC V2S 5Z5 CANADA
Tel: (604) 852-8771
Fax: (604) 859-1711
Web Site: www.shefieldgourmet.com
Mr. Wolfgang Lehmann, President

Contemporary retail outlet catering to coffee and tea lovers. Extensive selection of fresh-roasted gourmet coffees and gourmet teas, specialty drinks and pastries; complementary merchandise, including mugs and brewing equipment.

BACKGROUND:
Established: 1985; 1st Franchised: 1985
Franchised Units: 32
Company-Owned Units 1
Total Units: 32
Dist.: US-0; CAN-32; O'seas-0
North America: 7 Provinces

Density: 10 in ON, 8 in BC, 5 in AB
Projected New Units (12 Months): 2
Registered: AB
FINANCIAL/TERMS:
Cash Investment: $35-80K
Total Investment: $100-225K
Minimum Net Worth: $NR
Fees: Franchise - $25K
Royalty - 8%; Ad. - 0%
Earnings Claim Statement: NR
Term of Contract (Years): 5/5
Avg. # Of Employees: 2 FT, 3 PT
Passive Ownership: Discouraged
Encourage Conversions: Yes
Area Develop. Agreements: Yes
Sub-Franchising Contracts: No
Expand In Territory: NR
Space Needs: 300-500 SF; RM, SC
SUPPORT & TRAINING PROVIDED:
Financial Assistance Provided: No
Site Selection Assistance: Yes
Lease Negotiation Assistance: Yes
Co-Operative Advertising: N/A
Franchisee Assoc./Member: NR
Size Of Corporate Staff: 9
On-Going Support: C,D,E,G,I
Training: 1 Week On-Site.

SPECIFIC EXPANSION PLANS:
US: No
Canada: All Canada
Overseas: All Countries

◄◄ ►►

GRABBAJABBA
1121 Centre St. N., # 440
Calgary, AB T2E 7K6 CANADA
Tel: (800) 361-1151 (403) 230-1151
Fax: (403) 230-2182
Mr. Sheldon Jones, Franchise Development Manager

Up-scale European coffee house, specializing in over 50 varieties of Arabica whole bean and liquid coffees, cappuccino and other specialty coffees. European sandwiches, soups, salads, freshly-baked goods, decadent desserts and pastries.

BACKGROUND:
Established: 1987; 1st Franchised: 1990
Franchised Units: 59
Company-Owned Units 0
Total Units: 59
Dist.: US-0; CAN-59; O'seas-0
North America: 5 Provinces
Density: 30 in AB, 7 in BC, 13 in ON
Projected New Units (12 Months): 17
Registered: AB

FINANCIAL/TERMS:

Cash Investment:	$60-85K
Total Investment:	$150-225K
Minimum Net Worth:	$175K
Fees: Franchise -	$25K
Royalty - 8%;	Ad. - 0%
Earnings Claim Statement:	Yes
Term of Contract (Years):	10/10
Avg. # Of Employees:	2 FT, 4 PT
Passive Ownership:	Discouraged
Encourage Conversions:	Yes
Area Develop. Agreements:	No
Sub-Franchising Contracts:	No
Expand In Territory:	Yes
Space Needs: 1,100 SF; SF, SC, RM	

SUPPORT & TRAINING PROVIDED:

Financial Assistance Provided:	Yes(I)
Site Selection Assistance:	Yes
Lease Negotiation Assistance:	Yes
Co-Operative Advertising:	Yes
Franchisee Assoc./Member:	Yes
Size Of Corporate Staff:	12
On-Going Support:	C,D,E,f,G,h
Training: 14 Days Comprehensive Hands-On Training.	

SPECIFIC EXPANSION PLANS:

US:	No
Canada:	All Canada
Overseas:	No

◄◄ ►►

JAVA DAVE'S COFFEE

6239 E. 15th St.
Tulsa, OK 74112
Tel: (800) 725-7315 (918) 836-5570
Fax: (918) 835-4348
E-Mail: davesbeans@aol.com
Web Site: www.javadavescoffee.com
Mr. Mike Tiernan, National Franchise Manager

The JAVA DAVE'S COFFEE House System is a thrifty franchise that allows the franchisee an opportunity to participate in the higher level retail purveyance of products which includes the world's finest Arabica bean coffees, teas, cocoas and cappuccino mixes, as well as 200 other related products. The espresso and specialty drinks bar compliments the retail.

BACKGROUND: IFA MEMBER

Established: 1981; 1st Franchised: 1993	
Franchised Units:	13
Company-Owned Units	3
Total Units:	16
Dist.:	US-16; CAN-0; O'seas-0
North America:	1 State
Density:	16 in OK
Projected New Units (12 Months):	5-7
Qualifications:	4, 4, 2, 2, 4, 5
Registered:	

FINANCIAL/TERMS:

Cash Investment:	$120-150K
Total Investment:	$100-150K
Minimum Net Worth:	$200K
Fees: Franchise -	$17.5K
Royalty - 3%;	Ad. - 2%
Earnings Claim Statement:	No
Term of Contract (Years):	10/10
Avg. # Of Employees:	5 FT, 4 PT
Passive Ownership:	Discouraged
Encourage Conversions:	Yes
Area Develop. Agreements:	Yes/10
Sub-Franchising Contracts:	No
Expand In Territory:	Yes
Space Needs: 1,500-1,800 SF; SF, SC, RM	

SUPPORT & TRAINING PROVIDED:

Financial Assistance Provided:	Yes(D)
Site Selection Assistance:	Yes
Lease Negotiation Assistance:	Yes
Co-Operative Advertising:	Yes
Franchisee Assoc./Member:	Yes/Yes
Size Of Corporate Staff:	60
On-Going Support:	b,C,D,E,F,G,h,I
Training: 1 Week in Tulsa, OK; 1 Week On-Site.	

SPECIFIC EXPANSION PLANS:

US:	Midwest, Southwest
Canada:	No
Overseas:	No

◄◄ ►►

KELLY'S COFFEE & FUDGE FACTORY

9100 Wilshire Blvd.
Beverly Hills, CA 90212
Tel: (310) 786-8600
Fax: (310) 786-8606
Web Site: www.kellyscoffee.com
Mr. Barry A. Ogawa, Director of Sales

Gourmet, upscale coffee house that caters to entire family by offering fresh baked products, sandwiches and salads. Treats for children. An exciting, fun business with high profit items and minimal inventories required. Coffee franchising is a booming industry.

BACKGROUND:

Established: 1983; 1st Franchised: 1997	
Franchised Units:	35
Company-Owned Units	0
Total Units:	35
Dist.:	US-35; CAN-0; O'seas-0
North America:	3 States
Density:	32 in CA, 2 in AZ, 1 in MO
Projected New Units (12 Months):	12
Qualifications:	5, 5, 3, 3, 5, 5
Registered: CA	

FINANCIAL/TERMS:

Cash Investment:	$30K
Total Investment:	$120-180K
Minimum Net Worth:	$250K
Fees: Franchise -	$30K
Royalty - 6%;	Ad. - 2%
Earnings Claim Statement:	No
Term of Contract (Years):	10
Avg. # Of Employees:	2 FT, 4 PT
Passive Ownership:	Discouraged
Encourage Conversions:	No
Area Develop. Agreements:	Yes
Sub-Franchising Contracts:	No
Expand In Territory:	Yes
Space Needs: 1,000 SF; FS, SF, SC, RM	

SUPPORT & TRAINING PROVIDED:

Financial Assistance Provided:	Yes(I)
Site Selection Assistance:	Yes
Lease Negotiation Assistance:	Yes
Co-Operative Advertising:	Yes
Franchisee Assoc./Member:	Yes
Size Of Corporate Staff:	8
On-Going Support:	A,B,C,D,E,F,H,I
Training: 1 Week -- Location Varies.	

SPECIFIC EXPANSION PLANS:

US:	All United States
Canada:	No
Overseas:	NR

◄◄ ►►

NEW WORLD COFFEE

246 Industrial Way W.
Eatontown, NJ 07724
Tel: (800) 308-2457 (732) 544-0155
Fax: (732) 544-1315
E-Mail: roccof@bgls.com
Web Site: www.manhattanbagel.com
Mr. Rocco Fiorentino, VP Franchise Development

Full service bagel bakery - Manhattan Bagel. Upscale coffee bar/espresso - New World Coffee.

BACKGROUND: IFA MEMBER

Established: 1987; 1st Franchised: 1990	
Franchised Units:	380

Company-Owned Units	5
Total Units:	385
Dist.:	US-380; CAN-0; O'seas-5
North America:	NR
Density:	NR
Projected New Units (12 Months):	40
Qualifications:	5, 3, 1, 1, 4, 5
Registered: All States	

FINANCIAL/TERMS:

Cash Investment:	$50-75K
Total Investment:	$150-350K
Minimum Net Worth:	$225K+
Fees: Franchise -	$20K
Royalty - 5%;	Ad. - 2.5-4%
Earnings Claim Statement:	No
Term of Contract (Years):	10/10
Avg. # Of Employees:	3 FT, 5 PT
Passive Ownership:	Allowed
Encourage Conversions:	Yes
Area Develop. Agreements:	Yes
Sub-Franchising Contracts:	No
Expand In Territory:	Yes
Space Needs: NR SF; FS, SF, SC, RM	

SUPPORT & TRAINING PROVIDED:

Financial Assistance Provided:	Yes(I)
Site Selection Assistance:	Yes
Lease Negotiation Assistance:	Yes
Co-Operative Advertising:	Yes
Franchisee Assoc./Member:	Yes
Size Of Corporate Staff:	200+
On-Going Support:	C,D,E,G,H
Training: NR	

SPECIFIC EXPANSION PLANS:

US:	All United States
Canada:	All Canada
Overseas:	All Countries

<< >>

P. J.'S COFFEE & TEA

500 N. Hagan Ave.
New Orleans, LA 70119
Tel: (800) 749-5547 (504) 486-2827
Fax: (504) 486-2345
E-Mail: pjs@pjscoffee.com
Web Site: www.pjscoffee.com
Mr. Bryan K. O'Rourke, CEO

P. J.'S COFFEE & TEA has long been regarded as a leader in the specialty coffee industry in the southeast. Our neighborhood-based cafes are set apart from others because we roast and distribute only the highest-quality coffee and serve it in warm, comfortable settings. Our customer base is extremely varied. We provide an unusually high level of service to our franchisees because quality is of the utmost importance to us.

BACKGROUND:

Established: 1978;	1st Franchised: 1987
Franchised Units:	18
Company-Owned Units	4
Total Units:	22
Dist.:	US-22; CAN-0; O'seas-0
North America:	4 States
Density:	17 in LA, 2 in MS, 2 in FL
Projected New Units (12 Months):	7
Qualifications:	5, 5, 3, 3, 2, 3
Registered: FL	

FINANCIAL/TERMS:

Cash Investment:	$30-40K
Total Investment:	$100-190K
Minimum Net Worth:	$120K
Fees: Franchise -	$20K
Royalty - 5%;	Ad. - 1%
Earnings Claim Statement:	No
Term of Contract (Years):	10/10
Avg. # Of Employees:	1 FT, 6 PT
Passive Ownership:	Allowed
Encourage Conversions:	Yes
Area Develop. Agreements:	Yes/Varies
Sub-Franchising Contracts:	No
Expand In Territory:	Yes
Space Needs: 1,200 SF; SF, SC	

SUPPORT & TRAINING PROVIDED:

Financial Assistance Provided:	No
Site Selection Assistance:	Yes
Lease Negotiation Assistance:	Yes
Co-Operative Advertising:	Yes
Franchisee Assoc./Member:	No
Size Of Corporate Staff:	74
On-Going Support:	B,C,D,E,G,h,I
Training: 2 Days Corporate Office; 10 Days Corporate Store; 3 Days On-Location Sites.	

SPECIFIC EXPANSION PLANS:

US:	Southeast
Canada:	No
Overseas:	No

<< >>

SECOND CUP, THE

175 Bloor St. E., S. Tower, # 801
Toronto, ON M4W 3R8 CANADA

Tel: (800) 569-6318 (416) 975-5541
Fax: (416) 975-5207
Web Site: www.secondcup.com
Ms. Kanita Hildebrand, Director of Franchising

As the largest retailer of specialty coffee in Canada with over 370 locations coast to coast, we are committed in attracting quality franchisees. Together, with outstanding location and store operations, we are dedicated to serving the best coffee in the world in an inviting atmosphere with uncompromising standards of customer service, quality and freshness.

BACKGROUND:

Established: 1975;	1st Franchised: 1975
Franchised Units:	391
Company-Owned Units	8
Total Units:	399
Dist.:	US-0; CAN-399; O'seas-0
North America:	10 Provinces
Density:	170 in ON, 55 in AB, 30 PQ
Projected New Units (12 Months):	40
Qualifications:	4, 5, 4, 4, 4, 5
Registered: AB	

FINANCIAL/TERMS:

Cash Investment:	$90-140K
Total Investment:	$~335K
Minimum Net Worth:	$N/A
Fees: Franchise -	$25K
Royalty - 9%;	Ad. - 23
Earnings Claim Statement:	No
Term of Contract (Years):	Lease
Avg. # Of Employees:	5 FT, 10 PT
Passive Ownership:	Not Allowed
Encourage Conversions:	Yes
Area Develop. Agreements:	No
Sub-Franchising Contracts:	No
Expand In Territory:	Yes
Space Needs: 1,000-1,500 SF; FS, SF, SC, RM, Power Center	

SUPPORT & TRAINING PROVIDED:

Financial Assistance Provided:	No
Site Selection Assistance:	Yes
Lease Negotiation Assistance:	Yes
Co-Operative Advertising:	Yes
Franchisee Assoc./Member:	Yes/Yes
Size Of Corporate Staff:	60
On-Going Support:	A,B,C,D,E,F,G,h,I
Training: 3 Weeks Toronto, ON.	

SPECIFIC EXPANSION PLANS:

US:	No
Canada:	All Canada
Overseas:	No

<< >>

SUPPLEMENTAL LISTING OF FRANCHISORS

Barnie's Coffee & Tea Company, 340 N. Primrose Dr., Orlando, FL 32803 ; (407) 898-5341; Mr. David Lane ; (407) 894-1416

Beaner's Gourmet Coffee, 206 E. Grand River, Lansing, MI 48906 ; (517) 482-8625; Mr. Michael McFall (877) 423-2637; (517) 482-8145

Blenz Coffee, 535 Thurlow St., # 300, Vancouver, BC V6E 3L2 CANADA; (604) 684-2542; Mr. Mark Zahodnik ; (604) 682-2995

Coffee Cavern, P.O. Box 6280, Moraga, CA 94570 ; (925) 376-6542; Mr. Steve Selover (800) LATTE 2-U; (925) 376-1109

Coffee Express Drive Thrus & Cafes, 4 Union Plaza, Bangor, ME 04401 ; (207) 990-1477; Ms. Laura Jean Eckard ; (207) 947-5101

Coffee Way, 123 Rexdale Blvd., Rexdale, ON M9W 1P3 CANADA; (416) 741-5878; Mr. Roger G. Garneau ; (416) 741-4144

Gloria Jean's Gourmet Coffees, 11480 Commercial Parkway, Castroville, CA 95012 ; (831) 633-3726; Mr. Adam Thomas (800) 333-0050; (831) 633-6300

Java's Brewin, 95 Boston Rd., North Bellerica, MA 01862 ; (617) 924-7202; Mr. Chris Gregoris (800) 413-2376; (718) 944-1757

McBeans, 1560 Church Ave., # 6, Victoria, BC V8P 2H1 CANADA; (250) 721-3213; Mr. Arne Andersson ; (250) 721-2411

Mr. Mugs, P.O. Box 20019 Global Courier, Brantford, ON N3P 2A4 CANADA; (519) 752-0978; Mr. Paul Cleave ; (519) 752-9890

P. A. M.'s Coffee & Tea Co., 2900 John St., # 202, Markham, ON L3R 5G3 CANADA; (905) 305-9597; Mr. Gregory MacCormack ; (905) 305-9595

Quikava, 190 Old Derby St., # 304, Hingham, MA 02043 ; (781) 749-7222; Mr. Gerry Pelissier (800) 381-6303; (781) 749-4242

Seattle's Best Coffee, Six Concourse Pkwy., # 1700, Atlanta, GA 30328 ; (770) 353-3312; Ms. Joy Robinson ; (770) 353-3363

Symposium Café, 43-A Lesmill Rd., Toronto, ON M3B 2T8 CANADA; (416) 449-6722; Mr. Simon Stern ; (416) 449-3611

For a full explanation of the data provided in the Franchisor Profiles, please refer to **Chapter 2, "How to Use the Data."**

FOOD: ICE CREAM/YOGURT INDUSTRY PROFILE

Total # Franchisors in Industry Group	43
Total # Franchised Units in Industry Group	16543
Total # Company-Owned Units in Industry Group	1,168
Total # Operating Units in Industry Group	17,711
Average # Franchised Units/Franchisor	384.7
Average # Company-Owned Units/Franchisor	27.2
Average # Total Units/Franchisor	411.9
Ratio of Total # Franchised Units/Total # Company-Owned Units	14.2:1
Industry Survey Participants	22
Representing % of Industry	51.2%
Average Franchise Fee*:	$21.7K
Average Total Investment*:	$200.8K
Average On-Going Royalty Fee*:	5.4%

If a range was provided, the mid-point of the range was used. See detailed profiles for actual ranges.

FIVE LARGEST PARTICIPANTS IN SURVEY

Company	# Fran-chised Units	# Co-Owned Units	# Total Units	Franchise Fee	On-Going Royalty	Total Investment
1. Baskin-Robbins	5,000	11	5,011	30K	5-6.9%	104-505K
2. Yogen Fruz Worldwide	4,900	82	4,982	25K	6%	130-250K
3. TCBY Treats	3,006	2	3,008	2.5-20K	4%	54.6-330K
4. I Can't Believe It's Yogurt	400	940	1,340	15K	0%	110-203K
5. Carvel Ice Cream Bakery	393	2	395	10K	$1.63/Gal.	185-240K

All of the data provided are proprietary and should not be quoted without acknowledging *Bond's Franchise Guide.*

ALL AMERICAN ICE CREAM & FROZEN YOGURT

812 SW Washington St., # 1110
Portland, OR 97205
Tel: (503) 224-6199
Fax: (503) 224-5042
Mr. C. R. Duffie, Jr., President

Owner/operator-oriented franchisor with retail ice cream and frozen yogurt shops located in shopping mall and strip centers. Unique contemporary design using a color scheme that appeals to consumers of frozen treats. Low food costs, extensive training programs and a fun business to own and operate.

BACKGROUND:
Established: 1986;   1st Franchised: 1988
Franchised Units: 27
Company-Owned Units   0
Total Units: 27
Dist.:   US-27; CAN-0; O'seas-0
  North America: 3 States
  Density: 19 in OR, 7 in WA, 1 IN tx
Projected New Units (12 Months):   4
Qualifications: 4, 3, 2, 3, 3, 4
Registered: CA,HI,OR,WA
FINANCIAL/TERMS:
Cash Investment: $25-35K
Total Investment: $81-153K
Minimum Net Worth: $125K
Fees: Franchise - $4-20K
  Royalty - 5%;   Ad. - 1%
Earnings Claim Statement: No
Term of Contract (Years):   10/0
Avg. # Of Employees: 1 FT, 6 PT
Passive Ownership: Discouraged
Encourage Conversions: Yes
Area Develop. Agreements: Yes/2
Sub-Franchising Contracts: No
Expand In Territory: Yes
Space Needs: 600-800 SF; SC, RM
SUPPORT & TRAINING PROVIDED:
Financial Assistance Provided: No
Site Selection Assistance: Yes
Lease Negotiation Assistance: Yes
Co-Operative Advertising: Yes
Franchisee Assoc./Member: No
Size Of Corporate Staff: 3
On-Going Support: B,C,D,E,F,G
Training: 1 Week Head Office in Portland,
  OR; 1 Week at Franchisee Location.
SPECIFIC EXPANSION PLANS:
US: West, Inter-Mountain, SW
Canada: No
Overseas: No

⪡ ⪢

Baskin (31) Robbins.

BASKIN-ROBBINS

14 Pacella Park Dr.
Randolph, MA 02368
Tel: (888) 782-4636 (781) 961-4000
Fax: (781) 963-2913
Web Site: www.dunkin-baskin-togos-com
Mr. Lee Sanders, Director of Franchising

World's largest franchisor of ice cream and frozen yogurt stores. Ranked # 2 in Entrepreneur Magazine's (1999) 20th Annual Franchise Top 500 (Frozen Desserts/Ice Cream Category).

BACKGROUND: IFA MEMBER
Established: 1945;   1st Franchised: 1948
Franchised Units: 5,000
Company-Owned Units   11
Total Units: 5,011
Dist.:   US-2,286; CAN-620; O'seas-2,105
  North America: 41 States
  Density: 554 in CA, 195 in IL, 181 NY
Projected New Units (12 Months):   27
Registered: All States
FINANCIAL/TERMS:
Cash Investment: $NR
Total Investment: $104-505K
Minimum Net Worth: $NR
Fees: Franchise - $30K
  Royalty - 5-6.9%;   Ad. - 5%
Earnings Claim Statement: No
Term of Contract (Years):   20
Avg. # Of Employees:
Passive Ownership: Allowed
Encourage Conversions: NR
Area Develop. Agreements: Yes
Sub-Franchising Contracts: No
Expand In Territory: Yes
Space Needs: NR SF; FS, SF, SC, RM
SUPPORT & TRAINING PROVIDED:
Financial Assistance Provided: Yes(I)
Site Selection Assistance: Yes
Lease Negotiation Assistance: Yes
Co-Operative Advertising: Yes
Franchisee Assoc./Member: NR
Size Of Corporate Staff:
On-Going Support:
Training: 27 Days Training Facility in
  Burbank, CA and OJT at Designated
  Training Restaurant.
SPECIFIC EXPANSION PLANS:
US: All United States
Canada: All Canada
Overseas: All Countries

⪡ ⪢

BASKIN-ROBBINS CANADA

50 Ronson Dr., # 131
Toronto, ON M9W 1B3 CANADA
Tel: (800) 268-4923 (416) 245-3131
Fax: (416) 245-3040
Development Department,

As part of Allied Domecq's team of international franchise leaders, BASKIN-ROBBINS CANADA joins DUNKIN' DONUTS and TOGO'S GREAT SANDWICHES in franchising for the future - multi-branding. Allied Domecq's strategic plan includes territorial development.

BACKGROUND:
Established: 1940;   1st Franchised: 1971
Franchised Units: 243
Company-Owned Units   0
Total Units: 243
Dist.:   US-0; CAN-252; O'seas-0
  North America: 7 Provinces
  Density: ON, BC, PQ
Projected New Units (12 Months):   12
Qualifications: 5, 5, 4, 4, 4, 5
Registered: AB
FINANCIAL/TERMS:
Cash Investment: $125-150K
Total Investment: $380-450K
Minimum Net Worth: $500K
Fees: Franchise - $25K
  Royalty - 4.9%;   Ad. - 5%
Earnings Claim Statement: No
Term of Contract (Years):   10/10
Avg. # Of Employees: 4 FT, 8 PT
Passive Ownership: Discouraged
Encourage Conversions: No
Area Develop. Agreements: Yes/3
Sub-Franchising Contracts: No
Expand In Territory: No
Space Needs: 1,400-4,400 SF; FS, SF, SC, RM
SUPPORT & TRAINING PROVIDED:
Financial Assistance Provided: No
Site Selection Assistance: Yes
Lease Negotiation Assistance: Yes
Co-Operative Advertising: No
Franchisee Assoc./Member: Yes/Yes
Size Of Corporate Staff: 30
On-Going Support: B,C,E,d,G,H,I
Training: 3 Weeks Burbank, CA.
SPECIFIC EXPANSION PLANS:
US: No
Canada: BC,ON,PQ
Overseas: No

⪡ ⪢

BEN & JERRY'S

30 Community Dr.
South Burlington, VT 05403
Tel: (802) 846-1500
Fax: (802) 846-1538
Web Site: www.benjerry.com
Ms. Sandy Julius, Manager of Franchise
Licensing

BEN & JERRY'S was started in 1978 in a renovated gas station in Burlington, VT, by childhood friends Ben Cohen and Jerry Greenfield. They soon became popular for their funky, chunky flavors, made from fresh Vermont milk and cream. The scoop shops feature a fun environment with a varied menu including cakes, gifts, baked goods and coffee drinks created from ice cream, frozen yogurt and sorbet flavors. Community involvement is an important element in being a successful BEN & JERRY'S franchisee.

BACKGROUND: IFA MEMBER
Established: 1978; 1st Franchised: 1981
Franchised Units: 225
Company-Owned Units 6
Total Units: 231
Dist.: US-211; CAN-4; O'seas-16
 North America: 28 States, 1 Province
 Density: 39 in CA, 21 in NY, 12 in MA
Projected New Units (12 Months): 60
Qualifications: 5, 5, 4, 4, 4, 5
Registered: CA,FL,IL,IN,MD,MI,MN,NY,
 OR,RI,VA,WA
FINANCIAL/TERMS:
Cash Investment: $86K+
Total Investment: $199-481K
Minimum Net Worth: $150K
Fees: Franchise - $30K
 Royalty - 0%; Ad. - 4%
Earnings Claim Statement: No
Term of Contract (Years): 10/10
Avg. # Of Employees: 2 FT, 10 PT
Passive Ownership: Not Allowed
Encourage Conversions: Yes
Area Develop. Agreements: No
Sub-Franchising Contracts: No
Expand In Territory: No
Space Needs: Avg. 1,000 SF; FS, SF, SC,
 RM, KI
SUPPORT & TRAINING PROVIDED:
Financial Assistance Provided: No
Site Selection Assistance: Yes

Lease Negotiation Assistance: No
Co-Operative Advertising: Yes
Franchisee Assoc./Member: No
Size Of Corporate Staff: 30
On-Going Support: C,D,E,F,G,H,I
Training: 10 Days in VT.
SPECIFIC EXPANSION PLANS:
US: Various Markets
Canada: Not Currently
Overseas: Call International Division

⪻ ⪼

BRUSTER'S OLD-FASHIONED ICE CREAM & YOGURT

730 Mulberry St.
Bridgewater, PA 15009
Tel: (724) 774-4250
Fax: (724) 774-0666
Web Site: www.brustersicecream.com
Mr. David Guido, President

BRUSTER'S ICE CREAM features fresh, delicious homemade ice cream which is made fresh daily on-site at each of our stores. Quality products and exceptional customer service are our main goals. Our products feature only the best ingredients - whole nuts, cherries and the best caramels and fudges. Homemade waffle cones are a great complement to our homemade ice cream.

BACKGROUND:
Established: 1989; 1st Franchised: 1993
Franchised Units: 42
Company-Owned Units 3
Total Units: 45
Dist.: US-45; CAN-0; O'seas-0
 North America: 8 States
 Density: 21 in PA, 15 in GA, 2 in OH
Projected New Units (12 Months): 30
Qualifications: 3, 2, 1, 1, 4, 4
Registered: IN,NY,VA
FINANCIAL/TERMS:
Cash Investment: $150K
Total Investment: $150-761K
Minimum Net Worth: $None
Fees: Franchise - $30K
 Royalty - 5%; Ad. - Up to 3%
Earnings Claim Statement: No
Term of Contract (Years): 10/10/10
Avg. # Of Employees: 2-3 FT, 25 PT
Passive Ownership: Discouraged

Encourage Conversions: No
Area Develop. Agreements: Yes/Varies
Sub-Franchising Contracts: No
Expand In Territory: Yes
Space Needs: 988 SF; FS
SUPPORT & TRAINING PROVIDED:
Financial Assistance Provided: No
Site Selection Assistance: Yes
Lease Negotiation Assistance: Yes
Co-Operative Advertising: Yes
Franchisee Assoc./Member: No
Size Of Corporate Staff: 10
On-Going Support: B,C,D,E,G,H
Training: 4 Weeks Western PA or Atlanta,
 GA.
SPECIFIC EXPANSION PLANS:
US: Eastern United States
Canada: No
Overseas: No

⪻ ⪼

CARVEL ICE CREAM BAKERY

20 Batterson Park Rd.
Farmington, CT 06032
Tel: (800) 322-4848 (860) 677-6811
Fax: (860) 677-8211
E-Mail: cdobosh@carvelcorp.com
Web Site: www.carvelcorp.com
Ms. Carla Dobosh, Franchise Recruiting
Manager

CARVEL ICE CREAM BAKERIES manufacture and sell ice cream and no-fat desserts through retail stores. CARVEL ICE CREAM cakes are designed to compete not only in the frozen dessert markets, but in the $13 billion dollar retail bakery market. Franchise operators can open additional branch units in malls, tourist areas and stadiums for no additional licensing fee. Franchisee can also purchase a license to sell products to supermarket through CARVEL Branded-Products Program.

BACKGROUND: IFA MEMBER
Established: 1934; 1st Franchised: 1947
Franchised Units: 393
Company-Owned Units 2
Total Units: 395
Dist.: US-392; CAN-3; O'seas-29
 North America: 12 States, 1 Province
 Density: 220 in NY, 63 in NJ, 37 FL
Projected New Units (12 Months): 20

Qualifications: 5, 5, 3, 3, 3, 5
Registered: CA,MD,NY,RI,VA
FINANCIAL/TERMS:
Cash Investment: $100-125K
Total Investment: $185-240K
Minimum Net Worth: $100K
Fees: Franchise - $10K
  Royalty - $1.63/Gal.; Ad. - $1.42/Gal.
Earnings Claim Statement: No
Term of Contract (Years): 10/5/5
Avg. # Of Employees: 2 FT, 6 PT
Passive Ownership: Not Allowed
Encourage Conversions: Yes
Area Develop. Agreements: Yes
Sub-Franchising Contracts: No
Expand In Territory: Yes
Space Needs: 1,200-1,500 SF; FS, SF, RM
SUPPORT & TRAINING PROVIDED:
Financial Assistance Provided: Yes(I)
Site Selection Assistance: Yes
Lease Negotiation Assistance: Yes
Co-Operative Advertising: Yes
Franchisee Assoc./Member: Yes/Yes
Size Of Corporate Staff: 50
On-Going Support: A,B,C,D,E,G,H,I
Training: 11 Days Farmington, CT.
SPECIFIC EXPANSION PLANS:
US: East Coast
Canada: All Canada
Overseas: China, Mexico, Caribbean

◀◀ ▶▶

COLD STONE CREAMERY

16101 N. 82nd St., # A-4
Scottsdale, AZ 85260
Tel: (480) 348-1704
Fax: (480) 348-1718
E-Mail:
sharris@coldstonecreamery.com.com
Web Site: www.coldstonecreamery.com
Mr. Sheldon Harris, VP Development

The phenomenal success of COLD STONE CREAMERY has been the result of our unique concept, our premium quality and our strong team of franchisees. We are well-positioned to capitalize on the growing trend of consumers who demand quality products, a wide variety of choices and an enjoyable entertainment experience. All ice cream and non-fat yogurt is custom mixed and folded on the cold stone. COLD STONE CREAMERY is a place where anyone can literally 'create their own happiness.'

BACKGROUND: IFA MEMBER
Established: 1988; 1st Franchised: 1995

Franchised Units: 76
Company-Owned Units: 3
Total Units: 79
Dist.: US-79; CAN-0; O'seas-0
  North America: 16 States
  Density: 30 in AZ, 21 in CA, 6 in NV
Projected New Units (12 Months): 30
Qualifications: 2, 3, 1, 1, 3, 5
Registered: All States
FINANCIAL/TERMS:
Cash Investment: $35K
Total Investment: $178-234K
Minimum Net Worth: $NR
Fees: Franchise - $21K
  Royalty - 6%; Ad. - 2%
Earnings Claim Statement: No
Term of Contract (Years): 10/5/5/5
Avg. # Of Employees: 3 FT, 9 PT
Passive Ownership: Discouraged
Encourage Conversions: NR
Area Develop. Agreements: No
Sub-Franchising Contracts: No
Expand In Territory: Yes
Space Needs: 1,200 SF; SC
SUPPORT & TRAINING PROVIDED:
Financial Assistance Provided: No
Site Selection Assistance: Yes
Lease Negotiation Assistance: Yes
Co-Operative Advertising: Yes
Franchisee Assoc./Member: No
Size Of Corporate Staff: 9
On-Going Support: C,D,E,G,H
Training: 9 Days Scottsdale, AZ; 2 Days
  Franchisee Location.
SPECIFIC EXPANSION PLANS:
US: All United States
Canada: All Canada
Overseas: All Countries

◀◀ ▶▶

EMACK & BOLIO'S ICE CREAM & YOGURT

P.O. Box 703
Brookline Village, MA 02447
Tel: (617) 739-7995
Fax: (617) 232-1102
E-Mail: enbic@aol.com
Mr. Robert Rook, President

Best Ice Cream in NYC - 2000; Best Buy in NYC - 1999 Zagat Survey; Best Ice Cream

Cape Cod; Best Ice Cream New Jersey; Best Ice Cream L.A. 1998; Best Smoothie in Boston 1999. We train in our Macy's NYC Store and give additional training in your store at opening. Manuals and videos provided, ad slicks. No fees or royalties. 25 years' experience.

BACKGROUND:
Established: 1975; 1st Franchised: 1977
Franchised Units: 34
Company-Owned Units: 5
Total Units: 39
Dist.: US-37; CAN-0; O'seas-0
  North America: 10 States
  Density: 13 in MA, 5 in NJ, 4 in NY
Projected New Units (12 Months): 6
Qualifications: 3, 3, 1, 2, 4, 4
Registered: All States
FINANCIAL/TERMS:
Cash Investment: $60-90K
Total Investment: $60-90K
Minimum Net Worth: $N/A
Fees: Franchise - $0
  Royalty - 0%; Ad. - 0%
Earnings Claim Statement: No
Term of Contract (Years): 20/10
Avg. # Of Employees: 2 FT, 4-10 PT
Passive Ownership: Discouraged
Encourage Conversions: Yes
Area Develop. Agreements: Yes/20
Sub-Franchising Contracts: Yes
Expand In Territory: Yes
Space Needs: 200-1,500 SF; SF
SUPPORT & TRAINING PROVIDED:
Financial Assistance Provided: No
Site Selection Assistance: No
Lease Negotiation Assistance: Yes
Co-Operative Advertising: No
Franchisee Assoc./Member: No
Size Of Corporate Staff: 3
On-Going Support: B,C,D,E,F,G
Training: 1 Week Macy's NYC.
SPECIFIC EXPANSION PLANS:
US: All United States
Canada: No
Overseas: No

◀◀ ▶▶

HAPPY & HEALTHY PRODUCTS

1600 S. Dixie Hwy., # 200
Boca Raton, FL 33432
Tel: (800) 764-6114 (561) 367-0739
Fax: (561) 368-5267
E-Mail: franchiseinfo@fruitfull.com
Web Site: www.fruitfull.com
Ms. Susan Scotts, VP Sales & Marketing

A wholesale distributorship for the sale of frozen fruit bars, FRUITFULL, through dedicated freezers placed in retail locations or in retailer's own freezers. Super Grand, Grand and Standard wholesale franchisees will receive the services of an independent marketing consultant who will provide on-site training in identifying and negotiating agreements to place freezers. Training includes stocking, collection and route service procedures dealing with frozen storage products.

BACKGROUND: IFA MEMBER
Established: 1991; 1st Franchised: 1993
Franchised Units: 113
Company-Owned Units 0
Total Units: 113
Dist.: US-113; CAN-0; O'seas-0
 North America: 39 States
 Density: 12 in CA, 11 in NJ, 9 in IL
Projected New Units (12 Months): 25
Qualifications: 5, 5, 3, 3, 3, 5
Registered: All States Except ND
FINANCIAL/TERMS:
Cash Investment: $23-54K
Total Investment: $23-54K
Minimum Net Worth: $23-54K
Fees: Franchise - $17-24K
 Royalty - 0%; Ad. - 0%
Earnings Claim Statement: No
Term of Contract (Years): 10/5
Avg. # Of Employees: 1 FT or 1 PT
Passive Ownership: Discouraged
Encourage Conversions: No
Area Develop. Agreements: No
Sub-Franchising Contracts: No
Expand In Territory: Yes
Space Needs: N/A SF; N/A
SUPPORT & TRAINING PROVIDED:
Financial Assistance Provided: No
Site Selection Assistance: N/A
Lease Negotiation Assistance: N/A
Co-Operative Advertising: N/A
Franchisee Assoc./Member: No
Size Of Corporate Staff: 10
On-Going Support: b,C,D,G,H

Training: 1 or 2 Weeks in Franchise MSA.
SPECIFIC EXPANSION PLANS:
US: All Except WA,LA,ND,ME
Canada: No
Overseas: No

≪ ≫

I CAN'T BELIEVE IT'S YOGURT
3361 Boyington Dr., # 240
Carrollton, TX 75006
Tel: (800) 861-9393 (972) 788-4788
Fax: (972) 788-5036
Web Site: www.yogenfruz.com
Ms. Gayle Longamore, Franchise Sales

We are the leading premier yogurt franchisor domestically and internationally. I CAN'T BELIEVE IT'S YOGURT is noted for developing smooth, creamy, sweet-tasting frozen yogurt in more than 100 self-serve flavor combinations in original, non-fat, and sugar- free varieties.

BACKGROUND:
Established: 1977; 1st Franchised: 1983
Franchised Units: 400
Company-Owned Units 940
Total Units: 1,340
Dist.: US-1,025; CAN-0; O'seas-317
 North America: 33 States
 Density: 33 in TX, 16 in NC, 15 in FL
Projected New Units (12 Months): NR
Qualifications: 4, 2, 3, 2, 2, 4
Registered: CA,IL,IN,MN,OR,RI,WA, WI,DC
FINANCIAL/TERMS:
Cash Investment: $50K
Total Investment: $110-203K
Minimum Net Worth: $200K
Fees: Franchise - $15K
 Royalty - 0%; Ad. - 2.3%
Earnings Claim Statement: NR
Term of Contract (Years): 10/10
Avg. # Of Employees: 2 FT, 6 PT
Passive Ownership: Discouraged
Encourage Conversions: Yes
Area Develop. Agreements: Yes
Sub-Franchising Contracts: Yes
Expand In Territory: Yes
Space Needs: 1,200 SF; SC, RM
SUPPORT & TRAINING PROVIDED:
Financial Assistance Provided: No
Site Selection Assistance: Yes
Lease Negotiation Assistance: Yes
Co-Operative Advertising: N/A
Franchisee Assoc./Member: Yes
Size Of Corporate Staff: 60
On-Going Support: E,G

Training: 10 Days Corporate Headquarters; 1 Week Store.
SPECIFIC EXPANSION PLANS:
US: All United States
Canada: No
Overseas: All Countries

≪ ≫

JULIE ANN'S FROZEN CUSTARD
4314 F Crystal Lake Rd.
McHenry, IL 60050
Tel: (815) 459-9193
Fax: (815) 459-9195
Web Site: www.julieanns.com
Mr. Peter Wisniewski, President

JULIE ANN'S FROZEN CUSTARD is famous for its freshly-made frozen custard. It's like ultra ice cream. We make our product into sundaes, shakes, cones and 40 flavors of carry-out flavors. Fast food is available for year-round business. Our recipe is believed to be the finest in the world. Voted 'Best of Chicago' by New City magazine.

BACKGROUND:
Established: 1985; 1st Franchised: 1997
Franchised Units: 4
Company-Owned Units 1
Total Units: 5
Dist.: US-5; CAN-0; O'seas-0
 North America: 1 State
 Density: 5 in IL
Projected New Units (12 Months): 5
Qualifications: 5, 2, 1, 3, 4, 5
Registered: IL
FINANCIAL/TERMS:
Cash Investment: $150-200K
Total Investment: $150-280K
Minimum Net Worth: $500K
Fees: Franchise - $25-35K
 Royalty - 4-4.5%; Ad. - 0-2%
Earnings Claim Statement: Yes
Term of Contract (Years): 10/5/5

178

Avg. # Of Employees:	3 FT, 22 PT
Passive Ownership:	Discouraged
Encourage Conversions:	No
Area Develop. Agreements:	Yes
Sub-Franchising Contracts:	No
Expand In Territory:	Yes
Space Needs: 22,000 SF; FS, SC, RM	

SUPPORT & TRAINING PROVIDED:

Financial Assistance Provided:	No
Site Selection Assistance:	Yes
Lease Negotiation Assistance:	Yes
Co-Operative Advertising:	Yes
Franchisee Assoc./Member:	No
Size Of Corporate Staff:	1
On-Going Support:	B,C,D,E,F
Training: 1-2 Weeks Chicago, IL; 1-2 Weeks Franchisee Location.	

SPECIFIC EXPANSION PLANS:

US:	IL Only
Canada:	No
Overseas:	No

<< >>

KOHR BROS. FROZEN CUSTARD
2115 Berkmar Dr.
Charlottesville, VA 22901
Tel: (888) 527-9783 (804) 975-1500
Fax: (804) 975-1505
E-Mail: dennis.poletti@kohrbros.com
Web Site: www.kohrbros.com
Mr. Dennis G. Poletti, Exec. Director

KOHR BROS. is the original frozen custard since 1919. Our stores, which are bright and easily maintained, offer a simple and unique frozen dessert concept.

BACKGROUND:	IFA MEMBER
Established: 1919;	1st Franchised: 1994
Franchised Units:	30
Company-Owned Units	11
Total Units:	41
Dist.:	US-39; CAN-0; O'seas-0
North America:	11 States
Density:	10 in NJ, 6 in VA, 5 in FL
Projected New Units (12 Months):	24
Qualifications:	5, 5, 2, 4, 4, 5
Registered: FL,MD,MI,NY,VA	

FINANCIAL/TERMS:

Cash Investment:	$75K
Total Investment:	$145.9-277.5K

Minimum Net Worth:	$300K
Fees: Franchise -	$27.5K
Royalty - 5%;	Ad. - 1%
Earnings Claim Statement:	No
Term of Contract (Years):	5/3/5
Avg. # Of Employees:	6 FT, 4 PT
Passive Ownership:	Allowed
Encourage Conversions:	Yes
Area Develop. Agreements:	Yes
Sub-Franchising Contracts:	No
Expand In Territory:	Yes
Space Needs: 500 SF; FS, SC, RM, Kiosk	

SUPPORT & TRAINING PROVIDED:

Financial Assistance Provided:	Yes(I)
Site Selection Assistance:	Yes
Lease Negotiation Assistance:	Yes
Co-Operative Advertising:	Yes
Franchisee Assoc./Member:	No
Size Of Corporate Staff:	11
On-Going Support:	A,B,C,D,E,F,G,H,I
Training: 6 Days in Corporate Offices; 3 Days at Franchisee Unit.	

SPECIFIC EXPANSION PLANS:

US:	All United States
Canada:	No
Overseas:	No

<< >>

LARRY'S ICE CREAM & YOGURT PARLOURS
3361 Boyington Dr., # 200
Carrollton, TX 75006
Tel: (800) 861-9393 (972) 788-4788
Fax: (972) 788-5036
Web Site: www.yogenfruz.com
Ms. Gayle Longamore, Franchise Sales

Multi-flavor specialty ice cream, yogurt, smoothie and treat shop. Co-branding available with I CAN'T BELIEVE ITS YOGURT and JAVA COAST FINE COFFEES.

BACKGROUND:

Established: 1983;	1st Franchised: 1983
Franchised Units:	11
Company-Owned Units	2
Total Units:	13
Dist.:	US-13; CAN-0; O'seas-0
North America:	3 States
Density:	TX, AZ, LA
Projected New Units (12 Months):	NR
Qualifications:	5, 3, 1, 3, 3, 5
Registered: FL,CA	

FINANCIAL/TERMS:

Cash Investment:	$30-50K
Total Investment:	$135-160K
Minimum Net Worth:	$NR

Fees: Franchise -	$19-25K
Royalty - 5-6%;	Ad. - 1%
Earnings Claim Statement:	No
Term of Contract (Years):	20/20
Avg. # Of Employees:	2 FT, 8 PT
Passive Ownership:	Discouraged
Encourage Conversions:	Yes
Area Develop. Agreements:	Yes/Varies
Sub-Franchising Contracts:	No
Expand In Territory:	No
Space Needs: 500-1,300 SF; SC, RM	

SUPPORT & TRAINING PROVIDED:

Financial Assistance Provided:	No
Site Selection Assistance:	Yes
Lease Negotiation Assistance:	Yes
Co-Operative Advertising:	Yes
Franchisee Assoc./Member:	Yes/No
Size Of Corporate Staff:	5
On-Going Support:	B,C,D,E,H
Training: Comprehensive Training Provided at Corporate Headquarters in Dallas, TX.	

SPECIFIC EXPANSION PLANS:

US:	Southwest, South, Southeast
Canada:	No
Overseas:	No

<< >>

MAGGIEMOO'S INTERNATIONAL
10290 Old Columbia Rd., #305
Columbia, MD 21046
Tel: (800) 949-8114 (410) 309-6001
Fax: (410) 309-6006
E-Mail: info@maggiemoos.com
Web Site: www.maggiemoos.com
Ms. Kimberly Chambers, Dir. Franchise Development

Unique and exciting retail shop, featuring homemade, super-premium ice cream, non-fat ice cream, custom-made cones, sorbet, smoothies, homemade fudge, plus a line of specialty merchandise. We make our ice cream fresh in the store and serve it in fresh- baked waffle cones. Featuring over 40 mix-ins and folded in on a frozen granite slab to create 1,000s of great combos. Association with a marketable spokes character - MAGGIE MOO - in a fun, contemporary store design.

BACKGROUND: IFA MEMBER
Established: 1996;   1st Franchised: 1996
Franchised Units: 50
Company-Owned Units   1
Total Units: 51
Dist.:   US-51; CAN-0; O'seas-0
  North America: 19 States
  Density: 6 in KS, 6 in MO, 4 in TX
Projected New Units (12 Months):   30
Qualifications: 4, 5, 3, 2, 3, 5
Registered: CA,FL,IL,MD,MI,OR,RI,
  VA,WA,WI,DC
FINANCIAL/TERMS:
Cash Investment: $50-70K
Total Investment: $150-285K
Minimum Net Worth: $250K
Fees: Franchise - $23K
  Royalty - 6%;   Ad. - 2%
Earnings Claim Statement: No
Term of Contract (Years):   10/5/5
Avg. # Of Employees: 3 FT, 8 PT
Passive Ownership: Discouraged
Encourage Conversions: Yes
Area Develop. Agreements: Yes/3
Sub-Franchising Contracts: No
Expand In Territory: Yes
Space Needs: 900-1,400 SF; SC
SUPPORT & TRAINING PROVIDED:
Financial Assistance Provided: No
Site Selection Assistance: Yes
Lease Negotiation Assistance: Yes
Co-Operative Advertising: Yes
Franchisee Assoc./Member: Yes/Yes
Size Of Corporate Staff: 14
On-Going Support: B,C,D,E,F,G,h,I
Training: 11 Days Alexandria, VA; 6 Days
  Grand Opening On-Site.
SPECIFIC EXPANSION PLANS:
US: All United States
Canada: No
Overseas: No

MARBLE SLAB CREAMERY
3100 S. Gessner Dr., # 305
Houston, TX 77063
Tel: (713) 780-3601
Fax: (713) 780-0264
E-Mail: marbleslab@marbleslab.com
Web Site: www.marbleslab.com
Mr. Chris Dull, Franchise Development

Retail ice cream stores, featuring super-premium homemade ice cream, cones baked fresh daily, frozen yogurt, frozen pies and cakes, homemade cookies and brownies and specialty coffees. Ice cream is custom-designed for customer on frozen marble slab and made daily in the store.

BACKGROUND: IFA MEMBER
Established: 1983;   1st Franchised: 1984
Franchised Units: 177
Company-Owned Units   1
Total Units: 178
Dist.:   US-178; CAN-0; O'seas-0
  North America: 20 States
  Density: 80 in TX, 9 in LA, 6 in AZ
Projected New Units (12 Months):   48
Qualifications: 5, 3, 1, 3, 3, 5
Registered: CA,FL,IL,IN,WA
FINANCIAL/TERMS:
Cash Investment: $40-60K
Total Investment: $178-238K
Minimum Net Worth: $250K
Fees: Franchise - $23K
  Royalty - 6%;   Ad. - 2%
Earnings Claim Statement: Yes
Term of Contract (Years):   10/10
Avg. # Of Employees: 2 FT, 8 PT
Passive Ownership: Discouraged
Encourage Conversions: Yes
Area Develop. Agreements: Yes/Varies
Sub-Franchising Contracts: No
Expand In Territory: No
Space Needs: 500-1,800 SF; SC, RM
SUPPORT & TRAINING PROVIDED:
Financial Assistance Provided: No
Site Selection Assistance: Yes
Lease Negotiation Assistance: Yes
Co-Operative Advertising: Yes
Franchisee Assoc./Member: Yes/No
Size Of Corporate Staff: 20
On-Going Support: B,C,D,E,H
Training: 10 Days Franchisor Location; 6
  Days Franchisee Site.
SPECIFIC EXPANSION PLANS:
US: SW,S,SE,W, Midwest,East

Canada: All Canada
Overseas: All Countries

**MORRONE'S ITALIAN ICES &
HOMEMADE ICE CREAM**
17 Mifflin Ave., # 202
Havertiwb, PA 19083
Tel: (888) MORRONES
Fax: (610) 446-8381
E-Mail: morronesices@cs.com
Web Site: www.morrones.com
Mr. Domenic Aleardi, Franchise Sales

Retail outlets selling Italian Ices and a special blend of homemade ice cream made right on the premises. Also offering walk-in, year- round operations - new for 1999.

BACKGROUND:
Established: 1910;   1st Franchised: 1995
Franchised Units: 28
Company-Owned Units   1
Total Units: 29
Dist.:   US-29; CAN-0; O'seas-0
  North America: 5 States
  Density: 21 in PA, 2 in DC, 2 in DE
Projected New Units (12 Months): 20-25
Qualifications: 5, 2, 2, 3, 5, 5
Registered: MD,VA
FINANCIAL/TERMS:
Cash Investment: $52K
Total Investment: $139.5-199.5K
Minimum Net Worth: $100K
Fees: Franchise - $20K
  Royalty - 5%;   Ad. - 3%
Earnings Claim Statement: No
Term of Contract (Years):   10/10
Avg. # Of Employees: 2 FT, 6 PT
Passive Ownership: Discouraged
Encourage Conversions: Yes
Area Develop. Agreements: Yes/10
Sub-Franchising Contracts: Yes
Expand In Territory: Yes
Space Needs: 500-1,000 SF; FS, SF, SC, RM

SUPPORT & TRAINING PROVIDED:

Financial Assistance Provided:	Yes(I)
Site Selection Assistance:	Yes
Lease Negotiation Assistance:	Yes
Co-Operative Advertising:	Yes
Franchisee Assoc./Member:	No
Size Of Corporate Staff:	8
On-Going Support:	A,C,D,E,F,G,I

Training: 20-30 Hours Corporate Store; 40-100 Hours at Franchisee's Location.

SPECIFIC EXPANSION PLANS:

US:	All United States
Canada:	No
Overseas:	No

<< >>

PETRUCCI'S ICE CREAM CO.
507 W. Corporate Dr.
Langhorne, PA 19047
Tel: (888) PETRUCCI (215) 860-4848
Fax: (215) 860-6123
E-Mail: mpmogul@aol.com
Web Site: www.petruccis.com
Mr. Mick Petrucci, President

Retailing '50' wild whirling flavors of soft ice cream, homemade fresh fruit Italian ices, frozen yogurt and premium hand-dipped ice cream. All shops feature custom decorated ice cream cakes and proprietary take home frozen novelties.

BACKGROUND: IFA MEMBER

Established: 1983;	1st Franchised: 1996
Franchised Units:	28
Company-Owned Units	0
Total Units:	28
Dist.:	US-0; CAN-0; O'seas-0
North America:	5 States
Density:	18 in PA, 8 in NJ, 2 in MD
Projected New Units (12 Months):	25
Registered: MD	

FINANCIAL/TERMS:

Cash Investment:	$20K
Total Investment:	$139.9-229.9K
Minimum Net Worth:	$150K
Fees: Franchise -	$20K

Royalty - 5%;	Ad. - 2%
Earnings Claim Statement:	No
Term of Contract (Years):	10/5
Avg. # Of Employees:	5 FT, 3 PT
Passive Ownership:	Discouraged
Encourage Conversions:	Yes
Area Develop. Agreements:	Yes/10
Sub-Franchising Contracts:	No
Expand In Territory:	Yes
Space Needs: 1,250 SF; FS, RM	

SUPPORT & TRAINING PROVIDED:

Financial Assistance Provided:	Yes
Site Selection Assistance:	Yes
Lease Negotiation Assistance:	Yes
Co-Operative Advertising:	Yes
Franchisee Assoc./Member:	Yes/Yes
Size Of Corporate Staff:	7
On-Going Support:	C,D,E,F,G,H

Training: 3 Days Langhorne, PA; 3 Days Local Shop Training; 3-4 Days at Your Location when Open.

SPECIFIC EXPANSION PLANS:

US:	NE,SE
Canada:	NR
Overseas:	NR

<< >>

RITA'S ITALIAN ICE
1525 Ford Rd.
Bensalem, PA 19020
Tel: (800) 677-RITA (215) 633-9899
Fax: (215) 633-9922
Web Site: www.ritasice.com
Mr. Steve Beagelman, Vice President Franchising

Retail outlets selling Italian ices.

BACKGROUND: IFA MEMBER

Established: 1984;	1st Franchised: 1989
Franchised Units:	222
Company-Owned Units	3
Total Units:	225
Dist.:	US-225; CAN-0; O'seas-0
North America:	9 States
Density:	104 in PA, 44 in NJ,10 in MD
Projected New Units (12 Months):	36
Qualifications:	5, 3, 2, 3, 5, 5
Registered: CA,MD,NY,VA	

FINANCIAL/TERMS:

Cash Investment:	$50-70K
Total Investment:	$135-242K
Minimum Net Worth:	$250K
Fees: Franchise -	$25K
Royalty - 6.5%;	Ad. - 2.5%
Earnings Claim Statement:	Yes
Term of Contract (Years):	10/10
Avg. # Of Employees:	1 FT, 9 PT
Passive Ownership:	Discouraged
Encourage Conversions:	Yes
Area Develop. Agreements:	Yes
Sub-Franchising Contracts:	No
Expand In Territory:	Yes
Space Needs: 600-1,500 SF; FS	

SUPPORT & TRAINING PROVIDED:

Financial Assistance Provided:	Yes(I)
Site Selection Assistance:	Yes
Lease Negotiation Assistance:	Yes
Co-Operative Advertising:	Yes
Franchisee Assoc./Member:	Yes/Yes
Size Of Corporate Staff:	33
On-Going Support:	B,C,D,E,G,h

Training: 6 Days Corporate Office; 2-4 Days On-Site.

SPECIFIC EXPANSION PLANS:

US:	FL,MD,OH,VA,PA,NE,SC,WV
Canada:	No
Overseas:	No

<< >>

SCOOPERS ICE CREAM
22 Woodrow Ave.
Youngstown, OH 44512-3306
Tel: (330) 758-3857
Fax: (330) 758-4405
Mr. Norman J. Hughes, Jr., President

SCOOPERS ICE CREAM is a made-fresh-daily concept at each location. Using only the finest ingredients in a homemade, low over-run, high-butterfat, gourmet ice cream. As many as 100 flavors and yogurts and sherbets are made fresh at your location.

BACKGROUND:

Established: 1981;	1st Franchised: 1991
Franchised Units:	8
Company-Owned Units	2
Total Units:	10
Dist.:	US-10; CAN-0; O'seas-0
North America:	3 States
Density:	7 in PA, 2 in OH, 1 in FL
Projected New Units (12 Months):	8
Qualifications:	2, 1, 1, 2, 3, 3
Registered: NR	

FINANCIAL/TERMS:

Cash Investment:	$50K

Total Investment:	$50-80K
Minimum Net Worth:	$75K
Fees: Franchise -	$15K
Royalty - 5%;	Ad. - 0%
Earnings Claim Statement:	No
Term of Contract (Years):	10/10
Avg. # Of Employees:	2 FT, 20 PT
Passive Ownership:	Allowed
Encourage Conversions:	Yes
Area Develop. Agreements:	Yes/5
Sub-Franchising Contracts:	Yes
Expand In Territory:	Yes
Space Needs: 700-1,200 SF; FS, SF, SC, RM	

SUPPORT & TRAINING PROVIDED:

Financial Assistance Provided:	No
Site Selection Assistance:	Yes
Lease Negotiation Assistance:	Yes
Co-Operative Advertising:	Yes
Franchisee Assoc./Member:	No
Size Of Corporate Staff:	5
On-Going Support:	E
Training: 2-4 Days at Main Store Location; 1 Day at Store Opening.	

SPECIFIC EXPANSION PLANS:

US:	All United States
Canada:	All Canada
Overseas:	NR

≪ ≫

SWEET LICKS

1525 Ashbury Ln.
Pittsburgh, PA 15237
Tel: (412) 366-6531
Fax: (412) 366-6531
E-Mail: sweetlicks77@hotmail.com
Mr. Tony Battaglia, President

SWEET LICKS features REAL soft ice cream, non-fat yogurt and over 40 flavors of premium, hand-packed ice cream. Our extensive variety of reasonably-priced products is second to none. Outstanding customer service is a result of our 'hands on' training. Delicious, elegant ice cream cakes and pies are made daily in our stores for all occasions. Spacious outdoor decks provide a relaxed atmosphere while our loyal customers enjoy our refreshing ice cream treats.

BACKGROUND:

Established: 1980;	1st Franchised: 1999
Franchised Units:	1
Company-Owned Units	2
Total Units:	3
Dist.:	US-3; CAN-0; O'seas-0
North America:	1 State

Density:	3 in PA
Projected New Units (12 Months):	10
Qualifications:	4, 3, 3, 3, 3, 5
Registered:	

FINANCIAL/TERMS:

Cash Investment:	$40-115K
Total Investment:	$115K
Minimum Net Worth:	$None
Fees: Franchise -	$20K
Royalty - 6%;	Ad. - 0%
Earnings Claim Statement:	No
Term of Contract (Years):	10/5
Avg. # Of Employees:	2-3 FT, 12-18 PT
Passive Ownership:	Discouraged
Encourage Conversions:	No
Area Develop. Agreements:	Yes/Varies
Sub-Franchising Contracts:	No
Expand In Territory:	Yes
Space Needs: 1,200-1,500 SF; FS	

SUPPORT & TRAINING PROVIDED:

Financial Assistance Provided:	Yes(I)
Site Selection Assistance:	Yes
Lease Negotiation Assistance:	Yes
Co-Operative Advertising:	No
Franchisee Assoc./Member:	No
Size Of Corporate Staff:	3
On-Going Support:	B,C,D,E,F,G
Training: 2 Weeks SWEET LICKS Stores in Western PA.	

SPECIFIC EXPANSION PLANS:

US:	Eastern United States
Canada:	No
Overseas:	No

≪ ≫

TCBY TREATS

2855 E. Cottonwood Pkwy., #400
Salt Lake City, UT 84121-7050
Tel: (800) 343-5377 (800) 343-5377
Fax: (801) 736-5936
E-Mail: develop@tcby.com
Web Site: www.tcby.com
Mr. Scott Moffitt, Senior VP of Development

TCBY TREATS shops offer yogurt, sorbet and ice cream products, as well as a complete line of pies and cakes. TCBY Systems, Inc. offers franchises for traditional locations, and for 'combined concept' locations, wherein TCBY TREATS shops are operated within another business.

BACKGROUND:

Established: 1981;	1st Franchised: 1982
Franchised Units:	3,006
Company-Owned Units	2
Total Units:	3,008
Dist.:	US-2,751; CAN-42; O'seas-215
North America:	50 States, 2 Provinces
Density:	NR
Projected New Units (12 Months):	N/A
Qualifications:	5, 3, 2, 2, 2, 4
Registered: All States and AB	

FINANCIAL/TERMS:

Cash Investment:	$N/A
Total Investment:	$54.6-330.2K
Minimum Net Worth:	$50-200K
Fees: Franchise -	$2.5-20K
Royalty - 4%;	Ad. - 3%
Earnings Claim Statement:	No
Term of Contract (Years):	5/10/5/10
Avg. # Of Employees:	2 FT, 8 PT
Passive Ownership:	Discouraged
Encourage Conversions:	Yes
Area Develop. Agreements:	No
Sub-Franchising Contracts:	No
Expand In Territory:	Yes
Space Needs: 100-2,000 SF; FS, SF, SC, RM, C-Store, QSR	

SUPPORT & TRAINING PROVIDED:

Financial Assistance Provided:	No
Site Selection Assistance:	Yes
Lease Negotiation Assistance:	No
Co-Operative Advertising:	Yes
Franchisee Assoc./Member:	Yes/Yes
Size Of Corporate Staff:	400+
On-Going Support:	C,D,E,G,H,I
Training: 6.5 Days Little Rock, AR.	

SPECIFIC EXPANSION PLANS:

US:	All United States
Canada:	All Canada
Overseas:	All Countries

≪ ≫

YOGEN FRUZ WORLDWIDE

8300 Woodbine Ave., 5th Fl.
Markham, ON L3R 9Y7 CANADA
Tel: (905) 479-8762
Fax: (905) 479-5235
E-Mail: yogenfruz@yogenfruz.com
Web Site: www.yogenfruz.com
Mr. Gerry Gordon, Director of Franchising

YOGEN FRUZ WORLDWIDE is a frozen yogurt franchise chain. Frozen yogurt and fresh fruit are blended in front of the customer's eyes! We also sell shakes, pies, juices, ice cream, smoothies and fruity ice.

BACKGROUND:

Established: 1986; 1st Franchised: 1987	
Franchised Units:	4900
Company-Owned Units	82
Total Units:	4982

Dist.:   US-2478; CAN-429; O'seas-1129
  North America: 50 States,10 Provinces
  Density: 357 in GA, 300 in ON, 170 TX
Projected New Units (12 Months):   500
Qualifications: 5, 4, 3, 4, 3, 5
Registered: All States and AB

FINANCIAL/TERMS:

Cash Investment:	$50% Total Inv
Total Investment:	$130-250K
Minimum Net Worth:	$200K
Fees: Franchise -	$25K
Royalty - 6%;	Ad. - 2%
Earnings Claim Statement:	No
Term of Contract (Years):	10/5
Avg. # Of Employees:	2 FT, 4 PT
Passive Ownership:	Not Allowed
Encourage Conversions:	Yes
Area Develop. Agreements:	Yes/10
Sub-Franchising Contracts:	Yes
Expand In Territory:	Yes
Space Needs: 150-1,500 SF; SC, RM	

SUPPORT & TRAINING PROVIDED:

Financial Assistance Provided:	Yes(I)
Site Selection Assistance:	Yes
Lease Negotiation Assistance:	Yes
Co-Operative Advertising:	Yes
Franchisee Assoc./Member:	Yes/No
Size Of Corporate Staff:	69
On-Going Support:	C,D,E,F,G,H,I

Training: 2 Weeks in Dallas, TX; 1.5 Weeks
  in Toronto, ON.

SPECIFIC EXPANSION PLANS:

US:	All United States
Canada:	All Canada
Overseas:	All Countries

◄◄   ►►

SUPPLEMENTAL LISTING
OF FRANCHISORS

Abbott's Frozen Custard, 4791 Lake Ave., Rochester, NY 14612 ; (716) 865-6034; Ms. Linda Crandall-Mars ; (716) 865-7400

Bresler's Ice Cream & Yogurt Shops, 3361 Boyington Dr., # 200, Carrollton, TX 75006 ; (972) 788-5036; Ms. Gayle Longamore (800) 423-2763; (972) 788-4788

Gelato Amare, 11504 Hyde Pl., Raleigh, NC 27614 ; ; Mr. John L. Franklin ; (919) 847-4435

Good For You! Yogurt, 24-4567 Lougheed Hwy., Burnaby, BC V5C 3Z6 CANADA; (604) 299-2797; Mr. Karim Rahemtulla ; (604) 570-0570

Haagen-Dazs, 200 S. 6th St., Pillsbury Company, Minneapolis, MN 55402-1464 ; (612) 330-7074; Mr. Stephen Scheide (800) 793-6872; (612) 317-1334

Heidi's Frozen Yogurt Shoppes, 4175 Veterans Hwy., Ronkonkoma, NY 11779 ; (516) 737-9792; Ms. Clarice Barrett (800) 528-0727; (516) 737-9700

Helen Hutchley Ice Cream Shoppes, 4719 Navarre Rd., Canton, OH 44708 ; (330) 477-5908; Mr. Bob Sharp (800) 683-2479; (330) 477-4515

Herrell's Ice Cream, Eight Old South St., Northampton, MA 01060 ; (413) 584-5320; Mr. Steve Herrell ; (413) 586-9700

Ice Cream Churn, 4175 Veterans Hwy., Ronkonkoma, NY 11779 ; (516) 737-9792; Mr. Lee Anderson ; (516) 737-9700

Ice Cream Club, The, 1580 High Ridge Rd., Boynton Beach, FL 33426 ; (561) 731-0311; Mr. Richard Draper (800) 535-7711; (561) 731-3331

Joe's Italian Ices, 8312 State Road, Rear Bldg., Philadelphia, PA 19136 ; (215) 338-7262; Mr. Joe Voci (800) 563-7423; (215) 338-0100

Perkits Yogurt Shops, P.O. Box 2862, Cleveland, TN 37320 ; (423) 559-9914; Mr. Stan Davis ; (423) 559-9505

Ritter's Frozen Custard, 1118 N. Main St., Suite B, Franklin, IN 46131 ; (317) 738-5669; Mr. John Ritter ; (317) 738-5686

Swensen's Ice Cream Company, 3361 Boyington Dr., # 240, Carrollton, TX 75006 ; (972) 788-5036; Ms. Gayle Longamore (800) 423-2763; (972) 788-4788

Yogurt & Such, 438 Woodbury Rd., Plainview, NY 11803 ; (516) 624-7108;

Mr. Al Spennato (800) YOG-SUCH; (516) 827-0200

Yogurteria, 1325 Franklin Ave., # 165, Garden City, NY 11530 ; (516) 742-4499; Mr. Robert Baskind (800) TILDENS; (516) 746-7911

FOOD: QUICK SERVICE/TAKE-OUT INDUSTRY PROFILE

Total # Franchisors in Industry Group	329
Total # Franchised Units in Industry Group	103,278
Total # Company-Owned Units in Industry Group	<u>24,836</u>
Total # Operating Units in Industry Group	128,114
Average # Franchised Units/Franchisor	313.9
Average # Company-Owned Units/Franchisor	<u>75.5</u>
Average # Total Units/Franchisor	389.4
Ratio of Total # Franchised Units/Total # Company-Owned Units	4.2:1
Industry Survey Participants	140
Representing % of Industry	42.6%
Average Franchise Fee*:	$20.2K
Average Total Investment*:	$335.4K
Average On-Going Royalty Fee*:	4.9%

If a range was provided, the mid-point of the range was used. See detailed profiles for actual ranges.

FIVE LARGEST PARTICIPANTS IN SURVEY

Company	# Fran- chised Units	# Co- Owned Units	# Total Units	Franchise Fee	On-Going Royalty	Total Investment
1. McDonald's	20,531	6,057	26,588	45K	12.5%	477.8K-1.4MM
2. Subway Restaurants	14,109	5	14,114	10K	8%	66.2-175K
3. KFC	6,663	2,975	9,638	25K	4%	700K-1.2MM
4. Taco Bell	4,600	3,044	7,644	45K	5.5%	236-503K
5. Dairy Queen	5,800	50	5,850	15-30K	4-5%	NR

All of the data provided are proprietary and should not be quoted without acknowledging *Bond's Franchise Guide.*

1 POTATO 2
955 E. Javelina Ave., # 106
Mesa, AZ 85204
Tel: (800) 711-4036 (480) 503-3363
Fax: (480) 503-1850
E-Mail: nybfoods@nybfoods.com
Web Site: www.newyorkburrito.com
Ms. Sharon Snyder,

1 POTATO 2 is a unique, quick-serve restaurant concept, specializing in fresh, made-to-order baked potato entrees and other menu items with potato as the primary ingredient. Perfect for today's consumer who craves variety and is looking for healthy alternatives. Franchises available in regional shopping centers, downtown centers and strip malls.

BACKGROUND: IFA MEMBER
Established: 1978; 1st Franchised: 1984
Franchised Units: 29
Company-Owned Units: 2
Total Units: 31
Dist.: US-40; CAN-0; O'seas-0
North America: 14 States
Density: 13 in MN, 8 in WI, 6 in CA
Projected New Units (12 Months): NR
Qualifications: 5, 4, 4, 3, 3, 4
Registered: CA,IL,IN,MN,WI
FINANCIAL/TERMS:
Cash Investment: $60-70K
Total Investment: $90-180K
Minimum Net Worth: $250K
Fees: Franchise - $20K
Royalty - 4.5%; Ad. - 1.75%
Earnings Claim Statement: Yes
Term of Contract (Years): 8-10/8-10
Avg. # Of Employees: 2-3 FT, 6-8 PT
Passive Ownership: Discouraged
Encourage Conversions: Yes
Area Develop. Agreements: Yes/Varies
Sub-Franchising Contracts: No
Expand In Territory: Yes
Space Needs: 450-700 SF; RM
SUPPORT & TRAINING PROVIDED:
Financial Assistance Provided: Yes(I)
Site Selection Assistance: Yes
Lease Negotiation Assistance: Yes
Co-Operative Advertising: Yes
Franchisee Assoc./Member: Yes/Yes
Size Of Corporate Staff: 9
On-Going Support: a,B,C,D,E,F,G,H,I
Training: 2 Weeks Minneapolis, MN.
SPECIFIC EXPANSION PLANS:
US: Midwest, West
Canada: All Canada
Overseas: No

A & W RESTAURANTS
One A&W Dr.
Farmington Hills, MI 48331
Tel: (888) 456-2929 (248) 669-2000
Fax: (248) 553-8728
E-Mail: PalmerL@awrestaurants.com
Web Site: www.awrestaurants.com
Mr. George Goulson, Exec. VP Franchise
Development

A & W has been a successful, all-American icon for more than 80 years. Since repositioning A & W as the home of 'All American Food' with a menu of hamburgers, hot dogs, coney dogs, french fires, onion rings, chicken strips, etc. and our signature A & W Root Beer and Root Beer floats, we have entered the ranks of the most rapidly-growing quick-service restaurants in the world. 'It is very simple - if our franchisees succeed, we succeed.' - Sidney Feltenstein, Chairman, CEO.

BACKGROUND: IFA MEMBER
Established: 1919; 1st Franchised: 1925
Franchised Units: 825
Company-Owned Units: 177
Total Units: 1,002
Dist.: US-638; CAN-177; O'seas-187
North America: 48 States
Density: 79 in CA
Projected New Units (12 Months): 150
Qualifications: 4, 5, 4, 2, 1, 5
Registered: All States Except DC,HI
FINANCIAL/TERMS:
Cash Investment: $20% Turn-Key
Total Investment: $90-500K
Minimum Net Worth: $100K
Fees: Franchise - $10-20K
Royalty - 4-6%; Ad. - 4%
Earnings Claim Statement: No
Term of Contract (Years): 20/10
Avg. # Of Employees: 50-60 FT & PT
Passive Ownership: Allowed
Encourage Conversions: Yes
Area Develop. Agreements: Yes/Varies
Sub-Franchising Contracts: Yes
Expand In Territory: Yes
Space Needs: 600+ SF; FS, SF, SC, RM, Non-Tradit.
SUPPORT & TRAINING PROVIDED:
Financial Assistance Provided: Yes(I)

Site Selection Assistance: Yes
Lease Negotiation Assistance: Yes
Co-Operative Advertising: Yes
Franchisee Assoc./Member: Yes/Yes
Size Of Corporate Staff: 120
On-Going Support: B,C,D,E,F,G,H,I
Training: 18 Days Corp. Training Facility, Dearborn, MI; 3-5 Days Prior and 3-5 Days after Opening.
SPECIFIC EXPANSION PLANS:
US: All United States
Canada: No
Overseas: All Countries

◁◁ ▷▷

A. L. VAN HOUTTE
8300 19th Ave.
Montreal, PQ H1Z 4G8 CANADA
Tel: (800) 361-5628 (514) 593-7711
Fax: (514) 593-8755
Mr. Paul-Andre Guillotte, President

A. L. VAN HOUTTE cafes and bistros offer healthy, no-fry meals, served at any time of day with a cup of the distinctive, high-quality coffee that has given A. L. VAN HOUTTE cafes and bistros the refinement of a European breakfast and the freshness of a light meal or well-deserved coffee break.

BACKGROUND:
Established: 1919; 1st Franchised: 1983
Franchised Units: 94
Company-Owned Units: 14
Total Units: 108
Dist.: US-0; CAN-108; O'seas-0
North America: 2 Provinces
Density: 104 in PQ, 4 in ON
Projected New Units (12 Months): 6
Qualifications: 4, 3, 4, 3, 4, 4
Registered: NR
FINANCIAL/TERMS:
Cash Investment: $80K
Total Investment: $200-250K
Minimum Net Worth: $80K
Fees: Franchise - $40K
Royalty - 5%; Ad. - 2%
Earnings Claim Statement: No
Term of Contract (Years): 10/5
Avg. # Of Employees: 4 FT, 8 PT
Passive Ownership: Discouraged
Encourage Conversions: Yes
Area Develop. Agreements: Yes/10
Sub-Franchising Contracts: No
Expand In Territory: No
Space Needs: 1,500 SF; FS, SF, SC, RM
SUPPORT & TRAINING PROVIDED:
Financial Assistance Provided: Yes(I)

◁◁ ▷▷

Site Selection Assistance: Yes
Lease Negotiation Assistance: Yes
Co-Operative Advertising: N/A
Franchisee Assoc./Member: No
Size Of Corporate Staff: 35
On-Going Support: B,C,D,E,G,H,I
Training: 2 Weeks Training School; 3 Weeks Training Store; 10 Days or 2 Weeks Actual Store.

SPECIFIC EXPANSION PLANS:

US: All United States
Canada: All Canada
Overseas: All Countries

◄◄ ►►

AMECI PIZZA & PASTA

6603 Independence Ave., #B
Canoga Park, CA 91303
Tel: (818) 712-0110
Fax: (818) 712-0792
Web Site: www.imal.com
Mr. Nick Andrisano, President

Italian fast foods, such as pizza, pasta, salads and subs.

BACKGROUND:

Established: 1979; 1st Franchised: 1987
Franchised Units: 41
Company-Owned Units: 2
Total Units: 43
Dist.: US-43; CAN-0; O'seas-0
  North America: 1 State
  Density: 43 in CA
Projected New Units (12 Months): 5
Qualifications: 5, 2, 1, 2, 2, 5
Registered: CA

FINANCIAL/TERMS:

Cash Investment: $185K
Total Investment: $135-235K
Minimum Net Worth: $250K
Fees: Franchise - $25K
  Royalty - 4%; Ad. - 2%
Earnings Claim Statement: No
Term of Contract (Years): 10/10
Avg. # Of Employees: 4 FT, 5 PT
Passive Ownership: Discouraged
Encourage Conversions: Yes
Area Develop. Agreements: Yes/10/10
Sub-Franchising Contracts: No
Expand In Territory: Yes
Space Needs: 1,200 SF; SC

SUPPORT & TRAINING PROVIDED:

Financial Assistance Provided: No
Site Selection Assistance: Yes
Lease Negotiation Assistance: Yes
Co-Operative Advertising: Yes
Franchisee Assoc./Member: No
Size Of Corporate Staff: 7

On-Going Support: A,B,C,D,E,F,G,H,I
Training: 4 Weeks of School at Home Office; 2 Weeks at Unit Location.

SPECIFIC EXPANSION PLANS:

US: NR
Canada: No
Overseas: All Latin Countries

◄◄ ►►

ANDERSON'S RESTAURANTS

6075 Main St.
Williamsville, NY 14221
Tel: (716) 633-2302
Fax: (716) 633-2671
E-Mail: info@andersonscustard.com
Web Site: www.andersonscustard.com
Mr. Kirk P. Wildermuth, President

A Western New York tradition, serving award-winning roast beef, BBQ, chicken and ham sandwiches. Also, we are famous for our one-of-a-kind frozen custard, plus homemade ice cream. We also specialize in ice cream cakes and pies. We are the Northeast's premium lunch, dinner and dessert fast casual concept.

BACKGROUND: IFA MEMBER

Established: 1946; 1st Franchised: 1996
Franchised Units: 6
Company-Owned Units: 3
Total Units: 9
Dist.: US-9; CAN-0; O'seas-0
  North America: 1 State
  Density: 9 in NY
Projected New Units (12 Months): NR
Registered:

FINANCIAL/TERMS:

Cash Investment: $100-200K
Total Investment: $900K-1.1MM
Minimum Net Worth: $500K
Fees: Franchise - $30K
  Royalty - 4%; Ad. - 2%
Earnings Claim Statement: No
Term of Contract (Years): 20
Avg. # Of Employees: 10 FT, 25 PT
Passive Ownership: Not Allowed
Encourage Conversions: NR
Area Develop. Agreements: Yes/20
Sub-Franchising Contracts: No
Expand In Territory: Yes
Space Needs: 3,800 SF; FS, End Cap

SUPPORT & TRAINING PROVIDED:

Financial Assistance Provided: NR
Site Selection Assistance: Yes
Lease Negotiation Assistance: Yes
Co-Operative Advertising: Yes
Franchisee Assoc./Member: No
Size Of Corporate Staff: 7

On-Going Support: B,C,D,E,G
Training: 12-16 Weeks Buffalo, NY.

SPECIFIC EXPANSION PLANS:

US: OH,NY,PA
Canada: NR
Overseas: NR

◄◄ ►►

ARBY'S

1000 Corporate Dr.
Ft. Lauderdale, FL 33334
Tel: (800) 487-2729 (954) 351-5200
Fax: (954) 351-6822
E-Mail: roshins@arby.com
Web Site: www.arby.com
Ms. Roni Oshins, VP Business Development

The leader in the roast beef segment, ARBY'S offers cut above menu options including a complete line of roast beef and chicken sandwiches, chicken fingers, a light sandwich menu, salads and three fry varieties. Development opportunities available. An experienced brand with over 3,200 locations.

BACKGROUND: IFA MEMBER

Established: 1964; 1st Franchised: 1965
Franchised Units: 3,201
Company-Owned Units: 0
Total Units: 3,201
Dist.: US-3,043; CAN-122; O'seas-36
  North America: 48 States, 8 Provinces
  Density: 248 in OH, 167 in CA, 166 MI
Projected New Units (12 Months): 150
Qualifications: 5, 5, 4, 3, 3, 5
Registered: All States

FINANCIAL/TERMS:

Cash Investment: $0-2,253,200
Total Investment: $212.9K-2.25MM
Minimum Net Worth: $1.0MM
Fees: Franchise - $37.5K
  Royalty - 4%; Ad. - Min 3.7%
Earnings Claim Statement: Yes
Term of Contract (Years): 20/Varies

Avg. # Of Employees: 15 FT, 25 PT
Passive Ownership: Allowed
Encourage Conversions: Yes
Area Develop. Agreements: Yes/Varies
Sub-Franchising Contracts: No
Expand In Territory: Yes
Space Needs: 2,000-3,000 SF; FS

SUPPORT & TRAINING PROVIDED:
Financial Assistance Provided: No
Site Selection Assistance: Yes
Lease Negotiation Assistance: No
Co-Operative Advertising: Yes
Franchisee Assoc./Member: Yes/Yes
Size Of Corporate Staff: 150
On-Going Support: B,C,D,E,G,I
Training: 5 Weeks MTP-Certified Training
    Locations.

SPECIFIC EXPANSION PLANS:
US: NE, W, S
Canada: All Canada
Overseas: Canada, Mexico, Australia,
    U.K., Middle East

‹‹ ››

ARTHUR TREACHER'S FISH & CHIPS

7400 Baymeadows Way, # 300
Jacksonville, FL 32256
Tel: (800) 321-3113 (904) 739-1200
Fax: (904) 739-2500
Mr. William Saculla, President

Fast-food fish and chips, chicken and seafood.

BACKGROUND:
Established: 1969;   1st Franchised: 1970
Franchised Units: 59
Company-Owned Units: <u>61</u>
Total Units: 120
Dist.: US-111; CAN-9; O'seas-0
  North America: 15 States
  Density: 51 in OH, 27 in PA, 25 in FL
Projected New Units (12 Months): 60
Qualifications: 4, 4, 3, 3, 3, 4
Registered: FL,MI,NY
FINANCIAL/TERMS:
Cash Investment: $50-80K
Total Investment: $80-210K
Minimum Net Worth: $N/A
Fees: Franchise - $19.5K
  Royalty - 6%; Ad. - 3%
Earnings Claim Statement: No
Term of Contract (Years): 20/20
Avg. # Of Employees: 3 FT, 12 PT
Passive Ownership: Discouraged
Encourage Conversions: Yes
Area Develop. Agreements: Yes/Varies
Sub-Franchising Contracts: Yes

Expand In Territory: Yes
Space Needs: 500-2,000 SF; FS, SF, SC, RM
SUPPORT & TRAINING PROVIDED:
Financial Assistance Provided: No
Site Selection Assistance: Yes
Lease Negotiation Assistance: Yes
Co-Operative Advertising: Yes
Franchisee Assoc./Member: No
Size Of Corporate Staff: 25
On-Going Support: B,C,D,E,F,G,H,I
Training: 3 Weeks Jacksonville, FL.
SPECIFIC EXPANSION PLANS:
US: Northeast, Southeast
Canada: No
Overseas: No

‹‹ ››

BACK YARD BURGERS

1657 N. Shelby Oaks Dr., #105
Memphis, TN 38134
Tel: (800) 292-6939 (901) 367-0888
Fax: (901) 367-0999
E-Mail: rjones@backyardburgers.com
Web Site: www.backyardburgers.com
Mr. Ray Jones, Dir. Franchise Development

BACK YARD BURGERS operates and franchises quick casual restaurants, serving 1/3 lb. gourmet hamburgers, boneless, skinless chicken fillet sandwiches, fresh lemonade, hand-dipped shakes and malts and other menu items. Our theme emphasizes charbroiled, fresh, great-tasting food as the customers would cook in their own back yard.

BACKGROUND:
Established: 1987;   1st Franchised: 1988
Franchised Units: 56
Company-Owned Units: <u>35</u>
Total Units: 91
Dist.: US-91; CAN-0; O'seas-0
  North America: 16 States
  Density: 32 in TN, 12 in AR, 10 in NC
Projected New Units (12 Months): 15
Qualifications: 4, 4, 3, 2, 1, 3
Registered: FL,IL,IN,MI,VA
FINANCIAL/TERMS:
Cash Investment: $200-300K
Total Investment: $400K-1MM

Minimum Net Worth: $300K
Fees: Franchise - $25K
  Royalty - 4%; Ad. - 3%
Earnings Claim Statement: No
Term of Contract (Years): 10/5
Avg. # Of Employees: 8 FT, 22 PT
Passive Ownership: Discouraged
Encourage Conversions: Yes
Area Develop. Agreements: Yes/10
Sub-Franchising Contracts: No
Expand In Territory: Yes
Space Needs: 2,500 SF; FS

SUPPORT & TRAINING PROVIDED:
Financial Assistance Provided: Yes(I)
Site Selection Assistance: Yes
Lease Negotiation Assistance: Yes
Co-Operative Advertising: Yes
Franchisee Assoc./Member: Yes/Yes
Size Of Corporate Staff: 30
On-Going Support: B,C,D,E,F,G,H
Training: 8 Weeks Corporate
    Headquarters.

SPECIFIC EXPANSION PLANS:
US: SE,MW, Mid-Atlantic, SW
Canada: No
Overseas: No

‹‹ ››

BALDINOS GIANT JERSEY SUBS

3823 Roswell Rd., # 204
Marietta, GA 30062
Tel: (770) 971-9441
Fax: (770) 977-1083
Mr. Bill Baer, President/CEO

Quality submarine sandwiches with in-store bakery. All subs sliced fresh as ordered in full view of customer, served on freshly-baked rolls. Built for volume business at a 'fast-food' pace by use of multi-production lines. Variety of 20 hot and cold subs and freshly-baked gourmet cookies.

BACKGROUND:
Established: 1975;   1st Franchised: 1984
Franchised Units: 13
Company-Owned Units: <u>6</u>
Total Units: 19
Dist.: US-19; CAN-0; O'seas-0
  North America: 3 States
  Density: 13 in GA, 5 in NC, 1 in SC
Projected New Units (12 Months): 3
Registered: FL
FINANCIAL/TERMS:
Cash Investment: $NR
Total Investment: $100-200K
Minimum Net Worth: $NR
Fees: Franchise - $10K
  Royalty - 4.5%; Ad. - 0.5%

Earnings Claim Statement: No
Term of Contract (Years): 15/10
Avg. # Of Employees: 8 FT, 12 PT
Passive Ownership: Not Allowed
Encourage Conversions: Yes
Area Develop. Agreements: Yes/15+
Sub-Franchising Contracts: Yes
Expand In Territory: Yes
Space Needs: 1,800-2,400 SF; FS

SUPPORT & TRAINING PROVIDED:
Financial Assistance Provided: No
Site Selection Assistance: Yes
Lease Negotiation Assistance: Yes
Co-Operative Advertising: Yes
Franchisee Assoc./Member: NR
Size Of Corporate Staff: 4
On-Going Support: B,C,D,E,F,G,H,I
Training: 4 Weeks Headquarters.

SPECIFIC EXPANSION PLANS:
US: GA,SC,NC
Canada: No
Overseas: No

BARBEQUE COUNTRY JAMBOREE

10208 Wendover Dr.
Vienna, VA 22181
Tel: (703) 281-4384
Fax: (703) 281-4292
E-Mail: bbqcountry@aol.com
Mr. George E. Hoffman, Jr., Sales Manager

BARBEQUE COUNTRY JAMBOREE restaurants feature genuine open-pit barbeque with outstanding customer response. We have earned the distinction of serving authentic barbeque pork, beef, chicken and ribs with outstanding quality and flavor.

BACKGROUND:
Established: 1989; 1st Franchised: 1994
Franchised Units: 3
Company-Owned Units 3
Total Units: 6
Dist.: US-6; CAN-0; O'seas-0
North America: 2 States
Density: NR
Projected New Units (12 Months): 2-3
Qualifications: 5, 5, 4, 2, 3, 5
Registered: MD,VA

FINANCIAL/TERMS:
Cash Investment: $50K
Total Investment: $110-190K
Minimum Net Worth: $200K
Fees: Franchise - $10K
 Royalty - 5%; Ad. - 2%

Earnings Claim Statement: No
Term of Contract (Years): 10/10
Avg. # Of Employees: 3 FT, 4 PT
Passive Ownership: Not Allowed
Encourage Conversions: Yes
Area Develop. Agreements: No
Sub-Franchising Contracts: No
Expand In Territory: Yes
Space Needs: 2,000 SF; SF, SC

SUPPORT & TRAINING PROVIDED:
Financial Assistance Provided: No
Site Selection Assistance: Yes
Lease Negotiation Assistance: Yes
Co-Operative Advertising: Yes
Franchisee Assoc./Member: No
Size Of Corporate Staff: 2
On-Going Support: B,C,D,E,F
Training: 30 Days Centreville, VA.

SPECIFIC EXPANSION PLANS:
US: Mid-Atlantic Region
Canada: No
Overseas: No

SUBS & SALADS

BLIMPIE SUBS AND SALADS

1775 The Exchange, # 600
Atlanta, GA 30339
Tel: (800) 447-6256 (770) 984-2707
Fax: (770) 980-9176
E-Mail: chuckt@blimpie.com
Web Site: www.blimpie.com
Mr. Chuck Taylor, National Business Dev.

National submarine sandwich chain, serving fresh-sliced, high-quality meats and cheeses on fresh-baked bread. Also offering an assortment of fresh-made salads and other quality products. Awarding more than 1 new franchise daily and opening a new restaurant every day. Single and multi-unit opportunities.

BACKGROUND: IFA MEMBER
Established: 1964; 1st Franchised: 1977
Franchised Units: 2,034
Company-Owned Units 0
Total Units: 2,034
Dist.: US-1,190; CAN-30; O'seas-14
North America: 47 States, 4 Provinces
Density: 195 in GA, 185 in FL, 134 TX
Projected New Units (12 Months): NA
Qualifications: 4, 3, 2, 2, 2, 5
Registered: CA,FL,HI,IL,IN,MI,MN,NY,
 ND,OR,RI,SD,WA,WI

FINANCIAL/TERMS:
Cash Investment: $25-100K
Total Investment: $60-200K
Minimum Net Worth: $100K
Fees: Franchise - $18K
 Royalty - 6%; Ad. - 4%
Earnings Claim Statement: No
Term of Contract (Years): 20/5
Avg. # Of Employees: 4 FT, 8 PT
Passive Ownership: Discouraged
Encourage Conversions: Yes
Area Develop. Agreements: Yes
Sub-Franchising Contracts: Yes
Expand In Territory: Yes
Space Needs: 1,500 SF; FS, SF, SC, RM

SUPPORT & TRAINING PROVIDED:
Financial Assistance Provided: Yes(I)
Site Selection Assistance: Yes
Lease Negotiation Assistance: Yes
Co-Operative Advertising: Yes
Franchisee Assoc./Member: Yes/Yes
Size Of Corporate Staff: 105
On-Going Support: B,C,D,E,F,G,H,I
Training: 80 Hours in Atlanta, GA; 40
 Hours in Local Franchise.

SPECIFIC EXPANSION PLANS:
US: All United States
Canada: All Canada
Overseas: All Except Anti-American
 Countries

BOARDWALK FRIES

9110 Red Branch Rd., # O
Columbia, MD 21045
Tel: (410) 720-0020
Fax: (410) 720-0024
Mr. David DiFerdinando, President

We specialize in serving gourmet fries, fresh-cut and cooked in peanut oil with assorted toppings, prepared on location. We also have hot dogs, drinks, fresh-squeezed lemonade. Our locations range from fries only to full-menu restaurants.

BACKGROUND:
Established: 1981; 1st Franchised: 1981
Franchised Units: 55
Company-Owned Units 5
Total Units: 60
Dist.: US-60; CAN-0; O'seas-0
North America: NR
Density: NR
Projected New Units (12 Months): 18-24
Qualifications: 4, 3, 3, 3, 5, 5
Registered: CA,MD

FINANCIAL/TERMS:
Cash Investment: $25-100K

Total Investment:	$42-195K
Minimum Net Worth:	$100K
Fees: Franchise -	$15-25K
Royalty - 5-7%;	Ad. - 0-2%
Earnings Claim Statement:	No
Term of Contract (Years):	10/10
Avg. # Of Employees:	Varies
Passive Ownership:	Not Allowed
Encourage Conversions:	Yes
Area Develop. Agreements:	Yes/10
Sub-Franchising Contracts:	No
Expand In Territory:	Yes
Space Needs: Varies SF; Sports/ Entertainment	

SUPPORT & TRAINING PROVIDED:

Financial Assistance Provided:	Yes(I)
Site Selection Assistance:	Yes
Lease Negotiation Assistance:	Yes
Co-Operative Advertising:	Yes
Franchisee Assoc./Member:	No
Size Of Corporate Staff:	21
On-Going Support:	C,D,E,F
Training: 6 Days in MD.	

SPECIFIC EXPANSION PLANS:

US:	All United States
Canada:	No
Overseas:	Europe, Far East

≪ ≫

BOJANGLES' FAMOUS CHICKEN 'N BISCUITS
P.O. Box 240239
Charlotte, NC 28224
Tel: (800) 366-9921 (704) 527-2675
Fax: (704) 523-6676
E-Mail: msandefer@bojangles.com
Web Site: www.bojangles.com
Mr. Mike Sandefer, Director Franchise Development

BOJANGLES OPERATES DURING ALL 3 DAY-PARTS. Breakfast items are available all day long. Our menu in unique, and flavorful, with chicken prepared either spicy or traditional Southern-style. Restaurants operate in traditional locations and non-traditional locations in convenience stores.

BACKGROUND: IFA MEMBER

Established: 1977;	1st Franchised: 1979
Franchised Units:	112
Company-Owned Units	158

Total Units:	270
Dist.:	US-267; CAN-0; O'seas-3
North America:	9 States
Density: 130 in NC, 55 in SC,18 in GA	
Projected New Units (12 Months):	30
Qualifications:	5, 4, 4, 3, 3, 5
Registered: FL,IL,MD,VA	

FINANCIAL/TERMS:

Cash Investment:	$225-350K
Total Investment:	$225K-1.2MM
Minimum Net Worth:	$500K
Fees: Franchise -	$12-20K
Royalty - 4%;	Ad. - 1%
Earnings Claim Statement:	No
Term of Contract (Years):	20/10
Avg. # Of Employees:	12 FT, 20 PT
Passive Ownership:	Discouraged
Encourage Conversions:	Yes
Area Develop. Agreements:	Yes/10
Sub-Franchising Contracts:	No
Expand In Territory:	Yes
Space Needs: 2,000+ SF; FS	

SUPPORT & TRAINING PROVIDED:

Financial Assistance Provided:	No
Site Selection Assistance:	Yes
Lease Negotiation Assistance:	No
Co-Operative Advertising:	Yes
Franchisee Assoc./Member:	Yes/Yes
Size Of Corporate Staff:	80
On-Going Support:	B,C,D,E,F,G,H,I
Training: 5 Weeks Training in Training Units.	

SPECIFIC EXPANSION PLANS:

US:	Southeast, Midwest
Canada:	No
Overseas:	Central America, Caribbean Areas

≪ ≫

BREADEAUX PIZZA
P.O. Box 6158
St. Joseph, MO 64506
Tel: (800) 835-6534 (816) 364-1088
Fax: (816) 364-3739
E-Mail: scott@breadeauxpizza.com
Web Site: www.breadeauxpizza.com
Mr. Scott J. Henze, VP Sales & Marketing

BREADEAUX PIZZA is a growing regional chain, stressing quality and service. Our acclaimed pizza is made with a double raised crust that is chewy and sweet like fine french bread and our meat toppings have no fillers or additives. We also offer pastas, subs, baked potatoes, hot wings and salads to give customers plenty of variety. Our customers say 'Best Pizza in Town.'

BACKGROUND:

Established: 1985;	1st Franchised: 1985
Franchised Units:	91
Company-Owned Units	2
Total Units:	93
Dist.:	US-90; CAN-3; O'seas-0
North America:	7 States, 1 Province
Density:	43 in IA, 21 MO, 8 KS
Projected New Units (12 Months):	20
Qualifications:	3, 5, 2, 2, 3, 5
Registered: IL,MI,MN,SD,WI	

FINANCIAL/TERMS:

Cash Investment:	$30-80K
Total Investment:	$58-313K
Minimum Net Worth:	$50K
Fees: Franchise -	$15K
Royalty - 5%;	Ad. - 3%
Earnings Claim Statement:	Yes
Term of Contract (Years):	15/15
Avg. # Of Employees:	2 FT, 12 PT
Passive Ownership:	Discouraged
Encourage Conversions:	Yes
Area Develop. Agreements:	Yes/10
Sub-Franchising Contracts:	Yes
Expand In Territory:	Yes
Space Needs: 1,200-2,500 SF; FS, SF, SC, RM	

SUPPORT & TRAINING PROVIDED:

Financial Assistance Provided:	Yes(I)
Site Selection Assistance:	Yes
Lease Negotiation Assistance:	Yes
Co-Operative Advertising:	Yes
Franchisee Assoc./Member:	Yes/Yes
Size Of Corporate Staff:	25
On-Going Support:	A,B,C,D,E,F,G,H,I
Training: 2 Weeks Corporate Headquarters; 1 Week Franchisee Location; On-Going as Needed.	

SPECIFIC EXPANSION PLANS:

US:	Midwest
Canada:	No
Overseas:	No

≪ ≫

BROWN'S CHICKEN & PASTA
1200 Jorie Blvd.
Oak Brook, IL 60523
Tel: (630) 571-5300
Fax: (630) 571-5378
Mr. Frank Portillo, President

High-quality, quick-service franchisor of

BROWN'S CHICKEN & PASTA RESTAURANTS. Featuring various fresh-made side dishes. Stores can have take-out, dine-in and drive-up service. Our products, service and franchisee support exceed both customer and franchisee expectations. Expanded into corporate and home catering. Oven-baked chicken and full-service grill and pan pasta catering.

BACKGROUND:
Established: 1965; 1st Franchised: 1965
Franchised Units: 63
Company-Owned Units   <u>11</u>
Total Units: 74
Dist.:   US-74; CAN-0; O'seas-0
  North America: 3 States
  Density: 80 in IL, 5 in FL
Projected New Units (12 Months):   3-5
Qualifications: 3, 3, 2, 3, 5, 5
Registered: FL,IL,IN
FINANCIAL/TERMS:
Cash Investment: $25K
Total Investment: $150-160K
Minimum Net Worth: $200K
Fees: Franchise - $25K
  Royalty - 5%;   Ad. - 4%
Earnings Claim Statement: Yes
Term of Contract (Years):   15/5
Avg. # Of Employees: 3 FT, 12 PT
Passive Ownership: Not Allowed
Encourage Conversions: Yes
Area Develop. Agreements: Yes/15
Sub-Franchising Contracts: No
Expand In Territory: No
Space Needs: 1,500 SF; FS, SC
SUPPORT & TRAINING PROVIDED:
Financial Assistance Provided: No
Site Selection Assistance: Yes
Lease Negotiation Assistance: Yes
Co-Operative Advertising: Yes
Franchisee Assoc./Member: Yes/Yes
Size Of Corporate Staff: 12
On-Going Support: B,C,D,E,F,G,H,I
Training: 6 Weeks Oakbrook, IL Corporate Office.
SPECIFIC EXPANSION PLANS:
US: FL,IL,IN
Canada: No
Overseas: Russia, Asia

<< >>

BUCK'S PIZZA
53 Industrial Dr., P.O. Box 405
DuBois, PA 15801
Tel: (800) 310-8848 (814) 371-3076

Fax: (814) 371-4214
E-Mail: buck@penn.com
Web Site: www.buckspizza.com
Mr. Neil Shindledecker, VP/Dir. of Sales

We at BUCK'S PIZZA pride ourselves on the best-quality pizza we can prepare. To do that, we buy only select ingredients and prepare them in our own special way. BUCK'S PIZZA is a delicious blend of natural ingredients delicately, flavored with special spices. We have expanded to 21 states in a few short years. Towns of any size offer the opportunity for BUCK'S low start-up costs and low overhead concept. When you are ready, BUCK'S is ready to train and then support you in your business!

BACKGROUND:
Established: 1994; 1st Franchised: 1994
Franchised Units: 72
Company-Owned Units   <u>0</u>
Total Units: 72
Dist.:   US-72; CAN-0; O'seas-0
  North America: 21 States
  Density: 15 in TX, 10 in GA, 9 in SC
Projected New Units (12 Months):   24
Qualifications: 3, 4, 5, 3, 3, 5
Registered: FL,IL,MD,MN,NY,VA,
  WA,WI
FINANCIAL/TERMS:
Cash Investment: $15-30K
Total Investment: $90-125K
Minimum Net Worth: $N/A
Fees: Franchise - $10K
  Royalty - 3%;   Ad. - 2%
Earnings Claim Statement: No
Term of Contract (Years):   10/10
Avg. # Of Employees: 4 FT, 11 PT
Passive Ownership: Discouraged
Encourage Conversions: Yes
Area Develop. Agreements: Yes/Varies
Sub-Franchising Contracts: No
Expand In Territory: Yes
Space Needs: 1,000 SF; FS, SF, SC
SUPPORT & TRAINING PROVIDED:
Financial Assistance Provided: Yes(I)
Site Selection Assistance: Yes
Lease Negotiation Assistance: Yes
Co-Operative Advertising: Yes
Franchisee Assoc./Member: No
Size Of Corporate Staff: 9
On-Going Support: B,C,d,E,F,h,I
Training: 1-2   Day(s)   Seminar   in
  Headquarters; 10-14 Days On-Site.
SPECIFIC EXPANSION PLANS:
US: All United States
Canada: No
Overseas: No

<< >>

BUMPERS DRIVE-IN
279 Soldiers Colony Rd.
Canton, MS 39046
Tel: (601) 855-0146
Fax: (601) 855-9305
Ms. Monica Harrigill, Vice President of Operations

Fast food drive-in providing quality hamburgers, chicken, catfish, hot dogs, ice creams, shakes, french fries, potato pearls (tots), soft drinks, tea, coffee and desserts, namely apple pies, banana splits, short cakes with various toppings with the friendliest service possible.

BACKGROUND:
Established: 1985; 1st Franchised: 1985
Franchised Units: 4
Company-Owned Units   <u>25</u>
Total Units: 29
Dist.:   US-29; CAN-0; O'seas-0
  North America: 3 States
  Density: 28 in MS, 1 in TN
Projected New Units (12 Months):   1
Registered:
FINANCIAL/TERMS:
Cash Investment: $75-125K
Total Investment: $350-425K
Minimum Net Worth: $300K
Fees: Franchise - $10K
  Royalty - 3%;   Ad. - 6%
Earnings Claim Statement: No
Term of Contract (Years):   10/10
Avg. # Of Employees: 8 FT, 12 PT
Passive Ownership: Not Allowed
Encourage Conversions: NR
Area Develop. Agreements: Yes/10
Sub-Franchising Contracts: No
Expand In Territory: Yes
Space Needs: 24,000 SF; FS
SUPPORT & TRAINING PROVIDED:
Financial Assistance Provided: NR
Site Selection Assistance: Yes
Lease Negotiation Assistance: Yes
Co-Operative Advertising: Yes
Franchisee Assoc./Member: No
Size Of Corporate Staff: 72
On-Going Support: A,B,C,D,E,F,G,H,I
Training: 6 Weeks at Bumpers of Pearl, MS.
SPECIFIC EXPANSION PLANS:
US: MS,AR,TN,TX,MO,NC,SC
Canada: NR
Overseas: NR

<< >>

BURGER KING (CANADA)

401 The West Mall, 7th Fl.
Etobicoke, ON M9C 5J4 CANADA
Tel: (416) 626-7423
Fax: (416) 626-6691
E-Mail: gheos@whopper.com
Web Site: www.burgerking.com
Mr. George Heos, Franchise Devel. Manager

Second largest hamburger chain in the world. BURGER KING is currently recruiting franchisees qualified to develop multiple units in markets throughout Canada.

BACKGROUND: IFA MEMBER
Established: 1954; 1st Franchised: 1969
Franchised Units: 190
Company-Owned Units 110
Total Units: 300
Dist.: US-0; CAN-256; O'seas-0
North America: 10 Provinces
Density: 143 in ON, 59 in PQ, 30 BC
Projected New Units (12 Months): 35
Qualifications: 5, 4, 2, 3, 2, 5
Registered: AB
FINANCIAL/TERMS:
Cash Investment: $150-250K
Total Investment: $300K-1.1MM
Minimum Net Worth: $800K
Fees: Franchise - $55K
Royalty - 4%; Ad. - 4%
Earnings Claim Statement: Yes
Term of Contract (Years): 20/20
Avg. # Of Employees: 15 FT, 35 PT
Passive Ownership: Allowed
Encourage Conversions: Yes
Area Develop. Agreements: Yes/1-5
Sub-Franchising Contracts: No
Expand In Territory: Yes
Space Needs: 3,000-3,800 SF; FS, SF, SC, RM
SUPPORT & TRAINING PROVIDED:
Financial Assistance Provided: N/A
Site Selection Assistance: Yes
Lease Negotiation Assistance: Yes
Co-Operative Advertising: Yes
Franchisee Assoc./Member: Yes
Size Of Corporate Staff: 70
On-Going Support: B,C,D,E,F,H
Training: 15 Weeks Combined Classroom and Restaurant Training in Various Locations.
SPECIFIC EXPANSION PLANS:
US: Throughout Canada
Canada: All Canada
Overseas: No

◄◄ ►►

CAPTAIN D'S SEAFOOD

1717 Elm Hill Pike, # A-10
Nashville, TN 37210
Tel: (800) 346-9637 (615) 231-2616
Fax: (615) 231-2650
E-Mail: quentin_murray@captainds.com
Web Site: www.shoneys.com
Mr. Quentin Murray, Director of Franchising

Quick-service, sit-down/take-out seafood restaurant, serving broiled, baked and fried fish, shrimp and crab entrees, as well as chicken, specialty salads and a wide range of vegetables and desserts.

BACKGROUND: IFA MEMBER
Established: 1969; 1st Franchised: 1969
Franchised Units: 207
Company-Owned Units 365
Total Units: 572
Dist.: US-593; CAN-0; O'seas-0
North America: 22 States
Density: 96 in GA, 81 in TN, 65 AL
Projected New Units (12 Months): 3
Registered: IL,IN,MD,MN,NY,VA
FINANCIAL/TERMS:
Cash Investment: $150K
Total Investment: $884K-1.3MM
Minimum Net Worth: $300K
Fees: Franchise - $20K
Royalty - 3%; Ad. - 5.25%
Earnings Claim Statement: Yes
Term of Contract (Years): 20/20
Avg. # Of Employees: 5 FT, 15 PT
Passive Ownership: Discouraged
Encourage Conversions: No
Area Develop. Agreements: Yes/Varies
Sub-Franchising Contracts: No
Expand In Territory: Yes
Space Needs: 2,424-2,715 SF; FS, C-Store, Food Court
SUPPORT & TRAINING PROVIDED:
Financial Assistance Provided: No
Site Selection Assistance: Yes
Lease Negotiation Assistance: No
Co-Operative Advertising: Yes
Franchisee Assoc./Member: Yes
Size Of Corporate Staff: NR
On-Going Support: C,D,e,G,h,I
Training: Approximately 6 Weeks Nashville, TN; Depends on Franchisee's Experience.
SPECIFIC EXPANSION PLANS:
US: South, Southeast
Canada: No
Overseas: No

◄◄ ►►

CAPTAIN TONY'S PIZZA & PASTA EMPORIUM

2607 S. Woodland Blvd, # 300
Deland, FL 32720
Tel: (800) 332-8669 (904) 736-9855
Fax: (904) 736-7237
E-Mail: captain-tonys@wati.com
Web Site: www.captain-tonys.wati.com
Mr. Michael J. Martella, President

We have pizza, pasta, etc. for take-out, delivery and dining-in.

BACKGROUND:
Established: 1985; 1st Franchised: 1985
Franchised Units: 10
Company-Owned Units 0
Total Units: 10
Dist.: US-8; CAN-0; O'seas-2
North America: NR
Density: 4 in CA, 2 in OH
Projected New Units (12 Months): NR
Qualifications: 3, 3, 2, 3, 3, 5
Registered: FL,NY
FINANCIAL/TERMS:
Cash Investment: $25-75K
Total Investment: $65-250K
Minimum Net Worth: $250K
Fees: Franchise - $10-20K
Royalty - $200-400/Wk; Ad. - 0%
Earnings Claim Statement: No
Term of Contract (Years): 20
Avg. # Of Employees: NR
Passive Ownership: Discouraged
Encourage Conversions: Yes
Area Develop. Agreements: NR
Sub-Franchising Contracts: NR
Expand In Territory: NR
Space Needs: 1,200 SF; NR
SUPPORT & TRAINING PROVIDED:
Financial Assistance Provided: Yes(I)
Site Selection Assistance: Yes
Lease Negotiation Assistance: Yes
Co-Operative Advertising: No
Franchisee Assoc./Member: No
Size Of Corporate Staff: NR
On-Going Support: D,E,I
Training: 3 Weeks Orlando, FL.
SPECIFIC EXPANSION PLANS:
US: All United States
Canada: No
Overseas: All Countries

◄◄ ►►

CHECKERS DRIVE-IN RESTAURANTS

14255 49th St. N., # 1
Clearwater, FL 33762
Tel: (800) 275-3628 (727) 519-2000

Fax: (727) 519-2001
Web Site: www.checkers.com
Mr. Dave Miller, VP Fran. Operations

Quick-service, fast-food restaurant (double drive-thru).

BACKGROUND: IFA MEMBER
Established: 1986;   1st Franchised: 1989
Franchised Units: 249
Company-Owned Units   232
Total Units: 481
Dist.:   US-481; CAN-0; O'seas-0
   North America: 24 States
   Density: 191 in FL, 85 in GA, 32 AL
Projected New Units (12 Months):   35
Qualifications: 5, 4, 5, 4, 4, 4
Registered: FL,IL,IN,MD,MI,MN,NY,
   VA,WA,WI,DC
FINANCIAL/TERMS:
Cash Investment: $100-250K
Total Investment: $382.1-522.7K
Minimum Net Worth: $500K
Fees: Franchise - $30K
   Royalty - 4%;   Ad. - 0.25%+4.75%
Earnings Claim Statement: No
Term of Contract (Years):   20/Agrmt.
Avg. # Of Employees: 10 FT, 20 PT
Passive Ownership: Not Allowed
Encourage Conversions: Yes
Area Develop. Agreements: Yes
Sub-Franchising Contracts: Yes
Expand In Territory: Yes
Space Needs: 15,000 SF; FS
SUPPORT & TRAINING PROVIDED:
Financial Assistance Provided: No
Site Selection Assistance: Yes
Lease Negotiation Assistance: N/A
Co-Operative Advertising: Yes
Franchisee Assoc./Member: Yes
Size Of Corporate Staff: ~100
On-Going Support: A,B,C,D,E,F,G,H,I
Training: 4-6 Weeks Atlanta, GA; 4-6
   Weeks Clearwater, FL.
SPECIFIC EXPANSION PLANS:
US: Eastern United States
Canada: No
Overseas: No

⊲⊲ ⊳⊳

CHEEBURGER CHEEBURGER
15951 McGregor Blvd.
Fort Myers, FL 33908
Tel: (800) 487-6211 (941) 437-1611
Fax: (941) 437-1512
E-Mail: cheeburger@minospring.com
Mr. Bruce Zicari, President/CEO

Full-service, gourmet, specialty-sandwich restaurant, serving high-quality, freshly-prepared products and featuring burgers in various sizes, fresh-cut fries and big, thick milk shakes.

BACKGROUND:
Established: 1986;   1st Franchised: 1990
Franchised Units: 14
Company-Owned Units   4
Total Units: 18
Dist.:   US-18; CAN-0; O'seas-0
   North America: 5 States
   Density: 11 in FL, 2 in AR
Projected New Units (12 Months):   6
Qualifications: 5, 5, 3, 3, 4, 5
Registered: MI,NY
FINANCIAL/TERMS:
Cash Investment: $150-200K
Total Investment: $180-280K
Minimum Net Worth: $350K Liquid
Fees: Franchise - $17.5K
   Royalty - 4.5%;   Ad. - 1%
Earnings Claim Statement: No
Term of Contract (Years):   10/5
Avg. # Of Employees: 5 FT, 10 PT
Passive Ownership: NR
Encourage Conversions: Yes
Area Develop. Agreements: Yes
Sub-Franchising Contracts: No
Expand In Territory: Yes
Space Needs: 2,000 SF; FS, SF, SC
SUPPORT & TRAINING PROVIDED:
Financial Assistance Provided: No
Site Selection Assistance: Yes
Lease Negotiation Assistance: Yes
Co-Operative Advertising: Yes
Franchisee Assoc./Member: Yes
Size Of Corporate Staff: 5
On-Going Support: C,D,E,F,H,I,G
Training: 17 Days.
SPECIFIC EXPANSION PLANS:
US: East of Mississippi
Canada: All Canada
Overseas: No

⊲⊲ ⊳⊳

CHICAGO'S PIZZA
1111 N. Broadway
Greenfield, IN 46140

Tel: (317) 462-9878
Fax: (317) 467-1877
E-Mail: colips@freewooeb.com
Mr. Robert L. McDonald, CEO

Franchise designed for owner/operator. Flexibility allowed to ensure success. Can be adapted to large and small operations. Inside dining/carry-out/delivery.

BACKGROUND:
Established: 1979;   1st Franchised: 1981
Franchised Units: 12
Company-Owned Units   0
Total Units: 12
Dist.:   US-12; CAN-0; O'seas-0
   North America: 4 States
   Density: 10 in IN, 2 in OH
Projected New Units (12 Months):   2
Qualifications: 4, 4, 4, 3, 4, 5
Registered: IN
FINANCIAL/TERMS:
Cash Investment: $25-50K
Total Investment: $100-300K
Minimum Net Worth: $50K
Fees: Franchise - $10K
   Royalty - 4%;   Ad. - 2%
Earnings Claim Statement: No
Term of Contract (Years):   10/10
Avg. # Of Employees: 3 FT, 12 PT
Passive Ownership: Not Allowed
Encourage Conversions: Yes
Area Develop. Agreements: Yes/Open
Sub-Franchising Contracts: No
Expand In Territory: Yes
Space Needs: 1,800-3,000 SF; FS, SC
SUPPORT & TRAINING PROVIDED:
Financial Assistance Provided: No
Site Selection Assistance: Yes
Lease Negotiation Assistance: Yes
Co-Operative Advertising: Yes
Franchisee Assoc./Member: No
Size Of Corporate Staff: 3
On-Going Support: C,D,E,F,H
Training: 2 Weeks at Existing Store.
SPECIFIC EXPANSION PLANS:
US: IN,OH,MI,KY,IL
Canada: No
Overseas: No

⊲⊲ ⊳⊳

CHICKEN DELIGHT
395 Berry St.
Winnipeg, MB R3J 1N6 CANADA
Tel: (204) 885-7570
Fax: (204) 831-6176
Mr. Otto Koch, President

CHICKEN DELIGHT has been in business for over 40 years, featuring our famous, pressure-fried chicken and fresh, deep-dish pizza, plus other tasty selections. We cater to the fast-food market with dine-in, take-out, delivery and drive-thru. Our focus on chicken and pizza broadens your market potential in the take-out and delivery fast-food segment.

BACKGROUND:
Established: 1952; 1st Franchised: 1952
Franchised Units: 33
Company-Owned Units   16
Total Units: 49
Dist.:   US-17; CAN-37; O'seas-2
  North America: 3 States, 4 Provinces
  Density: 34 in MB, 3 in SK, 1 in ON
Projected New Units (12 Months):   3
Qualifications: 4, 5, 3, 3, 4, 3
Registered: MI,MN,ND,AB
FINANCIAL/TERMS:
Cash Investment: $70-100K
Total Investment: $250-375K
Minimum Net Worth: $200K
Fees: Franchise - $20K
  Royalty - 5%;   Ad. - 2%
Earnings Claim Statement: Yes
Term of Contract (Years):   10/10
Avg. # Of Employees: 6 FT, 6 PT
Passive Ownership: Discouraged
Encourage Conversions: Yes
Area Develop. Agreements: Yes/10
Sub-Franchising Contracts: No
Expand In Territory: Yes
Space Needs: 1,800 SF; FS, SF, SC, RM
SUPPORT & TRAINING PROVIDED:
Financial Assistance Provided: No
Site Selection Assistance: Yes
Lease Negotiation Assistance: Yes
Co-Operative Advertising: Yes
Franchisee Assoc./Member: No
Size Of Corporate Staff: 25
On-Going Support: a,B,C,D,E,F,G,h
Training: 4 Weeks Winnipeg, MB.
SPECIFIC EXPANSION PLANS:
US: All United States
Canada: All Canada
Overseas: Any Master License

≪ ≫

CHURCHS CHICKEN
980 Hammond Dr. NE, # 1100
Atlanta, GA 30328
Tel: (800) 639-3495 (770) 350-3685
Fax: (770) 512-3972
E-Mail: jrobinson@afce.com
Web Site: www.churchs.com

Mr. Hannibal Myers, VP New Business Development

CHURCHS is the 2nd largest chicken restaurant chain in the country. CHURCHS offers Southern fried chicken with signature side items such as fried okra, corn-on-the-cob, jalapenos and honey butter biscuits. CHURCHS has a proven business system niche customer base, low square footage requirements (as little as 750 square feet) and world class franchise support.

BACKGROUND: IFA MEMBER
Established: 1952; 1st Franchised: 1972
Franchised Units: 1,011
Company-Owned Units   487
Total Units: 1,498
Dist.:   US-1,182; CAN-94; O'seas-222
  North America: 28 States
  Density: 400 in TX, 100 in GA, 50 CA
Projected New Units (12 Months):   125
Qualifications: 5, 4, 3, 3, 3, 5
Registered: All States
FINANCIAL/TERMS:
Cash Investment: $200K
Total Investment: $300-400K
Minimum Net Worth: $400K
Fees: Franchise - $15K
  Royalty - 5%;   Ad. - 4%
Earnings Claim Statement: No
Term of Contract (Years):   20/10
Avg. # Of Employees: 15 FT, 6 PT
Passive Ownership: Discouraged
Encourage Conversions: Yes
Area Develop. Agreements: Yes/Varies
Sub-Franchising Contracts: No
Expand In Territory: Yes
Space Needs: 750-22,000 SF; FS, C-Store
SUPPORT & TRAINING PROVIDED:
Financial Assistance Provided: No
Site Selection Assistance: Yes
Lease Negotiation Assistance: Yes
Co-Operative Advertising: Yes
Franchisee Assoc./Member: Yes/Yes
Size Of Corporate Staff: 70
On-Going Support: C,D,E,F,G,h,I
Training: 6 Weeks Regional.
SPECIFIC EXPANSION PLANS:
US: All United States
Canada: All Canada
Overseas: Europe, Asia, Middle East,
  Australia

≪ ≫

CICI'S PIZZA
1080 W. Bethel Rd.
Coppell, TX 75019

Tel: (972) 745-4200
Fax: (972) 745-4204
E-Mail: jsheahan@cicispizza.com
Web Site: www.cicispizza.com
Mr. Jim Sheahan, Dir. Franchise Sales

CICI'S PIZZA provides its guests with delicious pizza, pasta, salad bar and dessert on an all-you-can-eat buffet for only $3.99 for adults and $2.29 for kids (prices may vary by location). Our low price, combined with quality food, great service and sparkling clean restaurants is making CICI'S among the fastest-growing franchises in America!

BACKGROUND:
Established: 1985; 1st Franchised: 1987
Franchised Units: 322
Company-Owned Units   30
Total Units: 352
Dist.:   US-352; CAN-0; O'seas-0
  North America: 17 States
  Density: NR
Projected New Units (12 Months):   60
Qualifications: 5, 4, 1, 1, 3, 5
Registered: FL,IN,MI,VA
FINANCIAL/TERMS:
Cash Investment: $83-121K
Total Investment: $276-405K
Minimum Net Worth: $NR
Fees: Franchise - $30K
  Royalty - 4%;   Ad. - 3%/$2.3K
Earnings Claim Statement: Yes
Term of Contract (Years):   10
Avg. # Of Employees: 8 FT, 15 PT
Passive Ownership: Not Allowed
Encourage Conversions: No
Area Develop. Agreements: Yes
Sub-Franchising Contracts: No
Expand In Territory: Yes
Space Needs: 3,600-4,000 SF; FS, SC
SUPPORT & TRAINING PROVIDED:
Financial Assistance Provided: Yes(I)
Site Selection Assistance: Yes
Lease Negotiation Assistance: Yes
Co-Operative Advertising: Yes
Franchisee Assoc./Member: No
Size Of Corporate Staff: 48
On-Going Support: B,C,D,E,F,G,H
Training: 8 Weeks Dallas, TX.
SPECIFIC EXPANSION PLANS:
US: South, Southeast, N. Central

Canada: No
Overseas: No

<< >>

CLUCK-U CHICKEN
261 Raymond Rd.
Princeton, NJ 08540
Tel: (732) 438-1900
Fax: (732) 438-0055
Web Site: www.clucku.com
Mr. Bob Alex, VP Franchise Dev.

Our objective is to exceed the expectations of our customers and develop a system full of great people. We sell chicken, BBQ and related products.

BACKGROUND:
Established: 1985; 1st Franchised: 1991
Franchised Units: 34
Company-Owned Units   1
Total Units: 35
Dist.:   US-35; CAN-0; O'seas-0
 North America: 6 States
 Density: NJ, MO, PA
Projected New Units (12 Months):   12
Qualifications: 3, 4, 4, 3, 5, 5
Registered: CA,MD
FINANCIAL/TERMS:
Cash Investment: $50K
Total Investment: $125-225K
Minimum Net Worth: $200K
Fees: Franchise - $2.5K
 Royalty - 5%;   Ad. - 2%
Earnings Claim Statement: No
Term of Contract (Years):   20/10
Avg. # Of Employees: 8 FT
Passive Ownership: Not Allowed
Encourage Conversions: Yes
Area Develop. Agreements: No
Sub-Franchising Contracts: Yes
Expand In Territory: Yes
Space Needs: 1,500 SF; FS, SF, SC
SUPPORT & TRAINING PROVIDED:
Financial Assistance Provided: Yes(I)
Site Selection Assistance: Yes
Lease Negotiation Assistance: Yes
Co-Operative Advertising: Yes
Franchisee Assoc./Member: No
Size Of Corporate Staff: 5
On-Going Support: B,C,D,E,F,G,H,I
Training: 6 Weeks at DE, CA, or NJ.
SPECIFIC EXPANSION PLANS:
US: All United States
Canada: No
Overseas: No

<< >>

COUSINS SUBS
N83 W13400 Leon Rd.
Menomonee Falls, WI 53051
Tel: (800) 238-9736 (262) 253-7700
Fax: (262) 253-7705
E-Mail: dkilby@cousinssubs.com
Web Site: www.cousinssubs.com
Mr. Rich Hanson, Franchise Sales

COUSINS SUBS celebrates over 28 years as an exceptionally high-volume, fast service concept in up-scale, in-line, free-standing and non-traditional locations. # 1 sub sandwich chain for five years running (Income Opportunities Magazine). Midwest, Southwest and South development available for single, multiple and area developers.

BACKGROUND: IFA MEMBER
Established: 1972; 1st Franchised: 1985
Franchised Units: 120
Company-Owned Units   36
Total Units: 156
Dist.:   US-156; CAN-0; O'seas-0
 North America: NR
 Density: 90 in WI, 25 in AZ, 19 in MN
Projected New Units (12 Months):   39
Qualifications: 5, 4, 5, 3, 5, 5
Registered: CA,IL,IN,MI,MN,ND,SD,WI
FINANCIAL/TERMS:
Cash Investment: $47-76.6K
Total Investment: $160-268K
Minimum Net Worth: $200K
Fees: Franchise - $15K
 Royalty - 4-6%;   Ad. - 2%
Earnings Claim Statement: Yes
Term of Contract (Years):   10/10
Avg. # Of Employees: 3 FT, 17 PT
Passive Ownership: Not Allowed
Encourage Conversions: Yes
Area Develop. Agreements: Yes/10
Sub-Franchising Contracts: Yes
Expand In Territory: Yes
Space Needs: 1,800 SF; FS, SF, SC, C-Store
SUPPORT & TRAINING PROVIDED:
Financial Assistance Provided: Yes(I)
Site Selection Assistance: Yes
Lease Negotiation Assistance: Yes
Co-Operative Advertising: Yes
Franchisee Assoc./Member: Yes/Yes

Size Of Corporate Staff: 50
On-Going Support: B,C,D,E,F,G,H,I
Training: 1 Wk Corp. HQ;4 Wks Training
 Store;10 Days Franchisee's New Store;3
 Field Visits/Mo 1st yr
SPECIFIC EXPANSION PLANS:
US: Midwest, Southwest, West
Canada: All Canada
Overseas: No

<< >>

CROISSANT + PLUS
2020 St. Patrick
Montreal, PQ H3K 1A9 CANADA
Tel: (800) 267-4896 (514) 931-5550
Fax: (514) 931-3749
E-Mail: madi@toa.ca
Mr. Tony Vanvari, President

A fast-food chain, offering healthy menu items such as soups, salads, sandwiches, bake-off products and gourmet coffees.

BACKGROUND:
Established: 1980; 1st Franchised: 1981
Franchised Units: 19
Company-Owned Units   6
Total Units: 25
Dist.:   US-0; CAN-40; O'seas-0
 North America: 3 Provinces
 Density: 37 in PQ, 2 in ON, 1 in BC
Projected New Units (12 Months):   10
Qualifications: 4, 5, 2, 2, 4, 5
Registered: NR
FINANCIAL/TERMS:
Cash Investment: $50-75K
Total Investment: $100-200K
Minimum Net Worth: $80-150K
Fees: Franchise - $10-30K
 Royalty - 5%;   Ad. - 3%
Earnings Claim Statement: No
Term of Contract (Years):   10/5
Avg. # Of Employees: 2 FT, 3-5 PT
Passive Ownership: Discouraged
Encourage Conversions: N/A
Area Develop. Agreements: Yes/10/10
Sub-Franchising Contracts: Yes
Expand In Territory: Yes
Space Needs: 300-1,000 SF; FS, SF,SC,
 RM, Office Bldg.
SUPPORT & TRAINING PROVIDED:
Financial Assistance Provided: Yes(I)
Site Selection Assistance: Yes
Lease Negotiation Assistance: Yes
Co-Operative Advertising: Yes
Franchisee Assoc./Member: Yes/Yes
Size Of Corporate Staff: 10
On-Going Support: B,C,D,E,F,H,I

Training: 2-6 Weeks Montreal, PQ; 2-6 Weeks Quebec City, PQ.

SPECIFIC EXPANSION PLANS:

US: All United States
Canada: All Canada
Overseas: No

<< >>

CULTURES RESTAURANTS
8300 Woodbine Ave., 5th Floor
Markham, ON L3R 9Y7 CANADA
Tel: (905) 948-1195
Fax: (905) 948-1282
E-Mail: srishikof@compuserve.com
Web Site: www.culturesrestaurants.com
Mr. Stefan Rishikof, General Manager

CULTURES serves fresh food fast in a contemporary setting. Our menu is prepared fresh daily. We serve soups, salads, sandwiches, baked potatoes, baked goods and our famous Smoothie yogurt drink. Let us tantalize your taste buds.

BACKGROUND:

Established: 1977;   1st Franchised: 1981
Franchised Units: 27
Company-Owned Units   6
Total Units: 33
Dist.:   US-0; CAN-33; O'seas-0
  North America: 2 Provinces
  Density: 31 in ON, 2 in PQ
Projected New Units (12 Months):   5
Qualifications: 4, 4, 3, 3, 3, 5
Registered: None

FINANCIAL/TERMS:

Cash Investment: $125K
Total Investment: $230-250K
Minimum Net Worth: $150K
Fees: Franchise - $35K
  Royalty - 5%;   Ad. - 3%
Earnings Claim Statement: No
Term of Contract (Years):   10/0
Avg. # Of Employees: 6 FT, 5 PT
Passive Ownership: Discouraged
Encourage Conversions: Yes
Area Develop. Agreements: Yes/10
Sub-Franchising Contracts: Yes
Expand In Territory: Yes
Space Needs: 1,600 SF; RM, Office Tower

SUPPORT & TRAINING PROVIDED:

Financial Assistance Provided: No
Site Selection Assistance: Yes
Lease Negotiation Assistance: Yes
Co-Operative Advertising: Yes
Franchisee Assoc./Member: No
Size Of Corporate Staff: 20
On-Going Support: B,C,D,E,H
Training: 4 Weeks Toronto, ON.

SPECIFIC EXPANSION PLANS:

US: All United States
Canada: All Canada
Overseas: Europe

<< >>

CULVERS FRANCHISING SYSTEM
107 Berkley Blvd., # A
Baraboo, WI 53913
Tel: (608) 356-5938
Fax: (608) 356-9017
E-Mail: katee@baraboo.com
Web Site: www.culvers.com
Mr. Tom Wakefield, Franchise Sales

The menu at CULVERS FROZEN CUSTARD is a bit of a flashback to the simple, honest taste of the 1950's hamburger stand. We have converted our ideas about quality and freshness into a new kind of restaurant where the tastes of butterburgers and frozen custard keep customers coming back. By serving good food at a good value, we've managed to become the largest frozen custard establishment in the United States.

BACKGROUND:

Established: 1984;   1st Franchised: 1987
Franchised Units: 84
Company-Owned Units   3
Total Units: 87
Dist.:   US-87; CAN-0; O'seas-0
  North America: 10 States
  Density: 57 in WI, 6 in IL, 4 in MN
Projected New Units (12 Months):   30
Qualifications: 4, 3, 3, 3, 1, 5
Registered: Midwest States

FINANCIAL/TERMS:

Cash Investment: $100-300K
Total Investment: $800K-1.8MM
Minimum Net Worth: $400K
Fees: Franchise - $42.5K
  Royalty - 4%;   Ad. - 2%
Earnings Claim Statement: No
Term of Contract (Years):   15/15
Avg. # Of Employees: 10 FT, 35 PT
Passive Ownership: Not Allowed
Encourage Conversions: Yes

Area Develop. Agreements: No
Sub-Franchising Contracts: No
Expand In Territory: Yes
Space Needs: 50,000 SF; FS, SC, RM

SUPPORT & TRAINING PROVIDED:

Financial Assistance Provided: No
Site Selection Assistance: Yes
Lease Negotiation Assistance: Yes
Co-Operative Advertising: No
Franchisee Assoc./Member: No
Size Of Corporate Staff: 29
On-Going Support: C,D,E,G,H
Training: 16 Weeks in Central, WI.

SPECIFIC EXPANSION PLANS:

US: Midwest -- WI to TX
Canada: No
Overseas: No

<< >>

DAIRY BELLE FREEZE
780 Montague Expy., # 702
San Jose, CA 95131
Tel: (408) 433-9337
Fax: (408) 433-9395
E-Mail: stone557@aol.com
Web Site: www.dairybelle.com
Ms. Patricia (Pat) Souza, President

Locally-owned and operated since 1957, DAIRY BELLE restaurants have provided quality food that is cooked to order to ensure the satisfaction of each customer. Our menu has expanded from soft-serve cones, hamburgers, fries and soft drinks to now include specialty sandwiches, Mexican food and a variety of soft-serve desserts.

BACKGROUND:

Established: 1957;   1st Franchised: 1981
Franchised Units: 13
Company-Owned Units   0
Total Units: 13
Dist.:   US-13; CAN-0; O'seas-0
  North America: 1 State
  Density: 13 in CA
Projected New Units (12 Months):   2
Qualifications: 5, 3, 4, 2, 2, 5
Registered: CA

FINANCIAL/TERMS:

Cash Investment: $50-100K

Total Investment: $50-200K
Minimum Net Worth: $100K
Fees: Franchise - $12.5K
  Royalty - 4.5%/$600; Ad. - 2%
Earnings Claim Statement: Yes
Term of Contract (Years): 10/10
Avg. # Of Employees: 4 FT, 3-10 PT
Passive Ownership: Not Allowed
Encourage Conversions: Yes
Area Develop. Agreements: No
Sub-Franchising Contracts: No
Expand In Territory: Yes
Space Needs: 1,500 SF; FS

SUPPORT & TRAINING PROVIDED:
Financial Assistance Provided: Yes(I)
Site Selection Assistance: Yes
Lease Negotiation Assistance: Yes
Co-Operative Advertising: Yes
Franchisee Assoc./Member: No
Size Of Corporate Staff: 6
On-Going Support: B,C,D,E,H
Training: 2-3 Weeks at Existing Franchisee's
  Restaurant; 2-3 Weeks at New
  Franchisee's Restaurant.

SPECIFIC EXPANSION PLANS:
US: Northern CA
Canada: No
Overseas: No

◄◄ ►►

DAIRY QUEEN
P.O. Box 39286-0286
Minneapolis, MN 55439-0286
Tel: (800) 285-8515 (612) 830-0200
Fax: (612) 830-0450
Web Site: www.dairyqueen.com
Mr. Eric Lavanger, VP Franchise Sales

With the first opening in 1940, DAIRY QUEEN has a proven track record of 50 years of satisfying consumer demand for quick-service food and treat menu items. As a result, thousands of franchisees currently do business under the DAIRY QUEEN sign.

BACKGROUND: IFA MEMBER
Established: 1940; 1st Franchised: 1940
Franchised Units: 5,800
Company-Owned Units: 50
Total Units: 5,850
Dist.: US-5,027; CAN-474; O'seas-192
  North America: 49 States,10 Provinces
  Density: 786 in TX, 284 in IL, 273 OH
Projected New Units (12 Months): Unknown
Qualifications: 5, 4, 3, 3, 3, 4
Registered: CA,FL,IL,IN,MD,MI,MN,NY,
  OR,RI,WA,WI,DC

FINANCIAL/TERMS:
Cash Investment: $NR
Total Investment: $NR
Minimum Net Worth: $100-150K
Fees: Franchise - $15-30K
  Royalty - 4-5%; Ad. - 3-6%
Earnings Claim Statement: No
Term of Contract (Years): 10
Avg. # Of Employees: Varies
Passive Ownership: Discouraged
Encourage Conversions: Yes
Area Develop. Agreements: No
Sub-Franchising Contracts: Yes
Expand In Territory: No
Space Needs: 20,000 SF; FS, SC, RM

SUPPORT & TRAINING PROVIDED:
Financial Assistance Provided: No
Site Selection Assistance: Yes
Lease Negotiation Assistance: Yes
Co-Operative Advertising: Yes
Franchisee Assoc./Member: NR
Size Of Corporate Staff: 500
On-Going Support: C,D,E,G,H
Training: 3 Weeks Minneapolis, MN;
  On-Going, On-Site.

SPECIFIC EXPANSION PLANS:
US: All United States
Canada: All Canada
Overseas: Asia, South America

◄◄ ►►

DAIRY QUEEN CANADA
905 Century Dr., P.O. Box 430
Burlington, ON L7R 3Y3 CANADA
Tel: (905) 639-1492
Fax: (905) 681-3623
Ms. Sandy Tudor,

Fast-food restaurant, featuring soft-serve products.

BACKGROUND: IFA MEMBER
Established: 1940; 1st Franchised: 1950
Franchised Units: 505
Company-Owned Units: 0
Total Units: 505
Dist.: US-0; CAN-505; O'seas-0
  North America: 10 Provinces
  Density: 165 in ON, 95 in AB, 88 BC
Projected New Units (12 Months): 35
Qualifications: 5, 3, 3, 3, 3, 5
Registered: AB

FINANCIAL/TERMS:
Cash Investment: $150-350K
Total Investment: $400K-1.2MM
Minimum Net Worth: $NR
Fees: Franchise - $30K
  Royalty - 4%; Ad. - 3-6%
Earnings Claim Statement: No

Term of Contract (Years): N/A
Avg. # Of Employees: 20 FT, 40 PT
Passive Ownership: Discouraged
Encourage Conversions: Yes
Area Develop. Agreements: No
Sub-Franchising Contracts: No
Expand In Territory: Yes
Space Needs: 2,000-3,000 SF; FS

SUPPORT & TRAINING PROVIDED:
Financial Assistance Provided: Yes(I)
Site Selection Assistance: Yes
Lease Negotiation Assistance: Yes
Co-Operative Advertising: Yes
Franchisee Assoc./Member: Yes/Yes
Size Of Corporate Staff: 70
On-Going Support: A,B,C,D,E,F,G,H,I
Training: 3 Weeks Minneapolis, MN.

SPECIFIC EXPANSION PLANS:
US: All United States
Canada: All Canada
Overseas: All Countries

◄◄ ►►

DEL TACO
23041 Avenida de La Carlota
Laguna Hills, CA 92653
Tel: (949) 462-9300
Fax: (949) 462-7444
Web Site: www.deltaco.net
Mr. Paul Hitzel Berger, VP Franchising

Mexican-American fast-food restaurant.

BACKGROUND: IFA MEMBER
Established: 1964; 1st Franchised: 1967
Franchised Units: 97
Company-Owned Units: 204
Total Units: 301
Dist.: US-301; CAN-0; O'seas-0
  North America: 10 States
  Density: 265 in CA, 15 in NV, 9 in GA
Projected New Units (12 Months): 50
Qualifications: 4, 5, 5, 4, 4, 4
Registered: CA,IL,NY

FINANCIAL/TERMS:
Cash Investment: $250K
Total Investment: $466-679K
Minimum Net Worth: $2MM
Fees: Franchise - $25K
  Royalty - 5%; Ad. - 4%
Earnings Claim Statement: No
Term of Contract (Years): 20/15
Avg. # Of Employees: 2 FT, 24 PT
Passive Ownership: Not Allowed
Encourage Conversions: No
Area Develop. Agreements: Yes/Varies
Sub-Franchising Contracts: No
Expand In Territory: Yes
Space Needs: 2,100 SF; FS

196

SUPPORT & TRAINING PROVIDED:

Financial Assistance Provided:	No
Site Selection Assistance:	No
Lease Negotiation Assistance:	No
Co-Operative Advertising:	Yes
Franchisee Assoc./Member:	No
Size Of Corporate Staff:	120
On-Going Support:	C,D,E,f,G,H,I
Training: 5 Days Laguna Hills, CA; 6 Weeks in Restaurant, CA.	

SPECIFIC EXPANSION PLANS:

US:	SE,SW,NE,NW
Canada:	No
Overseas:	No

◄◄ ►►

DIAMOND DAVE'S TACO COMPANY

201 S. Clinton St., # 281
Iowa City, IA 52240
Tel: (319) 337-7690
Fax: (319) 337-4707
Web Site: www.diamonddaves.com
Mr. Stanley J. White, President

DIAMOND DAVE'S TACO COMPANY is a regional restaurant chain, featuring great family-priced Mexican/American cuisine. Opportunities include full-service restaurant/bar concept. Locations available in enclosed regional malls, strip centers and free-standing units.

BACKGROUND:

Established: 1980; 1st Franchised: 1981	
Franchised Units:	29
Company-Owned Units	2
Total Units:	31
Dist.:	US-36; CAN-0; O'seas-0
North America:	5 States
Density:	14 in IA, 9 in IL, 5 in WI
Projected New Units (12 Months):	2
Registered: IL,MN,SD,WI	

FINANCIAL/TERMS:

Cash Investment:	$50-75K
Total Investment:	$150-250K
Minimum Net Worth:	$NR
Fees: Franchise -	$15K
Royalty - 4%;	Ad. - 1%
Earnings Claim Statement:	No
Term Of Contract (Years):	10/10
Avg. # Of Employees:	5 FT, 15 PT
Passive Ownership:	Discouraged
Encourage Conversions:	Yes

Area Develop. Agreements:	Yes
Sub-Franchising Contracts:	No
Expand In Territory:	Yes
Space Needs: 2,000-3,000 SF; SC, RM	

SUPPORT & TRAINING PROVIDED:

Financial Assistance Provided:	N/A
Site Selection Assistance:	Yes
Lease Negotiation Assistance:	Yes
Co-Operative Advertising:	Yes
Franchisee Assoc./Member:	NR
Size Of Corporate Staff:	4
On-Going Support:	C,D,E,F,G,H
Training: 2-4 Weeks Local Restaurant.	

SPECIFIC EXPANSION PLANS:

US:	Midwest Only
Canada:	No
Overseas:	No

◄◄ ►►

DONATOS PIZZA

935 Taylor Station Rd.
Columbus, OH 43230
Tel: (800) 366-2867 (614) 864-2444
Fax: (614) 575-4480
Mr. Ed Binzel, Director of Franchising

DONATOS PIZZA is a retail outlet specializing in the sale of pizzas, subs and salads, featuring delivery, carryout and dine-in service. DONATOS is committed to serving the best pizza and promoting goodwill through product, principle and people. DONATOS PIZZA strives to be the best pizza on the block where the stores are located.

BACKGROUND: IFA MEMBER

Established: 1963; 1st Franchised: 1991	
Franchised Units:	42
Company-Owned Units	72
Total Units:	114
Dist.:	US-114; CAN-0; O'seas-0
North America:	4 States
Density:	94 in OH, 13 in IN, 4 in KY
Projected New Units (12 Months):	25
Qualifications:	5, 4, 5, 3, 2, 4
Registered: FL,IL,IN,MD,MI,MN,VA,DC	

FINANCIAL/TERMS:

Cash Investment:	$25% of Total
Total Investment:	$250-600K
Minimum Net Worth:	$350K
Fees: Franchise -	$30K
Royalty - 4%;	Ad. - 4%
Earnings Claim Statement:	Yes
Term Of Contract (Years):	20/5
Avg. # Of Employees:	15 FT, 20 PT
Passive Ownership:	Discouraged
Encourage Conversions:	Yes
Area Develop. Agreements:	Yes/Varies

Sub-Franchising Contracts:	No
Expand In Territory:	Yes
Space Needs: 2,000 SF; FS, SF, SC	

SUPPORT & TRAINING PROVIDED:

Financial Assistance Provided:	No
Site Selection Assistance:	Yes
Lease Negotiation Assistance:	Yes
Co-Operative Advertising:	Yes
Franchisee Assoc./Member:	No
Size Of Corporate Staff:	90
On-Going Support:	B,C,D,E,G,H,I
Training: 6-8 Weeks Columbus, OH.	

SPECIFIC EXPANSION PLANS:

US:	Midwest, Southeast
Canada:	No
Overseas:	No

◄◄ ►►

EAST OF CHICAGO PIZZA COMPANY

318 W. Walton
Willard, OH 44890
Tel: (419) 935-3033
Fax: (419) 935-3278
E-Mail: development@eastofchicago.com
Web Site: www.eastofchicago.com
Ms. Nina L. Blanton, Dev. Coor.

EAST OF CHICAGO PIZZA COMPANY is a young, determined franchising company that utilizes dine-in and delivery/carry-out units to achieve market dominance. Established in 1990, EOC has grown to over 100 units, with plans to expand. Combining proven marketing and operational systems, with ideal franchisee strategic partnerships, EOC meets demands of customers with unique products, which, when combined with superior customer service, creates an atmosphere of tremendous customer loyalty/repeat business.

BACKGROUND:

Established: 1990; 1st Franchised: 1991	
Franchised Units:	120
Company-Owned Units	8
Total Units:	128
Dist.:	US-128; CAN-0; O'seas-0
North America:	5 States
Density:	115 in OH, 9 in IN, 4 in PA

Projected New Units (12 Months): 30
Qualifications: 4, 3, 3, 3, 4, 4
Registered: FL,IN,VA
FINANCIAL/TERMS:
Cash Investment: $50K
Total Investment: $150-300K
Minimum Net Worth: $N/A
Fees: Franchise - $20K
  Royalty - 5%; Ad. - 2%
Earnings Claim Statement: Yes
Term of Contract (Years): 10/10
Avg. # Of Employees: 10 FT, 10 PT
Passive Ownership: Allowed
Encourage Conversions: Yes
Area Develop. Agreements: No
Sub-Franchising Contracts: No
Expand In Territory: No
Space Needs: 1,200-3,000 SF; FS, SC
SUPPORT & TRAINING PROVIDED:
Financial Assistance Provided: No
Site Selection Assistance: Yes
Lease Negotiation Assistance: No
Co-Operative Advertising: Yes
Franchisee Assoc./Member: Yes/Yes
Size Of Corporate Staff: 40
On-Going Support: A,B,C,D,E,F,G,H
Training: 4 Weeks in Willard, OH.
SPECIFIC EXPANSION PLANS:
US: OH,IN,PA,FL,VA only.
Canada: No
Overseas: No

≪ ≫

EL POLLO LOCO
3333 Michelson Dr., # 550
Irvine, CA 92612
Tel: (800) 99-POLLO (949) 399-2055
Fax: (949) 399-2025
E-Mail: elpolloloco@hotmail.com
Web Site: www.elpolloloco.com
Mr. Stephen Dunn, Dir. Franchise Dev.

The nation's leading flame-broiled chicken, quick-service restaurant, specializing in great tasting Mexican food that offers customers a wholesome alternative to traditional fast-food.

BACKGROUND: IFA MEMBER
Established: 1975; 1st Franchised: 1983

Franchised Units: 148
Company-Owned Units: 122
Total Units: 270
Dist.: US-270; CAN-0; O'seas-4
  North America: 4 States
  Density: 250 in CA, 9 in AZ, 7 in NV
Projected New Units (12 Months): 20
Qualifications: 5, 5, 5, 3, 3, 5
Registered: CA
FINANCIAL/TERMS:
Cash Investment: $300K minimum
Total Investment: $502K-1MM
Minimum Net Worth: $1MM
Fees: Franchise - $40K
  Royalty - 4%; Ad. - 4-5%
Earnings Claim Statement: Yes
Term of Contract (Years): 20
Avg. # Of Employees: 8 FT, 17 PT
Passive Ownership: Discouraged
Encourage Conversions: Yes
Area Develop. Agreements: Yes/Varies
Sub-Franchising Contracts: No
Expand In Territory: Yes
Space Needs: 2,600 SF; FS, SF, SC
SUPPORT & TRAINING PROVIDED:
Financial Assistance Provided: No
Site Selection Assistance: Yes
Lease Negotiation Assistance: No
Co-Operative Advertising: Yes
Franchisee Assoc./Member: Yes/Yes
Size Of Corporate Staff: 75
On-Going Support: B,C,D,E,F,H,I
Training: 6 Weeks in Southern CA.
SPECIFIC EXPANSION PLANS:
US: CA,AZ,NV,TX
Canada: No
Overseas: No

≪ ≫

Erbert & Gerbert's
SUBS & CLUBS

ERBERT & GERBERT'S SUBS & CLUBS
320 Graham Ave.
Eau Claire, WI 54701
Tel: (800) 283-5241 (715) 833-1375
Fax: (715) 833-8523
Mr. Kevin Schippers, President

ERBERT AND GERBERT'S SUBS & CLUBS offer the gourmet sandwich product in the fast-food niche. Growing rapidly, the market is wide open for this top-quality, service-oriented company. Immaculate shops and outstanding service complement the gourmet product.
BACKGROUND:
Established: 1987; 1st Franchised: 1992

Franchised Units: 14
Company-Owned Units: 1
Total Units: 15
Dist.: US-15; CAN-0; O'seas-0
  North America: 3 States
  Density: 8 in WI, 5 in MN, 1 in ND
Projected New Units (12 Months): 12
Qualifications: 4, 5, 1, 3, 4, 5
Registered: IL,MN,ND,WI
FINANCIAL/TERMS:
Cash Investment: $30-35K
Total Investment: $94.6-183.8K
Minimum Net Worth: $200K
Fees: Franchise - $9.5K
  Royalty - 6.5%; Ad. - 2%
Earnings Claim Statement: Yes
Term of Contract (Years): 15/5
Avg. # Of Employees: 2-3 FT, 10 PT
Passive Ownership: Discouraged
Encourage Conversions: Yes
Area Develop. Agreements: Yes/Varies
Sub-Franchising Contracts: No
Expand In Territory: NR
Space Needs: 1,000-2,000 SF; SF, SC
SUPPORT & TRAINING PROVIDED:
Financial Assistance Provided: Yes(I)
Site Selection Assistance: Yes
Lease Negotiation Assistance: Yes
Co-Operative Advertising: Yes
Franchisee Assoc./Member: No
Size Of Corporate Staff: 5
On-Going Support: C,D,d,E,G,H,I
Training: 2 Weeks Home Office; 1 Week
  On-Site during Opening.
SPECIFIC EXPANSION PLANS:
US: All U.S., Primarily Midwest
Canada: No
Overseas: No

≪ ≫

FAMILY PIZZA
318 105th St. E., Bay 10
Saskatoon, SK S7N 1Z3 CANADA
Tel: (306) 955-0215
Fax: (306) 955-0215
Mr. Hal Schmidt, President

2-for-1 gourmet pizza and pasta. Take-out and delivery - 39 minute guarantee or your order is free.

BACKGROUND:

Established: 1983; 1st Franchised: 1987
Franchised Units: 15
Company-Owned Units   7
Total Units: 22
Dist.:   US-0; CAN-18; O'seas-0
  North America: 3 Provinces
  Density: 12 in SK, 5 in AB, 4 in BC
Projected New Units (12 Months):   10
Qualifications: 3, 3, 2, 3, 3, 4
Registered: AB

FINANCIAL/TERMS:

Cash Investment: $40K
Total Investment: $75-100K
Minimum Net Worth: $50K
Fees: Franchise - $15K
  Royalty - 4%;   Ad. - 5%
Earnings Claim Statement: Yes
Term of Contract (Years):   5/5
Avg. # Of Employees: 5 FT, 10 PT
Passive Ownership: Discouraged
Encourage Conversions: No
Area Develop. Agreements: Yes/5
Sub-Franchising Contracts: No
Expand In Territory: Yes
Space Needs: 900-1,500 SF; FS, SC

SUPPORT & TRAINING PROVIDED:

Financial Assistance Provided: Yes(I)
Site Selection Assistance: Yes
Lease Negotiation Assistance: Yes
Co-Operative Advertising: Yes
Franchisee Assoc./Member: No
Size Of Corporate Staff: 3
On-Going Support: A,B,C,D,E,F,G,H
Training: 2-4 Weeks in Store.

SPECIFIC EXPANSION PLANS:

US: No
Canada: All Canada
Overseas: No

≪ ≫

FARMER BOYS HAMBURGERS
3435 14th St., # 102
Riverside, CA 92501
Tel: (888) 930-3276 (909) 275-9900
Fax: (909) 275-9930
E-Mail: fnieie@aol.com
Web Site: www.farmerboys.com
Mr. Don Tucker, Director of Franchising

FARMER BOYS RESTAURANTS fill a unique food service niche by offering greater choice to both fast food and traditional sit-down restaurant customers. Concept offers over 100 fresh breakfast, lunch or dinner items, prepared and cooked to order in 5 - 7 minutes - with a choice of sit-down, take-out or drive-thru service.

BACKGROUND:

Established: 1981; 1st Franchised: 1997
Franchised Units: 8
Company-Owned Units   8
Total Units: 16
Dist.:   US-16; CAN-0; O'seas-0
  North America: 1 State
  Density: 16 in CA
Projected New Units (12 Months):   6
Qualifications: 4, 4, 2, 3, 1, 5
Registered: CA

FINANCIAL/TERMS:

Cash Investment: $200K
Total Investment: $286.2-443.5K
Minimum Net Worth: $350K
Fees: Franchise - $30K
  Royalty - 5%;   Ad. - 2%
Earnings Claim Statement: Yes
Term of Contract (Years):   20/10/10
Avg. # Of Employees:7-10 FT, 10-15 PT
Passive Ownership: Allowed
Encourage Conversions: No
Area Develop. Agreements: Yes/Varies
Sub-Franchising Contracts: No
Expand In Territory: Yes
Space Needs: 2,500-3,000 SF; FS

SUPPORT & TRAINING PROVIDED:

Financial Assistance Provided: NR
Site Selection Assistance: Yes
Lease Negotiation Assistance: Yes
Co-Operative Advertising: Yes
Franchisee Assoc./Member: No
Size Of Corporate Staff: 12
On-Going Support: B,C,D,E,F,I
Training: 3 Months at Company-Operated
  Unit.

SPECIFIC EXPANSION PLANS:

US: CA Only
Canada: No
Overseas: No

≪ ≫

FATBURGER
1218 Third St. Promenade
Santa Monica, CA 90401-1308
Tel: (310) 319-1850
Fax: (310) 319-1863
Web Site: www.fatburger.net
Mrs. Angelina Morse, Dir. Franchise
  Relations

The classic hamburger stand, serving cooked-to-order burgers at an open grill since 1952. Also serving grilled chicken-breast sandwiches, freshly-made onion rings and real milkshakes in a fun environment with a unique R & B jukebox.

BACKGROUND: IFA MEMBER
Established: 1952; 1st Franchised: 1980
Franchised Units: 23
Company-Owned Units   13
Total Units: 36
Dist.:   US-36; CAN-0; O'seas-0
  North America: 3 States
  Density: 28 in CA, 7 in NV
Projected New Units (12 Months):   8
Qualifications: 4, 5, 3, 2, 5, 5
Registered: CA,IL,MD,NY,WA

FINANCIAL/TERMS:

Cash Investment: $150-250K
Total Investment: $370-730K
Minimum Net Worth: $NR
Fees: Franchise - $30K
  Royalty - 5%;   Ad. - 2%
Earnings Claim Statement: Yes
Term of Contract (Years):   15/10/10
Avg. # Of Employees: 16-40 PT
Passive Ownership: Allowed
Encourage Conversions: Yes
Area Develop. Agreements: Yes/5
Sub-Franchising Contracts: No
Expand In Territory: No
Space Needs: 1,800-2,000 SF; FS, SF, SC

SUPPORT & TRAINING PROVIDED:

Financial Assistance Provided: No
Site Selection Assistance: Yes
Lease Negotiation Assistance: No
Co-Operative Advertising: No
Franchisee Assoc./Member: No
Size Of Corporate Staff: 10
On-Going Support: C,D,E,H
Training: 10 Weeks Orange County, CA;
  7-10 Days On-Site.

SPECIFIC EXPANSION PLANS:

US: All United States
Canada: All Canada
Overseas: No

≪ ≫

FLAMERS CHARBROILED
HAMBURGERS & CHICKEN
500 S. 3rd St.
Jacksonville Beach, FL 32250
Tel: (800) 952-7645 (904) 241-3737

199

Fax: (904) 241-1301
E-Mail: flamersgrill@usa.com
Web Site: www.flamersgrill.com
Mr. Faszin Darabi, President

Gourmet, charbroiled hamburgers, chicken, grilled fish and steaks restaurant, which operates in both food-court environments and neighborhood open-air centers, featuring food products cooked over an open-flame, just like you would cook them on your own backyard grill.

BACKGROUND: IFA MEMBER
Established: 1987;   1st Franchised: 1988
Franchised Units: 76
Company-Owned Units   8
Total Units: 84
Dist.:   US-79; CAN-0; O'seas-5
   North America: 24 States
   Density: 21 in FL, 11 in DC, 7 in PA
Projected New Units (12 Months): 10-15
Qualifications: 5, 3, 3, 4, 3, 4
Registered: CA,FL,HI,IL,IN,MD,MI,NY,
   OR,RI,VA,WA,WI,DC
FINANCIAL/TERMS:
Cash Investment: $60-90K
Total Investment: $180-210K
Minimum Net Worth: $350K
Fees: Franchise - $25K
   Royalty - 5%;   Ad. - 1%
Earnings Claim Statement: No
Term of Contract (Years):   10/10/10
Avg. # Of Employees: 3-4 FT, 7-10 PT
Passive Ownership: Allowed
Encourage Conversions: Yes
Area Develop. Agreements: Yes/20
Sub-Franchising Contracts: Yes
Expand In Territory: Yes
Space Needs: 500-2,000 SF; SF, SC, RM
SUPPORT & TRAINING PROVIDED:
Financial Assistance Provided: Yes(I)
Site Selection Assistance: Yes
Lease Negotiation Assistance: Yes
Co-Operative Advertising: Yes
Franchisee Assoc./Member: No
Size Of Corporate Staff: 11
On-Going Support: a,B,C,D,E,F,G,H,I
Training: 2 Weeks at Company Unit in
   Boston, MA; 2 Weeks Franchisee's Store.
SPECIFIC EXPANSION PLANS:
US: All United States
Canada: All Canada
Overseas: Europe, Middle East

≪ ≫

FOUR STAR PIZZA

P.O. Box W
Claysville, PA 15323

Tel: (800) 628-3398 (724) 484-9235
Fax: (724) 484-9267
Web Site: www.fourstarpizza.com
Mr. David Roderick, President

FOUR STAR PIZZA's commitment to quality is evident in everything we do, from the "made fresh daily" ingredients to the intensive training and on-going support given by our franchise liaison team. We think our concept is so good we own 6 stores ourselves. And by owning our own stores, we know what it takes to make money. We are in the industry with you, helping you maximize your investment return. Just compare our franchise fee with others in the business.

BACKGROUND: IFA MEMBER
Established: 1981;   1st Franchised: 1985
Franchised Units: 38
Company-Owned Units   7
Total Units: 45
Dist.:   US-27; CAN-0; O'seas-18
   North America: 5 States
   Density: 15 in PA, 5 in MD, 2 in OH
Projected New Units (12 Months):   6
Qualifications: 3, 4, 2, 3, 1, 5
Registered: MD,NY,VA
FINANCIAL/TERMS:
Cash Investment: $20-30K
Total Investment: $48-70K
Minimum Net Worth: $NR
Fees: Franchise - $2K
   Royalty - 5%;   Ad. - 0%
Earnings Claim Statement: No
Term of Contract (Years):   10/10
Avg. # Of Employees: 3-4 FT, 8-10 PT
Passive Ownership: Discouraged
Encourage Conversions: Yes
Area Develop. Agreements: Yes/25
Sub-Franchising Contracts: No
Expand In Territory: Yes
Space Needs: 1,000 SF; FS, SF, SC
SUPPORT & TRAINING PROVIDED:
Financial Assistance Provided: Yes(I)
Site Selection Assistance: Yes
Lease Negotiation Assistance: Yes
Co-Operative Advertising: Yes
Franchisee Assoc./Member: No
Size Of Corporate Staff: 6
On-Going Support: B,C,D,E,F,G,H
Training: 2 Weeks Corporate Stores.
SPECIFIC EXPANSION PLANS:
US: PA,VA,MD,WV,OH,NJ,NY
Canada: No
Overseas: No

≪ ≫

FOX'S PIZZA DEN

3243 Old Frankstown Rd.
Pittsburgh, PA 15239
Tel: (800) 899-3697 (724) 733-7888
Fax: (724) 325-5479
E-Mail: foxs@alltel.net
Web Site: www.foxspizza.com
Mr. James R. Fox, President

FOX'S PIZZA DEN believes in one philosophy - you earned it, you keep it! FOX'S royalties are $200 a month - no percentages of sales. FOX'S PIZZA DENS offers the finest pizza, specialty sandwiches, salads and sides and our house special - the 'wedgie.'

BACKGROUND:
Established: 1971;   1st Franchised: 1974
Franchised Units: 205
Company-Owned Units   0
Total Units: 205
Dist.:   US-205; CAN-0; O'seas-0
   North America: 19 States
   Density: 105 in PA, 42 in WV, 12 OH
Projected New Units (12 Months):   30
Qualifications: 2, 4, 4, 2, 2, 5
Registered: FL,MD,MI,NY,VA
FINANCIAL/TERMS:
Cash Investment: $50-80K
Total Investment: $50-80K
Minimum Net Worth: $N/A
Fees: Franchise - $8K
   Royalty - $200/Mo.;   Ad. - 0%
Earnings Claim Statement: No
Term of Contract (Years):   5/5
Avg. # Of Employees: 2-3 FT, 8-10 PT
Passive Ownership: Discouraged
Encourage Conversions: Yes
Area Develop. Agreements: Yes
Sub-Franchising Contracts: Yes
Expand In Territory: Yes
Space Needs: 1,000-2,000 SF; FS, SF, SC
SUPPORT & TRAINING PROVIDED:
Financial Assistance Provided: Yes(I)
Site Selection Assistance: Yes
Lease Negotiation Assistance: No
Co-Operative Advertising: Yes
Franchisee Assoc./Member: NR
Size Of Corporate Staff: 8
On-Going Support: B,C,D,E,F,G,H,I
Training: 7 Days On-Site.
SPECIFIC EXPANSION PLANS:
US: All United States

Canada:	No
Overseas:	No

<< >>

FRULLATI CAFÉ & BAKERY
7730 E. Greenway Rd., #230
Scottsdale, AZ 85260
Tel: (800) 289-8291 (972) 401-9730
Fax: (972) 401-9731
E-Mail: comments@frullati.com
Web Site: www.frulatti.com
Ms. Nicole Rayborn, Franchise Director

FRULLATI CAFÉ & BAKERY, the fresh franchise alternative in fast food. Featuring something fresh for every taste, FRULLATI's lite fare menu includes: fruit smoothies, frozen yogurt, deli sandwiches, healthy snacks, fresh baked bread, cookies and gourmet coffee. If the taste of success by owning one or a chain of FRULLATI CAFÉs sounds appetizing, here's the opportunity for you. We have FRULLATI CAFÉ & BAKERY franchise opportunities coming to your neighborhood.

BACKGROUND:	IFA MEMBER
Established: 1985; 1st Franchised: 1994	
Franchised Units:	60
Company-Owned Units	40
Total Units:	100
Dist.:	US-100; CAN-0; O'seas-0
North America:	14 States
Density:	29 in TX, 12 in IL, 7 in FL
Projected New Units (12 Months):	28
Qualifications:	5, 4, , 3, , 5
Registered:	CA,FL,IL,IN,MD,MI,MN,
ND,OR,VA,WA,WI	

FINANCIAL/TERMS:	
Cash Investment:	$50K
Total Investment:	$150-275K
Minimum Net Worth:	$150K
Fees: Franchise -	$20K
Royalty - 6%;	Ad. - 1%
Earnings Claim Statement:	Yes
Term of Contract (Years):	10/10
Avg. # Of Employees:	3 FT, 5 PT
Passive Ownership:	Discouraged
Encourage Conversions:	Yes
Area Develop. Agreements:	Yes/Varies
Sub-Franchising Contracts:	No
Expand In Territory:	Yes
Space Needs: 600 SF; RM	

SUPPORT & TRAINING PROVIDED:	
Financial Assistance Provided:	Yes(I)
Site Selection Assistance:	Yes
Lease Negotiation Assistance:	Yes
Co-Operative Advertising:	Yes
Franchisee Assoc./Member:	Yes/Yes

Size Of Corporate Staff:	350
On-Going Support:	C,D,E,G,H,I
Training: 3 Weeks Dallas, TX.	

SPECIFIC EXPANSION PLANS:	
US:	All United States
Canada:	No
Overseas:	No

<< >>

GODFATHER'S PIZZA
9140 W. Dodge Rd., # 300
Omaha, NE 68114
Tel: (800) 456-8347 (402) 391-1452
Fax: (402) 255-2685
Web Site: www.godfathers.com
Mr. Bruce N. Cannon, VP Franchising

GODFATHER'S PIZZA is consistently recognized by consumers and independent research as having a superior quality product. Couple this with consistent operations, innovative new products, attention to service and full support services and GODFATHER'S PIZZA is positioned to retain its reputation for high quality and service.

BACKGROUND:	
Established: 1973; 1st Franchised: 1974	
Franchised Units:	480
Company-Owned Units	111
Total Units:	591
Dist.:	US-590; CAN-1; O'seas-0
North America:	38 States
Density:	67 in WA, 60 in IA, 39 in MN
Projected New Units (12 Months):	27
Qualifications:	5, 5, 5, 3, ,
Registered:	CA,FL,IL,IN,MD,MI,MN,
OR,SD,WA	

FINANCIAL/TERMS:	
Cash Investment:	$55-120K
Total Investment:	$82.5-358K
Minimum Net Worth:	$200K
Fees: Franchise -	$20K
Royalty - 5%;	Ad. - 0%
Earnings Claim Statement:	No
Term of Contract (Years):	15/10
Avg. # Of Employees:	6 FT, 20 PT
Passive Ownership:	Discouraged
Encourage Conversions:	Yes
Area Develop. Agreements:	Yes/5
Sub-Franchising Contracts:	No
Expand In Territory:	Yes
Space Needs: 3,500 SF; FS, SC	

SUPPORT & TRAINING PROVIDED:	
Financial Assistance Provided:	No
Site Selection Assistance:	Yes
Lease Negotiation Assistance:	No
Co-Operative Advertising:	Yes

Franchisee Assoc./Member:	Yes
Size Of Corporate Staff:	92
On-Going Support:	D,G,I
Training: 35 Days Omaha, NE.	

SPECIFIC EXPANSION PLANS:	
US:	All United States
Canada:	No
Overseas:	No

<< >>

GOLDEN CHICK
11488 Luna Rd., # 100B
Dallas, TX 75234
Tel: (972) 831-0911
Fax: (972) 831-0401
Mr. Joe Malec, Dir. Franchise Dev.

GOLDEN CHICK is a fast-food chicken restaurant, offering indoor dining, drive-thru, carry-out and delivery service. GC's menu consists of fresh, golden fried chicken, golden tenders, country-style biscuits, gravy, french fries, cole slaw, mashed potatoes, corn on the cob, sandwiches and fountain soft drinks.

BACKGROUND:	
Established: 1967; 1st Franchised: 1972	
Franchised Units:	84
Company-Owned Units	7
Total Units:	91
Dist.:	US-80; CAN-0; O'seas-4
North America:	3 States
Density:	76 in TX, 3 in OK, 4 in MX
Projected New Units (12 Months):	6
Qualifications:	4, 4, 5, 2, 2, 5
Registered: NR	

FINANCIAL/TERMS:	
Cash Investment:	$NR
Total Investment:	$400-750K
Minimum Net Worth:	$N/A
Fees: Franchise -	$15K
Royalty - 4%;	Ad. - 1%
Earnings Claim Statement:	Yes
Term of Contract (Years):	20/N/A
Avg. # Of Employees:	NR
Passive Ownership:	Not Allowed
Encourage Conversions:	No
Area Develop. Agreements:	No
Sub-Franchising Contracts:	No
Expand In Territory:	No
Space Needs: 1,800 SF; FS	

SUPPORT & TRAINING PROVIDED:	
Financial Assistance Provided:	No
Site Selection Assistance:	Yes
Lease Negotiation Assistance:	No
Co-Operative Advertising:	Yes
Franchisee Assoc./Member:	No
Size Of Corporate Staff:	22

On-Going Support: C,D,d,E,F,G,H
Training: 6 Weeks Dallas, TX.
SPECIFIC EXPANSION PLANS:
US: South, Southwest
Canada: No
Overseas: No

⋘ ⋙

GORIN'S HOMEMADE CAFE & GRILL

57 Executive Park S., # 440
Atlanta, GA 30329
Tel: (888) 489-7277 (404) 248-9900
Fax: (404) 248-0180
Web Site: www.gorins.com
Mr. Mark Kaplan, Chairman

GORIN'S offers a unique, high quality sandwich concept, featuring its proprietary Melt Sandwiches such as the Almond Chicken Melt, Turkey Bacon Melt and the Honey Ham Melt. Additionally, GORIN'S serves a full line of deli sandwiches, cheesesteaks, soups and a proprietary line of ice cream. Combines the comfort and quality of casual dining with the price and convenience of quick serve.

BACKGROUND: IFA MEMBER
Established: 1981; 1st Franchised: 1983
Franchised Units: 30
Company-Owned Units   <u>1</u>
Total Units: 31
Dist.:   US-30; CAN-0; O'seas-1
  North America: 4 States
  Density: 32 in GA, 4 in AL, 1 in NC
Projected New Units (12 Months): 8-10
Qualifications: 5, 4, 3, 3, 3, 4
Registered: FL
FINANCIAL/TERMS:
Cash Investment: $85-95K
Total Investment: $190-250K
Minimum Net Worth: $300K
Fees: Franchise - $17.5K
  Royalty - 5%;   Ad. - 0.5-2.5%
Earnings Claim Statement: No
Term of Contract (Years):   10/10
Avg. # Of Employees: 7 FT, 6 PT
Passive Ownership: Discouraged
Encourage Conversions: Yes
Area Develop. Agreements: Yes/Varies
Sub-Franchising Contracts: No
Expand In Territory: Yes
Space Needs: 1,800-2,400 SF; FS, SF, SC, RM, OB
SUPPORT & TRAINING PROVIDED:
Financial Assistance Provided: Yes(I)
Site Selection Assistance: Yes

Lease Negotiation Assistance: Yes
Co-Operative Advertising: Yes
Franchisee Assoc./Member: Yes/Yes
Size Of Corporate Staff: 11
On-Going Support: C,D,E,F,G
Training: 3 Weeks Atlanta, GA.
SPECIFIC EXPANSION PLANS:
US: Southeast
Canada: No
Overseas: Asia, Europe, Open Countries

⋘ ⋙

GRANDMA LEE'S BAKERY RESTAURANT

2059 Lakeshore Rd.
Burlington, ON L7R 1E1 CANADA
Tel: (800) 894-7063 (905) 634-4111
Fax: (905) 634-1101
E-Mail: info@heritageconceptsintl.com
Web Site: www.heritageconceptsintl.com
Mr. Ashley Kelly, VP of Restaurant Operations

GRANDMA LEE'S BAKERY CAFE is Canada's largest soup and sandwich franchise chain. We are a 25 year old Canadian public company with stores in Canada, the U. S. and Australia. Our new cafe concept represents the leading edge in Canada for the fastest-growing segment of the food industry.

BACKGROUND:
Established: 1971; 1st Franchised: 1971
Franchised Units: 36
Company-Owned Units   <u>0</u>
Total Units: 36
Dist.:   US-2; CAN-34; O'seas-0
  North America: 1 State, 5 Provinces
  Density: 11 in AB, 9 inON, 9 in SK
Projected New Units (12 Months): 5
Qualifications: 3, 3, 1, 2, 1, 5
Registered: AB
FINANCIAL/TERMS:
Cash Investment: $45-75K
Total Investment: $125-225K
Minimum Net Worth: $45K
Fees: Franchise - $25K
  Royalty - 6.5%;   Ad. - 1.5%
Earnings Claim Statement: No
Term of Contract (Years):   10/10
Avg. # Of Employees: 4 FT, 4 PT
Passive Ownership: Allowed
Encourage Conversions: Yes
Area Develop. Agreements: Yes/20
Sub-Franchising Contracts: Yes
Expand In Territory: Yes
Space Needs: NR SF; FS, SF, Office

Towers
SUPPORT & TRAINING PROVIDED:
Financial Assistance Provided: Yes
Site Selection Assistance: Yes
Lease Negotiation Assistance: Yes
Co-Operative Advertising: Yes
Franchisee Assoc./Member: Yes/Yes
Size Of Corporate Staff: 6
On-Going Support: B,C,D,E,F,G,H,I
Training: 6 Weeks Closest Approved Training Store.
SPECIFIC EXPANSION PLANS:
US: All United States
Canada: All Canada
Overseas: Asia, Pacific Rim

⋘ ⋙

GREAT OUTDOOR SUB SHOPS

900 E. Parker Rd.
Plano, TX 75074
Tel: (888) 260-3354 (972) 424-7823
Fax: (972) 424-7798
Ms. Gail Voelcker, President

G. O. FRANCHISE, INC. is a quick-service restaurant which offers freshly-prepared submarine sandwiches, salads and ice cream under the trade name GREAT OUTDOOR SUB SHOP. Over the last 26 years, we have excelled and perfected the system and are now offering G. O. FRANCHISE opportunities to qualified individuals who are interested in the franchise restaurant industry.

BACKGROUND:
Established: 1973; 1st Franchised: 1996
Franchised Units: 4
Company-Owned Units   <u>8</u>
Total Units: 12
Dist.:   US-12; CAN-0; O'seas-0
  North America: 1 State
  Density: 12 in TX
Projected New Units (12 Months): 3
Qualifications: 4, 5, 4, 2, 5, 5
Registered: NR
FINANCIAL/TERMS:
Cash Investment: $75-265K
Total Investment: $75-265K
Minimum Net Worth: $150K
Fees: Franchise - $25K
  Royalty - 4%;   Ad. - 3%
Earnings Claim Statement: Yes
Term of Contract (Years):   10/10
Avg. # Of Employees: 6 FT, 5 PT
Passive Ownership: Not Allowed
Encourage Conversions: Yes
Area Develop. Agreements: Yes/10

Sub-Franchising Contracts:	No
Expand In Territory:	Yes
Space Needs: 2,000 +/- SF; FS, SC	

SUPPORT & TRAINING PROVIDED:

Financial Assistance Provided:	No
Site Selection Assistance:	Yes
Lease Negotiation Assistance:	Yes
Co-Operative Advertising:	N/A
Franchisee Assoc./Member:	No
Size Of Corporate Staff:	8
On-Going Support:	C,d,e
Training: 6 Weeks Dallas, TX.	

SPECIFIC EXPANSION PLANS:

US:	All United States
Canada:	No
Overseas:	No

<< >>

GREAT WRAPS!

4 Executive Park E., # 315
Atlanta, GA 30329
Tel: (888) GT-WRAPS (404) 248-9900
Fax: (404) 248-0180
E-Mail: franchise@greatwraps.net
Web Site: www.greatwraps.net
Mr. Mark Kaplan, Chairman

GREAT WRAPS, the original and #1 'Wrap Sandwich' franchise is leading this explosive, new food category into malls, shopping centers, airports and business districts. Features full line of wraps, burritos, cheesesteaks and smoothies. GREAT WRAPS offers you a proven business system, excellent training, marketing support and tremendous growth potential.

BACKGROUND: IFA MEMBER

Established: 1978; 1st Franchised: 1986	
Franchised Units:	39
Company-Owned Units	1
Total Units:	40
Dist.:	US-40; CAN-0; O'seas-0
North America:	8 States
Density:	19 in GA, 9 in FL, 3 in NC
Projected New Units (12 Months):	8-10
Qualifications:	5, 3, 3, 3, 4, 4
Registered: FL,VA	

FINANCIAL/TERMS:

Cash Investment:	$70-80K
Total Investment:	$175-275K
Minimum Net Worth:	$250K

Fees: Franchise -	$17.5K
Royalty - 5%;	Ad. - 0.5-2%
Earnings Claim Statement:	No
Term of Contract (Years):	10/10
Avg. # Of Employees:	5 FT, 6 PT
Passive Ownership:	Discouraged
Encourage Conversions:	Yes
Area Develop. Agreements:	Yes/Varies
Sub-Franchising Contracts:	No
Expand In Territory:	Yes
Space Needs: 600-1,500 SF; RM, SC, Airport, Univer.	

SUPPORT & TRAINING PROVIDED:

Financial Assistance Provided:	Yes(I)
Site Selection Assistance:	Yes
Lease Negotiation Assistance:	Yes
Co-Operative Advertising:	Yes
Franchisee Assoc./Member:	Yes
Size Of Corporate Staff:	11
On-Going Support:	B,C,D,E,G,H
Training: 3 Weeks Atlanta, GA.	

SPECIFIC EXPANSION PLANS:

US:	NE,SE,SW,MW
Canada:	No
Overseas:	No

<< >>

GRECO PIZZA DONAIR

105 Walker St., P.O. Box 1040
Truro, NS B2N 5G9 CANADA
Tel: (902) 893-4141
Fax: (902) 895-7635
E-Mail: grinners@greco.ca
Web Site: www.greco.ca
Mr. Guy Gallant, Director of Development

Atlantic Canada's largest home delivery pizza chain, specializing in pizza, donair products, oven sub sandwiches and pita-wrapped sandwiches.

BACKGROUND:

Established: 1977; 1st Franchised: 1981	
Franchised Units:	54
Company-Owned Units	2
Total Units:	56
Dist.:	US-0; CAN-54; O'seas-0
North America:	4 Provinces
Density:	21 in NB, 23 in NS, 5 in NF
Projected New Units (12 Months):	5
Registered: NR	

FINANCIAL/TERMS:

Cash Investment:	$40K
Total Investment:	$150-180K
Minimum Net Worth:	$40K
Fees: Franchise -	$15K
Royalty - 5%;	Ad. - 3%
Earnings Claim Statement:	No

Term of Contract (Years):	10/5/5
Avg. # Of Employees:	5 FT, 10 PT
Passive Ownership:	Discouraged
Encourage Conversions:	Yes
Area Develop. Agreements:	Yes/Varies
Sub-Franchising Contracts:	Yes
Expand In Territory:	Yes
Space Needs: 1,200 SF; FS, SF, SC, RM	

SUPPORT & TRAINING PROVIDED:

Financial Assistance Provided:	No
Site Selection Assistance:	Yes
Lease Negotiation Assistance:	Yes
Co-Operative Advertising:	Yes
Franchisee Assoc./Member:	NR
Size Of Corporate Staff:	19
On-Going Support:	a,b,C,D,E,F,G,h,I
Training: 4 Weeks Correspondence; 2 Days Headquarters; 3 Weeks On-Site.	

SPECIFIC EXPANSION PLANS:

US:	No
Canada:	PQ, Atlantic Can
Overseas:	No

<< >>

HAMBURGER STAND

4440 Von Karman Ave., # 222
Newport Bech, CA 92660
Tel: (800) 764-9353 (949) 752-5800
Fax: (949) 851-2618
E-Mail: fcoyle@galardigroup.com
Web Site: www.hamburgerstand.com
Mr. Frank R. Coyle, Franchise Sales Director

HAMBURGER STAND has successfully positioned itself in the highly competitive quick-serve hamburger business by providing the highest-quality products at lower than market prices. As a Division of Galardi Group, HAMBURGER STAND is part of a network of over 300 restaurants.

BACKGROUND:

Established: 1982; 1st Franchised: 1982	
Franchised Units:	23
Company-Owned Units	0
Total Units:	23
Dist.:	US-23; CAN-0; O'seas-0
North America:	NR
Density:	NR
Projected New Units (12 Months):	1
Qualifications:	4, 3, 3, 2, 1, 4
Registered: CA	

FINANCIAL/TERMS:

Cash Investment:	$150-200K
Total Investment:	$250-800K
Minimum Net Worth:	$150K
Fees: Franchise -	$20K
Royalty - 5%;	Ad. - 5%

Earnings Claim Statement: No
Term of Contract (Years): 20
Avg. # Of Employees: 2 FT, 25-35 PT
Passive Ownership: Discouraged
Encourage Conversions: Yes
Area Develop. Agreements: Yes/5
Sub-Franchising Contracts: No
Expand In Territory: Yes
Space Needs: 20,000 SF; FS

SUPPORT & TRAINING PROVIDED:
Financial Assistance Provided: Yes(I)
Site Selection Assistance: Yes
Lease Negotiation Assistance: No
Co-Operative Advertising: Yes
Franchisee Assoc./Member: Yes/Yes
Size Of Corporate Staff: 48
On-Going Support: A,B,C,d,E,F,H,I
Training: 5 Weeks Denver, CO; 1 Week Newport Beach, CA.

SPECIFIC EXPANSION PLANS:
US: Denver, Tucson Only.
Canada: No
Overseas: No

<< >>

HAPPY JOE'S PIZZA & ICE CREAM PARLOR
2705 Happy Joe Dr.
Bettendorf, IA 52722
Tel: (319) 332-8811
Fax: (319) 332-5822
Web Site: www.happyjoes.com
Mr. Tim Anderson, Dir. of Franchising

Pizza and ice cream in a fun atmosphere. Birthday party packages available. Very involved with special programs for youth in the community. Diversified pizza, pasta, sandwiches, salad bar and ice cream menu, candy, soft drinks and beer. Several parlors offer Family Fun Centers with redemption games and adventure-style golf.

BACKGROUND:
Established: 1972; 1st Franchised: 1973
Franchised Units: 52
Company-Owned Units: 14
Total Units: 66
Dist.: US-64; CAN-0; O'seas-0
North America: 6 States, 1 Province
Density: 34 in IA, 12 in IL, 7 in WI
Projected New Units (12 Months): 3
Qualifications: 5, 4, 3, 3, 3, 4
Registered: IL,ND,WI

FINANCIAL/TERMS:
Cash Investment: $50K
Total Investment: $50K-1.5MM
Minimum Net Worth: $200K
Fees: Franchise - $20K

Royalty - 4.5%; Ad. - 1%
Earnings Claim Statement: No
Term of Contract (Years): 15/10
Avg. # Of Employees: 4 FT, 30 PT
Passive Ownership: Discouraged
Encourage Conversions: Yes
Area Develop. Agreements: Yes/15
Sub-Franchising Contracts: No
Expand In Territory: Yes
Space Needs: 3,500 SF; FS, SF, SC

SUPPORT & TRAINING PROVIDED:
Financial Assistance Provided: Yes(I)
Site Selection Assistance: Yes
Lease Negotiation Assistance: Yes
Co-Operative Advertising: Yes
Franchisee Assoc./Member: Yes/Yes
Size Of Corporate Staff: 30
On-Going Support: B,C,D,E,G,h
Training: 6-12 Weeks in IA.

SPECIFIC EXPANSION PLANS:
US: Midwest
Canada: No
Overseas: No

<< >>

HARDEE'S FOOD SYSTEMS
1233 Hardee's Blvd.
Rocky Mount, NC 27804-2815
Tel: (800) 997-8435 (252) 977-2000
Fax: (252) 450-8655
Web Site: www.hardeesrestaurants.com
Mr. Don McLean, Franchise Manager

Fast food.

BACKGROUND: IFA MEMBER
Established: 1960; 1st Franchised: 1961
Franchised Units: 1,466
Company-Owned Units: 1,418
Total Units: 2,884
Dist.: US-2,778; CAN-0; O'seas-106
North America: 38 States
Density: 315 in NC, 207 in VA,186 SC
Projected New Units (12 Months): 50-70
Qualifications: 5, 5, 5, 1, 1, 5
Registered: All States

FINANCIAL/TERMS:
Cash Investment: $300K
Total Investment: $1.19-1.25MM
Minimum Net Worth: $1MM
Fees: Franchise - $35K
Royalty - 4%; Ad. - 5%
Earnings Claim Statement: No
Term of Contract (Years): 20/5
Avg. # Of Employees: 40 PT Total
Passive Ownership: Allowed
Encourage Conversions: N/A
Area Develop. Agreements: Yes/Varies
Sub-Franchising Contracts: No

Expand In Territory: Yes
Space Needs: 2,000 SF; FS, SC, RM, Univer.

SUPPORT & TRAINING PROVIDED:
Financial Assistance Provided: No
Site Selection Assistance: Yes
Lease Negotiation Assistance: No
Co-Operative Advertising: Yes
Franchisee Assoc./Member: Yes/No
Size Of Corporate Staff: 300
On-Going Support: A,B,C,D,E,f,h,I
Training: 3 Days Local Restaurant Orientation; 360 Hours Formal Training.

SPECIFIC EXPANSION PLANS:
US: Southeast, Midwest
Canada: No
Overseas: Bahrain, Costa Rica, Hong Kong, Korea, Kuwait, Lebanon, Oman, Qatar, Saudi Arabia, United Arab Em.

<< >>

HARTZ CHICKEN
14451 Cornerstone Village Dr., # 250
Houston, TX 77014
Tel: (281) 583-0020
Fax: (281) 580-3752
E-Mail: hartz@hartz-chicken.com
Web Site: www.hartz-chicken.com
Mr. John Bergeron, Controller

All-you-can-eat chicken buffet restaurant, featuring crispy and rotisserie chicken, Southern-style fish, fresh steamed vegetables, cold salads, casseroles, homestyle desserts and fresh homemade yeast rolls. Drive-thru and take-out service available at units. Delivery available in 1/3 of the domestic units. International program expanding - units open in Malaysia, Indonesia and China.

BACKGROUND: IFA MEMBER
Established: 1972; 1st Franchised: 1975
Franchised Units: 50
Company-Owned Units: 1
Total Units: 51
Dist.: US-42; CAN-0; O'seas-9
North America: 2 States
Density: 41 in TX, 1 in MS
Projected New Units (12 Months): 20
Qualifications: 4, 5, 3, 1, 3, 5
Registered: NR

FINANCIAL/TERMS:
Cash Investment: $250K
Total Investment: $300K-1MM
Minimum Net Worth: $250K
Fees: Franchise - $20K
Royalty - 4%; Ad. - 2-3%

Earnings Claim Statement: Yes
Term of Contract (Years): 20/5
Avg. # Of Employees: 7 FT, 6 PT
Passive Ownership: Discouraged
Encourage Conversions: Yes
Area Develop. Agreements: Yes
Sub-Franchising Contracts: Yes
Expand In Territory: Yes
Space Needs: 3,000 SF; FS

SUPPORT & TRAINING PROVIDED:
Financial Assistance Provided: No
Site Selection Assistance: Yes
Lease Negotiation Assistance: Yes
Co-Operative Advertising: Yes
Franchisee Assoc./Member: Yes
Size Of Corporate Staff: 10
On-Going Support: B,C,D,E,G,I
Training: 6 Weeks in Houston, TX.

SPECIFIC EXPANSION PLANS:
US: South
Canada: No
Overseas: Far East, Asia

<< >>

HO-LEE-CHOW
658 Danforth Ave., # 201
Toronto, ON M4J 5B9 CANADA
Tel: (800)HO-LEE-CHOW (416)
778-6660
Fax: (416) 778-6818
Mr. Jake Cappiello, President

Great Chinese food delivered fast and fresh. Each entree in our restaurants is cooked-to-order with no added MSG or preservatives. Each order is delivered in under 45 minutes. All locations are brightly lit and have our open kitchen concept so customers can view their food being cooked in the most pristine kitchens.

BACKGROUND:
Established: 1989; 1st Franchised: 1989
Franchised Units: 19
Company-Owned Units 4
Total Units: 23
Dist.: US-1; CAN-22; O'seas-0
 North America: 1 State, 1 Province
 Density: 22 in ON
Projected New Units (12 Months): 15
Qualifications: 3, 3, 1, 2, 3, 5
Registered: NR
FINANCIAL/TERMS:
Cash Investment: $75-100K
Total Investment: $150-175K

Minimum Net Worth: $100K
Fees: Franchise - $Included
 Royalty - 6%; Ad. - 3%
Earnings Claim Statement: Yes
Term of Contract (Years): 5/15
Avg. # Of Employees: 3 FT, 1 PT
Passive Ownership: Discouraged
Encourage Conversions: Yes
Area Develop. Agreements: Yes/20
Sub-Franchising Contracts: Yes
Expand In Territory: Yes
Space Needs: 900 SF; FS, SF, SC

SUPPORT & TRAINING PROVIDED:
Financial Assistance Provided: Yes(I)
Site Selection Assistance: Yes
Lease Negotiation Assistance: Yes
Co-Operative Advertising: Yes
Franchisee Assoc./Member: Yes/Yes
Size Of Corporate Staff: 50+
On-Going Support: A,B,C,D,E,F,G,H,I
Training: 1 Week Head Office in Toronto, ON; 4 Weeks On-Site.

SPECIFIC EXPANSION PLANS:
US: All United States
Canada: ON
Overseas: No

<< >>

HUNGRY HOWIE'S PIZZA & SUBS
30300 Stephenson Highway, # 200
Madison Heights, MI 48071
Tel: (800) 624-8122 (248) 414-3300
Fax: (248) 414-3301
E-Mail:
franchiseinfo@hungryhowies.com
Web Site: www.hungryhowies.com
Mr. Bob Cuffaro, Franchise Development

HUNGRY HOWIE'S, the innovator of the award-winning Flavored-Crust Pizza, is the nation's 9th largest carry-out / delivery pizza company. Menu offerings include 8 varieties of Flavored-Crust pizzas, delicious oven-baked subs and fresh and crispy salads.

BACKGROUND: IFA MEMBER
Established: 1973; 1st Franchised: 1982
Franchised Units: 435
Company-Owned Units 0
Total Units: 435
Dist.: US-434; CAN-1; O'seas-0
 North America: 19 States, 1 Province
 Density: 180 in FL, 180 in MI, 15 CA
Projected New Units (12 Months): 20
Qualifications: 4, 3, 2, 3, 4, 5

Registered: CA,FL,IL,IN,MD,MI,MN,NY,
 OR,RI,VA,WA,WI,DC
FINANCIAL/TERMS:
Cash Investment: $50K
Total Investment: $85-125K
Minimum Net Worth: $150K
Fees: Franchise - $15K
 Royalty - 5%; Ad. - 3%
Earnings Claim Statement: No
Term of Contract (Years): 20/20
Avg. # Of Employees: 4 FT, 8 PT
Passive Ownership: Discouraged
Encourage Conversions: Yes
Area Develop. Agreements: Yes/20
Sub-Franchising Contracts: Yes
Expand In Territory: Yes
Space Needs: 1,200 SF; SC

SUPPORT & TRAINING PROVIDED:
Financial Assistance Provided: Yes(I)
Site Selection Assistance: Yes
Lease Negotiation Assistance: Yes
Co-Operative Advertising: Yes
Franchisee Assoc./Member: No
Size Of Corporate Staff: 20
On-Going Support: B,C,D,E,F,G,h
Training: 5 Weeks Madison Heights, MI.
SPECIFIC EXPANSION PLANS:
US: All United States
Canada: No
Overseas: No

<< >>

INTERSTATE DAIRY QUEEN
4601 Willard Ave.
Chevy Chase, MD 20815
Tel: (800) 423-6171 (301) 913-9800
Fax: (301) 913-5424
E-Mail: wtellegen@interstatedq.com
Web Site: www.interstatedq.com
Mr. Walt Tellegen, President

Treat and fast-food franchising specialist in highway fuel-stop locations. Unique marketing program to attract highway travelers. Over 20 years of experience in co-branding.

BACKGROUND:
Established: 1977; 1st Franchised: 1977
Franchised Units: 165
Company-Owned Units 0
Total Units: 165
Dist.: US-165; CAN-0; O'seas-0

North America: 28 States
Density: 21 in GA, 16 in FL, 13 in TN
Projected New Units (12 Months): 14
Qualifications: 3, 3, 2, 3, 1, 4
Registered: CA,FL,IL,IN,MD,MI,NY, RI,DC

FINANCIAL/TERMS:

Cash Investment: $75-150K
Total Investment: $150-500K
Minimum Net Worth: $Varies
Fees: Franchise - $25K
Royalty - 4-7%; Ad. - 3-6%
Earnings Claim Statement: No
Term of Contract (Years): Permanent
Avg. # Of Employees: 20-30 PT
Passive Ownership: Allowed
Encourage Conversions: Yes
Area Develop. Agreements: No
Sub-Franchising Contracts: No
Expand In Territory: Yes
Space Needs: Varies SF; N/A

SUPPORT & TRAINING PROVIDED:

Financial Assistance Provided: No
Site Selection Assistance: Yes
Lease Negotiation Assistance: Yes
Co-Operative Advertising: No
Franchisee Assoc./Member: Yes/Yes
Size Of Corporate Staff: 15
On-Going Support: a,B,C,D,e,F,G,H,I
Training: 3 Weeks in Minneapolis, MN.

SPECIFIC EXPANSION PLANS:

US: Most Interstate Highways
Canada: No
Overseas: No

<< >>

JERSEY MIKE'S SUBMARINES & SALADS

1973 Hwy. 34, # E 21
Wall, NJ 07719
Tel: (800) 321-7676 (732) 282-2323
Fax: (732) 282-2244
E-Mail: jmikes@injersey.com
Web Site: www.jerseymikes.com
Mr. Victor F. Merlo, Vice President Sales

JERSEY MIKE'S is a submarine sandwich franchise company which prides itself on producing the freshest submarine sandwich in the industry. They bake bread daily in the store. Roast beefs are cooked on premises and meats and cheeses are sliced in front of the customer. Awards include 'Best Sub' in Nashville, Charlotte, RTP, Wilmington, Greenville and Ocean/Monmouth, NJ.

BACKGROUND:

Established: 1956; 1st Franchised: 1986
Franchised Units: 125

Company-Owned Units 6
Total Units: 131
Dist.: US-131; CAN-0; O'seas-0
North America: 13 States
Density: 83 in NC, 25 in OH, 15 in TN
Projected New Units (12 Months): NR
Registered:

FINANCIAL/TERMS:

Cash Investment: $NR
Total Investment: $150-200K
Minimum Net Worth: $NR
Fees: Franchise - $18.5K
Royalty - 5.5%; Ad. - 3.5%
Earnings Claim Statement: NR
Term of Contract (Years): 10/10
Avg. # Of Employees: 7 FT, 8 PT
Passive Ownership: Discouraged
Encourage Conversions: NR
Area Develop. Agreements: Yes/10
Sub-Franchising Contracts: No
Expand In Territory: NR
Space Needs: 1,500 SF; FS, SC

SUPPORT & TRAINING PROVIDED:

Financial Assistance Provided: NR
Site Selection Assistance: Yes
Lease Negotiation Assistance: Yes
Co-Operative Advertising: Yes
Franchisee Assoc./Member: No
Size Of Corporate Staff: 30
On-Going Support: B,C,D,E,G,H,I
Training: 3-4 Weeks Nashville, TN.

SPECIFIC EXPANSION PLANS:

US: All United States
Canada: NR
Overseas: NR

<< >>

JIMMY JOHN'S GOURMET SANDWICH SHOPS

600 Tollgate Rd., # B
Elgin, IL 60123
Tel: (800) 546-6904 (847) 888-7206
Fax: (847) 888-7070
E-Mail: hmarks@jimmyjohns.com
Web Site: www.jimmyjohns.com
Mr. Howard Marks, VP Franchise Dev.

World's greatest gourmet sandwich shop. All the sandwiches are made on fresh-

baked french bread or 7-grain honey wheat bread. We only use the highest-quality meats available with garden fresh veggies that are brought in and sliced each morning.

BACKGROUND: IFA MEMBER
Established: 1983; 1st Franchised: 1993
Franchised Units: 88
Company-Owned Units 10
Total Units: 98
Dist.: US-91; CAN-0; O'seas-7
North America: 16 States
Density: 39 in IL, 12 in WI, 10 in MI
Projected New Units (12 Months): 25
Qualifications: 5, 4, 2, 4, 4, 5
Registered: FL,IL,IN,MI,MN,RI, VA,WI,DC

FINANCIAL/TERMS:

Cash Investment: $25-50K
Total Investment: $116-303K
Minimum Net Worth: $100K
Fees: Franchise - $15-25K
Royalty - 6%; Ad. - 4.5%
Earnings Claim Statement: Yes
Term of Contract (Years): 10/5/5
Avg. # Of Employees: 2 FT, 20 PT
Passive Ownership: Discouraged
Encourage Conversions: N/A
Area Develop. Agreements: Yes/Varies
Sub-Franchising Contracts: No
Expand In Territory: Yes
Space Needs: 800-1,200 SF; FS, SC, SF

SUPPORT & TRAINING PROVIDED:

Financial Assistance Provided: No
Site Selection Assistance: Yes
Lease Negotiation Assistance: No
Co-Operative Advertising: Yes
Franchisee Assoc./Member: Yes
Size Of Corporate Staff: 12
On-Going Support: C,D,E,F,G,H,I
Training: 3 Weeks in Champaign, IL.

SPECIFIC EXPANSION PLANS:

US: All United States
Canada: All Canada
Overseas: All Countries

<< >>

KFC

1441 Gardiner Ln.
Louisville, KY 40213
Tel: (502) 874-8300
Fax: (502) 874-8732
Web Site: www.kfc.com
Mrs. Nikki Weis, Franchise Specialist

World's largest quick-service restaurant with a chicken-dominant menu. KFC offers full-service restaurants and non-traditional express units for captive markets.

BACKGROUND: IFA MEMBER

Established: 1954;	1st Franchised: 1959
Franchised Units:	6,663
Company-Owned Units	2,975
Total Units:	9638

Dist.: US-3,122; CAN-3,555; O'seas-3192
North America: 50 States,10 Provinces

Density:	CA, TX, IL
Projected New Units (12 Months):	100
Qualifications:	5, 4, 5, 3, 3, 5
Registered: All States	

FINANCIAL/TERMS:

Cash Investment:	$500K
Total Investment:	$700K-1.2MM
Minimum Net Worth:	$1MM
Fees: Franchise -	$25K
Royalty - 4%;	Ad. - 4.5%
Earnings Claim Statement:	No
Term of Contract (Years):	20/10
Avg. # Of Employees:	2 FT, 22 PT
Passive Ownership:	Not Allowed
Encourage Conversions:	No
Area Develop. Agreements:	No
Sub-Franchising Contracts:	No
Expand In Territory:	Yes
Space Needs: 2,000-3,000 SF; FS	

SUPPORT & TRAINING PROVIDED:

Financial Assistance Provided:	No
Site Selection Assistance:	Yes
Lease Negotiation Assistance:	No
Co-Operative Advertising:	Yes
Franchisee Assoc./Member:	Yes/Yes
Size Of Corporate Staff:	820
On-Going Support:	C,d,E,G,h,I
Training: 14 Weeks at Varied Sites.	

SPECIFIC EXPANSION PLANS:

US:	All United States
Canada:	All Canada
Overseas:	All Countries

<< >>

KOYA JAPAN

720 Broadway, # 207
Winnipeg, MB R3G 0X1 CANADA
Tel: (888) KOYA-USA (204) 783-4433
Fax: (204) 783-1749
E-Mail: jo-ann@koyajapan.com
Web Site: www.koyajapan.com
Mr. Steve M. Sabbagh, President

Delicious Japanese food served fast from the freshest of ingredients and complimented by or unique sauce. What makes us successful is our cooking techniques, each meal is made to order in full view of the customer. KOYA JAPAN -- where freshness sizzles before your eyes.

BACKGROUND:

Established: 1985;	1st Franchised: 1986
Franchised Units:	24
Company-Owned Units	0
Total Units:	24

Dist.:   US-2; CAN-22; O'seas-0
North America: 6 Provinces

Density:	7 in BC, 6 in MB, 5 in ON
Projected New Units (12 Months):	12
Qualifications:	4, 4, 3, 2, 3, 5
Registered: FL	

FINANCIAL/TERMS:

Cash Investment:	$50% of Total
Total Investment:	$165-250K
Minimum Net Worth:	$100K
Fees: Franchise -	$25K
Royalty - 6-7%;	Ad. - 2%
Earnings Claim Statement:	No
Term of Contract (Years):	Up to 10
Avg. # Of Employees:	3 FT, 1 PT
Passive Ownership:	Allowed
Encourage Conversions:	Yes
Area Develop. Agreements:	Yes/20
Sub-Franchising Contracts:	No
Expand In Territory:	Yes
Space Needs: 300-400 SF; RM	

SUPPORT & TRAINING PROVIDED:

Financial Assistance Provided:	No
Site Selection Assistance:	Yes
Lease Negotiation Assistance:	Yes
Co-Operative Advertising:	Yes
Franchisee Assoc./Member:	No
Size Of Corporate Staff:	3
On-Going Support:	C,d,E,I
Training: Up to 1 Month in Operating Location; up to 1 Month On-Site; 2-3 Days at Head Office.	

SPECIFIC EXPANSION PLANS:

US:	All United States
Canada:	All Canada

Overseas: Bahrain, United Arab Emirates, Kuwait, Quatar, Saudi Arabia

<< >>

LA PIZZA LOCA

7920 Orangethorpe Ave., # 202
Buena Park, CA 90620
Tel: (800) 676-LOCA (714) 670-0934
Fax: (714) 670-7849
Mr. Armando Delgado, Controller/CFO

Pizza delivery and carry-out restaurant, featuring unique and distinctive Latin-flavored pizzas. LA PIZZA LOCA's special Hispanic niche in the delivery segment of the pizza industry capitalizes on three large and rapidly-growing markets - pizza, home delivery and the Hispanic community. Home of 'La Gigante' and 'La Mexicana' pizzas.

BACKGROUND:

Established: 1986;	1st Franchised: 1991
Franchised Units:	15
Company-Owned Units	35
Total Units:	50

Dist.:   US-53; CAN-0; O'seas-0
North America: 3 States

Density:	NR
Projected New Units (12 Months):	6
Registered: CA,FL	

FINANCIAL/TERMS:

Cash Investment:	$40K+
Total Investment:	$120-145K
Minimum Net Worth:	$175K
Fees: Franchise -	$10K
Royalty - 5%;	Ad. - 5%
Earnings Claim Statement:	No
Term of Contract (Years):	10/10
Avg. # Of Employees:	2 FT, 13 PT
Passive Ownership:	Allowed
Encourage Conversions:	Yes
Area Develop. Agreements:	Yes/5
Sub-Franchising Contracts:	No
Expand In Territory:	No
Space Needs: 1,000 SF; FS, SC	

SUPPORT & TRAINING PROVIDED:

Financial Assistance Provided:	No
Site Selection Assistance:	Yes
Lease Negotiation Assistance:	Yes
Co-Operative Advertising:	Yes
Franchisee Assoc./Member:	No
Size Of Corporate Staff:	25
On-Going Support:	B,C,D,e,H,I
Training: 4 Weeks Buena Park, CA; 2 Weeks On-Site; On-Going On-Site.	

SPECIFIC EXPANSION PLANS:

US:	Southwest
Canada:	No
Overseas:	No

<< >>

LA SALSA FRESH MEXICAN GRILL

3938 State St., # 200
Santa Barbara, CA 93105
Tel: (800) LA-SALSA (805) 563-3644
Fax: (805) 898-2365
Web Site: www.lasalsa.com
Mr. Frank Holdraker, Vice President Franchising

Quick-service fresh Mexican grill restaurant.

BACKGROUND:

Established: 1979; 1st Franchised: 1988	
Franchised Units:	64
Company-Owned Units	32
Total Units:	96
Dist.:	US-96; CAN-0; O'seas-0
North America:	NR
Density:	62 in CA, 7 in AZ, 6 in UT
Projected New Units (12 Months):	36
Qualifications:	4, 4, 4, 2, 2, 5
Registered: CA,FL,IL,IN,MD,MI,MN,NY, VA,WA,WI	

FINANCIAL/TERMS:

Cash Investment:	$NR
Total Investment:	$222-371K
Minimum Net Worth:	$Varies
Fees: Franchise -	$29.5K
Royalty - 5%;	Ad. - 1%
Earnings Claim Statement:	Yes
Term of Contract (Years):	10/10
Avg. # Of Employees:	12 FT, 4 PT
Passive Ownership:	Not Allowed
Encourage Conversions:	Yes
Area Develop. Agreements:	Yes/Varies
Sub-Franchising Contracts:	No
Expand In Territory:	No
Space Needs: 1,800-2,000 SF; SF, SC, RM	

SUPPORT & TRAINING PROVIDED:

Financial Assistance Provided:	No
Site Selection Assistance:	No
Lease Negotiation Assistance:	No
Co-Operative Advertising:	Yes
Franchisee Assoc./Member:	No
Size Of Corporate Staff:	NR
On-Going Support:	B,C,D,E,G,H,I
Training: 5-8 Weeks Los Angeles, CA.	

SPECIFIC EXPANSION PLANS:

US:	All United States
Canada:	All Canada
Overseas:	No

◄◄ ►►

LARRY'S GIANT SUBS
8616 Baymeadows Rd.
Jacksonville, FL 32256
Tel: (800) 358-6870 (904) 739-9069
Fax: (904) 739-1218
E-Mail: lgskong@aol.com
Web Site: www.larryssubs.com
Mr. Mitchell Raikes, Vice President

Upscale submarine sandwich shop. Trendy décor with one of a kind custom table tops + huge ape wall display. Use only the finest products - USDA choice roast beef, imported ham & cheese and 100% real turkey.

BACKGROUND:

Established: 1981; 1st Franchised: 1986	
Franchised Units:	81
Company-Owned Units	2
Total Units:	83
Dist.:	US-83; CAN-0; O'seas-1
North America:	4 States
Density:	71 in FL, 10 in GA, 2 in TX
Projected New Units (12 Months):	20
Qualifications:	3, 3, 2, 2, 1, 5
Registered: FL	

FINANCIAL/TERMS:

Cash Investment:	$25-40K
Total Investment:	$100-130K
Minimum Net Worth:	$150K
Fees: Franchise -	$17K
Royalty - 6%;	Ad. - 2%
Earnings Claim Statement:	No
Term of Contract (Years):	10/Varies
Avg. # Of Employees:	4 FT, 10 PT
Passive Ownership:	Discouraged
Encourage Conversions:	N/A
Area Develop. Agreements:	Yes/2
Sub-Franchising Contracts:	Yes
Expand In Territory:	Yes
Space Needs: 1,400 SF; FS, SF, SC	

SUPPORT & TRAINING PROVIDED:

Financial Assistance Provided:	No
Site Selection Assistance:	Yes
Lease Negotiation Assistance:	Yes
Co-Operative Advertising:	Yes
Franchisee Assoc./Member:	No
Size Of Corporate Staff:	6
On-Going Support:	B,C,D,E,F,G,H,I
Training: 30 Days at Corporate Office.	

SPECIFIC EXPANSION PLANS:

US:	Southeast
Canada:	No
Overseas:	No

◄◄ ►►

LE CROISSANT SHOP

LE CROISSANT SHOP
227 W. 40th St.
New York, NY 10018
Tel: (212) 719-5940
Fax: (212) 944-0269
E-Mail:
franchise_info@lecroissantshop.com
Web Site: www.lecroissantshop.com
Mr. Arnaud Thieffry, Vice President

French bakery cafe - specialty croissants, bread, soups, french sandwiches and gourmet salads. Breakfast-Lunch-Dinner.

BACKGROUND:

Established: 1981; 1st Franchised: 1984	
Franchised Units:	12
Company-Owned Units	3
Total Units:	15
Dist.:	US-15; CAN-0; O'seas-13
North America:	3 States
Density:	12 in NY, 1 in PA, 1 in FL
Projected New Units (12 Months):	2-3
Qualifications:	4, 4, 3, 3, 3, 5
Registered: FL,IL,MD,NY,VA	

FINANCIAL/TERMS:

Cash Investment:	$1/3 Invest.
Total Investment:	$140-576K
Minimum Net Worth:	$NR
Fees: Franchise -	$22.5K
Royalty - 5%;	Ad. - NR
Earnings Claim Statement:	No
Term of Contract (Years):	10/5/5
Avg. # Of Employees:	10 FT
Passive Ownership:	Allowed
Encourage Conversions:	No
Area Develop. Agreements:	Yes/10
Sub-Franchising Contracts:	No
Expand In Territory:	Yes
Space Needs: 500-2,000 SF; FS, SF, SC, RM	

SUPPORT & TRAINING PROVIDED:

Financial Assistance Provided:	No
Site Selection Assistance:	Yes
Lease Negotiation Assistance:	Yes
Co-Operative Advertising:	N/A
Franchisee Assoc./Member:	No
Size Of Corporate Staff:	6
On-Going Support:	C,D,E
Training: 2 Weeks Headquarters in NY.	

SPECIFIC EXPANSION PLANS:

US:	East Coast
Canada:	No
Overseas:	South America, India, Asia

◄◄ ►►

LEE'S
Famous Recipe Chicken

LEE'S FAMOUS RECIPE CHICKEN
6045 Barfield Rd.
Atlanta, GA 30328
Tel: (404) 459-5807
Fax: (404) 259-5797

E-Mail: kspencer@rtminc.com
Web Site: www.winners-international.com
Ms. Karen Spencer, VP Franchise Sales

Quick-service restaurant - chicken segment. Focused on the quick, convenient distribution of food.

BACKGROUND:

Established: 1966; 1st Franchised: 1995	
Franchised Units:	142
Company-Owned Units	18
Total Units:	160
Dist.:	US-155; CAN-5; O'seas-0
North America:	16 States, 1 Province
Density:	52 in KY, 46 in OH, 18 in IN
Projected New Units (12 Months):	5
Qualifications:	5, 4, 4, 2, 2, 5
Registered: IL,IN,VA,WA	

FINANCIAL/TERMS:

Cash Investment:	$10K
Total Investment:	$410K-1.1MM
Minimum Net Worth:	$500K
Fees: Franchise -	$20K
Royalty - 4-5%;	Ad. - 1%
Earnings Claim Statement:	No
Term of Contract (Years):	20/20
Avg. # Of Employees:	8-10 FT, 30 PT
Passive Ownership:	Discouraged
Encourage Conversions:	Yes
Area Develop. Agreements:	Yes
Sub-Franchising Contracts:	No
Expand In Territory:	Yes
Space Needs: 1,800 SF; FS	

SUPPORT & TRAINING PROVIDED:

Financial Assistance Provided:	No
Site Selection Assistance:	Yes
Lease Negotiation Assistance:	No
Co-Operative Advertising:	Yes
Franchisee Assoc./Member:	Yes/Yes
Size Of Corporate Staff:	40
On-Going Support:	C,D,E,G,H
Training: 6 Weeks Certified Training Units.	

SPECIFIC EXPANSION PLANS:

US:	Midwest
Canada:	All Canada
Overseas:	All Countries

≪ ≫

LINDY - GERTIE'S
8437 Park Ave.
Burr Ridge, IL 60521
Tel: (630) 323-8003
Fax: (630) 323-5449
Mr. Joseph Yesutis, President

LINDY-GERTIE restaurants sell LINDY's chili, the oldest (established in 1924) chili parlor in Chicago, and GERTIE'S Ice Cream (the oldest ice cream parlor in Chicago, established in 1901).

BACKGROUND:

Established: 1986; 1st Franchised: 1987	
Franchised Units:	9
Company-Owned Units	1
Total Units:	10
Dist.:	US-10; CAN-0; O'seas-0
North America:	1 State
Density:	10 in IL
Projected New Units (12 Months):	2
Qualifications:	4, 1, 1, 2, 4, 5
Registered: IL	

FINANCIAL/TERMS:

Cash Investment:	$40K
Total Investment:	$NR
Minimum Net Worth:	$100K
Fees: Franchise -	$9.5K
Royalty - 6%;	Ad. - 2%
Earnings Claim Statement:	No
Term of Contract (Years):	10/10
Avg. # Of Employees:	1 FT, 2 PT
Passive Ownership:	Not Allowed
Encourage Conversions:	Yes
Area Develop. Agreements:	No
Sub-Franchising Contracts:	No
Expand In Territory:	Yes
Space Needs: NR SF; FS, SF, SC, RM	

SUPPORT & TRAINING PROVIDED:

Financial Assistance Provided:	Yes(I)
Site Selection Assistance:	Yes
Lease Negotiation Assistance:	Yes
Co-Operative Advertising:	Yes
Franchisee Assoc./Member:	No
Size Of Corporate Staff:	1
On-Going Support:	D,E
Training: 1 Week 5858 S. Kedzie, Chicago, IL; 1 Week 3685 S. Archer, Chicago, IL.	

SPECIFIC EXPANSION PLANS:

US:	IL
Canada:	No
Overseas:	No

≪ ≫

LITTLE KING
11811 I St.
Omaha, NE 68137
Tel: (800) 788-9478 (402) 330-8019
Fax: (402) 330-3221
E-Mail: rw68137@aol.com
Web Site: www.littlekinginc.com
Mr. Sidney B. Wertheim, CEO

Deli and sub restaurant, featuring fresh, fast-food concept - sandwiches. Products are prepared in full view of customers, breads are all baked fresh on premises. All meats are sliced fresh to order. Top-of-the-line food quality, utilizing major nationally-known brands. Concept is adaptable to various locations and configurations.

BACKGROUND:

Established: 1977; 1st Franchised: 1978	
Franchised Units:	30
Company-Owned Units	0
Total Units:	30
Dist.:	US-30; CAN-0; O'seas-0
North America:	5 States
Density:	29 in NE, 3 in IA, 2 in SD
Projected New Units (12 Months):	5-7
Qualifications:	5, 4, 4, 4, 1, 5
Registered: NR	

FINANCIAL/TERMS:

Cash Investment:	$Varies
Total Investment:	$75-95K
Minimum Net Worth:	$100K
Fees: Franchise -	$12K
Royalty - 6%;	Ad. - 2.5%
Earnings Claim Statement:	No
Term of Contract (Years):	10/10
Avg. # Of Employees:	1-3 FT, 6-9 PT
Passive Ownership:	Discouraged
Encourage Conversions:	Yes
Area Develop. Agreements:	Yes
Sub-Franchising Contracts:	No
Expand In Territory:	Yes
Space Needs: 1,200-1,800 SF; FS, SF, SC	

SUPPORT & TRAINING PROVIDED:

Financial Assistance Provided:	Yes(I)
Site Selection Assistance:	Yes
Lease Negotiation Assistance:	Yes
Co-Operative Advertising:	Yes
Franchisee Assoc./Member:	No
Size Of Corporate Staff:	2
On-Going Support:	B,C,E,F,G,H,I
Training: 15 Days Omaha, NE Headquarters; 8 Days On-Site; Follow Up Training as Needed.	

SPECIFIC EXPANSION PLANS:

US:	All United States
Canada:	No
Overseas:	No

≪ ≫

LONG JOHN SILVER'S

P.O. Box 11988
Lexington, KY 40579
Tel: (800) 545-8360 (859) 543-6000
Fax: (859) 543-6190
E-Mail: fsales@ljsilvers.com
Web Site: www.ljsilvers.com
Mr. John Caldwell, VP Franchise
Operations

LONG JOHN SILVER'S is the largest, quick-service seafood restaurant chain in the world. We continue to aggressively grow with new units and sales. Opportunities are available in new and existing markets.

BACKGROUND: IFA MEMBER
Established: 1969;   1st Franchised: 1970
Franchised Units: 473
Company-Owned Units   760
Total Units: 1,233
Dist.:   US-1,262; CAN-0; O'seas-18
  North America: 35 States
  Density: 185 in TX, 114 in OH, 101 IN
Projected New Units (12 Months):   NR
Qualifications: 5, 5, 5, 4, 5, 5
Registered: NR
FINANCIAL/TERMS:
Cash Investment: $NR
Total Investment: $500-800K
Minimum Net Worth: $400K
Fees: Franchise - $20K
  Royalty - 4%;   Ad. - 5%
Earnings Claim Statement: NR
Term of Contract (Years):   15/5/5
Avg. # Of Employees: NR
Passive Ownership: NR
Encourage Conversions: NR
Area Develop. Agreements: Yes
Sub-Franchising Contracts: No
Expand In Territory: Yes
Space Needs: NR SF; FS, C-Store, Food
  Court
SUPPORT & TRAINING PROVIDED:
Financial Assistance Provided: No
Site Selection Assistance: Yes
Lease Negotiation Assistance: NR
Co-Operative Advertising: NR
Franchisee Assoc./Member: Yes
Size Of Corporate Staff: 250
On-Going Support: C,D,E,G,h,I
Training: 5 Weeks Closest Training Shop
  to Franchisee.
SPECIFIC EXPANSION PLANS:
US: All United States
Canada: No
Overseas: Asia, Europe, Caribbean, Latin
  America, Middle East

MAGIC WOK

2060 Laskey Rd.
Toledo, OH 43613
Tel: (419) 471-0696
Fax: (419) 471-0405
E-Mail: tpipatjz@pop3.utoledo.edu
Mr. Tommy Pipatjarasgit, Vice President

Quick-service, made-to-order, hot oriental concept. Stand alone, mall, drive-thru, delivery, school lunch and other non-traditional operations. Low barrier to entry, high return on investment. Domestic and international.

BACKGROUND:
Established: 1983;   1st Franchised: 1991
Franchised Units: 7
Company-Owned Units   7
Total Units: 14
Dist.:   US-11; CAN-0; O'seas-2
  North America: 5 States
  Density: 7 in OH, 3 in MI
Projected New Units (12 Months):   2
Qualifications: 3, 2, 2, 2, 2, 4
Registered: FL,IL,IN,MD,MI,VA
FINANCIAL/TERMS:
Cash Investment: $50K
Total Investment: $95-150K
Minimum Net Worth: $100K
Fees: Franchise - $12.5K
  Royalty - 5%;   Ad. - 3%
Earnings Claim Statement: No
Term of Contract (Years):   10/10
Avg. # Of Employees: 2 FT, 8 PT
Passive Ownership: Discouraged
Encourage Conversions: Yes
Area Develop. Agreements: Yes
Sub-Franchising Contracts: Yes
Expand In Territory: Yes
Space Needs: 1,600 SF; FS
SUPPORT & TRAINING PROVIDED:
Financial Assistance Provided: No
Site Selection Assistance: Yes
Lease Negotiation Assistance: Yes
Co-Operative Advertising: Yes
Franchisee Assoc./Member: No
Size Of Corporate Staff: 7
On-Going Support: C,D,E,F,H,I
Training: 3-4 Weeks Toledo, OH.
SPECIFIC EXPANSION PLANS:
US: Midwest
Canada: No
Overseas: Saudi Arabia, Mexico

◄◄ ►►

MAMMA ILARDO'S
3600 Clipper Mill Rd., # 260
Baltimore, MD 21211

Tel: (410) 662-1930
Fax: (410) 662-1936
Web Site: www.mammailardos.com
Mr. John A. Filipiak, VP Operations and
  Development

MAMMA ILARDO'S freshly prepares delicious pizza. Choose from a variety of whole pies and pizza by the slice, featuring New York-style and our signature pan pizza. We offer great side items to complement our pizza, including calzones, pasta, salads and subs. 2 types of franchise systems - Pizzeria and Express. Franchise fee, Investment and royalties significantly lower for Express.

BACKGROUND:
Established: 1976;   1st Franchised: 1984
Franchised Units: 53
Company-Owned Units   3
Total Units: 56
Dist.:   US-53; CAN-0; O'seas-3
  North America: 16 States, Wash. DC
  Density: 13 in MD, 7 in NV, 7 in IN
Projected New Units (12 Months):   40
Qualifications: 3, 4, 4, 4, 4, 5
Registered: CA,FL,HI,IL,MD,MI,
  NY,OR,DC
FINANCIAL/TERMS:
Cash Investment: $40-100K
Total Investment: $175-320K
Minimum Net Worth: $150K
Fees: Franchise - $4-25K
  Royalty - 5-8%;   Ad. - 2%
Earnings Claim Statement: No
Term of Contract (Years):   10/10
Avg. # Of Employees: 8 FT, 10 PT
Passive Ownership: Discouraged
Encourage Conversions: Yes
Area Develop. Agreements: Yes/10
Sub-Franchising Contracts: Yes
Expand In Territory: Yes
Space Needs: 350-1,200 SF; SF, RM, Cart
SUPPORT & TRAINING PROVIDED:
Financial Assistance Provided: Yes(I)
Site Selection Assistance: Yes
Lease Negotiation Assistance: Yes
Co-Operative Advertising: N/A
Franchisee Assoc./Member: No
Size Of Corporate Staff: 10
On-Going Support: B,C,D,E,F,G,H
Training: 3 Days to 3 Weeks at Corporate
  Office and Stores in Baltimore, MD.
SPECIFIC EXPANSION PLANS:
US: All United States
Canada: All Canada
Overseas: All Countries

◄◄ ►►

MANCHU WOK (USA)

816 S. Military Trail, # 6
Deerfield Beach, FL 33442
Tel: (800) 423-4009 (954) 481-9555
Fax: (954) 481-9670
E-Mail: alechudson@manchuwok.com
Web Site: www.manchuwok.com/
index2.html
Mr. Alec Hudson, Franchise Sales Mgr.

MANCHU WOK is one of the largest Chinese quick service franchises in North America. MANCHU WOK operates in over 225 food court locations in large regional malls. MANCHU WOK franchisees are enjoying profitable growth; many owning multiple locations.

BACKGROUND: IFA MEMBER
Established: 1980; 1st Franchised: 1980
Franchised Units: 142
Company-Owned Units 47
Total Units: 189
Dist.: US-111; CAN-76; O'seas-2
  North America: 28 States,10 Provinces
  Density: 45 in ON, 14 in FL, 13 in IL
Projected New Units (12 Months): 50
Qualifications: 4, 4, 4, 3, 4, 4
Registered: All States and AB
FINANCIAL/TERMS:
Cash Investment: $100-150K
Total Investment: $260-306K
Minimum Net Worth: $100-150K
Fees: Franchise - $20K
  Royalty - 7%; Ad. - 1%
Earnings Claim Statement: Yes
Term of Contract (Years): 5/5
Avg. # Of Employees: 2-3 FT, 6-10 PT
Passive Ownership: Discouraged
Encourage Conversions: Yes
Area Develop. Agreements: No
Sub-Franchising Contracts: No
Expand In Territory: Yes
Space Needs: 600 SF; RM
SUPPORT & TRAINING PROVIDED:
Financial Assistance Provided: Yes(I)
Site Selection Assistance: Yes
Lease Negotiation Assistance: Yes
Co-Operative Advertising: N/A
Franchisee Assoc./Member: No
Size Of Corporate Staff: 500

On-Going Support: B,C,D,E,F,G,H,I
Training: 3-4 Weeks at Corporate Site.
SPECIFIC EXPANSION PLANS:
US: Northeast, Southeast
Canada: All Canada
Overseas: All Countries

<< >>

MANNY AND OLGA'S PIZZA

13707 N. Gate Dr.
Silver Spring, MD 20906
Tel: (301) 588-2500
Fax: (301) 608-8203
E-Mail: mannyandolgas@webtvnt.com
Mr. Bobby Athanasakis, President

MANNY AND OLGA'S PIZZA offers a full menu of pizza, subs, salads, pasta, wings, gyros and desserts - everything made fresh daily. Delivery or carry-out.

BACKGROUND: IFA MEMBER
Established: 1983; 1st Franchised: 1998
Franchised Units: 2
Company-Owned Units 3
Total Units: 5
Dist.: US-5; CAN-0; O'seas-0
  North America: 3 States
  Density: NR
Projected New Units (12 Months): 4
Qualifications: 5, 2, 1, 3, 3, 3
Registered: MD,DC,VA
FINANCIAL/TERMS:
Cash Investment: $50K
Total Investment: $90-160K
Minimum Net Worth: $100K
Fees: Franchise - $15K
  Royalty - 5%; Ad. - 4%
Earnings Claim Statement: No
Term of Contract (Years): 10/10
Avg. # Of Employees: 3 FT, 3 PT
Passive Ownership: Not Allowed
Encourage Conversions: Yes
Area Develop. Agreements: Yes/10
Sub-Franchising Contracts: Yes
Expand In Territory: Yes
Space Needs: 700 SF; FS, SF, SC, RM
SUPPORT & TRAINING PROVIDED:
Financial Assistance Provided: No
Site Selection Assistance: Yes
Lease Negotiation Assistance: Yes
Co-Operative Advertising: Yes
Franchisee Assoc./Member: No
Size Of Corporate Staff: 8
On-Going Support: E
Training: 3 Weeks Silver Spring, MD.
SPECIFIC EXPANSION PLANS:
US: Northeast

Canada: No
Overseas: No

<< >>

Marco's Pizza

MARCO'S PIZZA

5252 Monroe St.
Toledo, OH 43623
Tel: (800) 262-7267 (419) 885-7000
Fax: (419) 885-5215
Web Site: www.marcos.com
Mr. Eric F. Schmitt, Dir. of Fran. Sales

MARCO'S PIZZA offers pizza, hot sub sandwiches, Cheezybread, salad and soft drinks. There are 3 crust style - hand spun, pan or crispy thin, and 2 types of crust flavors - garlic butter and parmesan. MARCO'S PIZZA offers carry-out and fast, hot delivery.

BACKGROUND:
Established: 1978; 1st Franchised: 1979
Franchised Units: 89
Company-Owned Units 41
Total Units: 130
Dist.: US-130; CAN-0; O'seas-0
  North America: 3 States
  Density: 83 in OH, 22 in MI, 6 in IN
Projected New Units (12 Months): 20-25
Qualifications: 5, 5, 5, 4, 3, 5
Registered: IN,MI
FINANCIAL/TERMS:
Cash Investment: $60-75K
Total Investment: $118.5-204.5K
Minimum Net Worth: $100K
Fees: Franchise - $15K
  Royalty - 3-5%; Ad. - 1%
Earnings Claim Statement: No
Term of Contract (Years): 10/10
Avg. # Of Employees: 6 FT, 10 PT
Passive Ownership: Not Allowed
Encourage Conversions: N/A
Area Develop. Agreements: Yes/10
Sub-Franchising Contracts: No
Expand In Territory: Yes
Space Needs: 1,200-1,400 SF; SF, SC
SUPPORT & TRAINING PROVIDED:
Financial Assistance Provided: Yes(I)
Site Selection Assistance: Yes
Lease Negotiation Assistance: Yes
Co-Operative Advertising: Yes
Franchisee Assoc./Member: No
Size Of Corporate Staff: 40
On-Going Support: B,C,D,E,F,H,I
Training: 2 Weeks Toledo, OH; 6 Weeks in Store.

SPECIFIC EXPANSION PLANS:

US: Midwest
Canada: No
Overseas: No

MAUI TACOS

1775 The Exchange, # 540
Atlanta, GA 30339
Tel: (888) 628-4822 (770) 226-8226
Fax: (770) 541-2300
E-Mail: normanw@mauitacos.com
Web Site: www.mauitacos.com
Mr. Norman D. Willden, VP Franchise
    Development

Fast-casual "Maui-Mex" restaurant featuring Mexican Foods created by internationally recognized chef Mark Ellmao, using pineapple and lime juice marinade with island spices. Char-grilled chicken, steak, and lean beef burritos topped with unique salsas is our mainstay. This food experience is like a vacation in Maui.

BACKGROUND: IFA MEMBER
Established: 1993;   1st Franchised: 1998
Franchised Units: 13
Company-Owned Units   1
Total Units: 14
Dist.:   US-14; CAN-0; O'seas-0
    North America: 2 States
    Density: 8 in HI, 3 in GA
Projected New Units (12 Months):   20
Qualifications: 4, 4, 3, 3, 4, 4
Registered: CA,FL,HI,IN,MD,MI,MN,NY,
    ND,OR,RI,VA,WA,WI,DC
FINANCIAL/TERMS:
Cash Investment: $60-125K
Total Investment: $180-375K
Minimum Net Worth: $300K
Fees: Franchise - $20K
    Royalty - 6%;   Ad. - 4%
Earnings Claim Statement: Yes
Term of Contract (Years):   20/20
Avg. # Of Employees: 4 FT, 10 PT
Passive Ownership: Discouraged
Encourage Conversions: Yes
Area Develop. Agreements: Yes/50
Sub-Franchising Contracts: Yes
Expand In Territory: Yes
Space Needs: 2,000 SF; FS, SF,SC, RM,
    HB, Open Air
SUPPORT & TRAINING PROVIDED:
Financial Assistance Provided: Yes(I)

Site Selection Assistance: Yes
Lease Negotiation Assistance: Yes
Co-Operative Advertising: Yes
Franchisee Assoc./Member: Yes/Yes
Size Of Corporate Staff: 6
On-Going Support: A,B,C,D,E,F,G,h,I
Training: 160 Hours in Atlanta, GA.
SPECIFIC EXPANSION PLANS:
US: All United States
Canada: All Canada
Overseas: All Countries

MAZZIO'S PIZZA

4441 S. 72nd E. Ave.
Tulsa, OK 74145-4692
Tel: (800) 827-1910 (918) 641-1248
Fax: (918) 641-1236
E-Mail: mlong@mazzios.com
Web Site: www.mazzios.com
Mr.   Mark   Long,   Manager   Brand
    Development/Lic.

MAZZIO'S PIZZA is an up-scale Italian restaurant, featuring 3 types of pizza, along with excellent pasta, calzone rings, sandwiches and salad. There is an emphasis on an attractive decor and surroundings as well as a distinctive exterior. Delivery is available from an existing dine-in unit.

BACKGROUND: IFA MEMBER
Established: 1961;   1st Franchised: 1979
Franchised Units: 140
Company-Owned Units   95
Total Units: 235
Dist.:   US-235; CAN-0; O'seas-0
    North America: 13 States
    Density: 116 in OK, 36 in AR, 29 MO
Projected New Units (12 Months):   5
Qualifications: 5, 5, 5, 4, 5, 5
Registered: CA,FL,IL,IN,MI,VA
FINANCIAL/TERMS:
Cash Investment: $200K
Total Investment: $309-976K
Minimum Net Worth: $400K
Fees: Franchise - $25K
    Royalty - 3%;   Ad. - 1%
Earnings Claim Statement: Yes
Term of Contract (Years):   20/5
Avg. # Of Employees: 2 FT, 25-35 PT
Passive Ownership: Discouraged
Encourage Conversions: Yes
Area Develop. Agreements: Yes/5
Sub-Franchising Contracts: No
Expand In Territory: Yes
Space Needs: 3,000 SF; FS, SF, SC
SUPPORT & TRAINING PROVIDED:
Financial Assistance Provided: No

Site Selection Assistance: Yes
Lease Negotiation Assistance: No
Co-Operative Advertising: Yes
Franchisee Assoc./Member: No
Size Of Corporate Staff: 75
On-Going Support: B,C,D,E,F,G,H,I
Training: 9   Weeks   at   Corporate
    Headquarters; 3.5 Weeks On-Site.
SPECIFIC EXPANSION PLANS:
US: South, SW, SE, Midwest
Canada: No
Overseas: No

MCDONALD'S

2915 Jorie Blvd.
Oak Brook, IL 60523
Tel: (630) 623-6196
Fax: (630) 623-5645
Web Site: www.mcdonalds.com
Franchise Department,

Quick-service restaurant.

BACKGROUND: IFA MEMBER
Established: 1955;   1st Franchised: 1956
Franchised Units: 20,531
Company-Owned Units   6,057
Total Units: 26,588
Dist.:US-12627; CAN-1125; O'seas-12836
    North America: 50 States
    Density: 1,204 in CA, 845 TX, 742 FL
Projected New Units (12 Months):   NR
Qualifications: 3, 5, 3, 3, 4, 4
Registered: All States
FINANCIAL/TERMS:
Cash Investment: $100K+
Total Investment: $477.8K-1.4MM
Minimum Net Worth: $N/A
Fees: Franchise - $45K
    Royalty - 12.5%;   Ad. - 4%
Earnings Claim Statement: No
Term of Contract (Years):   20/20
Avg. # Of Employees: NR
Passive Ownership: Not Allowed
Encourage Conversions: N/A
Area Develop. Agreements: No
Sub-Franchising Contracts: No
Expand In Territory: No
Space Needs: 2,000 SF; FS
SUPPORT & TRAINING PROVIDED:
Financial Assistance Provided: No

Site Selection Assistance:	N/A
Lease Negotiation Assistance:	N/A
Co-Operative Advertising:	Yes
Franchisee Assoc./Member:	Yes/Yes
Size Of Corporate Staff:	NR
On-Going Support:	b,C,d,E,G,h,I
Training: NR	

SPECIFIC EXPANSION PLANS:

US:	All United States
Canada:	All Canada
Overseas:	All Countries

≪ ≫

MICHEL'S BAGUETTE

16251 Dallas Parkway
Dallas, TX 75248
Tel: (972) 687-4091
Fax: (972) 687-4062
E-Mail: lboyd@richmont.com
Web Site: www.mmmuffins.com
Ms. Lori Boyd, Project Coordinator

European bakery/café, featuring authentic European breads, rolls, and pastries. In addition, we offer gourmet soups, salads, sandwiches, and hot entrees. We also serve a variety of beverages including espresso, gourmet coffee, teas and fruit juices. In addition to our full store, we have a "grab 'n' go" version as well.

BACKGROUND: IFA MEMBER

Established: 1980;	1st Franchised: 1984
Franchised Units:	13
Company-Owned Units	4
Total Units:	17
Dist.:	US-0; CAN-15; O'seas-0
North America:	3 Provinces
Density:	13 in ON, 3 in AB, 1 in BC
Projected New Units (12 Months):	10
Qualifications:	5, 4, 3, 3, 4, 5
Registered: AB	

FINANCIAL/TERMS:

Cash Investment:	$300K+
Total Investment:	$750-800K
Minimum Net Worth:	$500K
Fees: Franchise -	$40K
Royalty - 6%;	Ad. - 0.5%
Earnings Claim Statement:	No
Term of Contract (Years):	10/10
Avg. # Of Employees:	10 FT, 8-12 PT
Passive Ownership:	Not Allowed
Encourage Conversions:	Yes
Area Develop. Agreements:	Yes (Int'l.)
Sub-Franchising Contracts:	Yes
Expand In Territory:	Yes
Space Needs: 4,000 SF; SF, SC, RM	

SUPPORT & TRAINING PROVIDED:

Financial Assistance Provided:	No

Site Selection Assistance:	Yes
Lease Negotiation Assistance:	Yes
Co-Operative Advertising:	Yes
Franchisee Assoc./Member:	No
Size Of Corporate Staff:	35
On-Going Support:	A,B,C,D,E,F,G,h
Training: 3 Months Toronto, ON or Dallas, TX.	

SPECIFIC EXPANSION PLANS:

US:	N/A
Canada:	All Canada
Overseas:	Middle East, Europe, South America

≪ ≫

MOE'S ITALIAN SANDWICHES

15 Constitution Dr., # 140
Bedford, NH 03110
Tel: (800) 588-6637
Fax: (603) 472-8025
E-Mail: info@moesitaliansandwiches.com
Web Site:
www.moesitaliansandwiches.com
Mr. Stanley R. Dehold, President

High-quality sandwiches and soups, featuring our flagship sandwich 'The Original Moe.' We have a simply concept that has over 40 years of heritage in New England. Low overhead, turnkey system. Very flexible.

BACKGROUND:

Established: 1959;	1st Franchised: 1993
Franchised Units:	14
Company-Owned Units	0
Total Units:	14
Dist.:	US-14; CAN-0; O'seas-0
North America:	2 States
Density:	11 in NH, 3 in ME
Projected New Units (12 Months):	4
Qualifications:	4, 4, 3, 3, 4, 5
Registered: None	

FINANCIAL/TERMS:

Cash Investment:	$20-30K
Total Investment:	$35-100K
Minimum Net Worth:	$150K
Fees: Franchise -	$12.5K
Royalty - 5%;	Ad. - 1%
Earnings Claim Statement:	No
Term of Contract (Years):	10/5

Avg. # Of Employees:	2 FT, 4 PT
Passive Ownership:	Discouraged
Encourage Conversions:	Yes
Area Develop. Agreements:	No
Sub-Franchising Contracts:	No
Expand In Territory:	Yes
Space Needs: 1,000-1,400 SF; SF, SC, RM	

SUPPORT & TRAINING PROVIDED:

Financial Assistance Provided:	Yes(I)
Site Selection Assistance:	Yes
Lease Negotiation Assistance:	Yes
Co-Operative Advertising:	Yes
Franchisee Assoc./Member:	No
Size Of Corporate Staff:	2
On-Going Support:	C,D,E,F,G,H,I
Training: 2 Weeks in Store -- Various Locations; 3 Days in Class.	

SPECIFIC EXPANSION PLANS:

US:	NE. Expansion Outside 2002
Canada:	No
Overseas:	No

≪ ≫

MR. GOODCENTS SUBS & PASTAS

16210 W. 110th St.
Lenexa, KS 66219
Tel: (800) 648-2368 (913) 888-9800
Fax: (913) 888-8477
E-Mail: frandev@mrgoodcents.com
Web Site: www.mrgoodcents.com
Ms. Margot A. Bubien, Dir. Fran. Dev.

Quick-service lunch and dinner restaurant, serving freshly-sliced submarine sandwiches served on bread baked daily on premises, hot pasta dishes, delicious soups and fresh salads, quick-service restaurant for dine-in, carry-out, delivery or catering. Continued business consultant support and in-house 30-day training period.

BACKGROUND: IFA MEMBER

Established: 1989;	1st Franchised: 1990
Franchised Units:	135
Company-Owned Units	10
Total Units:	145
Dist.:	US-145; CAN-0; O'seas-0
North America:	13 States

Density: 43 in KS, 54 in MO, 8 in AZ
Projected New Units (12 Months): NR
Qualifications: 3, 3, 2, 2, 1, 5
Registered: All States

FINANCIAL/TERMS:

Cash Investment: $35-50K
Total Investment: $67.8-187.3K
Minimum Net Worth: $NR
Fees: Franchise - $12.5K
    Royalty - 5%; Ad. - 2.5%
Earnings Claim Statement: No
Term of Contract (Years): 10/10
Avg. # Of Employees: 1-3 FT, 10-20 PT
Passive Ownership: N/A
Encourage Conversions: Yes
Area Develop. Agreements: No
Sub-Franchising Contracts: No
Expand In Territory: Yes
Space Needs: 1,700-2,000 SF; FS, SC

SUPPORT & TRAINING PROVIDED:

Financial Assistance Provided: Yes(I)
Site Selection Assistance: Yes
Lease Negotiation Assistance: Yes
Co-Operative Advertising: Yes
Franchisee Assoc./Member: No
Size Of Corporate Staff: 40
On-Going Support: A,B,C,D,E,F,G,H,I
Training: 30 Days Kansas City, MO.

SPECIFIC EXPANSION PLANS:

US: All United States
Canada: No
Overseas: No

◁◁ ▷▷

MR. HERO
5755 Granger Rd., # 200
Independence, OH 44131-1410
Tel: (800) 837-9599 (216) 398-1101
Fax: (216) 398-0707
E-Mail: jalmrher@aol.com
Web Site: www.mrhero.com
Ms. Terri Sozio, Franchise Sales Admin.

MR. HERO is an exciting alternative to the typical quick-service restaurant. Our difference centers around the food. We have grill-based hot food offerings of Romanburgers, ribeye steak sandwiches, hot buttered cheesesteaks with waffer fries, cold subs and an assortment of sides and desserts. Café Morocco breakfast program included.

BACKGROUND: IFA MEMBER
Established: 1969; 1st Franchised: 1969
Franchised Units: 124
Company-Owned Units: 11
Total Units: 135
Dist.: US-135; CAN-0; O'seas-0
    North America: 7 States
    Density: 112 in OH, 5 in KY, 5 in MI
Projected New Units (12 Months): 15
Qualifications: 5, 3, 3, 2, 5, 4
Registered: IL,IN,MD,MI,NY,VA,DC

FINANCIAL/TERMS:

Cash Investment: $40-75K
Total Investment: $65-300K
Minimum Net Worth: $250K
Fees: Franchise - $16.5K
    Royalty - 5.5%; Ad. - 4.5%
Earnings Claim Statement: No
Term of Contract (Years): 20/20
Avg. # Of Employees: 4 Ft, 8 PT
Passive Ownership: Discouraged
Encourage Conversions: Yes
Area Develop. Agreements: Yes/3-5
Sub-Franchising Contracts: Yes
Expand In Territory: Yes
Space Needs: 1,500 SF; FS, SF, SC, RM, Co-Brand

SUPPORT & TRAINING PROVIDED:

Financial Assistance Provided: Yes(I)
Site Selection Assistance: Yes
Lease Negotiation Assistance: Yes
Co-Operative Advertising: Yes
Franchisee Assoc./Member: No
Size Of Corporate Staff: 40
On-Going Support: A,B,C,D,E,F,G,H,I
Training: 4 Weeks Cleveland, OH.

SPECIFIC EXPANSION PLANS:

US: NE, E, SE, S, MW
Canada: No
Overseas: No

◁◁ ▷▷

MR. JIM'S PIZZA
4276 Kellway Circle
Addison, TX 75001
Tel: (800) 583-5960 (972) 267-5467
Fax: (972) 267-5463
Web Site: www.mrjimspizza.net
Mr. Randall Wooley, Executive Director

Specializing in delivery and take-out operations. Low start-up cost of under $90,000, including franchise fee. Dallas, Ft. Worth's largest locally-owned pizza franchise.

BACKGROUND:
Established: 1974; 1st Franchised: 1976
Franchised Units: 64

Company-Owned Units: 0
Total Units: 64
Dist.: US-64; CAN-0; O'seas-0
    North America: NR
    Density: 58 in TX, 2 in LA, 2 in VA
Projected New Units (12 Months): 6
Qualifications: 4, 4, 5, 2, 3, 4
Registered: OR,VA

FINANCIAL/TERMS:

Cash Investment: $50K
Total Investment: $56-108K
Minimum Net Worth: $100K
Fees: Franchise - $10K
    Royalty - 5%; Ad. - 0%
Earnings Claim Statement: No
Term of Contract (Years): 15/15
Avg. # Of Employees: 5 FT, 15 PT
Passive Ownership: Discouraged
Encourage Conversions: Yes
Area Develop. Agreements: Yes
Sub-Franchising Contracts: No
Expand In Territory: Yes
Space Needs: 1,100 SF; SC

SUPPORT & TRAINING PROVIDED:

Financial Assistance Provided: No
Site Selection Assistance: Yes
Lease Negotiation Assistance: Yes
Co-Operative Advertising: Yes
Franchisee Assoc./Member: No
Size Of Corporate Staff: 6
On-Going Support: B,C,D,E,G,H
Training: 2 Months.

SPECIFIC EXPANSION PLANS:

US: All Except FL, MI
Canada: No
Overseas: No

◁◁ ▷▷

MRS. VANELLI'S FRESH ITALIAN FOODS
700 Kerr St.
Oakville, ON L6K 3W5 CANADA
Tel: (800) 555-5726 (905) 337-7777
Fax: (905) 337-0331
E-Mail: info@donatogroup.com
Web Site: www.mrsvanellis.com
Mr. Nik Jurkovic, Dir. New Business Development

Serving pizza, pasta, salad and sandwiches located in mall food courts, airports, universities, hospitals, theme parks and other similar high traffic settings.

BACKGROUND: IFA MEMBER
Established: 1981; 1st Franchised: 1983
Franchised Units: 93
Company-Owned Units 1
Total Units: 94
Dist.: US-0; CAN-87; O'seas-7
 North America: NR
 Density: 49 in ON, 14 in BC, 5 in AB
Projected New Units (12 Months): 8
Qualifications: 5, 2, 2, 2, 3, 4
Registered: IL,AB

FINANCIAL/TERMS:
Cash Investment: $50-100K
Total Investment: $175-250K
Minimum Net Worth: $200K
Fees: Franchise - $25K
 Royalty - 6%; Ad. - 1.5%
Earnings Claim Statement: No
Term of Contract (Years): 8-10/5-10
Avg. # Of Employees: 3 FT, 6 PT
Passive Ownership: Discouraged
Encourage Conversions: Yes
Area Develop. Agreements: Yes/15
Sub-Franchising Contracts: Yes
Expand In Territory: Yes
Space Needs: 400 SF; RM

SUPPORT & TRAINING PROVIDED:
Financial Assistance Provided: Yes(I)
Site Selection Assistance: Yes
Lease Negotiation Assistance: Yes
Co-Operative Advertising: N/A
Franchisee Assoc./Member: No/No
Size Of Corporate Staff: 40
On-Going Support: B,C,D,E,G,H,I
Training: 3-4 Days at Company HQ; 3-4
 Days at the Store; 1 Week during your
 Grand Opening.

SPECIFIC EXPANSION PLANS:
US: All United States
Canada: All Canada
Overseas: All Countries

⊰⊰ ⊱⊱

**MRS. WINNER'S CHICKEN &
BISCUITS**
6045 Barfield Rd.
Atlanta, GA 30328
Tel: (404) 459-5800
Fax: (404) 459-5797
E-Mail: kspencer@rtminc.com
Web Site: www.winners-international.com
Ms. Karen Spencer, VP Franchise Sales

Quick-service restaurant - chicken segment. Focused on the quick, convenient distribution of food.

BACKGROUND: IFA MEMBER
Established: 1977; 1st Franchised: 1989
Franchised Units: 44
Company-Owned Units 111
Total Units: 155
Dist.: US-155; CAN-0; O'seas-0
 North America: 5 States
 Density: 72 in GA, 51 in TN, 14 in AL
Projected New Units (12 Months): 8
Qualifications: 5, 4, 4, 2, 2, 5
Registered: FL,MD,VA

FINANCIAL/TERMS:
Cash Investment: $10K
Total Investment: $410K-1.1MM
Minimum Net Worth: $500K
Fees: Franchise - $20K
 Royalty - 4-5%; Ad. - 1%
Earnings Claim Statement: No
Term of Contract (Years): 20/20
Avg. # Of Employees: 8-10 FT, 30 PT
Passive Ownership: Discouraged
Encourage Conversions: Yes
Area Develop. Agreements: Yes
Sub-Franchising Contracts: No
Expand In Territory: Yes
Space Needs: 1,800 SF; FS

SUPPORT & TRAINING PROVIDED:
Financial Assistance Provided: No
Site Selection Assistance: Yes
Lease Negotiation Assistance: No
Co-Operative Advertising: Yes
Franchisee Assoc./Member: Yes/Yes
Size Of Corporate Staff: 40
On-Going Support: C,D,E,G,H
Training: 6 Weeks Certified Training
 Units.

SPECIFIC EXPANSION PLANS:
US: Southeast
Canada: All Canada
Overseas: All Countries

⊰⊰ ⊱⊱

MY FRIEND'S PLACE
106 Hammond Dr.
Atlanta, GA 30328
Tel: (404) 843-2803
Fax: (404) 843-0371
Mr. John Thomas, Dir. of Franchise Sales

A quality franchise opportunity for your financial independence and future. Our restaurants cater to the quality-oriented customer interested in a quick, yet light and healthy lunch, specializing in sandwiches, salads, soups and home-made desserts.

MY FRIEND'S PLACE is a 'Fresh Food Express!'

BACKGROUND:
Established: 1980; 1st Franchised: 1990
Franchised Units: 12
Company-Owned Units 1
Total Units: 13
Dist.: US-13; CAN-0; O'seas-0
 North America: 1 State
 Density: 13 in GA
Projected New Units (12 Months): 4
Qualifications: 3, 4, 3, 3, 2, 5
Registered: NR

FINANCIAL/TERMS:
Cash Investment: $95-175K
Total Investment: $95-175K
Minimum Net Worth: $200K
Fees: Franchise - $17.5K
 Royalty - Flat; Ad. - Flat
Earnings Claim Statement: No
Term of Contract (Years): 15/10
Avg. # Of Employees: 2 FT, 2 PT
Passive Ownership: Not Allowed
Encourage Conversions: Yes
Area Develop. Agreements: No
Sub-Franchising Contracts: Yes
Expand In Territory: Yes
Space Needs: 1,400 SF; SC, FS

SUPPORT & TRAINING PROVIDED:
Financial Assistance Provided: Yes(I)
Site Selection Assistance: Yes
Lease Negotiation Assistance: Yes
Co-Operative Advertising: Yes
Franchisee Assoc./Member: No
Size Of Corporate Staff: 4
On-Going Support: C,d,E,f
Training: 12 Business Days Headquarters;
 12 Business Days Franchisee Site.

SPECIFIC EXPANSION PLANS:
US: SE Only, GA,FL,AL,IN,SC,TX
Canada: No
Overseas: No

⊰⊰ ⊱⊱

NATHAN'S FAMOUS
1400 Old Country Rd., # 400
Westbury, NY 11590
Tel: (800) NATHANS (516) 338-8500
Fax: (516) 338-7220
E-Mail: nfidevel@webspan.net
Mr. Carl Paley, Senior Vice President

Fast-food restaurant, featuring premium-quality, all beef hot dogs, fresh-cut fries, plus a large variety of menu items - 9 prototypes, ranging from carts, counter modules, food courts and full-service restaurants. Franchise license and area development opportunities available worldwide.

BACKGROUND:
Established: 1916;   1st Franchised: 1979
Franchised Units: 189
Company-Owned Units   <u>25</u>
Total Units: 214
Dist.:   US-214; CAN-0; O'seas-0
  North America: 37 States
  Density: 27 in NY, 19 in NJ, 17 in FL
Projected New Units (12 Months):   35
Qualifications: 5, 3, 4, 2, 3, 5
Registered: CA,FL,HI,IL,IN,MD,MI,MN,
  NY,VA,WA,WI,DC
FINANCIAL/TERMS:
Cash Investment: $50-250K
Total Investment: $50-550K
Minimum Net Worth: $400K
Fees: Franchise - $15-30K
  Royalty - 4.5%;   Ad. - 2.5%
Earnings Claim Statement: No
Term of Contract (Years):   20/15
Avg. # Of Employees: 6-7 FT, 10-15 PT
Passive Ownership: Discouraged
Encourage Conversions: Yes
Area Develop. Agreements: Yes/Varies
Sub-Franchising Contracts: Yes
Expand In Territory: Yes
Space Needs: 500-2,500 SF; SF, RM
SUPPORT & TRAINING PROVIDED:
Financial Assistance Provided: Yes(I)
Site Selection Assistance: Yes
Lease Negotiation Assistance: Yes
Co-Operative Advertising: Yes
Franchisee Assoc./Member: No
Size Of Corporate Staff: 42
On-Going Support: B,C,D,E,F,G,H,I
Training: 2-4 Weeks in Long Island, NY
  and in Store.
SPECIFIC EXPANSION PLANS:
US: All United States
Canada: PQ,ON
Overseas: Europe, Asia

NATURE'S TABLE
800 N. Magnolia Ave.
Orlando, FL 32803
Tel: (800) 222-6090
Fax: (407) 843-6057
Mr. Michael W. Karr, Franchise Agent

NATURE'S TABLE is an expanding Florida-based chain with 20 years of experience. Our menu features healthy food such as vegetarian chili, homemade soups, harvest salads, frozen yogurt, smoothies and a variety of sandwiches.

BACKGROUND:
Established: 1977;   1st Franchised: 1985
Franchised Units: 42
Company-Owned Units   <u>6</u>
Total Units: 48
Dist.:   US-48; CAN-0; O'seas-0
  North America: 1 State
  Density: 34 in FL
Projected New Units (12 Months):   12
Qualifications: 5, 3, 3, 4, 5, 4
Registered: FL,MD,MI,MN,VA,WI,DC
FINANCIAL/TERMS:
Cash Investment: $100-175K
Total Investment: $100-175K
Minimum Net Worth: $100K
Fees: Franchise - $25K
  Royalty - 5%;   Ad. - 1%
Earnings Claim Statement: No
Term of Contract (Years):   10/5
Avg. # Of Employees: 2 FT, 2-4 PT
Passive Ownership: Allowed
Encourage Conversions: N/A
Area Develop. Agreements: Yes/10
Sub-Franchising Contracts: No
Expand In Territory: No
Space Needs: 500-750 SF; RM
SUPPORT & TRAINING PROVIDED:
Financial Assistance Provided: No
Site Selection Assistance: Yes
Lease Negotiation Assistance: Yes
Co-Operative Advertising: No
Franchisee Assoc./Member: Yes
Size Of Corporate Staff: 7
On-Going Support: C,D,E,F,G,h,I
Training: 2 Weeks Orlando, FL; On-Site.
SPECIFIC EXPANSION PLANS:
US: Southeast United States
Canada: No
Overseas: No

NEW YORK BURRITO GOURMET WRAPS
955 E. Javelina Ave., # 106
Mesa, AZ 85204
Tel: (800) 711-4036 (480) 503-3363
Fax: (480) 503-1850
E-Mail: nybfoods@nybfoods.com
Web Site: www.newyorkburrito.com
Ms. Sharon Snyder,

Casual/up-scale, quick-serve restaurants serving multi-cultural gourmet wraps (burritos). Some restaurants feature breakfast, fruit smoothies, and/or beer and wine. Menu items prepared daily with the highest-quality and variety meats and veggies. Giant tortillas offered in a variety of flavors: tomato basil, whole wheat, spinach, jalapeno and white flour. Low start-up cost and ease of operation. Join the hottest new food trend of the 90s with the leader of the pack.

BACKGROUND: IFA MEMBER
Established: 1995;   1st Franchised: 1996
Franchised Units: 78
Company-Owned Units   <u>1</u>
Total Units: 79
Dist.:   US-79; CAN-0; O'seas-0
  North America: 27 States
  Density: 8 in CA, 8 in CO, 5 in UT
Projected New Units (12 Months):   15
Qualifications: 4, 4, 2, 3, 3, 4
Registered: CA,FL,IN,MI,MN,NY,
  OR,SD,WI
FINANCIAL/TERMS:
Cash Investment: $25-35K
Total Investment: $75-135K
Minimum Net Worth: $Varies
Fees: Franchise - $15K
  Royalty - 7%;   Ad. - 4%
Earnings Claim Statement: No
Term of Contract (Years):   Perpetual
Avg. # Of Employees: Varies
Passive Ownership: Discouraged
Encourage Conversions: N/A
Area Develop. Agreements: Yes
Sub-Franchising Contracts: No
Expand In Territory: Yes
Space Needs: 1,500-2,500 SF; FS, SC, RM
SUPPORT & TRAINING PROVIDED:
Financial Assistance Provided: Yes
Site Selection Assistance: Yes
Lease Negotiation Assistance: Yes
Co-Operative Advertising: Yes
Franchisee Assoc./Member: No
Size Of Corporate Staff: 9+
On-Going Support: A,B,C,D,E,F,G,H,I
Training: 5 Days at Headquarters/Training
  Center; 5 Days at Franchise Store.
SPECIFIC EXPANSION PLANS:
US: All United States
Canada: All Except AB
Overseas: No

ORION FOOD SYSTEMS

2930 W. Maple Ave.
Sioux Falls, SD 57101
Tel: (800) 648-6227 (605) 336-6961
Fax: (605) 336-0141
Web Site: www.orionfoodsys.com
Mr. Tom Coyle, Nat'l. Development Mgr.

Franchise offers 9 separate brands covering all popular fast food categories: HOT STUFF PIZZA, EDDIE PEPPERS GREAT AMERICAN, CINNAMON STREET BAKERY + COFFEE COMPANY, MEAN GENE'S BURGERS, MACGREGOR'S MARKET SUBS, SMASH HITS SUBS, JOEY PAGODA'S ORIENTAL EXPRESS, CHIX THE CHICKEN STATION.

BACKGROUND: IFA MEMBER
Established: 1984;   1st Franchised: 1986
Franchised Units: 1,501
Company-Owned Units   12
Total Units: 1,513
Dist.:   US-1,493; CAN-7; O'seas-1
  North America: 50 States, 2 Provinces
  Density: 89 in MN, 38 in SD, 34 in WI
Projected New Units (12 Months):   240
Qualifications: 4, 4, 4, 3, 3, 5
Registered: All States and AB
FINANCIAL/TERMS:
Cash Investment: $20K
Total Investment: $35-300K
Minimum Net Worth: $30K
Fees: Franchise - $0
  Royalty - 0%;   Ad. - 0%
Earnings Claim Statement: No
Term of Contract (Years):   5/5
Avg. # Of Employees: 4 FT, 10 PT
Passive Ownership: Allowed
Encourage Conversions: Yes
Area Develop. Agreements: No
Sub-Franchising Contracts: No
Expand In Territory: Yes
Space Needs: 700 SF; RM
SUPPORT & TRAINING PROVIDED:
Financial Assistance Provided: Yes(I)
Site Selection Assistance: Yes
Lease Negotiation Assistance: Yes
Co-Operative Advertising: No
Franchisee Assoc./Member: Yes/Yes
Size Of Corporate Staff: 700
On-Going Support: B,C,D,E,F,G,I
Training: 2 Weeks at New Franchisee's Site.

SPECIFIC EXPANSION PLANS:
US: All United States
Canada: All Canada
Overseas: No

‹‹ ››

PANAGO PIZZA

33149 Mill Lake Rd.
Abbotsford, BC V2S 2A4 CANADA
Tel: (604) 859-6621
Fax: (604) 850-1244
E-Mail: reception@panago.com
Web Site: www.panago.com
Mr. Stojan Ninkovic, Franchise Development

Western Canada based chain of delivery and take out outlets offering pizza, salads, pasta, wings, etc. One number phone system, strong local and regional marketing support.

BACKGROUND:
Established: 1986;   1st Franchised: 1986
Franchised Units: 121
Company-Owned Units   4
Total Units: 125
Dist.:   US-0; CAN-125; O'seas-0
  North America: 4 Provinces
  Density: 82 in BC, 39 in AB, 3 in SK
Projected New Units (12 Months):   15
Qualifications: 5, 5, 4, 3, 1, 5
Registered: AB
FINANCIAL/TERMS:
Cash Investment: $80K
Total Investment: $214.5-280K
Minimum Net Worth: $80K
Fees: Franchise - $20K
  Royalty - 5%;   Ad. - 5%
Earnings Claim Statement: No
Term of Contract (Years):   Max. 5
Avg. # Of Employees: NR
Passive Ownership: Not Allowed
Encourage Conversions: N/A
Area Develop. Agreements: Yes/5
Sub-Franchising Contracts: Yes
Expand In Territory: Yes
Space Needs: 2,200 SF; SF
SUPPORT & TRAINING PROVIDED:
Financial Assistance Provided: Yes(I)
Site Selection Assistance: Yes
Lease Negotiation Assistance: No
Co-Operative Advertising: Yes
Franchisee Assoc./Member: No
Size Of Corporate Staff: NR
On-Going Support: C,D,E,h,I
Training: 6 Weeks in Abbotsford, BC.

SPECIFIC EXPANSION PLANS:
US: No
Canada: All Canada
Overseas: No

‹‹ ››

PASQUALE'S PIZZA & PASTA

983 Yeager Pkwy.
Pellham, AL 35124
Tel: (205) 664-1839
Mr. Millard Deason, President

PASQUALE'S specializes in the preparation and serving of oven-roasted Italian sandwiches, pizza and spaghetti. From day one, we are with you to help you succeed. Our mission is to build close alliances with franchisees that are dedicated to exceeding customer expectations by using the freshest ingredients, offering a uniquely diverse menu and unparalleled service.

BACKGROUND:
Established: 1990;   1st Franchised: 1990
Franchised Units: 32
Company-Owned Units   0
Total Units: 32
Dist.:   US-32; CAN-0; O'seas-0
  North America: 7 States
  Density: 13 in AL, 6 in IN, 5 in KY
Projected New Units (12 Months):   NR
Registered:
FINANCIAL/TERMS:
Cash Investment: $80.3-208K
Total Investment: $115.3-293K
Minimum Net Worth: $100K
Fees: Franchise - $5K
  Royalty - 5%/$150/Wk.; Ad. - 2% Max.
Earnings Claim Statement: No
Term of Contract (Years):   10/10
Avg. # Of Employees: 4-6 FT, 6-8 PT
Passive Ownership: Not Allowed
Encourage Conversions: NR
Area Develop. Agreements: No
Sub-Franchising Contracts: No
Expand In Territory: Yes
Space Needs: 2,000 SF; FS, SF, SC
SUPPORT & TRAINING PROVIDED:
Financial Assistance Provided: NR
Site Selection Assistance: Yes
Lease Negotiation Assistance: Yes
Co-Operative Advertising: Yes
Franchisee Assoc./Member: No
Size Of Corporate Staff: 4
On-Going Support: a,B,C,D,E,F,I
Training: 1 Day Financial Seminar, Pelham, AL; 10 Working Days at Actual Restaurant Location.

SPECIFIC EXPANSION PLANS:

US: AL,GA,MS,KY,IN,OH
Canada: NR
Overseas: NR

<< >>

PAUL REVERE'S PIZZA INTERNATIONAL

1574 42nd St. NE
Cedar Rapids, IA 52402
Tel: (800) 995-9437 (319) 395-9113
Fax: (319) 395-9115
E-Mail: patrickroof@mcleodusa.net
Web Site: www.paulreverespizza.com
Mr. Patrick Roof, Franchise Development

PAUL REVERE'S PIZZA is a low investment, high quality franchise. Our concept is designed to utilize low square footage buildings or spaces. Low overhead equals larger bottomlines. High quality menu items, competitive pricing and excellent service make PAUL REVERE'S PIZZA a great buy for a customer or prospective franchisee.

BACKGROUND:

Established: 1975;   1st Franchised: 1982
Franchised Units: 48
Company-Owned Units   0
Total Units: 48
Dist.:   US-0; CAN-0; O'seas-0
  North America: 4 States
  Density: 29 in IA; 15 in WI; 2 in MO
Projected New Units (12 Months):   NR
Registered:
FINANCIAL/TERMS:
Cash Investment: $25-75K
Total Investment: $110-210K
Minimum Net Worth: $70K
Fees: Franchise - $15K
  Royalty - 4%;   Ad. - 0%
Earnings Claim Statement: Yes
Term of Contract (Years):   10/10
Avg. # Of Employees: 6 FT, 8 PT
Passive Ownership: Discouraged
Encourage Conversions: NR
Area Develop. Agreements: Yes/10
Sub-Franchising Contracts: Yes
Expand In Territory: Yes
Space Needs: 1,100 SF; SF, SC
SUPPORT & TRAINING PROVIDED:
Financial Assistance Provided: NR
Site Selection Assistance: Yes
Lease Negotiation Assistance: Yes
Co-Operative Advertising: N/A
Franchisee Assoc./Member: No
Size Of Corporate Staff: 3
On-Going Support: B,C,D,d,E,F,G,H,I

Training: 10-14 Days in Cedar Rapids, IA.
SPECIFIC EXPANSION PLANS:
US: IA,WI,IL,MN,MO,AR,NE,KS
Canada: NR
Overseas: NR

<< >>

PENN STATION/EAST COAST SUBS

8276 Beechmont Ave.
Cincinnati, OH 45255-3153
Tel: (513) 474-5957
Fax: (513) 474-7116
Web Site: www.penn-station.com
Mr. Mark Partusch, Director Sales/Development

Retail sale of authentic 'East Coast-style' submarines, including the original Philadelphia cheesesteak, all prepared fresh before the customer. Fresh-cut fries, flash fried in peanut oil, and fresh-squeezed lemonade.

BACKGROUND:

Established: 1985;   1st Franchised: 1987
Franchised Units: 67
Company-Owned Units   3
Total Units: 70
Dist.:   US-70; CAN-0; O'seas-0
  North America: 4 States
  Density: 41 in OH, 14 in IN, 13 in KY
Projected New Units (12 Months):   25
Qualifications: 3, 5, 3, 4, 4, 5
Registered: IN
FINANCIAL/TERMS:
Cash Investment: $40-82.5K
Total Investment: $182.8-328.7K
Minimum Net Worth: $Varies
Fees: Franchise - $17.5K
  Royalty - 4-7.5%;   Ad. - 1%
Earnings Claim Statement: Yes
Term of Contract (Years):   5/5/5/5
Avg. # Of Employees: 11 FT, 10 PT
Passive Ownership: Allowed
Encourage Conversions: No
Area Develop. Agreements: Yes
Sub-Franchising Contracts: No
Expand In Territory: Yes
Space Needs: 1,600-1,800 SF; FS, SC
SUPPORT & TRAINING PROVIDED:
Financial Assistance Provided: No
Site Selection Assistance: Yes
Lease Negotiation Assistance: Yes
Co-Operative Advertising: Yes
Franchisee Assoc./Member: Yes/Yes
Size Of Corporate Staff: 13
On-Going Support: C,D,E,F,G,H
Training: 2 Weeks Penn Station in

Cincinnati, OH; 2-3 Days On-Site Training Prior to Grand Opening.
SPECIFIC EXPANSION PLANS:
US: Midwest, Southeast, South
Canada: No
Overseas: No

<< >>

PHILLY CONNECTION

120 Interstate N. Pkwy., E., # 112
Atlanta, GA 30339-2103
Tel: (800) 886-8826 (770) 952-6152
Fax: (770) 952-3168
E-Mail: phillycon@mindspring.com
Web Site: www.phillyconnection.com
Mr. John D. Pollock, SVP Franchise Development

Quick service restaurant and ice cream parlor. "The Cheesesteak Champion" serves fresh, high quality products prepared to order in front of customers. On premises, take out, drive though, delivery. May operate in strip shopping centers, convenience stores, free-standing buildings and "end cap" space. Franchisor helps in site location, lease negotiation, equipment purchasing, grand opening, initial and ongoing training, toll free helpline.

BACKGROUND: IFA MEMBER
Established: 1984;   1st Franchised: 1987
Franchised Units: 83
Company-Owned Units   2
Total Units: 85
Dist.:   US-85; CAN-0; O'seas-0
  North America: 5 States
  Density: 49 in GA, 13 in NC, 11 in FL
Projected New Units (12 Months):   30
Qualifications: 4, 5, 3, 3, 3, 5
Registered: FL
FINANCIAL/TERMS:
Cash Investment: $30-80K
Total Investment: $130-231K
Minimum Net Worth: $110K
Fees: Franchise - $20K
  Royalty - 5%;   Ad. - 5%
Earnings Claim Statement: No
Term of Contract (Years):   10/5
Avg. # Of Employees: 2 FT, 10 PT
Passive Ownership: Discouraged
Encourage Conversions: N/A
Area Develop. Agreements: Yes/3
Sub-Franchising Contracts: No
Expand In Territory: Yes
Space Needs: 1,000-1,600 SF; FS, SF, SC, C-Stores
SUPPORT & TRAINING PROVIDED:
Financial Assistance Provided: Yes(I)

Site Selection Assistance:	Yes
Lease Negotiation Assistance:	Yes
Co-Operative Advertising:	Yes
Franchisee Assoc./Member:	No
Size Of Corporate Staff:	14
On-Going Support:	a,B,C,D,E,F,G,H,I

Training: 2-6 Weeks Existing Restaurant;
    1 Week Corporate Headquarters.
SPECIFIC EXPANSION PLANS:

US:	Southeast
Canada:	All Canada
Overseas:	Europe

<< >>

PICKERMAN'S SOUP & SANDWICH SHOP

5714 Nordic Dr., #400
Cedar Falls, IA 50613
Tel: (800) 273-2172 (319) 266-7141
Fax: (319) 277-1201
E-Mail: bev@pickermans.com
Web Site: www.pickermans.com
Ms. Bev Bauer, Administrative Assistant

a high-end soup & sandwich shop which sells 12 specialty sandwiches, 15 gourmet soups and 3 gourmet salads. Catering available as well as in-house seating in a comfortable décor of oak and hunter green.

BACKGROUND:

Established: 1998; 1st Franchised: 1998	
Franchised Units:	25
Company-Owned Units	0
Total Units:	25
Dist.:	US-25; CAN-0; O'seas-0
North America:	5 States
Density:	11 in IA, 8 in IL, 2 in MN
Projected New Units (12 Months):	100
Qualifications:	2, 2, 1, 2, 3, 3
Registered: IL,MN	

FINANCIAL/TERMS:

Cash Investment:	$25-30K
Total Investment:	$110-130K
Minimum Net Worth:	$Not Required
Fees: Franchise -	$10K
Royalty - 4%;	Ad. - 0%
Earnings Claim Statement:	No
Term of Contract (Years):	10/10
Avg. # Of Employees:	3 FT, 4 PT
Passive Ownership:	Not Allowed
Encourage Conversions:	Yes
Area Develop. Agreements:	Yes/10
Sub-Franchising Contracts:	No
Expand In Territory:	Yes
Space Needs: 1,500 SF; SC	

SUPPORT & TRAINING PROVIDED:

Financial Assistance Provided:	Yes(I)

Site Selection Assistance:	Yes
Lease Negotiation Assistance:	Yes
Co-Operative Advertising:	No
Franchisee Assoc./Member:	No
Size Of Corporate Staff:	16
On-Going Support:	C,D,E,F,G,H,I

Training: 1 Week at Your Store; 1 Week
    Corporate Office.
SPECIFIC EXPANSION PLANS:

US:	All United States
Canada:	No
Overseas:	No

<< >>

PIZZA FACTORY

P.O. Box 989, 49430 Road 426
Oakhurst, CA 93644
Tel: (800) 654-4840 (559) 683-3377
Fax: (559) 683-6879
Web Site: www.pizzafactoryinc.com
Mr. Ron Willey, Vice President

We Toss 'Em, They're Awesome. PIZZA FACTORY has a proven track record with 90 restaurants in 12 states, The franchisee has a strong support system which includes site location, lease negotiating, on-site training and on-going support from headquarters. Call for brochure. Serving homemade pizza, pasta, sandwiches, beer and wine.

BACKGROUND:

Established: 1979; 1st Franchised: 1985	
Franchised Units:	93
Company-Owned Units	3
Total Units:	96
Dist.:	US-96; CAN-0; O'seas-0
North America:	12 States
Density:	53 in CA, 16 in WA, 8 in ID
Projected New Units (12 Months):	10
Qualifications:	5, 4, 4, 2, 2, 3
Registered:	AZ,CA,CO,FL,ID,MN, OR,SD,WA

FINANCIAL/TERMS:

Cash Investment:	$65-80K
Total Investment:	$130-226K
Minimum Net Worth:	$150K
Fees: Franchise -	$20K
Royalty - 4%;	Ad. - 1%
Earnings Claim Statement:	No
Term of Contract (Years):	20
Avg. # Of Employees:	3 FT, 12-15 PT
Passive Ownership:	Discouraged
Encourage Conversions:	Yes
Area Develop. Agreements:	Yes/Varies
Sub-Franchising Contracts:	No
Expand In Territory:	Yes
Space Needs: 2,400 SF; SC	

SUPPORT & TRAINING PROVIDED:

Financial Assistance Provided:	No
Site Selection Assistance:	Yes
Lease Negotiation Assistance:	Yes
Co-Operative Advertising:	Yes
Franchisee Assoc./Member:	NR
Size Of Corporate Staff:	7
On-Going Support:	C,D,E,G,H,I

Training: 325 Hours Training Stores,
    Training Fee: $2,500.
SPECIFIC EXPANSION PLANS:

US:	All United States
Canada:	All Canada
Overseas:	All Countries; China

<< >>

PIZZA MAN

6930 1/2 Tujunga Ave.
North Hollywood, CA 91605
Tel: (818) 766-4395
Fax: (818) 766-1496
Mr. Robert Ohanian, President/CEO

Pizza, chicken, ribs, Italian dishes. Delivery and fast food.

BACKGROUND:

Established: 1964; 1st Franchised: 1973	
Franchised Units:	50
Company-Owned Units	0
Total Units:	50
Dist.:	US-50; CAN-0; O'seas-0
North America:	1 State
Density:	50 in CA
Projected New Units (12 Months):	3
Qualifications:	3, 5, 5, 4, 5, 5
Registered: All States	

FINANCIAL/TERMS:

Cash Investment:	$70K
Total Investment:	$100K
Minimum Net Worth:	$150K
Fees: Franchise -	$25K
Royalty - 4%/$140/Wk.;	Ad. -
4%/$140/Wk.	
Earnings Claim Statement:	No
Term of Contract (Years):	1+/1+
Avg. # Of Employees:	3 FT, 2 PT
Passive Ownership:	Discouraged
Encourage Conversions:	Yes
Area Develop. Agreements:	Yes/2
Sub-Franchising Contracts:	No
Expand In Territory:	Yes
Space Needs: 1,000 SF; SF, SC	

SUPPORT & TRAINING PROVIDED:

Financial Assistance Provided:	Yes(I)
Site Selection Assistance:	Yes

219

Lease Negotiation Assistance: Yes
Co-Operative Advertising: Yes
Franchisee Assoc./Member: No
Size Of Corporate Staff: 8
On-Going Support: b,C,D,e,f,H
Training: 3 Weeks Los Angeles, CA.
SPECIFIC EXPANSION PLANS:
US: All United States
Canada: All Canada
Overseas: All Countries

≪ ≫

Good Things, Everyday!

PIZZA RANCH, THE
1121 Main St., Box 823
Hull, IA 51239
Tel: (800) 321-3401 (712) 439-1150
Fax: (712) 439-1125
E-Mail: pizzar@mtcnet.net
Web Site: www.pizza-ranch.com
Mr. Lawrence Vander Esch, Co-Founder

THE PIZZA RANCH is a family restaurant, specializing in pizza, pasta and chicken.

BACKGROUND:
Established: 1981;   1st Franchised: 1984
Franchised Units: 79
Company-Owned Units 6
Total Units: 85
Dist.: US-85; CAN-0; O'seas-0
  North America: 6 States
  Density: 40 in IA, 20 in MN, 16 in SD
Projected New Units (12 Months): 12
Qualifications: 3, 3, 3, 3, 2, 5
Registered: IL,MI,MN,ND,SD, WI
FINANCIAL/TERMS:
Cash Investment: $20-50K
Total Investment: $200-500K
Minimum Net Worth: $25K
Fees: Franchise - $10K
  Royalty - 4%; Ad. - $1.7-2.2K
Earnings Claim Statement: No
Term of Contract (Years): 10/10/10
Avg. # Of Employees: 2 FT, 20 PT
Passive Ownership: Allowed
Encourage Conversions: Yes
Area Develop. Agreements: Yes
Sub-Franchising Contracts: Yes
Expand In Territory: Yes
Space Needs: 4,000 SF; Any

SUPPORT & TRAINING PROVIDED:
Financial Assistance Provided: Yes(I)
Site Selection Assistance: Yes
Lease Negotiation Assistance: Yes
Co-Operative Advertising: Yes
Franchisee Assoc./Member: No
Size Of Corporate Staff: 15
On-Going Support: C,D,E,F,G,H,I
Training: 2 Weeks Sioux Center, IA.; 1
  Week On-Site.
SPECIFIC EXPANSION PLANS:
US: Midwest
Canada: No
Overseas: No

≪ ≫

CHICKEN & BISCUITS

POPEYES CHICKEN & BISCUITS
5555 Glenridge Connector NE, # 300
Atlanta, GA 30342
Tel: (800) 639-3780
Fax: (404) 459-4523
E-Mail: fphelps@afce.com
Web Site: www.popeyes.com
Mr. Tad Phelps, Director of Franchising

POPEYES CHICKEN & BISCUITS, the world's second-largest chicken chain, is owned by AFC Enterprises, Inc., one of the world's largest restaurant parent companies and the winner of the 1997 MUFSO Operator of the Year and Golden Chain awards. POPEYES is famous for its New Orleans-style chicken, buttermilk biscuits and signature side items. The brand name has a presence in 41 states and 20 countries worldwide. 1999 system sales were $1 billion+.

BACKGROUND: IFA MEMBER
Established: 1972;   1st Franchised: 1976
Franchised Units: 1,318
Company-Owned Units 163
Total Units: 1,481
Dist.: US-945; CAN-12; O'seas-257
  North America: 41 States, 2 Provinces
  Density: NR
Projected New Units (12 Months) 120
Qualifications: 5, 4, 5, 3, , 3
Registered: All States
FINANCIAL/TERMS:
Cash Investment: $600K

Total Investment: $500K-1.2MM
Minimum Net Worth: $1.2MM
Fees: Franchise - $20K
  Royalty - 5%; Ad. - 3%
Earnings Claim Statement: No
Term of Contract (Years): 20/10
Avg. # Of Employees: 15-25 FT
Passive Ownership: Discouraged
Encourage Conversions: Yes
Area Develop. Agreements: Varies
Sub-Franchising Contracts: No
Expand In Territory: Yes
Space Needs: 2,200 SF; FS, SC, RM,
  Airport, Univer.
SUPPORT & TRAINING PROVIDED:
Financial Assistance Provided: Yes(I)
Site Selection Assistance: Yes
Lease Negotiation Assistance: Yes
Co-Operative Advertising: Yes
Franchisee Assoc./Member: Yes/Yes
Size Of Corporate Staff: NR
On-Going Support: B,C,D,E,F,G,H,I
Training: 4 Weeks Atlanta, GA.
SPECIFIC EXPANSION PLANS:
US: All United States
Canada: All Canada
Overseas: All Countries

≪ ≫

PORT OF SUBS
5365 Mae Anne Ave., # A-29
Reno, NV 89523
Tel: (775) 747-0555
Fax: (775) 747-1510
Web Site: www.portofsubs.com
Mr. John Larsen, President

A fast-service restaurant, offering a wide variety of submarine-type sandwiches, hot sandwiches and related items. Sandwiches are made-to-order to customer's specifications, using the freshest-quality meats and cheeses and fresh bread baked on the premises.

BACKGROUND: IFA MEMBER
Established: 1972;   1st Franchised: 1986
Franchised Units: 102
Company-Owned Units 11
Total Units: 113
Dist.: US-113; CAN-0; O'seas-0
  North America: 5 States
  Density: 63 in NV, 39 in CA, 8 in WA
Projected New Units (12 Months): 15
Registered: CA,HI,WA

FINANCIAL/TERMS:

Cash Investment: $50-60K
Total Investment: $140-210K
Minimum Net Worth: $150-200K
Fees: Franchise - $16K
   Royalty - 5.5%; Ad. - 1%
Earnings Claim Statement: No
Term of Contract (Years): 10/10
Avg. # Of Employees: 2 FT, 4-6 PT
Passive Ownership: Discouraged
Encourage Conversions: Yes
Area Develop. Agreements: Yes/Varies
Sub-Franchising Contracts: No
Expand In Territory: Yes
Space Needs: 1,200-1,500 SF; FS, SF, SC

SUPPORT & TRAINING PROVIDED:

Financial Assistance Provided: Yes(I)
Site Selection Assistance: Yes
Lease Negotiation Assistance: Yes
Co-Operative Advertising: Yes
Franchisee Assoc./Member: Yes
Size Of Corporate Staff: 25
On-Going Support: B,C,D,E,F,G,H,I
Training: 2 Weeks Headquarters; 2 Weeks
   in Store.

SPECIFIC EXPANSION PLANS:

US: Northwest, Southwest
Canada: No
Overseas: No

POTTS DOGGIE SHOP

16305 San Carlos Blvd.
Fort Myers, FL 33908
Tel: (941) 466-7747
Fax:
Ms. Evelyn Potts, President

Fast food, specializing in hot dogs, Philly steak sandwiches, wings, burgers, etc., open for breakfast, lunch and dinner.

BACKGROUND:

Established: 1971; 1st Franchised: 1985
Franchised Units: 2
Company-Owned Units: 5
Total Units: 7
Dist.: US-7; CAN-0; O'seas-0
   North America: 3 States
   Density: 3 in FL, 3 in PA, 1 in NJ
Projected New Units (12 Months): 3
Qualifications: 5, 4, 4, 4, 4, 4
Registered: FL

FINANCIAL/TERMS:

Cash Investment: $60K
Total Investment: $60K
Minimum Net Worth: $100K
Fees: Franchise - $15K
   Royalty - 4%; Ad. - 2%

Earnings Claim Statement: No
Term of Contract (Years): 5/5
Avg. # Of Employees: 4 FT, 5 PT
Passive Ownership: Allowed
Encourage Conversions: N/A
Area Develop. Agreements: Yes/5
Sub-Franchising Contracts: No
Expand In Territory: Yes
Space Needs: 1,400 SF; FS, SF, SC, RM

SUPPORT & TRAINING PROVIDED:

Financial Assistance Provided: No
Site Selection Assistance: Yes
Lease Negotiation Assistance: Yes
Co-Operative Advertising: Yes
Franchisee Assoc./Member: No
Size Of Corporate Staff: 1
On-Going Support: None
Training: 2-3 Weeks Ft. Myers, FL.

SPECIFIC EXPANSION PLANS:

US: Eastern Seaboard
Canada: No
Overseas: No

PUDGIE'S FAMOUS CHICKEN

Five Dakota Dr., # 302
Lake Success, NY 11042
Tel: (800) PUDGIES (516) 358-0600
Fax: (516) 358-5076
E-Mail: steven.gardner@pudgies.org
Web Site: www.pudgies.org
Mr. Steven R. Gardner, Dir. Fran. Dev.

Our secret is premium skinless chicken and proprietary breading. 25% less fat and cholesterol . Strong commitment to our franchise owners. Low start-up costs and low rent mean greater profits. Owners receive comprehensive training and extensive operational and marketing support.

BACKGROUND: IFA MEMBER

Established: 1981; 1st Franchised: 1981
Franchised Units: 19
Company-Owned Units: 15
Total Units: 34
Dist.: US-33; CAN-0; O'seas-1
   North America: 7 States
   Density: 14 in NY, 2 in NJ, 2 in CT
Projected New Units (12 Months): 12
Qualifications: 4, 4, 2, 3, 4, 4
Registered: FL,NY,VA,DC

FINANCIAL/TERMS:

Cash Investment: $60-75K
Total Investment: $150-200K
Minimum Net Worth: $100K
Fees: Franchise - $30K
   Royalty - 5%; Ad. - 3%

Earnings Claim Statement: No
Term of Contract (Years): 10/10
Avg. # Of Employees: 4 FT, 6 PT
Passive Ownership: Discouraged
Encourage Conversions: Yes
Area Develop. Agreements: Yes
Sub-Franchising Contracts: No
Expand In Territory: Yes
Space Needs: 1,000 SF; SF SC

SUPPORT & TRAINING PROVIDED:

Financial Assistance Provided: Yes(I)
Site Selection Assistance: Yes
Lease Negotiation Assistance: Yes
Co-Operative Advertising: Yes
Franchisee Assoc./Member: Yes/Yes
Size Of Corporate Staff: 200
On-Going Support: A,B,C,D,e,F,G,H,I
Training: 1 Week to 10 Days Long Island,
   NY.

SPECIFIC EXPANSION PLANS:

US: Northeast, Southeast
Canada: No
Overseas: No

<< >>

ROLI BOLI

109 Main Street
Sayreville, NJ 08872
Tel: (732) 257-8100
Fax: (732) 257-3255
Mr. Anthony Felicetta, President

Specialty sandwich - combines a french bread dough stuffed with a selection of 24 different ingredients to choose from, along with related items.

BACKGROUND:

Established: 1987; 1st Franchised: 1987
Franchised Units: 11
Company-Owned Units: 3
Total Units: 14
Dist.: US-13; CAN-0; O'seas-0
   North America: 6 States
   Density: 8 in NJ, 1 in CA, 1 in NC
Projected New Units (12 Months): 6
Qualifications: 1, 1, 1, 1, 1, 1
Registered: CA,FL,NY

FINANCIAL/TERMS:

Cash Investment: $50-75K
Total Investment: $130-195K
Minimum Net Worth: $NR
Fees: Franchise - $20K
   Royalty - 5%; Ad. - 0%
Earnings Claim Statement: No
Term of Contract (Years): 10/10
Avg. # Of Employees: 2 FT, 4 PT
Passive Ownership: Not Allowed
Encourage Conversions: N/A

Area Develop. Agreements: Yes
Sub-Franchising Contracts: No
Expand In Territory: Yes
Space Needs: 600 SF; RM

SUPPORT & TRAINING PROVIDED:
Financial Assistance Provided: No
Site Selection Assistance: Yes
Lease Negotiation Assistance: Yes
Co-Operative Advertising: Yes
Franchisee Assoc./Member: NR
Size Of Corporate Staff: 6
On-Going Support: C,D,E,F,G
Training: 2 Weeks Company Store; 1 Week
 Franchisee Location.

SPECIFIC EXPANSION PLANS:
US: All United States
Canada: All Canada
Overseas: All Countries

≪ ≫

RONZIO PIZZA

Six Blackstone Valley Pl., Bldg. 202
Lincoln, RI 02865
Tel: (401) 334-9750
Fax: (401) 334-0030
E-Mail: pgassace@fortress.com
Mr. Julian Angelone, President

RONZIO PIZZA is a retail pizza and sub shop, with the main emphasis on delivery.

BACKGROUND:
Established: 1987; 1st Franchised: 1992
Franchised Units: 16
Company-Owned Units 0
Total Units: 16
Dist.: US-16; CAN-0; O'seas-0
 North America: 2 States
 Density: 15 in RI, 1 in MA
Projected New Units (12 Months): 5
Qualifications: 5, 5, 4, 2, 2, 5
Registered: RI

FINANCIAL/TERMS:
Cash Investment: $25K Minimum
Total Investment: $95-136K
Minimum Net Worth: $100K
Fees: Franchise - $10K
 Royalty - 4%; Ad. - 2%
Earnings Claim Statement: No
Term of Contract (Years): 10/10
Avg. # Of Employees: 2 FT, 13 PT
Passive Ownership: Allowed
Encourage Conversions: Yes
Area Develop. Agreements: Yes/10
Sub-Franchising Contracts: No
Expand In Territory: Yes
Space Needs: 1,000-1,400 SF; SF, SC

SUPPORT & TRAINING PROVIDED:
Financial Assistance Provided: Yes(I)

Site Selection Assistance: Yes
Lease Negotiation Assistance: Yes
Co-Operative Advertising: Yes
Franchisee Assoc./Member: Yes
Size Of Corporate Staff: 2
On-Going Support: B,C,D,E,F,G,H
Training: 2 Weeks in Cumberland, RI.

SPECIFIC EXPANSION PLANS:
US: RI,CT,MA
Canada: No
Overseas: No

≪ ≫

SELECT SANDWICH

1090 Don Mills Rd., # 401
North York, ON M3C 3R6 CANADA
Tel: (416) 391-1244
Fax: (416) 391-5244
E-Mail: carolkahn@selectsandwich.com
Ms. Carol Kahn, Director of Franchising

SELECT SANDWICH has custom-made sandwiches, soups, salads and hot, daily specials. We cater to businesses for lunch, breakfast and meetings, five days a week.

BACKGROUND:
Established: 1979; 1st Franchised: 1980
Franchised Units: 38
Company-Owned Units 1
Total Units: 39
Dist.: US-0; CAN-35; O'seas-0
 North America: NR
 Density: NR
Projected New Units (12 Months): 6
Qualifications: 5, 3, 2, 2, 4, 5
Registered: NR

FINANCIAL/TERMS:
Cash Investment: $80K
Total Investment: $240K
Minimum Net Worth: $NR
Fees: Franchise - $30K
 Royalty - 6%; Ad. - 2%
Earnings Claim Statement: No
Term of Contract (Years): 10/10
Avg. # Of Employees: 4 FT, 2 PT
Passive Ownership: Not Allowed
Encourage Conversions: Yes
Area Develop. Agreements: Yes/10
Sub-Franchising Contracts: Yes
Expand In Territory: Yes
Space Needs: NR SF; SF, RM, OB

SUPPORT & TRAINING PROVIDED:
Financial Assistance Provided: Yes(I)
Site Selection Assistance: Yes
Lease Negotiation Assistance: Yes
Co-Operative Advertising: Yes
Franchisee Assoc./Member: Yes
Size Of Corporate Staff: 8

On-Going Support: a,B,C,D,E,F,G,H,I
Training: 6 Weeks at Location to Be
 Determined.

SPECIFIC EXPANSION PLANS:
US: No
Canada: All Canada
Overseas: No

≪ ≫

SKYLINE CHILI

4180 Thunderbird Ln.
Fairfield, OH 45014
Tel: (800) 443-4371 (513) 874-1188
Fax: (513) 874-3591
Web Site: www.skylinechili.com
Mr. Rick C. Collamer, VP Restaurant/Fran.
 Operations

Fast-casual restaurant concept that delivers great Cincinnati style chili in the speed of fast food. Sit down unit with table service that is ideal for owner/operators. Concept has a fanatical following by consumers and is one of the simplest restaurant concepts to run.

BACKGROUND: IFA MEMBER
Established: 1949; 1st Franchised: 1965
Franchised Units: 75
Company-Owned Units 33
Total Units: 108
Dist.: US-0; CAN-0; O'seas-0
 North America: 5 States
 Density: 94 in OH, 5 in KY, 5 in FL
Projected New Units (12 Months): NR
Registered:

FINANCIAL/TERMS:
Cash Investment: $20%
Total Investment: $300K-1MM
Minimum Net Worth: $650K
Fees: Franchise - $20K
 Royalty - 4%; Ad. - 4%
Earnings Claim Statement: Yes
Term of Contract (Years): 20/20
Avg. # Of Employees: 15 FT, 20 PT
Passive Ownership: Allowed
Encourage Conversions: NR
Area Develop. Agreements: Yes/10
Sub-Franchising Contracts: No
Expand In Territory: Yes
Space Needs: NR SF; FS, SF, SC, End
 Cap

SUPPORT & TRAINING PROVIDED:
Financial Assistance Provided: NR
Site Selection Assistance: Yes
Lease Negotiation Assistance: Yes
Co-Operative Advertising: Yes
Franchisee Assoc./Member: Yes/Yes
Size Of Corporate Staff: 40

On-Going Support: a,B,C,D,E,G,H,I
Training: 5 Weeks in Cincinnati, OH.
SPECIFIC EXPANSION PLANS:
US: OH,KY,IN,FL
Canada: NR
Overseas: NR

≪ ≫

SMOOTHIE KING
2400 Veterans Blvd., # 110
Kenner, LA 70062
Tel: (800) 577-4200 (504) 467-4006
Fax: (504) 469-1274
E-Mail: erin@smoothieking.com
Web Site: www.smoothieking.com
Mr. Mike Powers, Franchise Sales

SMOOTHIE KING is the original nutritional smoothie bar and health marketplace since 1973. Our brand is recognized by Entrepreneur Magazine as being # 1 in our category for 11 consecutive years and has steadily grown to 264 stores. Brand loyalty and recognition, corporate support and innovation are some reasons why SMOOTHIE KING is in the front of the industry.

BACKGROUND: IFA MEMBER
Established: 1973; 1st Franchised: 1989
Franchised Units: 264
Company-Owned Units 1
Total Units: 265
Dist.: US-165; CAN-0; O'seas-0
 North America: 10 States
 Density: 37 in LA, 28 in TX, 14 in FL
Projected New Units (12 Months): 75
Qualifications: 3, 3, 3, 3, 4, 4
Registered: All States
FINANCIAL/TERMS:
Cash Investment: $40K
Total Investment: $120-220K
Minimum Net Worth: $100K
Fees: Franchise - $20K
 Royalty - 5%; Ad. - 1%
Earnings Claim Statement: No
Term of Contract (Years): 10/10
Avg. # Of Employees: 2 FT, 6 PT
Passive Ownership: Discouraged
Encourage Conversions: Yes
Area Develop. Agreements: Yes
Sub-Franchising Contracts: No
Expand In Territory: Yes
Space Needs: 800-1,000 SF; SC

SUPPORT & TRAINING PROVIDED:
Financial Assistance Provided: N/A
Site Selection Assistance: Yes
Lease Negotiation Assistance: Yes
Co-Operative Advertising: No
Franchisee Assoc./Member: No
Size Of Corporate Staff: 16
On-Going Support: C,D,E,F,G,h,I
Training: 7 Days New Orleans, LA.
SPECIFIC EXPANSION PLANS:
US: All United States
Canada: No
Overseas: No

≪ ≫

SNAPPY TOMATO PIZZA
7230 Turfway Rd.
Florence, KY 41042
Tel: (888) 463-7627 (606) 525-4680
Fax: (606) 525-4686
E-Mail: elliotst@bigplanet.com
Web Site: www.snappytomato.com
Mr. Jason Rummer, VP Franchising

We offer the best in pizza, subs and salads. We have a variety of concepts to offer to our franchisee. We are the pizza of choice in the new millennia.

BACKGROUND:
Established: 1982; 1st Franchised: 1985
Franchised Units: 46
Company-Owned Units 5
Total Units: 51
Dist.: US-38; CAN-4; O'seas-9
 North America: 7 States, 1 Province
 Density: 17 in KY, 5 in FL, 5 in TN
Projected New Units (12 Months): 20
Qualifications: 3, 3, 3, 2, 1, 3
Registered: FL,IN,IL
FINANCIAL/TERMS:
Cash Investment: $20-30K
Total Investment: $70-150K
Minimum Net Worth: $NR
Fees: Franchise - $15K
 Royalty - 5.5%/$200; Ad. - 2.5%
Earnings Claim Statement: Yes
Term of Contract (Years): 15/15
Avg. # Of Employees: 2 FT, 10 PT
Passive Ownership: Discouraged
Encourage Conversions: Yes
Area Develop. Agreements: Yes/15
Sub-Franchising Contracts: Yes
Expand In Territory: Yes
Space Needs: 400-2,000 SF; FS, SF, SC, RM, C-Store
SUPPORT & TRAINING PROVIDED:
Financial Assistance Provided: No
Site Selection Assistance: Yes

Lease Negotiation Assistance: Yes
Co-Operative Advertising: Yes
Franchisee Assoc./Member: No
Size Of Corporate Staff: 5
On-Going Support: A,B,C,D,E,G,H,I
Training: 3 Days to 2 Weeks KY, TN or FL..
SPECIFIC EXPANSION PLANS:
US: SE,SE, Mid-Atl., Midwest
Canada: All Canada
Overseas: Japan, China, Caribbean, Middle East

≪ ≫

SONIC DRIVE-IN
101 Park Ave., # 1400
Oklahoma City, OK 73102
Tel: (800) 569-6656 (405) 290-7487
Fax: (405) 280-7516
E-Mail: bvinson@sonicdrivein.com
Web Site: www.sonicdrivein.com
Mr. David Vernon, VP Franchise Sales

SONIC DRIVE-INS offer made-to-order hamburgers and other sandwiches, and feature signature items, such as extra-long cheese coneys, hand-breaded onion rings, tater tots, fountain favorites, including cherry limeades, slushes and a full ice-cream dessert menu.

BACKGROUND: IFA MEMBER
Established: 1953; 1st Franchised: 1959
Franchised Units: 1,759
Company-Owned Units 289
Total Units: 2,048
Dist.: US-1,684; CAN-0; O'seas-0
 North America: 27 States
 Density: 574 in TX, 205 in OK, 160 TN
Projected New Units (12 Months): 160
Qualifications: 5, 5, 5, 2, 2, 4
Registered: CA,FL,IN,OR,VA,WA,DC
FINANCIAL/TERMS:
Cash Investment: $300K
Total Investment: $500K-1.0MM
Minimum Net Worth: $1MM
Fees: Franchise - $30K
 Royalty - 1-5%; Ad. - 4%
Earnings Claim Statement: No
Term of Contract (Years): 20/10
Avg. # Of Employees: 35 FT
Passive Ownership: Not Allowed
Encourage Conversions: No
Area Develop. Agreements: Yes/Varies
Sub-Franchising Contracts: No
Expand In Territory: Yes
Space Needs: 1,450 SF; FS
SUPPORT & TRAINING PROVIDED:
Financial Assistance Provided: Yes(I)

Site Selection Assistance: Yes
Lease Negotiation Assistance: Yes
Co-Operative Advertising: Yes
Franchisee Assoc./Member: Yes/Yes
Size Of Corporate Staff: 210
On-Going Support: B,C,D,E,F,G,H,I
Training: 1 Week Oklahoma City, OK; 11 Weeks at Local Market.
SPECIFIC EXPANSION PLANS:
US: SW,SE, West, Midwest
Canada: No
Overseas: Mexico

◄◄ ►►

STEAK 'N SHAKE
36 S. Pennsylvania St., # 500
Indianapolis, IN 46204
Tel: (317) 633-4100
Fax: (317) 656-4500
Web Site: www.steaknshake.com
Mr. Jeffrey S. Ball, Franchise Development Admin.

STEAK N' SHAKE is a unique restaurant concept, serving the mid-scale, casual dining segment of the market with a menu that features steakburgers, thin and crispy french fries and hand-dipped milk shakes. STEAK N' SHAKE offers full waitress service with food served on china, 24 hours a day.

BACKGROUND:
Established: 1934; 1st Franchised: 1939
Franchised Units: 51
Company-Owned Units 222
Total Units: 273
Dist.: US-249; CAN-0; O'seas-0
North America: 14 States
Density: 60 in MO, 51 in IN, 46 in IL
Projected New Units (12 Months): 45
Qualifications: 4, 4, 5, 3, 3, 5
Registered: FL,IL,IN,MI,VA
FINANCIAL/TERMS:
Cash Investment: $200-400K
Total Investment: $1.1-2.4MM
Minimum Net Worth: $500K
Fees: Franchise - $30K
Royalty - 4%; Ad. - 5%
Earnings Claim Statement: No
Term of Contract (Years): 20/20
Avg. # Of Employees: 20-25 FT, 30-40 PT
Passive Ownership: NR
Encourage Conversions: No
Area Develop. Agreements: Yes/3-6
Sub-Franchising Contracts: No
Expand In Territory: Yes
Space Needs: 3,630 SF; FS

SUPPORT & TRAINING PROVIDED:
Financial Assistance Provided: No
Site Selection Assistance: No
Lease Negotiation Assistance: No
Co-Operative Advertising: No
Franchisee Assoc./Member: No
Size Of Corporate Staff: 60
On-Going Support: NR
Training: 6-8 Weeks Operating Steak n' Shake.
SPECIFIC EXPANSION PLANS:
US: Midwest, Southeast
Canada: No
Overseas: No

◄◄ ►►

STEAK ESCAPE, THE
222 Neilston St.
Columbus, OH 43215
Tel: (614) 224-0300
Fax: (614) 224-6460
E-Mail: lallen@steakescape.com
Web Site: www.steakescape.com
Mr. Lloyd Allen, Dir. Franchise Development

THE STEAK ESCAPE concept, founded in October, 1982, prides itself on serving 'made-to-order' grilled sandwiches, freshly-cut french fries, freshly-squeezed lemonade and the unique 'smashed potato.' All of these items are prepared in full view of the customers, using our own famous method of exhibition-style cooking. THE STEAK ESCAPE's signature item is the Genuine Philadelphia Cheesesteak Sandwich.

BACKGROUND:
Established: 1982; 1st Franchised: 1982
Franchised Units: 165
Company-Owned Units 2
Total Units: 167
Dist.: US-166; CAN-0; O'seas-1
North America: 35 States
Density: 10 in OH, 10 in CA, 8 in TN
Projected New Units (12 Months): 40-45
Qualifications: 4, 4, 3, 1, 3, 4
Registered: All States
FINANCIAL/TERMS:
Cash Investment: $80-100K
Total Investment: $263K-1.1MM
Minimum Net Worth: $350K
Fees: Franchise - $25K
Royalty - 5-6%; Ad. - 0.05%

Earnings Claim Statement: No
Term of Contract (Years): 20/20
Avg. # Of Employees: 4 FT, 12 PT
Passive Ownership: Allowed
Encourage Conversions: Yes
Area Develop. Agreements: Yes
Sub-Franchising Contracts: Yes
Expand In Territory: Yes
Space Needs: 600-2,200 SF; FS, SF, SC, RM
SUPPORT & TRAINING PROVIDED:
Financial Assistance Provided: Yes(I)
Site Selection Assistance: Yes
Lease Negotiation Assistance: Yes
Co-Operative Advertising: No
Franchisee Assoc./Member: Yes/Yes
Size Of Corporate Staff: 28
On-Going Support: A,B,C,D,e,F,G,H,I
Training: 3 Weeks in Colombus, OH.
SPECIFIC EXPANSION PLANS:
US: All United States
Canada: All Canada
Overseas: Southeast Asia, Middle East, Australia, Central and South America

◄◄ ►►

STUFT PIZZA
1040 Calle Cordillera, # 103
San Clemente, CA 92673
Tel: (949) 361-2522
Fax: (949) 361-2501
E-Mail: jbertstuft@aol.com
Web Site: www.stuftpizzafran.com
Mr. Jack S. Bertram, President

Take-outs to full service with pasta and micro-brewery.

BACKGROUND:
Established: 1976; 1st Franchised: 1985
Franchised Units: 29
Company-Owned Units 1
Total Units: 30
Dist.: US-30; CAN-0; O'seas-0
North America: 2 States
Density: 26 in CA, 4 in OR
Projected New Units (12 Months): 5
Qualifications: 4, 3, 2, 3, 3, 4
Registered: CA,OR

FINANCIAL/TERMS:

Cash Investment:	$75-150K
Total Investment:	$150-750K
Minimum Net Worth:	$250K
Fees: Franchise -	$25K
Royalty - 3%;	Ad. - 0%
Earnings Claim Statement:	No
Term of Contract (Years):	10/10
Avg. # Of Employees:	3 FT, 8+ PT
Passive Ownership:	Discouraged
Encourage Conversions:	Yes
Area Develop. Agreements:	Yes
Sub-Franchising Contracts:	Yes
Expand In Territory:	Yes
Space Needs: 1,800+ SF; FS, SF, SC, RM	

SUPPORT & TRAINING PROVIDED:

Financial Assistance Provided:	N/A
Site Selection Assistance:	Yes
Lease Negotiation Assistance:	Yes
Co-Operative Advertising:	No
Franchisee Assoc./Member:	No
Size Of Corporate Staff:	2
On-Going Support:	C,D,E,G,H
Training: 2 Weeks San Clemente, CA.	

SPECIFIC EXPANSION PLANS:

US:	West
Canada:	No
Overseas:	No

SUB STATION II

425 N. Main St.
Sumter, SC 29150
Tel: (800) 779-2970 (803) 773-4711
Fax: (803) 775-2220
Web Site: www.substationii.com
Ms. Susan H. Vaden, Vice President

SUB STATION II is a chain of submarine sandwich franchises. We currently have 90 stores located in 9 states. Our sandwich shops offer a variety of over 25 submarine sandwiches, along with specialty sandwiches and salads. We have developed an efficient method of preparing each sandwich to the customer's specifications. The emphasis is on high-quality food and cleanliness. We provide our franchisee's with training and on-going support, lay-out, etc.

BACKGROUND:

Established: 1975;	1st Franchised: 1976
Franchised Units:	89
Company-Owned Units	1
Total Units:	90
Dist.:	US-90; CAN-0; O'seas-0
North America:	9 States
Density:	40 in SC, 20 in NC, 15 in CA

Projected New Units (12 Months):	15
Qualifications:	5, 4, 2, 3, 2, 4
Registered: CA,FL,VA	

FINANCIAL/TERMS:

Cash Investment:	$40-70K
Total Investment:	$75-150K
Minimum Net Worth:	$200K
Fees: Franchise -	$10.5K
Royalty - 4%;	Ad. - 2%
Earnings Claim Statement:	No
Term of Contract (Years):	10/10
Avg. # Of Employees:	4 FT, 8 PT
Passive Ownership:	Allowed
Encourage Conversions:	Yes
Area Develop. Agreements:	No
Sub-Franchising Contracts:	Yes
Expand In Territory:	Yes
Space Needs: 1,500 SF; FS, SF, SC, RM	

SUPPORT & TRAINING PROVIDED:

Financial Assistance Provided:	Yes(I)
Site Selection Assistance:	Yes
Lease Negotiation Assistance:	Yes
Co-Operative Advertising:	Yes
Franchisee Assoc./Member:	No
Size Of Corporate Staff:	8
On-Going Support:	B,C,D,E,G,h
Training: 7-10 Days Corporate Store; 7-10 Days Franchisee Location.	

SPECIFIC EXPANSION PLANS:

US:	Southeast, Southern Calif.
Canada:	No
Overseas:	No

SUBMARINA

10225 Barnes Canyon Rd., # A-202
San Diego, CA 92121
Tel: (877) 714-SUBS (858) 784-0760
Fax: (858) 784-0765
Web Site: www.submarina.com
Mr. Jeffrey Warfield, President

SUBMARINA is the quality alternative to the national sub shop franchises. We combine the unique attributes of a back-East deli and the speed and convenience of a quick-serve restaurant. Our menu is filled with an ample variety of hot and cold subs and deli sandwiches containing the uncommon, such as prosciutto and capacolla, and the popular, turkey and avocado. Sliced to order and served in made-from-scratch bakery breads and rolls, with the customer's choice of 11 different toppings.

BACKGROUND:

Established: 1977;	1st Franchised: 1988
Franchised Units:	36

Company-Owned Units	3
Total Units:	39
Dist.:	US-39; CAN-0; O'seas-0
North America:	2 States
Density:	38 in CA, 1 in NV
Projected New Units (12 Months):	12
Qualifications:	3, 4, 1, 3, 3, 5
Registered: CA	

FINANCIAL/TERMS:

Cash Investment:	$25-50K
Total Investment:	$140-200K
Minimum Net Worth:	$200K
Fees: Franchise -	$20K
Royalty - 6%;	Ad. - 2%
Earnings Claim Statement:	Yes
Term of Contract (Years):	10/10
Avg. # Of Employees:	1 FT, 6 PT
Passive Ownership:	Not Allowed
Encourage Conversions:	Yes
Area Develop. Agreements:	Yes/10
Sub-Franchising Contracts:	No
Expand In Territory:	Yes
Space Needs: 1,200 SF; FS, SF, SC, RM	

SUPPORT & TRAINING PROVIDED:

Financial Assistance Provided:	Yes(I)
Site Selection Assistance:	Yes
Lease Negotiation Assistance:	Yes
Co-Operative Advertising:	Yes
Franchisee Assoc./Member:	No
Size Of Corporate Staff:	10
On-Going Support:	A,B,C,D,E,F,G,H
Training: 2 Weeks Corporate Office/ Training Store; 2 Weeks Their Store.	

SPECIFIC EXPANSION PLANS:

US:	Southern CA,AZ,NV
Canada:	No
Overseas:	No

SUBWAY RESTAURANTS

325 Bic Dr.
Milford, CT 06460-3059
Tel: (800) 888-4848 (203) 877-4281
Fax: (203) 876-6688
E-Mail: franchise@subway.com
Web Site: www.subway.com
Franchise Development Team,

The world's largest and fastest-growing submarine sandwich and salad franchise. At SUBWAY, we take pride in offering one of the most reasonable, well-structured franchise programs available. Our concept is low investment, simple operation and delicious fast food. We now have over 13,480 stores in 68 countries.

BACKGROUND:　　　IFA MEMBER
Established: 1965;　1st Franchised: 1974
Franchised Units:　　　　　　14,109
Company-Owned Units　　　　　5
Total Units:　　　　　　　　14,114
Dist.: US-11,879; CAN-1,352; O'seas-883
　North America:　All States & Provinces
　Density:　　　　　　　CA, TX, FL
Projected New Units (12 Months): 1,000+
Qualifications:　　　　4, 3, 1, 3, 3, 5
Registered: All States
FINANCIAL/TERMS:
Cash Investment:　　　　　$30-75K
Total Investment:　　　　$66.2-175K
Minimum Net Worth:　　　　$66.2K
Fees: Franchise -　　　　　　$10K
　Royalty - 8%;　　　　Ad. - 3.5%
Earnings Claim Statement:　　　No
Term of Contract (Years):　　20/20
Avg. # Of Employees:　2-3 FT, 6-10 PT
Passive Ownership:　　Not Allowed
Encourage Conversions:　　　N/A
Area Develop. Agreements:　Yes/20
Sub-Franchising Contracts:　　No
Expand In Territory:　　　　Yes
Space Needs: 500-1,500 SF; FS, SF, SC,
　RM, C-Store
SUPPORT & TRAINING PROVIDED:
Financial Assistance Provided:　Yes(D)
Site Selection Assistance:　　Yes
Lease Negotiation Assistance:　Yes
Co-Operative Advertising:　　No
Franchisee Assoc./Member:　Yes/Yes
Size Of Corporate Staff:　　　550
On-Going Support:　A,B,C,D,E,F,G,H,I
Training: 2 Weeks in Milford, CT (Foreign
　Training in Costa Rica or Australia).
SPECIFIC EXPANSION PLANS:
US:　　　　　　　All United States
Canada:　　　　　　　All Canada
Overseas:　　　　　　All Countries

TACO BELL

17901 Von Karman Ave.
Irvine, CA 92614
Tel: (714) 863-4500
Fax: (714) 863-4136
Web Site: www.tacobell.com
Mr. Patrick J. Flanagan, Chief Franchising
　Officer

TACO BELL has been the world's largest Mexican quick-service franchise for the past 38 years.

BACKGROUND:　　　IFA MEMBER
Established: 1962;　1st Franchised: 1964
Franchised Units:　　　　　　4,600
Company-Owned Units　　　　3,044
Total Units:　　　　　　　　7,644
Dist.:　US-1,597; CAN-600; O'seas-5447
　North America:　　　　50 States
　Density: 232 in CA, 151 in OH, 150 FL
Projected New Units (12 Months):　NR
Registered: All States
FINANCIAL/TERMS:
Cash Investment:　　　　　　$NR
Total Investment:　　　　$236-503K
Minimum Net Worth:　　　　　$NR
Fees: Franchise -　　　　　　$45K
　Royalty - 5.5%;　　　　Ad. - 4.5
Earnings Claim Statement:　　　No
Term of Contract (Years):　　　20
Avg. # Of Employees:
Passive Ownership:　　　　Allowed
Encourage Conversions:　　　NR
Area Develop. Agreements:　　Yes
Sub-Franchising Contracts:　　No
Expand In Territory:　　　　Yes
Space Needs: NR SF; FS, SF, RM, Other
SUPPORT & TRAINING PROVIDED:
Financial Assistance Provided:　Yes
Site Selection Assistance:　　Yes
Lease Negotiation Assistance:　Yes
Co-Operative Advertising:　　Yes
Franchisee Assoc./Member:　　NR
Size Of Corporate Staff:
On-Going Support:
Training: 18 Weeks at Approved Training
　Restaurant.
SPECIFIC EXPANSION PLANS:
US:　　　　　　　All United States
Canada:　　　　　　　All Canada
Overseas:　　　　　　All Countries

TACO CASA

P.O. Box 4542
Topeka, KS 66604
Tel: (785) 267-2548
Fax: (785) 267-2652
Mr. James F. Reiter, President

TACO CASA offers Mexican fast-food restaurants, serving tacos, tostados, burritos, sanchos, enchiladas, sachiladas, chili, chili burritos and various other entree items. Operates primarily in enclosed shopping centers. Free-standing units have drive-thru facilities. The attractive initial investment greatly enhances the return on investment.

BACKGROUND:
Established: 1964;　1st Franchised: 1976
Franchised Units:　　　　　　16
Company-Owned Units　　　　2
Total Units:　　　　　　　　18
Dist.:　　　US-18; CAN-0; O'seas-0
　North America:　　　　6 States
　Density:　5 in MS, 4 in FL, 3 in KY
Projected New Units (12 Months):　4
Registered: FL
FINANCIAL/TERMS:
Cash Investment:　　　　　$30-70K
Total Investment:　　　　$90-400K
Minimum Net Worth:　　　　$150K
Fees: Franchise -　　　　　　$15K
　Royalty - 4%;　　　　Ad. - 1.5%
Earnings Claim Statement:　　　No
Term of Contract (Years):　　　20
Avg. # Of Employees:　　3 FT, 15 PT
Passive Ownership:　　Discouraged
Encourage Conversions:　　　Yes
Area Develop. Agreements:　Yes/Varies
Sub-Franchising Contracts:　　No
Expand In Territory:　　　　Yes
Space Needs: NR SF; FS, SC, RM
SUPPORT & TRAINING PROVIDED:
Financial Assistance Provided:　No
Site Selection Assistance:　　Yes
Lease Negotiation Assistance:　Yes
Co-Operative Advertising:　　Yes
Franchisee Assoc./Member:　　NR
Size Of Corporate Staff:　　　5
On-Going Support:　a,B,C,D,E,F,G,h,I
Training: 2 Weeks Headquarters.
SPECIFIC EXPANSION PLANS:
US:　　　　　　　　　Southeast
Canada:　　　　　　　　　No
Overseas:　　　　　　　　　No

◄◄　►►

TACO JOHN'S INTERNATIONAL

808 W. 20th St.
Cheyenne, WY 82001
Tel: (800) 854-0819 (307) 635-0101
Fax: (307) 638-0603
Web Site: www.tacojohns.com
Mr. Gene Van Horne, VP of Development

Mexican fast-food restaurant franchisor.

BACKGROUND:　　　IFA MEMBER
Established: 1968;　1st Franchised: 1985
Franchised Units:　　　　　　443
Company-Owned Units　　　　17
Total Units:　　　　　　　　460
Dist.:　　　US-460; CAN-0; O'seas-0
　North America:　　　　25 States

226

Density: 71 in IA, 70 in MN, 37 in SD
Projected New Units (12 Months):   30
Qualifications: 4, 5, 3, 3, 1, 5
Registered: All States Except DC
FINANCIAL/TERMS:
Cash Investment: $25-200K
Total Investment: $100-550K
Minimum Net Worth: $100-250K
Fees: Franchise - $10-19.5K
  Royalty - 4%;   Ad. - 3.5%
Earnings Claim Statement: Yes
Term of Contract (Years):   20/10/10
Avg. # Of Employees: NR
Passive Ownership: Discouraged
Encourage Conversions: Yes
Area Develop. Agreements: Yes/Varies
Sub-Franchising Contracts: No
Expand In Territory: Yes
Space Needs: 1,200-1,600 SF; FS, SF
SUPPORT & TRAINING PROVIDED:
Financial Assistance Provided: No
Site Selection Assistance: Yes
Lease Negotiation Assistance: No
Co-Operative Advertising: NR
Franchisee Assoc./Member: NR
Size Of Corporate Staff: 75
On-Going Support: a,C,d,E,h
Training: NR
SPECIFIC EXPANSION PLANS:
US: Upper Midwest, Rockies
Canada: No
Overseas: No

≪ ≫

TACO MAYO
10405 Greenbriar Pl.
Oklahoma City, OK 73159
Tel: (405) 691-8226
Fax: (405) 691-2572
E-Mail: franchising@tacomayo.com
Web Site: www.tacomayo.com
Ms. Debbie Jackson, Qualification Specialist

Southwest-based, privately-held chain of quick-service restaurants, serving Tex-Mex favorites, including tacos, nachos, salads, burritos, etc. Over 100 restaurants in 8 states, with active advertising co-ops, centralized purchasing, distribution, training and field service representatives. Free-standing limits (conversion and remodeled) feature drive-thru and dining room seating.

BACKGROUND:
Established: 1978;   1st Franchised: 1980
Franchised Units: 69
Company-Owned Units   <u>34</u>
Total Units: 103
Dist.:   US-103; CAN-0; O'seas-0
  North America: 8 States
  Density: 86 in OK, 9 in TX, 3 in KS
Projected New Units (12 Months):   18
Qualifications: 5, 4, 2, 3, 5, 5
Registered: NR
FINANCIAL/TERMS:
Cash Investment: $80K
Total Investment: $99-499K
Minimum Net Worth: $200K
Fees: Franchise - $15K
  Royalty - 4%;   Ad. - 3%
Earnings Claim Statement: No
Term of Contract (Years):   10/10
Avg. # Of Employees: 5 FT, 16 PT
Passive Ownership: Not Allowed
Encourage Conversions: Yes
Area Develop. Agreements: Yes/10
Sub-Franchising Contracts: No
Expand In Territory: Yes
Space Needs: 900-2,200 SF; FS
SUPPORT & TRAINING PROVIDED:
Financial Assistance Provided: Yes(I)
Site Selection Assistance: Yes
Lease Negotiation Assistance: Yes
Co-Operative Advertising: Yes
Franchisee Assoc./Member: Yes/Yes
Size Of Corporate Staff: 23
On-Going Support: a,B,C,D,E,G,H
Training: 3 Weeks at Store in Tulsa or Oklahoma City, OK; 2 Weeks at Franchise Store.
SPECIFIC EXPANSION PLANS:
US: OK,KS,AR,MO,LA,N.TX
Canada: No
Overseas: No

≪ ≫

TACO PALACE
814 E. Hwy. 60, P. O. Box 87
Monett, MO 65708
Tel: (417) 235-1150
Fax: (417) 235-1150
E-Mail: larry@tacopalace.com
Web Site: www.tacopalace.com
Mr. Larry Faria, President

No franchise fee; 1 year contract commitment; very low investment concept; low royalty fees; unlimited training at headquarters; franchise concept is targeted at people that normally cold not afford the cost and expense that other franchises require; Sunday closings.

BACKGROUND:
Established: 1986;   1st Franchised: 1997
Franchised Units: 10
Company-Owned Units   <u>2</u>
Total Units: 12
Dist.:   US-0; CAN-0; O'seas-0
  North America: 2 States
  Density: 10 in MO, 2 in KS
Projected New Units (12 Months):   NR
Registered:
FINANCIAL/TERMS:
Cash Investment: $34-49K
Total Investment: $34-49K
Minimum Net Worth: $50K
Fees: Franchise - $0
  Royalty - 3-6%;   Ad. - 1%
Earnings Claim Statement: No
Term of Contract (Years):   1/1
Avg. # Of Employees: 3 FT, 5 PT
Passive Ownership: Discouraged
Encourage Conversions: NR
Area Develop. Agreements: No
Sub-Franchising Contracts: No
Expand In Territory: Yes
Space Needs: 1,000+ SF; FS, SF, SC, RM
SUPPORT & TRAINING PROVIDED:
Financial Assistance Provided: NR
Site Selection Assistance: Yes
Lease Negotiation Assistance: Yes
Co-Operative Advertising: Yes
Franchisee Assoc./Member: No
Size Of Corporate Staff: 2
On-Going Support: B,C,D,E,F,G,H
Training: 20 Days in Monett, MO; 20 Days with Trainers at Franchisee's Location.
SPECIFIC EXPANSION PLANS:
US: MO,AR,TN,OK,KS,MS,KY,LA
Canada: NR
Overseas: NR

≪ ≫

TACO TIME INTERNATIONAL
3880 W. 11th Ave.
Eugene, OR 97402
Tel: (800) 547-8907 (541) 687-8222
Fax: (541) 343-5208
E-Mail: bobn@tacotime.com
Web Site: www.tacotime.com
Mr. Bob Newton, Dir. of Franchise Development

TACO TIME continues to provide and improve our system for quick-service Mexican restaurants that have stood the test of time for 40 years. TACO TIME quality, focus on customer service, franchisee support and existing new products make us the innovative leader of high-quality Mexican food.

BACKGROUND:

Established: 1959; 1st Franchised: 1960
Franchised Units: 311
Company-Owned Units 4
Total Units: 315
Dist.: US-194; CAN-112; O'seas-9
  North America: 14 States, 7 Provinces
  Density: 74 in OR, 42 in UT, 34 in BC
Projected New Units (12 Months): 20
Qualifications: 5, 4, 3, 4, 5, 5
Registered: All States Except MD,RI,AB

FINANCIAL/TERMS:

Cash Investment: $100K
Total Investment: $150-200K
Minimum Net Worth: $300K
Fees: Franchise - $25K
  Royalty - 5%; Ad. - 4%
Earnings Claim Statement: No
Term of Contract (Years): 15/10
Avg. # Of Employees: 2-3 FT, 15-20 PT
Passive Ownership: Not Allowed
Encourage Conversions: Yes
Area Develop. Agreements: Yes
Sub-Franchising Contracts: Yes
Expand In Territory: Yes
Space Needs: 1,500-2,160 SF; FS, RM

SUPPORT & TRAINING PROVIDED:

Financial Assistance Provided: No
Site Selection Assistance: Yes
Lease Negotiation Assistance: Yes
Co-Operative Advertising: Yes
Franchisee Assoc./Member: Yes/Yes
Size Of Corporate Staff: 25
On-Going Support: B,C,D,E,F,G,h,I
Training: Up to 6 Weeks at Corporate Office.

SPECIFIC EXPANSION PLANS:

US: All United States
Canada: Western Province
Overseas: Master Licensing Agreement -- Asia

TACONE WRAPS

4223 Glencoe Ave., # C-200
Marina Del Rey, CA 90292
Tel: (877) 482-2663 (310) 574-8177
Fax: (310) 574-8179
E-Mail: craig@tacone.com
Web Site: www.tacone.com
Mr. Craig Albert, President

Franchisor of quick-service restaurants serving fresh soups, sandwiches, salads, smoothies and catering.

BACKGROUND:

Established: 1995; 1st Franchised: 1998
Franchised Units: 8
Company-Owned Units 9
Total Units: 17
Dist.: US-0; CAN-0; O'seas-0
  North America: 6 States
  Density: 9 in CA, 2 in MA, 1 in NJ
Projected New Units (12 Months): NR
Registered:

FINANCIAL/TERMS:

Cash Investment: $50K
Total Investment: $125-300K
Minimum Net Worth: $100K
Fees: Franchise - $25K
  Royalty - 6%/3K/Mo.; Ad. - 2%
Earnings Claim Statement: Yes
Term of Contract (Years): 10
Avg. # Of Employees: 1 FT, 5-7 PT
Passive Ownership: Discouraged
Encourage Conversions: NR
Area Develop. Agreements: Yes/10
Sub-Franchising Contracts: Yes
Expand In Territory: No
Space Needs: 400-1,500 SF; SF, SC, RM

SUPPORT & TRAINING PROVIDED:

Financial Assistance Provided: NR
Site Selection Assistance: Yes
Lease Negotiation Assistance: Yes
Co-Operative Advertising: Yes
Franchisee Assoc./Member: No
Size Of Corporate Staff: 10
On-Going Support: A,B,C,D,E,F,G,H,I
Training: 6 Weeks Los Angeles, CA.

SPECIFIC EXPANSION PLANS:

US: All United States
Canada: NR
Overseas: NR

<< >>

TASTEE-FREEZ

48380 Van Dyke Ave.
Utica, MI 48317
Tel: (810) 739-5520
Fax: (810) 739-8351
E-Mail: tfiint@aol.com
Web Site: www.tastee-freez.com
Ms. Lauren Rice, Director of Marketing

Restaurant franchise with the flexibility to offer a full menu from chicken, burgers and fries plus hand-dipped and soft serve ice cream treats to offering a very streamlined soft serve treats-only menu for a co-brand or limited space location.

BACKGROUND: IFA MEMBER
Established: 1950; 1st Franchised: 1950
Franchised Units: 260
Company-Owned Units 0
Total Units: 260
Dist.: US-253; CAN-0; O'seas-7
  North America: NR
  Density: NR
Projected New Units (12 Months): 40-50
Qualifications: 3, 3, 3, 3, 3, 3
Registered: CA,FL,IN,MD,MI,MN, ND,VA,WI

FINANCIAL/TERMS:

Cash Investment: $20-250K
Total Investment: $30K-1MM
Minimum Net Worth: $N/A
Fees: Franchise - $5-15K
  Royalty - 4-5%; Ad. - 1%
Earnings Claim Statement: No
Term of Contract (Years): 10/10
Avg. # Of Employees: Varies
Passive Ownership: Discouraged
Encourage Conversions: Yes
Area Develop. Agreements: N/A
Sub-Franchising Contracts: N/A
Expand In Territory: Possible
Space Needs: NR SF; FS, SF, SC, Co-Brand

SUPPORT & TRAINING PROVIDED:

Financial Assistance Provided: No
Site Selection Assistance: No
Lease Negotiation Assistance: No
Co-Operative Advertising: No
Franchisee Assoc./Member: No
Size Of Corporate Staff: 7
On-Going Support: B,C,D,E,F,G,H
Training: Varies.

SPECIFIC EXPANSION PLANS:

US: All United States
Canada: No
Overseas: No

<< >>

THUNDERCLOUD SUBS

1102 W. 6th St.
Austin, TX 78703
Tel: (800) 256-7895 (512) 479-8805
Fax: (512) 479-8806
E-Mail: thunder@onr.com
Web Site: www.ThunderCloud.com
Mr. David E. Cohen, Director of Franchising

Fresh, fast and healthy sub sandwiches, salads, soup, etc. in a casual atmosphere without the fast-food look. A distinctive trademark, system and product, each store having a unique decor that ties in to the local community. Definitely not a cookie cutter franchise. We train our people to capture the essence of the THUNDERCLOUD experience. The customer service and atmosphere play a large part in overall customer satisfaction. We offer a great value.

BACKGROUND:

Established: 1975; 1st Franchised: 1989	
Franchised Units:	30
Company-Owned Units	8
Total Units:	38
Dist.:	US-38; CAN-0; O'seas-0
North America:	2 States
Density:	37 in TX
Projected New Units (12 Months):	8-12
Qualifications:	4, 4, 3, 3, 4, 5
Registered: NR	

FINANCIAL/TERMS:

Cash Investment:	$25-50K
Total Investment:	$60-100K
Minimum Net Worth:	$100K
Fees: Franchise -	$10K
Royalty - 4%;	Ad. - Varies
Earnings Claim Statement:	No
Term of Contract (Years):	10+8/4/4
Avg. # Of Employees:	2 FT, 6-12 PT
Passive Ownership:	Discouraged
Encourage Conversions:	Yes
Area Develop. Agreements:	Yes/Varies
Sub-Franchising Contracts:	No
Expand In Territory:	Yes
Space Needs: 1,000-1,500 SF; FS, SF, SC	

SUPPORT & TRAINING PROVIDED:

Financial Assistance Provided:	No
Site Selection Assistance:	Yes
Lease Negotiation Assistance:	Yes
Co-Operative Advertising:	N/A
Franchisee Assoc./Member:	No
Size Of Corporate Staff:	5
On-Going Support:	C,D,E,F,G,h,I
Training: 1-2 Weeks at Corporate Headquarters in Austin, TX; 5-10 Days at Franchisee's Store.	

SPECIFIC EXPANSION PLANS:

US:	Primarily Southwest
Canada:	No
Overseas:	No

◁◁ ▷▷

TIPPY'S TACO HOUSE

5025 Falcon Hollow
McKinney, TX 75070
Tel: (972) 547-0888
Fax: (972) 547-0888
Mr. W. L. (Jack) Locklier, Owner
Excellent Tex-Mex food. Eat-in/take-out/drive-thru/delivery. Chuckwagon chili enchiladas, tacos, burritos, wraps of all

kinds, armadillo eggs, chimichongos, nachos, fried jalapenos, tortilla soup, quesadillas and guacamole.

BACKGROUND:

Established: 1958; 1st Franchised: 1968	
Franchised Units:	15
Company-Owned Units	0
Total Units:	15
Dist.:	US-15; CAN-0; O'seas-0
North America:	5 States
Density:	VA, NC
Projected New Units (12 Months):	NR
Qualifications:	1, 3, 2, 2, 5, 5
Registered: NR	

FINANCIAL/TERMS:

Cash Investment:	$20% of Total
Total Investment:	$150K+
Minimum Net Worth:	$150K
Fees: Franchise -	$20K
Royalty - 3%;	Ad. - 0.03%
Earnings Claim Statement:	No
Term of Contract (Years):	20/20
Avg. # Of Employees:	5 FT, 3 PT
Passive Ownership:	Discouraged
Encourage Conversions:	Yes
Area Develop. Agreements:	Yes/Varies
Sub-Franchising Contracts:	Yes
Expand In Territory:	Yes
Space Needs: 1,500-2,000 SF; FS, SF, SC	

SUPPORT & TRAINING PROVIDED:

Financial Assistance Provided:	No
Site Selection Assistance:	Yes
Lease Negotiation Assistance:	Yes
Co-Operative Advertising:	No
Franchisee Assoc./Member:	No
Size Of Corporate Staff:	2
On-Going Support:	B,D,E,F,G,H
Training: 1 Week at Closest Approved Unit.	

SPECIFIC EXPANSION PLANS:

US:	Southwest, Southeast, North
Canada:	No
Overseas:	No

◁◁ ▷▷

TUBBY'S SUB SHOPS

6029 East 14 Mile Rd.
Sterling Heights, MI 48312-5801
Tel: (800) 752-0644 (810) 978-8829
Fax: (810) 977-8083
E-Mail: tony@tubby.com
Web Site: www.tubby.com
Mr. Tony Noga, VP Franchise Dev.

We serve a variety of cold and grilled-to-perfection submarine sandwiches, using only the finest ingredients. We also offer a wide selection of side items, including

soups, salads and desserts. TUBBY'S offers many different concepts - each of which easily adapts to any location. Area development territories are available.

BACKGROUND: IFA MEMBER

Established: 1968; 1st Franchised: 1978	
Franchised Units:	94
Company-Owned Units	3
Total Units:	97
Dist.:	US-97; CAN-0; O'seas-0
North America:	4 States
Density:	80 in MI, 4 in OH, 3 in NJ
Projected New Units (12 Months):	36
Qualifications:	5, 5, 2, 2, 3, 5
Registered: All States	

FINANCIAL/TERMS:

Cash Investment:	$25-50K
Total Investment:	$110-300K
Minimum Net Worth:	$150K
Fees: Franchise -	$8-15K
Royalty - 4-6%;	Ad. - 1%
Earnings Claim Statement:	No
Term of Contract (Years):	10/10
Avg. # Of Employees:	2 FT, 3 PT
Passive Ownership:	Discouraged
Encourage Conversions:	Yes
Area Develop. Agreements:	Yes
Sub-Franchising Contracts:	Yes
Expand In Territory:	Yes
Space Needs: 600-1,200 SF; FS, SF, SC, RM, C-Store	

SUPPORT & TRAINING PRCVIDED:

Financial Assistance Provided:	Yes(I)
Site Selection Assistance:	Yes
Lease Negotiation Assistance:	Yes
Co-Operative Advertising:	Yes
Franchisee Assoc./Member:	No
Size Of Corporate Staff:	13
On-Going Support:	C,D,E,G,H,I
Training: 3 Weeks Headquarters and Training Store.	

SPECIFIC EXPANSION PLANS:

US:	All United States
Canada:	All Canada
Overseas:	All Countries

◁◁ ▷▷

229

VILLA PIZZA/COZZOLI'S

17 Elm St.
Morristown, NJ 07960
Tel: (973) 285-4800
Fax: (973) 285-5252
E-Mail: atorine@villapizza.com
Web Site: www.villapizza.com
Mr. Adam Torine, Dir. Business Dev.

Quick-service pizza and Italian restaurant chain, primarily located in regional malls and outlet centers either in food courts or in-line locations. We use only the freshest cheeses, seasonings, vegetables, homemade sauces and other ingredients. Our large, tantalizing food display offers customers a wide variety of homemade dishes.

BACKGROUND:

Established: 1964; 1st Franchised: 1995	
Franchised Units:	70
Company-Owned Units	120
Total Units:	190
Dist.: US-116; CAN-0; O'seas-4	
North America:	38 States
Density: 11 in TX, 10 in PA, 7 in VA	
Projected New Units (12 Months):	25
Qualifications:	4, 4, 5, 3, 3, 4
Registered: CA,FL,IL,KY,MI,NE,NY,ND, RI,SD,TX,UT,VA,WA,WI	

FINANCIAL/TERMS:

Cash Investment:	$100-250K
Total Investment:	$190-400K
Minimum Net Worth:	$150K
Fees: Franchise -	$25K
Royalty - 5%;	Ad. - 0%
Earnings Claim Statement:	No
Term of Contract (Years):	10
Avg. # Of Employees:	2 FT, 4-7 PT
Passive Ownership:	Not Allowed
Encourage Conversions:	Yes
Area Develop. Agreements:	No
Sub-Franchising Contracts:	No
Expand In Territory:	Yes
Space Needs: 650-2,500 SF; RM, Non-Traditional	

SUPPORT & TRAINING PROVIDED:

Financial Assistance Provided:	Yes(I)
Site Selection Assistance:	Yes
Lease Negotiation Assistance:	Yes
Co-Operative Advertising:	N/A
Franchisee Assoc./Member:	No

Size Of Corporate Staff:	25
On-Going Support:	B,C,D,E,F,G,I
Training: 2 Weeks.	

SPECIFIC EXPANSION PLANS:

US:	All United States
Canada:	All Canada
Overseas:	England, Italy and Spain

◄◄ ►►

WARD'S RESTAURANTS

Seven Professional Pkwy.
Hattiesburg, MS 39402
Tel: (800) 748-9273 (601) 268-9273
Fax: (601) 268-9283
E-Mail: wfsinc@netdoor.com
Web Site: www.wardsrestaurants.com
Mr. Kenneth R. Hrdlica, President

Fast-food restaurant, both traditional and non-traditional, featuring chili-burgers, chili-dogs and frosted mugs of homemade root beer. Menu is complemented by full breakfast line and a variety of sandwiches, side orders and beverages. Seating of up to 60 and drive-thru facilities are part of the building package.

BACKGROUND:

Established: 1985; 1st Franchised: 1985	
Franchised Units:	18
Company-Owned Units	2
Total Units:	20
Dist.: US-20; CAN-0; O'seas-0	
North America:	2 States
Density: 15 in MS, 5 in AL	
Projected New Units (12 Months):	2
Qualifications:	5, 4, 3, 3, 3, 4
Registered: NR	

FINANCIAL/TERMS:

Cash Investment:	$100K
Total Investment:	$250-400K
Minimum Net Worth:	$100K
Fees: Franchise -	$20K
Royalty - 4-5%;	Ad. - NR
Earnings Claim Statement:	No
Term of Contract (Years):	20/10
Avg. # Of Employees:	8 FT, 17 PT
Passive Ownership:	Discouraged
Encourage Conversions:	Yes
Area Develop. Agreements:	Yes/Varies
Sub-Franchising Contracts:	No
Expand In Territory:	Yes
Space Needs: 2,000 SF; FS	

SUPPORT & TRAINING PROVIDED:

Financial Assistance Provided:	No
Site Selection Assistance:	Yes
Lease Negotiation Assistance:	No
Co-Operative Advertising:	No
Franchisee Assoc./Member:	No
Size Of Corporate Staff:	4
On-Going Support:	a,C,D,E,f,G,h,I
Training: 4 Weeks Home Office.	

SPECIFIC EXPANSION PLANS:

US:	All United States, Southeast
Canada:	No
Overseas:	No

◄◄ ►►

WE'RE ROLLING PRETZEL COMPANY

2500 W. State St., P. O. Box 6106
Alliance, OH 44601
Tel: (888) 549-7655 (330) 823-0575
Fax: (330) 821-8908
E-Mail: kkrabill@wererolling.com
Web Site: www.wererolling.com
Mr. Kevin Krabill, President

A unique soft pretzel company designed for mall kiosks and in-line food service locations. Unique and innovative products and promotions. Featuring fresh-made pretzels, food products and beverages. Full corporate office training and support. Absentee owner permitted. Capitalize on the healthy aspect of pretzel snacks with your own WE'RE ROLLING PRETZEL COMPANY franchise.

BACKGROUND:

Established: 1996; 1st Franchised: 1998	
Franchised Units:	2
Company-Owned Units	2
Total Units:	4
Dist.: US-4; CAN-0; O'seas-0	
North America:	2 States
Density: 3 in OH, 1 in PA	
Projected New Units (12 Months):	15
Qualifications:	3, 3, 2, 3, 2, 5
Registered: FL,MI	

FINANCIAL/TERMS:

Cash Investment:	$40-70K
Total Investment:	$55.5-109.2K
Minimum Net Worth:	$150K
Fees: Franchise -	$15K
Royalty - 5%;	Ad. - 1%
Earnings Claim Statement:	No
Term of Contract (Years):	5/5
Avg. # Of Employees:	3 FT, 3 PT

Passive Ownership: Allowed
Encourage Conversions: Yes
Area Develop. Agreements: Yes/5
Sub-Franchising Contracts: No
Expand In Territory: Yes
Space Needs: 300-600 SF; RM, Non-
Traditional
SUPPORT & TRAINING PROVIDED:
Financial Assistance Provided: No
Site Selection Assistance: Yes
Lease Negotiation Assistance: Yes
Co-Operative Advertising: N/A
Franchisee Assoc./Member: No
Size Of Corporate Staff: 5
On-Going Support: B,C,D,E,F,G,H,I
Training: 5 Days Corporate Office; 3 Days
Franchise Location.
SPECIFIC EXPANSION PLANS:
US: All Except Registered States
Canada: No
Overseas: No

WENDY'S RESTAURANTS OF
CANADA
240 Wyecroft Rd.
Oakville, ON L6K 2G7 CANADA
Tel: (905) 849-7685
Fax: (905) 849-5545
E-Mail: ed_mayne@wendys.com
Web Site: www.wendy.com
Mr. Ed Mayne, Director of Development

Our mission is to deliver total quality in our restaurants worldwide by excelling in quality, variety, atmosphere, competitive prices, consistency, a predictable experience and convenience., Customer satisfaction is our first priority every day of the year. That means serving the best hamburgers in the business, as well as offering a wide variety of complementary products - fish, chicken, baked potatoes, prepackaged salads, chili and fresh stuffed pitas.

BACKGROUND:
Established: 1969; 1st Franchised: 1975
Franchised Units: 179
Company-Owned Units 96
Total Units: 275
Dist.: US-0; CAN-260; O'seas-0
North America: 10 Provinces
Density: 128 in ON, 47 in AB, 38 BC
Projected New Units (12 Months): 45
Qualifications: 5, 5, 4, 4, 3, 5
Registered: AB
FINANCIAL/TERMS:
Cash Investment: $250K
Total Investment: $590K-1.4MM

Minimum Net Worth: $500K
Fees: Franchise - $40K
Royalty - 4%/$350; Ad. - 4%
Earnings Claim Statement: No
Term of Contract (Years): 20/10
Avg. # Of Employees: 4 FT, 60 PT
Passive Ownership: Not Allowed
Encourage Conversions: Yes
Area Develop. Agreements: Yes/1
Sub-Franchising Contracts: No
Expand In Territory: Yes
Space Needs: 41,000 SF; FS, RM
SUPPORT & TRAINING PROVIDED:
Financial Assistance Provided: No
Site Selection Assistance: Yes
Lease Negotiation Assistance: Yes
Co-Operative Advertising: Yes
Franchisee Assoc./Member: Yes/Yes
Size Of Corporate Staff: 106
On-Going Support: C,D,E,G,h,I
Training: 20 Weeks in Training Centers.
SPECIFIC EXPANSION PLANS:
US: No
Canada: ON
Overseas: No

WIENERSCHNITZEL
4440 Von Karman Ave., # 222
Newport Beach, CA 92660
Tel: (800) 764-9353 (949) 851-2609
Fax: (949) 851-2618
E-Mail: fcoyle@galardigroup.com
Web Site: www.wienerschnitzel.com
Mr. Frank R. Coyle, Franchise Sales
Director

WIENERSCHNITZEL is the world's largest quick service hot dog restaurant chain with over 300 locations selling 70 million hot dogs annually. We are interested in developing new locations throughout California, the Southwest and Pacific Northwest.

BACKGROUND:
Established: 1961; 1st Franchised: 1965

Franchised Units: 316
Company-Owned Units 0
Total Units: 316
Dist.: US-316; CAN-0; O'seas-0
North America: 11 States
Density: 220 in CA, 30 in TX, 7 in NM
Projected New Units (12 Months): 35
Qualifications: 4, 3, 3, 2, 1, 4
Registered: CA,IL,OR,WA
FINANCIAL/TERMS:
Cash Investment: $100-200K
Total Investment: $250K-1.2MM
Minimum Net Worth: $150K
Fees: Franchise - $20K
Royalty - 5%; Ad. - 3-5%
Earnings Claim Statement: No
Term of Contract (Years): 20/1-20
Avg. # Of Employees: 1-3 FT, 25-30 PT
Passive Ownership: Discouraged
Encourage Conversions: Yes
Area Develop. Agreements: Yes/1
Sub-Franchising Contracts: No
Expand In Territory: Yes
Space Needs: 20,000 SF; FS, RM
SUPPORT & TRAINING PROVIDED:
Financial Assistance Provided: Yes(I)
Site Selection Assistance: Yes
Lease Negotiation Assistance: No
Co-Operative Advertising: Yes
Franchisee Assoc./Member: Yes/Yes
Size Of Corporate Staff: 48
On-Going Support: A,B,C,d,E,F,G,H,I
Training: 30 Days Plano, TX; 30 Days
Gilroy, CA; 7 Days Corporate Office.
SPECIFIC EXPANSION PLANS:
US: NW,SW,SE,NE
Canada: No
Overseas: No

WILLY DOG
120 Clarence St., # 1141
Kingston, ON K7L 4Y5 CANADA
Tel: (800) 915-4683 (613) 549-7366
Fax: (613) 549-4108
Mr. Will R. Hodgekiss, President

A self-contained hot dog and fast-food cart that looks like a giant hot dog. All support, licensing, set-up and on-going support included. Unit has hot and cold running water, BBQ, ice box, etc. and runs from propane only. Fully towable behind any car. (We speak Spanish.)

BACKGROUND:
Established: 1989; 1st Franchised: 1993
Franchised Units: 105
Company-Owned Units 16

Total Units: 121
Dist.: US-0; CAN-0; O'seas-0
North America: 2 States
Density: 5 in NY, 5 in VT
Projected New Units (12 Months): NR
Registered:
FINANCIAL/TERMS:
Cash Investment: $4.5K
Total Investment: $4.5K
Minimum Net Worth: $10K
Fees: Franchise - $4.5K
Royalty - $500/Yr.; Ad. - 0%
Earnings Claim Statement: Yes
Term of Contract (Years): 10/10
Avg. # Of Employees: 1 FT, 1 PT
Passive Ownership: Discouraged
Encourage Conversions: NR
Area Develop. Agreements: Yes/10
Sub-Franchising Contracts: Yes
Expand In Territory: Yes
Space Needs: 30 SF; Outside, Self-Contained
SUPPORT & TRAINING PROVIDED:
Financial Assistance Provided: NR
Site Selection Assistance: Yes
Lease Negotiation Assistance: Yes
Co-Operative Advertising: Yes
Franchisee Assoc./Member: No
Size Of Corporate Staff: 5
On-Going Support: B,C,D,E,F,G,H,I
Training: On-Site as Needed.
SPECIFIC EXPANSION PLANS:
US: All United States
Canada: NR
Overseas: NR

⪡ ⪢

WING ZONE
1718 Peachtree St., NW, # 1070
Atlanta, GA 30309
Tel: (877) 333-9464 (404) 875-5045
Fax: (404) 875-6631
E-Mail: matt@wingzone.com
Web Site: www.wingzone.com
Mr. Scott C. Bigelow, National Sales Mgr.

WING ZONE is a Buffalo-style chicken wing restaurant that offers 25 homemade flavors of jumbo wings, salads, grilled sandwiches, appetizers and desserts. We offer take-out and delivery, and have anchored our stores around large college populations.

BACKGROUND: IFA MEMBER
Established: 1993; 1st Franchised: 1999

Franchised Units: 14
Company-Owned Units: 6
Total Units: 20
Dist.: US-20; CAN-0; O'seas-0
North America: 8 States
Density: 3 in FL, 2 in GA, 2 in SC
Projected New Units (12 Months): 24
Qualifications: 4, 3, 2, 2, 3, 5
Registered: FL
FINANCIAL/TERMS:
Cash Investment: $40-75K
Total Investment: $115-165K
Minimum Net Worth: $125K
Fees: Franchise - $20K
Royalty - 5%; Ad. - 0.5%
Earnings Claim Statement: No
Term of Contract (Years): 10/10
Avg. # Of Employees: 6 FT, 15 PT
Passive Ownership: Discouraged
Encourage Conversions: Yes
Area Develop. Agreements: No
Sub-Franchising Contracts: No
Expand In Territory: Yes
Space Needs: 1,200-1,500 SF; SF, SC
SUPPORT & TRAINING PROVIDED:
Financial Assistance Provided: No
Site Selection Assistance: Yes
Lease Negotiation Assistance: Yes
Co-Operative Advertising: Yes
Franchisee Assoc./Member: No
Size Of Corporate Staff: 4
On-Going Support: a,b,C,D,E,F,I
Training: 1 Week Home Office in Atlanta, GA; 1-2 Weeks Franchisee's Location.
SPECIFIC EXPANSION PLANS:
US: All United States
Canada: All Canada
Overseas: All Countries

⪡ ⪢

WINGSTOP
1234 Northwest Hwy.
Garland, TX 75041
Tel: (972) 686-6500
Fax: (972) 686-6502
E-Mail: jim@wingstop.com
Web Site: www.wingstop.com
Mr. James P. Deering, Vice President

The Arlington Morning News wrote: 'With the somewhat rough-and-ready air of an early century barnstormers' aircraft hanger, WINGSTOP treads the line between neighborhood hang and a casual, laid-back

dinner-snack spot. The place's signature chicken wings, however, are righteously assertive, distinctive and anything but bland . . ' WINGSTOP is fun! WINGSTOP is focused! WINGSTOP is growing fast!

BACKGROUND: IFA MEMBER
Established: 1994; 1st Franchised: 1997
Franchised Units: 25
Company-Owned Units: 1
Total Units: 26
Dist.: US-26; CAN-0; O'seas-0
North America: 5 States
Density: 21 in TX, 1 in LA, 1 in AL
Projected New Units (12 Months): 25
Qualifications: 3, 3, 2, 2, 1, 4
Registered: All States
FINANCIAL/TERMS:
Cash Investment: $40-50K
Total Investment: $215K
Minimum Net Worth: $100K
Fees: Franchise - $20K
Royalty - 5%; Ad. - 2%
Earnings Claim Statement: Yes
Term of Contract (Years): 10/10
Avg. # Of Employees: 2 FT, 4 PT
Passive Ownership: Allowed
Encourage Conversions: No
Area Develop. Agreements: Yes/Negot.
Sub-Franchising Contracts: No
Expand In Territory: Yes
Space Needs: 1,200-1,400 SF; SC
SUPPORT & TRAINING PROVIDED:
Financial Assistance Provided: Yes(I)
Site Selection Assistance: Yes
Lease Negotiation Assistance: Yes
Co-Operative Advertising: Yes
Franchisee Assoc./Member: No
Size Of Corporate Staff: 7
On-Going Support: A,B,C,D,E,H
Training: 2 Weeks Corporate Store; 1 Week Franchise Store.
SPECIFIC EXPANSION PLANS:
US: All United States
Canada: All Canada
Overseas: All Countries

⪡ ⪢

YAYA'S FLAME BROILED CHICKEN
521 S. Dort Hwy.
Flint, MI 48503
Tel: (800) 754-1242 (810) 235-6550
Fax: (810) 235-5210
Web Site: www.yayas.com
Mr. John D. Chinonis, President

Flamed-broiled chicken, health oriented with great flavor. No freezers or fryers in restaurant. Dine-in or take-out. Locations in strips centers or free-standing buildings.

BACKGROUND: IFA MEMBER
Established: 1985; 1st Franchised: 1988
Franchised Units: 10
Company-Owned Units 8
Total Units: 18
Dist.: US-20; CAN-0; O'seas-0
North America: 2 States
Density: 14 in MI, 6 in FL
Projected New Units (12 Months): 5
Qualifications: 4, 4, 3, 3, 4, 4
Registered: FL,MI,MN
FINANCIAL/TERMS:
Cash Investment: $233-336K
Total Investment: $233-336K
Minimum Net Worth: $500K
Fees: Franchise - $15K
Royalty - 4%; Ad. - 4%
Earnings Claim Statement: No
Term of Contract (Years): 10/10
Avg. # Of Employees: 7 FT, 7 PT
Passive Ownership: Not Allowed
Encourage Conversions: N/A
Area Develop. Agreements: Yes/10
Sub-Franchising Contracts: No
Expand In Territory: Yes
Space Needs: 2,800 SF; FS, SF, SC
SUPPORT & TRAINING PROVIDED:
Financial Assistance Provided: No
Site Selection Assistance: N/A
Lease Negotiation Assistance: N/A
Co-Operative Advertising: Yes
Franchisee Assoc./Member: No
Size Of Corporate Staff: 6
On-Going Support: C,D,E,F,H,I
Training: 3 Weeks Flint, MI.
SPECIFIC EXPANSION PLANS:
US: All United States
Canada: All Canada
Overseas: No

ZERO'S SUBS

2106 Pacific Ave.
Virginia Beach, VA 23451
Tel: (800) 588-0782 (757) 425-8306
Fax: (757) 422-9157
E-Mail: zeros@norfolk.infi.net
Web Site: www.zeros.com
Mr. Charles J. McCotter, Executive VP

Specializes in hot, oven-baked submarine sandwiches made-to-order with quality ingredients. We also serve pizzas, salads, soups, kids meals, meal deals and desserts. All priced for today's budget. Catering and party subs complement any special event. The uniqueness of ZERO'S SUBS will bring customers back.

BACKGROUND: IFA MEMBER
Established: 1969; 1st Franchised: 1990
Franchised Units: 51
Company-Owned Units 6
Total Units: 57
Dist.: US-55; CAN-0; O'seas-2
North America: 5 States
Density: 42 in VA, 8 in NC, 2 in AZ
Projected New Units (12 Months): 25
Qualifications: 3, 4, 3, 3, 4, 5
Registered: AZ,FL,IL,KY,NC,OH, SC,VA,WV
FINANCIAL/TERMS:
Cash Investment: $30-50K
Total Investment: $120-170K
Minimum Net Worth: $125K
Fees: Franchise - $15K
Royalty - 6%; Ad. - 2%
Earnings Claim Statement: No
Term of Contract (Years): 15/15
Avg. # Of Employees: 4 FT, 3 PT
Passive Ownership: Discouraged
Encourage Conversions: Yes
Area Develop. Agreements: Yes/25
Sub-Franchising Contracts: Yes
Expand In Territory: Yes
Space Needs: 1,400 SF; FS, SC, RM, Destination Center
SUPPORT & TRAINING PROVIDED:
Financial Assistance Provided: Yes(I)
Site Selection Assistance: Yes
Lease Negotiation Assistance: Yes
Co-Operative Advertising: Yes
Franchisee Assoc./Member: Yes/Yes
Size Of Corporate Staff: 10
On-Going Support: B,C,D,E,F,G,H,I
Training: 3-6 Weeks in Virginia Beach, VA.
SPECIFIC EXPANSION PLANS:
US: SE,NE,MW, Mid-Atl., AZ
Canada: No
Overseas: China

SUPPLEMENTAL LISTING OF FRANCHISORS

A & W Food Services of Canada, 171 W. Esplanade, # 300, North Vancouver, BC V7M 3K9 CANADA; (604) 988-0553; Ms. Betty Johnson ; (604) 988-2141

Angelo's Pizza, 100 7th Ave. S., South St. Paul, MN 55075 ; ; Mr. John Burbank ; (612) 450-1270

Anntony's Caribbean Cafe, 145 Brevard Ct., Charlotte, NC 28202 ; (704) 339-0353; Ms. Debra Gomfalves ; (704) 339-0303

Antone's Famous Po' Boys & Deli, 13100 Northwest Fwy., # 160, Houston, TX 77040 ; (713) 934-2200; Mr. Rick Arnold (800) 934-6734; (713) 934-2100

Arby's (Canada), 6299 Airport Rd., # 200, Mississauga, ON L4V 1N3 CANADA; (905) 672-2755; Mr. Mike Brown (800) 263-7040; (905) 672-2729

Arctic Circle, P.O. Box 339, Midvale, UT 84047 ; (801) 561-9646; Mr. George D. Morgan ; (801) 561-3620

Aurelio's Is Pizza, 18162 Harwood Ave., Homewood, IL 60430 ; (708) 798-6692; Mr. Joseph Aurelio ; (708) 798-8050

Bassett's Original Turkey, 2300 Computer Ave., Bldg. 1, # 9, Willow Grove, PA 19090 ; (215) 659-6329; Mr. Mark Meller (800) 282-8875; (215) 675-9670

Bennett's Pit Bar-B-Que, 6551 S. Revere Pkwy., # 285, Englewood, CO 80111 ; (303) 792-5801; Ms. Judy Shotwell ; (303) 792-3088

Big Town Hero, 912 SW Third, Portland, OR 97204 ; (503) 497-1055; Mr. James Jeter ; (503) 228-HERO

Box Lunch, The, 50 Briar Ln., Wellfleet, MA 02667 ; (508) 349-3661; Mr. Owen MacNutt ; (508) 349-3509

Boz Hot Dogs, 770 E. 142nd St., Dolton, IL 60419 ; (708) 841-4770; Mr. Harry Banks ; (708) 841-3747

Brigham's, 30 Mill St., Millbrook Park, Arlington, MA 02476 ; (781) 646-0507; Mr. George Trafton (800) BRIGHAM; (781) 648-9000

Broadway Station Restaurants, 1818 Woodda'., Dr., Woodbury, MN 55125 ; (651) 731-9609; Mr. Jim Kruizenga ; (651) 731-0800

Brown Baggers, 1919 S. 40th St., # 202, Lincoln, NE 68506-5248 ; (402) 434-5624; Mr. Jack L. Rediger (800) 865-2378; (402) 434-5020

Buddy's Bar-B-Q, 5806 Kingston Pk., Knoxville, TN 37919 ; (423) 588-7211;

Mr. Todd Wolf (800) 368-9208; (423) 588-0051

Bullets Corporation of America, 9201 Forest Hill Ave., # 109, Richmond, VA 23235 ; (804) 330-5405; Mr. Daniel H. McMurtie (800) 472-0933; (804) 330-0837

Burger King Corporation, 17777 Old Cutler Rd., Miami, FL 33157; (305) 378-7721; Mr. Mike Deegan; (305) 378-3581

Buscemi's International, 30362 Gratiot Ave., Roseville, MI 48066 ; (810) 296-3366; Mr. Anthony P. Buscemi ; (810) 296-5560

Café Paradiso, 253 Hanover St., Boston, MA 02113 ; (617) 742-7317; Mr. Oscar De Stefano (888) 742-1768; (617) 742-1768

Cafe Supreme, 1233 Rue de la Montagne, # 201, Montreal, PQ H3G 1Z2 CANADA; (514) 875-9899; Mr. Raymond Croubalian ; (514) 875-9803

Cap'n Taco, 16099 Brookpark Rd., Brookpark, OH 44142 ; (216) 676-9830; Mr. Raymond Brown ; (216) 621-3777

Carbone's Pizza, 680 E. 7th St., Saint Paul, MN 55106 ; (651) 771-3320; Mr. Tom Carbone ; (651) 771-5553

Carl's Jr. Restaurants, 1200 N. Harbor Blvd., Anaheim, CA 92803-4349 ; (714) 520-4409; Mr. Craig Hopkins (800) 422-4141; (714) 774-5796

Central Park USA, 300 High St., Chattanooga, TN 37403 ; (423) 267-4361; Mr. Robert Fisher ; (423) 267-6575

Charlie Williams' Pinecrest, 1 Pinecrest Lodge Rd., Athens, GA 30605 ; (706) 548-2205; Mr. Mike Williams (800) 551-4267; (706) 353-2606

Chick-Fil-A, 5200 Buffington Rd., Atlanta, GA 30349-2998 ; (404) 765-8942; Ms. LeShawn Davis (800) 232-2677; (404) 765-2571

Chicken & Rib Crib, The, P.O. Box 802216, Dallas, TX 75380 ; (972) 716-9913; Mr. Paul Stewart (800) 460-9000; (972) 716-9931

Chicken Out Rotisserie, 15952 Shady Grove Rd., Gaithersburg, MD 20877 ; (301) 548-0024; Mr. Mark Bucher ; (301) 921-0600

Chicken Shack Systems, 725 Lettsworth St., Baton Rouge, LA 70802 ; (225) 383-3973; Ms. Jill Delpit ; (225) 343-1687

Chico's Famous Chicken 'N Pizza, 584 Voutrait Rd., RR # 2, Mill Bay, BC V0R 2P0 CANADA; (250) 743-9623; Mr. Michael Moisson ; (250) 743-9609

Chico's Tacos, P.O. Box 891269, Temecula, CA 92589-1269 ; (909) 676-6104; Mr. Daniel J. Rush (800) 772-4426; (909) 676-3204

Choice Picks Food Court, 10750 Columbia Pike, Silver Spring, MD 20901-4447 ; (301) 598-6205; Mr. Michael Parent (800) 503-2212; (301) 592-6296

Club Sandwich, 107 Cherry St., New Canaan, CT 06840 ; (203) 849-0405; Mr. Michael G. DeVito (800) 428-2675; (203) 348-1232

Cocina De Mino Restaurante, 325 SE 29th, Oklahoma City, OK 73129 ; (405) 632-8102; Mr. Skip Jordan ; (405) 632-1036

Cookies by George Bakery, Café & Gifts, 650 Bath Rd., Kingston, ON K7M 4X6 CANADA; (613) 634-1556; Mr. Don Landon ; (613) 634-1069

Copelands of New Orleans, 1405 Airline Hwy., Metairie, LA 70001 ; (504) 830-1038; Mr. William A. Copeland (800) 401-0401; (504) 830-1000

Corky's Rib and BBQ, 1210 Briarville Rd., Bldg. E, Madison, TN 37115 ; (615) 865-8864; Mr. Mickey Skelton (800) 342-1705; (615) 860-7188

Couch's Barbeque, 5323 27 E. Nettleton, Jonesboro, AR 72401 ; (870) 932-0730; Ms. Beth Couch ; (870) 932-0710

County Line, The, 3345 Bee Cave Rd., #150, Austin, TX 78746 ; (512) 327-2622; Mr. Bruce Walcutt ; (512) 327-1959

Cowboy Chicken, 17437 Preston Rd., Dallas, TX 75006 ; (972) 732-6284; Mr. Phil Sanders ; (972) 732-6281

Cozzoli Pizza Systems, 4770 Biscayne Blvd., #1400, Miami, FL 33137 ; (305) 576-8831; Mr. Merrill Lamb ; (305) 576-1922

D'Angelo Sandwich Shops, 600 Providence Hwy., Dedham, MA 02626 ; (781) 461-1896; Mr. Larry Flarherty (800) 242-1437; (781) 461-1200

Del's Lemonade, 1260 Oaklawn Ave., Cranston, RI 02920 ; (401) 463-7931; Mr. Joseph J. N. Padula ; (401) 463-6190

Desi's Famous Pizza, 438 Hazle Ave., # 200, Wilkes-Barre, PA 18702 ; (717) 829-3264; Mr. Frank Desiderio (800) 694-DESI; (717) 829-3374

Di Lallo Management, 2851 Allard, Montreal, PQ H4E 2M1 CANADA; (514) 368-1005; Mr. Lou Di Lallo ; (514) 368-1005

Dino's Pizza, P.O. Box 97244, Raleigh, NC 27621 ; ; Mr. John E. Ray ; (919) 676-1080

Dominic's of New York, 4949 Cox Rd., Suite B, Glen Allen, VA 23060 ; (804) 273-0152; Mr. Nick DiMartino (888) DOM-OFNY; (804) 273-0600

Edwardo's Natural Pizza Restaurants, 205 W. Wacker Dr., # 1800, Chicago, IL 60606 ; (312) 346-2115; Mr. Bill Bronner (800) 944-3393; (312) 346-5455

Fast Eddie's, 129 Wellington St., # 102, Brantford, ON N3T 5Z9 CANADA; (519) 758-1393; Mr. Mike Gorski ; (519) 758-0111

Fazoli's Systems, 2470 Palumbo Dr., Lexington, KY 40509 ; (606) 268-2263; Mr. Gordon R. Doyle ; (606) 268-1668

Figaro's Italian Kitchen, 1500 Liberty St., S. E., # 160, Salem, OR 97302 ; (503) 363-5364; Mr. Max Bennett (888) FIG-AROS; (503) 371-9318

Fluky's, 5225 W. Touhy Ave., # 103, Skokie, IL 60077-3266 ; (847) 329-1454; Mr. Jack Drexler ; (847) 329-1409

Fosters Freeze International, 3701 S. Higuera St. , # 102, San Luis Obispo, CA 93401 ; (805) 781-6106; Mr. Randy Fritchie ; (805) 781-6100

Frank & Stein Dogs & Drafts, P.O. Box 20608, Roanoke, VA 24018-0061 ; (540)-389-1780; Mr. C. Gregory Caldwell ; (540) 389-8435

Frankies Franchise Systems, 643 Lakewood Rd., Waterbury, CT 06704 ; (203) 757-5361; Mr. Gerald Caiazzo ; (203) 756-2935

Gerald M. Liss Co., 203 N. Main St., Bowling Green, OH 43402; (419) 354-1402; Mr. Jake Hinton; (419) 352-5166

Giff's Sub Shop, 634 NE Eglin Pkwy., Fort Walton Beach, FL 32548 ; ; Mr. Rick Arnette ; (850) 864-5468

Gina's Pizza, 420 Iris Ave., Corona Del Mar, CA 92625 ; (949) 673-3598; Mr. Andrew Costa ; (949) 673-4297

Golden Fried Chicken, 11488 Luna Rd., #100B, Dallas, TX 75234 ; (972) 831-0401; Ms. Pam Gould ; (972) 831-0911

Golden Skillet, USA, P.O. Box 905, Ahoskie, NC 27910 ; (252) 332-7557; Mr. David Shields ; (252) 332-5248

Gondola Pizza Incomparable, 115 De Baets St., Winnipeg, MB R2J 3R9 CANADA; (204) 661-9036; Mr. Derek Loewen ; (204) 661-2851

Grand Roasters Limited, 419 Occidental Ave. So., #207, Seattle, WA 98104 ; (206) 625-9820; Ms. Mary Flemming ; (206) 625-0598

Grandy's, 997 Grandy's Ln., Lewisville, TX 75077 ; (972) 317-8174; Mr. Monty Whitehurst (800) 320-1404; (972) 317-8143

Gumby's Pizza International, 5217 SW 91st Dr., Gainesville, FL 32608 ; (352) 377-2592; Mr. Chance Hippler (800) 354-8629; (352) 375-8084

Hamburger Mary's, P.O. Box 633, Corona Del Mar, CA 92625 ; (949) 675-9979; Mr. Stan Sax (888) 83-4-MARY;

Health First Restaurants, 3321 Greenhill Ln., # 310, Louisville, KY 40207 ; (510) 547-3245; Ms. Roberta L. Bondo ; (510) 839-5471

Heavy Duty Pizza, 14 Northrop., # 4, St. Catharines, ON L2M 7N7 CANADA; (905) 646-1912; Mr. Denis Blanchard ; (905) 641-1117

Hobee's California Restaurants, 4224 El Camino Real, Palo Alto, CA 94306 ;

(650) 493-0756; Mr. Edward Fike (800) 462-3376; (650) 493-7823

Hot 'N Now Hamburgers, 4205 Charlar, #3, Holt, MI 48842 ; (517) 694-6370; Mr. Taul Warren ; (517) 694-4240

Hot Dog On A Stick, 5601 Palmer Way, Carlsbad, CA 92008-7242 ; (619) 755-5809; Ms. Fredrica L. Thode (800) 321-8400; (619) 775-3049

Icebox/Soupbox, 2943 N. Broadway, Chicago, IL 60657 ; ; Mr. J. Taerbaum ; (773) 935-9800

Izzy's Pizza Restaurant, 110 3rd Ave., SE, Albany, OR 97321 ; (541) 928-8127; Mr. Fred Jansen ; (541) 926-8693

J. Brenner's Chicken & Cheesesteaks, 57 Executive Park S., # 440, Atlanta, GA 30329 ; (404) 248-0180; Mr. Mark Kaplan ; (404) 248-9900

Jake's Over The Top, P.O. Box 150650, Ogden, UT 84415 ; (801) 476-9788; Mr. Corey King (800) 207-5804; (801) 476-9780

Jake's Pizza, 1911-C Rohlwing Rd., Rolling Meadows, IL 60008-4502 ; (847) 368-1995; Mr. John Flowers (800) 4-A-JAKES; (847) 368-1990

Januzzi's Pizza, 120 Academy St., Wilkes Barre, PA 18702 ; (570) 823-2043; Mr. Jack Januzzi ; (717) 823-8857

Jerry's Subs & Pizza, 15942 Shady Grove Rd., Gaithersburg, MD 20877 ; (301) 948-3508; Mr. Jordan Fainberg ; (301) 921-8777

Jets Pizza, 37177 Mound Rd., Sterling Heights, MI 48310-4116 ; (810) 268-6762; Mr. Jim Galloway (800) 446-5870; (810) 268-5870

Jimboy's Tacos, 1485 Response Rd., # 110, Sacramento, CA 95815 ; (916) 564-0802; Mr. Todd Rapisura (800) JIM-BOYS; (916) 564-8226

Jimmy's Pizza, 2015 First St. S., #119, Willmar, MN 56201 ; (320) 235-7837; Mr. Fred Gordon ; (320) 235-7844

Johnny Rockets, The Original Hamburger, 15635 Alton Pkwy., # 350, Irvine, CA

92618 ; (949) 789-7588; Ms. Lisa Lake (888) 236-9100; (949) 789-7575

KFC Canada, 10 Carlson Court, # 400, Rexdale, ON M9W 6L2 CANADA; (416) 674-2697; Mr. Steve Figiola (800) 268-5435; (416) 674-0367

Kojax, 8150 Marco Polo, Riviere des Prairies, PQ H1E 5Y7 CANADA; (514) 494-8988; Mr. Giovanni Fiorino ; (514) 494-2526

Krystal Company, The, One Union Square, 10th Fl., Chattanooga, TN 37402 ; (423) 757-1590; Ms. Christie Sherlin (800) 458-5912; (423) 757-1550

Lamppost Pizza, 3002 Dow Ave., #320, Tustin, CA 92780 ; (714) 731-0951; Mr. Tom Barro ; (714) 731-6171

Larosa's Pizzerias, 2334 Boudinot Ave., Cincinnati, OH 45238 ; (513) 922-2776; Mr. Kevin Burrill ; (513) 347-5660

Ledo Pizza System, 2568A Riva Rd., # 202, Annapolis, MD 21401 ; (410) 266-6888; Mr. Robert M. Beall ; (410) 721-6887

Linda's Rotisserie & Chicken, 220 Lenox Ave., Westfield, NJ 07090-5101 ; (908) 276-0552; Mr. Peter Weissbrod (800) LINDA-21; (908) 276-2080

Little Caesars Pizza, 2211 Woodward Ave., Detroit, MI 48201-3400 ; (313) 983-6197; Mr. Bob Mazziotti (800) 553-5776; (313) 983-6000

Loeb, 1430 Blair Pl., Box 8387, Ottawa, ON K1G 3K8 CANADA; (613) 747-3304; Mr. Mike Milobar ; (613) 747-3305

Mark Pi's China Gate, 3960-G Brown park Dr., Hillard, OH 43026 ; (614) 771-5134; Mr. Danny Wann ; (614) 771-5120

Mary Brown's Fried Chicken, 250 Shields Court, # 7, Markham, ON L3R 9W7 CANADA; (905) 513-0050; Mr. Nigel Beattie ; (905) 513-0044

Mary's Pizza Shack, P.O. Box 1049, Boyes Hot Springs, CA 95416 ; (707) 938-5976; Mr. Cullen Williamson (800) 938-3602; (707) 938-3602

Mash Hoagies/Mash Subs & Salads, 3164 Lake Washington Rd., Melbourne, FL

32934 ; (321) 752-6026; Mr. Alan Lee ; (321) 242-2066

McDonald's Restaurants of Canada, McDonald's Place, Toronto, ON M3C 3L4 CANADA; (416) 446-3429; Mr. John Piper ; (416) 443-1000

Mellow Mushroom Pizza, 695 North Ave. NE, Atlanta, GA 30308 ; (404) 223-5419; Mr. Mike Nicholson ; (404) 524-6133

Mexandale California Mexican Grill, 225 SE 15th Terrace, Cove Center, Deerfield Beach, FL 33441 ; (954) 425-7832; Mr. Eric Chavez (877) 426-3253; (954) 425-0845

Miami Subs Grill, 6300 NW 31st Ave., Ft. Lauderdale, FL 33309 ; (954) 973-7616; Ms. Mollty Hoepfner ; (954) 973-0000

Mio's Pizzeria, 6930 Madisonville Rd., Cincinnati, OH 45227 ; (513) 271-8749; Mr. Jim Shaner ; (513) 271-1100

Mr. Chicken, P.O. Box 23051, Cleveland, OH 44123 ; (440) 585-4815; Mr. Michael D. Simens ; (440) 585-4800

Mr. Gatti's, 444 Sidney Baker S., P. O. Box 1522, Kerrville, TX 78028 ; (830) 257-2003; Ms. Jody Tolman ; (830) 792-5700

Mr. Pita, 48238 lake Valley Circle, Shelby Township, MI 48317 ; (810) 323-3625; Mr. Frank Lombardo ; (810) 323-3624

Mr. Topper's Pizza, 311 Elm St. W., # 3, Sudbury, ON P3C 1V6 CANADA; (705) 674-5302; Mr. Keith Toppazzini; (705) 674-0703

My Family Food Court, 3331 Viking Way, # 7, Richmond, BC V6V 1X7 CANADA; (604) 270-6560; Mr. Duncan Williams ; (604) 270-2360

Nacho Nana's Worldwide, 6005 S. Ash Ave., Tempe, AZ 85283 ; (602) 897-4815; Mr. Al Slaten ; (602) 897-4445

Orange Julius, P.O. Box 39286, Minneapolis, MN 55439-0286 ; (612) 830-0450; Mr. Eric Lavanger (800) JULIUS-9; (612) 830-0200

Orange Julius Canada, 5245 Harvester Rd., P.O. Box 430, Burlington, ON L7R 3Y3 CANADA; (905) 639-8877; Mr. Wayne Vanderhorst (800) 268-9169; (905) 639-1492

Original Hamburger Stand, P.O. Box 7460, Newport Beach, CA 92658 ; (949) 851-2615; Mr. Frank R. Coyle ; (949) 752-5800

Owner's Auto Mart, 3100 W. 12 St. # 108, Sioux Fall, SD 57104 ; (605) 336-7357; Mr. Mike Wosje (800) 437-7228;

Panchero's Mexican Grill, P.O. Box 1786, Iowa City, IA 52244 ; (319) 358-6435; Mr. James Manura (888) MEX-BEST; (319) 351-4551

Papa Gino's, 600 Providence Hwy., Dedham, MA 02026 ; (781) 461-1896; Mr. Larry Flaherty (800) 242-1437; (781) 461-1200

Papa John's Pizza, P.O. Box 99900, Louisville, KY 40269-0900 ; (502) 263-7352; Mr. Hart Boesel ; (502) 266-5200

Pasta Lovers Trattorias, 201 West First St., Sanford, FL 32771 ; (407) 321-3077; Ms. Sheryl Panion ; (407) 321-1101

Pastel's Café, 1121 Centre St. N., # 440, Calgary, AB T2E 7K6 CANADA; (403) 230-2182; Mr. Sheldon Jones (800) 361-1151; (403) 230-1151

Pedro's Tacos of California, 2313 S. El Camino Real, San Clemente, CA 92670 ; (949) 493-0562; Mr. Edward McNary ; (949) 498-5904

Peter Piper Pizza, 6263 N. Scottsdale Rd., # 100, Scottsdale, AZ 85250 ; (602) 609-6522; Mr. Vaughn Berg (888) 912-1333; (602) 609-6400

Piccadilly Circus Pizza, 1009 Okoboji Ave., Box # 188, Milford, IA 51351 ; (712) 338-2263; Mr. Jon Snow (800) 338-4340; (712) 338-2771

Pie's The Limit, The, 145 Rodeo Dr., Thornhill, ON L4J 4Y6 CANADA; (905) 709-9176; Mr. B. M. Bloch ; (416) 861-9820

Pier 49 San Francisco Sourdough Pizza, 2400 E. 7000 South, Salt Lake City, UT 84121 ; (801) 947-9561; Mr. Mike Dicou (800) 748-4149; (801) 947-9161

Pizza Inn, 5050 Quorum Dr., # 500, Dallas, TX 75240-7020 ; (972) 702-0009;

Mr. Bryan Haley (800) 880-9955; (972) 701-9955

Pizza Outlet, 2101 Greentree Rd., # A-202, Pittsburgh, PA 15220 ; (412) 279-9781; Mr. Joseph M. Bullian (888) 816-2116; (412) 279-9100

Pizza Pipeline, The, 418 W. Sharp, Spokane, WA 99201 ; (509) 326-3017; Mr. Mike Kite ; (509) 326-1977

Pizza Pizza International, 580 Jarvis St., Toronto, ON M4Y 2H9 CANADA; (416) 967-0891; Mr. Sebastian Fushini (800) 263-5556; (416) 967-1010

Pizza Pro, 2107 North 2nd St., Cabot, AR 72023 ; (501) 605-1204; Mr. John Campbell (800) 777-7554; (501) 605-1175

Pizza Royale, 650 Graham Bell, # 217, Sainte-Foy, PQ G1N 4H5 CANADA; (418) 682-2684; Mr. Rejean Samson ; (418) 682-5744

Pollo Tropical, 7300 N. Kendall Dr., # 800, Miami, FL 33156 ; (305) 670-6403; Ms. Lissette Zamora ; (305) 670-7696

Potatoes Plus, P.O. Box 14007, Oklahoma City, OK 73113 ; (405) 478-7331; Ms. Shirley Grace ; (405) 478-7653

Pudgies Pizza & Sub Shops, 524 530 N. Main St., Elmira, NY 14901 ; ; Ms. Bernadette Cleary ; (607) 734-3366

Ranch *1, 130 W. 42nd St., 21st Fl., New York, NY 10036 ; (212) 730-4444; Mr. Gary Occhiogrosso (800) 372-6241; (212) 354-6666

Renzios, 4690 S. Yosemite St., Greenwood Village, CO 80111 ; (303) 267-0088; Mr. Thomas D. Rentzios (800) 892-3441; (303) 267-0300

Restaurant Systems International, 1000 South Ave., Staten Island, NY 10314-3403 ; (718) 494-8776; Mr. Steve Beagelman (800) 205-6050; (718) 494-8888

Rocky Rococo Pizza & Pasta, 105 E. Wisconsin Ave., #101, Oconomowoc, WI 53066 ; (262) 569-5591; Mr. Thomas R. Hester ; (262) 569-5580

Rollo Pollo Rotisserie Chicken, 4975 Shelbyville Rd., Louisville, KY 40207 ;

(502) 894-0268; Mr. Richard Jeffrey ; (502) 894-0012

Rotelli Pizza & Pasta, P.O. Box 83-2062, Delray Beach, FL 33483 ; (561) 272-6922; Mr. Robert A. Spuck (800) 839-4931; (561) 483-9699

Roy Rogers, 7272 Park Circle Dr., Bldg. 270, Hanover, MD 21076-1333 ; (410) 782-2077; Mr. Roy Murphy ; (410) 782-2013

Rubio's Baja Grill, 1902 Wright Place, #300, Carlsbad, CA 92008 ; (760) 929-8203; Mr. John Ramsey (800) 354-4199; (760) 929-8226

Ruby's, 110 Newport Center Dr., # 110, Newport Beach, CA 92660 ; (714) 644-4625; Mr. Michael Milligan (800) HAY-RUBY; (714) 644-7829

Ruffage, 3380 S. Service Rd., Burlington, ON L7N 3J5 CANADA; (905) 637-7745; Mr. Andrew Diveky ; (905) 681-8448

Salubre-Pizza, Subsation's Sandwiches, 2337 Perimeter Park Dr., #200, Chamblee, GA 30341 ; (770) 457-2404; Mr. Doug Moran (800) 310-9640; (770) 457-7611

Sandwich Board, The, 10 Plastics Ave., Etobicoke, ON M8Z 4B7 CANADA; (416) 255-8086; Mr. Rudolph Dieter Hoefel ; (416) 255-0898

Schoop's Hamburgers, 215 Ridge Rd., Munster, IN 46321; Mr. Mark Schooper; (219) 836-6233

Simple Simon's Pizza, 6650 S. Lewis, Tulsa, OK 74136 ; (918) 493-6916; Mr. Todd Miller ; (918) 496-1272

Sneaky Pete's Hot Dogs, 100 Centerview Dr., # 191, Birmingham, AL 35126 ; (205) 824-0852; Mr. Benny D'Amico ; (205) 824-0855

Steak Around, 515 King St., # 440, Alexandria, VA 22314 ; (703) 683-7966; Mr. Dan Rowe (888) 327-8325; (703) 683-8545

Straya California Creole Café, 1405 Airline Hwy., Metairie, LA 70001 ; (504) 832-8918; Mr. Alvin Copeland (800) 401-0401; (504) 830-1000

Subs Plus, 173 Queenston St., St. Catharines, ON L2R 3A2 CANADA; (905)

641-3696; Sampson & Associates (888) 549-7777; (905) 641-3696

Taco Bell (Canada), 10 Carlson Court, # 400, Rexdale, ON M9W 6L2 CANADA; (416) 674-2697; Mr. Steve Figliola ; (416) 674-0367

Taco Grande, P.O. Box 780066, Wichita, KS 67278 ; (316) 744-0299; Mr. John G. Wylie ; (316) 744-0200

Taco Maker, The, 4605 Harrison Blvd., 3rd Fl., Ogden, UT 84403 ; (801) 476-9788; Mr. Corey King (800) 207-5804; (801) 476-9780

Taco Villa, 3710 Chesswood Dr., # 220, North York, ON M3J 2W4 CANADA; (416) 636-9162; Ms. Wendy J. MacKinnon (800) 608-8226; (416) 636-9348

Tasty Tacos, 1420 E. Grand Ave., Des Moines, IA 50316 ; (515) 263-8828; Ms. Linda Blair ; (515) 262-3940

This is It! Bar-B-Q & Seafood, 4405 Mall Blvd., # 320, Union City, GA 30291 ; (770) 964-8539; Ms. Shelly Anthony ; (770) 964-1668

Togo's Eatery, 14 Pacella Park Dr., Randolph, MA 02368 ; (781) 963-2913; Mr. Lee Sanders (888) 782-4636; (781) 961-4000

Togo's Great Sandwiches, 50 Ronson Dr., # 131, Toronto, ON M9W 1B3 CANADA; (416) 245-3040; Franchise Development (800) 268-4923; (416) 245-3131

Tom's House of Pizza, 7730 Macleod Trail S., Calgary, AB T2H 0L9 CANADA; (403) 255-3209; Director of Franchising ; (403) 252-0111

Wendy's International, 4288 W. Dublin-Granville Rd., P.O. Box 256, Dublin, OH 43017 ; (614) 764-6894; Ms. Barbara E. Langsdon (800) 443-7266; (614) 764-3100

Wetzel's Pretzels, 65 N. Raymond Ave., # 310, Pasadena, CA 91103 ; (626) 432-6904; Mr. Anthony Parete ; (626) 432-6900

WG Grinders, 220 W. Bridge St., #200, Dublin, OH 43017 ; (614) 766-4030; Mr. Peter Ortiz ; (614) 766-2313

Whataburger, 4600 Parkdale, Corpus Christi, TX 78411 ; (361) 878-0473; Mr.

Wayne Powell ; (361) 878-0650

White Castle International, 555 W. Goodale St., Columbus, OH 43216-1498 ; (614) 461-4033; Mr. James Sipp ; (614) 559-2510

Windmill Gourmet Fast Foods, 200 Ocean Ave., Long Branch, NJ 07740 ; (732) 870-9613; Ms. Rona Levine Levy (800) 874-8282; (732) 870-8282

Wing Machine, 234B Parliament St., Toronto, ON M5A 3A4 CANADA; (416) 362-8217; Mr. Frank Schiavone ; (416) 362-5555

Wing Wagon, 71 Public Square, Watertown, NY 13601 ; (315) 788-4580; Mr. Charles G. Wert (800) 836-7815; (315) 788-4580

Wingers - An American Diner, 404 E. 4500 South, # A12, Salt Lake City, UT 84107 ; (801) 261-1615; Mr. Jeff Chivers ; (801) 261-3700

Wings To Go, 170 Jennifer Rd., # 250, Annapolis, MD 21401 ; (410) 224-5635; Mr. Jim Tisack (800) 552-WING; (410) 224-5631

Wok To U Express, 3331 Viking Way, # 7, Richmond, BC V6V 1X7 CANADA; (604) 270-6560; Mr. Duncan Williams ; (604) 270-2360

Woody's Hot Dogs Hawaii, P.O. Box 600, Makaha, HI 96792 ; (808) 696-5481; Mr. Coe D. Meyer ; (808) 696-5483

Wrap & Roll Café, 1405 Airline Hwy., Metairie, LA 70001 ; (504) 832-8918; Mr. Bryan White (800) 401-0401; (504) 830-1000

Wrapsters, 4944 Lower Roswell Rd., # 523, Marietta, GA 30068 ; ; Director of Franchising ; (770) 645-7771x

Yasin's Homestyle Seafood, 1987 W. 111th St., Chicago, IL 60643 ; (773) 238-3152; Mr. Dennis Robinson ; (773) 238-3100

Zeppe's Pizzeria, 10 Alpha Park, Highland Heights, OH 44143 ; (440) 442-4655; Mr. Joseph T. Ciresi ; (440) 442-9898

FOOD: RESTAURANTS/FAMILY-STYLE INDUSTRY PROFILE

Total # Franchisors in Industry Group	163
Total # Franchised Units in Industry Group	16,571
Total # Company-Owned Units in Industry Group	<u>11,154</u>
Total # Operating Units in Industry Group	27,725
Average # Franchised Units/Franchisor	101.7
Average # Company-Owned Units/Franchisor	<u>68.4</u>
Average # Total Units/Franchisor	170.1
Ratio of Total # Franchised Units/Total # Company-Owned Units	1.5:1
Industry Survey Participants	70
Representing % of Industry	42.9%
Average Franchise Fee*:	$35.5K
Average Total Investment*:	$888.8K
Average On-Going Royalty Fee*:	4.4%

If a range was provided, the mid-point of the range was used. See detailed profiles for actual ranges.

FIVE LARGEST PARTICIPANTS IN SURVEY

Company	# Fran- chised Units	# Co- Owned Units	# Total Units	Franchise Fee	On-Going Royalty	Total Investment
1. Denny's	1,060	756	1,816	35K	4%	858K-1.5MM
2. Applebee's International	852	257	1,109	35K	4%	1.7-3.2MM
3. Sbarro	286	634	920	45K	6%	250-850K
4. Friendly's Restaurant	111	504	615	35K	4%	875K-1.5MM
5. Carlson Restaurants Worldwide	360	180	540	75K	4%	1.7-4MM

All of the data provided are proprietary and should not be quoted without acknowledging *Bond's Franchise Guide.*

APPLEBEE'S INTERNATIONAL

4551 W. 107th St., # 100
Overland Park, KS 66207
Tel: (913) 967-4000
Fax: (913) 967-4135
Web Site: www.aplebees.com
Mr. Larry M. Bader, Director Franchise
Development

Everyone's favorite neighbor is definitely APPLEBEE'S neighborhood grill and bar. This distinguished casual-dining restaurant has a comfortable individuality which reflects the neighborhood in which it is located, making the APPLEBEE'S concept appealing wherever it is built.

BACKGROUND: IFA MEMBER
Established: 1980;   1st Franchised: 1988
Franchised Units: 852
Company-Owned Units   257
Total Units: 1,109
Dist.:   US-889; CAN-5; O'seas-8
  North America: 47 States, 3 Provinces
  Density: 62 in FL, 54 in CA, 48 in OH
Projected New Units (12 Months):   125
Qualifications: 5, 5, 5, , , 5
Registered: All Except AB
FINANCIAL/TERMS:
Cash Investment: $1MM-50% Liq.
Total Investment: $1.74-3.17MM
Minimum Net Worth: $NR
Fees: Franchise - $35K/Unit
  Royalty - 4%;   Ad. - 3%
Earnings Claim Statement: No
Term of Contract (Years):   20/5
Avg. # Of Employees: 75-100 FT
Passive Ownership: Not Allowed
Encourage Conversions: No
Area Develop. Agreements: Yes
Sub-Franchising Contracts: No
Expand In Territory: Yes
Space Needs: 5,000-5,400 SF; FS, SC, RM
SUPPORT & TRAINING PROVIDED:
Financial Assistance Provided: No
Site Selection Assistance: Yes
Lease Negotiation Assistance: Yes
Co-Operative Advertising: Yes
Franchisee Assoc./Member: Yes
Size Of Corporate Staff: 300
On-Going Support: A,B,C,D,E,G,H,I
Training: 8-12 Weeks Certified Training
  Unit; 3-Day Seminars at Headquarters.
SPECIFIC EXPANSION PLANS:
US: NY,LA,HI,AK
Canada: All Canada
Overseas: All Countries

≪ ≫

BEEF O'BRADY'S

505 E. Jackson, # 308
Tampa, FL 33602
Tel: (800) 728-8878 (813) 226-2333
Fax: (813) 226-0030
Web Site: www.beefofradys.com
Mr. Nick Vojnovic, VP of Franchising

BEEF O'BRADY'S is a neighborhood sports pub, geared for families. The pub has beer and wine only and video games. Their signature items are buffalo wings (26 million sold every year), sandwiches, salads and burgers.

BACKGROUND: IFA MEMBER
Established: 1985;   1st Franchised: 1998
Franchised Units: 42
Company-Owned Units   0
Total Units: 42
Dist.:   US-42; CAN-0; O'seas-0
  North America: 1 State
  Density: 42 in FL
Projected New Units (12 Months):   16
Qualifications: 3, 4, 2, 2, 4, 4
Registered: FL
FINANCIAL/TERMS:
Cash Investment: $10-100K
Total Investment: $200-300K
Minimum Net Worth: $100K
Fees: Franchise - $20K
  Royalty - 3%;   Ad. - 1.5%
Earnings Claim Statement: No
Term of Contract (Years):   10/10
Avg. # Of Employees: 12FT, 8PT
Passive Ownership: Not Allowed
Encourage Conversions: Yes
Area Develop. Agreements: Yes/10
Sub-Franchising Contracts: No
Expand In Territory: Yes
Space Needs: 3,000 SF; SC
SUPPORT & TRAINING PROVIDED:
Financial Assistance Provided: Yes(I)
Site Selection Assistance: Yes
Lease Negotiation Assistance: Yes
Co-Operative Advertising: Yes
Franchisee Assoc./Member: No/No
Size Of Corporate Staff: 6
On-Going Support: B,C,D,E,H,I
Training: 5 Weeks in Tampa, FL.
SPECIFIC EXPANSION PLANS:
US: Southeast
Canada: No
Overseas: No

≪ ≫

BENIHANA OF TOKYO

8685 NW 53rd Ter.
Miami, FL 44166

Tel: (800) 327-3369 (305) 593-0770
Fax: (305) 471-5866
E-Mail: benihana@bellsouth.net
Mr. Tom Vrabel, Director of Franchising

BENIHANA is not only an internationally famous Japanese steak and seafood restaurant, it is also a genuine 'dining experience.' Both first-time and frequent visitors to BENIHANA are immediately drawn to the unique table top hibachi-style of cuisine, where mouth-watering dishes are prepared before their very eyes.

BACKGROUND:
Established: 1964;   1st Franchised: 1970
Franchised Units: 22
Company-Owned Units   0
Total Units: 22
Dist.:   US-57; CAN-1; O'seas-8
  North America: 20 States, 1 Province
  Density: 15 in CA, 6 in FL, 3 in IL
Projected New Units (12 Months):   3
Qualifications: 5, 4, 3, 2, 2, 4
Registered: CA,HI,NY
FINANCIAL/TERMS:
Cash Investment: $550-650K
Total Investment: $1.3-1.8MM
Minimum Net Worth: $1K
Fees: Franchise - $50K
  Royalty - 6%;   Ad. - 0.5%
Earnings Claim Statement: No
Term of Contract (Years):   15/Varies
Avg. # Of Employees: 35 FT, 7 PT
Passive Ownership: Discouraged
Encourage Conversions: Yes
Area Develop. Agreements: Yes/15
Sub-Franchising Contracts: No
Expand In Territory: No
Space Needs: 6,000+ SF; FS
SUPPORT & TRAINING PROVIDED:
Financial Assistance Provided: No
Site Selection Assistance: Yes
Lease Negotiation Assistance: N/A
Co-Operative Advertising: Yes
Franchisee Assoc./Member: No
Size Of Corporate Staff: 51
On-Going Support: a,C,d,E,F,H,I
Training: 12-15 Weeks in Miami, FL.
SPECIFIC EXPANSION PLANS:
US: PA,MD,MI,NC,OH,AZ,TX,NY
Canada: All Canada
Overseas: Europe, Pacific Rim

≪ ≫

BENNIGAN'S

6500 International Pkwy., # 1000
Plano, TX 75093
Tel: (800) 543-9670 (972) 588-5762

Fax: (972) 588-5806
E-Mail: lmckee@metrogroup.com
Web Site: www.bennigans.com
Ms. Lynette McKee, VP Domestic Fran.
Devel.

BENNIGAN'S is a leading casual restaurant chain known for the warm hospitality of an Irish pub and the great taste of fun American foods. Established in 1976, BENNIGAN'S helped create the casual dining segment in the restaurant industry. BENNIGAN'S has expanded beyond its original tavern image to become more food-focused. Today, each restaurant serves a wide assortment of moderately-priced, quality food, as well as a wide selection of beverages.

BACKGROUND: IFA MEMBER
Established: 1976; 1st Franchised: 1995
Franchised Units: 92
Company-Owned Units 163
Total Units: 255
Dist.: US-139; CAN-0; O'seas-16
North America: 32 States
Density: 56 in TX, 42 in FL, 19 in IL
Projected New Units (12 Months): N/A
Qualifications: 5, 5, 5, 3, 3, 3
Registered: All States
FINANCIAL/TERMS:
Cash Investment: $750K
Total Investment: $1.1-2.1MM
Minimum Net Worth: $3MM
Fees: Franchise - $65K
Royalty - 4%; Ad. - 4%
Earnings Claim Statement: No
Term of Contract (Years): 15/15
Avg. # Of Employees: NR
Passive Ownership: Discouraged
Encourage Conversions: Yes
Area Develop. Agreements: Yes
Sub-Franchising Contracts: No
Expand In Territory: Yes
Space Needs: 6,500 SF; FS
SUPPORT & TRAINING PROVIDED:
Financial Assistance Provided: No
Site Selection Assistance: Yes
Lease Negotiation Assistance: No
Co-Operative Advertising: Yes
Franchisee Assoc./Member: Yes/No
Size Of Corporate Staff: 400

On-Going Support: B,C,E,G,h
Training: Managers -- 1 Week Home Office and 11 Weeks in Unit; Employees -- 2-4 Weeks in Unit.
SPECIFIC EXPANSION PLANS:
US: All United States
Canada: All Canada
Overseas: All Countries

◄◄ ►►

BIG BOY RESTAURANT & BAKERY
4199 Marcy Dr.
Warren, MI 48091
Tel: (800) 837-3003 (810) 755-8114
Fax: (810) 757-4737
Web Site: www.bigboy.com
Mr. Ronald E. Johnston, Executive Vice President

Full-service family restaurant with over 60 years of success. BIG BOY'S comprehensive menu features a daily breakfast and fruit buffet, soup, salad and fruit bar, in-store bakery and award-winning desserts, in addition to traditional favorites. Industry leader in managed profitability.

BACKGROUND:
Established: 1936; 1st Franchised: 1952
Franchised Units: 405
Company-Owned Units 68
Total Units: 473
Dist.: US-373; CAN-0; O'seas-100
North America: 17 States
Density: 142 in MI, 102 in OH, 25 KY
Projected New Units (12 Months): 7
Qualifications: 5, 5, 4, 3, 4, 5
Registered: All States
FINANCIAL/TERMS:
Cash Investment: $250K
Total Investment: $600K-1.8MM
Minimum Net Worth: $700K
Fees: Franchise - $40K
Royalty - 3%; Ad. - 3%
Earnings Claim Statement: Yes
Term of Contract (Years): 20
Avg. # Of Employees: 10 FT, 25 PT
Passive Ownership: Discouraged
Encourage Conversions: Yes
Area Develop. Agreements: Yes/20
Sub-Franchising Contracts: No
Expand In Territory: Yes
Space Needs: 5,200 SF; FS
SUPPORT & TRAINING PROVIDED:
Financial Assistance Provided: Yes(I)
Site Selection Assistance: Yes

Lease Negotiation Assistance: Yes
Co-Operative Advertising: Yes
Franchisee Assoc./Member: Yes/Yes
Size Of Corporate Staff: 165
On-Going Support: A,B,C,D,E,F,G,H,I
Training: 6-8 Weeks In-Unit; 1-2 Weeks at Corporate Headquarters.
SPECIFIC EXPANSION PLANS:
US: All United States
Canada: All Canada
Overseas: All Countries

◄◄ ►►

BOBBY RUBINO'S PLACE FOR RIBS
1990 E. Sunrise Blvd.
Ft. Lauderdale, FL 33304
Tel: (800) 997-7427 (954) 763-9871
Fax: (954) 467-1192
E-Mail: rubinosusa@att.net
Ms. Kay Ferrara, Director Franchise Operations

Full-service, including full liquor service. Specializing in BBQ. BOBBY RUBINO'S PLACE FOR RIBS also has a large menu including steak, seafood, salads, etc. served in a casual atmosphere. A kiddie menu is available.

BACKGROUND:
Established: 1978; 1st Franchised: 1982
Franchised Units: 10
Company-Owned Units 0
Total Units: 10
Dist.: US-9; CAN-0; O'seas-1
North America: 5 States
Density: 4 in FL, 1 in CA, 1 in NY
Projected New Units (12 Months): 3
Qualifications: 5, 5, 3, 3, 3, 3
Registered: FL,MI,NY,WI
FINANCIAL/TERMS:
Cash Investment: $200K
Total Investment: $450-650K
Minimum Net Worth: $750K
Fees: Franchise - $50K
Royalty - 4%; Ad. - 3%
Earnings Claim Statement: No
Term of Contract (Years): 15/10
Avg. # Of Employees: 20 FT, 20 PT
Passive Ownership: Discouraged
Encourage Conversions: Yes
Area Develop. Agreements: Yes/Negot.

Sub-Franchising Contracts: No
Expand In Territory: Yes
Space Needs: 6,000 SF; FS, SF, SC, RM
SUPPORT & TRAINING PROVIDED:
Financial Assistance Provided: No
Site Selection Assistance: Yes
Lease Negotiation Assistance: Yes
Co-Operative Advertising: Yes
Franchisee Assoc./Member: No
Size Of Corporate Staff: 1
On-Going Support: a,C,d,E,F,h,I
Training: 6-8 Weeks Ft. Lauderdale, FL.
SPECIFIC EXPANSION PLANS:
US: All United States
Canada: All Canada
Overseas: All Countries

≪ ≫

BOSTON PIZZA
5500 Parkwood Way, #200
Richmond, BC V6V 2M4 CANADA
Tel: (800) 887-7757 (604) 270-1108
Fax: (604) 270-4168
E-Mail: franchising@bostonpizza.com
Web Site: www.bostonpizza.com
Mr. Rick Villalpando, Director of Franchising

BOSTON PIZZA is Canada's most successful casual dining pizza and pasta franchise operation, with over 100 locations and system-wide sales in excess of $200 million. Boston Pizza appeals to four sectors: families at early evening; business people at lunch; after movies; and take-out and delivery.

BACKGROUND: IFA MEMBER
Established: 1963; 1st Franchised: 1968
Franchised Units: 130
Company-Owned Units: 2
Total Units: 132
Dist.: US-3; CAN-129; O'seas-0
North America: 3 States, 5 Provinces
Density: 59 in AB, 44 in BC, 10 in SK
Projected New Units (12 Months): 12
Qualifications: 5, 5, 3, 3, 3, 4
Registered: ND,WA,AB
FINANCIAL/TERMS:
Cash Investment: $300-400K
Total Investment: $900K-1MM
Minimum Net Worth: $1MM
Fees: Franchise - $45-55K
Royalty - 7%; Ad. - 3%
Earnings Claim Statement: Yes
Term of Contract (Years): 10/10

Avg. # Of Employees: 30 FT, 40 PT
Passive Ownership: Not Allowed
Encourage Conversions: No
Area Develop. Agreements: Yes/10
Sub-Franchising Contracts: No
Expand In Territory: Yes
Space Needs: 5,000-6,600 SF; FS
SUPPORT & TRAINING PROVIDED:
Financial Assistance Provided: Yes(I)
Site Selection Assistance: Yes
Lease Negotiation Assistance: Yes
Co-Operative Advertising: Yes
Franchisee Assoc./Member: Yes/Yes
Size Of Corporate Staff: 79
On-Going Support: B,C,D,E,F,G,H
Training: 8 Weeks Richmond, BC, Corporate Training Centre.
SPECIFIC EXPANSION PLANS:
US: Northwest, Southwest, South
Canada: All Canada
Overseas: All Countries

≪ ≫

BUFFALO WILD WINGS GRILL & BAR
1919 Interchange Tower 600 S. Hwy. 169
Minneapolis, MN 55426
Tel: (800) 499-9586 (952) 593-9943
Fax: (952) 593-9787
E-Mail: bill@buffalowildwings.com
Web Site: www.buffalowildwings.com
Mr. Bill McClintock, VP Franchise Dev.

Sports theme, family-friendly restaurant, world-famous buffalo wings with 12 proprietary sauces, great burgers & sandwiches, full bar, 25+ TV's, National Trivia Network.

BACKGROUND: IFA MEMBER
Established: 1982; 1st Franchised: 1991
Franchised Units: 96
Company-Owned Units: 37
Total Units: 133
Dist.: US-133; CAN-0; O'seas-0
North America: 20 States
Density: 55 in OH, 11 in IN, 7 in KY
Projected New Units (12 Months): 40
Qualifications: 5, 4, 4, 3, 3, 5
Registered: All States

FINANCIAL/TERMS:
Cash Investment: $200K
Total Investment: $586-896K
Minimum Net Worth: $600K
Fees: Franchise - $25-30K
Royalty - 5%; Ad. - 3%
Earnings Claim Statement: Yes
Term of Contract (Years): 10/2/5
Avg. # Of Employees: 3 FT, 50 PT
Passive Ownership: Not Allowed
Encourage Conversions: Yes
Area Develop. Agreements: Yes/10
Sub-Franchising Contracts: No
Expand In Territory: Yes
Space Needs: 5,000-6,000 SF; FS, SC
SUPPORT & TRAINING PROVIDED:
Financial Assistance Provided: Yes
Site Selection Assistance: Yes
Lease Negotiation Assistance: Yes
Co-Operative Advertising: Yes
Franchisee Assoc./Member: Yes/Yes
Size Of Corporate Staff: 65
On-Going Support: A,B,C,D,E,F,G,H,I
Training: 3 Weeks in Store.
SPECIFIC EXPANSION PLANS:
US: All United States
Canada: No
Overseas: No

≪ ≫

BUFFALO'S CAFE
707 Whitlock Ave. SW, Bldg. H-13
Marietta, GA 30064
Tel: (800) 459-4647 (770) 420-1800
Fax: (770) 420-1811
E-Mail: kculkin@buffaloscafe.com
Web Site: www.buffaloscafe.com
Mr. Kevin Culkin, Director of Franchising

BUFFALO'S CAFE offers casual family dining in an 'Old West' cafe atmosphere. Menu is based on a fresh-food concept, featuring Buffalo-style chicken-wings, rotisserie chicken and other charbroiled specialties. Complete training is offered both initially and on-going.

BACKGROUND: IFA MEMBER
Established: 1985; 1st Franchised: 1991
Franchised Units: 42
Company-Owned Units: 6
Total Units: 48

Dist.: US-46; CAN-0; O'seas-2
 North America: 6 States, Puerto Rico
 Density: 35 in GA, 5 in SC, 2 in FL
Projected New Units (12 Months): 20
Qualifications: 4, 4, 2, 2, 4, 4
Registered: FL

FINANCIAL/TERMS:

Cash Investment: $200K
Total Investment: $450K-1.5MM
Minimum Net Worth: $500K
Fees: Franchise - $35K
 Royalty - 5%; Ad. - 2%
Earnings Claim Statement: No
Term of Contract (Years): 10/10/10
Avg. # Of Employees: 20 FT, 30 PT
Passive Ownership: Allowed
Encourage Conversions: No
Area Develop. Agreements: Yes/Varies
Sub-Franchising Contracts: No
Expand In Territory: Yes
Space Needs: 4,000-5,000 SF; FS, SC

SUPPORT & TRAINING PROVIDED:

Financial Assistance Provided: Yes(I)
Site Selection Assistance: Yes
Lease Negotiation Assistance: Yes
Co-Operative Advertising: Yes
Franchisee Assoc./Member: Yes
Size Of Corporate Staff: 20
On-Going Support: B,C,D,E,F,G,H,I
Training: 30 Days Corporate Store; 2
 Weeks Franchisee's Store -- Pre & Post
 Opening.

SPECIFIC EXPANSION PLANS:

US: All United States
Canada: All Canada
Overseas: All Countries

<< >>

BULLWINKLE'S RESTAURANT & THE FAMILY FUN CENTERS

18300 Von Karman, # 900
Irvine, CA 92612
Tel: (949) 261-0404
Fax: (949) 261-1414
Web Site: www.bullwinkles.com
Mr. Mickey Kanolzer, VP of Food and
 Beverage

There's only one family entertainment concept that combines great food and fun center attractions. 'Gadzooks', you say? Well, all this plus merchandise, animated shows, go-karts, soft play areas, miniature golf, games and hard rides, too.

BACKGROUND:

Established: 1982; 1st Franchised: 1994
Franchised Units: 2

Company-Owned Units 7
Total Units: 9
Dist.: US-8; CAN-0; O'seas-1
 North America: 2 States
 Density: 6 in CA, 1 in OR
Projected New Units (12 Months): 3
Qualifications: 4, 5, 3, 4, 4, 4
Registered: CA,FL,NY,OR,

FINANCIAL/TERMS:

Cash Investment: $40%
Total Investment: $1.1-5.5MM
Minimum Net Worth: $650K
Fees: Franchise - $25-75K
 Royalty - 4%; Ad. - 3.5%
Earnings Claim Statement: Yes
Term of Contract (Years): 15/15
Avg. # Of Employees: 40 PT, 40 FT
Passive Ownership: Discouraged
Encourage Conversions: Yes
Area Develop. Agreements: Yes/15
Sub-Franchising Contracts: No
Expand In Territory: No
Space Needs: 10,000 SF; FS

SUPPORT & TRAINING PROVIDED:

Financial Assistance Provided: Yes(I)
Site Selection Assistance: Yes
Lease Negotiation Assistance: Yes
Co-Operative Advertising: Yes
Franchisee Assoc./Member: No
Size Of Corporate Staff: 6
On-Going Support: A,C,D,E,F,G,H
Training: 5 Weeks Upland, CA; 3 Weeks
 On-Site.

SPECIFIC EXPANSION PLANS:

US: All United States
Canada: All Canada
Overseas: Middle East

<< >>

CAFÉ SANTA FE

4004 N. College, # I
Fayetteville, AR 72703
Tel: (800) 909-4898 (501) 444-9001
Fax: (501) 444-0434
E-Mail: info@cafesantafe.com
Web Site: www.cafesantafe.com
Mr. Tom D. Flores, President

A unique blend of old-style Mexican food and new wave Southwest fare. CAFÉ SANTA FE is a contemporary Southwest-style concept that appeals to the young and

old. It sets itself apart by not yielding to the 'Village' look. Bright, airy and festive! 'Come away with CAFÉ SANTA FE and taste the Southwest.'

BACKGROUND:

Established: 1982; 1st Franchised: 1996
Franchised Units: 11
Company-Owned Units 4
Total Units: 15
Dist.: US-15; CAN-0; O'seas-0
 North America: 2 States
 Density: 13 in AR, 2 in MO
Projected New Units (12 Months): 7
Qualifications: 3, 5, 3, 3, 5, 5
Registered:

FINANCIAL/TERMS:

Cash Investment: $200-250K
Total Investment: $1.1MM
Minimum Net Worth: $300K
Fees: Franchise - $35K
 Royalty - 4.5%; Ad. - 1%
Earnings Claim Statement: No
Term of Contract (Years): 10/10
Avg. # Of Employees: 10 FT, 25 PT
Passive Ownership: Not Allowed
Encourage Conversions: Yes
Area Develop. Agreements: Yes/10
Sub-Franchising Contracts: No
Expand In Territory: Yes
Space Needs: 4,500 SF; FS, SC

SUPPORT & TRAINING PROVIDED:

Financial Assistance Provided: No
Site Selection Assistance: Yes
Lease Negotiation Assistance: Yes
Co-Operative Advertising: Yes
Franchisee Assoc./Member: No
Size Of Corporate Staff: 8
On-Going Support: A,B,C,D,E,F,G
Training: 4-6 Weeks in Springdale, AR --
 Corporate Training; 2 Weeks, On-Site.

SPECIFIC EXPANSION PLANS:

US: AR,MO,KS,OK
Canada: No
Overseas: No

<< >>

CARLSON RESTAURANTS WORLDWIDE

7540 LBJ Fwy., # 100
Dallas, TX 75251
Tel: (800) FRIDAYS (972) 450-5400
Fax: (972) 450-5784
Web Site: www.tgifridays.com
Mr. Bill Alexander, Executive Director
 Franchising

Casual-theme, full-service restaurants.

BACKGROUND:

Established: 1965;   1st Franchised: 1970
Franchised Units: 360
Company-Owned Units   180
Total Units: 540
Dist.:   US-414; CAN-1; O'seas-93
  North America: 45 States
  Density: 49 in FL, 42 in TX, 35 in CA
Projected New Units (12 Months):   100+
Qualifications: 5, 4, 5, 3, 5, 5
Registered: All States

FINANCIAL/TERMS:

Cash Investment: $1MM
Total Investment: $1.7-4MM
Minimum Net Worth: $3MM
Fees: Franchise - $75K
  Royalty - 4%;   Ad. - 2-4%
Earnings Claim Statement: Yes
Term of Contract (Years):   20/Varies
Avg. # Of Employees: 100-125
Passive Ownership: Discouraged
Encourage Conversions: Yes
Area Develop. Agreements: Yes/5
Sub-Franchising Contracts: No
Expand In Territory: Yes
Space Needs: 6,800 SF; FS

SUPPORT & TRAINING PROVIDED:

Financial Assistance Provided: No
Site Selection Assistance: Yes
Lease Negotiation Assistance: No
Co-Operative Advertising: No
Franchisee Assoc./Member: Yes/Yes
Size Of Corporate Staff: 300+
On-Going Support: b,c,d,e,h,I
Training: 2 Weeks in Dallas, TX.

SPECIFIC EXPANSION PLANS:

US: All United States
Canada: All Canada
Overseas: All Countries

‹‹ ››

CASEY'S BAR/GRILL
10 Kingsbridge Garden Circle, # 600
Mississauga, ON L5R 3K6 CANADA
Tel: (905) 568-0000
Fax: (905) 568-0080
Web Site: www.primerestaurants.com
Mr. H. Ross R. Bain, VP Admin./Legal
  Counsel

Casual dining, grilled food, burgers,
wraps.

BACKGROUND:

Established: 1979;   1st Franchised: 1979
Franchised Units: 22
Company-Owned Units   12
Total Units: 34

Dist.:   US-0; CAN-34; O'seas-0
North America: 2 Provinces
Density: 28 in ON, 6 in PQ
Projected New Units (12 Months):   4
Qualifications: 5, 3, 3, 2, 5, 5
Registered: None

FINANCIAL/TERMS:

Cash Investment: $250-350K
Total Investment: $995K
Minimum Net Worth: $500K
Fees: Franchise - $40K
  Royalty - 5%;   Ad. - 2%/2% Local
Earnings Claim Statement: No
Term of Contract (Years):   10/5
Avg. # Of Employees: 35 FT, 25 PT
Passive Ownership: Discouraged
Encourage Conversions: Yes
Area Develop. Agreements: Yes
Sub-Franchising Contracts: No
Expand In Territory: No
Space Needs: 5,168 SF; FS, SC, RM

SUPPORT & TRAINING PROVIDED:

Financial Assistance Provided: No
Site Selection Assistance: Yes
Lease Negotiation Assistance: Yes
Co-Operative Advertising: Yes
Franchisee Assoc./Member: Yes/Yes
Size Of Corporate Staff: 100
On-Going Support: B,C,D,E,h
Training: 6 Weeks in Store; 1 Week at Head
  Office.

SPECIFIC EXPANSION PLANS:

US: Canada Only
Canada: All Canada
Overseas: No

‹‹ ››

CHARLEY'S STEAKERY
6610 Busch Blvd., # 100
Columbus, OH 43229
Tel: (800) 437-8325 (614) 847-8100
Fax: (614) 847-8110
E-Mail:
franchising@charleyssteakery.com
Web Site: www.charleyssteakery.com
Mr. Richard A. Page, Vice President
  Development

CHARLEY'S STEAKERY is a progressive
quick-service restaurant with over 100
locations across the United States and

Canada. The heart of CHARLEY'S menu
consists of freshly-grilled Steak and
Chicken Subs, fresh-cut fries and freshly
squeezed lemonade. CHARLEY'S open
kitchen environment and freshly-prepared
products are unique in the fast-food
industry.

BACKGROUND: IFA MEMBER

Established: 1986;   1st Franchised: 1991
Franchised Units: 96
Company-Owned Units   10
Total Units: 106
Dist.:   US-96; CAN-8; O'seas-2
  North America: 27 States, 1 Province
  Density: 15 in OH, 8 in FL,8 in ON
Projected New Units (12 Months):   60
Qualifications: 4, 5, 2, 2, 2, 5
Registered: CA,FL,HI,IL,IN,MD,MI,
  NY,VA,WI

FINANCIAL/TERMS:

Cash Investment: $NR
Total Investment: $124.5-294.5K
Minimum Net Worth: $200K
Fees: Franchise - $19.5K
  Royalty - 5% or $200/Mo.; Ad. - 0.25%
Earnings Claim Statement: Yes
Term of Contract (Years):   10/10
Avg. # Of Employees: NR
Passive Ownership: Discouraged
Encourage Conversions: Yes
Area Develop. Agreements: Yes/10
Sub-Franchising Contracts: Yes
Expand In Territory: Yes
Space Needs: NR SF; SC, RM

SUPPORT & TRAINING PROVIDED:

Financial Assistance Provided: Yes(I)
Site Selection Assistance: Yes
Lease Negotiation Assistance: Yes
Co-Operative Advertising: Yes
Franchisee Assoc./Member: Yes/Yes
Size Of Corporate Staff: 18
On-Going Support:
  B,C,D,e(required),G,h,I
Training: 3 Weeks at Columbus, OH.

SPECIFIC EXPANSION PLANS:

US: All United States
Canada: ON
Overseas: No

‹‹ ››

CHEDDAR'S CASUAL CAFÉ
616 Six Flags Dr., # 116
Arlington, TX 76011
Tel: (817) 640-4344
Fax: (817) 633-4452
Mr. Larry D. Zimmerman, Director
  Franchise Development

Full-service restaurant. Terrific price/value, with traditional menu, in pleasing ambiance.

BACKGROUND:

Established: 1978;   1st Franchised: 1984
Franchised Units: 16
Company-Owned Units   14
Total Units: 30
Dist.:   US-30; CAN-0; O'seas-0
  North America: 10 States
  Density: 12 in TX, 6 in IL, 3 in OH
Projected New Units (12 Months):   5-7
Qualifications: 5, 4, 5, 2, 3, 5
Registered:

FINANCIAL/TERMS:

Cash Investment: $300K
Total Investment: $1.5-1.9MM+
Minimum Net Worth: $750K
Fees: Franchise - $30K
  Royalty - 3%;   Ad. - 0%
Earnings Claim Statement: No
Term of Contract (Years):   20/20
Avg. # Of Employees: 60FT, 40 PT
Passive Ownership: Not Allowed
Encourage Conversions: NR
Area Develop. Agreements: Yes/Varies
Sub-Franchising Contracts: No
Expand In Territory: NR
Space Needs: 7,700 SF; FS

SUPPORT & TRAINING PROVIDED:

Financial Assistance Provided: No
Site Selection Assistance: Yes
Lease Negotiation Assistance: Yes
Co-Operative Advertising: No
Franchisee Assoc./Member: No
Size Of Corporate Staff: 20
On-Going Support: B,C,D,E,F,G,H
Training: 12 Weeks Arlington, TX.

SPECIFIC EXPANSION PLANS:

US: All United States
Canada: All Canada
Overseas: All Countries

⋘   ⋙

COLTER'S BAR-B-Q

5910 N. Central Expy., # 1355
Dallas, TX 75206
Tel: (888) 265-8377 (214) 987-5910
Fax: (214) 987-5938
E-Mail: anne@colter's
Web Site: www.coltersbbq.com
Ms. Marie Bernat, Vice President

Casual, family, cafeteria-style barbeque restaurant, serving Texas barbeque in a western setting.

BACKGROUND:

Established: 1982;   1st Franchised: 1994
Franchised Units: 8
Company-Owned Units   5
Total Units: 13
Dist.:   US-13; CAN-0; O'seas-0
  North America: 1 State
  Density: 13 in TX
Projected New Units (12 Months):   2-4
Qualifications: 5, 4, 4, 3, 4, 3
Registered: NR

FINANCIAL/TERMS:

Cash Investment: $156-250K
Total Investment: $730K-1.03MM
Minimum Net Worth: $1-1.5MM
Fees: Franchise - $30K
  Royalty - 4%;   Ad. - 0.5%
Earnings Claim Statement: No
Term of Contract (Years):   20/10-20
Avg. # Of Employees: 3 FT, 25 PT
Passive Ownership: Discouraged
Encourage Conversions: No
Area Develop. Agreements: Yes/Open
Sub-Franchising Contracts: No
Expand In Territory: Yes
Space Needs: 4,600 SF; FS

SUPPORT & TRAINING PROVIDED:

Financial Assistance Provided: Yes(I)
Site Selection Assistance: Yes
Lease Negotiation Assistance: N/A
Co-Operative Advertising: Yes
Franchisee Assoc./Member: No
Size Of Corporate Staff: 10
On-Going Support: B,C,D,E,F,H,I
Training: 8 Weeks at Dallas, TX.

SPECIFIC EXPANSION PLANS:

US: Southwest, Northeast
Canada: No
Overseas: No

⋘   ⋙

DAMON'S INTERNATIONAL

4645 Executive Dr.
Columbus, OH 43220
Tel: (614) 442-7900
Fax: (614) 538-2521

E-Mail: kclark@damons.com
Web Site: www.damons.com
Mr. Ed Williams, VP of Development

DAMON'S... A dining event in a casual dining restaurant, dedicated to exceeding your expectations in all areas of operation. The 128-unit chain is famous for its award-winning BBQ ribs, prime rib and onion loaf. DAMON'S features 10' screens and is a state-of-the-art electronic sports/entertainment facility.

BACKGROUND:

Established: 1979;   1st Franchised: 1982
Franchised Units: 114
Company-Owned Units   21
Total Units: 135
Dist.:   US-133; CAN-0; O'seas-2
  North America: NR
  Density: 33 in OH, 11 in IN, 11 in MI
Projected New Units (12 Months):   25
Qualifications: 5, 4, 4, 3, 3, 5
Registered: CA,FL,IL,IN,MD,MI,MN,
  NY,OR,RI,SD,VA,WA,WI

FINANCIAL/TERMS:

Cash Investment: $300K Minimum
Total Investment: $940K-2.7MM
Minimum Net Worth: $1MM
Fees: Franchise - $50K
  Royalty - 4%;   Ad. - 0.5%
Earnings Claim Statement: Yes
Term of Contract (Years):   10/3-5
Avg. # Of Employees: 30 FT, 50 PT
Passive Ownership: Discouraged
Encourage Conversions: Yes
Area Develop. Agreements: Yes/Varies
Sub-Franchising Contracts: No
Expand In Territory: Yes
Space Needs: 6,500 Min. SF; FS, SC, RM,
  Hotel

SUPPORT & TRAINING PROVIDED:

Financial Assistance Provided: Yes(I)
Site Selection Assistance: Yes
Lease Negotiation Assistance: Yes
Co-Operative Advertising: Yes
Franchisee Assoc./Member: Yes
Size Of Corporate Staff: 53
On-Going Support: a,B,C,D,E,F,h
Training: 8 Weeks in Restaurant Training.

SPECIFIC EXPANSION PLANS:

US: Southwest, TX,CA,CO
Canada: No
Overseas: Orient, Europe, Central
  America

⋘   ⋙

DENNY'S

203 E. Main St.
Spartanburg, SC 29319-9912
Tel: (800) 304-0222 (864) 597-8938
Fax: (864) 597-7708
E-Mail: B_Cauthan@Advantica-Dine.Com
Web Site: www.dennys.com/franchise
Ms. Beth Cauthan, Administrator

From its beginning in 1953, DENNY'S has grown into one of America's largest full-service restaurant chains, serving nearly 1 million customers a day at its nearly 1,800 restaurants worldwide. Today, DENNY'S is going back to its roots with the DENNY'S Diner 2000 reimaging program for existing restaurants. DENNY'S is well known for its around-the-clock breakfast entrees and is the only full-service restaurant chain where most restaurants are open 24 hours a day, 7 days a week.

BACKGROUND: IFA MEMBER
Established: 1953;   1st Franchised: 1963
Franchised Units: 1,060
Company-Owned Units   756
Total Units: 1,816
Dist.:   US-1,745; CAN-48; O'seas-23
 North America: 49 States, 4 Provinces
 Density: 207 in CA, 135 in FL, 100 TX
Projected New Units (12 Months):   NR
Qualifications: 5, 5, 5, 2, 2, 5
Registered: All States
FINANCIAL/TERMS:
Cash Investment: $250K
Total Investment: $858K-1.5MM
Minimum Net Worth: $750K
Fees: Franchise - $35K
 Royalty - 4%;   Ad. - 5%
Earnings Claim Statement: Yes
Term of Contract (Years):   20/N/A
Avg. # Of Employees: 80 FT
Passive Ownership: Discouraged
Encourage Conversions: Yes
Area Develop. Agreements: Yes
Sub-Franchising Contracts: No
Expand In Territory: Yes
Space Needs: 30,000-38,364 SF; FS, SC,
 Other
SUPPORT & TRAINING PROVIDED:
Financial Assistance Provided: Yes(I)

Site Selection Assistance: Yes
Lease Negotiation Assistance: No
Co-Operative Advertising: Yes
Franchisee Assoc./Member: Yes/No
Size Of Corporate Staff: 18
On-Going Support: C,D,E,G,H,I
Training: Up to 10 Weeks at Various
 Geographical Areas.
SPECIFIC EXPANSION PLANS:
US: All United States
Canada: All Canada
Overseas: No

≪ ≫

DESERT MOON CAFÉ

612 Corporate Wy., #1M
Valley Cottage, NY 10989
Tel: (877) JOIN-DMC (914) 267-3300
Fax: (914) 267-2548
E-Mail: desertmooncafe@msn.com
Web Site: www.desertmooncafe.com
Mr. Gary Occhiogrosso, VP of
 Franchising

Fast casual Southwestern / Fresh-Mex Grille in a fun, bold environment.

BACKGROUND:
Established: 1998;   1st Franchised: 1999
Franchised Units: 5
Company-Owned Units   5
Total Units: 10
Dist.:   US-10; CAN-0; O'seas-0
 North America: 50 States
 Density: 3 in NY, 2 in CT
Projected New Units (12 Months):   15
Qualifications: 5, 3, 4, 1, 3, 5
Registered: FL,MD,MI,NY,RI,VA,DC
FINANCIAL/TERMS:
Cash Investment: $60K
Total Investment: $190-350K
Minimum Net Worth: $200K
Fees: Franchise - $25K
 Royalty - 5%;   Ad. - 3%
Earnings Claim Statement: No
Term of Contract (Years):   10/5
Avg. # Of Employees: 2 FT, 4 PT
Passive Ownership: Discouraged
Encourage Conversions: Yes
Area Develop. Agreements: Yes/3
Sub-Franchising Contracts: No
Expand In Territory: Yes
Space Needs: 1,800 SF; SC
SUPPORT & TRAINING PROVIDED:
Financial Assistance Provided: Yes(I)

Site Selection Assistance: Yes
Lease Negotiation Assistance: Yes
Co-Operative Advertising: Yes
Franchisee Assoc./Member: Yes/Yes
Size Of Corporate Staff: 6
On-Going Support: C,D,E,F,G,I
Training: 4 Weeks Corporate Training; 2
 Weeks On-Site.
SPECIFIC EXPANSION PLANS:
US: Northeast, Florida
Canada: No
Overseas: No

≪ ≫

DICKEY'S BARBECUE PIT RESTAURANTS

P.O. Box 802216
Dallas, TX 75380
Tel: (800) 460-9000 (972) 716-9931
Fax: (972) 716-9913
Mr. Paul J. Stewart, Dir. Franchise
 Development

Original Texas-style, slow-smoked barbecue. 8 meats and 15 hot and cold veggie dishes made fresh every day. Average 4,000 SF, seating 120-140. In-line, conversions and new buildings. Custom exteriors.

BACKGROUND:
Established: 1941;   1st Franchised: 1994
Franchised Units: 17
Company-Owned Units   4
Total Units: 21
Dist.:   US-21; CAN-0; O'seas-0
 North America: 3 States
 Density: 18 in TX, 2 in CO, 1 in CA
Projected New Units (12 Months):   40
Qualifications: 5, 4, 1, 4, 1, 5
Registered: CA,FL,RI
FINANCIAL/TERMS:
Cash Investment: $150-250K
Total Investment: $450K-1.3MM
Minimum Net Worth: $500K
Fees: Franchise - $25K
 Royalty - 4%;   Ad. - 2%
Earnings Claim Statement: Yes
Term of Contract (Years):   10/20
Avg. # Of Employees: 10 FT, 8 PT
Passive Ownership: Discouraged
Encourage Conversions: Yes
Area Develop. Agreements: Yes/5
Sub-Franchising Contracts: No
Expand In Territory: No
Space Needs: 4,000 SF; FS, SC, RM,
 Conversions
SUPPORT & TRAINING PROVIDED:

Financial Assistance Provided: Yes(I)
Site Selection Assistance: Yes
Lease Negotiation Assistance: Yes
Co-Operative Advertising: Yes
Franchisee Assoc./Member: No
Size Of Corporate Staff: 10
On-Going Support: B,C,D,E,F,h,I
Training: 30 Days Dallas, TX.
SPECIFIC EXPANSION PLANS:
US: West, Tidewater
Canada: No
Overseas: Pacific Rim

◄◄ ►►

DOG n SUDS DRIVE-IN
RESTAURANTS
188 N. State Road 267, # 102
Avon, IN 46123
Tel: (800) DOGNSUDS (317) 272-1000
Fax: (317) 272-1002
E-Mail: dognsudscorp@juno.com
Web Site: www.DOGnSUDS.net
Mr. Richard T. Morath, President/CEO

Classic, carhop, curb-service QSR with optional inside dining and drive-thru service. DOG n SUDS serves coney dogs, chilidogs, hamburgers and the world's creamiest root beer.

BACKGROUND:
Established: 1953; 1st Franchised: 1954
Franchised Units: 16
Company-Owned Units: <u>10</u>
Total Units: 26
Dist.: US-26; CAN-0; O'seas-0
  North America: 3 States
  Density: 22 in IN, 2 in IL, 2 in KY
Projected New Units (12 Months): 5
Qualifications: 4, 4, 2, 3, 3, 4
Registered: FL,IL,IN
FINANCIAL/TERMS:
Cash Investment: $150K
Total Investment: $600K-1.0MM
Minimum Net Worth: $750K
Fees: Franchise - $25K
  Royalty - 3-5%; Ad. - 3%
Earnings Claim Statement: No
Term of Contract (Years): 15/5
Avg. # Of Employees: 15 FT, 10 PT
Passive Ownership: Allowed
Encourage Conversions: Yes
Area Develop. Agreements: Yes/Open
Sub-Franchising Contracts: No
Expand In Territory: Yes
Space Needs: 40,000 SF; FS
SUPPORT & TRAINING PROVIDED:
Financial Assistance Provided: N/A

Site Selection Assistance: Yes
Lease Negotiation Assistance: Yes
Co-Operative Advertising: Yes
Franchisee Assoc./Member: No
Size Of Corporate Staff: 8
On-Going Support: B,C,D,E,F,I
Training: 6 Weeks Indianapolis, IN.
SPECIFIC EXPANSION PLANS:
US: All United States
Canada: No
Overseas: No

◄◄ ►►

An American Italian Eatery

EAST SIDE MARIO'S
10 Kingsbridge Garden Circle, # 600
Mississauga, ON L5R 3K6 CANADA
Tel: (800) 361-3111 (905) 568-0000
Fax: (905) 568-0080
Web Site: www.primerestaurants
Mr. H. Ross Bain, VP Admin./Legal Counsel

American-Italian.

BACKGROUND:
Established: 1979; 1st Franchised: 1989
Franchised Units: 79
Company-Owned Units: <u>7</u>
Total Units: 86
Dist.: US-9; CAN-77; O'seas-0
  North America: 7 States, 4 Provinces
  Density: 58 in ON, 12 in PQ, 3 in AB
Projected New Units (12 Months): 10
Qualifications: 5, 3, 3, 2, 5, 5
Registered: NR
FINANCIAL/TERMS:
Cash Investment: $300-400K
Total Investment: $1.08MM
Minimum Net Worth: $750K
Fees: Franchise - $50K
  Royalty - 5%; Ad. - 3%/1% Local
Earnings Claim Statement: No
Term of Contract (Years): 10/5
Avg. # Of Employees: 50 FT, 25 PT
Passive Ownership: Discouraged
Encourage Conversions: Yes
Area Develop. Agreements: Yes
Sub-Franchising Contracts: No
Expand In Territory: No
Space Needs: 5,314 SF; FS, SC, RM

SUPPORT & TRAINING PROVIDED:
Financial Assistance Provided: No
Site Selection Assistance: Yes
Lease Negotiation Assistance: Yes
Co-Operative Advertising: Yes
Franchisee Assoc./Member: Yes/Yes
Size Of Corporate Staff: 100
On-Going Support: B,C,D,E,h
Training: 6 Weeks in Store; 1 Week at Head
  Office.
SPECIFIC EXPANSION PLANS:
US: Only Canada
Canada: All Canada
Overseas: No

◄◄ ►►

EDO JAPAN
4838 32nd St. SE
Calgary, AB T2B 2S6 CANADA
Tel: (403) 215-8800
Fax: (403) 215-8801
E-Mail: edo@edojapan.com
Web Site: www.edojapan.com
Ms. Colleen Pickard, Manager, Legal/
  Admin.

EDO JAPAN originated the concept of preparing Japanese Teppan Meals inexpensively through fast-food outlets more than 20 years ago. Since that time, EDO has maintained its popularity in the food courts due to EDO's menu placing emphasis on freshness, nutrition, service and very reasonable prices.

BACKGROUND:
Established: 1977; 1st Franchised: 1986
Franchised Units: 95
Company-Owned Units: <u>9</u>
Total Units: 104
Dist.: US-46; CAN-55; O'seas-3
  North America: 13 States, 5 Provinces
  Density: 28 in AB, 16 in ON, 14 in CA
Projected New Units (12 Months): 6
Qualifications: 5, 4, 4, 3, 4, 5
Registered: CA,FL,HI,MD,OR,WA,AB
FINANCIAL/TERMS:
Cash Investment: $NR
Total Investment: $160-350K
Minimum Net Worth: $NR
Fees: Franchise - $20K
  Royalty - 6%; Ad. - 0-2%
Earnings Claim Statement: No

Term of Contract (Years): Lease
Avg. # Of Employees: 2 FT, 4 PT
Passive Ownership: Discouraged
Encourage Conversions: N/A
Area Develop. Agreements: Yes/Varies
Sub-Franchising Contracts: Yes
Expand In Territory: Yes
Space Needs: 350-650 SF; RM
SUPPORT & TRAINING PROVIDED:
Financial Assistance Provided: No
Site Selection Assistance: Yes
Lease Negotiation Assistance: Yes
Co-Operative Advertising: Yes
Franchisee Assoc./Member: No
Size Of Corporate Staff: 10
On-Going Support: B,C,D,E,F,G,H
Training: 2 Weeks Calgary, AB; 10 Days
    Opening Assistance On-Site.
SPECIFIC EXPANSION PLANS:
US: All United States
Canada: No
Overseas: No

<< >>

ELMER'S BREAKFAST/LUNCH/DINNER

P.O. Box 16938
Portland, OR 97292-0938
Tel: (800) 325-5188 (503) 252-1485
Fax: (503) 257-7448
Web Site: www.elmers-restaurants.com
Mr. Bruce Davis, President

Full-service, family-oriented restaurant serving three meals a day. All menu items served all day. Banquet facilities.

BACKGROUND:
Established: 1960; 1st Franchised: 1966
Franchised Units: 18
Company-Owned Units: 11
Total Units: 29
Dist.: US-29; CAN-0; O'seas-0
    North America: 6 States
Density: 12 in OR, 5 in WA, 4 in ID
Projected New Units (12 Months): NR
Qualifications: 5, 5, 3, 3, 4, 5
Registered: CA,OR,WA
FINANCIAL/TERMS:
Cash Investment: $200K
Total Investment: $N/A
Minimum Net Worth: $Varies
Fees: Franchise - $35K
    Royalty - 4%; Ad. - 1%
Earnings Claim Statement: No
Term of Contract (Years): 25/Varies
Avg. # Of Employees: 15 FT, 35 PT
Passive Ownership: Not Allowed

Encourage Conversions: No
Area Develop. Agreements: Yes/5
Sub-Franchising Contracts: No
Expand In Territory: Yes
Space Needs: 6,800 SF; FS
SUPPORT & TRAINING PROVIDED:
Financial Assistance Provided: No
Site Selection Assistance: Yes
Lease Negotiation Assistance: No
Co-Operative Advertising: N/A
Franchisee Assoc./Member: No
Size Of Corporate Staff: 11
On-Going Support: B,C,D,E,G,h
Training: 8-12 Weeks Portland, OR.
SPECIFIC EXPANSION PLANS:
US: Northwest
Canada: No
Overseas: No

<< >>

FRIENDLY'S RESTAURANT

1855 Boston Rd.
Wilbraham, MA 01095
Tel: (888) 342-7776 (413) 543-2400
Fax: (413) 543-1015
Web Site: www.friendlys.com
Mr. Tim O. Andereck, VP Franchise Sales

FRIENDLY'S is a full-service restaurant chain with ice cream a key point of difference. FRIENDLY'S has enjoyed five years of comparable store sales increases and five years of guest check average increases. The franchise will receive full support for success, including training, marketing, site selection, store openings and on-going operational assistance.

BACKGROUND:
Established: 1935; 1st Franchised: 1997
Franchised Units: 111
Company-Owned Units: 504
Total Units: 615
Dist.: US-615; CAN-0; O'seas-0
    North America: 17 States
Density: 164 in NY, 153 in MA, 67 CT
Projected New Units (12 Months): 41
Registered: FL,IL,IN,MD,MI,NY,
    RI,VA,WI
FINANCIAL/TERMS:
Cash Investment: $300-400K
Total Investment: $875K-1.5MM
Minimum Net Worth: $1MM (400Liq)
Fees: Franchise - $35K
    Royalty - 4%; Ad. - 3%
Earnings Claim Statement: Yes
Term of Contract (Years): 20/10-20
Avg. # Of Employees: 40 FT, 35 PT

Passive Ownership: Allowed
Encourage Conversions: Yes
Area Develop. Agreements: Yes
Sub-Franchising Contracts: No
Expand In Territory: Yes
Space Needs: 4,100-5,000 SF; FS
SUPPORT & TRAINING PROVIDED:
Financial Assistance Provided: No
Site Selection Assistance: Yes
Lease Negotiation Assistance: Yes
Co-Operative Advertising: Yes
Franchisee Assoc./Member: No
Size Of Corporate Staff: 400
On-Going Support: A,b,c,d,E,F,G
Training: 12 Weeks at the Corporate Training Center and in individual training units.
SPECIFIC EXPANSION PLANS:
US: SE,NE, Mid-Atlantic
Canada: No
Overseas: All Countries

<< >>

FUDDRUCKERS

66 Cherry Hill Rd., #200
Beverly, MA 01915
Tel: (860) 651-4421
Fax: (860) 651-5218
E-Mail: craig.ahrens@fuddruckers.com
Web Site: www.fuddruckers.com
Mr. Craig Ahrens,

It's an exciting time at FUDDRUCKERS. Our relentless commitment to freshness makes us "Home of the World's Greatest Hamburgers". Our in-house butcher shops and bakeries provide our guests with the freshest products available. FUDDRUCKERS' menu includes not only our famous 1/3 and 1/2 pound hamburgers but now features a 1-lb. burger. We have also added Big Bowl salads, new Steakhouse Platters and fantastic desserts like our Brownie Blast Sundae. We also have a new 50's and 60's rock and roll image.

BACKGROUND: IFA MEMBER
Established: 1980; 1st Franchised: 1982
Franchised Units: 106
Company-Owned Units: 106

Total Units:	212
Dist.:	US-199; CAN-1; O'seas-12
North America:	30 States, 1 Province
Density:	37 in TX, 12 in VA, 11 in IL
Projected New Units (12 Months):	12
Qualifications:	5, 5, 4, 3, 2, 5

Registered: CA,FL,HI,IL,IN,MD,MI,MN,
NY,ND,OR,RI,SD,VA,WA,DC,AB

FINANCIAL/TERMS:

Cash Investment:	$300K
Total Investment:	$650K-1.28MM
Minimum Net Worth:	$1MM
Fees: Franchise -	$50K
Royalty - 5%;	Ad. - 0-3%
Earnings Claim Statement:	No
Term of Contract (Years):	20/20
Avg. # Of Employees:	15 FT, 30 PT
Passive Ownership:	Discouraged
Encourage Conversions:	Yes
Area Develop. Agreements:	Yes/Varies
Sub-Franchising Contracts:	No
Expand In Territory:	Yes
Space Needs: 6,800 SF; FS	

SUPPORT & TRAINING PROVIDED:

Financial Assistance Provided:	No
Site Selection Assistance:	Yes
Lease Negotiation Assistance:	No
Co-Operative Advertising:	NR
Franchisee Assoc./Member:	No
Size Of Corporate Staff:	70
On-Going Support:	C,D,E

Training: 8 Weeks at Regional Training
Locations.

SPECIFIC EXPANSION PLANS:

US:	All United States
Canada:	All Canada
Overseas:	All Countries

≪≪ ≫≫

GARFIELD'S RESTAURANT & PUB

1220 S. Santa Fe Ave.
Edmond, OK 73003
Tel: (405) 705-5077
Fax: (405) 705-5005
E-Mail: laurenceb@eats-inc.com
Web Site: www.eats-inc.com
Mr. Laurence Bader, VP Franchise
Development

A friendly casual dining restaurant serving an American menu of convenience, quality and value.

BACKGROUND:	IFA MEMBER
Established: 1984;	1st Franchised: 1987
Franchised Units:	7
Company-Owned Units	49

Total Units:	56
Dist.:	US-56; CAN-0; O'seas-0
North America:	22 States
Density:	6 in OK, 6 in IN, 4 in MO
Projected New Units (12 Months):	6
Qualifications:	5, 3, 5, 3, 3, 5

Registered: CA,FL,IL,IN,MD,MI,MN,
NY,ND,OR,RI,SD,VA,WA,WI

FINANCIAL/TERMS:

Cash Investment:	$300-500K
Total Investment:	$860K-1.63MM
Minimum Net Worth:	$1MM
Fees: Franchise -	$30K
Royalty - 4%;	Ad. - 3.5%
Earnings Claim Statement:	No
Term of Contract (Years):	20/5
Avg. # Of Employees:	40 FT, 20 PT
Passive Ownership:	Not Allowed
Encourage Conversions:	Yes
Area Develop. Agreements:	Yes/Negot.
Sub-Franchising Contracts:	No
Expand In Territory:	Yes
Space Needs: 4,500-5,000 SF; FS,SC,RM	

SUPPORT & TRAINING PROVIDED:

Financial Assistance Provided:	No
Site Selection Assistance:	Yes
Lease Negotiation Assistance:	No
Co-Operative Advertising:	Yes
Franchisee Assoc./Member:	No
Size Of Corporate Staff:	48
On-Going Support:	a,C,D,E

Training: 8 Weeks in Edmond, OK.

SPECIFIC EXPANSION PLANS:

US:	All United States
Canada:	No
Overseas:	No

≪≪ ≫≫

GOLDEN CORRAL FAMILY STEAKHOUSE

5151 Glenwood Ave., # 300
Raleigh, NC 27612
Tel: (800) 284-5673 (919) 881-4647
Fax: (919) 881-5252
Web Site: www.goldencorralrest.com
Mr. Peter Charland, VP Franchise
Development

We offer nearly 25 years of proven success in the family steakhouse market segment. The metromarket concept features in-store bakery, dessert bar and our Golden Choice Buffet, in addition to our up-dated core menu. The layout of our metro market restaurant, as well as our expanded food offering, enables each customer to define his own experience each time he visits a GOLDEN CORRAL.

BACKGROUND:	IFA MEMBER
Established: 1973;	1st Franchised: 1986
Franchised Units:	297
Company-Owned Units	152
Total Units:	449
Dist.:	US-449; CAN-0; O'seas-0
North America:	38 States
Density:	TX, OK, NC
Projected New Units (12 Months):	50
Registered: All States	

FINANCIAL/TERMS:

Cash Investment:	$300K
Total Investment:	$1.2-3.3MM
Minimum Net Worth:	$1500K
Fees: Franchise -	$40K
Royalty - 4%;	Ad. - 2%
Earnings Claim Statement:	Yes
Term of Contract (Years):	15/5
Avg. # Of Employees:	80 FT, 40 PT
Passive Ownership:	Not Allowed
Encourage Conversions:	No
Area Develop. Agreements:	Yes/Varies
Sub-Franchising Contracts:	No
Expand In Territory:	Yes
Space Needs: 8,500-11,000 SF; FS	

SUPPORT & TRAINING PROVIDED:

Financial Assistance Provided:	No
Site Selection Assistance:	Yes
Lease Negotiation Assistance:	No
Co-Operative Advertising:	Yes
Franchisee Assoc./Member:	NR
Size Of Corporate Staff:	190
On-Going Support:	C,D,E,G

Training: 12 Weeks Headquarters and Field.

SPECIFIC EXPANSION PLANS:

US:	All United States
Canada:	All Canada
Overseas:	Mexico, Puerto Rico

≪≪ ≫≫

GOLDEN GRIDDLE FAMILY RESTAURANTS

505 Consumers Rd., # 1000
North York, ON M2J 4V8 CANADA
Tel: (416) 493-3800
Fax: (416) 493-3889
E-Mail: gogrill@interlog.com
Web Site: www.goldengriddlecorp.com
Mr. W. W. Hood, President

Full-service, licensed family restaurant, serving all day. We are located primarily in hotels and are totally franchised.

BACKGROUND:

Established: 1964; 1st Franchised: 1976
Franchised Units: 42
Company-Owned Units   0
Total Units: 42
Dist.:   US-1; CAN-41; O'seas-0
  North America: 1 State, 3 Provinces
  Density: 39 in ON, 3 in BC, 1 in MI
Projected New Units (12 Months):   14
Qualifications: 5, 4, 3, 3, 2, 5
Registered:

FINANCIAL/TERMS:

Cash Investment: $50-100K
Total Investment: $100-500K
Minimum Net Worth: $100K
Fees: Franchise - $17.5-25K
  Royalty - 5%;   Ad. - 3%
Earnings Claim Statement: No
Term of Contract (Years):   10/10
Avg. # Of Employees: 3-6 FT, 10-30 PT
Passive Ownership: Discouraged
Encourage Conversions: Yes
Area Develop. Agreements: Yes/5
Sub-Franchising Contracts: No
Expand In Territory: Yes
Space Needs: 3,000 SF; FS, SF, SC, RM

SUPPORT & TRAINING PROVIDED:

Financial Assistance Provided: No
Site Selection Assistance: Yes
Lease Negotiation Assistance: Yes
Co-Operative Advertising: Yes
Franchisee Assoc./Member: No
Size Of Corporate Staff: 20
On-Going Support: B,C,D,d,E,G,H,h
Training: 3-5 Days at Head Offoce; 14-28
  Days at Training Store.

SPECIFIC EXPANSION PLANS:

US: Northeast, Southeast
Canada: All Canada
Overseas: No

⊲⊲ ⊳⊳

**GREAT STEAK & POTATO
COMPANY**
188 N. Brookwood Ave.
Hamilton, OH 45013
Tel: (513) 896-9695
Fax: (513) 896-3750

E-Mail: franchiseinfo@thegreatsteak.com
Web Site: www.thegreatsteak.com
Mr. Roger Burrin, Dir. Franchise
  Development

Signature   items   include   genuine
Philadelphia cheesesteak sandwiches, hand-
cut French fries (cooked in peanut oil)
and freshly-squeezed lemonade. Additional
sandwich items include chicken, ham and
vegetarian 'Philadelphias.' Other offerings
include baked potatoes with toppings.

BACKGROUND:

Established: 1982;   1st Franchised: 1984
Franchised Units: 215
Company-Owned Units   20
Total Units: 235
Dist.:   US-219; CAN-12; O'seas-4
  North America: 31 States, 2 Provinces
  Density: 33 in OH, 25 in CA, 24 in IL
Projected New Units (12 Months):   35
Qualifications: 5, 3, 3, 3, 3, 3
Registered: All States

FINANCIAL/TERMS:

Cash Investment: $50-100K
Total Investment: $200-750K
Minimum Net Worth: $200K
Fees: Franchise - $20K
  Royalty - 5%;   Ad. - 2%
Earnings Claim Statement: No
Term of Contract (Years):   10/10
Avg. # Of Employees: 2 FT, 15 PT
Passive Ownership: Allowed
Encourage Conversions: Yes
Area Develop. Agreements: Yes/10
Sub-Franchising Contracts: Yes
Expand In Territory: Yes
Space Needs: 600-2,000 SF; SC

SUPPORT & TRAINING PROVIDED:

Financial Assistance Provided: No
Site Selection Assistance: Yes
Lease Negotiation Assistance: Yes
Co-Operative Advertising: Yes
Franchisee Assoc./Member: No
Size Of Corporate Staff: 25
On-Going Support: a,B,C,D,E,F,G
Training: 2 Weeks Cincinnati, OH.

SPECIFIC EXPANSION PLANS:

US: All United States
Canada: All Canada
Overseas: All Countries

⊲⊲ ⊳⊳

GROUND ROUND RESTAURANTS
P.O. Box 859078
Braintree, MA 02184-9078
Tel: (800) 229-7005 (781) 380-3100

Fax: (781) 380-3168
E-Mail: kandereck@ahconcepts.com
Web Site: www.groundround.com
Mr. Kim Andereck, SVP Franchising

Full-service,   casual   theme,   family
restaurant.   Variety of menu offerings -
sandwiches, seafood, appetizers, steaks,
ribs, chicken and burgers. Alcoholic
beverages are available.

BACKGROUND:

Established: 1969;   1st Franchised: 1970
Franchised Units: 41
Company-Owned Units   136
Total Units: 177
Dist.:   US-176; CAN-1; O'seas-0
  North America: 24 States, 1 Province
  Density: 30 in NY, 27 in MA, 19 in OH
Projected New Units (12 Months):   15
Qualifications: 5, 4, 5, 3, 3, 4
Registered: CA,FL,IL,IN,MD,MI,MN,NY,
  ND,OR,RI,SD,VA,WI,DC

FINANCIAL/TERMS:

Cash Investment: $250-500K
Total Investment: $500K-1.3MM
Minimum Net Worth: $1MM
Fees: Franchise - $40K
  Royalty - 4%;   Ad. - 2.5%
Earnings Claim Statement: No
Term of Contract (Years):   20/20
Avg. # Of Employees: 75 FT, 25 PT
Passive Ownership: Allowed
Encourage Conversions: Yes
Area Develop. Agreements: Yes
Sub-Franchising Contracts: No
Expand In Territory: Yes
Space Needs: 5,500-6,000 SF; FS, SF, SC,
  RM

SUPPORT & TRAINING PROVIDED:

Financial Assistance Provided: No
Site Selection Assistance: Yes
Lease Negotiation Assistance: No
Co-Operative Advertising: Yes
Franchisee Assoc./Member: Yes/No
Size Of Corporate Staff: 70
On-Going Support: B,C,D,E,h,I
Training: 6-10 Weeks at Regional Training
  Unit.

SPECIFIC EXPANSION PLANS:

US: NE, MW, Atl. States, Grt Lks
Canada: No
Overseas: No

⊲⊲ ⊳⊳

HARVEY'S RESTAURANTS
6303 Airport Rd.
Mississauga, ON L4V 1R8 CANADA

Tel: (905) 405-6771
Fax: (905) 405-6667
E-Mail: ifong@cara.com
Web Site: www.cara.com
Mr. Claus Etzler, Franchise Manager

Foodservice. Quick-service restaurants.

BACKGROUND:
Established: 1900; 1st Franchised: 1982
Franchised Units: 330
Company-Owned Units   39
Total Units: 369
Dist.:   US-0; CAN-350; O'seas-0
  North America: NR
  Density: ON, PQ, AB
Projected New Units (12 Months):   42
Qualifications: 5, 4, 3, 3, 1, 5
Registered: AB
FINANCIAL/TERMS:
Cash Investment: $155-200K
Total Investment: $510-600K
Minimum Net Worth: $300K
Fees: Franchise - $50-75K
  Royalty - 5%;   Ad. - 4%
Earnings Claim Statement: Yes
Term of Contract (Years):   20/5x4
Avg. # Of Employees: 3 FT, 40 PT
Passive Ownership: Not Allowed
Encourage Conversions: Yes
Area Develop. Agreements: No
Sub-Franchising Contracts: No
Expand In Territory: Yes
Space Needs: 2,600 SF; FS
SUPPORT & TRAINING PROVIDED:
Financial Assistance Provided: N/A
Site Selection Assistance: Yes
Lease Negotiation Assistance: Yes
Co-Operative Advertising: Yes
Franchisee Assoc./Member: Yes/Yes
Size Of Corporate Staff: 200
On-Going Support: C,D,E,G,h,I
Training: 6-8 Weeks Toronto, ON.
SPECIFIC EXPANSION PLANS:
US: No
Canada: All Canada
Overseas: No

⋘ ⋙

**HOULIHAN'S RESTAURANT
GROUP**
2 Brush Creek Blvd., P. O. Box 16000
Kansas City, MO 64112

Tel: (816) 756-2200
Fax: (816) 561-2842
E-Mail: bgrams@houlihans.com
Web Site: www.houlihans.com
Ms. Bridget Grams, Dir. Franchise Sales

HOULIHAN'S is the ONE casual dining restaurant and bar with a varied menu catering to adults.

BACKGROUND:
Established: 1972; 1st Franchised: 1987
Franchised Units: 50
Company-Owned Units   60
Total Units: 110
Dist.:   US-110; CAN-0; O'seas-0
  North America: 24 States
  Density: NJ, PA
Projected New Units (12 Months):   10
Qualifications: 4, 4, 5, 3, 3, 4
Registered: All States
FINANCIAL/TERMS:
Cash Investment: $1MM
Total Investment: $NR
Minimum Net Worth: $4MM
Fees: Franchise - $40K
  Royalty - 4%;   Ad. - 1.5%
Earnings Claim Statement: Yes
Term of Contract (Years):   20/10
Avg. # Of Employees: 40 FT, 80 PT
Passive Ownership: Allowed
Encourage Conversions: Yes
Area Develop. Agreements: Yes/Varies
Sub-Franchising Contracts: No
Expand In Territory: NR
Space Needs: 5,000 SF; FS, SF, SC, RM
SUPPORT & TRAINING PROVIDED:
Financial Assistance Provided: No
Site Selection Assistance: Yes
Lease Negotiation Assistance: Yes
Co-Operative Advertising: Yes
Franchisee Assoc./Member: No
Size Of Corporate Staff: 120
On-Going Support: B,C,D,E,F,H,I
Training: 90-120 Days in Various Locations
  in U.S.
SPECIFIC EXPANSION PLANS:
US: All United States
Canada: No
Overseas: No

⋘ ⋙

HUBB'S PUB
1231 Florida Ave.
Rockledge, FL 32955
Tel: (407) 639-5080
Fax: (407) 639-8050
Web Site: www.hubbspub.com

Mr. Frank Riggio, Vice President
The Home of Colossal Sandwiches - specializing in imported beers from around the world. Each unit has 39 taps for draft beer and over 200 bottled brands. "HUBB'S - Where You Always Meet a Friend".

BACKGROUND:
Established: 1982; 1st Franchised: 1992
Franchised Units: 3
Company-Owned Units   3
Total Units: 6
Dist.:   US-6; CAN-0; O'seas-0
  North America: 2 States
  Density: 4 in FL, 2 in WA
Projected New Units (12 Months):   20
Registered: FL,WA
FINANCIAL/TERMS:
Cash Investment: $100-150K
Total Investment: $320-450K
Minimum Net Worth: $NR
Fees: Franchise - $50K
  Royalty - 2-4%;   Ad. - NR
Earnings Claim Statement: No
Term of Contract (Years):   20/5
Avg. # Of Employees: 6 FT, 10 PT
Passive Ownership: Discouraged
Encourage Conversions: No
Area Develop. Agreements: Yes/20
Sub-Franchising Contracts: Yes
Expand In Territory: Yes
Space Needs: 4,000-5,000 SF; FS, SF, SC
SUPPORT & TRAINING PROVIDED:
Financial Assistance Provided: Yes(I)
Site Selection Assistance: Yes
Lease Negotiation Assistance: NR
Co-Operative Advertising: NR
Franchisee Assoc./Member: No
Size Of Corporate Staff: 6
On-Going Support: A,B,C,D,E,F,G,H
Training: 6-8 Weeks Headquarters.
SPECIFIC EXPANSION PLANS:
US: All United States
Canada: All Canada
Overseas: Europe, Central America,
  Pacific Rim

⋘ ⋙

HUDDLE HOUSE RESTAURANTS
2969 E. Ponce de Leon Ave.
Decatur, GA 30030

Tel: (800) 418-9555 (404) 377-5700
Fax: (404) 377-0497
E-Mail: franchise@huddlehouse.com
Web Site: www.huddlehouse.com
Mr. Cory Durden, Dir. Franchise Dev.

HUDDLE HOUSE RESTAURANTS are open 24 hours a day, serving delicious meals, cooked to order - a place where hungry folks gather to enjoy good food, good friends and good hospitality. HUDDLE HOUSE RESTAURANTS offer any meal, any time from our broad menu of breakfast, lunch and dinner entrees, featuring, 'Big House' platters, which are our signature 'Big Meals for Big Appetites.'

BACKGROUND: IFA MEMBER
Established: 1964;   1st Franchised: 1966
Franchised Units: 330
Company-Owned Units   30
Total Units: 360
Dist.:   US-360; CAN-0; O'seas-0
  North America: 13 States
  Density: 166 in GA, 60 in SC, 34 AL
Projected New Units (12 Months):   40
Qualifications: 5, 5, 4, 3, 3, 4
Registered: FL,IL,IN,VA
FINANCIAL/TERMS:
Cash Investment: $120-500K
Total Investment: $120-500K
Minimum Net Worth: $200K
Fees: Franchise - $20K
  Royalty - 4%;   Ad. - 1%
Earnings Claim Statement: No
Term of Contract (Years):   15/5x3
Avg. # Of Employees: 18 FT, 6 PT
Passive Ownership: Discouraged
Encourage Conversions: Yes
Area Develop. Agreements: Yes/Varies
Sub-Franchising Contracts: Yes
Expand In Territory: Yes
Space Needs: 2,000 SF; FS,SF,SC,
  Co-Brand, C-Stores
SUPPORT & TRAINING PROVIDED:
Financial Assistance Provided: No
Site Selection Assistance: Yes
Lease Negotiation Assistance: Yes
Co-Operative Advertising: Yes
Franchisee Assoc./Member: Yes/No
Size Of Corporate Staff: 120
On-Going Support: b,C,D,E,f,h,I
Training: 5-6 Weeks Metro Atlanta, GA;
  1-2 Weeks On-Site Pre-Opening; 1
  Week Training Store.
SPECIFIC EXPANSION PLANS:
US: Southeast, Midwest
Canada: No
Overseas: No
◄◄ ►►

HUDSON'S GRILL OF AMERICA
16970 Dallas Pkwy., # 402
Dallas, TX 75248-1928
Tel: (972) 931-9237
Fax: (972) 931-1326
E-Mail: sacco@hudsonsgrill.com
Web Site: www.hudsonsgrill.com
Mr. David L. Osborn, President

A casual-style, full-service, high-energy, late 50's and early 60's rock 'n' roll theme restaurant and bar. Burgers, chicken sandwiches, salads, desserts and specialty items, such as fajitas. TV monitors throughout restaurant and bar show sporting events while the bubbling Wurlitzer juke box beats out Elvis Presley and Beatles' tunes, bridging the past with the present.

BACKGROUND:
Established: 1985;   1st Franchised: 1986
Franchised Units: 14
Company-Owned Units   3
Total Units: 17
Dist.:   US-17; CAN-0; O'seas-0
  North America: 4 States
  Density: 10 in CA, 4 in TX, 2 in MI
Projected New Units (12 Months):   4
Qualifications: 5, 3, 1, 3, 3, 5
Registered: All Except RI
FINANCIAL/TERMS:
Cash Investment: $125K
Total Investment: $100K-1MM
Minimum Net Worth: $250K
Fees: Franchise - $25K
  Royalty - 4%;   Ad. - 1%
Earnings Claim Statement: Yes
Term of Contract (Years):   20/20
Avg. # Of Employees: 12 FT, 38 PT
Passive Ownership: Allowed
Encourage Conversions: No
Area Develop. Agreements: Yes/5
Sub-Franchising Contracts: Yes
Expand In Territory: Yes
Space Needs: 4,500 SF; FS
SUPPORT & TRAINING PROVIDED:
Financial Assistance Provided: Yes(I)
Site Selection Assistance: Yes
Lease Negotiation Assistance: Yes
Co-Operative Advertising: Yes
Franchisee Assoc./Member: No
Size Of Corporate Staff: 7
On-Going Support: B,C,D,E,F,H
Training: 5-6 Weeks CA; 5-6 Weeks TX.
SPECIFIC EXPANSION PLANS:
US: All United States
Canada: BC,AB,ON,PQ,NS
Overseas: Latin America, South America,
  Pacific Rim, Europe

◄◄ ►►

HUMPTY'S FAMILY RESTAURANT
2505 Macleod Trail S.
Calgary, AB T2G 5J4 CANADA
Tel: (800) 661-7589 (403) 269-4675
Fax: (403) 266-1973
E-Mail: humpty@cadvision.com
Web Site: www.humptys.com
Mr. Don Koenig, President

A full-service, family-oriented restaurant, offering a varied menu that includes an extensive breakfast menu. Available 24 hours a day at most locations. Many restaurants are highway-located and include gas and convenience-store service.

BACKGROUND:
Established: 1977;   1st Franchised: 1982
Franchised Units: 55
Company-Owned Units   5
Total Units: 60
Dist.:   US-0; CAN-52; O'seas-0
  North America: 4 Provinces
  Density: 30 in AB, 9 in SK, 9 in BC
Projected New Units (12 Months):   17
Qualifications: 5, 4, 2, 3, 4, 5
Registered: AB
FINANCIAL/TERMS:
Cash Investment: $130-200K
Total Investment: $400-500K
Minimum Net Worth: $400K
Fees: Franchise - $25K
  Royalty - 5%;   Ad. - 2%
Earnings Claim Statement: No
Term of Contract (Years):   10/2-5
Avg. # Of Employees: 26 FT, 8 PT
Passive Ownership: Not Allowed
Encourage Conversions: Yes
Area Develop. Agreements: Yes/20
Sub-Franchising Contracts: No
Expand In Territory: Yes
Space Needs: 4,000 SF; FS, SC
SUPPORT & TRAINING PROVIDED:
Financial Assistance Provided: Yes(I)
Site Selection Assistance: Yes
Lease Negotiation Assistance: Yes
Co-Operative Advertising: Yes
Franchisee Assoc./Member: Yes/Yes
Size Of Corporate Staff: 12
On-Going Support: B,C,D,E,F,G,H,I
Training: 3 Weeks Calgary, AB; 4 Weeks
  On-Location.
SPECIFIC EXPANSION PLANS:
US: Northwest
Canada: All Canada
Overseas: No
◄◄ ►►

JOEY'S ONLY SEAFOOD RESTAURANT
514 42nd Ave. SE
Calgary, AB T2G 1Y6 CANADA
Tel: (800) 661-2123 (403) 243-4584
Fax: (403) 243-8989
Mr. David Mossey, Senior Partner

JOEY'S ONLY is a sit down, family-style seafood restaurant, specializing in fish and chips, licensed for beer and wine. Casual atmosphere, affordable prices, high-quality, high-volume restaurants with a wide selection of popular seafood dishes.

BACKGROUND:
Established: 1985; 1st Franchised: 1992	
Franchised Units:	60
Company-Owned Units	1
Total Units:	61
Dist.:	US-6; CAN-55; O'seas-0
North America:	4 States, 5 Provinces
Density:	20 in AB, 2 in MT, 2 in ND
Projected New Units (12 Months):	10
Qualifications:	4, 4, 3, 3, 5, 5
Registered: CA,FL,ND,AB	

FINANCIAL/TERMS:
Cash Investment:	$40-80K
Total Investment:	$149-202.5K
Minimum Net Worth:	$200K
Fees: Franchise -	$25K
Royalty - 4.5%;	Ad. - 1%
Earnings Claim Statement:	No
Term of Contract (Years):	10/5
Avg. # Of Employees:	5 FT, 15 PT
Passive Ownership:	Discouraged
Encourage Conversions:	Yes
Area Develop. Agreements:	Yes/20
Sub-Franchising Contracts:	Yes
Expand In Territory:	Yes
Space Needs: 2,000-2,400 SF; FS, SF, SC	

SUPPORT & TRAINING PROVIDED:
Financial Assistance Provided:	No
Site Selection Assistance:	Yes
Lease Negotiation Assistance:	Yes
Co-Operative Advertising:	No
Franchisee Assoc./Member:	Yes/Yes
Size Of Corporate Staff:	11
On-Going Support:	C,D,E,F,G,H,I
Training: 5 Weeks in Franchise Office and in Corporate Store.	

SPECIFIC EXPANSION PLANS:
US:	All United States
Canada:	All Canada
Overseas:	No

<< >>

KELSEY'S RESTAURANTS
450 S. Service Rd. W.
Oakville, ON L6K 2H4 CANADA
Tel: (800) 982-1682 (905) 842-5510
Fax: (905) 842-9048
E-Mail: lsantolini@hq.kelseys.ca
Web Site: www.kelseys.ca
Mr. Larry Santolini, Director of Franchising

Approaching its 20th anniversary, KELSEY'S has been bringing outstanding food, unrivaled service and its celebrated 'good times' to communities throughout Canada since 1998. KELSEY'S new menu features more than 100 exciting items. KELSEY'S warm, friendly decor and fast service make it an appealing place for lunch crowds, the after work gang, as well as families at dinner and late evening adult patrons who come for the good times in a neighborhood atmosphere.

BACKGROUND:
Established: 1978; 1st Franchised: 1983	
Franchised Units:	28
Company-Owned Units	77
Total Units:	105
Dist.:	US-0; CAN-54; O'seas-0
North America:	5 Provinces
Density:	42 in ON, 8 in AB, 1 in SK
Projected New Units (12 Months):	10
Qualifications:	5, 4, 4, 2, 2, 5
Registered: AB	

FINANCIAL/TERMS:
Cash Investment:	$250-300K
Total Investment:	$600-750K
Minimum Net Worth:	$600K
Fees: Franchise -	$40K
Royalty - 5%;	Ad. - 0.5%
Earnings Claim Statement:	No
Term of Contract (Years):	10/5/5
Avg. # Of Employees:	70-90 FT & PT
Passive Ownership:	Not Allowed
Encourage Conversions:	No
Area Develop. Agreements:	NR
Sub-Franchising Contracts:	No
Expand In Territory:	Yes
Space Needs: 5,000 SF; FS	

SUPPORT & TRAINING PROVIDED:
Financial Assistance Provided:	Yes(I)
Site Selection Assistance:	Yes
Lease Negotiation Assistance:	Yes
Co-Operative Advertising:	Yes
Franchisee Assoc./Member:	Yes/Yes
Size Of Corporate Staff:	30
On-Going Support:	a,B,C,D,E,F,G,I
Training: 12 Weeks in Restaurant; 1 Week Office.	

SPECIFIC EXPANSION PLANS:
US:	N/A
Canada:	ON,AB,BC
Overseas: Philippines, Western Europe, Australia	

<< >>

LE PEEP
4 W. Dry Creek Circle, # 201
Littleton, CO 80120
Tel: (303) 730-6300
Fax: (303) 730-7105
E-Mail: lepeep4w@ad.com
Web Site: www.lepeep.com
Ms. Allison Wilson, Licensing Manager

LE PEEP is a licenser of a breakfast, brunch and lunch concept, featuring an award-winning menu, decor and coffee and juice bar.

BACKGROUND:
Established: 1992; 1st Franchised: 1981	
Franchised Units:	64
Company-Owned Units	8
Total Units:	72
Dist.:	US-72; CAN-0; O'seas-0
North America:	13 States
Density:	25 in CO, 8 in TX, 5 in GA
Projected New Units (12 Months):	8
Qualifications:	5, 3, 5, 3, 3, 5
Registered: N/A	

FINANCIAL/TERMS:
Cash Investment:	$100-350K
Total Investment:	$100-550K
Minimum Net Worth:	$100K
Fees: Franchise -	$0
Royalty - 3%;	Ad. - 1%
Earnings Claim Statement:	Yes
Term of Contract (Years):	15/10
Avg. # Of Employees:	10 FT, 10 PT
Passive Ownership:	N/A
Encourage Conversions:	Yes
Area Develop. Agreements:	No
Sub-Franchising Contracts:	No
Expand In Territory:	Yes
Space Needs: 2,500-3,500 SF; FS, SF, SC	

SUPPORT & TRAINING PROVIDED:
Financial Assistance Provided:	No
Site Selection Assistance:	No
Lease Negotiation Assistance:	No
Co-Operative Advertising:	No
Franchisee Assoc./Member:	No
Size Of Corporate Staff:	9
On-Going Support:	b,c,d,e
Training: 8 Weeks in Denver, CO.	

SPECIFIC EXPANSION PLANS:
US:	All United States

Canada: All Canada
Overseas: U.K., France, Australia

MADE IN JAPAN...A TERIYAKI EXPERIENCE

700 Kerr St.
Oakville, ON L6K 3W5 CANADA
Tel: (800) 555-5726 (905) 337-7777
Fax: (905) 337-0331
E-Mail: info@donatogroup.com
Web Site: www.madein-japan.com
Mr. Nik Jurkovic, Dir. New Business Development

Japanese quick service restaurant located in major mall food courts, airports, universities, hospitals, theme parks, strip plazas and other similar high traffic settings.

BACKGROUND: IFA MEMBER
Established: 1986; 1st Franchised: 1987
Franchised Units: 53
Company-Owned Units 2
Total Units: 55
Dist.: US-0; CAN-50; O'seas-5
 North America: 4 Provinces
 Density: 36 in ON, 7 in PQ, 4 in BC
Projected New Units (12 Months): 6
Qualifications: 5, 2, 2, 2, 3, 4
Registered: IL,AB
FINANCIAL/TERMS:
Cash Investment: $50-100K
Total Investment: $175-250K
Minimum Net Worth: $200K
Fees: Franchise - $25K
 Royalty - 6%; Ad. - 1.5%
Earnings Claim Statement: No
Term of Contract (Years): 8-10/5-10
Avg. # Of Employees: 3 FT, 6 PT
Passive Ownership: Discouraged
Encourage Conversions: Yes
Area Develop. Agreements: Yes/15
Sub-Franchising Contracts: Yes
Expand In Territory: Yes
Space Needs: 400-1,800 SF; SC, RM
SUPPORT & TRAINING PROVIDED:
Financial Assistance Provided: Yes(I)
Site Selection Assistance: Yes
Lease Negotiation Assistance: Yes
Co-Operative Advertising: N/A
Franchisee Assoc./Member: No/No

Size Of Corporate Staff: 40
On-Going Support: B,C,D,E,G,H,I
Training: 3-4 Days at Company HQ; 3-4 Days at the Store; 1 Week during your Grand Opening.
SPECIFIC EXPANSION PLANS:
US: All United States
Canada: All Canada
Overseas: All Countries

MAX & ERMA'S RESTAURANTS

4849 Evanswood Dr.
Columbus, OH 43229
Tel: (614) 431-5800
Fax: (614) 431-4111
E-Mail: rob@max-ermas.com
Web Site: www.max-ermas.com
Mr. Rob Lindeman, Director of Franchising

MAX & ERMA'S RESTAURANTS is famous for gourmet burgers, overstuffed sandwiches, homemade pasta dishes, chargrilled chicken specialties, super salads and taste-tempting munchies. Antiques artifacts and local paraphernalia make MAX & ERMA'S a fun, unique place to take friends and family. We work hard every day to help our guests enjoy their total dining experience so they can't wait to come back. And, we believe that experience starts with our food. We use only the freshest, highest-quality ingredients.

BACKGROUND: IFA MEMBER
Established: 1972; 1st Franchised: 1997
Franchised Units: 4
Company-Owned Units 53
Total Units: 57
Dist.: US-57; CAN-0; O'seas-0
 North America: 9 States
 Density: 20 in OH, 8 in MI, 7 in IL
Projected New Units (12 Months): 10
Qualifications: 3, 4, 4, 2, 3, 5
Registered: VA,WI
FINANCIAL/TERMS:
Cash Investment: $400-500K
Total Investment: $800K-2.7MM
Minimum Net Worth: $3MM
Fees: Franchise - $40K
 Royalty - 4%; Ad. - 2%
Earnings Claim Statement: No
Term of Contract (Years): 20/10
Avg. # Of Employees: 40 FT, 50 PT
Passive Ownership: Allowed

Encourage Conversions: Yes
Area Develop. Agreements: Yes
Sub-Franchising Contracts: No
Expand In Territory: Yes
Space Needs: 5,000-6,900 SF; FS, RM
SUPPORT & TRAINING PROVIDED:
Financial Assistance Provided: No
Site Selection Assistance: Yes
Lease Negotiation Assistance: Yes
Co-Operative Advertising: N/A
Franchisee Assoc./Member: No
Size Of Corporate Staff: 55
On-Going Support: B,C,D,E,F,G,H
Training: 14 Weeks Manager Training; 2-6 Weeks Staff Training; 2-3 Weeks Opening Training.
SPECIFIC EXPANSION PLANS:
US: All United States
Canada: No
Overseas: No

MIKES RESTAURANTS

8250 Decarie Blvd., # 310
Montreal, PQ H4P 2P5 CANADA
Tel: (514) 341-5544
Fax: (514) 341-5635
Web Site: www.mikes.ca
Mr. Carmen Starnino, Vice President Operations

MIKES RESTAURANTS is the dominant purveyor, in its market area, of Italian-style specialties, featuring pizzas, sandwiches and pastas. Each unit features a very attractive and welcoming decor. MIKES RESTAURANTS also provide a full dessert and alcohol menu.

BACKGROUND:
Established: 1967; 1st Franchised: 1972
Franchised Units: 103
Company-Owned Units 24
Total Units: 127
Dist.: US-0; CAN-127; O'seas-0
 North America: 3 Provinces
 Density: 125 in PQ, 1 in ON, 1 in NB
Projected New Units (12 Months): 5-7
Qualifications: 4, 5, 3, 3, 5, 5
Registered: NR
FINANCIAL/TERMS:
Cash Investment: $75-175K
Total Investment: $275-550K
Minimum Net Worth: $NR
Fees: Franchise - $45K
 Royalty - 8%; Ad. - 0%
Earnings Claim Statement: No
Term of Contract (Years): 20/20

Avg. # Of Employees:	25 FT, 10 PT
Passive Ownership:	Not Allowed
Encourage Conversions:	Yes
Area Develop. Agreements:	Yes/20
Sub-Franchising Contracts:	No
Expand In Territory:	Yes
Space Needs: 3,500 SF; FS, SC	

SUPPORT & TRAINING PROVIDED:

Financial Assistance Provided:	Yes(I)
Site Selection Assistance:	Yes
Lease Negotiation Assistance:	Yes
Co-Operative Advertising:	Yes
Franchisee Assoc./Member:	Yes
Size Of Corporate Staff:	36
On-Going Support:	B,C,D,E,F,H
Training: 6-8 Weeks Montreal, PQ.	

SPECIFIC EXPANSION PLANS:

US:	Northeast
Canada:	ON,NB,NS,NF
Overseas:	No

◄◄ ►►

**MONTANA'S COOKHOUSE
SALOON**

450 S. Sarvis Rd. W.
Oakville, ON L6K 2H4 CANADA
Tel: (913) 696-0815
Fax: (913) 696-0815
E-Mail: acg696@aol.com
Web Site: www.kelseys.ca
Mr. Andy Gunkler, VP of Franchise Dev.

Montana's offers the guest a rustic, Western lodge setting with fresh country-style cooking. Montana's offers guests a menu of approximately 60 selections featuring rotisserie chicken, turkey, beef and pork. The average adult check is $9-12 with kid's meals starting at $2.99. Montana's is casual dining at affordable prices.

BACKGROUND:

Established: 1978;	1st Franchised: 1983
Franchised Units:	36
Company-Owned Units	83
Total Units:	119
Dist.:	US-1; CAN-118; O'seas-0
North America:	1 State, 5 Provinces
Density:	42 in ON, 8 in AB, 2 in NY
Projected New Units (12 Months):	22
Qualifications:	5, , 5, 1, 2, 5
Registered:	

FINANCIAL/TERMS:

Cash Investment:	$300-400K
Total Investment:	$400K-1.2MM
Minimum Net Worth:	$5 MM
Fees: Franchise -	$35K
Royalty - 4%;	Ad. - 1.5%
Earnings Claim Statement:	No
Term of Contract (Years):	20/10
Avg. # Of Employees:	70-90 FT & PT
Passive Ownership:	Discouraged
Encourage Conversions:	Yes
Area Develop. Agreements:	Yes
Sub-Franchising Contracts:	No
Expand In Territory:	Yes
Space Needs: 5,200 SF; FS	

SUPPORT & TRAINING PROVIDED:

Financial Assistance Provided:	Yes(I)
Site Selection Assistance:	Yes
Lease Negotiation Assistance:	No
Co-Operative Advertising:	Yes
Franchisee Assoc./Member:	No
Size Of Corporate Staff:	50
On-Going Support:	B,C,D,E,F,G,h
Training: 12 Weeks in Toronto, ON.	

SPECIFIC EXPANSION PLANS:

US:	All United States
Canada:	All Canada
Overseas:	No

◄◄ ►►

MOUNTAIN MIKE'S PIZZA

4212 N. Freeway Blvd., # 6
Sacramento, CA 95834
Tel: (916) 929-3946
Fax: (916) 929-6018
Mr. Randy Vogel, President

Casual dining in a family-oriented restaurant, featuring counter service, delivery and take-out, lunch buffet, self-service beverages and video game room. Our pizzas are made-to-order, using only the freshest-quality ingredients available.

BACKGROUND:

Established: 1978;	1st Franchised: 1978
Franchised Units:	79
Company-Owned Units	0
Total Units:	79
Dist.:	US-79; CAN-0; O'seas-0
North America:	6 States
Density:	63 in CA, 1 in NV, 1 in OR
Projected New Units (12 Months):	40
Qualifications:	4, 4, 2, 2, 3, 5
Registered:	CA,FL,IL,IN,MD,MI, MN,OR,VA,WI

FINANCIAL/TERMS:

Cash Investment:	$75-100K

Total Investment:	$150-250K
Minimum Net Worth:	$150K
Fees: Franchise -	$20K
Royalty - 5%/$1K;	Ad. - 3%
Earnings Claim Statement:	Yes
Term of Contract (Years):	15/15
Avg. # Of Employees:	2 FT, 15 PT
Passive Ownership:	Not Allowed
Encourage Conversions:	Yes
Area Develop. Agreements:	Yes/15
Sub-Franchising Contracts:	No
Expand In Territory:	Yes
Space Needs: 2,500 SF; SF, SC	

SUPPORT & TRAINING PROVIDED:

Financial Assistance Provided:	Yes(I)
Site Selection Assistance:	Yes
Lease Negotiation Assistance:	Yes
Co-Operative Advertising:	Yes
Franchisee Assoc./Member:	No
Size Of Corporate Staff:	10
On-Going Support:	A,B,C,D,E,F,H,I
Training: 3 Weeks Boulder, CO/Northern CA; 2 Weeks On-Site at Opening.	

SPECIFIC EXPANSION PLANS:

US:	All United States
Canada:	No
Overseas:	No

◄◄ ►►

NANCY'S PIZZERIA

8200 W. 185th St., # J
Tinley Park, IL 60477
Tel: (800) NANCYS7 (708) 444-4411
Fax: (708) 444-4422
E-Mail: geonordstrom@chicagofranchise.com
Web Site: www.chicagofranchise.com
Mr. George Nordstrom, VP Franchise Development

NANCY'S PIZZERIA is expanding nationally; we have 66 franchisees with stores located in Illinois, Iowa and Michigan. More coming soon in Florida and Indiana. We offer the following advantages: original inventor of stuffed pizza, protected territories, comprehensive classroom and in-store training, pre and past-opening support provided by our "operations" support staff, teamed with the product voted "The Best Pizza in Chicago" by Chicago Magazine and lauded by other publications.

BACKGROUND:
Established: 1974; 1st Franchised: 1993
Franchised Units: 66
Company-Owned Units   0
Total Units: 66
Dist.:   US-66; CAN-0; O'seas-0
  North America: 3 States
  Density: 36 in IL, 1 in IA, 1 in MI
Projected New Units (12 Months):   12
Qualifications: 5, 4, 3, 3, 5, 5
Registered: CA,FL,IL,IN,MD,MI,VA,WI
FINANCIAL/TERMS:
Cash Investment: $50-120K
Total Investment: $190-250K
Minimum Net Worth: $250K
Fees: Franchise - $20K
  Royalty - 5%;   Ad. - 2%
Earnings Claim Statement: No
Term of Contract (Years):   10/10
Avg. # Of Employees: 3 FT, 15 PT
Passive Ownership: Discouraged
Encourage Conversions: Yes
Area Develop. Agreements: Yes/1-5
Sub-Franchising Contracts: No
Expand In Territory: Yes
Space Needs: 800-1,400 SF; SF
SUPPORT & TRAINING PROVIDED:
Financial Assistance Provided: No
Site Selection Assistance: Yes
Lease Negotiation Assistance: Yes
Co-Operative Advertising: Yes
Franchisee Assoc./Member: No
Size Of Corporate Staff: 12
On-Going Support: b,C,D,E,F,G,H
Training: 230 Hours of Hands-On
  Training; 40 Hours Office Training.
SPECIFIC EXPANSION PLANS:
US: All United States
Canada: No
Overseas: No

◄◄ ►►

PEPE'S MEXICAN RESTAURANT
1325 W. 15th St.
Chicago, IL 60608
Tel: (312) 733-2500
Fax: (312) 733-2564
Mr. Edwin A. Ptak, Corporate Counsel

A full-service Mexican restaurant, serving a complete line of Mexican food, with liquor, beer and wine. Complete training and help in remodeling, site selection, equipment purchasing and running the restaurant provided.

BACKGROUND:
Established: 1967; 1st Franchised: 1968

Franchised Units: 56
Company-Owned Units   1
Total Units: 57
Dist.:   US-57; CAN-0; O'seas-0
  North America: 3 States
  Density: 43 in IL, 13 in IN, 1 in VA
Projected New Units (12 Months):   4
Qualifications: 3, 3, 2, 2, 1, 4
Registered: IL,IN,VA
FINANCIAL/TERMS:
Cash Investment: $30-100K
Total Investment: $75-300K
Minimum Net Worth: $NR
Fees: Franchise - $15K
  Royalty - 4%;   Ad. - 3%
Earnings Claim Statement: Yes
Term of Contract (Years):   20
Avg. # Of Employees: 8 FT, 5 PT
Passive Ownership: Discouraged
Encourage Conversions: Yes
Area Develop. Agreements: Yes/Varies
Sub-Franchising Contracts: No
Expand In Territory: No
Space Needs: 3,000 SF; FS, SF, SC
SUPPORT & TRAINING PROVIDED:
Financial Assistance Provided: No
Site Selection Assistance: Yes
Lease Negotiation Assistance: Yes
Co-Operative Advertising: Yes
Franchisee Assoc./Member: NR
Size Of Corporate Staff: 15
On-Going Support: B,C,D,E,F,G,H
Training: 4 Weeks Headquarters.
SPECIFIC EXPANSION PLANS:
US: Midwest
Canada: No
Overseas: No

◄◄ ►►

PERKINS RESTAURANT &
BAKERY
6075 Poplar Ave., # 800
Memphis, TN 38119-4709
Tel: (800) 877-7375 (901) 766-6400
Fax: (901) 766-6482
E-Mail:
franchise@perkinsrestaurants.com
Web Site: www.perkinsrestaurants.com
Mr. Robert J. Winters, VP Franchise
  Development

Full-service family-style restaurant, offering breakfast, lunch and dinner, along with proprietary bakery items at moderate prices.

BACKGROUND: IFA MEMBER
Established: 1958; 1st Franchised: 1958
Franchised Units: 339
Company-Owned Units   145
Total Units: 484
Dist.:   US-469; CAN-15; O'seas-0
  North America: 35 States
  Density: 75 in MN, 54 in PA, 51 in OH
Projected New Units (12 Months):   35
Qualifications: 5, 3, 5, 3, 3, 4
Registered: All States Except RI
FINANCIAL/TERMS:
Cash Investment: $100-600K
Total Investment: $1.0-2.0MM
Minimum Net Worth: $750K
Fees: Franchise - $40K
  Royalty - 4%;   Ad. - 3%
Earnings Claim Statement: Yes
Term of Contract (Years):   10-20/20
Avg. # Of Employees: 20 FT, 40 PT
Passive Ownership: Discouraged
Encourage Conversions: Yes
Area Develop. Agreements: Yes/3-8
Sub-Franchising Contracts: No
Expand In Territory: Yes
Space Needs: 5,000 SF; FS, SC
SUPPORT & TRAINING PROVIDED:
Financial Assistance Provided: No
Site Selection Assistance: Yes
Lease Negotiation Assistance: Yes
Co-Operative Advertising: Yes
Franchisee Assoc./Member: No
Size Of Corporate Staff: 224
On-Going Support: a,B,C,D,E,F,G,H,I
Training: 8-12 Weeks Management Training
  at Various Locations.
SPECIFIC EXPANSION PLANS:
US: All United States
Canada: All Canada
Overseas: No

◄◄ ►►

PIZZA DELIGHT
331 Elmwood Dr., 2nd Fl., P.O. Box
23070
Moncton, NB E1A 6S8 CANADA
Tel: (506) 853-0990
Fax: (506) 853-4131
E-Mail: opportunity@pizzadelight.ca
Web Site: www.pizzadelight.com
Mr. Bernard Imbeault, Chief Executive
  Officer

255

Our will and purpose is to get and keep customers. It can be realized through our mission: to be the best pizza place in town! We are a multi-brand organization operating as: PIZZA DELIGHT and LE COQ ROTI (rotisserie chicken).

BACKGROUND:

Established: 1968; 1st Franchised: 1970
Franchised Units: 144
Company-Owned Units   3
Total Units: 147
Dist.:   US-0; CAN-145; O'seas-2
  North America: 6 Provinces
  Density: NB, NF, NS
Projected New Units (12 Months):   15
Qualifications: 5, 3, 2, 2, 4, 5
Registered: None

FINANCIAL/TERMS:

Cash Investment: $50-150K
Total Investment: $150-350K
Minimum Net Worth: $250K
Fees: Franchise - $10-30K
  Royalty - 4-6%;   Ad. - 4.5%
Earnings Claim Statement: No
Term of Contract (Years):   10/5
Avg. # Of Employees: 5-10 FT, 5-10 PT
Passive Ownership: Discouraged
Encourage Conversions: Yes
Area Develop. Agreements: Yes/20
Sub-Franchising Contracts: Yes
Expand In Territory: Yes
Space Needs: 1,000-4,000 SF; Varies

SUPPORT & TRAINING PROVIDED:

Financial Assistance Provided: Yes(I)
Site Selection Assistance: Yes
Lease Negotiation Assistance: Yes
Co-Operative Advertising: Yes
Franchisee Assoc./Member: No
Size Of Corporate Staff: 25
On-Going Support: a,B,C,D,E,F,G,H,i
Training: 12 Days Head Office; 10 Days
  On-the-Job Training; 3 Days a Year of
  Continuous Training.

SPECIFIC EXPANSION PLANS:

US: No
Canada: Central, East
Overseas: No

⋖⋖ ⋗⋗

PIZZERIA UNO CHICAGO BAR & GRILL
100 Charles Park Rd.
Boston, MA 02132-4985
Tel: (800) 449-8667 (617) 323-9200
Fax: (617) 218-5376
E-Mail: randy.clifton@pizzeriauno.com
Web Site: www.pizzeriauno.com

Mr. Randy M. Clifton, VP Worldwide Franchising

A casual theme restaurant with a brand name signature product - UNO's Original Chicago Deep Dish Pizza. A full, varied menu with broad appeal and a flair for fun and comfortable decor in a facility that attracts guests of all ages.

BACKGROUND: IFA MEMBER

Established: 1943; 1st Franchised: 1979
Franchised Units: 70
Company-Owned Units   105
Total Units: 175
Dist.:   US-171; CAN-0; O'seas-4
  North America: 43 States
  Density: 27 in MA
Projected New Units (12 Months):   40
Qualifications: 5, 5, 3, 2, 3, 4
Registered: All States

FINANCIAL/TERMS:

Cash Investment: $700K
Total Investment: $900K-1.7MM
Minimum Net Worth: $2MM
Fees: Franchise - $35K
  Royalty - 5%;   Ad. - 1%
Earnings Claim Statement: Yes
Term of Contract (Years):   15/10
Avg. # Of Employees: 30 FT, 35 PT
Passive Ownership: Allowed
Encourage Conversions: Yes
Area Develop. Agreements: Yes/Negot.
Sub-Franchising Contracts: No
Expand In Territory: Yes
Space Needs: 5,500 SF; FS, SC, RM

SUPPORT & TRAINING PROVIDED:

Financial Assistance Provided: Yes(I)
Site Selection Assistance: Yes
Lease Negotiation Assistance: Yes
Co-Operative Advertising: Yes
Franchisee Assoc./Member: Yes/Yes
Size Of Corporate Staff: 135
On-Going Support: a,B,C,D,E,F,G,H,I
Training: 8 Weeks in a Training Restaurant;
  2 Weeks On-Site Staff Training.

SPECIFIC EXPANSION PLANS:

US: All United States
Canada: All Canada
Overseas: Asia, South and Central
  America, Europe

⋖⋖ ⋗⋗

PONDEROSA/BONANZA STEAKHOUSES
6500 International Pkwy.
Plano, TX 75093
Tel: (800) 543-9670 (972) 588-5887

Fax: (972) 588-5806
E-Mail: franchise@metrogroup.com
Web Site:
www.metromediarestaurants.com
Mr. Lawrence F. Stein, Dir. Franchise Dev.

PONDEROSA Steakhouse

PONDEROSA and BONANZA FAMILY STEAKHOUSES serve great-tasting, family-priced steaks and entrees, accompanied by a large variety of all-you-can-eat salad items, soups, appetizers, hot vegetables, breads, sundae and dessert bar and other tasty food. All steaks and entrees come with the salad bar, buffet and dessert bar at no extra cost.

BACKGROUND: IFA MEMBER

Established: 1965; 1st Franchised: 1966
Franchised Units: 378
Company-Owned Units   145
Total Units: 523
Dist.:   US-461; CAN-14; O'seas-48
  North America: 29 States
  Density: 97 in OH, 52 in IN, 45 in NY
Projected New Units (12 Months): N/A
Qualifications: 5, 5, 4, 3, 4, 5
Registered: All States and AB

FINANCIAL/TERMS:

Cash Investment: $300K Liquid
Total Investment: $810K-1.9MM
Minimum Net Worth: $1.0MM
Fees: Franchise - $40K
  Royalty - 4%;   Ad. - 4%
Earnings Claim Statement: No
Term of Contract (Years):   20
Avg. # Of Employees: Varies
Passive Ownership: Discouraged
Encourage Conversions: Yes
Area Develop. Agreements: Yes/Varies
Sub-Franchising Contracts: No
Expand In Territory: Yes
Space Needs: 6,000-8,800 SF; FS, SC, RM

SUPPORT & TRAINING PROVIDED:

Financial Assistance Provided: No
Site Selection Assistance: Yes
Lease Negotiation Assistance: Yes
Co-Operative Advertising: Yes
Franchisee Assoc./Member: Yes/No
Size Of Corporate Staff: 400
On-Going Support: C,D,E,F,G,H,I
Training: 9 Weeks Headquarters in Plano,
  TX and Restaurant in Field.

SPECIFIC EXPANSION PLANS:

US: All United States

Canada:	All Canada
Overseas:	All Countries

R. J. BOAR'S BBQ

3127 Brady St., # 3
Davenport, IA 52803
Tel: (319) 322-2627
Fax: (319) 322-1947
Web Site: www.rjboars.com
Mr. Schuyler (Skip) Moore, Director of
Franchise Sales

R. J. BOAR'S is awarding franchise opportunities in the Midwest to qualified individuals. We specialize in hickory-smoked ribs, chicken and beef. As a niche player in the casual theme restaurant category, we realized very early on that a broad and varied menu of popular items was a crucial factor in determining our formula. That's why R. J. BOAR'S has such a diverse menu, including signature appetizers, specialty salads, fresh fish, tender steaks and award-winning hickory-smoked BBQ.

BACKGROUND:

Established: 1993;	1st Franchised: 1998
Franchised Units:	1
Company-Owned Units	<u>4</u>
Total Units:	5
Dist.:	US-4; CAN-0; O'seas-0
North America:	2 States
Density:	3 in IA, 2 in IL
Projected New Units (12 Months):	6-8
Qualifications:	4, 4, 5, 2, 2, 4
Registered: IL,IN,MN,SD,WI	

FINANCIAL/TERMS:

Cash Investment:	$175-300K
Total Investment:	$378-909K
Minimum Net Worth:	$1.5MM
Fees: Franchise -	$35K
Royalty - 4%;	Ad. - 3%

Earnings Claim Statement:	No
Term of Contract (Years):	10/5/5
Avg. # Of Employees:	10 FT, 60 PT
Passive Ownership:	Not Allowed
Encourage Conversions:	Yes
Area Develop. Agreements:	Yes/Varies
Sub-Franchising Contracts:	No
Expand In Territory:	Yes
Space Needs: 5,500 SF; FS	

SUPPORT & TRAINING PROVIDED:

Financial Assistance Provided:	No
Site Selection Assistance:	Yes
Lease Negotiation Assistance:	No
Co-Operative Advertising:	Yes
Franchisee Assoc./Member:	No
Size Of Corporate Staff:	4
On-Going Support:	B,C,D,E,f, h
Training: 8-10 Weeks Bettendorf, IA.	

SPECIFIC EXPANSION PLANS:

US:	Midwest
Canada:	No
Overseas:	No

RED HOT & BLUE

1701 Clarendon Blvd., # 105
Arlington, VA 22209
Tel: (800) 723-0745 (703) 276-8833
Fax: (703) 528-4789
E-Mail: dknutsen@rhbri.com
Web Site: www.redhotandbluebbq.com
Mr. Dave Knutsen, Director Franchise
Operations

RED HOT & BLUE restaurants serve Memphis-style ribs, pork, beef, chicken plus salads, burgers and a full menu in a casual dining environment, featuring blues memorabilia and recorded blues music. Service is Southern hospitality.

BACKGROUND:

Established: 1988;	1st Franchised: 1991
Franchised Units:	32
Company-Owned Units	<u>3</u>
Total Units:	35
Dist.:	US-35; CAN-0; O'seas-0
North America:	10 States
Density:	6 in NC, 5 in TX, 5 in VA
Projected New Units (12 Months):	6
Qualifications:	5, 5, 5, 4, 3, 5
Registered: All States Except RI,SD	

FINANCIAL/TERMS:

Cash Investment:	$347.7-868K
Total Investment:	$397.75K
Minimum Net Worth:	$1MM
Fees: Franchise -	$35K
Royalty - 5%;	Ad. - $375/Mo.

Earnings Claim Statement:	No
Term of Contract (Years):	20/10
Avg. # Of Employees:	30 FT, 20 PT
Passive Ownership:	Not Allowed
Encourage Conversions:	Yes
Area Develop. Agreements:	Yes/Varies
Sub-Franchising Contracts:	No
Expand In Territory:	No
Space Needs: 2,400-5,000 SF; FS, SC	

SUPPORT & TRAINING PROVIDED:

Financial Assistance Provided:	No
Site Selection Assistance:	Yes
Lease Negotiation Assistance:	No
Co-Operative Advertising:	Yes
Franchisee Assoc./Member:	Yes/Yes
Size Of Corporate Staff:	18
On-Going Support:	C,D,E,f,G,h
Training: 3 Weeks at Home Office; 2 Weeks On-Site.	

SPECIFIC EXPANSION PLANS:

US:	All United States
Canada:	All Canada
Overseas:	No

SANDELLA'S CAFÉ

9 Brookside Pl.
West Redding, CT 06896
Tel: (888) 544-9984 (203) 544-9984
Fax: (203) 544-7749
E-Mail: bmajor@sandellas.com
Web Site: www.sandellas.com
Mr. Bruce J. Major, Chief Development
Officer

Positioned in the explosive wrap market, SANDELLA'S is carving a market niche in fresh, distinctive food at affordable prices. The SANDELLA'S concept combines the convenience and value of quick-service concepts with the quality, freshness and variety associated with up-scale, casual full-service dining.

BACKGROUND: IFA MEMBER

Established: 1994;	1st Franchised: 1998
Franchised Units:	10
Company-Owned Units	<u>3</u>
Total Units:	13
Dist.:	US-9; CAN-0; O'seas-0
North America:	5 States
Density:	5 in NY, 2 in TX, 2 in CT
Projected New Units (12 Months):	45
Qualifications:	5, 5, 2, 3, 3, 5
Registered: HI	

FINANCIAL/TERMS:

Cash Investment:	$50-100K
Total Investment:	$145-245K

Minimum Net Worth:	$250K
Fees: Franchise -	$20K
Royalty - 6%;	Ad. - 3 + 1%
Earnings Claim Statement:	No
Term of Contract (Years):	10/10
Avg. # Of Employees:	4 FT, 4 PT
Passive Ownership:	Discouraged
Encourage Conversions:	Yes
Area Develop. Agreements:	Yes/Varies
Sub-Franchising Contracts:	Yes
Expand In Territory:	Yes
Space Needs: 1,500 +/- SF; FS, SF, SC, RM	

SUPPORT & TRAINING PROVIDED:

Financial Assistance Provided:	Yes(I)
Site Selection Assistance:	Yes
Lease Negotiation Assistance:	Yes
Co-Operative Advertising:	Yes
Franchisee Assoc./Member:	No
Size Of Corporate Staff:	25
On-Going Support:	A,B,C,D,E,F,G,H,I
Training: 6 Days Georgetown, CT; 10 Days in Store.	

SPECIFIC EXPANSION PLANS:

US:	All United States
Canada:	All Canada
Overseas:	All Countries

SANDWICH TREE RESTAURANTS

535 Thurlow St., # 300
Vancouver, BC V6E 3L2 CANADA
Tel: (800) 663-8733 (604) 684-3314
Fax: (604) 684-2542
Web Site: www.sandwichtree.ca
Mr. Tony Cardarelli, Director of Operations

Famous for our custom sandwiches, creative salads, hearty soups, catering and much more, SANDWICH TREE is a limited-hours operation located in shopping centres, commercial towers and industrial centres. Our quality food, served in our attractive surroundings, makes SANDWICH TREE a number one investment opportunity.

BACKGROUND:

Established: 1978;	1st Franchised: 1979
Franchised Units:	31
Company-Owned Units	0
Total Units:	31
Dist.:	US-0; CAN-43; O'seas-0
North America:	6 Provinces
Density:	19 in BC, 7 in NS, 5 in ON
Projected New Units (12 Months):	4
Registered: NR	

FINANCIAL/TERMS:

Cash Investment:	$35-55K
Total Investment:	$90-120K
Minimum Net Worth:	$NR
Fees: Franchise -	$10-17.5K
Royalty - 5%;	Ad. - 3%
Earnings Claim Statement:	Yes
Term of Contract (Years):	5/5
Avg. # Of Employees:	4 FT, 7 PT
Passive Ownership:	Discouraged
Encourage Conversions:	Yes
Area Develop. Agreements:	Yes/10
Sub-Franchising Contracts:	Yes
Expand In Territory:	Yes
Space Needs: 300+ SF; SF, RM, Industrial Park	

SUPPORT & TRAINING PROVIDED:

Financial Assistance Provided:	Yes(I)
Site Selection Assistance:	Yes
Lease Negotiation Assistance:	Yes
Co-Operative Advertising:	Yes
Franchisee Assoc./Member:	NR
Size Of Corporate Staff:	6
On-Going Support:	a,B,C,D,E,F,G,H,I
Training: 2 Weeks Headquarters.	

SPECIFIC EXPANSION PLANS:

US:	No
Canada:	All Canada
Overseas:	All Countries

SBARRO

401 Broadhollow Rd.
Melville, NY 11747
Tel: (800) 766-4949 (631) 715-4100
Fax: (631) 715-4183
E-Mail: communications@sbarro.com
Web Site: www.sbarro.com
Ms. Meryl Jacovsky, Franchise Communications Coord

The # 1 quick-service Italian restaurant around the world. Family-owned and operated, SBARRO prides itself on its use of fresh ingredients, innovative recipes and a commitment to quality service known the world over.

BACKGROUND: IFA MEMBER

Established: 1959;	1st Franchised: 1979
Franchised Units:	286
Company-Owned Units	634
Total Units:	920
Dist.:	US-817; CAN-4; O'seas-99
North America:	30 States, 1 Province
Density:	25 in Il, 24 in NY, 16 in FL
Projected New Units (12 Months):	NR
Qualifications:	5, 4, 5, 3, 3, 3

Registered:	CA,HI,IL,MD,MI,MN, NY,ND,VA,WI

FINANCIAL/TERMS:

Cash Investment:	$150K
Total Investment:	$250-850K
Minimum Net Worth:	$250K
Fees: Franchise -	$45K
Royalty - 6%;	Ad. - 0%
Earnings Claim Statement:	No
Term of Contract (Years):	10/10
Avg. # Of Employees:8-10 FT, 10-15 PT	
Passive Ownership:	Not Allowed
Encourage Conversions:	N/A
Area Develop. Agreements:	Yes/10
Sub-Franchising Contracts:	No
Expand In Territory:	Yes
Space Needs: 800-1,000 SF; RM	

SUPPORT & TRAINING PROVIDED:

Financial Assistance Provided:	No
Site Selection Assistance:	No
Lease Negotiation Assistance:	No
Co-Operative Advertising:	Yes
Franchisee Assoc./Member:	Yes/Yes
Size Of Corporate Staff:	250
On-Going Support:	A,B,C,E,G,I
Training: 3 Weeks Walt Whitman Mall, Huntington, NY.	

SPECIFIC EXPANSION PLANS:

US:	NE,SE, Midwest, Southwest
Canada:	All Canada
Overseas:	All Countries

SHOOTERS INTERNATIONAL

3033 NE 32nd Ave.
Ft. Lauderdale, FL 33308
Tel: (954) 566-3044
Fax: (954) 566-2953
Mr. Melvin A. Burge, Executive Vice President

SHOOTERS INTERNATIONAL is an up-scale, waterfront, family-style restaurant and entertainment complex, catering to singles, family and boating clientele, offering valet service for boat docking and autos. We have outside dining, a patio, swimming pool, plus over 100 menu items.

BACKGROUND:

Established: 1982;	1st Franchised: 1985
Franchised Units:	5
Company-Owned Units	1
Total Units:	6
Dist.:	US-6; CAN-0; O'seas-1
North America:	3 States
Density:	3 in FL, 1 in OH

Projected New Units (12 Months): 2
Qualifications: 5, 4, 5, 4, 4, 5
Registered: CA,FL,IL,IN,NY,RI,VA
FINANCIAL/TERMS:
Cash Investment: $1.3-1.6MM
Total Investment: $NR
Minimum Net Worth: $1.3-1.6MM
Fees: Franchise - $75K
  Royalty - 4%; Ad. - NR
Earnings Claim Statement: No
Term of Contract (Years): 15/15
Avg. # Of Employees: 120 FT
Passive Ownership: Discouraged
Encourage Conversions: Yes
Area Develop. Agreements: No
Sub-Franchising Contracts: No
Expand In Territory: Yes
Space Needs: 7,000 SF; FS, Waterfront
SUPPORT & TRAINING PROVIDED:
Financial Assistance Provided: No
Site Selection Assistance: Yes
Lease Negotiation Assistance: Yes
Co-Operative Advertising: Yes
Franchisee Assoc./Member: No
Size Of Corporate Staff: 10
On-Going Support: C,d,e,H
Training: 4 Months Ft. Lauderdale, FL.
SPECIFIC EXPANSION PLANS:
US: All United States
Canada: ON
Overseas: Mexico, Middle East, Europe,
  Latin America

◄◄ ►►

SIRLOIN STOCKADE FAMILY STEAKHOUSES

2908 N. Plum St.
Hutchinson, KS 67502
Tel: (316) 669-9372
Fax: (316) 669-0531
Mr. Dan Spitz, Dir. Franchise Sales

SIRLOIN STOCKADE FAMILY STEAKHOUSES feature a selection of top-quality steaks, chicken and fish, a self-service salad bar, hot food buffet and display bakery at affordable prices. Free-standing buildings of approximately 10,000 square feet, seating 360-400; 70,000 square feet of land required.

BACKGROUND:
Established: 1984; 1st Franchised: 1984
Franchised Units: 66
Company-Owned Units 6
Total Units: 72
Dist.: US-64; CAN-0; O'seas-8
  North America: 10 States

Density: 18 in TX, 15 in KS, 8 in OK
Projected New Units (12 Months): 4
Registered: IL,IN,VA
FINANCIAL/TERMS:
Cash Investment: $350-500K
Total Investment: $1.2-2.3MM
Minimum Net Worth: $NR
Fees: Franchise - $15K
  Royalty - 3%; Ad. - 1%
Earnings Claim Statement: No
Term of Contract (Years): 15/15 USA
Avg. # Of Employees: 20 FT, 50 PT
Passive Ownership: Discouraged
Encourage Conversions: Yes
Area Develop. Agreements: Yes/Varies
Sub-Franchising Contracts: No
Expand In Territory: Yes
Space Needs: 10,000 SF; FS
SUPPORT & TRAINING PROVIDED:
Financial Assistance Provided: No
Site Selection Assistance: Yes
Lease Negotiation Assistance: No
Co-Operative Advertising: No
Franchisee Assoc./Member: NR
Size Of Corporate Staff: 16
On-Going Support: B,C,D,E,G,h,i
Training: 8-12 Weeks Training Store;
  Opening Week at Site; On-Going Site.
SPECIFIC EXPANSION PLANS:
US: All United States
Canada: No
Overseas: Mexico

◄◄ ►►

SMITTY'S RESTAURANTS

501 18th Ave. SW, # 600
Calgary, AB T2S 0C7 CANADA
Tel: (403) 229-3838
Fax: (403) 229-3899
E-Mail: ptomlinson@smittys.ca
Web Site: www.smittys.ca
Mr. Paul Tomlinson, VP Franchise
  Development

Specializing in ALL-DAY breakfast, featuring lunch and dinner menus with a special senior's menu. A truly family restaurant.

BACKGROUND:
Established: 1960; 1st Franchised: 1960
Franchised Units: 107
Company-Owned Units 12
Total Units: 119
Dist.: US-0; CAN-119; O'seas-0
  North America: 8 Provinces
  Density: 38 in AB, 18 in BC, 18 in SK
Projected New Units (12 Months): 10

Qualifications: 3, 4, 3, 3, 4, 4
Registered: AB
FINANCIAL/TERMS:
Cash Investment: $150K
Total Investment: $300-500K
Minimum Net Worth: $NR
Fees: Franchise - $35K
  Royalty - 5%; Ad. - 0%
Earnings Claim Statement: Yes
Term of Contract (Years): 20/10
Avg. # Of Employees: 15 FT, 15 PT
Passive Ownership: Discouraged
Encourage Conversions: Yes
Area Develop. Agreements: Yes/20+
Sub-Franchising Contracts: No
Expand In Territory: Yes
Space Needs: 4,300-5,000 SF; FS, SF, RM,
  Hotel
SUPPORT & TRAINING PROVIDED:
Financial Assistance Provided: Yes(I)
Site Selection Assistance: Yes
Lease Negotiation Assistance: Yes
Co-Operative Advertising: Yes
Franchisee Assoc./Member: No
Size Of Corporate Staff: 20
On-Going Support: C,D,E,F,G,h
Training: 3-4 Weeks Calgary, AB; 2-3
  Weeks Restaurant Location.
SPECIFIC EXPANSION PLANS:
US: HI
Canada: All Canada
Overseas: No

◄◄ ►►

SONNY'S REAL PIT BAR-B-Q

2605 Maitland Center Pkwy., # C
Maitland, FL 32751
Tel: (407) 660-8888
Fax: (407) 660-9050
Ms. Barbara C. Crain, Director Franchise
  Services

SONNY'S is the largest Bar-B-Q chain and concentrates in the Southeast U. S. SONNY'S is a full-service restaurant, specializing in Bar-B-Q beef, pork, chicken and ribs, as well as fast and friendly service.

BACKGROUND:
Established: 1968; 1st Franchised: 1976
Franchised Units: 102
Company-Owned Units 11
Total Units: 113
Dist.: US-113; CAN-0; O'seas-0
  North America: 6 States
  Density: 66 in FL, 18 in GA, 4 in NC
Projected New Units (12 Months): 10

259

Qualifications: 3, 4, 5, 2, 3, 4
Registered: FL,VA

FINANCIAL/TERMS:
Cash Investment: $NR
Total Investment: $600K-1.1MM
Minimum Net Worth: $1MM
Fees: Franchise - $25K
  Royalty - 3.5%; Ad. - 1%
Earnings Claim Statement: No
Term of Contract (Years): 20/10
Avg. # Of Employees: 25 FT, 15 PT
Passive Ownership: Discouraged
Encourage Conversions: No
Area Develop. Agreements: Yes/Varies
Sub-Franchising Contracts: No
Expand In Territory: Yes
Space Needs: 5,500 SF; FS

SUPPORT & TRAINING PROVIDED:
Financial Assistance Provided: No
Site Selection Assistance: Yes
Lease Negotiation Assistance: No
Co-Operative Advertising: Yes
Franchisee Assoc./Member: Yes/Yes
Size Of Corporate Staff: 17
On-Going Support: a,b,c,d,e,G,h,I
Training: 400-500 Hours or 10-13 Weeks
  at Orlando, FL.

SPECIFIC EXPANSION PLANS:
US: Southeast
Canada: No
Overseas: No

<< >>

ST. HUBERT BAR-B-Q
1515 Chomedey Blvd., # 250
Laval, PQ H7V 3Y7 CANADA
Tel: (450) 688-6500
Fax: (450) 688-3900
Web Site: www.st-hubert.qc.ca
Mr. Jacques Guilbert, Vice President
  Development

ST. HUBERT is a family-style restaurant, offering roasted chicken and Bar-B-Q ribs. We have table service, take-out and home delivery in certain areas.

BACKGROUND:
Established: 1951; 1st Franchised: 1967
Franchised Units: 81
Company-Owned Units: 13
Total Units: 94
Dist.: US-0; CAN-94; O'seas-0
  North America: 3 Provinces
  Density: 82 in PQ, 10 in ON, 2 in NB
Projected New Units (12 Months): 2
Qualifications: 4, 4, 4, 3, 4, 5
Registered: NR

FINANCIAL/TERMS:
Cash Investment: $200-400K
Total Investment: $700K-1.3MM
Minimum Net Worth: $200-400K
Fees: Franchise - $60K
  Royalty - 4%; Ad. - 3%
Earnings Claim Statement: No
Term of Contract (Years): 10/10
Avg. # Of Employees: 35 FT, 35 PT
Passive Ownership: Not Allowed
Encourage Conversions: N/A
Area Develop. Agreements: No
Sub-Franchising Contracts: No
Expand In Territory: Yes
Space Needs: 6,500 SF; FS, SC

SUPPORT & TRAINING PROVIDED:
Financial Assistance Provided: No
Site Selection Assistance: Yes
Lease Negotiation Assistance: No
Co-Operative Advertising: Yes
Franchisee Assoc./Member: No
Size Of Corporate Staff: 80
On-Going Support: a,b,C,d,e,f,G,H,I
Training: 7 Weeks Laval, PQ.

SPECIFIC EXPANSION PLANS:
US: No
Canada: No
Overseas: No

<< >>

STEAK AND ALE
6500 International Pkwy.
Plano, TX 75093
Tel: (800) 543-9670 (972) 588-5657
Fax: (972) 588-5806
E-Mail: franchise@metrogroup.com
Web Site: www.mrg.net
Mr. Art Kilmer, VP of Franchising

STEAK AND ALE is an up-scale restaurant that features a variety of distinctive tastes, such as prime rib, steaks and a fresh salad bar served in a casually elegant atmosphere.

BACKGROUND: IFA MEMBER
Established: 1966; 1st Franchised: 1998
Franchised Units: 1
Company-Owned Units: 112
Total Units: 113
Dist.: US-113; CAN-0; O'seas-0
  North America: 24 States
  Density: 27 in FL, 25 in TX, 7 in NJ
Projected New Units (12 Months): N/A
Qualifications: 5, 5, 4, 3, 4, 5
Registered: All States

FINANCIAL/TERMS:
Cash Investment: $500K

Total Investment: $1.0-2.0MM
Minimum Net Worth: $1MM
Fees: Franchise - $50K
  Royalty - 4%; Ad. - 4%
Earnings Claim Statement: No
Term of Contract (Years): 20/Varies
Avg. # Of Employees: NR
Passive Ownership: Discouraged
Encourage Conversions: Yes
Area Develop. Agreements: Yes/20
Sub-Franchising Contracts: No
Expand In Territory: Yes
Space Needs: 6,300 SF; FS

SUPPORT & TRAINING PROVIDED:
Financial Assistance Provided: No
Site Selection Assistance: Yes
Lease Negotiation Assistance: No
Co-Operative Advertising: Yes
Franchisee Assoc./Member: Yes/No
Size Of Corporate Staff: 375
On-Going Support: A,B,C,D,E,G,h
Training: Headquarters at Plano, TX; in
  Unit.

SPECIFIC EXPANSION PLANS:
US: All United States
Canada: All Canada
Overseas: All Countries

<< >>

STRAW HAT PIZZA
6400 Village Pkwy.
Dublin, CA 94568
Tel: (925) 829-1500
Fax: (925) 829-9533
E-Mail: info@strawhatpizza.com
Web Site: www.strawhatpizza.com
Mr. Joshua V. Richman, President/CEO

STRAW HAT PIZZA is a cooperative owned by a membership made up of individual store owners. Royalty fees are very low and more than offset by purchasing, insurance and marketing advantages. Stores operate under a detailed system, yet are allowed a great deal of flexibility. Store owners participate in the operation of the parent company.

BACKGROUND: IFA MEMBER
Established: 1959; 1st Franchised: 1969
Franchised Units: 50
Company-Owned Units: 0
Total Units: 50
Dist.: US-50; CAN-0; O'seas-0

North America: 2 States
Density: 47 in CA, 3 in NV
Projected New Units (12 Months):   6
Qualifications: 3, 3, 4, 3, 4, 5
Registered: CA,HI,WA

FINANCIAL/TERMS:
Cash Investment: $100-150K
Total Investment: $150-600K
Minimum Net Worth: $250K
Fees: Franchise - $10K
  Royalty - 2%;   Ad. - 0.8%
Earnings Claim Statement: No
Term of Contract (Years):   10/10
Avg. # Of Employees: 3-5 FT, 8-15 PT
Passive Ownership: Discouraged
Encourage Conversions: Yes
Area Develop. Agreements: No
Sub-Franchising Contracts: No
Expand In Territory: Yes
Space Needs: 4,000 SF; SC

SUPPORT & TRAINING PROVIDED:
Financial Assistance Provided: Yes(I)
Site Selection Assistance: No
Lease Negotiation Assistance: No
Co-Operative Advertising: Yes
Franchisee Assoc./Member: No
Size Of Corporate Staff: 5
On-Going Support: B,C,D,F,G,H
Training: 4 Weeks in Long Beach, CA.

SPECIFIC EXPANSION PLANS:
US: West
Canada: No
Overseas: No

⊲⊲ ⊳⊳

STRINGS ITALIAN CAFE

11344 Coloma Rd., # 545
Gold River, CA 95670
Tel: (916) 635-3990
Fax: (916) 631-9775
Mr. Al DeCaprio, President

STRINGS ITALIAN CAFE is a full-service, casual restaurant, with a menu focusing on a variety of pasta entrees, pizza, salads, desserts and espresso. A central kitchen/commissary provides most of the product requirements.

BACKGROUND:
Established: 1987;   1st Franchised: 1989
Franchised Units: 17
Company-Owned Units   3
Total Units: 20
Dist.:   US-18; CAN-2; O'seas-0
  North America: 3 States, 1 Province
  Density: 24 in CA, 2 in PQ, 1 in NV
Projected New Units (12 Months):   4

Qualifications: 4, 4, 5, 3, 3, 4
Registered: CA,FL,OR,WA

FINANCIAL/TERMS:
Cash Investment: $100K
Total Investment: $325K
Minimum Net Worth: $400K
Fees: Franchise - $37.5K
  Royalty - 5%;   Ad. - 2%
Earnings Claim Statement: No
Term of Contract (Years):   10/5
Avg. # Of Employees: 4-6 FT, 15 PT
Passive Ownership: Discouraged
Encourage Conversions: Yes
Area Develop. Agreements: Yes/5
Sub-Franchising Contracts: No
Expand In Territory: Yes
Space Needs: 2,500 SF; SC, RM

SUPPORT & TRAINING PROVIDED:
Financial Assistance Provided: No
Site Selection Assistance: Yes
Lease Negotiation Assistance: Yes
Co-Operative Advertising: Yes
Franchisee Assoc./Member: No
Size Of Corporate Staff: 12
On-Going Support: C,D,E,F,G,H
Training: 6 Weeks Gold River, CA; 3 Weeks
  On-Site.

SPECIFIC EXPANSION PLANS:
US: All United States
Canada: No
Overseas: No

⊲⊲ ⊳⊳

SUNSHINE CAFE

7112 Zionsville Rd.
Indianapolis, IN 46268-4153
Tel: (800) 808-4774 (317) 299-3391
Fax: (317) 299-3390
E-Mail: sqsinc@aol.com
Mr. James Frederick, Chief Executive Officer

A bright and cheerful, casual restaurant which reflects family dining at its best. Full table service is offered. Menu offers breakfast, lunch and dinner fare available throughout the day with local special entrees each day. Widely varied menu features American, Mexican, Italian and Oriental fare with fresh salad selections, signature items and desserts. Franchise has option to offer alcoholic beverages (beer, wine only) as market demands.

BACKGROUND:
Established: 1965;   1st Franchised: 1985
Franchised Units: 12
Company-Owned Units   2

Total Units: 14
Dist.:   US-14; CAN-0; O'seas-0
  North America: 2 States
  Density: 13 in IN, 1 in OH
Projected New Units (12 Months):   6
Qualifications: 5, 5, 5, 2, 4, 5
Registered: IL,IN,MI,WI

FINANCIAL/TERMS:
Cash Investment: $150K+
Total Investment: $150K-1MM
Minimum Net Worth: $500K
Fees: Franchise - $25K
  Royalty - 4%;   Ad. - 3%
Earnings Claim Statement: No
Term of Contract (Years):   5/5
Avg. # Of Employees: 50 FT, 10 PT
Passive Ownership: Allowed
Encourage Conversions: Yes
Area Develop. Agreements: Yes/Varies
Sub-Franchising Contracts: No
Expand In Territory: Yes
Space Needs: 4,400-5,600 SF; FS, SC, SF

SUPPORT & TRAINING PROVIDED:
Financial Assistance Provided: Yes(I)
Site Selection Assistance: Yes
Lease Negotiation Assistance: Yes
Co-Operative Advertising: Yes
Franchisee Assoc./Member: No
Size Of Corporate Staff: 16
On-Going Support: B,C,D,E,F,G,H
Training: 7 Weeks Indianapolis, IN.

SPECIFIC EXPANSION PLANS:
US: Midwest, N. Central U.S.
Canada: No
Overseas: No

⊲⊲ ⊳⊳

SWISS CHALET/SWISS CHALET PLUS RESTAURANTS

6303 Airport Rd.
Mississauga, ON L4V 1R8 CANADA
Tel: (905) 405-6500
Fax: (905) 405-6777
Ms. Irene Fong, Dir. of Franchise Admin.

Foodservice family restaurants.

BACKGROUND:
Established: 1900;   1st Franchised: 1984
Franchised Units: 173
Company-Owned Units   38
Total Units: 211
Dist.:   US-7; CAN-146; O'seas-0
  North America: NR
  Density: ON, PQ, AB
Projected New Units (12 Months):   20
Qualifications: 5, 4, 3, 3, 1, 5
Registered: AB

FINANCIAL/TERMS:

Cash Investment:	$300-360K
Total Investment:	$1-1.2MM
Minimum Net Worth:	$600K
Fees: Franchise -	$75-90K
Royalty - 5%;	Ad. - 4%
Earnings Claim Statement:	Yes
Term of Contract (Years):	20/5x4
Avg. # Of Employees:	6 FT, 80 PT
Passive Ownership:	Not Allowed
Encourage Conversions:	Yes
Area Develop. Agreements:	No
Sub-Franchising Contracts:	No
Expand In Territory:	Yes
Space Needs: 6,000 SF; FS	

SUPPORT & TRAINING PROVIDED:

Financial Assistance Provided:	No
Site Selection Assistance:	Yes
Lease Negotiation Assistance:	Yes
Co-Operative Advertising:	Yes
Franchisee Assoc./Member:	Yes/Yes
Size Of Corporate Staff:	200
On-Going Support:	C,D,E,G,h,I
Training: 10-12 Weeks Toronto, ON.	

SPECIFIC EXPANSION PLANS:

US:	No
Canada:	All Canada
Overseas:	No

◁◁ ▷▷

TAXI'S RESTAURANTS INTERNATIONAL

1840 San Miguel Dr., # 206
Walnut Creek, CA 94596
Tel: (877) 448-8294 (925) 939-5021
Fax: (925) 937-7227
E-Mail: franchise@taxis1.com
Web Site: www.taxishamburgers.com
Mr. Jeffery Neustadt, President/CEO

TAXI'S RESTAURANTS is a chain of fast/casual restaurants, offering a varied menu of gourmet hamburgers, over-sized sandwiches, salads, soups, shakes and a Top-Your-Own Baked Potato Bar. The restaurants feature a lively atmosphere, complete with jukebox music set in the theme of a taxi garage. TAXI'S is open for lunch and dinner and Company unit sales average over $1 million annually.

BACKGROUND: IFA MEMBER

Established: 1991;	1st Franchised: NR
Franchised Units:	0
Company-Owned Units	5
Total Units:	5
Dist.:	US-5; CAN-0; O'seas-0
North America:	1 State
Density:	5 in CA
Projected New Units (12 Months):	7
Qualifications:	4, 5, 5, 3, 1, 4
Registered: CA,WA	

FINANCIAL/TERMS:

Cash Investment:	$N/A
Total Investment:	$395-450K
Minimum Net Worth:	$N/A
Fees: Franchise -	$25K
Royalty - 4%;	Ad. - 3.75%
Earnings Claim Statement:	No
Term of Contract (Years):	20/N/A
Avg. # Of Employees:	10 FT, 15 PT
Passive Ownership:	Not Allowed
Encourage Conversions:	Yes
Area Develop. Agreements:	Yes
Sub-Franchising Contracts:	No
Expand In Territory:	Yes
Space Needs: 2,500 SF; FS, SF, SC, RM	

SUPPORT & TRAINING PROVIDED:

Financial Assistance Provided:	No
Site Selection Assistance:	Yes
Lease Negotiation Assistance:	No
Co-Operative Advertising:	No
Franchisee Assoc./Member:	No
Size Of Corporate Staff:	4
On-Going Support:	C,D,E,G,H,I
Training: 4 Weeks Walnut Creek, CA.	

SPECIFIC EXPANSION PLANS:

US:	NR
Canada:	No
Overseas:	No

◁◁ ▷▷

VILLAGE INN RESTAURANTS

400 W. 48th Ave., P. O. Box 16601
Denver, CO 80216
Tel: (800) 891-9978 (303) 296-2121
Fax: (303) 672-2212
Web Site: www.vicorpinc.com
Ms. Maxine Crogle, Qualifications Specialist

Full-service, family-style restaurants, offering a variety of menu items and bi-monthly features, emphasizing our breakfast heritage in all dayparts.

BACKGROUND: IFA MEMBER

Established: 1958;	1st Franchised: 1961
Franchised Units:	114
Company-Owned Units	104
Total Units:	218
Dist.:	US-218; CAN-0; O'seas-0
North America:	21 States
Density:	45 in CO, 25 in FL, 23 AZ
Projected New Units (12 Months):	12
Qualifications:	5, 4, 5, 3, 1, 5
Registered:	CA,FL,IL,MD,MN,MS,
ND,SD,UT,VA,WA	

FINANCIAL/TERMS:

Cash Investment:	$Varies
Total Investment:	$512K-2.4MM
Minimum Net Worth:	$750K
Fees: Franchise -	$35K
Royalty - 4%;	Ad. - 0%
Earnings Claim Statement:	No
Term of Contract (Years):	25/10
Avg. # Of Employees:	20 FT, 40 PT
Passive Ownership:	Discouraged
Encourage Conversions:	Yes
Area Develop. Agreements:	Yes/Varies
Sub-Franchising Contracts:	No
Expand In Territory:	Yes
Space Needs: 5,200 SF; FS, SC, RM	

SUPPORT & TRAINING PROVIDED:

Financial Assistance Provided:	No
Site Selection Assistance:	Yes
Lease Negotiation Assistance:	No
Co-Operative Advertising:	No
Franchisee Assoc./Member:	No
Size Of Corporate Staff:	200
On-Going Support:	C,d,E,F,G,h,I
Training: Approximately 10-12 Weeks Denver, CO.	

SPECIFIC EXPANSION PLANS:

US:	Mid-Atlantic,MW,NE,SE
Canada:	No
Overseas:	No

◁◁ ▷▷

WESTERN SIZZLIN'

317 Kimball Ave.
Roanoke, VA 24016
Tel: (800) 642-2157 (540) 345-3195
Fax: (540) 345-0831

E-Mail: wsinc@feist.com
Web Site: www.western-sizzlin.com
Mr. John Mash, Director Franchise
  Development

WESTERN SIZZLIN' restaurants operate a full line of steak-chicken-seafood entrees, as well as a full expanded food bar, featuring proteins, vegetables and bakery items, along with an expanded salad bar. Our focus is on making a quality statement with excellent price/value. Also offering franchises for Great American Steak & Buffet and Austin's Steakhouse and Saloon.

BACKGROUND: IFA MEMBER
Established: 1962; 1st Franchised: 1976
Franchised Units: 210
Company-Owned Units   26
Total Units: 236
Dist.:   US-236; CAN-0; O'seas-0
  North America: NR
  Density: 31 in AR, 24 in VA, 21 in GA
Projected New Units (12 Months):   NR
Qualifications: 5, 4, 2, 3, 2, 5
Registered: CA,FL,IL,IN,MD,VA
FINANCIAL/TERMS:
Cash Investment: $NR
Total Investment: $811K-2.3MM
Minimum Net Worth: $NR
Fees: Franchise - $30K
  Royalty - 2% Gross; Ad. - 1% Gross
Earnings Claim Statement: No
Term of Contract (Years):   20/10
Avg. # Of Employees: 25 FT, 50 PT
Passive Ownership: NR
Encourage Conversions: Yes
Area Develop. Agreements: Yes/Negot.
Sub-Franchising Contracts: NR
Expand In Territory: Yes
Space Needs: 7,500-8,500 SF; FS
SUPPORT & TRAINING PROVIDED:
Financial Assistance Provided: No
Site Selection Assistance: Yes
Lease Negotiation Assistance: No
Co-Operative Advertising: No
Franchisee Assoc./Member: Yes
Size Of Corporate Staff: 40
On-Going Support: C,D,E,F,G,h,I
Training: 6 Weeks Training Center in
  Manassas, VA, Knoxville, TN, Little
  Rock, AR.
SPECIFIC EXPANSION PLANS:
US: All United States
Canada: No
Overseas: No

≪ ≫

WORLDLY WRAPS
221 Sequoia Rd., # 222
Louisville, KY 40207
Tel: (510) 839-5462
Fax: (510) 839-2104
Ms. Anna L. Barley, President

Truly the world's best wraps! 17 different varieties. Also, smoothies and health drinks. Low start-up cost. Exceptional training and on-going support. This is a new market that has not yet been tapped. Take advantage of our concept and our growth program. Option to expand within territory.

BACKGROUND:
Established: 1994; 1st Franchised: 1995
Franchised Units: 24
Company-Owned Units   6
Total Units: 30
Dist.:   US-21; CAN-0; O'seas-0
  North America: 6 States
  Density: 10 in KY, 4 in TN, 2 in IN
Projected New Units (12 Months):   4
Registered: CA,FL,IL,MN,WA
FINANCIAL/TERMS:
Cash Investment: $90-120K
Total Investment: $200-280K
Minimum Net Worth: $100K
Fees: Franchise - $19.5K
  Royalty - 6%;   Ad. - 1%
Earnings Claim Statement: No
Term of Contract (Years):   10/10
Avg. # Of Employees: 2 FT, 8 PT
Passive Ownership: Not Allowed
Encourage Conversions: Yes
Area Develop. Agreements: Yes/10
Sub-Franchising Contracts: No
Expand In Territory: No
Space Needs: 3,000-4,000 SF; FS
SUPPORT & TRAINING PROVIDED:
Financial Assistance Provided: Yes(I)
Site Selection Assistance: Yes
Lease Negotiation Assistance: Yes
Co-Operative Advertising: Yes
Franchisee Assoc./Member: NR
Size Of Corporate Staff: 21
On-Going Support: A,B,C,D,E,F,G,H,I
Training: 8 Weeks Headquarters; 3 Weeks
  Pre-Opening; On-Going.
SPECIFIC EXPANSION PLANS:
US: South, Southeast
Canada: No
Overseas: No

≪ ≫

**SUPPLEMENTAL LISTING
OF FRANCHISORS**

ABC Country Restaurants, 15373 Fraser Hwy., #202, Surrey, BC V3S 6B4 CANADA; (604) 583-8488; Ms. Joan Overin ; (604) 583-2919

Albert's Family Restaurant, 10544 - 144 St., Edmonton, AB T5H 3J7 CANADA; (403) 426-7391; Mr. Mark Siderson ; (403) 429-1259

Arrow Neighborhood Pub Group, The, 173 Woolwich St., # 201, Guelph, ON N1H 3V4 CANADA; (519) 836-6749; Mr. Bob Desautels ; (519) 836-3948

Aunt Sarah's Pancake House, P.O. Box 9504, Richmond, VA 23228; (804) 266-1255; Mr. Glen Dankos; (804) 264-9189

Banners Restaurants, 1965 W. Fourth Ave., # 203, Vancouver, BC V6J 1M8 CANADA; (604) 737-7993; Mr. Irwin Woodrow ; (604) 737-7748

BJ's Kountry Kitchen, 4325 N. Golden State Blvd., # 102, Fresno, CA 93722 ; (209) 275-8786; Mr. Gary Honeycutt ; (209) 275-1981

Boston Beanery Restaurant & Tavern, 2931-B University Avenue, Morgantown, WV 26505 ; (304)-598-7201; Mr. Dave Seman ; (304) 598-8828

Boston Pizza International, 5500 Parkwood Way, #200, Richmond, BC V6V 2M4 CANADA; (604) 270-4168; Mr. Rick Villalpando ; (604) 270-1108

Bridgeman's Restaurants, 5700 Smetana Dr., # 110, Minnetonka, MN 55343 ; (612) 931-3199; Mr. Steven H. Lampi (800) 297-5050; (612) 931-3099

Bud's Broiler, 2337 Tulane Ave., New Orleans, LA 70119 ; (504) 821-3810; Mr. Joseph Catalano ; (504) 821-3598

Buffalo Wings & Rings, 900 Adams Crossing, #B, Cincinnati, OH 45202 ; (513) 723-0465; Ms. Linda D. Biciocchi (800) 501-2865; (513) 723-1886

Cafe Med, 4699 Keele St., # 1, Downsview, ON M3J 2N8 CANADA; (416) 661-9706; Mr. M. Mayerson ; (416) 661-9916

Caz's Fish & Chip Shoppe/Sea Grille, 200 N. Service Rd. W., # 1, Ste. 600, Oakville, ON L6M 2Y1 CANADA; (905) 825-0774; Mr. Douglas E. Casimiri ; (905) 847-7424

Coco's/Carrows, 3355 Michelson Dr., # 350, Irvine, CA 92612 ; (949) 251-5231; Mr. Robert Curry ; (949) 251-5700

Columbia Steak House, 261 Midland Ave., Lexington, KY 40508 ; (606) 231-0012; Mr. Greg D. Penn ; (606) 231-0008

Corporate Cafe, One Corporate Dr., Andover, MA 01810 ; (978) 682-9683; Mr. Mark E. Capomaccio (800) 562-9665; (978) 682-9665

Country Kitchen International, P.O. Box 44434, Madison, WI 53744-4434 ; (608) 274-9999; Mr. Charles Myers ; (608) 274-5030

Cucos Mexican Café, 110 Veterans Blvd., # 222, Metairie, LA 70005 ; (504) 835-0336; Mr. Vincent Liuzza (800) 888-2826; (504) 835-0306

Don Cherry's Grapevine Restaurants, 500 Ray Lawson Blvd., Brampton, ON l6y 5b3 CANADA; (905) 451-1980; Mr. Richard J. Scully ; (905) 451-5197

Durango Steak House, 2325 Ulmerton Rd., # 20, Clearwater, FL 33762 ; (727) 572-8342; Mr. Fred B. Bullard III (800) 525-8643; (727) 540-0009 X103

Eat at Joe's, P.O. Box 500, Yonkers, NY 10704 ; (914) 725-8663; Mr. Joe Fiore (800) 899-5637; (914) 337-6584

El Chico Restaurants, 12200 Stemmons Fwy., # 100, Dallas, TX 75234 ; (214) 888-8198; Ms. Elizabeth Clark ; (972) 241-5500

El Torito Restaurants, P.O. Box 19561, Irvine, CA 92623-9561 ; (949) 724-9914; Mr. Michael Malanga ; (949) 757-7900

Embers America, 1664 University Ave., St. Paul, MN 55104 ; (651) 645-6866; Mr. Greg Poling (888) 805-3448; (651) 645-6473

Famous Dave's of America, 7657 Anagram Dr., Eden Prairie, MN 55344 ; (612) 833-9388; Mr. Victor Salamone (800) 210-4040; (612) 833-9301

Fish Cove Franchising, 1802 Teall Ave., Syracuse, NY 13206 ; (315) 463-1038; Mr. Joseph Falcone ; (315) 463-6990

Friday's Front Row Sports Grill, 7540 LBJ Fwy., # 100, Dallas, TX 75251 ; (214) 450-5503; Ms. Kelly Smith (800) 374-3297;

FT Restaurants, 6032 Fieldstone, #H, Baton Rouge, LA 70809 ; (225) 751-2963; Mr. Mitch Richardson ; (225) 751-2960

Geppetto's Pizza & Ribs, 3314 Warren Rd., Cleveland, OH 44111 ; (216) 251-8960; Mr. Michael O'Malley ; (216) 251-1354

Gigglebees, 519 S. Minnesota Ave., Sioux Falls, SD 57104 ; (605) 334-4514; Mr. Brett Eble ; (605) 331-4242

Goldies Patio Grill, 8332 E. 73rd St. S., Tulsa, OK 74133 ; ; Mr. Richard Harkey ; (918) 254-8100

Good Times Drive Thru, 601 Corporate Cir., Golden, CO 80401 ; (303) 273-0177; Mr. Boyd Hoback ; (303) 384-1400

Granny Feelgood's Natural Food Restaurant, 25 W. Flagler St., City National Bank Bldg, Miami, FL 33130 ; (305) 579-2106; Mr. Irving Fields ; (305) 377-9600

Hooters of America, 1815 The Exchange, Atlanta, GA 30339 ; (770) 980-2452; Mr. Greg Michael ; (770) 951-2040

International House of Pancakes/IHOP, 525 N. Brand Blvd., 3rd Fl., Glendale, CA 91203-1903 ; (818) 240-0270; Ms. Anna Ulvan ; (818) 240-6055

Iron Skillet Restaurants, The, 6080 Surety Dr., El Paso, TX 79905 ; (915) 774-7391; Mr. Larry Glines (800) 331-8809; (915) 779-4711

Jack Astor's Bar& Grill, 4405 Knoll View Dr., Plano, TX 75024 ; (972) 801-9415; Mr. Wayne J. Shanahan ; (972) 801-9376

JB's Family Restaurant, 2207 S. 48th St., # A, Tempe, AZ 85282 ; (602) 426-0480; Mr. Bill Boger (800) 995-7555; (602) 426-2660

Johnny's New York Style Pizza, 834 Virginia Ave., Hapeville, GA 30354 ;

(404) 766-3727; Mr. Scott Allen ; (404) 766-3727

K-Bob's Steakhouses, 3700 Rio Grande NW, # 6, Albuquerque, NM 87107 ; (505) 341-2490; Ms. Susan Rosulek (800) 225-8403; (505) 341-2504

Keg Restaurants, 10760 Shellbridge Way, # 150, Richmond, BC V6X 3H1 CANADA; (604) 276-2681; Mr. James Henderson ; (604) 276-0242

Kettle Restaurants, P.O. Box 2964, Houston, TX 77252 ; (713) 263-1240; Mr. Mark Shackelford (800) 929-2391; (713) 263-1237

Koo Koo Roo Enterprises, Inc., P.O. Box 19561, Irvine, CA 92623-9561 ; (714) 757-3047; Mr. Kevin Relyea ; (949) 757-8015

Le Wok Imperial, 1168 St. Catherine West, # 207, Montreal, PQ H3A 1K1 CANADA; ; Mr. Steve Quan ; (514) 397-9886

Loop, The, One San Jose Pl., # 3, Jacksonville, FL 32257 ; (904) 268-5809; Mr. Eddie Fink (800) 329-5667; (904) 268-2609

Mandarin Restaurant, 239 Queen St. E., # 18, Brampton, ON L6W 2B6 CANADA; (905) 456-3411; Mr. James Chiu ; (905) 451-4100

Maurice's Gourmet Barbeque, 1600 Charleston Hwy., West Columbia, SC 29169 ; (803) 791-8707; Mr. Julian Bosworth (800) 628-7423; (803) 791-5887

Melting Pot Restaurants, The, P.O. Box 270059, Tampa, FL 33688-0059 ; (813) 889-9361; Ms. Kathy Hardy (800) 783-0867; (813) 881-0055

Morgan's Forest Restaurant, 18196 Deep Passage Ln., Fort Myers Beach, FL 33931 ; (941) 466-5830; Mr. Mike McGuigan ; (941) 466-5830

Mr. Mike's Grill, 611 Columbia St., New Westminster, BC V3M 1A7 CANADA; (604) 515-1197; Mr. Bill Outhwait ; (604) 515-1190

MY Mother's Delicacies Café, 501 S. Washington Ave., Scranton, PA 18505 ;

(570) 961-8861; Ms. Susan Herlands ; (570) 343-5266

O'Brien's Irish Sandwich Bar, 223 E. Wacker Dr., #3610, Chicago, IL 60601 ; (312) 893-3625; Mr. Jerrold Radu ; (312) 893-3625

Old Chicago Franchising, 248 Centinnel Pwky. #100, Louisville, CO 80027 ; (303) 664-4007; Mr. Bill Hope ; (303) 664-4200

Old San Francisco Steakhouse, 9809 McCullough, San Antonio, TX 78216 ; (210) 341-3585; Mr. Barry Cohen ; (210) 341-3189

Ottomanelli's Café, 1549 York Ave., New York, NY 10028 ; (212) 772-8436; Mr. Nicolo Ottomanelli ; (212) 772-8423

Pantry Family Restaurants, The, 1812 152nd St., # 203, South Surrey, BC V4A 4N5 CANADA; (604) 536-4103; Mr. Mike K. Hoffmann ; (604) 536-4111

Pat O'Brien's International Inc., 718 St. Peter St., New Orleans, LA 70116 ; (504) 582 6909; Mr. William H. Warshauer ; (504) 582-6910

Pizza Hut, 14841 Dallas Pkwy., Dallas, TX 75093 ; (972) 338-7998; Ms. Carol Hague ; (972) 338-8286

Prime Restaurant Group, 10 Kingsbridge Garden Cir., # 600, Mississauga, ON L5R 3K6 CANADA; (905) 568-0080; Ms. Debbie Daniel (800) 361-3111; (905) 568-0000

R. J. Gator's Florida Food N' Fun, 609 Hepburn Ave., # 103, Jupiter, FL 33058 ; (561) 575-9220; Mr. Reginald L. Timoteo (800) 438-4286; (561) 575-0326

Red Robin International, 5575 DTC Pkwy., # 110, Englewood, CO 80111 ; (303) 846-6013; Mr. Mike Woods ; (303) 846-6000

Red's Backwoods BBQ, 2255 Glades Rd., # 110E, Boca Raton, FL 33431 ; (561) 998-2249; Ms. Maxine Taylor (888) 311-7337; (561) 998-2250

Restaurant Developers Corp., 5755 Granger Rd., Cleveland, OH 44131 ; (216) 398-0707; Mr. Jim LeSeuer (800) 837-9599; (216) 398-1101

Restaurants Giorgio (Amerique), 222 St-Laurent Blvd., Montreal, PQ H2Y 2Y3 CANADA; (514) 844-0071; Ms. Magalie Brazier ; (514) 845-4221

Ricky's Restaurants, 7565 132nd St., # 201, Surrey, BC V3W 1K5 CANADA; (604) 597-8874; Mr. Frank DiBenedetto (888) 597-7272; (604) 597-7272

Round Table Pizza Restaurant, 2175 N. California Blvd., # 400, Walnut Creek, CA 94596 ; (925) 974-3978; Mr. Peter Hultgren (800) 866-5866; (925) 274-1700

Royal Fork Restaurant, 6874 Fairview Ave., Boise, ID 83704 ; (208) 322-0149; Mr. Meryln Knight ; (208) 322-5600

Royal Waffle King, P.O. Box 1025, Alpharetta, GA 30009 ; (770) 475-0763; Mr. Charlie Crowder ; (770) 442-3800

Ruby Tuesday, 150 W. Church Ave., Maryville, TN 37801 ; (423) 379-6817; Mr. Mark Ingram (800) 325-0755; (423) 379-5700

Runza Family Steak House, 5931 S. 58th St., #D, Lincoln, NE 68516 ; (402) 423-5726; Mr. Donald Everett, Jr. ; (402) 423-2394

Russ' Restaurants, 390 E. 8th St., Holland, MI 49423 ; (616) 396-6755; Mr. John Bouws (800) 521-1778; (616) 396-6571

Salvatore Scallopini Restaurants, 1650 E. 12th Mile Rd., Madison Heights, MI 48071 ; (248) 542-9168; Mr. Lawrence J. Bongiovanni ; (248) 542-9150

Samuel Mancino's Italian Eatery, 1595 W. Centre, Portage, MI 49024 ; (616) 327-6807; Mr. Samuel Mancino, Jr. (888) 792-8181; (616) 327-6800

Samurai Sam's Teriyaki Grill, 7720 E. Evans, Scottsdale, AZ 85260 ; (480) 483-4621; Mr. John Young ; (480) 483-8602

Shakey's Pizza Restaurants, 2201 DuPont Dr., # 100, Irvine, CA 92612 ; (714) 757-2757; Mr. Madison Jobe (888) 444-6686; (714) 757-4200

Sheik Restaurant, The, 7361 103rd St., Jacksonville, FL 32210 ; (904) 778-1866; Mr. Mike Sheik ; (904) 778-4805

Shoney's Restaurants, 1727 Elm Hill Pike, # B-3, Nashville, TN 37210 ; (615) 231-2009; Mr. Robert Nicoletti (800) 346-9637; (615) 231-2605

Sizzler International, 6101 W. Centinela Ave., # 200, Culver City, CA 90230-6337 ; (310) 568-8255; Mr. Mike Wildmen ; (310) 568-0135

Staggering Ox, 400 Euclid-Lundy Ct., Helena, MT 59601 ; (406) 443-1732; Mr. Keith Clevenger ; (406) 443-1732

Taco Cabana, 8918 Tesoro Dr., # 200, San Antonio, TX 78217 ; (210) 804-2135; Mr. David Lloyd (800) 842-0556; (210) 804-0990

Tony Roma's - A Place For Ribs, 9304 Forest Ln., # 200, Dallas, TX 75243 ; (214) 343-2680; Mr. Wayne Vineyard (800) 286-7662; (214) 343-7800

WaffleWorld, 3110 High St., Portsmouth, VA 23707 ; (757) 483-2074; Mr. Paris Zambis ; (757) 399-6612

Wall Street Deli, One Independence Plaza, # 100, Birmingham, AL 35209-2628 ; (205) 868-0875; Mr. Ken Myres (888) 351-2514; (205) 868-2566

We Love Sushi, 2800 W. Sahara Ave., Unit 6C, Las Vegas, NV 89102 ; (702) 364-0451; Mr. Ted Kovacic (888) 447-8744; (702) 364-0384

Western Steer Family Steakhouse/WSMP, 3437 E. Main St., P. O. Box 399, Claremont, NC 28610-9771 ; (828) 459-3114; Mr. Kenneth L. Moser (800) 222-9771; (828) 459-7626

White Spot Restaurants, 1126 SE Marine Dr., Vancouver, BC V5X 2V7 CANADA; (604) 325-1499; Mr. Amir Mulji ; (604) 321-6631

FOOD: SPECIALTY FOODS INDUSTRY PROFILE

Total # Franchisors in Industry Group	92
Total # Franchised Units in Industry Group	7,100
Total # Company-Owned Units in Industry Group	<u>915</u>
Total # Operating Units in Industry Group	8,015
Average # Franchised Units/Franchisor	77.2
Average # Company-Owned Units/Franchisor	<u>9.9</u>
Average # Total Units/Franchisor	87.1
Ratio of Total # Franchised Units/Total # Company-Owned Units	7.8:1
Industry Survey Participants	38
Representing % of Industry	41.3%
Average Franchise Fee*:	$23.4K
Average Total Investment*:	$236.9K
Average On-Going Royalty Fee*:	5.3%

If a range was provided, the mid-point of the range was used. See detailed profiles for actual ranges.

FIVE LARGEST PARTICIPANTS IN SURVEY

Company	# Fran-chised Units	# Co-Owned Units	# Total Units	Franchise Fee	On-Going Royalty	Total Investment
1. Quizno's Classic Subs	944	28	972	20K	7%	170-225K
2. Schlotzky's Deli	760	23	783	30K	6%	1.3-2.3MM
3. Auntie Anne's	561	18	579	30K	6%	252K
4. Papa Murphy's	540	12	552	25K	5%	149-200K
5. Candy Bouquet International	400	1	401	3.5-25K	0%	7-43K

All of the data provided are proprietary and should not be quoted without acknowledging *Bond's Franchise Guide*.

ATLANTA BREAD COMPANY
1200 A Wilson Way, # 100
Smyrna, GA 30082
Tel: (800) 398-3728 (770) 432-0933
Fax: (770) 444-1991
E-Mail: franchise-div@atlantabread.com
Web Site: www.atlantabread.com
Mr. John J. Byron, VP Franchise
    Development

Let's make some bread together! The concept behind the ATLANTA BREAD COMPANY BAKERY AND CAFE is simple: an upscale neighborhood café serving soups, salads, sandwiches, breads, pastries, and delicious hot dinners. ATLANTA BREAD COMPANY is riding the crest of the hottest food concept around - and we've experienced over 450% growth in just 12 months. ABC provides a full spectrum of support, from business plans to real estate assistance. Franchise offer made by prospectus only.

BACKGROUND: IFA MEMBER
Established: 1993;   1st Franchised: 1995
Franchised Units: 125
Company-Owned Units   1
Total Units: 126
Dist.:   US-101; CAN-0; O'seas-0
  North America: 23 States
  Density: GA, NC, SC
Projected New Units (12 Months):   40
Qualifications: 5, 3, 3, 3, 4, 4
Registered: FL,IL,IN,MD,MI,MN,NY,
    OR,RI,VA,WI,DC
FINANCIAL/TERMS:
Cash Investment: $100-120K
Total Investment: $400-500K
Minimum Net Worth: $350-400K
Fees: Franchise - $40K
  Royalty - 5%;   Ad. - 2%
Earnings Claim Statement: No
Term of Contract (Years):   10/10
Avg. # Of Employees: 9 FT, 9 PT
Passive Ownership: Discouraged
Encourage Conversions: N/A
Area Develop. Agreements: No

Sub-Franchising Contracts: No
Expand In Territory: No
Space Needs: 3,500-5,000 SF; FS, SF, SC,
    RM
SUPPORT & TRAINING PROVIDED:
Financial Assistance Provided: Yes(I)
Site Selection Assistance: Yes
Lease Negotiation Assistance: Yes
Co-Operative Advertising: N/A
Franchisee Assoc./Member: No
Size Of Corporate Staff: 18
On-Going Support: B,C,D,E,F,H,I
Training: 6 Weeks Atlanta, GA
SPECIFIC EXPANSION PLANS:
US: All United States
Canada: All Canada
Overseas: All Countries

◄◄ ►►

AUNTIE ANNE'S
160-A, Rt. 41, P. O. Box 529
Gap, PA 17527
Tel: (717) 442-4766
Fax: (717) 442-4139
Web Site: www.auntieannes.com
Ms. Terry Wisdo, VP Franchise Dev.

As the founder and leader of what Entrepreneur Magazine calls the pretzel retailing revolution, AUNTIE ANNE'S supports over 600 locations. Customers love to watch our pretzels being rolled, twisted and baked. They choose our pretzels not only for the variety and taste, but also for our commitment to providing a nutritious snack alternative to mall treats. Our innovative mall-based concept has made AUNTIE ANNE'S one of the most sought-after franchises in the industry today.

BACKGROUND:
Established: 1988;   1st Franchised: 1989
Franchised Units: 561
Company-Owned Units   18
Total Units: 579
Dist.:   US-520; CAN-0; O'seas-30
  North America: 42 States
  Density: 81 in PA, 41 in CA, 40 in FL
Projected New Units (12 Months):   70
Qualifications: 5, 3, 3, 2, , 5
Registered: All States
FINANCIAL/TERMS:
Cash Investment: $156-252K
Total Investment: $252K
Minimum Net Worth: $300K
Fees: Franchise - $30K
  Royalty - 6%;   Ad. - 1%
Earnings Claim Statement: No

Term of Contract (Years):   1-5/5
Avg. # Of Employees: 3 FT, 12 PT
Passive Ownership: Discouraged
Encourage Conversions: N/A
Area Develop. Agreements: No
Sub-Franchising Contracts: No
Expand In Territory: Yes
Space Needs: 400-800 SF; RM
SUPPORT & TRAINING PROVIDED:
Financial Assistance Provided: No
Site Selection Assistance: Yes
Lease Negotiation Assistance: Yes
Co-Operative Advertising: No
Franchisee Assoc./Member: Yes/No
Size Of Corporate Staff: 135
On-Going Support: A,B,C,D,E,G,h
Training: 7-14   Days   Corporate
    Headquarters, Gap, PA.
SPECIFIC EXPANSION PLANS:
US: Parts of MW, SE, West. Regns
Canada: All Canada
Overseas: All Countries
    Except Singapore, Thailand, Indonesia,
    Malaysia and Philipines

◄◄ ►►

**BAHAMA BUCK'S ORIGINAL
SHAVED ICE CO.**
1741 W. University Dr., # 148
Tempe, AZ 85281
Tel: (800) 382-8257 (480) 894-4408
Fax: (480) 894-4409
Mr. Eric Lee, Treasurer

BAHAMA BUCK'S offers a unique, low-cost opportunity for anyone interested in a fun, family-oriented business. We concentrate on offering quality products and great customer service. Set in a tropical atmosphere, BAHAMA BUCK'S offers 61 flavors of soft, creamy shaved ice, plus over 14 non-alcoholic tropical drinks. Store layouts and sizes vary and are extremely flexible, but typically range from 1200-1500 square feet.

BACKGROUND:
Established: 1990;   1st Franchised: 1992
Franchised Units: 5
Company-Owned Units   5

Total Units:	10
Dist.:	US-10; CAN-0; O'seas-0
North America:	2 States
Density:	5 in AZ, 5 in TX
Projected New Units (12 Months):	6
Qualifications:	4, 3, 1, 3, 4, 4
Registered:	NR

FINANCIAL/TERMS:

Cash Investment:	$35K
Total Investment:	$60-140K
Minimum Net Worth:	$120K
Fees: Franchise -	$15K
Royalty - 6%;	Ad. - 1%
Earnings Claim Statement:	No
Term of Contract (Years):	10/10
Avg. # Of Employees:	1 FT, 12 PT
Passive Ownership:	Allowed
Encourage Conversions:	Yes
Area Develop. Agreements:	Yes/10
Sub-Franchising Contracts:	No
Expand In Territory:	Yes
Space Needs: 1,000-1,500 SF; FS, SC	

SUPPORT & TRAINING PROVIDED:

Financial Assistance Provided:	Yes(I)
Site Selection Assistance:	Yes
Lease Negotiation Assistance:	Yes
Co-Operative Advertising:	Yes
Franchisee Assoc./Member:	No
Size Of Corporate Staff:	5
On-Going Support:	B,C,d,E,G,H,I
Training: 60-80 Hours Tempe, AZ; 2 Days On-Site.	

SPECIFIC EXPANSION PLANS:

US:	Southwest, South
Canada:	No
Overseas:	No

◄◄ ►►

BAKER STREET ARTISAN BREADS & CAFE

847 W. Lancaster Ave.
Bryn Mawr, PA 19010-3337
Tel: (610) 520-2920
Fax: (610) 520-3199
Ms. Whitney Myrus, Vice President Franchising

Authentic artisan hand-crafted bread store, with emphasis on pastries, espresso and sandwiches in a cafe setting.

BACKGROUND:

Established: 1992;	1st Franchised: 1992
Franchised Units:	3
Company-Owned Units	7
Total Units:	10
Dist.:	US-10; CAN-0; O'seas-0
North America:	NR
Density:	NR

Projected New Units (12 Months):	30
Qualifications:	4, 4, 3, 4, 3, 5
Registered: All States	

FINANCIAL/TERMS:

Cash Investment:	$30-60K
Total Investment:	$300-600K
Minimum Net Worth:	$500K
Fees: Franchise -	$30K
Royalty - 4%;	Ad. - 2%
Earnings Claim Statement:	Yes
Term of Contract (Years):	10/10
Avg. # Of Employees:	5 FT, 10 PT
Passive Ownership:	Allowed
Encourage Conversions:	Yes
Area Develop. Agreements:	Yes
Sub-Franchising Contracts:	No
Expand In Territory:	Yes
Space Needs: 2,000 SF; FS, SF, SC	

SUPPORT & TRAINING PROVIDED:

Financial Assistance Provided:	Yes(D)
Site Selection Assistance:	Yes
Lease Negotiation Assistance:	Yes
Co-Operative Advertising:	Yes
Franchisee Assoc./Member:	Yes/Yes
Size Of Corporate Staff:	10
On-Going Support:	C,D,E,F,G,H,I
Training: 3 Weeks Philadelphia, PA; 7 Days Store Location.	

SPECIFIC EXPANSION PLANS:

US:	All United States
Canada:	All Canada
Overseas:	Europe, Asia

◄◄ ►►

BEAVERTAILS PASTRY

112 Nelson St., Unit 101 C
Ottawa, ON K1N 7R5 CANADA
Tel: (800) 704-0351 (613) 789-4940
Fax: (613) 789-5158
E-Mail: info@beavertailsinc.com
Web Site: www.beavertailsinc.com
Mr. Robert Libbey, President/CEO

BEAVERTAILS are a unique, wholesome pastry cooked fresh at leisure sites. We offer low entry investment, interesting locations and excellent strategic support. We are interested in development opportunities at amusement parks, sports venues, tourist destinations and ski hills across North America.

BACKGROUND:

Established: 1978;	1st Franchised: 1989
Franchised Units:	100
Company-Owned Units	3
Total Units:	103
Dist.:	US-4; CAN-99; O'seas-0
North America:	4 States, 4 Provinces

Density:	1 in FL, 1 in CO, 1 in WV
Projected New Units (12 Months):	NR
Registered:	

FINANCIAL/TERMS:

Cash Investment:	$30-50K
Total Investment:	$85-150K
Minimum Net Worth:	$50K
Fees: Franchise -	$20K
Royalty - 5%;	Ad. - 3%
Earnings Claim Statement:	Yes
Term of Contract (Years):	5/15
Avg. # Of Employees:	1 FT, 2-3 PT
Passive Ownership:	Discouraged
Encourage Conversions:	NR
Area Develop. Agreements:	Yes
Sub-Franchising Contracts:	Yes
Expand In Territory:	Yes
Space Needs: 200-300 SF; FS, SF, RM, Amusement.Recr.	

SUPPORT & TRAINING PROVIDED:

Financial Assistance Provided:	NR
Site Selection Assistance:	Yes
Lease Negotiation Assistance:	Yes
Co-Operative Advertising:	Yes
Franchisee Assoc./Member:	Yes/Yes
Size Of Corporate Staff:	10
On-Going Support:	A,B,C,D,E,F,G,I
Training: 14 Days Ottawa, ON; 3 Days On-Site.	

SPECIFIC EXPANSION PLANS:

US:	Southeast, Southwest
Canada:	NR
Overseas:	NR

◄◄ ►►

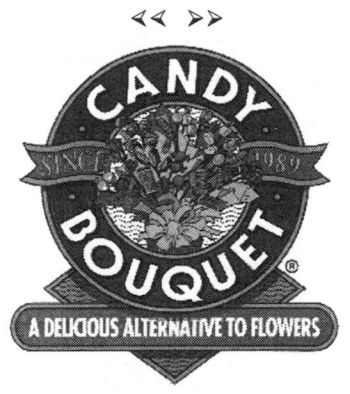

CANDY BOUQUET INTERNATIONAL

423 E. 3rd St.
Little Rock, AR 72201
Tel: (877) CANDY01 (501) 375-9990
Fax: (501) 375-9998
E-Mail: yumyum@candybouquet.com
Web Site: www.candybouquet.com
Mrs. Margaret M. McEntire, President/CEO

A CANDY BOUQUET is a full-scale candy store and a store of arrangements designed like flowers that is crafted from candies and the finest of chocolates. Each bouquet includes a burst of accessories, bright cellophane accents and unique containers. CANDY BOUQUETS are fun to give, fun to receive and fun to eat. They are perfect as corporate gifts and can be shipped anywhere.

BACKGROUND: IFA MEMBER
Established: 1989; 1st Franchised: 1994
Franchised Units: 400
Company-Owned Units: 1
Total Units: 401
Dist.: US-329; CAN-42; O'seas-30
 North America: 47 States, 10 Provinces
 Density: 34 in AR, 26 in CA, 28 in TX
Projected New Units (12 Months): 150
Qualifications: 5, 5, 5, 5, 5, 5
Registered: All States and AB
FINANCIAL/TERMS:
Cash Investment: $7.5-43K
Total Investment: $7-43K
Minimum Net Worth: $N/A
Fees: Franchise - $3.5-25K
 Royalty - 0%; Ad. - 0%
Earnings Claim Statement: No
Term of Contract (Years): 5/5
Avg. # Of Employees: 1 FT, 2 PT
Passive Ownership: Not Allowed
Encourage Conversions: N/A
Area Develop. Agreements: Yes/10
Sub-Franchising Contracts: Yes
Expand In Territory: Yes
Space Needs: Appox. 1,000 SF; HB, SF
SUPPORT & TRAINING PROVIDED:
Financial Assistance Provided: No
Site Selection Assistance: Yes
Lease Negotiation Assistance: No
Co-Operative Advertising: Yes
Franchisee Assoc./Member: No
Size Of Corporate Staff: 27
On-Going Support: b,c,d,D,e,G,h,I
Training: 5 Days Little Rock, AR.
SPECIFIC EXPANSION PLANS:
US: All United States
Canada: All Canada
Overseas: All Countries

CANDY EXPRESS
10480 Little Patuxent Pkwy, # 400
Columbia, MD 21044
Tel: (800) 511-4438 (410) 964-5500
Fax: (410) 964-6404
E-Mail: jrosenberg@candyexpress.com
Web Site: www.candyexpress.com
Mr. Joel Rosenberg, President

America's Candy Store™

The number-one ranked retail candy store franchise, offering over 1,000 varieties of candy and confections in a self-serve format. This international franchise company provides franchisees with a total turn-key opportunity that is profitable and easy to operate.

BACKGROUND:
Established: 1989; 1st Franchised: 1989
Franchised Units: 43
Company-Owned Units: 5
Total Units: 48
Dist.: US-40; CAN-0; O'seas-8
 North America: 17 States
 Density: 6 in MD, 5 in GA, 4 in VA
Projected New Units (12 Months): 15
Qualifications: 5, 2, 1, 1, 2, 3
Registered: All States
FINANCIAL/TERMS:
Cash Investment: $25-75K
Total Investment: $125-175K
Minimum Net Worth: $200K
Fees: Franchise - $25K
 Royalty - 6%; Ad. - 1%
Earnings Claim Statement: No
Term of Contract (Years): 10/10
Avg. # Of Employees: 1 FT, 3 PT
Passive Ownership: Allowed
Encourage Conversions: Yes
Area Develop. Agreements: Yes/20
Sub-Franchising Contracts: Yes
Expand In Territory: Yes
Space Needs: 1,000 SF; SF, RM, Airport
SUPPORT & TRAINING PROVIDED:
Financial Assistance Provided: Yes(I)
Site Selection Assistance: Yes
Lease Negotiation Assistance: Yes
Co-Operative Advertising: Yes
Franchisee Assoc./Member: Yes/No
Size Of Corporate Staff: 10
On-Going Support: A,B,C,D,E,F,G,H
Training: 2 Weeks MD.
SPECIFIC EXPANSION PLANS:
US: All United States
Canada: All Canada
Overseas: All Countries

FROZEN FUSION FRUIT SMOOTHIES
8900 E. Chaparrel Rd., # 1000
Scottsdale, AZ 85250
Tel: (800) 385-3765 (480) 367-5600
Fax: (480) 367-5676
Web Site: www.frozenfusion.com
Mr. Michael A. Kiick, VP Franchise Expansion

FROZEN FUSION is a tantalizing blend of fresh fruit and creamy non-fat yogurt. As a healthy snack or a satisfying meal, these fruit-based smoothies appeal to every taste. From the weight conscious, to the taste conscious, to the time conscious. There are a variety of tempting choices, including today's most popular nutritional supplements. They quench thirsts. They build energy. They even tame the sweetest tooth. FROZEN FUSION is perfect for any time of the day.

BACKGROUND: IFA MEMBER
Established: 1995; 1st Franchised: 1996
Franchised Units: 20
Company-Owned Units: 4
Total Units: 24
Dist.: US-24; CAN-0; O'seas-0
 North America: 9 States
 Density: 5 in AZ, 4 in DC, 3 in CA
Projected New Units (12 Months): 27
Qualifications: 5, 5, 3, 1, 3, 5
Registered: CA,FL,HI,IL,IN,MD,MI,MN, NY,OR,RI,VA,WA,WI,DC
FINANCIAL/TERMS:
Cash Investment: $75K
Total Investment: $180-250K
Minimum Net Worth: $250K
Fees: Franchise - $25-30K
 Royalty - 5%; Ad. - 1.5%
Earnings Claim Statement: No
Term of Contract (Years): 10/10
Avg. # Of Employees: 4 FT, 10 PT
Passive Ownership: Discouraged
Encourage Conversions: N/A
Area Develop. Agreements: Yes/10
Sub-Franchising Contracts: No
Expand In Territory: Yes
Space Needs: 500-1,000 SF; FS, SF, RM
SUPPORT & TRAINING PROVIDED:
Financial Assistance Provided: Yes(I)
Site Selection Assistance: Yes
Lease Negotiation Assistance: Yes
Co-Operative Advertising: Yes
Franchisee Assoc./Member: No
Size Of Corporate Staff: 13
On-Going Support: A,B,C,D,E,F,G,H,I
Training: 1 Week Headquarters in Scottsdale, AZ; 1 Week On-Site.

SPECIFIC EXPANSION PLANS:

US:	All United States
Canada:	All Canada
Overseas:	All Countries

FUDGE CO.

103 Belvedere Ave.
Charlevoix, MI 49720
Tel: (231) 547-9941
Fax: (231) 547-4612
Mr. Robert L. Hoffman, President

Handmade fudge cooked in copper kettles, using only natural ingredients and no preservatives, cooled and creamed on marble slabs in view of the public.

BACKGROUND:

Established: 1978;	1st Franchised: 1981
Franchised Units:	8
Company-Owned Units	1
Total Units:	9
Dist.:	US-7; CAN-0; O'seas-2
North America:	3 States
Density:	2 in AZ, 2 in AL, 2 in VA
Projected New Units (12 Months):	2-4
Qualifications:	4, 4, 1, 3, 4, 4
Registered: FL,HI,MI,OR	

FINANCIAL/TERMS:

Cash Investment:	$NR
Total Investment:	$28-35K
Minimum Net Worth:	$100K
Fees: Franchise -	$12.5-15K
Royalty - 3%;	Ad. - 0%
Earnings Claim Statement:	Yes
Term of Contract (Years):	10/10
Avg. # Of Employees:	2 FT, 2 PT
Passive Ownership:	Discouraged
Encourage Conversions:	N/A
Area Develop. Agreements:	Yes
Sub-Franchising Contracts:	NR
Expand In Territory:	Yes
Space Needs: 300-600 SF; FS, RM, Resort Areas	

SUPPORT & TRAINING PROVIDED:

Financial Assistance Provided:	No
Site Selection Assistance:	Yes
Lease Negotiation Assistance:	No
Co-Operative Advertising:	Yes
Franchisee Assoc./Member:	No
Size Of Corporate Staff:	NR
On-Going Support:	b,c,D,E
Training: 10-14 Days in AZ.	

SPECIFIC EXPANSION PLANS:

US:	All United States
Canada:	All Canada
Overseas:	All Countries

GREAT EARTH VITAMINS

11478 Mission Vista Dr.
Rancho Cucamonga, CA 91730
Tel: (800) 374-7328 (909) 987-8892
Fax: (909) 941-3472
Web Site: www.greatearth.com
Mr. Christopher Barr, National Development Director

Franchise company that understands consumers' needs and lifestyles, enabling franchisees to personalize a program of vitamins and nutritional supplements for consumers based upon the training we conduct for new franchise owners in our own school. This sets us apart from all other vitamin and nutrient supplement franchise systems.

BACKGROUND:

Established: 1971;	1st Franchised: 1974
Franchised Units:	150
Company-Owned Units	1
Total Units:	151
Dist.:	US-142; CAN-8; O'seas-1
North America:	15 States
Density:	77 in CA, 11 in TX
Projected New Units (12 Months):	25
Qualifications:	2, 1, 3, 3, 2, 2
Registered: All States	

FINANCIAL/TERMS:

Cash Investment:	$NR
Total Investment:	$75-135K
Minimum Net Worth:	$100K
Fees: Franchise -	$30K
Royalty - 6%;	Ad. - $150/Mo.
Earnings Claim Statement:	No
Term of Contract (Years):	10/5
Avg. # Of Employees:	2 FT, 2 PT
Passive Ownership:	Discouraged
Encourage Conversions:	Yes
Area Develop. Agreements:	Yes/Varies
Sub-Franchising Contracts:	Yes
Expand In Territory:	Yes
Space Needs: 650-1,400 SF; SC, RM	

SUPPORT & TRAINING PROVIDED:

Financial Assistance Provided:	Yes(D)
Site Selection Assistance:	Yes
Lease Negotiation Assistance:	Yes
Co-Operative Advertising:	Yes
Franchisee Assoc./Member:	Yes
Size Of Corporate Staff:	12
On-Going Support:	B,C,D,E,G,h,I
Training: 3 Weeks Cerritos, CA.	

SPECIFIC EXPANSION PLANS:

US:	All United States
Canada:	All Canada
Overseas:	NR

HARD TIMES CAFÉ

515 King St., # 440
Alexandria, VA 22314
Tel: (800) 422-2435 (703) 683-8545
Fax: (703) 683-7966
E-Mail: danr@hardtimes.com
Web Site: www.hardtimes.com
Mr. Dan A. Rowe, Chief Executive Officer

Authentic western-style chili parlor. Featuring chili, burgers and beer.

BACKGROUND: IFA MEMBER

Established: 1980;	1st Franchised: 1992
Franchised Units:	10
Company-Owned Units	4
Total Units:	14
Dist.:	US-0; CAN-0; O'seas-0
North America:	3 States
Density:	6 in VA, 6 in MD, 2 in NC
Projected New Units (12 Months):	NR
Registered:	

FINANCIAL/TERMS:

Cash Investment:	$100-200K
Total Investment:	$400-500K
Minimum Net Worth:	$250K
Fees: Franchise -	$30K
Royalty - 4%;	Ad. - 1%
Earnings Claim Statement:	No
Term of Contract (Years):	10/10
Avg. # Of Employees:	6 FT, 20 PT
Passive Ownership:	Not Allowed
Encourage Conversions:	NR
Area Develop. Agreements:	Yes/20
Sub-Franchising Contracts:	Yes
Expand In Territory:	Yes
Space Needs: NR SF; FS, SC	

SUPPORT & TRAINING PROVIDED:

Financial Assistance Provided:	NR
Site Selection Assistance:	Yes
Lease Negotiation Assistance:	Yes
Co-Operative Advertising:	Yes
Franchisee Assoc./Member:	No
Size Of Corporate Staff:	10
On-Going Support:	a,C,D,E,F,G,H,I
Training: 4 Weeks in Washington, DC Area.	

SPECIFIC EXPANSION PLANS:

US:	East Coast, Mid-Atlantic
Canada:	NR
Overseas:	NR

HEAVENLY HAM

1100 Old Ellis Rd., # 100
Roswell, GA 30076
Tel: (800) 899-2228 (770) 752-1999
Fax: (770) 752-4653
E-Mail: info@heavenlyham.com
Web Site: www.heavenlyham.com
Mr. Roger Flynn, Director of Franchising

The innovative opportunity in high quality specialty foods. Ownership benefits include: minimal labor, low start-up costs, extensive training, marketing support, site selection assistance and more. HEAVEN.Y HAM focuses primarily on two businesses: specialty meats and lunch. We offer signature spiral-sliced, honey and spice glazed ham and delicious tender-smoked turkeys. Other specialty meats include pork chops, hickory smoked ribs, bacon and steaks.

BACKGROUND: IFA MEMBER
Established: 1984; 1st Franchised: 1984
Franchised Units: 201
Company-Owned Units 1
Total Units: 202
Dist.: US-202; CAN-0; O'seas-0
  North America: 32 States
  Density: 17 in FL, 13 in NC, 13 in IN
Projected New Units (12 Months): 30
Qualifications: 5, 2, 1, 2, 3, 5
Registered: CA,FL,IL,IN,MD,MI,MN,NY, OR,RI,VA,WA,WI,DC
FINANCIAL/TERMS:
Cash Investment: $NR
Total Investment: $184.9-289K
Minimum Net Worth: $250K
Fees: Franchise - $30K
  Royalty - 5%; Ad. - 1%
Earnings Claim Statement: Yes
Term of Contract (Years): 10/10
Avg. # Of Employees: 2 FT, 2 PT
Passive Ownership: Not Allowed
Encourage Conversions: No
Area Develop. Agreements: No
Sub-Franchising Contracts: No
Expand In Territory: Yes
Space Needs: 2,500 SF; FS, SC
SUPPORT & TRAINING PROVIDED:
Financial Assistance Provided: Yes(I)
Site Selection Assistance: Yes
Lease Negotiation Assistance: Yes
Co-Operative Advertising: Yes
Franchisee Assoc./Member: No
Size Of Corporate Staff: 30
On-Going Support: C,D,E,F,G,H,I
Training: 10 Days Atlanta, GA.
SPECIFIC EXPANSION PLANS:
US: All United States
Canada: No
Overseas: No

HOT SAM'S PRETZEL BAKERY

2855 E. Cottonwood Pkwy., # 400
Salt Lake City, UT 84121
Tel: (800) 677-3435 (801) 736-5600
Fax: (801) 736-5970
E-Mail: franchise@mrsfields.com
Web Site: www.mrsfields.com
Mr. Scott Moffitt, VP Franchising

HOT SAM'S specializes in fresh, baked-on-the-premises pretzels, complemented by a selected line of tantalizing toppings. Providing a variety of items that have proven appeal, HOT SAM'S offers hand-rolled and twisted, sweet dough-style available in several flavors and is famous for its Bavarian-style pretzels, selling over 12 million a year. Our fresh-squeezed lemonade can't be beat. HOT SAM'S is a division of Mrs. Fields' Original Cookies, Inc.

BACKGROUND:
Established: 1967; 1st Franchised: 1996
Franchised Units: 0
Company-Owned Units 100
Total Units: 100
Dist.: US-100; CAN-0; O'seas-0
  North America: 22 States
  Density: 25 in OH, 9 in IN, 9 in MI
Projected New Units (12 Months): 15
Qualifications: 3, 4, 3, 2, 3, 5
Registered: All States
FINANCIAL/TERMS:
Cash Investment: $10-50K
Total Investment: $20-238K
Minimum Net Worth: $150K
Fees: Franchise - $25K
  Royalty - 6%; Ad. - 1%
Earnings Claim Statement: No
Term of Contract (Years): 17/7/5/5
Avg. # Of Employees: 1 FT, 4 PT
Passive Ownership: Discouraged
Encourage Conversions: Yes
Area Develop. Agreements: Yes/17
Sub-Franchising Contracts: No
Expand In Territory: Varies
Space Needs: NR SF; RM, Non-Traditional
SUPPORT & TRAINING PROVIDED:
Financial Assistance Provided: Yes(I)
Site Selection Assistance: Yes
Lease Negotiation Assistance: Yes
Co-Operative Advertising: No
Franchisee Assoc./Member: Yes/Yes
Size Of Corporate Staff: 70
On-Going Support: A,B,C,D,E,F,G,H,I
Training: 6 Days Salt Lake City, UT.
SPECIFIC EXPANSION PLANS:
US: All United States
Canada: All Canada
Overseas: All Countries

I. B. NUTS & FRUIT TOO

1206 N. Business Loop, 70 W.
Columbia, MO 65202
Tel: (573) 875-2998
Fax: (573) 449-8971
E-Mail: heckett@ibnuts.com
Web Site: www.ibnuts.com
Mr. David D. Hockett, President

Our franchise opportunities are two-fold. We have specialty food stores and routes that provide our customers with fine fruits, nuts and candies. Our store facilities also offer a wide array of Agri-State and gourmet foods with an extensive line of baskets, tins, crates and numerous accessory items to complement the gift-giving connoisseur. The route-store combination is the perfect one-two punch!

BACKGROUND:
Established: 1990; 1st Franchised: 1993
Franchised Units: 14
Company-Owned Units 1
Total Units: 15
Dist.: US-15; CAN-0; O'seas-0
  North America: 2 States
  Density: 9 in MO, 1 in IA
Projected New Units (12 Months): 6
Qualifications: 2, 4, 3, 2, 3, 5
Registered: All States
FINANCIAL/TERMS:
Cash Investment: $7K

Total Investment:	$12-20K
Minimum Net Worth:	$20K
Fees: Franchise -	$5.5K
Royalty - 0%;	Ad. - 0%
Earnings Claim Statement:	Yes
Term of Contract (Years):	5/5
Avg. # Of Employees:	2 FT, 2 PT
Passive Ownership:	Discouraged
Encourage Conversions:	N/A
Area Develop. Agreements:	Yes/On-going
Sub-Franchising Contracts:	No
Expand In Territory:	Yes
Space Needs: 750 SF; SF, HB, RM	

SUPPORT & TRAINING PROVIDED:

Financial Assistance Provided:	Yes(I)
Site Selection Assistance:	Yes
Lease Negotiation Assistance:	Yes
Co-Operative Advertising:	Yes
Franchisee Assoc./Member:	No
Size Of Corporate Staff:	4
On-Going Support:	C,D,E,F,H,I
Training: 2 Days Columbia, MO; 2-3 Days Franchise Location.	

SPECIFIC EXPANSION PLANS:

US:	Midwest
Canada:	No
Overseas:	No

JOE CORBI'S ® PIZZA KIT FUNDRAISING PROGRAM
1430 Desoto Rd.
Baltimore, MD 21230
Tel: (800) 587-7677 (410) 525-8331
Fax: (412) 851-1733
Web Site: www.joecorbi.com
Mr. Joseph Violi,

Specializing in the sale of fund-raising pizza kits, breads and other food items, as well as related goods and ancillary services, which are marketed to charitable, municipal, civic and other organizations.

BACKGROUND:

Established: 1984;	1st Franchised: 1999
Franchised Units:	2
Company-Owned Units	6

Total Units:	8
Dist.:	US-8; CAN-0; O'seas-0
North America:	7 States
Density:	2 in PA, 1 in MD, 1 in VA
Projected New Units (12 Months):	6
Qualifications:	5, 3, 3, 3, 5, 5
Registered: MD,NY	

FINANCIAL/TERMS:

Cash Investment:	$40-85K
Total Investment:	$50.4-105.5K
Minimum Net Worth:	$50.4K
Fees: Franchise -	$25-50K
Royalty - 0%;	Ad. - 0%
Earnings Claim Statement:	No
Term of Contract (Years):	10/10
Avg. # Of Employees:	2 FT
Passive Ownership:	Discouraged
Encourage Conversions:	Yes
Area Develop. Agreements:	No
Sub-Franchising Contracts:	No
Expand In Territory:	Yes
Space Needs: N/A SF; HB	

SUPPORT & TRAINING PROVIDED:

Financial Assistance Provided:	No
Site Selection Assistance:	Yes
Lease Negotiation Assistance:	No
Co-Operative Advertising:	No
Franchisee Assoc./Member:	No
Size Of Corporate Staff:	7
On-Going Support:	C,d,F,G,H
Training: 3 Days at Operating Unit.	

SPECIFIC EXPANSION PLANS:

US:	Eastern United States
Canada:	No
Overseas:	No

So Good To Come Home To.

M&M MEAT SHOPS
640 Trillium Dr., P.O. Box 2488
Kitchener, ON N2H 6M3 CANADA
Tel: (519) 895-1075
Fax: (519) 895-0762
E-Mail: johannaj@mmms.ca
Web Site: www.mmmeatshops.com
Ms. Johanna Jamnik, Executive Assistant

Canada's largest specialty frozen food chain, providing high-quality meats and specialty frozen food items to the public at reasonable prices. Recipient of 1992 and 1995 Canadian Franchise Association Award of Excellence, 1994 Hall of Fame Award and 1999 Corporate Citizenship Award. Our product caters to a variety of lifestyles - homemakers, seniors, professionals and trades people.

BACKGROUND: IFA MEMBER

Established: 1980;	1st Franchised: 1981
Franchised Units:	312
Company-Owned Units	3
Total Units:	315
Dist.:	US-0; CAN-315; O'seas-0
North America:	10 Provinces
Density: 175 in ON, 38 in PQ,33 in AB	
Projected New Units (12 Months):	34
Registered: AB	

FINANCIAL/TERMS:

Cash Investment:	$150K
Total Investment:	$300K
Minimum Net Worth:	$300K
Fees: Franchise -	$30K
Royalty - 3%;	Ad. - 1.5%
Earnings Claim Statement:	Yes
Term of Contract (Years):	10/10
Avg. # Of Employees:	2 FT, 1 PT
Passive Ownership:	Not Allowed
Encourage Conversions:	Yes
Area Develop. Agreements:	No
Sub-Franchising Contracts:	No
Expand In Territory:	Yes
Space Needs: 1,400 SF; SC	

SUPPORT & TRAINING PROVIDED:

Financial Assistance Provided:	Yes(I)
Site Selection Assistance:	Yes
Lease Negotiation Assistance:	Yes
Co-Operative Advertising:	Yes
Franchisee Assoc./Member:	Yes/Yes
Size Of Corporate Staff:	80
On-Going Support:	B,C,D,E,F,G,H,I
Training: 2 Weeks Kitchener, ON.	

SPECIFIC EXPANSION PLANS:

US:	No
Canada:	All Canada
Overseas:	No

MAUI WOWI SMOOTHIES
39 Viking Dr.
Englewood, CO 80110
Tel: (888) 862-8555 (303) 781-7800

Fax: (303) 781-2438
E-Mail: crm@concentric.net
Web Site: www.mauiwowi.com
Ms. Stacy Swift, President

MAIU WOWI is a home-based business using our unique kiosks and carts in mall and high traffic venues. Work when and where you would like using a system which has been proven for 18 years. Perfect for retirees, teachers and people who want to keep their current jobs to start. Healthy and high-end product for schools, events, malls, etc.

BACKGROUND: IFA MEMBER
Established: 1983;   1st Franchised: 1997
Franchised Units: 56
Company-Owned Units   2
Total Units: 58
Dist.:   US-56; CAN-0; O'seas-1
  North America: 14 States
  Density: 10 in CO, 6 in WA, 3 in UT
Projected New Units (12 Months):   30
Qualifications: 2, 2, 1, 1, 1, 5
Registered:
FINANCIAL/TERMS:
Cash Investment: $17-37K
Total Investment: $21-54K
Minimum Net Worth: $100K
Fees: Franchise - $20K
  Royalty - 0%;   Ad. - 5%
Earnings Claim Statement: No
Term of Contract (Years):   5/5
Avg. # Of Employees: 2 PT
Passive Ownership: Allowed
Encourage Conversions: Yes
Area Develop. Agreements: Yes/20
Sub-Franchising Contracts: Yes
Expand In Territory: Yes
Space Needs: 100 SF; HB
SUPPORT & TRAINING PROVIDED:
Financial Assistance Provided: Yes(I)
Site Selection Assistance: Yes
Lease Negotiation Assistance: Yes
Co-Operative Advertising: Yes
Franchisee Assoc./Member: No
Size Of Corporate Staff: 5
On-Going Support: B,C,D,E,F,G,H,I
Training: 1.5 Days at Your Location.
SPECIFIC EXPANSION PLANS:
US: All United States
Canada: All Canada
Overseas: Europe

≪ ≫

MCALISTER'S DELI
731 S. Pear Orchard Rd., # 51
Ridgeland, MS 39157

Tel: (888) 855-3354 (601) 952-1100
Fax: (601) 952-1138
E-Mail: pwalls@usa.net
Web Site: www.mcallistersdeli.com
Mr. Patrick K. Walls, Dir. of Franchising

Fast, casual restaurant, featuring a complete menu of gourmet deli foods, including hot and cold deli sandwiches, super-stuffed baked potatoes, salads, soups, desserts, iced tea and other food and beverage products.

BACKGROUND:
Established: 1989;   1st Franchised: 1994
Franchised Units: 55
Company-Owned Units   10
Total Units: 65
Dist.:   US-65; CAN-0; O'seas-0
  North America: 11 States
  Density: 19 in MS, 9 in TN, 8 in AL
Projected New Units (12 Months):   25
Qualifications: 5, 5, 4, 3, 1, 3
Registered: All States
FINANCIAL/TERMS:
Cash Investment: $80-250K
Total Investment: $147K-1.2MM
Minimum Net Worth: $500K
Fees: Franchise - $30K
  Royalty - 5%;   Ad. - 2%
Earnings Claim Statement: Yes
Term of Contract (Years):   10/5/5
Avg. # Of Employees: 5 FT, 35 PT
Passive Ownership: Allowed
Encourage Conversions: Yes
Area Develop. Agreements: Yes/Varies
Sub-Franchising Contracts: No
Expand In Territory: No
Space Needs: 3,600 SF; FS, SC
SUPPORT & TRAINING PROVIDED:
Financial Assistance Provided: Yes(I)
Site Selection Assistance: Yes
Lease Negotiation Assistance: Yes
Co-Operative Advertising: Yes
Franchisee Assoc./Member: No
Size Of Corporate Staff: 23
On-Going Support: a,B,C,D,E,F,G,H,I
Training: 10 Weeks Jackson, MS; 10 Days
  Franchisee Location.
SPECIFIC EXPANSION PLANS:
US: All United States
Canada: All Canada
Overseas: No

≪ ≫

MOM'S BAKE AT HOME PIZZA
4457 Main St.
Philadelphia, PA 19127
Tel: (800) 311-MOMS (215) 482-1044
Fax: (215) 482-0402

E-Mail: bakehome@aol.com
Mrs. Gwenn C. Bair, President

MOM'S PIZZA franchise 'Bake at Home' pizza stores. The franchisee purchases his or her supplies from the main office. The franchisee then retails a fresh, hand-made gourmet pizza, which is baked at the customer's convenience, in the convenience of his or her home.

BACKGROUND:
Established: 1961;   1st Franchised: 1981
Franchised Units: 17
Company-Owned Units   0
Total Units: 17
Dist.:   US-18; CAN-0; O'seas-0
  North America: 2 States
  Density: 12 in PA, 6 in NJ
Projected New Units (12 Months):   2
Registered: NR
FINANCIAL/TERMS:
Cash Investment: $50K
Total Investment: $50K
Minimum Net Worth: $NR
Fees: Franchise - $15K
  Royalty - 0%;   Ad. - 0%
Earnings Claim Statement: No
Term of Contract (Years):   On-going
Avg. # Of Employees: 1 FT, 2 PT
Passive Ownership: Not Allowed
Encourage Conversions: No
Area Develop. Agreements: No
Sub-Franchising Contracts: No
Expand In Territory: No
Space Needs: 800 SF; SC
SUPPORT & TRAINING PROVIDED:
Financial Assistance Provided: No
Site Selection Assistance: Yes
Lease Negotiation Assistance: Yes
Co-Operative Advertising: No
Franchisee Assoc./Member: No
Size Of Corporate Staff: 12
On-Going Support: B,C,D,E
Training: 7 Days Existing Franchise.
SPECIFIC EXPANSION PLANS:
US: PA,NJ
Canada: No
Overseas: No

≪ ≫

NEW YORK FRIES
1220 Yonge St., # 400
Toronto, ON M4T 1W1 CANADA
Tel: (416) 963-5005
Fax: (416) 963-4920
E-Mail: mail@newyorkfries.com
Web Site: www.newyorkfries.com
Mr. Warren Price, Executive VP

Exceptional product and simplicity of operations make NEW YORK FRIES an outstanding opportunity. Our concept is simple - our standards are high. We start with fresh potatoes, hand-cut, on-site everyday. We cook them in 100% vegetable oil, using our own special process. Runner-up for 1994 Franchise of the Year award by CFA and winner of many marketing awards. It's an excellent opportunity for a multi-unit operator with a respected system.

BACKGROUND:

Established: 1984;   1st Franchised: 1984
Franchised Units: 145
Company-Owned Units   10
Total Units: 155
Dist.:   US-0; CAN-153; O'seas-2
  North America: 9 Provinces
  Density: 78 in ON, 25 in BC, 22 in AB
Projected New Units (12 Months):   12
Qualifications: 4, 4, 4, 3, 1, 5
Registered: AB
FINANCIAL/TERMS:
Cash Investment: $40-65K
Total Investment: $125-175K
Minimum Net Worth: $NR
Fees: Franchise - $30K
  Royalty - 6%;   Ad. - 1.5%
Earnings Claim Statement: No
Term of Contract (Years):   10/5/5
Avg. # Of Employees: 2 FT, 6 PT
Passive Ownership: Allowed
Encourage Conversions: N/A
Area Develop. Agreements: No
Sub-Franchising Contracts: No
Expand In Territory: Yes
Space Needs: 200-300 SF; RM
SUPPORT & TRAINING PROVIDED:
Financial Assistance Provided: No
Site Selection Assistance: Yes
Lease Negotiation Assistance: Yes
Co-Operative Advertising: Yes
Franchisee Assoc./Member: No
Size Of Corporate Staff: 15
On-Going Support: B,C,d,E,G,h
Training: 1 Week Toronto, ON; 1 Week
  On-Site.
SPECIFIC EXPANSION PLANS:
US: All United States
Canada: All Canada
Overseas: Pacific Rim

◁◁ ▷▷

PAPA MURPHY'S
8000 NE Parkway Dr., # 350
Vancouver, WA 98662
Tel: (800) 257-7272 (360) 260-7272

Fax: (360) 260-0050
E-Mail: franchise@papamurphys.com
Web Site: www.papamurphys.com
Mr. Jerry Kenney, Senior VP of Development

PAPA MURPHY'S produces a great pizza made from top-quality ingredients. Letting customers bake it themselves is smart business. Put the 2 together and you get the largest, fastest-growing Take 'N' Bake franchise in the world. PAPA MURPHY'S now has 565 stores with another 175 stores expected to open in 2000.

BACKGROUND: IFA MEMBER
Established: 1981;   1st Franchised: 1982
Franchised Units: 540
Company-Owned Units   12
Total Units: 552
Dist.:   US-552; CAN-0; O'seas-0
  North America: 19 States
  Density: 150 in CA,114 in WA,84 in OR
Projected New Units (12 Months):   175
Qualifications: 4, 3, 2, 3, 3, 5
Registered: CA,IL,IN,MI,MN,ND,
  OR,SD,WA,WI
FINANCIAL/TERMS:
Cash Investment: $80K
Total Investment: $148.8-199.5K
Minimum Net Worth: $250K
Fees: Franchise - $25K
  Royalty - 5%;   Ad. - 1%
Earnings Claim Statement: No
Term of Contract (Years):   10/5
Avg. # Of Employees: 2 FT, 8-10 PT
Passive Ownership: Not Allowed
Encourage Conversions: Yes
Area Develop. Agreements: No
Sub-Franchising Contracts: No
Expand In Territory: Yes
Space Needs: 1,200-1,400 SF; FS, SF, SC
SUPPORT & TRAINING PROVIDED:
Financial Assistance Provided: Yes(I)
Site Selection Assistance: Yes
Lease Negotiation Assistance: Yes
Co-Operative Advertising: Yes
Franchisee Assoc./Member: Yes/No
Size Of Corporate Staff: 106
On-Going Support: B,C,D,E,G,H,I
Training: 3 Days/30 Hours in the Closest
  Training Store; 6 Weeks in Store; 6 Days
  Corporate Office.
SPECIFIC EXPANSION PLANS:
US: Midwest
Canada: No
Overseas: No

◁◁ ▷▷

PIZZA NOVA
2247 Midland Ave.
Scarborough, ON M1P 4R1 CANADA
Tel: (416) 439-0051
Fax: (416) 299-3558
Mr. Frank Macri, Franchise Director

PIZZA NOVA specializes in traditional Italian pizza, pastas and chicken wings. All menu items are prepared fresh daily and are available for take-out or delivery. We pride ourselves on quality and service.

BACKGROUND:
Established: 1963;   1st Franchised: 1969
Franchised Units: 85
Company-Owned Units   2
Total Units: 87
Dist.:   US-1; CAN-80; O'seas-6
  North America: 1 State, 1 Province
  Density: 80 in ON
Projected New Units (12 Months):   10
Qualifications: 4, 4, 4, 2, 4, 5
Registered: NR
FINANCIAL/TERMS:
Cash Investment: $40K
Total Investment: $125-135K
Minimum Net Worth: $NR
Fees: Franchise - $N/A
  Royalty - 6%;   Ad. - 4%
Earnings Claim Statement: Yes
Term of Contract (Years):   5/5
Avg. # Of Employees: 4 FT, 6 PT
Passive Ownership: Not Allowed
Encourage Conversions: Yes
Area Develop. Agreements: No
Sub-Franchising Contracts: No
Expand In Territory: Yes
Space Needs: 800-1,100 SF; SF, SC, RM
SUPPORT & TRAINING PROVIDED:
Financial Assistance Provided: No
Site Selection Assistance: Yes
Lease Negotiation Assistance: Yes
Co-Operative Advertising: Yes
Franchisee Assoc./Member: Yes
Size Of Corporate Staff: 18
On-Going Support: A,B,C,D,E,F,G,H
Training: 3 Weeks.
SPECIFIC EXPANSION PLANS:
US: NR
Canada: ON
Overseas: All Countries

◁◁ ▷▷

POTATO SACK, THE
201 Monroeville Mall
Monroeville, PA 15146
Tel: (800) 828-3770 (412) 373-0850
Fax: (412) 373-4497

Mr. Buzz Pasquini, Owner

THE POTATO SACK has gourmet-topped baked potatoes, fresh-cut french fries and potato skins. Mall food courts are where our operation thrives. Our food is healthy, nutritious and what the customer of the 90's is looking for. Aggressive, customer service-oriented team players, who can follow a proven success formula, are our target franchisees.

BACKGROUND:
Established: 1980; 1st Franchised: 1992
Franchised Units: 4
Company-Owned Units   2
Total Units: 6
Dist.:   US-6; CAN-0; O'seas-0
  North America: 2 States
  Density: 4 in PA, 2 in FL
Projected New Units (12 Months):   0
Qualifications: 4, 4, 4, 3, 3, 4
Registered: FL,NY,VA
FINANCIAL/TERMS:
Cash Investment: $50-75K
Total Investment: $200-275K
Minimum Net Worth: $250K
Fees: Franchise - $20K
  Royalty - 5%;   Ad. - 1%
Earnings Claim Statement: No
Term of Contract (Years):   10/5
Avg. # Of Employees: 3 FT, 10 PT
Passive Ownership: Not Allowed
Encourage Conversions: Yes
Area Develop. Agreements: No
Sub-Franchising Contracts: No
Expand In Territory: No
Space Needs: NR SF; RM
SUPPORT & TRAINING PROVIDED:
Financial Assistance Provided: No
Site Selection Assistance: Yes
Lease Negotiation Assistance: Yes
Co-Operative Advertising: Yes
Franchisee Assoc./Member: No
Size Of Corporate Staff: 3
On-Going Support: C,D,E,F,G,h,I
Training: 5-10 Days Corporate Store in PA
  or FL.
SPECIFIC EXPANSION PLANS:
US: PA, FL
Canada: No
Overseas: No

⊰⊰ ⊱⊱

POWER SMOOTHIE
160 S. University Dr., # B
Plantation, FL 33324
Tel: (888) 818-POWER (954) 370-3913
Fax: (954) 370-3902

Mr. Michael Genovese, President

POWER SMOOTHIE offers 'delicious nutrition' with a fast, up-beat atmosphere. We serve healthy smoothies, juices, sandwiches, nutritional supplements and low-fat snacks in a clean, non-cooking environment.

BACKGROUND:
Established: 1991; 1st Franchised: 1994
Franchised Units: 14
Company-Owned Units   0
Total Units: 14
Dist.:   US-14; CAN-0; O'seas-0
  North America: 3 States
  Density: 11 in FL, 2 in NV, 1 in TX
Projected New Units (12 Months): 20
Qualifications: 2, 2, 2, 2, 2, 5
Registered: FL
FINANCIAL/TERMS:
Cash Investment: $80-120K
Total Investment: $80-120K
Minimum Net Worth: $50K
Fees: Franchise - $20K
  Royalty - 5%;   Ad. - 1.5-3%
Earnings Claim Statement: No
Term of Contract (Years):   10/10
Avg. # Of Employees: 2 FT, 5 PT
Passive Ownership: Allowed
Encourage Conversions: Yes
Area Develop. Agreements: Yes/Negot.
Sub-Franchising Contracts: No
Expand In Territory: Yes
Space Needs: 800-1,500 SF; SC, RM
SUPPORT & TRAINING PROVIDED:
Financial Assistance Provided: Yes(I)
Site Selection Assistance: Yes
Lease Negotiation Assistance: Yes
Co-Operative Advertising: Yes
Franchisee Assoc./Member: No
Size Of Corporate Staff: 5
On-Going Support: C,D,E,F,I
Training: 2 Weeks Plantation, FL.
SPECIFIC EXPANSION PLANS:
US: All United States
Canada: No
Overseas: All Countries

⊰⊰ ⊱⊱

PRETZEL MAKER
2855 E. Cottonwood Pkwy., # 400
Salt Lake City, UT 84121-7050
Tel: (800) 348-6311 (801) 736-5600
Fax: (888) 867-7343
Web Site: www.mrsfields.com
Franchise   Development,   Franchise
  Development Manager

The 'World's Best Soft Pretzels,' hand-rolled and served hot with high consumer acceptance, precision portion control and available in combination store configurations. May be operated in both traditional and non-traditional venues.

BACKGROUND: IFA MEMBER
Established: 1991; 1st Franchised: 1992
Franchised Units: 154
Company-Owned Units   4
Total Units: 158
Dist.:   US-209; CAN-14; O'seas-1
  North America: 39 States, 9 Provinces
  Density: 21 in CA, 13 in UT, 11 in CO
Projected New Units (12 Months): 80
Qualifications: 4, 4, 3, 2, 2, 5
Registered: All States
FINANCIAL/TERMS:
Cash Investment: $10-30K
Total Investment: $90-160K
Minimum Net Worth: $150K
Fees: Franchise - $20K
  Royalty - 5%;   Ad. - 1.5%
Earnings Claim Statement: No
Term of Contract (Years):   10/10
Avg. # Of Employees: 5 FT, 7 PT
Passive Ownership: Discouraged
Encourage Conversions: Yes
Area Develop. Agreements: Yes/3
Sub-Franchising Contracts: No
Expand In Territory: Yes
Space Needs: 500-700 SF; FS, SC, RM
SUPPORT & TRAINING PROVIDED:
Financial Assistance Provided: Yes(I)
Site Selection Assistance: Yes
Lease Negotiation Assistance: Yes
Co-Operative Advertising: Yes
Franchisee Assoc./Member: No
Size Of Corporate Staff: 37
On-Going Support: B,C,D,E,F,G,H
Training: 5 Days Denver, CO.
SPECIFIC EXPANSION PLANS:
US: All United States
Canada: All Canada
Overseas: Asia, Australia

⊰⊰ ⊱⊱

PRETZEL TIME
2855 E. Cottonwood Pkwy., # 400
Salt Lake City, UT 84121
Tel: (800) 348-6311 (801) 736-5600
Fax: (888) 867-7343
Web Site: www.pretzeltime.com
Franchise   Development,   Franchise
  Development Manager

'Freshness With A Twist.' Retail pretzel stores, offering a healthy snack alternative that is freshly mixed, rolled and baked. Unique combination store options are available for traditional and non-traditional venues.

BACKGROUND: IFA MEMBER
Established: 1991;   1st Franchised: 1992
Franchised Units: 143
Company-Owned Units   86
Total Units: 229
Dist.:   US-218; CAN-2; O'seas-0
 North America: 41 States, 2 Provinces
 Density: 29 in CA, 20 in NY, 19 in TX
Projected New Units (12 Months):   100
Registered: All States
FINANCIAL/TERMS:
Cash Investment: $175-250K
Total Investment: $175-250K
Minimum Net Worth: $250K
Fees: Franchise - $25K
 Royalty - 9%;   Ad. - 1%
Earnings Claim Statement: No
Term of Contract (Years):   20/5
Avg. # Of Employees: 3 FT, 9 PT
Passive Ownership: Allowed
Encourage Conversions: Yes
Area Develop. Agreements: Yes
Sub-Franchising Contracts: No
Expand In Territory: Yes
Space Needs: 400-1,000 SF; RM
SUPPORT & TRAINING PROVIDED:
Financial Assistance Provided: No
Site Selection Assistance: Yes
Lease Negotiation Assistance: Yes
Co-Operative Advertising: No
Franchisee Assoc./Member: No
Size Of Corporate Staff: 26
On-Going Support: B,C,D,E,F,G,H,I
Training: 5 Days Corporate Training Center; 5 Days On-Site.
SPECIFIC EXPANSION PLANS:
US: All United States
Canada: All Canada
Overseas: Europe, Japan, Mexico, Australia, Israel

PRETZEL TWISTER, THE
2706 S. Horseshoe Dr., # 112
Naples, FL 34102
Tel: (888) 638-8806 (941) 643-2075
Fax: (941) 353-6479
E-Mail: keith@pretzeltwister.com
Web Site: www.pretzeltwister.com
Mr. Keith Johnson, President

THE PRETZEL TWISTER is a gourmet, hand-rolled soft pretzel franchise. Other products sold are fresh, hand squeezed lemonade, frozen fruit smoothies and soft drinks. The pretzels are served fresh and hot and are available in a wide variety of flavors.

BACKGROUND:
Established: 1992;   1st Franchised: 1993
Franchised Units: 30
Company-Owned Units   0
Total Units: 30
Dist.:   US-25; CAN-5; O'seas-0
 North America: 11 States, 4 Provinces
 Density: 9 in FL, 7 in NC, 3 in SC
Projected New Units (12 Months):   NR
Registered:
FINANCIAL/TERMS:
Cash Investment: $NR
Total Investment: $82.7-140.2K
Minimum Net Worth: $NR
Fees: Franchise - $17.5K
 Royalty - 5%;   Ad. - 0.25-1%
Earnings Claim Statement: No
Term of Contract (Years):   NR
Avg. # Of Employees: NR
Passive Ownership: Allowed
Encourage Conversions: NR
Area Develop. Agreements: No
Sub-Franchising Contracts: No
Expand In Territory: Yes
Space Needs: 300-900 SF; RN, Kiosk or In-Line
SUPPORT & TRAINING PROVIDED:
Financial Assistance Provided: NR
Site Selection Assistance: No
Lease Negotiation Assistance: Yes
Co-Operative Advertising: No
Franchisee Assoc./Member: NR
Size Of Corporate Staff: NR
On-Going Support: C,D,E,G,h,I
Training: NR
SPECIFIC EXPANSION PLANS:
US: All United States
Canada: NR
Overseas: NR

"HOME OF THE BUTTER DIPPED SOFT PRETZEL"
PRETZELS PLUS
639 Frederick St.
Hanover, PA 17331
Tel: (800) 559-7927 (717) 633-7927

Fax: (717) 633-5078
E-Mail: pretzelsplus@pretzelsplus.com
Web Site: www.pretzelsplus.com
Mr. Alan Harbaugh, Dir. of Franchising

PRETZELS PLUS stores sell soft, hand-rolled pretzels, soups and hearty sandwiches made on our famous pretzel dough rolls. Our mall-based stores provide ample seating for about twenty people in the cafe-styled environment. With our sandwich menu along with our pretzels, we're definitely a twist above the competition.

BACKGROUND:
Established: 1990;   1st Franchised: 1991
Franchised Units: 30
Company-Owned Units   0
Total Units: 30
Dist.:   US-30; CAN-0; O'seas-0
 North America: 9 States
 Density: 13 in PA, 5 in VA, 3 in NC
Projected New Units (12 Months):   24
Qualifications: 5, 2, 1, 1, 2, 2
Registered: MD,VA
FINANCIAL/TERMS:
Cash Investment: $70-90K
Total Investment: $70-90K
Minimum Net Worth: $N/A
Fees: Franchise - $12K
 Royalty - 4%;   Ad. - 0%
Earnings Claim Statement: No
Term of Contract (Years):   10/10
Avg. # Of Employees: 5 FT, 4 PT
Passive Ownership: Allowed
Encourage Conversions: Yes
Area Develop. Agreements: No
Sub-Franchising Contracts: No
Expand In Territory: Yes
Space Needs: 1,000 SF; RM
SUPPORT & TRAINING PROVIDED:
Financial Assistance Provided: No
Site Selection Assistance: Yes
Lease Negotiation Assistance: No
Co-Operative Advertising: No
Franchisee Assoc./Member: No
Size Of Corporate Staff: 3
On-Going Support: B,D,E,I
Training: 3 Days before Opening.
SPECIFIC EXPANSION PLANS:
US: Eastern United States
Canada: All Canada
Overseas: No

QUIZNO'S CLASSIC SUBS
1415 Larimer St.
Denver, CO 80202

Tel: (800) 335-4782 (303) 291-0999
Fax: (720) 359-3393
Web Site: www.quiznos.com
Ms. Patricia Meyer, Dir. Franchise Sales

Quizno's 🍞 SUBS

QUIZNO'S CLASSIC SUBS is an up-scale, Italian-theme sub sandwich restaurant that features 'the best sandwich you will ever eat.' QUIZNO'S subs are oven-baked and made with our special recipe bread, QUIZNO'S special dressing and the highest-quality meats and cheeses. With over 900 units open across the U. S., Canada and Puerto Rico, our success will continue as we double the number of units open in the coming year. Franchisees are supported at both the corporate level and by one of our 80 area owners.

BACKGROUND: IFA MEMBER
Established: 1981;   1st Franchised: 1984
Franchised Units: 944
Company-Owned Units   28
Total Units: 972
Dist.:   US-860; CAN-106; O'seas-6
 North America: NR
 Density: CO, IL, TX
Projected New Units (12 Months):   400
Qualifications: 5, 4, 2, 2, 2, 5
Registered: All States
FINANCIAL/TERMS:
Cash Investment: $60K
Total Investment: $170-225K
Minimum Net Worth: $125K
Fees: Franchise - $20K
 Royalty - 7%;   Ad. - 1-3%
Earnings Claim Statement: No
Term of Contract (Years):   15
Avg. # Of Employees: 2 FT, 6 PT
Passive Ownership: Discouraged
Encourage Conversions: Yes
Area Develop. Agreements: Yes/10
Sub-Franchising Contracts: No
Expand In Territory: Yes
Space Needs: 1,400 SF; SC, RM
SUPPORT & TRAINING PROVIDED:
Financial Assistance Provided: Yes(I)
Site Selection Assistance: Yes
Lease Negotiation Assistance: Yes
Co-Operative Advertising: Yes
Franchisee Assoc./Member: No
Size Of Corporate Staff: 103
On-Going Support: C,D,E,F,G,H,I
Training: 11 Days Regional Market; 11
 Days Corporate Office Denver, CO.
SPECIFIC EXPANSION PLANS:
US: All United States

Canada: All Canada
Overseas: All Countries

<< >>

ROCKY MOUNTAIN CHOCOLATE FACTORY

265 Turner Dr.
Durango, CO 81303
Tel: (800) 438-7623 (970) 259-0554
Fax: (970) 259-5895
Web Site: www.rmcf.com
Mr. Greg L. Pope, VP Franchise Dev.

Retail sale of packaged and bulk chocolates, brittles, truffles, sauces, cocoas, coffees, assorted hard candies and related chocolate and non-chocolate items. In-store preparation of fudges, caramel apples and dipped fruits via interactive cooking demonstrations. Complete line of gift and holiday items. Supplemental retail sale of soft drinks, ice cream, cookies and brewed coffee.

BACKGROUND:
Established: 1981;   1st Franchised: 1982
Franchised Units: 183
Company-Owned Units   38
Total Units: 221
Dist.:   US-202; CAN-17; O'seas-1
 North America: 41 States, 3 Provinces
 Density: 36 in CA, 22 in CO, 12 BC
Projected New Units (12 Months): 12-15
Registered: CA,FL,HI,IL,IN,MD,MI,MN,
 NY,OR,SD,VA,WA,WI
FINANCIAL/TERMS:
Cash Investment: $50K
Total Investment: $113-213K
Minimum Net Worth: $250K
Fees: Franchise - $19.5K
 Royalty - 5%;   Ad. - 1%
Earnings Claim Statement: No
Term of Contract (Years):   5/5
Avg. # Of Employees: 2 FT, 4 PT
Passive Ownership: Discouraged
Encourage Conversions: N/A
Area Develop. Agreements: No
Sub-Franchising Contracts: No
Expand In Territory: Yes
Space Needs: 800-1,200 SF; Factory
 Outlet
SUPPORT & TRAINING PROVIDED:
Financial Assistance Provided: Yes(I)
Site Selection Assistance: Yes

Lease Negotiation Assistance: Yes
Co-Operative Advertising: No
Franchisee Assoc./Member: Yes
Size Of Corporate Staff: 12
On-Going Support: B,C,D,E,F,G,H,I
Training: 7 Days Durango, CO; 5 Days
 Store Site.
SPECIFIC EXPANSION PLANS:
US: All United States
Canada: No
Overseas: All Countries

<< >>

SCHLOTZSKY'S DELI

203 Colorado St.
Austin, TX 78701
Tel: (800) 846-2867 (512) 236-3600
Fax: (512) 236-3650
Web Site: www.schlotzskys.com
Ms. Laura Bernstein, Public Relations

SCHLOTZSKY'S DELI is a franchised restaurant, serving a menu of sandwiches, pizza and salads on SCHLOTZSKY'S baked-fresh-daily sourdough bread. Restaurants are designed to provide fresh, clean environments with an in-store bakery.

BACKGROUND:
Established: 1971;   1st Franchised: 1977
Franchised Units: 760
Company-Owned Units   23
Total Units: 783
Dist.:   US-764; CAN-0; O'seas-19
 North America: 37 States
 Density: 224 in TX, 38 in TN, 27 AZ
Projected New Units (12 Months):   40
Qualifications: 5, 5, 3, 3, 4, 5
Registered: All States
FINANCIAL/TERMS:
Cash Investment: $173-754K
Total Investment: $1.3-2.3MM
Minimum Net Worth: $250K
Fees: Franchise - $30K
 Royalty - 6%;   Ad. - 1%
Earnings Claim Statement: Yes
Term of Contract (Years):   20/10
Avg. # Of Employees: 5 FT, 20 PT
Passive Ownership: Not Allowed
Encourage Conversions: No
Area Develop. Agreements: Yes/50
Sub-Franchising Contracts: Yes
Expand In Territory: Yes
Space Needs: 3,200 SF; FS
SUPPORT & TRAINING PROVIDED:
Financial Assistance Provided: Yes
Site Selection Assistance: Yes
Lease Negotiation Assistance: Yes

Co-Operative Advertising: Yes
Franchisee Assoc./Member: Yes/No
Size Of Corporate Staff: 243
On-Going Support: B,C,D,E,F,G,H,I
Training: 3 Weeks in Austin, TX.
SPECIFIC EXPANSION PLANS:
US: All United States
Canada: All Canada
Overseas: Europe, Latin America, Pacific Rim

<< >>

SEATTLE SUTTON'S HEALTHY EATING

1500 Boyce Memorial Dr.
Ottawa, IL 61350
Tel: (888) 442-3438 (815) 433-4444
Fax: (815) 795-3493
E-Mail: info@sshe.com
Web Site: www.sshe.com
Mr. Seattle Sutton, President

We do healthy, freshly-prepared meals (21 per week). SEATTLE SUTTON'S meal plan is low fat, low cholesterol and sodium-restricted. The meals are for anyone interested in eating freshly-prepared, healthy meals without shopping, planning, cooking or cleaning up.

BACKGROUND:
Established: 1991; 1st Franchised: 1997
Franchised Units: 0
Company-Owned Units: 1
Total Units: 1
Dist.: US-1; CAN-0; O'seas-0
North America: 1 State
Density: 1 in IL
Projected New Units (12 Months): 1-2
Qualifications: 5, 4, 3, 2, 2, 5
Registered:
FINANCIAL/TERMS:
Cash Investment: $400-800K
Total Investment: $400-800K
Minimum Net Worth: $400-800K
Fees: Franchise - $35K
Royalty - 5%; Ad. - 0%
Earnings Claim Statement: Yes
Term of Contract (Years): 10/10
Avg. # Of Employees: 20 FT, 15 PT
Passive Ownership: Not Allowed
Encourage Conversions: N/A

Area Develop. Agreements: No
Sub-Franchising Contracts: No
Expand In Territory: Yes
Space Needs: 10,000 SF; FS
SUPPORT & TRAINING PROVIDED:
Financial Assistance Provided: No
Site Selection Assistance: No
Lease Negotiation Assistance: No
Co-Operative Advertising: No
Franchisee Assoc./Member: No
Size Of Corporate Staff: 4
On-Going Support:
Training: 5 Weeks in Ottawa, IL.
SPECIFIC EXPANSION PLANS:
US: All United States
Canada: No
Overseas: No

<< >>

STEAK-OUT CHAR-BROILED DELIVERY

6801 Governors Lake Pkwy., #100
Norcross, GA 30071
Tel: (678) 533-6000
Fax: (678) 291-0222
E-Mail: jmccord@steakout.com
Web Site: www.steakout.com
Mr. Joseph M. McCord, Vice President

STEAK-OUT franchising specializes in home and office deliveries of charbroiled steaks, chicken and burgers - other menu items include salads and desserts. The only full meal delivery service expanding nationwide. Customers absolutely love our combination of quality food and delivery service. America's finest delivery.

BACKGROUND: IFA MEMBER
Established: 1986; 1st Franchised: 1987
Franchised Units: 91
Company-Owned Units: 2
Total Units: 93
Dist.: US-93; CAN-0; O'seas-0
North America: 17 States
Density: 18 in AL, 12 in TN, 8 in GA
Projected New Units (12 Months): 12
Qualifications: 4, 5, 3, 3, 3, 5
Registered: CA,FL,IL,IN,MD,MI,MN, NY,OR,SD,VA,WI
FINANCIAL/TERMS:
Cash Investment: $50-75K
Total Investment: $232.3-330.2K
Minimum Net Worth: $300K

Fees: Franchise - $24.5K
Royalty - 5%; Ad. - 2%
Earnings Claim Statement: Yes
Term of Contract (Years): 10/10
Avg. # Of Employees: 2 FT, 25-30 PT
Passive Ownership: Discouraged
Encourage Conversions: Yes
Area Develop. Agreements: Yes/Varies
Sub-Franchising Contracts: No
Expand In Territory: Yes
Space Needs: 1,600 SF; FS, SF, SC
SUPPORT & TRAINING PROVIDED:
Financial Assistance Provided: Yes(I)
Site Selection Assistance: Yes
Lease Negotiation Assistance: Yes
Co-Operative Advertising: N/A
Franchisee Assoc./Member: No
Size Of Corporate Staff: 25
On-Going Support: B,C,D,E,G,H,I
Training: 4-5 Weeks Training Center at Atlanta, GA.
SPECIFIC EXPANSION PLANS:
US: SE,MW,NE
Canada: No
Overseas: No

<< >>

STUCKEY'S EXPRESS

4601 Willard Ave.
Chevy Chase, MD 20815
Tel: (800) 423-6171 (301) 913-9800
Fax: (301) 913-5424
Mr. Mike Bolin, Dir. of Business Dev.

An innovative way to add the STUCKEY'S name and product line to an existing or new location with minimal investment and no build-ons necessary!!

BACKGROUND:
Established: 1930; 1st Franchised: 1960
Franchised Units: 155
Company-Owned Units: 2
Total Units: 157
Dist.: US-132; CAN-0; O'seas-0
North America: 21 States
Density: 10 in MS, 8 in SC, 6 in TN
Projected New Units (12 Months): 12
Qualifications: 5, 4, 4, 2, 1, 4
Registered: CA,IL,IN,MD,MI,VA,DC
FINANCIAL/TERMS:
Cash Investment: $10-25K
Total Investment: $28-135K
Minimum Net Worth: $NR
Fees: Franchise - $2.5K
Royalty - $250/Mo.; Ad. - 0.5%
Earnings Claim Statement: No
Term of Contract (Years): 20/10
Avg. # Of Employees: Varies

Passive Ownership:	Allowed
Encourage Conversions:	Yes
Area Develop. Agreements:	No
Sub-Franchising Contracts:	No
Expand In Territory:	Yes
Space Needs: Varies SF; Fuel Center	

SUPPORT & TRAINING PROVIDED:

Financial Assistance Provided:	No
Site Selection Assistance:	Yes
Lease Negotiation Assistance:	Yes
Co-Operative Advertising:	No
Franchisee Assoc./Member:	Yes/Yes
Size Of Corporate Staff:	12
On-Going Support:	B,C,D,E,G,H,I
Training: 1 Week in Store.	

SPECIFIC EXPANSION PLANS:

US:	All United States
Canada:	No
Overseas:	No

◁◁ ▷▷

SUCKERS CANDY CO.
1111 Flint Rd., #36
Downsview, ON M3J 3C7 CANADA
Tel: (416) 226-3437
Fax: (416) 665-8839
E-Mail: suckers@interlog.com
Mr. Jack Green, President

Candies, toys. Nostalgic. Appealing to the child in all of us.

BACKGROUND:

Established: 1998; 1st Franchised: 1998	
Franchised Units:	1
Company-Owned Units	2
Total Units:	3
Dist.:	US-0; CAN-3; O'seas-0
North America:	1 Province
Density:	3 in ON
Projected New Units (12 Months):	30
Qualifications:	4, 3, 2, 2, 3, 4
Registered: NR	

FINANCIAL/TERMS:

Cash Investment:	$75K
Total Investment:	$150-250K
Minimum Net Worth:	$60-75K
Fees: Franchise -	$25K
Royalty - 6%;	Ad. - 2%
Earnings Claim Statement:	No
Term of Contract (Years):	5/5
Avg. # Of Employees:	1 FT, 6 PT
Passive Ownership:	Discouraged
Encourage Conversions:	No

Area Develop. Agreements:	No
Sub-Franchising Contracts:	No
Expand In Territory:	Yes
Space Needs: 1,000 SF; FS, SF, RM	

SUPPORT & TRAINING PROVIDED:

Financial Assistance Provided:	Yes(I)
Site Selection Assistance:	Yes
Lease Negotiation Assistance:	Yes
Co-Operative Advertising:	Yes
Franchisee Assoc./Member:	No
Size Of Corporate Staff:	15
On-Going Support:	B,C,D,E,F,G,H
Training: 2 Weeks in Toronto, ON.	

SPECIFIC EXPANSION PLANS:

US:	All United States
Canada:	All Canada
Overseas:	All Countries

◁◁ ▷▷

SWEETS FROM HEAVEN
1830 Forbes Ave.
Pittsburgh, PA 15219-5836
Tel: (412) 434-6711
Fax: (412) 434-6718
E-Mail: sfheaven@aol.com
Web Site: www.sweetsfromheaven.com
Mr. Mark R. Lando, President

Self-serve candy stores with unique selection of international candies. Part of an international chain of over 300 stores.

BACKGROUND: IFA MEMBER

Established: 1992; 1st Franchised: 1993	
Franchised Units:	287
Company-Owned Units	16
Total Units:	303
Dist.:	US-59; CAN-0; O'seas-124
North America:	16 States
Density:	6 in TX, 5 in FL, 6 in PA
Projected New Units (12 Months):	24
Qualifications:	5, 3, 1, 3, 3, 4
Registered: CA,IL,NY,VA	

FINANCIAL/TERMS:

Cash Investment:	$50K
Total Investment:	$125-232K
Minimum Net Worth:	$125K
Fees: Franchise -	$30K
Royalty - 6%;	Ad. - 0%
Earnings Claim Statement:	No
Term of Contract (Years):	10/5
Avg. # Of Employees:	4 FT, 3 PT
Passive Ownership:	Allowed
Encourage Conversions:	Yes
Area Develop. Agreements:	Yes/10
Sub-Franchising Contracts:	Yes
Expand In Territory:	Yes
Space Needs: 800-1,000 SF; SF, RM, Tourist Areas	

SUPPORT & TRAINING PROVIDED:

Financial Assistance Provided:	No
Site Selection Assistance:	Yes
Lease Negotiation Assistance:	Yes
Co-Operative Advertising:	No
Franchisee Assoc./Member:	No
Size Of Corporate Staff:	13
On-Going Support:	B,C,D,E,F,G
Training: 1 Week Corporate Office; 1 Week Company Store; 1 Week Franchisee's Store.	

SPECIFIC EXPANSION PLANS:

US:	All United States
Canada:	All Canada
Overseas:	All Countries

◁◁ ▷▷

TROPICAL SMOOTHIE
51 3rd St., # 5
Shalimar, FL 32579-1700
Tel: (888) 292-2522 (850) 609-6022
Fax: (850) 609-6023
E-Mail: tsi@tropicalsmoothie.com
Web Site: www.tropicalsmoothie.com
Mr. Eric Jenrich, President

TROPICAL SMOOTHIE has created a high energy, low-fat, natural sweetener based beverage which is made from real fruits. Our smoothies are customized with nutritional supplements upon request. We also offer fresh juice as well as supplements for resale. TROPICAL SMOOTHIE Café offers a variety of sandwiches, wraps and specialty coffee.

BACKGROUND:

Established: 1997; 1st Franchised: 1997	
Franchised Units:	43
Company-Owned Units	3
Total Units:	46
Dist.:	US-46; CAN-0; O'seas-0
North America:	5 States
Density:	24 in FL, 16 in AL, 3 in GA
Projected New Units (12 Months):	30
Qualifications:	4, 3, 3, 3, 4, 5
Registered: FL,VA,DC	

FINANCIAL/TERMS:

Cash Investment:	$20-50K
Total Investment:	$60-120K
Minimum Net Worth:	$50K
Fees: Franchise -	$10K
Royalty - 6%;	Ad. - 3%
Earnings Claim Statement:	No
Term of Contract (Years):	20/20
Avg. # Of Employees:	2 FT, 6 PT
Passive Ownership:	Discouraged
Encourage Conversions:	Yes
Area Develop. Agreements:	Yes/50

Sub-Franchising Contracts: Yes
Expand In Territory: Yes
Space Needs: 1,000 SF; SC
SUPPORT & TRAINING PROVIDED:
Financial Assistance Provided: Yes(I)
Site Selection Assistance: Yes
Lease Negotiation Assistance: Yes
Co-Operative Advertising: Yes
Franchisee Assoc./Member: No
Size Of Corporate Staff: 3
On-Going Support: A,B,C,D,E,F,G,H,I
Training: 1 Week On-Site; At Local Stores
    until franchisee shows ability to work.
SPECIFIC EXPANSION PLANS:
US: All United States
Canada: All Canada
Overseas: All Countries

≺≺ ≻≻

WINE NOT INTERNATIONAL
15 Heritage Rd., Unit 1
Markham, ON M5N 1G5 CANADA
Tel: (888) 946-3668 (905) 294-6121
Fax: (905) 294-7772
E-Mail: winenot@global.com
Web Site: www.winenot.com
Mr. Kerry Baskey, VP Sales & Marketing

Turn-key commercial custom wineries, wine pubs and u-vint operations in which we provide equipment and supplies for the on-premises winemaker and provide wine pub services and equipment for restaurants and hotels.

BACKGROUND:
Established: 1993; 1st Franchised: 1993
Franchised Units: 38
Company-Owned Units: 0
Total Units: 38
Dist.: US-0; CAN-38; O'seas-0
  North America: 1 Province
  Density: 38 in ON
Projected New Units (12 Months): 16
Qualifications: 4, 3, 2, 2, 3, 5
Registered: CA,FL,HI,IL,IN,MD,MI,MN,
  ND,OR,RI,SD,WA,WI
FINANCIAL/TERMS:
Cash Investment: $40-150K
Total Investment: $110-375K
Minimum Net Worth: $100-500K
Fees: Franchise - $25-35K
  Royalty - 5%; Ad. - 2%

Earnings Claim Statement: Yes
Term of Contract (Years): 5/5/5
Avg. # Of Employees: 2 FT, 2 PT
Passive Ownership: Discouraged
Encourage Conversions: Yes
Area Develop. Agreements: Yes
Sub-Franchising Contracts: Yes
Expand In Territory: Yes
Space Needs: 1,200-3,000 SF; FS, SC
SUPPORT & TRAINING PROVIDED:
Financial Assistance Provided: Yes(I)
Site Selection Assistance: Yes
Lease Negotiation Assistance: Yes
Co-Operative Advertising: Yes
Franchisee Assoc./Member: Yes/Yes
Size Of Corporate Staff: 10
On-Going Support: A,B,C,D,E,F,G,H,I
Training: 2 Weeks Home Study; 6 Days
  Head Office; 1-2 Week on Location.
SPECIFIC EXPANSION PLANS:
US: All United States
Canada: All Canada
Overseas: U.K., Thailand, Japan,
  Caribbean

≺≺ ≻≻

**SUPPLEMENTAL LISTING
OF FRANCHISORS**

AmeriCandy, 1401 Lexington Rd., Louisville, KY 40206-1928 ; (502) 583-6627; Mr. Omar L. Tatum ; (502) 583-1776

Antonello's, 2886 Brooklyn Rd., Jackson, MI 49203-4805 ; (517) 768-1300; Mr. Mike Siciliano (888) 575-5494; (517) 768-9227

Bain's Deli, 1415 Larimer St., Denver, CO 80202 ; (303) 291-0909; Director of Franchising (800) 205-6050; (303) 291-0999

Betsy Ann Chocolates, 322 Perry Hwy., Pittsburgh, PA 15229 ; (412) 931-9777; Franchise Department (888) 4-TRUFFL; (412) 931-4288

Bevmax, The Wine & Liquor Superstore, 17 Cedar St., Stamford, CT 06902 ; (203) 316-0627; Mr. Martin Sudy (877) 4BE-VMAX; (203) 674-0705

Bon Appetit Int'l. Gourmet Foods, 1409 S. 900 East, Salt Lake City, UT 84105 ; (801) 463-1903; Mr. Mick Chandler (888) 278-FOOD; (801) 463-9917

Bourbon Street Candy Company, 266 Elmwood Ave., # 287, Buffalo, NY 14222 ; (905) 894-3072; Mr. Blaine McGrath (800) 949-5115; (905) 894-4819

Bunnies Fresh Juice & Smoothie Bar, 2045 Highway 9, P. O. Box 880, Mandeville, LA 70470-0880 ; (504) 624-9449; Mr. Tim Goux (800) 240-0002; (504) 626-0180

Candy Blossoms, 7511 Lemont Rd., Darien, IL 60561 ; (603) 985-6469; Mr. Sam Norton (800) 572-5931; (603) 985-9406

Canopy, The, 3275 Bethany Ln., # 1, Ellicott City, MD 21042 ; (410) 750-1254; Mr. Kevin Cooney ; (410) 750-1252

Carole's Cheesecake Company, 1272 Castlefield Ave., Toronto, ON M6B 1G3 CANADA; (416) 256-0001; Mr. Michael Ogus ; (416) 256-0000

Cassano's Pizza & Subs, 1700 E. Stroop Rd., Dayton, OH 45429 ; (937) 294-8107; Mr. Vic Cassano, Jr. ; (937) 294-8400

Different Twist Pretzel Co., The, 6052 Route 8, P.O. Box 334, Bakerstown, PA 15007 ; (724) 443-7287; Mr. August P. Maggio ; (724) 443-8010

Edelweiss Deli Express, 3331 Viking Way, # 7, Richmond, BC V6V 1X7 CANADA; (604) 270-6560; Mr. Duncan Williams ; (604) 270-2360

Erik's Delicafe, 365 Coral St., Santa Cruz, CA 95060 ; (831) 458-9797; Ms. Pam Gruen ; (831) 458-1818

Fire Glazed Ham Store and Cafe, 1112 - 7th Ave., Monroe, WI 53566 ; (608) 324-4516; Ms. Donna Bartley (800) 356-8119; (608) 328-8555

Giuliano's Deli Express, 1117 E. Walnut St., Carson, CA 90746 ; (310) 537-7981; Ms. Nancy Giuliano ; (310) 537-7700

Gourmax Market, 2699 E. Oakland Park Blvd., Ft. Lauderdale, FL 33306 ; (954) 396-4997; Mr. Robert A. Spuck (800) 839-4931; (954) 396-4991

Guacamole's Mexican Delivery & Carryout, 107 Woodwind Station Dr., Woodstock, GA 30189 ; (770) 591-9476; Mr. Steve Warres ; (770) 993-7979

HBH of Georgia Franchise Company, The, 2830 Dresden Dr., Atlanta, GA 30341 ; (770) 936-7108; Mr. Bob Faller ; (770) 936-7131

Hickory Farms of Ohio, 1505 Holland Rd., Maumee, OH 43537 ; (419) 893-0164; Mr. Geoff Smith (800) 433-6008; (419) 893-7611

Jason's Deli, 2400 Broadway, Beaumont, TX 77702 ; (409) 832-9994; Mr. Michael Neil (800) 444-4825; (409) 832-5055 X5

Jerky Hut, P.O. Box 308, Hubbard, OR 97032 ; (503) 981-7692; Mr. Stephen R. Risch (800) 2BF-JRKY;

Juice Kitchen, 1050 17th St., #B195, Denver, CO 80265 ; (303) 573-7055; Ms. Katie Yockey (888) 697-1671; (303) 573-7060

Juice Works, 1200 TCBY Tower, 425 W. Capitol Ave., Little Rock, AR 72201 ; (501) 688-8549; Mr. Jerry Butterbaugh (800) 449-5842; (501) 688-8267

Karmelkorn, P.O. Box 39286, Minneapolis, MN 55439-0286 ; (612) 830-0498; Mr. Eric Lavanger (800) 285-8515; (612) 830-0200

Kernels Popcorn, 40 Eglinton Ave. E., # 250, Toronto, ON M4P 3A2 CANADA; (416) 487-3920; Ms. Bernice Sinopoli (800) CORN-COB; (416) 487-4194

Kilwin's Chocolates, 355 N. Division Rd., Petoskey, MI 48079 ; (231) 347-6951; Mr. Don McCarthy (888) 454-5946; (231) 347-3800

Logan Farms Honey Glazed Hams, 10001 Westheimer Rd., #1040, Houston, TX 77042 ; (713) 977-0532; Mr. Pink Logan (800) 833-4267; (713) 781-3773

Maison Du Popcorn, 188 Washington St., Norwich, CT 06360 ; (203) 886-0360; Mr. William A. Abate ; (203) 886-0360

Mayan Jamma Juice, P.O. Box 150650, Ogden, UT 84415 ; (801) 476-9788; Mr. Corey King (800) 207-5804; (801) 476-9780

Mountain Man Nut & Fruit Co., 10338 S. Progress Way, Parker, CO 80134 ; (303) 841-4100; Mr. Mike Conner ; (303) 841-4041

New Yorker Deli, 322 Pharr Rd., Atlanta, GA 30305 ; (404) 240-0890; Mr. Chris Casper ; (404) 240-0260

Papa Romano's, 24581 Crestview Court, Farmington Hills, MI 48335 ; (248) 888-0011; Mr. Daniel J. Morelli (800) 427-2727; (248) 888-7272

Pizza Delight International, 331 Elmwood Dr. Box 23970, Moncton, NB E1A 6S8 CANADA; (905) 477-2207; Mr. C. Tom Rollert ; (905) 477-1600

Planet Smoothie, 3060 Peachtree Rd., #340, Buckhead Plaza, Atlanta, GA 30305 ; (770) 850-8522; Ms. Elizabeth Kane ; (770) 850-8500

Pop'N Stuff, 1303 Celebrity Circle, # 125, Myrtle Beach, SC 29577-7498 ; (843) 946-6813; Mr. Larry G. Hammond (800) 735-5440; (843) 444-4680

Poultry King, 30 E. Beaver Creek Rd., # 206, Richmond Hill, ON L4B 1J2 CANADA; (905) 886-8904; Mr. Michael Aychental (800) 942-5351; (905) 886-8900

Sammi's Deli, 114 Wilton Hill Rd., Columbia, SC 29212 ; (803) 771-7958; Mr. Hassan Addahoumi ; (803) 256-7763

Schakolad Chocolate Factory, 509 S. Semoran Blvd., Winter Park, FL 32792 ; (407) 677-4118; Mr. Edgar Schaked ; (407) 677-4114

Smoothie Island, 1775 The Exchange, # 540, Atlanta, GA 30339 ; (770) 226-8226; Mr. Norman D. Willden (888) 628-4822; (770) 226-8226

South Bend Chocolate Company, 3300 W. Sample, South Bend, IN 46619 ; (219) 233-3150; Mr. Mark Tarner ; (219) 233-2577

Surf City Squeeze, 7730 E. Greenway Rd. #203, Scottsdale, AZ 85260 ; (602) 443-1972; Ms. Nicole Rayborn ; (602) 443-0200

Sweet City, 1604 Hilltop West, # 204, Virginia Beach, VA 23451 ; (757) 491-5543; Mr. Robert L. Chapman ; (757) 422-3061

The Old Fashioned Egg Cream Company, The, 3350 NW 2nd Ave., # A28, Boca Raton, FL 33431 ; (561) 417-6888; Mr. Mark Streisfeld ; (561) 417-6800

Toarmina's Pizza, 673 Barbara St., Westland, MI 48185 ; (734) 727-1882; Mr. Louis Toarmina ; (734) 729-9067

Tropik Sun Fruit & Nut, 37 Sherwood Terrace, # 101, Lake Bluff, IL 60044 ; (847) 234-3856; Ms. Barbara J. Wellard ; (847) 234-3407

Tudor's Biscuit World, 209 1st Ave. S., Nitro, WV 25143 ; (304) 727-1111; Mr. Mark Dawson (800) 727-1111; (304) 343-4026

Vitamin Logic, 557 Burbank St., # K, Broomfield, CO 80122 ; (303) 438-0700; Mr. David W. Coker ; (303) 438-1600

HAIRSTYLING SALONS INDUSTRY PROFILE

Total # Franchisors in Industry Group	29
Total # Franchised Units in Industry Group	5,700
Total # Company-Owned Units in Industry Group	<u>876</u>
Total # Operating Units in Industry Group	6,576
Average # Franchised Units/Franchisor	196.6
Average # Company-Owned Units/Franchisor	<u>30.2</u>
Average # Total Units/Franchisor	226.8
Ratio of Total # Franchised Units/Total # Company-Owned Units	6.5:1
Industry Survey Participants	11
Representing % of Industry	37.9%
Average Franchise Fee*:	$17.8K
Average Total Investment*:	$105.0K
Average On-Going Royalty Fee*:	5.6%

If a range was provided, the mid-point of the range was used. See detailed profiles for actual ranges.

FIVE LARGEST PARTICIPANTS IN SURVEY

Company	# Fran-chised Units	# Co-Owned Units	# Total Units	Franchise Fee	On-Going Royalty	Total Investment
1. Great Clips	1,400	14	1,414	17.5K	6%/$200/Wk.	87.2-162K
2. Fantastic Sams	1,339	11	1,350	20-30K	$200/Wk.	75-165K
3. Supercuts	812	485	1,297	12.5-22.5K	4-6%Yr.1	90-164K
4. Cost Cutters Family Hair Care	710	112	822	12.5-19.5	6/4%	67.7-124K
5. First Choice Haircutters	180	126	306	10-25K	5-7%	92.5-121K

All of the data provided are proprietary and should not be quoted without acknowledging *Bond's Franchise Guide*.

CITY LOOKS SALONS INTERNATIONAL

7201 Metro Blvd.
Edina, MN 55439-2130
Tel: (888) 888-7778 (952) 947-7777
Fax: (952) 947-7300
Web Site: www.regiscorp.com
Mr. Steve Bonniwell, Dir. Franchise Dev.

CITY LOOKS SALONS INTERNATIONAL provides private, individual consultation and styling in tasteful, comfortable surroundings, filling a need for clients who place a strong emphasis on full-service, personalized hair care. CITY LOOKS franchises generate deep customer loyalty and up-scale sales.

BACKGROUND:	IFA MEMBER
Established: 1963;	1st Franchised: 1967
Franchised Units:	49
Company-Owned Units	1
Total Units:	50
Dist.:	US-35; CAN-0; O'seas-15
North America:	8 States
Density:	25 in MN, 8 in IA
Projected New Units (12 Months):	10
Qualifications:	5, 5, 3, 3, 1, 5
Registered: All States	

FINANCIAL/TERMS:

Cash Investment:	$Varies
Total Investment:	$60-126K
Minimum Net Worth:	$250K
Fees: Franchise -	$19.5K
Royalty - 4%;	Ad. - 4%
Earnings Claim Statement:	No
Term of Contract (Years):	15/15
Avg. # Of Employees:	10 FT
Passive Ownership:	Allowed
Encourage Conversions:	Yes
Area Develop. Agreements:	Yes/Varies
Sub-Franchising Contracts:	No
Expand In Territory:	Yes
Space Needs: 1,000 SF; SF, SC, RM	

SUPPORT & TRAINING PROVIDED:

Financial Assistance Provided:	Yes(I)
Site Selection Assistance:	Yes
Lease Negotiation Assistance:	Yes
Co-Operative Advertising:	Yes
Franchisee Assoc./Member:	Yes/Yes
Size Of Corporate Staff:	66
On-Going Support:	C,d,e,G,h,I
Training: 1 Week Headquarters; 10 Days On-Site.	

SPECIFIC EXPANSION PLANS:

US:	All United States
Canada:	All Canada
Overseas:	All Countries

≪ ≫

COST CUTTERS®
FAMILY HAIR CARE
We're your style:

COST CUTTERS FAMILY HAIR CARE

7201 Metro Blvd.
Edina, MN 55439-2130
Tel: (888) 888-7778 (952) 947-7777
Fax: (952) 947-7300
E-Mail: jennifer.kiewel@regiscorp.com
Web Site: www.costcutters.com
Mr. Steve Bonniwell, Dir. Franchise Development

COST CUTTERS FAMILY HAIR CARE is a value-priced, family hair salon chain with over 850 locations in 45 states. COST CUTTERS offers its customers high-quality hair care services and products in an attractive atmosphere and at affordable prices.

BACKGROUND:	IFA MEMBER
Established: 1968;	1st Franchised: 1982
Franchised Units:	710
Company-Owned Units	112
Total Units:	822
Dist.:	US-822; CAN-0; O'seas-0
North America:	45 States
Density:	115 in WI, 82 in MN, 81 CO
Projected New Units (12 Months):	100
Qualifications:	5, 5, 1, 4, 2, 5
Registered: All States	

FINANCIAL/TERMS:

Cash Investment:	$75K
Total Investment:	$67.7K-123.8K
Minimum Net Worth:	$250K
Fees: Franchise -	$12.5-19.5K
Royalty - 6%/4% Yr. 1;	Ad. - 5%
Earnings Claim Statement:	Yes
Term of Contract (Years):	15/15
Avg. # Of Employees:	6 FT, 3 PT
Passive Ownership:	Discouraged
Encourage Conversions:	Yes
Area Develop. Agreements:	Yes/Varies
Sub-Franchising Contracts:	No
Expand In Territory:	Yes
Space Needs: 1,000 SF; SC	

SUPPORT & TRAINING PROVIDED:

Financial Assistance Provided:	Yes(I)
Site Selection Assistance:	Yes
Lease Negotiation Assistance:	Yes
Co-Operative Advertising:	Yes
Franchisee Assoc./Member:	No
Size Of Corporate Staff:	55
On-Going Support:	C,D,E,G,h,I
Training: 1 Week at National HQ; 1 Week On-Site; Several On-Site Visits Prior to Opening.	

SPECIFIC EXPANSION PLANS:

US:	All United States
Canada:	All Canada
Overseas:	All Countries

≪ ≫

Fantastic Sams

FANTASTIC SAMS

1400 N. Kellogg, # E
Anaheim, CA 92807
Tel: (800) 441-6588 (714) 701-3471
Fax: (714) 779-3422
E-Mail: franchise@fantasticsams.com
Web Site: www.fantasticsams.com
Mr. Terry Cooper, Senior VP Franchise Licensing

FANTASTIC SAMS is the world's largest hair care franchise, with over 1,350 salons represented throughout 5 countries. Our full service salons offer quality hair care services for the entire family, including cuts, perms and color. When you join the FANTASTIC SAMS family of franchisees, you'll receive both local and national support through on-going management training, educational programs and national conferences, as well as advertising and other benefits. No hair care experience required.

BACKGROUND:	IFA MEMBER
Established: 1974;	1st Franchised: 1976
Franchised Units:	1,339
Company-Owned Units	11
Total Units:	1,350
Dist.:	US-1,251; CAN-15; O'seas-84
North America:	43 States, 4 Provinces
Density:	219 in CA, 131 in FL, 96 MI
Projected New Units (12 Months):	120
Qualifications:	2, 4, 1, 3, 1, 4
Registered: All States	

FINANCIAL/TERMS:

Cash Investment:	$20-30K
Total Investment:	$75-165K
Minimum Net Worth:	$Varies
Fees: Franchise -	$20-30K
Royalty - $200/Wk.;	Ad. - $100/Wk.
Earnings Claim Statement:	No
Term of Contract (Years):	10/10
Avg. # Of Employees:	8 FT
Passive Ownership:	Allowed
Encourage Conversions:	Yes

Area Develop. Agreements: Yes/10
Sub-Franchising Contracts: Yes
Expand In Territory: Yes
Space Needs: 1,200 SF; SC

SUPPORT & TRAINING PROVIDED:
Financial Assistance Provided: Yes(I)
Site Selection Assistance: Yes
Lease Negotiation Assistance: Yes
Co-Operative Advertising: Yes
Franchisee Assoc./Member: No
Size Of Corporate Staff: 42
On-Going Support: C,d,E,G,h
Training: 6 Days in Anaheim, CA; On-Going within Region.

SPECIFIC EXPANSION PLANS:
US: All United States
Canada: All Canada
Overseas: Pacific Rim

◄◄ ►►

FIRST CHOICE HAIRCUTTERS
6465 Millcreek Dr., # 210
Mississauga, ON L5N 5R6 CANADA
Tel: (800) 617-3961 (905) 821-8555
Fax: (905) 567-7000
E-Mail: info@firstchoice.com
Web Site: www.firstchoice.com
Ms. Martha Lawrence, Franchise Sales Rep.

We're a cutting-edge chain of price-value family hair care salons with over 300 locations across Canada and the US. Since 1980, we've built a strong, growing base of loyal customers - over 6 million last year alone. And you don't even have to have any hair experience or become a stylist. We'll provide all the training, tools and on-going support you'll need to manage your thriving salon business. At FIRST CHOICE HAIRCUTTERS, our philosophy is simple: your success is our success.

BACKGROUND: IFA MEMBER
Established: 1980;   1st Franchised: 1982
Franchised Units: 180
Company-Owned Units   <u>126</u>
Total Units: 306
Dist.:   US-63; CAN-243; O'seas-0
   North America: 2 States, 8 Provinces
   Density: 164 in ON, 43 in FL, 24 AB
Projected New Units (12 Months):   40
Registered: N/A

FINANCIAL/TERMS:
Cash Investment: $46-61K
Total Investment: $92.5-121.2K
Minimum Net Worth: $NR
Fees: Franchise - $10-25K
   Royalty - 5-7%;   Ad. - 3% Fund
Earnings Claim Statement: No
Term of Contract (Years):   10/5
Avg. # Of Employees: 5-7 FT, 2-4 PT
Passive Ownership: Not Allowed
Encourage Conversions: Yes
Area Develop. Agreements: Yes/10
Sub-Franchising Contracts: No
Expand In Territory: Yes
Space Needs: 800-1,000 SF; SC

SUPPORT & TRAINING PROVIDED:
Financial Assistance Provided: Yes(I)
Site Selection Assistance: Yes
Lease Negotiation Assistance: Yes
Co-Operative Advertising: Yes
Franchisee Assoc./Member: No
Size Of Corporate Staff: 20
On-Going Support: B,C,D,E,G,H,I
Training: 1 Week Classroom; 10 Days On-Site. Annual Staff Refresher.

SPECIFIC EXPANSION PLANS:
US: OH,MI, Southeast
Canada: All Canada
Overseas: No

◄◄ ►►

GREAT CLIPS
3800 W. 80th St., # 400
Minneapolis, MN 55431-4419
Tel: (800) 947-1143
Fax: (952) 844-3443
E-Mail: franchise@greatclips.com
Web Site: www.greatclipsfranchise.com
Mr. Charles Simpson, VP Franchise Development

High-volume haircutting salon, specializing in haircuts for the entire family. Unique, attractive decor, with quality, comprehensive advertising programs. Strong, local support to franchisees, excellent training programs. We offer real value to our customers. Tremendous growth opportunities.

BACKGROUND: IFA MEMBER
Established: 1982;   1st Franchised: 1983
Franchised Units: 1,400
Company-Owned Units   <u>14</u>

Total Units: 1,414
Dist.:   US-1,366; CAN-48; O'seas-0
   North America: 32 States, 2 Provinces
   Density: 115 in MN, 107 in CA, 95 OH
Projected New Units (12 Months):   180
Qualifications: 5, 4, 1, 3, 3, 5
Registered: CA,FL,IL,IN,MD,MI,MN,NY, ND,OR,SD,VA,WA,WI,DC,AB

FINANCIAL/TERMS:
Cash Investment: $70-100K
Total Investment: $87.2-161.5K
Minimum Net Worth: $150K
Fees: Franchise - $17.5K
   Royalty - 6%;   Ad. - 5%
Earnings Claim Statement: Yes
Term of Contract (Years):   10/5/5
Avg. # Of Employees: 3 FT, 5 PT
Passive Ownership: Discouraged
Encourage Conversions: No
Area Develop. Agreements: Yes
Sub-Franchising Contracts: No
Expand In Territory: Yes
Space Needs: 1,000-1,200 SF; SF, SC

SUPPORT & TRAINING PROVIDED:
Financial Assistance Provided: Yes(I)
Site Selection Assistance: Yes
Lease Negotiation Assistance: Yes
Co-Operative Advertising: Yes
Franchisee Assoc./Member: Yes/Yes
Size Of Corporate Staff: 180
On-Going Support: A,B,C,D,E,f,G,H,I
Training: 5 Days Minneapolis, MN; 2.5 Weeks Local Market.

SPECIFIC EXPANSION PLANS:
US: All United States
Canada: Western Canada
Overseas: No

◄◄ ►►

LEMON TREE - A UNISEX HAIRCUTTING EST.
3301 Hempstead Tpk.
Levittown, NY 11756
Tel: (800) 345-9156 (516) 735-2828
Fax: (516) 735-1851
E-Mail: lemontree@lemontree.com
Web Site: www.lemontree.com
Mr. Glen Yaris, Vice President Sales

LEMON TREE serves the haircare needs of all people, offering the entire family affordable prices and quality service. Lemon Tree uses only name brand quality products. Lemon Tree is open from early morning to late evening, 7 days per week. We provide a strong, hands-on training program to each franchisee.

BACKGROUND:

Established: 1975; 1st Franchised: 1975	
Franchised Units:	66
Company-Owned Units	0
Total Units:	66
Dist.: US-66; CAN-0; O'seas-0	
North America:	5 States
Density: 60 in NY, 2 in PA, 1 in CT	
Projected New Units (12 Months):	8-10
Qualifications:	4, 4, 1, 2, 1, 5
Registered: FL,MD,NY	

FINANCIAL/TERMS:

Cash Investment:	$25-30K
Total Investment:	$40-75K
Minimum Net Worth:	$40K
Fees: Franchise -	$15K
Royalty - 6%;	Ad. - $400/Mo.
Earnings Claim Statement:	No
Term of Contract (Years):	15/15
Avg. # Of Employees:	4-6 FT, 3 PT
Passive Ownership:	Discouraged
Encourage Conversions:	Yes
Area Develop. Agreements:	Yes/Varies
Sub-Franchising Contracts:	No
Expand In Territory:	Yes
Space Needs: 800-1,200 SF; FS, SF, SC, RM	

SUPPORT & TRAINING PROVIDED:

Financial Assistance Provided:	Yes(D)
Site Selection Assistance:	Yes
Lease Negotiation Assistance:	Yes
Co-Operative Advertising:	Yes
Franchisee Assoc./Member:	No
Size Of Corporate Staff:	6
On-Going Support:	C,D,E,F,H,I
Training: 1 Week at Headquarters; 1 Week plus whatever needed at Store Location.	

SPECIFIC EXPANSION PLANS:

US:	East Coast
Canada:	No
Overseas:	No

◄◄ ►►

LORD'S & LADY'S HAIR SALONS
450 Belgrade Ave.
West Roxbury, MA 02132
Tel: (617) 323-4714
Fax: (617) 323-4059
Mr. Michael Barsamian, President

Service and retail mall locations which normally do 50% men and 50% women in sales.

BACKGROUND:

Established: 1975; 1st Franchised: 1980	
Franchised Units:	22
Company-Owned Units	0
Total Units:	22
Dist.: US-22; CAN-0; O'seas-0	
North America:	3 States
Density: 18 in MA, 3 in NH, 1 in CT	
Projected New Units (12 Months):	3
Qualifications:	3, 4, 5, 3, 4, 4
Registered: NR	

FINANCIAL/TERMS:

Cash Investment:	$50-175K
Total Investment:	$50-175K
Minimum Net Worth:	$200K
Fees: Franchise -	$25K
Royalty - 6%;	Ad. - 0%
Earnings Claim Statement:	No
Term of Contract (Years):	10/10
Avg. # Of Employees:	6 FT, 8 PT
Passive Ownership:	Discouraged
Encourage Conversions:	Yes
Area Develop. Agreements:	No
Sub-Franchising Contracts:	No
Expand In Territory:	Yes
Space Needs: 1,500 SF; RM	

SUPPORT & TRAINING PROVIDED:

Financial Assistance Provided:	Yes(I)
Site Selection Assistance:	Yes
Lease Negotiation Assistance:	Yes
Co-Operative Advertising:	Yes
Franchisee Assoc./Member:	No
Size Of Corporate Staff:	6
On-Going Support:	A,B,C,D,E,F,H,I
Training: 2-5 Days in Boston, MA.	

SPECIFIC EXPANSION PLANS:

US:	Northeast
Canada:	No
Overseas:	No

◄◄ ►►

PRO-CUTS
500 Grapevine Hwy., # 400
Hurst, TX 76054-2708
Tel: (888) PRO-CUTS (817) 788-8000
Fax: (817) 788-0000
E-Mail: gopro@pro-cuts.com
Web Site: www.pro-cuts.com
Mr. James Franks, Director of Development

PRO-CUTS provides professional haircuts for the whole family at affordable prices. PRO-CUTS exhibits a friendly, yet professional atmosphere. Our franchisees

are provided with support and training in ALL phases of operation, as well as on-going training and support for employees.

BACKGROUND: IFA MEMBER

Established: 1982; 1st Franchised: 1983	
Franchised Units:	185
Company-Owned Units	25
Total Units:	210
Dist.: US-210; CAN-0; O'seas-0	
North America:	12 States
Density: 160 in TX, 18 in OK, 9 OH	
Projected New Units (12 Months):	25
Qualifications:	4, 5, 1, 3, 3, 4
Registered: CA	

FINANCIAL/TERMS:

Cash Investment:	$15-60K
Total Investment:	$100-130K
Minimum Net Worth:	$150K
Fees: Franchise -	$10-25K
Royalty - 6%;	Ad. - 5%
Earnings Claim Statement:	No
Term of Contract (Years):	10/10
Avg. # Of Employees:	6 FT, 2 PT
Passive Ownership:	Discouraged
Encourage Conversions:	No
Area Develop. Agreements:	Yes
Sub-Franchising Contracts:	Yes
Expand In Territory:	Yes
Space Needs: 1,000-1,200 SF; FS, SC	

SUPPORT & TRAINING PROVIDED:

Financial Assistance Provided:	Yes(I)
Site Selection Assistance:	Yes
Lease Negotiation Assistance:	Yes
Co-Operative Advertising:	Yes
Franchisee Assoc./Member:	Yes/Yes
Size Of Corporate Staff:	28
On-Going Support:	b,C,D,E,G,h,I
Training: 3 Days Franchise Support Office; 1 Week Field Training.	

SPECIFIC EXPANSION PLANS:

US:	All United States
Canada:	No
Overseas:	No

◄◄ ►►

SNIP N' CLIP HAIRCUT SHOPS
7910 Quivira Rd.
Lenexa, KS 66215
Tel: (800) 944-7182 (913) 438-1200
Fax: (913) 438-3456
Mr. Steve Lidskin, VP Franchise Director

Family haircut shops. Fast service, low price, no appointments. Strip mall shopping centers. Least expensive cpt. turn key

BACKGROUND:

Established: 1976;	1st Franchised: 1986
Franchised Units:	51
Company-Owned Units	55
Total Units:	106
Dist.:	US-106; CAN-0; O'seas-0
North America:	16 States
Density:	36 in KS, 27 in MO, 6 in AR
Projected New Units (12 Months):	7
Qualifications:	4, 3, 1, 3, , 4
Registered: All States	

FINANCIAL/TERMS:

Cash Investment:	$51.8K
Total Investment:	$60-80K
Minimum Net Worth:	$100K
Fees: Franchise -	$10K
Royalty - 5%;	Ad. - 0%
Earnings Claim Statement:	No
Term of Contract (Years):	5/5
Avg. # Of Employees:	4 FT, 2 PT
Passive Ownership:	Allowed
Encourage Conversions:	N/A
Area Develop. Agreements:	Yes
Sub-Franchising Contracts:	No
Expand In Territory:	Yes
Space Needs: 1,000 SF; SF, SC	

SUPPORT & TRAINING PROVIDED:

Financial Assistance Provided:	Yes(I)
Site Selection Assistance:	Yes
Lease Negotiation Assistance:	Yes
Co-Operative Advertising:	N/A
Franchisee Assoc./Member:	Yes
Size Of Corporate Staff:	10
On-Going Support:	C,D,E,G,H,I
Training: 5 Days On-Site.	

SPECIFIC EXPANSION PLANS:

US:	Midwest, West, Southwest
Canada:	No
Overseas:	No

◁◁ ▷▷

SPORT CLIPS

PMB 266, P.O. Box 3000
Georgetown, TX 78627-3000
Tel: (800) 872-4247 (512) 869-1201
Fax: (512) 869-0366
E-Mail: sportclpsz@aol.com
Web Site: www.sportclips.com
Ms. Beth Boecker, Market Dev. Coord.

Sports-themed haircutting salons, appealing primarily to men and boys. Unique design, proprietary haircutting system and complete support at the unit level. Retail sale of Paul Mitchell hair care products, sports apparel and memorabilia.

BACKGROUND:

Established: 1995;	1st Franchised: 1995
Franchised Units:	32
Company-Owned Units	7
Total Units:	39
Dist.:	US-39; CAN-0; O'seas-0
North America:	4 States
Density:	32 in TX, 5 in NY, 1 in CO
Projected New Units (12 Months):	40
Qualifications:	5, 3, 1, 1, 3, 5
Registered: UT,TX	

FINANCIAL/TERMS:

Cash Investment:	$30-50K
Total Investment:	$100-150K
Minimum Net Worth:	$250K
Fees: Franchise -	$15K
Royalty - 6%;	Ad. - $250/Wk.
Earnings Claim Statement:	Yes
Term of Contract (Years):	5/5
Avg. # Of Employees:	8 FT, 4 PT
Passive Ownership:	Allowed
Encourage Conversions:	No
Area Develop. Agreements:	Yes
Sub-Franchising Contracts:	Yes
Expand In Territory:	Yes
Space Needs: 1,200 SF; SC	

SUPPORT & TRAINING PROVIDED:

Financial Assistance Provided:	No
Site Selection Assistance:	Yes
Lease Negotiation Assistance:	Yes
Co-Operative Advertising:	Yes
Franchisee Assoc./Member:	No
Size Of Corporate Staff:	15
On-Going Support:	B,C,D,E,F,G,H,I
Training: 3 Days in Georgetown, TX for	
Franchisee + 2 Weeks Locally; 2 Weeks	
Locally for Manager.	

SPECIFIC EXPANSION PLANS:

US:	TX,UT,CO,NM
Canada:	No
Overseas:	No

◁◁ ▷▷

SUPERCUTS

7201 Metro Blvd.
Edina, MN 55439-2130
Tel: (888) 888-7778 (952) 947-7777
Fax: (952) 947-7300
Web Site: www.supercuts.com
Mr. Steve Bonniwell, Dir. Franchise
Development

Top quality, affordable haircare salons.

BACKGROUND: IFA MEMBER

Established: 1975;	1st Franchised: 1977
Franchised Units:	812
Company-Owned Units	485
Total Units:	1,297
Dist.:	US-1,329; CAN-9; O'seas-0
North America:	50 States
Density:	NR
Projected New Units (12 Months):	100
Qualifications:	5, 5, 1, 3, 4, 5
Registered: All States and AB	

FINANCIAL/TERMS:

Cash Investment:	$75K
Total Investment:	$90-164.1K
Minimum Net Worth:	$250K
Fees: Franchise -	$12.5-22.5K
Royalty - 4-6% Yr. 1;	Ad. - 5%
Earnings Claim Statement:	No
Term of Contract (Years):	Evergreen
Avg. # Of Employees:	6 FT, 4 PT
Passive Ownership:	Discouraged
Encourage Conversions:	Yes
Area Develop. Agreements:	Yes
Sub-Franchising Contracts:	No
Expand In Territory:	Yes
Space Needs: 1,200 SF; SC	

SUPPORT & TRAINING PROVIDED:

Financial Assistance Provided:	Yes(D)
Site Selection Assistance:	Yes
Lease Negotiation Assistance:	Yes
Co-Operative Advertising:	Yes
Franchisee Assoc./Member:	Yes/Yes
Size Of Corporate Staff:	50
On-Going Support:	B,C,D,E,G,H
Training: 4 Days Minneapolis, MN.	

SPECIFIC EXPANSION PLANS:

US:	All United States
Canada:	Toronto,Vancouve
Overseas:	No

◁◁ ▷▷

**SUPPLEMENTAL LISTING
OF FRANCHISORS**

Americuts Family Barber Shops, 41 Durant Ave., # 103, Bethel, CT 06801 ; (203) 792-3990; Ms. Veronica Perrone (800) 718-2887; (203) 792-9955

Beaners Fun Cuts For Kids, 31200 407 2nd St., SW, Calgary, AB T2P 2Y3 CANADA; (403) 264-2197; Ms. Saundra Shapiro (888) BEA-NERS; (403) 261-8600

City Looks Salons International, 7201 Metro Blvd., Edina, MN 55439-2130 ;

(952) 947-7300; Mr. Steve Bonniwell (888) 888-7778; (952) 947-7777

Cookie Cutter's Haircuts For Kids, 15268 Story Creek Way, Noblesville, IN 46060 ; (317) 773-9295; Mr. Larry Shelton ; (317) 464-8346

Great Cuts, 271 Great Rd., #29, Acton, MA 01729 ; (978) 929-9667; Ms. Tina Forster ; (978) 929-9670

Great Expectations / Haircrafters, 6900 Jericho Tpk., Syosset, NY 11711 ; (516) 677-0319; Mr. Don von Liebermann (800) 992-0139; (516) 677-0320

Hair Club For Men, 1515 S. Federal Hwy., # 401, Boca Raton, FL 33432 ; (561) 361-7685; Mr. Richard T. Gurley ; (561) 361-7600

Hair Performers, The, 7201 Metro Blvd., Edina, MN 55439-2130 ; (952) 947-7300; Mr. Steve Bonniwell (888) 888-7778; (952) 947-7777

Hair Replacement Center, 1971 W. 190th St., # 200, Torrance, CA 90504 ; (818) 820-5048; Mr. Scott Bernhardt (800) 899-4472; (310) 516-6614

Hair Replacement Systems, 400 S. Dixie Highway, Hallandale, FL 33009 ; (305) 457-0054; Mr. Kevin A. Maggs (800) 327-7971; (305) 457-0050

Hairlines, 656 E. Golf Rd., Arlington Heights, IL 60005-4061 ; (847) 593-7955; Mr. Paul V. Finamore (800) 424-7911; (847) 593-7900

Headstart Hair Care Salons, 248 Cahaba Valley Pkwy,, Pellham, AL 35124 ; (205) 988-3046; Mr. Charles Bruno (800) 783-7915; (205) 988-4995

Kids Super Salon, 7408 W. Commercial Blvd., Lauderhill, FL 33319 ; (954) 746-5119; Mr. Carlos M. Fluxa (800) 405-9466; (954) 355-2589

Les Consultants Chev'Hair, 221 St. Georges, St-Barnabe Nord, PQ G0X 2K0 CANADA; (819) 264-2075; Mr. Gaston Gelinas ; (819) 264-2116

Magicuts (Canada), 3780 14th Ave., # 106, Markham, ON L3R 9Y5 CANADA; (905)

470-8174; Ms. Susan Clark (800) 542-4247; (905) 470-7850

Men's Hair Now, 515 Madison Ave., # 300, New York, NY 10022 ; (212) 832-0942; Mr. Joseph S. Pierro (800) 835-HAIR; (212) 832-0707

We Care Hair, 7201 Metro Blvd., Edina, MN 55439-2130 ; (952) 947-7300; Mr. Steve Bonniwell (888) 888-7778; (952) 947-7777

HEALTH/FITNESS/BEAUTY INDUSTRY PROFILE

Total # Franchisors in Industry Group	53
Total # Franchised Units in Industry Group	9,413
Total # Company-Owned Units in Industry Group	1,701
Total # Operating Units in Industry Group	11,114
Average # Franchised Units/Franchisor	177.6
Average # Company-Owned Units/Franchisor	32.1
Average # Total Units/Franchisor	209.7
Ratio of Total # Franchised Units/Total # Company-Owned Units	5.5:1
Industry Survey Participants	23
Representing % of Industry	43.4%
Average Franchise Fee*:	$18.5K
Average Total Investment*:	$155.7K
Average On-Going Royalty Fee*:	6.6%

If a range was provided, the mid-point of the range was used. See detailed profiles for actual ranges.

FIVE LARGEST PARTICIPANTS IN SURVEY

Company	# Franchised Units	# Co-Owned Units	# Total Units	Franchise Fee	On-Going Royalty	Total Investment
1. Jazzercise	5,076	2	5,078	.7K	20%	1.5-20K
1. Merle Norman Cosmetics	1,942	5	1,947	0K	0%	35-170K
2. Jenny Craig Weight Loss Centres	133	637	770	50K	7%	160-315K
3. Diet Center	250	0	250	15K	8%/100/Wk.	16.4-34.9K
4. Lady of America	193	0	193	12.5K	10%	40-75K

All of the data provided are proprietary and should not be quoted without acknowledging *Bond's Franchise Guide*.

ALOETTE COSMETICS
4900 Highlands Pkwy.
Smyrna, GA 30082
Tel: (800) ALOETTE (678) 444-2563
Fax: (678) 444-2564
Mr. Scott May, VP Franchise Operations

ALOETTE is a direct marketer of Aloe Vera-based skin care products. Franchises provide career opportunities to beauty consultants who sell the products through home shows.

BACKGROUND:
Established: 1978; 1st Franchised: 1978
Franchised Units: 79
Company-Owned Units   3
Total Units: 82
Dist.:   US-50; CAN-32; O'seas-0
  North America: 36 States,10 Provinces
  Density: 18 in ON, 4 in BC, 3 in PQ
Projected New Units (12 Months):   10
Qualifications: 1, 2, 5, 2, 1, 2
Registered: NR
FINANCIAL/TERMS:
Cash Investment: $10-20K
Total Investment: $55-86.3K
Minimum Net Worth: $10K
Fees: Franchise - $20K
  Royalty - 5%;   Ad. - N/A
Earnings Claim Statement: No
Term of Contract (Years):   5/10
Avg. # Of Employees: 3 FT
Passive Ownership: Discouraged
Encourage Conversions: N/A
Area Develop. Agreements: No
Sub-Franchising Contracts: No
Expand In Territory: Yes
Space Needs: 1,000 SF; HB, Light
  Industrial, Retail
SUPPORT & TRAINING PROVIDED:
Financial Assistance Provided: Yes(D)
Site Selection Assistance: No
Lease Negotiation Assistance: No
Co-Operative Advertising: No
Franchisee Assoc./Member: No
Size Of Corporate Staff: 25
On-Going Support: C,D,E,h
Training: 2 Days Operations Training at
  Franchise; 2 Days Sales Training at
  Franchise.
SPECIFIC EXPANSION PLANS:
US: All United States
Canada: ON
Overseas: No

<< >>

BEAUTY BRANDS SALON-SPA-SUPERSTORE
4600 Madison, # 400
Kansas City, MO 64112
Tel: (888) 725-6608 (816) 531-2266
Fax: (816) 531-7122
E-Mail: franchising@beautybrands.com
Web Site: www.beautybrands.com
Mr. Steve Eckman, VP Corp. Devel./
  Franchising

BEAUTY BRANDS SALON/SPA/ SUPERSTORE is the cutting-edge concept that offers consumers a "total beauty" experience. We have brought together a full-service salon and spa and have showcased it in a dynamic 6,000-7,000 square-foot retail environment offering nearly 50,000 units of product representing the top salon brands for hair, skin and nails.

BACKGROUND: IFA MEMBER
Established: 1995;   1st Franchised: 1998
Franchised Units: 0
Company-Owned Units   13
Total Units: 13
Dist.:   US-13; CAN-0; O'seas-0
  North America: 5 States
  Density: 4 in KS, 3 in TX, 2 in MO
Projected New Units (12 Months):   12
Qualifications: 5, 5, 1, 1, 1, 4
Registered: All States
FINANCIAL/TERMS:
Cash Investment: $100-200K
Total Investment: $594.5-936K
Minimum Net Worth: $3MM
Fees: Franchise - $5-40K
  Royalty - 0-4%;   Ad. - 1-2%
Earnings Claim Statement: No
Term of Contract (Years):   10/10
Avg. # Of Employees: 5 FT, 25 PT
Passive Ownership: Not Allowed
Encourage Conversions: Yes
Area Develop. Agreements: Yes/Varies
Sub-Franchising Contracts: No
Expand In Territory: Yes
Space Needs: 5,000-7,000 SF; FS, SC
SUPPORT & TRAINING PROVIDED:
Financial Assistance Provided: No
Site Selection Assistance: Yes
Lease Negotiation Assistance: Yes

Co-Operative Advertising: Yes
Franchisee Assoc./Member: Yes
Size Of Corporate Staff: 50
On-Going Support: A,B,C,D,E,F,h,I
Training: 4-6 Weeks Kansas City, MO.
SPECIFIC EXPANSION PLANS:
US: All United States
Canada: All Canada
Overseas: No

<< >>

BENEFICIAL HEALTH & BEAUTY
1780 West 500 South
Salt Lake City, UT 84104
Tel: (800) 367-0990 (801) 973-7778
Fax: (801) 973-8836
Ms. Linda T. Nelson, President

BENEFICIAL HEALTH & BEAUTY CENTERS are urban mini-health spas, offering a total wellness and fitness program in each local community. We offer programs that aid in body cleansing, weight-loss, nutrition, body contouring, skin care, massage, personal exercise trainers and many complementary programs.

BACKGROUND:
Established: 1981;   1st Franchised: 1990
Franchised Units: 26
Company-Owned Units   2
Total Units: 28
Dist.:   US-10; CAN-0; O'seas-18
  North America: 3 States
  Density: 6 in CA, 2 in HI, 2 in WI
Projected New Units (12 Months):   10
Qualifications: 5, 5, 3, 3, 4, 4
Registered: CA,HI,IL,MI,MN,NY,ND,
  OR,WA,WI
FINANCIAL/TERMS:
Cash Investment: $30-80K
Total Investment: $100K
Minimum Net Worth: $NR
Fees: Franchise - $15K
  Royalty - 3%;   Ad. - 4%
Earnings Claim Statement: No
Term of Contract (Years):   10/5
Avg. # Of Employees: 2 FT, 2 PT
Passive Ownership: Discouraged
Encourage Conversions: Yes
Area Develop. Agreements: Yes/10
Sub-Franchising Contracts: No
Expand In Territory: Yes
Space Needs: 1,200-2,500 SF; FS, SC, SF,
  HB
SUPPORT & TRAINING PROVIDED:
Financial Assistance Provided: Yes(I)

289

Site Selection Assistance: Yes
Lease Negotiation Assistance: Yes
Co-Operative Advertising: Yes
Franchisee Assoc./Member: NR
Size Of Corporate Staff: 7
On-Going Support: B,C,D,E,f,G,H,I
Training: 2 Days Local Area; 4 Days Practical Salt Lake City, UT; Weekly On-Site.

SPECIFIC EXPANSION PLANS:
US: All United States
Canada: All Canada
Overseas: All Countries

≪ ≫

BEVERLY HILLS WEIGHT LOSS & WELLNESS

20 Airport Rd.
Gilford, NH 03246
Tel: (800) 825-4500
Fax: (603) 524-8771
E-Mail: bhw/w@wsii.com
Web Site: www.beverlyhillsintl.com
Mr. Ralph Cutillo, President

Medically supervised weight loss clinics.

BACKGROUND:
Established: 1986;   1st Franchised: 1989
Franchised Units: 53
Company-Owned Units 0
Total Units: 53
Dist.: US-53; CAN-0; O'seas-0
 North America: NR
 Density: NR
Projected New Units (12 Months): 12
Qualifications: 4, 5, 3, 3, 4, 4
Registered: CA,FL,IN,MN,NY,RI,VA
FINANCIAL/TERMS:
Cash Investment: $15-25K
Total Investment: $50-55K
Minimum Net Worth: $N/A
Fees: Franchise - $15K
 Royalty - 6%; Ad. - Sugg. 2-4%
Earnings Claim Statement: No
Term of Contract (Years): 5/5-20
Avg. # Of Employees: 2 FT, 1-2 PT
Passive Ownership: Discouraged
Encourage Conversions: Yes
Area Develop. Agreements: Yes/5
Sub-Franchising Contracts: Yes
Expand In Territory: Yes
Space Needs: 2,000 SF; SF, SC
SUPPORT & TRAINING PROVIDED:
Financial Assistance Provided: Yes(D)
Site Selection Assistance: Yes
Lease Negotiation Assistance: Yes
Co-Operative Advertising: Yes

Franchisee Assoc./Member: No
Size Of Corporate Staff: 5
On-Going Support: B,C,D,E,F,G,H,I
Training: 2 Weeks Regional Location.
SPECIFIC EXPANSION PLANS:
US: All United States
Canada: ON
Overseas: No

≪ ≫

DIET CENTER

395 Springside Dr.
Akron, OH 44333-2496
Tel: (800) 656-3294 (330) 666-7952
Fax: (330) 666-2197
E-Mail: info@dietcenterworldwide.com
Web Site: www.dietcenterworldwide.com
Mr. Kenneth M. Massey, Dir. Fran. Dev.

DIET CENTER offers innovative weight management programs.

BACKGROUND:
Established: 1972;   1st Franchised: 1972
Franchised Units: 250
Company-Owned Units 0
Total Units: 250
Dist.: US-238; CAN-11; O'seas-1
 North America: 44 States, 4 Provinces
 Density: 28 in NY, 19 in NC, 18 in CA
Projected New Units (12 Months): 8-10
Qualifications: 3, 3, 3, 2, 3, 5
Registered: All States
FINANCIAL/TERMS:
Cash Investment: $16.4-34.9K
Total Investment: $16.4-34.9K
Minimum Net Worth: $50-75K
Fees: Franchise - $15K
 Royalty - 8%/$100/Wk.; Ad. - 8%/$500/Mo.
Earnings Claim Statement: No
Term of Contract (Years): 5/5
Avg. # Of Employees: 2 FT, 1 PT
Passive Ownership: Discouraged
Encourage Conversions: Yes
Area Develop. Agreements: No
Sub-Franchising Contracts: No
Expand In Territory: Yes
Space Needs: 700-1,200 SF; FS, SF, SC
SUPPORT & TRAINING PROVIDED:
Financial Assistance Provided: No
Site Selection Assistance: Yes
Lease Negotiation Assistance: Yes
Co-Operative Advertising: No
Franchisee Assoc./Member: No
Size Of Corporate Staff: 40
On-Going Support: C,D,E,G,H,I
Training: 3 Weeks in Akron, OH.

SPECIFIC EXPANSION PLANS:
US: All United States
Canada: All Canada
Overseas: No

≪ ≫

DIET LIGHT WEIGHT LOSS SYSTEM

300 Market St., # 101
Lebanon, OR 97352
Tel: (800) 248-7712 (541) 259-3573
Fax: (541) 259-3506
E-Mail: dietlight@juno.com
Web Site: www.busdir.com/dietlight
Ms. Kathy Bengtson, President

A complete weight loss system that incorporates individual counseling with delicious, gourmet meals. The Delight Entrees are vacuum-sealed, contain no preservatives, and require no refrigeration. One day a week clients can eat out or plan their own meals. Some of the centers have incorporated a fitness area with workout equipment for women.

BACKGROUND:
Established: 1983;   1st Franchised: 1989
Franchised Units: 5
Company-Owned Units 10
Total Units: 15
Dist.: US-18; CAN-0; O'seas-0
 North America: 4 States
 Density: 11 in OR, 4 in CA, 2 in TN
Projected New Units (12 Months): 6
Qualifications: 3, 3, 3, 2, 3, 3
Registered: All States
FINANCIAL/TERMS:
Cash Investment: $10K
Total Investment: $10-20K
Minimum Net Worth: $25K
Fees: Franchise - $5K
 Royalty - 0%; Ad. - 0%
Earnings Claim Statement: Yes
Term of Contract (Years): NR
Avg. # Of Employees: 1 FT, 2 PT
Passive Ownership: Discouraged
Encourage Conversions: Yes
Area Develop. Agreements: No
Sub-Franchising Contracts: No
Expand In Territory: Yes
Space Needs: 500-1,000 SF; SC
SUPPORT & TRAINING PROVIDED:
Financial Assistance Provided: No
Site Selection Assistance: Yes

Lease Negotiation Assistance: Yes
Co-Operative Advertising: No
Franchisee Assoc./Member: No
Size Of Corporate Staff: 3
On-Going Support: a,b,c,d,e,F,h,I
Training: 3 Days Lebanon, OR.
SPECIFIC EXPANSION PLANS:
US: All United States
Canada: All Canada
Overseas: No

<< >>

EXECUTIVE TANS
4800 Wadsworth Blvd., # 100
Wheat Ridge, CO 80033
Tel: (877) 393-2826 (303) 403-1000
Fax: (303) 403-9109
E-Mail: sales@executivetans.com
Web Site: www.executivetans.com
Mr. Wayne Smeal, President

Indoor tanning salons along with related products and services.

BACKGROUND:
Established: 1991; 1st Franchised: 1995
Franchised Units: 25
Company-Owned Units 1
Total Units: 26
Dist.: US-26; CAN-0; O'seas-0
  North America: 1 State
  Density: 26 in CO
Projected New Units (12 Months): 10
Qualifications: 3, 3, 3, 4, 3, 3
Registered: IL,FL,WI
FINANCIAL/TERMS:
Cash Investment: $40-60K
Total Investment: $130-150K
Minimum Net Worth: $175K
Fees: Franchise - $15K
  Royalty - $795-1,895/Mo; Ad. -
$315/Mo
Earnings Claim Statement: No
Term of Contract (Years): 3/3
Avg. # Of Employees: 2 FT, 3 PT
Passive Ownership: Discouraged
Encourage Conversions: Yes
Area Develop. Agreements: Yes/5
Sub-Franchising Contracts: Yes
Expand In Territory: Yes
Space Needs: 1,500-6,000 SF; SC
SUPPORT & TRAINING PROVIDED:
Financial Assistance Provided: Yes(I)

Site Selection Assistance: Yes
Lease Negotiation Assistance: Yes
Co-Operative Advertising: Yes
Franchisee Assoc./Member: No
Size Of Corporate Staff: 4
On-Going Support: B,C,d,E,G,h,I
Training: 1 Week at Corporate Offices; 1
  Week on Location.
SPECIFIC EXPANSION PLANS:
US: All United States
Canada: No
Overseas: No

<< >>

FABUTAN SUN TAN STUDIOS
5925 3rd St. SE
Calgary, AB T2H 1K3 CANADA
Tel: (800) 565-3658 (403) 640-2100
Fax: (403) 640-2116
E-Mail: MAIL@fabutan.com
Web Site: www.fabutan.com
Mr. Will Hoes, Director of Franchising

North America's largest indoor tanning company, chosen as # 1 tanning franchise by Entrepreneur Magazine. Marketing indoor tanning and related services with a proven system over 20 years. Site location, lease negotiation, construction, full training, post-opening support, financial assistance and a fantastic growing company to assist in your success included.

BACKGROUND:
Established: 1979; 1st Franchised: 1985
Franchised Units: 87
Company-Owned Units 12
Total Units: 99
Dist.: US-1; CAN-98; O'seas-0
  North America: 1 State, 5 Provinces
  Density: 45 in AB, 18 in ON, 15 in BC
Projected New Units (12 Months): 25-30
Qualifications: 3, 3, 1, 1, 4, 4
Registered: AB
FINANCIAL/TERMS:
Cash Investment: $20-30K
Total Investment: $60-85K
Minimum Net Worth: $NR
Fees: Franchise - $7.5-15K
  Royalty - 6%; Ad. - 1%
Earnings Claim Statement: Yes
Term of Contract (Years): 10/5
Avg. # Of Employees: 2 FT, 3 PT
Passive Ownership: Allowed

Encourage Conversions: No
Area Develop. Agreements: Yes
Sub-Franchising Contracts: Yes
Expand In Territory: Yes
Space Needs: 700-1,000 SF; FS, SC
SUPPORT & TRAINING PROVIDED:
Financial Assistance Provided: Yes(I)
Site Selection Assistance: Yes
Lease Negotiation Assistance: Yes
Co-Operative Advertising: yes
Franchisee Assoc./Member: Yes/Yes
Size Of Corporate Staff: 22
On-Going Support: C,D,G,H,I
Training: 3-5 Days Calgary, AB; 1-2 Days
  Franchisee Site.
SPECIFIC EXPANSION PLANS:
US: All United States
Canada: All Canada
Overseas: No

<< >>

f

FACES
FACES
3425 Laird Rd, # 5
Mississauga, ON L5L 5R8 CANADA
Tel: (905) 569-8989
Fax: (905) 569-8998
E-Mail: stevensont@faces-cosmetics.com
Web Site: www.faces-cosmetics.com
Ms. Tamara Stevenson, Director of
  Franchising

FACES is a retail cosmetics business featuring in-mall, stand-alone boutiques selling FACES' own extensive, affordable and distinct brand of prestige color cosmetics and bath, body and skin care. Twenty-five years of operating history and extensive market research enables FACES to successfully service a critical gap between mass-market merchandisers and expensive department store brands.

BACKGROUND: IFA MEMBER
Established: 1974; 1st Franchised: 1980
Franchised Units: 75
Company-Owned Units 22
Total Units: 97
Dist.: US-0; CAN-67; O'seas-30

North America: 9 Provinces
Density: 38 in PQ, 19 in ON
Projected New Units (12 Months): NR
Qualifications: 3, 4, 3, 3, 3, 5
Registered: FL,MI,MN,NY,ND,OR, RI,SD,VA,WA,WI,DC

FINANCIAL/TERMS:
Cash Investment: $25-30K
Total Investment: $85-90K
Minimum Net Worth: $Varies
Fees: Franchise - $16.3K
　Royalty - 5%; Ad. - 2%
Earnings Claim Statement: No
Term of Contract (Years): 10/10
Avg. # Of Employees: 1 FT, 3-4 PT
Passive Ownership: Allowed
Encourage Conversions: Yes
Area Develop. Agreements: Yes/10
Sub-Franchising Contracts: Yes
Expand In Territory: Yes
Space Needs: 230 SF; SF, SC, RM

SUPPORT & TRAINING PROVIDED:
Financial Assistance Provided: Yes(I)
Site Selection Assistance: Yes
Lease Negotiation Assistance: Yes
Co-Operative Advertising: No
Franchisee Assoc./Member: No
Size Of Corporate Staff: 70
On-Going Support: A,B,D,E,G,h
Training: 4 Weeks Toronto, ON.

SPECIFIC EXPANSION PLANS:
US: All United States
Canada: All Canada
Overseas: All Countries in a Master Franchisee capacity

◁◁ ▷▷

FIT AMERICA
401 Fairway Dr., # 200
Deerfield Beach, FL 33441
Tel: (800) 221-1186 (954) 570-3211
Fax: (954) 570-8608
E-Mail: jackfarland@fitamerica.com
Web Site: www.fitamerica.com
Mr. Jack Farland, Dir. Franchise Development

Retail store operation offering the finest all-natural herbal products, comprehensive education and training, and unparalleled, free customer service, as well as motivation to help people lose weight.

BACKGROUND: IFA MEMBER
Established: 1992; 1st Franchised: 1996
Franchised Units: 72
Company-Owned Units: 0
Total Units: 72
Dist.: US-72; CAN-0; O'seas-0
　North America: 13 States
　Density: 18 in NJ, 12 in FL, 12 in NY
Projected New Units (12 Months): 20
Qualifications: 4, 4, 1, 2, 3, 3
Registered: CA,FL,IL,MI,NY,VA

FINANCIAL/TERMS:
Cash Investment: $25-45K
Total Investment: $25-45K
Minimum Net Worth: $N/A
Fees: Franchise - $8.4K
　Royalty - $400/Mo.; Ad. - $165/Mo.
Earnings Claim Statement: No
Term of Contract (Years): 2/2
Avg. # Of Employees: 3 FT
Passive Ownership: Discouraged
Encourage Conversions: Yes
Area Develop. Agreements: No
Sub-Franchising Contracts: No
Expand In Territory: Yes
Space Needs: 800-1,200 SF; SC

SUPPORT & TRAINING PROVIDED:
Financial Assistance Provided: No
Site Selection Assistance: Yes
Lease Negotiation Assistance: Yes
Co-Operative Advertising: Yes
Franchisee Assoc./Member: Yes/Yes
Size Of Corporate Staff: 32
On-Going Support: A,B,C,D,E,F,G,h,I
Training: 3 Days Corporate Headquarters; 1 Week at Already Existing Site; 2 Weeks Franchisee's Store

SPECIFIC EXPANSION PLANS:
US: All United States
Canada: No
Overseas: No

◁◁ ▷▷

FORM-YOU-3 INTERNATIONAL
395 Springside Dr.
Akron, OH 44333-2496
Tel: (800) 525-6315 (330) 668-1461
Fax: (330) 666-2197
Web Site: www.formyou3.com
Mr. Kenneth M. Massey, Director Franchise Development

Assisting individuals in weight loss and maintenance by utilizing a proprietary multi-level diet plan, individual and group behavior life modification programs, diet-related products and maintenance programs.

BACKGROUND:
Established: 1982; 1st Franchised: 1983
Franchised Units: 34
Company-Owned Units: 0
Total Units: 34
Dist.: US-34; CAN-0; O'seas-0
　North America: 12 States
　Density: 12 in OH, 7 in MI, 5 in NC
Projected New Units (12 Months): 10
Qualifications: 5, 4, 3, 3, , 5
Registered: None

FINANCIAL/TERMS:
Cash Investment: $23.1-33.7K
Total Investment: $33-43K
Minimum Net Worth: $100K
Fees: Franchise - $15K
　Royalty - 6%/$150/Wk.; Ad. - 6%
Earnings Claim Statement: No
Term of Contract (Years): 5/5/5/5
Avg. # Of Employees: 2-5 FT
Passive Ownership: Not Allowed
Encourage Conversions: Yes
Area Develop. Agreements: No
Sub-Franchising Contracts: No
Expand In Territory: Yes
Space Needs: 700-1,200 SF; SC

SUPPORT & TRAINING PROVIDED:
Financial Assistance Provided: N/A
Site Selection Assistance: Yes
Lease Negotiation Assistance: Yes
Co-Operative Advertising: Yes
Franchisee Assoc./Member: No
Size Of Corporate Staff: 45
On-Going Support: A,B,c,d,E,G,H,I
Training: 3 Weeks in Akron, OH; 1-3 Days On-Site.

SPECIFIC EXPANSION PLANS:
US: All United States
Canada: No
Overseas: No

◁◁ ▷▷

HOMECARE AMERICA
50 Washington St., # 201
Norwalk, CT 06854
Tel: (800) 452-6664 (203) 354-3775
Fax: (203) 354-3797
E-Mail: boconnell@homecareamerica.com
Web Site: www.homecareamerica.com
Ms. Bonnie O'Connell, Asst. to President

HOMECARE AMERICA is the nation's premier retailer of home health care and healthy lifestyle products. Consistent with a mission to help everyone live better, the uniqueness of the store is found in the extensive selection of products for sleep comfort, body and active care and mobility. HOMECARE AMERICA is the culmination of a consistent progression toward the need in the marketplace for a true and complete home health care product and information source.

BACKGROUND: IFA MEMBER
Established: 1986;   1st Franchised: 1986
Franchised Units: 12
Company-Owned Units 0
Total Units: 12
Dist.: US-12; CAN-0; O'seas-0
  North America: 4 States
  Density: 5 in NY, 3 in NJ, 2 in FL
Projected New Units (12 Months): 10
Qualifications: 4, 4, 3, 3, 3, 4
Registered: All States
FINANCIAL/TERMS:
Cash Investment: $75K
Total Investment: $350-650K
Minimum Net Worth: $100K
Fees: Franchise - $45K
  Royalty - 6%; Ad. - 2%
Earnings Claim Statement: Yes
Term of Contract (Years): 10/10
Avg. # Of Employees: 3 FT, 2 PT
Passive Ownership: Allowed
Encourage Conversions: Yes
Area Develop. Agreements: Yes/Varies
Sub-Franchising Contracts: No
Expand In Territory: Yes
Space Needs: 3,000 SF; FS, SF, SC
SUPPORT & TRAINING PROVIDED:
Financial Assistance Provided: Yes(I)
Site Selection Assistance: Yes
Lease Negotiation Assistance: Yes
Co-Operative Advertising: Yes
Franchisee Assoc./Member: No
Size Of Corporate Staff: 18
On-Going Support: A,B,C,D,E,F,G,H,I
Training: 6 Weeks in CT; 2 Weeks On-Site.
SPECIFIC EXPANSION PLANS:
US: All United States
Canada: All Canada
Overseas: All Countries

◁◁ ▷▷

JAZZERCISE
2808 Roosevelt St.
Carlsbad, CA 92008
Tel: (800) FIT IS IT (760) 434-2101
Fax: (760) 434-8958
E-Mail: jazzinc@jazzercise.com
Web Site: www.jazzercise.com
Mr. Kenny Harvey, Public Relations Director

JAZZERCISE is the world's leading international dance fitness franchisor, with a video service division and mail-order catalog business at 1-800-FIT-IS-IT, specializing in active wear and accessories.

BACKGROUND:
Established: 1969;   1st Franchised: 1983
Franchised Units: 5,076
Company-Owned Units 2
Total Units: 5,078
Dist.: US-3,961; CAN-101; O'seas-860
  North America: 50 States, 5 Provinces
  Density: 642 in CA, 386 in OH, 302 TX
Projected New Units (12 Months): 600
Qualifications: 1, 2, 4, 2, 5, 5
Registered: All States
FINANCIAL/TERMS:
Cash Investment: $1.5-3K
Total Investment: $1.5-20K
Minimum Net Worth: $N/A
Fees: Franchise - $0.7K
  Royalty - 20%; Ad. - N/A
Earnings Claim Statement: No
Term of Contract (Years): 5/5
Avg. # Of Employees: NR
Passive Ownership: Allowed
Encourage Conversions: N/A
Area Develop. Agreements: No
Sub-Franchising Contracts: No
Expand In Territory: Yes
Space Needs: 3,000 SF; Community Building
SUPPORT & TRAINING PROVIDED:
Financial Assistance Provided: No
Site Selection Assistance: No
Lease Negotiation Assistance: No
Co-Operative Advertising: Yes
Franchisee Assoc./Member: No
Size Of Corporate Staff: 135
On-Going Support: C,D,G,H,I
Training: 3 Days Various Locations.
SPECIFIC EXPANSION PLANS:
US: All United States
Canada: All Canada
Overseas: All Countries

◁◁ ▷▷

JENNY CRAIG WEIGHT LOSS CENTRES
11355 N. Torrey Pines Rd.
La Jolla, CA 92038
Tel: (800) 583-6151 (858) 812-7000
Fax: (858) 812-2711
Web Site: www.jennycraig.com
Ms. Jeanine Vigeant, Sr. Director of Franchising

JENNY CRAIG INTERNATIONAL is one of the largest weight-management service companies in the world. We believe the key to success in our weight management program lies in a strong emphasis on personalized service, quality products and a highly-trained and motivated staff. We are seeking unique, highly-qualified individuals to meet our expansion plans.

BACKGROUND: IFA MEMBER
Established: 1983;   1st Franchised: 1987
Franchised Units: 133
Company-Owned Units 637
Total Units: 770
Dist.: US-623; CAN-30; O'seas-117
  North America: 46 States, 3 Provinces
  Density: NR
Projected New Units (12 Months): 10
Qualifications: 5, 5, 4, 4, 5, 5
Registered: All States
FINANCIAL/TERMS:
Cash Investment: $150K
Total Investment: $160-315K
Minimum Net Worth: $250K
Fees: Franchise - $50K
  Royalty - 7%; Ad. - 0%
Earnings Claim Statement: No
Term of Contract (Years): 10/10
Avg. # Of Employees: 4 FT
Passive Ownership: Discouraged
Encourage Conversions: N/A
Area Develop. Agreements: Yes/10
Sub-Franchising Contracts: No
Expand In Territory: Yes
Space Needs: 1,200-1,500 SF; SC
SUPPORT & TRAINING PROVIDED:
Financial Assistance Provided: No
Site Selection Assistance: Yes
Lease Negotiation Assistance: Yes
Co-Operative Advertising: N/A
Franchisee Assoc./Member: No
Size Of Corporate Staff: 250
On-Going Support: A,B,C,D,E,F,H,I
Training: 2-3 Days Corporate Office; 2 Weeks Regional Training Sites.

SPECIFIC EXPANSION PLANS:
US: All United States
Canada: All Canada
Overseas: No

<< >>

LADY OF AMERICA

2400 E. Commercial Blvd., # 808
Ft. Lauderdale, FL 33308
Tel: (800) 833-5239 (954) 492-1201
Fax: (954) 492-1187
E-Mail: landman1@gate.net
Web Site: www.ladyofamerica.com
Mr. Chuck Cououto, Sales Director

Ladies-only health club, specializing in aerobics, weight training, personal training and the sales of related products and services.

BACKGROUND:
Established: 1984;   1st Franchised: 1985
Franchised Units: 193
Company-Owned Units   0
Total Units: 193
Dist.:   US-145; CAN-0; O'seas-0
  North America: 25 States, 4 Countries
  Density: 46 in FL, 25 in TX, 15 in PA
Projected New Units (12 Months):   25
Qualifications: 5, 4, 1, 3, 4, 4
Registered: CA,FL,NY
FINANCIAL/TERMS:
Cash Investment: $20-30K
Total Investment: $40-75K
Minimum Net Worth: $50K
Fees: Franchise - $12.5K
  Royalty - 10%;   Ad. - 0%
Earnings Claim Statement: No
Term of Contract (Years):   10/5
Avg. # Of Employees: 2 FT, 6 PT
Passive Ownership: Allowed
Encourage Conversions: Yes
Area Develop. Agreements: Yes/10
Sub-Franchising Contracts: Yes
Expand In Territory: Yes
Space Needs: 4,500 SF; SC
SUPPORT & TRAINING PROVIDED:
Financial Assistance Provided: Yes
Site Selection Assistance: Yes
Lease Negotiation Assistance: Yes
Co-Operative Advertising: Yes
Franchisee Assoc./Member: Yes/No
Size Of Corporate Staff: 25
On-Going Support: A,B,C,D,E,F,G,H,I
Training: 2-3 Weeks On-Site; 1-2 Weeks at
  Corporate Headquarters.
SPECIFIC EXPANSION PLANS:
US: All United States

Canada: All Canada
Overseas: All Countries

<< >>

MADAME ET MONSIEUR

8157 Santa Monica Blvd.
West Hollywood, CA 90046
Tel: (310) 275-8901
Fax: (310) 275-8906
Mr. Robey Taute, President

World leaders in bodyshaping, cellulite and weight loss using non-physical computerized machine programs.

BACKGROUND:
Established: 1983;   1st Franchised: 1983
Franchised Units: 81
Company-Owned Units   2
Total Units: 83
Dist.:   US-9; CAN-0; O'seas-74
  North America: 1 State
  Density: NR
Projected New Units (12 Months):   50
Qualifications: 2, 5, 3, 3, 2, 5
Registered: CA,NY
FINANCIAL/TERMS:
Cash Investment: $60K
Total Investment: $160K
Minimum Net Worth: $100K
Fees: Franchise - $NR
  Royalty - $300/Mo.;   Ad. - Negotiable
Earnings Claim Statement: Yes
Term of Contract (Years):   5-10/5-10
Avg. # Of Employees: 3 FT
Passive Ownership: Discouraged
Encourage Conversions: No
Area Develop. Agreements: No
Sub-Franchising Contracts: NR
Expand In Territory: Yes
Space Needs: 1,000+ SF; SF, RM
SUPPORT & TRAINING PROVIDED:
Financial Assistance Provided: Yes(I)
Site Selection Assistance: Yes
Lease Negotiation Assistance: Yes
Co-Operative Advertising: Yes
Franchisee Assoc./Member: No
Size Of Corporate Staff: 40
On-Going Support: B,D,E,H,i
Training: 40-60 Hours/2-3 Weeks Beverly
  Hills, CA.
SPECIFIC EXPANSION PLANS:
US: All United States
Canada: All Canada
Overseas: Europe

<< >>

MERLE NORMAN
COSMETICS

MERLE NORMAN COSMETICS

9130 Bellanca Ave.
Los Angeles, CA 90045
Tel: (800) 421-6648 (310) 641-3000
Fax: (310) 337-2370
Web Site: www.merlenorman.com
Ms.   Carol   LaPorta,   VP   Studio
  Development

MERLE NORMAN COSMETICS is a specialty retail store, selling scientifically-developed, state-of-the-art cosmetic products, using the 'free make over' and 'try before you buy' complete customer satisfaction methods of selling.

BACKGROUND: IFA MEMBER
Established: 1931;   1st Franchised: 1989
Franchised Units: 1,942
Company-Owned Units   5
Total Units: 1,947
Dist.:   US-1,845; CAN-93; O'seas-9
  North America: 50 States, 9 Provinces
  Density: 270 in TX, 98 in GA, 97 AL
Projected New Units (12 Months):   56
Qualifications: 3, 4, 3, 3, 4, 4
Registered: All States
FINANCIAL/TERMS:
Cash Investment: $15-65K
Total Investment: $35-170K
Minimum Net Worth: $NR
Fees: Franchise - $0
  Royalty - 0%;   Ad. - 0%
Earnings Claim Statement: No
Term of Contract (Years):   Unlimited
Avg. # Of Employees: 2 FT, 2-5 PT
Passive Ownership: Discouraged
Encourage Conversions: No
Area Develop. Agreements: No
Sub-Franchising Contracts: No
Expand In Territory: Yes
Space Needs: 450-800 SF; SC, RM
SUPPORT & TRAINING PROVIDED:
Financial Assistance Provided: Yes(I)
Site Selection Assistance: Yes
Lease Negotiation Assistance: Yes
Co-Operative Advertising: Yes
Franchisee Assoc./Member: No
Size Of Corporate Staff: 640
On-Going Support: a,B,C,D,E,F,G,H,I
Training: 2 Weeks Los Angeles, CA.
SPECIFIC EXPANSION PLANS:
US: All United States
Canada: AB,BC,MB,ON,SK
Overseas: No

≪ ≫

MIRAGE TANNING CENTERS

15965 Jeanette St.
Southfield, MI 48075
Tel: (248) 559-1415
Fax: (248) 557-7931
E-Mail: wfcnet@cris.com
Web Site: www.wfcnet.com
Dr. Geoffrey Stebbins, President

MIRAGE TANNING offers their customers the most innovative technology in indoor tanning. Indoor tanning is quickly becoming a very high-tech mega-industry. MIRAGE TANNING provides a market feasibility study, professional consultation, customized design, construction and much more.

BACKGROUND:

Established: 1989; 1st Franchised: 1993	
Franchised Units:	10
Company-Owned Units	6
Total Units:	16
Dist.:	US-16; CAN-0; O'seas-0
North America:	1 State
Density:	16 in MI
Projected New Units (12 Months):	8
Qualifications:	3, 3, 2, 3, 3, 4
Registered: NR	

FINANCIAL/TERMS:

Cash Investment:	$50K
Total Investment:	$200-500K
Minimum Net Worth:	$200K
Fees: Franchise -	$15K
Royalty - 8%;	Ad. - NR
Earnings Claim Statement:	NR
Term of Contract (Years):	NR
Avg. # Of Employees:	NR
Passive Ownership:	Allowed
Encourage Conversions:	Yes
Area Develop. Agreements:	NR
Sub-Franchising Contracts:	Yes
Expand In Territory:	Yes
Space Needs: NR SF; FS, SF, SC	

SUPPORT & TRAINING PROVIDED:

Financial Assistance Provided:	Yes(I)
Site Selection Assistance:	Yes
Lease Negotiation Assistance:	Yes
Co-Operative Advertising:	Yes
Franchisee Assoc./Member:	NR
Size Of Corporate Staff:	NR
On-Going Support:	D,E
Training: NR	

SPECIFIC EXPANSION PLANS:

US:	All United States
Canada:	All Canada
Overseas:	All Countries

≪ ≫

PHYSICIANS WEIGHT LOSS CENTERS OF AMERICA

395 Springside Dr.
Akron, OH 44333-2496
Tel: (800) 205-7887 (330) 666-7952
Fax: (330) 666-2197
E-Mail: info@pwlc.com
Web Site: www.pwlc.com
Mr. Kenneth M. Massey, Dir. Fran. Dev.

Supervised weight reduction business, offering the customer a comprehensive program, utilizing individual treatment, personal care, counseling and weight management.

BACKGROUND:

Established: 1979; 1st Franchised: 1980	
Franchised Units:	54
Company-Owned Units	2
Total Units:	56
Dist.:	US-56; CAN-0; O'seas-0
North America:	12 States
Density: 20 in OH, 10 in SC, 4 in NC	
Projected New Units (12 Months):	10
Qualifications:	5, 4, 3, 3, , 5
Registered: All States Except CA,HI,NY	

FINANCIAL/TERMS:

Cash Investment:	$21.04-52.1K
Total Investment:	$38-70K
Minimum Net Worth:	$100K
Fees: Franchise -	$20K
Royalty - 5.5%/$115/Wk.;	Ad. -
7%/$600/Wk.	
Earnings Claim Statement:	No
Term of Contract (Years):	5/5/5
Avg. # Of Employees:	2 FT, 2 PT
Passive Ownership:	Not Allowed
Encourage Conversions:	Yes
Area Develop. Agreements:	No
Sub-Franchising Contracts:	No
Expand In Territory:	Yes
Space Needs: 1,200 SF; SC	

SUPPORT & TRAINING PROVIDED:

Financial Assistance Provided:	No
Site Selection Assistance:	Yes
Lease Negotiation Assistance:	Yes
Co-Operative Advertising:	Yes
Franchisee Assoc./Member:	No
Size Of Corporate Staff:	45
On-Going Support:	A,B,c,d,E,G,H,I
Training: 3 Weeks Akron, OH; 1-3 Days On-Site.	

SPECIFIC EXPANSION PLANS:

US:	All United States
Canada:	No
Overseas:	No

≪ ≫

SANGSTER'S HEALTH CENTRES

2218 Hanselman Ave.
Saskatoon, SK S7L 6A4 CANADA
Tel: (306) 653-4481
Fax: (306) 653-4688
E-Mail: sangsters@sangsters.com
Web Site: www.sangsters.com
Ms. Wendy Sangster, VP of Franchising

With 30 years of experience, SANGSTER'S HEALTH CENTRES has grown to become Canada's top health and vitamin franchise, with 50 stores from coast to coast. A comprehensive support package, along with quality vitamins and herbs have made SANGSTER'S the industry leaders since 1971. Over 300 carefully-selected items offer terrific prices, the best quality and exclusivity. Share in the terrific success of this industry by becoming part of the SANGSTER'S HEALTH CENTRES team.

BACKGROUND:

Established: 1971; 1st Franchised: 1978	
Franchised Units:	44
Company-Owned Units	4
Total Units:	48
Dist.:	US-0; CAN-48; O'seas-0
North America:	7 Provinces
Density: 14 in SK, 11 in ON, 8 in AB	
Projected New Units (12 Months):	8
Qualifications:	3, 3, 4, 2, 3, 4
Registered: AB	

FINANCIAL/TERMS:

Cash Investment:	$30-50K
Total Investment:	$125-160K
Minimum Net Worth:	$50K
Fees: Franchise -	$25K
Royalty - 5%;	Ad. - 2%
Earnings Claim Statement:	No
Term of Contract (Years):	5/2-5
Avg. # Of Employees:	2 FT, 1 PT
Passive Ownership:	Discouraged
Encourage Conversions:	Yes
Area Develop. Agreements:	No
Sub-Franchising Contracts:	No
Expand In Territory:	Yes
Space Needs: 600-1,000 SF; SC, RM	

SUPPORT & TRAINING PROVIDED:

Financial Assistance Provided:	Yes(D)
Site Selection Assistance:	Yes

Lease Negotiation Assistance:	Yes
Co-Operative Advertising:	Yes
Franchisee Assoc./Member:	No
Size Of Corporate Staff:	13
On-Going Support:	B,C,D,E,F,G,H

Training: 2 Weeks in Saskatoon, SK; Minimum of 1 Week at Franchisee Location.

SPECIFIC EXPANSION PLANS:

US:	All United States
Canada:	All Canada
Overseas:	Europe, Asia

<< >>

TOP OF THE LINE FRAGRANCES

515 Bath Ave.
Long Branch, NJ 07740
Tel: (800) 929-3083 (732) 229-0014
Fax: (732) 222-1762
E-Mail: info@tolfranchise.com
Web Site: www.tolfranchise.com
Mr. Steven Ciaverelli, Vice President

T.O.L. specializes in the retail sale of designer fragrances at the lowest discounted prices.

BACKGROUND:

Established: 1987;	1st Franchised: 1987
Franchised Units:	3
Company-Owned Units	1
Total Units:	4
Dist.:	US-4; CAN-0; O'seas-0
North America:	3 States
Density:	2 in FL, 1 in TN, 1 in PA
Projected New Units (12 Months):	3
Qualifications:	5, 3, 3, 1, 1, 4
Registered:	

FINANCIAL/TERMS:

Cash Investment:	$150-200K
Total Investment:	$150-200K
Minimum Net Worth:	$150K
Fees: Franchise -	$20K
Royalty - 5%;	Ad. - N/A
Earnings Claim Statement:	No
Term of Contract (Years):	10/5
Avg. # Of Employees:	3 FT, 3 PT
Passive Ownership:	Discouraged
Encourage Conversions:	Yes
Area Develop. Agreements:	Yes/10
Sub-Franchising Contracts:	No
Expand In Territory:	Yes
Space Needs: 700-1,200 SF; SC, RM, Outlet Ctr.	

SUPPORT & TRAINING PROVIDED:

Financial Assistance Provided:	Yes(I)
Site Selection Assistance:	Yes
Lease Negotiation Assistance:	Yes

Co-Operative Advertising:	N/A
Franchisee Assoc./Member:	No
Size Of Corporate Staff:	5
On-Going Support:	B,C,d,E,F,I
Training: 7-10 Days at Franchise Location.	

SPECIFIC EXPANSION PLANS:

US:	East
Canada:	No
Overseas:	No

<< >>

TROPI-TAN FRANCHISING

5152 Commerce Rd.
Flint, MI 48507
Tel: (800) 642-4826 (810) 230-6789
Fax: (810) 230-1115
Ms. Carol Mills, Franchise Director

In business for 19 years, TROPI-TAN indoor sun-tanning salons are international design and decor award winners. One of the most progressive salon chains, TROPI-TAN salons also feature a full line of tanning lotions, clothing, and related accessories.

BACKGROUND: IFA MEMBER

Established: 1979;	1st Franchised: 1985
Franchised Units:	5
Company-Owned Units	6
Total Units:	11
Dist.:	US-11; CAN-0; O'seas-0
North America:	1 State
Density:	11 in MI
Projected New Units (12 Months):	25
Qualifications:	3, 3, 1, 3, 3, 5
Registered: MI	

FINANCIAL/TERMS:

Cash Investment:	$50-100K
Total Investment:	$175-250K
Minimum Net Worth:	$150K
Fees: Franchise -	$20K
Royalty - 5%;	Ad. - 3%
Earnings Claim Statement:	No
Term of Contract (Years):	10/5
Avg. # Of Employees:	1 FT, 3 PT
Passive Ownership:	Discouraged
Encourage Conversions:	Yes
Area Develop. Agreements:	Yes/5

Sub-Franchising Contracts:	No
Expand In Territory:	Yes
Space Needs: 2,500 SF; FS, SC	

SUPPORT & TRAINING PROVIDED:

Financial Assistance Provided:	Yes(I)
Site Selection Assistance:	Yes
Lease Negotiation Assistance:	Yes
Co-Operative Advertising:	Yes
Franchisee Assoc./Member:	No
Size Of Corporate Staff:	30
On-Going Support:	A,B,C,D,E,F,G,H,I
Training: 80 Hours at Corporate Training Center; 40 Hours On-Site.	

SPECIFIC EXPANSION PLANS:

US:	All United States
Canada:	All Canada
Overseas:	All Countries

<< >>

WOMEN'S 17-MINUTE WORKOUT

4790 Douglas Circle, NW
Canton, OH 44718
Tel: (888) 832-1717 (330) 305-1717
Fax: (330) 497-6453
E-Mail: WO17MINUTE@aol.com
Web Site:
www.womens17minuteworkout.com
Mr. Kenneth Massey, VP Franchise Development

A totally unique women-only fitness club franchise opportunity. Backed by 25 years of experience, our proprietary system teaches women the truth about women's fitness and offers the fitness-minded entrepreneur the opportunity to own a very lucrative results-oriented business. Our members' results are incredible...and that spells success for everyone involved.

BACKGROUND: IFA MEMBER

Established: 1996;	1st Franchised: 1998
Franchised Units:	5
Company-Owned Units	6
Total Units:	11
Dist.:	US-6; CAN-0; O'seas-0
North America:	1 State
Density:	6 in OH
Projected New Units (12 Months):	12
Qualifications:	3, 3, 4, 2, 2, 5
Registered:	FL,IL,IN,MD,MI,MN, NY,RI,VA,WI,DC

FINANCIAL/TERMS:

Cash Investment:	$45K

Total Investment:	$158-197K
Minimum Net Worth:	$200K
Fees: Franchise -	$22.5K
Royalty - 6%/1.85K/Mo.;	Ad. - 1%
Earnings Claim Statement:	No
Term of Contract (Years):	5/5
Avg. # Of Employees:	4 FT, 4 PT
Passive Ownership:	Discouraged
Encourage Conversions:	Yes
Area Develop. Agreements:	Yes/5
Sub-Franchising Contracts:	No
Expand In Territory:	Yes
Space Needs: 1,800 SF; SC	

SUPPORT & TRAINING PROVIDED:

Financial Assistance Provided:	No
Site Selection Assistance:	Yes
Lease Negotiation Assistance:	Yes
Co-Operative Advertising:	N/A
Franchisee Assoc./Member:	No
Size Of Corporate Staff:	10
On-Going Support:	A,B,C,D,E,F,G,H,I
Training: 3-4 Weeks Canton, OH.	

SPECIFIC EXPANSION PLANS:

US:	All United States
Canada:	No
Overseas:	No

SUPPLEMENTAL LISTING
OF FRANCHISORS

A. T. C. Healthcare Services, 1983 Marcus Ave., # 200, Lake Success, NY 11042 ; (516) 358-3678; Mr. Ed Teixeira (800) 444-4633; (516) 358-1000

Bally Total Fitness Center, 8700 Bryn Mawr, 2nd Fl., Chicago, IL 60631 ; (773) 693-2982; Ms. Michelle Lange ; (773) 399-1300

Beaux Visages European Skin Care Centers, 270 Mount Hope Dr., Albany, NY 12202 ; (518) 465-0364; Mr. John Dennis ; (518) 465-1420

Body Shop, The, P.O. Box 1409, Wake Forest, NC 27588-1409 ; (919) 554-4361; Ms. Rita Murphy-Johnson ; (919) 554-4900

Contempo Women's Workout World, 16015 Harlem Ave., Tinley Park, IL 60477 ; (708) 429-9741; Ms. Shari Whitley ; (708) 429-7766

Copa Ca Tana Tanning Salons, 222 N. Sepulveda Blvd., #2000, El Segundo, CA 90245 ; (310) 364-5245; Mr. Joe Donnini ; (310) 364-5220

Curves For Women, 400 Schroeder Dr., Waco, TX 76710 ; (254) 399-9731; Mr. Gary Findley (800) 848-1096; (254) 399-9285

Doctors & Nurses Weight Control Center, 1386 Shoreline Dr., Gulf Breeze, FL 32561 ; (850) 934-0340; Ms. Sharon Colbert (800) 367-6391; (850) 934-8006

Fitness Centers of America, 221 Bonita Ave., # 712, Piedmont, CA 94611 ; (510) 547-3245; Ms. Les L. Antonius ; (510) 839-5471

Great American Backrub, The, 4500 140th Ave. N., # 221, Clearwater, FL 33762 ; (813) 532-4737; Mr. Jim Dibe (800) BACK-RUB; (813) 532-4818

Hollywood Weight Loss Centre, P.O. Box 1070, College Station, Fredericksburg, VA 22402 ; (724) 438-3903; Mr. Loyd Liming (888) 477-LOSE; (540)891-7494

I Natural, 32-02 Queens Blvd., Long Island City, NY 11101 ; (718) 786-3204; Ms. Victoria Perrella (800) 9-MAKEUP; (718) 729-2929

Inches A Weigh, P.O. Box 59346, Birmingham, AL 35209 ; (205) 879-2106; Mr. Scott Simcik (800) 241-8663; (205) 879-8663

Irly Bird, 7846 128th St., P.O. Box 9010, Surrey, BC V3T 4X7 CANADA; (604) 597-3693; Mr. Stuart Joule ; (604) 596-1551

Jeneal Studios, 3798 Westchase, Houston, TX 77042 ; (713) 789-8585; Dr. Jerry O'Neal, Ph.D (800) 7JE-NEAL; (713) 781-2263

LA Weight Loss, 255 Business Center Dr., # 150, Horshan, PA 19044 ; (215) 328-9251; Ms. Karen Siegel (888) 411-THIN; (215) 328-9250

Let's Make Up, 25 E. Northfield Rd., Livingston, NJ 07039 ; (973) 992-5150; Ms. Sandy Silverman ; (973) 992-2585

Nectar Bath & Body Shops, 143 32nd Ave., La Chine, PQ H8T 3J1 CANADA; (514) 631-8520; Mr. Jeff de Leeuw ; (514) 631-3333

Nu-Best Diagnostic Labs, 4159 Corporate Ct., Palm Harbor, FL 34683 ; (727) 943-7198; Mr. Ron Edwards (800) 839-6757; (727) 942-8324

Our Weigh, 3637 Park Ave., # 201, Memphis, TN 38111-5614 ; ; Ms. Helen K. Seale ; (901) 458-7546

Pearle Vision, 1925 Enterprise Pkwy., Twinsburg, OH 44087 ; (330) 486-3931; Mr. Greg Helwig (800) 282-3931; (330) 486-4000

Physicians Weight Loss Centers (Canada), 395 Springside Dr., Akron, OH 44333 ; (330) 666-2197; Mr. Ken Massey (800) 205-7887; (330) 666-7952

Planet Beach, 3910 General Degaulle, New Orleans, LA 70114 ; (504) 361-5540; Ms. Nancy Price (888) 290-8266; (504) 361-5550

State Beauty Supply, 10405-B E. 55th Place, Tulsa, OK 74146 ; (918) 627-8660; Mr. Frederic H. Harms ; (918) 627-8000

Sunbanque Island Tanning, 2533A Yonge St., Toronto, ON M4P 2H9 CANADA; (416) 488-3712; Mr. Joel Giusto ; (416) 488-5838

Sunchain Tanning Centers, 8102 E. McDowell, #2C, Scottsdale, AZ 85257 ; (480) 994-5162; Mr. Edward Chaney ; (480) 421-9630

Tan World, 1919 S. 40th St., # 202, Lincoln, NE 68506-5248 ; (402) 434-5624; Mr. Jack L. Rediger (800) 865-2378; (402) 434-5620

U.S. Fitness Products, 3072 Wake Forest Rd., Raleigh, NC 27609 ; (919) 875 8010; Mr. David Thomas ; (919) 875-1900

Volpe Nails, P.O. Box 19979, Sarasota, FL 34276-2979 ; (941) 925-7213; Mr. Gary Donson (800) 848-6573; (941) 925-7410

LAUNDRY & DRY CLEANING INDUSTRY PROFILE

Total # Franchisors in Industry Group	21
Total # Franchised Units in Industry Group	1,978
Total # Company-Owned Units in Industry Group	937
Total # Operating Units in Industry Group	2,915
Average # Franchised Units/Franchisor	94.2
Average # Company-Owned Units/Franchisor	44.6
Average # Total Units/Franchisor	138.8
Ratio of Total # Franchised Units/Total # Company-Owned Units	2.1:1
Industry Survey Participants	10
Representing % of Industry	47.6%
Average Franchise Fee*:	$19.6K
Average Total Investment*:	$152.3K
Average On-Going Royalty Fee*:	6.8%

If a range was provided, the mid-point of the range was used. See detailed profiles for actual ranges.

FIVE LARGEST PARTICIPANTS IN SURVEY

Company	# Franchised Units	# Co-Owned Units	# Total Units	Franchise Fee	On-Going Royalty	Total Investment
1. Martinizing Dry Cleaning	763	0	763	30K	4%	210-300K
2. Comet One-Hour Cleaners	333	13	346	20K	0%	200-300K
3. Pressed 4 Time	133	0	133	12.5K	6%	15.2-22.3K
4. Wedding Gown Specialists	119	1	120	N/A	20% Fee	2.5K+
5. Eagle Cleaners	92	0	92	15K	5%/$195	200-250K

All of the data provided are proprietary and should not be quoted without acknowledging *Bond's Franchise Guide*.

1-800-DRYCLEAN

3948 Ranchero Dr.
Ann Arbor, MI 48108
Tel: (888) 239-2532
Fax: (734) 822-6888
E-Mail: inor@1800dryclean.com
Web Site: www.1800dryclean.com
Mr. Marc A. Kiekenapp, Vice President

Without being a drycleaner, you can be a leader in this $10 billion market. The consumer wants convenience - the industry is not providing it. 1-800-DRYCLEAN delivers the solution! Big business does not necessarily mean big investment. For under $25,000, your 1-800-DRYCLEAN pick up and delivery service can be well on its way to becoming a fleet operation.

BACKGROUND: IFA MEMBER
Established: 2000;   1st Franchised: 2000
Franchised Units: 18
Company-Owned Units   0
Total Units: 18
Dist.:   US-18; CAN-0; O'seas-0
  North America: 9 States
  Density: 5 in FL, 2 in MI, 2 in AL
Projected New Units (12 Months):   25
Qualifications: 3, 3, 1, 3, 4, 5
Registered: CA,FL,IL,IN,MD,MI,MN,NY,
  OR,RI,VA,WA,WI,DC
FINANCIAL/TERMS:
Cash Investment: $20K
Total Investment: $16.8-27.2K
Minimum Net Worth: $100K
Fees: Franchise - $6.9K
  Royalty - 7%;   Ad. - 0%
Earnings Claim Statement: No
Term of Contract (Years):   10/10
Avg. # Of Employees: 5 FT
Passive Ownership: Discouraged
Encourage Conversions: Yes
Area Develop. Agreements: No
Sub-Franchising Contracts: No
Expand In Territory: Yes
Space Needs: 200 SF; HB
**SUPPORT & TRAINING PRO-
VIDED:**
Financial Assistance Provided: Yes(I)
Site Selection Assistance: Yes
Lease Negotiation Assistance: No
Co-Operative Advertising: No
Franchisee Assoc./Member: NR

Size Of Corporate Staff: 17
On-Going Support: C,D,E,G,h,I
Training: 5 Days Home Office; 4 Days
  Franchise Location; 6 Months Field
  Right-Start Program.
SPECIFIC EXPANSION PLANS:
US: All United States
Canada: All Canada
Overseas: All Countries

⊰⊰ ⊱⊱

AWC COMMERCIAL WINDOW COVERINGS

825 W. Williamson
Fullerton, CA 92832
Tel: (800) 252-2280 (714) 879-3880
Fax: (714) 879-8419
Web Site: www.ibos.com/pub/ibos/awc
Mr. Leland B. Daniels, President

Mobile non-toxic drapery dry cleaning services provided on location for commercial customers; as well as sales, installation & repairs of all types of window coverings at competitive prices through centralized buying. Nationwide accounts will be serviced by the franchisees as they are established. Utilizing the customer base, references and reputation of the franchisor, developed over the past 37 years makes this an exceptional opportunity with endless possibilities and immediate credibility.

BACKGROUND:
Established: 1963;   1st Franchised: 1992
Franchised Units: 10
Company-Owned Units   4
Total Units: 14
Dist.:   US-14; CAN-0; O'seas-0
  North America: 5 States
  Density: 6 in CA, 1 in MD, 1 in NV
Projected New Units (12 Months):   3
Qualifications: 3, 4, 3, 3, 4, 4
Registered: CA,DC,MD
FINANCIAL/TERMS:
Cash Investment: $25-50K
Total Investment: $112.5-181.4K
Minimum Net Worth: $N/A
Fees: Franchise - $25K
  Royalty - 5-12.5%;   Ad. - 2.5%
Earnings Claim Statement: No
Term of Contract (Years):   10/10

Avg. # Of Employees: 1 FT, PT
As Needed
Passive Ownership: Not Allowed
Encourage Conversions: Yes
Area Develop. Agreements: Yes
Sub-Franchising Contracts: No
Expand In Territory: Yes
Space Needs: N/A SF; HB
SUPPORT & TRAINING PROVIDED:
Financial Assistance Provided: Yes(I)
Site Selection Assistance: N/A
Lease Negotiation Assistance: Yes
Co-Operative Advertising: Yes
Franchisee Assoc./Member: No
Size Of Corporate Staff: 8
On-Going Support: A,B,C,D,F,h,I
Training: 2 Weeks at Plant and On-Site;
  On-Going.
SPECIFIC EXPANSION PLANS:
US: All United States
Canada: All Canada
Overseas: All Countries

⊰⊰ ⊱⊱

CLEAN 'N' PRESS AMERICA

500 Airport Blvd., # 100
Burlingame, CA 94010
Tel: (800) 237-1711 (650) 344-2377
Fax: (650) 344-2545
Mr. Alan Block, President

Dry cleaning and laundry service utilizing a central plant with satellite stores and pick-up and delivery service, providing quality for less. We provide you with a complete and highly-efficient system, including marketing programs, ranging from a single van to a multiple plant/store combination. You are given full training and support through an extensive hands-on training program with detailed manuals.

BACKGROUND:
Established: 1991;   1st Franchised: 1991
Franchised Units: 30
Company-Owned Units   0
Total Units: 30
Dist.:   US-40; CAN-0; O'seas-0
  North America: 3 States
  Density: 40 in MN
Projected New Units (12 Months):   20
Qualifications: 4, 4, 1, 3, 3, 5
Registered: CA,MN
FINANCIAL/TERMS:
Cash Investment: $150K
Total Investment: $20-400K
Minimum Net Worth: $365K

Fees: Franchise - $9.5-40K
   Royalty - 5%;   Ad. - Varies
Earnings Claim Statement: No
Term of Contract (Years):   10/10
Avg. # Of Employees: Varies
Passive Ownership: Discouraged
Encourage Conversions: Yes
Area Develop. Agreements: Yes/Varies
Sub-Franchising Contracts: Yes
Expand In Territory: Yes
Space Needs: 850-3,500 SF; HB, SF, SC

SUPPORT & TRAINING PROVIDED:
Financial Assistance Provided: Yes(I)
Site Selection Assistance: Yes
Lease Negotiation Assistance: Yes
Co-Operative Advertising: N/A
Franchisee Assoc./Member: No
Size Of Corporate Staff: 6
On-Going Support: C,D,E,F,I
Training: 1-3 Weeks Phoenix, AZ or Other
   Location.

SPECIFIC EXPANSION PLANS:
US: All United States
Canada: All Canada
Overseas: Asia, Europe, North and South
   America

◄◄ ►►

COMET ONE-HOUR CLEANERS
406 W. Division St.
Arlington, TX 76011
Tel: (817) 461-3555
Fax: (817) 861-4779
E-Mail: sgregory@airmail.net
Web Site: www.comet-cleaners.com
Mr. Jack D. Godfrey, Jr., Vice President

We offer a turn-key opportunity in the laundry and dry-cleaning business. Site evaluation, complete training and installation are just a few of the services that COMET offers. There is only a one-time-per-year franchise fee of $2,000 required, as opposed to other franchisors that require a percent of your gross income per year.

BACKGROUND: IFA MEMBER
Established: 1960;   1st Franchised: 1967
Franchised Units: 333
Company-Owned Units   13
Total Units: 346
Dist.:   US-329; CAN-0; O'seas-13
   North America: 15 States
   Density: 212 in TX, 21 in AR, 16 TN
Projected New Units (12 Months):   20
Qualifications: 4, 4, 1, 3, 3, 4
Registered: CA

FINANCIAL/TERMS:
Cash Investment: $60-100K
Total Investment: $200-300K
Minimum Net Worth: $80K
Fees: Franchise - $20K
   Royalty - 0%;   Ad. - N/A
Earnings Claim Statement: No
Term of Contract (Years):   5/5/5
Avg. # Of Employees: 6 FT, 2-3 PT
Passive Ownership: Discouraged
Encourage Conversions: No
Area Develop. Agreements: No
Sub-Franchising Contracts: No
Expand In Territory: Yes
Space Needs: 1,800-2,000 SF; SC

SUPPORT & TRAINING PROVIDED:
Financial Assistance Provided: Yes(I)
Site Selection Assistance: Yes
Lease Negotiation Assistance: Yes
Co-Operative Advertising: No
Franchisee Assoc./Member: Yes/Yes
Size Of Corporate Staff: 12
On-Going Support: c,d,D,E,G
Training: 1 Week in Waco, TX; 1 Week in
   Store.

SPECIFIC EXPANSION PLANS:
US: All United States
Canada: No
Overseas: No

◄◄ ►►

DRY CLEANING STATION
8301 Golden Valley Rd., # 230
Golden Valley, MN 55427
Tel: (800) 655-8134 (612) 541-0832
Fax: (612) 542-2246
E-Mail: johnca@franchisemasters.com
Mr. John A. Campbell, Chief Executive
   Officer

A high-quality, lower priced dry cleaner and shirt laundry, offering a special niche in the industry, including environmentally efficient equipment, proprietary unique software/computer systems and attractively-designed, high-traffic stores.

BACKGROUND:
Established: 1987;   1st Franchised: 1993
Franchised Units: 11
Company-Owned Units   3
Total Units: 14
Dist.:   US-14; CAN-0; O'seas-0
   North America: 7 States
   Density: 5 in MN, 4 in NE
Projected New Units (12 Months):   10
Qualifications: 5, 3, 1, 2, 2, 5
Registered: FL,IL,MI,MN

FINANCIAL/TERMS:
Cash Investment: $40-80K
Total Investment: $190-270K
Minimum Net Worth: $250K
Fees: Franchise - $22.5K
   Royalty - 2-5%;   Ad. - 0%
Earnings Claim Statement: Yes
Term of Contract (Years):   15/2-5
Avg. # Of Employees: 4 FT, 2 PT
Passive Ownership: Discouraged
Encourage Conversions: No
Area Develop. Agreements: Yes/Open
Sub-Franchising Contracts: No
Expand In Territory: Yes
Space Needs: 2,200-4,000 SF; FS, SF, SC

SUPPORT & TRAINING PROVIDED:
Financial Assistance Provided: Yes(I)
Site Selection Assistance: Yes
Lease Negotiation Assistance: Yes
Co-Operative Advertising: Yes
Franchisee Assoc./Member: No
Size Of Corporate Staff: 5
On-Going Support: B,C,D,E,G,H,I
Training: 10-15 Days at a Store and
   Headquarters.

SPECIFIC EXPANSION PLANS:
US: All United States
Canada: All Canada
Overseas: All Countries

◄◄ ►►

EAGLE CLEANERS
1750 University Dr., # 111
Coral Springs, FL 33071
Tel: (800) 275-9751 (954) 346-9501
Fax: (954) 346-9505
Mr. Gerard J. Teeven, President

Franchisor of state-of-the-art dry-cleaning stores, offering turn-key plants and drop stores, complete training, site evaluation and a marketing strategy that separates us from the rest of the dry cleaning industry.

BACKGROUND: IFA MEMBER
Established: 1991;   1st Franchised: 1993
Franchised Units: 92
Company-Owned Units   0
Total Units: 92
Dist.:   US-92; CAN-0; O'seas-0
   North America: 16 States
   Density: CT, NY, FL
Projected New Units (12 Months):   40
Qualifications: 4, 5, 1, 4, 5, 4
Registered: FL,IL,MI,NY

FINANCIAL/TERMS:
Cash Investment: $75-110K
Total Investment: $200-250K

Minimum Net Worth:	$250K
Fees: Franchise -	$15K
Royalty - 5%/$195;	Ad. - 3%
Earnings Claim Statement:	No
Term of Contract (Years):	10/10
Avg. # Of Employees:	3 FT, 1 PT
Passive Ownership:	Discouraged
Encourage Conversions:	No
Area Develop. Agreements:	Yes/10
Sub-Franchising Contracts:	Yes
Expand In Territory:	Yes
Space Needs: 1,800-2,200 SF; FS, SC	

SUPPORT & TRAINING PROVIDED:

Financial Assistance Provided:	Yes(I)
Site Selection Assistance:	Yes
Lease Negotiation Assistance:	Yes
Co-Operative Advertising:	N/A
Franchisee Assoc./Member:	No
Size Of Corporate Staff:	16
On-Going Support:	A,C,D,E,F,G,H,I
Training: 3 Weeks Coral Springs, FL; 1 Week Opening; 90-120 Post-Opening.	

SPECIFIC EXPANSION PLANS:

US:	East, Midwest
Canada:	No
Overseas: Mexico, South America, Latin America	

MARTINIZING DRY CLEANING
2005 Ross Ave.
Cincinnati, OH 45212-2021
Tel: (800) 827-0345 (513) 351-6211
Fax: (513) 731-0818
E-Mail: cleanup@martinizing.com
Web Site: www.martinizing.com
Mr. Jerald E. Laesser, Vice President

New franchisees receive the full benefit of MARTINIZING DRY CLEANING's 50 plus years of experience in site selection, training and marketing. MARTINIZING focuses totally on assisting its franchisees before, during and after opening. MARTINIZING is the most recognized name in dry-cleaning. We're rated # 1 in our industry by Entrepreneur Magazine.

BACKGROUND: IFA MEMBER

Established: 1949;	1st Franchised: 1949
Franchised Units:	763
Company-Owned Units	0
Total Units:	763
Dist.:	US-522; CAN-36; O'seas-205
North America:	41 States, 6 Provinces
Density:	10 in MI, 82 in CA, 40 in TX

Projected New Units (12 Months):	25
Qualifications:	5, 4, 1, 3, 1, 5
Registered: All States	

FINANCIAL/TERMS:

Cash Investment:	$80K
Total Investment:	$210-300K
Minimum Net Worth:	$180K
Fees: Franchise -	$30K
Royalty - 4%;	Ad. - 0.5%
Earnings Claim Statement:	No
Term of Contract (Years):	20
Avg. # Of Employees:	2 FT, 4 PT
Passive Ownership:	Discouraged
Encourage Conversions:	Yes
Area Develop. Agreements:	Yes/3-20
Sub-Franchising Contracts:	Yes
Expand In Territory:	Yes
Space Needs: 1,500-2,000 SF; FS, SC	

SUPPORT & TRAINING PROVIDED:

Financial Assistance Provided:	Yes(I)
Site Selection Assistance:	Yes
Lease Negotiation Assistance:	Yes
Co-Operative Advertising:	Yes
Franchisee Assoc./Member:	Yes/Yes
Size Of Corporate Staff:	16
On-Going Support:	C,D,E,G,H,I
Training: 1 Week Classroom; 2 Weeks In-Store.	

SPECIFIC EXPANSION PLANS:

US:	All United States
Canada:	All Except AB
Overseas:	Europe, Far and Middle East

NU-LOOK 1-HR. CLEANERS
15 NE Second Ave.
Deerfield Beach, FL 33441-3503
Tel: (800) 413-7881 (954) 426-1111
Fax: (954) 570-6248
Mr. Karl N. Dickey, President/CEO

Retail dry cleaner.

BACKGROUND:

Established: 1967;	1st Franchised: 1967
Franchised Units:	53
Company-Owned Units	1
Total Units:	54
Dist.:	US-52; CAN-0; O'seas-2
North America:	4 States
Density:	24 in FL, 12 in MD, 10 in VA
Projected New Units (12 Months):	25
Qualifications:	2, 4, 2, 2, 3, 4
Registered: FL,MD,VA	

FINANCIAL/TERMS:

Cash Investment:	$45-75K
Total Investment:	$125-200K+
Minimum Net Worth:	$150K

Fees: Franchise -	$20K
Royalty - 2%;	Ad. - 3%
Earnings Claim Statement:	No
Term of Contract (Years):	20/10
Avg. # Of Employees:	2 FT, 2 PT
Passive Ownership:	Discouraged
Encourage Conversions:	Yes
Area Develop. Agreements:	Yes
Sub-Franchising Contracts:	Yes
Expand In Territory:	Yes
Space Needs: 1,200-1,400 SF; FS, SC	

SUPPORT & TRAINING PROVIDED:

Financial Assistance Provided:	Yes(I)
Site Selection Assistance:	Yes
Lease Negotiation Assistance:	Yes
Co-Operative Advertising:	Yes
Franchisee Assoc./Member:	No
Size Of Corporate Staff:	4
On-Going Support:	C,D,E,G,H
Training: 4 Weeks Deerfield Beach, FL.	

SPECIFIC EXPANSION PLANS:

US:	All United States
Canada:	All Canada
Overseas:	All Countries

PRESSED 4 TIME
124 Boston Post Rd.
Sudbury, MA 01776
Tel: (800) 423-8711 (978) 443-9200
Fax: (978) 443-0709
E-Mail: franchiseinfo@pressed4time.com
Web Site: www.pressed4time.com
Mr. Randy Erb, Dir. Franchise Development

The nation's first and foremost dry-cleaning/shoe repair, pick-up and delivery franchise. Coast to coast, more than 50,000 customers smile when they see our franchisees. Dry-cleaning and shoe repair are performed by local merchants. Experience in the 7 billion-dollar dry-cleaning industry is not needed. If you like people and can work on your own, then this leading home-based, mobile franchise is probably for you!

BACKGROUND: IFA MEMBER

Established: 1987;	1st Franchised: 1990
Franchised Units:	133
Company-Owned Units	0
Total Units:	133
Dist.:	US-107; CAN-4; O'seas-22

North America: 31 States, 2 Provinces
Density: 13 in PA, 7 in OH, 7 in MA
Projected New Units (12 Months): 36
Qualifications: 2, 1, 1, 3, 3, 3
Registered: CA,FL,IL,IN,MD,MI,MN, NY,OR,RI,VA,WA,WI

FINANCIAL/TERMS:
Cash Investment: $15.2-22.3K
Total Investment: $15.2-22.3K
Minimum Net Worth: $N/A
Fees: Franchise - $12.5K
Royalty - 6%; Ad. - None
Earnings Claim Statement: No
Term of Contract (Years): 10/10
Avg. # Of Employees: 1 FT
Passive Ownership: Not Allowed
Encourage Conversions: Yes
Area Develop. Agreements: No
Sub-Franchising Contracts: No
Expand In Territory: Yes
Space Needs: N/A SF; HB

SUPPORT & TRAINING PROVIDED:
Financial Assistance Provided: No
Site Selection Assistance: Yes
Lease Negotiation Assistance: N/A
Co-Operative Advertising: N/A
Franchisee Assoc./Member: No
Size Of Corporate Staff: 5
On-Going Support: a,b,C,D,E,G,H,I
Training: 2 Days Corporate at Sudbury, MA; 2 Days at Franchise; 1 Day at Franchise.

SPECIFIC EXPANSION PLANS:
US: All United States
Canada: All Canada
Overseas: No

<< >>

WEDDING GOWN SPECIALISTS/ RESTORATION

1270 Cedars Rd.
Lawrenceville, GA 30045
Tel: (800) 543-8987 (770) 998-3111
Fax: (770) 682-8736
Mr. Garah (Gary) I. Webster, Founder

Chemically restores discolored/stained wedding and christening gowns to true color without damage to fabric or dye. We also treat museum items, old quilts, etc.

BACKGROUND:
Established: 1987; 1st Franchised: 1987
Franchised Units: 119
Company-Owned Units 1
Total Units: 120
Dist.: US-100; CAN-10; O'seas-10
North America: 35 States, 4 Provinces

Density: 7 in OH, 5 in CA, 5 in NC
Projected New Units (12 Months): 15
Qualifications: 3, 3, 3, 3, 3, 3
Registered: NR

FINANCIAL/TERMS:
Cash Investment: $2.5K+
Total Investment: $2.5K+
Minimum Net Worth: $N/A
Fees: Franchise - $N/A
Royalty - 20% Fee; Ad. - 0%
Earnings Claim Statement: No
Term of Contract (Years): 1-Ind./1
Avg. # Of Employees: 1 FT, 1 PT
Passive Ownership: Discouraged
Encourage Conversions: No
Area Develop. Agreements: Yes/1-Indef.
Sub-Franchising Contracts: No
Expand In Territory: Yes
Space Needs: 500-1,000 SF; FS, SF, SC, RM, HB

SUPPORT & TRAINING PROVIDED:
Financial Assistance Provided: No
Site Selection Assistance: No
Lease Negotiation Assistance: No
Co-Operative Advertising: Yes
Franchisee Assoc./Member: Yes/Yes
Size Of Corporate Staff: 3
On-Going Support: b,c,d,G,h,I
Training: Not Required.

SPECIFIC EXPANSION PLANS:
US: All United States
Canada: All Canada
Overseas: All Free Nations

<< >>

SUPPLEMENTAL LISTING OF FRANCHISORS

A-1 Discount Cleaners, 8301 Golden Valley Rd., # 230, Golden Valley, MN 55427-4410 ; (612) 542-2246; Mr. John Campbell (800) 234-3726; (612) 541-1385

America's Wash-N-Stor, 201 Barton Springs Rd., Austin, TX 78704 ; (512) 472-2905; Mr. Matt Stillwell ; (512) 457-1337

Business Opportunities, LA., 466 Arthur Ave., Shreveport, LA 71105 ; (318) 861-7367; Mr. Ken F. Kreeger (800) 357-7367; (318) 861-7367

Champion Cleaners, 5117 Hwy. 153, Chattanooga, TN 37343 ; (423) 870-2039; Mr. Ray Oldham (800) 357-0797; (423) 876-7430

Dryclean - U.S.A., 290 NE 68th Street, Miami, FL 33138 ; (305) 754-8010; Mr. Jorge Salvat (800) 746-4583; (305) 754-9966

Harvey Washbangers, 106 29th Ave. N., P.O. Box 50582, Nashville, TN 37205 ; (615) 298-1696; Mr. David Harvey ; (615) 298-5547

London Cleaners, 21 Amber St., # 12, Markham, ON L3R 4Z3 CANADA; (905) 475-7249; Mr. Mark Kuzu ; (905) 475-1350

Lucy's Laundrymart, 3812 Sepulveda Blvd., #510, Torrance, CA 90505 ; (310) 378-6264; Mr. Robert Pardo (877) GO-LUCYS; (310) 378-2620

LAWN & GARDEN INDUSTRY PROFILE

Total # Franchisors in Industry Group	20
Total # Franchised Units in Industry Group	1,185
Total # Company-Owned Units in Industry Group	<u>150</u>
Total # Operating Units in Industry Group	1,335
Average # Franchised Units/Franchisor	59.3
Average # Company-Owned Units/Franchisor	<u>7.5</u>
Average # Total Units/Franchisor	66.8
Ratio of Total # Franchised Units/Total # Company-Owned Units	7.9:1
Industry Survey Participants	12
Representing % of Industry	60.0%
Average Franchise Fee*:	$23.8K
Average Total Investment*:	$65.6K
Average On-Going Royalty Fee*:	7.5%

If a range was provided, the mid-point of the range was used. See detailed profiles for actual ranges.

FIVE LARGEST PARTICIPANTS IN SURVEY

Company	# Fran- chised Units	# Co- Owned Units	# Total Units	Franchise Fee	On-Going Royalty	Total Investment
1. Lawn Doctor	380	0	380	0	10%	41K
2. Weed Man	130	2	132	20-34K	$7.9K/Vehicle	75K
3. Nitro-Green	40	53	93	19.5K	7-8.5%	35-50K
4. U.S. Lawns	82	0	82	29K	3-4%	40-70K
5. Naturalawn of America	52	2	54	29.5K	7-9%	50-125K

All of the data provided are proprietary and should not be quoted without acknowledging *Bond's Franchise Guide*.

CLINTAR GROUNDSKEEPING SERVICES

70 Esna Park Dr., # 1
Markham, ON L3R 1E3 CANADA
Tel: (800) 361-3542 (905) 943-9530
Fax: (905) 943-9529
E-Mail: info@clintar.com
Web Site: www.clintar.com
Mr. Robert C. Wilton, President

Company provides a full-service, year-round grounds care service to Fortune 500 clients and government agencies. The average size business is $1,000,000. It provides landscape maintenance services, power sweeping, and snow and ice control services.

BACKGROUND:

Established: 1973; 1st Franchised: 1984
Franchised Units: 8
Company-Owned Units: 1
Total Units: 9
Dist.: US-0; CAN-9; O'seas-0
North America: 1 Province
Density: 9 in ON
Projected New Units (12 Months): 2
Qualifications: 4, 5, 2, 3, 4, 5
Registered: NR

FINANCIAL/TERMS:

Cash Investment: $50-75K
Total Investment: $90-150K
Minimum Net Worth: $100K
Fees: Franchise - $30K
Royalty - 8%; Ad. - 0%
Earnings Claim Statement: No
Term of Contract (Years): 10/5
Avg. # Of Employees: 10 FT, 15 PT
Passive Ownership: Not Allowed
Encourage Conversions: Yes
Area Develop. Agreements: Yes
Sub-Franchising Contracts: No
Expand In Territory: Yes
Space Needs: 3,000 SF; FS, Multi-Unit Industrial

SUPPORT & TRAINING PROVIDED:

Financial Assistance Provided: Yes(I)
Site Selection Assistance: Yes
Lease Negotiation Assistance: Yes
Co-Operative Advertising: Yes
Franchisee Assoc./Member: Yes/Yes
Size Of Corporate Staff: 9
On-Going Support: a,B,C,D,E,F,H,I
Training: 2 Weeks in Toronto, ON.

SPECIFIC EXPANSION PLANS:

US: Northwest (Great Lakes Area)
Canada: All Canada
Overseas: No

≪ ≫

JIM'S MOWING

210 Lark Ln.
Euless, TX 76039
Tel: (817) 684-0192
E-Mail: jmhstn@swbell.net
Web Site: www.jims.com.au
Mr. Peter Barley, Regional Franchisor

JIM'S MOWING is the worlds largest lawn and garden care franchisee with over 1500 units in 4 countries. We offer full office support in training, marketing, live call answering and automated paging system.

BACKGROUND:

Established: 1982; 1st Franchised: 1989
Franchised Units: 4
Company-Owned Units: 2
Total Units: 6
Dist.: US-0; CAN-0; O'seas-0
North America: 1 State
Density: 6 in TX
Projected New Units (12 Months): NR
Registered:

FINANCIAL/TERMS:

Cash Investment: $12-16K
Total Investment: $12-20K
Minimum Net Worth: $N/A
Fees: Franchise - $8K
Royalty - 6%; Ad. - $30/Mo.
Earnings Claim Statement: No
Term of Contract (Years): 10/10
Avg. # Of Employees: 2 FT
Passive Ownership: Discouraged
Encourage Conversions: NR
Area Develop. Agreements: No
Sub-Franchising Contracts: No
Expand In Territory: Yes
Space Needs: N/A SF; N/A

SUPPORT & TRAINING PROVIDED:

Financial Assistance Provided: NR
Site Selection Assistance: N/A
Lease Negotiation Assistance: N/A
Co-Operative Advertising: Yes
Franchisee Assoc./Member: Yes/Yes
Size Of Corporate Staff: 37
On-Going Support: A,B,C,D,G,H,I
Training: 3 Days On-Site; 2 Days Office

SPECIFIC EXPANSION PLANS:

US: TX Only
Canada: NR
Overseas: NR

≪ ≫

LAWN DOCTOR

142 State Route 34
Holmdel, NJ 07733-2092
Tel: (800) 631-5660 (732) 946-0029
Fax: (732) 946-9089
Web Site: www.lawndoctor.com
Mr. Edward L. Reid, National Franchise Sales Dir.

LAWN DOCTOR is an automated lawn care service. We use all natural and regular fertilization, plus control application, using our exclusive Turf Tamer equipment, manufactured and used only by LAWN DOCTOR, supplemented by a broad range of cultural care practices, utilizing integrated Pest Control Management to develop the health and beauty of turf and landscape areas with environmentally-balanced care.

BACKGROUND: IFA MEMBER

Established: 1967; 1st Franchised: 1967
Franchised Units: 380
Company-Owned Units: 0
Total Units: 380
Dist.: US-350; CAN-0; O'seas-0
North America: 34 States
Density: 63 in NJ, 37 in NY, 35 in PA
Projected New Units (12 Months): 30
Qualifications: 3, 1, 1, 2, 1, 5
Registered: FL,IL,IN,MD,MI,MN,NY, RI,SD,VA,WI,DC

FINANCIAL/TERMS:

Cash Investment: $22K
Total Investment: $41K
Minimum Net Worth: $50K
Fees: Franchise - $0
Royalty - 10%; Ad. - 10%
Earnings Claim Statement: No
Term of Contract (Years): 20/5/5
Avg. # Of Employees: 2 PT
Passive Ownership: Discouraged
Encourage Conversions: Yes
Area Develop. Agreements: No
Sub-Franchising Contracts: No
Expand In Territory: Yes
Space Needs: N/A SF; HB

SUPPORT & TRAINING PROVIDED:

Financial Assistance Provided: Yes(D)
Site Selection Assistance: N/A
Lease Negotiation Assistance: No
Co-Operative Advertising: Yes
Franchisee Assoc./Member: Yes/Yes
Size Of Corporate Staff: 50
On-Going Support: B,C,D,G,H,I
Training: 2 Weeks NJ.

SPECIFIC EXPANSION PLANS:
US:	All Except CA,WA,OR
Canada:	No
Overseas:	No

<< >>

LIQUI-GREEN LAWN & TREE CARE

9601 N. Allen Rd.
Peoria, IL 61615
Tel: (800) 747-5211 (309) 243-5815
Fax: (309) 243-5247
Mr. C. Millard Dailey, Director

This is a full-service lawn and tree care company, applying fertilizers, weed killers, soil sterilants, insecticides, growth regulators, secondary micro-elements, tree inspections, spraying and soil amendments such as liquid lime.

BACKGROUND:
Established: 1971;	1st Franchised: 1979
Franchised Units:	31
Company-Owned Units	1
Total Units:	32
Dist.:	US-31; CAN-1; O'seas-32
North America:	NR
Density:	NR
Projected New Units (12 Months):	3
Registered: IL,IN,VA,WA	

FINANCIAL/TERMS:
Cash Investment:	$NR
Total Investment:	$NR
Minimum Net Worth:	$Varies
Fees: Franchise -	$NR
Royalty - NR;	Ad. - NR
Earnings Claim Statement:	No
Term of Contract (Years):	10/5-10
Avg. # Of Employees:	1 PT
Passive Ownership:	NR
Encourage Conversions:	N/A
Area Develop. Agreements:	NR
Sub-Franchising Contracts:	Yes
Expand In Territory:	Yes
Space Needs: N/A SF; NR	

SUPPORT & TRAINING PROVIDED:
Financial Assistance Provided:	Yes(I)
Site Selection Assistance:	Yes
Lease Negotiation Assistance:	N/A
Co-Operative Advertising:	N/A
Franchisee Assoc./Member:	Yes/Yes
Size Of Corporate Staff:	NR
On-Going Support:	b,C,G,H,I
Training: NR	

SPECIFIC EXPANSION PLANS:
US:	Northwest, Southwest
Canada:	No
Overseas:	No

<< >>

NATURALAWN OF AMERICA

1 E. Church St.
Frederick, MD 21701
Tel: (800) 989-5444 (301) 694-5440
Fax: (301) 846-0320
E-Mail: natlawn@erols.com
Web Site: www.nl-amer.com
Mr. Randy Loeb, VP Franchise Development

NATURALAWN of America is the only nationwide lawn care franchise offering an environmentally friendly lawn care service incorporating natural, organic-based fertilizers and biological controls. Our franchise owners provide residential and commercial customers with fertilization, weed control, insect control, disease control and lawn diagnosis services using safer and healthier products, eliminating the need for harsh chemicals and pesticides.

BACKGROUND:
Established: 1987;	1st Franchised: 1989
Franchised Units:	52
Company-Owned Units	2
Total Units:	54
Dist.:	US-53; CAN-1; O'seas-0
North America:	19 States
Density:	6 in MD, 5 in PA, 5 in VA
Projected New Units (12 Months):	10-12
Qualifications:	5, 4, 2, 3, 4, 5
Registered: CA,FL,IL,IN,MD,MI,MN,NY, OR,RI,VA,WA,WI	

FINANCIAL/TERMS:
Cash Investment:	$30K
Total Investment:	$50-125K
Minimum Net Worth:	$125K
Fees: Franchise -	$29.5K
Royalty - 7-9%;	Ad. - 0%
Earnings Claim Statement:	Yes
Term of Contract (Years):	5/10
Avg. # Of Employees:	2 FT, 4-6 PT
Passive Ownership:	Discouraged
Encourage Conversions:	Yes
Area Develop. Agreements:	No
Sub-Franchising Contracts:	No
Expand In Territory:	Yes
Space Needs: 1,200-1,500 SF; Warehouse	

SUPPORT & TRAINING PROVIDED:
Financial Assistance Provided:	Yes(B)
Site Selection Assistance:	N/A
Lease Negotiation Assistance:	Yes
Co-Operative Advertising:	N/A
Franchisee Assoc./Member:	No
Size Of Corporate Staff:	14
On-Going Support:	B,C,D,E,F,G,H,I
Training: 1 Week + 3 Days + 3 Days Corporate Headquarters; 2 Days Regionally 3-4 Times Per Year.	

SPECIFIC EXPANSION PLANS:
US:	All United States
Canada:	All Canada
Overseas:	Western Europe, Southeast Asia

<< >>

NITRO-GREEN PROFESSIONAL LAWN & TREE CARE

2100 W. Drake, # 128
Ft. Collins, CO 80526
Tel: (800) 982-5296 (970) 204-9681
Fax: (970) 204-9020
Mr. Roger Albrecht, Dir. Franchise Development

We award lawn and tree care franchises to qualified individuals who are willing to become an active partner with us. Our automated residential and commercial services are natural and organic and may be provided pesticide-free. Our mission is to make the customer the focus of everything we do.

BACKGROUND:
Established: 1977;	1st Franchised: 1979
Franchised Units:	40
Company-Owned Units	53
Total Units:	93
Dist.:	US-93; CAN-0; O'seas-0
North America:	14 States
Density:	8 in MT, 5 in ND, 5 in CA
Projected New Units (12 Months):	10
Qualifications:	5, 3, 2, 1, 4, 4
Registered: CA	

FINANCIAL/TERMS:
Cash Investment:	$35-40K
Total Investment:	$35-50K
Minimum Net Worth:	$50K
Fees: Franchise -	$19.5K
Royalty - 7-8.5%;	Ad. - N/A
Earnings Claim Statement:	No
Term of Contract (Years):	20/10
Avg. # Of Employees:	1 FT, 1-2 PT
Passive Ownership:	Allowed
Encourage Conversions:	Yes
Area Develop. Agreements:	No
Sub-Franchising Contracts:	No
Expand In Territory:	Yes
Space Needs: NR SF; FS, HB	

SUPPORT & TRAINING PROVIDED:

Financial Assistance Provided:	Yes(I)
Site Selection Assistance:	N/A
Lease Negotiation Assistance:	N/A
Co-Operative Advertising:	No
Franchisee Assoc./Member:	Yes/Yes
Size Of Corporate Staff:	16
On-Going Support:	C,D,E,G,H,I
Training: 6 Days Fairfield, CA.	

SPECIFIC EXPANSION PLANS:

US:	All United States
Canada:	No
Overseas:	No

≪ ≫

NUTRI-LAWN, ECOLOGY-FRIENDLY LAWN CARE

5397 Eglinton Ave. W., # 110
Toronto, ON M9C 5K6 CANADA
Tel: (800) 396-6096 (416) 620-7100
Fax: (416) 620-7771
E-Mail: nli@nutrilawn.com
Web Site: www.nutrilawn.com
Mr. Larry Maydonik, President

NUTRI-LAWN offers ecology-friendly lawn care to meet increasing consumer demand. We focus on fertilization and reduced control product usage through our spot treating and integrated pest management approach. We create large lawn care operations through our proven program and systems.

BACKGROUND: IFA MEMBER

Established: 1985; 1st Franchised: 1987	
Franchised Units:	37
Company-Owned Units	0
Total Units:	37
Dist.:	US-2; CAN-34; O'seas-1
North America:	2 States, 8 Provinces
Density:	20 in ON, 7 in BC
Projected New Units (12 Months):	6
Qualifications:	5, 4, 1, 3, 3, 5
Registered: VA	

FINANCIAL/TERMS:

Cash Investment:	$30-60K
Total Investment:	$50-100K
Minimum Net Worth:	$100K
Fees: Franchise -	$25K
Royalty - 6%;	Ad. - 1.5%

Earnings Claim Statement:	No
Term of Contract (Years):	5/10
Avg. # Of Employees:	1 FT
Passive Ownership:	Not Allowed
Encourage Conversions:	Yes
Area Develop. Agreements:	Yes
Sub-Franchising Contracts:	No
Expand In Territory:	Yes
Space Needs: 0 SF; SC	

SUPPORT & TRAINING PROVIDED:

Financial Assistance Provided:	No
Site Selection Assistance:	Yes
Lease Negotiation Assistance:	Yes
Co-Operative Advertising:	Yes
Franchisee Assoc./Member:	Yes/Yes
Size Of Corporate Staff:	4
On-Going Support:	B,C,D,E,G,H
Training: 1 Week Toronto, ON.	

SPECIFIC EXPANSION PLANS:

US:	Northeast, Northwest
Canada:	All Canada
Overseas:	All Countries

≪ ≫

NUTRITE HYDRO AGRI CANADA

P.O. Box 1000
Brossard, PQ J4Z 3N2 CANADA
Tel: (800) 561-7449 (450) 462-2555
Fax: (450) 462-3634
E-Mail: Jacques.Cardinal@hydro.com
Mr. M. Jacques Cardinal, Director of Franchising

Your venture - If you dream of starting your own business, or want to add new services to an existing business, you should think seriously about owning a NUTRITE LAWN CARE franchise. The bottom line is - A NUTRITE franchise is a wise investment. Join the NUTRITE group now!

BACKGROUND:

Established: 1967; 1st Franchised: 1984	
Franchised Units:	43
Company-Owned Units	0
Total Units:	43
Dist.:	US-0; CAN-44; O'seas-0
North America:	3 Provinces
Density:	37 in PQ, 5 in ON, 2 in NB
Projected New Units (12 Months):	3
Registered: CA	

FINANCIAL/TERMS:

Cash Investment:	$40K
Total Investment:	$40K
Minimum Net Worth:	$NR
Fees: Franchise -	$10K
Royalty - $3.5K/Yr.;	Ad. - 0%

Earnings Claim Statement:	Yes
Term of Contract (Years):	5/5
Avg. # Of Employees:	2 FT
Passive Ownership:	Allowed
Encourage Conversions:	Yes
Area Develop. Agreements:	No
Sub-Franchising Contracts:	No
Expand In Territory:	No
Space Needs: NR SF; NR	

SUPPORT & TRAINING PROVIDED:

Financial Assistance Provided:	No
Site Selection Assistance:	Yes
Lease Negotiation Assistance:	No
Co-Operative Advertising:	No
Franchisee Assoc./Member:	NR
Size Of Corporate Staff:	30
On-Going Support:	A,B,C,D,F,G,h,i
Training: No Limit on Location.	

SPECIFIC EXPANSION PLANS:

US:	No
Canada:	All Canada
Overseas:	No

≪ ≫

SCOTTS LAWN SERVICE

14111 Scottslawn Rd.
Marysville, OH 43041
Tel: (800) 221-1760 (937) 644-7297
Fax: (937) 644-7422
E-Mail:
jim_miller@scottslawnservice.com
Web Site: www.scottslawnservice.com
Mr. Jim Miller, Director of Franchising

SCOTTS, the leading marketer of home lawn and garden products, has entered the lawn service business, the result ... SCOTTS LAWN SERVICE. As a franchise system, we offer very strong brand name awareness, powerful sales and marketing programs, extensive training and premium products.

BACKGROUND:

Established: 1998; 1st Franchised: 1998	
Franchised Units:	20
Company-Owned Units	12
Total Units:	32
Dist.:	US-32; CAN-0; O'seas-0
North America:	NR
Density:	4 in OH, 3 in GA
Projected New Units (12 Months):	5
Qualifications:	4, 3, 3, 2, 2, 5

Registered: FL,IL,IN,MD,MI,MN,ND, OR,SD,VA,WA,WI

FINANCIAL/TERMS:

Cash Investment:	$30K
Total Investment:	$64.9-146K
Minimum Net Worth:	$100K
Fees: Franchise -	$20-65K
Royalty - 6-10%;	Ad. - 0%
Earnings Claim Statement:	No
Term of Contract (Years):	10/10
Avg. # Of Employees:	2+ FT
Passive Ownership:	Discouraged
Encourage Conversions:	Yes
Area Develop. Agreements:	No
Sub-Franchising Contracts:	No
Expand In Territory:	Yes

Space Needs: 400 SF; FS, HB

SUPPORT & TRAINING PROVIDED:

Financial Assistance Provided:	Yes(I)
Site Selection Assistance:	N/A
Lease Negotiation Assistance:	No
Co-Operative Advertising:	N/A
Franchisee Assoc./Member:	No
Size Of Corporate Staff:	12
On-Going Support:	B,C,D,E,F,H,I

Training: 2 Weeks in Marysville, OH.

SPECIFIC EXPANSION PLANS:

US:	All United States
Canada:	No
Overseas:	No

≪ ≫

SUPER LAWNS
15901Derwood Rd., P. O. Box 5677
Rockville, MD 20855
Tel: (800) 44-LAWN1 (301) 948-8181
Fax: (301) 948-8461
Web Site: www.superlawns.com
Mr. Ron Miller, Vice President

Our system is a modern, profitable approach to lawn care. One person or many, depending upon your desire to succeed. We offer complete training and constant assistance in all areas of business. We'll try to keep you 'One step ahead of the competition.'

BACKGROUND:

Established: 1975;	1st Franchised: 1979
Franchised Units:	22
Company-Owned Units	1
Total Units:	23
Dist.:	US-23; CAN-0; O'seas-0
North America:	5 States
Density:	8 in MD, 5 in VA, 3 in DE
Projected New Units (12 Months):	4
Qualifications:	3, 3, 2, 2, 4, 5
Registered: MD,VA	

FINANCIAL/TERMS:

Cash Investment:	$30K
Total Investment:	$60-70K
Minimum Net Worth:	$60K
Fees: Franchise -	$17.5K
Royalty - 10% Decreasing;	Ad. - 0%
Earnings Claim Statement:	No
Term of Contract (Years):	20/5
Avg. # Of Employees:	1 FT
Passive Ownership:	Discouraged
Encourage Conversions:	N/A
Area Develop. Agreements:	No
Sub-Franchising Contracts:	No
Expand In Territory:	Yes

Space Needs: N/A SF; N/A

SUPPORT & TRAINING PROVIDED:

Financial Assistance Provided:	Yes(B)
Site Selection Assistance:	N/A
Lease Negotiation Assistance:	N/A
Co-Operative Advertising:	Yes
Franchisee Assoc./Member:	No
Size Of Corporate Staff:	3
On-Going Support:	B,C,D,F,I

Training: 7-10 Days Rockville, MD or Elkton, MD and as Needed.

SPECIFIC EXPANSION PLANS:

US:	East of Mississippi
Canada:	No
Overseas:	No

≪ ≫

U. S. LAWNS
4777 Old Winter Garden Rd.
Orlando, FL 33811
Tel: (800) US-LAWNS (407) 522-1630
Fax: (407) 522-1669
E-Mail: info@uslawns.com
Web Site: www.uslawns.com
Mr. Kenneth Hutcheson, Vice President

Train and support franchisees in a commercial landscape market.

BACKGROUND: IFA MEMBER

Established: 1986;	1st Franchised: 1987
Franchised Units:	82

Company-Owned Units	0
Total Units:	82
Dist.:	US-82; CAN-0; O'seas-0
North America:	14 States
Density:	FL, MD, CA
Projected New Units (12 Months):	36
Qualifications:	2, 4, 3, 2, 3, 5
Registered: CA,FL,IL,MD,MI,VA,WI	

FINANCIAL/TERMS:

Cash Investment:	$10-40K
Total Investment:	$40-70K
Minimum Net Worth:	$50K
Fees: Franchise -	$29K
Royalty - 3-4%;	Ad. - 1%
Earnings Claim Statement:	No
Term of Contract (Years):	5/5
Avg. # Of Employees:	8-10 FT
Passive Ownership:	Discouraged
Encourage Conversions:	Yes
Area Develop. Agreements:	Yes
Sub-Franchising Contracts:	No
Expand In Territory:	Yes

Space Needs: NR SF; N/A

SUPPORT & TRAINING PROVIDED:

Financial Assistance Provided:	Yes
Site Selection Assistance:	Yes
Lease Negotiation Assistance:	Yes
Co-Operative Advertising:	Yes
Franchisee Assoc./Member:	Yes/Yes
Size Of Corporate Staff:	18
On-Going Support:	A,b,C,D,G,H,I

Training: 5 Days in FL; 5 Days at Your Location.

SPECIFIC EXPANSION PLANS:

US:	PA,NJ,CT,MA,FL,CA,NC,SC
Canada:	No
Overseas:	No

≪ ≫

WEED MAN
2399 Royal Windsor Dr.
Mississauga, ON L5J 1K9 CANADA
Tel: (905) 823-8550
Fax: (905) 823-4594
E-Mail: weedman@netcom.ca
Web Site: www.weed-man.com
Mr. Michael J. Kernaghan, Vice President

Professional lawn care services.

BACKGROUND:

Established: 1970;	1st Franchised: 1976
Franchised Units:	130
Company-Owned Units	2
Total Units:	132
Dist.:	US-6; CAN-126; O'seas-0
North America:	6 States, 10 Provinces
Density:	NR

Projected New Units (12 Months): 5
Qualifications: 3, 4, 1, 3, 3, 4
Registered: IL,IN,MI,MN,NY,OR,WA,WI

FINANCIAL/TERMS:

Cash Investment: $25K
Total Investment: $75K
Minimum Net Worth: $50K
Fees: Franchise - $20-34K
 Royalty - $7.9K/Vehcl.; Ad. - 20%
Royalty
Earnings Claim Statement: Yes
Term of Contract (Years): 10/10
Avg. # Of Employees: 5 FT
Passive Ownership: Discouraged
Encourage Conversions: Yes
Area Develop. Agreements: Yes
Sub-Franchising Contracts: No
Expand In Territory: Yes
Space Needs: NR SF; HB, SC

SUPPORT & TRAINING PROVIDED:

Financial Assistance Provided: No
Site Selection Assistance: Yes
Lease Negotiation Assistance: No
Co-Operative Advertising: Yes
Franchisee Assoc./Member: No
Size Of Corporate Staff: 9
On-Going Support: B,C,D,F,G,H
Training: 1 Week Mississauga, ON.

SPECIFIC EXPANSION PLANS:

US: Northwest, Central and East
Canada: All Canada
Overseas: Australia

SUPPLEMENTAL LISTING OF FRANCHISORS

Bobby Lawn Care, P.O. Box 35082, London, ON N5W 5Z6 CANADA; (519) 455-5915; Mr. Ron Vanderheide (800) 265-7521; (519) 455-5912

Enviro Masters Lawn Care, P.O. Box 178, Caledon East, ON L0N 1E0 CANADA; (905) 584-0402; Mr. Martin Fielding ; (905) 584-9592

Greenland Irrigation, 150 Ambleside Dr., London, ON N6G 4R1 CANADA; (519) 433-9780; Mr. Barry Smith ; (519) 439-0220

Servistar Home & Garden Showplace, 8600 W. Bryn Mawr Ave., Chicago, IL 60631 ; (773) 695-7049; Mr. Dave Meder (888) 474-9752; (773) 695-5379

Spring-Green Lawn Care, 11909 Spaulding School Dr., Plainfield, IL 60544 ; (815) 436-9056; Ms. Nancy Babyar (800) 435-4051; (815) 436-8777

Terra Systems, 1515 Cliffwood Place, Charlotte, NC 28203 ; (704) 342-0317; Mr. Kevin G. Robke ; (704) 342-0310

Lodging Chapter

23

LODGING INDUSTRY PROFILE

Total # Franchisors in Industry Group	69
Total # Franchised Units in Industry Group	23,700
Total # Company-Owned Units in Industry Group	<u>2,825</u>
Total # Operating Units in Industry Group	26,525
Average # Franchised Units/Franchisor	343.5
Average # Company-Owned Units/Franchisor	<u>40.9</u>
Average # Total Units/Franchisor	384.4
Ratio of Total # Franchised Units/Total # Company-Owned Units	8.4:1
Industry Survey Participants	24
Representing % of Industry	34.8%
Average Franchise Fee*:	$37.3K
Average Total Investment*:	$8,226.6K
Average On-Going Royalty Fee*:	4.3%

If a range was provided, the mid-point of the range was used. See detailed profiles for actual ranges.

FIVE LARGEST PARTICIPANTS IN SURVEY

Company	# Franchised Units	# Co-Owned Units	# Total Units	Franchise Fee	On-Going Royalty	Total Investment
1. Choice Hotels Int'l.	4,371	0	4,371	25-50K	3.5-5.25%	4MM-6MM
2. Bass Hotels & Resorts	2,685	189	2,874	$500/Rm.	5%	40-150K/Rm.
3. Hampton Inn	844	17	861	45K Min.	4%Gross Rm.	3-5MM
4. Motel 6	134	722	856	25K	4%	1-3MM
5. Kampgrounds of Amer.	496	12	508	25K	8%	200K-4MM

All of the data provided are proprietary and should not be quoted without acknowledging *Bond's Franchise Guide.*

AMERICINN INTERNATIONAL

18202 Minnetonka Blvd.
Deephaven, MN 55391
Tel: (612) 476-9020
Fax: (612) 476-7601
E-Mail: franchise@americinn.com
Web Site: www.americinn.com
Mr. Jon D Kennedy, VP Mktg./Fran. Dev.

AMERICINN is an up-scale, limited-service, value-oriented chain. Currently, AMERICINN has over 170 franchises and continues to grow. Typically, the motels are located along major highways in cities with populations of between 10,000 and 300,000. AMERICINN has been successful with both travelers and vacationers because of their up-scale amenities and economy rates.

BACKGROUND:

Established: 1984;   1st Franchised: 1984
Franchised Units: 166
Company-Owned Units   4
Total Units: 170
Dist.:   US-170; CAN-0; O'seas-0
  North America: 17 States
  Density: 64 in MN, 35 in WI,16 in IA
Projected New Units (12 Months):   200
Qualifications: 5, 5, 4, 4, 4,
Registered: All States

FINANCIAL/TERMS:

Cash Investment: $25% Budget
Total Investment: $1.83MM
Minimum Net Worth: $1MM
Fees: Franchise - $30K
  Royalty - 5%;   Ad. - 2%
Earnings Claim Statement: No
Term of Contract (Years):   20
Avg. # Of Employees: 20 FT, 9 PT
Passive Ownership: Allowed
Encourage Conversions: N/A
Area Develop. Agreements: No
Sub-Franchising Contracts: No
Expand In Territory: Yes
Space Needs: 60,000 SF; FS

SUPPORT & TRAINING PROVIDED:

Financial Assistance Provided: Yes(I)
Site Selection Assistance: Yes
Lease Negotiation Assistance: Yes
Co-Operative Advertising: Yes
Franchisee Assoc./Member: Yes/Yes
Size Of Corporate Staff: 50
On-Going Support: a,b,C,D,E,G,H,I
Training: 3 Different Properties, 1 Week at
  Each.

SPECIFIC EXPANSION PLANS:

US: All United States
Canada: All Canada
Overseas: All Countries

BASS HOTELS & RESORTS

3 Ravinia Dr., # 2900
Atlanta, GA 30346
Tel: (770) 604-2166
Fax: (770) 604-2107
E-Mail: hifranchise@basshotels.com
Web Site: www.basshotels.com
Mr. Brown Kessler, VP Franchise Sales

BASS HOTELS & RESORTS, the hotel business of Bass PLC of the United Kingdom, operates or franchises more than 3,000 hotels and 490,000 guest rooms in more than 100 countries and territories. Franchisor of HOLLIDAY INN/EXPRESS, CROWNE PLAZA, STAYBRIDGE SUITES and INTER-CONTINENTAL HOTELS.

BACKGROUND: IFA MEMBER

Established: 1952;   1st Franchised: 1952
Franchised Units: 2,685
Company-Owned Units   189
Total Units: 2,874
Dist.:   US-0; CAN-0; O'seas-0
  North America: 50 States
  Density: 169 in CA,155 in FL,168 TX
Projected New Units (12 Months):   NR
Registered:

FINANCIAL/TERMS:

Cash Investment: $1-20MM
Total Investment: $40-150K/Room
Minimum Net Worth: $Varies
Fees: Franchise - $500/Rm,40Kmin
  Royalty - 5%;   Ad. - 2.5-3%
Earnings Claim Statement: Yes
Term of Contract (Years):   10
Avg. # Of Employees: Varies
Passive Ownership: Allowed
Encourage Conversions: Yes
Area Develop. Agreements: No
Sub-Franchising Contracts: No
Expand In Territory: Yes
Space Needs: NR SF; FS

SUPPORT & TRAINING PROVIDED:

Financial Assistance Provided: NR
Site Selection Assistance: No
Lease Negotiation Assistance: Yes
Co-Operative Advertising: Yes
Franchisee Assoc./Member: Yes
Size Of Corporate Staff: 1,000
On-Going Support: B,c,d,e,G,h
Training: Varying Fees Required. Programs
  Supported by Franchisor.

SPECIFIC EXPANSION PLANS:

US: All United States
Canada: All Canada
Overseas: All Countries

BAYMONT INNS & SUITES

250 E. Wisconsin Ave., # 1750
Milwaukee, WI 53202-1750
Tel: (414) 905-2000
Fax: (414) 905-2496
E-Mail: gilsimon@baymontinns.com
Web Site: www.baymontinns.com
Mr. Gilbert S. Simon, Natl. Director
  Franchise Sales

BAYMONT INNS AND SUITES is positioned to appeal to both business and leisure travelers offering many amenities - frequent travelers' rewards, complimentary breakfast, voice mail, coffee makers and much more for $49.00 - 69.00.

BACKGROUND: IFA MEMBER

Established: 1935;   1st Franchised: 1986
Franchised Units: 76
Company-Owned Units   96
Total Units: 172
Dist.:   US-172; CAN-0; O'seas-0
  North America: 30 States
  Density: 20 in MI, 18 in IL, 17 in WI
Projected New Units (12 Months):   40
Qualifications: 5, 5, 3, 2, 1, 3
Registered: All States

FINANCIAL/TERMS:

Cash Investment: $70%
Total Investment: $3.5MM+
Minimum Net Worth: $3MM
Fees: Franchise - $35K
  Royalty - 5%;   Ad. - 2%
Earnings Claim Statement: Yes
Term of Contract (Years):   20/10
Avg. # Of Employees: 4 FT, 12-18 PT
Passive Ownership: Allowed
Encourage Conversions: Yes
Area Develop. Agreements: Yes
Sub-Franchising Contracts: No
Expand In Territory: No
Space Needs: 2 Acres SF; FS

SUPPORT & TRAINING PROVIDED:

Financial Assistance Provided: Yes(I)
Site Selection Assistance: Yes
Lease Negotiation Assistance: No
Co-Operative Advertising: Yes

Franchisee Assoc./Member: Yes/Yes
Size Of Corporate Staff: 76
On-Going Support: C,D,E,G,H,I
Training: 1-2 Weeks Milwaukee, WI.
SPECIFIC EXPANSION PLANS:
US: All United States
Canada: All Canada
Overseas: No

≪ ≫

BEST INNS & SUITES
13 Corporate Sq., # 250
Atlanta, GA 30329
Tel: (800) TELL-US5 (404) 321-4045
Fax: (404) 321-4482
E-Mail: franchise.info@usfsi.com
Web Site: www.bestinn.com
Mr. Mike Muir, SVP Franchise Sales

BEST INNS & SUITES is a high-quality, mid-level, limited service hotel brand. With 145 hotels open, 31 under construction and another 26 signed agreements, BEST continues to expand around the country. BEST INNS & SUITES is primarily a conversion brand for existing hotel owners looking for a better way to do business. U. S. Franchise Sustems, franchisor of the brand, is a recognized leader in the hotel industry, with 3 growing brands and a reputation for treating our franchisees fairly.

BACKGROUND: IFA MEMBER
Established: 1995; 1st Franchised: 1995
Franchised Units: 145
Company-Owned Units   <u>0</u>
Total Units: 145
Dist.:   US-145; CAN-0; O'seas-0
  North America: 35 States
  Density: 17 in CA, 11 in IL, 9 in OR
Projected New Units (12 Months):   50
Qualifications: 3, 4, 4, 2, 2, 3
Registered: All States
FINANCIAL/TERMS:
Cash Investment: $190-330K
Total Investment: $190K-2.0MM
Minimum Net Worth: $N/A
Fees: Franchise - $35K
  Royalty - 3-5%;   Ad. - 2.5%

Earnings Claim Statement: Yes
Term of Contract (Years):   20/10
Avg. # Of Employees: 10-25 FT
Passive Ownership: Allowed
Encourage Conversions: Yes
Area Develop. Agreements: No
Sub-Franchising Contracts: No
Expand In Territory: Yes
Space Needs: NR SF; FS
SUPPORT & TRAINING PROVIDED:
Financial Assistance Provided: Yes(I)
Site Selection Assistance: No
Lease Negotiation Assistance: Yes
Co-Operative Advertising: Yes
Franchisee Assoc./Member: Yes/Yes
Size Of Corporate Staff: 135
On-Going Support: B,C,D,E,G,H,I
Training: 5 Days Atlanta, GA; 2-5 Days
  On-Site at Hotel.
SPECIFIC EXPANSION PLANS:
US: All United States
Canada: No
Overseas: No

≪ ≫

CANDLEWOOD SUITES/
CAMBRIDGE SUITES
8621 E. 21st St. N., # 200
Wichita, KS 67206
Tel: (316) 631-1361
Fax: (316) 631-1333
E-Mail: bgordon@candlewoodsuites.com
Web Site: www.candlewoodsuites.com
Mr. Chuck Armstrong, VP Franchise
  Sales

CANDLEWOOD SUITES is a unique, high-quality, mid-priced hotel brand designed to deliver exceptional value to both owners and guests. CAMBRIDGE SUITES, established in 1998, is another tremendous opportunity to build or convert an existing hotel into the newest concept in lodging for the up-scale traveler.

BACKGROUND: IFA MEMBER
Established: 1995; 1st Franchised: 1996
Franchised Units: 17
Company-Owned Units   <u>71</u>
Total Units: 88
Dist.:   US-88; CAN-0; O'seas-0

North America: 30 States
Density: 14 in TX, 8 in IL, 8 in CA
Projected New Units (12 Months):   NR
Qualifications: 3, 3, 2, 2, 2, 3
Registered: All States Except HI
FINANCIAL/TERMS:
Cash Investment: $700K-2MM
Total Investment: $3-7MM
Minimum Net Worth: $N/A
Fees: Franchise - $400/Key/40K
  Royalty - 4-5%RR;   Ad. - 1.5%RR
Earnings Claim Statement: Yes
Term of Contract (Years):   20
Avg. # Of Employees: 6-13 FT
Passive Ownership: Allowed
Encourage Conversions: Yes
Area Develop. Agreements: No
Sub-Franchising Contracts: No
Expand In Territory: Yes
Space Needs: 56,628-108,90 SF; FS
SUPPORT & TRAINING PROVIDED:
Financial Assistance Provided: NR
Site Selection Assistance: No
Lease Negotiation Assistance: Yes
Co-Operative Advertising: No
Franchisee Assoc./Member: Yes/Yes
Size Of Corporate Staff: 100
On-Going Support: C,D,G,H,I
Training: Extensive Training Program.
SPECIFIC EXPANSION PLANS:
US: All United States
Canada: All Canada
Overseas: All Countries

≪ ≫

CHOICE HOTELS CANADA
5090 Explorer Dr., # 500
Mississauga, ON L4W 4T9 CANADA
Tel: (905) 602-2222
Fax: (905) 624-7796
E-Mail: franchising@choicehotels.ca
Web Site: www.choicehotels.ca
Mr. Scott T. Duff, VP Franchise Dev.

Canada's largest hotel chain, with over 235 locations open and under development. We franchise 7 brands: CLARION, QUALITY, COMFORT, SLEEP INN, RODEWAY INN, ECONO LODGE & MAINSTAY.

BACKGROUND:
Established: 1993; 1st Franchised: 1993

Franchised Units: 250
Company-Owned Units: 0
Total Units: 250
Dist.: US-0; CAN-250; O'seas-0
  North America: 10 Provinces
  Density: 100 in ON, 45 in PQ, 20 in A
Projected New Units (12 Months): 15
Qualifications: 4, 5, 4, 3, 3, 4
Registered: AB

FINANCIAL/TERMS:
Cash Investment: $500K-1.0MM
Total Investment: $2-30MM
Minimum Net Worth: $1MM
Fees: Franchise - $25-100K
  Royalty - 3-5%; Ad. - 1.7%
Earnings Claim Statement: No
Term of Contract (Years): 20/10
Avg. # Of Employees: 15 FT, 5 PT
Passive Ownership: Allowed
Encourage Conversions: Yes
Area Develop. Agreements: No
Sub-Franchising Contracts: No
Expand In Territory: No
Space Needs: 60,000 SF; FS

SUPPORT & TRAINING PROVIDED:
Financial Assistance Provided: Yes(I)
Site Selection Assistance: Yes
Lease Negotiation Assistance: No
Co-Operative Advertising: Yes
Franchisee Assoc./Member: Yes/Yes
Size Of Corporate Staff: 45
On-Going Support: A,B,C,D,e,G,h
Training: 3 Days to 1 Week On-Site
  Opening; 1-2 Day Seminar On-Going
  On-Site.

SPECIFIC EXPANSION PLANS:
US: No
Canada: All Canada
Overseas: All Countries

<< >>

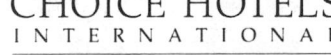

CHOICE HOTELS
INTERNATIONAL
10750 Columbia Pike
Silver Spring, MD 20901-4447
Tel: (800) 547-0007 (301) 592-5000
Fax: (301) 592-6205
E-Mail: franchiseinfo@choicehotels.com
Web Site: www.choicehotels.com
Mr. Steven T. Schultz, Executive VP

CHOICE HOTELS INTERNATIONAL is one of the largest hotel franchises in the world with more than 4,000 hotels, inns, all-suite hotels and resorts in 36 countries: COMFORT, QUALITY, CLARION, SLEEP, RODEWAY, ECONO LODGE and MAINSTAY SUITES.

BACKGROUND: IFA MEMBER
Established: 1980; 1st Franchised: 1981
Franchised Units: 4,371
Company-Owned Units: 0
Total Units: 4,371
Dist.: US-3,234; CAN-234; O'seas-903
  North America: 50 States,10 Provinces
  Density: 223 in TX, 222 in CA, 191 FL
Projected New Units (12 Months): 300
Qualifications: 4, 4, 4, 2, 1, 1
Registered: All States

FINANCIAL/TERMS:
Cash Investment: $10-35% dev. $
Total Investment: $4-6MM
Minimum Net Worth: $Varies
Fees: Franchise - $25-50K
  Royalty - 3.5-5.25%; Ad. - 1-3.5% Rev.
Earnings Claim Statement: Yes
Term of Contract (Years): 20/None
Avg. # Of Employees: Varies
Passive Ownership: Allowed
Encourage Conversions: Yes
Area Develop. Agreements: No
Sub-Franchising Contracts: No
Expand In Territory: No
Space Needs: 31,000-33,000 SF; FS

SUPPORT & TRAINING PROVIDED:
Financial Assistance Provided: Yes(B)
Site Selection Assistance: No
Lease Negotiation Assistance: N/A
Co-Operative Advertising: N/A
Franchisee Assoc./Member: Yes/Yes
Size Of Corporate Staff: 2,025
On-Going Support: C,D,E,G,h,I
Training: 1 Week in Silver Spring, MD.

SPECIFIC EXPANSION PLANS:
US: All United States
Canada: All Canada
Overseas: All Countries

<< >>

COUNTRY INNS & SUITES BY
CARLSON
P.O. Box 59159, Carlson Pkwy.
Minneapolis, MN 55459-8203
Tel: (800) 456-4000 (763) 212-2525
Fax: (763) 212-1338
E-Mail: njohnson@countryinns.com
Web Site: www.countryinns.com
Ms. Nancy Johnson, SVP of Development

A cozy stay at a comfortable price®

COUNTRY INNS & SUITES locations feature traditional architecture and sophisticated residential interior design with hardwood flooring and decorative ceiling borders. Each hotel welcomes guests with traditional furnishings that blend rich woods and elegant patterned fabrics. The brand is known for its consistently high-quality accommodations and personal, warm hospitality.

BACKGROUND: IFA MEMBER
Established: 1987; 1st Franchised: 1987
Franchised Units: 238
Company-Owned Units: 4
Total Units: 242
Dist.: US-220; CAN-13; O'seas-9
  North America: 34 States, 6 Provinces
  Density: 38 in MN, 21 in WI, 19 in GA
Projected New Units (12 Months): 54
Qualifications: 5, 5, 5, 3, 5, 5
Registered: All States

FINANCIAL/TERMS:
Cash Investment: $780K-1.45MM
Total Investment: $3.1-5.4MM
Minimum Net Worth: $775K
Fees: Franchise - $40K
  Royalty - 3.5-4.5%; Ad. - 2-3%
Earnings Claim Statement: Yes
Term of Contract (Years): 15/0
Avg. # Of Employees: 10 FT, 6 PT
Passive Ownership: Allowed
Encourage Conversions: Yes
Area Develop. Agreements: No
Sub-Franchising Contracts: No
Expand In Territory: No
Space Needs: 65,340 SF; FS

SUPPORT & TRAINING PROVIDED:
Financial Assistance Provided: Yes(I)
Site Selection Assistance: No
Lease Negotiation Assistance: No
Co-Operative Advertising: Yes
Franchisee Assoc./Member: No
Size Of Corporate Staff: 41
On-Going Support: B,C,D,E,G,H
Training: 1 Week Minneapolis, MN (Brand Orientation); 3 Days Opening On-Site; 3 Days New Franchisee.

SPECIFIC EXPANSION PLANS:
US: All United States
Canada: All Canada
Overseas: Europe, Asia

‹‹ ››

DOUBLETREE HOTEL SYSTEMS

755 Crossover Ln.
Memphis, TN 38117
Tel: (901) 374-5000
Fax: (901) 374-5051
Web Site: www.doubletreehotels.com
Mr. Steve Bollenbach, President

DOUBLETREE HOTELS CORPOR-ATION, headquartered in Phoenix, is one of the nation's leading hotel management and franchising companies, with more than 170 hotels in 37 states, the District of Columbia and Mexico. DOUBLETREE properties currently extend into 3 market segments: DOUBLETREE HOTELS - upscale, first-class, full-service hotels; DOUBLETREE GUEST SUITES - first-class, full-service all suite hotels and CLUB HOTELS BY DOUBLETREE.

BACKGROUND:

Established: 1989; 1st Franchised: 1989	
Franchised Units:	128
Company-Owned Units	127
Total Units:	255
Dist.:	US-251; CAN-1; O'seas-3
North America:	29 States
Density:	25 in CA, 18 in FL, 11 in TX
Projected New Units (12 Months): 10-20	
Qualifications:	5, 5, 5, 2, 3, 5
Registered: All States	

FINANCIAL/TERMS:

Cash Investment:	$10-15MM
Total Investment:	$20-38MM
Minimum Net Worth:	$N/A
Fees: Franchise -	$25-50K
Royalty - 2-4%;	Ad. - 3.5%
Earnings Claim Statement:	No
Term of Contract (Years):	10/10
Avg. # Of Employees:	100 FT
Passive Ownership:	Allowed
Encourage Conversions:	Yes
Area Develop. Agreements:	Yes/Varies
Sub-Franchising Contracts:	No
Expand In Territory:	Yes
Space Needs: 5-10 Acres SF; FS	

SUPPORT & TRAINING PROVIDED:

Financial Assistance Provided:	No
Site Selection Assistance:	No
Lease Negotiation Assistance:	No
Co-Operative Advertising:	Yes
Franchisee Assoc./Member:	No
Size Of Corporate Staff:	300
On-Going Support:	A,b,c,d,h
Training: NR	

SPECIFIC EXPANSION PLANS:

US:	All United States
Canada:	All Canada
Overseas:	No

‹‹ ››

EMBASSY SUITES®

A DESIGN *for* LIVING®

EMBASSY SUITES HOTELS

9336 Civic Center Dr.
Beverly Hills, CA 90210
Tel: (800) 286-0645
Fax: (310) 205-7655
Web Site: www.embassy-suites.com
Mr. Bill Fortier, SVP Franchise Dev.

Hilton Hotels Corp. is the franchisor/ operator of the DOUBLETREE HOTELS, EMBASSY SUITES HOTELS, HAMPTON INN & SUITES, HOME-WOOD SUITES, DOUBLETREE CLUB, RED LION HOTELS. The company franchises, operates or owns hotels throughout the United States, Canada, Mexico and Latin America. Promus is headquartered in Memphis, Tennessee and has approximately 40,000 employees.

BACKGROUND: IFA MEMBER

Established: 1983; 1st Franchised: 1983	
Franchised Units:	63
Company-Owned Units	85
Total Units:	148
Dist.:	US-0; CAN-0; O'seas-0
North America:	38 States
Density:	32 in CA, 26 in TX, 23 in FL
Projected New Units (12 Months): NR	
Registered:	

FINANCIAL/TERMS:

Cash Investment:	$3MM
Total Investment:	$15-30MM
Minimum Net Worth:	$3MM
Fees: Franchise -	$100K Min.
Royalty - 4% Gross Rm. Rev;Ad. - 3.5% Rm.Rev	
Earnings Claim Statement:	No
Term of Contract (Years):	20
Avg. # Of Employees:	75 FT
Passive Ownership:	Allowed
Encourage Conversions:	NR
Area Develop. Agreements:	No
Sub-Franchising Contracts:	No
Expand In Territory:	Yes
Space Needs: 153,000 SF; NR	

SUPPORT & TRAINING PROVIDED:

Financial Assistance Provided:	NR
Site Selection Assistance:	No
Lease Negotiation Assistance:	Yes
Co-Operative Advertising:	Yes
Franchisee Assoc./Member:	No
Size Of Corporate Staff:	850
On-Going Support:	A,b,C,D,E,G,h
Training: 2 Weeks in Memphis, TN.	

SPECIFIC EXPANSION PLANS:

US:	All United States
Canada:	NR
Overseas:	NR

‹‹ ››

HAMPTON INN

755 Crossover Ln.
Memphis, TN 38117
Tel: (800) HAMPTON (901) 374-5000
Fax: (901) 374-5008
Web Site: www.hampton-inn.com
Mr. Mickey Powell, SVP Franchise Dev.

Promus Hotel Corporation is the franchisor/ operator of the DOUBLETREE HOTELS, EMBASSY SUITES, HAMP-TON INN & SUITES, HOMEWOOD SUITES, DOUBLETREE CLUB, RED LION HOTELS. The company franchises, operates or owns hotels throughout the United States, Canada, Mexico and Latin America. Promus is headquartered in Memphis, Tennessee and has approximately 40,000 employees.

BACKGROUND: IFA MEMBER

Established: 1983; 1st Franchised: 1983	
Franchised Units:	844
Company-Owned Units	17
Total Units:	861
Dist.:	US-0; CAN-0; O'seas-0
North America:	48 States
Density:	110 in FL,88 in TX,78 in NC
Projected New Units (12 Months): NR	
Registered:	

FINANCIAL/TERMS:

Cash Investment:	$750K
Total Investment:	$3-5MM
Minimum Net Worth:	$1.5 MM
Fees: Franchise -	$45K Min.
Royalty - 4% Gross Rm. Rev; Ad. - 4% Rm. Rev.	
Earnings Claim Statement:	No
Term of Contract (Years):	20
Avg. # Of Employees:	20 FT
Passive Ownership:	Allowed
Encourage Conversions:	NR
Area Develop. Agreements:	No
Sub-Franchising Contracts:	No

Expand In Territory: Yes
Space Needs: 110 SF; NR
SUPPORT & TRAINING PROVIDED:
Financial Assistance Provided: NR
Site Selection Assistance: No
Lease Negotiation Assistance: Yes
Co-Operative Advertising: Yes
Franchisee Assoc./Member: No
Size Of Corporate Staff: 850
On-Going Support: A,b,C,D,E,G,h
Training: 2 Weeks Memphis, TN.
SPECIFIC EXPANSION PLANS:
US: All United States
Canada: NR
Overseas: NR

<< >>

HAWTHORN SUITES®

HAWTHORN SUITES HOTELS INTERNATIONAL

13 Corporate Sq., # 250
Atlanta, GA 30329
Tel: (888) 777-7511 (404) 321-4045
Fax: (404) 321-4482
E-Mail: franchise.info@usfsi.com
Web Site: www.hawthorn.com
Mr. Tim Muir, SVP Franchise Sales

HAWTHORN SUITES is one of the fastest-growing suite-oriented hotel brands in the US. With 140 hotels open, 23 under construction and another 115 executed agreements in place, HAWTHORN continues to expand in major and tertiary markets. The Hyatt reservations systems provides reservations referrals for HAWTHORN when a Hyatt is unavailable in the same market. Proven track record of successful development, strong operating performance and sustainable growth in mid- to upper-level market.

BACKGROUND: IFA MEMBER
Established: 1995; 1st Franchised: 1995
Franchised Units: 140
Company-Owned Units 0
Total Units: 140
Dist.: US-139; CAN-0; O'seas-1
 North America: 26 States
 Density: 13 in TX, 11 in OR, 10 in IL
Projected New Units (12 Months): 25
Qualifications: 4, 4, 4, 2, 2, 3
Registered: All States
FINANCIAL/TERMS:
Cash Investment: $200K-2.0MM

Total Investment: $3.1-6.9MM
Minimum Net Worth: $N/A
Fees: Franchise - $40K
 Royalty - 5%; Ad. - 2.5%
Earnings Claim Statement: Yes
Term of Contract (Years): 20/10
Avg. # Of Employees: 20-100FT
Passive Ownership: Allowed
Encourage Conversions: Yes
Area Develop. Agreements: No
Sub-Franchising Contracts: No
Expand In Territory: Yes
Space Needs: NR SF; FS
SUPPORT & TRAINING PROVIDED:
Financial Assistance Provided: Yes(I)
Site Selection Assistance: No
Lease Negotiation Assistance: Yes
Co-Operative Advertising: Yes
Franchisee Assoc./Member: Yes/Yes
Size Of Corporate Staff: 135
On-Going Support: B,C,D,E,G,H,I
Training: 5 Days Training in Atlanta, GA;
 5 Days Sales Training in Atlanta, GA.
SPECIFIC EXPANSION PLANS:
US: All United States
Canada: All Canada
Overseas: Europe, South America, Latin
 America.

<< >>

HILTON INNS

9336 Civic Center Dr.
Beverly Hills, CA 90210
Tel: (800) 286-0645 (310) 278-4321
Fax: (310) 205-7655
E-Mail: christine_cook@hilton.com
Web Site: www.hilton.com
Mr. James Abrahamson, SVP Franchise
 Development

Internationally-recognized hotel brand. Travelers the world over equate the name "HILTON" with an outstanding lodging experience. We continue to provide solid, innovative operations and have set an industry standard for training and development. We offer franchisees a highly-successful, centralized, reservation-referral system backed by aggressive national marketing programs.

BACKGROUND: IFA MEMBER
Established: 1919; 1st Franchised: 1967
Franchised Units: 177
Company-Owned Units 68
Total Units: 245
Dist.: US-228; CAN-0; O'seas-17
 North America: 40 States
 Density: 33 in CA, 23 in FL, 20 in TX

Projected New Units (12 Months): 48
Qualifications: 5, 5, 5, 3, 1, 3
Registered: CA,FL,IN,MD,MI,NY,ND,
 OR,RI,WA,WI,DC
FINANCIAL/TERMS:
Cash Investment: $3-5MM
Total Investment: $15-25MM
Minimum Net Worth: $N/A
Fees: Franchise - $20K+
 Royalty - 5%; Ad. - 1%
Earnings Claim Statement: No
Term of Contract (Years): 10/5
Avg. # Of Employees: 150 FT
Passive Ownership: Allowed
Encourage Conversions: Yes
Area Develop. Agreements: No
Sub-Franchising Contracts: No
Expand In Territory: Yes
Space Needs: 135,000 SF; NR
SUPPORT & TRAINING PROVIDED:
Financial Assistance Provided: No
Site Selection Assistance: N/A
Lease Negotiation Assistance: No
Co-Operative Advertising: Yes
Franchisee Assoc./Member: No
Size Of Corporate Staff: 600
On-Going Support: b,C,D,d,G,H
Training: 4 Days Dallas, TX; 3 Days
 Beverly Hills, CA; 3 Days Regional
 Office.
SPECIFIC EXPANSION PLANS:
US: All United States
Canada: All Canada
Overseas: Mexico

<< >>

HOMEWOOD SUITES HOTEL

HOMEWOOD SUITES BY HILTON

9336 Civic Center Dr.
Beverly Hills, CA 90210
Tel: (800) 286-0645 (310) 278-4321
Fax: (310) 205-7655
E-Mail: bill-fortier@hilton.com
Web Site: www.homewoodfranchise.com
Mr. Bill Fortier, SVP Franchise Dev.

Hilton Hotels Corp. develops, owns, manages or franchises 1,800 hotels, resorts and vacation ownership properties. Its portfolio includes HILTON, DOUBLE-

TREE, EMBASSY SUITES HOTELS, HAMPTON INN, HAMPTON INNS & SUITES, HARRISON CONFERENCE CENTERS, HILTON CAMDEN INN, HOMEWOOD SUITES BY HILTON, RED LION HOTELS & INNS and CONRAD INTERNATIONAL

BACKGROUND: IFA MEMBER
Established: 1988;   1st Franchised: 1988
Franchised Units: 64
Company-Owned Units   30
Total Units: 94
Dist.:   US-94; CAN-0; O'seas-0
  North America: 32 States
  Density: 25 in TX, 9 in FL, 8 IN nc
Projected New Units (12 Months):   19
Registered:
FINANCIAL/TERMS:
Cash Investment: $1.5MM
Total Investment: $6-12MM
Minimum Net Worth: $1.5MM
Fees: Franchise - $45K Min.
  Royalty - 4% Gross Rm. Rev; Ad. - 4% Rm. Rev.
Earnings Claim Statement: No
Term of Contract (Years):   20/20
Avg. # Of Employees: 25 FT
Passive Ownership: Allowed
Encourage Conversions: Yes
Area Develop. Agreements: No
Sub-Franchising Contracts: No
Expand In Territory: Yes
Space Needs: 110,000 SF; N/A
SUPPORT & TRAINING PROVIDED:
Financial Assistance Provided: N/A
Site Selection Assistance: No
Lease Negotiation Assistance: Yes
Co-Operative Advertising: Yes
Franchisee Assoc./Member: No
Size Of Corporate Staff: 850
On-Going Support: A,b,C,D,E,G,h
Training: 2 Weeks in Memphis, TN.
SPECIFIC EXPANSION PLANS:
US: All United States
Canada: All Canada
Overseas: All Countries

≪   ≫

HOSPITALITY INTERNATIONAL
1726 Montreal Circle
Tucker, GA 30084
Tel: (800) 892-8405 (770) 270-1180
Fax: (770) 270-1077

E-Mail: hospitality@reservahost.com
Web Site: www.reservahost.com
Ms. Chhaya Patel, Franchise Dev. Coor.

Hotel franchisor of MASTER HOSTS INNS AND RESORTS, RED CARPET INN, SCOTTISH INNS, PASSPORT INN, DOWNTOWNER INNS and SUNDOWNER INNS, with over 232 franchised properties. HOSPITALITY INTERNATIONAL is proud of the fact that approximately 75% of its current franchisees are minorities. The company is actively pursuing the addition of new minority-owned franchises in all of the U.S.

BACKGROUND:
Established: 1982;   1st Franchised: 1982
Franchised Units: 232
Company-Owned Units   0
Total Units: 232
Dist.:   US-232; CAN-0; O'seas-0
  North America: 35 States
  Density: 34 in FL, 40 in GA, 16 in TN
Projected New Units (12 Months):   25
Qualifications: 3, 5, 4, 3, 2, 5
Registered: All States Except HI,WA
FINANCIAL/TERMS:
Cash Investment: $70-200K
Total Investment: $1.0-5.0MM
Minimum Net Worth: $Varies
Fees: Franchise - $2.5-5K
  Royalty - $2-3.5K;   Ad. - 2%
Earnings Claim Statement: No
Term of Contract (Years):   5
Avg. # Of Employees: 6 FT, 3 PT
Passive Ownership: Allowed
Encourage Conversions: Yes
Area Develop. Agreements: No
Sub-Franchising Contracts: No
Expand In Territory: N/A
Space Needs: 288/Guest SF; N/A
SUPPORT & TRAINING PROVIDED:
Financial Assistance Provided: Yes(I)
Site Selection Assistance: Yes
Lease Negotiation Assistance: Yes
Co-Operative Advertising: Yes
Franchisee Assoc./Member: Yes/Yes
Size Of Corporate Staff: 36
On-Going Support: B,C,D,E,G,H,I
Training: 2 Days in Tucker, GA.
SPECIFIC EXPANSION PLANS:
US: All United States
Canada: All Canada
Overseas: Mexico, Asia, South America

≪   ≫

KAMPGROUNDS OF AMERICA/ KOA
P.O. Box 30558
Billings, MT 59114
Tel: (800) 548-7239 (406) 248-7444
Fax: (406) 254-7440
E-Mail: licensing@koa.net
Web Site: www.koakampgrounds.com
Mr. Arthur Peterson, CEO

KAMPGROUNDS OF AMERICA is North America's largest franchise system of open-to-the public campgrounds; no membership fees or annual dues are required. All KOA campgrounds offer RV and tent sites; 90% also offer Kamping Kabins. Nearly 2 million copies of the KOA directory are printed and distributed to campers. KOA campgrounds are located in 45 of the contiguous United States, 8 Canadian Provinces, Mexico and Japan.

BACKGROUND: IFA MEMBER
Established: 1961;   1st Franchised: 1962
Franchised Units: 496
Company-Owned Units   12
Total Units: 508
Dist.:   US-463; CAN-34; O'seas-11
  North America: 45 States, 8 Provinces
  Density: 30 in CA, 30 in FL, 29 in CO
Projected New Units (12 Months):   8
Qualifications: 5, 3, 2, 3, 4, 4
Registered: All States
FINANCIAL/TERMS:
Cash Investment: $100-500K
Total Investment: $200K-4MM
Minimum Net Worth: $200K
Fees: Franchise - $25K
  Royalty - 8%;   Ad. - 2%
Earnings Claim Statement: Yes
Term of Contract (Years):   10/10
Avg. # Of Employees: 5 PT (Varies)
Passive Ownership: Discouraged
Encourage Conversions: Yes
Area Develop. Agreements: No

315

Sub-Franchising Contracts: No
Expand In Territory: Yes
Space Needs: 5+ acres SF; NR
SUPPORT & TRAINING PROVIDED:
Financial Assistance Provided: No
Site Selection Assistance: Yes
Lease Negotiation Assistance: Yes
Co-Operative Advertising: Yes
Franchisee Assoc./Member: Yes/Yes
Size Of Corporate Staff: 65
On-Going Support: A,B,C,D,E,F,G,h,I
Training: 2 Days at Customer Location; 3
Days at Billings, MT; 5 Days at Billings,
MT.
SPECIFIC EXPANSION PLANS:
US: All United States
Canada: All Canada
Overseas: Europe, Central America,
Mexico

≪ ≫

MICROTEL INNS & SUITES
13 Corporate Square, # 250
Atlanta, GA 30329
Tel: (888) 771-7171 (404) 321-4045
Fax: (404) 231-4482
E-Mail: franchise.info@usfsi.com
Web Site: www.microtelinn.com
Mr. Tim Muir, SVP Franchise Sales

MICROTEL INNS & SUITES is one of
the fastest-growing, all-new construction
budget hotel franchise brands in the
US. With nearly 215 hotels open, 37
under construction and another 226 signed
agreements in place, MICROTEL is
positioned for continued growth.
MICROTEL offers a proven track record
of successful development, strong
operating performance and sustainable
growth in the budget market. If you are
looking to build a budget hotel, you need
to look into MICROTEL.

BACKGROUND: IFA MEMBER
Established: 1995; 1st Franchised: 1995
Franchised Units: 215
Company-Owned Units 0
Total Units: 215

Dist.: US-212; CAN-0; O'seas-3
North America: 46 States
Density: 15 in TX, 12 in NC, 11 in TN
Projected New Units (12 Months): 35
Qualifications: 3, 4, 4, 2, 2, 3
Registered: All States
FINANCIAL/TERMS:
Cash Investment: $200-500K
Total Investment: $2.5-3.4MM
Minimum Net Worth: $N/A
Fees: Franchise - $35K
Royalty - 4-6%; Ad. - 2-3%
Earnings Claim Statement: Yes
Term of Contract (Years): 20/10
Avg. # Of Employees: 10-25 FT
Passive Ownership: Allowed
Encourage Conversions: No
Area Develop. Agreements: No
Sub-Franchising Contracts: No
Expand In Territory: Yes
Space Needs: NR SF; FS
SUPPORT & TRAINING PROVIDED:
Financial Assistance Provided: Yes(I)
Site Selection Assistance: No
Lease Negotiation Assistance: Yes
Co-Operative Advertising: Yes
Franchisee Assoc./Member: Yes/Yes
Size Of Corporate Staff: 135
On-Going Support: B,C,D,E,G,H,I
Training: 5 Days Training in Atlanta, GA.
SPECIFIC EXPANSION PLANS:
US: All United States
Canada: All Canada
Overseas: Europe, South America

≪ ≫

MOTEL 6
14651 Dallas Pkwy., # 500
Dallas, TX 75240
Tel: (888) 842-2942 (972) 702-6951
Fax: (972) 386-4107
E-Mail: arcioto@airmail.net
Web Site: www.motel6.com
Mr. Dean Savas, Vice President Franchise

Quality product, proven operational results,
easy to operate. Many open motels
available. Well-established brand. Part of
Accor organization, largest owner/
operator of economy lodging in the U.S.

BACKGROUND: IFA MEMBER
Established: 1962; 1st Franchised: 1996
Franchised Units: 134
Company-Owned Units 722
Total Units: 856
Dist.: US-856; CAN-0; O'seas-0
North America: 48 States
Density: 172 in CA, 95 in TX, 44 AZ

Projected New Units (12 Months): 50
Qualifications: 5, 5, 4, 1, 4, 4
Registered: All States
FINANCIAL/TERMS:
Cash Investment: $100-500K
Total Investment: $1-3MM
Minimum Net Worth: $N/A
Fees: Franchise - $25K
Royalty - 4%; Ad. - 3.5%
Earnings Claim Statement: Yes
Term of Contract (Years): 10-15/10
Avg. # Of Employees: 2-4 FT, 4-10 PT
Passive Ownership: Allowed
Encourage Conversions: Yes
Area Develop. Agreements: Yes/2-5
Sub-Franchising Contracts: No
Expand In Territory: No
Space Needs: 69,000 SF; FS
SUPPORT & TRAINING PROVIDED:
Financial Assistance Provided: No
Site Selection Assistance: No
Lease Negotiation Assistance: No
Co-Operative Advertising: N/A
Franchisee Assoc./Member: Yes/No
Size Of Corporate Staff: 500
On-Going Support: B,C,D,G,I
Training: 1.5 Weeks Dallas, TX for Owners
and Managers.
SPECIFIC EXPANSION PLANS:
US: All U.S. -- Emphasis on East
Canada: All Canada
Overseas: No

≪ ≫

RADISSON HOTELS
WORLDWIDE
P.O. Box 59159, Carlson Pkwy.
Minneapolis, MN 55459-8204
Tel: (800) 333-3333 (612) 212-5526
Fax: (612) 212-3400
E-Mail: abender@carlson.com
Web Site: www.radisson.com
Mr. T. Peter Blyth, SVP Development

RADISSON HOTELS WORLDWIDE is
a leader in the hotel industry which operates,
manages and franchises nearly 400 up-scale
hotels and resorts in 52 countries.

BACKGROUND: IFA MEMBER
Established: 1962; 1st Franchised: 1987
Franchised Units: 391
Company-Owned Units 7
Total Units: 398
Dist.: US-398; CAN-0; O'seas-0
North America: 45 States
Density: 30 in CA, 35 in FL, 17 in TX
Projected New Units (12 Months): NR
Registered:

FINANCIAL/TERMS:
Cash Investment: $50K
Total Investment: $22-44MM
Minimum Net Worth: $Varies
Fees: Franchise - $50K
  Royalty - 4%; Ad. - 3.75%
Earnings Claim Statement: Yes
Term of Contract (Years): 15/0
Avg. # Of Employees: Varies
Passive Ownership: NR
Encourage Conversions: NR
Area Develop. Agreements: No
Sub-Franchising Contracts: No
Expand In Territory: Yes
Space Needs: 150,000 SF; Hotel

SUPPORT & TRAINING PROVIDED:
Financial Assistance Provided: NR
Site Selection Assistance: No
Lease Negotiation Assistance: No
Co-Operative Advertising: No
Franchisee Assoc./Member: No
Size Of Corporate Staff: 72
On-Going Support: b,C,D,E,G,h,I
Training: GM Certification, Yes I Can
  Training.

SPECIFIC EXPANSION PLANS:
US: All United States
Canada: NR
Overseas: NR

≪≫

RAMADA FRANCHISE CANADA, INC.
36 Toronto St., # 750
Toronto, ON M5C 2C5 CANADA
Tel: (416) 361-1010
Fax: (416) 361-9050
Web Site: www.ramada.ca
Mr. Timothy M. Whitehead, Vice
  President

Multi-tiered hotel franchise organization, with representation across Canada. 41 PLAZA INN and limited properties comprising good rooms nationwide. Franchise offers marketing, training, advertising, loyalty programs and site selection.

BACKGROUND: IFA MEMBER
Established: 1991; 1st Franchised: 1992
Franchised Units: 41
Company-Owned Units 0
Total Units: 41
Dist.: US-0; CAN-41; O'seas-0
  North America: 8 Provinces
  Density: 20 in ON, 12 in BC, 4 in PQ
Projected New Units (12 Months): 8-10

Qualifications: 5, 4, 1, 5, 1, 5
Registered: AB
FINANCIAL/TERMS:
Cash Investment: $1-7MM
Total Investment: $2-20MM
Minimum Net Worth: $Varies
Fees: Franchise - $35K
  Royalty - 3%; Ad. - 4%
Earnings Claim Statement: No
Term of Contract (Years): 5/5/5/5
Avg. # Of Employees: 0.4/Room; 80FT, 20PT
Passive Ownership: Allowed
Encourage Conversions: Yes
Area Develop. Agreements: Yes/5
Sub-Franchising Contracts: No
Expand In Territory: Yes
Space Needs: NR SF; FS

SUPPORT & TRAINING PROVIDED:
Financial Assistance Provided: N/A
Site Selection Assistance: Yes
Lease Negotiation Assistance: Yes
Co-Operative Advertising: Yes
Franchisee Assoc./Member: Yes/Yes
Size Of Corporate Staff: 15
On-Going Support: A,B,C,D,E,G,H,I
Training: 3-5 Days On-Site.

SPECIFIC EXPANSION PLANS:
US: No
Canada: All Canada
Overseas: No

≪≫

RED ROOF INNS
14651 Dallas Pkwy., # 500
Dallas, TX 75240
Tel: (888) 842-2942 (972) 702-5963
Fax: (972) 702-3610
E-Mail: arcinfo@airmail.net
Web Site: www.redroofinns.com
Mr. Dean Savas, VP Franchise

RED ROOF is a strong, proven brand, delivering excellent results. Now a part of Accor, the world's leading owner/operator in economy lodging. Through franchising, this brand offers many opportunities to interested entrepreneurs in open markets throughout the U.S.

BACKGROUND: IFA MEMBER
Established: 1972; 1st Franchised: 1996
Franchised Units: 70
Company-Owned Units 258
Total Units: 328
Dist.: US-328; CAN-0; O'seas-0
  North America: 39 States
  Density: 35 in OH, 29 in TX, 23 in MI

Projected New Units (12 Months): NR
Registered:
FINANCIAL/TERMS:
Cash Investment: $100-500K
Total Investment: $2.6-5.0MM
Minimum Net Worth: $N/A
Fees: Franchise - $30K
  Royalty - 4.5%; Ad. - 4%
Earnings Claim Statement: Yes
Term of Contract (Years): 20/10
Avg. # Of Employees: 2-4 FT, 4-10 PT
Passive Ownership: Allowed
Encourage Conversions: NR
Area Develop. Agreements: Yes
Sub-Franchising Contracts: No
Expand In Territory: No
Space Needs: 93,000+ SF; Hotel

SUPPORT & TRAINING PROVIDED:
Financial Assistance Provided: NR
Site Selection Assistance: N/A
Lease Negotiation Assistance: N/A
Co-Operative Advertising: N/A
Franchisee Assoc./Member: Yes/Yes
Size Of Corporate Staff: 500
On-Going Support: B,C,D,e,g,H,I
Training: 1.5 Weeks for Owners and
  Managers in Dallas, TX.

SPECIFIC EXPANSION PLANS:
US: All United States
Canada: NR
Overseas: NR

≪≫

U. S. FRANCHISE SYSTEMS
13 Corporate Square, # 250
Atlanta, GA 30329
Tel: (404) 321-4045
Fax: (404) 235-7460
E-Mail: steve.romaniello@usfsi.com
Web Site: www.usfsi.com
Mr. Steve Romaniello, EVP Franchise
  Sales/Admin.

Hotel franchisor of MICROTEL INNS & SUITES, BEST INNS & SUITES and HAWTHORN SUITES brands. MICROTEL -- all new construction, budget. BEST INNS -- middle level limited service. HAWTHORN -- upscale, suite-oriented brand. USFS is known as the "fair franchisor" with the most 2-sided agreement, lower than average fee structure, and no-hidden fees. Brands range from low-capital requirements (MICROTEL) to high (HAWTHORN).

BACKGROUND:
Established: 1995; 1st Franchised: 1995

Franchised Units: 350
Company-Owned Units 0
Total Units: 350
Dist.: US-267; CAN-0; O'seas-2
North America: 49 States
Density: NR
Projected New Units (12 Months): 200
Qualifications: 4, 4, 4, 3, 3, 4
Registered: All States
FINANCIAL/TERMS:
Cash Investment: $300K-2MM
Total Investment: $1.2-7MM
Minimum Net Worth: $N/A
Fees: Franchise - $35-40K
Royalty - 5-6%; Ad. - 2.5%
Earnings Claim Statement: Yes
Term of Contract (Years): 20/10
Avg. # Of Employees: 10-25 FT
Passive Ownership: Allowed
Encourage Conversions: Yes
Area Develop. Agreements: No
Sub-Franchising Contracts: No
Expand In Territory: Yes
Space Needs: 45,000 SF; FS, Raw land for
development
SUPPORT & TRAINING PROVIDED:
Financial Assistance Provided: Yes(I)
Site Selection Assistance: No
Lease Negotiation Assistance: Yes
Co-Operative Advertising: No
Franchisee Assoc./Member: Yes
Size Of Corporate Staff: 150
On-Going Support: B,C,D,E,G,H,I
Training: 3-4 Days Atlanta, GA; On-Site
as Needed.
SPECIFIC EXPANSION PLANS:
US: All United States
Canada: All Canada
Overseas: All Countries

≪≪ ≫≫

WOODFIELD SUITES
250 E. Wisconsin Ave., # 1750
Milwaukee, WI 53202
Tel: (414) 905-1382
Fax: (414) 905-2000
E-Mail: gilsimon@baymontinns.com
Web Site: www.marcuscorp.com
Mr. Gil Simon, Director of Franchise
Sales

WOODFIELD SUITES is positioned to appeal to both business and longer term business travelers offering many amenities - complimentary executive continental breakfast, complimentary hospitality and Jacuzzi suites and fully-equipped kitchens available in all suites, including a microwave, oven, refrigerator, coffeemaker. Suites also include an ironing board, hair dryer and voice mail.

BACKGROUND: IFA MEMBER
Established: 1988; 1st Franchised: 1998
Franchised Units: 0
Company-Owned Units 8
Total Units: 8
Dist.: US-8; CAN-0; O'seas-0
North America: 5 States
Density: 3 in WI, 1 in IL, 1 in TX
Projected New Units (12 Months): 0
Qualifications: 5, 5, 3, 2, 1, 3
Registered: All States
FINANCIAL/TERMS:
Cash Investment: $70%
Total Investment: $8.6-9.8MM
Minimum Net Worth: $8-9MM
Fees: Franchise - $30K
Royalty - 4.5%; Ad. - 1%
Earnings Claim Statement: No
Term of Contract (Years): 20/0
Avg. # Of Employees: 9 FT, 18-23 PT
Passive Ownership: Allowed
Encourage Conversions: Yes
Area Develop. Agreements: No
Sub-Franchising Contracts: No
Expand In Territory: Yes
Space Needs: 130,680 (3ac) SF; FS
SUPPORT & TRAINING PROVIDED:
Financial Assistance Provided: No
Site Selection Assistance: Yes
Lease Negotiation Assistance: No
Co-Operative Advertising: Yes
Franchisee Assoc./Member: No
Size Of Corporate Staff: 4
On-Going Support: C,d,e,h,I
Training: 1 Week in Milwaukee, WI.
SPECIFIC EXPANSION PLANS:
US: All United States
Canada: No
Overseas: No

≪≪ ≫≫

**YOGI BEAR JELLYSTONE PARK
CAMP-RESORTS**
50 W. TechnaCentre Dr., # G
Milford, OH 45150-9798
Tel: (800) 626-3720 (513) 831-2100
Fax: (513) 2576-8670

Web Site: www.campjellystone.com
Mr. Robert E. Schutter, Jr., President/
COO

A unique recreation camp-resort for the entire family. YOGI and friends offer daily activities with a full amenity package, clean restrooms and YOGI souvenirs. Each camp-resort is independently owned and operated and maintains system standards.

BACKGROUND:
Established: 1969; 1st Franchised: 1969
Franchised Units: 71
Company-Owned Units 0
Total Units: 71
Dist.: US-66; CAN-5; O'seas-0
North America: 25 States, 2 Provinces
Density: 8 in IN, 7 in MI, 7 in WI
Projected New Units (12 Months): 4
Registered: CA,FL,IL,IN,MD,MI,MN,
NY,VA,WI
FINANCIAL/TERMS:
Cash Investment: $28K+
Total Investment: $28K+
Minimum Net Worth: $NR
Fees: Franchise - $18-28K
Royalty - 6%; Ad. - 1%
Earnings Claim Statement: NR
Term of Contract (Years): 5-20/5-10
Avg. # Of Employees: 3 FT, 25 PT
Passive Ownership: Discouraged
Encourage Conversions: Yes
Area Develop. Agreements: No
Sub-Franchising Contracts: No
Expand In Territory: No
Space Needs: NR SF; NR
SUPPORT & TRAINING PROVIDED:
Financial Assistance Provided: Yes(D)
Site Selection Assistance: Yes
Lease Negotiation Assistance: Yes
Co-Operative Advertising: Yes
Franchisee Assoc./Member: NR
Size Of Corporate Staff: 6
On-Going Support: B,C,D,E,G,H,I
Training: 2-3 Days Site; 3-4 Days
Headquarters; 1-3 Days/Year On-Site.
SPECIFIC EXPANSION PLANS:
US: All United States
Canada: All Canada
Overseas: No

≪≪ ≫≫

SUPPLEMENTAL LISTING OF FRANCHISORS

AmeriSuites, 700 Route 46 E., P.O. Box 2700, Fairfield, NJ 07007 ; (973) 882-1991; Mr. Terry O'Leary (888) 778-3111; (973) 882-1010

Cendant Corporation, Six Sylvan Way, Parsippany, NJ 07054 ; (973) 496-5351; Mr. Tom Bernardo (800) 758-8999; (973) 428-9700

Club Hotels By Double Tree, 755 Crossover Ln., Memphis, TN 38117 ; (901) 374-5008; Mr. Mickey Powell ; (901) 374-5000

Clubhouse Inns of America, 1950 Stemmons Fwy., # 6001, Dallas, TX 75207 ; (214) 863-1665; Mr. Paul Nussbaum ; (214) 863-1000

Condotels International, 2000 Highway 17 S., North Myrtle Beach, SC 29582-4125 ; (843) 272-6556; Mr. Thomas Taylor (800) 852-6636; (843) 272-8400

Country Hearth Inn, 7000 Central Pkwy. NE, #850, Atlanta, GA 30328 ; (770) 393-2480; Mr. Chetan Patel (800) 432-7992; (770) 393-2662

Courtyard by Marriott, 1 Marriott Dr., Dept. 514.01, Washington, DC 20058 ; (301) 380-6699; Mr. Daryl A. Nickel ; (301) 380-7658

Days Inns of America, Six Sylvan Way, Parsippany, NJ 07054 ; (973) 496-5351; Mr. Tom Bernardo ; (973) 496-5236

Downtowner Inns, 1726 Montreal Circle, Tucker, GA 30084 ; (770) 270-1077; Ms. Amy Foy (800) 892-8405; (770) 270-1180

Fairfield Inn by Marriott, 1 Marriott Dr., Dept. 514.01, Washington, DC 20058 ; (301) 380-6699; Mr. Daryl A. Nickel ; (301) 380-5237

Family Inns of America, P.O. Box 10, Pigeon Forge, TN 37868 ; (615) 428-1500; Ms. Dee Lundy (800) 472-1188; (615) 453-1766

HomeGate Franchising, 700 Route 46 E., P.O. Box 2700, Fairfield, NJ 07007 ; (973) 882-1991; Ms. Terry O'Leary (888) 778 3111; (973) 882-1010

Howard Johnson Franchise Systems, Six Sylvan Way, Parsippany, NJ 07054 ; (973) 496-2305; Mr. Tom Bernardo (800) 932-6726; (973) 428-9700

Howard Johnson Hotels (Canada), 36 Toronto St. #750, Toronto, ON M5C 2C5 CANADA; (416) 361-9050; Mr. Glen Blake (800) 249-4656; (416) 361-1010

Inn Development & Management, 17100 S. Halsted St., Harvey, IL 60426 ; (708) 225-7447; Mr. Ace Lanahan ; (708) 333-3120

Inn Suites Hotels, 1615 E. Northern, # 105, Phoenix, AZ 85020 ; (602) 491-1008; Ms. Kim Soard (800) 842-4242; (602) 997-6285

ITT Sheraton Canada, 45 Church St., Stoney Creek, ON L8E 2X7 CANADA; (905) 664-1113; Mr. David Oliver ; (905) 664-3337

Kee West Inns, # 1 Office Park Circle, # 210, Birmingham, AL 35223 ; (205) 879-1281; Mr. Cary Jackson, Jr. (800) 833-0555; (205) 879-1241

Knights Franchise System, 339 Jefferson Rd., Parsippany, NJ 07054 ; ; Mr. Michael O'Hara (800) 932-3300; (973) 496-1591

Mainstay Suites, 10750 Columbia Pike, Silver Spring, MD 20901 ; (301) 592-6205; Mr. Steve Shultz (800) 547-0007; (301) 592-5000

National 9 Inns, Suites, Motels, 2285 S. Main St., Salt Lake City, UT 84115 ; (801) 466-9856; Mr. Kevin Howell ; (801) 466-9826

Park Inns International, 6263 N. Scottsdale Rd., # 200, Scottsdale, AZ 85250 ; (602) 951-3050; Mr. Manfred Gerling (800) 600-7275; (602) 951-3335

Park Plaza International, 6263 N. Scottsdale Rd., # 200, Scottsdale, AZ 85250 ; (602) 951-3050; Mr. Manfred Gerling (800) 600-7275; (602) 951-3335

Prime Hospitality Corp, 700 Route 46 E., P. O. Box 2700, Fairfield, NJ 07007-2700 ; (973) 882-1991; Ms. Terry P. O'Leary ; (973) 882-1010

Promus Hotels, 755 Crossover Ln., Memphis, TN 38117 ; (901) 374-5051; Mr. Thomas L. Keltner ; (901) 374-5000

Ramada Inns, 339 Jefferson Rd., P. O. Box 278, Parsippany, NJ 07054-0278 ; (973) 496-5351; Mr. John Osborne (800) 932-6726; (973) 428-9700

Residence Inn by Marriott, 1 Marriott Dr., Dept. 514.01, Washington, DC 20058 ; (301) 380-8957; Mr. Daryl A. Nickel ; (301) 380-9000

Shoney's Inns, 130 Maple Dr. North, Hendersonville, TN 37075 ; (615) 264-3497; Mr. John Buttolph (800) 222-2222; (615) 264-8000

Starwood Hotels & Resorts Worldwide, 100 Galleria Parkway, # 1350, Atlanta, GA 30339 ; (770) 857-2041; Mr. Sam Winterbottom ; (770) 857-2000

Super 8 Motels, 1 Sylvan Way, Parsippany, NJ 07054 ; (973) 496-5351; Mr. Michael O'Hara (800) 889-8847; (973) 496-5250

Thompson Hospitality, 1191 Freedom Dr., # 260, Reston, VA 20190 ; (703) 709-0292; Mr. Ali Azima ; (703) 709-0145

Travelodge / Thriftlodge, 1 Sylvan Way, Parsippany, NJ 07054 ; (973) 496-2219; Mr. Mike O'Hara ; (973) 428-9700

Villager Lodge, 339 Jefferson Rd., Parsippany, NJ 07054 ; (973) 496-5902; Mr. Ken Rogers (800) 843-1960; (973) 496-9700

Wandlyn Inns, P.O. Box 430, Fredericton, NB E3B 5P8 CANADA; (506) 452-8894; Mr. Gary Llewellyn (800) 561-0000; (506) 462-4401

Wellesley Inns, 700 Route 46 E., P.O. Box 2700, Fairfield, NJ 07007 ; (973) 882-1991; Ms. Terry O'Leary (888) 778 3111; (973) 882-1010

Wingate Inn, One Sylvan Way, Parsippany, NJ 07054-0278 ; (973) 496-1354; Mr. Anthony Falor (800) 567-4283; (973) 428-9700

Woodfin Suite Hotels, 12730 High Bluff Dr., # 250, San Diego, CA 92130 ; (619) 794-2348; Ms. Tana Farrell ; (619) 794-2338

Maid Service & Home Cleaning Industry Profile

Total # Franchisors in Industry Group	26
Total # Franchised Units in Industry Group	3,697
Total # Company-Owned Units in Industry Group	<u>132</u>
Total # Operating Units in Industry Group	3,829
Average # Franchised Units/Franchisor	142.3
Average # Company-Owned Units/Franchisor	<u>5.1</u>
Average # Total Units/Franchisor	147.4
Ratio of Total # Franchised Units/Total # Company-Owned Units	28.0:1
Industry Survey Participants	16
Representing % of Industry	61.5%
Average Franchise Fee*:	$14.4K
Average Total Investment*:	$49.3K
Average On-Going Royalty Fee*:	5.4%

If a range was provided, the mid-point of the range was used. See detailed profiles for actual ranges.

Five Largest Participants in Survey

Company	# Fran-chised Units	# Co-Owned Units	# Total Units	Franchise Fee	On-Going Royalty	Total Investment
1. Merry Maids	1,201	30	1,231	13.5-21.5K	5-7%	24.9-41.4K
2. Molly Maid	540	7	547	6.9K	7-3%	36-65K
3. Maids, The	378	50	428	17.5K	3.3-7%	56-245K
4. Maid Brigade Services	252	3	255	18.5K	3-7%	43.5K+
5. Maid To Perfection	175	0	175	9K	5-7%	35-40k

All of the data provided are proprietary and should not be quoted without acknowledging *Bond's Franchise Guide.*

CLASSY MAIDS USA
P.O. Box 8552
Madison, WI 53708
Tel: (800) 445-5238 (608) 242-8943
Fax: (608) 242-1788
E-Mail: franchiseguy@home.com
Mr. William D. Olday, Vice President
    Franchising

Multi-service cleaning franchise. Choose one or all of the following services: maid service, light janitorial, carpet cleaning, window washing, move-in/move-out. One week training program (your location or ours). Special conversion program available ($250 fee). Financing assistance and more. Area development territories available.

BACKGROUND:
Established: 1980;   1st Franchised: 1985
Franchised Units: 8
Company-Owned Units   0
Total Units: 8
Dist.:   US-8; CAN-0; O'seas-0
  North America: 5 States
  Density: 2 in MN, 2 in WI, 1 in TN
Projected New Units (12 Months):   3
Qualifications: 2, 3, 1, 1, 5, 3
Registered: None
FINANCIAL/TERMS:
Cash Investment: $7K
Total Investment: $12K
Minimum Net Worth: $15K
Fees: Franchise - $9.9K
  Royalty - 6%;   Ad. - 0%
Earnings Claim Statement: No
Term of Contract (Years):   10/10
Avg. # Of Employees: 1 FT, 5-8 PT
Passive Ownership: Allowed
Encourage Conversions: Yes
Area Develop. Agreements: No
Sub-Franchising Contracts: No
Expand In Territory: Yes
Space Needs: NR SF; HB
SUPPORT & TRAINING PRO-VIDED:
Financial Assistance Provided: Yes(D)
Site Selection Assistance: N/A
Lease Negotiation Assistance: N/A
Co-Operative Advertising: Yes
Franchisee Assoc./Member: No
Size Of Corporate Staff: 3

On-Going Support: a,b,c,d,e,G,h,I
Training: 3-5 Days Madison, WI, or 3-5
    Days at Franchisee Location ($1,200).
SPECIFIC EXPANSION PLANS:
US: All United States
Canada: No
Overseas: No

◄◄ ►►

CLEANING AUTHORITY, THE
9017 Red Branch Rd., # G
Columbia, MD 21045
Tel: (800) 783-6243 (410) 740-1900
Fax: (410) 740-1906
E-Mail: tim@thecleaningauthority.com
Web Site: www.thecleaningauthority.com
Mr. Tim Evankovich, COO

THE CLEANING AUTHORITY offers franchisees new and innovative methods in developing a successful maid service. Our unique, high-response marketing, coupled with our state-of-the-art proprietary software system, sets us far above the competition in supporting the franchisee. Join us to make your future more successful. Member Platinum 200.

BACKGROUND: IFA MEMBER
Established: 1978;   1st Franchised: 1996
Franchised Units: 35
Company-Owned Units   1
Total Units: 36
Dist.:   US-36; CAN-0; O'seas-0
  North America: 15 States
  Density: 6 in MD, 5 in FL, 4 in TX
Projected New Units (12 Months):   12
Qualifications: 2, 3, 1, 1, 2, 5
Registered: CA,FL,MD,MI,VA
FINANCIAL/TERMS:
Cash Investment: $15-25K
Total Investment: $40-60K
Minimum Net Worth: $50K
Fees: Franchise - $18-28K
  Royalty - 4-6%;   Ad. - 2%
Earnings Claim Statement: No
Term of Contract (Years):   10/5
Avg. # Of Employees: Varies
Passive Ownership: Not Allowed
Encourage Conversions: Yes
Area Develop. Agreements: No
Sub-Franchising Contracts: No
Expand In Territory: Yes
Space Needs: 800-1,200 SF; Industrial

SUPPORT & TRAINING PROVIDED:
Financial Assistance Provided: Yes(I)
Site Selection Assistance: Yes
Lease Negotiation Assistance: No
Co-Operative Advertising: Yes
Franchisee Assoc./Member: Yes/Yes
Size Of Corporate Staff: 8
On-Going Support: b,C,D,G,H,I
Training: 2 Weeks Corporate Office in
    Columbia, MD.
SPECIFIC EXPANSION PLANS:
US: All United States
Canada: All Canada
Overseas: No

◄◄ ►►

COTTAGECARE
6323 W. 110th St.
Overland Park, KS 66211
Tel: (800) 469-6303 (913) 469-8778
Fax: (913) 469-0822
E-Mail: bnagel@cottagecare.com
Web Site: www.cottagecare.com
Mr. Brian W. Nagel, Franchise Licensing

Big business approach to housecleaning. We do the marketing and sign up new customers for you! You retain customers and manage the business, not clean houses. "Jumbo" exclusive territories are 4 times larger than industry standards, leading to 'Jumbo' sales.

BACKGROUND: IFA MEMBER
Established: 1988;   1st Franchised: 1989
Franchised Units: 53
Company-Owned Units   1
Total Units: 54
Dist.:   US-48; CAN-6; O'seas-0
  North America: 22 States, 2 Provinces
  Density: 5 in TX, 3 in AB
Projected New Units (12 Months):   15
Qualifications: 4, 4, 2, 2, 1, 5
Registered: All States
FINANCIAL/TERMS:
Cash Investment: $15-25K
Total Investment: $35-70K
Minimum Net Worth: $N/A
Fees: Franchise - $7.5-19.5K
  Royalty - 5.5%;   Ad. - As needed
Earnings Claim Statement: Yes
Term of Contract (Years):   10/10
Avg. # Of Employees: 1 FT, 16 PT
Passive Ownership: Discouraged
Encourage Conversions: No
Area Develop. Agreements: No

Sub-Franchising Contracts: No
Expand In Territory: Yes
Space Needs: 400 SF; FS, SF, SC

SUPPORT & TRAINING PROVIDED:
Financial Assistance Provided: Yes(I)
Site Selection Assistance: Yes
Lease Negotiation Assistance: Yes
Co-Operative Advertising: N/A
Franchisee Assoc./Member: No
Size Of Corporate Staff: 14
On-Going Support: C,D,G,H
Training: 2 Weeks Kansas City, KS
  Headquarters.

SPECIFIC EXPANSION PLANS:
US: All United States
Canada: All Canada
Overseas: No

≪ ≫

DIAMOND HOME CLEANING SERVICES
4887 E. La Palma Ave., # 708
Anaheim, CA 92807
Tel: (800) 393-6243 (714) 701-9771
Fax: (714) 693-8106
E-Mail: mtgi@diamondhomecleaning.com
Web Site: www.diamondhomecleaning.com
Mr. Tom Devlin, President

3 franchise concepts - 1 franchise fee when you join the DIAMOND HOME CLEANING SERVICES franchise system. After completion of our extensive training program, you will be an expert in maid services, carpet cleaning and window cleaning services. Benefits include explosive 20% annual customer growth demand; home-based business; no weekends (have a life!); low investment of $25-60K, including start-up/working capital; and prime territories available.

BACKGROUND: IFA MEMBER
Established: 1993; 1st Franchised: 1997
Franchised Units: 26
Company-Owned Units 8
Total Units: 24
Dist.: US-34; CAN-0; O'seas-0
  North America: 2 States
  Density: 13 in CA
Projected New Units (12 Months): 12
Qualifications: 5, 3, 1, 3, 3, 5
Registered: CA

FINANCIAL/TERMS:
Cash Investment: $25K
Total Investment: $25-61K
Minimum Net Worth: $100K
Fees: Franchise - $5K
  Royalty - 4-6%; Ad. - 0%
Earnings Claim Statement: No
Term of Contract (Years): 10/5
Avg. # Of Employees: 3 FT, 24 PT
Passive Ownership: Discouraged
Encourage Conversions: Yes
Area Develop. Agreements: No
Sub-Franchising Contracts: No
Expand In Territory: Yes
Space Needs: 500 SF; HB

SUPPORT & TRAINING PROVIDED:
Financial Assistance Provided: Yes(I)
Site Selection Assistance: Yes
Lease Negotiation Assistance: Yes
Co-Operative Advertising: No
Franchisee Assoc./Member: No
Size Of Corporate Staff: 6
On-Going Support: B,C,D,E,F,G,H,I
Training: 1 Week Anaheim, CA.

SPECIFIC EXPANSION PLANS:
US: Southwest
Canada: No
Overseas: No

≪ ≫

HOME CLEANING CENTERS OF AMERICA
P.O. Box 11427
Overland Park, KS 66207-1427
Tel: (800) 767-1118 (913) 327-5227
Fax: (913) 327-5272
E-Mail: mcalhoon@aol.com
Web Site: www.homecleaninginc.com
Mr. Mike Calhoon, President

Very large franchise zones. Quality Quality Quality. Owners do not clean houses. Every corporate policy is made by the franchise owners. Each and every owner is hand picked - having money is not enough. Corporate 'Mission Statement' is to have the largest grossing, highest-quality offices in the industry.

BACKGROUND: IFA MEMBER
Established: 1981; 1st Franchised: 1984
Franchised Units: 25
Company-Owned Units 0
Total Units: 25
Dist.: US-25; CAN-0; O'seas-0
  North America: 9 States

Density: 7 in MO, 4 in KS, 4 in CO
Projected New Units (12 Months): 3
Qualifications: 3, 3, 1, 3, 5, 5
Registered: CA,IL,IN,MI,MN,NY,OR

FINANCIAL/TERMS:
Cash Investment: $20-30K
Total Investment: $30-50K
Minimum Net Worth: $N/A
Fees: Franchise - $9.5K
  Royalty - 4.5-5%; Ad. - 0%
Earnings Claim Statement: Yes
Term of Contract (Years): 10/10
Avg. # Of Employees: 12 FT
Passive Ownership: Discouraged
Encourage Conversions: No
Area Develop. Agreements: No
Sub-Franchising Contracts: No
Expand In Territory: Yes
Space Needs: 500 SF; Non-Retail

SUPPORT & TRAINING PROVIDED:
Financial Assistance Provided: No
Site Selection Assistance: Yes
Lease Negotiation Assistance: Yes
Co-Operative Advertising: No
Franchisee Assoc./Member: Yes/Yes
Size Of Corporate Staff: 2
On-Going Support: b,C,D,E,F,G,H,I
Training: 5 Days Denver, CO or 5 days at
  St. Louis, MO.

SPECIFIC EXPANSION PLANS:
US: All United States
Canada: No
Overseas: No

≪ ≫

MAID BRIGADE SERVICES
Four Concourse Pkwy., # 200
Atlanta, GA 30328
Tel: (800) 722-6243 (770) 551-9630
Fax: (770) 391-9092
E-Mail: chay@maidbrigade.com
Web Site: www.maidbrigade.com
Ms. Cathy Hay, VP Franchise
  Development

MAID BRIGADE offers the best opportunity in the industry with our 3 new Large, Major and Regional Market Franchises. Our exclusive territory sizes range from 20,000 to 150,000 qualified households. We provide unparalleled support, business development and the latest technology in the industry. Our focus is to build strong businesses. Master franchises available outside the USA.

BACKGROUND: IFA MEMBER
Established: 1979; 1st Franchised: 1984
Franchised Units: 252
Company-Owned Units 3
Total Units: 255
Dist.: US-168; CAN-85; O'seas-2
North America: 28 States,10 Provinces
Density: VA, TX, WA
Projected New Units (12 Months): 20
Qualifications: 4, 3, 2, 3, 2, 5
Registered: CA,FL,HI,IL,MD,MI,MN,NY,
OR,VA,WA,WI,DC

FINANCIAL/TERMS:
Cash Investment: $43.5K+
Total Investment: $43.5K+
Minimum Net Worth: $100K
Fees: Franchise - $18.5K
Royalty - 3-7%; Ad. - 2%
Earnings Claim Statement: Yes
Term of Contract (Years): 10/10
Avg. # Of Employees: 15 FT
Passive Ownership: Allowed
Encourage Conversions: Yes
Area Develop. Agreements: Yes/5
Sub-Franchising Contracts: Yes
Expand In Territory: Yes
Space Needs: 500-1,000 SF; HB, SF, SC

SUPPORT & TRAINING PROVIDED:
Financial Assistance Provided: Yes(I)
Site Selection Assistance: Yes
Lease Negotiation Assistance: Yes
Co-Operative Advertising: Yes
Franchisee Assoc./Member: Yes/Yes
Size Of Corporate Staff: 13
On-Going Support: A,B,C,D,E,F,G,H,I
Training: 5 Days in Atlanta, GA; 10 Days
On-Site Week of Opening; Training
Videos/Manuals.

SPECIFIC EXPANSION PLANS:
US: All United States
Canada: All Canada
Overseas: All Countries

MAID TO PERFECTION
7133 Rutherford Rd., # 105
Baltimore, MD 21244
Tel: (800) 648-6243 (410) 944-6466
Fax: (410) 944-6469
E-Mail: maidsvc@aol.com
Web Site: www.maidtoperfectioncorp.com
Mr. Todd Cearfoss, Sales Director

MAID TO PERFECTION ® is the only major cleaning franchise that provides access to every residential and commercial service

dollar, within an exclusive territory. Ranked #1 for franchisee support/satisfaction in Success, April, 1999; cited as one of only 15 Great, Low-Investment franchises by Black Enterprise, September, 1999.

BACKGROUND: IFA MEMBER
Established: 1980; 1st Franchised: 1990
Franchised Units: 175
Company-Owned Units 0
Total Units: 175
Dist.: US-205; CAN-2; O'seas-0
North America: 22 States, 2 Provinces
Density: 50 in MD, 33 in PA, 20 in CA
Projected New Units (12 Months): 50
Qualifications: 5, 5, 2, 4, 4, 5
Registered: CA,FL,IL,IN,MD,MI,MN,NY,
ND,OR,RI,VA,WA,WI,DC

FINANCIAL/TERMS:
Cash Investment: $15-20K
Total Investment: $35-40K
Minimum Net Worth: $80K
Fees: Franchise - $9K
Royalty - 5-7%; Ad. - 0%
Earnings Claim Statement: No
Term of Contract (Years): 5/5
Avg. # Of Employees: 15 FT, 5 PT
Passive Ownership: Discouraged
Encourage Conversions: Yes
Area Develop. Agreements: Yes/5
Sub-Franchising Contracts: No
Expand In Territory: Yes
Space Needs: 400-500 SF; FS, HB, Non-Retail

SUPPORT & TRAINING PROVIDED:
Financial Assistance Provided: Yes(B)
Site Selection Assistance: Yes
Lease Negotiation Assistance: Yes
Co-Operative Advertising: No
Franchisee Assoc./Member: Yes/No
Size Of Corporate Staff: 7
On-Going Support: C,D,E,G,H,I
Training: 1 Week at Corporate
Headquarters; 1 Week On-Site.

SPECIFIC EXPANSION PLANS:
US: All United States
Canada: All Canada
Overseas: All Countries

MaidPro®

MAIDPRO
180 Canal St.
Boston, MA 02114
Tel: (888) MAIDPRO (617) 742-8787
Fax: (617) 720-0700
E-Mail: info@maidpro.com
Web Site: www.maidpro.com
Mr. Richard Sparacio, Dir. Franchise Dev.

MAIDPRO is setting the trend in the home and office cleaning industry. MAIDPRO has a contemporary approach to this high-growth service. With unmatched graphic design and marketing, a completely paperless office and the ability for clients to request service on the Internet, MAIDPRO's franchisees have become successful in running a larger business.

BACKGROUND:
Established: 1991; 1st Franchised: 1997
Franchised Units: 16
Company-Owned Units 2
Total Units: 18
Dist.: US-18; CAN-0; O'seas-0
North America: 10 States
Density: 8 in MA, 2 in FL, 1 in CT
Projected New Units (12 Months): 15
Qualifications: 3, 3, 1, 2, 4, 5
Registered: All States

FINANCIAL/TERMS:
Cash Investment: $10-15K
Total Investment: $24.4-42.4K
Minimum Net Worth: $N/A
Fees: Franchise - $7.9K
Royalty - 3-6%; Ad. - N/A
Earnings Claim Statement: No
Term of Contract (Years): 10/5
Avg. # Of Employees: 15 FT, 3 PT
Passive Ownership: Not Allowed
Encourage Conversions: Yes
Area Develop. Agreements: No
Sub-Franchising Contracts: No
Expand In Territory: Yes
Space Needs: 500-1,500 SF; SF, OB

SUPPORT & TRAINING PROVIDED:
Financial Assistance Provided: Yes(I)
Site Selection Assistance: Yes
Lease Negotiation Assistance: Yes
Co-Operative Advertising: Yes
Franchisee Assoc./Member: No
Size Of Corporate Staff: 5
On-Going Support: C,d,E,G,h,I
Training: 2 Weeks in Boston, MA.

SPECIFIC EXPANSION PLANS:
US: All United States
Canada: No
Overseas: No

≪ ≫

MAIDS, THE
4820 Dodge St.
Omaha, NE 68132-4820
Tel: (800) 843-6243 (402) 558-5555
Fax: (402) 558-4112
E-Mail: jbasden@navix.net
Web Site: www.maids.com
Mr. Michael P. Fagen, Executive VP

AMERICA'S MAID SERVICE - THE MAIDS is the premier residential cleaning franchise. Our cleaning system is the most thorough in the industry and sets us ahead of all competition. We offer low investment, comprehensive training and on-going support that set the industry standard. Call THE MAIDS today and discover why we are AMERICA'S MAID SERVICE.

BACKGROUND: IFA MEMBER
Established: 1979; 1st Franchised: 1980
Franchised Units: 378
Company-Owned Units   50
Total Units: 428
Dist.:   US-415; CAN-13; O'seas-0
  North America: 40 States, 5 Provinces
  Density: 34 in CA, 23 in NY, 20 in IL
Projected New Units (12 Months):   40
Qualifications: 4, 4, 1, 3, 1, 4
Registered: All States
FINANCIAL/TERMS:
Cash Investment: $14-61K
Total Investment: $56-245K
Minimum Net Worth: $180-350K
Fees: Franchise - $17.5K
  Royalty - 3.3-7%;   Ad. - 1%
Earnings Claim Statement: Yes
Term of Contract (Years):   20/20
Avg. # Of Employees: 1-2 FT, 8-12 PT
Passive Ownership: Discouraged
Encourage Conversions: Yes
Area Develop. Agreements: No
Sub-Franchising Contracts: Yes
Expand In Territory: Yes
Space Needs: 200 SF; FS, SC, SF
SUPPORT & TRAINING PROVIDED:
Financial Assistance Provided: Yes(I)
Site Selection Assistance: Yes
Lease Negotiation Assistance: No
Co-Operative Advertising: Yes
Franchisee Assoc./Member: Yes/Yes
Size Of Corporate Staff: 35

On-Going Support: A,B,C,D,G,H,I
Training: 8 Days Each in Both Managerial
  and Technical Training at Headquarters;
  90 Days On-Site.
SPECIFIC EXPANSION PLANS:
US: All United States
Canada: All Canada
Overseas: All Countries

≪ ≫

MERRY MAIDS
860 Ridge Lake Blvd.
Memphis, TN 38120
Tel: (800) 798-8000 (901) 537-8100
Fax: (901) 537-8140
Web Site: www.merrymaids.com
Mr. Rob Sanders, Franchise Sales Mgr.

MERRY MAIDS is the largest and most recognized company in the home cleaning industry. The company's commitment to training and on-going support is unmatched. MERRY MAIDS is highly-ranked as the hottest and fastest-growing franchise opportunity according to leading national publications. We offer low investment, cross-selling promotions with our partner companies, research and development and commitment to quality.

BACKGROUND:
Established: 1979;   1st Franchised: 1980
Franchised Units: 1,201
Company-Owned Units   30
Total Units: 1,231
Dist.:   US-852; CAN-40; O'seas-339
  North America: 49 States, 7 Provinces
  Density: 114 in CA, 45 in TX, 45 IL
Projected New Units (12 Months):   40
Qualifications: 5, 3, 1, 3, 4, 5
Registered: All States
FINANCIAL/TERMS:
Cash Investment: $11.4-19.4K
Total Investment: $24.9-41.4K
Minimum Net Worth: $Varies
Fees: Franchise - $13.5-21.5K
  Royalty - 5-7%;   Ad. - 0.25-1%
Earnings Claim Statement: No
Term of Contract (Years):   5/5
Avg. # Of Employees: 2 FT, 12 PT
Passive Ownership: Discouraged
Encourage Conversions: Yes
Area Develop. Agreements: No

Sub-Franchising Contracts: No
Expand In Territory: Yes
Space Needs: 800 SF; FS
SUPPORT & TRAINING PROVIDED:
Financial Assistance Provided: Yes(D)
Site Selection Assistance: No
Lease Negotiation Assistance: No
Co-Operative Advertising: N/A
Franchisee Assoc./Member: Yes/No
Size Of Corporate Staff: 55
On-Going Support: C,D,G,H,I
Training: 8 Days Headquarters, Memphis,
  TN.
SPECIFIC EXPANSION PLANS:
US: All United States
Canada: All Canada
Overseas: All Countries

≪ ≫

MERRY MAIDS OF CANADA
6540 Tomken Rd.
Mississauga, ON L5T 2E9 CANADA
Tel: (800) 263-5928 (905) 670-0000
Fax: (905) 670-0077
E-Mail: thould@svm.com
Web Site: www.svm.com
Ms. Terry Hould, Franchise Director

Largest company in the residential cleaning industry. The company's commitment to training and on-going support is unmatched. Highly ranked as the hottest and fastest-growing franchise opportunity according to leading national publications.

BACKGROUND:
Established: 1991;   1st Franchised: 1991
Franchised Units: 53
Company-Owned Units   1
Total Units: 54
Dist.:   US-800; CAN-54; O'seas-1300
  North America: 9 Provinces
  Density: 25 in ON, 7 in BC
Projected New Units (12 Months):   15
Qualifications: 2, 3, 1, 2, 3, 4
Registered: AB
FINANCIAL/TERMS:
Cash Investment: $17.5-24.5K
Total Investment: $40-50K
Minimum Net Worth: $50K
Fees: Franchise - $17.5-24.5K
  Royalty - 5-7%;   Ad. - 0%
Earnings Claim Statement: No

Term of Contract (Years): 5/5
Avg. # Of Employees: 2 FT, 2 PT
Passive Ownership: Discouraged
Encourage Conversions: Yes
Area Develop. Agreements: No
Sub-Franchising Contracts: No
Expand In Territory: Yes
Space Needs: 300-500 SF; Warehouse
SUPPORT & TRAINING PROVIDED:
Financial Assistance Provided: Yes
Site Selection Assistance: No
Lease Negotiation Assistance: No
Co-Operative Advertising: No
Franchisee Assoc./Member: Yes/CFA
Size Of Corporate Staff: 50
On-Going Support: B,C,D,G,h,I
Training: 8 Days Memphis, TN.
SPECIFIC EXPANSION PLANS:
US: N/A
Canada: All Canada
Overseas: N/A

<< >>

**MINI MAID SERVICE SYSTEMS
OF CANADA**
192 Shorting Rd.
Scarborough, ON M1S 3S7 CANADA
Tel: (800) 363-MAID (416) 298-7288
Fax: (416) 298-8445
Mr. David Dugas, President

A team of 4 maids clean, using own supplies and equipment. All fully-trained, uniformed, insured and bonded. Arrive at customer homes in identifiable station wagons for professional image. Strong support programs from home office assures successful operation.

BACKGROUND:
Established: 1979; 1st Franchised: 1979
Franchised Units: 80
Company-Owned Units: 21
Total Units: 101
Dist.: US-0; CAN-101; O'seas-0
North America: 7 Provinces
Density: 20 in ON, 16 in BC, 9 in PQ
Projected New Units (12 Months): 3
Registered: AB
FINANCIAL/TERMS:
Cash Investment: $14K
Total Investment: $14K
Minimum Net Worth: $NR
Fees: Franchise - $10K
Royalty - 6%; Ad. - 2%
Earnings Claim Statement: No
Term of Contract (Years): 10/10
Avg. # Of Employees: 6 FT

Passive Ownership: Not Allowed
Encourage Conversions: No
Area Develop. Agreements: Yes/5
Sub-Franchising Contracts: Yes
Expand In Territory: Yes
Space Needs: NR SF; NR
SUPPORT & TRAINING PROVIDED:
Financial Assistance Provided: No
Site Selection Assistance: Yes
Lease Negotiation Assistance: N/A
Co-Operative Advertising: Yes
Franchisee Assoc./Member: NR
Size Of Corporate Staff: 5
On-Going Support: B,C,D,G,H,I
Training: 1 Week Headquarters; Annual Seminars.
SPECIFIC EXPANSION PLANS:
US: No
Canada: All Canada
Overseas: No

<< >>

MOLLY MAID
3948 Ranchero Dr.
Ann Arbor, MI 48108
Tel: (800) 665-5962 (734) 822-6800
Fax: (734) 822-6888
E-Mail: info@mollymaid.com
Web Site: www.mollymaid.com
Mr. Marc A. Kiekenapp, Vice President

MOLLY MAID is # 1 in the industry in residential cleaning and home care service. Ranked in INC 500, Entrepreneur's Top 100, Platinum 200, Entrepreneur 509 and Business Start-Ups As Top 200 Hottest Franchises. MOLLY MAID's technology won The Windows Worldwide Open in 1995 sponsored by Bill Gates.

BACKGROUND: IFA MEMBER
Established: 1979; 1st Franchised: 1979
Franchised Units: 540
Company-Owned Units: 7
Total Units: 547
Dist.: US-280; CAN-167; O'seas-100
North America: 36 States, 3 Provinces
Density: 146 in ON, 52 in CA, 22 MI
Projected New Units (12 Months): 40
Qualifications: 3, 3, 1, 3, 4, 5
Registered: CA,FL,IL,IN,MD,MI,MN,NY,
OR,RI,VA,WA,WI,DC

FINANCIAL/TERMS:
Cash Investment: $15-25K
Total Investment: $36-65K
Minimum Net Worth: $150K
Fees: Franchise - $6.9K
Royalty - 7-3%; Ad. - $75/Qtr.
Earnings Claim Statement: Yes
Term of Contract (Years): 10/10
Avg. # Of Employees: 12 FT
Passive Ownership: Discouraged
Encourage Conversions: Yes
Area Develop. Agreements: No
Sub-Franchising Contracts: No
Expand In Territory: Yes
Space Needs: 400 SF; Other
SUPPORT & TRAINING PROVIDED:
Financial Assistance Provided: Yes(I)
Site Selection Assistance: Yes
Lease Negotiation Assistance: No
Co-Operative Advertising: Yes
Franchisee Assoc./Member: Yes/Yes
Size Of Corporate Staff: 33
On-Going Support: C,D,F,G,h,I
Training: 5 Days in Home Office; 6 Months in Right Start Program; 2 Days at Franchise Location.
SPECIFIC EXPANSION PLANS:
US: All United States
Canada: All Canada
Overseas: Japan, United Kingdom

<< >>

OTHER WOMAN, THE
9136 NE Glisan St.
Portland, OR 97220
Tel: (800) 846-6052 (503) 252-4336
Fax: (503) 252-9259
E-Mail: cindy@theotherwoman.com
Web Site: www.theotherwoman.com
Ms. Cindy Wells, President

The Other Woman professional cleaning service is now offering franchise opportunities in limited states and territories of the United States. This has become one of the most sought after franchises in the U.S. This is due in part to the low financial investment required and the growing need of families with two working adults to have an outside party clean their homes.

BACKGROUND:

Established: 1988; 1st Franchised: 1998	
Franchised Units:	0
Company-Owned Units	3
Total Units:	3
Dist.:	US-3; CAN-0; O'seas-0
North America:	2 States
Density:	2 in OR, 1 in WA
Projected New Units (12 Months):	3-5
Qualifications:	3, 3, 1, 2, 3, 3
Registered: CA,FL,NY,OR,WA	

FINANCIAL/TERMS:

Cash Investment:	$2-10K
Total Investment:	$18-34K
Minimum Net Worth:	$N/A
Fees: Franchise -	$15K
Royalty - 3-6%;	Ad. - 0%
Earnings Claim Statement:	No
Term of Contract (Years):	7/5
Avg. # Of Employees:	1-? PT
Passive Ownership:	Not Allowed
Encourage Conversions:	No
Area Develop. Agreements:	No
Sub-Franchising Contracts:	No
Expand In Territory:	N/A
Space Needs: Varies SF; HB, OB	

SUPPORT & TRAINING PROVIDED:

Financial Assistance Provided:	No
Site Selection Assistance:	N/A
Lease Negotiation Assistance:	No
Co-Operative Advertising:	No
Franchisee Assoc./Member:	Yes/Yes
Size Of Corporate Staff:	3
On-Going Support:	B,C,D,E,G,I
Training: 1-2 Weeks in Portland, OR.	

SPECIFIC EXPANSION PLANS:

US:	Mostly West Coast
Canada:	No
Overseas:	No

⋘ ⋙

SERVICEMASTER RESIDENTIAL/ COMMERCIAL (CANADA)

6540 Tomken Rd.
Mississauga, ON L5T 2E9 CANADA
Tel: (800) 263-5928 (905) 670-0000
Fax: (905) 670-0077
Web Site: www.svm.com
Mr. David Messenger, VP Franchise Market Devel.

One of Canada's oldest and best-respected franchise opportunities. SERVICEMAS-TER provides clean-up and reconstruction services after fire and floods, janitorial services, commercial carpet cleaning and residential carpet and upholstery cleaning services.

BACKGROUND:

Established: 1947; 1st Franchised: 1947	
Franchised Units:	160
Company-Owned Units	0
Total Units:	160
Dist.:	US-0; CAN-160; O'seas-0
North America:	10 Provinces
Density: 80 in ON, 19 in BC, 11 in AB	
Projected New Units (12 Months):	9
Qualifications:	3, 3, 1, 2, 3, 4
Registered: AB	

FINANCIAL/TERMS:

Cash Investment:	$11.5-28.5K
Total Investment:	$20-49K
Minimum Net Worth:	$145K
Fees: Franchise -	$11.5-28.5K
Royalty - 4-9%;	Ad. - 1%
Earnings Claim Statement:	No
Term of Contract (Years):	5/5
Avg. # Of Employees:	Varies
Passive Ownership:	Not Allowed
Encourage Conversions:	Yes
Area Develop. Agreements:	No
Sub-Franchising Contracts:	No
Expand In Territory:	Yes
Space Needs: NR SF; N/A	

SUPPORT & TRAINING PROVIDED:

Financial Assistance Provided:	Yes(D)
Site Selection Assistance:	N/A
Lease Negotiation Assistance:	N/A
Co-Operative Advertising:	Yes
Franchisee Assoc./Member:	Yes
Size Of Corporate Staff:	100
On-Going Support:	B,C,D,G,h,I
Training: 2 Weeks Memphis, TN.	

SPECIFIC EXPANSION PLANS:

US:	All United States
Canada:	All Canada
Overseas:	No

⋘ ⋙

SUPPLEMENTAL LISTING OF FRANCHISORS

Buckets & Bows Maid Service, 3700 Forums Dr., # 111, Flower Mound, TX 75028 ; (972) 355-0598; Ms. Deborah Sardone (888) 258-5540; (972) 539-9270

Custom Maids, 1019 W. 10th St., Amarillo, TX 79101 ; (806) 373-6246; Mr. William R. Mangiameli (800) 530-4778; (806) 373-6243

Maids Plus, 977 E. Cherry St., Canal Fulton, OH 44614 ; (216) 854-3001; Mr. Robert L. Pickens (800) 523-MAID; (216) 854-3651

Maids To Order, 919 E. Cherry St., Canal Fulton, OH 44614 ; ; Mr. Joe Jeffreys (800) 701-6243;

Mini Maid, 2727 Canton Rd., # 550, Marietta, GA 30066 ; (770) 794-1877; Ms. Laurie Ackerly (800) 627-6464; (770) 794-9938

Modernistic Carpet & Upholstery Cleaning, 1460 Rankin St., Troy, MI 48083; (248) 589-1700; Mr. Vic Koppang (800) 609-1000; (248) 589-2660

Molly Maid International, 1340 Eisenhower Pl., Ann Arbor, MI 48108 ; (734) 975-9000; Ms. Mary A. Kiekenapp (800) 665-5962; (800) MOLLYMAID

Our Maid Service, 15449 Middlebelt, Livonia, MI 48154 ; (734) 421-4936; Mr. Jerry Grabowski (800) 968-9182; (734) 421-4733

Sparkling Maid, 7936 E. Arapahoe Ct., # 2400, Englewood, CO 80112 ; (303) 843-0276; Ms. Eileen T. Martin ; (303) 770-6059

Swisher Maids, 6849 Fairview Rd., Charlotte, NC 28210-3363 ; (704) 365-8941; Mr. Bruce Mullan (800) 444-4138; (704) 364-7707

Workenders, 4400 N. Federal Hwy., # 210, Boca Raton, FL 33431 ; (561) 477-5321; Mr. Gary D. Goranson (888) 249-0074; (561) 477-5352

MAINTENANCE/CLEANING/SANITATION INDUSTRY PROFILE

Total # Franchisors in Industry Group	118
Total # Franchised Units in Industry Group	34,605
Total # Company-Owned Units in Industry Group	<u>567</u>
Total # Operating Units in Industry Group	35,172
Average # Franchised Units/Franchisor	293.3
Average # Company-Owned Units/Franchisor	<u>4.8</u>
Average # Total Units/Franchisor	298.1
Ratio of Total # Franchised Units/Total # Company-Owned Units	61.0:1
Industry Survey Participants	66
Representing % of Industry	55.9%
Average Franchise Fee*:	$17.2K
Average Total Investment*:	$60.9K
Average On-Going Royalty Fee*:	7.8%

If a range was provided, the mid-point of the range was used. See detailed profiles for actual ranges.

FIVE LARGEST PARTICIPANTS IN SURVEY

Company	# Fran-chised Units	# Co-Owned Units	# Total Units	Franchise Fee	On-Going Royalty	Total Investment
1. Coverall Cleaning Concepts	5,941	0	5,941	6-32.2K	5%	6.2-35.9K
2. ServiceMaster Clean	4,403	0	4,403	13.5-27.5K	4-10%	21.9-72.1K
3. Chem-Dry	3,903	0	3,903	19.9K	$198/Mo.	6.9-27.6K
4. Cleannet USA	1,718	7	1,725	2-25.5K	3%	2.9-37.5K
5. Tower Cleaning Systems	1,270	0	1,270	4-33.6K	3%	3.4-34K

All of the data provided are proprietary and should not be quoted without acknowledging *Bond's Franchise Guide*.

1-800-GOT-JUNK?
NORTH AMERICA'S LARGEST JUNK REMOVAL SERVICE

1-800-GOT-JUNK?
201-2182 W. 12th Ave.
Vancouver, BC V6K 2N4 CANADA
Tel: (877) 408-5865 (604) 731-5782
Fax: (801) 751-0634
E-Mail: wmaillet@1800gotjunk.com
Web Site: www.1800gotjunk.com
Mr. Wayne Millet, VP Development

1-800-GOT-JUNK? has revolutionized customer service in junk removal for over 10 years. By setting the mark for service standards and professionalism, an industry that once operated without set rates, price lists or receipts, now has top service standards. You will have the expert advice and support that is key to success. Our intensive training program will get you on track; our on-going support and continuing education will keep you there. Centralized call center allows you to focus on your business.

BACKGROUND: IFA MEMBER
Established: 1989;   1st Franchised: 1999
Franchised Units: 20
Company-Owned Units   1
Total Units: 21
Dist.:   US-11; CAN-10; O'seas-0
  North America: 7 States, 3 Provinces
  Density: 5 in CA, 5 in ON, 2 in WA
Projected New Units (12 Months):   36
Qualifications: 5, 5, 1, 2, 4, 5
Registered: All States
FINANCIAL/TERMS:
Cash Investment: $45-70K
Total Investment: $45-70K
Minimum Net Worth: $50K
Fees: Franchise - $28K
  Royalty - 8%;   Ad. - 1%
Earnings Claim Statement: No
Term of Contract (Years):   5/15
Avg. # Of Employees: 6 FT, 4 PT
Passive Ownership: Discourged
Encourage Conversions: No
Area Develop. Agreements: No
Sub-Franchising Contracts: No
Expand In Territory: Yes
Space Needs: 350 SF; OB
SUPPORT & TRAINING PROVIDED:
Financial Assistance Provided: Yes(I)
Site Selection Assistance: N/A
Lease Negotiation Assistance: N/A
Co-Operative Advertising: Yes
Franchisee Assoc./Member: Yes/Yes
Size Of Corporate Staff: 18

On-Going Support: a,B,C,D,G,H,I
Training: 5-10 Days Vancouver, BC; 3-5
  Days in Assigned Territory.
SPECIFIC EXPANSION PLANS:
US: All United States
Canada: No
Overseas: No

◄◄ ►►

**AEROWEST & WESTAIR
SANITATION SERVICES**
3882 Del Amo Blvd., # 602
Torrance, CA 90503
Tel: (310) 793-4242
Fax: (310) 793-4250
E-Mail: westsaninc@aol.com
Web Site: www.members.aol.com/
  westsaninc
Mr. Chris Ratay, Franchise Manager

WEST provides unique odor counteractant dispensers and fluids at cost to franchisees for their service work in the 'high end' market, including hospitals, offices, government and municipal buildings, etc. Administrative support is performed by WEST on behalf of the franchisee, including billings and collections (gross franchise income is advanced at time of billing), allowing franchisees to concentrate on sales and service.

BACKGROUND: IFA MEMBER
Established: 1983;   1st Franchised: 1983
Franchised Units: 46
Company-Owned Units   29
Total Units: 75
Dist.:   US-75; CAN-0; O'seas-0
  North America: 30 States
  Density: 13 in CA, 9 in NY, 7 in IL
Projected New Units (12 Months):   8
Qualifications: 2, 3, 3, 2, 2, 4
Registered: CA,KY,MD,IL,NY,WA,MI
FINANCIAL/TERMS:
Cash Investment: $3-10K
Total Investment: $3-40K
Minimum Net Worth: $10K
Fees: Franchise - $2K

Royalty - 35%;   Ad. - 0%
Earnings Claim Statement: Yes
Term of Contract (Years):   5/1
Avg. # Of Employees: 1 FT
Passive Ownership: Discouraged
Encourage Conversions: N/A
Area Develop. Agreements: N/A
Sub-Franchising Contracts: No
Expand In Territory: Yes
Space Needs: N/A SF; HB
SUPPORT & TRAINING PROVIDED:
Financial Assistance Provided: Yes(D)
Site Selection Assistance: N/A
Lease Negotiation Assistance: N/A
Co-Operative Advertising: N/A
Franchisee Assoc./Member: No
Size Of Corporate Staff: 12
On-Going Support: A,B,C,D,G,H,I
Training: 1-2 Weeks Local, Near
  Franchisee's Home.
SPECIFIC EXPANSION PLANS:
US: All United States
Canada: No
Overseas: Europe, Asia

◄◄ ►►

AIRE-MASTER OF AMERICA
1821 N. Highway CC, P.O. Box 2310
Nixa, MO 65714
Tel: (800) 525-0957 (417) 725-2691
Fax: (417) 725-5737
E-Mail: aire@airemaster.com
Web Site: www.airemaster.com
Mr. Jim M. Roudenis, Franchise Director

AIRE-MASTER is a unique system of odor control and restroom fixture cleaning. Unlike the majority of 'air-fresheners' on the market, AIRE-MASTER deodorizers and deodorant products actually eliminate odors by oxidation. You don't need prior experience in the odor control/sanitary supply industry to qualify for an AIRE-MASTER franchise. Customer base is built by making sales calls and providing good customer service. Complete training.

BACKGROUND:

Established: 1958; 1st Franchised: 1977	
Franchised Units:	46
Company-Owned Units	5
Total Units:	51
Dist.: US-50; CAN-1; O'seas-0	
North America: 34 States, 1 Province	
Density: 4 in MO, 3 in CA, 3 in NJ	
Projected New Units (12 Months):	10
Qualifications:	5, 5, 5, 5, 5, 5
Registered: CA,IL,MD,NY	

FINANCIAL/TERMS:

Cash Investment:	$30K
Total Investment:	$30-80K
Minimum Net Worth:	$NR
Fees: Franchise -	$22K
Royalty - 5%;	Ad. - 0%
Earnings Claim Statement:	No
Term of Contract (Years):	20/3
Avg. # Of Employees:	2-3 FT
Passive Ownership:	Discouraged
Encourage Conversions:	Yes
Area Develop. Agreements:	No
Sub-Franchising Contracts:	No
Expand In Territory:	N/A
Space Needs: N/A SF; HB	

SUPPORT & TRAINING PROVIDED:

Financial Assistance Provided:	Yes(D)
Site Selection Assistance:	N/A
Lease Negotiation Assistance:	Yes
Co-Operative Advertising:	Yes
Franchisee Assoc./Member:	Yes/Yes
Size Of Corporate Staff:	70
On-Going Support:	a,B,C,D,E,G,h,I
Training: 5 Days Headquarters, Nixa, MO;	
5 Days Franchisee's Location.	

SPECIFIC EXPANSION PLANS:

US:	All United States
Canada:	All Canada
Overseas:	No

<< >>

AMERICAN LEAK DETECTION
888 Research Dr., # 100, P.O. Box 1701
Palm Springs, CA 92263
Tel: (800) 755-6697 (760) 320-9991
Fax: (760) 320-1288
E-Mail: sbangs@ leakbusters.com
Web Site: www.leakbusters.com
Ms. Sheila T. Bangs, Director of Franchise
Sales

Electronic detection of water, drain, waste, sewer and gas leaks under concrete slabs of homes, commercial buildings, pools, spas, fountains, etc. with equipment commissioned/manufactured by company.

BACKGROUND: IFA MEMBER

Established: 1974; 1st Franchised: 1985	
Franchised Units:	303
Company-Owned Units	2
Total Units:	305
Dist.: US-229; CAN-8; O'seas-68	
North America: 38 States, 3 Provinces	
Density: 63 in CA, 29 in FL, 17 in TX	
Projected New Units (12 Months):	8
Qualifications:	3, 3, 2, 2, 2, 3
Registered: CA,FL,HI,IL,IN,MD,MI,MN,	
NY,OR,RI,VA,WA,WI,DC,AB	

FINANCIAL/TERMS:

Cash Investment:	$45-120K
Total Investment:	$75-150K
Minimum Net Worth:	$Varies
Fees: Franchise -	$49.5K+
Royalty - 8-10%;	Ad. - N/A
Earnings Claim Statement:	No
Term of Contract (Years):	10/10
Avg. # Of Employees:	1-4 FT, 2 PT
Passive Ownership:	Discouraged
Encourage Conversions:	N/A
Area Develop. Agreements:	No
Sub-Franchising Contracts:	No
Expand In Territory:	Yes
Space Needs: NR SF; NR	

SUPPORT & TRAINING PROVIDED:

Financial Assistance Provided:	Yes(D)
Site Selection Assistance:	N/A
Lease Negotiation Assistance:	N/A
Co-Operative Advertising:	Yes
Franchisee Assoc./Member:	Yes/Yes
Size Of Corporate Staff:	42
On-Going Support:	a,B,C,D,f,G,H,I
Training: 6-10 Weeks Palm Springs, CA.	

SPECIFIC EXPANSION PLANS:

US:	Northeast, Midwest
Canada:	MB,SK,AB
Overseas: Western Europe, Far East,	
South America, Middle East	

<< >>

**AMERICARE RESTROOM
HYGIENE & SUPPLY**
225 Laura Dr., #A
Addison, IL 60101
Tel: (800) 745-6191 (630) 458-1990
Fax: (630) 458-1994
Mr. Richard F. Gac, President

Aroma enhancement plus infection control systems for retail, commercial and industrial manufacturing, specializing in full line of high profit products and services for germ killing, restroom supplies and maintenance.

BACKGROUND:

Established: 1990; 1st Franchised: 1993	
Franchised Units:	21
Company-Owned Units	20
Total Units:	41
Dist.: US-41; CAN-0; O'seas-0	
North America:	3 States
Density: 36 in IL, 3 in IN, 2 in WI	
Projected New Units (12 Months):	4
Qualifications:	3, 2, 1, 2, 3, 5
Registered: IL,WI	

FINANCIAL/TERMS:

Cash Investment:	$5K
Total Investment:	$9.5-95K
Minimum Net Worth:	$100K
Fees: Franchise -	$9.5K
Royalty - 15%;	Ad. - NR
Earnings Claim Statement:	No
Term of Contract (Years):	10/10
Avg. # Of Employees:	1 FT, 2 PT
Passive Ownership:	Not Allowed
Encourage Conversions:	N/A
Area Develop. Agreements:	Yes
Sub-Franchising Contracts:	Yes
Expand In Territory:	Yes
Space Needs: N/A SF; HB	

SUPPORT & TRAINING PROVIDED:

Financial Assistance Provided:	Yes
Site Selection Assistance:	N/A
Lease Negotiation Assistance:	N/A
Co-Operative Advertising:	Yes
Franchisee Assoc./Member:	No
Size Of Corporate Staff:	10
On-Going Support:	A,B,C,D,E,F,G,H,I
Training: 2 Weeks in Addison, IL.	

SPECIFIC EXPANSION PLANS:

US:	IL,IN,MI,WI
Canada:	No
Overseas:	No

<< >>

BIOLOGIX
8503 Mid-County Industrial Dr.
St. Louis, MO 63114
Tel: (800) 747-1885 (314) 423-1945
Fax: (314) 423-4394
Mr. James C. Jones, Vice President/
Director

BIOLOGIX provides guaranteed environmental waste elimination services to clients in the food service and hospitality industry. This is a ground floor opportunity to purchase exclusive rights to a territory in the Biotechnology/Environmental service field. Business-to-business sales, renewable income and a positive environmental impact make BIOLOGIX a tremendous opportunity.

BACKGROUND: IFA MEMBER

Established: 1989;	1st Franchised: 1995
Franchised Units:	19
Company-Owned Units	2
Total Units:	21
Dist.:	US-2; CAN-0; O'seas-0
North America:	12 States
Density:	4 in MO, 3 in OH, 2 in TX
Projected New Units (12 Months):	22
Qualifications:	4, 4, 3, 4, 4, 5
Registered: IL,IN,MD,MI,RI,VA,WI	

FINANCIAL/TERMS:

Cash Investment:	$23.9-43.6K
Total Investment:	$NR
Minimum Net Worth:	$30K
Fees: Franchise -	$12.5K
Royalty - 4%;	Ad. - N/A
Earnings Claim Statement:	No
Term of Contract (Years):	5/5
Avg. # Of Employees:	2 FT, 2 PT
Passive Ownership:	Discouraged
Encourage Conversions:	N/A
Area Develop. Agreements:	No
Sub-Franchising Contracts:	No
Expand In Territory:	Yes
Space Needs: NR SF; HB	

SUPPORT & TRAINING PROVIDED:

Financial Assistance Provided:	No
Site Selection Assistance:	N/A
Lease Negotiation Assistance:	N/A
Co-Operative Advertising:	N/A
Franchisee Assoc./Member:	No
Size Of Corporate Staff:	30
On-Going Support:	A,B,C,D,F,G,H,I
Training: 1 Week St. Louis, MO.	

SPECIFIC EXPANSION PLANS:

US:	All United States
Canada:	No
Overseas:	NR

<< >>

BONUS BUILDING CARE

4950 Keller Springs, # 190
Addison, TX 75001
Tel: (800) 931-1102 (972) 789-9400
Fax: (972) 789-9399
E-Mail: bonusinc@aol.com

Web Site: www.bonusbuildingcare.com
Ms. Margaret A. Masterson, President

BONUS
BUILDING CARE

Commercial cleaning. Turn-key operation, with customers, training, operations assistance, equipment, business insurance and clerical support. Best cleaning franchise on the market today because of lower fees, personalized support, less restrictions and quicker start-up. We're not the biggest, but we are the best. Master franchises available. IFA Member.

BACKGROUND: IFA MEMBER

Established: 1996;	1st Franchised: 1996
Franchised Units:	211
Company-Owned Units	4
Total Units:	215
Dist.:	US-215; CAN-0; O'seas-0
North America:	4 States
Density:	TN, MO, TX
Projected New Units (12 Months):	100
Qualifications:	1, 1, 2, 2, 3, 3
Registered: IL	

FINANCIAL/TERMS:

Cash Investment:	$Varies
Total Investment:	$Varies
Minimum Net Worth:	$N/A
Fees: Franchise -	$6.5K
Royalty - 10%;	Ad. - 0%
Earnings Claim Statement:	No
Term of Contract (Years):	20/20
Avg. # Of Employees:	Varies
Passive Ownership:	Discouraged
Encourage Conversions:	Yes
Area Develop. Agreements:	No
Sub-Franchising Contracts:	Yes
Expand In Territory:	No
Space Needs: N/A SF; BH	

SUPPORT & TRAINING PROVIDED:

Financial Assistance Provided:	Yes(D)
Site Selection Assistance:	N/A
Lease Negotiation Assistance:	N/A
Co-Operative Advertising:	N/A
Franchisee Assoc./Member:	Yes/No
Size Of Corporate Staff:	6
On-Going Support:	B,C,D,I
Training: Minimum 20 Hours On-Site; Minimum 10 Hours Classroom; as Needed Self-Study.	

SPECIFIC EXPANSION PLANS:

US:	All United States
Canada:	All Canada
Overseas:	All Countries

<< >>

BRITE SITE

4616 W. Fullerton Ave.
Chicago, IL 60639-1816
Tel: (773) 772-7300
Fax: (773) 772-7631
Mr. Andreas Vassilos, President

BRITE SITE specializes in cleaning retail stores. We offer a proven system of operations, backed by over 25 years of experience. Our existing client base includes regional and national chain stores. Exclusive territories available. No experience necessary.

BACKGROUND:

Established: 1971;	1st Franchised: 1993
Franchised Units:	6
Company-Owned Units	1
Total Units:	7
Dist.:	US-7; CAN-0; O'seas-0
North America:	3 States
Density:	6 in IL, 1 in IN, 1 in WI
Projected New Units (12 Months):	5
Qualifications:	2, 3, 3, 1, 1, 5
Registered: IL,IN	

FINANCIAL/TERMS:

Cash Investment:	$5-50K
Total Investment:	$8-100K
Minimum Net Worth:	$15K
Fees: Franchise -	$5-15K+
Royalty - 10%;	Ad. - 0-2%
Earnings Claim Statement:	No
Term of Contract (Years):	10/10
Avg. # Of Employees:	NR
Passive Ownership:	Discouraged
Encourage Conversions:	Yes
Area Develop. Agreements:	Yes/10
Sub-Franchising Contracts:	Yes
Expand In Territory:	Yes
Space Needs: NR SF; SF, HB, Industrial Park	

SUPPORT & TRAINING PROVIDED:

Financial Assistance Provided:	Yes(B)
Site Selection Assistance:	N/A
Lease Negotiation Assistance:	Yes
Co-Operative Advertising:	Yes
Franchisee Assoc./Member:	Yes/Yes
Size Of Corporate Staff:	6
On-Going Support:	A,B,C,D,E,G,H,I
Training: 3-14 Days Home Office and Field.	

SPECIFIC EXPANSION PLANS:

US:	Midwest
Canada:	No
Overseas:	No

<< >>

BUILDING SERVICES OF AMERICA
11900 W. 87th St., # 135
Lenexa, KS 66215
Tel: (913) 599-6200
Fax: (913) 599-4441
Mr. Howard Capps, President

Franchised commercial cleaning.

BACKGROUND:
Established: 1992;   1st Franchised: 1992
Franchised Units: 31
Company-Owned Units   1
Total Units: 32
Dist.:   US-32; CAN-0; O's eas-0
  North America: 2 States
  Density: 14 in KS, 18 in MO
Projected New Units (12 Months):   6
Qualifications: 2, 2, 1, 2, 2, 2
Registered: NR

FINANCIAL/TERMS:
Cash Investment: $1.5-15K
Total Investment: $7.5-20K
Minimum Net Worth: $0
Fees: Franchise - $1.5-15K
  Royalty - 8%;   Ad. - 0%
Earnings Claim Statement: No
Term of Contract (Years):   10/10
Avg. # Of Employees: Varies
Passive Ownership: Not Allowed
Encourage Conversions: N/A
Area Develop. Agreements: No
Sub-Franchising Contracts: No
Expand In Territory: Yes
Space Needs: NR SF; N/A

SUPPORT & TRAINING PROVIDED:
Financial Assistance Provided: Yes(D)
Site Selection Assistance: No
Lease Negotiation Assistance: No
Co-Operative Advertising: No
Franchisee Assoc./Member: Yes/Yes
Size Of Corporate Staff: 7
On-Going Support: A,C,D,G,H
Training: 1-2 Weeks at Corporate Office.

SPECIFIC EXPANSION PLANS:
US: All United States
Canada: No
Overseas: No

<< >>

CAPITAL CARPET CLEANING
1306 Coral Park Ln.
Vero Beach, FL 32963
Tel: (561) 234-3707
Mr. Robert Campbell, President

CAPITAL CARPET CLEANING was developed out of an unquestionable need in the carpet and upholstery cleaning industry to provide a superior, ultra-high powered, carpet and upholstery cleaning system.

BACKGROUND:
Established: 1983;   1st Franchised: 1990
Franchised Units: 12
Company-Owned Units   2
Total Units: 14
Dist.:   US-14; CAN-0; O's eas-0
  North America: 3 States
  Density: 7 in FL, 4 in MN, 3 in CA
Projected New Units (12 Months):   10
Qualifications: 1, 3, 1, 3, 3, 5
Registered: CA,FL,MN

FINANCIAL/TERMS:
Cash Investment: $0-5K
Total Investment: $35-45K
Minimum Net Worth: $NR
Fees: Franchise - $1-10K
  Royalty - 0%;   Ad. - 0%
Earnings Claim Statement: No
Term of Contract (Years):   5/5
Avg. # Of Employees: 1 FT, 1 PT
Passive Ownership: Allowed
Encourage Conversions: Yes
Area Develop. Agreements: No
Sub-Franchising Contracts: No
Expand In Territory: Yes
Space Needs: NR SF; HB

SUPPORT & TRAINING PROVIDED:
Financial Assistance Provided: Yes(B)
Site Selection Assistance: Yes
Lease Negotiation Assistance: Yes
Co-Operative Advertising: Yes
Franchisee Assoc./Member: No
Size Of Corporate Staff: 2
On-Going Support: C,D,E,G,H
Training: 2 Weeks FL.

SPECIFIC EXPANSION PLANS:
US: All United States
Canada: All Canada
Overseas: All Countries

<< >>

CEILING DOCTOR
17810 Davenport Rd., # 108
Dallas, TX 75252
Tel: (800) 992-6299 (972) 250-3311
Fax: (972) 250-3929
Mr. Rob Forrest, Chairman

CEILING DOCTOR provides high-quality, specialty cleaning services to office buildings, retail stores and restaurants.

Complete training and on-going support will ensure your success when you follow our proven operations and marketing systems.

BACKGROUND:
Established: 1984;   1st Franchised: 1985
Franchised Units: 110
Company-Owned Units   1
Total Units: 111
Dist.:   US-52; CAN-20; O's eas-39
  North America: 16 States, 7 Provinces
  Density: 7 in ON, 5 in OH, 4 in PA
Projected New Units (12 Months):   4
Qualifications: 3, 4, 2, 3, 5, 5
Registered: CA,FL,HI,IL,IN,MI,
  NY,VA,WA

FINANCIAL/TERMS:
Cash Investment: $35K
Total Investment: $35K
Minimum Net Worth: $50K
Fees: Franchise - $12.5K
  Royalty - 8%;   Ad. - 2%
Earnings Claim Statement: No
Term of Contract (Years):   5/45
Avg. # Of Employees: 1 FT, 2 PT
Passive Ownership: Discouraged
Encourage Conversions: Yes
Area Develop. Agreements: Yes/50
Sub-Franchising Contracts: No
Expand In Territory: Yes
Space Needs: 150 SF; HB

SUPPORT & TRAINING PROVIDED:
Financial Assistance Provided: No
Site Selection Assistance: N/A
Lease Negotiation Assistance: N/A
Co-Operative Advertising: N/A
Franchisee Assoc./Member: No
Size Of Corporate Staff: 4
On-Going Support: C,D,E,F,G,H,I
Training: 7 Days Dallas, TX.

SPECIFIC EXPANSION PLANS:
US: All United States
Canada: All Canada
Overseas: All Countries

<< >>

CHEM-DRY CANADA
8472 Harvard Pl.
Chilliwack, BC V2P 7Z5 CANADA
Tel: (888) CHEM-DRY (604) 795-9918
Fax: (604) 795-7071
E-Mail: chemdry@chemdry.ca
Web Site: www.chemdry.ca

Ms. Trudy V. Miller, Fran. Marketing/ Licensing

The world's largest carpet & upholstery franchise rated 'The Best of the Best' by Entrepreneur magazine for 12 consecutive years. Our unique patented, non-toxic, heated carbonating cleaner allows most carpets to dry in one hour. State-of-the-art equipment, 22 years experience, on-going research, in-field training, technical support, a monthly newsletter and annual conventions makes a CHEM-DRY franchise a good business.

BACKGROUND:
Established: 1977;   1st Franchised: 1978
Franchised Units: 135
Company-Owned Units   0
Total Units: 135
Dist.:   US-0; CAN-135; O'seas-0
  North America: 10 Provinces
  Density: 48 in ON, 28 in BC, 18 in AB
Projected New Units (12 Months):   20
Qualifications: 3, 1, 1, 1, 1, 1
Registered: AB
FINANCIAL/TERMS:
Cash Investment: $17-25K
Total Investment: $37.9K
Minimum Net Worth: $40K
Fees: Franchise - $11K
  Royalty - $310/Mo.;   Ad. - $0
Earnings Claim Statement: No
Term of Contract (Years):   5/5
Avg. # Of Employees: 1-5 FT, 2-4 PT
Passive Ownership: Discouraged
Encourage Conversions: N/A
Area Develop. Agreements: No
Sub-Franchising Contracts: No
Expand In Territory: Yes
Space Needs: 500 SF; HB
SUPPORT & TRAINING PROVIDED:
Financial Assistance Provided: Yes(D)
Site Selection Assistance: N/A
Lease Negotiation Assistance: No
Co-Operative Advertising: No
Franchisee Assoc./Member: Yes/Yes
Size Of Corporate Staff: 14
On-Going Support: B,C,D,G,H,I
Training: 1 Week Head Office.
SPECIFIC EXPANSION PLANS:
US: N/A
Canada: All Canada
Overseas: No

⋘ ⋙

CHEM-DRY CARPET & UPHOLSTERY CLEANING
1530 North 1000 West
Logan, UT 84321
Tel: (800) 841-6583 (435) 755-0099
Fax: (435) 755-0021
E-Mail: charlie@chemdry.com
Web Site: www.chemdry.com
Mr. Mark S. Coon, National Franchise Director

We have over 20 years of experience, state-of-the-art, patented equipment, on-going research and development and technical support. CHEM-DRY lets you offer a unique, patented, hot carbonating carpet and upholstery cleaning service that is second-to-none! Entrepreneur Magazine has rated us #1 in our field for the past 10 years.

BACKGROUND:
Established: 1977;   1st Franchised: 1978
Franchised Units: 3,903
Company-Owned Units   0
Total Units: 3,903
Dist.:   US-2,505; CAN-124; O'seas-1330
  North America: 50 States, 11Provinces
  Density: 433 in CA, 177 in TX, 151 FL
Projected New Units (12 Months):
                                     225-250
Qualifications: 2, 3, 1, 1, 3, 5
Registered: All States
FINANCIAL/TERMS:
Cash Investment: $7K Down Pay.
Total Investment: $6.9-27.6K
Minimum Net Worth: $N/A
Fees: Franchise - $19.9K
  Royalty - $198/Mo.;   Ad. - 0%
Earnings Claim Statement: No
Term of Contract (Years):   5/5
Avg. # Of Employees: 3 FT
Passive Ownership: Allowed
Encourage Conversions: N/A
Area Develop. Agreements: No
Sub-Franchising Contracts: No
Expand In Territory: No
Space Needs: N/A SF; N/A
SUPPORT & TRAINING PROVIDED:
Financial Assistance Provided: Yes(D)
Site Selection Assistance: N/A
Lease Negotiation Assistance: N/A
Co-Operative Advertising: Yes
Franchisee Assoc./Member: Yes/No

Size Of Corporate Staff: 60
On-Going Support: B,C,D,G,H,I
Training: 5 Days Logan, UT; 8 Hour Home
  Study with Video.
SPECIFIC EXPANSION PLANS:
US: All United States
Canada: All Canada
Overseas: Most Countries

⋘ ⋙

CHEMSTATION INTERNATIONAL
3400 Encrete Ln.
Dayton, OH 45439
Tel: (877) 999-8265 (937) 294-8265
Fax: (937) 534-0426
E-Mail: customerservice@chemstation.com
Web Site: www.chemstation.com
Mr. George Homan, President

CHEMSTATION is an affiliation of manufacturing centers which offer their customers the unique service of custom manufactured cleaning chemicals delivered in bulk to refillable containers that eliminate the waste and inefficiencies of drums.

BACKGROUND: IFA MEMBER
Established: 1983;   1st Franchised: 1984
Franchised Units: 40
Company-Owned Units   2
Total Units: 42
Dist.:   US-42; CAN-0; O'seas-0
  North America: 27 States
  Density: 5 in OH, 3 in MI, 3 in IN
Projected New Units (12 Months):   2
Qualifications: 5, 4, 3, 2, 1, 5
Registered: NR
FINANCIAL/TERMS:
Cash Investment: $150-300K
Total Investment: $500-700K
Minimum Net Worth: $NR
Fees: Franchise - $45K
  Royalty - 4%;   Ad. - 2%
Earnings Claim Statement: No
Term of Contract (Years):   10/5
Avg. # Of Employees: 6 FT
Passive Ownership: Discouraged
Encourage Conversions: N/A
Area Develop. Agreements: No
Sub-Franchising Contracts: No
Expand In Territory: Yes
Space Needs: 6,000 SF; Commercial/
  Industrial

332

SUPPORT & TRAINING PROVIDED:

Financial Assistance Provided:	No
Site Selection Assistance:	Yes
Lease Negotiation Assistance:	Yes
Co-Operative Advertising:	Yes
Franchisee Assoc./Member:	Yes
Size Of Corporate Staff:	35
On-Going Support:	A,B,C,D,E,F,G,H,I

Training: 1 Week Dayton, OH and On-Going.

SPECIFIC EXPANSION PLANS:

US:	West, NY, Northeast
Canada:	All Canada
Overseas:	All Countries

◄◄ ►►

CLEANING CONSULTANT SERVICES

3693 E. Marginal Way S.
Seattle, WA 98134
Tel: (206) 682-9748
Fax: (206) 622-6876
E-Mail:
wgriffin@cleaningconsultants.com
Web Site: www.cleaningconsultants.com
Mr. William R. Griffin, President

Our licensed consultants provide services and information to institutional and industrial companies, as well as the self-employed who are involved with professional cleaning and building maintenance. They sell books, videos, software, consulting and seminars.

BACKGROUND:

Established: 1976;	1st Franchised: 1979
Franchised Units:	5
Company-Owned Units	4
Total Units:	9
Dist.:	US-8; CAN-1; O'seas-0
North America:	3 States, 1 Province
Density:	NR
Projected New Units (12 Months):	10
Qualifications:	, 5, 5, , ,
Registered: NR	

FINANCIAL/TERMS:

Cash Investment:	$5K
Total Investment:	$5K
Minimum Net Worth:	$20K
Fees: Franchise -	$2.5K
Royalty - 0%;	Ad. - 0%
Earnings Claim Statement:	No
Term of Contract (Years):	3/2
Avg. # Of Employees:	1 FT
Passive Ownership:	Not Allowed
Encourage Conversions:	No
Area Develop. Agreements:	No

Sub-Franchising Contracts:	No
Expand In Territory:	No
Space Needs: NR SF; N/A	

SUPPORT & TRAINING PROVIDED:

Financial Assistance Provided:	N/A
Site Selection Assistance:	N/A
Lease Negotiation Assistance:	No
Co-Operative Advertising:	Yes
Franchisee Assoc./Member:	No
Size Of Corporate Staff:	3
On-Going Support:	d

Training: 3 Days Seattle, WA; 3 Days On-Site.

SPECIFIC EXPANSION PLANS:

US:	All United States
Canada:	All Canada
Overseas:	All Countries

◄◄ ►►

CLEANNET USA

9861 Broken Land Pkwy., # 208
Columbia, MD 21046
Tel: (800) 735-8838 (410) 720-6444
Fax: (410) 720-5307
Web Site: www.cleannetusa.com
Mr. Dennis M. Urner, Executive Vice President

Full-service, turn-key commercial office cleaning franchise, offering guaranteed customer accounts, training equipment, supplies, local office support, quality control backup, billing/invoicing and guaranteed payment for services provided. Company also sells master licenses for markets with metropolitan populations of 500,000 and up.

BACKGROUND:

Established: 1987;	1st Franchised: 1988
Franchised Units:	1,718
Company-Owned Units	7
Total Units:	1,725
Dist.:	US-1,725; CAN-0; O'seas-0
North America:	13 States
Density: 366 in MD, 308 in NJ, 195 PA	
Projected New Units (12 Months):	400
Qualifications:	4, 3, 2, 1, 3, 4
Registered: CA,FL,IL,MD,MI,VA	

FINANCIAL/TERMS:

Cash Investment:	$0-25K
Total Investment:	$2.9-35.7K
Minimum Net Worth:	$0-100K
Fees: Franchise -	$2-25.5K
Royalty - 3%;	Ad. - 0%
Earnings Claim Statement:	No

Term of Contract (Years):	20/20
Avg. # Of Employees:	2 FT, 10 PT
Passive Ownership:	Discouraged
Encourage Conversions:	N/A
Area Develop. Agreements:	Yes/20
Sub-Franchising Contracts:	Yes
Expand In Territory:	Yes
Space Needs: 2,000 SF; Multi-Tenant	

SUPPORT & TRAINING PROVIDED:

Financial Assistance Provided:	Yes(D)
Site Selection Assistance:	Yes
Lease Negotiation Assistance:	Yes
Co-Operative Advertising:	No
Franchisee Assoc./Member:	No
Size Of Corporate Staff:	75
On-Going Support:	A,B,C,D,E,G,H,I

Training: 8 Days to 2 Weeks Company Offices; 4 Days to 3 Weeks Job Site or Master Offices.

SPECIFIC EXPANSION PLANS:

US:	All United States
Canada:	All Canada

Overseas: South Africa, Korea, Southeast Asia, Europe, Australia, U.K.

◄◄ ►►

COIT SERVICES

897 Hinckley Rd.
Burlingame, CA 94010
Tel: (800) 243-8797 (650) 697-5471
Fax: (650) 697-6117
E-Mail: craig@coit.com
Web Site: www.coit.com
Mr. Craig Ratkovich, Director Franchise Development

Granting large, exclusive territories, COIT SERVICES provides a proven opportunity in the carpet, upholstery, drapery, area rug air-duct cleaning and hard surface renewal business. COIT franchisees enjoy use of a universal 800# (1-800-FOR-COIT), along with successful marketing and business development that have been developed in 50 years of operational experience.

BACKGROUND: IFA MEMBER

Established: 1950;	1st Franchised: 1963
Franchised Units:	60
Company-Owned Units	10
Total Units:	70
Dist.:	US-66; CAN-3; O'seas-1
North America:	26 States, 2 Provinces
Density:	16 in CA, 4 in WA, 4 in OH

Projected New Units (12 Months):   51
Qualifications: 3, 5, 4, 3, 1, 5
Registered: All States
FINANCIAL/TERMS:
Cash Investment: $40-60K
Total Investment: $100K
Minimum Net Worth: $No Minimum
Fees: Franchise - $25K
  Royalty - 2-6%;   Ad. - 0%
Earnings Claim Statement: Yes
Term of Contract (Years):   10/10
Avg. # Of Employees: 2 FT, 1 PT
Passive Ownership: Discouraged
Encourage Conversions: Yes
Area Develop. Agreements: No
Sub-Franchising Contracts: No
Expand In Territory: Yes
Space Needs: 1,000 SF; Industrial
SUPPORT & TRAINING PROVIDED:
Financial Assistance Provided: Yes(D)
Site Selection Assistance: Yes
Lease Negotiation Assistance: Yes
Co-Operative Advertising: Yes
Franchisee Assoc./Member: Yes/Yes
Size Of Corporate Staff: 19
On-Going Support: A,a,B,C,D,E,G,H,I
Training: 7 Days Corporate Headquarters;
  1-2 Weeks in Field.
SPECIFIC EXPANSION PLANS:
US: Northeast, Southeast,Midwest
Canada: All Canada
Overseas: All Countries

◄◄ ►►

COUSTIC-GLO INTERNATIONAL
7115 Ohms Ln. #7111
Minneapolis, MN 55439
Tel: (800) 388-6347 (612) 835-1338
Fax: (612) 835-1395
E-Mail: info@coutic-glo.com
Web Site: www.coustic-glo.com
Mr. Scott L. Smith, Dir. Franchise
  Marketing

Building restoration products which enable
you to clean and restore all types of ceiling
and wall areas. Very specialized market
which is growing as buildings age and the
indoor environmental concerns continue
to grow nationwide.

BACKGROUND: IFA MEMBER
Established: 1975;   1st Franchised: 1984
Franchised Units: 110
Company-Owned Units   1
Total Units: 111
Dist.:   US-210; CAN-26; O'seas-26
  North America: NR

Density: 12 in GA, 6 in FL, 5 in TX
Projected New Units (12 Months):   50
Qualifications: 4, 4, 3, 3, 3, 3
Registered: All States
FINANCIAL/TERMS:
Cash Investment: $12-25K
Total Investment: $12-25K
Minimum Net Worth: $20K
Fees: Franchise - $12K
  Royalty - 5%;   Ad. - 1%
Earnings Claim Statement: Yes
Term of Contract (Years):   10/5
Avg. # Of Employees: 1 FT
Passive Ownership: Allowed
Encourage Conversions: N/A
Area Develop. Agreements: Yes/10
Sub-Franchising Contracts: Yes
Expand In Territory: Yes
Space Needs: N/A SF; N/A
SUPPORT & TRAINING PROVIDED:
Financial Assistance Provided: Yes(I)
Site Selection Assistance: N/A
Lease Negotiation Assistance: N/A
Co-Operative Advertising: Yes
Franchisee Assoc./Member: Yes/Yes
Size Of Corporate Staff: 20
On-Going Support: B,C,D,G,H,I
Training: 2 Weeks On-Location.
SPECIFIC EXPANSION PLANS:
US: All United States
Canada: All Canada
Overseas: All Countries

◄◄ ►►

COVERALL NORTH AMERICA
500 W. Cypress Creek Rd., # 580
Ft. Lauderdale, FL 33309
Tel: (800) 537-3371 (954) 351-1110
Fax: (954) 492-5044
E-Mail: jcaughey@coverall.com
Web Site: www.coverall.com
Mr. Jack Caughey, VP Franchise Dev.

Comprehensive janitorial franchise which
includes state-of-the-art training, franchise
development, equipment and supplies,
billing and collection services, as well as
customer assistance services. Additional
training, bulk volume-buying power,
insurance and benefit packages also
available. Master franchises also available.
Master insurance plans offered.

BACKGROUND: IFA MEMBER
Established: 1985;   1st Franchised: 1985

Franchised Units: 5,941
Company-Owned Units   0
Total Units: 5,941
Dist.:   US-5,676; CAN-88; O'seas-177
  North America: 32 States, 2 Provinces
  Density: 807 in CA, 714 in FL, 445 OH
Projected New Units (12 Months): 1,782
Qualifications: 3, 3, 2, 2, 3, 5
Registered: All States Except SD
FINANCIAL/TERMS:
Cash Investment: $1.5-25.5K
Total Investment: $6.2-35.9K
Minimum Net Worth: $1.5K
Fees: Franchise - $6-32.2K
  Royalty - 5%;   Ad. - 2%
Earnings Claim Statement: No
Term of Contract (Years):   20/20
Avg. # Of Employees: 1-2 FT, 2-3 PT
Passive Ownership: Allowed
Encourage Conversions: Yes
Area Develop. Agreements: Yes/20
Sub-Franchising Contracts: Yes
Expand In Territory: Yes
Space Needs: N/A SF; N/A
SUPPORT & TRAINING PROVIDED:
Financial Assistance Provided: Yes(D)
Site Selection Assistance: Yes
Lease Negotiation Assistance: No
Co-Operative Advertising: Yes
Franchisee Assoc./Member: No/No
Size Of Corporate Staff: 60
On-Going Support: A,B,C,D,G,H,I
Training: Approximately 40 Hours at Local
  Regional Office; Training Varies with
  Type of Franchise.
SPECIFIC EXPANSION PLANS:
US: All United States
Canada: All Canada
Overseas: All Countries

◄◄ ►►

DURACLEAN INTERNATIONAL
220 Campus Dr.
Arlington Heights, IL 60006
Tel: (800) 251-7070 (847) 704-7100
Fax: (847) 704-7101
E-Mail: mhiggins@duraclean.com
Web Site: www.duraclean.com
Mr. Michael Higgins, VP Global Expansion

DURACLEAN offers distinct services,
markets and revenue center packages to
fit your needs for independence and
growth. Carpet cleaning, ceiling and wall
cleaning, upholstery and drapery cleaning,
fire/smoke/water restoration, janitorial,
pressure washing, hard surface floor care,
duct cleaning and ultrasonic cleaning are

all services that we offer. We are the most diversified cleaning franchise in the world.

BACKGROUND: IFA MEMBER
Established: 1930;   1st Franchised: 1945
Franchised Units: 347
Company-Owned Units   1
Total Units: 348
Dist.:   US-267; CAN-22; O'seas-59
  North America: 50 States
  Density: 38 in FL, 34 in IL, 30 in CA
Projected New Units (12 Months):   30
Qualifications: 4, 4, 3, 3, 3, 3
Registered: All States
FINANCIAL/TERMS:
Cash Investment: $25K
Total Investment: $54-70K
Minimum Net Worth: $N/A
Fees: Franchise - $10K
  Royalty - 6-8%;   Ad. - 0%
Earnings Claim Statement: No
Term of Contract (Years):   5/5
Avg. # Of Employees: 2 FT, 1 PT
Passive Ownership: Discouraged
Encourage Conversions: Yes
Area Develop. Agreements: No
Sub-Franchising Contracts: No
Expand In Territory: Yes
Space Needs: N/A SF; HB
SUPPORT & TRAINING PROVIDED:
Financial Assistance Provided: Yes(D)
Site Selection Assistance: N/A
Lease Negotiation Assistance: N/A
Co-Operative Advertising: No
Franchisee Assoc./Member: Yes/No
Size Of Corporate Staff: 25
On-Going Support: C,D,G,H,I
Training: 6 Days Success Institute, Corp.
  Office; 2 Days On-Site Cleaning; Home
  Study Program.
SPECIFIC EXPANSION PLANS:
US: All United States
Canada: All Canada
Overseas: All Countries

≪ ≫

E. P. I. C. SYSTEMS
402 E. Maryland
Evansville, IN 47711
Tel: (800) 230-3742 (812) 428-7750
Fax: (812) 428-4162
E-Mail: jrschaperjohn@netzero.net
Mr. Craig Wargel, Franchise Support Rep.

Complete janitorial service franchising master units for $25,000 per million population, single units for $6,500. We can assist with financing with good credit.

BACKGROUND:
Established: 1993;   1st Franchised: 1994
Franchised Units: 7
Company-Owned Units   0
Total Units: 7
Dist.:   US-7; CAN-0; O'seas-0
  North America: 2 States
  Density: 4 in KY, 3 in IN
Projected New Units (12 Months):   6
Qualifications: 5, 3, 4, 3, 5, 4
Registered: FL,IN,MI
FINANCIAL/TERMS:
Cash Investment: $6.5-28.5K
Total Investment: $6.5-60K
Minimum Net Worth: $10.2-28.5K
Fees: Franchise - $6.5K
  Royalty - 4-10%;   Ad. - N/A
Earnings Claim Statement: No
Term of Contract (Years):   10/10
Avg. # Of Employees: 1 FT, 5 PT
Passive Ownership: Discouraged
Encourage Conversions: Yes
Area Develop. Agreements: Yes/10
Sub-Franchising Contracts: Yes
Expand In Territory: Yes
Space Needs: 250-1,000 SF; HB, OB
SUPPORT & TRAINING PROVIDED:
Financial Assistance Provided: Yes(D)
Site Selection Assistance: Yes
Lease Negotiation Assistance: No
Co-Operative Advertising: No
Franchisee Assoc./Member: No
Size Of Corporate Staff: 4
On-Going Support: c,D,I
Training: 2 Weeks at Headquarters.
SPECIFIC EXPANSION PLANS:
US: Midwest, Southeast
Canada: No
Overseas: No

≪ ≫

EARTH-CLEAN.COM
7649 Old Georgetown Rd., # 200A
Bethesda, MD 20814
Tel: (800) 571-5422 (301) 654-4986

Fax: (301) 654-4476
E-Mail: andrew@earth-clean.com
Web Site: www.earth-clean.com
Mr. Andrew Drykerman, Director Business
  Development

Earthclean.com is a full-service powerwashing and exterior maintenance franchise. We serve both commercial and residential customers. We offer quality services such as pressure washing and sealing decks, siding, concrete, gutters and awnings. We also provide a full line of landscaping services such as design, irrigation, seeding, planting and lawn care.

BACKGROUND:
Established: 1997;   1st Franchised: 1997
Franchised Units: 6
Company-Owned Units   1
Total Units: 7
Dist.:   US-7; CAN-0; O'seas-0
  North America: 3 States
  Density: 4 in MD, 2 in VA, 1 in DC
Projected New Units (12 Months):   5
Qualifications: 2, 4, 3, 2, 5, 5
Registered:
FINANCIAL/TERMS:
Cash Investment: $5K
Total Investment: $5-18K
Minimum Net Worth: $10-20K
Fees: Franchise - $5K
  Royalty - 6-12%;   Ad. - 0%
Earnings Claim Statement: No
Term of Contract (Years):   5/5
Avg. # Of Employees: 2 FT
Passive Ownership: Allowed
Encourage Conversions: N/A
Area Develop. Agreements: Yes/5
Sub-Franchising Contracts: Yes
Expand In Territory: Yes
Space Needs: N/A SF; N/A
SUPPORT & TRAINING PROVIDED:
Financial Assistance Provided: Yes(D)
Site Selection Assistance: Yes
Lease Negotiation Assistance: N/A
Co-Operative Advertising: Yes

Franchisee Assoc./Member: Yes/Yes
Size Of Corporate Staff: 4
On-Going Support: A,B,C,D,E,F,H,I
Training: 1 Day in each DC, MD and VA.
SPECIFIC EXPANSION PLANS:
US: All States, Concent. East
Canada: No
Overseas: No

<< >>

ENVIRONMENTAL BIOTECH
1701 Biotech Way
Sarasota, FL 34243
Tel: (800) 314-6263 (941) 358-9112
Fax: (941) 359-9744
E-Mail: info@environmentalbiotech.com
Web Site: www.environmentalbiotech.com
Global Development Dept.,

Business-to-business service company. Utilizing the latest proprietary bio-technologies, we provide maintenance services to eliminate waste build-up in drain lines. Our target is the commercial and industrial food-service market, as well as hospitals and other producers of grease, oil, sugar, starch and gelatin waste.

BACKGROUND: IFA MEMBER
Established: 1991;   1st Franchised: 1991
Franchised Units: 66
Company-Owned Units   0
Total Units: 66
Dist.:   US-40; CAN-1; O'seas-25
   North America: 22 States, 1 Province
   Density: 11 in FL, 5 in TX, 4 in PA
Projected New Units (12 Months):   20
Qualifications: 5, 5, 4, 4, 5, 5
Registered: CA,FL,IL,IN,MD,MI,MN,
   NY,VA,WA,WI
FINANCIAL/TERMS:
Cash Investment: $45-56.6K
Total Investment: $80-91.6K
Minimum Net Worth: $300K
Fees: Franchise - $35K
   Royalty - 5%;   Ad. - 1%
Earnings Claim Statement: No
Term of Contract (Years):   5/5/5
Avg. # Of Employees: 2 FT, 1 PT
Passive Ownership: Not Allowed
Encourage Conversions: No
Area Develop. Agreements: No
Sub-Franchising Contracts: No
Expand In Territory: No

Space Needs: 1,000 SF; Warehouse/ Office
SUPPORT & TRAINING PROVIDED:
Financial Assistance Provided: No
Site Selection Assistance: No
Lease Negotiation Assistance: No
Co-Operative Advertising: No
Franchisee Assoc./Member: Yes/Yes
Size Of Corporate Staff: 30
On-Going Support: b,C,D,G,h
Training: 2 Consecutive Weeks E.B.I. Headquarters; 3+ Weeks in Field.
SPECIFIC EXPANSION PLANS:
US: All United States
Canada: All Canada
Overseas: Most Countries

<< >>

FABRI-ZONE CLEANING SYSTEMS
3135 Universal Dr., # 6
Mississauga, ON L4X 2E2 CANADA
Tel: (888) 781-1123 (905) 602-7691
Fax: (905) 602-7821
E-Mail: headoffice@fabrizone.com
Web Site: www.fabrizone.com
Mr. David S. Collier, President

FABRI-ZONE offers a full-service franchise concept to start with a turn-key system with an environmentally-sensitive cleaning program, a patented dry cleaning and purification carpet cleaning process. FABRI-restore steam finishing process cleans upholstery, drapery and ceilings. Professional marketing, sales and financial support. Recommended by carpet manufacturers.

BACKGROUND:
Established: 1981;   1st Franchised: 1984
Franchised Units: 39
Company-Owned Units   1
Total Units: 40
Dist.:   US-7; CAN-30; O'seas-3
   North America: NR
   Density: NR
Projected New Units (12 Months):   8
Qualifications: 3, 4, 1, 4, 4, 4
Registered: NR
FINANCIAL/TERMS:
Cash Investment: $6K
Total Investment: $15-30K
Minimum Net Worth: $NR
Fees: Franchise - $5K
   Royalty - 6%;   Ad. - 0%
Earnings Claim Statement: NR
Term of Contract (Years):   3/3

Avg. # Of Employees: 2 FT, 4 PT
Passive Ownership: Not Allowed
Encourage Conversions: Yes
Area Develop. Agreements: Yes
Sub-Franchising Contracts: NR
Expand In Territory: NR
Space Needs: NR SF; N/A
SUPPORT & TRAINING PROVIDED:
Financial Assistance Provided: Yes
Site Selection Assistance: N/A
Lease Negotiation Assistance: N/A
Co-Operative Advertising: N/A
Franchisee Assoc./Member: No
Size Of Corporate Staff: 20
On-Going Support: B,C,d,e,G,H,I
Training: 8 Days Toronto, ON.
SPECIFIC EXPANSION PLANS:
US: NR
Canada: All Canada
Overseas: All Countries

<< >>

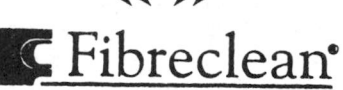

FIBRECLEAN SUPPLIES
1 - 3611 27 St. N.E.
Calgary, AB T1Y 5E4 CANADA
Tel: (403) 291-2870
Fax: (403) 291-3786
E-Mail: kbrown@fibreclean.com
Web Site: www.fibreclean.com
Ms. Kathy Brown, Fran. Operations Mgr.

FIBRECLEAN SUPPLIES distributes specialty wholesale supplies to the rapidly-expanding cleaning industry. We are the leading soft fibre supplier in Canada, with product lines that are recognizable throughout the industry. FIBRECLEAN offers franchisees existing sales to start with, exclusive territories, comprehensive training, customized software, in-house marketing department, centralized purchasing, certified instructors, product R & D, national and local mailers and much more.

BACKGROUND:
Established: 1977;   1st Franchised: 1996
Franchised Units: 4
Company-Owned Units   4
Total Units: 8
Dist.:   US-0; CAN-8; O'seas-0
   North America: 5 Provinces
   Density: 3 in BC, 2 in AB, 1 in ON
Projected New Units (12 Months):   3
Qualifications: 5, 5, 2, 2, 2, 5
Registered: AB

FINANCIAL/TERMS:

Cash Investment:	$75-125K
Total Investment:	$100-200K
Minimum Net Worth:	$100K
Fees: Franchise -	$Varies
Royalty - 5%;	Ad. - 1.25%
Earnings Claim Statement:	No
Term of Contract (Years):	5/5
Avg. # Of Employees:	3 FT
Passive Ownership:	Discouraged
Encourage Conversions:	Yes
Area Develop. Agreements:	Yes/Varies
Sub-Franchising Contracts:	Yes
Expand In Territory:	yes
Space Needs: 2,500 SF; Industrial Storefront	

SUPPORT & TRAINING PROVIDED:

Financial Assistance Provided:	No
Site Selection Assistance:	Yes
Lease Negotiation Assistance:	Yes
Co-Operative Advertising:	Yes
Franchisee Assoc./Member:	No
Size Of Corporate Staff:	31
On-Going Support:	B,C,D,E,F,h
Training: 2 Weeks Calgary, AB; 1 Week On-Site.	

SPECIFIC EXPANSION PLANS:

US:	No
Canada:	MB,PQ, Maritime
Overseas:	No

≪ ≫

**FISH WINDOW CLEANING
SERVICES**

148 #G Chesterfield Industrial Blvd.
Chesterfield, MO 63005
Tel: (877) 707-FISH (636) 530-7334
Fax: (636) 530-7856
E-Mail: info@fishwindowcleaning.com
Web Site: www.fishwindowcleaning.com
Ms. Linda Merrick, Vice President

FISH WINDOW CLEANING provides 22 years of experience that gives the franchisee the keys to successfully manage his/her own business. FWC specializes in year-round residential and ground-level commercial window cleaning. The turnkey operation includes all equipment, proprietary software, managerial techniques, guaranteed accounts and lots of hands-on support in the franchisee's large, protected territory to jumpstart business.

BACKGROUND: IFA MEMBER

Established: 1978;	1st Franchised: 1998
Franchised Units:	24
Company-Owned Units	1
Total Units:	25
Dist.:	US-25; CAN-0; O'seas-0
North America:	11 States
Density:	5 in OH, 4 in MO, 3 in KY
Projected New Units (12 Months):	30
Qualifications:	4, 4, 1, 2, 3, 5
Registered: CA,FL,HI,IL,IN,MI,MN,NY, OR,RI,SD,VA,WA,WI,AB	

FINANCIAL/TERMS:

Cash Investment:	$20-100K
Total Investment:	$29.6-35.6K
Minimum Net Worth:	$50K
Fees: Franchise -	$18.5-24.5K
Royalty - 5.5-8%;	Ad. - 0%
Earnings Claim Statement:	No
Term of Contract (Years):	10/5
Avg. # Of Employees:	2-12 FT
Passive Ownership:	Discouraged
Encourage Conversions:	Yes
Area Develop. Agreements:	No
Sub-Franchising Contracts:	No
Expand In Territory:	Yes
Space Needs: N/A SF; HB	

SUPPORT & TRAINING PROVIDED:

Financial Assistance Provided:	Yes(D)
Site Selection Assistance:	N/A
Lease Negotiation Assistance:	N/A
Co-Operative Advertising:	Yes
Franchisee Assoc./Member:	No
Size Of Corporate Staff:	5
On-Going Support:	A,C,D,G,H,I
Training: 8 Days in Chesterfield, MO.	

SPECIFIC EXPANSION PLANS:

US:	All United States
Canada:	All Canada
Overseas:	No

≪ ≫

**HEAVEN'S BEST CARPET/
UPHOLST. CLEANING**

247 N. 1st E., P. O. Box 607
Rexburg, ID 83440
Tel: (800) 359-2095 (208) 359-1106
Fax: (208) 359-1236
Web Site: www.heavensbest.com
Mr. Cody Howard, CEO

Unique low moisture cleaning process. There is no better franchise opportunity than this. Our franchisees are happy, our customers are happy. Our franchise is very affordable. Call for our free video.

BACKGROUND:

Established: 1983;	1st Franchised: 1983
Franchised Units:	504
Company-Owned Units	0
Total Units:	504
Dist.:	US-491; CAN-4; O'seas-9
North America:	28 States
Density:	48 in CA, 46 in ID, 25 in CO
Projected New Units (12 Months):	100
Registered: CA,IL,IN,MN,OR,WA	

FINANCIAL/TERMS:

Cash Investment:	$7.5-20K
Total Investment:	$16-40K
Minimum Net Worth:	$10K
Fees: Franchise -	$2.9K
Royalty - $80/Mo.;	Ad. - NR
Earnings Claim Statement:	No
Term of Contract (Years):	5/5
Avg. # Of Employees:	1 FT
Passive Ownership:	Allowed
Encourage Conversions:	Yes
Area Develop. Agreements:	No
Sub-Franchising Contracts:	Yes
Expand In Territory:	Yes
Space Needs: N/A SF; N/A	

SUPPORT & TRAINING PROVIDED:

Financial Assistance Provided:	Yes
Site Selection Assistance:	N/A
Lease Negotiation Assistance:	N/A
Co-Operative Advertising:	Yes
Franchisee Assoc./Member:	Yes/Yes
Size Of Corporate Staff:	7
On-Going Support:	A,B,F,G,H,I
Training: 4 Days Rexburg, ID.	

SPECIFIC EXPANSION PLANS:

US:	All United States
Canada:	All Canada
Overseas:	All Countries

≪ ≫

**HYDRO PHYSICS PIPE
INSPECTION**

1855 W. Union Ave., # N
Englewood, CO 80110
Tel: (800) 781-3164 (303) 781-2474
Fax: (303) 781-0477
E-Mail: hydrophys@aol.com
Mr. Thomas J. Suiter, President

HYDRO PHYSICS specializes in the video inspection of underground pipes. By seeing exactly what and where the problems are located, we can save our customers thousands of dollars in unnecessary repair costs. We are the only franchise specializing in this type of work.

BACKGROUND:

Established: 1991;   1st Franchised: 1998
Franchised Units: 9
Company-Owned Units 1
Total Units: 10
Dist.:   US-10; CAN-0; O'seas-0
  North America: 4 States
  Density: 1 in CO, 1 in ID, 1 in MO
Projected New Units (12 Months):   15
Qualifications: 4, 3, 2, 2, 2, 5
Registered: CA,VA

FINANCIAL/TERMS:

Cash Investment: $25-80K
Total Investment: $68-125K
Minimum Net Worth: $250K
Fees: Franchise - $19.5K
  Royalty - 7.5%;   Ad. - 2%
Earnings Claim Statement: No
Term of Contract (Years):   10/10
Avg. # Of Employees: 1 FT
Passive Ownership: Not Allowed
Encourage Conversions: N/A
Area Develop. Agreements: Yes/10
Sub-Franchising Contracts: No
Expand In Territory: Yes
Space Needs: NR SF; N/A

SUPPORT & TRAINING PROVIDED:

Financial Assistance Provided: Yes(I)
Site Selection Assistance: N/A
Lease Negotiation Assistance: N/A
Co-Operative Advertising: N/A
Franchisee Assoc./Member: No
Size Of Corporate Staff: 2
On-Going Support: B,C,D,e,F,G,H,I
Training: 2 Weeks in Englewood, CO.

SPECIFIC EXPANSION PLANS:

US: All United States
Canada: No
Overseas: No

⋘ ⋙

JAN-PRO CLEANING SYSTEMS
383 Strand Industrial Dr.
Little River, SC 29566
Tel: (800) 668-1001 (843) 399-9895
Fax: (843) 399-9890
E-Mail: janpro1@aol.com
Web Site: www.jan-pro.com
Ms. Carol McLennan, Vice President

JAN-PRO has built a solid reputation as a quality franchise organization within the commercial cleaning industry. We have

been highly ranked in magazines such as Entrepreneur, Income Opportunities, Home Business and Business Start-Up. JAN-PRO franchise owners are in business for themselves, but not by themselves.

BACKGROUND:

Established: 1991;   1st Franchised: 1992
Franchised Units: 570
Company-Owned Units 100
Total Units: 670
Dist.:   US-0; CAN-0; O'seas-0
  North America: 16 States
  Density: 75 in NJ, 55 in GA, 45 in IL
Projected New Units (12 Months):   NR
Registered:

FINANCIAL/TERMS:

Cash Investment: $1-35K
Total Investment: $2.8-44K
Minimum Net Worth: $3K
Fees: Franchise - $1-35K
  Royalty - 8%;   Ad. - 0%
Earnings Claim Statement: No
Term of Contract (Years):   10/20
Avg. # Of Employees: 2 FT, 2 PT
Passive Ownership: Allowed
Encourage Conversions: NR
Area Develop. Agreements: No
Sub-Franchising Contracts: Yes
Expand In Territory: Yes
Space Needs: NR SF; HB

SUPPORT & TRAINING PROVIDED:

Financial Assistance Provided: NR
Site Selection Assistance: N/A
Lease Negotiation Assistance: N/A
Co-Operative Advertising: N/A
Franchisee Assoc./Member: No
Size Of Corporate Staff:
On-Going Support: A,B,C,D,G,H
Training: 5 On-Site Training Sessions.

SPECIFIC EXPANSION PLANS:

US: All United States
Canada: NR
Overseas: NR

⋘ ⋙

JANTIZE AMERICA
15449 Middlebelt
Livonia, MI 48154
Tel: (800) 968-9182 (734) 421-4733
Fax: (734) 421-4936
E-Mail: asi500@aol.com
Mr. Jerry Grabowski, President

You can own your own business for less than the cost of a new car! A JANTIZE commercial office cleaning franchise has it all - computerized procedures, audio/ visual training, on-going assistance and more!

BACKGROUND:

Established: 1985;   1st Franchised: 1988
Franchised Units: 12
Company-Owned Units 2
Total Units: 14
Dist.:   US-14; CAN-0; O'seas-0
  North America: 2 States
  Density: 13 in MI, 1 in NV
Projected New Units (12 Months):   5
Qualifications: 4, 4, 3, 2, 2, 5
Registered: MI

FINANCIAL/TERMS:

Cash Investment: $9-11.5K
Total Investment: $20K
Minimum Net Worth: $NR
Fees: Franchise - $3.5-16K
  Royalty - 9%;   Ad. - 0%
Earnings Claim Statement: No
Term of Contract (Years):   10/10
Avg. # Of Employees: 3-20 PT
Passive Ownership: Discouraged
Encourage Conversions: Yes
Area Develop. Agreements: No
Sub-Franchising Contracts: Yes
Expand In Territory: No
Space Needs: NR SF; NR

SUPPORT & TRAINING PROVIDED:

Financial Assistance Provided: Yes(D)
Site Selection Assistance: Yes
Lease Negotiation Assistance: No
Co-Operative Advertising: No
Franchisee Assoc./Member: NR
Size Of Corporate Staff: 8
On-Going Support: a,D,E,G,H,I
Training: 3-6 Days Headquarters; 3 Days
  Franchisee Location.

SPECIFIC EXPANSION PLANS:

US: All United States
Canada: All Canada
Overseas: No

⋘ ⋙

JDI CLEANING SYSTEMS
3390 South Service Rd.
Burlington, ON L7N 3J5 CANADA
Tel: (800) 567-5091 (905) 634-5228
Fax: (905) 634-8790
E-Mail: info@jdicleaning.com
Web Site: www.jdicleaning.com
Mr. Joseph Imbrogno, President

Commercial and residential janitorial franchisor, specializing in service to small- and medium-sized accounts. Tested marketing and customer service systems that ensure success. Regional and master programs available.

BACKGROUND:

Established: 1992;   1st Franchised: 1992
Franchised Units: 26
Company-Owned Units 1
Total Units: 27
Dist.:   US-0; CAN-27; O'seas-0
   North America: 1 Province
   Density: 27 in ON
Projected New Units (12 Months):   12
Qualifications: 3, 2, 1, 2, 4, 5
Registered: NR

FINANCIAL/TERMS:

Cash Investment: $10.5K
Total Investment: $18.5K
Minimum Net Worth: $20K
Fees: Franchise - $10.5K
   Royalty - 13%;   Ad. - 2%
Earnings Claim Statement: Yes
Term of Contract (Years):   5/5
Avg. # Of Employees: 1 FT, 2 PT
Passive Ownership: Discouraged
Encourage Conversions: Yes
Area Develop. Agreements: Yes/10
Sub-Franchising Contracts: No
Expand In Territory: Yes
Space Needs: NR SF; N/A

SUPPORT & TRAINING PROVIDED:

Financial Assistance Provided: Yes(D)
Site Selection Assistance: N/A
Lease Negotiation Assistance: N/A
Co-Operative Advertising: N/A
Franchisee Assoc./Member: No
Size Of Corporate Staff: 4
On-Going Support: A,B,C,D,G,H,i
Training: 2 Days Head Office; 30 Days
   On-Site.

SPECIFIC EXPANSION PLANS:

US: Northeastern United States
Canada: All Canada
Overseas: No

≪   ≫

JOY CARPET DRY CLEANING
1301 W. Parker Rd., # 116
Plano, TX 75023
Tel: (800) 959-5136 (972) 881-4678
Fax: (972) 379-6444
E-Mail: joycarpt@flash.net
Web Site: www.flash.net/~joycarpt.com
Mr. Bill Swingler, President

Specializing in REAL carpet dry cleaning which is dry & can be used immediately. We guarantee that the spots removed do not return. Unique ways of getting business without telemarketing gets tremendous referrals and repeat business. This proven 17 year old business offers extensive individual training and on-going support in carpet dry cleaning, upholstery & drapery cleaning, air duct cleaning & water damage restoration.

BACKGROUND:

Established: 1983;   1st Franchised: 1998
Franchised Units: 2
Company-Owned Units 1
Total Units: 3
Dist.:   US-3; CAN-0; O'seas-0
   North America: 1 State
   Density: 3 in TX
Projected New Units (12 Months): 10-20
Qualifications: 3, 4, 1, 1, 2, 5
Registered:

FINANCIAL/TERMS:

Cash Investment: $15-20K
Total Investment: $30-50K
Minimum Net Worth: $Varies
Fees: Franchise - $12.5K
   Royalty - 5%;   Ad. - 1%
Earnings Claim Statement: No
Term of Contract (Years):   10/10
Avg. # Of Employees: 4 FT
Passive Ownership: Allowed
Encourage Conversions: No
Area Develop. Agreements: Yes
Sub-Franchising Contracts: Yes
Expand In Territory: Yes
Space Needs: NR SF; SF, SC, HB

SUPPORT & TRAINING PROVIDED:

Financial Assistance Provided: Yes(I)
Site Selection Assistance: Yes
Lease Negotiation Assistance: No
Co-Operative Advertising: No
Franchisee Assoc./Member: No
Size Of Corporate Staff: 2
On-Going Support: B,C,D,F,G,H,I
Training: 2 Weeks in Plano, TX.

SPECIFIC EXPANSION PLANS:

US: SW, Southeast, Midwest
Canada: All Canada
Overseas: No

≪   ≫

KWIK DRY INTERNATIONAL
25665 Caton Farm Rd.
Plainfield, IL 60544
Tel: (815) 436-0333
Fax: (815) 436-7519
Mr. Jim Boyd, Operations Manager

You would control your time and income, be new, yet run a business with 30 years of experience, using the dry extraction method of cleaning both carpets and furniture. KWIK DRY is very user-friendly (easy on the operator), utilizing an all natural cleaner. We put great emphasis on marketing (getting the jobs). Ideal as a second income business. Choice locations available.

BACKGROUND:

Established: 1967;   1st Franchised: 1995
Franchised Units: 12
Company-Owned Units 0
Total Units: 12
Dist.:   US-12; CAN-0; O'seas-0
   North America: 5 States
   Density: 6 in IL, 3 in MO
Projected New Units (12 Months):   20
Qualifications: 1, 1, 1, 1, 4, 5
Registered: IL

FINANCIAL/TERMS:

Cash Investment: $5.7K
Total Investment: $11.7K
Minimum Net Worth: $10K
Fees: Franchise - $6K
   Royalty - $175/Mo.;   Ad. - 0%
Earnings Claim Statement: No
Term of Contract (Years):   5/5
Avg. # Of Employees: 1 FT
Passive Ownership: Allowed
Encourage Conversions: N/A
Area Develop. Agreements: No
Sub-Franchising Contracts: No
Expand In Territory: Yes
Space Needs: NR SF; HB

SUPPORT & TRAINING PROVIDED:

Financial Assistance Provided: Yes(D)
Site Selection Assistance: N/A
Lease Negotiation Assistance: N/A
Co-Operative Advertising: N/A
Franchisee Assoc./Member: No
Size Of Corporate Staff: NR
On-Going Support: B,G,h
Training: 5 Days Plainsfield, IL.

SPECIFIC EXPANSION PLANS:

US: All United States
Canada: No
Overseas: No

≪   ≫

LANGENWALTER CARPET DYEING
1111 S. Richfield Rd.
Placentia, CA 92870-6790
Tel: (800) 422-4370 (714) 528-7610
Fax: (714) 528-7620

E-Mail: langdy@aol.com
Web Site: www.home.Navisoft.com/
langenwalter
Mr. John Langenwalter, Vice President

We offer complete carpet color correction. The franchisees are carpet color correction experts. They can take care of problems such as sunfading, pet stains, bleach spots, chemical stains, etc. Complete color changes are also done to save the customer 85% of carpet replacement costs.

BACKGROUND:

Established: 1975;	1st Franchised: 1981
Franchised Units:	170
Company-Owned Units	3
Total Units:	173
Dist.:	US-152; CAN-19; O's-2
North America:	25 States, 3 Provinces
Density:	75 in CA, 10 in BC, 9 in MA
Projected New Units (12 Months):	50
Qualifications:	3, 2, 1, 1, 2, 4
Registered:	CA,FL,IN,MD,MI,MN,NY, OR,RI,VA,WA,WI,AB

FINANCIAL/TERMS:

Cash Investment:	$30K
Total Investment:	$30K
Minimum Net Worth:	$30K
Fees: Franchise -	$18K
Royalty - $110/Mo.;	Ad. - 0%
Earnings Claim Statement:	No
Term of Contract (Years):	3/3
Avg. # Of Employees:	1 PT
Passive Ownership:	Not Allowed
Encourage Conversions:	No
Area Develop. Agreements:	No
Sub-Franchising Contracts:	No
Expand In Territory:	Yes
Space Needs: NR SF; HB	

SUPPORT & TRAINING PROVIDED:

Financial Assistance Provided:	No
Site Selection Assistance:	N/A
Lease Negotiation Assistance:	N/A
Co-Operative Advertising:	Yes
Franchisee Assoc./Member:	No
Size Of Corporate Staff:	10
On-Going Support:	G,h,I
Training: 5 Days Placentia, CA.	

SPECIFIC EXPANSION PLANS:

US:	All United States
Canada:	All Canada
Overseas:	All Countries

<< >>

MAINTAIN CLEANING SYSTEMS
927 State Rte. 28
Milford, OH 45150

Tel: (800) 861-4168 (513) 576-6622
Fax: (800) 867-0056
Mr. Allen Atkinson, President

Operate your own commercial cleaning service with outstanding local support. We will train and support you every step of the way.

BACKGROUND:

Established: 1993;	1st Franchised: 1993
Franchised Units:	49
Company-Owned Units	0
Total Units:	49
Dist.:	US-49; CAN-0; O's-0
North America:	2 States
Density:	40 in OH, 9 in KY
Projected New Units (12 Months):	40
Qualifications:	3, 3, 3, 3, 5, 5
Registered: NR	

FINANCIAL/TERMS:

Cash Investment:	$1-5K
Total Investment:	$8.5-25K
Minimum Net Worth:	$N/A
Fees: Franchise -	$7K
Royalty - 5%;	Ad. - N/A
Earnings Claim Statement:	No
Term of Contract (Years):	5/2
Avg. # Of Employees:	1 PT
Passive Ownership:	Not Allowed
Encourage Conversions:	Yes
Area Develop. Agreements:	No
Sub-Franchising Contracts:	No
Expand In Territory:	N/A
Space Needs: NR SF; N/A	

SUPPORT & TRAINING PROVIDED:

Financial Assistance Provided:	Yes(B)
Site Selection Assistance:	N/A
Lease Negotiation Assistance:	N/A
Co-Operative Advertising:	N/A
Franchisee Assoc./Member:	No
Size Of Corporate Staff:	10
On-Going Support:	A,C,D,E,H,I
Training: 2 Days Cincinnati, OH.	

SPECIFIC EXPANSION PLANS:

US:	Midwest Only
Canada:	No
Overseas:	No

<< >>

MASTER CARE
555 6th St., # 327
New Westminster, BC V3L 4Y4
CANADA
Tel: (800) 889-2799 (604) 525-8221
Fax: (604) 526-2235
E-Mail: gerhard@direct.ca
Mr. Gerhard Hoffman, President

Commercial janitorial services.

BACKGROUND:

Established: 1960;	1st Franchised: 1987
Franchised Units:	107
Company-Owned Units	1
Total Units:	108
Dist.:	US-0; CAN-108; O's-0
North America:	1 Province
Density:	108 in BC
Projected New Units (12 Months):	30
Qualifications:	3, 3, 1, 1, 2, 3
Registered: NR	

FINANCIAL/TERMS:

Cash Investment:	$2-75K
Total Investment:	$5-200K
Minimum Net Worth:	$25K
Fees: Franchise -	$4.5-125K
Royalty - 5-15%;	Ad. - 1%
Earnings Claim Statement:	No
Term of Contract (Years):	5/5
Avg. # Of Employees:	2 FT
Passive Ownership:	Discouraged
Encourage Conversions:	Yes
Area Develop. Agreements:	Yes/10
Sub-Franchising Contracts:	Yes
Expand In Territory:	Yes
Space Needs: NR SF; N/A	

SUPPORT & TRAINING PROVIDED:

Financial Assistance Provided:	Yes(D)
Site Selection Assistance:	Yes
Lease Negotiation Assistance:	N/A
Co-Operative Advertising:	Yes
Franchisee Assoc./Member:	Yes/Yes
Size Of Corporate Staff:	4
On-Going Support:	A,B,C,D,E,G,h,I
Training: 1-6 Weeks at Head Office.	

SPECIFIC EXPANSION PLANS:

US:	Master Franchises Only
Canada:	Master Franchise
Overseas:	No

<< >>

MAXCARE PROFESSIONAL CLEANING SYSTEMS
210 Town Park Dr.
Kennesaw, GA 30144
Tel: (800) 707-4332 (678) 355-4407
Fax: (678) 355-4977
E-Mail: kkaplan@maximgp.com
Web Site: www.maxcarecleaning.com
Mr. Ken Kaplan, VP Franchise Development

All surfaces floor maintenance featuring state-of-the-art equipment, such as 'dust free' wood refinishing, and interior powerwashing of tile surfaces with no overspray. Many pre-established relationships with insurance companies, retailers, home improvement centers and real estate companies.

BACKGROUND: IFA MEMBER
Established: 1997; 1st Franchised: 1997
Franchised Units: 85
Company-Owned Units 0
Total Units: 85
Dist.: US-28; CAN-0; O'seas-0
  North America: 34 States
  Density: 11 in FL, 8 in TX, 6 in IL
Projected New Units (12 Months): 100
Qualifications: 3, 3, 3, 2, 3, 3
Registered: All States
FINANCIAL/TERMS:
Cash Investment: $NR
Total Investment: $12.5-50K
Minimum Net Worth: $50K
Fees: Franchise - $8.7K
  Royalty - 6%; Ad. - 2%
Earnings Claim Statement: No
Term of Contract (Years): 10/10
Avg. # Of Employees: 3 FT
Passive Ownership: Allowed
Encourage Conversions: N/A
Area Develop. Agreements: No
Sub-Franchising Contracts: No
Expand In Territory: Yes
Space Needs: NR SF; HB
SUPPORT & TRAINING PROVIDED:
Financial Assistance Provided: Yes(D)
Site Selection Assistance: N/A
Lease Negotiation Assistance: N/A
Co-Operative Advertising: N/A
Franchisee Assoc./Member: No
Size Of Corporate Staff: 12
On-Going Support: B,C,D,E,G,H,I
Training: 10-16 Days Atlanta, GA.
SPECIFIC EXPANSION PLANS:
US: All United States
Canada: All Canada
Overseas: No

≪ ≫

**MILLICARE COMMERCIAL
CARPET CARE**
201 Lukken Industrial Dr., W.
LaGrange, GA 30240
Tel: (888) 88M-CARE (706) 880-3377
Fax: (706) 880-3279
E-Mail: millicare@millicare.com
Web Site: www.millicare.com
Mr. Michael McDonald, VP of Business
  Management

Buy into experience and professionalism.

MILLICARE ENVIRONMENTAL SERVICES is currently seeking to select people to become franchisees in select cities in North America. The MILLICARE system includes a variety of services provided to commercial facility managers including carpet maintenance, carpet recycling, panel and upholstery cleaning and entryway systems. Franchisees receive world-class training, sales and marketing programs from a strong, experienced global franchisor.

BACKGROUND: IFA MEMBER
Established: 1984; 1st Franchised: 1996
Franchised Units: 80
Company-Owned Units 0
Total Units: 80
Dist.: US-71; CAN-7; O'seas-2
  North America: NR
  Density: NR
Projected New Units (12 Months): 15-20
Qualifications: 5, 4, 3, 3, 4, 5
Registered: CA,FL,HI,IL,IN,MD,MI,MN,
  NY,OR,RI,VA,WA,WI,DC,AB
FINANCIAL/TERMS:
Cash Investment: $30-50K
Total Investment: $70-170K
Minimum Net Worth: $100K
Fees: Franchise - $20K
  Royalty - 6%; Ad. - 2%
Earnings Claim Statement: No
Term of Contract (Years): 5/5
Avg. # Of Employees: 1-20 FT
Passive Ownership: Allowed
Encourage Conversions: No
Area Develop. Agreements: Poss.
Sub-Franchising Contracts: No
Expand In Territory: Possible
Space Needs: 2,000 SF; Warehouse
SUPPORT & TRAINING PROVIDED:
Financial Assistance Provided: Yes(I)
Site Selection Assistance: No
Lease Negotiation Assistance: N/A
Co-Operative Advertising: Yes
Franchisee Assoc./Member: Yes
Size Of Corporate Staff: 6
On-Going Support: C,D,E,G,H,I
Training: 3 Days La Grange, GA; 3 Days

Model Franchise Location, DE; 2 Days
Franchisee's Location.
SPECIFIC EXPANSION PLANS:
US: All Major 2ndary Metro Areas
Canada: Toronto,Montreal
Overseas: Mexico

≪ ≫

MR. ROOTER CORP.
1020 N. University Parks Dr.
Waco, TX 76707
Tel: (800) 583-8003 (254) 745-2500
Fax: (254) 745-2501
Web Site: www.mrrooter.com
Mr. Mike Hawkins, VP Franchising

Full-service plumbing and sewer/drain cleaning. Franchise specializing in conversion of existing trades people to our method of doing business.

BACKGROUND: IFA MEMBER
Established: 1968; 1st Franchised: 1972
Franchised Units: 252
Company-Owned Units 0
Total Units: 252
Dist.: US-174; CAN-18; O'seas-60
  North America: 41 States, 4 Provinces
  Density: 35 in CA, 18 in ON, 17 in TX
Projected New Units (12 Months): 40
Qualifications: 3, 3, 5, 2, 3, 4
Registered: All States
FINANCIAL/TERMS:
Cash Investment: $NR
Total Investment: $NR
Minimum Net Worth: $Varies
Fees: Franchise - $19.5K
  Royalty - 3-6%; Ad. - 2%
Earnings Claim Statement: No
Term of Contract (Years): 10/5
Avg. # Of Employees: Depends on Sales
Passive Ownership: Not Allowed
Encourage Conversions: Yes
Area Develop. Agreements: Yes/10
Sub-Franchising Contracts: Yes
Expand In Territory: Yes
Space Needs: NR SF; N/A
SUPPORT & TRAINING PROVIDED:
Financial Assistance Provided: Yes(I)
Site Selection Assistance: N/A
Lease Negotiation Assistance: N/A
Co-Operative Advertising: No

Franchisee Assoc./Member: No
Size Of Corporate Staff: 13
On-Going Support: C,D,E,F,G,H,I
Training: 1 Week Waco, TX.
SPECIFIC EXPANSION PLANS:
US: Uncovered Areas
Canada: All Canada
Overseas: All Countries

◅◅ ▻▻

NATIONAL MAINTENANCE CONTRACTORS

1801 130th Ave. NE
Bellevue, WA 98005
Tel: (800) 347-7844 (425) 881-0500
Fax: (425) 883-4785
Mr. Lyle R. Graddon, President

NATIONAL MAINTENANCE CONTRACTORS is a janitorial business.

BACKGROUND:
Established: 1975; 1st Franchised: 1978
Franchised Units: 409
Company-Owned Units 0
Total Units: 409
Dist.: US-409; CAN-0; O'seas-0
  North America: 2 States
  Density: 275 in WA, 139 in OR
Projected New Units (12 Months): 25
Qualifications: 5, 2, 5, 1, 1, 5
Registered: OR,WA
FINANCIAL/TERMS:
Cash Investment: $1-20K
Total Investment: $2-22K
Minimum Net Worth: $N/A
Fees: Franchise - $1-20K
  Royalty - 6%; Ad. - 0%
Earnings Claim Statement: No
Term of Contract (Years): 5/5
Avg. # Of Employees: 1-4 FT
Passive Ownership: Discouraged
Encourage Conversions: Yes
Area Develop. Agreements: No
Sub-Franchising Contracts: No
Expand In Territory: Yes
Space Needs: N/A SF; NR
SUPPORT & TRAINING PROVIDED:
Financial Assistance Provided: Yes(D)
Site Selection Assistance: N/A
Lease Negotiation Assistance: N/A
Co-Operative Advertising: N/A
Franchisee Assoc./Member: No
Size Of Corporate Staff: 32
On-Going Support: A,C,D,G,H,I
Training: 5 Days Headquarters.
SPECIFIC EXPANSION PLANS:
US: WA,OR Only

Canada: No
Overseas: No

◅◅ ▻▻

NaturZОne Pest Control

NATURZONE PEST CONTROL
1899 Porter Lake Dr., #103
Sarasota, FL 34240
Tel: (877) 3-NOPEST (941) 378-3334
Fax: (941) 378-8584
E-Mail: travis@naturzone.com
Web Site: www.naturzone.com
Mr. Travis Wellbrock, President

Natural, non-allergenic pest control + lawn care/fertilization. Serves both commercial units and residential homes.

BACKGROUND:
Established: 1988; 1st Franchised: 1999
Franchised Units: 3
Company-Owned Units 1
Total Units: 4
Dist.: US-4; CAN-0; O'seas-0
  North America: 2 States
  Density: 3 in FL, 1 in KY
Projected New Units (12 Months): 10
Qualifications: 3, 3, 2, 1, 3, 4
Registered: FL
FINANCIAL/TERMS:
Cash Investment: $5K
Total Investment: $25K
Minimum Net Worth: $50K
Fees: Franchise - $15K
  Royalty - 5%; Ad. - N/A
Earnings Claim Statement: No
Term of Contract (Years): On-going
Avg. # Of Employees: 3 FT
Passive Ownership: Discouraged
Encourage Conversions: Yes
Area Develop. Agreements: Yes
Sub-Franchising Contracts: No
Expand In Territory: Yes
Space Needs: NR SF; FS, HB, SC
SUPPORT & TRAINING PROVIDED:
Financial Assistance Provided: Yes(I)
Site Selection Assistance: No
Lease Negotiation Assistance: No
Co-Operative Advertising: Yes
Franchisee Assoc./Member: No
Size Of Corporate Staff: 10
On-Going Support: C,D,h
Training: 2-3 Weeks in Sarasota, FL.
SPECIFIC EXPANSION PLANS:
US: All United States

Canada: All Canada
Overseas: All Countries

◅◅ ▻▻

O.P.E.N. CLEANING SYSTEMS

OPENWORKS
2777 E. Camelback Rd., # 350
Phoenix, AZ 85016
Tel: (800) 777-6736 (602) 224-0440
Fax: (602) 468-3788
E-Mail: info@openworksweb.com
Web Site: www.openworksweb.com
Ms. Shelly Cahill, Director of Marketing

OPENWORKS has been granting commercial cleaning franchises since 1983. Our program is centered around on-going training and support in addition to guaranteed initial customers. All franchises include a customer base, equipment and advanced business training. We also offer Master Franchises on an exclusive basis for certain metropolitan areas.

BACKGROUND: IFA MEMBER
Established: 1983; 1st Franchised: 1983
Franchised Units: 387
Company-Owned Units 3
Total Units: 390
Dist.: US-390; CAN-0; O'seas-0
  North America: 3 States
  Density: 187 in AZ, 125 in WA, 75 CA
Projected New Units (12 Months): 100
Qualifications: 3, 3, 1, 2, 4, 4
Registered: CA,IL,WA
FINANCIAL/TERMS:
Cash Investment: $5-150K
Total Investment: $14-150K
Minimum Net Worth: $10-500K
Fees: Franchise - $9-45K
  Royalty - 10%; Ad. - 1%
Earnings Claim Statement: No
Term of Contract (Years): 10/10
Avg. # Of Employees: 3+ FT
Passive Ownership: Discouraged
Encourage Conversions: Yes

Area Develop. Agreements: Yes/20
Sub-Franchising Contracts: Yes
Expand In Territory: Yes
Space Needs: 3,000(master) SF; Master

SUPPORT & TRAINING PROVIDED:
Financial Assistance Provided: Yes(D)
Site Selection Assistance: No
Lease Negotiation Assistance: Yes
Co-Operative Advertising: N/A
Franchisee Assoc./Member: No
Size Of Corporate Staff: 40
On-Going Support: A,B,C,D,E,G,H,I
Training: 2 Wks. Regional Office (Janitorial); 4 Wks. Regional Off. & 3 Wks. Master's Off. (Master).

SPECIFIC EXPANSION PLANS:
US: All United States
Canada: All Canada
Overseas: All Countries

≪ ≫

P.E.S.T. MACHINE TEAM, THE
3616 Lake Rd.
Ponca City, OK 74604-5100
Tel: (800) 654-4541 (580) 762-6614
Fax: (580) 765-4613
E-Mail: parke1@hit.net
Mr. Brad Parker, President

Using patented P.E.S.T. ® Machine, treat homes for cockroaches one time with a one year guarantee. Other clients include apartment complexes (especially low rent), restaurants and health care facilities. Can also offer all other aspects of pest control.

BACKGROUND:
Established: 1963;   1st Franchised: 1987
Franchised Units: 3
Company-Owned Units   <u>6</u>
Total Units: 9
Dist.:   US-0; CAN-0; O'seas-0
   North America: 3 States
   Density: 1 in OK, 1 in KS, 1 in CA
Projected New Units (12 Months):   NR
Registered:

FINANCIAL/TERMS:
Cash Investment: $N/A
Total Investment: $25-75K
Minimum Net Worth: $NR
Fees: Franchise - $25K
   Royalty - 8%/150/Mo.;   Ad. - N/A
Earnings Claim Statement: No
Term of Contract (Years):   5/5
Avg. # Of Employees: 1 FT
Passive Ownership: Discouraged
Encourage Conversions: NR

Area Develop. Agreements: No
Sub-Franchising Contracts: No
Expand In Territory: Yes
Space Needs: NR SF; HB

SUPPORT & TRAINING PROVIDED:
Financial Assistance Provided: NR
Site Selection Assistance: N/A
Lease Negotiation Assistance: N/A
Co-Operative Advertising: No
Franchisee Assoc./Member: No
Size Of Corporate Staff: 15
On-Going Support: A,a,B,C,c,D,d,E,F,G,I
Training: 3 Weeks in Ponca City, OK; 1 Week at Franchisee's Location.

SPECIFIC EXPANSION PLANS:
US: All United States
Canada: NR
Overseas: NR

≪ ≫

"professional polish"
A Total Franchise System

PROFESSIONAL POLISH
5450 East Loop, 820 S.
Fort Worth, TX 76119
Tel: (800) 255-0488 (817) 572-7353
Fax: (817) 561-6193
E-Mail: info@professionalpolish.com
Mr. Carren Cavanaugh, President

Janitorial, lawn and building repair. Alto distributor.

BACKGROUND:
Established: 1981;   1st Franchised: 1986
Franchised Units: 30
Company-Owned Units   <u>2</u>
Total Units: 32
Dist.:   US-32; CAN-0; O'seas-0
   North America: 3 States
   Density: 30 in TX, 1 in NC, 1 in AL
Projected New Units (12 Months):   4
Qualifications: 5, 5, 1, 3, 3, 5
Registered: FL

FINANCIAL/TERMS:
Cash Investment: $6K
Total Investment: $14.5K
Minimum Net Worth: $6K
Fees: Franchise - $5K
   Royalty - 15%;   Ad. - 0%
Earnings Claim Statement: Yes
Term of Contract (Years):   25/25
Avg. # Of Employees: 5 FT, 3 PT
Passive Ownership: Not Allowed
Encourage Conversions: N/A
Area Develop. Agreements: Yes/25
Sub-Franchising Contracts: No

Expand In Territory: Yes
Space Needs: 1,000 SF; OB

SUPPORT & TRAINING PROVIDED:
Financial Assistance Provided: Yes(D)
Site Selection Assistance: Yes
Lease Negotiation Assistance: Yes
Co-Operative Advertising: Yes
Franchisee Assoc./Member: No
Size Of Corporate Staff: 8
On-Going Support: A,B,C,D,E,F,G,H,I
Training: 10 Days Fort Worth, TX; 30 Days Franchise City.

SPECIFIC EXPANSION PLANS:
US: Southwest, Southeast
Canada: No
Overseas: No

≪ ≫

PROPERTY DAMAGE APPRAISERS
6100 Southwest Blvd., # 200
Fort Worth, TX 76109-3964
Tel: (800) 749-7324 (817) 731-5555
Fax: (817) 731-5550
Web Site: www.pdahomeoffice.com
Mr. Rick Cutler, Dir.Training and Development

The industry's largest, franchised appraisal company, with national marketing support, a computerized office management system, training and on-going management assistance. No initial franchise fee is required - only a royalty on completed business. Automobile damage appraising experience a pre-requisite.

BACKGROUND:
Established: 1963;   1st Franchised: 1963
Franchised Units: 256
Company-Owned Units   <u>0</u>
Total Units: 256
Dist.:   US-263; CAN-0; O'seas-0
   North America: 47 States
   Density: 25 in TX, 21 in CA, 15 in FL
Projected New Units (12 Months):   20
Qualifications: 3, 3, 5, 3, , 5
Registered: All States

FINANCIAL/TERMS:
Cash Investment: $9.2-23K
Total Investment: $9.2-23K
Minimum Net Worth: $NR
Fees: Franchise - $0
   Royalty - 15%;   Ad. - 0%
Earnings Claim Statement: No
Term of Contract (Years):   3/5
Avg. # Of Employees: 2 FT
Passive Ownership: Not Allowed

Encourage Conversions: Yes
Area Develop. Agreements: No
Sub-Franchising Contracts: No
Expand In Territory: Yes
Space Needs: NR SF; N/A

SUPPORT & TRAINING PROVIDED:
Financial Assistance Provided: No
Site Selection Assistance: Yes
Lease Negotiation Assistance: N/A
Co-Operative Advertising: Yes
Franchisee Assoc./Member: No
Size Of Corporate Staff: 36
On-Going Support: A,C,D,G,H,I
Training: 1 Week Corporate Headquarters;
4 Days On-Site.

SPECIFIC EXPANSION PLANS:
US: All United States
Canada: No
Overseas: No

≪ ≫

RACS INTERNATIONAL
9302 N. Meridian St., # 355
Indianapolis, IN 46269
Tel: (317) 844-8152
Fax: (317) 844-2270
Web Site: www.racsclean.com
Mr. Chuck Morrison, President

RACS INTERNATIONAL is a name known for quality, integrity and outstanding service, with over 20 years of commercial cleaning experience. Currently, it is among the top 20 franchises in terms of low investment start-up costs. RACS has developed a highly-trained network of commercial cleaning franchises with excellent ratings.

BACKGROUND: IFA MEMBER
Established: 1989; 1st Franchised: 1991
Franchised Units: 8
Company-Owned Units: 9
Total Units: 17
Dist.: US-42; CAN-0; O'seas-0
North America: 2 States
Density: 23 in FL, 11 in IN
Projected New Units (12 Months): 25
Registered: FL,IN

FINANCIAL/TERMS:
Cash Investment: $1.5-28K
Total Investment: $4.4-43.1K
Minimum Net Worth: $N/A

Fees: Franchise - $3-31.5K
Royalty - 5%; Ad. - 1%
Earnings Claim Statement: No
Term of Contract (Years): 20/20
Avg. # Of Employees: 5 FT
Passive Ownership: Not Allowed
Encourage Conversions: Yes
Area Develop. Agreements: Yes/10
Sub-Franchising Contracts: Yes
Expand In Territory: Yes
Space Needs: 1,500 SF; HB, Other

SUPPORT & TRAINING PROVIDED:
Financial Assistance Provided: Yes(D)
Site Selection Assistance: Yes
Lease Negotiation Assistance: Yes
Co-Operative Advertising: Yes
Franchisee Assoc./Member: No
Size Of Corporate Staff: 11
On-Going Support: A,b,C,D,G,I
Training: 18 Hours RACS Office; 12 Hours On-the-Job.

SPECIFIC EXPANSION PLANS:
US: All United States
Canada: No
Overseas: No

≪ ≫

RAINBOW INTERNATIONAL
CARPET CARE & RESTORATION
1010 N. University Parks Dr.
Waco, TX 76707
Tel: (800) 583-9100 (254) 745-2444
Fax: (254) 745-2592
E-Mail: rainbowintl@dwyergroup.com
Web Site: www.rainbowintl.com
Mr. Mike Hawkins, Vice President Franchising

Nationally acclaimed carpet care and restoration franchisor, with 16 years of experienced, positioned to help franchisees tap into the expanding insurance restoration industry, only one of the more than ten profit centers from which franchisees can gain competitive advantage. Success of our franchisees is attributed to our proven niche marketing methods, comprehensive 12-hour technical support and consumer awareness of RAINBOW. Featured in Entrepreneur's Top 100.

BACKGROUND: IFA MEMBER
Established: 1980; 1st Franchised: 1981
Franchised Units: 449
Company-Owned Units: 0
Total Units: 449
Dist.: US-294; CAN-15; O'seas-140
North America: 42 States, 6 Provinces

Density: 50 in TX, 20 in CA, 15 in FL
Projected New Units (12 Months): 24
Qualifications: 3, 2, 1, 2, 3, 5
Registered: All States

FINANCIAL/TERMS:
Cash Investment: $15-20K
Total Investment: $28.9-86K
Minimum Net Worth: $30K
Fees: Franchise - $15.9K
Royalty - 7%; Ad. - 2%
Earnings Claim Statement: No
Term of Contract (Years): 10/5
Avg. # Of Employees: 2 FT, 1 PT
Passive Ownership: Discouraged
Encourage Conversions: No
Area Develop. Agreements: No
Sub-Franchising Contracts: No
Expand In Territory: Yes
Space Needs: NR SF; HB

SUPPORT & TRAINING PROVIDED:
Financial Assistance Provided: Yes(D)
Site Selection Assistance: N/A
Lease Negotiation Assistance: No
Co-Operative Advertising: No
Franchisee Assoc./Member: No
Size Of Corporate Staff: 14
On-Going Support: A,b,C,D,G,H,I
Training: 2 Weeks at Corporate Headquarters.

SPECIFIC EXPANSION PLANS:
US: All United States
Canada: All Canada
Overseas: Japan, Middle East, Europe, Latin America

≪ ≫

ROTO-ROOTER
300 Ashworth Rd.
West Des Moines, IA 50265
Tel: (800) 575-7737 (515) 223-1343
Fax: (515) 223-6109
Web Site: www.entremkt.com/rotorooter
Mr. Larry Rothman, Director of Franchising

World's largest plumbing repair and sewer and drain cleaning company, providing service to residential, commercial and municipal customers.

BACKGROUND: IFA MEMBER

Established: 1935;   1st Franchised: 1935
Franchised Units: 518
Company-Owned Units   103
Total Units: 621
Dist.:   US-598; CAN-23; O'seas-0
 North America: 50 States, 5 Provinces
 Density: 44 in CA, 28 in TX, 24 in FL
Projected New Units (12 Months):   2
Qualifications: 3, 4, 5, 2, 2, 2
Registered: All States and AB
FINANCIAL/TERMS:
Cash Investment: $15-75K
Total Investment: $25-99K
Minimum Net Worth: $N/A
Fees: Franchise - $5K
 Royalty - Varies;   Ad. - Varies
Earnings Claim Statement: No
Term of Contract (Years):   10/10
Avg. # Of Employees: NR
Passive Ownership: Discouraged
Encourage Conversions: Yes
Area Develop. Agreements: No
Sub-Franchising Contracts: No
Expand In Territory: Yes
Space Needs: NR SF; N/A
SUPPORT & TRAINING PROVIDED:
Financial Assistance Provided: Yes(I)
Site Selection Assistance: N/A
Lease Negotiation Assistance: N/A
Co-Operative Advertising: Yes
Franchisee Assoc./Member: Yes/No
Size Of Corporate Staff: 25
On-Going Support: B,G,h,I
Training: N/A
SPECIFIC EXPANSION PLANS:
US: No
Canada: No
Overseas: All Countries

≪ ≫

ROTO-STATIC INTERNATIONAL
90 Delta Park Blvd., Bldg. A
Brampton, ON L6T 5E7 CANADA
Tel: (905) 458-7002
Fax: (905) 458-8650
E-Mail: success@rotostatic.com
Web Site: www.rotostatic.com
Mr. Greg Inkster, Vice President

Profit from offering 6 services, including a unique system of carpet cleaning, , using Static Attraction principle, water damage restoration and odor removal services. Complete training in head office. On-going support systems. A company with a proven past.

BACKGROUND:
Established: 1977;   1st Franchised: 1977
Franchised Units: 141
Company-Owned Units   0
Total Units: 141
Dist.:   US-0; CAN-141; O'seas-0
 North America: 9 Provinces
 Density: ON, PQ, BC
Projected New Units (12 Months):   10
Registered: AB
FINANCIAL/TERMS:
Cash Investment: $39K
Total Investment: $39K
Minimum Net Worth: $NR
Fees: Franchise - $14.5K
 Royalty - 5%;   Ad. - 2%
Earnings Claim Statement: No
Term of Contract (Years):   25/25
Avg. # Of Employees: 1-2 FT
Passive Ownership: Discouraged
Encourage Conversions: NR
Area Develop. Agreements: Yes
Sub-Franchising Contracts: Yes
Expand In Territory: No
Space Needs: NR SF; NR
SUPPORT & TRAINING PROVIDED:
Financial Assistance Provided: No
Site Selection Assistance: N/A
Lease Negotiation Assistance: N/A
Co-Operative Advertising: N/A
Franchisee Assoc./Member: Yes
Size Of Corporate Staff: 7
On-Going Support: C,D,E,F,G,H,I
Training: 4 Days Toronto, ON.
SPECIFIC EXPANSION PLANS:
US: All United States
Canada: All Canada
Overseas: U.K., Germany, France,
 Australia, Japan, Mexico, Spain

≪ ≫

SANIBRITE
9040 Leslie St., # 218
Richmond Hill, ON L4B 3M4 CANADA
Tel: (416) 410-7264
Fax: (416) 410-7264
E-Mail: sanibrit@idirect.com
Web Site: www.sanibrite.on.ca
Mr. Hossein Companieh, President

SANIBRITE is a unique company that is embarking on one of the most dynamic and totally new ideas in Canada. We have combined the success rate of franchising with a profitable and growing field of commercial cleaning. As a weary investor, SANIBRITE will provide you with the best business investment available for

your money. It is a business that will be immune to economic problems, such as depreciation, recession and inflation.

BACKGROUND:
Established: 1987;   1st Franchised: 1989
Franchised Units: 45
Company-Owned Units   1
Total Units: 46
Dist.:   US-1; CAN-44; O'seas-1
 North America: 2 States
 Density: 44 in ON, 1 in PQ
Projected New Units (12 Months):   5
Qualifications: 4, 3, 4, 3, 3, 4
Registered: NR
FINANCIAL/TERMS:
Cash Investment: $2-20K
Total Investment: $2-20K
Minimum Net Worth: $NR
Fees: Franchise - $0.95-15K
 Royalty - 9.5%;   Ad. - 4%
Earnings Claim Statement: Yes
Term of Contract (Years):   10/5/5
Avg. # Of Employees: 2 FT, 1 PT
Passive Ownership: Not Allowed
Encourage Conversions: Yes
Area Develop. Agreements: Yes/10/5
Sub-Franchising Contracts: Yes
Expand In Territory: No
Space Needs: 700-1,000 SF; Varies
SUPPORT & TRAINING PROVIDED:
Financial Assistance Provided: Yes(D)
Site Selection Assistance: Yes
Lease Negotiation Assistance: Yes
Co-Operative Advertising: Yes
Franchisee Assoc./Member: Yes
Size Of Corporate Staff: 5
On-Going Support: A,B,C,D,E,G,H,I
Training: 3 Hours Head Office; 5 Days
 On-Site.
SPECIFIC EXPANSION PLANS:
US: All United States
Canada: All Canada
Overseas: All Countries

≪ ≫

SCRUBWAY
1880 Markley St., 2nd Fl.
Morristown, PA 19401
Tel: (800) 355-3000 (610) 278-9000
Fax: (610) 275-7360
E-Mail: towerclean@aol.com
Mr. Adam Beck, Vice President

Building on the reputation of our affiliate company, TOWER CLEANING SYSTEMS, SCRUBWAY provides revolutionary hygiene service to the commercial restroom hygiene industry. Our tested and proven franchise program includes: start-up inventory, complete step-by-step/on-going training, profession-al administrative support. SCRUBWAY's unique products ensure customer satisfaction while our exclusive sales territory policy ensures limited competition.

BACKGROUND:

Established: 1994; 1st Franchised: 1994	
Franchised Units:	5
Company-Owned Units	1
Total Units:	6
Dist.: US-6; CAN-0; O'seas-0	
North America:	5 States
Density:	2 in PA
Projected New Units (12 Months):	20
Qualifications:	5, 5, 2, 4, 4, 5
Registered: All States	

FINANCIAL/TERMS:

Cash Investment:	$10-60K
Total Investment:	$25-80K
Minimum Net Worth:	$100K
Fees: Franchise -	$10-15K
Royalty - 6%;	Ad. - 2%
Earnings Claim Statement:	No
Term of Contract (Years):	10/10
Avg. # Of Employees:	1-5 FT, 2-3 PT
Passive Ownership:	Allowed
Encourage Conversions:	N/A
Area Develop. Agreements:	Yes/10
Sub-Franchising Contracts:	No
Expand In Territory:	Yes
Space Needs: NR SF; N/A	

SUPPORT & TRAINING PROVIDED:

Financial Assistance Provided:	Yes(D)
Site Selection Assistance:	N/A
Lease Negotiation Assistance:	N/A
Co-Operative Advertising:	N/A
Franchisee Assoc./Member:	No
Size Of Corporate Staff:	50+
On-Going Support:	A,B,C,D,E,F,G,I
Training: 1 Week Headquarters; 1 Week On-Site.	

SPECIFIC EXPANSION PLANS:

US:	All United States
Canada:	No
Overseas:	No

SERV U-1ST
2706 NE Sandy Blvd.
Portland, OR 97219
Tel: (503) 244-7628
Fax: (503) 234-3989
Mr. Robert D. Rosenkranz, President

SERV U-1ST owners clean up with know-how. We serve you with on-going instruction in janitorial services for buildings. We teach proven technologies for procuring, servicing and keeping your clients. We offer 20 years' experience and our honest reputation.

BACKGROUND:

Established: 1988; 1st Franchised: 1988	
Franchised Units:	11
Company-Owned Units	0
Total Units:	11
Dist.: US-11; CAN-0; O'seas-0	
North America:	1 State
Density:	11 in OR
Projected New Units (12 Months):	2
Qualifications:	3, 3, 1, 2, 3, 5
Registered: OR	

FINANCIAL/TERMS:

Cash Investment:	$4-8K
Total Investment:	$6.5-13.5K
Minimum Net Worth:	$9K
Fees: Franchise -	$2.3K
Royalty - 6-15%;	Ad. - 0%
Earnings Claim Statement:	No
Term of Contract (Years):	10/10
Avg. # Of Employees:	1 or 2 FT
Passive Ownership:	Not Allowed
Encourage Conversions:	Yes
Area Develop. Agreements:	No
Sub-Franchising Contracts:	No
Expand In Territory:	Yes
Space Needs: N/A SF; HB	

SUPPORT & TRAINING PROVIDED:

Financial Assistance Provided:	Yes
Site Selection Assistance:	N/A
Lease Negotiation Assistance:	N/A
Co-Operative Advertising:	N/A
Franchisee Assoc./Member:	Yes
Size Of Corporate Staff:	2
On-Going Support:	C,D,E,H
Training: 20 2-Hour Sessions, Portland, OR.	

SPECIFIC EXPANSION PLANS:

US:	Oregon Only
Canada:	No
Overseas:	No

SERVICE ONE
5104 N. Orange Blossom Tr., # 114
Orlando, FL 32810
Tel: (800) 522-7111 (407) 293-7645
Fax: (407) 299-4306
Ms. Judi Clem, Franchise Director

We are a janitorial franchise, delivering

supplies, equipment, training and customers.

BACKGROUND:

Established: 1965; 1st Franchised: 1985	
Franchised Units:	140
Company-Owned Units	0
Total Units:	140
Dist.: US-140; CAN-0; O'seas-0	
North America:	20 States
Density: 87 in FL, 5 in AZ, 13 in NC	
Projected New Units (12 Months):	24
Registered: FL	

FINANCIAL/TERMS:

Cash Investment:	$3-9K
Total Investment:	$6.1-19.3K
Minimum Net Worth:	$NR
Fees: Franchise -	$6-18.3K
Royalty - $175/Mo.;	Ad. - 0%
Earnings Claim Statement:	NR
Term of Contract (Years):	10/10
Avg. # Of Employees:	NR
Passive Ownership:	Not Allowed
Encourage Conversions:	N/A
Area Develop. Agreements:	No
Sub-Franchising Contracts:	No
Expand In Territory:	No
Space Needs: NR SF; N/A	

SUPPORT & TRAINING PROVIDED:

Financial Assistance Provided:	Yes(D)
Site Selection Assistance:	N/A
Lease Negotiation Assistance:	N/A
Co-Operative Advertising:	N/A
Franchisee Assoc./Member:	No
Size Of Corporate Staff:	6
On-Going Support:	A,E,G,I
Training: 2 Days Where Convenient.	

SPECIFIC EXPANSION PLANS:

US:	Non-Registration States
Canada:	No
Overseas:	No

SERVICE-TECH CORPORATION
7589 First Pl.
Cleveland, OH 44146-6711
Tel: (800) 992-9302 (440) 735-1505
Fax: (440) 735-1433
Web Site: www.servicetechcorp.com
Mr. Alan J. Sutton, President

Indoor air quality. Opportunity to join 36 years of experience in solving the growing concerns of indoor air pollution. Services offered include air duct cleaning, kitchen exhaust cleaning, vacuum cleaning and specialized cleaning, plus more, to industrial and commercial customers.

BACKGROUND:

Established: 1960;   1st Franchised: 1988
Franchised Units: 3
Company-Owned Units   4
Total Units: 7
Dist.:   US-8; CAN-0; O'seas-0
  North America: 4 States
  Density: 4 in OH, 1 in MI, 1 in FL
Projected New Units (12 Months):   3
Qualifications: 4, 3, 2, 3, 3, 5
Registered: FL,IL,MI

FINANCIAL/TERMS:

Cash Investment: $20-50K
Total Investment: $59-89K
Minimum Net Worth: $NR
Fees: Franchise - $19K
  Royalty - 4-6%;   Ad. - 1%
Earnings Claim Statement: No
Term of Contract (Years):   10/10+
Avg. # Of Employees: 4 FT, 2 PT
Passive Ownership: Not Allowed
Encourage Conversions: N/A
Area Develop. Agreements: No
Sub-Franchising Contracts: No
Expand In Territory: Yes
Space Needs: 2,000 SF; HB

SUPPORT & TRAINING PROVIDED:

Financial Assistance Provided: Yes(I)
Site Selection Assistance: N/A
Lease Negotiation Assistance: N/A
Co-Operative Advertising: N/A
Franchisee Assoc./Member: NR
Size Of Corporate Staff: 35
On-Going Support: B,C,D,E,H,I
Training: 2 Weeks Headquarters; 1 Week
  Franchisee Location.

SPECIFIC EXPANSION PLANS:

US: All United States
Canada: No
Overseas: No

SERVICEMASTER CLEAN

860 Ridge Lake Blvd.
Memphis, TN 38120-9792
Tel: (800) 230-2360 (901) 684-7500
Fax: (901) 684-7580
E-Mail: dcoopwood@smrescom.com
Web Site: www.ownafranchise.com
Mr. Dan Kellow, Vice President

SERVICEMASTER provides heavy-duty cleaning services to both residential and commercial customers. Services include carpet, upholstery, window, drapery, disaster restoration and janitorial cleaning that is recognized around the world. With over 50 years experience,

SERVICEMASTER offers state-of-the-art equipment, research and development, continuous training, cross-selling promotions with our partner companies and a strong franchise relations base.

BACKGROUND: IFA MEMBER

Established: 1947;   1st Franchised: 1952
Franchised Units: 4,403
Company-Owned Units   0
Total Units: 4,403
Dist.:   US-2,835; CAN-170; O'seas-1398
  North America: 50 States, 9 Provinces
  Density: 214 in IL, 156 in CA, 145 OH
Projected New Units (12 Months):   120
Qualifications: 5, 3, 2, 2, 3, 5
Registered: All States and AB

FINANCIAL/TERMS:

Cash Investment: $10-20K
Total Investment: $21.9-72.1K
Minimum Net Worth: $100K
Fees: Franchise - $13.5-27.5K
  Royalty - 4-10%;   Ad. - 0.5-1%
Earnings Claim Statement: No
Term of Contract (Years):   5/5
Avg. # Of Employees: 3 FT, 2 PT
Passive Ownership: Discouraged
Encourage Conversions: Yes
Area Develop. Agreements: No
Sub-Franchising Contracts: Yes
Expand In Territory: Yes
Space Needs: N/A SF; N/A

SUPPORT & TRAINING PROVIDED:

Financial Assistance Provided: Yes(D)
Site Selection Assistance: No
Lease Negotiation Assistance: No
Co-Operative Advertising: Yes
Franchisee Assoc./Member: Yes/Yes
Size Of Corporate Staff: 200
On-Going Support: A,B,C,D,F,G,H,I
Training: 2 Weeks Memphis, TN; 1 Week
  on Location.

SPECIFIC EXPANSION PLANS:

US: All United States
Canada: All Canada
Overseas: All Countries

SERVPRO

575 Airport Blvd.
Gallatin, TN 37066
Tel: (800) 826-9586 (615) 451-0200
Fax: (615) 451-4861

E-Mail: franchise@servpronet.com
Web Site: www.servpro.com
Mr. Kevin Brown, Dir. Fran. Expansion

SERVPRO

A completely diversified cleaning and restoration business, with multiple income opportunities. The insurance restoration market (fire, smoke and water damages) is our main focus. We also specialize in commercial and residential cleaning. SERVPRO teaches effective management, marketing and technical skills. We are seeking qualified individuals with the desire to own their own business and become part of the SERVPRO team. If you want to be the best, join the best team. Call 1-800-826-9586.

BACKGROUND:

Established: 1967;   1st Franchised: 1969
Franchised Units: 1,031
Company-Owned Units   0
Total Units: 1,031
Dist.:   US-1,031; CAN-0; O'seas-0
  North America: 49 States
  Density: 105 in CA, 78 in FL, 50 OH
Projected New Units (12 Months):   80
Qualifications: 3, 4, 1, 3, 4, 4
Registered: All States

FINANCIAL/TERMS:

Cash Investment: $30-50K
Total Investment: $59-95K
Minimum Net Worth: $50K
Fees: Franchise - $45K
  Royalty - 8-10%;   Ad. - Up to 3%
Earnings Claim Statement: No
Term of Contract (Years):   5/5
Avg. # Of Employees: 4 FT, Varied PT
Passive Ownership: Discouraged
Encourage Conversions: Yes
Area Develop. Agreements: No
Sub-Franchising Contracts: No
Expand In Territory: No
Space Needs: NR SF; N/A

SUPPORT & TRAINING PROVIDED:

Financial Assistance Provided: Yes(D)
Site Selection Assistance: N/A
Lease Negotiation Assistance: No
Co-Operative Advertising: No
Franchisee Assoc./Member: No
Size Of Corporate Staff: 85
On-Going Support: B,C,D,E,G,H
Training: 2 Weeks Gallatin, TN; 1 Week
  Franchisee's Business Location.

SPECIFIC EXPANSION PLANS:

US: All United States

Canada:	No
Overseas:	No

<< >>

SPARKLE WASH

26851 Richmond Rd.
Bedford Heights, OH 44146
Tel: (800) 321-0770 (216) 464-4212
Fax: (216) 464-8869
E-Mail: pfunku@en.com
Web Site: www.sparklewash.com
Mr. Hans G. Funk, President

SPARKLE WASH provides mobile power-cleaning and restoration, providing broad market opportunities to our franchisees for the commercial, industrial, residential and fleet markets. SPARKLE WASH franchisees can also provide special services, including wood restoration, all using our environmentally-friendly products.

BACKGROUND: IFA MEMBER
Established: 1965; 1st Franchised: 1967
Franchised Units: 171
Company-Owned Units: 1
Total Units: 172
Dist.: US-93; CAN-0; O'seas-79
  North America: 32 States
  Density: 13 in OH, 13 in PA, 8 in NY
Projected New Units (12 Months): 10
Qualifications: 3, 3, 1, 2, 4, 5
Registered: All States

FINANCIAL/TERMS:
Cash Investment: $19.3-21.3K
Total Investment: $50K
Minimum Net Worth: $60K
Fees: Franchise - $15K
  Royalty - 3-5%; Ad. - 0%
Earnings Claim Statement: Yes
Term of Contract (Years): Continual
Avg. # Of Employees: 2 FT, 2 PT
Passive Ownership: Allowed
Encourage Conversions: Yes
Area Develop. Agreements: No
Sub-Franchising Contracts: No
Expand In Territory: Yes
Space Needs: NR SF; N/A

SUPPORT & TRAINING PROVIDED:
Financial Assistance Provided: Yes(B)
Site Selection Assistance: N/A
Lease Negotiation Assistance: N/A
Co-Operative Advertising: No
Franchisee Assoc./Member: Yes/Yes
Size Of Corporate Staff: 15
On-Going Support: B,C,D,G,H,I
Training: 1 Week Headquarters; 3 Days

Franchisee Location; 3 Days National/Regional Meetings.

SPECIFIC EXPANSION PLANS:
US: All United States
Canada: All Canada
Overseas: All Countries

<< >>

STEAMATIC

303 Arthur St.
Fort Worth, TX 76107
Tel: (800) 527-1295 (817) 332-1575
Fax: (817) 332-5349
E-Mail: cclark@steamatic.com
Web Site: www.steamatic.com
Mr. Chris S. Clark, Vice President

The total cleaning and restoration franchise, serving the residential, commercial and industrial markets. Greatest emphasis is on combating many of the problems associated with indoor air pollution, such as cleaning/sanitation of the HVAC system, air ducts and coils, carpet cleaning, etc. Emphasis also on water/storm damage cleaning and restoration of residential/commercial buildings. Plus, general residential and commercial cleaning.

BACKGROUND: IFA MEMBER
Established: 1946; 1st Franchised: 1968
Franchised Units: 312
Company-Owned Units: 8
Total Units: 320
Dist.: US-193; CAN-72; O'seas-21
  North America: 50 States,10 Provinces
  Density: 19 in TX, 15 in FL, 8 in IL
Projected New Units (12 Months): 40
Registered: All States

FINANCIAL/TERMS:
Cash Investment: $35-100K
Total Investment: $25-75K
Minimum Net Worth: $NR
Fees: Franchise - $5-18K
  Royalty - 5-8%; Ad. - 0%
Earnings Claim Statement: No
Term of Contract (Years): 10/5
Avg. # Of Employees: 5-40 FT, 3-10 PT
Passive Ownership: Discouraged
Encourage Conversions: Yes
Area Develop. Agreements: No
Sub-Franchising Contracts: No
Expand In Territory: No
Space Needs: NR SF; Warehouse

SUPPORT & TRAINING PROVIDED:
Financial Assistance Provided: Yes(D)
Site Selection Assistance: N/A
Lease Negotiation Assistance: N/A

Co-Operative Advertising:	N/A
Franchisee Assoc./Member:	Yes/Yes
Size Of Corporate Staff:	32

On-Going Support: A,B,C,D,E,F,G,H,I
Training: 2 Weeks Ft. Worth, TX.

SPECIFIC EXPANSION PLANS:
US: All United States
Canada: All Canada
Overseas: All Countries

<< >>

TOWER CLEANING SYSTEMS

P.O. Box 2468
South Eastern, PA 19399
Tel: (800) 355-4000
Fax: (610) 275-7662
E-Mail: towerclean@aol.com
Web Site: www.toweronline.com
Mr. Chuck Lomagro, Vice President

TOWER CLEANING was rated in the top 100 franchises by "Entrepreneur"; "Inc. Magazine" says we are one of the country's fastest-growing franchises of 1997. We feature a tested, proven program with your initial clients already obtained; full start-up package, complete step-by-step and on-going training; professional administrative support (customer relations, accounting, invoicing, on-going marketing).

BACKGROUND:
Established: 1988; 1st Franchised: 1990
Franchised Units: 1,270
Company-Owned Units: 0
Total Units: 1,270
Dist.: US-1,270; CAN-0; O'seas-0
  North America: 19 States
  Density: 480 in PA, 235 in NJ, 225 WA
Projected New Units (12 Months): 500
Qualifications: 3, 3, 3, 2, 1, 5
Registered: All States

FINANCIAL/TERMS:
Cash Investment: $1.5-25K
Total Investment: $3.4-34K
Minimum Net Worth: $10K
Fees: Franchise - $4-33.6K
  Royalty - 3%; Ad. - 0%
Earnings Claim Statement: No
Term of Contract (Years): 10/10
Avg. # Of Employees: 1-5 FT
Passive Ownership: Allowed
Encourage Conversions: Yes
Area Develop. Agreements: Yes/10
Sub-Franchising Contracts: No
Expand In Territory: Yes
Space Needs: N/A SF; NR

SUPPORT & TRAINING PROVIDED:
Financial Assistance Provided: Yes(D)
Site Selection Assistance: N/A
Lease Negotiation Assistance: N/A
Co-Operative Advertising: N/A
Franchisee Assoc./Member: No
Size Of Corporate Staff: 50+
On-Going Support: A,B,C,D,G,H,I
Training: 1 Week Local Office; 2-3 Days On-Site.

SPECIFIC EXPANSION PLANS:
US: All United States
Canada: All Canada
Overseas: No

TRULY NOLEN

6375 E. Tanque Verde, # 270
Tucson, AZ 85715
Tel: (800) 458-3664 (520) 977-5817
Fax: (520) 546-2511
E-Mail: truly@truly.com
Web Site: www.truly.com
Mr. Truly W. (Bill) Nolen, Director of Franchising

Innovative pest control and pest control marketing - pest, termite, lawn and inspection services.

BACKGROUND: IFA MEMBER
Established: 1938; 1st Franchised: 1996
Franchised Units: 7
Company-Owned Units: 80
Total Units: 87
Dist.: US-87; CAN-0; O'seas-0
North America: NR
Density: 34 in FL, 15 in AZ, 6 in CA
Projected New Units (12 Months): 10
Qualifications: 2, 2, 2, 2, 4, 5
Registered: CA,MI,NY,VA,WA
FINANCIAL/TERMS:
Cash Investment: $5K
Total Investment: $100-300K
Minimum Net Worth: $25K
Fees: Franchise - $35K
Royalty - 9%; Ad. - 0%
Earnings Claim Statement: No
Term of Contract (Years): 5/5
Avg. # Of Employees: 10 FT
Passive Ownership: Discouraged
Encourage Conversions: Yes
Area Develop. Agreements: Yes/5
Sub-Franchising Contracts: No
Expand In Territory: Yes
Space Needs: NR SF; N/A
SUPPORT & TRAINING PROVIDED:
Financial Assistance Provided: N/A

Site Selection Assistance: No
Lease Negotiation Assistance: No
Co-Operative Advertising: Yes
Franchisee Assoc./Member: No
Size Of Corporate Staff: 35
On-Going Support: a,b,C,D,E,f,G,h,I
Training: 1 Week in Orlando FL; On-Site as determined.

SPECIFIC EXPANSION PLANS:
US: All States Except AZ
Canada: All Canada
Overseas: No

UNICLEAN SYSTEMS

1010 W. Cleans Rd., #200
North Vancouver, BC V7R 4S9
CANADA
Tel: (604) 986-4750
Fax: (604) 987-6838
Mr. Jack B. Karpowicz, President

Commercial office cleaning on a long-term contract basis.

BACKGROUND:
Established: 1976; 1st Franchised: 1981
Franchised Units: 398
Company-Owned Units: 1
Total Units: 399
Dist.: US-48; CAN-347; O'seas-0
North America: 12 States, 5 Provinces
Density: 167 in BC, 89 in ON, 35 PQ
Projected New Units (12 Months): 20
Qualifications: 2, 3, 2, 2, 4, 5
Registered: CL,IL,OR,WA
FINANCIAL/TERMS:
Cash Investment: $5.5-16.5K
Total Investment: $5.5-16.5K
Minimum Net Worth: $N/A
Fees: Franchise - $1.5K
Royalty - 15%; Ad. - 0-5%
Earnings Claim Statement: No
Term of Contract (Years): 3/3
Avg. # Of Employees: N/A
Passive Ownership: Discouraged
Encourage Conversions: No
Area Develop. Agreements: Yes/10
Sub-Franchising Contracts: Yes
Expand In Territory: Yes
Space Needs: N/A SF; HB
SUPPORT & TRAINING PROVIDED:
Financial Assistance Provided: Yes(I)
Site Selection Assistance: N/A
Lease Negotiation Assistance: No
Co-Operative Advertising: Yes
Franchisee Assoc./Member: No
Size Of Corporate Staff: 8

On-Going Support: A,b,c,D,G,H
Training: 1-2 Weeks Home Office. North Vancouver, BC.
SPECIFIC EXPANSION PLANS:
US: All United States
Canada: All Except AB
Overseas: No

VALUE LINE MAINTENANCE SYSTEMS

P.O. Box 6450
Great Falls, MT 59406
Tel: (800) 824-4838 (406) 761-4471
Fax: (406) 761-4486
Mr. Jerome McAllister, General Manager

VALUE LINE MAINTENANCE offers janitorial service to large retail outlets. VALUE LINE offers technical support, sales support and maintains a supply and machine facility to help franchisees stay up to date on product development and maintain their equipment.

BACKGROUND:
Established: 1959; 1st Franchised: 1982
Franchised Units: 22
Company-Owned Units: 3
Total Units: 25
Dist.: US-25; CAN-0; O'seas-0
North America: 5 States
Density: MT, CA, WY
Projected New Units (12 Months): 2
Qualifications: 3, 4, 2, 3, 4, 4
Registered: CA
FINANCIAL/TERMS:
Cash Investment: $25K
Total Investment: $50K
Minimum Net Worth: $50K
Fees: Franchise - $30K
Royalty - 10%; Ad. - 0%
Earnings Claim Statement: No
Term of Contract (Years): 10/10
Avg. # Of Employees: 2 FT
Passive Ownership: Discouraged
Encourage Conversions: N/A
Area Develop. Agreements: No
Sub-Franchising Contracts: No
Expand In Territory: Yes
Space Needs: NR SF; N/A
SUPPORT & TRAINING PROVIDED:
Financial Assistance Provided: Yes(D)
Site Selection Assistance: Yes
Lease Negotiation Assistance: N/A
Co-Operative Advertising: N/A
Franchisee Assoc./Member: Yes
Size Of Corporate Staff: 12

On-Going Support: A,B,C,D,E,F,I
Training: 1 Week Corporate; 2 Weeks On-Location.
SPECIFIC EXPANSION PLANS:
US: CA
Canada: No
Overseas: No

◄◄ ►►

VANGUARD CLEANING SYSTEMS
3 Twin Dolphin Dr., # 295
Redwood City, CA 94065
Tel: (800) 654-6422 (650) 594-1500
Fax: (650) 591-1545
E-Mail: rlee@vanguardcleaning.com
Web Site: www.vanguardcleaning.com
Mr. Raymond C. Lee, President

VANGUARD CLEANING SYSTEMS has been successfully franchising in the commercial cleaning industry since 1984. VANGUARD is currently seeking unit and master franchisees in the United States. A VANGUARD Master has 2 key responsibilities: recruiting individual unit franchisees and securing commercial cleaning accounts for them.

BACKGROUND: IFA MEMBER
Established: 1984; 1st Franchised: 1984
Franchised Units: 220
Company-Owned Units: 2
Total Units: 222
Dist.: US-180; CAN-0; O'seas-0
 North America: 1 State
 Density: 181 in CA
Projected New Units (12 Months): 40
Qualifications: 3, 5, 1, 3, 4, 5
Registered: CA,FL
FINANCIAL/TERMS:
Cash Investment: $37.5K(Master)
Total Investment: $100-470K(M)
Minimum Net Worth: $100K (Master)
Fees: Franchise - $75K (Master)
 Royalty - 4% (Master); Ad. - 1.5%(M)
Earnings Claim Statement: No

Term of Contract (Years): 20/10
Avg. # Of Employees: 5 FT, 2 PT
Passive Ownership: Discouraged
Encourage Conversions: Yes
Area Develop. Agreements: No
Sub-Franchising Contracts: Yes
Expand In Territory: Yes
Space Needs: N/A SF; N/A
SUPPORT & TRAINING PROVIDED:
Financial Assistance Provided: Yes(D)
Site Selection Assistance: N/A
Lease Negotiation Assistance: N/A
Co-Operative Advertising: N/A
Franchisee Assoc./Member: No
Size Of Corporate Staff: 14
On-Going Support: A,b,C,D,G,I
Training: 3 Weeks+ Redwood City, CA.
SPECIFIC EXPANSION PLANS:
US: All United States
Canada: All Canada
Overseas: All Countries

◄◄ ►►

WINDOW BUTLER
6355 E. Kemper Rd., # 250
Cincinnati, OH 45241
Tel: (800) 808-6470 (513) 489-4000
Fax: (513) 469-2226
E-Mail: wbutler@one.net
Web Site: www.windowbutler.com
Mr. Jim Young, President

Home services are in demand! A WINDOW BUTLER franchise provides busy homeowners with window cleaning and all the maintenance services they need. It is a business built around managing people, not doing the work yourself. Our complete package was developed by the founders of 2 highly successful service-related franchises with over 500 units collectively.

BACKGROUND: IFA MEMBER
Established: 1997; 1st Franchised: 1997
Franchised Units: 23

Company-Owned Units: 0
Total Units: 23
Dist.: US-23; CAN-0; O'seas-0
 North America: 14 States
 Density: 3 in OH, 2 in KS, 3 in TN
Projected New Units (12 Months): 12
Qualifications: 3, 4, 1, 2, 3, 5
Registered: CA,FL,IL,IN,MD,MI,NY, OR,VA,DC
FINANCIAL/TERMS:
Cash Investment: $10-20K
Total Investment: $17.5-35K
Minimum Net Worth: $10K
Fees: Franchise - $7.9-22.9K
 Royalty - 6%; Ad. - 3%
Earnings Claim Statement: No
Term of Contract (Years): 10/10/10
Avg. # Of Employees: 3 FT
Passive Ownership: Discouraged
Encourage Conversions: Yes
Area Develop. Agreements: No
Sub-Franchising Contracts: No
Expand In Territory: No
Space Needs: N/A SF; HB
SUPPORT & TRAINING PROVIDED:
Financial Assistance Provided: Yes(D)
Site Selection Assistance: Yes
Lease Negotiation Assistance: N/A
Co-Operative Advertising: N/A
Franchisee Assoc./Member: No
Size Of Corporate Staff: 5
On-Going Support: C,D,E,G,H,I
Training: 1 Week Cincinnati, OH.
SPECIFIC EXPANSION PLANS:
US: All United States
Canada: No
Overseas: No

◄◄ ►►

WINDOW GANG

WINDOW GANG
6509 Aviation Pkwy.
Morrisville, NC 27560
Tel: (800) 849-2308 (252) 728-7444
Fax: (252) 728-4246
E-Mail: gang@mail.clis.com
Web Site: www.windowgang.com
Mr. Tim McCullen, President

Residential/commercial window, gutter, pressure and blind cleaning company. Large, extensive markets.

BACKGROUND: IFA MEMBER
Established: 1986; 1st Franchised: 1996
Franchised Units: 82
Company-Owned Units: 1

Total Units: 83
Dist.: US-83; CAN-0; O'seas-0
  North America: 4 States
  Density: 44 in NC, 23 in SC, 8 in VA
Projected New Units (12 Months): NR
Registered:
FINANCIAL/TERMS:
Cash Investment: $50K
Total Investment: $50K
Minimum Net Worth: $50K
Fees: Franchise - $20K
  Royalty - 6%; Ad. - 0%
Earnings Claim Statement: No
Term of Contract (Years): 10/10
Avg. # Of Employees: 4 FT
Passive Ownership: Discouraged
Encourage Conversions: NR
Area Develop. Agreements: NR
Sub-Franchising Contracts: No
Expand In Territory: Yes
Space Needs: NR SF; HB, Warehouse
SUPPORT & TRAINING PROVIDED:
Financial Assistance Provided: NR
Site Selection Assistance: Yes
Lease Negotiation Assistance: Yes
Co-Operative Advertising: No
Franchisee Assoc./Member: No
Size Of Corporate Staff:
On-Going Support: B,C,D,e,G,H,I
Training: 5-10 Days Morrisville, NC.
SPECIFIC EXPANSION PLANS:
US: All United States
Canada: NR
Overseas: NR

≪ ≫

WINDOW GENIE
700 W. Pete Rose Way, Longworth Hall
Cincinnati, OH 45203
Tel: (800) 700-0022 (513) 241-8443
Fax: (513) 412-7760
E-Mail: squeegeepro@aol.com
Web Site: www.windowgenie.com
Mr. Richard Nonelle, President

Residential window cleaning and pressure washing business.

BACKGROUND:
Established: 1994; 1st Franchised: 1998
Franchised Units: 20
Company-Owned Units 1
Total Units: 21

Dist.: US-21; CAN-0; O'seas-0
  North America: 7 States
  Density: 6 in OH, 1 in KY, 1 in PA
Projected New Units (12 Months): 19
Qualifications: 4, 4, 1, 3, 3, 5
Registered: CA,FL,IN,MI
FINANCIAL/TERMS:
Cash Investment: $10-15K
Total Investment: $28-42K
Minimum Net Worth: $Varies
Fees: Franchise - $15K
  Royalty - 6%; Ad. - 1%
Earnings Claim Statement: No
Term of Contract (Years): 10/5
Avg. # Of Employees: 2 FT, 2 PT
Passive Ownership: Discouraged
Encourage Conversions: Yes
Area Develop. Agreements: No
Sub-Franchising Contracts: No
Expand In Territory: Yes
Space Needs: N/A SF; N/A
SUPPORT & TRAINING PROVIDED:
Financial Assistance Provided: Yes(D)
Site Selection Assistance: N/A
Lease Negotiation Assistance: N/A
Co-Operative Advertising: N/A
Franchisee Assoc./Member: No
Size Of Corporate Staff: 3
On-Going Support: B,C,D,E,F,G,H,I
Training: 5 Days Corporate, Cincinnati, OH; 5 Days On-Site.
SPECIFIC EXPANSION PLANS:
US: All United States
Canada: All Canada
Overseas: No

≪ ≫

SUPPLEMENTAL LISTING OF FRANCHISORS

Advanced Cleaning Systems, 3501 W. Vine St., #341, Kissimmee, FL 34741 ; (407) 847-4265; Mr. Paul Svejda ; (407) 870-9800

American Air Care, 4751 Lydell Rd., Cheverly, MD 20781 ; (301) 322-8446; Mr. Eric C. Moreno ; (301) 772-2000

American Carpet Cleaning Systems, 3501 SE 16 PL, Cape Corral, FL 33904 ; (941) 945-7744; Director of Franchising ; (941) 945-7744

Arodal, 6171 Conin Dr., Mississauga, ON L4V 1N8 CANADA; (905) 678-6967; Mr. Al Fisher ; (905) 678-6888

Bee-Clean, 4505 101st, Edmonton, AB T6E 5C6 CANADA; (780) 436-9528; Mr. Brian Gingras ; (780) 462-0069

Buster's Enterprises, 29160 U.S. Hwy. 19 N., Clearwater, FL 33761 ; (813) 789-0060; Mr. Ken Ray ; (813) 787-7087

Cleaning Ideas, P.O. Box 7269, San Antonio, TX 78207 ; (210) 227-0002; Mr. Charles Davis ; (210) 227-9161

Dririte, 4000 Dow Rd., # 10, Melbourne, FL 32934-9276 ; ; Mr. Gilbert L'Hommedieu (800) 462-5845; (407) 422-6688

Ductbusters, 29160 U. S. Hwy. 19 N., Clearwater, FL 33761 ; (727) 789-0060; Mr. Ken Ray (800) SUN-DUCT; (727) 787-7087

Energy Wise, 708 Gravenstein Hwy., North # 101, Sebastopol, CA 95472 ; (707) 824-8775; Mr. Michael Gross (800) 553-6800; (707) 824-8775

Envirobate, 3301 E. 26th St., Minneapolis, MN 55406 ; (612) 729-1021; Mr. Scott Larson (800) 926-1776; (612) 729-1080

Fiber-Seal Services International, 10254 Miller Rd., Dallas, TX 75238 ; (214) 349-7818; Mr. Kurt Falvey (800) 883-7325; (214) 349-8374

Fibrenew International Ltd., Box 33, Site 16, Rural Rt. 8, Calgary, AB T2J 2T9 CANADA; (403) 278-1434; Mr. Michael Wilson ; (403) 278-7818

H. Jack's Plumbing & Home Comfort Co., 1523 Cascade St., Erie, PA 16502-1549 ; (814) 459-7484; Mr. William Krause (888) 454-8462; (814) 836-0286

International Master Care Janitorial, 555 6th St., # 327, New Westminster, BC V3L 5H1 CANADA; (604) 526-2235; Mr. Gerard Hoffman (800) 889-2799; (604) 525-8221

Jani-King (Canada), 23 Cornwallis St., Kentville, NS B4N 2E2 CANADA; (902) 678-3500; Mr. Bruce Tupper (800) 565-1873; (902) 678-3200

Jani-King International, 16885 Dallas Pkwy., Addison, TX 75001 ; (972)

503-0866; Mr. Jerry L. Crawford (800) 552-5264; (972) 991-0900

Laser Chem Advanced Carpet & Upholstery Dryclean., 1301 Arizona Ave., # 4, Parker, AZ 85344 ; (520) 669-5488; Mr. Rick Waggoner (800) 272-2741; (520) 669-5488

Laser Chem White Glove Commercial Cleaning, 1301 Arizona Ave., # 4, Parker, AZ 85344 ; (520) 669-5488; Mr. Rick Waggoner (800) 272-2741; (520) 669-5488

National Homecraft, 4441 SE 53rd Ave., P. O. Box 830157, Ocala, FL 34483-0157 ; (352) 694-6939; Mr. Gerald W. McKinney ; (352) 694-2580

Omex International, 3905 Hartzdale Dr., # 506, Camp Hill, PA 17011 ; (717) 737-9271; Mr. Steve Thomas (800) 827-OMEX; (717) 737-7311

Paul W. Davis Systems, 1 Independent Dr., # 2300, Jacksonville, FL 32202 ; (904) 730-8972; Mr. Tim Robinson (800) 294-1517; (904) 737-2779

Paul's Restorations, 1640 Upper Ottowa St., Hamilton, ON L8W 3P2 CANADA; (905) 388-7478; Mr. David Sebastianutti (800) 363-PAUL; (905) 388-7285

Potty Doctor Plumbing Service, 424 N. Dixie Hwy., Lake Worth, FL 33460 ; (561) 585-8136; Mr. Bernard Guthrie ; (561) 582-0571

Professional Carpet Systems, 5182 Old Dixie Hwy., Forest Park, GA 30050 ; (404) 363-0103; Mr. Scott Cooper (800) 925-5055; (404) 362-2300

Purofirst International, 5350 NW 35th Ave., Ft. Lauderdale, FL 33309 ; (800) 995-8527; Mr. Rory O'Dwyer (800) 247-9047; (954) 777-2431

Remodeling Contractors & Cleaning, 13845 W. 107th St., Lenexa, KS 66215 ; (913) 327-8701; Mr. William Sutter (800) 289-1389; (913) 327-8700

Rooter Man, 268 Rangeway Rd., North Billerica, MA 01862 ; (978) 663-3976; Mr. Donald McDonald (800) 698-2244; (978) 667-1144

Sabercorps, P. O. Box 17, Sussex, WI 53089 ; (262) 246-4528; Ms. LaVonne Beecher (888) 773-9234; (262) 246-4521

SealMaster, 2520 S. Campbell St., Sandusky, OH 44870 ; (419) 626-5477; Mr. Roger Auker (800) 395-7325; (419) 626-4375

ServiceMaster of Canada, 6540 Tomken Rd., Mississauga, ON L5T 2E9 CANADA; (905) 670-0077; Mr. Duane MacNeill ; (905) 670-0000

Stanley Steemer Carpet Cleaner, 5500 Stanley Steemer Pkwy., Dublin, OH 43016 ; (614) 717-9223; Mr. Philip P. Ryser (800) 848-7496; (614) 764-2007

Steam Brothers Professional Cleaning & Restoration, 933 1/2 Basin Ave., Bismarck, ND 58504 ; (701) 222-1372; Mr. Adam Leier (800) 767-5064; (701) 222-1263

Steam Masters, 413 Litchfield Dr., Windsor Locks, CT 06096 ; (860) 623-9274; Mr. Donald Michaud (800) 448-5871; (860) 623-9274

Swisher Hygiene, 6849 Fairview Rd., Charlotte, NC 28210 ; (704) 364-1202; Mr. Bruce Mullan (800) 444-4138; (704) 364-7707

Swisher Pest Control, 6849 Fairview Rd., Charlotte, NC 28210; (704) 365-8941; Mr. Tom Busch (800) 444-4138; (704) 364-7707

Thee Chimney Sweep, 36 Vernon Rd. NE, Rome, GA 30165 ; (706) 235-6758; Mr. Gary Trotter ; (706) 232-5261

Town & Country Office & Carpet Care, 2570 San Ramon Valley Blvd. # A-102, San Ramon, CA 94583 ; (925) 867-2756; Mr. Theodore F. Prince ; (925) 867-3850

Tri-Color Carpet Dyeing and Cleaning, 603 W. Main St., Glasgow, KY 42141 ; (502) 651-6048; Mr. Randy Raines (800) 452-9065; (502) 651-7879

Vehex, 4581 Patterson, Grand Rapids, MI 49512 ; ; Mr. Mikel Muffley (800) 271-7077; (616) 975-2767

Window King, 1045 Garden of the Gods, # O, Colorado Springs, CO 80907 ; (719) 522-0441; Mr. Mel Gobel (877) 522-0100; (719) 522-0100

MEDICAL/OPTICAL/DENTAL PRODUCTS & SERVICES INDUSTRY PROFILE

Total # Franchisors in Industry Group	21
Total # Franchised Units in Industry Group	2,248
Total # Company-Owned Units in Industry Group	<u>354</u>
Total # Operating Units in Industry Group	2,602
Average # Franchised Units/Franchisor	107.0
Average # Company-Owned Units/Franchisor	<u>16.9</u>
Average # Total Units/Franchisor	123.9
Ratio of Total # Franchised Units/Total # Company-Owned Units	6.4:1
Industry Survey Participants	7
Representing % of Industry	33.3%
Average Franchise Fee*:	$28.9K
Average Total Investment*:	$189.0K
Average On-Going Royalty Fee*:	5.0%

If a range was provided, the mid-point of the range was used. See detailed profiles for actual ranges.

FIVE LARGEST PARTICIPANTS IN SURVEY

Company	# Fran-chised Units	# Co-Owned Units	# Total Units	Franchise Fee	On-Going Royalty	Total Investment
1. Miracle-Ear	1,374	162	1,536	28-60K	$46.50/Unit	100-200K
2. Option Care	147	31	178	15-35K	Varies	NR
3. Amigo Mobility Center	42	5	47	20K	2-5%	65-89K
4. Henry Ford Optimeyes	15	22	37	10K	8%	150-250K
5. Hemorrhiod Clinic, The	32	1	33	25K	6%	140-225K

All of the data provided are proprietary and should not be quoted without acknowledging *Bond's Franchise Guide.*

AMIGO MOBILITY CENTER

6693 Dixie Hwy.
Bridgeport, MI 48722-0402
Tel: (800) 821-2710
Fax: (517) 777-6537
Web Site: www.concentric.net/nmchihq
Ms. Sue Wheeler, Franchise Support

An AMIGO MOBILITY CENTER is a sales and service outlet, specializing in mobility products for mobility-impaired individuals or anyone with difficulty walking. Our Centers sell and service a variety of items, including battery-powered scooters, wheelchairs and conversion vans to the home health care market.

BACKGROUND: IFA MEMBER
Established: 1968; 1st Franchised: 1984
Franchised Units: 42
Company-Owned Units: 5
Total Units: 47
Dist.: US-47; CAN-0; O'seas-0
 North America: 16 States
 Density: 9 in MI, 5 in FL, 5 in OH
Projected New Units (12 Months): 10
Qualifications: 4, 2, 2, 2, 3, 5
Registered: FL,IL,IN,MI,NY,MN
FINANCIAL/TERMS:
Cash Investment: $40-50K
Total Investment: $65-89K
Minimum Net Worth: $NR
Fees: Franchise - $20K
 Royalty - 2-5%; Ad. - 1%
Earnings Claim Statement: Yes
Term of Contract (Years): 10/5
Avg. # Of Employees: 2 FT, 2 PT
Passive Ownership: Discouraged
Encourage Conversions: Yes
Area Develop. Agreements: Yes
Sub-Franchising Contracts: No
Expand In Territory: Yes
Space Needs: 1,600 SF; Upper-Scale
 Industrial Park
SUPPORT & TRAINING PROVIDED:
Financial Assistance Provided: Yes(I)
Site Selection Assistance: Yes
Lease Negotiation Assistance: Yes
Co-Operative Advertising: Yes
Franchisee Assoc./Member: Yes
Size Of Corporate Staff: 9
On-Going Support: A,B,C,D,E,F,G,H,I
Training: 14 Days Corporate Headquarters;
 14-18 Days Franchise Center.
SPECIFIC EXPANSION PLANS:
US: Midwest, SW, NE and Sunbelt
Canada: No
Overseas: All Countries

<< >>

HEMORRHOID CLINIC, THE

P.O. Box 12488
Oakland, CA 94604
Tel: (510) 839-5471
Fax: (510) 547-3245
Dr. Roberto L. Anning, President

Highly efficient and automated out-patient clinics for hemorrhoid and related rectal procedures. Proprietary laser techniques developed by Dr. Anning insure painless, 20-minute procedure and minimal recuperative discomfort. Lucrative business that takes advantage of the fact that 1 in 8 adults requires rectal surgery. 12 week training at headquarters clinic. All procedures on video. Excellent opportunity to work with the best!

BACKGROUND:
Established: 1987; 1st Franchised: 1988
Franchised Units: 32
Company-Owned Units: 1
Total Units: 33
Dist.: US-27; CAN-3; O'seas-3
 North America: 10 States, 2 Provinces
 Density: 5 in OH, 2 in KY, 2 in MS
Projected New Units (12 Months): 2
Registered: NR
FINANCIAL/TERMS:
Cash Investment: $80-125K
Total Investment: $140-225K
Minimum Net Worth: $NR
Fees: Franchise - $25K
 Royalty - 6%; Ad. - 1%
Earnings Claim Statement: Yes
Term of Contract (Years): 10/10
Avg. # Of Employees: 3 FT, 4 PT
Passive Ownership: Not Allowed
Encourage Conversions: Yes
Area Develop. Agreements: Yes/10
Sub-Franchising Contracts: Yes
Expand In Territory: Yes
Space Needs: 1,500-2,000 SF; FS, SF
SUPPORT & TRAINING PROVIDED:
Financial Assistance Provided: Yes(I)
Site Selection Assistance: Yes
Lease Negotiation Assistance: Yes
Co-Operative Advertising: Yes
Franchisee Assoc./Member: NR
Size Of Corporate Staff: 12
On-Going Support: C,D,E,G,H,I
Training: 12 Weeks Anning Clinic; 3 Weeks
 On-Site; On-Going Video Training
 Procedures.
SPECIFIC EXPANSION PLANS:
US: All United States

Canada: ON Only
Overseas: No

<< >>

HENRY FORD OPTIMEYES

655 W. 13 Mile Rd.
Madison Heights, MI 48071
Tel: (877) OPTIMEYES (248) 588-9300
Fax: (248) 588-3355
Web Site: www.optimeyes.com
Dr. Donald M. Borsand, CEO

Sale of primary vision care services and products to correct and improve vision. Three user vision correction centers for refractive surgery, sale of eye glasses and contact lenses.

BACKGROUND:
Established: 1980; 1st Franchised: 1981
Franchised Units: 15
Company-Owned Units: 22
Total Units: 37
Dist.: US-37; CAN-0; O'seas-0
 North America: 1 State
 Density: NR
Projected New Units (12 Months): 5
Qualifications: 5, 3, 5, 5, 5, 5
Registered: MI
FINANCIAL/TERMS:
Cash Investment: $100K
Total Investment: $150-250K
Minimum Net Worth: $200K
Fees: Franchise - $10K
 Royalty - 8%; Ad. - 5%
Earnings Claim Statement: Yes
Term of Contract (Years): 10/5
Avg. # Of Employees: 5 FT, 2 PT
Passive Ownership: Not Allowed
Encourage Conversions: Yes
Area Develop. Agreements: Yes/10
Sub-Franchising Contracts: Yes
Expand In Territory: Yes
Space Needs: 2,000 SF; FS, SD, SC, RM
SUPPORT & TRAINING PROVIDED:
Financial Assistance Provided: Yes(I)
Site Selection Assistance: Yes
Lease Negotiation Assistance: Yes
Co-Operative Advertising: Yes
Franchisee Assoc./Member: Yes
Size Of Corporate Staff: 25
On-Going Support: A,B,C,D,E,G,H,I
Training: 2 Weeks Roseville, MI; On-Going
 Field Training.

SPECIFIC EXPANSION PLANS:
US: Michigan Only
Canada: No
Overseas: No

≪≫

MIRACLE-EAR
4101 Dahlberg Dr.
Golden Valley, MN 55422
Tel: (800) 234-7714 (612) 520-9500
Fax: (612) 520-9520
Web Site: www.miracle-ear.com
Mr. Tim Kuehn, Director Franchise
   Licensing

Manufacturer and world's largest retailer of hearing systems, with 1,287 offices nationally. MIRACLE-EAR also has master franchisors in 20 foreign countries.

BACKGROUND: IFA MEMBER
Established: 1948;   1st Franchised: 1983
Franchised Units: 1,374
Company-Owned Units   162
Total Units: 1,536
Dist.:   US-1,267; CAN-0; O'seas-20
   North America: 50 States
   Density: 96 in CA, 39 in TX, 74 in FL
Projected New Units (12 Months):   125
Qualifications: 4, 4, 2, 3, 4, 4
Registered: All States
FINANCIAL/TERMS:
Cash Investment: $50-150K
Total Investment: $100-200K
Minimum Net Worth: $100K
Fees: Franchise - $28-60K
   Royalty - $46.50/Unit;Ad. - $26/Inquiry
Earnings Claim Statement: No
Term of Contract (Years):   5/5
Avg. # Of Employees: 2 FT, 1 PT
Passive Ownership: Not Allowed
Encourage Conversions: N/A
Area Develop. Agreements: Yes/1-1.5
Sub-Franchising Contracts: No
Expand In Territory: Yes
Space Needs: 750 SF; FS, SF, SC, RM
SUPPORT & TRAINING PROVIDED:
Financial Assistance Provided: N/A
Site Selection Assistance: N/A
Lease Negotiation Assistance: No
Co-Operative Advertising: Yes
Franchisee Assoc./Member: No
Size Of Corporate Staff: 3
On-Going Support: A,C,D,E,G,h,I
Training: 2 Weeks Corporate Headquarters;
   10 Weeks On-Site.
SPECIFIC EXPANSION PLANS:
US: West, Midwest

Canada: No
Overseas: All Countries

≪≫

OPTION CARE
100 Corporate North, # 212
Bannockburn, IL 60015
Tel: (800) 879-6137 (847) 615-1690
Fax: (847) 615-0326
Mr. Jeff Vigh, VP Sales & Marketing

We offer franchises for the establishment of outpatient health care businesses which operate under the service mark of OPTION CARE. Our franchises specialize in what is sometimes referred to as home infusion therapy, but the services encompass many aspects of health care in home and other outpatient settings.

BACKGROUND:
Established: 1979;   1st Franchised: 1984
Franchised Units: 147
Company-Owned Units   31
Total Units: 178
Dist.:   US-178; CAN-0; O'seas-0
   North America: 37 States
   Density: 16 in CA, 13 in FL, 13 in OH
Projected New Units (12 Months):   10
Qualifications: 3, 5, 5, 4, 2, 3
Registered: CA,HI,IL,IN,MD,MI,MN,
   NY,ND,RI,SD,VA,WA,WI
FINANCIAL/TERMS:
Cash Investment: $243.7-541.8K
Total Investment: $NR
Minimum Net Worth: $NR
Fees: Franchise - $15-35K
   Royalty - Varies;   Ad. - 1.5%
Earnings Claim Statement: No
Term of Contract (Years):   20/10
Avg. # Of Employees: NR
Passive Ownership: Allowed
Encourage Conversions: Yes
Area Develop. Agreements: No
Sub-Franchising Contracts: No
Expand In Territory: Yes
Space Needs: 1,500 SF; FS, SF, SC
SUPPORT & TRAINING PROVIDED:
Financial Assistance Provided: No
Site Selection Assistance: No
Lease Negotiation Assistance: No
Co-Operative Advertising: No
Franchisee Assoc./Member: No
Size Of Corporate Staff: 64
On-Going Support: B,G,H,I
Training: 4 Days Clinical Operations
   Chicago, IL; 4 Days Sales/Business
   Development Chicago, IL.

SPECIFIC EXPANSION PLANS:
US: All United States
Canada: No
Overseas: No

≪≫

TOTAL MEDICAL COMPLIANCE
99 NW Miami Gardens Dr., #206
North Miami Beach, FL 33169
Tel: (800) 840-6742 (305) 690-9890
Fax: (305) 690-9992
E-Mail: tmcfran@aol.com
Web Site: www.centercourt.com/tmc
Mr. Chuck Weiss, President

TOTAL MEDICAL COMPLIANCE franchisees work in the growing health care industry, providing consultant services to health care providers such as doctors, dentists and clinics. Every health care provider must comply with federal and state health related laws. The TMC system allows you to provide this consulting service even if you do not have a medical background.

BACKGROUND:
Established: 1993;   1st Franchised: 1995
Franchised Units: 5
Company-Owned Units   2
Total Units: 7
Dist.:   US-7; CAN-0; O'seas-0
   North America: 7 States
   Density: 4 in FL, 2 in TX, 1 in NC
Projected New Units (12 Months):   8
Qualifications: 5, 4, 4, 4, 5, 5
Registered: All States
FINANCIAL/TERMS:
Cash Investment: $35-80K
Total Investment: $50-100K
Minimum Net Worth: $200K
Fees: Franchise - $35-80K
   Royalty - 2%;   Ad. - 0.25%
Earnings Claim Statement: Yes
Term of Contract (Years):   5/5
Avg. # Of Employees: 2 FT, 1 PT
Passive Ownership: Allowed
Encourage Conversions: N/A
Area Develop. Agreements: No
Sub-Franchising Contracts: No
Expand In Territory: Yes
Space Needs: NR SF; N/A
SUPPORT & TRAINING PROVIDED:
Financial Assistance Provided: No
Site Selection Assistance: N/A
Lease Negotiation Assistance: N/A
Co-Operative Advertising: N/A
Franchisee Assoc./Member: No

Size Of Corporate Staff: 5
On-Going Support: b,C,D,G,h,I
Training: 1 Week Home Office; 1 Week
    Franchisee Territory.
SPECIFIC EXPANSION PLANS:
US: All United States
Canada: No
Overseas: No

<< >>

WOMEN'S HEALTH BOUTIQUE

12715 Telge Rd.
Cypress, TX 77429
Tel: (888) 280-2053 (281) 256-4100
Fax: (281) 256-4178
E-Mail: w-h-bsales@w-h-b.com
Web Site: www.w-h-b.com
Mr. Bob Dolan, VP Franchise Sales

One-stop shopping for women with special needs in a tasteful environment, attended by knowledgeable, highly trained, compassionate saleswomen. Real products and services for post breast surgery, pre- and post-natal, post-mastectomy, compression therapy, hair loss, incontinence, skin care, wigs and turbans and personal care.

BACKGROUND: IFA MEMBER
Established: 1988; 1st Franchised: 1993
Franchised Units: 15
Company-Owned Units 3
Total Units: 18
Dist.: US-18; CAN-0; O'seas-0
    North America: 10 States
    Density: 5 in TX, 3 in MI, 2 in GA
Projected New Units (12 Months): 12
Qualifications: 4, 4, 3, 2, 5, 5
Registered: All Except HI,ND,SD
FINANCIAL/TERMS:
Cash Investment: $55K
Total Investment: $214.7-234.7K
Minimum Net Worth: $200K
Fees: Franchise - $20.8K
    Royalty - 4-7%; Ad. - 0%
Earnings Claim Statement: No
Term of Contract (Years): 10/10
Avg. # Of Employees: 2-3 FT
Passive Ownership: Not Allowed
Encourage Conversions: N/A
Area Develop. Agreements: No
Sub-Franchising Contracts: No
Expand In Territory: Yes
Space Needs: 1,500 SF; SC, Medical
    Center
SUPPORT & TRAINING PROVIDED:
Financial Assistance Provided: Yes(I)

Site Selection Assistance: Yes
Lease Negotiation Assistance: Yes
Co-Operative Advertising: No
Franchisee Assoc./Member: Yes/Yes
Size Of Corporate Staff: NR
On-Going Support: C,D,E,G,H,I
Training: Approximately 5 Weeks.
SPECIFIC EXPANSION PLANS:
US: All United States
Canada: No
Overseas: No

<< >>

SUPPLEMENTAL LISTING
OF FRANCHISORS

American Alternative Hospitals, 8940 SVL Box, Victorville, CA 92392 ; (760) 242-3502; Mr. Venkat R. Vangala (800) 800-1605; (760) 946-6000

American Physical Rehabilitation Network, 4747 Holland Sylvania Rd., 2nd Fl., Sylvania, OH 43560 ; (419) 824-3435; Mr. Harvey Bowles (800) 331-3058; (419) 824-3434

Cohen's Fashion Optical, 1500 Hempstead Turnpike, East Meadow, NY 11554-1558 ; (516) 465-6930; Ms. Norma Scalzulli ; (516) 599-5500

Dentist's Choice, The, 1171 W. Shaw Ave., # 103, Fresno, CA 93711 ; (559) 241-7175; Mr. Steve Everhart (800) 757-1333; (559) 241-7171

Diversified Dental Services, 10641 First St. E., # 204, Treasure Island, FL 33706 ; (727) 367-9751; Ms. Dorothy Moore (800) 374-6273; (727) 367-6801

Electric Mobility Center, 1 Mobility Plaza, Sewell, NJ 08080 ; (609) 468-3426; Ms. Sue Baush Sarda (800) 662-4548; (609) 468-0270

Optometric Eye Care Center, P.O. Box 7185, Rocky Mount, NC 27804 ; (252) 937-6358; Dr. Blair Harrold (800) 334-3937; (252) 937-6650

ProCare Vision Centers, 926 N. 21st St., Newark, OH 43055 ; (614) 366-5453; Dr. Eva K. Pound-Bickle (800) 837-5569; (614) 366-7011

Sterling Optical, 1500 Hempstead Turnpike, East Meadow, NY 11554 ; (516) 390-2111; Mr. Jerry Darnel (800) 332-6302; (516) 390-2100

Texas State Optical, 4925 W. Cardinal Dr., Beaumont, TX 77705 ; (409) 842-3522; Mr. Keith Albright ; (409) 842-4113

PACKAGING & MAILING INDUSTRY PROFILE

Total # Franchisors in Industry Group	18
Total # Franchised Units in Industry Group	8,560
Total # Company-Owned Units in Industry Group	<u>26</u>
Total # Operating Units in Industry Group	8,586
Average # Franchised Units/Franchisor	475.6
Average # Company-Owned Units/Franchisor	<u>1.4</u>
Average # Total Units/Franchisor	477.0
Ratio of Total # Franchised Units/Total # Company-Owned Units	329.2:1
Industry Survey Participants	11
Representing % of Industry	61.1%
Average Franchise Fee*:	$26.0K
Average Total Investment*:	$95.9K
Average On-Going Royalty Fee*:	6.2%

If a range was provided, the mid-point of the range was used. See detailed profiles for actual ranges.

FIVE LARGEST PARTICIPANTS IN SURVEY

Company	# Fran-chised Units	# Co-Owned Units	# Total Units	Franchise Fee	On-Going Royalty	Total Investment
1. Mail Boxes Etc.	4,074	0	4,074	29.9K	5%	118-119K
2. Postnet Postal & Business Centers	712	0	712	26.9K	4%	91-122K
3. Packaging and Shipping Specialists	518	6	524	24.5K	0%	56-85K
4. Pak Mail	400	0	400	28K	5% Sliding	70-115K
5. Handle With Care Packaging	325	0	325	21.5K	5%	48.5-51K

All of the data provided are proprietary and should not be quoted without acknowledging *Bond's Franchise Guide.*

AIM MAIL CENTERS

15550-D Rockfield Blvd.
Irvine, CA 92618
Tel: (800) 669-4246 (949) 837-4151
Fax: (949) 837-4537
E-Mail: mherrera@aimmailcenters.com
Web Site: www.aimmailcenters.com
Mr. Michael R. Herrera, VP of Franchise
 Development

AIM MAIL CENTERS take care of all business service needs. AIM's services include renting mailboxes, buying stamps, sending faxes, notary, making copies and passport photos. AIM is also an authorized UPS and FedEx Shipping Outlet. It's like having a post office, office supply store, gift shop, and copy shop all rolled into one. We are so confident of our franchise program that we offer a money-back guarantee.

BACKGROUND: IFA MEMBER
Established: 1985;   1st Franchised: 1989
Franchised Units: 60
Company-Owned Units   0
Total Units: 60
Dist.:   US-60; CAN-0; O'seas-0
 North America: 7 States
 Density: 46 in CA, 2 in WA, 2 in AZ
Projected New Units (12 Months):   36
Qualifications: 4, 1, 1, 3, 4, 5
Registered: All States
FINANCIAL/TERMS:
Cash Investment: $30-35K
Total Investment: $95-105K
Minimum Net Worth: $125K
Fees: Franchise - $23.9K
 Royalty - 5%;   Ad. - 2%
Earnings Claim Statement: Yes
Term of Contract (Years):   15
Avg. # Of Employees: 1 FT, 2 PT
Passive Ownership: Discouraged
Encourage Conversions: Yes
Area Develop. Agreements: Yes/5
Sub-Franchising Contracts: No
Expand In Territory: Yes
Space Needs: 1,000 SF; SF, SC, Anchored
 Center

SUPPORT & TRAINING PROVIDED:
Financial Assistance Provided: Yes(I)
Site Selection Assistance: Yes
Lease Negotiation Assistance: Yes
Co-Operative Advertising: Yes
Franchisee Assoc./Member: Yes
Size Of Corporate Staff: 10
On-Going Support: C,D,E,G,H,I
Training: 2 Weeks Corporate Headquarters;
 3 Days in Store.
SPECIFIC EXPANSION PLANS:
US: All United States
Canada: All Except AB
Overseas: All Countries

<< >>

CRATERS & FREIGHTERS

7000 E. 47th Ave., # 100
Denver, CO 80216
Tel: (800) 949-9931 (303) 399-8190
Fax: (303) 393-7644
E-Mail:
Franchising@CratersAndFreighters.com
Web Site: www.CratersAndFreighters.com
Mr. Bob Molnar, Dir. of Franchise
 Development

As specialty freight handlers, CRATERS & FREIGHTERS is the best-niched concept in the industry. We're the exclusive source for reliable, affordable specialty shipping services for pieces that are too big for UPS and too small for movers. We provide high-demand packing, crating and shipping with iron-clad insurance to an up-scale clientele. Serve your large territory from low overhead warehouse space.

BACKGROUND: IFA MEMBER
Established: 1990;   1st Franchised: 1991
Franchised Units: 59
Company-Owned Units   0
Total Units: 59
Dist.:   US-59; CAN-0; O'seas-0
 North America: 29 States
 Density: 6 in CA, 5 in FL, 5 in TX
Projected New Units (12 Months):   14
Qualifications: 5, 4, 2, 1, 3, 5
Registered: CA,FL,MD,MI
FINANCIAL/TERMS:
Cash Investment: $NR
Total Investment: $54-77K
Minimum Net Worth: $100K

Fees: Franchise - $24.8K
 Royalty - 5%;   Ad. - 1%
Earnings Claim Statement: No
Term of Contract (Years):   10/10
Avg. # Of Employees: 3 FT
Passive Ownership: Discouraged
Encourage Conversions: N/A
Area Develop. Agreements: No
Sub-Franchising Contracts: No
Expand In Territory: Yes
Space Needs: 1,800-2,000 SF; Warehouse
SUPPORT & TRAINING PROVIDED:
Financial Assistance Provided: Yes(I)
Site Selection Assistance: Yes
Lease Negotiation Assistance: Yes
Co-Operative Advertising: Yes
Franchisee Assoc./Member: Yes/No
Size Of Corporate Staff: 12
On-Going Support: A,B,C,D,E,G,h,I
Training: 7 Days Home Office in Denver,
 CO.
SPECIFIC EXPANSION PLANS:
US: All United States
Canada: All Canada
Overseas: All Countries

<< >>

HANDLE WITH CARE PACKAGING STORE

5675 DTC Blvd., # 280
Englewood, CO 80111-9845
Tel: (800) 525-6309 (303) 741-6626
Fax: (303) 741-6653
Web Site: www.packstore.com
Mr. Don Romines, Dir. Franchise
 Development

HANDLE WITH CARE PACKAGING STORES specialize in FLAV, those items that are fragile, large, awkward or valuable - from 1 - 1,000 pounds. Known as the packaging and shipping experts, HANDLE WITH CARE PACKAGING STORES often receive referrals from other postal service centers to package and ship items like artwork, antiques, furniture and electronics. They have the skill, the equipment and the knowledge to get such jobs done right.

BACKGROUND:
Established: 1980;   1st Franchised: 1984
Franchised Units: 325
Company-Owned Units   0
Total Units: 325
Dist.:   US-315; CAN-1; O'seas-9
 North America: 41 States, 1 Province
 Density: 57 in CA, 25 in FL, 20 in VA

Projected New Units (12 Months): 30-40
Qualifications: 4, 4, 2, 3, 1, 4
Registered: All States

FINANCIAL/TERMS:

Cash Investment: $48.5-51K
Total Investment: $48.5-51K
Minimum Net Worth: $NR
Fees: Franchise - $21.5K
   Royalty - 5%;   Ad. - 3%
Earnings Claim Statement: No
Term of Contract (Years):   Perpetual
Avg. # Of Employees: 1-2 FT, 1-2 PT
Passive Ownership: Not Allowed
Encourage Conversions: Yes
Area Develop. Agreements: Yes/Open
Sub-Franchising Contracts: No
Expand In Territory: No
Space Needs: 1,200-1,500 SF; SC

SUPPORT & TRAINING PROVIDED:

Financial Assistance Provided: Yes(D)
Site Selection Assistance: Yes
Lease Negotiation Assistance: No
Co-Operative Advertising: Yes
Franchisee Assoc./Member: No
Size Of Corporate Staff: 20
On-Going Support: C,D,E,G,H,I
Training: 2 Weeks Denver, CO; 3 Days
   On-Site at Opening.

SPECIFIC EXPANSION PLANS:

US: All United States
Canada: All Canada
Overseas: No

◄◄ ►►

MAIL BOXES ETC.®
MAKING BUSINESS EASIER.® WORLDWIDE.

MAIL BOXES ETC.

6060 Cornerstone Ct. W.
San Diego, CA 92121-3795
Tel: (800) 280-9229 (858) 455-8800
Fax: (858) 546-7488
E-Mail: fransale@mbe.com
Web Site: www.mbe.com
Mr. John Dring, Dir. Domestic Franchise
   Sales

MAIL BOXES ETC. (MBE) is the world's
largest franchisor of independently-owned
and operated business, communication and
postal service centers. MBE Centers serve
a large customer group of small and home-
based businesses and general consumers.

Products and services include: mailbox
services, copies, faxes, U. S. Postal services,
shipping (FedEx, UPS, etc.), freight
shipping, packaging, office and mailing
supplies, printing services and more.

BACKGROUND: IFA MEMBER
Established: 1980;   1st Franchised: 1980
Franchised Units: 4,074
Company-Owned Units   0
Total Units: 4,074
Dist.:   US-3,380; CAN-232; O'seas-462
   North America: 50 States,10 Provinces
   Density: 505 in CA, 263 in FL, 166 TX
Projected New Units (12 Months):   200
Qualifications: 5, 4, 3, 3, 3, 5
Registered: All States

FINANCIAL/TERMS:

Cash Investment: $45K
Total Investment: $118-199K
Minimum Net Worth: $150K
Fees: Franchise - $29.9K
   Royalty - 5%;   Ad. - 3.5%
Earnings Claim Statement: No
Term of Contract (Years):   10/10
Avg. # Of Employees: 2 Min. FT
Passive Ownership: Allowed
Encourage Conversions: Yes
Area Develop. Agreements: Yes/10
Sub-Franchising Contracts: No
Expand In Territory: Yes
Space Needs: 1,200-1,800 SF; FS, SF, SC,
   RM, Non-Tradit.

SUPPORT & TRAINING PROVIDED:

Financial Assistance Provided: Yes
Site Selection Assistance: No
Lease Negotiation Assistance: Yes
Co-Operative Advertising: Yes
Franchisee Assoc./Member: Yes/Yes
Size Of Corporate Staff: 260
On-Going Support: B,C,D,E,G,H,I
Training: 5 Days Local Market; 2 Weeks
   San Diego, CA; 5 Days Local Market.

SPECIFIC EXPANSION PLANS:

US: All United States
Canada: All Canada
Overseas: All Countries

◄◄ ►►

MAIL BOXES ETC. (CANADA)

505 Iroquois Shore Rd., # 4
Oakville, ON L6H 2R3 CANADA
Tel: (800) 661-MBEC (905) 338-9754
Fax: (905) 338-7491
E-Mail: dwarren@ca.mbe.com
Web Site: www.mbe.com
Mr. Ralph Askar, Executive Vice President/
   COO

Business and communication services.

BACKGROUND:

Established: 1990;   1st Franchised: 1990
Franchised Units: 255
Company-Owned Units   2
Total Units: 257
Dist.:   US-0; CAN-216; O'seas-0
   North America: 9 Provinces
   Density: NR
Projected New Units (12 Months):   50
Qualifications: 5, 4, 3, 3, 3, 4
Registered: NR

FINANCIAL/TERMS:

Cash Investment: $60K
Total Investment: $110-135K
Minimum Net Worth: $125K
Fees: Franchise - $29.9K
   Royalty - 6%;   Ad. - 2%
Earnings Claim Statement: No
Term of Contract (Years):   10/10
Avg. # Of Employees: 2 FT, 1 PT
Passive Ownership: Discouraged
Encourage Conversions: Yes
Area Develop. Agreements: Yes/10
Sub-Franchising Contracts: No
Expand In Territory: Yes
Space Needs: 1,200 SF; FS, SF, SC

SUPPORT & TRAINING PROVIDED:

Financial Assistance Provided: Yes
Site Selection Assistance: Yes
Lease Negotiation Assistance: Yes
Co-Operative Advertising: Yes
Franchisee Assoc./Member: Yes/No
Size Of Corporate Staff: 20
On-Going Support: a,B,C,D,e,G,h
Training: 2 Weeks at Corporate Office; 1.5
   Weeks in Center.

SPECIFIC EXPANSION PLANS:

US: All United States
Canada: All Canada
Overseas: U.K. and Ireland

◄◄ ►►

PACKAGING AND SHIPPING SPECIALIST

5211 85th St., # 104
Lubbock, TX 79424
Tel: (800) 877-8884 (806) 794-9996
Fax: (806) 794-9997
E-Mail: packship@arn.net
Web Site: www.packship.com
Mr. Mike Gallagher, President

We are the only company that does not
charge royalties and one of the most
affordable and knowledgeable companies
in this industry. A complete copy center

and mail center with an array of related retail items for the consumer.

BACKGROUND:
Established: 1981;   1st Franchised: 1988
Franchised Units: 518
Company-Owned Units   <u>6</u>
Total Units: 524
Dist.:   US-480; CAN-10; O'seas-34
  North America: 37 States,10 Provinces
  Density: 75 in TX, 20 in NY, 12 in IL
Projected New Units (12 Months):   70
Qualifications: 2, 1, 1, 1, 2, 1
Registered: All States
FINANCIAL/TERMS:
Cash Investment: $20-30K
Total Investment: $56-85K
Minimum Net Worth: $100K
Fees: Franchise - $24.5K
  Royalty - 0%;   Ad. - 0%
Earnings Claim Statement: No
Term of Contract (Years):   5/5
Avg. # Of Employees: 2 FT, 2 PT
Passive Ownership: Allowed
Encourage Conversions: Yes
Area Develop. Agreements: Yes/10
Sub-Franchising Contracts: No
Expand In Territory: Yes
Space Needs: 1,000-2,000 SF; SF, SC
SUPPORT & TRAINING PROVIDED:
Financial Assistance Provided: Yes(I)
Site Selection Assistance: Yes
Lease Negotiation Assistance: Yes
Co-Operative Advertising: No
Franchisee Assoc./Member: No
Size Of Corporate Staff: 20
On-Going Support: B,C,D,E,G,h,I
Training: 10-14 Days in Raleigh, NC; 10-14
  Days in Dallas, TX.
SPECIFIC EXPANSION PLANS:
US: All United States
Canada: All Canada
Overseas: All Countries

◄◄ ►►

PAK MAIL
CENTERS OF AMERICA

PAK MAIL
7173 S. Havana St., # 600
Englewood, CO 80112
Tel: (800) 833-2821 (303) 957-1000
Fax: (800) 336-7363
E-Mail: sales@pakmail.com
Web Site: www.pakmail.com
Mr. Chuck Prentner, Licensing Manager

PAK MAIL is a convenient center for packaging, shipping and business support services, offering both residential and commercial customers air, ground, and ocean carriers, custom packaging and crating, private mailbox rental, mail services, packaging and moving supplies, copy and fax service and internet access and related services. We ship anything, anywhere.

BACKGROUND: IFA MEMBER
Established: 1983;   1st Franchised: 1984
Franchised Units: 400
Company-Owned Units   <u>0</u>
Total Units: 400
Dist.:   US-370; CAN-8; O'seas-22
  North America: 42 States
  Density: 91 in FL, 41 in GA, 22 in CA
Projected New Units (12 Months):   50
Qualifications: 3, 2, 2, 2, 2, 5
Registered: All States and AB
FINANCIAL/TERMS:
Cash Investment: $30-108K
Total Investment: $70-115K
Minimum Net Worth: $100K
Fees: Franchise - $28K
  Royalty - 5% Sliding;   Ad. - 2%
Earnings Claim Statement: Yes
Term of Contract (Years):   10/10
Avg. # Of Employees: 1 FT, 1 PT
Passive Ownership: Discouraged
Encourage Conversions: Yes
Area Develop. Agreements: Yes/5
Sub-Franchising Contracts: No
Expand In Territory: Yes
Space Needs: 1,200 SF; SC
SUPPORT & TRAINING PROVIDED:
Financial Assistance Provided: Yes(I)
Site Selection Assistance: Yes
Lease Negotiation Assistance: Yes
Co-Operative Advertising: Yes
Franchisee Assoc./Member: Yes/Yes
Size Of Corporate Staff: 22
On-Going Support: B,C,D,E,F,G,H,I
Training: 10 Days in Englewood, CO; 3

Days in Existing Center; 3 Days In New Center at Opening.
SPECIFIC EXPANSION PLANS:
US: All United States
Canada: All Canada
Overseas: All Countries

◄◄ ►►

POSTAL ANNEX+
7580 Metropolitan Dr., # 200
San Diego, CA 92108
Tel: (800) 456-1525 (619) 563-4800
Fax: (619) 563-9850
Web Site: www.postalannex.com
Mr. John Goodell, Director Franchise
  Development

Retail business service center, providing: packaging, shipping, copying, postal, mail box rental, printing fax, notary, office supplies and more.

BACKGROUND: IFA MEMBER
Established: 1985;   1st Franchised: 1986
Franchised Units: 238
Company-Owned Units   <u>0</u>
Total Units: 238
Dist.:   US-237; CAN-0; O'seas-1
  North America: NR
  Density: 120 in CA, 15 in OR, 15 MI
Projected New Units (12 Months):   36
Qualifications: 5, 3, 1, 1, 3, 3
Registered: CA,FL,IL,MD,MI,NY,
  OR,WA,WI,DC
FINANCIAL/TERMS:
Cash Investment: $30-50K
Total Investment: $108.9-158.4K
Minimum Net Worth: $200K
Fees: Franchise - $27.9K
  Royalty - 5%;   Ad. - 2%
Earnings Claim Statement: Yes
Term of Contract (Years):   15/15
Avg. # Of Employees: 1 FT, 2 PT
Passive Ownership: Allowed
Encourage Conversions: Yes
Area Develop. Agreements: Yes/15
Sub-Franchising Contracts: Yes
Expand In Territory: Yes
Space Needs: 1,200 SF; SF, SC
SUPPORT & TRAINING PROVIDED:
Financial Assistance Provided: Yes(I)
Site Selection Assistance: Yes
Lease Negotiation Assistance: Yes
Co-Operative Advertising: Yes
Franchisee Assoc./Member: Yes/Yes
Size Of Corporate Staff: 18
On-Going Support: A,B,C,D,E,F,G,h,I
Training: 2 Weeks San Diego, CA.

SPECIFIC EXPANSION PLANS:

US:	All United States
Canada:	All Canada
Overseas:	All Countries

≪ ≫

POSTAL CONNECTIONS OF AMERICA

287 S. Robertson Blvd.
Beverly Hills, CA 90211
Tel: (310) 360-1215
Fax: (310) 360-6765
E-Mail: info@postalconnections.com
Web Site: www.postalconnections.com
Ms. Maryhelen Molina, Director Franchise Sales

Since 1985, we have specialized in a variety of services, including packing, shipping, mailbox rentals, copying, notary and more. We have recently introduced, through our CyberCenter package, features such as high-speed Internet access, video conferencing and conference rooms, truly making these locations 'virtual offices.'

BACKGROUND:

Established: 1985;	1st Franchised: 1995
Franchised Units:	19
Company-Owned Units	6
Total Units:	25
Dist.:	US-25; CAN-0; O'seas-0
North America:	6 States
Density:	7 in AZ, 5 in CA, 3 in OR
Projected New Units (12 Months):	50
Qualifications:	3, 5, 3, 3, 4, 5
Registered: All States	

FINANCIAL/TERMS:

Cash Investment:	$30-40K
Total Investment:	$80-120K
Minimum Net Worth:	$N/A
Fees: Franchise -	$18.9K
Royalty - 5% (Grad);	Ad. - 2%
Earnings Claim Statement:	Yes
Term of Contract (Years):	10/10
Avg. # Of Employees:	2 FT, 1 PT
Passive Ownership:	Discouraged
Encourage Conversions:	N/A
Area Develop. Agreements:	Yes/10
Sub-Franchising Contracts:	No
Expand In Territory:	Yes
Space Needs: 1,200 SF; SF, SC	

SUPPORT & TRAINING PROVIDED:

Financial Assistance Provided:	Yes(I)
Site Selection Assistance:	Yes
Lease Negotiation Assistance:	Yes
Co-Operative Advertising:	No
Franchisee Assoc./Member:	No
Size Of Corporate Staff:	7
On-Going Support:	AS,B,C,D,E,F,G,h,I

Training: 7 Days Headquarters in Beverly Hills, CA; 10 Days after Opening at New Location.

SPECIFIC EXPANSION PLANS:

US:	All United States
Canada:	All Canada
Overseas:	Asia, Europe, South America

≪ ≫

POSTNET POSTAL & BUSINESS CENTERS

2501 N. Green Valley Pkwy., # 101
Henderson, NV 89014
Tel: (800) 841-7171 (702) 792-7100
Fax: (702) 792-7115
E-Mail: info@postnet.net
Web Site: www.postnet.net
Mr. Ken Ross, VP Global Franchise Dev't.

Become a POSTNET Pro! POSTNET's franchise opportunity offers a proven method of marketing products and services, which consumers need on a daily basis. The opportunity to get in on the ground floor of a rapidly expanding business is a rarity -- POSTNET's domestic and international franchisees have the opportunity to tap into the world market, offering personal and business services including UPS and FedEx Shipping, B/W and color copy services, private mail boxes, fax, printing and much more.

BACKGROUND: IFA MEMBER

Established: 1985;	1st Franchised: 1993
Franchised Units:	712
Company-Owned Units	0
Total Units:	712
Dist.:	US-392; CAN-61; O'seas-314
North America:	39 States, 2 Provinces
Density:	17 in CA, 14 in IL, 11 in FL
Projected New Units (12 Months):	60
Qualifications:	4, 3, 2, 3, 4, 5
Registered: All States and AB	

FINANCIAL/TERMS:

Cash Investment:	$35-50K
Total Investment:	$91-122K
Minimum Net Worth:	$150K
Fees: Franchise -	$26.9K
Royalty - 4%;	Ad. - 1%
Earnings Claim Statement:	No
Term of Contract (Years):	10/10
Avg. # Of Employees:	2 FT, 1 PT
Passive Ownership:	Not Allowed
Encourage Conversions:	Yes
Area Develop. Agreements:	Yes/10
Sub-Franchising Contracts:	No
Expand In Territory:	Yes
Space Needs: 1,200 SF; SC	

SUPPORT & TRAINING PROVIDED:

Financial Assistance Provided:	Yes(I)
Site Selection Assistance:	Yes
Lease Negotiation Assistance:	Yes
Co-Operative Advertising:	No
Franchisee Assoc./Member:	Yes
Size Of Corporate Staff:	30
On-Going Support:	C,D,E,G,H,I

Training: 1 Week Henderson, NV; 1 Week at Store Opening; 2-3 Days Follow-Up.

SPECIFIC EXPANSION PLANS:

US:	All United States
Canada:	All Canada
Overseas:	All Countries

≪ ≫

UNISHIPPERS ASSOCIATION

746 E. Winchester St., # 200
Salt Lake City, UT 84107
Tel: (800) 999-8721 (801) 487-0600
Fax: (801) 487-0623
E-Mail: john_lund@unishippers.com
Web Site: www.unishippers.com
Mr. John Lund, Dir. Internt'l Franchise Sales

UNISHIPPERS, the largest reseller of transportation services in the United States, is looking for goal-oriented Master Franchisees as it expands into the global market. UNISHIPPERS combines the shipping volumes of thousands of businesses to obtain discounts and benefits from major overnight express and other transportation service carriers. These discounts and benefits, usually available only to large corporations, are then passed on to our customers, primarily small- to medium-sized businesses.

BACKGROUND: IFA MEMBER

Established: 1987;	1st Franchised: 1987
Franchised Units:	305

Company-Owned Units	<u>0</u>
Total Units:	305
Dist.:	US-296; CAN-0; O'seas-1
North America:	48 States
Density:	27 in CA, 20 in NY, 20 in TX
Projected New Units (12 Months):	4
Qualifications:	4, 5, 1, 1, 5, 5
Registered:	CA,FL,HI,IN,MD,MI,MN, NY,ND,OR,RI,SD,VA,WA,WI,DC

FINANCIAL/TERMS:

Cash Investment:	$10-50K
Total Investment:	$10-100K
Minimum Net Worth:	$N/A
Fees: Franchise -	$10-50K
Royalty - 16.5%;	Ad. - 1% Gross
Earnings Claim Statement:	Yes
Term of Contract (Years):	5/5
Avg. # Of Employees:	1 FT
Passive Ownership:	Allowed
Encourage Conversions:	N/A
Area Develop. Agreements:	No
Sub-Franchising Contracts:	Yes
Expand In Territory:	No
Space Needs: NR SF; N/A	

SUPPORT & TRAINING PROVIDED:

Financial Assistance Provided:	Yes
Site Selection Assistance:	N/A
Lease Negotiation Assistance:	No
Co-Operative Advertising:	N/A
Franchisee Assoc./Member:	No
Size Of Corporate Staff:	35
On-Going Support:	C,D,G,h,I
Training: 1 Week Salt Lake City, UT; 2 Days at Franchisee's Location.	

SPECIFIC EXPANSION PLANS:

US:	No
Canada:	All Canada
Overseas:	Western Europe, Pacific Rim

SUPPLEMENTAL LISTING OF FRANCHISORS

CGI Worldwide Express Services, 2501 Cedar Springs Rd. #450, Dallas, TX 75201-1451 ; (219) 220-1046; Mr. David Kiger (800) 758-7447; (214) 965-9965

Packy the Shipper/Pack 'N Ship/PNS, 6115 Washington Ave., 2nd Fl., Racine, WI 53408 ; (414) 504-2499; Ms. Becky Hoffman (800) 547-2259; (414) 504-2490

Parcel Plus, 2661 Riva Rd., Bldg. 1000, Suite 102, Annapolis, MD 21401-8405 ; (410) 266-3266; Ms. Kelle Barchanowicz (800) 662-5553; (410) 266-3200

Pilot Air Freight Corporation, 314 N. Middletown Rd., Lima, PA 19037 ; (610) 891-9341; Mr. Richard J. Morris (800) 447-4568; (610) 891-8100

Worldwide Express, P.O. Box 132518, Dallas, TX 75313 ; (214) 720-2446; Mr. Roger MacDonnell (800) 758-7447; (214) 720-2400

For a full explanation of the data provided in the Franchisor Profiles, please refer to **Chapter 2, "How to Use the Data."**

PRINTING & GRAPHICS INDUSTRY PROFILE

Total # Franchisors in Industry Group	26
Total # Franchised Units in Industry Group	4,841
Total # Company-Owned Units in Industry Group	<u>55</u>
Total # Operating Units in Industry Group	4,896
Average # Franchised Units/Franchisor	186.2
Average # Company-Owned Units/Franchisor	<u>2.1</u>
Average # Total Units/Franchisor	188.3
Ratio of Total # Franchised Units/Total # Company-Owned Units	88.0:1
Industry Survey Participants	16
Representing % of Industry	61.5%
Average Franchise Fee*:	$25.4K
Average Total Investment*:	$254.1
Average On-Going Royalty Fee*:	5.6%

If a range was provided, the mid-point of the range was used. See detailed profiles for actual ranges.

FIVE LARGEST PARTICIPANTS IN SURVEY

Company	# Fran-chised Units	# Co-Owned Units	# Total Units	Franchise Fee	On-Going Royalty	Total Investment
1. Minuteman Press International	890	0	890	44.5K	6%	100-120K
2. Kwik-Copy Printing	773	0	773	25K	4-8%	296-358 K
3. Sir Speedy	755	17	772	20K	4-6%	316-391K
4. American Speedy Printing Centers	400	0	400	9.5K	3.6-6%	30-200K
5. Alphagraphics Print Shops	343	1	344	25.9K	1.5-8%	256-448K

alphagraphics®
DESIGN ■ COPY ■ PRINT

ALPHAGRAPHICS PRINTSHOPS OF THE FUTURE

3760 N. Commerce Dr., Suite 100
Tucson, AZ 85705
Tel: (800) 528-4885 (520) 293-9200
Fax: (520) 887-2850
E-Mail: opportunity@alphagraphics.com
Web Site: www.alphagraphics.com
Mr. Allen Daniel, VP of Int'l Operations

ALPHAGRAPHICS PRINTSHOPS OF THE FUTURE are the leading providers of print-related and digital publishing services for business worldwide. Our mission is to enable our customers to easily and effectively communicate in any publishing medium - anywhere in the world, any time. Our franchisees enjoy an average $949,477 in annual sales, the industry's highest. Services include design, high-speed duplication, single and multi-color printing, digital publishing, binding, CD-ROM and Web site services.

BACKGROUND: IFA MEMBER
Established: 1970;   1st Franchised: 1980
Franchised Units: 343
Company-Owned Units   1
Total Units: 344
Dist.:   US-261; CAN-2; O'seas-81
   North America: 42 States, 1 Province
   Density: 33 in AZ, 29 in TX, 25 in IL
Projected New Units (12 Months):   40
Qualifications: 5, 5, 1, 4, 3, 5
Registered: CA,FL,IL,IN,MD,MI,MN, NY,OR,RI,VA,WA,WI
FINANCIAL/TERMS:
Cash Investment: $100-150K
Total Investment: $256.4-447.9K
Minimum Net Worth: $350K
Fees: Franchise - $25.9K
   Royalty - 1.5-8%;   Ad. - 2.5%
Earnings Claim Statement: Yes
Term of Contract (Years):   20/20
Avg. # Of Employees: 5 FT
Passive Ownership: Not Allowed
Encourage Conversions: Yes
Area Develop. Agreements: Yes/N/A
Sub-Franchising Contracts: No
Expand In Territory: Yes
Space Needs: 2,000-2,400 SF; FS, SC
SUPPORT & TRAINING PROVIDED:
Financial Assistance Provided: Yes(I)
Site Selection Assistance: Yes
Lease Negotiation Assistance: No

Co-Operative Advertising: Yes
Franchisee Assoc./Member: Yes
Size Of Corporate Staff: 99
On-Going Support: B,C,D,E,G,h,I
Training: 4 Weeks Tucson Service Center; 1 Week Field Location.
SPECIFIC EXPANSION PLANS:
US: All United States
Canada: All Canada
Overseas: All Countries

<< >>

AMERICAN SPEEDY PRINTING CENTERS

1800 W. Maple Rd.
Troy, MI 48084
Tel: (800) 726-9050 (248) 614-3700
Fax: (248) 614-3719
E-Mail: conniel@americanspeedy.com
Web Site: www.allegrabizop.com
Ms. Connie Lilley, Development Coor.

AMERICAN SPEEDY PRINTING CENTERS currently offers four color digital printing, desktop publishing, high speed and color copying. They also offer their customers on-line ordering capabilities and assistance to their franchisees in web page developments.

BACKGROUND: IFA MEMBER
Established: 1976;   1st Franchised: 1977
Franchised Units: 400
Company-Owned Units   0
Total Units: 400
Dist.:   US-320; CAN-66; O'seas-14
   North America: 40 States, 2 Provinces
   Density: 85 in MI, 29 in IL, 27 in CA
Projected New Units (12 Months):   0
Qualifications: 5, 4, 1, 2, 2, 5
Registered: CA,FL,HI,IN,MD,MI,NY,ND, OR,RI,SD,VA,WA,WI,DC
FINANCIAL/TERMS:
Cash Investment: $30-200K
Total Investment: $30-200K
Minimum Net Worth: $N/A
Fees: Franchise - $9.5K
   Royalty - 3.6-6%;   Ad. - 1%
Earnings Claim Statement: No
Term of Contract (Years):   20/20
Avg. # Of Employees: 3 FT, 1 PT

Passive Ownership: Discouraged
Encourage Conversions: Yes
Area Develop. Agreements: No
Sub-Franchising Contracts: Yes
Expand In Territory: Yes
Space Needs: 1,500 SF; FS, SF, SC, RM
SUPPORT & TRAINING PROVIDED:
Financial Assistance Provided: Yes(I)
Site Selection Assistance: Yes
Lease Negotiation Assistance: Yes
Co-Operative Advertising: Yes
Franchisee Assoc./Member: Yes/Yes
Size Of Corporate Staff: 70
On-Going Support: A,C,D,E,F,G,H,I
Training: 2 Weeks at Home Office; 1 Week On-Site.
SPECIFIC EXPANSION PLANS:
US: MI
Canada: AB
Overseas: No

<< >>

AMERICAN WHOLESALE THERMOGRAPHERS / AWT

12715 Telge Rd.
Cypress, TX 77429-0777
Tel: (888) 280-2053 (281) 256-4100
Fax: (281) 256-4178
E-Mail: awtsales@awt.com
Web Site: www.awt.com
Mr. Bob Dolan, VP Franchise Sales

Wholesale printing, providing next-day raised-letter printed materials to retail printers, copy centers and business service centers. Products include quality business cards, stationery, announcements and invitations.

BACKGROUND: IFA MEMBER
Established: 1980;   1st Franchised: 1981
Franchised Units: 20
Company-Owned Units   0
Total Units: 20
Dist.:   US-16; CAN-4; O'seas-0
   North America: 14 States, 2 Provinces
   Density: 3 in ON, 2 in OK, 2 in CA
Projected New Units (12 Months):   2
Qualifications: 5, 4, 1, 2, 1, 5
Registered: FL,IL,IN,MI,NY,VA,WI
FINANCIAL/TERMS:
Cash Investment: $90K
Total Investment: $340-352K
Minimum Net Worth: $250K
Fees: Franchise - $30K
   Royalty - 5%;   Ad. - NR
Earnings Claim Statement: Yes
Term of Contract (Years):   25/25
Avg. # Of Employees: 9 FT, 4 PT

Passive Ownership: Not Allowed
Encourage Conversions: No
Area Develop. Agreements: No
Sub-Franchising Contracts: No
Expand In Territory: Yes
Space Needs: 2,500-3,000 SF; Business Park, Warehouse

SUPPORT & TRAINING PROVIDED:
Financial Assistance Provided: Yes(B)
Site Selection Assistance: Yes
Lease Negotiation Assistance: Yes
Co-Operative Advertising: Yes
Franchisee Assoc./Member: Yes/Yes
Size Of Corporate Staff: NR
On-Going Support: B,C,D,E,G,h,I
Training: 2 Weeks Headquarters; 2 Weeks Operating Store; 2 Weeks On-Site.

SPECIFIC EXPANSION PLANS:
US: All United States
Canada: All Canada
Overseas: No

BCT
3000 NE 30th Pl., 5th Floor
Ft. Lauderdale, FL 33306
Tel: (800) 627-9998 (954) 563-1224
Fax: (954) 565-0742
E-Mail: rsa@herald.infi.net
Web Site: www.bct-net.com
Mr. Robert S. Anderson, Franchise Development Director

Join the 24-year old industry-leading wholesale, manufacturing franchise with the competitive advantage. We are recession-resistant, high-volume, quick-turn around, wholesale only manufacturers, specializing in next-day delivery of thermographed and offset-printed products and rubber stamps to retail printers, mailing centers, office supply stores and other retailers. Comprehensive training, excellent support and nationally praised.

BACKGROUND: IFA MEMBER
Established: 1975; 1st Franchised: 1977
Franchised Units: 92
Company-Owned Units 1
Total Units: 93
Dist.: US-86; CAN-7; O'seas-1
North America: 38 States, 5 Provinces
Density: 16 in CA, 7 in FL, 5 in NY
Projected New Units (12 Months): 2
Qualifications: 4, 4, 3, 3, 3, 5
Registered: All States
FINANCIAL/TERMS:
Cash Investment: $115-151K

Total Investment: $354-441K
Minimum Net Worth: $250K
Fees: Franchise - $35K
Royalty - 6%; Ad. - N/A
Earnings Claim Statement: No
Term of Contract (Years): 25/10
Avg. # Of Employees: 10 FT, 6 PT
Passive Ownership: Not Allowed
Encourage Conversions: Yes
Area Develop. Agreements: No
Sub-Franchising Contracts: No
Expand In Territory: No
Space Needs: 4,000+ SF; FS, SC, Commercial Park

SUPPORT & TRAINING PROVIDED:
Financial Assistance Provided: Yes(I)
Site Selection Assistance: Yes
Lease Negotiation Assistance: Yes
Co-Operative Advertising: No
Franchisee Assoc./Member: Yes
Size Of Corporate Staff: 32
On-Going Support: a,B,C,d,E,G,h,I
Training: 2 Weeks Ft. Lauderdale, FL; 1 Week Pre-Opening at New-Site; 2 Weeks after and On-Going.

SPECIFIC EXPANSION PLANS:
US: NJ,NE
Canada: No
Overseas: No

COPY CLUB
12715 Telge Rd.
Cypress, TX 77429-0777
Tel: (888) 280-2053 (281) 256-4100
Fax: (281) 256-4178
E-Mail: ccsales@copyclub.com
Web Site: www.copyclub.com
Mr. Bob Dolan, VP Franchise Sales

High-visibility, high-traffic digital imaging and copying and business/communications center, open 24 hours a day. Dynamic retail environment. Also offering self-service copying and computer rental.

BACKGROUND: IFA MEMBER
Established: 1992; 1st Franchised: 1994
Franchised Units: 14
Company-Owned Units 0
Total Units: 14
Dist.: US-14; CAN-0; O'seas-0
North America: 4 States
Density: TX, CA, GA
Projected New Units (12 Months): 5
Qualifications: 5, 5, 3, 1, 1, 4
Registered: CA,FL,IL,NY,VA,WA
FINANCIAL/TERMS:
Cash Investment: $95K

Total Investment: $361.6-495.4K
Minimum Net Worth: $500K
Fees: Franchise - $30K
Royalty - 7%; Ad. - 0%
Earnings Claim Statement: Yes
Term of Contract (Years): 25/25
Avg. # Of Employees: 8 FT, 5 PT
Passive Ownership: Allowed
Encourage Conversions: No
Area Develop. Agreements: Yes/10
Sub-Franchising Contracts: Yes
Expand In Territory: Yes
Space Needs: 4,000 SF; FS

SUPPORT & TRAINING PROVIDED:
Financial Assistance Provided: Yes(I)
Site Selection Assistance: Yes
Lease Negotiation Assistance: Yes
Co-Operative Advertising: No
Franchisee Assoc./Member: Yes/Yes
Size Of Corporate Staff: NR
On-Going Support: C,D,E,G,h,I
Training: 3 Weeks in Classroom; 2 Weeks On-Site.

SPECIFIC EXPANSION PLANS:
US: All United States
Canada: No
Overseas: No

FRANKLIN'S SYSTEMS
12715 Telge Rd.
Cypress, TX 77429
Tel: (888) 280-2053 (281) 256-4100
Fax: (281) 256-4178
E-Mail: fgsales@franklin's-printing.com
Web Site: www.franklins-printing.com
Mr. Bob Dolan, VP Franchise Sales

Part of the ICED family of franchises, now in our 30th year, with over 1,000 franchises in 21 countries. We maintain a position of leadership in our traditional printing and digital publishing, including Webpage design and maintenance, as well as legendary outside sales consultant training. Your corporate management skills are transferable in our business-to-business environment.

BACKGROUND:
Established: 1971; 1st Franchised: 1977
Franchised Units: 66
Company-Owned Units 0
Total Units: 66
Dist.: US-66; CAN-0; O'seas-0
North America: 14 States
Density: 22 in GA, 11 in FL, 7 in TN
Projected New Units (12 Months): 5
Registered: FL,VA

FINANCIAL/TERMS:
Cash Investment: $84K
Total Investment: $296.4-359.8K
Minimum Net Worth: $250K
Fees: Franchise - $25K
  Royalty - 4-8%; Ad. - 0%
Earnings Claim Statement: No
Term of Contract (Years): 25/25
Avg. # Of Employees: 3-7 FT, 1 PT
Passive Ownership: Not Allowed
Encourage Conversions: No
Area Develop. Agreements: No
Sub-Franchising Contracts: No
Expand In Territory: Yes
Space Needs: 1,500-2,000 SF; SC, SF, Business Park

SUPPORT & TRAINING PROVIDED:
Financial Assistance Provided: Yes(I)
Site Selection Assistance: Yes
Lease Negotiation Assistance: Yes
Co-Operative Advertising: No
Franchisee Assoc./Member: Yes/Yes
Size Of Corporate Staff: NR
On-Going Support: B,C,D,E,G,h,I
Training: 5 Weeks Training (Lodging and Airfare Included.)

SPECIFIC EXPANSION PLANS:
US: All United States
Canada: No
Overseas: No

◄◄ ►►

INK WELL, THE
12715 Telge Rd.
Cypress, TX 77429
Tel: (888) 280-2053 (281) 256-4100
Fax: (281) 256-4178
E-Mail: iwsales@iwa.com
Web Site: www.iwa.com
Mr. Bob Dolan, VP Franchise Sales

THE INK WELL printing centers are positioned to provide high-quality, full-service printing and copying, typesetting and design services to the business community.

BACKGROUND: IFA MEMBER
Established: 1972; 1st Franchised: 1981
Franchised Units: 40
Company-Owned Units 0
Total Units: 40
Dist.: US-40; CAN-0; O'seas-0
  North America: 8 States
  Density: 24 in OH, 5 in IL, 3 in FL
Projected New Units (12 Months): 4
Qualifications: 5, 4, 1, 2, 1, 5
Registered: FL

FINANCIAL/TERMS:
Cash Investment: $84K

Total Investment: $296.4-357.8K
Minimum Net Worth: $250K
Fees: Franchise - $25K
  Royalty - 4-6%; Ad. - 2%
Earnings Claim Statement: No
Term of Contract (Years): 25/25
Avg. # Of Employees: 4-6 FT, 1 PT
Passive Ownership: Not Allowed
Encourage Conversions: No
Area Develop. Agreements: No
Sub-Franchising Contracts: No
Expand In Territory: Yes
Space Needs: 1,500-2,000 SF; SC, SC, Business Park

SUPPORT & TRAINING PROVIDED:
Financial Assistance Provided: Yes(D)
Site Selection Assistance: Yes
Lease Negotiation Assistance: Yes
Co-Operative Advertising: Yes
Franchisee Assoc./Member: Yes/Yes
Size Of Corporate Staff: NR
On-Going Support: B,C,D,E,G,h,I
Training: 5 Weeks Headquarters; 1 Week in Field; 8 Days On-Site.

SPECIFIC EXPANSION PLANS:
US: All United States
Canada: No
Overseas: No

◄◄ ►►

KWIK-KOPY PRINTING
12715 Telge Rd.
Cypress, TX 77429
Tel: (888) 280-2053 (281) 256-4100
Fax: (281) 256-4178
E-Mail: kksales@kwikkopy.com
Web Site: www.kwikkopy.com
Mr. Bob Dolan, VP Franchise Sales

Part of the ICED family of franchises, now in our 30th year, with over 1,000 franchises in 21 countries. As a member of the ICED family of franchises, we maintain a position of leadership with our traditional printing and digital publishing, including Website design and maintenance, as well as legendary outside sales consultant training. Your corporate management skills are transferable in our business-to-business environment.

BACKGROUND: IFA MEMBER
Established: 1967; 1st Franchised: 1967
Franchised Units: 773
Company-Owned Units 0
Total Units: 773
Dist.: US-365; CAN-76; O'seas-332
  North America: 39 States, 6 Provinces
  Density: 147 in TX, 32 in IL, 27 CA
Projected New Units (12 Months): 8
Registered: All Except SD,ND,HI

FINANCIAL/TERMS:
Cash Investment: $84K
Total Investment: $296.4-357.8K
Minimum Net Worth: $250K
Fees: Franchise - $25K
  Royalty - 4-8%; Ad. - 0%
Earnings Claim Statement: Yes
Term of Contract (Years): 25/25
Avg. # Of Employees: 3-7 FT, 1 PT
Passive Ownership: Not Allowed
Encourage Conversions: No
Area Develop. Agreements: No
Sub-Franchising Contracts: No
Expand In Territory: Yes
Space Needs: 1,500-2,000 SF; SC, SF, Business Park

SUPPORT & TRAINING PROVIDED:
Financial Assistance Provided: Yes(D)
Site Selection Assistance: Yes
Lease Negotiation Assistance: Yes
Co-Operative Advertising: No
Franchisee Assoc./Member: Yes/Yes
Size Of Corporate Staff: NR
On-Going Support: B,C,D,E,G,h,I
Training: 5 Weeks for 2 People, Lodging Included; $1,500 Allowance for Meals/Airfare; Other Credits.

SPECIFIC EXPANSION PLANS:
US: All United States
Canada: All Canada
Overseas: All Countries

◄◄ ►►

KWIK-KOPY PRINTING CANADA
1550 16th Ave.
Richmond Hill, ON L4B 3K9 CANADA
Tel: (800) 387-9725 (416) 798-7007
Fax: (905) 780-0575
E-Mail: kkpcc@kwikkopy.ca
Web Site: www.kwikkopy.ca
Mr. C. John Woodburn, Dir. of Franchising

Full-service print franchise, on-site printing, copying and digital printing/copying. Canada's largest and most successful print franchise. Strong support and training programs -- no industry experience necessary -- over 1,000 outlets worldwide.

BACKGROUND:

Established: 1979; 1st Franchised: 1979
Franchised Units: 73
Company-Owned Units   5
Total Units: 78
Dist.:   US-0; CAN-78; O'seas-0
  North America: 9 Provinces
  Density: 55 in ON, 5 in AB, 5 in BC
Projected New Units (12 Months):   6
Qualifications: 3, 4, 1, 3, 4, 5
Registered: All States and AB

FINANCIAL/TERMS:

Cash Investment: $80K
Total Investment: $175-200K
Minimum Net Worth: $200K
Fees: Franchise - $29.5K
  Royalty - 7%;   Ad. - 3%
Earnings Claim Statement: No
Term of Contract (Years):   10/10
Avg. # Of Employees: 2 FT
Passive Ownership: Not Allowed
Encourage Conversions: Yes
Area Develop. Agreements: Yes/10
Sub-Franchising Contracts: No
Expand In Territory: Yes
Space Needs: 800-1,500 SF; FS, Office
  Tower, Ind. Park

SUPPORT & TRAINING PROVIDED:

Financial Assistance Provided: Yes(I)
Site Selection Assistance: Yes
Lease Negotiation Assistance: Yes
Co-Operative Advertising: Yes
Franchisee Assoc./Member: Yes/No
Size Of Corporate Staff: 15
On-Going Support: C,D,E,G,h,I
Training: 3 Weeks Houston, TX; 1 Week
  Toronto, ON; 1 Week On-Site.

SPECIFIC EXPANSION PLANS:

US: N/A
Canada: All Canada
Overseas: Middle East, India, Asian
  Pacific Rim, Africa

◄◄ ►►

LAZERQUICK
27375 SW Parkway Ave., # 200
Wilsonville, OR 97070
Tel: (800) 477-2679 (503) 682-1322
Fax: (503) 682-7816
E-Mail: mhart@lazerquick.com
Web Site: www.lazerquick.com
Mr. Michael Hart, Vice President of
  Franchising

LAZERQUICK centers are complete, one-stop printing and copying centers. All centers feature state-of-the-art electronic publishing, digital graphics and imaging services that support our range of quality, fast-service offset printing, high-speed copying and related bindery and finishing services. The LAZERQUICK franchise is based on value and performance. Affiliates benefit from our unique and innovative programs.

BACKGROUND: IFA MEMBER

Established: 1968; 1st Franchised: 1990
Franchised Units: 25
Company-Owned Units   22
Total Units: 47
Dist.:   US-47; CAN-0; O'seas-0
  North America: 7 States
  Density: 29 in OR, 13 in WA, 1 in CA
Projected New Units (12 Months):   6
Qualifications: 4, 3, 2, 3, 3, 5
Registered: CA,FL,IL,IN,MD,MI,MN,
  NY,OR,VA,WA,WI

FINANCIAL/TERMS:

Cash Investment: $51.8-82.5K
Total Investment: $172.5-275K
Minimum Net Worth: $N/A
Fees: Franchise - $25K
  Royalty - 3-5%/$500; Ad. - 1.5%/$250
Earnings Claim Statement: Yes
Term of Contract (Years):   7/7/7
Avg. # Of Employees: 2 FT, 2 PT
Passive Ownership: Not Allowed
Encourage Conversions: Yes
Area Develop. Agreements: Yes/Varies
Sub-Franchising Contracts: No
Expand In Territory: No
Space Needs: 1,400-1,800 SF; SC

SUPPORT & TRAINING PROVIDED:

Financial Assistance Provided: Yes(I)
Site Selection Assistance: Yes
Lease Negotiation Assistance: Yes
Co-Operative Advertising: N/A
Franchisee Assoc./Member: No
Size Of Corporate Staff: 32
On-Going Support: C,D,E,G,I
Training: 5-7 Weeks at Corporate
  Headquarters.

SPECIFIC EXPANSION PLANS:

US: All United States
Canada: All Exc. AB,PQ
Overseas: No

◄◄ ►►

**MINUTEMAN PRESS
INTERNATIONAL**
1640 New Highway
Farmingdale, NY 11735

Tel: (800) 645-3006 (516) 249-1370
Fax: (516) 249-5618
E-Mail: MPIHQ@aol.com
Web Site: www.minuteman-press.com
Mr. Gary Titus, VP

Full-service printing and graphic centers, specializing in multi-color commercial printing at instant print prices. A one-stop printing and graphics business.

BACKGROUND: IFA MEMBER

Established: 1975; 1st Franchised: 1975
Franchised Units: 890
Company-Owned Units   0
Total Units: 890
Dist.:   US-770; CAN-70; O'seas-50
  North America: 46 States, 5 Provinces
  Density: 75 in CA, 66 in NY, 58 in TX
Projected New Units (12 Months):   50
Qualifications: 1, 1, 1, 1, 2, 5
Registered: All States and AB

FINANCIAL/TERMS:

Cash Investment: $35-60K
Total Investment: $100-120K
Minimum Net Worth: $NR
Fees: Franchise - $44.5K
  Royalty - 6%;   Ad. - 0%
Earnings Claim Statement: Yes
Term of Contract (Years):   35/10
Avg. # Of Employees: 3 FT to Start
Passive Ownership: Discouraged
Encourage Conversions: Yes
Area Develop. Agreements: No
Sub-Franchising Contracts: No
Expand In Territory: Yes
Space Needs: 1,200 SF; FS, SF, SC

SUPPORT & TRAINING PROVIDED:

Financial Assistance Provided: Yes(I)
Site Selection Assistance: Yes
Lease Negotiation Assistance: Yes
Co-Operative Advertising: No
Franchisee Assoc./Member: No
Size Of Corporate Staff: 160
On-Going Support: b,C,D,E,F,G,H,I
Training: 3 Weeks New York; On-Site As
  Needed.

SPECIFIC EXPANSION PLANS:

US: All United States
Canada: All Canada
Overseas: U.K., South Africa, Australia

◄◄ ►►

PRINT THREE
160 Nashdene Rd.
Chatham, ON M1V 4CA CANADA
Tel: (800) 335-5918 (416) 754-8700
Fax: (416) 754-8441
E-Mail: john@printthree.com

Web Site: www.printthree.com
Mr. John Johnson, Director Franchise Development

Franchise opportunities are available in urban centers across Canada. Canada's premier award winning digital printing franchise. We serve Canada's corporate community, large and small, offering a complete line of digital printing services. We feature desktop publishing, digital wide format, digital color, digital B&W reproduction, direct mail fulfillment services and selected binding and laminating services.

BACKGROUND:
Established: 1970;   1st Franchised: 1980
Franchised Units: 50
Company-Owned Units   0
Total Units: 50
Dist.:   US-0; CAN-50; O'seas-0
  North America: 3 Provinces
  Density: 46 in ON, 3 in AB, 1 in NF
Projected New Units (12 Months):   10
Qualifications: 5, 4, 1, 5, 1, 5
Registered:
FINANCIAL/TERMS:
Cash Investment: $65K
Total Investment: $270-300K
Minimum Net Worth: $150K
Fees: Franchise - $20K
  Royalty - 6%;   Ad. - 1%
Earnings Claim Statement: No
Term of Contract (Years):   25/0
Avg. # Of Employees: 3 FT
Passive Ownership: Not Allowed
Encourage Conversions: Yes
Area Develop. Agreements: Yes
Sub-Franchising Contracts: Yes
Expand In Territory: Yes
Space Needs: 1,000 SF; High-Core
  Locales
SUPPORT & TRAINING PROVIDED:
Financial Assistance Provided: Yes(I)
Site Selection Assistance: Yes
Lease Negotiation Assistance: Yes
Co-Operative Advertising: N/A
Franchisee Assoc./Member: Yes/Yes
Size Of Corporate Staff: 14
On-Going Support: C,D,E,f,G,H,I
Training: 2 Weeks at the Head Office in
  Scarborough, ON; 1 Week On-Site.

SPECIFIC EXPANSION PLANS:
US: No
Canada: BC,AB,SK,MB,ON
Overseas: No

≪≪ ≫≫

PROFORMA
8800 E. Pleasant Valley Rd.
Cleveland, OH 44131
Tel: (800) 825-1525 (216) 520-8400
Fax: (216) 520-8444
E-Mail: johnh@proforma.com
Web Site: www.proforma.com
Mr. Gregory Muzzillo, President

Home-based franchise. Franchise owners market and distribute printing and promotional products to other businesses. Major player in a $150 billion industry! Low overhead. Full marketing and administrative support. $9,500 initial investment. Expanding rapidly throughout North America.

BACKGROUND: IFA MEMBER
Established: 1978;   1st Franchised: 1985
Franchised Units: 314
Company-Owned Units   0
Total Units: 314
Dist.:   US-260; CAN-20; O'seas-0
  North America: 42 States, 2 Provinces
  Density: 18 in CA, 10 in OH, 10 in NY
Projected New Units (12 Months):   75
Qualifications: 3, 5, 1, 3, 1, 5
Registered: All States
FINANCIAL/TERMS:
Cash Investment: $5-10K
Total Investment: $22-27K
Minimum Net Worth: $100K
Fees: Franchise - $19.5K
  Royalty - 9%;   Ad. - 1%
Earnings Claim Statement: No
Term of Contract (Years):   10/10
Avg. # Of Employees: 1 FT
Passive Ownership: Not Allowed
Encourage Conversions: Yes
Area Develop. Agreements: No
Sub-Franchising Contracts: No
Expand In Territory: N/A
Space Needs: NR SF; HB
SUPPORT & TRAINING PROVIDED:
Financial Assistance Provided: Yes(D)
Site Selection Assistance: N/A
Lease Negotiation Assistance: N/A
Co-Operative Advertising: Yes
Franchisee Assoc./Member: NR
Size Of Corporate Staff: 140
On-Going Support: A,C,D,F,G,H,I

Training: 1 Week Headquarters; 2 Days
  Regional 2 Days National; 2 Days Field
  Visit.
SPECIFIC EXPANSION PLANS:
US: All United States
Canada: All Canada
Overseas: No

≪≪ ≫≫

SCREEN PRINTING USA
534 W. Shawnee Ave.
Plymouth, PA 18651-2009
Tel:
Fax:
Mr. Russell Owens, President

Full-service silk screen printing. Hats, shirts, jackets, signs, posters, decals. Full ASI services. Computer artwork and design.

BACKGROUND:
Established: 1988;   1st Franchised: 1988
Franchised Units: 32
Company-Owned Units   0
Total Units: 32
Dist.:   US-30; CAN-2; O'seas-0
  North America: 5 States, 1 Province
  Density: PA, NY
Projected New Units (12 Months):   12
Registered: FL,MN,NY,VA
FINANCIAL/TERMS:
Cash Investment: $10K
Total Investment: $40-60K
Minimum Net Worth: $NR
Fees: Franchise - $25K
  Royalty - 6%;   Ad. - 2%
Earnings Claim Statement: No
Term of Contract (Years):   10/10
Avg. # Of Employees: 2 FT, 1 PT
Passive Ownership: Discouraged
Encourage Conversions: No
Area Develop. Agreements: Yes/10
Sub-Franchising Contracts: Yes
Expand In Territory: Yes
Space Needs: 1,500 SF; FS, SF, HB
SUPPORT & TRAINING PROVIDED:
Financial Assistance Provided: Yes(D)
Site Selection Assistance: Yes
Lease Negotiation Assistance: Yes
Co-Operative Advertising: Yes
Franchisee Assoc./Member: Yes/Yes
Size Of Corporate Staff: 4
On-Going Support: B,C,D,E,G,H
Training: 2 Weeks Plymouth, PA.
SPECIFIC EXPANSION PLANS:
US: All United States
Canada: All Canada
Overseas: No

◄◄ ►►

SIGNAL GRAPHICS PRINTING

6789 S. Yosemite St., # 100
Englewood, CO 80112
Tel: (800) 852-6336 (303) 779-6789
Fax: (303) 779-8445
E-Mail: SAMPACORP@ aol.com
Web Site: www.signalgraphics.com
Mr. Michael Latham, Director Franchise
  Development

A full range of services places SIGNAL GRAPHICS PRINTING ahead of the competition. Our franchising program will enable the owner having no previous printing experience to market quick printing, copying, desktop publishing, digital services, typesetting and high-quality commercial printing to a wide range of customers in the business community. Just the right size system to offer prime locations and personalized support.

BACKGROUND: IFA MEMBER
Established: 1974; 1st Franchised: 1982
Franchised Units: 47
Company-Owned Units   2
Total Units: 49
Dist.:   US-46; CAN-0; O'seas-3
  North America: 18 States
  Density: 18 in CO, 3 in CA, 5 in TX
Projected New Units (12 Months):   10
Registered: All States Except ND,SD
FINANCIAL/TERMS:
Cash Investment: $60K Minimum
Total Investment: $190-230K
Minimum Net Worth: $NR
Fees: Franchise - $18K
  Royalty - 0-5%;   Ad. - $100/Mo.
Earnings Claim Statement: Yes
Term of Contract (Years):   25/25
Avg. # Of Employees: 4 FT, 1 PT
Passive Ownership: Discouraged
Encourage Conversions: Yes
Area Develop. Agreements: No
Sub-Franchising Contracts: No
Expand In Territory: Yes
Space Needs: 1,500 SF; SC
SUPPORT & TRAINING PROVIDED:
Financial Assistance Provided: Yes(I)
Site Selection Assistance: Yes
Lease Negotiation Assistance: Yes
Co-Operative Advertising: Yes
Franchisee Assoc./Member: Yes/Yes
Size Of Corporate Staff: NR
On-Going Support: B,C,d,E,G,H,I
Training: 3 Weeks Headquarters; 2 Weeks
  On-Site.

SPECIFIC EXPANSION PLANS:
US: All United States
Canada: All Canada
Overseas: All Countries

◄◄ ►►

SIR SPEEDY

26722 Plaza Dr.
Mission Viejo, CA 92672
Tel: (800) 854-3321 (949) 348-5000
Fax: (949) 348-5068
E-Mail: fdelucia@sirspeedy.com
Web Site: www.sirspeedy.com
Mr. Frank A. de Lucia, VP Franchise
  Development

A Monday through Friday business-to-business service, it provides copying, printing, digital communication and graphic design for a diverse range of corporate clients. It's global digital link facilitates instantaneous communication and transfer of material between all centers in the group.

BACKGROUND: IFA MEMBER
Established: 1968; 1st Franchised: 1968
Franchised Units: 755
Company-Owned Units   17
Total Units: 772
Dist.:   US-752; CAN-5; O'seas-125
  North America: 47 States, 1 Province
  Density: 86 in CA, 72 in FL, 41 in IL
Projected New Units (12 Months):   40
Qualifications: 5, 4, 1, 3, 3, 5
Registered: All States
FINANCIAL/TERMS:
Cash Investment: $100-150K
Total Investment: $316-391K
Minimum Net Worth: $300K
Fees: Franchise - $20K
  Royalty - 4-6%;   Ad. - 1-2%
Earnings Claim Statement: Yes
Term of Contract (Years):   20/10
Avg. # Of Employees: 5+ FT
Passive Ownership: Discouraged
Encourage Conversions: Yes
Area Develop. Agreements: No
Sub-Franchising Contracts: No
Expand In Territory: Yes
Space Needs: 2,000-12,000 SF; FS, SC
SUPPORT & TRAINING PROVIDED:
Financial Assistance Provided: Yes(I)
Site Selection Assistance: Yes
Lease Negotiation Assistance: Yes
Co-Operative Advertising: No
Franchisee Assoc./Member: No
Size Of Corporate Staff: 50

On-Going Support: B,C,D,E,F,G,H,I
Training: 3 Weeks in Mission Viejo, CA; 6
  Weeks at Franchisee's Site.
SPECIFIC EXPANSION PLANS:
US: All United States
Canada: ON
Overseas: Most Countries

◄◄ ►►

SUPPLEMENTAL LISTING
OF FRANCHISORS

BCX Printing Centers, 613 E. Indian School Rd., Phoenix, AZ 85012 ; (602) 241-0841; Mr. Gene Cufone (800) 736-8047; (602) 241-1231

Franklin's Printing, Digital Imaging and Copying, 12715 Telge Rd., Cypress, TX 77410-0777 ; (281) 245-4178; Mr. Bob Dolan (888) 280 2053; (281) 256-4100

Insta-Pak, 5025 Dorr St., Toledo, OH 43615 ; (419) 537-1511; Mr. Steve Harding (800) 444-7525; (419) 537-1555

Insty-Prints, 15155 Technology Dr., Eden Prairie, MN 55344 ; (612) 975-6262; Mr. Todd Hendrickson (800) 779-1000; (612) 975-6200

Made 'N-A-Minute Printers, 2050 Rosser Ave., Burnaby, BC V5C 5Y1 CANADA; (604) 291-2337; Mr. Paul McCrea ; (604) 688-2381

PIP Printing, 27001 Agoura Rd., # 200, Agoura Hills, CA 91301-5339 ; (818) 880-3989; Mr. Tom Cunningham (800) 292-4747; (818) 880-3804

Sure Graphics, 101, 12465-82 Ave., Surrey, BC V3W 3E8 CANADA; (604) 594-8320; Mr. Zul Mitha ; (604) 594-8334

PUBLICATIONS INDUSTRY PROFILE

Total # Franchisors in Industry Group	23
Total # Franchised Units in Industry Group	927
Total # Company-Owned Units in Industry Group	<u>232</u>
Total # Operating Units in Industry Group	959
Average # Franchised Units/Franchisor	40.3
Average # Company-Owned Units/Franchisor	<u>1.4</u>
Average # Total Units/Franchisor	41.7
Ratio of Total # Franchised Units/Total # Company-Owned Units	29.0:1
Industry Survey Participants	7
Representing % of Industry	30.4%
Average Franchise Fee*:	$13.1K
Average Total Investment*:	$28.8K
Average On-Going Royalty Fee*:	7.0%

If a range was provided, the mid-point of the range was used. See detailed profiles for actual ranges.

FIVE LARGEST PARTICIPANTS IN SURVEY

Company	# Fran-chised Units	# Co-Owned Units	# Total Units	Franchise Fee	On-Going Royalty	Total Investment
1. Coffee News	276	3	279	2K	$20-75/Wk.	2.5K
2. Bingo Bugle Newspaper	71	0	71	1.5-10K	10%	1.5-10K
3. Perfect Wedding Guide, The	19	3	22	25-35K	6%	35-50K
4. Finderbinder/Sourcebook	18	1	19	1K	5-10%	10-15K
5. Homesteader	13	2	15	3.4K	10%	3.3-22K

All of the data provided are proprietary and should not be quoted without acknowledging *Bond's Franchise Guide*.

BINGO BUGLE NEWSPAPER
P.O. Box 527
Vashon Island, WA 98070
Tel: (800) 327-6437 (206) 463-5656
Fax: (206) 463-5630
E-Mail: roger@bingobugle.com
Web Site: www.bingobugle.com
Mr. Roger Snowden, President

THE BINGO BUGLE is North America's largest network of newspapers devoted to bingo & gaming. Circulation over 1 million copies monthly. Listed in Entrepreneur's Annual Franchise 500 as one of the lowest cost franchise opportunities. Franchise fees range from $1,500 to $7,000. Complete training and support. Modest investment. Call 1-800-327-6437 for details.

BACKGROUND:
Established: 1981; 1st Franchised: 1983
Franchised Units: 71
Company-Owned Units: 0
Total Units: 71
Dist.: US-66; CAN-5; O'seas-0
 North America: 30 States, 2 Provinces
 Density: 12 in CA, 6 in NY, 5 in FL
Projected New Units (12 Months): 6
Qualifications: 2, 4, 4, 2, 2, 1
Registered: IL,FL,SD,VA
FINANCIAL/TERMS:
Cash Investment: $1.5-6K
Total Investment: $1.5-10K
Minimum Net Worth: $NR
Fees: Franchise - $1.5-10K
 Royalty - 10%; Ad. - 0%
Earnings Claim Statement: No
Term of Contract (Years): 5/5
Avg. # Of Employees: 0
Passive Ownership: Allowed
Encourage Conversions: No
Area Develop. Agreements: No
Sub-Franchising Contracts: No
Expand In Territory: No
Space Needs: N/A SF; N/A
SUPPORT & TRAINING PROVIDED:
Financial Assistance Provided: No
Site Selection Assistance: N/A
Lease Negotiation Assistance: No
Co-Operative Advertising: No
Franchisee Assoc./Member: Yes/Yes
Size Of Corporate Staff: 2
On-Going Support: NR
Training: 2.5 Days Seattle, WA.
SPECIFIC EXPANSION PLANS:
US: Northeast, Central US, NC

Canada: All Canada
Overseas: No

‹‹ ››

COFFEE NEWS
P.O. Box 8444
Bangor, ME 04402-8444
Tel: (207) 941-0860
Fax: (207) 941-0860
E-Mail: bill@coffeenewsusa.com
Web Site: www.coffeenewsusa.com
Mr. William A. Buckley, President

COFFEE NEWS is an international, fun-filled weekly publication produced and delivered free of charge by local franchisors to restaurants, coffee shops and the hospitality industry. Each issue contains short stories, trivia, horoscopes, interesting facts and jokes, plus a local event section edited by the franchisee. Income is derived from the sale of ads to small businesses in each community.

BACKGROUND:
Established: 1994; 1st Franchised: 1996
Franchised Units: 276
Company-Owned Units: 3
Total Units: 279
Dist.: US-109; CAN-135; O'seas-35
 North America: NR
 Density: 31 in BC, 28 in ME, 23 in ON
Projected New Units (12 Months): 100
Qualifications: 1, 5, 5, 3, 3, 3
Registered: CA,FL,HI,MN,NY,OR, SD,WI,AB
FINANCIAL/TERMS:
Cash Investment: $2.5K
Total Investment: $2.5K
Minimum Net Worth: $None
Fees: Franchise - $2K
 Royalty - $20-75/Wk.; Ad. - 0%
Earnings Claim Statement: No
Term of Contract (Years): 4/4
Avg. # Of Employees: 1 FT, 1 PT
Passive Ownership: Discouraged
Encourage Conversions: N/A
Area Develop. Agreements: No
Sub-Franchising Contracts: No
Expand In Territory: Yes
Space Needs: N/A SF; N/A
SUPPORT & TRAINING PROVIDED:
Financial Assistance Provided: No
Site Selection Assistance: Yes
Lease Negotiation Assistance: No
Co-Operative Advertising: No

Franchisee Assoc./Member: No
Size Of Corporate Staff: 5
On-Going Support: G
Training: Quarterly Sales Meetings in ME.
SPECIFIC EXPANSION PLANS:
US: All United States
Canada: All Canada
Overseas: All Countries

‹‹ ››

FINDERBINDER/SOURCEBOOK DIRECTORIES
8546 Chevy Chase Dr.
La Mesa, CA 91941-5325
Tel: (800) 255-2575 (619) 463-5050
Fax: (619) 463-5097
Web Site: www.marketing-tactics.com
Mr. Gary Beals, President

The FINDERBINDER News Media Directory and the SOURCEBOOK Directory of Clubs and Associations are locally-produced reference books created by existing communications firms, such as an advertising agency or public relations consultants. It is an added profit center that builds public awareness for the local company.

BACKGROUND:
Established: 1974; 1st Franchised: 1978
Franchised Units: 18
Company-Owned Units: 1
Total Units: 19
Dist.: US-22; CAN-0; O'seas-0
 North America: 15 States
 Density: 4 in CA
Projected New Units (12 Months): 3
Registered: CA
FINANCIAL/TERMS:
Cash Investment: $NR
Total Investment: $10-15K
Minimum Net Worth: $30K
Fees: Franchise - $1K
 Royalty - 5-10%; Ad. - N/A
Earnings Claim Statement: No
Term of Contract (Years): Open
Avg. # Of Employees: 2 FT, 1 PT
Passive Ownership: Discouraged
Encourage Conversions: No
Area Develop. Agreements: No
Sub-Franchising Contracts: No
Expand In Territory: Yes
Space Needs: N/A SF; N/A
SUPPORT & TRAINING PROVIDED:
Financial Assistance Provided: No
Site Selection Assistance: N/A
Lease Negotiation Assistance: N/A
Co-Operative Advertising: Yes

Franchisee Assoc./Member: No
Size Of Corporate Staff: 3
On-Going Support: C,D,E,G,H,I
Training: 1 Day in San Diego.
SPECIFIC EXPANSION PLANS:
US: All United States
Canada: All Canada
Overseas: U.K., Australia, New Zealand

≪ ≫

The Publication for New Homeowners

HOMESTEADER
P.O. Box 2824
Framingham, MA 01703
Tel: (800) 941-9907 (508) 820-4311
Fax: (508) 820-0280
Web Site: www.thehomesteader.com
Mr. Allen Nitschelm, President

THE HOMESTEADER is a publication direct-mailed to new homeowners, one of the best target markets for businesses to reach. This is a low-cost, home-based opportunity with great income potential for anyone with a sales, publishing or business background.

BACKGROUND:
Established: 1990; 1st Franchised: 1993
Franchised Units: 13
Company-Owned Units 2
Total Units: 15
Dist.: US-17; CAN-0; O'seas-0
North America: 4 States
Density: 11 in MA, 4 in CT, 1 in NY
Projected New Units (12 Months): 6-10
Qualifications: 3, 3, 4, 2, 4, 2
Registered: CA,FL,NY,VA
FINANCIAL/TERMS:
Cash Investment: $3.3-22K
Total Investment: $3.3-22K
Minimum Net Worth: $10K
Fees: Franchise - $3.4K
 Royalty - 10%; Ad. - 0-2%
Earnings Claim Statement: Yes
Term of Contract (Years): 10/10
Avg. # Of Employees: 1 FT
Passive Ownership: Allowed
Encourage Conversions: N/A
Area Develop. Agreements: No
Sub-Franchising Contracts: No
Expand In Territory: No
Space Needs: NR SF; HB
SUPPORT & TRAINING PROVIDED:
Financial Assistance Provided: Yes(I)

Site Selection Assistance: N/A
Lease Negotiation Assistance: N/A
Co-Operative Advertising: N/A
Franchisee Assoc./Member: No
Size Of Corporate Staff: 4
On-Going Support: d,H
Training: 2-3 Days Framingham, MA.
SPECIFIC EXPANSION PLANS:
US: All United States
Canada: All Canada
Overseas: No

≪ ≫

PERFECT WEDDING GUIDE, THE
1206 N C.R. 427
Longwood, FL 32750
Tel: (888) 22-BRIDE (407) 331-6212
Fax: (407) 331-5004
E-Mail:
orlando@perfectweddingguide.com
Web Site: www.perfectweddingguide.com
Mr. Patrick J. McGroder, President

THE PERFECT WEDDING GUIDE is a comprehensive buyers' guide to wedding and honeymoon products and services. As the owner of a PERFECT WEDDING GUIDE, you will publish a magazine that thousands of people will read every day. With the guidance of the nation's premier wedding magazine publisher, you will own and manage your own business!

BACKGROUND: IFA MEMBER
Established: 1991; 1st Franchised: 1998
Franchised Units: 19
Company-Owned Units 3
Total Units: 22
Dist.: US-22; CAN-0; O'seas-0
North America: 6 States
Density: 4 in FL, 2 in TX
Projected New Units (12 Months): 24
Qualifications: 4, 3, 3, 3, 5, 5
Registered: FL
FINANCIAL/TERMS:
Cash Investment: $30-50K
Total Investment: $35-50K

Minimum Net Worth: $50K
Fees: Franchise - $25-35K
 Royalty - 6%; Ad. - 1%
Earnings Claim Statement: No
Term of Contract (Years): 10/10
Avg. # Of Employees: 2 FT
Passive Ownership: Discouraged
Encourage Conversions: NR
Area Develop. Agreements: No
Sub-Franchising Contracts: No
Expand In Territory: Yes
Space Needs: N/A SF; HB
SUPPORT & TRAINING PROVIDED:
Financial Assistance Provided: Yes(D)
Site Selection Assistance: N/A
Lease Negotiation Assistance: N/A
Co-Operative Advertising: No
Franchisee Assoc./Member: No
Size Of Corporate Staff: 7
On-Going Support: a,b,C,d,G,h,I
Training: 5 Days Longwood, FL; 5 Days Franchise Territory.
SPECIFIC EXPANSION PLANS:
US: All United States
Canada: All Canada
Overseas: No

≪ ≫

PICKET FENCE PREVIEW
One Kennedy Dr., # 5
South Burlington, VT 05403
Tel: (800) 201-0338 (802) 660-3167
Fax: (802) 863-8965
Web Site: www.picketfence-vtfsbo.com
Mr. William F. Supple, Jr., President

We publish color, for-sale-by-owner real estate magazines. Business comes to you because homeowners want to avoid spending thousands on real estate commissions. These magazines outperform the realtors! It is a turn-key system: magazine and internet publishing, yard signs, instructional videos and books and mortgage services - all you need to succeed.

BACKGROUND:
Established: 1993; 1st Franchised: 1994
Franchised Units: 5
Company-Owned Units 1
Total Units: 6
Dist.: US-6; CAN-0; O'seas-0
North America: 5 States
Density: NR
Projected New Units (12 Months): 15
Qualifications: 3, 4, 3, 2, 5, 4
Registered: All States

FINANCIAL/TERMS:

Cash Investment:	$50-75K
Total Investment:	$50-90K
Minimum Net Worth:	$35K
Fees: Franchise -	$25K/Territory
Royalty - 0-3%;	Ad. - 0%
Earnings Claim Statement:	Yes
Term of Contract (Years):	5/5
Avg. # Of Employees:	2 FT
Passive Ownership:	Discouraged
Encourage Conversions:	No
Area Develop. Agreements:	Yes
Sub-Franchising Contracts:	No
Expand In Territory:	Yes
Space Needs: 800 SF; SF	

SUPPORT & TRAINING PROVIDED:

Financial Assistance Provided:	Yes
Site Selection Assistance:	Yes
Lease Negotiation Assistance:	No
Co-Operative Advertising:	No
Franchisee Assoc./Member:	Yes/Yes
Size Of Corporate Staff:	7
On-Going Support:	B,C,D,E,H,I
Training: 4-5 Days Burlington, VT.	

SPECIFIC EXPANSION PLANS:

US:	All United States
Canada:	All Canada
Overseas:	No

◄◄ ►►

TV AMERICA

333 Glen St.
Glen Falls, NY 2801
Tel: (800) 833-9581 (518) 792-9914
Fax: (518) 798-4188
E-Mail: franchiseinfo@tvdata.com
Web Site: www.tvamericafranchise.com
Ms. Deborah Flack, VP Marketing

The TV AMERICA franchise is a way for ambitious, sales-savvy individuals to build a strong entertainment publishing business in their community. The TV AMERICA listings magazine, and its Internet counterpart, can be operated as a home-based business. TV AMERICA provides continuous support and training to ensure its franchisees have the tools necessary to reach their goals.

BACKGROUND:

Established: 1997;	1st Franchised: 2000
Franchised Units:	2

Company-Owned Units	0
Total Units:	2
Dist.:	US-2; CAN-0; O'seas-0
North America:	1 State
Density:	2 in NY
Projected New Units (12 Months):	20
Qualifications:	3, 3, 2, 2, 5, 5
Registered: All States	

FINANCIAL/TERMS:

Cash Investment:	$25K
Total Investment:	$43-68K
Minimum Net Worth:	$No Minimum
Fees: Franchise -	$25K
Royalty - 7%;	Ad. - 1%
Earnings Claim Statement:	No
Term of Contract (Years):	5/5
Avg. # Of Employees:	1 FT, 1 PT
Passive Ownership:	Not Allowed
Encourage Conversions:	Yes
Area Develop. Agreements:	No
Sub-Franchising Contracts:	No
Expand In Territory:	Yes
Space Needs: N/A SF; N/A	

SUPPORT & TRAINING PROVIDED:

Financial Assistance Provided:	No
Site Selection Assistance:	N/A
Lease Negotiation Assistance:	N/A
Co-Operative Advertising:	N/A
Franchisee Assoc./Member:	No
Size Of Corporate Staff:	5
On-Going Support:	b,c,D,E
Training: 5 Days Glen Falls, NY.	

SPECIFIC EXPANSION PLANS:

US:	All United States
Canada:	All Canada
Overseas:	No

◄◄ ►►

SUPPLEMENTAL LISTING OF FRANCHISORS

4 Seasons Publishing Inc., # 9 3151 Lakeshore Rd., #112, Kelowna, BC V1W 2S9 CANADA; (250) 868-0730; Mr. Glen Thompson ; (250) 868-0728

A Wonderful Wedding, P.O. Box 38037, Charleston, SC 29414 ; (843) 769-0269; Mr. Ken Thomason (800) 661-9135; (843) 556-1500

Buying & Dining Guide, 80 Eighth Ave., New York, NY 10011 ; (212) 243-7457; Mr. Allan Horwitz ; (212) 243-6800

Fiesta Cartoon Maps, 942 N. Orlando, Mesa, AZ 85205 ; (480) 981-3570; Ms. Sheri Eddy (800) 541-4963; (480) 396-8226

Home Guide Magazine, 1600 Capital Cir., SW, Tallahassee, FL 32310 ; (850) 574-2525; Mr. Lou Gonzalez (800) 726-6683; (850) 574-2111

Homes & Land Magazine, 1600 Capital Circle SW, Tallahassee, FL 32310 ; (850) 574-2525; Mr. Ben Sadler (800) 726-6683; (850) 574-2111

K & O Publishing, 5744 NE 61st St., P.O. Box 51189, Seattle, WA 98115-1189 ; (206) 527-9756; Mr. Warren Kraft (800) 447-1958; (206) 527-4958

Musclemag International, 5775 McLaughlin Rd., Mississauga, ON L5R 3P7 CANADA; (905) 507-3064; Ms. Maryanne Butler ; (905) 507-3545

Pennysaver, 80 Eighth Ave., New York, NY 10011 ; (212) 243-7457; Mr. Allan Horwitz ; (212) 243-6800

Small City Business Journals, 110 Merchants Row, Rutland, VT 06701 ; (802) 775-0650; Mr. Richard Rohe ; (802) 775-9500

Television & Entertainment Publications, Liberty Square, Danvers, MA 01923 ; (978) 595-9237; Ms. Joan Gallagher (888) 977-4666; (978) 777-4666

Television + Entertainment Publications, Liberty Square, Danvers, MA 01923 ; (781) 595-9237; Ms. Joan Gallagher (888) 977-4666; (781) 777-9225

Today's Seniors, 467 Spears Rd., Oakville, ON L6K 3S4 CANADA; (905) 337-5571; Mr. Don Wall (800) 387-7682; (905) 815-0017

Town Planner, 16600 Sprague Rd., # 440, Cleveland, OH 44130 ; (440) 243-1299; Mr. Larry Paulozzi (800) 383-1253; (440) 243-1229

TV News Magazine, 80 Eighth Ave., New York, NY 10011 ; (212) 243-7457; Mr. Allan Horwitz ; (212) 243-6800

373

REAL ESTATE INSPECTION SERVICES INDUSTRY PROFILE

Total # Franchisors in Industry Group	23
Total # Franchised Units in Industry Group	2,058
Total # Company-Owned Units in Industry Group	386
Total # Operating Units in Industry Group	2,444
Average # Franchised Units/Franchisor	89.5
Average # Company-Owned Units/Franchisor	16.8
Average # Total Units/Franchisor	106.3
Ratio of Total # Franchised Units/Total # Company-Owned Units	5.3:1
Industry Survey Participants	10
Representing % of Industry	43.5%
Average Franchise Fee*:	$20.1K
Average Total Investment*:	$34.3K
Average On-Going Royalty Fee*:	7.5%

If a range was provided, the mid-point of the range was used. See detailed profiles for actual ranges.

FIVE LARGEST PARTICIPANTS IN SURVEY

Company	# Franchised Units	# Co-Owned Units	# Total Units	Franchise Fee	On-Going Royalty	Total Investment
1. Terminix Termite & Pest Control	265	320	585	25-50K	7%	25-50K
2. Housemaster Home Inspection	382	0	382	8.5-24K	7.5%	14.3-47.5K
3. Amerispec Home Inspection	345	1	346	13.9-23.9K	7%	18.9-59.5K
4. Hometeam Inspection Service	297	0	297	11.9-29.9K	6%	17.5-45K
5. Pillar to Post	267	0	267	13.9-23.9K	7%/$200	20.9-42.9K

All of the data provided are proprietary and should not be quoted without acknowledging *Bond's Franchise Guide*.

AMERISPEC HOME INSPECTION SERVICE
860 Ridge Lake Blvd.
Memphis, TN 38120
Tel: (800) 426-2270 (901) 820-8509
Fax: (901) 820-8520
E-Mail: sales@amerispec.net
Web Site: www.amerispecfranchise.com
Mr. Thomas Jeffries, Franchise Sales Mgr.

AMERISPEC delivers productivity enhancing tools to our owners like AMERISPEC HOME INSPECTOR (R), proprietary home inspection software loaded on an affordable hand-held computer and our E&O Insurance policy, which protects real estate agents against negligent referral claims. A private intranet permits two-way communication with and among our owners. Consider our extensive training, the acclaimed and recognized 'AMERISPEC report,' our ongoing educational support and the package is complete.

BACKGROUND: IFA MEMBER
Established: 1987;   1st Franchised: 1988
Franchised Units: 345
Company-Owned Units   1
Total Units: 346
Dist.:   US-275; CAN-71; O'seas-0
  North America: 48 States, 8 Provinces
  Density: 23 in CA, 15 in FL, 11 in IL
Projected New Units (12 Months):   40
Qualifications: 3, 3, 3, 3, 1, 5
Registered: All States
FINANCIAL/TERMS:
Cash Investment: $10-15K
Total Investment: $18.9-59.5K
Minimum Net Worth: $25K
Fees: Franchise - $13.9-23.9K
  Royalty - 7%;   Ad. - 3%
Earnings Claim Statement: No
Term of Contract (Years):   5/5
Avg. # Of Employees: 1 FT, 2 PT
Passive Ownership: Allowed
Encourage Conversions: Yes
Area Develop. Agreements: No
Sub-Franchising Contracts: No
Expand In Territory: Yes
Space Needs: N/A SF; HB
SUPPORT & TRAINING PROVIDED:
Financial Assistance Provided: Yes(D)
Site Selection Assistance: N/A
Lease Negotiation Assistance: N/A

Co-Operative Advertising: N/A
Franchisee Assoc./Member: No
Size Of Corporate Staff: 30
On-Going Support: C,D,E,G,h,I
Training: 2 Weeks Memphis, TN.
SPECIFIC EXPANSION PLANS:
US: All United States
Canada: All Canada
Overseas: No

≪ ≫

BRICKKICKER, THE
849 N. Ellsworth
Naperville, IL 60563
Tel: (800) 821-1820 (630) 420-9900
Fax: (630) 420-2270
Web Site: www.brickkicker.com
Mr. Ron Ewald, President

Home and building inspections. Operating our own business since 1989 gives us a unique insight into the entrepreneurial aspects required to be an impact player in the industry. We've packaged our experience into a dynamic, aggressive program, including a heavy emphasis on 'live,' on-the-job training. Every BRICKKICKER benefits from the roll up our sleeves attitude in which we operate.

BACKGROUND:
Established: 1989;   1st Franchised: 1995
Franchised Units: 77
Company-Owned Units   2
Total Units: 79
Dist.:   US-79; CAN-0; O'seas-0
  North America: 7 States
  Density: 16 in MI, 8 in WI, 7 in IN
Projected New Units (12 Months):   45
Qualifications: 3, 4, 2, 3, 3, 4
Registered: All States
FINANCIAL/TERMS:
Cash Investment: $9.4-24.9K
Total Investment: $19.4-39.9K
Minimum Net Worth: $10K
Fees: Franchise - $6.9-12.9K
  Royalty - 6%;   Ad. - 2%
Earnings Claim Statement: No
Term of Contract (Years):   7/20
Avg. # Of Employees: 1 FT
Passive Ownership: Discouraged
Encourage Conversions: Yes
Area Develop. Agreements: No
Sub-Franchising Contracts: No
Expand In Territory: Yes
Space Needs: NR SF; NR
SUPPORT & TRAINING PROVIDED:
Financial Assistance Provided: Yes(D)
Site Selection Assistance: N/A

Lease Negotiation Assistance: N/A
Co-Operative Advertising: N/A
Franchisee Assoc./Member: Yes/Yes
Size Of Corporate Staff: 7
On-Going Support: B,C,D,E,G,H,I
Training: 10 Days, Naperville, IL; 3 Days
  On-Site.
SPECIFIC EXPANSION PLANS:
US: All United States
Canada: All Canada
Overseas: No

≪ ≫

CRITTER CONTROL

CRITTER CONTROL
9435 E. Cherry Bend Rd.
Traverse City, MI 49684
Tel: (800) 451-6544 (231) 947-2400
Fax: (231) 947-9440
E-Mail: crittercontrol @ coslink.net
Web Site: www.crittercontrol.com
Mr. Sean Carruth, Staff Biologist

Urban Wildlife Management Specialists. Nation's leading animal control firm. Humane animal removal, prevention and repairs of animal damage.

BACKGROUND:
Established: 1983;   1st Franchised: 1988
Franchised Units: 71
Company-Owned Units   25
Total Units: 96
Dist.:   US-95; CAN-1; O'seas-0
  North America: NR
  Density: 10 in MI, 9 in FL, 7 in OH
Projected New Units (12 Months):   10
Qualifications: 2, 3, 3, 3, 3, 4
Registered: CA,IN,MD,MI,NY,VA,WI
FINANCIAL/TERMS:
Cash Investment: $3-5K
Total Investment: $5-25K
Minimum Net Worth: $N/A
Fees: Franchise - $15-24K
  Royalty - 6-16%;   Ad. - 1-2%
Earnings Claim Statement: No
Term of Contract (Years):   10/10
Avg. # Of Employees: 2 FT, 1 PT
Passive Ownership: Discouraged
Encourage Conversions: N/A
Area Develop. Agreements: No
Sub-Franchising Contracts: No
Expand In Territory: Yes
Space Needs: NR SF; HB
SUPPORT & TRAINING PROVIDED:
Financial Assistance Provided: No

Site Selection Assistance: Yes
Lease Negotiation Assistance: N/A
Co-Operative Advertising: Yes
Franchisee Assoc./Member: Yes/Yes
Size Of Corporate Staff: 7
On-Going Support: C,D,G,H,I
Training: 1 Week Columbus, OH.

SPECIFIC EXPANSION PLANS:
US: All United States
Canada: All Canada
Overseas: No

<< >>

THE HOMETEAM
INSPECTION SERVICE, INC.

HOMETEAM INSPECTION SERVICE, THE

6355 E. Kemper Rd., # 250
Cincinnati, OH 45241
Tel: (800) 598-5297 (513) 469-2100
Fax: (513) 469-2226
E-Mail: hometean@one.net
Web Site: www.hmteam.com
Mr. Greg Hashett, VP of Operations

Ranked #1 fastest-growing home inspection franchise in North America. Unique and field-proven marketing system that produces leads and appointments. Exclusive, protected territory. Extensive and continuous training. Sales hotline to build your business. Financing provided.

BACKGROUND: IFA MEMBER
Established: 1992; 1st Franchised: 1992
Franchised Units: 297
Company-Owned Units: 0
Total Units: 297
Dist.: US-292; CAN-5; O'seas-0
 North America: 48 States, 2 Provinces
 Density: 29 in FL, 20 in OH, 16 in MI
Projected New Units (12 Months): 29
Qualifications: 2, 3, 2, 3, 3, 5
Registered: CA,FL,IL,IN,MD,MI,MN,NY,
 ND,OR,RI,SD,VA,WA,WI,DC
FINANCIAL/TERMS:
Cash Investment: $6.5-15.7K
Total Investment: $17.5-45K
Minimum Net Worth: $N/A
Fees: Franchise - $11.9-29.9K
 Royalty - 6%; Ad. - 3%
Earnings Claim Statement: No
Term of Contract (Years): 10/10/10
Avg. # Of Employees: 1 FT
Passive Ownership: Discouraged
Encourage Conversions: N/A
Area Develop. Agreements: No
Sub-Franchising Contracts: No

Expand In Territory: Yes
Space Needs: N/A SF; N/A
SUPPORT & TRAINING PROVIDED:
Financial Assistance Provided: Yes(D)
Site Selection Assistance: N/A
Lease Negotiation Assistance: N/A
Co-Operative Advertising: Yes
Franchisee Assoc./Member: Yes/Yes
Size Of Corporate Staff: 20
On-Going Support: A,B,C,D,G,H,I
Training: 2 Weeks Corporate Headquarters,
 Cincinnati, OH.
SPECIFIC EXPANSION PLANS:
US: All United States
Canada: All Canada
Overseas: No

<< >>

HouseMaster®

"The Home Inspection Professionals"®

HOUSEMASTER HOME INSPECTIONS

421 W. Union Ave.
Bound Brook, NJ 08805
Tel: (800) 526-3939 (732) 469-6565
Fax: (732) 469-7405
E-Mail: jgranito@housemaster.com
Web Site: www.housemaster.com
Mr. John J. Granito, Director of Franchise
 Sales

HOUSEMASTER is the oldest and most experienced home inspection franchise. HOUSEMASTER is the recognized authority on home inspections and has been featured as such on CNN, CNBC, Our Home Show and many more! You will be impressed with the level of expertise and the unsurpassed level of support that HOUSEMASTER franchise owners enjoy.

BACKGROUND: IFA MEMBER
Established: 1979; 1st Franchised: 1979
Franchised Units: 382
Company-Owned Units: 0
Total Units: 382
Dist.: US-349; CAN-33; O'seas-0
 North America: 48 States, 10 Provinces
 Density: 23 in NJ, 20 in NY, 18 in FL
Projected New Units (12 Months): 72
Qualifications: 4, 3, 2, 2, 5, 5
Registered: All States
FINANCIAL/TERMS:
Cash Investment: $12-35K
Total Investment: $14.3-47.5K
Minimum Net Worth: $75K

Fees: Franchise - $8.5-24K
 Royalty - 7.5%; Ad. - 2.5%
Earnings Claim Statement: No
Term of Contract (Years): 5/5
Avg. # Of Employees: Varies
Passive Ownership: Allowed
Encourage Conversions: N/A
Area Develop. Agreements: No
Sub-Franchising Contracts: No
Expand In Territory: Yes
Space Needs: N/A SF; HB
SUPPORT & TRAINING PROVIDED:
Financial Assistance Provided: Yes(D)
Site Selection Assistance: N/A
Lease Negotiation Assistance: N/A
Co-Operative Advertising: N/A
Franchisee Assoc./Member: Yes/Yes
Size Of Corporate Staff: 22
On-Going Support: D,G,H,I
Training: 2-3 Weeks Bound Brook, NJ.
SPECIFIC EXPANSION PLANS:
US: All United States
Canada: All Canada
Overseas: Most Countries

<< >>

NATIONAL PROPERTY INSPECTIONS

11620 Arbor St., # 100
Omaha, NE 68144-2935
Tel: (800) 333-9807 (402) 333-9807
Fax: (402) 333-9780
Web Site: www.npiweb.com
Ms. Julie Erickson, Dir. of Franchise Sales

Nationally-acclaimed residential and commercial property inspection franchise. Low start-up costs. Exclusive territories. Expansion encouraged. Award-winning national referral program. Intensive, interactive, 2-week training course. Ongoing marketing management and technical support. Fee includes state-of-the-art computer package and everything needed for first year of business

BACKGROUND:
Established: 1987; 1st Franchised: 1987
Franchised Units: 86
Company-Owned Units: 0
Total Units: 86
Dist.: US-85; CAN-1; O'seas-0
 North America: 37 States, 1 Province
 Density: 7 in IL, 5 in WI, 5 in NY
Projected New Units (12 Months): 24
Qualifications: 3, 3, 4, 3, 4, 4
Registered: All States and AB
FINANCIAL/TERMS:
Cash Investment: $5-8K

Total Investment:	$17.8-25.8K
Minimum Net Worth:	$NR
Fees: Franchise -	$17.8-25.8K
Royalty - 8%;	Ad. - 0%
Earnings Claim Statement:	No
Term of Contract (Years):	5/5
Avg. # Of Employees:	1 FT
Passive Ownership:	Discouraged
Encourage Conversions:	Yes
Area Develop. Agreements:	Yes
Sub-Franchising Contracts:	No
Expand In Territory:	Yes
Space Needs: NR SF; N/A	

SUPPORT & TRAINING PROVIDED:

Financial Assistance Provided:	Yes(D)
Site Selection Assistance:	N/A
Lease Negotiation Assistance:	N/A
Co-Operative Advertising:	N/A
Franchisee Assoc./Member:	No
Size Of Corporate Staff:	18
On-Going Support:	D,G,H,I
Training: 2 Weeks Omaha, NE in NPI Corporate Office.	

SPECIFIC EXPANSION PLANS:

US:	All United States
Canada:	All Canada
Overseas:	No

<< >>

PESTMASTER SERVICES
137 E. South St.
Bishop, CA 93514
Tel: (800) 525-8866 (760) 873-8100
Fax: (760) 873-5618
E-Mail: pestmaster@worldnet.att.net
Web Site: www.pestmaster.com
Ms. Carol MacAfee, Franchise Coordinator

PESTMASTER SERVICES provides a strategic advantage in the battle for pest control market share by maximizing your business potential while minimizing administrative hassles. Training in a diverse service menu. This diversity helps to insulate our business from the seasonal fluctuations that affect so many other pest control businesses. As a PESTMASTER franchise owner, you may build a solid foundation of pest control accounts that involve year-round activity.

BACKGROUND:

Established: 1990;	1st Franchised: 1997
Franchised Units:	11
Company-Owned Units	15
Total Units:	26
Dist.:	US-26; CAN-0; O'seas-0
North America:	5 States

Density:	19 in CA, 2 in NV, 2 in FL
Projected New Units (12 Months):	2
Qualifications:	4, 5, 4, 3, 4, 5
Registered: None	

FINANCIAL/TERMS:

Cash Investment:	$NR
Total Investment:	$60.8-109.8K
Minimum Net Worth:	$NR
Fees: Franchise -	$22.5K
Royalty - 9%;	Ad. - 0.5%
Earnings Claim Statement:	No
Term of Contract (Years):	10/10
Avg. # Of Employees:	2 FT, 1 PT
Passive Ownership:	Not Allowed
Encourage Conversions:	Yes
Area Develop. Agreements:	NR
Sub-Franchising Contracts:	No
Expand In Territory:	Yes
Space Needs: N/A SF; NR	

SUPPORT & TRAINING PROVIDED:

Financial Assistance Provided:	Yes(I)
Site Selection Assistance:	Yes
Lease Negotiation Assistance:	N/A
Co-Operative Advertising:	Yes
Franchisee Assoc./Member:	No
Size Of Corporate Staff:	15
On-Going Support:	NR
Training: 2 Weeks Corporate Office; 2 Weeks Franchise Location.	

SPECIFIC EXPANSION PLANS:

US:	All United States
Canada:	No
Overseas:	No

<< >>

PILLAR TO POST
13902 N. Dale Mabry Hwy., # 212
Tampa, FL 33618
Tel: (877) 963-3129 (813) 962-4461
Fax: (813) 963-5301
E-Mail: frandey@pillartopost.com
Web Site: www.pillartopost.com
Mr. Allen Castleman, Dir. of Franchising

PILLAR TO POST is the #1 home inspection franchise in the U.S. PTP offers a proven system of home inspection with training and support that has no equal. Successful and imaginative marketing programs. Materials, technical support and operational advice are provided. Husband and wife teams do very well.

BACKGROUND: IFA MEMBER

Established: 1994;	1st Franchised: 1994
Franchised Units:	267
Company-Owned Units	0
Total Units:	267
Dist.:	US-177; CAN-90; O'seas-0
North America:	40 States, 8 Provinces
Density:	15 in OH, 12 in NY, 11 in FL
Projected New Units (12 Months):	90
Qualifications:	3, 3, 3, 3, 3, 3
Registered: All States	

FINANCIAL/TERMS:

Cash Investment:	$13.9-23.9K
Total Investment:	$20.9-42.9K
Minimum Net Worth:	$50K
Fees: Franchise -	$13.9-23.9K
Royalty - 7%/$200;	Ad. - 2%/$100
Earnings Claim Statement:	No
Term of Contract (Years):	5/5
Avg. # Of Employees:	1 FT, 1 PT
Passive Ownership:	Not Allowed
Encourage Conversions:	N/A
Area Develop. Agreements:	N/A
Sub-Franchising Contracts:	No
Expand In Territory:	No
Space Needs: N/A SF; N/A	

SUPPORT & TRAINING PROVIDED:

Financial Assistance Provided:	No
Site Selection Assistance:	N/A
Lease Negotiation Assistance:	N/A
Co-Operative Advertising:	N/A
Franchisee Assoc./Member:	No
Size Of Corporate Staff:	15
On-Going Support:	b,C,D,F,G,h,I
Training: 2 Weeks Corporate Head Office.	

SPECIFIC EXPANSION PLANS:

US:	All United States
Canada:	All Canada
Overseas:	Europe

<< >>

TERMINIX TERMITE & PEST CONTROL
860 Ridge Lake Blvd.
Memphis, TN 38120
Tel: (800) 654-7848 (901) 766-1376
Fax: (901) 766-1208
Web Site: www.terminix.com
Mr. William Cochran, Mgr. Fran. Operations

Termite and pest control company.

BACKGROUND: IFA MEMBER

Established: 1927;	1st Franchised: 1927
Franchised Units:	265
Company-Owned Units	320
Total Units:	585
Dist.:	US-524; CAN-0; O'seas-61
North America:	45 States

Density: 58 in CA, 49 in TX, 47 in FL
Projected New Units (12 Months):   5
Qualifications: 4, 5, 5, 3, , 5
Registered: CA,IL,IN,MD,MI,MN,NY,
    ND,OR,RI,SD,VA,WA,WI

FINANCIAL/TERMS:

Cash Investment: $7.1-25.55K
Total Investment: $25-50K
Minimum Net Worth: $Varies
Fees: Franchise - $25-50K
    Royalty - 7%;   Ad. - 2%
Earnings Claim Statement: No
Term of Contract (Years):   5-7/5
Avg. # Of Employees: Varies on Size
Passive Ownership: Discouraged
Encourage Conversions: Yes
Area Develop. Agreements: NR
Sub-Franchising Contracts: No
Expand In Territory: Yes
Space Needs: N/A SF; NR

SUPPORT & TRAINING PROVIDED:

Financial Assistance Provided: Yes
Site Selection Assistance: N/A
Lease Negotiation Assistance: N/A
Co-Operative Advertising: Yes
Franchisee Assoc./Member: Yes/No
Size Of Corporate Staff: 7215
On-Going Support: B,C,D,G,h,I
Training: 5-6 Days in Memphis, TN
    (Initial);   6   Weeks   On-Location
    Training.

SPECIFIC EXPANSION PLANS:

US: All United States
Canada: All Canada
Overseas: Central America, China, Japan

◄◄ ►►

SUPPLEMENTAL LISTING
OF FRANCHISORS

Advantage Radon Control Centers, 804
Second St. Pike, Southampton, PA 18966 ;
(215) 953-8837; Mr. Perry S. Ecksel (800)
535-8378; (215) 953-9200

AllerClean, 6400 Blackhorse Pk., Egg
Harbor Township, NJ 08234 ; (609)
641-0988; Mr. Ray Hurley (800) 745-5631;

Ambic Building Inspection Consultants,
1200 Rt. 130, Robbinsville, NJ 08691 ;
(609) 426-1230; Mr. W. David Goldstein
(800) 88-AMBIC; (609) 448-3900

American Lead Consultants, 200 S. Broad
St., 6th Fl., Philadelphia, PA 19102 ; (215)
732-9559; Mr. Perry Safian (800) 441-5323;
(215) 732-9449

AmeriSpec of Canada, 6540 Tomken Rd.,
Mississauga, ON L5T 2E9 CANADA;
(905) 670-0077; Mr. David Messenger
(800) 263-5928; (905) 670-0000

Criterium Engineers, 22 Monument Square,
#600, Portland, ME 04101 ; (207)
775-4405; Mr. Peter E. Hollander (800)
242-1969; (207) 828-1969

Envirofree Inspections, 4763 S. Old U.S.
23, # A, Brighton, MI 48114-8685 ;
(810) 220-2772; Mr. Chuck Filippone (800)
220-0013; (810) 220-2767

Grassroots - Home Inspection Specialists,
214 Martindale Rd., St. Catharines, ON
L2R 6P9 CANADA; (905) 685-8125; Mr.
Harry Salomons (800) 774-2538; (905)
687-1925

Inspect-It 1st Property Inspection, 16042
N. 32nd St., #B-5, Phoenix, AZ 85032 ;
(602) 992-3127; Ms. Angela Raydo (800)
510-9100; (602) 971-9400

Westland Services Corp., 18 Lyman St.,
K, Westborough, MA 01581 ; (508)
836-2601; Mr. Philip G. Haddad, Jr. (800)
622-0772; (508) 836-2600

World Inspection Network, 6500 6th Ave.
NW, Seattle, WA 98117 ; (206) 441-3655;
Mr. Kurt Kempfer (800) 967-8127; (206)
728-8100

REAL ESTATE SERVICES INDUSTRY PROFILE

Total # Franchisors in Industry Group	50
Total # Franchised Units in Industry Group	21,851
Total # Company-Owned Units in Industry Group	206
Total # Operating Units in Industry Group	22,060
Average # Franchised Units/Franchisor	437.0
Average # Company-Owned Units/Franchisor	4.1
Average # Total Units/Franchisor	441.1
Ratio of Total # Franchised Units/Total # Company-Owned Units	106.1:1
Industry Survey Participants	23
Representing % of Industry	46.0%
Average Franchise Fee*:	$14.4K
Average Total Investment*:	$69.3K
Average On-Going Royalty Fee*:	5.9%

If a range was provided, the mid-point of the range was used. See detailed profiles for actual ranges.

FIVE LARGEST PARTICIPANTS IN SURVEY

Company	# Fran-chised Units	# Co-Owned Units	# Total Units	Franchise Fee	On-Going Royalty	Total Investment
1. Century 21 Real Estate	6,200	0	6,200	12.5-25K	6%	50-200K
2. RE/MAX International	3,713	0	3,713	7.5-25K	Varies	20-150K
3. Coldwell Banker Residential	2,954	0	2,954	7.5-20K	6%	15.1-57K
4. ERA Franchise Systems	2,600	0	2,600	12.5-20K	6%	NR
5. Better Homes & Gardens Real Estate	1,599	0	1,599	3.9K	1-5%	Varies

All of the data provided are proprietary and should not be quoted without acknowledging *Bond's Franchise Guide*.

APARTMENT SELECTOR

P.O. Box 8355
Dallas, TX 75205-0060
Tel: (800) 324-3733 (214) 361-4420
Fax: (214) 361-8677
E-Mail: aptsel@aptselector.com
Web Site: www.aptselector.com
Mr. Kendall A. Laughlin, President

APARTMENT SELECTOR is the nation's oldest and largest FREE apartment and home rental service. Our fee is paid by apartment owners. Extensive training systems for agents and management. Referral network called Official Relocation Network.

BACKGROUND:

Established: 1959;	1st Franchised: 1983
Franchised Units:	21
Company-Owned Units	0
Total Units:	21
Dist.:	US-21; CAN-0; O'seas-0
North America:	6 States
Density:	8 in TX
Projected New Units (12 Months):	2
Qualifications:	3, 3, 4, 3, 1, 1
Registered: All States	

FINANCIAL/TERMS:

Cash Investment:	$3K+
Total Investment:	$NR
Minimum Net Worth:	$N/A
Fees: Franchise -	$2.5-10K
Royalty - 5%;	Ad. - 1%
Earnings Claim Statement:	No
Term of Contract (Years):	3/3
Avg. # Of Employees:	3 FT, 3 PT
Passive Ownership:	Discouraged
Encourage Conversions:	Yes
Area Develop. Agreements:	No
Sub-Franchising Contracts:	No
Expand In Territory:	No
Space Needs: 250 SF; SC	

SUPPORT & TRAINING PROVIDED:

Financial Assistance Provided:	No
Site Selection Assistance:	Yes
Lease Negotiation Assistance:	No
Co-Operative Advertising:	No
Franchisee Assoc./Member:	No
Size Of Corporate Staff:	3
On-Going Support:	c,d,E,g,h,I
Training: 1 Week Dallas, TX.	

SPECIFIC EXPANSION PLANS:

US:	Southeast, West
Canada:	No
Overseas:	No

<< >>

ASSIST-2-SELL

1610 Meadow Wood Ln.
Reno, NV 89502
Tel: (800) 528-7816 (775) 688-6060
Fax: (775) 688-6069
E-Mail: info@assist2sell.com
Web Site: www.assist2sell.com
Mr. Lyle Martin, Vice President

America's 'full service with sav' discount real estate franchise. Real estate license required. The future of real estate will focus around a 'menu of services' concept. Lower commissions will be the norm. Don't be left behind: catch our vision and step into the future.

BACKGROUND:

Established: 1987;	1st Franchised: 1993
Franchised Units:	125
Company-Owned Units	0
Total Units:	125
Dist.:	US-125; CAN-0; O'seas-0
North America:	33 States
Density:	17 in CO, 14 in CA, 9 in MA
Projected New Units (12 Months):	35
Qualifications:	2, 4, 5, 2, 3, 4
Registered: CA,FL,IL,IN,MD,MN,NY,ND, OR,RI,SD,VA,WA,WI	

FINANCIAL/TERMS:

Cash Investment:	$0
Total Investment:	$25.5-52K
Minimum Net Worth:	$N/A
Fees: Franchise -	$10K
Royalty - 5%;	Ad. - 0%
Earnings Claim Statement:	No
Term of Contract (Years):	7/7
Avg. # Of Employees:	3 FT
Passive Ownership:	Discouraged
Encourage Conversions:	Yes
Area Develop. Agreements:	No
Sub-Franchising Contracts:	No
Expand In Territory:	Yes
Space Needs: 150 SF; OB	

SUPPORT & TRAINING PROVIDED:

Financial Assistance Provided:	No
Site Selection Assistance:	Yes
Lease Negotiation Assistance:	Yes
Co-Operative Advertising:	No
Franchisee Assoc./Member:	No
Size Of Corporate Staff:	6
On-Going Support:	d,G,H,I
Training: 4 Days in Reno, NV.	

SPECIFIC EXPANSION PLANS:

US:	All United States
Canada:	All Canada
Overseas:	All Countries

<< >>

BETTER HOMES & GARDENS REAL ESTATE SERV.

1912 Grand Ave.
Des Moines, IA 50309
Tel: (800) 274-7653 (515) 284-2711
Fax: (515) 284-3801
Web Site: www.bhg-real-estate.com
Mr. Scott Hale, National Marketing Director

BETTER HOMES AND GARDENS is an extension of the renowned magazine, and since its debut in 1978, has become one of the nation's largest real estate franchisors, with more than 1,599 offices in all 50 states. The 25,758 sales professionals in the network generated more than $35.2 billion in residential sales volume in 1997. The real estate franchise is an operating group of Meredith Corporation and is based in Des Moines, IA.

BACKGROUND: IFA MEMBER

Established: 1902;	1st Franchised: 1978
Franchised Units:	1,599
Company-Owned Units	0
Total Units:	1,599
Dist.:	US-1,599; CAN-0; O'seas-0
North America:	50 States
Density:	106 in CA, 48 in IL, 78 NY
Projected New Units (12 Months):	120
Qualifications:	3, 4, 5, 3, 3,
Registered: All States	

FINANCIAL/TERMS:

Cash Investment:	$Varies
Total Investment:	$Varies
Minimum Net Worth:	$Varies
Fees: Franchise -	$3.9K
Royalty - 1-5%;	Ad. - 2.2%
Earnings Claim Statement:	No
Term of Contract (Years):	5/5
Avg. # Of Employees:	NR
Passive Ownership:	Allowed
Encourage Conversions:	Yes
Area Develop. Agreements:	No
Sub-Franchising Contracts:	No
Expand In Territory:	Yes
Space Needs: NR SF; N/A	

SUPPORT & TRAINING PROVIDED:

Financial Assistance Provided:	Yes
Site Selection Assistance:	No
Lease Negotiation Assistance:	No

Co-Operative Advertising: Yes
Franchisee Assoc./Member: No
Size Of Corporate Staff: 132
On-Going Support: b,C,d,e,G,h,I
Training: 2 Days, Des Moines, IA.
SPECIFIC EXPANSION PLANS:
US: All United States
Canada: All Canada
Overseas: Japan, Australia

≪ ≫

Each office is independently owned and operated.

BETTER HOMES REALTY

1777 Botelho Dr., # 390
Walnut Creek, CA 94596
Tel: (800) 642-4428 (925) 937-9001
Fax: (925) 988-2770
E-Mail: flo@bhrcorp.com
Web Site: www.bhr.com
Ms. Florence Stevens, Vice President

Established identity, legal hot line support, no institutional advertising fee, franchise cap each calendar year, excellent corporate support, free DRE renewal, corporate advertising, hands-on regional support.

BACKGROUND:
Established: 1964;   1st Franchised: 1969
Franchised Units: 39
Company-Owned Units 0
Total Units: 39
Dist.: US-40; CAN-0; O'seas-0
 North America: 1 State
 Density: 39 in CA
Projected New Units (12 Months): 10
Qualifications: 3, 3, 3, 2, 1, 1
Registered: CA
FINANCIAL/TERMS:
Cash Investment: $10-60K
Total Investment: $N/A
Minimum Net Worth: $N/A
Fees: Franchise - $9.95K
 Royalty - 6% w/Cap/4.5%; Ad. - 0%
Earnings Claim Statement: Yes
Term of Contract (Years): 5/5
Avg. # Of Employees: N/A
Passive Ownership: Allowed
Encourage Conversions: Yes
Area Develop. Agreements: NR

Sub-Franchising Contracts: Yes
Expand In Territory: Yes
Space Needs: N/A SF; N/A
SUPPORT & TRAINING PROVIDED:
Financial Assistance Provided: Yes(I)
Site Selection Assistance: N/A
Lease Negotiation Assistance: N/A
Co-Operative Advertising: Yes
Franchisee Assoc./Member: No
Size Of Corporate Staff: 7
On-Going Support: b,C,D,G,H,I
Training: Varies. 0.5-1 Day.
SPECIFIC EXPANSION PLANS:
US: West
Canada: No
Overseas: No

≪ ≫

BUYER'S AGENT, THE

1255 A Lynnfield Rd., # 273
Memphis, TN 38119
Tel: (800) 766-8728 (901) 767-1077
Fax: (901) 767-3577
E-Mail: rebuyragt@aol.com
Web Site: www.forbuyers.com
Mr. Tom Hathaway, President

The nation's oldest and largest real estate franchise in the business of exclusive buyer representation.

BACKGROUND:
Established: 1988;   1st Franchised: 1988
Franchised Units: 70
Company-Owned Units 0
Total Units: 70
Dist.: US-70; CAN-0; O'seas-0
 North America: 28 States
 Density: 8 in FL, 8 in CA, 5 in TN
Projected New Units (12 Months): 50
Qualifications: 3, 3, 2, 3, 3, 3
Registered: CA,FL,HI,IN,MD,MI,MN,
 NY,OR,RI,VA,WA,WI
FINANCIAL/TERMS:
Cash Investment: $20-30K
Total Investment: $25-50K
Minimum Net Worth: $50K
Fees: Franchise - $14.9K
 Royalty - 5%; Ad. - 1%
Earnings Claim Statement: No
Term of Contract (Years): 5/5
Avg. # Of Employees: 5-15 FT
Passive Ownership: Discouraged
Encourage Conversions: Yes
Area Develop. Agreements: Consider
Sub-Franchising Contracts: No
Expand In Territory: Yes
Space Needs: 2,000 SF; FS, SF, SC

SUPPORT & TRAINING PROVIDED:
Financial Assistance Provided: Yes(I)
Site Selection Assistance: Yes
Lease Negotiation Assistance: Yes
Co-Operative Advertising: Yes
Franchisee Assoc./Member: No
Size Of Corporate Staff: 12
On-Going Support: A,B,C,D,E,G,H,I
Training: 5 Days Memphis, TN.
SPECIFIC EXPANSION PLANS:
US: All United States
Canada: All Canada
Overseas: No

≪ ≫

BUYER'S RESOURCE INTERNATIONAL

393 Hanover Center Blvd.
Etna, NH 03750
Tel: (800) 359-4092 (603) 643-9300
Fax: (603) 643-0404
E-Mail: info@buyersresource.com
Web Site: www.buyersresource.com
Mr. George Spitzer, Vice President

An exclusive buyer agency franchise system, offering support in training, management and consumer referrals.

BACKGROUND:
Established: 1989;   1st Franchised: 1989
Franchised Units: 20
Company-Owned Units 0
Total Units: 20
Dist.: US-20; CAN-0; O'seas-0
 North America: 11 States
 Density: NR
Projected New Units (12 Months): 200
Qualifications: 4, 4, 3, 3, 3, 5
Registered: Selected States
FINANCIAL/TERMS:
Cash Investment: $25-50K
Total Investment: $25-50K
Minimum Net Worth: $N/A
Fees: Franchise - $5-14K
 Royalty - 5%; Ad. - 2%/$125/Mo.
Earnings Claim Statement: No
Term of Contract (Years): 5/5
Avg. # Of Employees: Varies
Passive Ownership: Discouraged
Encourage Conversions: Yes
Area Develop. Agreements: Yes/5
Sub-Franchising Contracts: Yes
Expand In Territory: Yes
Space Needs: N/A SF; FS, SF, SC, RM
SUPPORT & TRAINING PROVIDED:
Financial Assistance Provided: N/A
Site Selection Assistance: No

Lease Negotiation Assistance: No	Site Selection Assistance: Yes	Site Selection Assistance: Yes
Co-Operative Advertising: Yes	Lease Negotiation Assistance: No	Lease Negotiation Assistance: No
Franchisee Assoc./Member: No	Co-Operative Advertising: Yes	Co-Operative Advertising: Yes
Size Of Corporate Staff: 4	Franchisee Assoc./Member: No	Franchisee Assoc./Member: No
On-Going Support: b,c,D,e,G,h,I	Size Of Corporate Staff: 357	Size Of Corporate Staff: 26
Training: 3-4 Days in NH.	On-Going Support: C,d,G,h,I	On-Going Support: A,C,d,E,G,H,I
	Training: 4.5 Days Irvine, CA.	Training: Varies.

SPECIFIC EXPANSION PLANS: (column 1)

US:	All United States
Canada:	All Canada
Overseas:	All Countries

SPECIFIC EXPANSION PLANS: (column 2)

US:	All United States
Canada:	All Canada
Overseas:	All Countries

SPECIFIC EXPANSION PLANS: (column 3)

US:	No
Canada:	All Canada
Overseas:	No

≺≺ ≻≻

CENTURY 21 REAL ESTATE

Six Sylvan Way
Parsippany, NJ 07054
Tel: (800) 826-8083 (973) 496-7221
Fax: (973) 496-4981
Web Site: www.century21.com
Mr. Rick Del Sontro, SVP Franchise Sales

World's largest residential real estate franchising organization: provides a marketing support system for independently-owned and operated real estate brokerage offices. Offering international advertising, VIP referral system, residential and commercial sales training and other real estate related services.

BACKGROUND: IFA MEMBER
Established: 1971; 1st Franchised: 1972
Franchised Units: 6,200
Company-Owned Units 0
Total Units: 6,200
Dist.: US-4,493; CAN-265; O'seas-1,442
North America: All States & Provinces
Density: 520 in CA, 348 in FL, 314 IL
Projected New Units (12 Months): 417
Qualifications: 4, 4, 5, 4, 4, 4
Registered: All States
FINANCIAL/TERMS:
Cash Investment: $NR
Total Investment: $50-200K
Minimum Net Worth: $25K
Fees: Franchise - $12.5-25K
Royalty - 6%; Ad. - 2%
Earnings Claim Statement: No
Term of Contract (Years): 5-10/5-10
Avg. # Of Employees: Varies
Passive Ownership: Discouraged
Encourage Conversions: Yes
Area Develop. Agreements: No
Sub-Franchising Contracts: No
Expand In Territory: Yes
Space Needs: Varies SF; FS, SF, SC
SUPPORT & TRAINING PROVIDED:
Financial Assistance Provided: No

≺≺ ≻≻

COLDWELL BANKER AFFILIATES (CANADA)

1 Richmond St. W., # 701
Toronto, ON M5H 3W4 CANADA
Tel: (800) 268-9599 (416) 947-9229
Fax: (416) 777-4604
Web Site: www.coldwellbanker.ca
Mr. Gacy Hockey, SVP of Business
    Development

The most complete full-service real estate franchise in Canada. Offering unsurpassed revenue generating capabilities, leading-edge technology and outstanding support services consistent with our trademark of 'ultimate service.'

BACKGROUND:
Established: 1989; 1st Franchised: 1989
Franchised Units: 230
Company-Owned Units 0
Total Units: 230
Dist.: US-0; CAN-230; O'seas-0
North America: 9 Provinces
Density: 136 in ON, 36 in BC, 25 AB
Projected New Units (12 Months): 30
Qualifications: 4, 4, 5, 2, 4, 4
Registered: AB
FINANCIAL/TERMS:
Cash Investment: $10-100K
Total Investment: $10-200K
Minimum Net Worth: $Varies
Fees: Franchise - $7.5-18K
Royalty - 6%; Ad. - $40/Person
Earnings Claim Statement: No
Term of Contract (Years): 5-10/5-10
Avg. # Of Employees: 3 FT, 1 PT
Passive Ownership: Discouraged
Encourage Conversions: Yes
Area Develop. Agreements: No
Sub-Franchising Contracts: No
Expand In Territory: Yes
Space Needs: Varies SF; All Possible
SUPPORT & TRAINING PROVIDED:
Financial Assistance Provided: No

≺≺ ≻≻

COLDWELL BANKER RESIDENTIAL AFFILIATES

Six Sylvan Way
Parsippany, NJ 07054
Tel: (973) 496-5757
Fax: (973) 496-5908
Web Site: www.coldwellbanker.com
Mr. Jose Perez, SVP Franchise Sales

Established in 1906, the company has 91 years of real estate experience. The system includes over 2,565 franchised offices and more than 52,000 sales associates and employees in North America. COLDWELL BANKER has maintained a steadfast commitment to leadership in customer service. International real estate franchising.

BACKGROUND: IFA MEMBER
Established: 1906; 1st Franchised: 1982
Franchised Units: 2,954
Company-Owned Units 0
Total Units: 2,954
Dist.: US-2,341; CAN-224; O'seas-0
North America: 50 States, 11 Provinces
Density: 237 in CA, 138 in IL, 125 FL
Projected New Units (12 Months): 225
Qualifications: 4, 4, 5, 3, 2, 4
Registered: All States
FINANCIAL/TERMS:
Cash Investment: $11.1-55.4K
Total Investment: $15.1-56.8K
Minimum Net Worth: $N/A
Fees: Franchise - $7.5-20K
Royalty - 6%; Ad. - 2.5%
Earnings Claim Statement: No
Term of Contract (Years): 10/10
Avg. # Of Employees: NR
Passive Ownership: Not Allowed
Encourage Conversions: Yes
Area Develop. Agreements: No
Sub-Franchising Contracts: No
Expand In Territory: Yes
Space Needs: N/A SF; FS, SF, SC

SUPPORT & TRAINING PROVIDED:

Financial Assistance Provided:	Yes(D)
Site Selection Assistance:	No
Lease Negotiation Assistance:	N/A
Co-Operative Advertising:	Yes
Franchisee Assoc./Member:	Yes
Size Of Corporate Staff:	200
On-Going Support:	C,d,G,h,I

Training: 1 Week Coldwell Banker Systems Orientation.

SPECIFIC EXPANSION PLANS:

US:	All United States
Canada:	All Canada
Overseas:	All Countries

COMMISSION EXPRESS
8306 Professional Hill Dr.
Fairfax, VA 22031
Tel: (888) 560-5501 (703) 560-5500
Fax: (703) 560-5502
E-Mail: manager@commissionexpress.com
Web Site: www.commissionexpress.com
Mr. John L. Stedman, President

We are a true 'white collar' franchise. We offer 'exclusive' territories with professional customers. 9 to 5, no holidays or late nights, a normal life. High profit margin per transaction and a high 80% repeat factor.

BACKGROUND:

Established: 1992;	1st Franchised: 1996
Franchised Units:	24
Company-Owned Units	1
Total Units:	25
Dist.:	US-25; CAN-0; O'seas-0
North America:	12 States
Density:	4 in VA, 3 in GA, 3 in NJ
Projected New Units (12 Months):	10
Qualifications:	4, 5, 3, 3, 3, 4
Registered:	CA,FL,IL,IN,MD,MI,NY, VA,WA

FINANCIAL/TERMS:

Cash Investment:	$34.4-43.7K
Total Investment:	$80-150K
Minimum Net Worth:	$100K
Fees: Franchise -	$7.5-20K
Royalty - 4.5-9%;	Ad. - 1%
Earnings Claim Statement:	Yes
Term of Contract (Years):	10/5
Avg. # Of Employees:	1 FT
Passive Ownership:	Discouraged
Encourage Conversions:	N/A

Area Develop. Agreements:	No
Sub-Franchising Contracts:	No
Expand In Territory:	Yes
Space Needs: 400 SF; N/A	

SUPPORT & TRAINING PROVIDED:

Financial Assistance Provided:	Yes(D)
Site Selection Assistance:	Yes
Lease Negotiation Assistance:	No
Co-Operative Advertising:	Yes
Franchisee Assoc./Member:	No
Size Of Corporate Staff:	4
On-Going Support:	C,D,G,H,I

Training: 5 Days Fairfax, VA.

SPECIFIC EXPANSION PLANS:

US:	All United States
Canada:	All Canada
Overseas:	No

ELLIOTT & COMPANY APPRAISERS
Seven Oak Branch Dr., #C
Greensboro, NC 27407
Tel: (800) 854-5889 (336) 854-3075
Fax: (336) 854-7734
E-Mail: elliottco@elliottco.com
Web Site: www.elliottco.com
Mr. Charlie W. Elliott, Jr., President

The franchisor provides a comprehensive package of services designed to assist the franchisee in marketing residential and commercial appraisals and managing the appraisal office.

BACKGROUND:

Established: 1985;	1st Franchised: 1994
Franchised Units:	10
Company-Owned Units	4
Total Units:	14
Dist.:	US-10; CAN-0; O'seas-0
North America:	2 States
Density:	7 in NC, 3 in SC
Projected New Units (12 Months):	4
Qualifications:	3, , 5, , , 4
Registered: FL,VA	

FINANCIAL/TERMS:

Cash Investment:	$5.1-17.1K
Total Investment:	$5.1-17.1K
Minimum Net Worth:	$N/A
Fees: Franchise -	$7.5K
Royalty - 8%/$200 Min.; Ad. - 2%/$50 Min.	
Earnings Claim Statement:	No
Term of Contract (Years):	5/5
Avg. # Of Employees:	1 FT
Passive Ownership:	Allowed
Encourage Conversions:	No

Area Develop. Agreements:	No
Sub-Franchising Contracts:	No
Expand In Territory:	Yes
Space Needs: N/A SF; Commercial Office	

SUPPORT & TRAINING PROVIDED:

Financial Assistance Provided:	Yes(D)
Site Selection Assistance:	Yes
Lease Negotiation Assistance:	Yes
Co-Operative Advertising:	Yes
Franchisee Assoc./Member:	No
Size Of Corporate Staff:	3
On-Going Support:	C,D,E,h,I

Training: 2 Days Greensboro, NC.

SPECIFIC EXPANSION PLANS:

US:	All United States
Canada:	No
Overseas:	No

ERA FRANCHISE SYSTEMS
Six Sylvan Way
Parsippany, NJ 07054
Tel: (973) 496-5828
Fax: (973) 496-5904
E-Mail: jack.frost@gem.com
Web Site: www.ERA.com
Mr. Jack Frost, SVP Franchise Sales

International real estate franchising. Over 25 years' experience in developing consumer-oriented products and services. The network includes more than 2,600 independently-owned sales associates throughout the U. S. and 20 countries.

BACKGROUND: IFA MEMBER

Established: 1971;	1st Franchised: 1972
Franchised Units:	2,600
Company-Owned Units	0
Total Units:	2,600
Dist.:	US-1,300; CAN-0; O'seas-1,300
North America:	NR
Density:	NR
Projected New Units (12 Months):	NR
Registered: NR	

FINANCIAL/TERMS:

Cash Investment:	$NR
Total Investment:	$NR
Minimum Net Worth:	$NR
Fees: Franchise -	$12.5-20K
Royalty - 6%;	Ad. - 2%
Earnings Claim Statement:	No
Term of Contract (Years):	10/10
Avg. # Of Employees:	NR
Passive Ownership:	NR
Encourage Conversions:	NR
Area Develop. Agreements:	No

Sub-Franchising Contracts:	No
Expand In Territory:	NR
Space Needs: NR SF; NR	

SUPPORT & TRAINING PROVIDED:

Financial Assistance Provided:	NR
Site Selection Assistance:	NR
Lease Negotiation Assistance:	NR
Co-Operative Advertising:	NR
Franchisee Assoc./Member:	NR
Size Of Corporate Staff:	NR
On-Going Support:	NR
Training: NR	

SPECIFIC EXPANSION PLANS:

US:	All United States
Canada:	All Canada
Overseas:	Central and South America

≪ ≫

GROUP TRANS-ACTION BROKERAGE SERVICES

550 Sherbrooke St. W., # 775, W. Tower
Montreal, PQ H3A 1B9 CANADA
Tel: (514) 288-6777
Fax: (514) 288-7543
Mr. Jean-Louis Bernard, General Manager

Group of independent real estate brokers everywhere in Quebec. Complete real estate services.

BACKGROUND:

Established: 1979; 1st Franchised: 1982	
Franchised Units:	64
Company-Owned Units	0
Total Units:	64
Dist.:	US-0; CAN-64; O'seas-0
North America:	1 Province
Density:	55 in PQ
Projected New Units (12 Months):	6
Registered: AB	

FINANCIAL/TERMS:

Cash Investment:	$10K
Total Investment:	$10-50K
Minimum Net Worth:	$NR
Fees: Franchise -	$6-17K
Royalty - Flat;	Ad. - Flat
Earnings Claim Statement:	No
Term of Contract (Years):	5/1
Avg. # Of Employees:	10 FT
Passive Ownership:	Not Allowed
Encourage Conversions:	N/A
Area Develop. Agreements:	Yes
Sub-Franchising Contracts:	No
Expand In Territory:	Yes
Space Needs: 1,000 SF; FS, SF	

SUPPORT & TRAINING PROVIDED:

Financial Assistance Provided:	Yes(I)
Site Selection Assistance:	Yes

Lease Negotiation Assistance:	Yes
Co-Operative Advertising:	Yes
Franchisee Assoc./Member:	NR
Size Of Corporate Staff:	4
On-Going Support:	a,b,c,D,E,f,G,H,i
Training: 1 Week Headquarters.	

SPECIFIC EXPANSION PLANS:

US:	No
Canada:	All Canada
Overseas:	No

≪ ≫

HELP-U-SELL

6800 Jericho Tpk., # 208E
Syosset, NY 11791
Tel: (800) 366-1177 (516) 364-9650
Fax: (516) 364-8757
E-Mail: husann@aol.com
Web Site: www.helpusell.net
Ms. Ann Reynolds, VP Franchise Sales

HELP-U-SELL is the largest and oldest consumer-focused real estate company in North America. Consumers can receive comprehensive professional assistance in marketing and selling their home while saving thousands of dollars. Proven marketing system generate continuous buyer and seller leads.

BACKGROUND:

Established: 1976; 1st Franchised: 1976	
Franchised Units:	147
Company-Owned Units	0
Total Units:	147
Dist.:	US-145; CAN-2; O'seas-0
North America:	29 States, 1 Province
Density:	45 in CA, 19 in FL, 6 in MD
Projected New Units (12 Months):	50
Qualifications:	4, 4, 5, 3, 3, 4
Registered:	CA,FL,HI,IN,MD,MI,OR, RI,SD,WA,WI,DC,AB

FINANCIAL/TERMS:

Cash Investment:	$4.5K
Total Investment:	$15-45K
Minimum Net Worth:	$N/A
Fees: Franchise -	$4.5K
Royalty - 3-5.5%;	Ad. - 1%
Earnings Claim Statement:	No
Term of Contract (Years):	5/5
Avg. # Of Employees:	4-10 FT
Passive Ownership:	Discouraged
Encourage Conversions:	Yes
Area Develop. Agreements:	No
Sub-Franchising Contracts:	Yes
Expand In Territory:	No
Space Needs: 1,000 SF; FS, SF, SC, RM, Exec. Suite	

SUPPORT & TRAINING PROVIDED:

Financial Assistance Provided:	No
Site Selection Assistance:	Yes
Lease Negotiation Assistance:	No
Co-Operative Advertising:	No
Franchisee Assoc./Member:	No
Size Of Corporate Staff:	NR
On-Going Support:	c,D,e,G,h,I
Training: 4 Days San Bernadino, CA Headquarters.	

SPECIFIC EXPANSION PLANS:

US:	All United States
Canada:	All Canada
Overseas:	Asia

≪ ≫

HER REAL ESTATE

4656 Executive Dr.
Columbus, OH 43220
Tel: (800) 848-7400 (614) 459-7400
Fax: (614) 442-2880
Web Site: www.herrealtors.com
Ms. Karen S. Workman, Director of Franchising

Personalized approach to real estate financing. Brokers keep their own identity and marks of franchisor do not detract or dominate. On-location educational opportunities. Franchisee offered exclusive territory, test-marketed, award-winning marketing tools and techniques. Support program through field representation, continuing education and other unique educational opportunities.

BACKGROUND:

Established: 1976; 1st Franchised: 1981	
Franchised Units:	11
Company-Owned Units	21
Total Units:	32
Dist.:	US-32; CAN-0; O'seas-0
North America:	1 State
Density:	32 in OH
Projected New Units (12 Months):	6
Registered: NR	

FINANCIAL/TERMS:

Cash Investment:	$NR
Total Investment:	$9.3-103K
Minimum Net Worth:	$NR
Fees: Franchise -	$2.5-80K
Royalty - 5%;	Ad. - 1%
Earnings Claim Statement:	Yes
Term of Contract (Years):	5/5
Avg. # Of Employees:	NR
Passive Ownership:	Not Allowed
Encourage Conversions:	Yes
Area Develop. Agreements:	No

Sub-Franchising Contracts: Yes
Expand In Territory: Yes
Space Needs: NR SF; N/A

SUPPORT & TRAINING PROVIDED:
Financial Assistance Provided: Yes(I)
Site Selection Assistance: N/A
Lease Negotiation Assistance: No
Co-Operative Advertising: Yes
Franchisee Assoc./Member: NR
Size Of Corporate Staff: 22
On-Going Support: D,E,F,G,H,I
Training: 2 Weeks Headquarters.

SPECIFIC EXPANSION PLANS:
US: OH Only
Canada: No
Overseas: No

HOMEOWNERS CONCEPT

611 N. Mayfair Rd.
Wauwatosa, WI 53226
Tel: (800) 800-9890 (414) 258-7778
Fax: (414) 258-8276
Mr. Peter M. Skanavis, President

HOMEOWNERS CONCEPT offers a unique flat fee real estate program of consulting/sales. Extremely efficient, high-volume, very profitable operation on the cutting edge of providing "value" to the consumer. Large, exclusive territory.

BACKGROUND:
Established: 1982; 1st Franchised: 1984
Franchised Units: 39
Company-Owned Units 0
Total Units: 39
Dist.: US-38; CAN-1; O'seas-0
North America: 8 States, 1 Province
Density: 7 in WI, 6 in OH, 4 in TX
Projected New Units (12 Months): 15
Qualifications: 2, 4, 3, 2, 4, 5
Registered: IL,WI,NY,FL,WA

FINANCIAL/TERMS:
Cash Investment: $16-20K
Total Investment: $16-20K
Minimum Net Worth: $50K
Fees: Franchise - $4.5K
Royalty - 3%; Ad. - NR
Earnings Claim Statement: No
Term of Contract (Years): 10/10
Avg. # Of Employees: 5 FT
Passive Ownership: Not Allowed
Encourage Conversions: Yes
Area Develop. Agreements: No
Sub-Franchising Contracts: No
Expand In Territory: Yes
Space Needs: 700 SF; OB

SUPPORT & TRAINING PROVIDED:
Financial Assistance Provided: No
Site Selection Assistance: Yes
Lease Negotiation Assistance: No
Co-Operative Advertising: No
Franchisee Assoc./Member: No
Size Of Corporate Staff: 2
On-Going Support: d,G,H,I
Training: 1 Week Milwaukee, WI.

SPECIFIC EXPANSION PLANS:
US: All United States
Canada: All Canada
Overseas: No

≪ ≫

HOMEVESTORS OF AMERICA

11910 Greenville Ave., # 300
Dallas, TX 75243
Tel: (888) 701-3888 (972) 761-0046
Fax: (972) 761-9022
E-Mail: hvmarketing@homevestors.com
Web Site: www.homevestors.com
Mr. L. T. Jasper, Dir. Franchise Dev.

HOMEVESTORS franchise owners are real estate investors that specialize in buying and selling single-family houses. The franchise provides a system to by houses wholesale; financing to purchase houses; training and other services.

BACKGROUND:
Established: 1989; 1st Franchised: 1996
Franchised Units: 33
Company-Owned Units 0
Total Units: 33
Dist.: US-33; CAN-0; O'seas-0
North America: 6 States
Density: 13 in TX, 3 in FL, 3 in MO
Projected New Units (12 Months): 15
Qualifications: 4, 4, 3, 2, 4, 5
Registered:

FINANCIAL/TERMS:
Cash Investment: $75-125K
Total Investment: $151-180K
Minimum Net Worth: $100K
Fees: Franchise - $25-35K
Royalty - $775/Transaction; Ad. - $125/Trans.
Earnings Claim Statement: No
Term of Contract (Years): 5/5
Avg. # Of Employees: 3 FT, 1 PT
Passive Ownership: Discouraged
Encourage Conversions: Yes
Area Develop. Agreements: No
Sub-Franchising Contracts: No
Expand In Territory: No
Space Needs: 500 SF; SF

SUPPORT & TRAINING PROVIDED:
Financial Assistance Provided: No
Site Selection Assistance: Yes
Lease Negotiation Assistance: No
Co-Operative Advertising: No
Franchisee Assoc./Member: No
Size Of Corporate Staff: 14
On-Going Support: A,C,D,E,G,H
Training: 5 Days in Dallas, TX; 2 Days at Franchise Location.

SPECIFIC EXPANSION PLANS:
US: Southwest, Southeast
Canada: No
Overseas: No

≪ ≫

NATIONAL TENANT NETWORK

525 SW First, # 105, P.O. Box 1664
Lake Oswego, OR 97034
Tel: (800) 228-0989 (503) 635-1118
Fax: (503) 638-2450
E-Mail: ntn@ntnnet.com
Web Site: www.ntnnet.com
Mr. Edward F. Byczynski, President

NATIONAL TENANT NETWORK (NTN) is a network providing tenant screening services to the real estate industry. Through the NTN centralized data system of nationally networked servers, subscribers have instant access to the data maintained exclusively by NTN in 18 states. We provide automated, 24-hour a day, 7 days a week access through phone, fax, PC and modem and over the Internet. On-line service provides tenant performance data, retail credit reports, analysis and scoring as well as other information.

BACKGROUND:
Established: 1980; 1st Franchised: 1987
Franchised Units: 22
Company-Owned Units 3
Total Units: 25
Dist.: US-25; CAN-0; O'seas-0
North America: 18 States
Density: 4 in TX, 2 in CA, 2 in NJ
Projected New Units (12 Months): 4

Qualifications: 2, 3, 2, 4, 4, 3
Registered: CA,FL,IL,IN,OR,VA,WA,AB
FINANCIAL/TERMS:
Cash Investment: $40-65K
Total Investment: $80-100K
Minimum Net Worth: $N/A
Fees: Franchise - $25K
  Royalty - 10%; Ad. - 2%
Earnings Claim Statement: No
Term of Contract (Years): 10/10
Avg. # Of Employees: 2 FT, 1 PT
Passive Ownership: Discouraged
Encourage Conversions: N/A
Area Develop. Agreements: Yes/10
Sub-Franchising Contracts: No
Expand In Territory: Yes
Space Needs: 300-500 SF; FS
SUPPORT & TRAINING PROVIDED:
Financial Assistance Provided: Yes(D)
Site Selection Assistance: No
Lease Negotiation Assistance: No
Co-Operative Advertising: Yes
Franchisee Assoc./Member: No
Size Of Corporate Staff: 10
On-Going Support: a,B,C,D,E,G,H,I
Training: 2 Weeks Franchisee Location.
SPECIFIC EXPANSION PLANS:
US: All United States
Canada: All Canada
Overseas: No

◄◄ ►►

RE/MAX INTERNATIONAL
P.O. Box 3907
Englewood, CO 80155-3907
Tel: (800) 525-7452 (303) 770-5531
Fax: (303) 796-3599
E-Mail: echols@remax.net
Web Site: www.remax.com
Mr. Bill Echols, VP Public Relations

The RE/MAX real estate franchise network, now in its 29th year of consecutive growth, is a global system of more than 3,700 independently-owned and operated offices in 35 countries, engaging 64,000

members. RE/MAX sales associates lead the industry in professional designations, experience and production while providing real estate services in residential, commercial, referral, relocation and asset management. For more information visit www.remax.com.

BACKGROUND: IFA MEMBER
Established: 1973; 1st Franchised: 1975
Franchised Units: 3,713
Company-Owned Units: 0
Total Units: 3,713
Dist.: US-2,738; CAN-531; O'seas-444
  North America: 50 States,12 Provinces
  Density: 275 in CA, 211 in ON, 151 TX
Projected New Units (12 Months): 400
Qualifications: 3, 4, 5, 1, 4, 4
Registered: All States
FINANCIAL/TERMS:
Cash Investment: $20-200K
Total Investment: $20-150K
Minimum Net Worth: $Varies
Fees: Franchise - $10-25K
  Royalty - Varies; Ad. - Varies
Earnings Claim Statement: No
Term of Contract (Years): 5/5
Avg. # Of Employees: 2-4 FT, 1 PT
Passive Ownership: Discouraged
Encourage Conversions: Yes
Area Develop. Agreements: No
Sub-Franchising Contracts: Yes
Expand In Territory: Varies
Space Needs: Varies SF; FS, SF, SC, RM
SUPPORT & TRAINING PROVIDED:
Financial Assistance Provided: Yes(D)
Site Selection Assistance: Yes
Lease Negotiation Assistance: Yes
Co-Operative Advertising: N/A
Franchisee Assoc./Member: No
Size Of Corporate Staff: 250
On-Going Support: C,D,G,h,I
Training: 40+ Hours at Headquarters in
  Englewood, CO.
SPECIFIC EXPANSION PLANS:
US: All United States
Canada: All Canada
Overseas: All Free World Countries.
  Already in 75 countries. Yet to open in
  Japan.

◄◄ ►►

REALTY EXECUTIVES
INTERNATIONAL
4427 N. 36th St., # 100
Phoenix, AZ 85018
Tel: (800) 252-3366 (602) 957-0747
Fax: (602) 224-5542

E-Mail: billpowers@realtyexecutives.com
Web Site: www.realtyexecutives.com
Mr. William A. Powers, Chief Operating
  Officer

The originators of the 100% Commission Concept. Awarding franchises to use the REALTY EXECUTIVES' name.

BACKGROUND:
Established: 1965; 1st Franchised: 1987
Franchised Units: 624
Company-Owned Units: 0
Total Units: 624
Dist.: US-564; CAN-35; O'seas-25
  North America: 45 States, 5 Provinces
  Density: NR
Projected New Units (12 Months): 150
Qualifications: 4, 5, 5, 2, 3, 4
Registered:
FINANCIAL/TERMS:
Cash Investment: $25K
Total Investment: $25-82.5K
Minimum Net Worth: $30-50K
Fees: Franchise - $15K
  Royalty - $35-50/agent/mo;Ad. - $5-10/
Agent
Earnings Claim Statement: No
Term of Contract (Years): 5/5
Avg. # Of Employees: 1 FT
Passive Ownership: Allowed
Encourage Conversions: Yes
Area Develop. Agreements: Yes/5
Sub-Franchising Contracts: Yes
Expand In Territory: Yes
Space Needs: NR SF; N/A
SUPPORT & TRAINING PROVIDED:
Financial Assistance Provided: No
Site Selection Assistance: No
Lease Negotiation Assistance: No
Co-Operative Advertising: Yes
Franchisee Assoc./Member: No
Size Of Corporate Staff: 12
On-Going Support: G,h,I
Training: 4 Days at Company Headquarters
  in Phoenix.
SPECIFIC EXPANSION PLANS:
US: All United States
Canada: All Canada
Overseas: All Countries

◄◄ ►►

REMERICA REAL ESTATE
40500 Ann Arbor Rd., # 102
Plymouth, MI 48170
Tel: (800) REM-ERICA (734) 459-4500
Fax: (734) 459-1566
E-Mail: jim.preston@remerica.com
Web Site: www.remerica.com
Mr. James R. Preston, Senior VP

A cutting-edge residential real estate franchising organization. We offer broker, agent (experience and new), training, secretarial training, assist in recruiting, your own dynamic and interactive Website, intranet, technical support, TV and print advertising. See www.remerica.com.

BACKGROUND:
Established: 1988;   1st Franchised: 1990
Franchised Units: 34
Company-Owned Units   0
Total Units: 34
Dist.:   US-34; CAN-0; O'seas-0
  North America: 1 State
  Density: 34 in MI
Projected New Units (12 Months):   10
Qualifications: 5, 4, 5, 4, 2, 5
Registered: NR
FINANCIAL/TERMS:
Cash Investment: $15-70K
Total Investment: $20-100K
Minimum Net Worth: $25-100K
Fees: Franchise - $10K
  Royalty - 6%;   Ad. - 2%
Earnings Claim Statement: No
Term of Contract (Years):   5/5
Avg. # Of Employees: NR
Passive Ownership: Discouraged
Encourage Conversions: Yes
Area Develop. Agreements: No
Sub-Franchising Contracts: No
Expand In Territory: Yes
Space Needs: NR SF; FS, SF, SC, RM
SUPPORT & TRAINING PROVIDED:
Financial Assistance Provided: Yes(I)
Site Selection Assistance: Yes
Lease Negotiation Assistance: Yes
Co-Operative Advertising: Yes
Franchisee Assoc./Member: No
Size Of Corporate Staff: 12
On-Going Support: A,B,C,D,E,F,G,H,I
Training: 20+ Hours Plymouth, MI.

SPECIFIC EXPANSION PLANS:
US: All United States
Canada: All Canada
Overseas: No

◄◄ ►►

SHOWHOMES OF AMERICA
3010 LBJ Fwy., # 555
Dallas, TX 75234
Tel: (972) 243-1900
Fax: (972) 243-3909
E-Mail: showhomes@airmail.net
Web Site: www.showhomes.com
Ms. Judy Windle, Business Manager

SHOWHOMES is a dynamic, innovative marketing strategy for selling vacant homes. This is accomplished by placing a carefully selected person, with just the right furniture, to live in and present in model home conditions for sale while the home is on the market.

BACKGROUND:
Established: 1986;   1st Franchised: 1994
Franchised Units: 21
Company-Owned Units   3
Total Units: 24
Dist.:   US-24; CAN-0; O'seas-0
  North America: NR
  Density: 4 in FL, 3 in TX
Projected New Units (12 Months):   10
Qualifications: 3, 3, 4, 4, 4, 5
Registered: CA,IL,NY,VA
FINANCIAL/TERMS:
Cash Investment: $NR
Total Investment: $25-50K
Minimum Net Worth: $25K
Fees: Franchise - $15-25K
  Royalty - 10%;   Ad. - 0% Now
Earnings Claim Statement: No
Term of Contract (Years):   10/5/5
Avg. # Of Employees: 3-4 FT
Passive Ownership: Discouraged
Encourage Conversions: N/A
Area Develop. Agreements: No
Sub-Franchising Contracts: No
Expand In Territory: Yes
Space Needs: NR SF; Varies
SUPPORT & TRAINING PROVIDED:
Financial Assistance Provided: Yes(I)
Site Selection Assistance: Yes
Lease Negotiation Assistance: No

Co-Operative Advertising: Yes
Franchisee Assoc./Member: No
Size Of Corporate Staff: 5
On-Going Support: B,c,D,E,G,h
Training: 5-6 Days Dallas, TX.
SPECIFIC EXPANSION PLANS:
US: Most United States
Canada: All Canada
Overseas: No

◄◄ ►►

TUCKER ASSOCIATES
9279 N. Meridian St.
Indianapolis, IN 46260
Tel: (800) 659-0432 (317) 571-2200
Fax: (317) 571-2204
Web Site: www.talktotucker.com
Mr. Mark Bush, Senior Vice President

Real estate franchisor for the State of Indiana, offering marketing, recruiting, training and relocation leads for franchisees. Number one company in Indiana and recently named # 10 brand name of independently-owned companies.

BACKGROUND:
Established: 1918;   1st Franchised: 1989
Franchised Units: 19
Company-Owned Units   14
Total Units: 33
Dist.:   US-33; CAN-0; O'seas-0
  North America: 1 State
  Density: 33 in IN
Projected New Units (12 Months):   3-4
Qualifications: 5, 5, 5, 3, 4, 5
Registered: IL,IN
FINANCIAL/TERMS:
Cash Investment: $100-200K
Total Investment: $125-250K
Minimum Net Worth: $25K
Fees: Franchise - $0
  Royalty - 6%;   Ad. - 0%
Earnings Claim Statement: No
Term of Contract (Years):   6/5
Avg. # Of Employees: 1-2 FT, 3 PT
Passive Ownership: Discouraged

387

Encourage Conversions: Yes
Area Develop. Agreements: No
Sub-Franchising Contracts: No
Expand In Territory: Yes
Space Needs: 1,500 SF; FS, SF, SC

SUPPORT & TRAINING PROVIDED:

Financial Assistance Provided: Yes
Site Selection Assistance: Yes
Lease Negotiation Assistance: Yes
Co-Operative Advertising: N/A
Franchisee Assoc./Member: No
Size Of Corporate Staff: 3
On-Going Support: a,B,C,D,E,G,h
Training: 2 Weeks Indianapolis, IN.

SPECIFIC EXPANSION PLANS:

US: IN, Surrounding States
Canada: No
Overseas: No

≪ ≫

SUPPLEMENTAL LISTING
OF FRANCHISORS

America's Choice, 636 N. French, # 10, Amherst, NY 14228 ; (716) 691-0650; Mr. David Schembri (800) 831-2493; (716) 691-0596

Buck-A-Stall Parking Lot Painting, P.O. Box 100945, Denver, CO 80250-0945 ; (303) 806-0288; Mr. Jim Shafer (800) 321-BUCK; (303) 806-0288

Buy Owner, 5757 N. Andrews Way, Ft. Lauderdale, FL 33309 ; (954) 771-8187; Mr. Charles Eckert (800) 771-7777; (954) 771-7777

Castles Unlimited, 837 Beacon St., Newton Centre, MA 02159 ; (617) 244-5847; Mr. James D. Lowenstern ; (617) 964-3300

Century 21 Real Estate Canada, 700-1199 W. Pender St., Vancouver, BC V6E 2R1 CANADA; (604) 606-2125; Mr. C. Brian Rushton ; (604) 606-2100

Comreal International, 8725 NW 18th Ter., # 105, Miami, FL 33172 ; (305) 591-9704; Mr. Stephen H. Smith ; (305) 591-3044

Empire World Realty, 336 Harris Hill Rd., Buffalo, NY 14221 ; (716) 677-0955; Mr. Nicholas R. Gugliuzza ; (716) 677-5229

EWM, Inc., 4760 Route 9, S., Howell, NJ 07731 ; (732) 905-8606; Ms. Mary P. Muldaur (800) 396-4621; (732) 364-5900

Fair Realty Executives Company, 320 N. Lake St., Aurora, IL 60506 ; (630) 897-7750; Mr. Roy Fair (800) 553-3247; (630) 897-7600

Keller Williams Realtors, 3701 Bee Cave Rd., # 200, Austin, TX 78746 ; (512) 328-1433; Ms. Annie Osborn ; (512) 327-3070

Mortgage Services Associates (MSA), 19 Thompson St., East Haven, CT 06513 ; (203) 468-2587; Mr. Joseph D. Raffone ; (203) 468-6612

National Apartment Services, 7644-B Fullerton Rd., Springfield, VA 22153 ; (703) 455-3475; Mr. Dave Walker (888) 356-3535;

National Real Estate Service, 4100 Newport Pl., # 730, Newport Beach, CA 92660 ; (949) 660-1910; Mr. Andrew Cimerman (800) 654-7653; (949) 660-1919

Property Investment Group Services, 312 12th St., NW, Canton, OH 44703 ; (330) 453-5420; Mr. Steve Vandegrift (800) 949-7447; (330) 453-5406

Prudential Real Estate Affiliates, 3333 Michelson Dr., #1000, Irvine, CA 92612 ; (949) 794-7031; Ms. Linda Haley (800) 477-7732; (949) 794-7900

Qpoint Home Mortgage Network, 10900 NE 4th St., #1040, Bellevue, WA 98004 ; (425) 462-4691; Ms. Minday E. Greene ; (425) 462-6562

RE/MAX Ontario/Atlantic, 7101 Syntex Dr., Mississauga, ON L5N 6H5 CANADA; (905) 542-2318; Mr. Michael Polzler (888) 542-2499; (905) 542-2400

Real Estate One, 521 Randolph, Traverse City, MI 49684 ; (616) 946-4339; Mr. Gary L. Pownall ; (616) 946-4040

Realty 3 of America, 1278 San Antonio Creek Rd., Santa Barbara, CA 93111 ; (805) 683-1179; Mr. Mack Maho ; (805) 683-2044

Realty 500, 4600 Kietzke Ln, # M247, Reno, NV 89502-5046 ; (775) 689-8546; Mr. Mark Ashworth (800) 554-0823; (775) 689-8545

Realty One, 7310 Potomac Dr., Boise, ID 83704 ; (208) 322-2756; Mr. David W. Dildine (800) REALTY-1; (208) 322-2700

Realty World, 4100 Newport Place, # 720, Newport Beach, CA 92660 ; (949) 251-1066; Ms. Annie Garzon (800) 685-4984; (949) 251-0745

Sears Termite & Pest Control, 6359 Edgewater Dr,, Orlando, FL 32810 ; (407) 523-9888; Mr. Kurt Miller (800) 528-7287;

State Wide Real Estate Services, P.O. Box 297, Escanaba, MI 49829 ; (906) 786-1388; Mr. Richard J. Langley (800) 682-9123; (906) 786-8392

RECREATION & ENTERTAINMENT INDUSTRY PROFILE

Total # Franchisors in Industry Group	36
Total # Franchised Units in Industry Group	2,247
Total # Company-Owned Units in Industry Group	<u>132</u>
Total # Operating Units in Industry Group	2,379
Average # Franchised Units/Franchisor	62.4
Average # Company-Owned Units/Franchisor	<u>3.7</u>
Average # Total Units/Franchisor	66.1
Ratio of Total # Franchised Units/Total # Company-Owned Units	17.0:1
Industry Survey Participants	12
Representing % of Industry	33.3%
Average Franchise Fee*:	$17.3K
Average Total Investment*:	$366.7K
Average On-Going Royalty Fee*:	8.5%

If a range was provided, the mid-point of the range was used. See detailed profiles for actual ranges.

FIVE LARGEST PARTICIPANTS IN SURVEY

Company	# Fran-chised Units	# Co-Owned Units	# Total Units	Franchise Fee	On-Going Royalty	Total Investment
1. World Gym	260	0	260	12.8K	$6.5K/Yr.	221-632K
2. American Poolplayers Association	234	1	234	Varies	20%	4.3-6.2K
3. Putt-Putt Golf Courses	201	6	207	5-30K	5%	100K-5MM
4. Complete Music	148	1	149	15.5K	8%	15.5-35K
5. Outdoor Connection	81	2	83	8.5K	2-5%	9.2-13K

All of the data provided are proprietary and should not be quoted without acknowledging *Bond's Franchise Guide.*

AMERICAN DARTERS ASSOCIATION

1000 Lake Saint Louis Blvd., # 310
Lake St. Louis, MO 63367
Tel: (888) 327-8752 (636) 625-8621
Fax: (636) 625-2975
E-Mail: adadarts@inlink.com
Web Site: www.adadarters.com
Mr. Glenn Remick, President

ADA franchisees offer recreational dart leagues using the Neutralizer, a copyrighted handicap system that neutralizes play. The league currently consists of 15,000 members who compete in year-round weekly play. Franchisees receive customized software, complete training, technical updates, support and networking opportunities at the national convention.

BACKGROUND:

Established: 1990;	1st Franchised: 1991
Franchised Units:	75
Company-Owned Units	0
Total Units:	75
Dist.:	US-75; CAN-0; O'seas-0
North America:	26 States
Density:	TX, IL, MO
Projected New Units (12 Months):	12
Qualifications:	3, 3, 3, 3, 3, 2
Registered: All States Except OR,AB

FINANCIAL/TERMS:

Cash Investment:	$1-2.3K
Total Investment:	$1.5-2.8K
Minimum Net Worth:	$Varies
Fees: Franchise -	$By Population
Royalty - 20%;	Ad. - N/A
Earnings Claim Statement:	No
Term of Contract (Years):	1.5/5
Avg. # Of Employees:	Varies
Passive Ownership:	Not Allowed
Encourage Conversions:	N/A
Area Develop. Agreements:	No
Sub-Franchising Contracts:	No
Expand In Territory:	Yes
Space Needs: N/A SF; N/A

SUPPORT & TRAINING PROVIDED:

Financial Assistance Provided:	No
Site Selection Assistance:	Yes
Lease Negotiation Assistance:	N/A
Co-Operative Advertising:	No
Franchisee Assoc./Member:	No
Size Of Corporate Staff:	2
On-Going Support:	A,B,C,D,F,G,H,I
Training: 3 Days Lake Saint Louis, MO.

SPECIFIC EXPANSION PLANS:

US:	All United States
Canada:	No
Overseas:	No

<< >>

AMERICAN MOBILE SOUND

600 Ward Dr., # A-1
Santa Barbara, CA 93111
Tel: (800) 788-9007 (805) 681-8132
Fax: (805) 681-8134
Mr. Tad Clark, Franchise Dev. Coordinator

Each franchisee receives a comprehensive, step-by-step, customer-oriented training program enabling him or her to provide the highest-quality, most consistent, affordable disc jockey service, utilizing state-of-the art, high-quality sound and with professionally-trained DJ's for any event, as well as a complete music library with updates - 'Imagine...a career you can truly enjoy.'

BACKGROUND:

Established: 1991;	1st Franchised: 1994
Franchised Units:	31
Company-Owned Units	0
Total Units:	31
Dist.:	US-28; CAN-0; O'seas-0
North America:	12 States
Density:	9 in CA, 5 in CO, 3 in TX
Projected New Units (12 Months):	12
Qualifications:	2, 2, 1, 1, 3, 5
Registered: CA

FINANCIAL/TERMS:

Cash Investment:	$10-87K
Total Investment:	$10-87K
Minimum Net Worth:	$10K
Fees: Franchise -	$6-15K
Royalty - 7%/$150;	Ad. - 0%
Earnings Claim Statement:	No
Term of Contract (Years):	10/10
Avg. # Of Employees:	5 PT
Passive Ownership:	Allowed
Encourage Conversions:	N/A
Area Develop. Agreements:	No
Sub-Franchising Contracts:	No
Expand In Territory:	Yes
Space Needs: 250 SF; HB, OB

SUPPORT & TRAINING PROVIDED:

Financial Assistance Provided:	Yes
Site Selection Assistance:	Yes
Lease Negotiation Assistance:	Yes
Co-Operative Advertising:	N/A
Franchisee Assoc./Member:	Yes/Yes
Size Of Corporate Staff:	2
On-Going Support:	b,C,D,d,E,G,H,I
Training: 9 Days Santa Barbara, CA.

SPECIFIC EXPANSION PLANS:

US:	All United States
Canada:	No
Overseas:	No

<< >>

THE GOVERNING BODY OF AMATEUR POOL ®

AMERICAN POOLPLAYERS ASSOCIATION

1000 Lake St. Louis Blvd., # 325
Lake St. Louis, MO 63367
Tel: (800) 3-RACKEM (636) 625-8611
Fax: (636) 625-2975
E-Mail: khinkebein@poolplayers.com
Web Site: www.poolplayers.com
Franchise Development Manager,

APA franchisees operate recreational pool leagues utilizing "The Equalizer", a unique handicap system that equalizes play. The League, previously known as the Bud Light Pool League or the Camel pool League and now known nationally as the "APA Pool League", currently consists of over 170,000 members who compete in year-round weekly play. Franchisees receive customized software, technical updates, complete training, marketing support and networking opportunities at the annual convention.

BACKGROUND: IFA MEMBER

Established: 1980;	1st Franchised: 1982
Franchised Units:	234
Company-Owned Units	0
Total Units:	234
Dist.:	US-220; CAN-14; O'seas-0
North America:	46 States, 5 Provinces
Density:	14 in IL, 16 in FL, 13 in CA
Projected New Units (12 Months):	20
Qualifications:	2, 4, 2, 3, 3, 5
Registered: CA,FL,HI,IL,IN,MD,MI,MN, NY,ND,RI,SD,VA,WA,WI

FINANCIAL/TERMS:

Cash Investment:	$4.3-6.2K
Total Investment:	$4.3-6.2K
Minimum Net Worth:	$N/A
Fees: Franchise -	$Varies
Royalty - 20%;	Ad. - N/A
Earnings Claim Statement:	No
Term of Contract (Years):	2/5/10
Avg. # Of Employees:	Varies
Passive Ownership:	Not Allowed
Encourage Conversions:	N/A
Area Develop. Agreements:	No

Sub-Franchising Contracts: No
Expand In Territory: N/A
Space Needs: N/A SF; HB
SUPPORT & TRAINING PROVIDED:
Financial Assistance Provided: Yes(D)
Site Selection Assistance: Yes
Lease Negotiation Assistance: N/A
Co-Operative Advertising: Yes
Franchisee Assoc./Member: Yes/No
Size Of Corporate Staff: 40+
On-Going Support: A,D,G,H
Training: 6 Days APA Home Office.
SPECIFIC EXPANSION PLANS:
US: All United States
Canada: All Canada
Overseas: No

◄◄ ►►

7270 ROSWELL ROAD • (770) 395-0724

CINEMA GRILL
P.O. Box 28467
Atlanta, GA 30319
Tel: (404) 250-9536
Fax: (404) 256-1569
E-Mail: cinegrill@aol.com
Web Site: www.cinemagrill.com
Mr. John J. Duffy, Vice President

CINEMA GRILL, with the contemporary décor, wide beverage selection and tempting food offered by our hospitable staff bring together the theatre of the past with an unforgettable dining experience. We welcome you to a unique idea, a very special environment and an affordable and enjoyable evening out.

BACKGROUND: IFA MEMBER
Established: 1995; 1st Franchised: 1995
Franchised Units: 25
Company-Owned Units: 1
Total Units: 26
Dist.: US-26; CAN-0; O'seas-0
North America: 9 States
Density: 3 in VA, 3 in MD, 2 in NC
Projected New Units (12 Months): 10
Qualifications: 4, 4, 2, 2, 4, 4
Registered: All States
FINANCIAL/TERMS:
Cash Investment: $100K
Total Investment: $500K
Minimum Net Worth: $100-250K
Fees: Franchise - $30K
Royalty - 3%; Ad. - 0%

Earnings Claim Statement: No
Term of Contract (Years): 10/10
Avg. # Of Employees: 40 FT
Passive Ownership: Allowed
Encourage Conversions: Yes
Area Develop. Agreements: Yes/10
Sub-Franchising Contracts: No
Expand In Territory: Yes
Space Needs: 10,000-25,000 SF; FS, SC, RM
SUPPORT & TRAINING PROVIDED:
Financial Assistance Provided: Yes(I)
Site Selection Assistance: Yes
Lease Negotiation Assistance: Yes
Co-Operative Advertising: No
Franchisee Assoc./Member: Yes/Yes
Size Of Corporate Staff: 12
On-Going Support: C,E,f,G,H,I
Training: 3 Weeks Corporate Store.
SPECIFIC EXPANSION PLANS:
US: All United States
Canada: All Canada
Overseas: All Countries

◄◄ ►►

COMPLETE MUSIC
7877 L St.
Omaha, NE 68127
Tel: (800) 843-3866 (402) 339-0001
Fax: (402) 339-1285
E-Mail: comucorp@aol.com
Web Site: www.cmusic.com
Mr. Kem Matthews, Franchise Director

COMPLETE MUSIC is the leader in disc jockey entertainment, providing dance music for over 1 million people each year. The uniqueness of this business allows owners, who need not be entertainers, to use their skills in management to hire and book their own musically-trained DJ's for all types of special events.

BACKGROUND:
Established: 1972; 1st Franchised: 1982
Franchised Units: 148
Company-Owned Units: 1
Total Units: 149
Dist.: US-140; CAN-4; O'seas-0
North America: 31 States, 1 Province
Density: 21 in TX, 11 in NE, 8 in CO
Projected New Units (12 Months): 6-12
Qualifications: 3, 4, 1, 4, 4, 3
Registered: CA,FL,IL,IN,MD,MI,MN, OR,SD,WA,WI
FINANCIAL/TERMS:
Cash Investment: $9.5-24.5K
Total Investment: $15.5-35K

Minimum Net Worth: $N/A
Fees: Franchise - $15.5K
Royalty - 8%; Ad. - 4%
Earnings Claim Statement: Yes
Term of Contract (Years): Lifetime
Avg. # Of Employees: 2 FT, 5-40 PT
Passive Ownership: Discouraged
Encourage Conversions: Yes
Area Develop. Agreements: No
Sub-Franchising Contracts: No
Expand In Territory: Yes
Space Needs: N/A SF; HB
SUPPORT & TRAINING PROVIDED:
Financial Assistance Provided: Yes(D)
Site Selection Assistance: Yes
Lease Negotiation Assistance: Yes
Co-Operative Advertising: Yes
Franchisee Assoc./Member: Yes/Yes
Size Of Corporate Staff: 5
On-Going Support: B,c,D,E,F,G,h,i
Training: 9 Days Omaha, NE; 4 Days On-Site.
SPECIFIC EXPANSION PLANS:
US: All United States
Canada: All Canada
Overseas: No

◄◄ ►►

DUFFERIN GAME ROOM STORE
3770 Nashua Dr.
Mississauga, ON L4V 1M6 CANADA
Tel: (800) 268-2597 (905) 677-7665
Fax: (800) 387-3157
Ms. Sarah Stone, Contract Manager

Canada's premier retailer of family games, specializing in high-quality DUFFERIN billiard equipment and 3,000 other games to enjoy quality time with family and friends.

BACKGROUND:
Established: 1986; 1st Franchised: 1987
Franchised Units: 18
Company-Owned Units: 26
Total Units: 44
Dist.: US-0; CAN-44; O'seas-0
North America: 7 Provinces
Density: 20 in ON, 9 in AB, 6 in BC
Projected New Units (12 Months): 2-3
Qualifications: 5, 4, 3, 3, 3, 5
Registered: AB
FINANCIAL/TERMS:
Cash Investment: $143K
Total Investment: $357K
Minimum Net Worth: $TBA
Fees: Franchise - $28.6K
Royalty - 5%; Ad. - 2%

Earnings Claim Statement:	No
Term of Contract (Years):	10/5
Avg. # Of Employees:	3 FT, 6 PT
Passive Ownership:	Not Allowed
Encourage Conversions:	No
Area Develop. Agreements:	No
Sub-Franchising Contracts:	No
Expand In Territory:	No
Space Needs: 3,000-3,500 SF; FS, SC, RM	

SUPPORT & TRAINING PROVIDED:

Financial Assistance Provided:	No
Site Selection Assistance:	Yes
Lease Negotiation Assistance:	Yes
Co-Operative Advertising:	Yes
Franchisee Assoc./Member:	Yes/Yes
Size Of Corporate Staff:	300
On-Going Support:	C,D,E,F,G,h,I
Training: Head Office.	

SPECIFIC EXPANSION PLANS:

US:	No
Canada:	No
Overseas:	No

<< >>

HOOP MOUNTAIN

130 Centre St., # 7
Danvers, MA 01923
Tel: (800) 819-8445
Fax: (978) 774-8628
Mr. Steven Gibbs, President

Basketball camp. Manage tournaments. Manage all-star games. Manage exposure events.

BACKGROUND:

Established: 1985;	1st Franchised: 1996
Franchised Units:	8
Company-Owned Units	1
Total Units:	9
Dist.:	US-5; CAN-2; O'seas-0
North America:	14 States
Density:	2 in MA, 2 in CT, 2 in RI
Projected New Units (12 Months):	3-5
Qualifications:	3, 4, 1, 4, 3, 4
Registered: FL	

FINANCIAL/TERMS:

Cash Investment:	$10K
Total Investment:	$10-20K
Minimum Net Worth:	$50K
Fees: Franchise -	$10K
Royalty - 8%;	Ad. - N/A
Earnings Claim Statement:	Yes
Term of Contract (Years):	10/10
Avg. # Of Employees:	1 FT or 1 PT
Passive Ownership:	Not Allowed
Encourage Conversions:	No
Area Develop. Agreements:	Yes

Sub-Franchising Contracts:	Yes
Expand In Territory:	Yes
Space Needs: N/A SF; N/A	

SUPPORT & TRAINING PROVIDED:

Financial Assistance Provided:	Yes
Site Selection Assistance:	Yes
Lease Negotiation Assistance:	Yes
Co-Operative Advertising:	No
Franchisee Assoc./Member:	No
Size Of Corporate Staff:	1
On-Going Support:	A,B,C,D,F,I
Training: 2 Weeks in Boston, MA.	

SPECIFIC EXPANSION PLANS:

US:	NR
Canada:	No
Overseas:	All Countries

<< >>

OUTDOOR CONNECTION

108 W. Rutledge, P.O. Box 307
Yates Center, KS 66783
Tel: (316) 625-3466
Fax: (316) 625-3494
Web Site: www.outdoor-connection.com
Mr. Marc Glades, President

Market fishing and hunting trips. Trips are in North and Central America.

BACKGROUND:

Established: 1988;	1st Franchised: 1989
Franchised Units:	81
Company-Owned Units	2
Total Units:	83
Dist.:	US-83; CAN-0; O'seas-0
North America:	NR
Density:	13 in MN, 9 in IL, 7 in IA
Projected New Units (12 Months):	15
Qualifications:	3, 2, 2, 2, 3, 2
Registered: CA,FL,IL,IN,,MD,MI,MN,NY, ND,OR,VA,WA,WI	

FINANCIAL/TERMS:

Cash Investment:	$8.5-11.5K
Total Investment:	$9.2-13K
Minimum Net Worth:	$None
Fees: Franchise -	$8.5K
Royalty - 2-5%;	Ad. - 1%

Earnings Claim Statement:	No
Term of Contract (Years):	5/5
Avg. # Of Employees:	1 FT, 1 PT
Passive Ownership:	Not Allowed
Encourage Conversions:	N/A
Area Develop. Agreements:	No
Sub-Franchising Contracts:	No
Expand In Territory:	Yes
Space Needs: N/A SF; N/A	

SUPPORT & TRAINING PROVIDED:

Financial Assistance Provided:	Yes(D)
Site Selection Assistance:	No
Lease Negotiation Assistance:	N/A
Co-Operative Advertising:	Yes
Franchisee Assoc./Member:	No
Size Of Corporate Staff:	6
On-Going Support:	D,E,G,H
Training: 1.5 Days at Yates Center, KS (Home Office); 1.5 Days Franchisee Site (If Appropriate).	

SPECIFIC EXPANSION PLANS:

US:	All United States
Canada:	All Canada
Overseas:	No

<< >>

PUTT-PUTT GOLF COURSES OF AMERICA

3007 Ft. Bragg Rd.
Fayetteville, NC 28303-0237
Tel: (910) 485-7131
Fax: (910) 485-1122
Web Site: www.putt-putt.com
Mr. Scott Anderson, National Franchise Director

PUTT-PUTT GOLF is now in its 44th year of operation. It is the oldest and largest operator/franchisor of miniature golf and family entertainment centers in the world. PUTT-PUTT GOLF operates in 28 states and in 8 foreign countries and specializes in the development of PUTT-PUTT GOLF, gamerooms, batting cages, bumpercars, go-carts, laser tag and total play.

BACKGROUND:

Established: 1954;	1st Franchised: 1955
Franchised Units:	201
Company-Owned Units	6
Total Units:	207
Dist.:	US-186; CAN-1; O'seas-21
North America:	28 States, 1 Province
Density:	28 in TX, 25 in NC, 21 in OH
Projected New Units (12 Months):	12
Qualifications:	4, 5, 2, 3, 3, 4
Registered: All States and AB	

FINANCIAL/TERMS:

Cash Investment:	$30K-1MM
Total Investment:	$100K-5MM
Minimum Net Worth:	$100K
Fees: Franchise -	$5-30K
Royalty - 5%;	Ad. - 2%
Earnings Claim Statement:	No
Term of Contract (Years):	40
Avg. # Of Employees:	NR
Passive Ownership:	Allowed
Encourage Conversions:	N/A
Area Develop. Agreements:	No
Sub-Franchising Contracts:	No
Expand In Territory:	No
Space Needs: 3-7 acres SF; N/A	

SUPPORT & TRAINING PROVIDED:

Financial Assistance Provided:	Yes(I)
Site Selection Assistance:	Yes
Lease Negotiation Assistance:	Yes
Co-Operative Advertising:	No
Franchisee Assoc./Member:	No
Size Of Corporate Staff:	24
On-Going Support:	C,D,G,H,I
Training: 1 Week in Fayetteville, NC; 3-7 Days at Franchisee's Location.	

SPECIFIC EXPANSION PLANS:

US:	All United States
Canada:	All Canada
Overseas:	South America

<< >>

GROVE RECREATIONS INCORPORATED

(803) 236-4733
Fax (803) 236-0336

THEMED MINIATURE GOLF COURSES

P.O. Box 2435
Myrtle Beach, SC 29578-2435
Tel: (843) 236-4733
Fax: (843) 249-2118
E-Mail: chgrove@sccoast.net
Mr. Charles H. Grove, President

Themed, contoured adventure-type miniature golf courses with lakes, streambeds and waterfalls. Lush landscaping and the very finest designed, unique, playable holes that invite repeat participation. We also design and build complete family entertainment centers.

BACKGROUND:

Established: 1977;	1st Franchised: 1985
Franchised Units:	12
Company-Owned Units	4

Total Units:	16
Dist.:	US-16; CAN-0; O'seas-0
North America:	10 States
Density:	SC, FL, TX
Projected New Units (12 Months):	5
Qualifications:	5, 4, 2, 2, 3, 4
Registered: NR	

FINANCIAL/TERMS:

Cash Investment:	$62.5K-100K
Total Investment:	$250-400K
Minimum Net Worth:	$N/A
Fees: Franchise -	$N/A
Royalty - N/A;	Ad. - N/A
Earnings Claim Statement:	No
Term of Contract (Years):	Unlimited
Avg. # Of Employees:	2 FT, 2 PT
Passive Ownership:	Allowed
Encourage Conversions:	N/A
Area Develop. Agreements:	No
Sub-Franchising Contracts:	No
Expand In Territory:	Yes
Space Needs: 30,000 SF; FS	

SUPPORT & TRAINING PROVIDED:

Financial Assistance Provided:	N/A
Site Selection Assistance:	Yes
Lease Negotiation Assistance:	Yes
Co-Operative Advertising:	No
Franchisee Assoc./Member:	Yes/Yes
Size Of Corporate Staff:	5
On-Going Support:	B,C,D
Training: NR	

SPECIFIC EXPANSION PLANS:

US:	All United States
Canada:	All Canada
Overseas:	No

<< >>

WOODY'S WOOD SHOPS

1814 Franklin St., # 820
Oakland, CA 94612
Tel: (510) 839-5462
Fax: (510) 839-2104
Dr. Christo L. Bruiser, President

WOODY'S WOOD SHOPS offer instruction and use of virtually all shop tools in a fully-outfitted wood shop. After detailed instruction and testing, members have full use of shop and related facilities. Open 15 hours/day, 7 days/week. Also sell small tools and all power equipment at cost plus 5%. Members pay front-end fees plus dues.

BACKGROUND:

Established: 1978;	1st Franchised: 1980
Franchised Units:	28
Company-Owned Units	14

Total Units:	42
Dist.:	US-33; CAN-6; O'seas-0
North America:	7 States, 2 Provinces
Density:	16 in CA, 8 in OR, 3 in WA
Projected New Units (12 Months):	4
Registered: NR	

FINANCIAL/TERMS:

Cash Investment:	$72K
Total Investment:	$85-185K
Minimum Net Worth:	$NR
Fees: Franchise -	$22K
Royalty - 6%;	Ad. - 2%
Earnings Claim Statement:	Yes
Term of Contract (Years):	15/15
Avg. # Of Employees:	1 FT, 4 PT
Passive Ownership:	Discouraged
Encourage Conversions:	Yes
Area Develop. Agreements:	Yes/15
Sub-Franchising Contracts:	Yes
Expand In Territory:	No
Space Needs: 2,800-3,400 SF; FS, Warehouse	

SUPPORT & TRAINING PROVIDED:

Financial Assistance Provided:	Yes(D)
Site Selection Assistance:	Yes
Lease Negotiation Assistance:	Yes
Co-Operative Advertising:	Yes
Franchisee Assoc./Member:	NR
Size Of Corporate Staff:	21
On-Going Support:	A,C,D,g,H,i
Training: 3 Weeks Headquarters; 2 Weeks On-Site; On-Going.	

SPECIFIC EXPANSION PLANS:

US:	All United States
Canada:	ON Only
Overseas:	No

<< >>

WORLD GYM

3223 Washington Blvd.
Marina Del Rey, CA 90405
Tel: (800) 544-7441 (310) 827-6355
Fax: (310) 827-7705
E-Mail: info@worldgym.com
Web Site: www.worldgym.com
Mr. Mike Uretz, Chief Executive Officer

The franchise originally started with hard-core bodybuilding gyms and has evolved into fitness centers. We encourage franchisees to purchase state-of-the-art equipment catering to all types of members - from individual members, to families, to corporate memberships. The business involves the sale of gym memberships, clothing, accessories and food and vitamin supplements.

BACKGROUND:

Established: 1977; 1st Franchised: 1985
Franchised Units: 260
Company-Owned Units 0
Total Units: 260
Dist.: US-244; CAN-3; O'seas-13
  North America: 36 States, 2 Provinces
  Density: 32 in FL, 25 in CA, 22 in NY
Projected New Units (12 Months): 50
Registered: CA,FL,HI,IL,IN,MD,MI,MN,
  NY,ND,RI,SD,VA,WA

FINANCIAL/TERMS:

Cash Investment: $221.3K
Total Investment: $221.3-632K
Minimum Net Worth: $300K
Fees: Franchise - $12.75K
  Royalty - $6.5K/Yr.; Ad. - 0%
Earnings Claim Statement: No
Term of Contract (Years): 5/5
Avg. # Of Employees: 3-5 FT, 3 PT
Passive Ownership: Allowed
Encourage Conversions: Yes
Area Develop. Agreements: Yes/6
Sub-Franchising Contracts: Yes
Expand In Territory: Yes
Space Needs: 10,000-15,000 SF; SC, RM

SUPPORT & TRAINING PROVIDED:

Financial Assistance Provided: No
Site Selection Assistance: Yes
Lease Negotiation Assistance: Yes
Co-Operative Advertising: No
Franchisee Assoc./Member: No
Size Of Corporate Staff: 4
On-Going Support: d,G,H,I
Training: 4 WORLD GYM Universities
  per Year.

SPECIFIC EXPANSION PLANS:

US: All United States
Canada: All Canada
Overseas: All Countries

**SUPPLEMENTAL LISTING
OF FRANCHISORS**

A Corporate A'fair, 1922 Lynn Brook Pl., Memphis, TN 38116 ; (901) 398-5081; Mr. David F. Martin, Sr. (800) 783-8386; (901) 398-4386

Advantage Golf Tournament Service, 3728 Realty Rd., Addison, TX 75001 ; (972) 243-4694; Mr. Michael Price (800) 659-2815; (972) 243-6209

Amacade Centers, P.O. Box 24, Fayetteville, AR 72702 ; (501) 443-4024; Mr. Henry Nwauwa ; (501) 443-6791

Arnold Palmer Golf Management International, 6751 Forum Dr., # 200, Orlando, FL 32821 ; (407) 926-2550; Ms. Staci Killam (888) 532-1131; (407) 926-2500

ATEC Grand Slam U.S.A., 10931 Crabapple Rd. # 103A, Rosell, GA 30075 ; (707) 552-3503; Mr. Ken Hinson (800) 775-2607;

Body Balance For Performance, 3923 Foothill Blvd., La Crescenta, CA 91214 ; (818) 957-9343; Mr. Scott Tregurtha (800) 473-6211;

Canadian Pool League, 200 McNab St., # 201, P.O. Box 722, Walkerton, ON N0G 2V0 CANADA; (519) 881-2520; Mr. Lindsay Dobson (877) 919-7665; (519) 881-2196

Fred Astaire Dance Studios, 7900 Glades Rd., # 630, Boca Raton, FL 33434 ; (561) 218-3299; Ms. Linda Milo (800) 278-2473; (561) 218-3237

Gold's Gym, 358 Hampton Dr., Venice, CA 90291 ; (310) 392-4680; Mr. Paul Grymkowski ; (310) 392-3005

National Athletic Club, 709 Johnnie Dodds, Mount Pleasant, SC 29464 ; ; Mr. Michael Mason (888) TAN-CLUB; (843) 849-3000

Pump Radio Network, 2820 Jefferson Ave., Midland, MI 48640 ; (517) 837-3597; Mr. Richard Zimmer (877) 682-5537; (517) 837-2460

Scorecaster, P.O. Box 5, Westwood, MA 02090 ; (781) 329-2217; Mr. Chris Thompson ; (781) 461-1717

Side Pockets, 13320 W. 87th St. Pkwy., Lenexa, KS 66215 ; (913) 888-8869; Mr. Richard Hawkins (800) 490-9810; (913) 888-POOL

Table For Eight, 60 Thackeray Rd., Wellesley, MA 02481 ; (781) 431-0106; Ms. Johanna S. Noyes (888) 8-TABLE8; (781) 239-3370

Team Golf, 1776 Woodstead Ct., # 213, The Woodlands, TX 77380 ; (713) 362-8888; Mr. Jim Mainer (800) 282-8326; (713) 362-7777

Together Dating Service, 5026 Dorsey Hall, #205, Ellicott City, MD 21024 ; (410) 992-6910; Mr. Brad Megahan (877) 730-8866; (410) 730-8866

U Paint Design Studios, 7855 E. Evans, Scottsdale, AZ 85260 ; (602) 922-7283; Mr. John Hall ; (602) 922-9959

Ultrazone, 2880 E. Flamingo Rd., # E, Las Vegas, NV 89121 ; (702) 734-3618; Mr. Brian Sweet (800) 628-2829; (702) 734-3617

Villari's Self Defense Centers, 101 Cedar Grove Ln., # 105, Somerset, NJ 08873 ; (732) 563-0325; Mr. Anthony R. Biele ; (732) 563-0707

RENTAL SERVICES INDUSTRY PROFILE

Total # Franchisors in Industry Group	11
Total # Franchised Units in Industry Group	2,478
Total # Company-Owned Units in Industry Group	<u>3,578</u>
Total # Operating Units in Industry Group	2,856
Average # Franchised Units/Franchisor	225.3
Average # Company-Owned Units/Franchisor	<u>34.4</u>
Average # Total Units/Franchisor	259.7
Ratio of Total # Franchised Units/Total # Company-Owned Units	6.6:1
Industry Survey Participants	8
Representing % of Industry	72.7%
Average Franchise Fee*:	$16.7K
Average Total Investment*:	$199.6
Average On-Going Royalty Fee*:	5.0%

If a range was provided, the mid-point of the range was used. See detailed profiles for actual ranges.

FIVE LARGEST PARTICIPANTS IN SURVEY

Company	# Fran-chised Units	# Co-Owned Units	# Total Units	Franchise Fee	On-Going Royalty	Total Investment
1. Grand Rental Station/Taylor	1,272	0	1,272	1.5K	1.3%	225-250K
2. Aaron's Sales & Lease Ownership	186	238	424	35K	5%	207-440K
3. Nation-Wide General Rental	376	1	377	0K	0%	80-178K
4. Colortyme	352	0	352	25K	4%	272-479K
5. Gingiss Formal Wear	189	49	238	15K	6%	99-243K

All of the data provided are proprietary and should not be quoted without acknowledging *Bond's Franchise Guide.*

Aaron's

AARON'S SALES & LEASE OWNERSHIP

309 E. Paces Ferry Rd., N. E.
Atlanta, GA 30305-2377
Tel: (800) 551-6015 (404) 237-4016
Fax: (404) 240-6540
E-Mail: jimsteger@aaronsfranchise.com
Web Site: www.aaronsfranchise.com
Mr. Jim Steger, Director Franchise Development

AARON'S SALES & LEASE OWNERSHIP is one of the fastest-growing rental purchase companies in the U.S., specializing in furniture, electronics and appliances. AARON'S SALES & LEASE OWNERSHIP offers franchisees the expertise, advantages and support of a well-established company, plus the opportunity to realize a significant financial return in a booming market segment.

BACKGROUND: IFA MEMBER
Established: 1955;   1st Franchised: 1992
Franchised Units: 186
Company-Owned Units: 238
Total Units: 424
Dist.: US-424; CAN-0; O'seas-0
  North America: 35 States
  Density: TX, FL, GA
Projected New Units (12 Months): 50
Qualifications: 5, 5, 1, 4, 5, 5
Registered: CA,FL,HI,IL,IN,MI,NY,ND, OR,RI,SD,VA,WA,WI
FINANCIAL/TERMS:
Cash Investment: $200K
Total Investment: $207-439.9K
Minimum Net Worth: $350K
Fees: Franchise - $35K
  Royalty - 5%; Ad. - 2.5%
Earnings Claim Statement: Yes
Term of Contract (Years): 10/10
Avg. # Of Employees: 6 FT
Passive Ownership: Allowed
Encourage Conversions: N/A
Area Develop. Agreements: Yes/Varies
Sub-Franchising Contracts: No
Expand In Territory: Yes
Space Needs: 8,000 SF; SC
SUPPORT & TRAINING PROVIDED:
Financial Assistance Provided: Yes(I)
Site Selection Assistance: Yes
Lease Negotiation Assistance: Yes
Co-Operative Advertising: Yes
Franchisee Assoc./Member: Yes
Size Of Corporate Staff: 3,500

On-Going Support: A,B,C,D,E,F,H,I
Training: 3 Weeks Corporate Headquarters; 2 Weeks Minimum On-Site; On-Going Varies.
SPECIFIC EXPANSION PLANS:
US: All United States
Canada: All Canada
Overseas: No

COLORTYME

5700 Tennyson Pkwy., # 180
Plano, TX 75024
Tel: (800) 411-8963 (972) 608-5376
Fax: (972) 403-4936
Web Site: www.colortyme.com
Mr. Pat Sumner, Director Franchise Dev.

The nation's largest rental-purchase franchise company, specializing in electronics, furniture, appliances and computers. We help our customers find what's right for them and give our franchisees the support needed to be successful, at the best profit margins in the industry.

BACKGROUND: IFA MEMBER
Established: 1979;   1st Franchised: 1981
Franchised Units: 352
Company-Owned Units: 0
Total Units: 352
Dist.: US-352; CAN-0; O'seas-0
  North America: 42 States
  Density: 56 in TX, 18 in IN, 18 in KS
Projected New Units (12 Months): 52
Qualifications: 4, 4, 4, 3, 3, 4
Registered: CA,FL,HI,IL,IN,MD,MI,NY, ND,OR,RI,SD,VA,WA,WI,DC
FINANCIAL/TERMS:
Cash Investment: $120-140K
Total Investment: $272-479K
Minimum Net Worth: $300K
Fees: Franchise - $25K
  Royalty - 4%; Ad. - $250/Mo.
Earnings Claim Statement: Yes
Term of Contract (Years): 5-10/5-10
Avg. # Of Employees: 6 FT
Passive Ownership: Allowed
Encourage Conversions: Yes
Area Develop. Agreements: Yes/5
Sub-Franchising Contracts: No
Expand In Territory: Yes
Space Needs: 3,500 SF; FS, SF, SC, RM

SUPPORT & TRAINING PROVIDED:
Financial Assistance Provided: Yes(I)
Site Selection Assistance: Yes
Lease Negotiation Assistance: Yes
Co-Operative Advertising: Yes
Franchisee Assoc./Member: Yes/No
Size Of Corporate Staff: 21
On-Going Support: B,C,D,E,F,G,H
Training: 4 Weeks Varied Training.
SPECIFIC EXPANSION PLANS:
US: All United States
Canada: No
Overseas: No

GENT'S FORMAL WEAR

404 E. Wright St.
Pensacola, FL 32501
Tel: (850) 434-3272
Fax: (850) 439-2177
E-Mail: gentsformalwear@aol.com
Web Site: www.gentsformalwear.com
Mr. Richard Crenshaw, President

Men's formal wear, rental and sales.

BACKGROUND:
Established: 1981;   1st Franchised: 1991
Franchised Units: 2
Company-Owned Units: 1
Total Units: 3
Dist.: US-3; CAN-0; O'seas-0
  North America: 2 States
  Density: 2 in FL, 1 in MS
Projected New Units (12 Months): 2
Qualifications: 3, 3, 2, 2, 4, 4
Registered: FL
FINANCIAL/TERMS:
Cash Investment: $45K
Total Investment: $45-75K
Minimum Net Worth: $150K
Fees: Franchise - $10-15K
  Royalty - 8%; Ad. - NR
Earnings Claim Statement: Yes
Term of Contract (Years): 5/5
Avg. # Of Employees: 2 FT, 1 PT
Passive Ownership: Discouraged
Encourage Conversions: Yes
Area Develop. Agreements: No
Sub-Franchising Contracts: Yes
Expand In Territory: Yes

Space Needs: 1,000 SF; FS, SC

SUPPORT & TRAINING PROVIDED:

Financial Assistance Provided:	No
Site Selection Assistance:	Yes
Lease Negotiation Assistance:	Yes
Co-Operative Advertising:	No
Franchisee Assoc./Member:	Yes/Yes
Size Of Corporate Staff:	2
On-Going Support:	A,B,C,d,E,F,h

Training: 2 Weeks Home Office; 1 Week On-Site.

SPECIFIC EXPANSION PLANS:

US:	Southeast
Canada:	No
Overseas:	No

≪ ≫

GINGISS FORMALWEAR

2101 Executive Dr.
Addison, IL 60101-1482
Tel: (800) 621-7125 (630) 620-9050
Fax: (630) 620-8840
E-Mail: gingiss@gingiss.com
Web Site: www.gingiss.com
Mr. Tom Ryan, VP of Franchise Development

GINGISS FORMALWEAR specializes in the rental and sale of men's and boys' tuxedos and related accessories. GINGISS is the leader in the formalwear wedding industry that does not go out of style, and is the only national formalwear chain that can coordinate groomsmen from coast to coast. GINGISS manufactures its own proprietary lines of formalwear, including exclusive designers such as Oleg Cassini.

BACKGROUND:	IFA MEMBER
Established: 1936;	1st Franchised: 1968
Franchised Units:	189
Company-Owned Units	49
Total Units:	238
Dist.:	US-238; CAN-0; O'seas-0
North America:	30 States
Density:	38 in TX, 38 in IL, 33 in CA
Projected New Units (12 Months):	15
Qualifications:	3, 3, 3, 3, 3, 3
Registered: CA,FL,IL,IN,MD,MI,MN,NY, OR,RI,VA,WA,WI,DC	

FINANCIAL/TERMS:

Cash Investment:	$59-107K

Total Investment:	$98.7-242.7K
Minimum Net Worth:	$NR
Fees: Franchise -	$15K
Royalty - 6%;	Ad. - 2%
Earnings Claim Statement:	Yes
Term of Contract (Years):	10/10
Avg. # Of Employees:	2 FT, 4 PT
Passive Ownership:	Discouraged
Encourage Conversions:	Yes
Area Develop. Agreements:	Yes
Sub-Franchising Contracts:	No
Expand In Territory:	Yes
Space Needs: 1,100-1,200 SF; FS, SF, SC, RM	

SUPPORT & TRAINING PROVIDED:

Financial Assistance Provided:	Yes(I)
Site Selection Assistance:	Yes
Lease Negotiation Assistance:	Yes
Co-Operative Advertising:	Yes
Franchisee Assoc./Member:	Yes/Yes
Size Of Corporate Staff:	50
On-Going Support:	B,C,D,E,F,G,H

Training: 1 Week Corporate Headquarters; 1 Week Company Operated Store; On-Going on Location.

SPECIFIC EXPANSION PLANS:

US:	All United States
Canada:	All Canada
Overseas:	No

≪ ≫

GRAND RENTAL STATION/ TAYLOR RENTAL

P.O. Box 1510
Butler, PA 16003
Tel: (800) 833-3004 (724) 284-6676
Fax: (724) 284-6489
E-Mail: edetrich@truserv.com
Web Site: www.grandrental.com
Mr. Ed Detrich, National Sales Manager

Complete equipment rental operation, specializing in light contractor, home owner and party/special occasion rentals. We provide a complete support program including market/site evaluation, store design, inventory customization, hands-on-training and on-going field and technical support.

BACKGROUND:	IFA MEMBER
Established: 1910;	1st Franchised: 1985
Franchised Units:	1,272
Company-Owned Units	0
Total Units:	1,272

Dist.:	US-1,272; CAN-0; O'seas-0
North America:	42 States
Density:	MA, PA, NY
Projected New Units (12 Months):	60
Qualifications:	4, 4, 1, 1, 2, 4
Registered: All States	

FINANCIAL/TERMS:

Cash Investment:	$75-150K
Total Investment:	$225-250K
Minimum Net Worth:	$100K
Fees: Franchise -	$1.5K
Royalty - 1.3%;	Ad. - $30/Mo.
Earnings Claim Statement:	No
Term of Contract (Years):	10/10
Avg. # Of Employees:	3 FT, 3 PT
Passive Ownership:	Discouraged
Encourage Conversions:	Yes
Area Develop. Agreements:	No
Sub-Franchising Contracts:	No
Expand In Territory:	Yes
Space Needs: 5,000 SF; FS, SC	

SUPPORT & TRAINING PROVIDED:

Financial Assistance Provided:	No
Site Selection Assistance:	Yes
Lease Negotiation Assistance:	Yes
Co-Operative Advertising:	Yes
Franchisee Assoc./Member:	Yes/Yes
Size Of Corporate Staff:	16
On-Going Support:	B,C,D,E,F,G,H,I

Training: 1 Week in Gary, IL.

SPECIFIC EXPANSION PLANS:

US:	All United States
Canada:	All Canada
Overseas:	All Countries

≪ ≫

JOE RENT ALL/LOUE TOUT

28 Vanier St.
Chateauguay, PQ J6J 3W8 CANADA
Tel: (800) 361-2020 (450) 692-6268
Fax: (450) 692-2848
E-Mail: mrjoe@cam.org
Web Site: www.joelouetout.ca
Mr. Ray Bellerose, Network Development

Equipment rental in 4 different options: tools, recreational vehicles, special events, motorcycles. Full operating support, including school. Buying group with central billing. Specific insurance plans. Own computer program.

BACKGROUND:

Established: 1979; 1st Franchised: 1982	
Franchised Units:	75
Company-Owned Units	0
Total Units:	75
Dist.:	US-0; CAN-85; O'seas-0
North America:	5 Provinces
Density:	66 in PQ
Projected New Units (12 Months):	8
Qualifications:	4, 4, 3, 4, 2, 4
Registered: NR	

FINANCIAL/TERMS:

Cash Investment:	$25K
Total Investment:	$100-500K
Minimum Net Worth:	$50K
Fees: Franchise -	$20K
Royalty - 4%;	Ad. - 3%
Earnings Claim Statement:	No
Term of Contract (Years):	5/5
Avg. # Of Employees:	2 FT, 2 PT
Passive Ownership:	Discouraged
Encourage Conversions:	Yes
Area Develop. Agreements:	No
Sub-Franchising Contracts:	No
Expand In Territory:	Yes
Space Needs: 2,500 SF; FS, SF	

SUPPORT & TRAINING PROVIDED:

Financial Assistance Provided:	Yes(I)
Site Selection Assistance:	Yes
Lease Negotiation Assistance:	No
Co-Operative Advertising:	No
Franchisee Assoc./Member:	No
Size Of Corporate Staff:	5
On-Going Support:	B,C,D,E,F,H,I

Training: 1 Full Week Head Office School; 1 Week with Existing Successful Operator.

SPECIFIC EXPANSION PLANS:

US:	As Master Franchisor
Canada:	All Canada
Overseas:	Yes, As Master Franchisor

◄◄ ►►

NATION-WIDE GENERAL RENTAL CENTERS

5510 Hwy. 9 N.
Alpharetta, GA 30004
Tel: (800) 227-1643 (770) 664-7765
Fax: (770) 664-0052
E-Mail: office@nation-widerental.com
Web Site: www.nation-widerental.com
Mr. Ike Goodvin, President

Tool and equipment rental business (since 1976) for homeowners, party and contractors. A complete turn-key package with proven equipment. No franchise fee or royalties. A complete training program with a buy-back agreement. This may be your business opportunity - act now! See our Website.

BACKGROUND:

Established: 1976; 1st Franchised: 1976	
Franchised Units:	376
Company-Owned Units	1
Total Units:	377
Dist.:	US-375; CAN-0; O'seas-2
North America:	29 States
Density:	NR
Projected New Units (12 Months):	18
Qualifications:	2, 1, 1, 2, 1, 5
Registered: NR	

FINANCIAL/TERMS:

Cash Investment:	$40-50K
Total Investment:	$80-178K
Minimum Net Worth:	$40-50K
Fees: Franchise -	$0
Royalty - 0%;	Ad. - 0%
Earnings Claim Statement:	Yes
Term of Contract (Years):	3/1
Avg. # Of Employees:	1 PT
Passive Ownership:	Discouraged
Encourage Conversions:	No
Area Develop. Agreements:	No
Sub-Franchising Contracts:	No
Expand In Territory:	Yes
Space Needs: 2,500 SF; FS, SF, SC	

SUPPORT & TRAINING PROVIDED:

Financial Assistance Provided:	Yes
Site Selection Assistance:	Yes
Lease Negotiation Assistance:	Yes
Co-Operative Advertising:	No
Franchisee Assoc./Member:	Yes/Yes
Size Of Corporate Staff:	NR
On-Going Support:	B,C,D,E,F,I

Training: 7 Days Atlanta, GA.

SPECIFIC EXPANSION PLANS:

US:	All United States
Canada:	All Canada
Overseas:	No

◄◄ ►►

SUPPLEMENTAL LISTING OF FRANCHISORS

Al's Formal Wear, P.O. Box 379, Bedford, TX 76095 ; (817) 355-4455; Mr. Larry Gatell (800) 879-1777; (817) 355-4444

Baby's Away, 14023 E. Hampden Pl., Aurora, CO 80014; (303) 596-8864; Mr. John Wierzba (800) 984-9030; (303) 750-6668

JMB Linen, 276 Hamilton St., Rahway, NJ 07065 ; (732) 388-0371; Mr. Gerald Hughes (800) 221-6948; (732) 388-3388

President Tuxedo, 32185 Hollingsworth, Warren, MI 48092 ; (810) 264-7119; Mr. Michael Sbrocca, Jr. (800) 837-TUXS; (810) 264-0600

RETAIL: ART, ART SUPPLIES & FRAMING INDUSTRY PROFILE

Total # Franchisors in Industry Group	11
Total # Franchised Units in Industry Group	737
Total # Company-Owned Units in Industry Group	<u>34</u>
Total # Operating Units in Industry Group	771
Average # Franchised Units/Franchisor	67.0
Average # Company-Owned Units/Franchisor	<u>3.1</u>
Average # Total Units/Franchisor	70.1
Ratio of Total # Franchised Units/Total # Company-Owned Units	21.7:1
Industry Survey Participants	6
Representing % of Industry	54.5%
Average Franchise Fee*:	$26.7K
Average Total Investment*:	$142.0K
Average On-Going Royalty Fee*:	5.8%

If a range was provided, the mid-point of the range was used. See detailed profiles for actual ranges.

FIVE LARGEST PARTICIPANTS IN SURVEY

Company	# Fran-chised Units	# Co-Owned Units	# Total Units	Franchise Fee	On-Going Royalty	Total Investment
1. Fastframe USA	198	7	205	25K	7.5%	94-124K
2. Deck the Walls	181	1	182	35K	6%	226-275K
3. Great Frame Up, The	118	0	118	25K	6%	97-138K
4. Framing & Art Centre	53	0	53	25K	6%	110-160K
5. Color Me Mine	44	4	48	20K	5%	125-165K

All of the data provided are proprietary and should not be quoted without acknowledging *Bond's Franchise Guide*.

BUDGET FRAMER
4313 E. Tradewinds Ave.
Ft. Lauderdale, FL 33308
Tel: (954) 491-0129
Fax: (954) 491-0129
E-Mail: thadden@aol.com
Web Site: www.budgetframerinc.com
Ms. Terie Hadden, CEO

Complete turnkey operation with low costs and low royalty. Training is located in your store, which means no traveling to the franchisor. Franchisees conduct reasonable business hours, usually in a strip center setting. They will receive continual support from the BUDGET FRAMER with site selection and lease negotiation.

BACKGROUND:
Established: 1986;   1st Franchised: 1992
Franchised Units: 25
Company-Owned Units   1
Total Units: 26
Dist.:   US-26; CAN-0; O'seas-0
  North America: 6 States
  Density: NR
Projected New Units (12 Months):   5
Qualifications: 4, 3, 1, 5, 4, 5
Registered: FL
FINANCIAL/TERMS:
Cash Investment: $35K min.
Total Investment: $95K
Minimum Net Worth: $300K
Fees: Franchise - $30K
  Royalty - 4%;   Ad. - 0%
Earnings Claim Statement: No
Term of Contract (Years):   5/5
Avg. # Of Employees: 2 FT, 1 PT
Passive Ownership: Discouraged
Encourage Conversions: NR
Area Develop. Agreements: No
Sub-Franchising Contracts: No
Expand In Territory: Yes
Space Needs: 1,000-1,200 SF; SC
SUPPORT & TRAINING PROVIDED:
Financial Assistance Provided: Yes(D)
Site Selection Assistance: Yes
Lease Negotiation Assistance: Yes
Co-Operative Advertising: No
Franchisee Assoc./Member: No
Size Of Corporate Staff: 1
On-Going Support: G
Training: 5-7 Days in Your Franchise
  Store.
SPECIFIC EXPANSION PLANS:
US: Eastern Seaboard
Canada: No
Overseas: No

‹‹ ››

COLOR ME MINE
14721 Califa St.
Van Nuys, CA 91411
Tel: (888) 265-6764 (818) 989-8404
Fax: (818) 780-1442
E-Mail: maria@colormemine.com
Web Site: www.colormemine.com
Ms. Maria Baker, Director of Franchise Sales

COLOR ME MINE is the world's leader in contemporary ceramics and crafts studios. Our comprehensive training and support system includes glazing, firing and design techniques, construction marketing, accounting services and manufacturing plants to ensure consistency and supply.

BACKGROUND: IFA MEMBER
Established: 1992;   1st Franchised: 1996
Franchised Units: 44
Company-Owned Units   4
Total Units: 48
Dist.:   US-48; CAN-0; O'seas-48
  North America: 10 States
  Density: 22 in CA, 5 in PA, 4 in NJ
Projected New Units (12 Months):   25
Qualifications: 4, 3, 2, 3, 5, 5
Registered: CA,FL,HI,IL,IN,MD,MI,MN,
  NY,OR,VA,WA,WI,DC,AB
FINANCIAL/TERMS:
Cash Investment: $50K
Total Investment: $125-165K
Minimum Net Worth: $150K
Fees: Franchise - $20K
  Royalty - 5%;   Ad. - 1%
Earnings Claim Statement: No
Term of Contract (Years):   5/5
Avg. # Of Employees: 2 FT, 4 PT
Passive Ownership: Discouraged
Encourage Conversions: Yes
Area Develop. Agreements: No
Sub-Franchising Contracts: No
Expand In Territory: Yes
Space Needs: 1,300-2,000 SF; SF, SC, RM,
  Entertainment Cent
SUPPORT & TRAINING PROVIDED:
Financial Assistance Provided: No
Site Selection Assistance: Yes
Lease Negotiation Assistance: Yes
Co-Operative Advertising: No
Franchisee Assoc./Member: No
Size Of Corporate Staff: 48
On-Going Support: A,B,C,D,E,F,G,H,I
Training: 2 Weeks at Home Office in
  Van Nuys, CA; 5-7 Days at Franchised
  Location.

SPECIFIC EXPANSION PLANS:
US: All United States
Canada: All Canada
Overseas: All countries

‹‹ ››

Specialists in Art, Custom Framing and Design

DECK THE WALLS
100 Glenborough Dr., # 1450
Houston, TX 77067
Tel: (800) 543-3325 (281) 775-5200
Fax: (281) 775-5250
E-Mail: annn@deckthewalls.com
Web Site: www.deckthewalls.com/
  franchise/index.html
Ms. Ann Nance, Franchise Development
  Manager

DECK THE WALLS is the world's largest franchisor of art, custom framing & wall décor. Each store carries a large selection of limited & open edition prints, custom frame moulding & mats. Easy to learn & operate; exceptional training & support; national buying power & proven marketing programs. Stores located in high-traffic regional malls & shopping centers. Rewarding business in a growing industry.

BACKGROUND: IFA MEMBER
Established: 1979;   1st Franchised: 1981
Franchised Units: 181
Company-Owned Units   1
Total Units: 182
Dist.:   US-182; CAN-0; O'seas-0
  North America: 38 States
  Density: 26 in TX, 15 in PA, 12 in FL
Projected New Units (12 Months):   15
Qualifications: 5, 3, 3, 3, 4, 5
Registered: CA,FL,IL,IN,MD,MI,MN,NY,
  ND,OR,RI,SD,VA,WA,WI
FINANCIAL/TERMS:
Cash Investment: $125K
Total Investment: $226-275K
Minimum Net Worth: $300K
Fees: Franchise - $35K
  Royalty - 6%;   Ad. - 2%
Earnings Claim Statement: No
Term of Contract (Years):   10/10
Avg. # Of Employees: 2 FT, 3 PT
Passive Ownership: Allowed
Encourage Conversions: Yes
Area Develop. Agreements: No
Sub-Franchising Contracts: No
Expand In Territory: Yes
Space Needs: 1,500-2,000 SF; RM

SUPPORT & TRAINING PROVIDED:

Financial Assistance Provided:	Yes(I)
Site Selection Assistance:	Yes
Lease Negotiation Assistance:	Yes
Co-Operative Advertising:	Yes
Franchisee Assoc./Member:	Yes/Yes
Size Of Corporate Staff:	48
On-Going Support:	B,C,D,E,F,G,H,I
Training: 2 Weeks in Houston, TX.	

SPECIFIC EXPANSION PLANS:

US:	All United States
Canada:	All Canada
Overseas:	No

≪ ≫

If it's important to you,

It's important to us.

FASTFRAME USA

1200 Lawrence Dr., # 300
Newbury Park, CA 91320-1234
Tel: (888) TO-FRAME (805) 498-4463
Fax: (805) 498-8983
E-Mail: fastframe@fastframe.com
Web Site: www.fastframe.com
Ms. Brenda Hales, Franchise Development

Over the past 14 years, FASTFRAME USA has captured its share of the market with its 200+ franchises within the US, along with affiliates in Brazil, Japan, Australia and the UK. FASTFRAME has emerged as a leader in the custom picture framing industry. FASTFRAME has built it foundation and reputation by providing high-quality craftsmanship, in a variety of products, at competitive prices, with immediate turn-around capabilities while guaranteeing customer satisfaction.

BACKGROUND: IFA MEMBER

Established: 1986;	1st Franchised: 1987
Franchised Units:	198
Company-Owned Units	7
Total Units:	205
Dist.:	US-196; CAN-0; O'seas-9
North America:	23 States
Density:	94 in CA, 18 in IL, 11 in GA
Projected New Units (12 Months):	30
Qualifications:	5, 4, 1, 1, 1, 5
Registered: CA,HI,IL,IN,MN,NY,VA	

FINANCIAL/TERMS:

Cash Investment:	$30K
Total Investment:	$93.5-124K
Minimum Net Worth:	$93.5K
Fees: Franchise -	$25K
Royalty - 7.5%;	Ad. - 3%
Earnings Claim Statement:	No
Term of Contract (Years):	10/10
Avg. # Of Employees:	1 FT, 2 PT
Passive Ownership:	Not Allowed
Encourage Conversions:	Yes
Area Develop. Agreements:	Yes/5
Sub-Franchising Contracts:	Yes
Expand In Territory:	Yes
Space Needs: 1,200-1,400 SF; FS, SF, SC	

SUPPORT & TRAINING PROVIDED:

Financial Assistance Provided:	Yes(I)
Site Selection Assistance:	Yes
Lease Negotiation Assistance:	Yes
Co-Operative Advertising:	Yes
Franchisee Assoc./Member:	Yes/Yes
Size Of Corporate Staff:	16
On-Going Support:	A,b,C,D,E,F,G,H,I
Training: 2 Weeks at Corporate Headquarters; 1 Week at Franchisee Location.	

SPECIFIC EXPANSION PLANS:

US:	All United States
Canada:	No
Overseas:	All Countries

≪ ≫

FRAMING & ART CENTRE

1800 Appleby Line
Burlington, ON L7L 6A1 CANADA
Tel: (800) 563-7263 (905) 332-6116
Fax: (905) 335-5377
E-Mail: framing@worldchat.com
Ms. Diane Howatt, Franchise Coordinator

FRAMING & ART CENTRE is Canada's only national art & custom framing store, specializing in a hands-on, artistic environment. Each store offers a large selection of design samples, prints and posters with custom framing in a creative atmosphere. Easy to learn and operate, exceptional training and support, national buying power and proven marketing programs. Air Miles offered.

BACKGROUND:

Established: 1974;	1st Franchised: 1977
Franchised Units:	53
Company-Owned Units	0
Total Units:	53
Dist.:	US-0; CAN-53; O'seas-0
North America:	5 Provinces
Density:	29 in ON, 12 in BC, 6 in AB
Projected New Units (12 Months):	5
Qualifications:	4, 3, 3, 3, 3, 5
Registered: AB	

FINANCIAL/TERMS:

Cash Investment:	$30K
Total Investment:	$110-160K
Minimum Net Worth:	$150K
Fees: Franchise -	$25K
Royalty - 6%;	Ad. - 1%
Earnings Claim Statement:	No
Term of Contract (Years):	10/5
Avg. # Of Employees:	2 FT, 2 PT
Passive Ownership:	Discouraged
Encourage Conversions:	Yes
Area Develop. Agreements:	Yes
Sub-Franchising Contracts:	No
Expand In Territory:	Yes
Space Needs: 1,000-1,200 SF; SF, SC	

SUPPORT & TRAINING PROVIDED:

Financial Assistance Provided:	Yes(I)
Site Selection Assistance:	Yes
Lease Negotiation Assistance:	Yes
Co-Operative Advertising:	Yes
Franchisee Assoc./Member:	No
Size Of Corporate Staff:	4
On-Going Support:	A,B,C,D,E,F,G,H,I
Training: 10 Days Burlington, ON.	

SPECIFIC EXPANSION PLANS:

US:	No
Canada:	All Canada
Overseas:	No

≪ ≫

The Great Frame Up

YOU MAKE IT OR WE MAKE IT. THAT'S WHAT MAKES IT GREAT.

GREAT FRAME UP, THE

100 Glenborough Dr., #1450
Houston, TX 77067
Tel: (800) 443-3325 (281) 775-5262
Fax: (281) 775-5250
E-Mail: annn@franchiseconceptsinc.com
Web Site: www.thegreatframeup.com/franchise.html
Ms. Ann Nance, Franchise Development Manager

THE GREAT FRAME UP is part of the world's largest retail franchisor of affordable, high-quality custom framing. Specializing in custom framing in a hands-on, artistic environment featuring wide selections of custom frame mouldings & mat styles, a proprietary framing system, superior design center & more. Easy to learn & operate; exceptional training & support; national buying power & proven marketing programs. Growth industry.

BACKGROUND: IFA MEMBER
Established: 1971;   1st Franchised: 1975
Franchised Units: 118
Company-Owned Units   0
Total Units: 118
Dist.:   US-118; CAN-0; O'seas-0
 North America: 26 States
 Density: 25 in IL, 16 in GA, 15 in CA
Projected New Units (12 Months):   20
Qualifications: 5, 3, 3, 3, 4, 5
Registered: All States
FINANCIAL/TERMS:
Cash Investment: $50K
Total Investment: $97-138K
Minimum Net Worth: $250K
Fees: Franchise - $25K
 Royalty - 6%;   Ad. - 2%
Earnings Claim Statement: No
Term of Contract (Years):   10/10
Avg. # Of Employees: 3 FT, 2 PT
Passive Ownership: Allowed
Encourage Conversions: Yes
Area Develop. Agreements: No
Sub-Franchising Contracts: No
Expand In Territory: Yes
Space Needs: 1,500-2,000 SF; SC
SUPPORT & TRAINING PROVIDED:
Financial Assistance Provided: Yes(I)
Site Selection Assistance: Yes
Lease Negotiation Assistance: Yes
Co-Operative Advertising: Yes
Franchisee Assoc./Member: Yes/Yes
Size Of Corporate Staff: 38
On-Going Support: B,C,D,E,F,G,H,I
Training: 2 Weeks in Houston, TX.
SPECIFIC EXPANSION PLANS:
US: All United States
Canada: No
Overseas: No

<< >>

**SUPPLEMENTAL LISTING
OF FRANCHISORS**

Frame & Save, 27 Spiral Dr., Florence, KY 41042 ; (606) 647-4405; Mr. Patrick Karlosky (800) 543-5464; (606) 647-4400

Framing & Art Centres (U. S.), 1800 Appleby Line, Burlington, ON L7L 6A1 CANADA; (905) 335-5377; Ms. Dianne Howatt (800) 563-7263; (905) 332-6116

Kennedy Studios, 140 Tremont St., Boston, MA 02111 ; (617) 695-0957; Mr. Ted Kennedy (800) 448-0027; (617) 542-0868

Malibu Gallery, 1919 S. 40th St., # 202, Lincoln, NE 68506-5248 ; (402) 434-5624; Mr. Jack L. Rediger (800) 865-2378; (402) 434-5620

For a full explanation of the data provided in the Franchisor Profiles, please refer to **Chapter 2, "How to Use the Data."**

RETAIL: ATHLETIC WEAR/SPORTING GOODS INDUSTRY PROFILE

Total # Franchisors in Industry Group	21
Total # Franchised Units in Industry Group	2,157
Total # Company-Owned Units in Industry Group	<u>4,743</u>
Total # Operating Units in Industry Group	2,600
Average # Franchised Units/Franchisor	102.7
Average # Company-Owned Units/Franchisor	<u>21.1</u>
Average # Total Units/Franchisor	123.8
Ratio of Total # Franchised Units/Total # Company-Owned Units	4.9:1
Industry Survey Participants	14
Representing % of Industry	66.7%
Average Franchise Fee*:	$27.7K
Average Total Investment*:	$277.4K
Average On-Going Royalty Fee*:	4.2%

If a range was provided, the mid-point of the range was used. See detailed profiles for actual ranges.

FIVE LARGEST PARTICIPANTS IN SURVEY

Company	# Fran- chised Units	# Co- Owned Units	# Total Units	Franchise Fee	On-Going Royalty	Total Investment
1. Athlete's Foot, The	462	279	741	25K	5%	175-350K
2. Play It Again Sports	734	4	734	25K	5%	170-205K
3. Pro Golf of America	157	0	157	24.5-49.5K	2.5-3%	400-600K
4. Golf USA	112	4	116	30-40K	2%	172-313K
5. Bike Line	55	17	72	24.5K	4%	130-176K

All of the data provided are proprietary and should not be quoted without acknowledging *Bond's Franchise Guide*.

A. J. BARNES BICYCLE EMPORIUM

9014 Rocky Pt.
Cordova, TN 38018
Tel: (901) 685-1936
E-Mail: ajbarnes1@ajbarnes.com
Web Site: www.ajbarnes.com
Mr. Rob Richey, Dir. of Franchise Sales

A. J. BARNES BICYCLE EMPORIUM is a full-service bicycle retail franchise chain with a fun, old-fashioned theme. Featuring major brands and an innovative open-kitchen-style service area so customers can actually watch their bicycle being serviced. A. J. BARNES is the premium-quality bicycle retail franchise, offering top-flite business operations training and on-going support from a highly-experienced management team with years of franchise operation.

BACKGROUND:

Established: 1989;	1st Franchised: 1992
Franchised Units:	34
Company-Owned Units	0
Total Units:	34
Dist.:	US-34; CAN-0; O'seas-0
North America:	3 States
Density:	11 in FL, 2 in GA, 1 in TN
Projected New Units (12 Months):	20
Qualifications:	3, 3, 1, 1, 1, 5
Registered: FL	

FINANCIAL/TERMS:

Cash Investment:	$40K
Total Investment:	$100-115K
Minimum Net Worth:	$100K
Fees: Franchise -	$25K
Royalty - 6%;	Ad. - 0%
Earnings Claim Statement:	No
Term of Contract (Years):	10/10
Avg. # Of Employees:	2 FT, 1 PT
Passive Ownership:	Allowed
Encourage Conversions:	No
Area Develop. Agreements:	Yes/10
Sub-Franchising Contracts:	No
Expand In Territory:	Yes
Space Needs: 2,000 SF; SC	

SUPPORT & TRAINING PROVIDED:

Financial Assistance Provided:	Yes(I)
Site Selection Assistance:	Yes
Lease Negotiation Assistance:	Yes
Co-Operative Advertising:	Yes
Franchisee Assoc./Member:	Yes/Yes
Size Of Corporate Staff:	5
On-Going Support:	A,C,D,E,F,G,H,I
Training: 14 Days Total at West Palm Beach, FL; 3 Days on Location.	

SPECIFIC EXPANSION PLANS:

US:	All United States
Canada:	No
Overseas:	Western Europe

‹‹ ››

ATHLETE'S FOOT, THE

1950 Vaughn Rd.
Kennesaw, GA 30144
Tel: (800) 524-6444 (770) 514-4721
Fax: (770) 514-4903
E-Mail: rsmith@theathletesfoot.com
Web Site: www.theathletesfoot.com
Mr. Jeff Shafritz, Director Franchise Sales

THE ATHLETE'S FOOT, with more than 650 stores, is the leading international franchisor of name-brand athletic footwear. As a franchisee, you will benefit from headquarters' support, including training, advertising, product selection, special vendor discount programs, continual footwear research at our exclusive-wear test center and much more.

BACKGROUND: IFA MEMBER

Established: 1971;	1st Franchised: 1972
Franchised Units:	462
Company-Owned Units	279
Total Units:	741
Dist.:	US-739; CAN-2; O'seas-0
North America:	49 States, 1 Province
Density:	NR
Projected New Units (12 Months):	110
Qualifications:	4, 5, 3, 3, 2, 5
Registered: All States	

FINANCIAL/TERMS:

Cash Investment:	$75-125K
Total Investment:	$175-350K
Minimum Net Worth:	$100K
Fees: Franchise -	$25K
Royalty - 5%;	Ad. - 0.6%
Earnings Claim Statement:	No
Term of Contract (Years):	10/5
Avg. # Of Employees:	2 FT, 6 PT
Passive Ownership:	Discouraged
Encourage Conversions:	Yes
Area Develop. Agreements:	Yes/10
Sub-Franchising Contracts:	No
Expand In Territory:	Yes
Space Needs: 1,200 SF; FS, SF, SC, RM	

SUPPORT & TRAINING PROVIDED:

Financial Assistance Provided:	Yes(I)
Site Selection Assistance:	Yes
Lease Negotiation Assistance:	Yes
Co-Operative Advertising:	No
Franchisee Assoc./Member:	Yes/Yes
Size Of Corporate Staff:	180
On-Going Support:	B,C,D,E,f,G,H,I
Training: 1 Wk. at Headquarters in Atlanta; 1 Wk. Prior to and during Opening on Location; On-Going.	

SPECIFIC EXPANSION PLANS:

US:	All United States
Canada:	All Canada
Overseas:	All Countries

‹‹ ››

BIKE LINE

1035 Andrew Dr.
West Chester, PA 19380
Tel: (800) 537-2654 (610) 429-4370
Fax: (610) 429-4295
E-Mail: jpalmer@bikeline.com
Web Site: www.bikeline.com
Mr. Chris Zorger, Dir. Franchise Dev.

BIKE LINE, the nation's largest chain of specialty bicycle and fitness retailers, can get your career rolling in a new direction which can be both challenging and rewarding. Our time-proven program guides you through the pitfalls of new business creation and focuses on your success. Call for a comprehensive information package today.

BACKGROUND:

Established: 1983;	1st Franchised: 1991
Franchised Units:	55
Company-Owned Units	17
Total Units:	72
Dist.:	US-72; CAN-0; O'seas-0
North America:	18 States
Density:	23 in PA, 6 in NJ, 3 in MD
Projected New Units (12 Months):	12
Qualifications:	5, 5, 3, 3, 5, 5
Registered: FL,IL,MD,MI,MN,VA	

FINANCIAL/TERMS:

Cash Investment:	$25-45K
Total Investment:	$130-176K
Minimum Net Worth:	$200K
Fees: Franchise -	$24.5K
Royalty - 4%;	Ad. - 3%
Earnings Claim Statement:	Yes
Term of Contract (Years):	10/10
Avg. # Of Employees:	1 FT, 2 PT
Passive Ownership:	Discouraged
Encourage Conversions:	Yes
Area Develop. Agreements:	No
Sub-Franchising Contracts:	No
Expand In Territory:	Yes
Space Needs: 3,000 SF; SF, SC	

SUPPORT & TRAINING PROVIDED:

Financial Assistance Provided:	Yes(I)
Site Selection Assistance:	Yes
Lease Negotiation Assistance:	Yes
Co-Operative Advertising:	Yes
Franchisee Assoc./Member:	No
Size Of Corporate Staff:	12
On-Going Support:	B,C,D,E,F,G,H,I
Training: 2 Weeks Westchester, PA.	

SPECIFIC EXPANSION PLANS:

US:	All United States
Canada:	No
Overseas:	No

◄◄ ►►

EMPOWERED™
WOMEN'S GOLF

EMPOWERED WOMEN'S GOLF SHOPS
5344 Belt Line Rd.
Dallas, TX 75240-2216
Tel: (800) 533-7309 (972) 253-8807
Fax: (972) 233-9079
E-Mail: empowrdgolf@earthlink.net
Web Site: www.empoweredgolf.com
Mr. Barry Dixon, VP of Operations

Golf retailer for women only.

BACKGROUND:

Established: 1993; 1st Franchised: 1997	
Franchised Units:	4
Company-Owned Units	2
Total Units:	6
Dist.:	US-6; CAN-0; O'seas-0
North America:	5 States
Density:	2 in TX, 1 in AR, 1 in NV
Projected New Units (12 Months):	4
Qualifications:	5, 5, 1, 3, 3, 5
Registered: CA,FL	

FINANCIAL/TERMS:

Cash Investment:	$100-200K
Total Investment:	$350-450K
Minimum Net Worth:	$500K
Fees: Franchise -	$25K
Royalty - 3%;	Ad. - 1%
Earnings Claim Statement:	No
Term of Contract (Years):	5/10
Avg. # Of Employees:	2 FT, 1 PT
Passive Ownership:	Allowed
Encourage Conversions:	N/A
Area Develop. Agreements:	Yes/10
Sub-Franchising Contracts:	No
Expand In Territory:	Yes
Space Needs: 2,800 SF; SC	

SUPPORT & TRAINING PROVIDED:

Financial Assistance Provided:	N/A
Site Selection Assistance:	Yes

Lease Negotiation Assistance:	Yes
Co-Operative Advertising:	Yes
Franchisee Assoc./Member:	Yes
Size Of Corporate Staff:	3
On-Going Support:	C,D,e,F,g
Training: 2 Weeks in Dallas, TX.	

SPECIFIC EXPANSION PLANS:

US:	All United States
Canada:	No
Overseas:	No

◄◄ ►►

FIELD OF DREAMS
5017 Hiatas Rd.
Sunrise, FL 33351
Tel: (800) 989-0956 (800) 959-0956
Fax: (954) 742-8544
Ms. Beth Mueller, Assistant to Chairman

FIELD OF DREAMS, the ultimate sports and celebrity gift store.

BACKGROUND:

Established: 1990; 1st Franchised: 1991	
Franchised Units:	25
Company-Owned Units	0
Total Units:	25
Dist.:	US-23; CAN-1; O'seas-1
North America:	18 States
Density:	3 in GA, 3 in CA, 2 in TX
Projected New Units (12 Months):	10
Qualifications:	5, 4, 5, 4, 5, 5
Registered: CA,FL,MI,OR	

FINANCIAL/TERMS:

Cash Investment:	$60-245K
Total Investment:	$160-225K
Minimum Net Worth:	$150K
Fees: Franchise -	$32.5K
Royalty - 6%;	Ad. - 3%
Earnings Claim Statement:	No
Term of Contract (Years):	Lease
Avg. # Of Employees:	1 FT, 2 PT
Passive Ownership:	Discouraged
Encourage Conversions:	N/A
Area Develop. Agreements:	Yes
Sub-Franchising Contracts:	No
Expand In Territory:	Yes
Space Needs: 900-1,400 SF; RM	

SUPPORT & TRAINING PROVIDED:

Financial Assistance Provided:	Yes(I)
Site Selection Assistance:	Yes
Lease Negotiation Assistance:	Yes
Co-Operative Advertising:	Yes
Franchisee Assoc./Member:	No
Size Of Corporate Staff:	9
On-Going Support:	C,D,E,h,I
Training: 10 Days Orlando, FL.	

SPECIFIC EXPANSION PLANS:

US:	All United States

Canada:	All Canada
Overseas:	All Countries

◄◄ ►►

GOLF AUGUSTA PRO SHOPS
217 Bobby Jones Expwy.
Augusta, GA 30907
Tel: (800) GOLF-051 (706) 863-9905
Fax: (706) 863-9909
E-Mail:
sbyrd@GolfAugustaProShops.com
Web Site: www.golfaugustaproshops.com
Mr. Brad Salmons, Dir. of Franchise
Development

At GOLF AUGUSTA PRO SHOPS, we're 'The Lower Your Score Store!' Founded in 1994, GOLF AUGUSTA shops are the foremost indoor teaching/ custom clubmaking/retail club centers in the world. A GOLF AUGUSTA franchise is unlike any other. Utilizing state-of-the-art technology, we specialize in providing golfers of all levels with lessons and properly fit golf clubs to maximize their abilities.

BACKGROUND: IFA MEMBER

Established: 1994; 1st Franchised: 1995	
Franchised Units:	11
Company-Owned Units	1
Total Units:	12
Dist.:	US-12; CAN-0; O'seas-0
North America:	9 States
Density:	3 in NC, 2 in PA
Projected New Units (12 Months):	12
Qualifications:	4, 5, 2, 2, 4, 4
Registered: FL,IN,MI,MN,NY,VA,WI	

FINANCIAL/TERMS:

Cash Investment:	$315K
Total Investment:	$375K
Minimum Net Worth:	$500K
Fees: Franchise -	$25K
Royalty - 4%;	Ad. - 2%
Earnings Claim Statement:	No
Term of Contract (Years):	5/5
Avg. # Of Employees:	3 FT, 4 PT
Passive Ownership:	Discouraged
Encourage Conversions:	Yes
Area Develop. Agreements:	Yes/Varies
Sub-Franchising Contracts:	No
Expand In Territory:	Yes
Space Needs: 4,000 SF; FS, SF, SC	

SUPPORT & TRAINING PROVIDED:

Financial Assistance Provided:	No
Site Selection Assistance:	Yes
Lease Negotiation Assistance:	Yes
Co-Operative Advertising:	No
Franchisee Assoc./Member:	No

Size Of Corporate Staff: 10
On-Going Support: B,E,G,I
Training: 2 Weeks Augusta, GA.
SPECIFIC EXPANSION PLANS:
US: All United States
Canada: All Canada
Overseas: All Countries

<< >>

GOLF ETC. OF AMERICA

710 E. Hwy. 337
Granbury, TX 76048
Tel: (800) 806-8633 (817) 279-7888
Fax: (817) 279-9882
E-Mail: sales@golfetc.com
Web Site: www.golfetc.com
Mr. Shane Hunt, Chief Executive Officer

Total turn-key golf pro shop franchise. Retail center for golf equipment, accessories, gift items and furniture. Service center built inside for precision custom fitting and repair of golf clubs. Exciting and fun sports and entertainment industry.

BACKGROUND:
Established: 1992; 1st Franchised: 1996
Franchised Units: 29
Company-Owned Units 1
Total Units: 30
Dist.: US-30; CAN-0; O'seas-0
 North America: 18 States
 Density: 10 in TX, 5 in FL, 4 in NC
Projected New Units (12 Months): NR
Registered:
FINANCIAL/TERMS:
Cash Investment: $25-40K
Total Investment: $130-145K
Minimum Net Worth: $130-145K
Fees: Franchise - $NR
 Royalty - NR; Ad. - N/A
Earnings Claim Statement: No
Term of Contract (Years): NR
Avg. # Of Employees: 1 FT, 2 PT
Passive Ownership: Allowed
Encourage Conversions: NR
Area Develop. Agreements: NR
Sub-Franchising Contracts: No
Expand In Territory: NR
Space Needs: 2,000-2,500 SF; SF, SC, RM
SUPPORT & TRAINING PROVIDED:
Financial Assistance Provided: NR
Site Selection Assistance: Yes
Lease Negotiation Assistance: Yes
Co-Operative Advertising: No
Franchisee Assoc./Member: No
Size Of Corporate Staff: 11
On-Going Support: b,D,E,G,H,I
Training: 1 Week Granbury, TX.

SPECIFIC EXPANSION PLANS:
US: All United States
Canada: NR
Overseas: NR

<< >>

GOLF USA

3705 W. Memorial Rd., # 801
Oklahoma City, OK 73134
Tel: (800) 488-1107 (405) 751-0015
Fax: (405) 755-0065
E-Mail: franchise@gusahq.com
Web Site: www.golfusainc.com
Mr. Rick Benson, VP Franchising

Discount golf retail stores, complete with name-brand, pro-line equipment, apparel and accessories. Indoor driving range/swing analyzer.

BACKGROUND: IFA MEMBER
Established: 1986; 1st Franchised: 1989
Franchised Units: 112
Company-Owned Units 4
Total Units: 116
Dist.: US-102; CAN-4; O'seas-10
 North America: 37 States, 3 Provinces
 Density: 7 in FL, 6 in TX, 6 in NE
Projected New Units (12 Months): 12
Qualifications: 4, 5, 2, 2, 2, 3
Registered: CA,FL,HI,IL,IN,MD,MI,
 MN,NY,OR,RI,SD,VA,WA,WI
FINANCIAL/TERMS:
Cash Investment: $50-100K
Total Investment: $172-313K
Minimum Net Worth: $100K
Fees: Franchise - $30-40K
 Royalty - 2%; Ad. - 1%
Earnings Claim Statement: No
Term of Contract (Years): 20/20
Avg. # Of Employees: 2 FT, 1 PT
Passive Ownership: Discouraged
Encourage Conversions: Yes
Area Develop. Agreements: Yes/4
Sub-Franchising Contracts: Yes
Expand In Territory: Yes
Space Needs: 2,500-4,500 SF; FS, SF, SC
SUPPORT & TRAINING PROVIDED:
Financial Assistance Provided: No
Site Selection Assistance: Yes
Lease Negotiation Assistance: Yes
Co-Operative Advertising: Yes

Franchisee Assoc./Member: No
Size Of Corporate Staff: 15
On-Going Support: A,B,C,D,E,F,G,H,I
Training: 1 Week Oklahoma City, OK; 5
 Days at New Location.
SPECIFIC EXPANSION PLANS:
US: All United States
Canada: All Canada
Overseas: All Countries

<< >>

LAS VEGAS GOLF & TENNIS

2701 Crimson Canyon Dr.
Las Vegas, NV 89128
Tel: (800) 873-5110 (702) 798-5500
Fax: (702) 798-6847
E-Mail: franchise@lvgtcorp.com
Web Site: www.lvgolf.com
Ms. Staci Behnke, Franchise Dev. Mgr.

Country club service at the off-course price. Our retail stores specialize in a wide variety of name brand pro-line golf and tennis equipment and apparel, as well as our own Vision line and merchandise. Our operational staff, store development department, in-house advertising agency, computerization system and 2-week training course, along with the on-going support proves to be well above the rest.

BACKGROUND: IFA MEMBER
Established: 1974; 1st Franchised: 1984
Franchised Units: 40
Company-Owned Units 7
Total Units: 47
Dist.: US-445; CAN-0; O'seas-2
 North America: 18 States
 Density: 10 in CA, 5 in MI
Projected New Units (12 Months): 8
Qualifications: 5, 3, 1, 2, 2, 4
Registered: CA,FL,HI,IL,IN,MD,MI,MN,
 NY,OR,VA,WA,WI
FINANCIAL/TERMS:
Cash Investment: $250K
Total Investment: $537-774K
Minimum Net Worth: $750K
Fees: Franchise - $39K
 Royalty - 3%; Ad. - 2%
Earnings Claim Statement: Yes
Term of Contract (Years): 15/15
Avg. # Of Employees: 5 FT, 2-3 PT
Passive Ownership: Discouraged
Encourage Conversions: Yes

Area Develop. Agreements:	Yes
Sub-Franchising Contracts:	No
Expand In Territory:	Yes
Space Needs: 6,000-10,000 SF; FS, SF, SC, RM, End Cap	

SUPPORT & TRAINING PROVIDED:

Financial Assistance Provided:	Yes(I)
Site Selection Assistance:	Yes
Lease Negotiation Assistance:	Yes
Co-Operative Advertising:	Yes
Franchisee Assoc./Member:	No
Size Of Corporate Staff:	36
On-Going Support:	A,B,C,D,e,F,G,h,I
Training: 2 Weeks Corporate Headquarters in Las Vegas, NV.	

SPECIFIC EXPANSION PLANS:

US:	All United States
Canada:	E & W Canada
Overseas:	All Countries

PLAY IT AGAIN SPORTS

4200 Dahlberg Dr.
Minneapolis, MN 55422
Tel: (800) 592-8046 (612) 520-8500
Fax: (612) 520-8501
Web Site: www.playitagainsports.com
Ms. Angie Dahl, Franchise Sales Consultant

Our retail stores blend the sale of used and new, name-brand sports equipment along with promoting trade-in discounts. This sales mix creates ultra-high value for the customer while providing significantly higher gross profit margins than traditional retailers.

BACKGROUND: IFA MEMBER

Established: 1983; 1st Franchised: 1988	
Franchised Units:	734
Company-Owned Units	4
Total Units:	734
Dist.: US-623; CAN-69; O'seas-1	
North America: 50 States,10 Provinces	
Density: 67 in CA, 38 in ON, 34 in MI	
Projected New Units (12 Months):	35
Qualifications:	5, 3, 2, 1, 1, 5
Registered: All States	

FINANCIAL/TERMS:

Cash Investment:	$60-70K
Total Investment:	$170-205K
Minimum Net Worth:	$225K
Fees: Franchise -	$25K
Royalty - 5%;	Ad. - 5%
Earnings Claim Statement:	Yes
Term of Contract (Years):	10/10
Avg. # Of Employees:	3 FT, 2 PT
Passive Ownership:	Discouraged

Encourage Conversions:	Yes
Area Develop. Agreements:	No
Sub-Franchising Contracts:	No
Expand In Territory:	Yes
Space Needs: 2,500-3,000 SF; FS, SC	

SUPPORT & TRAINING PROVIDED:

Financial Assistance Provided:	Yes(I)
Site Selection Assistance:	Yes
Lease Negotiation Assistance:	Yes
Co-Operative Advertising:	Yes
Franchisee Assoc./Member:	NR
Size Of Corporate Staff:	283
On-Going Support:	B,C,D,E,F,G,H,I
Training: 2 1/2 Days Minneapolis, MN; 2 1/2 Days Minneapolis, M; 5 Days Minneapolis, MN.	

SPECIFIC EXPANSION PLANS:

US:	All United States
Canada:	All Canada
Overseas:	No

PRO GOLF OF AMERICA

32751 Middlebelt Rd.
Farmington Hills, MI 48334-1726
Tel: (800) 521-6388 (248) 737-0553
Fax: (248) 737-9077
Web Site: www.progolfamerica.com
Mr. Steve Gossard, VP of Sales & Development

PRO GOLF offers the best opportunity to make money among the golf franchise stores available today. We have the best training, the largest selection of private label and exclusive products to sell and the best name - PRO GOLF. Come visit PRO GOLF and learn how a successful retail golf store should operate.

BACKGROUND: IFA MEMBER

Established: 1962; 1st Franchised: 1974	
Franchised Units:	157
Company-Owned Units	0
Total Units:	157
Dist.: US-130; CAN-22; O'seas-5	
North America: 29 States, 4 Provinces	
Density: 14 in MI, 12 in CA, 10 in FL	
Projected New Units (12 Months):	20
Qualifications:	5, 4, 3, 4, , 5
Registered: All States	

FINANCIAL/TERMS:

Cash Investment:	$200-350K
Total Investment:	$400-600K
Minimum Net Worth:	$450K
Fees: Franchise -	$24.5-49.5K
Royalty - 2.5-3%;	Ad. - 0%
Earnings Claim Statement:	No
Term of Contract (Years):	15/10

Avg. # Of Employees:	4 FT, 3 PT
Passive Ownership:	Discouraged
Encourage Conversions:	Yes
Area Develop. Agreements:	Yes/Negot.
Sub-Franchising Contracts:	No
Expand In Territory:	Yes
Space Needs: 4,000-6,000 SF; FS, SC	

SUPPORT & TRAINING PROVIDED:

Financial Assistance Provided:	Yes(I)
Site Selection Assistance:	Yes
Lease Negotiation Assistance:	Yes
Co-Operative Advertising:	Yes
Franchisee Assoc./Member:	No
Size Of Corporate Staff:	20
On-Going Support:	B,C,D,E,F,G,H,I
Training: 8-12 Days at the Corporate Office in MI; 4-6 Days at Your Location.	

SPECIFIC EXPANSION PLANS:

US:	All United States
Canada:	All Canada
Overseas:	All That Have Golfers

SOCCER POST INTERNATIONAL

111 Melrose Dr.
New Rochelle, NY 10804
Tel: (914) 235-9161
Fax: (914) 636-8434
E-Mail: soccerpost@msn.com
Web Site: www.soccerpost.com
Mr. Jerome L. Kellert, President/CEO

A soccer specialty retail business, featuring top-of-the-line, cutting-edge soccer equipment from Adidas, Nike, Reebok, Xara, etc. Owner of store will become the center of soccer activity in the communities they serve. Must be soccer savvy!

BACKGROUND:

Established: 1978; 1st Franchised: 1991	
Franchised Units:	25
Company-Owned Units	7
Total Units:	32
Dist.: US-32; CAN-0; O'seas-0	
North America:	NR
Density: 8 in PA 7 in NJ, 2 in IL	
Projected New Units (12 Months):	12
Qualifications:	5, 3, 1, 3, 4, 5
Registered: CA,FL,IL,IN,MD.MI,NY, RI,WA	

FINANCIAL/TERMS:

Cash Investment:	$190-250K
Total Investment:	$190-250K
Minimum Net Worth:	$300K

Fees: Franchise - $19.5K
  Royalty - 3-5%;   Ad. - 1.5-3%
Earnings Claim Statement: Yes
Term of Contract (Years):   5/5
Avg. # Of Employees: 1 FT, 2-4 PT
Passive Ownership: Allowed
Encourage Conversions: Yes
Area Develop. Agreements: Yes/10
Sub-Franchising Contracts: Yes
Expand In Territory: Yes
Space Needs: 3,200 SF; SC

SUPPORT & TRAINING PROVIDED:
Financial Assistance Provided: Yes
Site Selection Assistance: Yes
Lease Negotiation Assistance: Yes
Co-Operative Advertising: Yes
Franchisee Assoc./Member: No
Size Of Corporate Staff: 9
On-Going Support: C,D,E,F,G,h,I
Training: 2 Weeks Plus Store, Voorhees, NJ.

SPECIFIC EXPANSION PLANS:
US: All United States
Canada: No
Overseas: No

≪ ≫

THE SPORT SHOE

SPORT SHOE, THE

1770 Corporate Dr., # 500
Norcross, GA 30093
Tel: (800) 944-7463 (770) 279-7494
Fax: (770) 279-7180
E-Mail: franchise@thesportshoe.com
Web Site: www.thesportshoe.com
Mrs. Jan Judd, Director of Franchising

For over 25 years, THE SPORT SHOE has been one of America's premier athletic shoe stores and sports-related activewear. THE SPORT SHOE offers continuing professional support, including site selection, lease negotiation, in-store operation and product knowledge, marketing and merchandising assistance, in-store set up and grand opening assistance.

BACKGROUND: IFA MEMBER
Established: 1974;   1st Franchised: 1989
Franchised Units: 7
Company-Owned Units   <u>25</u>
Total Units: 32
Dist.:   US-32; CAN-0; O'seas-0
  North America: 4 States
  Density: 4 in GA, 1 in NC, 1 in AL
Projected New Units (12 Months):   6

Qualifications: 5, 5, 4, 4, 4, 4
Registered: FL,IN,MI
FINANCIAL/TERMS:
Cash Investment: $150K
Total Investment: $300K+
Minimum Net Worth: $300K
Fees: Franchise - $25K
  Royalty - 4%;   Ad. - N/A
Earnings Claim Statement: No
Term of Contract (Years):   10/5/5
Avg. # Of Employees: 2-4 FT, 6-8 PT
Passive Ownership: Allowed
Encourage Conversions: Yes
Area Develop. Agreements: Yes
Sub-Franchising Contracts: No
Expand In Territory: Yes
Space Needs: 3,000 SF; FS, SC

SUPPORT & TRAINING PROVIDED:
Financial Assistance Provided: No
Site Selection Assistance: Yes
Lease Negotiation Assistance: Yes
Co-Operative Advertising: Yes
Franchisee Assoc./Member: No
Size Of Corporate Staff: 60
On-Going Support: C,D,E,H,I
Training: 6-8 Weeks Corporate Office and Store.

SPECIFIC EXPANSION PLANS:
US: All United States
Canada: No
Overseas: No

≪ ≫

SUPPLEMENTAL LISTING OF FRANCHISORS

Fan-A-Mania Sports and Entertainment, 3855 S. 500 W., # R, Salt Lake City, UT 84115 ; (801) 288-9210; Mr. Mark Helean (800) 770-9120; (801) 288-9120

Fleet Feet, 2311 J St., Sacramento, CA 95816 ; (916) 557-1010; Mr. Tom Raynor ; (916) 557-1000

International Golf, 9101 N. Thornydale Rd., Tucson, AZ 85742; (520) 744-2076; Ms. Sheila J. White (800) 204-2600; (520) 744-1840

Ottawa Algonquin Travel, 657 Bronson Ave., Ottawa, ON K1S 4E7 CANADA; (613) 233-7805; Mr. Mark Dyer (800) 668-1743; (613) 233-7713

Pro Image, The, 563 West 500 S., # 330, Bountiful, UT 84010 ; (801) 296-1319; Mr. Ryan Laws (888) 477-6326; (801) 296-9999

Sports FANtastic!, 1919 S. 40th St., # 202, Lincoln, NE 68506-5248 ; (402) 434-5624; Mr. Jack L. Rediger (800) 865-2378; (402) 434-5620

Sports Traders, 508 Discovery St., Victoria, BC V8T 1G8 CANADA; (250) 383-2853; Mr. Patrick Mellett (800) 792-3111; (250) 383-6443

RETAIL: CLOTHING/SHOES/ACCESSORIES INDUSTRY PROFILE

Total # Franchisors in Industry Group	10
Total # Franchised Units in Industry Group	122
Total # Company-Owned Units in Industry Group	<u>389</u>
Total # Operating Units in Industry Group	511
Average # Franchised Units/Franchisor	12.2
Average # Company-Owned Units/Franchisor	<u>38.9</u>
Average # Total Units/Franchisor	51.1
Ratio of Total # Franchised Units/Total # Company-Owned Units	0.3:1
Industry Survey Participants	3
Representing % of Industry	30.0%
Average Franchise Fee*:	$20.0K
Average Total Investment*:	$46.2K
Average On-Going Royalty Fee*:	6.0%

If a range was provided, the mid-point of the range was used. See detailed profiles for actual ranges.

FIVE LARGEST PARTICIPANTS IN SURVEY

Company	# Fran-chised Units	# Co-Owned Units	# Total Units	Franchise Fee	On-Going Royalty	Total Investment
1. Elegance Jewelry	1	265	266	0	0%	$99/Kit
2. Panda Shoes	41	5	46	25K	4%	80-125K
3. Mainstream Fashions	4	15	19	15K	8%	31.5-40.3K

All of the data provided are proprietary and should not be quoted without acknowledging *Bond's Franchise Guide.*

ELEGANCE JEWELRY
12 Conran St.
St. John's, NF AIB 5G8 CANADA
Tel: (709) 745-8070
Mr. Melvin Slade, President

Home-based fashion jewelry sales. Excellent compensation and profit sharing plans.

BACKGROUND:

Established: 1990; 1st Franchised: 1995	
Franchised Units:	1
Company-Owned Units	265
Total Units:	266
Dist.:	US-1; CAN-265; O'seas-0
North America:	1 State, 8 Provinces
Density:	1 in NF
Projected New Units (12 Months):	1,000
Qualifications:	3, 3, 4, 1, 2, 4
Registered: NR	

FINANCIAL/TERMS:

Cash Investment:	$99/Kit
Total Investment:	$99/Kit
Minimum Net Worth:	$N/A
Fees: Franchise -	$0
Royalty - 0%;	Ad. - 0%
Earnings Claim Statement:	Yes
Term of Contract (Years):	5/5
Avg. # Of Employees:	1 FT
Passive Ownership:	Allowed
Encourage Conversions:	N/A
Area Develop. Agreements:	No
Sub-Franchising Contracts:	No
Expand In Territory:	Yes
Space Needs: NR SF; HB	

SUPPORT & TRAINING PROVIDED:

Financial Assistance Provided:	No
Site Selection Assistance:	N/A
Lease Negotiation Assistance:	N/A
Co-Operative Advertising:	No
Franchisee Assoc./Member:	No
Size Of Corporate Staff:	1
On-Going Support:	NR
Training: By Mail.	

SPECIFIC EXPANSION PLANS:

US:	All United States
Canada:	All Canada
Overseas:	No

≪ ≫

MAINSTREAM FASHIONS
13877 Elkhart Rd.
Apple Valley, MN 55124
Tel: (612) 423-6254
Fax: (612) 322-1923
E-Mail: nick.denicola@mainstreamfashions.com
Web Site: www.mainstreamfashions.com
Mr. Nick DeNicola, VP Franchise Development

MAINSTREAM FASHIONS is a home-based business which markets contemporary women's and children's clothing through home and office shows. We're looking for entrepreneur-minded individuals with some business experience and a passion for fashion. Must be motivated to succeed in a fun, flexible and rewarding business environment.

BACKGROUND: IFA MEMBER

Established: 1991; 1st Franchised: 1998	
Franchised Units:	4
Company-Owned Units	15
Total Units:	19
Dist.:	US-19; CAN-0; O'seas-0
North America:	4 States
Density:	15 in MN, 2 in IA, 1 in WI
Projected New Units (12 Months):	NR
Registered:	

FINANCIAL/TERMS:

Cash Investment:	$31.5-40.3K
Total Investment:	$31.5-40.3K
Minimum Net Worth:	$40K
Fees: Franchise -	$15K
Royalty - 8%;	Ad. - 0-2%
Earnings Claim Statement:	Yes
Term of Contract (Years):	10/10
Avg. # Of Employees:	1 FT
Passive Ownership:	Discouraged
Encourage Conversions:	NR
Area Develop. Agreements:	No
Sub-Franchising Contracts:	No
Expand In Territory:	Yes
Space Needs: N/A SF; HB	

SUPPORT & TRAINING PROVIDED:

Financial Assistance Provided:	NR
Site Selection Assistance:	N/A
Lease Negotiation Assistance:	N/A
Co-Operative Advertising:	N/A
Franchisee Assoc./Member:	No
Size Of Corporate Staff:	3
On-Going Support:	B,C,D,E,G,H
Training: Approximately 3 Days Apple Valley, MN; 2-3 Days in Territory.	

SPECIFIC EXPANSION PLANS:

US:	Most States
Canada:	NR
Overseas:	NR

≪ ≫

PANDA SHOES
305 Marc Aurele Fortin Blvd.
Laval, PQ H7L 2A3 CANADA
Tel: (450) 622-4833
Fax: (450) 622-2939
E-Mail: info@pandashoes.com
Web Site: www.pandashoes.com
Ms. Linda Goulet, President

Children's shoe specialist - locations in major malls across Canada - 62 stores. Complete training program, including selling, merchandising, administration, etc. National advertising. Best selection of footwear for kids.

BACKGROUND:

Established: 1972; 1st Franchised: 1974	
Franchised Units:	41
Company-Owned Units	5
Total Units:	46
Dist.:	US-0; CAN-62; O'seas-0
North America:	6 Provinces
Density:	38 in PQ, 12 in ON, 9 in BC
Projected New Units (12 Months):	2
Registered: NR	

FINANCIAL/TERMS:

Cash Investment:	$60K
Total Investment:	$80-125K
Minimum Net Worth:	$NR
Fees: Franchise -	$25K
Royalty - 4%;	Ad. - 0.5%
Earnings Claim Statement:	No
Term of Contract (Years):	5/Lease
Avg. # Of Employees:	3 FT, 2 PT
Passive Ownership:	Discouraged
Encourage Conversions:	Yes
Area Develop. Agreements:	No
Sub-Franchising Contracts:	No
Expand In Territory:	Yes
Space Needs: 800 SF; RM	

SUPPORT & TRAINING PROVIDED:

Financial Assistance Provided:	No
Site Selection Assistance:	Yes
Lease Negotiation Assistance:	Yes
Co-Operative Advertising:	Yes
Franchisee Assoc./Member:	NR
Size Of Corporate Staff:	8
On-Going Support:	B,C,D,E,F,G,H
Training: 2 Weeks Toronto, ON; 2 Weeks On-Site (at Opening).	

SPECIFIC EXPANSION PLANS:

US:	No
Canada:	All Except AB
Overseas:	No

≪ ≫

SUPPLEMENTAL LISTING OF FRANCHISORS

Faux Pas International, 5817 Kavanaugh Blvd., Little Rock, AR 72207 ; (501)

614-8777; Ms. Betty Brinkley ; (501) 225-4848

Happydays Handbag & Luggage Company, 1441 Craigflower Rd., #409, Victoria, BC V9A 2Y9 CANADA; (250) 595-8935; Mr. Reed Sumina ; (250) 595-8934

Krug's Big & Tall, 16 N. Washington Ave., Bergenfield, NJ 07621-2126 ; (201) 387-1619; Mr. Neil Rubin (800) 367-5784; (201) 387-0100

Le Bateau Blanc, 710 Rue Bouvier, # 175, Charlesbourg, PQ G2J 1H7 CANADA; (418) 627-4125; Mrs. Lisette Poulin ; (418) 627-1846

Mark's Work Wearhouse, 1035 64th Ave. SE, # 30, Calgary, AB T2H 2J7 CANADA; (403) 255-6005; Ms. Tammy Allen (800) 663-6275; (403) 255-9220

Petticoat Box, 2011050 W. 14th St., North Vancouver, BC V7P 3P3 CANADA; (604) 985-3937; Ms. Maria Collen (888) 988-2444; (604) 985-4996

RETAIL: CONVENIENCE STORES/SUPERMARKETS/DRUGS INDUSTRY PROFILE

Total # Franchisors in Industry Group	31
Total # Franchised Units in Industry Group	31,257
Total # Company-Owned Units in Industry Group	6,094
Total # Operating Units in Industry Group	37,351
Average # Franchised Units/Franchisor	1,008.3
Average # Company-Owned Units/Franchisor	196.6
Average # Total Units/Franchisor	1,204.9
Ratio of Total # Franchised Units/Total # Company-Owned Units	5.1:1
Industry Survey Participants	11
Representing % of Industry	35.4%
Average Franchise Fee*:	$17.7K
Average Total Investment*:	$731.9K
Average On-Going Royalty Fee*:	4.4%

If a range was provided, the mid-point of the range was used. See detailed profiles for actual ranges.

FIVE LARGEST PARTICIPANTS IN SURVEY

Company	# Fran-chised Units	# Co-Owned Units	# Total Units	Franchise Fee	On-Going Royalty	Total Investment
1. 7-Eleven, Inc.	15,572	2,666	18,238	54K Avg.	N/A	Varies
2. Circle K	3,300	2,400	5,700	15-30K	3.5%	400K-1.5MM
3. Health Mart	600	0	600	50K	0%	150-300K
4. Star Mart	96	345	441	30K	4%	2-4MM
5. Convenient Food Mart	256	50	306	18K	5%$	197-298K

All of the data provided are proprietary and should not be quoted without acknowledging *Bond's Franchise Guide*.

7-ELEVEN, INC.
2711 N. Haskell Ave., Box 711
Dallas, TX 75204
Tel: (800) 255-0711 (214) 841-6800
Fax: (214) 841-6776
Web Site: www.7-eleven.com
Ms. Joanne Webb-Joyce, National Franchise
  Manager

7-ELEVEN stores were born from the simple concept of giving people 'what they want, when and where they want it.' This idea gave rise to the entire convenience store industry. While this formula still works today, customers' needs are changing at an accelerating pace. We are meeting this challenge with an infrastructure of daily distribution of fresh perishables, regional production of fresh foods and pastries and an information system that greatly improves ordering and merchandising decisions.

BACKGROUND: IFA MEMBER
Established: 1927; 1st Franchised: 1964
Franchised Units: 15,572
Company-Owned Units 2666
Total Units: 18,238
Dist.: US-5,591; CAN-475; O'seas-12,172
  North America: 36 States, 5 Provinces
  Density: 1,172 in CA, 604 VA, 452 FL
Projected New Units (12 Months): 150
Qualifications: 4, 4, 3, 3, 5, 5
Registered: CA,IL,IN,MD,MI,NY,
  OR,RI,VA,WA
FINANCIAL/TERMS:
Cash Investment: $76K Avg.
Total Investment: $Varies
Minimum Net Worth: $10K
Fees: Franchise - $54K Avg.
  Royalty - N/A; Ad. - N/A
Earnings Claim Statement: No
Term of Contract (Years): 10
Avg. # Of Employees: 4 FT, 4 PT
Passive Ownership: Not Allowed

Encourage Conversions: N/A
Area Develop. Agreements: No
Sub-Franchising Contracts: No
Expand In Territory: No
Space Needs: 2,400 SF; FS, SC
SUPPORT & TRAINING PROVIDED:
Financial Assistance Provided: Yes(D)
Site Selection Assistance: N/A
Lease Negotiation Assistance: N/A
Co-Operative Advertising: No
Franchisee Assoc./Member: Yes/No
Size Of Corporate Staff: 1,000
On-Going Support: A,B,C,D,E,F,G,H,I
Training: 6 Weeks at Various Training
  Stores throughout US.
SPECIFIC EXPANSION PLANS:
US: NW,SW,MW,NE, Great Lakes
Canada: No
Overseas: No

ARROW PRESCRIPTION CENTER
312 Farmington Ave.
Farmington, CT 06032
Tel: (800) 203-2776 (860) 676-1222
Fax: (860) 676-1499
Web Site: www.arrowrx.com
Mr. Chip Caney, VP Marketing &
  Development

ARROW CORPORATION is one of the nation's largest franchisors of retail pharmacies, offering opportunities in traditional and alternative settings. At the core of ARROW'S philosophy is the delivery of pharmacy services directly to the patient by the pharmacist.

BACKGROUND: IFA MEMBER
Established: 1989; 1st Franchised: 1990
Franchised Units: 56
Company-Owned Units 3
Total Units: 59
Dist.: US-59; CAN-0; O'seas-0
  North America: 6 States
  Density: 42 in CT, 5 in MI, 5 in MA
Projected New Units (12 Months): 16
Qualifications: 4, 4, 5, 5, 4, 4
Registered: NR
FINANCIAL/TERMS:
Cash Investment: $20% of Total
Total Investment: $Varies
Minimum Net Worth: $100K
Fees: Franchise - $15K
  Royalty - 6%; Ad. - Varies
Earnings Claim Statement: No
Term of Contract (Years): 20/10
Avg. # Of Employees: 2 FT, 1-6 PT

Passive Ownership: Discouraged
Encourage Conversions: Yes
Area Develop. Agreements: Yes/5
Sub-Franchising Contracts: No
Expand In Territory: No
Space Needs: 1,500 SF; FS, SC
SUPPORT & TRAINING PROVIDED:
Financial Assistance Provided: Yes(B)
Site Selection Assistance: Yes
Lease Negotiation Assistance: No
Co-Operative Advertising: Yes
Franchisee Assoc./Member: Yes
Size Of Corporate Staff: 30
On-Going Support: A,C,D,E,F,G,H,I
Training: 1-2 Weeks Corporate Training
  Center.
SPECIFIC EXPANSION PLANS:
US: All United States
Canada: No
Overseas: No

CIRCLE K
1500 N. Priest Dr.
Tempe, AZ 85281
Tel: (800) 813-7677 (602) 728-8000
Fax: (602) 728-5248
E-Mail: mrials@tosco.com
Web Site: www.TMCFranchise.tosco.com
Mr. Mike Rials, Director of Franchising

Unlike any other convenience store and petroleum company, we offer you a CIRCLE K license opportunity that helps to build a business with leading brands in both the convenience store and petroleum industries (CIRCLE K/76/BP). Licensing leading brands in these industries provides you with the ability to offer your customers a one-of-a-kind convenience experience. We also offer superior business systems, extensive training and effective promotional tools. This unique combination is the Tosco advantage.

BACKGROUND: IFA MEMBER
Established: 1951; 1st Franchised: 1995
Franchised Units: 3,300
Company-Owned Units 2,400

Total Units: 5,700
Dist.: US-2,700; CAN-0; O'seas-3,000
  North America: 37 States
  Density: 550 in AZ, 400 in FL, 200 CA
Projected New Units (12 Months): 100
Qualifications: 5, 4, 5, 3, 3, 5
Registered: CA,FL,HI,MD,OR,VA,WA
FINANCIAL/TERMS:
Cash Investment: $300-450K
Total Investment: $400K-1.5MM
Minimum Net Worth: $500K
Fees: Franchise - $15-30K
  Royalty - 3-5%; Ad. - 2%
Earnings Claim Statement: Yes
Term of Contract (Years): 10/5/5
Avg. # Of Employees: 8 FT, 4 PT
Passive Ownership: Discouraged
Encourage Conversions: Yes
Area Develop. Agreements: Yes/10
Sub-Franchising Contracts: No
Expand In Territory: Yes
Space Needs: 3,000 SF; FS
SUPPORT & TRAINING PROVIDED:
Financial Assistance Provided: Yes(I)
Site Selection Assistance: Yes
Lease Negotiation Assistance: Yes
Co-Operative Advertising: N/A
Franchisee Assoc./Member: No
Size Of Corporate Staff: 1,200
On-Going Support: B,C,D,E,F,G,H,I
Training: 4-6 Weeks at Location to Be
  Determined.
SPECIFIC EXPANSION PLANS:
US: WA,OR,CA,HI
Canada: No
Overseas: Asia, South America, Europe

◄◄ ►►

CONVENIENT FOOD MART
467 North State St.
Painesville, OH 44077
Tel: (800) 860-4844 (440) 639-6515
Fax: (440) 639-6526
Web Site: www.convenientfoodmart.com
Ms. Barb Mahoney, Director of
  Franchising

CONVENIENT FOOD MART offers an
expanded approval to convenience with
a fresh approach. Our system provides
the opportunity to build equity as part
of a strong franchise system. Stores
average 3,000 square feet, carrying extended
produce, deli and hot and cold prepared
items.

BACKGROUND:
Established: 1958; 1st Franchised: 1959

Franchised Units: 256
Company-Owned Units 50
Total Units: 306
Dist.: US-306; CAN-0; O'seas-0
  North America: 9 States
  Density: 121 in OH, 47 in NY, 40 IL
Projected New Units (12 Months): 15
Qualifications: 5, 4, 3, 3, 5, 5
Registered: Pending in IL,IN,NY
FINANCIAL/TERMS:
Cash Investment: $30-180K
Total Investment: $197-298K
Minimum Net Worth: $150K
Fees: Franchise - $18K
  Royalty - 5%; Ad. - Included
Earnings Claim Statement: No
Term of Contract (Years): 20/20
Avg. # Of Employees: 6 FT, 4 PT
Passive Ownership: Discouraged
Encourage Conversions: Yes
Area Develop. Agreements: No
Sub-Franchising Contracts: Yes
Expand In Territory: Yes
Space Needs: 3,000 SF; FS, SF, SC
SUPPORT & TRAINING PROVIDED:
Financial Assistance Provided: No
Site Selection Assistance: Yes
Lease Negotiation Assistance: Yes
Co-Operative Advertising: Yes
Franchisee Assoc./Member: Yes/No
Size Of Corporate Staff: 50
On-Going Support: A,C,D,E,H,I
Training: 2 Weeks at Training Center; 1
  Week at Actual Store.
SPECIFIC EXPANSION PLANS:
US: OH,NY
Canada: No
Overseas: No

◄◄ ►►

**EXPRESS MART CONVENIENT
STORE**
6567 Kinne Rd., P.O. Box 46
DeWitt, NY 13214
Tel: (315) 446-0125
Fax: (315) 446-1355
Mr. Mark E. Maher, Director of
  Franchising

Convenience-store franchise with
petroleum emphasis, currently offering
development territories and master
franchise agreements for U.S. and foreign
countries.

BACKGROUND: IFA MEMBER
Established: 1975; 1st Franchised: 1990
Franchised Units: 20

Company-Owned Units 47
Total Units: 67
Dist.: US-67; CAN-0; O'seas-0
  North America: 4 States
  Density: 56 in NY, 8 in MA, 2 in CT
Projected New Units (12 Months): 3
Qualifications: 4, 3, 3, 3, 4, 4
Registered: CT,NY
FINANCIAL/TERMS:
Cash Investment: $40-60K
Total Investment: $136-460K
Minimum Net Worth: $Varies
Fees: Franchise - $15K
  Royalty - 4%; Ad. - 1%
Earnings Claim Statement: No
Term of Contract (Years): 5/5/5/5
Avg. # Of Employees: 6 FT, 4 PT
Passive Ownership: Allowed
Encourage Conversions: Yes
Area Develop. Agreements: No
Sub-Franchising Contracts: Yes
Expand In Territory: Yes
Space Needs: 800-5,000 SF; FS
SUPPORT & TRAINING PROVIDED:
Financial Assistance Provided: Yes
Site Selection Assistance: Yes
Lease Negotiation Assistance: Yes
Co-Operative Advertising: Yes
Franchisee Assoc./Member: Yes
Size Of Corporate Staff: 300
On-Going Support: B,C,D,E,F
Training: 1 Week Corporate Headquarters;
  1 Week Store Training.
SPECIFIC EXPANSION PLANS:
US: All United States
Canada: All Canada
Overseas: No

◄◄ ►►

HEALTH MART
1 Post St.
San Francisco, CA 94104
Tel: (800) 369-5467 (415) 983-8300
Fax: (415) 983-9353
Mr. Jerry Josephson, Director of Franchise
  Services

The largest full-line pharmacy franchise
for independent store owners.

BACKGROUND:
Established: 1981; 1st Franchised: 1983
Franchised Units: 600
Company-Owned Units 0
Total Units: 600
Dist.: US-600; CAN-0; O'seas-0
  North America: 34 States
  Density: 83 in IL, 64 in MO, 59 in LA

Projected New Units (12 Months): 100
Qualifications: 3, 4, 5, 5, 1, 3
Registered: All States
FINANCIAL/TERMS:
Cash Investment: $5-15K
Total Investment: $150-300K
Minimum Net Worth: $NR
Fees: Franchise - $500K
  Royalty - 0%; Ad. - $150/Mo.
Earnings Claim Statement: Yes
Term of Contract (Years): 5/5
Avg. # Of Employees: 2 FT, 1 PT
Passive Ownership: Allowed
Encourage Conversions: Yes
Area Develop. Agreements: No
Sub-Franchising Contracts: No
Expand In Territory: Yes
Space Needs: 500+ SF; FS, SF, SC, RM
SUPPORT & TRAINING PROVIDED:
Financial Assistance Provided: N/A
Site Selection Assistance: No
Lease Negotiation Assistance: No
Co-Operative Advertising: Yes
Franchisee Assoc./Member: No
Size Of Corporate Staff: 5
On-Going Support: b,C,D,e,G,h,I
Training: 1-3 Days On-Site.
SPECIFIC EXPANSION PLANS:
US: All United States
Canada: No
Overseas: No

⨞⨞ ⨟⨟

JACKPOT CONVENIENCE STORES

2737 W. Commorde Way
Seattle, WA 98199
Tel: (800) 772-5765 (206) 285-2400
Fax: (206) 283-8036
Mr. Steven C. Gray, Franchise Manager

JACKPOT offers a franchise that includes a system of retail grocery services. JACKPOT licenses to franchisees its business system, know-how and its licensed trade name and service marks. JACKPOT provides training, continuing support, administration and marketing and promotion services.

BACKGROUND:
Established: 1981; 1st Franchised: 1990
Franchised Units: 104
Company-Owned Units: 10
Total Units: 114
Dist.: US-114; CAN-0; O'seas-0
  North America: NR
  Density: NR

Projected New Units (12 Months): NR
Qualifications: 5, 4, 5, 1, 3, 4
Registered: CA,OR,WA
FINANCIAL/TERMS:
Cash Investment: $40-75K
Total Investment: $75-250K
Minimum Net Worth: $60K
Fees: Franchise - $5K
  Royalty - 0.5%; Ad. - 1%
Earnings Claim Statement: No
Term of Contract (Years): 3/3
Avg. # Of Employees: No
Recommendation
Passive Ownership: Not Allowed
Encourage Conversions: N/A
Area Develop. Agreements: No
Sub-Franchising Contracts: No
Expand In Territory: No
Space Needs: NR SF; N/A
SUPPORT & TRAINING PROVIDED:
Financial Assistance Provided: No
Site Selection Assistance: N/A
Lease Negotiation Assistance: N/A
Co-Operative Advertising: N/A
Franchisee Assoc./Member: Yes/Yes
Size Of Corporate Staff: NR
On-Going Support: A,C,D,E,F,G,h,I
Training: 4 Weeks Seattle, WA.
SPECIFIC EXPANSION PLANS:
US: WA,OR,CA,NV,ID
Canada: No
Overseas: No

⨞⨞ ⨟⨟

MEDICAP PHARMACY

4700 Westown Pkwy, # 300
West Des Moines, IA 50266-6730
Tel: (800) 445-2244 (515) 224-8400
Fax: (515) 224-8415
Web Site: www.medicapRX.com
Mr. Calvin C. James, VP Franchise
  Development

MEDICAP PHARMACY - convenient, low-cost, professional pharmacies. The stores operate in an average of 1,500 square feet. We average 90% RX and the remaining 10% over-the-counter products, including MEDICAP-brand private label. We specialize in starting new stores and converting existing full-line drug stores and independent pharmacies to the MEDICAP concept. We teach independent pharmacists how to survive in today's marketplace.

BACKGROUND: IFA MEMBER
Established: 1971; 1st Franchised: 1974
Franchised Units: 182
Company-Owned Units: 15
Total Units: 197
Dist.: US-197; CAN-0; O'seas-0
  North America: 38 States
  Density: 50 in IA, 11 in SC, 10 in IL
Projected New Units (12 Months): 25
Qualifications: 3, 1, 4, 5, 3, 5
Registered: CA,FL,IL,IN,MD,MN,ND, OR,SD,WA,WI
FINANCIAL/TERMS:
Cash Investment: $10K-45K
Total Investment: $20-324.7K
Minimum Net Worth: $NR
Fees: Franchise - $8.5-15K
  Royalty - 2-4%; Ad. - 1%
Earnings Claim Statement: Yes
Term of Contract (Years): 20/20
Avg. # Of Employees: 2 FT
Passive Ownership: Allowed
Encourage Conversions: Yes
Area Develop. Agreements: No
Sub-Franchising Contracts: No
Expand In Territory: Yes
Space Needs: 1,500 SF; FS, SF, SC
SUPPORT & TRAINING PROVIDED:
Financial Assistance Provided: Yes(I)
Site Selection Assistance: Yes
Lease Negotiation Assistance: Yes
Co-Operative Advertising: N/A
Franchisee Assoc./Member: NR
Size Of Corporate Staff: 52
On-Going Support: B,C,D,E,F,G,H,I
Training: 5 Days Headquarters; 3 Days On-Site; 3 Days Computer.
SPECIFIC EXPANSION PLANS:
US: All United States
Canada: All Canada
Overseas: All Countries

⨞⨞ ⨟⨟

OPEN PANTRY FOOD MARTS

817 S. Main St.
Racine, WI 53403-1522
Tel: (800) 242-1018 (262) 632-3161
Fax: (262) 632-1463
E-Mail: RABuhler@clmail.com
Web Site: www.openpantry.com
Mr. John Schonert, VP Franchise Operations

Convenience store operations.

BACKGROUND: IFA MEMBER

Established: 1966; 1st Franchised: 1966	
Franchised Units:	38
Company-Owned Units	16
Total Units:	54
Dist.:	US-54; CAN-0; O'seas-0
North America:	2 States
Density:	53 in WI, 1 in IL
Projected New Units (12 Months):	6
Qualifications:	5, 5, 5, 4, 4, 5
Registered: WI	

FINANCIAL/TERMS:

Cash Investment:	$15-30K
Total Investment:	$NR
Minimum Net Worth:	$75K
Fees: Franchise -	$10K
Royalty - NR;	Ad. - NR
Earnings Claim Statement:	No
Term of Contract (Years):	NR
Avg. # Of Employees:	3 FT, 3 PT
Passive Ownership:	Not Allowed
Encourage Conversions:	No
Area Develop. Agreements:	No
Sub-Franchising Contracts:	No
Expand In Territory:	NR
Space Needs: NR SF; FS, SF, SC	

SUPPORT & TRAINING PROVIDED:

Financial Assistance Provided:	Yes(I)
Site Selection Assistance:	No
Lease Negotiation Assistance:	N/A
Co-Operative Advertising:	Yes
Franchisee Assoc./Member:	No
Size Of Corporate Staff:	18
On-Going Support:	C,D,E,G,H,I
Training: NR	

SPECIFIC EXPANSION PLANS:

US:	NR
Canada:	No
Overseas:	NR

<< >>

STAR MART
12700 Northborough, MFB 132
Houston, TX 77067
Tel: (281) 874-3970
Fax: (281) 874-8209
E-Mail: argirndt@equilon.com
Web Site: www.euilon.com
Mr. Allen Girndt, Manager Franchise Development

STAR MART is a proprietary convenience store offering of the Texaco system.

They offer strong marketing, advertising and operations support coupled with the strength of Texaco "clean system" fuel.

BACKGROUND: IFA MEMBER

Established: 1926; 1st Franchised: 1992	
Franchised Units:	96
Company-Owned Units	345
Total Units:	441
Dist.:	US-441; CAN-0; O'seas-0
North America:	15 States
Density:	111 CA, 93 in AZ, 51 in CO
Projected New Units (12 Months):	40
Qualifications:	5, 5, 4, 3, 3, 5
Registered: CA,OR,SD,WA,WI	

FINANCIAL/TERMS:

Cash Investment:	$250-325K
Total Investment:	$2-4MM
Minimum Net Worth:	$600K
Fees: Franchise -	$30K
Royalty - 4%;	Ad. - 2%
Earnings Claim Statement:	No
Term of Contract (Years):	10/10
Avg. # Of Employees:	10FT, 20 PT
Passive Ownership:	Discouraged
Encourage Conversions:	Yes
Area Develop. Agreements:	No
Sub-Franchising Contracts:	No
Expand In Territory:	Yes
Space Needs: 3,000+ SF; FS	

SUPPORT & TRAINING PROVIDED:

Financial Assistance Provided:	Yes(D)
Site Selection Assistance:	Yes
Lease Negotiation Assistance:	No
Co-Operative Advertising:	Yes
Franchisee Assoc./Member:	Yes/Yes
Size Of Corporate Staff:	15
On-Going Support:	B,C,D,E,F,G,H,I
Training: 3 Weeks in Buena Park, CA.	

SPECIFIC EXPANSION PLANS:

US:	AZ,CA,CO,WA,OR,Kansas City
Canada:	No
Overseas:	No

<< >>

UNCLESAM'S CONVENIENT STORE
P.O. Box 870
Elsa, TX 78543-0870
Tel: (888) 786-7373 (956) 262-7273
Fax: (956) 262-7290
E-Mail: uscs12@aol.com
Web Site: www.unclesamscstore.com
Mr. Jackie L. Thomas, Executive Vice President

A turn-key convenience store franchise program available in 31 states. Affiliated with major fuel and merchandise suppliers. Attractive financing available to qualified candidates. Training, site evaluation, store design, operations manual, software package, advertising, promotions, security systems, deli, car wash and many more benefits.

BACKGROUND:

Established: 1970; 1st Franchised: 1997	
Franchised Units:	1
Company-Owned Units	52
Total Units:	53
Dist.:	US-52; CAN-0; O'seas-0
North America:	1 State
Density:	52 in TX
Projected New Units (12 Months):	10
Qualifications:	4, 5, 3, 4, 3, 5
Registered: FL,OR	

FINANCIAL/TERMS:

Cash Investment:	$100K+
Total Investment:	$800K+
Minimum Net Worth:	$300K
Fees: Franchise -	$25K
Royalty - 5%;	Ad. - 1%
Earnings Claim Statement:	No
Term of Contract (Years):	5/5/5/5/5
Avg. # Of Employees:	6 FT, 2 PT
Passive Ownership:	Discouraged
Encourage Conversions:	Yes
Area Develop. Agreements:	Yes/5
Sub-Franchising Contracts:	No
Expand In Territory:	Yes
Space Needs: 2,500+ SF; FS	

SUPPORT & TRAINING PROVIDED:

Financial Assistance Provided:	Yes(I)
Site Selection Assistance:	Yes
Lease Negotiation Assistance:	Yes
Co-Operative Advertising:	Yes
Franchisee Assoc./Member:	Yes/No
Size Of Corporate Staff:	6
On-Going Support:	a,B,C,d,E,F,I
Training: 4 Weeks at Corporate Headquarters.	

SPECIFIC EXPANSION PLANS:

US:	South, SW, SE, East, West
Canada:	No
Overseas:	No

<< >>

WHITE HEN PANTRY
3003 Butterfield Rd.
Oak Brook, IL 60523
Tel: (800) PANTRY-1 (630) 366-3000

Fax: (630) 366-3447
Web Site: www.clarkretail.com
Ms. Gail M. Bosch, Franchising Manager

WHITE HEN PANTRY is a neighborhood convenience store, specializing in fresh-brewed coffee, full-service deli, custom-made sandwiches and salads, fresh produce and a bakery.

BACKGROUND: IFA MEMBER
Established: 1965; 1st Franchised: 1965
Franchised Units: 295
Company-Owned Units 0
Total Units: 295
Dist.: US-295; CAN-0; O'seas-0
 North America: 4 States
 Density: 233 in IL, 56 in MA, 6 in IN
Projected New Units (12 Months): 10
Qualifications: 2, 4, 3, 2, 3, 5
Registered: IL,IN
FINANCIAL/TERMS:
Cash Investment: $56.8K+
Total Investment: $Flexible
Minimum Net Worth: $N/A
Fees: Franchise - $25K
 Royalty - 8%+; Ad. - Included
Earnings Claim Statement: Yes
Term of Contract (Years): 10/10
Avg. # Of Employees: 2 FT, 12 PT
Passive Ownership: Not Allowed
Encourage Conversions: N/A
Area Develop. Agreements: No
Sub-Franchising Contracts: No
Expand In Territory: No
Space Needs: 2,500 SF; SC
SUPPORT & TRAINING PROVIDED:
Financial Assistance Provided: Yes(D)
Site Selection Assistance: Yes
Lease Negotiation Assistance: Yes
Co-Operative Advertising: N/A
Franchisee Assoc./Member: Yes
Size Of Corporate Staff: 260
On-Going Support: A,C,D,E,F,G,H,I
Training: 1 Week Corporate Office; 2
 Weeks On-Site.
SPECIFIC EXPANSION PLANS:
US: IL,IN,MA,NH Only
Canada: No
Overseas: No

≪ ≫

SUPPLEMENTAL LISTING OF FRANCHISORS

Drug Emporium, 155 Hidden Ravines Dr., Powell, OH 43065 ; (740) 548-6541; Mr. Tim Dargush ; (740) 548-7080

Food Giant/IGA/Mayfair/Red Rooster, 6355 Viscount Rd., Mississauga, ON L4V 1W2 CANADA; (905) 671-5179; Mr. Dale Sallows ; (905) 672-6633

Food-N-Fuel, 4366 Round Lake Rd. W., Arden Hills, MN 55112 ; (651) 633-0015; Mr. Edward Bird (800) 282-6844; (651) 633-7863

Giant Eagle, 101 Kappa Dr., Pittsburgh, PA 15238 ; (412) 963-0374; Mr. John Lucot ; (412) 963-2560

Giant Tiger Stores, 2480 Walkley Rd., Ottawa, ON K1G 6A9 CANADA; (613) 521-4474; Mr. Svend Pederson ; (613) 521-8222

IGA Canada, 304 The East Mall, # 700, Etobicoke, ON M9B 6E2 CANADA; (416) 234-7013; Mr. Ted Moore ; (416) 232-2880

J. J. Pepper's Food Store, 121 E. Grand Ave., Northlake, IL 60164 ; (708) 409-0003; Mr. Ed Sayre ; (708) 409-0001

Johnny Quik Food Stores, 5816 E. Shields Ave., Fresno, CA 93727 ; (559) 291-1656; Ms. Joanne Thibodeaux ; (559) 291-7136

Medicine Shoppe, The, 1100 N. Lindbergh Blvd., St. Louis, MO 63132 ; (314) 872-5500; Mr. L. Mike Rice (800) 325-1397; (314) 993-6000

Piggly Wiggly, P.O. Box 1719, Memphis, TN 38101 ; (901) 395-8475; Mr. John Kugele (800) 800-8215; (901) 395-8215

Quickway, 44 Grand St., Sidney, NY 13838 ; (607) 563-1460; Mr. Harry Pratt (800) 934-9480; (607) 561-2700

Quik Stop Markets, 4567 Enterprise St., Fremont, CA 94538 ; ; Mr. William L. Rankin ; (510) 657-1544

Sav-Mor Drug Stores, 43155 W. Nine Mile Rd., Novi, MI 48376 ; (248) 348-4316; Mr. Gerald Katchman ; (248) 348-1570

Shoppers Drug Mart, 225 Yorkland Blvd., Willowdale, ON M2J 4Y7 CANADA; (416) 490-2700; Ms. Bryana Goldberg ; (416) 490-2648

Sugar Creek Convenience Stores & Fuel, 760 Brooks Ave., Rochester, NY 14619 ; (716) 328-7374; Mr. Tim Hardy ; (716) 436-2691

Tedeschi Food Shops, 14 Howard St., Rockland, MA 02370 ; (281) 874-7863; Mr. Richard Roth (800) 833-3724; (281)874-4887

Retail: Home Furnishings   Chapter

38

RETAIL: HOME FURNISHINGS INDUSTRY PROFILE

Total # Franchisors in Industry Group	44
Total # Franchised Units in Industry Group	2,612
Total # Company-Owned Units in Industry Group	<u>150</u>
Total # Operating Units in Industry Group	2,762
Average # Franchised Units/Franchisor	59.4
Average # Company-Owned Units/Franchisor	<u>3.4</u>
Average # Total Units/Franchisor	62.8
Ratio of Total # Franchised Units/Total # Company-Owned Units	17.4:1
Industry Survey Participants	15
Representing % of Industry	34.1%
Average Franchise Fee*:	$18.6K
Average Total Investment*:	$123.2K
Average On-Going Royalty Fee*:	4.1%

If a range was provided, the mid-point of the range was used. See detailed profiles for actual ranges.

FIVE LARGEST PARTICIPANTS IN SURVEY

Company	# Fran- chised Units	# Co- Owned Units	# Total Units	Franchise Fee	On-Going Royalty	Total Investment
1. Floor Coverings International	226	0	226	16K	5%/$325/Mo.	31.1-41.3K
2. Budget Blinds	208	3	211	25K	4-5%	50-90K
3. Verlo Mattress Factory Stores	65	2	67	30K	5%	100-150K
4. Slumberland International	44	23	67	12.5K	3%	100-400K
5. Floor To Ceiling	62	1	63	3-6K	$350+/Mo.	Varies

All of the data provided are proprietary and should not be quoted without acknowledging *Bond's Franchise Guide*.

A SHADE BETTER
3615 Superior Ave., Bldg. # 42
Cleveland, OH 44114
Tel: (800) 722-8676 (216) 391-5267
Fax: (216) 391-8118
E-Mail: franchdev@ashadebetter.com
Web Site: www.ashadebetter.com
Franchise Office,

Distinctive retail stores selling beautiful lamp shades, lamps and accessories. Franchisees will also have the opportunity to develop and service the wholesale market in their exclusive territory.

BACKGROUND:
Established: 1988;   1st Franchised: 1993
Franchised Units: 9
Company-Owned Units   9
Total Units: 18
Dist.:   US-18; CAN-0; O'seas-0
 North America: 7 States
 Density: 5 in OH, 3 in IL, 2 in TX
Projected New Units (12 Months):   12
Qualifications: 4, 4, 2, 2, 3, 5
Registered: CA,FL,IL,IN,MD,MI,WI
FINANCIAL/TERMS:
Cash Investment: $75-100K
Total Investment: $114-156K
Minimum Net Worth: $300K
Fees: Franchise - $35K
 Royalty - 6%;   Ad. - 1%
Earnings Claim Statement: No
Term of Contract (Years):   5/5/5/5
Avg. # Of Employees: 2 FT, 2 PT
Passive Ownership: Discouraged
Encourage Conversions: Yes
Area Develop. Agreements: Yes/Varies
Sub-Franchising Contracts: No
Expand In Territory: Yes
Space Needs: 1,800 SF; SC
SUPPORT & TRAINING PROVIDED:
Financial Assistance Provided: No
Site Selection Assistance: Yes
Lease Negotiation Assistance: Yes
Co-Operative Advertising: No
Franchisee Assoc./Member: No
Size Of Corporate Staff: 6
On-Going Support: B,C,D,E,h,I

Training: 6 Days Cleveland, OH or Phoenix, AZ; 6 Days On-Site.
SPECIFIC EXPANSION PLANS:
US: Midwest , Southwest
Canada: No
Overseas: No

⋘ ⋙

BIG BOB'S NEW & USED CARPET SHOPS
9320 W. 75th Street
Shawnee Mission, KS 66204
Tel: (877) 644-2627 (913) 789-7773
Fax: (913) 789-7126
E-Mail: BBB97INC@aol.com
Web Site: www.bigbobscarpet.com
Mr. David Elyachar, President

To provide an affordable opportunity to franchise, drawing from the unique used, second, promotionals, and private lines of flowing and in turn providing an excellent margin and excellent prices to the franchisee and the customer. BIG BOB'S uses unique and proven advertising. There will be full training and counsel when needed.

BACKGROUND:
Established: 1983;   1st Franchised: 1993
Franchised Units: 33
Company-Owned Units   3
Total Units: 36
Dist.:   US-36; CAN-0; O'seas-0
 North America: 19 States
 Density: 6 in OH, 5 in TX, 4 in FL
Projected New Units (12 Months):   7
Qualifications: 2, 3, 3, 2, 4, 4
Registered: CA,FL,IL,IN,MD,MI,
 MN,NY,VA,WA
FINANCIAL/TERMS:
Cash Investment: $60-140K
Total Investment: $60-140K
Minimum Net Worth: $Not Required
Fees: Franchise - $7.5K
 Royalty - 1-5%;   Ad. - N/A
Earnings Claim Statement: No
Term of Contract (Years):   5/5
Avg. # Of Employees: 3-5 FT
Passive Ownership: Discouraged
Encourage Conversions: Yes
Area Develop. Agreements: No
Sub-Franchising Contracts: No
Expand In Territory: Yes
Space Needs: 7,000-12,000 SF; FS, SF
SUPPORT & TRAINING PROVIDED:
Financial Assistance Provided: Yes(I)
Site Selection Assistance: Yes
Lease Negotiation Assistance: No
Co-Operative Advertising: No

Franchisee Assoc./Member: No
Size Of Corporate Staff: 4
On-Going Support: B,C,D,E,F,G,H,I
Training: 1 Week in Kansas City, KS; Other Optional Areas.
SPECIFIC EXPANSION PLANS:
US: All United States
Canada: No
Overseas: No

⋘ ⋙

BUDGET BLINDS
733 W. Taft Ave.
Orange, CA 92865
Tel: (800) 800-9250 (714) 637-2100
Fax: (714) 637-1400
E-Mail: bbinfo@budgetblinds.com
Web Site: www.budgetblinds.com
Mr. Timothy Ranallo, Mgr. Sales/Marketing

BUDGET BLINDS trains individuals to own and operate a home-based business that sells and installs window coverings, via a well-equipped mobile showroom. What makes our franchise unique is that we actually teach people how to run a business, versus teaching people how to do a job. By business we mean hiring, monitoring and maintaining employees, working from cash flow, profit loss and balance statements, We teach what business owners need to know, not what job operators want to know.

BACKGROUND: IFA MEMBER
Established: 1992;   1st Franchised: 1994
Franchised Units: 156
Company-Owned Units   3
Total Units: 159
Dist.:   US-159; CAN-0; O'seas-0
 North America: 33 States
 Density: 47 in CA, 14 in AZ, 8 in GA
Projected New Units (12 Months):   200
Qualifications: 2, 4, 1, 2, 3, 5
Registered: All States
FINANCIAL/TERMS:
Cash Investment: $21.8-49.2K
Total Investment: $21.8-49.2K
Minimum Net Worth: $21.8K
Fees: Franchise - $15K
 Royalty - 4-5%;   Ad. - $300
Earnings Claim Statement: No
Term of Contract (Years):   5/5
Avg. # Of Employees: 4 FT
Passive Ownership: Allowed

Encourage Conversions:	Yes
Area Develop. Agreements:	Yes
Sub-Franchising Contracts:	Yes
Expand In Territory:	Yes
Space Needs: NR SF; HB	

SUPPORT & TRAINING PROVIDED:

Financial Assistance Provided:	Yes(I)
Site Selection Assistance:	Yes
Lease Negotiation Assistance:	N/A
Co-Operative Advertising:	Yes
Franchisee Assoc./Member:	Yes/No
Size Of Corporate Staff:	15
On-Going Support:	b,C,D,G,H,I
Training: 2 Weeks in Southern CA.	

SPECIFIC EXPANSION PLANS:

US:	All United States
Canada:	All Canada
Overseas:	No

◄◄ ►►

CARPET NETWORK

109 Gaither Dr., # 302
Mount Laurel, NJ 08054
Tel: (800) 428-1067 (856) 273-9393
Fax: (856) 273-0160
E-Mail: info@carpetnetwork.com
Web Site: www.carpetnetwork.com
Mr. Leonard Rankin, President

'The Traveling Floor and Window Store.' A mobile business offering carpet, area rugs, laminate, wood, vinyl flooring and window treatments in the convenience of the consumer's home or business. Over 4,000 selections from leading manufacturers, serving today's 'time starved' consumer. Large exclusive territories, marketing strategy - training - 24-hour support and much more.

BACKGROUND:

Established: 1991; 1st Franchised: 1992	
Franchised Units:	46
Company-Owned Units	1
Total Units:	47
Dist.:	US-47; CAN-0; O'seas-0
North America:	18 States
Density:	8 in PA, 4 in NY, 3 in NJ
Projected New Units (12 Months):	24
Qualifications:	3, 3, 1, 3, 3, 5
Registered: FL,IN,MN,NY	

FINANCIAL/TERMS:

Cash Investment:	$13K
Total Investment:	$13K
Minimum Net Worth:	$13K
Fees: Franchise -	$9.9K

Royalty - 2-7%;		Ad. - $165/Mo.
Earnings Claim Statement:		No
Term of Contract (Years):		15/15
Avg. # Of Employees:		1 FT, 1 PT
Passive Ownership:		Discouraged
Encourage Conversions:		N/A
Area Develop. Agreements:		Yes
Sub-Franchising Contracts:		No
Expand In Territory:		Yes
Space Needs: N/A SF; HB		

SUPPORT & TRAINING PROVIDED:

Financial Assistance Provided:	Yes(D)
Site Selection Assistance:	N/A
Lease Negotiation Assistance:	N/A
Co-Operative Advertising:	N/A
Franchisee Assoc./Member:	Yes/Yes
Size Of Corporate Staff:	5
On-Going Support:	C,D,G,h,I
Training: 6 Days at Corporate Office, Mt. Laurel, NJ.	

SPECIFIC EXPANSION PLANS:

US:	All United States
Canada:	No
Overseas:	No

◄◄ ►►

DECOR-AT-YOUR-DOOR INTERNATIONAL

23 Heather Green Ct.
Ocoee, FL 34761
Tel: (800) 936-3326 (407) 877-3033
Fax: (407) 877-8088
E-Mail: info@decor-at-your-door.com
Web Site: www.decor-at-your-door.com
Ms. Lori Marshall, President/CEO

Assist business and home owners in choosing and purchasing window treatments, wall coverings and floor coverings. We offer quality service, the top brands and the most reasonable franchise fees in the industry. Check the competition and compare DECOR-AT-YOUR-DOOR is listed among the Top 50 New Franchises by Entrepreneur Magazine.

BACKGROUND:

Established: 1995; 1st Franchised: 2000	
Franchised Units:	16
Company-Owned Units	0

Total Units:	16
Dist.:	US-16; CAN-0; O'seas-0
North America:	15 States
Density:	2 in CA
Projected New Units (12 Months):	5
Qualifications:	1, 3, 3, 2, 2, 5
Registered: FL	

FINANCIAL/TERMS:

Cash Investment:		$5-25K
Total Investment:		$5-25K
Minimum Net Worth:		$NR
Fees: Franchise -		$5K
Royalty - 1%/$100;		Ad. - 1%
Earnings Claim Statement:		No
Term of Contract (Years):		10/10
Avg. # Of Employees:		1 FT, 1 PT
Passive Ownership:		Discouraged
Encourage Conversions:		N/A
Area Develop. Agreements:		No
Sub-Franchising Contracts:		No
Expand In Territory:		Yes
Space Needs: NR SF; HB		

SUPPORT & TRAINING PROVIDED:

Financial Assistance Provided:	No
Site Selection Assistance:	N/A
Lease Negotiation Assistance:	No
Co-Operative Advertising:	Yes
Franchisee Assoc./Member:	No
Size Of Corporate Staff:	1
On-Going Support:	b,E,G,h
Training: 1 Week or 5 Days in Orlando, FL.	

SPECIFIC EXPANSION PLANS:

US:	All United States, Target SE
Canada:	No
Overseas:	No

◄◄ ►►

DRAPERY WORKS SYSTEMS

4640 Western Ave.
Lisle, IL 60532
Tel: (800) 353-7273 (630) 963-2820
Fax: (630) 963-1370
Ms. Sheila Muehling, President

The DRAPERY WORKS is a custom drapery and soft bedding accessories mobile business, unique for its own custom workroom which fabricates orders for the franchisee. We offer expertise and successful selling practices from fifteen years of business through training and on-going support. Create your own hours. Appointments become enjoyable through profitable visits with new and old customers.

BACKGROUND:

Established: 1978; 1st Franchised: 1993	
Franchised Units:	6
Company-Owned Units	1

Total Units:	7
Dist.:	US-7; CAN-0; O'seas-0
North America:	2 States
Density:	6 in IL, 1 in NC
Projected New Units (12 Months):	10
Qualifications:	3, 1, 4, 5, 2,
Registered: FL,IL,KY,TX,WI	

FINANCIAL/TERMS:

Cash Investment:	$25K
Total Investment:	$25-53K
Minimum Net Worth:	$NR
Fees: Franchise -	$14.5K
Royalty - 6%;	Ad. - 2%
Earnings Claim Statement:	No
Term of Contract (Years):	10/10
Avg. # Of Employees:	1 FT
Passive Ownership:	N/A
Encourage Conversions:	No
Area Develop. Agreements:	Yes/10
Sub-Franchising Contracts:	Yes
Expand In Territory:	Yes
Space Needs: N/A SF; Mobile	

SUPPORT & TRAINING PROVIDED:

Financial Assistance Provided:	Yes(I)
Site Selection Assistance:	Yes
Lease Negotiation Assistance:	N/A
Co-Operative Advertising:	N/A
Franchisee Assoc./Member:	Yes
Size Of Corporate Staff:	4
On-Going Support:	C,D,e,G,H,I
Training: 2 Weeks Lisle, IL; 6 Weeks Field.	

SPECIFIC EXPANSION PLANS:

US:	All United States
Canada:	No
Overseas:	No

≪ ≫

EXPRESSIONS IN FABRICS

401 11th St., NW
Hickory, NC 28601
Fax: (704) 328-2176
Web Site: www.expressions-furniture.com
Mr. Bob Berman, VP Fran. Marketing

EXPRESSIONS is a chain of franchised retail stores offering consumers a unique home furnishing concept - a dramatically different approach to fabric selection, design, pricing, delivery and service. With more than 50 Stores nationwide, we are the leader of the custom upholstery category of the $42 billion home furnishings industry - a category that EXPRESSIONS created 20 years ago with our first New Orleans store.

BACKGROUND:

Established: 1978; 1st Franchised: 1983	
Franchised Units:	49
Company-Owned Units	4

Total Units:	53
Dist.:	US-53; CAN-0; O'seas-0
North America:	30 States
Density:	5 in CA, 5 in TX, 4 in MI
Projected New Units (12 Months):	10
Qualifications:	5, 4, 3, 4, 3, 5
Registered: All States	

FINANCIAL/TERMS:

Cash Investment:	$50-100K
Total Investment:	$296-449K
Minimum Net Worth:	$500K
Fees: Franchise -	$30K
Royalty - 3.5%;	Ad. - 2%
Earnings Claim Statement:	No
Term of Contract (Years):	10/10
Avg. # Of Employees:	7 FT
Passive Ownership:	Allowed
Encourage Conversions:	Yes
Area Develop. Agreements:	Yes/3
Sub-Franchising Contracts:	No
Expand In Territory:	Yes
Space Needs: 5,000 SF; FS, SF, SC	

SUPPORT & TRAINING PROVIDED:

Financial Assistance Provided:	Yes(I)
Site Selection Assistance:	Yes
Lease Negotiation Assistance:	Yes
Co-Operative Advertising:	Yes
Franchisee Assoc./Member:	Yes/Yes
Size Of Corporate Staff:	35
On-Going Support:	a,B,C,D,E,H
Training: 10 Days Corporate Store.	

SPECIFIC EXPANSION PLANS:

US:	All United States
Canada:	No
Overseas:	No

≪ ≫

FLOOR COVERINGS INTERNATIONAL

5182 Old Dixie Hwy., #B
Forest Park, GA 30297
Tel: (800) 955-4324 (404) 361-5047
Fax: (404) 366-4606
E-Mail: lmcbride@carpetvan.com
Web Site: www.floorcoveringsintl.com
Mr. Mac McBride, VP of Marketing Dev.

FLOOR COVERINGS INTERNATIONAL is the 'Flooring Store at your Door.' FCI is the first and leading mobile 'shop at home' flooring store. Customers can select from over 3,000 styles and colors of flooring right in their own home! All the right ingredients are there to simplify a buying decision. We offer all the brand names you and your customers will be familiar with. We carry all types of flooring, as well as window blinds.

BACKGROUND:

Established: 1988; 1st Franchised: 1989	
Franchised Units:	226
Company-Owned Units	0
Total Units:	226
Dist.:	US-150; CAN-16; O'seas-60
North America:	43 States, 5 Provinces
Density:	15 in PA, 11 in OH, 9 in IL
Projected New Units (12 Months):	45
Qualifications:	5, 5, 4, 3, 4, 4
Registered: All States	

FINANCIAL/TERMS:

Cash Investment:	$25-35K
Total Investment:	$31.1-41.3K
Minimum Net Worth:	$50K
Fees: Franchise -	$16K
Royalty - 5%/$325/Mo.;	Ad. -
2%/$130/Mo.	
Earnings Claim Statement:	No
Term of Contract (Years):	10/10
Avg. # Of Employees:	1 FT, 1PT
Passive Ownership:	Discouraged
Encourage Conversions:	Yes
Area Develop. Agreements:	Yes/10
Sub-Franchising Contracts:	No
Expand In Territory:	Yes
Space Needs: NR SF; Mobile Van	

SUPPORT & TRAINING PROVIDED:

Financial Assistance Provided:	Yes(D)
Site Selection Assistance:	Yes
Lease Negotiation Assistance:	N/A
Co-Operative Advertising:	Yes
Franchisee Assoc./Member:	Yes
Size Of Corporate Staff:	15
On-Going Support:	A,B,C,D,E,G,H,I
Training: 2 Weeks Home Study; 2 Weeks Atlanta, GA.	

SPECIFIC EXPANSION PLANS:

US:	All United States
Canada:	All Canada
Overseas:	U.K.

≪ ≫

FLOOR TO CEILING

2999 W. Country Rd. 42, # 145
Burnsville, MN 55306
Tel: (952) 890-8979
Fax: (952) 890-3818
E-Mail: mscherer@floortoceiling.com
Web Site: www.floortoceiling.com
Mr. Mike Scherer, Franchise Sales Dir.

FLOOR TO CEILING offers a comprehensive retail franchise opportunity in the fast-growing home decorating market. FTC franchisees benefit from national buying power in floorcovering, kitchen and bath and decorative products from the nation's leading manufacturers.

Our service is complete with software, advertising, rebates, insurance, consumer financing, HR and much more!

BACKGROUND:
Established: 1990;   1st Franchised: 1996
Franchised Units: 62
Company-Owned Units   1
Total Units: 63
Dist.:   US-63; CAN-0; O'seas-0
  North America: 9 States
  Density: 23 in MN, 14 in WI, 6 in IL
Projected New Units (12 Months): 15-20
Qualifications: 5, 4, 5, 3, 4, 5
Registered: IL,IN,MN,ND,SD,WA,WI
FINANCIAL/TERMS:
Cash Investment: $Varies
Total Investment: $Varies
Minimum Net Worth: $Varies
Fees: Franchise - $3-6K
  Royalty - $350+/Mo.;   Ad. - 0%
Earnings Claim Statement: Yes
Term of Contract (Years):   5/5-10
Avg. # Of Employees: 4 FT, 2 PT
Passive Ownership: Allowed
Encourage Conversions: Yes
Area Develop. Agreements: Yes/Varies
Sub-Franchising Contracts: NR
Expand In Territory: Yes
Space Needs: 8,000-14,000 SF; FS, SF, SC
SUPPORT & TRAINING PROVIDED:
Financial Assistance Provided: N/A
Site Selection Assistance: No
Lease Negotiation Assistance: No
Co-Operative Advertising: Yes
Franchisee Assoc./Member: Yes/Yes
Size Of Corporate Staff: 10
On-Going Support: A,C,D,E,G,H
Training: Variable Amount of Time at
  Home Office.
SPECIFIC EXPANSION PLANS:
US: All United States
Canada: No
Overseas: No

<< >>

LIVING LIGHTING
4699 Keele St., # 2
Downsview, ON M3J 2N8 CANADA
Tel: (416) 661-9916
Fax: (416) 661-9706
Mr. Michael Mayerson, VP Leasing and
  Franchising

Full line of retail lighting, home lighting and home decorating centers.

BACKGROUND:
Established: 1968;   1st Franchised: 1970

Franchised Units: 28
Company-Owned Units   0
Total Units: 28
Dist.:   US-0; CAN-28; O'seas-0
  North America: 2 Provinces
  Density: 27 in ON, 1 in BC
Projected New Units (12 Months):   NR
Registered: AB
FINANCIAL/TERMS:
Cash Investment: $80K
Total Investment: $200-225K
Minimum Net Worth: $NR
Fees: Franchise - $30K
  Royalty - 4%;   Ad. - 1%
Earnings Claim Statement: Yes
Term of Contract (Years):   NR
Avg. # Of Employees: NR
Passive Ownership: NR
Encourage Conversions: NR
Area Develop. Agreements: NR
Sub-Franchising Contracts: NR
Expand In Territory: NR
Space Needs: NR SF; NR
SUPPORT & TRAINING PROVIDED:
Financial Assistance Provided: No
Site Selection Assistance: Yes
Lease Negotiation Assistance: Yes
Co-Operative Advertising: Yes
Franchisee Assoc./Member: Yes/Yes
Size Of Corporate Staff: 18
On-Going Support: NR
Training: NR
SPECIFIC EXPANSION PLANS:
US: NR
Canada: All Canada
Overseas: No

<< >>

MORE SPACE PLACE, THE
12555 Enterprise Blvd., # 101
Largo, FL 33773
Tel: (888) 731-3051 (727) 539-1611
Fax: (727) 524-6382
Web Site: www.morsspaceplace.com
Mr. Ben Swift, Dir. Franchise Dev.

Quality storage and space utilization systems. A collection of unique furniture, Murphy Beds, Pocket Office Desk System, custom closets and more. TMSP is poised to help consumers and business save one of today's most precious commodities: SPACE.

BACKGROUND: IFA MEMBER
Established: 1989;   1st Franchised: 1993
Franchised Units: 18
Company-Owned Units   1
Total Units: 19

Dist.:   US-19; CAN-0; O'seas-0
  North America: 2 States
  Density: 18 in FL, 1 in MI
Projected New Units (12 Months):   12
Qualifications: 4, 4, 1, 3, 2, 5
Registered: FL,MI
FINANCIAL/TERMS:
Cash Investment: $85-153.8K
Total Investment: $85-153.8K
Minimum Net Worth: $250K
Fees: Franchise - $22.5K
  Royalty - 4.5%/$250/W;   Ad. -
2.5%/$500/M
Earnings Claim Statement: No
Term of Contract (Years):   10/10
Avg. # Of Employees: 3 FT, 1 PT
Passive Ownership: Discouraged
Encourage Conversions: Yes
Area Develop. Agreements: Yes/10
Sub-Franchising Contracts: No
Expand In Territory: Yes
Space Needs: 2,500 SF; FS, SF, SC
SUPPORT & TRAINING PROVIDED:
Financial Assistance Provided: No
Site Selection Assistance: Yes
Lease Negotiation Assistance: Yes
Co-Operative Advertising: Yes
Franchisee Assoc./Member: No
Size Of Corporate Staff: 16
On-Going Support: B,C,D,E,F,H
Training: 2 Weeks Headquarters Largo,
  FL.; 3 Days On-Site.
SPECIFIC EXPANSION PLANS:
US: All United States
Canada: No
Overseas: No

<< >>

NAKED FURNITURE
1157 Lackawanna Trail, P. O. Box F
Clarks Summit, PA 18411
Tel: (800) 352-2522 (570) 587-7800
Fax: (570) 586-8587
E-Mail: nkdfurn@epix.net
Web Site: www.nakedfurniture.com
Mr. Bruce C. MacGowan, President

NAKED FURNITURE is the nation's largest retailer of custom-finished and ready-to-finish solid wood home furnishings. We offer a wide range of innovative and affordable choices. We serve our markets with attractive, professionally-run stores and a diverse selection of quality furniture and accessories that allow our store owners to maintain their leadership position in the rapidly-growing specialty furniture market.

BACKGROUND: IFA MEMBER
Established: 1972;   1st Franchised: 1979
Franchised Units: 34
Company-Owned Units   3
Total Units: 37
Dist.:   US-37; CAN-0; O'seas-0
  North America: 12 States
  Density: 9 in MI, 8 in IL, 5 in PA
Projected New Units (12 Months):   6
Qualifications: 4, 3, 1, 1, 3, 5
Registered: CA,FL,IL,IN,MD,MI,MN,
  ND,NY,RI,VA,WA,WI
FINANCIAL/TERMS:
Cash Investment: $72-123K
Total Investment: $143-245K
Minimum Net Worth: $NR
Fees: Franchise - $19.5K
  Royalty - 4%;   Ad. - 1%
Earnings Claim Statement: No
Term of Contract (Years):   10/10
Avg. # Of Employees: 3 FT, 2 PT
Passive Ownership: Allowed
Encourage Conversions: Yes
Area Develop. Agreements: Yes
Sub-Franchising Contracts: No
Expand In Territory: Yes
Space Needs: 6,500+ SF; FS, SF, SC, RM
SUPPORT & TRAINING PROVIDED:
Financial Assistance Provided: Yes
Site Selection Assistance: Yes
Lease Negotiation Assistance: Yes
Co-Operative Advertising: No
Franchisee Assoc./Member: Yes/Yes
Size Of Corporate Staff: 19
On-Going Support: a,B,C,D,E,F,G,h,I
Training: 1 Week Headquarters; 1 Week
  On-Site.
SPECIFIC EXPANSION PLANS:
US: All United States
Canada: No
Overseas: No

≪ ≫

**SLUMBERLAND
INTERNATIONAL**
3060 Centerville Rd.
Little Canada, MN 55117
Tel: (651) 482-7500
Fax: (651) 490-0479
Web Site: www.slumberland.com
Mr. Keith Freeburg, Franchise Director

SLUMBERLAND is a home furnishings specialty retailer, featuring name-brand mattresses, sleep sofas, reclining chairs, sofas and chairs, daybeds and related bedroom furniture. SLUMBERLAND is a market-driven retailer that outpaces national averages in sales/SF and gross margins.

BACKGROUND: IFA MEMBER
Established: 1967;   1st Franchised: 1978
Franchised Units: 44
Company-Owned Units   23
Total Units: 67
Dist.:   US-67; CAN-0; O'seas-0
  North America: 7 States
  Density: 33 in MN, 12 in IA, 8 in SD
Projected New Units (12 Months):   8
Registered: IL,MN,ND,SD,WI
FINANCIAL/TERMS:
Cash Investment: $NR
Total Investment: $100-400K
Minimum Net Worth: $NR
Fees: Franchise - $12.5K
  Royalty - 3%;   Ad. - 2%
Earnings Claim Statement: No
Term of Contract (Years):   10/10
Avg. # Of Employees: 4 FT, 2 PT
Passive Ownership: Discouraged
Encourage Conversions: Yes
Area Develop. Agreements: No
Sub-Franchising Contracts: No
Expand In Territory: Yes
Space Needs: 15,000 SF; FS, SC
SUPPORT & TRAINING PROVIDED:
Financial Assistance Provided: No
Site Selection Assistance: No
Lease Negotiation Assistance: Yes
Co-Operative Advertising: N/A
Franchisee Assoc./Member: NR
Size Of Corporate Staff: NR
On-Going Support: B,c,d,G,H,i
Training: 3 Days Headquarters; 2 Weeks
  On-Site.
SPECIFIC EXPANSION PLANS:
US: Central Midwest
Canada: No
Overseas: No

≪ ≫

**VERLO MATTRESS FACTORY
STORES**
W3130 Route 4 Hwy 59, P.O. Box 298
Whitewater, WI 53190
Tel: (800) 229-8957 (414) 473-8957
Fax: (414) 473-4623

Web Site: www.verlo.com
Mr. James M. Young, Dir. of Fran. Awards

VERLO MATTRESS FACTORY STORES (R) is the nation's largest CRAFTSMAN DIRECT (R) retailer. Each franchise assembles hand-crafted mat-tresses to the customer's specifics. With unparalleled support and an operating system in place to take us into the next century, this is an opportunity you will need to investigate.

BACKGROUND: IFA MEMBER
Established: 1958;   1st Franchised: 1981
Franchised Units: 65
Company-Owned Units   2
Total Units: 67
Dist.:   US-67; CAN-0; O'seas-0
  North America: 8 States
  Density: 26 in IL, 21 in WI, 5 in MO
Projected New Units (12 Months):   12
Qualifications: 4, 3, 2, 3, 4, 5
Registered: FL,IL,IN,MD,MI,MN,NY,
  ND,SD,VA,WI,DC
FINANCIAL/TERMS:
Cash Investment: $100-150K
Total Investment: $100-150K
Minimum Net Worth: $400K
Fees: Franchise - $30K
  Royalty - 5%;   Ad. - $300/Mo.
Earnings Claim Statement: No
Term of Contract (Years):   5/5
Avg. # Of Employees: 3+ FT
Passive Ownership: Allowed
Encourage Conversions: Yes
Area Develop. Agreements: Yes/Varies
Sub-Franchising Contracts: No
Expand In Territory: Yes
Space Needs: 3,000-10,000 SF; FS, SF,
  Store Within a Store
SUPPORT & TRAINING PROVIDED:
Financial Assistance Provided: No
Site Selection Assistance: Yes
Lease Negotiation Assistance: Yes
Co-Operative Advertising: No
Franchisee Assoc./Member: Yes/Yes
Size Of Corporate Staff: 20
On-Going Support: B,C,D,E,G,H,i
Training: 12 Days Corporate Office; 7
  Days On-Site; On-Going.
SPECIFIC EXPANSION PLANS:
US: All United States
Canada: No
Overseas: No

≪ ≫

WINDOW WORKS
7167 Shady Oak Rd.
Eden Prairie, MN 55344-3516

Tel: (800) 326-2659 (952) 943-4353
Fax: (952) 943-9050
E-Mail: jspelbrink@windowworks.net
Web Site: www.windowworks.net
Ms. Joanne Spelbrink, VP Operations

WINDOW WORKS showroom and mini-plant concept retails custom window treatments and accessories all within a 1,000 to 1,500 SF facility. Designers offer in-home consultation service, selling top-quality drapery, shutters, cellular shades, wood blinds and verticals. Exclusive Windcom software tracks day-to-day business and generates 27 reports from marketing to sales tax.

BACKGROUND:

Established: 1978;	1st Franchised: 1979
Franchised Units:	8
Company-Owned Units	0
Total Units:	8
Dist.:	US-8; CAN-0; O'seas-0
North America:	7 States
Density:	1 in MI, 1 in CO
Projected New Units (12 Months):	3-4
Qualifications:	3, 2, 1, 2, 3, 4
Registered: IL,IN,MD,MI,MN,VA,WA,WI	

FINANCIAL/TERMS:

Cash Investment:	$15-25K
Total Investment:	$39-67K
Minimum Net Worth:	$75K
Fees: Franchise -	$17.5K
Royalty - 4%;	Ad. - 1%
Earnings Claim Statement:	No
Term of Contract (Years):	15/15
Avg. # Of Employees:	2 FT, 1 PT
Passive Ownership:	Discouraged
Encourage Conversions:	No
Area Develop. Agreements:	No
Sub-Franchising Contracts:	No
Expand In Territory:	No
Space Needs: 1,000-1,500 SF; SC	

SUPPORT & TRAINING PROVIDED:

Financial Assistance Provided:	Yes(I)
Site Selection Assistance:	Yes
Lease Negotiation Assistance:	Yes
Co-Operative Advertising:	Yes
Franchisee Assoc./Member:	No
Size Of Corporate Staff:	3
On-Going Support:	C,D,E,G,H,I

Training: 1-2 Weeks Corporate Window Works -- MN; Store Site, as Needed.

SPECIFIC EXPANSION PLANS:

US:	Most Areas; Not CA or NY
Canada:	No
Overseas:	No

<< >>

SUPPLEMENTAL LISTING OF FRANCHISORS

Abbey Carpet Company, 3471 Bonita Bay Blvd., Bonita Springs, FL 34134 ; (941) 948-0999; Mr. Steve Silverman (800) USE-ABBEY; (941) 948-0900

Affordable Window Coverings, 27715 Jefferson Ave., #103, Temecula, CA 92590 ; (909) 308-0059; Ms. Lisa Thompson (800) 700-4947; (909) 506-2339

Attic, Ltd., The, 3605 N. Willow Knolls Rd., Peoria, IL 61615 ; ; Mr. James M. Tedford ; (309) 692-3317

Carpet Master, 179 Christopher St., New York, NY 10014 ; (516) 795-3545; Mr. Jay Larson (800) 596-7847; (516) 798-7000

Carpet Pro Systems, 317 East U. S. Hwy 70, Garner, NC 27529 ; (919) 662-4054; Mr. John Jones (888) 45-GO-PRO; (919) 662-3776

Carpeteria, 25322 Rye Canyon Rd., Valencia, CA 91355-1151 ; (805) 257-4958; Mrs. Ruth Dugan (800) 356-6763; (805) 295-1000

Carpetland USA, 8201 Calumet Ave., Munster, IN 46321 ; (773) 978-0595; Mr. Jeff Bernstein ; (219) 836-5555

CarpetMax, 210 Town Park Dr., Kennesaw, GA 30144 ; (678) 355-4995; Mr. Ken Kaplan (800) 331-1744; (678) 355-4000

Classy Closets Etc., 1235 S. Akimel Ln., # 5063, Chandler, AZ 85226-5170 ; (602) 438-2304; Mr. Duane Standage (800) 992-2448; (602) 967-2200

Closets To Go, 9540 SW Tigard St., Tigard, OR 97223 ; (503) 679-7068; Mr. Jeff Turner (800) 312-7424; (503) 639-5089

Décor & You, 900 Main St. S., Bldg. # 2, Southbury, CT 06488 ; (203) 264-3516; Ms. Karen Powell (800) 477-3326; (203) 264-3500

Decorating Den Interiors, 19100 Montgomery Village Ave., # 200, Montgomery Village, MD 20886 ; (301) 272-1520; Ms. Alice Flester (800) DEC-DENS; (301) 272-1500

Designs of the Interior, 205 Lageschulte, Barrington, IL 60010 ; (847) 382-9804; Mr. Jim Evanger (888) 382-7488; (847) 382-7488

Furniture Rep's Warehouse, 294 Carlton Dr., Carol Stream, IL 60188 ; (630) 588-1754; Ms. Marianne Barkowski ; (630) 588-9270

GCO Carpet Outlet, 210 Town Park Dr., Kennesaw, GA 30144 ; (678) 355-4981; Mr. Ray Livi (800) 279-8345; (678) 355-4436

Horizon, USA, 2701 Lisenby Ave., Panama City, FL 32405 ; (850) 769-1122; Mr. Darrell Pierce (800) 476-3246; (850) 785-1994

Lifestyle Mobile Carpet Showroom, P.O. Box 3876, Dalton, GA 30721 ; (706) 278-7711; Mr. Phil Moran (800) 346-4531; (706) 278-7919

Nationwide Floor & Window Coverings, 828 E. Broadway, # 800, Milwaukee, WI 53202 ; (414) 765-1300; Mr. Greg Schmich (800) 366-8088; (414) 765-9900

Norwalk - The Furniture Idea, 815 Crocker Rd., # 5, Westlake, OH 44145 ; (440) 871-6057; Mr. Mike Turbeville (888) NORWALK; (419) 668-4461

Panhandler, The, 4699 Keele St., # 2, Downsview, ON M3J QN8 CANADA; (416) 661-9706; Mr. Michael Mayerson ; (416) 661-9916

Sears Carpet & Upholstery Care, 640 Enterprise Dr., #A, Lewis Center, OH 43035 ; (614) 847-4055; Mr. Ted Witcher ; (614) 847-1603

Spring Crest Drapery Centers, 4375 Prado Rd., Unit 104, Corona, CA 91720 ; (909) 340-2078; Mr. Jack W. Long (800) 552-5523; (909) 340-2293

Yesterday's Furniture & Country Store, 2000 S. Seven Highway, Blue Springs, MO 64014 ; (816) 229-1233; Mr. Chris Belcher (888) 228-0800; (816) 228-7227

RETAIL: HOME IMPROVEMENT & HARDWARE INDUSTRY PROFILE

Total # Franchisors in Industry Group	14
Total # Franchised Units in Industry Group	10,449
Total # Company-Owned Units in Industry Group	<u>412</u>
Total # Operating Units in Industry Group	10,861
Average # Franchised Units/Franchisor	746.4
Average # Company-Owned Units/Franchisor	<u>29.4</u>
Average # Total Units/Franchisor	775.8
Ratio of Total # Franchised Units/Total # Company-Owned Units	25.4:1
Industry Survey Participants	5
Representing % of Industry	35.7%
Average Franchise Fee*:	$30.6K
Average Total Investment*:	$157.3K
Average On-Going Royalty Fee*:	6.0%

If a range was provided, the mid-point of the range was used. See detailed profiles for actual ranges.

FIVE LARGEST PARTICIPANTS IN SURVEY

Company	# Fran-chised Units	# Co-Owned Units	# Total Units	Franchise Fee	On-Going Royalty	Total Investment
1. Snap-On Tools	4,298	189	4,487	5K	$50/Mo.	166-232K
2. Matco Tools	1,329	31	1,360	0K	0%	54-147K
3. Stained Glass Overlay	285	0	285	45K	5%	80K
3. Color Your World	44	130	174	35-80K	7%	180-300K
5. Wallpapers To Go	40	16	56	15K	6%	139-194K

All of the data provided are proprietary and should not be quoted without acknowledging *Bond's Franchise Guide*.

COLOR YOUR WORLD

2600 Steeles Ave. W.
Concord, ON L4K 3C8 CANADA
Tel: (800) 387-7311 (905) 738-7477
Fax: (905) 738-9723
Mr. Bob Crookston, Franchise Sales Mgr.

Canada's largest paint and wallpaper retailer, selling to the do-it-yourself and trade markets.

BACKGROUND:
Established: 1912;   1st Franchised: 1977
Franchised Units: 44
Company-Owned Units   130
Total Units: 174
Dist.:   US-0; CAN-276; O'seas-0
  North America: 10 Provinces
  Density: ON, BC, AB
Projected New Units (12 Months):   NR
Qualifications: 5, 5, 2, 3, 4, 5
Registered: AB
FINANCIAL/TERMS:
Cash Investment: $90-150K
Total Investment: $180-300K
Minimum Net Worth: $N/A
Fees: Franchise - $35-80K
  Royalty - 7%;   Ad. - 4%
Earnings Claim Statement: No
Term of Contract (Years):   10/5
Avg. # Of Employees: 4 FT, 3 PT
Passive Ownership: Discouraged
Encourage Conversions: N/A
Area Develop. Agreements: No
Sub-Franchising Contracts: No
Expand In Territory: No
Space Needs: 3,000 SF; FS
SUPPORT & TRAINING PROVIDED:
Financial Assistance Provided: N/A
Site Selection Assistance: N/A
Lease Negotiation Assistance: N/A
Co-Operative Advertising: N/A
Franchisee Assoc./Member: Yes/No
Size Of Corporate Staff: NR
On-Going Support: A,B,C,D,F,G,h,I
Training: 8 Weeks at Various Locations.
SPECIFIC EXPANSION PLANS:
US: No
Canada: All Canada
Overseas: No

MATCO TOOLS

4403 Allen Rd.
Stow, OH 44224-1096
Tel: (800) 368-6651 (330) 929-4949
Fax: (330) 926-5325
Web Site: www.matcotools.com
Ms. Angie McCartney, Fran. Sales Admin.

Mobile distributors of "World Class" MATCO TOOLS, diagnostic computers and service equipment to professional automotive technicians at their place of employment.

BACKGROUND: IFA MEMBER
Established: 1978;   1st Franchised: 1993
Franchised Units: 1,329
Company-Owned Units   31
Total Units: 1,360
Dist.:   US-1,360; CAN-0; O'seas-0
  North America: 50 States
  Density: NR
Projected New Units (12 Months):   290
Qualifications: 3, 2, 2, 1, 2, 5
Registered: All States
FINANCIAL/TERMS:
Cash Investment: $15.5-26K
Total Investment: $54-147K
Minimum Net Worth: $15K
Fees: Franchise - $0
  Royalty - 0%;   Ad. - 0%
Earnings Claim Statement: No
Term of Contract (Years):   10/10
Avg. # Of Employees: 1 FT
Passive Ownership: Allowed
Encourage Conversions: Yes
Area Develop. Agreements: No
Sub-Franchising Contracts: No
Expand In Territory: Yes
Space Needs: N/A SF; N/A
SUPPORT & TRAINING PROVIDED:
Financial Assistance Provided: Yes(D)
Site Selection Assistance: N/A
Lease Negotiation Assistance: N/A
Co-Operative Advertising: N/A
Franchisee Assoc./Member: Yes/Yes
Size Of Corporate Staff: 180
On-Going Support: A,B,C,D,E,F,G,H,I
Training: 6 Day Classroom Stow, OH; 3
  Weeks On-Site.
SPECIFIC EXPANSION PLANS:
US: All United States
Canada: No
Overseas: No

SNAP-ON TOOLS

2801 80th St.
Kenosha, WI 53141
Tel: (800) 786-6600 (414) 656-6516
Fax: (414) 656-5088
E-Mail: franchise@snapon.com
Web Site: www.snapon.com
Mr. M. Raymond Moore, Dir. of Franchise
  Operations

The premier solutions provider to the vehicle service industry. Premium quality products, delivered and sold with premium service. We are proud of our heritage and boldly addressing the future needs of our customers with improved efficiency, creating products and services from hand tools to data and management systems. Contact us today for discussion.

BACKGROUND: IFA MEMBER
Established: 1920;   1st Franchised: 1991
Franchised Units: 4,298
Company-Owned Units   189
Total Units: 4,487
Dist.:   US-3,259; CAN-384; O'seas-844
  North America: All States & Provinces
  Density: 323 in CA, 226 in TX, 176 PA
Projected New Units (12 Months):   313
Qualifications: 3, 4, 2, 2, 5, 5
Registered: All States
FINANCIAL/TERMS:
Cash Investment: $37.4K Minimum
Total Investment: $166.4-232.4K
Minimum Net Worth: $30K
Fees: Franchise - $5K
  Royalty - $50/Mo.;   Ad. - 0%
Earnings Claim Statement: Yes
Term of Contract (Years):   10/5
Avg. # Of Employees: 1 FT
Passive Ownership: Not Allowed
Encourage Conversions: Yes
Area Develop. Agreements: No
Sub-Franchising Contracts: No
Expand In Territory: Yes
Space Needs: NR SF; N/A
SUPPORT & TRAINING PROVIDED:
Financial Assistance Provided: Yes(D)
Site Selection Assistance: N/A
Lease Negotiation Assistance: N/A
Co-Operative Advertising: N/A
Franchisee Assoc./Member: No
Size Of Corporate Staff: NR
On-Going Support: A,B,C,D,E,F,G,h,I
Training: 1 Week at Branch or Regional
  Office; 1 Week at Branch; 3 Weeks
  On-the-Job.

SPECIFIC EXPANSION PLANS:
US: All United States
Canada: All Canada
Overseas: Japan, United Kingdom,
  Germany, Australia, New Zealand

≪≪ ≫≫

STAINED GLASS OVERLAY
1827 N. Case St.
Orange, CA 92865
Tel: (800) 994-4746 (714) 974-6124
Fax: (714) 974-6529
E-Mail: marketing@sgoinc.com
Web Site: www.sgoinc.com
Mr. Tom Wood, Franchise Development

We are the leading decorative glass
franchisor in the world. Combine our
patented technology and proven format
into a great business. Design works of
SGO, for homes, business and religious
institutions. We don't require that you have
an artistic of glass industry backgroung.
We provide training in all required skills.

BACKGROUND: IFA MEMBER
Established: 1981;   1st Franchised: 1982
Franchised Units: 285
Company-Owned Units   0
Total Units: 285
Dist.:   US-141; CAN-14; O'seas-130
  North America: 39 States, 6 Provinces
  Density: 26 in CA, 7 in IL, 6 in FL
Projected New Units (12 Months):   25
Qualifications: 4, 2, 2, 3, 4, 5
Registered: All States and AB
FINANCIAL/TERMS:
Cash Investment: $80K
Total Investment: $80K
Minimum Net Worth: $200K
Fees: Franchise - $45K
  Royalty - 5%;   Ad. - 2%
Earnings Claim Statement: No
Term of Contract (Years):   5/5
Avg. # Of Employees: 3 FT, 1 PT
Passive Ownership: Discouraged
Encourage Conversions: Yes
Area Develop. Agreements: No
Sub-Franchising Contracts: Yes
Expand In Territory: Yes

Space Needs: 1,200 SF; HB, Ind. Space
SUPPORT & TRAINING PROVIDED:
Financial Assistance Provided: Yes(I)
Site Selection Assistance: Yes
Lease Negotiation Assistance: No
Co-Operative Advertising: No
Franchisee Assoc./Member: Yes/Yes
Size Of Corporate Staff: 17
On-Going Support: B,C,d,e,F,G,h,I
Training: 2 x 1 Week Sessions at
  Headquarters in Orange, CA.
SPECIFIC EXPANSION PLANS:
US: All United States
Canada: All Canada
Overseas: Western Europe

≪≪ ≫≫

WALLPAPERS TO GO
14560 Midway Rd.
Dallas, TX 75244
Tel: (800) 843-7094 (972) 503-8688
Fax: (972) 503-8737
E-Mail: tonym@wallpapertodo.com
Web Site: www.wallpapertogo.com
Mr. Tony Martinez, President

World's largest specialty decorating chain in
wallcoverings, window treatments, fabric,
installation and related decorative
accessories. A major participant in the
growing $100 billion home remodeling
industry, WALLPAPERS TO GO is the
5th largest retail purchaser of wallcoverings
in the U. S.

BACKGROUND: IFA MEMBER
Established: 1973;   1st Franchised: 1986
Franchised Units: 40
Company-Owned Units   16
Total Units: 56
Dist.:   US-56; CAN-0; O'seas-0
  North America: 16 States
  Density: 14 in CA, 13 in TX, 4 in WA
Projected New Units (12 Months):   5
Qualifications: 5, 4, 2, 3, 3, 5
Registered: NR
FINANCIAL/TERMS:
Cash Investment: $65K
Total Investment: $139-194K
Minimum Net Worth: $NR
Fees: Franchise - $15K
  Royalty - 6%;   Ad. - 5%
Earnings Claim Statement: No
Term of Contract (Years):   10/10
Avg. # Of Employees: 3 FT, 3 PT
Passive Ownership: Not Allowed
Encourage Conversions: Yes
Area Develop. Agreements: No
Sub-Franchising Contracts: No

Expand In Territory: Yes
Space Needs: 3,500 SF; FS, SC
SUPPORT & TRAINING PROVIDED:
Financial Assistance Provided: No
Site Selection Assistance: Yes
Lease Negotiation Assistance: Yes
Co-Operative Advertising: Yes
Franchisee Assoc./Member: No
Size Of Corporate Staff: 81
On-Going Support: C,D,E,G,h,I
Training: 8 Days Corporate Offices; 5 Days
  Corporate Store.
SPECIFIC EXPANSION PLANS:
US: TX,AZ,CA,WA,OR,CO,MI,OH,IN
Canada: No
Overseas: No

≪≪ ≫≫

**SUPPLEMENTAL LISTING
OF FRANCHISORS**

Ace Hardware, 2200 Kensington Court,
Oak Brook, IL 60544 ; (630) 571-0977;
Mr. Bill Jablonowski (800) 4-ACE-HDW;
(630) 472-4041

American Heritage Shutters, 6655 Poplar
Ave., # 204, Germantown, TN 38138-0643
; (901) 755-8666; Mr. Tom Crutcher ; (901)
751-1000

Austin Hardwoods, 2119 Goodrich, Austin,
TX 78704 ; (512) 441-6444; Mr. Carl
Lasner ; (512) 442-4001

Do It Best Corp., Nelson Rd., P.O. Box 868,
Fort Wayne, IN 46801 ; (219) 748-5478;
Ms. Kelly Koeneman (888) 364-8237; (219)
748-5300

Feather River Wood & Glass, 2365 Forest
Ave., Chico, CA 95928 ; (530) 895-9207;
Mr. Paul Wolfe (800) 395-3667; (530)
895-0762

Floortastic, 1638 S. Research Loop Rd.,
#160, Tuscon, AZ 85710 ; (520)296-4393;
Mr. Dale R. Young (800)332-7397; (520)
722-9781

Snap-On Tools (Canada), 2325 Skymark
Ave., Mississauga, ON L4W 5A9
CANADA; (905) 238-9658; Mr. Tommy
Clark (800) 665-8665; (905) 624-0066

United States Seamless, 2001 1st Ave. N.,
Fargo, ND 58102-2426 ; (701) 241-9999;
Mr. David E. Hedman (800) 615-9318;
(701) 241-8888

RETAIL: PET PRODUCTS & SERVICES INDUSTRY PROFILE

Total # Franchisors in Industry Group	18
Total # Franchised Units in Industry Group	1,023
Total # Company-Owned Units in Industry Group	<u>153</u>
Total # Operating Units in Industry Group	1,176
Average # Franchised Units/Franchisor	56.8
Average # Company-Owned Units/Franchisor	<u>8.5</u>
Average # Total Units/Franchisor	65.3
Ratio of Total # Franchised Units/Total # Company-Owned Units	6.7:1
Industry Survey Participants	9
Representing % of Industry	50.0%
Average Franchise Fee*:	$17.4K
Average Total Investment*:	$90.4K
Average On-Going Royalty Fee*:	6.2%

If a range was provided, the mid-point of the range was used. See detailed profiles for actual ranges.

FIVE LARGEST PARTICIPANTS IN SURVEY

Company	# Fran-chised Units	# Co-Owned Units	# Total Units	Franchise Fee	On-Going Royalty	Total Investment
1. Pet Valu International	333	95	428	20K	N/A	85.4-208K
2. Petland	144	1	145	25K	4.5%	180-500K
3. Whiskers & Paw Catering	98	0	98	19.5K	0%	60-75K
4. Pet Pantry International	38	1	39	20K	0%	65K
5. Aussie Pet Mobile	36	0	36	25K	8%	30K

All of the data provided are proprietary and should not be quoted without acknowledging *Bond's Franchise Guide.*

AUSSIE PET MOBILE

7545 Irvine Center Dr., # 200
Irvine, CA 92618
Tel: (888) 677-7387 (949) 623-8390
Fax: (949) 623-8391
E-Mail: iwm@aussiepetmobile.com
Web Site: www.aussiepetmobile.com
Mr. Ian W. Moses, President

AUSSIE PET MOBILE is an internationally proven franchise system of mobile pet grooming with new U.S. headquarters in Orange County, CA. We pride ourselves on our innovative trailer design, heated hydrobath and a 15-step grooming maintenance process. No experience is required. The AUSSIE PET MOBILE franchise package includes a comprehensive training course. Franchisees enjoy a protected territory with regional and national advertising support.

BACKGROUND: IFA MEMBER

Established: 1996;	1st Franchised: 1997
Franchised Units:	36
Company-Owned Units	0
Total Units:	36
Dist.:	US-1; CAN-0; O'seas-35
North America:	1 State
Density:	NR
Projected New Units (12 Months):	50
Qualifications:	2, 1, 1, 3, 3, 5
Registered: CA,FL,MI,OR	

FINANCIAL/TERMS:

Cash Investment:	$10K
Total Investment:	$30K
Minimum Net Worth:	$10K
Fees: Franchise -	$25K
Royalty - 8%;	Ad. - 4%
Earnings Claim Statement:	No
Term of Contract (Years):	10/10+10
Avg. # Of Employees:	1 FT
Passive Ownership:	Not Allowed
Encourage Conversions:	No
Area Develop. Agreements:	Yes/10
Sub-Franchising Contracts:	Yes
Expand In Territory:	Yes
Space Needs: NR SF; N/A	

SUPPORT & TRAINING PROVIDED:

Financial Assistance Provided:	Yes(I)
Site Selection Assistance:	N/A
Lease Negotiation Assistance:	N/A
Co-Operative Advertising:	Yes
Franchisee Assoc./Member:	Yes/Yes
Size Of Corporate Staff:	2
On-Going Support:	A,B,C,D,E,F,G,H,I
Training: 2 Weeks in Orange County, CA.	

SPECIFIC EXPANSION PLANS:

US:	All United States
Canada:	All Canada
Overseas:	All Countries

◀◀ ▶▶

BONE APPETIT BAKERY, THE

925 L
Lincoln, NE 68508
Tel: (800) 865-2378 (402) 434-5620
Fax: (402) 434-5624
E-Mail: tina@boneappetitbakery.com
Web Site: www.boneappetitbakery.com
Ms. Tina Busch,

At THE BONE APPETIT BAKERY, we take our pet treats very seriously! We have created a unique business concept built around what we believe to be the world's finest treat for your dog or cat. Our wholesome all-natural treats are hand-cut and freshly baked. We want to share our success formula with franchise owners who are interested in the multi-billion dollar pet industry. Site-selection, complete training and full franchisor support are provided.

BACKGROUND:

Established: 1996;	1st Franchised: 1997
Franchised Units:	20
Company-Owned Units	0
Total Units:	20
Dist.:	US-20; CAN-0; O'seas-0
North America:	13 States
Density:	3 in TX, 2 in IN, 2 in FL
Projected New Units (12 Months):	10
Qualifications:	4, 2, 2, 2, 2, 4
Registered: FL,IN,MD,NY,VA,WA,WI	

FINANCIAL/TERMS:

Cash Investment:	$25K
Total Investment:	$50-108K
Minimum Net Worth:	$100K
Fees: Franchise -	$17.5K
Royalty - 6%;	Ad. - 1%
Earnings Claim Statement:	No
Term of Contract (Years):	10/5/5
Avg. # Of Employees:	1 FT, 2 PT
Passive Ownership:	Discouraged
Encourage Conversions:	Yes
Area Develop. Agreements:	Yes/5
Sub-Franchising Contracts:	No
Expand In Territory:	Yes
Space Needs: 1,200 SF; FS, SC	

SUPPORT & TRAINING PROVIDED:

Financial Assistance Provided:	Yes(I)
Site Selection Assistance:	Yes
Lease Negotiation Assistance:	Yes
Co-Operative Advertising:	No
Franchisee Assoc./Member:	No
Size Of Corporate Staff:	5
On-Going Support:	B,C,D,E,h,I
Training: 5-10 Days in Lincoln, NE; 1-3 Franchisee's Location.	

SPECIFIC EXPANSION PLANS:

US:	All United States
Canada:	All Canada
Overseas:	No

◀◀ ▶▶

CRITTER CARE OF AMERICA

1519 Kirkwood Ave.
Nashville, TN 37221
Tel: (800) 256-3014 (615) 850-2273
Fax: (615) 463-8527
Web Site: www.crittercare.com
Mr. Stan W. Bumgarner, President

The CRITTER CARE OF AMERICA franchise concept offers any pet lover an excellent opportunity to achieve personal and financial fulfillment being a professional pet sitter. As the superior alternative to kennels or cages, you'll care for pets in the comfort and familiarity of their own home. We provide you superior training, continuing education and on-going corporate support. You'll enjoy the benefits of a growing nationwide network of franchisees who share ideas and experiences.

BACKGROUND:

Established: 1984;	1st Franchised: 1987
Franchised Units:	15
Company-Owned Units	1
Total Units:	16
Dist.:	US-16; CAN-0; O'seas-0
North America:	NR
Density:	3 in CO, 2 in CA, 2 in TN
Projected New Units (12 Months):	6
Qualifications:	3, 3, 3, 3, 5, 5
Registered: CA,NY	

FINANCIAL/TERMS:

Cash Investment:	$10-25K
Total Investment:	$20-40K
Minimum Net Worth:	$25K
Fees: Franchise -	$10K
Royalty - 6%;	Ad. - N/A
Earnings Claim Statement:	No
Term of Contract (Years):	10/5/5
Avg. # Of Employees:	2 FT, 4-10 PT
Passive Ownership:	Not Allowed
Encourage Conversions:	Yes
Area Develop. Agreements:	Yes/5
Sub-Franchising Contracts:	No
Expand In Territory:	Yes
Space Needs: N/A SF; NR	

SUPPORT & TRAINING PROVIDED:

Financial Assistance Provided:	Yes(D)
Site Selection Assistance:	No
Lease Negotiation Assistance:	N/A
Co-Operative Advertising:	Yes
Franchisee Assoc./Member:	NR
Size Of Corporate Staff:	3
On-Going Support:	C,D,h

Training: 5 Days in Nashville, TN or Denver, CO; 2 Days On-Site.

SPECIFIC EXPANSION PLANS:

US:	Southeast, CO
Canada:	No
Overseas:	No

PET NANNY OF AMERICA

310 N. Clippert St., # 5
Lansing, MI 48912
Tel: (517) 336-8622
Fax: (517) 336-8624
E-Mail: petnanny@arc.net
Web Site: www.petnanny.com
Ms. Rebecca Ann Brevitz, President

PET NANNY, the professional pet-sitting business system, was developed in 1983 specifically for full-time, serious operators in the fascinating pet care world. Our program gives specialists the quality competitive edge necessary to dominate in any market. In training, all areas of operation are covered including pet development and training, marketing, advertising, newsletters and contracts.

BACKGROUND:

Established: 1987;	1st Franchised: 1988
Franchised Units:	17
Company-Owned Units	0
Total Units:	17
Dist.:	US-17; CAN-0; O'seas-0
North America:	NR

Density:	3 in MI, 1 in FL, 1 in AZ
Projected New Units (12 Months):	6
Qualifications:	1, 3, 3, 3, 5, 5
Registered: FL,MI,OR	

FINANCIAL/TERMS:

Cash Investment:	$2.9-6.8K
Total Investment:	$5.3-6.8K
Minimum Net Worth:	$50K
Fees: Franchise -	$4.8K
Royalty - 5%/Min. $25/wk;	Ad. - 2%
Earnings Claim Statement:	No
Term of Contract (Years):	5/5
Avg. # Of Employees:	1 FT, 6 PT
Passive Ownership:	Discouraged
Encourage Conversions:	Yes
Area Develop. Agreements:	No
Sub-Franchising Contracts:	No
Expand In Territory:	Yes
Space Needs: N/A SF; HB	

SUPPORT & TRAINING PROVIDED:

Financial Assistance Provided:	Yes(D)
Site Selection Assistance:	N/A
Lease Negotiation Assistance:	N/A
Co-Operative Advertising:	Yes
Franchisee Assoc./Member:	No
Size Of Corporate Staff:	5
On-Going Support:	a,B,c,D,G,h

Training: 3-5 Days in Lansing, MI.

SPECIFIC EXPANSION PLANS:

US:	Most States
Canada:	ON
Overseas:	U.K.

PET PANTRY INTERNATIONAL, THE

1657 Highway 395, # 202
Minden, NV 89423
Tel: (800) 381-7387 (775) 783-9722
Fax: (775) 783-9513
Mr. Don Lockman, Chairman/CEO

THE PET PANTRY can offer you a spectacular growth opportunity because the forecast calls for it to continue reigning cats and dogs! No royalties; protected marketing areas; little competition; advertising and marketing support; comprehensive, ongoing educational and training programs; on-going business development support. Our free home delivery of super-premium dog and cat food is a profitable way to build your future. Call 1-800-381-7387.

BACKGROUND:

Established: 1995;	1st Franchised: 1995
Franchised Units:	38

Company-Owned Units	1
Total Units:	39
Dist.:	US-39; CAN-0; O'seas-0
North America:	22 States
Density:	8 in CA, 4 in WA, 2 in PA
Projected New Units (12 Months):	50
Qualifications:	4, 3, 1, 2, 1, 5
Registered: All States	

FINANCIAL/TERMS:

Cash Investment:	$20K
Total Investment:	$65K
Minimum Net Worth:	$100K
Fees: Franchise -	$20K
Royalty - 0%;	Ad. - 0%
Earnings Claim Statement:	No
Term of Contract (Years):	7/7
Avg. # Of Employees:	1 FT
Passive Ownership:	Allowed
Encourage Conversions:	No
Area Develop. Agreements:	No
Sub-Franchising Contracts:	No
Expand In Territory:	Yes
Space Needs: 600 SF; HB	

SUPPORT & TRAINING PROVIDED:

Financial Assistance Provided:	No
Site Selection Assistance:	Yes
Lease Negotiation Assistance:	No
Co-Operative Advertising:	Yes
Franchisee Assoc./Member:	No
Size Of Corporate Staff:	13
On-Going Support:	B,C,D,F,g,H,I

Training: 5 Days in Minden, NV at Corporate Office.

SPECIFIC EXPANSION PLANS:

US:	All United States
Canada:	All Canada
Overseas:	All as Master Franchisor

PET VALU INTERNATIONAL

992 Old Eeagle School Rd., # 902
Wayne, PA 19087
Tel: (888) 564-6784 (610) 225-0800
Fax: (610) 225-0822
E-Mail: petvalu@aol.com
Web Site: www.petvalu.com
Mr. David J. Wheat, VP Franchise Development

Discount retailer of pet foods and supplies. 'Your Neighborhood Store With Superstore Prices.'

BACKGROUND: IFA MEMBER

Established: 1976;	1st Franchised: 1987
Franchised Units:	333
Company-Owned Units	95
Total Units:	428

Dist.: US-95; CAN-328; O'seas-0
 North America: 5 States, 2 Provinces
 Density: 227 in ON, 30 in PA,26 in NJ
Projected New Units (12 Months): TBD
Qualifications: 4, 3, 2, 3, 4, 5
Registered: MD,NY,VA
FINANCIAL/TERMS:
Cash Investment: $15-95K
Total Investment: $85.4-207.9K
Minimum Net Worth: $40-160K
Fees: Franchise - $20K
 Royalty - N/A; Ad. - N/A
Earnings Claim Statement: No
Term of Contract (Years): 10/5/5
Avg. # Of Employees: 2 FT, 2 PT
Passive Ownership: Not Allowed
Encourage Conversions: No
Area Develop. Agreements: No
Sub-Franchising Contracts: No
Expand In Territory: No
Space Needs: 2,000-3,000 SF; SC
SUPPORT & TRAINING PROVIDED:
Financial Assistance Provided: Yes(B)
Site Selection Assistance: N/A
Lease Negotiation Assistance: Yes
Co-Operative Advertising: Yes
Franchisee Assoc./Member: Yes
Size Of Corporate Staff: 59
On-Going Support: A,C,E,F,I
Training: 1 Day at Head Office, Wayne, PA;
 3 Weeks at Head Office and Operating
 Store.
SPECIFIC EXPANSION PLANS:
US: Northeast
Canada: MB,ON
Overseas: No

≪ ≫

PETLAND
250 Riverside St.., P. O. Box 1606
Chillicothe, OH 45601-5606
Tel: (800) 221-5935 (740) 775-2464
Fax: (740) 775-2575
Web Site: www.petlandinc.com
Mr. Jim Whitman, Director of
 Franchising

PETLAND is a full-service, pet retail
store that features live animals, including
tropical fish, marine fish, small mammals,
reptiles, amphibians, tropical, domestically-
bred birds, puppies and kittens. The
PETLAND concept also features over
4,000 merchandise items to support the
pets sold to or already in the homes of its

customers. Over 1,500 merchandise items
are PETLAND brands, sold exclusively
through PETLAND retail stores.

BACKGROUND:
Established: 1967; 1st Franchised: 1972
Franchised Units: 144
Company-Owned Units 1
Total Units: 145
Dist.: US-93; CAN-46; O'seas-6
 North America: 32 States, 5 Provinces
 Density: 19 in OH, 14 in FL, 11 in IL
Projected New Units (12 Months): 18
Qualifications: 3, 5, 1, 3, 4, 5
Registered: AB
FINANCIAL/TERMS:
Cash Investment: $60-120K
Total Investment: $180-500K
Minimum Net Worth: $250K
Fees: Franchise - $25K
 Royalty - 4.5%; Ad. - N/A
Earnings Claim Statement: No
Term of Contract (Years): 20/20
Avg. # Of Employees: 5 FT, 7 PT
Passive Ownership: Discouraged
Encourage Conversions: Yes
Area Develop. Agreements: No
Sub-Franchising Contracts: No
Expand In Territory: Yes
Space Needs: 5,000 SF; FS, SC, RM
SUPPORT & TRAINING PROVIDED:
Financial Assistance Provided: Yes(I)
Site Selection Assistance: Yes
Lease Negotiation Assistance: Yes
Co-Operative Advertising: Yes
Franchisee Assoc./Member: No
Size Of Corporate Staff: 38
On-Going Support: B,C,D,E,F,G,H,I
Training: 1.5 Weeks Training Store,
 Chillicothe, OH; 1 Week Classroom; 2
 Weeks New Store Location.
SPECIFIC EXPANSION PLANS:
US: All United States
Canada: All Canada
Overseas: Western Europe, Australia,
 South America

≪ ≫

PETS ARE INN
7723 Tanglewood Ct., #150
Minneapolis, MN 55439
Tel: (800) 248-PETS (952) 944-8298
Fax: (952) 829-3828
E-Mail: jplatt@petsareinn.com
Web Site: www.petsareinn.com
Mr. Jim Platt, Director Franchise
 Operations

Pets Are Inn

When a family goes on vacation, they
prefer to have their pet cared for in a
loving - caring - home environment. We
are looking for individuals that recognize
the need for PETS ARE INN in their
area. An individual that has a proven track
record as a professional in other areas but
has made a conscious decision to change
career paths - to be involved in business
and in the community. Our unique niche
in the hospitality/travel industry provides
our customers and their pets with worry
free services.

BACKGROUND:
Established: 1982; 1st Franchised: 1992
Franchised Units: 17
Company-Owned Units 0
Total Units: 17
Dist.: US-17; CAN-0; O'seas-0
 North America: NR
 Density: 6 in MN, 3 in TX, 2 in WA
Projected New Units (12 Months): 4
Qualifications: 5, 4, 3, 5, 5, 4
Registered: CA,HI,IL,IN,MD,MI,MN,WA
FINANCIAL/TERMS:
Cash Investment: $20K
Total Investment: $35-65K
Minimum Net Worth: $NR
Fees: Franchise - $15K
 Royalty - 5-10%; Ad. - 1%
Earnings Claim Statement: Yes
Term of Contract (Years): 10/10
Avg. # Of Employees: 2 FT, 4 PT
Passive Ownership: Not Allowed
Encourage Conversions: N/A
Area Develop. Agreements: No
Sub-Franchising Contracts: No
Expand In Territory: No
Space Needs: NR SF; HB
SUPPORT & TRAINING PROVIDED:
Financial Assistance Provided: No
Site Selection Assistance: Yes
Lease Negotiation Assistance: Yes
Co-Operative Advertising: Yes
Franchisee Assoc./Member: No

Size Of Corporate Staff: 5
On-Going Support: A,B,C,D,E,G,H,I
Training: 5 Days in Minneapolis, MN.
SPECIFIC EXPANSION PLANS:
US: Central Time Zone
Canada: No
Overseas: No

WHISKERS & PAWS CATERING
896 W. Nye Ln., #201
Carson City, NV 89703
Tel: (877) 583-9800 (775) 841-6000
Fax: (775) 841-6420
Web Site: www.whiskersandpaws.com
Mr. Kenneth Wright, Chairman

Our franchisees offer free home delivery of
our "Best Friends Choice" super premium
pet foods and supplies. We offer a 100%
satisfaction guarantee and of course "old-
fashioned service."

BACKGROUND: IFA MEMBER
Established: 1998;   1st Franchised: 1998
Franchised Units: 98
Company-Owned Units   0
Total Units: 98
Dist.:   US-81; CAN-17; O'seas-0
  North America: 15 States, 4 Provinces
  Density: 8 in NC, 7 in CA, 5 in NV
Projected New Units (12 Months):   60
Qualifications: 2, 3, 1, 2, 3, 5
Registered: CA,FL,HI,IL,IN,MD,MI,MN,
   NY,ND,OR,RI,SD,VA,WA,WI,DC
FINANCIAL/TERMS:
Cash Investment: $60K
Total Investment: $60-75K
Minimum Net Worth: $100K
Fees: Franchise - $19.5K
  Royalty - 0%;   Ad. - 0%
Earnings Claim Statement: No
Term of Contract (Years):   10/10
Avg. # Of Employees: 2 FT, 4 PT
Passive Ownership: Allowed
Encourage Conversions: N/A
Area Develop. Agreements: No
Sub-Franchising Contracts: No
Expand In Territory: No
Space Needs: NR SF; N/A

SUPPORT & TRAINING PROVIDED:
Financial Assistance Provided: N/A
Site Selection Assistance: Yes
Lease Negotiation Assistance: N/A
Co-Operative Advertising: N/A
Franchisee Assoc./Member: No
Size Of Corporate Staff: 12
On-Going Support: A,B,C,D,E,F,G,H,I
Training: 5 Days in Carson City, NV.
SPECIFIC EXPANSION PLANS:
US: All United States
Canada: All Except PQ
Overseas: Britain, Germany, Italy, the
   Netherlands, France

SUPPLEMENTAL LISTING
OF FRANCHISORS

Animal Adventure Pets, 5453 S. 76th St.,
Greendale, WI 53129 ; (414) 423-7351; Mr.
Mike Edwards (800) 289-5665;

Canine Counselors, 1660 Southern Blvd.
A, West Palm Beach, FL 33406 ; (561)
640-3973; Ms. Robert Ward (800)
456-DOGS; (561) 640-3970

Canusa (Brant) Pet Products, 175 Ashgrove
Ave., Brantford, ON N3R 7C6 CANADA;
(519)-752-2752; Mr. John Di Sabatino ;
(519) 752-7866

Pet City, 1325 S. Cherokee St., Denver, CO
80223 ; (303) 777-5762; Mr. Steve Waugh
(800) 526-7387; (303) 744-6131

Pet Habitat, 6921 Heather St., Vancouver,
BC V6P 3P5 CANADA; (604) 266-5880;
Mr. Ernest Ang ; (604) 266-2721

Pet Valu International (Canada), 7300
Warden Ave., # 400, Markham, ON L3R
9Z6 CANADA; (905) 946-0659; Mr. Wade
Jamieson (888) 564-6784; (905) 946-1200

PetPeople, 722 Genevieve St., # E, Solana
Beach, CA 92075; (619) 481-3337; Mr. Gregory
S. Morris (800) 655-6595; (619) 481-3335

Ruffin's Pet Centres, 109 Industrial Dr.,
Dunnville, ON N1A 2X5 CANADA; (905)
774-1096; Mr. Mark Reynolds ; (905)
774-7079

U-Wash Doggie, 1056 W. Alameda,
Burbank, CA 91506 ; (661) 297-2029; Mr.
Fransisco R. Gamero (888) 820-7900;

Retail: Photographic Products & Services

Chapter

41

RETAIL: PHOTOGRAPHIC PRODUCTS & SERVICES INDUSTRY PROFILE

Total # Franchisors in Industry Group	15
Total # Franchised Units in Industry Group	911
Total # Company-Owned Units in Industry Group	<u>84</u>
Total # Operating Units in Industry Group	995
Average # Franchised Units/Franchisor	60.7
Average # Company-Owned Units/Franchisor	<u>5.6</u>
Average # Total Units/Franchisor	66.3
Ratio of Total # Franchised Units/Total # Company-Owned Units	10.8:1
Industry Survey Participants	4
Representing % of Industry	426.7%
Average Franchise Fee*:	$21.4K
Average Total Investment*:	$153.3K
Average On-Going Royalty Fee*:	6.0%

If a range was provided, the mid-point of the range was used. See detailed profiles for actual ranges.

FIVE LARGEST PARTICIPANTS IN SURVEY

Company	# Fran-chised Units	# Co-Owned Units	# Total Units	Franchise Fee	On-Going Royalty	Total Investment
1. Motophoto (SM)	371	49	420	15K	6%	310K
4. One Hour Motophoto (Canada)	53	3	56	35K	6%	225-250K
5. I.N.V.U. Portraits	51	0	51	12K	6%	28-66K
4. Visual Image, The	15	5	20	23.5K	0%	35-40K

All of the data provided are proprietary and should not be quoted without acknowledging *Bond's Franchise Guide.*

I.N.V.U. PORTRAITS

563 West 500 S., # 250
Bountiful, UT 84010
Tel: (801) 292-4688
Fax: (801) 299-1625
E-Mail: randy@invuportraits.com
Web Site: www.invuportraits.com
Mr. Randy S. Olson, Franchise Sales

I.N.V.U. PORTRAITS combine heart-warming, one-of-a-kind photography with the up-scale creative touch of hand coloring and sepia toning. The resulting combination is a cherished piece. If you've ever considered owning your own home-based business and are able to put your creative talents and energies into an exciting and rewarding industry, we want to speak with you.

BACKGROUND:

Established: 1995; 1st Franchised: 1996
Franchised Units: 51
Company-Owned Units   0
Total Units: 51
Dist.:   US-51; CAN-0; O'seas-0
    North America: 30 States
    Density: 4 in CA, 4 in FL, 3 in VA
Projected New Units (12 Months):   60
Qualifications: 5, 4, 2, 1, 4, 5
Registered: CA,FL,IL,IN,MD,MI,MN,
    NY,OR,RI,VA,WA,WI,DC
FINANCIAL/TERMS:
Cash Investment: $28-66K
Total Investment: $28-66K
Minimum Net Worth: $50K
Fees: Franchise - $12K
    Royalty - 6%;   Ad. - 2%
Earnings Claim Statement: No
Term of Contract (Years):   10/5
Avg. # Of Employees: 4 FT
Passive Ownership: Not Allowed
Encourage Conversions: No
Area Develop. Agreements: No
Sub-Franchising Contracts: No
Expand In Territory: Yes
Space Needs: N/A SF; HB
SUPPORT & TRAINING PROVIDED:
Financial Assistance Provided: No
Site Selection Assistance: N/A
Lease Negotiation Assistance: N/A
Co-Operative Advertising: N/A
Franchisee Assoc./Member: No
Size Of Corporate Staff: 45
On-Going Support: b,C,D,G,h
Training: 5 Days Salt Lake City, UT.
SPECIFIC EXPANSION PLANS:
US: All United States
Canada: All Canada
Overseas: No

≪   ≫

MOTOPHOTO

MOTOPHOTO (SM)

4444 Lake Center Dr.
Dayton, OH 45426-0096
Tel: (800) 733-6686 (937) 854-6686
Fax: (937) 854-0140
E-Mail: franchise@motophoto.com
Web Site: www.motophoto.com
Mr. Paul Pieschel, SVP Franchise Development

MOTOPHOTO is an up-scale specialty retailer in the $14 billion and still-growing photo processing and portrait industries. MOTOPHOTO stores feature on-site processing, portrait studios, select merchandise and digital applications. This is a happy, clean and up-scale business, operating with a small, professional staff and requiring a modest inventory investment with strong profit potential. Ranked #4 in Income Opporunties' Platinum 2000 and # 15 in Success Franchise Gold 100.

BACKGROUND: IFA MEMBER
Established: 1981;   1st Franchised: 1982
Franchised Units: 371
Company-Owned Units   49
Total Units: 420
Dist.:   US-335; CAN-38; O'seas-47
    North America: 27 States, 1 Province
    Density: 50 in NJ, 44 in ON, 27 in IL
Projected New Units (12 Months):   20
Qualifications: 5, 4, 1, 4, 3, 5
Registered: CA,FL,HI,IL,IN,MD,MI,NY,
    RI,VA,WI,DC
FINANCIAL/TERMS:
Cash Investment: $60K
Total Investment: $310K
Minimum Net Worth: $150K
Fees: Franchise - $15K
    Royalty - 6%;   Ad. - 0.5%
Earnings Claim Statement: Yes
Term of Contract (Years):   10/10
Avg. # Of Employees: 3 FT, 3 PT
Passive Ownership: Allowed
Encourage Conversions: Yes
Area Develop. Agreements:Yes/5/5/5/5
Sub-Franchising Contracts: No
Expand In Territory: Yes
Space Needs: 1,200-1,400 SF; FS, SF, SC,
    RM
SUPPORT & TRAINING PROVIDED:
Financial Assistance Provided: Yes(D)
Site Selection Assistance: Yes

Lease Negotiation Assistance: Yes
Co-Operative Advertising: Yes
Franchisee Assoc./Member: No
Size Of Corporate Staff: 70
On-Going Support: B,C,D,E,G,H,I
Training: 3 Weeks Dayton, OH; 3 Weeks
    Local Market.
SPECIFIC EXPANSION PLANS:
US: All United States
Canada: ON, W Provinces
Overseas: All Countries

≪   ≫

ONE HOUR MOTOPHOTO & PORTRAIT STUDIO (CANADA)

1315 Lawrence Ave. E., # 509
Don Mills, ON M3A 3R3 CANADA
Tel: (416) 443-1900
Fax: (416) 443-1653
E-Mail: franchise@motophoto.com
Web Site: www.motophoto.com
Mr. John Blatchly, Franchise Dev.

Own a franchise that's fun to run! MOTOPHOTO is an up-scale, specialty retail concept featuring one hour processing, photo-related merchandise and a portrait studio. We're dedicated to enhancing our customers' enjoyment of their imaging experiences better than any other provider.

BACKGROUND:
Established: 1986;   1st Franchised: 1987
Franchised Units: 53
Company-Owned Units   3
Total Units: 56
Dist.:   US-0; CAN-56; O'seas-26
    North America: 1 Province
    Density: 56 in ON
Projected New Units (12 Months):   6-8
Qualifications: 5, 5, 1, 4, 4, 5
Registered: NR
FINANCIAL/TERMS:
Cash Investment: $85-90K
Total Investment: $225-250K
Minimum Net Worth: $250K
Fees: Franchise - $35K
    Royalty - 6%;   Ad. - 6%
Earnings Claim Statement: Yes
Term of Contract (Years):   10/2-5
Avg. # Of Employees: 3 FT, 2 PT
Passive Ownership: Not Allowed
Encourage Conversions: Yes
Area Develop. Agreements: No
Sub-Franchising Contracts: No
Expand In Territory: Yes
Space Needs: 1,000-1,200 SF; SF, SC, RM

SUPPORT & TRAINING PROVIDED:

Financial Assistance Provided:	Yes(I)
Site Selection Assistance:	Yes
Lease Negotiation Assistance:	Yes
Co-Operative Advertising:	Yes
Franchisee Assoc./Member:	Yes/Yes
Size Of Corporate Staff:	10
On-Going Support:	A,B,C,D,E,F,G,H
Training: 3 Weeks Corporate Training.	

SPECIFIC EXPANSION PLANS:

US:	N/A
Canada:	ON,BC
Overseas:	No

<< >>

VISUAL IMAGE, THE

523 Highland Ave.
Maryville, TN 37803
Tel: (800) 344-0323 (865) 981-1270
Fax: (865) 681-0279
E-Mail: thevip@mindspring.com
Web Site: www.thevisualimageinc.com
Mr. Donald Holman, Vice President

VISUAL IMAGE combines the advantages of high mark-up photography with the low overhead of home-based business. Because we do all our photography on location, you save the high cost of retailspace and the confinement of retail hours! We go to pre-schools and pet shops and take portraits for busy, working parents. Because we do studio-quality portraiture, preschools love our work and invite us back season after season. Creative, fulfilling work, financial and physical rewards.

BACKGROUND:

Established: 1984; 1st Franchised: 1994	
Franchised Units:	15
Company-Owned Units	5
Total Units:	20
Dist.:	US-20; CAN-0; O'seas-0
North America:	12 States
Density:	4 in FL, 4 in TN, 2 in NC
Projected New Units (12 Months):	3
Qualifications:	3, 4, 1, 1, 3, 5
Registered: FL,MI	

FINANCIAL/TERMS:

Cash Investment:	$30-40K
Total Investment:	$35-40K
Minimum Net Worth:	$50K
Fees: Franchise -	$23.5K
Royalty - 0%;	Ad. - 0%
Earnings Claim Statement:	Yes
Term of Contract (Years):	3/5
Avg. # Of Employees:	1 FT, 1 PT
Passive Ownership:	Discouraged

Encourage Conversions:	N/A
Area Develop. Agreements:	No
Sub-Franchising Contracts:	No
Expand In Territory:	Yes
Space Needs: N/A SF; HB	

SUPPORT & TRAINING PROVIDED:

Financial Assistance Provided:	Yes(I)
Site Selection Assistance:	N/A
Lease Negotiation Assistance:	N/A
Co-Operative Advertising:	Yes
Franchisee Assoc./Member:	Yes
Size Of Corporate Staff:	3
On-Going Support:	B,C,D,G,h,I
Training: 1 Week Home Base; 1 Week Training Center; I Week Training Center/Your Location.	

SPECIFIC EXPANSION PLANS:

US:	All United States
Canada:	No
Overseas:	No

<< >>

SUPPLEMENTAL LISTING
OF FRANCHISORS

Action Sports Photos, 4220 N. May Ave., Oklahoma City, OK 73112 ; (405) 942-0555; Mr. Gary L. Fearnow ; (405) 942-7007

Contempo Portraits, 1235 S. Gilbert Rd., # 16, Mesa, AZ 85204 ; (602) 926-2382; Mrs. Cheri Silard/ Sandy Eniss ; (602) 926-2216

Glamour Shots, 1300 Metropolitan Ave., Oklahoma City, OK 73108 ; (405) 951-7343; Ms. Kim McElroy (800) 336-4550; (405) 947-8747

IPI - Insta-Pak, 5025 Dorr St., Toledo, OH 43615 ; (419) 537-1511; Mr. Steve Hardin (800) 444-7525; (419) 537-1555

Japan Camera Centre 1 Hour Photo, 205 Riviera Dr., # 1, Markham, ON L3R 5J8 CANADA; (416) 445-0519; Ms. Wendy Maul (800) 268-7740; (416) 445-1481

Master Photography, P.O. Box 2239, Aspen, CO 81612 ; (970) 927-2522; Mr. Gary Crabtree (800) 482-2505; (970) 927-2505

Photoarts Etc., 323 E. Broadway, Vista, CA 92084 ; (760) 806-1851; Mr. William Lange (800) 699-7468; (760) 806-9760

Pixarts, 9420 Mira Mesa Blvd., # C, San Diego, CA 92126-4848 ; (858) 578-2750; Mr. Anthony M. Napoli (800) 865-4333; (858) 578-7200

Sports Section, The, 3871 Lakefield Dr., # 100, Suwanee, GA 30024 ; (770) 622-4949; Mr. Larry R. Cranford (800) 321-9127; (770) 622-4900

Zaio.Com, 93 Center Pointe Dr., St. Charles, MO 63304 ; (636) 498-0293; Mr. Dennis G. Fuller (877) 233-9563; (636) 447-4429

RETAIL: SPECIALTY INDUSTRY PROFILE

Total # Franchisors in Industry Group	116
Total # Franchised Units in Industry Group	6,698
Total # Company-Owned Units in Industry Group	<u>3,716</u>
Total # Operating Units in Industry Group	10,414
Average # Franchised Units/Franchisor	57.7
Average # Company-Owned Units/Franchisor	<u>32.0</u>
Average # Total Units/Franchisor	89.7
Ratio of Total # Franchised Units/Total # Company-Owned Units	1.8:1
Industry Survey Participants	49
Representing % of Industry	42.2%
Average Franchise Fee*:	$23.3K
Average Total Investment*:	$176.4K
Average On-Going Royalty Fee*:	5.5%

If a range was provided, the mid-point of the range was used. See detailed profiles for actual ranges.

FIVE LARGEST PARTICIPANTS IN SURVEY

Company	# Franchised Units	# Co-Owned Units	# Total Units	Franchise Fee	On-Going Royalty	Total Investment
1. General Nutrition Centers	1,636	2,812	4,448	32.5K	6%	130-180K
2. Book Rack, The	283	1	284	6K	$75/Mo.	18K+
3. Wild Birds Unlimited	281	0	281	18K	4%/$8K Min.	80-140K
4. Wicks n' Sticks	218	4	222	25K	6%	154-249K
5. Computer Renaissance	211	1	212	20K	3%	180-225K

All of the data provided are proprietary and should not be quoted without acknowledging *Bond's Franchise Guide*.

....IT STORE

1111 Flint Rd.,# 36
Downsview, ON M3J 3C7 CANADA
Tel: (416) 665-3471
Fax: (416) 665-8839
E-Mail: fun@itstore.com
Web Site: www.itstore.com
Mr. Jack Green, President

Gifts from the perfectly practical to the absolutely ridiculous. Contemporary greeting cards, gifts, novelties - specializing in cutting edge.

BACKGROUND:

Established: 1981; 1st Franchised: 1982	
Franchised Units:	31
Company-Owned Units	18
Total Units:	49
Dist.:	US-0; CAN-49; O'seas-0
North America:	NR
Density:	29 in ON, 3 in NB, 1 in NS
Projected New Units (12 Months):	5
Qualifications:	4, 3, 2, 2, 3, 4
Registered: FL,IL,IN,ND,MI,MN,NY,WI	

FINANCIAL/TERMS:

Cash Investment:	$75K
Total Investment:	$150-225K
Minimum Net Worth:	$150K
Fees: Franchise -	$25K
Royalty - 6%;	Ad. - 2%
Earnings Claim Statement:	No
Term of Contract (Years):	5/5
Avg. # Of Employees:	1 FT, 6 PT
Passive Ownership:	Discouraged
Encourage Conversions:	N/A
Area Develop. Agreements:	No
Sub-Franchising Contracts:	No
Expand In Territory:	Yes
Space Needs: 1,200-1,400 SF; RM	

SUPPORT & TRAINING PROVIDED:

Financial Assistance Provided:	Yes(I)
Site Selection Assistance:	Yes
Lease Negotiation Assistance:	Yes
Co-Operative Advertising:	Yes
Franchisee Assoc./Member:	No
Size Of Corporate Staff:	15
On-Going Support:	B,C,D,E,F,G,H,I
Training: NR	

SPECIFIC EXPANSION PLANS:

US:	All United States
Canada:	All Canada
Overseas:	All Countries

<< >>

ASHLEY AVERY'S COLLECTABLES

100 Glenborough Dr., #1450
Houston, TX 77067
Tel: (800) 543-3325 (281) 775-5290
Fax: (281) 775-5250
E-Mail: annn@shopaac.com
Web Site: www.shopaac.com
Ms. Ann Nance, Franchise Dev. Mgr.

ASHLEY AVERY'S COLLECTABLES is one of America's finest retailers of beautiful gifts & collectables, featuring exclusive pieces from world-renowned names such as Swarovski, Armani, Ilardo, Hummel and many more. Each store features an elegant, gallery-like atmosphere with fascinating works of all kinds. Located in up-scale regional malls. Easy to learn & operate; exceptional training and support; national buying power & proven marketing programs.

BACKGROUND: IFA MEMBER

Established: 1981; 1st Franchised: 1981	
Franchised Units:	38
Company-Owned Units	1
Total Units:	39
Dist.:	US-39; CAN-0; O'seas-0
North America:	13 States
Density:	17 in TX, 5 in FL, 2 in GA
Projected New Units (12 Months):	10
Qualifications:	5, 3, 3, 3, 4, 5
Registered: CA,FL,IL,IN,MD,MI,MN, NY,ND,RI,SD,VA,WA,WI	

FINANCIAL/TERMS:

Cash Investment:	$200K
Total Investment:	$266-397K
Minimum Net Worth:	$400K
Fees: Franchise -	$30K
Royalty - 6%;	Ad. - 2%
Earnings Claim Statement:	No
Term of Contract (Years):	10
Avg. # Of Employees:	2 FT, 2 PT
Passive Ownership:	Allowed
Encourage Conversions:	Yes
Area Develop. Agreements:	No
Sub-Franchising Contracts:	No
Expand In Territory:	Yes
Space Needs: 900-1,200 SF; RM, Kiosk (200sf)	

SUPPORT & TRAINING PROVIDED:

Financial Assistance Provided:	Yes(I)
Site Selection Assistance:	Yes
Lease Negotiation Assistance:	Yes
Co-Operative Advertising:	Yes
Franchisee Assoc./Member:	Yes/Yes
Size Of Corporate Staff:	7
On-Going Support:	A,B,C,D,E,F,G,H,I
Training: 7 Days in Houston, TX.	

SPECIFIC EXPANSION PLANS:

US:	All United States
Canada:	No
Overseas:	No

<< >>

BOOK RACK, THE

2715 E. Commercial Blvd.
Ft. Lauderdale, FL 33308
Tel: (954) 984-1918
Fax:
Mr. Fred M. Darnell, President

New and used paperback books.

BACKGROUND:

Established: 1963; 1st Franchised: 1966	
Franchised Units:	283
Company-Owned Units	1
Total Units:	284
Dist.:	US-283; CAN-1; O'seas-0
North America:	NR
Density:	TX, FL, TN
Projected New Units (12 Months):	19
Qualifications:	3, 3, 5, 3, 1, 2
Registered: All States Except ND,SD	

FINANCIAL/TERMS:

Cash Investment:	$16-34K
Total Investment:	$18K+
Minimum Net Worth:	$16K
Fees: Franchise -	$6K
Royalty - $75/Mo.;	Ad. - 0%
Earnings Claim Statement:	No
Term of Contract (Years):	Lifetime
Avg. # Of Employees:	1 FT, 1 PT
Passive Ownership:	Allowed
Encourage Conversions:	Yes
Area Develop. Agreements:	No
Sub-Franchising Contracts:	No
Expand In Territory:	Yes
Space Needs: 1,200-6,000 SF; SC	

SUPPORT & TRAINING PROVIDED:

Financial Assistance Provided:	No
Site Selection Assistance:	Yes
Lease Negotiation Assistance:	Yes
Co-Operative Advertising:	No
Franchisee Assoc./Member:	No
Size Of Corporate Staff:	8
On-Going Support:	C,D,E,F,G,H
Training: 7-10 Days Ft. Lauderdale, FL.	

SPECIFIC EXPANSION PLANS:

US:	All United States
Canada:	All Canada
Overseas:	No

≺≺ ≻≻

BUTTERFIELDS, ETC.

1040 Wm. Hilton Pkwy., Circle Bldg.
Hilton Head Island, SC 29928
Tel: (843) 842-6000
Fax: (843) 842-6999
Mr. Jim Lunceford, President

Retail gourmet kitchen store, located in up-scale malls. Our merchandise mix includes high-quality cookware, largest assortment of kitchen gadgets, cookbooks, decorative ceramics, linens, cutlery and fresh-roasted coffee beans.

BACKGROUND:

Established: 1979; 1st Franchised: 1986	
Franchised Units:	26
Company-Owned Units	0
Total Units:	26
Dist.:	US-26; CAN-0; O'seas-0
North America:	NR
Density:	NR
Projected New Units (12 Months):	NR
Registered: NR	

FINANCIAL/TERMS:

Cash Investment:	$50K
Total Investment:	$150-225K
Minimum Net Worth:	$250K
Fees: Franchise -	$20K
Royalty - 4-5%;	Ad. - NR
Earnings Claim Statement:	No
Term of Contract (Years):	10
Avg. # Of Employees:	NR
Passive Ownership:	Not Allowed
Encourage Conversions:	Yes
Area Develop. Agreements:	NR
Sub-Franchising Contracts:	NR
Expand In Territory:	NR
Space Needs: NR SF; NR	

SUPPORT & TRAINING PROVIDED:

Financial Assistance Provided:	Yes(I)
Site Selection Assistance:	Yes
Lease Negotiation Assistance:	Yes
Co-Operative Advertising:	No
Franchisee Assoc./Member:	No
Size Of Corporate Staff:	NR
On-Going Support:	NR
Training: 2 Weeks.	

SPECIFIC EXPANSION PLANS:

US:	NR
Canada:	No
Overseas:	No

≺≺ ≻≻

CANDLEMAN CORPORATION

1021 Industrial Park Rd.
Brainerd, MN 56401
Tel: (800) 328-3453 (218) 829-0592
Fax: (218) 825-2449
E-Mail: info@candleman.com
Web Site: www.candleman.com
Ms. Sara Wise, Vice President

Franchisor of focused, up-scale retail stores, offering the most overwhelming assortment of candles anywhere. Our management team has years of successful experience in retail and franchising. Stores are located in the best regional malls nationwide. One-of-a-kind niche business. Proprietary computer system tracks all aspects of sales and inventory and generates precision management reports.

BACKGROUND:

Established: 1991; 1st Franchised: 1992	
Franchised Units:	60
Company-Owned Units	2
Total Units:	62
Dist.:	US-57; CAN-5; O'seas-0
North America:	33 States, 2 Provinces
Density:	8 in OH, 7 in MN, 6 in FL
Projected New Units (12 Months):	15
Qualifications:	4, 4, 2, 2, 4, 5
Registered: All States	

FINANCIAL/TERMS:

Cash Investment:	$70K
Total Investment:	$150-350K
Minimum Net Worth:	$200K
Fees: Franchise -	$25K
Royalty - 6%;	Ad. - 100/Mo.
Earnings Claim Statement:	No
Term of Contract (Years):	10/10
Avg. # Of Employees:	1 FT, 4-5 PT
Passive Ownership:	Not Allowed
Encourage Conversions:	No
Area Develop. Agreements:	No
Sub-Franchising Contracts:	No
Expand In Territory:	No
Space Needs: 800-1,200 SF; RM	

SUPPORT & TRAINING PROVIDED:

Financial Assistance Provided:	Yes(I)
Site Selection Assistance:	Yes
Lease Negotiation Assistance:	Yes
Co-Operative Advertising:	No
Franchisee Assoc./Member:	Yes/Yes
Size Of Corporate Staff:	24
On-Going Support:	C,D,E,F,G,H,I

Training: 5 Days in Headquarters; 3-5 Days On-Site.

SPECIFIC EXPANSION PLANS:

US:	All United States
Canada:	All Canada
Overseas: Europe, Middle East, Australia, South America	

≺≺ ≻≻

CAR PHONE STORE, THE

2608 Berlin Turnpike
Newington, CT 06109
Tel: (860) 571-7600
Fax: (860) 257-1818
E-Mail: info@thecarphonestore.com
Web Site: www.thecarphonestore.com
Mr. Keith Sinclair, President

THE CAR PHONE STORE/WIRELESS ZONE is a retail store chain dedicated to the sale of cellular phones, accessories and other wireless products. Volume discounted merchandise from a full-service warehouse, training, on-going support and advertising are available, enabling franchisees to concentrate on selling product and taking advantage of the wireless industry's continuing fast growth.

BACKGROUND:

Established: 1988; 1st Franchised: 1988	
Franchised Units:	83
Company-Owned Units	2
Total Units:	85
Dist.:	US-85; CAN-0; O'seas-0
North America:	11 States
Density:	29 in MA, 28 in CT, 9 in MD
Projected New Units (12 Months):	NR
Registered:	

FINANCIAL/TERMS:

Cash Investment:	$N/A
Total Investment:	$22.9-125.8K
Minimum Net Worth:	$N/A
Fees: Franchise -	$7.5-25K
Royalty - 10-20%;	Ad. - Varies
Earnings Claim Statement:	NR
Term of Contract (Years):	7/7
Avg. # Of Employees:	2 FT, 1 PT
Passive Ownership:	Discouraged
Encourage Conversions:	NR
Area Develop. Agreements:	No
Sub-Franchising Contracts:	Yes
Expand In Territory:	Yes
Space Needs: 1,200-2000 SF; SC	

SUPPORT & TRAINING PROVIDED:

Financial Assistance Provided:	NR
Site Selection Assistance:	Yes
Lease Negotiation Assistance:	Yes
Co-Operative Advertising:	Yes

Franchisee Assoc./Member: No
Size Of Corporate Staff: 41
On-Going Support: b,C,D,E,G,H
Training: 5 Days Newington, CT or 5 Days Columbia, MD.
SPECIFIC EXPANSION PLANS:
US: Northeast, Mid-Atlantic
Canada: NR
Overseas: NR

≪ ≫

CHRISTMAS DECOR
206 23rd St., P. O. Box 5946
Lubbock, TX 79404
Tel: (800) 687-9551 (806) 772-1225
Fax: (806) 722-9627
Web Site: www.christmasdecor.net
Mr. Blake K. Smith, President

Holiday and event decorating services provided to homes and businesses. Fun, high-margin business that offers annual income by working only 4-6 months of the year. Also, an excellent add-on business for landscape, pool and spa, electrical and other seasonal service contractors. Landscape lighting franchise available also to create year round business.

BACKGROUND: IFA MEMBER
Established: 1986; 1st Franchised: 1996
Franchised Units: 210
Company-Owned Units 0
Total Units: 210
Dist.: US-160; CAN-5; O'seas-0
North America: 44 States, 2 Provinces
Density: 23 in TX, 14 in OH, 13 in MI
Projected New Units (12 Months): 100
Qualifications: 2, 4, 2, 3, 3, 4
Registered: All States and AB
FINANCIAL/TERMS:
Cash Investment: $6.6-9.5K
Total Investment: $15.9-31.9K
Minimum Net Worth: $N/A
Fees: Franchise - $9.5-15.9K
Royalty - 2-4.5%; Ad. - $180/Yr.
Earnings Claim Statement: No
Term of Contract (Years): 5/5
Avg. # Of Employees: 2-4 FT, 3-20 PT
Passive Ownership: Discouraged
Encourage Conversions: N/A
Area Develop. Agreements: No
Sub-Franchising Contracts: No
Expand In Territory: No
Space Needs: Varies SF; HB, Many Add-On Businesses
SUPPORT & TRAINING PROVIDED:
Financial Assistance Provided: Yes(D)
Site Selection Assistance: Yes

Lease Negotiation Assistance: No
Co-Operative Advertising: No
Franchisee Assoc./Member: Yes/Yes
Size Of Corporate Staff: 18
On-Going Support: A,B,D,G,h,I
Training: 3 Days Major Cities in US; 2 Days of Continuing Education in Major Cities.
SPECIFIC EXPANSION PLANS:
US: All United States
Canada: All Canada
Overseas: All Christian Countries

≪ ≫

COMPUTER DOCTOR
12 2nd Ave. SW
Aberdeen, SD 57401
Tel: (888) 297-2292 (605) 225-4122
Fax: (605) 225-5176
E-Mail: sales @cdfs.com
Web Site: www.cdfs.com
Ms. Lisa Hinz, Director Franchise Dev.

COMPUTER DOCTOR retail stores buy, trade-in, resell used computer parts and systems, sell new computer parts, systems, printers, and components, sell computer supplies, cables, and adapters, combined with mobile on-site or in-store computer and printer repair services and upgrades. A multiple profit center in one franchise with unlimited market potential.

BACKGROUND: IFA MEMBER
Established: 1992; 1st Franchised: 1996
Franchised Units: 104
Company-Owned Units 1
Total Units: 105
Dist.: US-105; CAN-0; O'seas-0
North America: 14 States
Density: 6 in IA, 5 in SD, 4 in ND
Projected New Units (12 Months): 50
Qualifications: 2, 3, 1, 2, 2, 5
Registered: CA,FL,IN,MN,ND,OR, SD,VA
FINANCIAL/TERMS:
Cash Investment: $15-50K
Total Investment: $16.6-170.7K
Minimum Net Worth: $100K
Fees: Franchise - $5-20K
Royalty - 3%; Ad. - 2%
Earnings Claim Statement: No
Term of Contract (Years): 5/5
Avg. # Of Employees:

Passive Ownership: Discouraged
Encourage Conversions: Yes
Area Develop. Agreements: Yes/10
Sub-Franchising Contracts: Yes
Expand In Territory: Yes
Space Needs: 300-1,500 SF; FS, SF, SC
SUPPORT & TRAINING PROVIDED:
Financial Assistance Provided: Yes(I)
Site Selection Assistance: Yes
Lease Negotiation Assistance: Yes
Co-Operative Advertising: No
Franchisee Assoc./Member: Yes/Yes
Size Of Corporate Staff: 10
On-Going Support: B,C,D,E,F,G,H,I
Training: 2 Weeks Aberdeen, SD.
SPECIFIC EXPANSION PLANS:
US: All United States
Canada: All Canada
Overseas: No

≪ ≫

computer moms
We do Windows !!!!
www.computermoms.com

COMPUTER MOMS INTERNATIONAL
3925 West Braker Ln., # 1000
Austin, TX 78759
Tel: (888) 447-3666 (512) 477-6667
Fax: (512) 305-0132
E-Mail: inquiry@computermoms.com
Web Site: www.computermoms.com
Mr. Russell Harrell, COO

Home-based business providing one-on-one computer training and support at the client's home or office on their computer with their applications. Prospective franchisees should have an intermediate level of Windows literacy and proficiency in common PC applications. Master franchises available now.

BACKGROUND: IFA MEMBER
Established: 1994; 1st Franchised: 1998
Franchised Units: 54
Company-Owned Units 1
Total Units: 55
Dist.: US-55; CAN-0; O'seas-0
North America: 2 States
Density: 54 in TX, 1 in OK
Projected New Units (12 Months): 36-72
Qualifications: 2, 3, 4, 2, 4, 4
Registered: NR
FINANCIAL/TERMS:
Cash Investment: $8.76-95.25K

Total Investment:	$9.75-100K
Minimum Net Worth:	$N/A
Fees: Franchise -	$9.75K
Royalty - 14%;	Ad. - 3%/$25/Wk.
Earnings Claim Statement:	No
Term of Contract (Years):	7/7
Avg. # Of Employees:	1 FT, 0-10 PT
Passive Ownership:	Not Allowed
Encourage Conversions:	Yes
Area Develop. Agreements:	Yes/5
Sub-Franchising Contracts:	Yes
Expand In Territory:	Yes
Space Needs: NR SF; N/A	

SUPPORT & TRAINING PROVIDED:

Financial Assistance Provided:	Yes(D)
Site Selection Assistance:	N/A
Lease Negotiation Assistance:	N/A
Co-Operative Advertising:	N/A
Franchisee Assoc./Member:	No
Size Of Corporate Staff:	8
On-Going Support:	A,B,C,d,H,I
Training: Two 1-Week Sessions in Austin, TX.	

SPECIFIC EXPANSION PLANS:

US:	All United States
Canada:	No
Overseas:	No

◄◄ ►►

COMPUTER RENAISSANCE

4200 Dahlberg Dr.
Minneapolis, MN 55422-4837
Tel: (800) 645-7297 (612) 520-8500
Fax: (612) 520-8599
E-Mail: jleffler@cr1.com
Web Site: www.cr1.com
Mr. John Leffler, Senior Franchise Sales

COMPUTER RENAISSANCE stores buy previously-owned computers from a variety of sources. We then offer them to home users, small business and schools, who are looking for the most computing power for their dollar. Not all computer users need, want, or can afford brand new computer equipment. COMPUTER RENAISSANCE provides a way to meet these users' computing needs while spending less money than new. This dynamically growing concept is in the able hands of an established and proven franchise company.

BACKGROUND: **IFA MEMBER**

Established: 1988;	1st Franchised: 1993
Franchised Units:	211
Company-Owned Units	1
Total Units:	212
Dist.:	US-147; CAN-5; O'seas-0

North America:	32 States, 5 Provinces
Density:	12 in IL, 11 in WA, 10 in MN
Projected New Units (12 Months):	10
Qualifications:	4, 4, 2, 2, 1, 4
Registered: All States	

FINANCIAL/TERMS:

Cash Investment:	$75-100K
Total Investment:	$180-225K
Minimum Net Worth:	$100K
Fees: Franchise -	$20K
Royalty - 3%;	Ad. - 0.6%
Earnings Claim Statement:	Yes
Term of Contract (Years):	10/10
Avg. # Of Employees:	4 FT, 2 PT
Passive Ownership:	Discouraged
Encourage Conversions:	Yes
Area Develop. Agreements:	Yes
Sub-Franchising Contracts:	No
Expand In Territory:	No
Space Needs: 2,000 SF; SC	

SUPPORT & TRAINING PROVIDED:

Financial Assistance Provided:	Yes(I)
Site Selection Assistance:	Yes
Lease Negotiation Assistance:	Yes
Co-Operative Advertising:	No
Franchisee Assoc./Member:	Yes/Yes
Size Of Corporate Staff:	20
On-Going Support:	B,C,D,E,F,G
Training: 2 Weeks at Minneapolis, MN; 2 Days in Store.	

SPECIFIC EXPANSION PLANS:

US:	All United States
Canada:	All Canada
Overseas:	No

◄◄ ►►

CONNOISSEUR, THE

201 Torrance Blvd.
Redondo Beach, CA 90277
Tel: (310) 374-9768
Fax: (310) 372-9097
E-Mail: info@giftsofwine.com
Web Site: www.giftsofwine.com
Mr. Sandy French, President

Personalized gifts of fine wines, champagnes, gourmet, crystal and special occasion items.

BACKGROUND:

Established: 1975;	1st Franchised: 1989
Franchised Units:	6
Company-Owned Units	1
Total Units:	7
Dist.:	US-7; CAN-0; O'seas-0
North America:	5 States
Density:	2 in CO, 2 in CA, 1 in IL
Projected New Units (12 Months):	25
Registered: All States	

FINANCIAL/TERMS:

Cash Investment:	$175K
Total Investment:	$175K
Minimum Net Worth:	$NR
Fees: Franchise -	$29.5K
Royalty - 6%;	Ad. - 1%
Earnings Claim Statement:	No
Term of Contract (Years):	10/10
Avg. # Of Employees:	1 FT, 2 PT
Passive Ownership:	Discouraged
Encourage Conversions:	No
Area Develop. Agreements:	Yes/10/10
Sub-Franchising Contracts:	Yes
Expand In Territory:	Yes
Space Needs: 2,000 SF; FS, SC, RM	

SUPPORT & TRAINING PROVIDED:

Financial Assistance Provided:	No
Site Selection Assistance:	Yes
Lease Negotiation Assistance:	Yes
Co-Operative Advertising:	No
Franchisee Assoc./Member:	NR
Size Of Corporate Staff:	4
On-Going Support:	A,B,C,D,E,F,H
Training: 1 Week Headquarters.	

SPECIFIC EXPANSION PLANS:

US:	All United States
Canada:	No
Overseas:	No

◄◄ ►►

COUNTRY CLUTTER

3333 Vaca Valley Pkwy., # 900
Vacaville, CA 95688
Tel: (800) 425-8883 (707) 451-6890
Fax: (707) 451-0410
E-Mail: franchiseinfo@countryclutter.com
Web Site: www.countryclutter.com
Mr. Terry Odneal, VP Franchise Dev.

A charming country store for gifts, collectibles and home decor. A unique business that offers old fashioned quality, selection and customer service. A complete franchise program professionally designed, computerized and planned to sell a perfected blend of country merchandise made by primarily American manufacturers and crafters. Rich arrangements and displays of textures, colors and aromas make shopping at COUNTRY CLUTTER a true sensory delight.

BACKGROUND: IFA MEMBER

Established: 1991; 1st Franchised: 1992	
Franchised Units:	52
Company-Owned Units	2
Total Units:	54
Dist.:	US-54; CAN-0; O'seas-0
North America:	23 States
Density:	16 in CA, 4 in GA, 5 in TX
Projected New Units (12 Months):	15
Qualifications:	5, 3, 3, 3, 4, 5
Registered: CA,FL,HI,IL,IN,MD,MI,NY,	
OR,RI,VA,WA, WI, DC	

FINANCIAL/TERMS:

Cash Investment:	$70-85K
Total Investment:	$155-307K
Minimum Net Worth:	$250K
Fees: Franchise -	$25K
Royalty - 5.5%;	Ad. - 1%
Earnings Claim Statement:	Yes
Term of Contract (Years):	5/5
Avg. # Of Employees:	2 FT, 5 PT
Passive Ownership:	Discouraged
Encourage Conversions:	Yes
Area Develop. Agreements:	Yes/Open
Sub-Franchising Contracts:	No
Expand In Territory:	No
Space Needs: 1,800-2,400 SF; RM, Factory	
Outlets	

SUPPORT & TRAINING PROVIDED:

Financial Assistance Provided:	No
Site Selection Assistance:	Yes
Lease Negotiation Assistance:	Yes
Co-Operative Advertising:	No
Franchisee Assoc./Member:	Yes/Yes
Size Of Corporate Staff:	19
On-Going Support:	C,D,E,F,G,h,I
Training: 3-5 Days Headquarters; 3-5 Days	
On-Site; 40 Hours Home Training with	
Computer.	

SPECIFIC EXPANSION PLANS:

US:	All United States
Canada:	No
Overseas:	No

<< >>

CROWN TROPHY

9 Skyline Dr.
Hawthorne, NY 10532
Tel: (800) 583-8228 (914) 347-8106
Fax: (914) 347-0211
E-Mail: scott@crowntrophy.com
Web Site: www.crownfranchise.com
Mr. Scott Kelly, Executive Vice President

The only franchise of its kind in America, CROWN TROPHY is the largest supplier and fastest growing retailer of trophies and awards in the country. Crown offers a full-service facility utilizing state-of-the-art equipment along with the most innovative product line in the industry. CROWN TROPHY is truly a one of a kind, unique franchise opportunity.

BACKGROUND: IFA MEMBER

Established: 1978; 1st Franchised: 1987	
Franchised Units:	92
Company-Owned Units	1
Total Units:	93
Dist.:	US-93; CAN-0; O'seas-0
North America:	27 States
Density:	13 in NY, 6 in NJ, 6 in PA
Projected New Units (12 Months):	20
Qualifications:	2, 2, 1, 3, 5, 5
Registered: CA,FL,IL,IN,MD,MI,MN,	
ND,NY,OR,SD,WI	

FINANCIAL/TERMS:

Cash Investment:	$80K
Total Investment:	$120-130K
Minimum Net Worth:	$100K
Fees: Franchise -	$32K
Royalty - 5%;	Ad. - None
Earnings Claim Statement:	No
Term of Contract (Years):	10/5/5
Avg. # Of Employees:	1 FT, 2 PT
Passive Ownership:	Not Allowed
Encourage Conversions:	Yes
Area Develop. Agreements:	No
Sub-Franchising Contracts:	No
Expand In Territory:	Yes
Space Needs: 1,500-1,600 SF; SF, SC	

SUPPORT & TRAINING PROVIDED:

Financial Assistance Provided:	Yes(I)
Site Selection Assistance:	Yes
Lease Negotiation Assistance:	Yes
Co-Operative Advertising:	No
Franchisee Assoc./Member:	No
Size Of Corporate Staff:	10
On-Going Support:	C,D,E,F,H,I
Training: 10 Days Corporate Office; 5	
Days On-Site.	

SPECIFIC EXPANSION PLANS:

US:	All United States
Canada:	No
Overseas:	No

<< >>

D' VINE WINE

514 Camden Cir.
Mississauga, ON L4Z 2P2 CANADA
Tel: (888) 464-9463 (905) 501-8520
Fax: (905) 712-3871
E-Mail: franchise@dvinewind.com

Web Site: www.dvinewind.com
Mr. Dennis W. Mogg, President

D'VINE WINE is an exciting franchise opportunity in a new growth industry, where customers can come into a beautiful European decor gift shop and browse for interesting accessories, everything from cork screws to decanters, glasses, trays, jugs, wine coolers and all their needs for wine making at home. D'VINE WINE has special packages for birthdays, weddings, anniversaries and corporate events. We also have gift baskets, wine exchange programs, gift certificates, custom labels and quantity discounts.

BACKGROUND:

Established: 1999; 1st Franchised: 2000	
Franchised Units:	1
Company-Owned Units	0
Total Units:	1
Dist.:	US-0; CAN-1; O'seas-0
North America:	NR
Density:	NR
Projected New Units (12 Months):	10
Qualifications:	4, 4, 3, 4, 4, 5
Registered: FL,MI	

FINANCIAL/TERMS:

Cash Investment:	$40-50K
Total Investment:	$85-125K
Minimum Net Worth:	$150K
Fees: Franchise -	$25K
Royalty - 6%;	Ad. - 4%
Earnings Claim Statement:	No
Term of Contract (Years):	10/10
Avg. # Of Employees:	1 FT, 1 PT
Passive Ownership:	Not Allowed
Encourage Conversions:	N/A
Area Develop. Agreements:	Yes/5
Sub-Franchising Contracts:	Yes
Expand In Territory:	Yes
Space Needs: 1,000 SF; SC	

SUPPORT & TRAINING PROVIDED:

Financial Assistance Provided:	No
Site Selection Assistance:	Yes
Lease Negotiation Assistance:	Yes
Co-Operative Advertising:	Yes
Franchisee Assoc./Member:	No
Size Of Corporate Staff:	6
On-Going Support:	B,C,D,E,f,G,h,I
Training: 5-10 Days in ON or MI.	

SPECIFIC EXPANSION PLANS:

US:	Some States

Canada: Some Provinces
Overseas: Some Countries

≪≪ ≫≫

DESKTOP VISUAL PRODUCTS

411 W. 400 South
Salt Lake City, UT 84101
Tel: (800) 748-5332 (801) 359-5808
Fax: (801) 359-5809
E-Mail: rickf@desktopvisuals.com
Web Site: www.desktopvisuals.com
Mr. Rick Frandsen, President

DESKTOP VISUAL franchises support the presentation industry, selling and renting portable LCD projectors and computers. It is a high-technology marketplace that is dynamic, growing and moving. The business in multi-faceted. We represent manufacturers of LCD projectors. We sell and rent projectors to industry, government and education. Clear advantages include an exclusive territory, cooperative inventory purchasing and extensive technical and operational training and support. Investment from $75K - 110K.

BACKGROUND:

Established: 1990;   1st Franchised: 1998
Franchised Units: 1
Company-Owned Units   2
Total Units: 3
Dist.:   US-3; CAN-0; O'seas-0
  North America: 1 State
  Density: 3 in OR
Projected New Units (12 Months):   6
Qualifications: 4, 3, 1, 3, 3, 5
Registered: IL,OR,WA

FINANCIAL/TERMS:

Cash Investment: $35K
Total Investment: $75-110K
Minimum Net Worth: $75K
Fees: Franchise - $20K
  Royalty - 20%;   Ad. - 3%
Earnings Claim Statement: No
Term of Contract (Years):   10/10
Avg. # Of Employees: 1 FT
Passive Ownership: Discouraged
Encourage Conversions: No
Area Develop. Agreements: No
Sub-Franchising Contracts: No
Expand In Territory: Yes
Space Needs: 400 SF; OB

SUPPORT & TRAINING PROVIDED:

Financial Assistance Provided: No
Site Selection Assistance: Yes
Lease Negotiation Assistance: No
Co-Operative Advertising: Yes

Franchisee Assoc./Member: Yes
Size Of Corporate Staff: 5
On-Going Support: B,C,D,E,f,G,H,I
Training: 1 Week Salt Lake City, UT; 1
  Week On-Site.

SPECIFIC EXPANSION PLANS:

US: West
Canada: No
Overseas: No

≪≪ ≫≫

EARFUL OF BOOKS

9430 Research Blvd., # 130, Echelon II
Austin, TX 78759
Tel: (888) EAR-FULS (512) 343-2620
Fax: (512) 343-2751
E-Mail: contactus@earful.com
Web Site: www.earfulcom
Mr. Jim Grant, VP Franchise Dev.

Rental and sale of audio books in cassette and CD format.

BACKGROUND:

Established: 1991;   1st Franchised: 1998
Franchised Units: 7
Company-Owned Units   6
Total Units: 13
Dist.:   US-13; CAN-0; O'seas-0
  North America: 5 States
  Density: 7 in TX, 3 in NC
Projected New Units (12 Months):   20
Qualifications: 5, 4, 3, 4, 5, 5
Registered: CA,IL,MD,NY,VA,WA,WI,DC

FINANCIAL/TERMS:

Cash Investment: $100K
Total Investment: $225-275K
Minimum Net Worth: $250K
Fees: Franchise - $25K
  Royalty - 4%;   Ad. - 1%
Earnings Claim Statement: No
Term of Contract (Years):   10/5
Avg. # Of Employees: 2 FT, 4 PT
Passive Ownership: Allowed
Encourage Conversions: Yes
Area Develop. Agreements: Yes
Sub-Franchising Contracts: No
Expand In Territory: Yes
Space Needs: 2,000-2,500 SF; SC

SUPPORT & TRAINING PROVIDED:

Financial Assistance Provided: No
Site Selection Assistance: Yes
Lease Negotiation Assistance: Yes
Co-Operative Advertising: Yes
Franchisee Assoc./Member: Yes/Yes
Size Of Corporate Staff: 10
On-Going Support: D,E,F,I
Training: 1 Week at Home Office; 1 Week
  On-Site.

SPECIFIC EXPANSION PLANS:

US: All United States
Canada: Yes, Considered
Overseas: No

≪≪ ≫≫

ECOSMARTE PLANET FRIENDLY

730 West 78th St.
Richfield, MN 55423
Tel: (800) 466-7946 (612) 866-1200
Fax: (612) 866-0152
E-Mail: ecosmarte@visi.com
Web Site: www.ecosmarte.com
Mr. Joe Cantin, No. American Sales Mgr.

Environmental technology retail store, specializing in non-chlorine, non-brine water systems for home, business pool and spa. Oxygen and natural products.

BACKGROUND:

Established: 1994;   1st Franchised: 1996
Franchised Units: 5
Company-Owned Units   2
Total Units: 7
Dist.:   US-7; CAN-0; O'seas-0
  North America: 6 States
  Density: 3 in MN, 1 in AZ, 1 in TX
Projected New Units (12 Months):   6
Qualifications: 3, 3, 1, 4, 3, 4
Registered: NR

FINANCIAL/TERMS:

Cash Investment: $75-245K
Total Investment: $100-245K
Minimum Net Worth: $250K
Fees: Franchise - $15-30K
  Royalty - 0%;   Ad. - 0%
Earnings Claim Statement: No
Term of Contract (Years):   5/5
Avg. # Of Employees: 2 FT, 4 PT
Passive Ownership: Discouraged
Encourage Conversions: No
Area Develop. Agreements: Yes/5
Sub-Franchising Contracts: No
Expand In Territory: Yes
Space Needs: 1,500 SF; SF, SC, HB

SUPPORT & TRAINING PROVIDED:

Financial Assistance Provided: Yes(I)
Site Selection Assistance: Yes

Lease Negotiation Assistance: Yes
Co-Operative Advertising: Yes
Franchisee Assoc./Member: No
Size Of Corporate Staff: 20
On-Going Support: B,C,D,e,h,I
Training: 10 Days at Phoenix, AZ; 7 Days Minneapolis, MN.

SPECIFIC EXPANSION PLANS:
US: Southwest, Northeast
Canada: All Canada
Overseas: All Countries

≪ ≫

ELEPHANT HOUSE
3007 Longhorn Blvd., # 101
Austin, TX 78758
Tel: (800) 729-2273 (512) 339-3004
Fax: (512) 339-7990
E-Mail: jscott@elephanthouse.com
Web Site: www.elephanthouse.com
Ms. Julia Scott, National Sales Director

THE ELEPHANT HOUSE system is a proven, home-based greeting card franchise, where you can be your own boss. Independent retail stores are your clients, and we teach you our successful method of obtaining these clients and keeping them happy. The investment is inventory-based and includes all fees. Training is provided at your home.

BACKGROUND:
Established: 1991; 1st Franchised: 1995
Franchised Units: 47
Company-Owned Units: 1
Total Units: 48
Dist.: US-0; CAN-0; O'seas-0
  North America: NR
  Density: 7 in CA, 5 in FL, 5 in TX
Projected New Units (12 Months): NR
Registered:
FINANCIAL/TERMS:
Cash Investment: $Total
Total Investment: $16-26.5K
Minimum Net Worth: $50K
Fees: Franchise - $5K
  Royalty - 0%; Ad. - 0%
Earnings Claim Statement: No
Term of Contract (Years): 7/7
Avg. # Of Employees: 1 FT
Passive Ownership: Allowed
Encourage Conversions: NR
Area Develop. Agreements: No
Sub-Franchising Contracts: No
Expand In Territory: N/A
Space Needs: NR SF; N/A
SUPPORT & TRAINING PROVIDED:
Financial Assistance Provided: NR

Site Selection Assistance: N/A
Lease Negotiation Assistance: N/A
Co-Operative Advertising: N/A
Franchisee Assoc./Member: No
Size Of Corporate Staff: 5
On-Going Support: C,D,E,G,I
Training: 5 Days in Franchisee's Territory.

SPECIFIC EXPANSION PLANS:
US: All United States
Canada: NR
Overseas: NR

≪ ≫

ELEPHANT WALK
318 N. Carson St., # 214
Carson City, NV 89701
Tel: (800) 654-5156 (775) 882-1963
Fax: (800) 654-5161
Mr. John (Jack) D. Pomeroy, President

CAPTURE THE BEAUTY! You'll love owning an ELEPHANT WALK Gift Gallery. Unique, handcrafted, nature-themed gifts...sculptures, jewelry, home decorative products and more. Developed and refined in Hawaii... Now rapidly reaching malls across the nation.

BACKGROUND:
Established: 1983; 1st Franchised: 1996
Franchised Units: 0
Company-Owned Units: 9
Total Units: 9
Dist.: US-9; CAN-0; O'seas-0
  North America: 2 States
  Density: 8 in HI, 1 in NV
Projected New Units (12 Months): 4
Qualifications: 3, 3, 2, 3, 4, 5
Registered: HI
FINANCIAL/TERMS:
Cash Investment: $75-100K
Total Investment: $145-195K
Minimum Net Worth: $250K
Fees: Franchise - $25K
  Royalty - 6%; Ad. - 1%
Earnings Claim Statement: No
Term of Contract (Years): 5/5/5/5
Avg. # Of Employees: 1 FT, 4 PT
Passive Ownership: Discouraged
Encourage Conversions: Yes
Area Develop. Agreements: No
Sub-Franchising Contracts: No
Expand In Territory: Yes
Space Needs: 1,000 SF; SF, RM, Airport, Resort Area
SUPPORT & TRAINING PROVIDED:
Financial Assistance Provided: N/A
Site Selection Assistance: Yes
Lease Negotiation Assistance: Yes

Co-Operative Advertising: No
Franchisee Assoc./Member: No
Size Of Corporate Staff: 6
On-Going Support: C,D,E,F,G,H,I
Training: 10 Days Honolulu, HI (I.E.L. University).

SPECIFIC EXPANSION PLANS:
US: All United States
Canada: No
Overseas: No

≪ ≫

FAST-FIX JEWELRY REPAIRS
1750 N. Florida Mango Rd. # 103
West Palm Beach, FL 33409
Tel: (800) 359-0407 (561) 478-5292
Fax: (561) 478-5291
E-Mail: fastfix@bellsouth.net
Web Site: www.fastfix.com
Mr. Mark Goldstein, VP Franchise Dev.

FAST-FIX JEWELRY REPAIRS ® is a proven business with a 15-year track record in the multi-billion dollar jewelry and watch repair industry. FAST-FIX stores operate only in major regional malls, which guarantees high visibility and traffic. Most repairs can be completed within an hour while customers watch or enjoy shopping. FAST-FIX JEWELRY REPAIRS ® has more than 100 franchise locations nationwide. The chain's innovative and complete training program is conducted at the site of each new store.

BACKGROUND: IFA MEMBER
Established: 1984; 1st Franchised: 1987
Franchised Units: 101
Company-Owned Units: 0
Total Units: 101
Dist.: US-101; CAN-0; O'seas-0
  North America: NR
  Density: 16 in FL, 16 in TX, 11 in CA
Projected New Units (12 Months): 25
Qualifications: 3, 5, 1, 1, 1, 4
Registered: CA,FL,IL,MD,NY,VA,WA
FINANCIAL/TERMS:
Cash Investment: $35-50K
Total Investment: $102-170K
Minimum Net Worth: $N/A
Fees: Franchise - $25K
  Royalty - 5%; Ad. - 0%
Earnings Claim Statement: No

Term of Contract (Years): 10/10
Avg. # Of Employees: 3 FT, 1 PT
Passive Ownership: Discouraged
Encourage Conversions: NR
Area Develop. Agreements: Yes/10
Sub-Franchising Contracts: No
Expand In Territory: Yes
Space Needs: 150-850 SF; RM
SUPPORT & TRAINING PROVIDED:
Financial Assistance Provided: Yes(I)
Site Selection Assistance: Yes
Lease Negotiation Assistance: Yes
Co-Operative Advertising: N/A
Franchisee Assoc./Member: Yes/Yes
Size Of Corporate Staff: 9
On-Going Support: B,C,D,E,G,H,I
Training: 6 Days On-Site.
SPECIFIC EXPANSION PLANS:
US: All United States
Canada: All Canada
Overseas: No

≪ ≫

FOLIAGE DESIGN SYSTEMS
4496 35th St.
Orlando, FL 32811-6504
Tel: (800) 933-7351 (407) 245-7776
Fax: (407) 245-7533
E-Mail: fdsfc@worldnet.att.net
Web Site: www.foliagedesign.com
Mr. John S. Hagood, Chairman

FOLIAGE DESIGN SYSTEMS is one of the largest interior plant maintenance companies in the U. S., according to Interiorscape Magazine. FOLIAGE DESIGN franchisees learn the business from the ground up in an intensive training program followed by training sessions in the field. Franchisees are taught design, sales and maintenance of interior foliage plants.

BACKGROUND:
Established: 1971; 1st Franchised: 1980
Franchised Units: 45
Company-Owned Units 3
Total Units: 48
Dist.: US-45; CAN-1; O'seas-1
 North America: 17 States, 1 Province

Density: 19 in FL, 4 in SC, 3 in MS
Projected New Units (12 Months): 3
Registered: FL,HI,VA
FINANCIAL/TERMS:
Cash Investment: $15-50K
Total Investment: $35-150K
Minimum Net Worth: $NR
Fees: Franchise - $20-100K
 Royalty - 6%; Ad. - 0%
Earnings Claim Statement: No
Term of Contract (Years): 20/5
Avg. # Of Employees: 4 FT, 2 PT
Passive Ownership: Discouraged
Encourage Conversions: No
Area Develop. Agreements: No
Sub-Franchising Contracts: Yes
Expand In Territory: Yes
Space Needs: 200 SF; Greenhouse, Warehouse
SUPPORT & TRAINING PROVIDED:
Financial Assistance Provided: No
Site Selection Assistance: Yes
Lease Negotiation Assistance: No
Co-Operative Advertising: No
Franchisee Assoc./Member: NR
Size Of Corporate Staff: 6
On-Going Support: a,B,C,D,F,G,H,I
Training: 2 Weeks Headquarters; 3-5 Days in Field.
SPECIFIC EXPANSION PLANS:
US: All United States
Canada: All Canada
Overseas: Europe, Asia, Mexico, South America

≪ ≫

FOOT SOLUTIONS HQ
1730 Cumberland Point Dr., # 5
Marietta, GA 30067
Tel: (866) 338-2597 (770) 955-0099
Fax: (770) 933-8268
E-Mail: info@footsolutions.com
Web Site: www.footsolutions.com
Mr. John E. Hellriegel, Chief Operating Officer

FOOT SOLUTIONS provides a much-needed service to the rapidly-growing percentage of people who experience sore and tired feet. Specialized, computerized foot scanning to make custom insoles and orthodics ensures a perfect fit. Sell 10 lines of comfort shoes for work, dress and play

BACKGROUND:
Established: 2000; 1st Franchised: 2000
Franchised Units: 4
Company-Owned Units 0
Total Units: 4

Dist.: US-4; CAN-0; O'seas-0
 North America: 3 States
 Density: 2 in OR, 1 in OH, 1 in GA
Projected New Units (12 Months): 40
Qualifications: 4, 4, 3, 3, 3, 4
Registered: None.
FINANCIAL/TERMS:
Cash Investment: $40K
Total Investment: $110-150K
Minimum Net Worth: $250K
Fees: Franchise - $20K
 Royalty - 5%; Ad. - 4%
Earnings Claim Statement: No
Term of Contract (Years): 20/10/10
Avg. # Of Employees: 1 FT, 2-3 PT
Passive Ownership: Allowed
Encourage Conversions: No
Area Develop. Agreements: No
Sub-Franchising Contracts: No
Expand In Territory: Yes
Space Needs: NR SF; SF, SC
SUPPORT & TRAINING PROVIDED:
Financial Assistance Provided: No
Site Selection Assistance: Yes
Lease Negotiation Assistance: Yes
Co-Operative Advertising: No
Franchisee Assoc./Member: No
Size Of Corporate Staff: 9
On-Going Support: B,C,D,E,H,I
Training: 1 Week Marietta, GA; 8 Days San Jose, CA.
SPECIFIC EXPANSION PLANS:
US: Southeast, Midwest, NW
Canada: All Canada
Overseas: No

≪ ≫

GENERAL NUTRITION CENTERS
300 Sixth Ave.
Pittsburgh, PA 15222
Tel: (800) 766-7099 (412) 288-2043
Fax: (412) 288-2033
E-Mail: franchising@gnc-hq.com
Web Site: www.gncfranchising.com
Director of Franchising,

GNC is the leading national specialty retailer of vitamins, minerals, herbs and sports nutrition supplements and is uniquely positioned to capitalize on the accelerating self-care trend. As the leading provider of products and information for personal health enhancement, the company holds the largest specialty-retail share of the nutritional supplement market.

GNC was ranked America's #1 retail franchise in 1998/1999 by Entrepreneur International.

BACKGROUND: IFA MEMBER
Established: 1935; 1st Franchised: 1988
Franchised Units: 1,636
Company-Owned Units <u>2,812</u>
Total Units: 4,448
Dist.: US-4,088; CAN-134; O'seas-266
North America: 50 States, 1 Province
Density: 408 in CA, 340 in FL, 293 TX
Projected New Units (12 Months): NR
Qualifications: 5, 5, 1, 1, 1, 4
Registered: All States
FINANCIAL/TERMS:
Cash Investment: $60K
Total Investment: $130.2-179.5K
Minimum Net Worth: $100K
Fees: Franchise - $32.5K
Royalty - 6%; Ad. - 3%
Earnings Claim Statement: Yes
Term of Contract (Years): 10/5
Avg. # Of Employees: 1 FT, 3-5 PT
Passive Ownership: Not Allowed
Encourage Conversions: Yes
Area Develop. Agreements: Yes/Varies
Sub-Franchising Contracts: No
Expand In Territory: Yes
Space Needs: 1,402 (avg.) SF; SC, RM
SUPPORT & TRAINING PROVIDED:
Financial Assistance Provided: Yes(D)
Site Selection Assistance: Yes
Lease Negotiation Assistance: Yes
Co-Operative Advertising: Yes
Franchisee Assoc./Member: Yes/Yes
Size Of Corporate Staff: 700+
On-Going Support: A,B,C,D,E,F,G,H,I
Training: 1 Wk. On-Site in Local Corporate Store; 1 Wk. in Pittsburgh, PA; 1 Wk. opening assistance.
SPECIFIC EXPANSION PLANS:
US: All United States
Canada: PQ Only
Overseas: Middle East, Japan, Malaysia, New Zealand, Africa.

≪ ≫

GROWER DIRECT FRESH CUT FLOWERS
4220 - 98 St., # 301
Edmonton, AB T6E 6A1 CANADA
Tel: (800) 567-7258 (780) 436-7774
Fax: (780) 436-3336
Mr. John Paton, Franchise Coordinator

As the largest floral chain retailer, our independently operated franchise locations sell the world's highest-quality fresh cut roses and other flowers in a unique 'boutique-style' setting. Product is sourced directly from the finest producers known and transported weekly to our stores via GROWER DIRECT's distribution system. Rapid product sales translate into 50-60 inventory turns annually and help make the enjoyment of FRESH CUT FLOWERS an affordable and everyday event for our customers.

BACKGROUND:
Established: 1991; 1st Franchised: 1991
Franchised Units: 121
Company-Owned Units <u>1</u>
Total Units: 122
Dist.: US-0; CAN-122; O'seas-0
North America: 10 Provinces
Density: 38 in AB, 22 in ON, 15 in BC
Projected New Units (12 Months): 12
Qualifications: 4, 4, 2, 2, 4, 4
Registered: AB
FINANCIAL/TERMS:
Cash Investment: $40K
Total Investment: $35-40K
Minimum Net Worth: $50K
Fees: Franchise - $25K
Royalty - $240/Wk.; Ad. - $15/Wk.
Earnings Claim Statement: No
Term of Contract (Years): 10/10
Avg. # Of Employees: 1 FT, 2 PT
Passive Ownership: Discouraged
Encourage Conversions: Yes
Area Develop. Agreements: No
Sub-Franchising Contracts: Yes
Expand In Territory: Yes
Space Needs: 400-1,000 SF; SC
SUPPORT & TRAINING PROVIDED:
Financial Assistance Provided: No
Site Selection Assistance: Yes
Lease Negotiation Assistance: Yes
Co-Operative Advertising: Yes
Franchisee Assoc./Member: Yes/Yes
Size Of Corporate Staff: 14
On-Going Support: b,C,D,E,G,H,I
Training: 5 Days in Store; 5 Days in Classroom; 5 Days Industry Tours.
SPECIFIC EXPANSION PLANS:
US: No
Canada: All Canada
Overseas: No

≪ ≫

HEALTHY BACK
P.O. Box 1296
Newington, VA 22122-1296
Tel: (703) 339-1300
Fax: (703) 339-0671
Web Site: www.healthyback.com
Mr. Howard J. Margolis, Franchise Mgr.

Healthy Back

The Healthy Back is a retail store which specializes in selling ergonomically designed products such as office chairs, recliners, beds, pillows, supports, massagers, desks, foot rests, books, videos and other products which help prevent and relieve back/neck and improve a person's daily comfort.

BACKGROUND:
Established: 1993; 1st Franchised: 1999
Franchised Units: 12
Company-Owned Units <u>10</u>
Total Units: 22
Dist.: US-22; CAN-0; O'seas-0
North America: 19 States
Density: 4 in CO, 1 in Each of rest
Projected New Units (12 Months): 6
Qualifications: 5, 4, 3, 4, 2, 5
Registered:
FINANCIAL/TERMS:
Cash Investment: $100K
Total Investment: $167.1-279.9K
Minimum Net Worth: $650K
Fees: Franchise - $25K
Royalty - 5%; Ad. - 1.5%
Earnings Claim Statement: No
Term of Contract (Years): 5/5
Avg. # Of Employees: 2 PT
Passive Ownership: Not Allowed
Encourage Conversions: N/A
Area Develop. Agreements: No
Sub-Franchising Contracts: No
Expand In Territory: No
Space Needs: 2,500 SF; SC
SUPPORT & TRAINING PROVIDED:
Financial Assistance Provided: Yes(I)
Site Selection Assistance: Yes
Lease Negotiation Assistance: Yes
Co-Operative Advertising: No
Franchisee Assoc./Member: Yes/Yes
Size Of Corporate Staff: 16
On-Going Support: C,D,E,F,G,h,I
Training: 9 Days in Washington, DC area.
SPECIFIC EXPANSION PLANS:
US: All United States
Canada: No
Overseas: No

≪ ≫

INTERNATIONAL NEWS
2000 Argentia Rd., Plaza 1, # 270
Mississauga, ON L5N 1P7 CANADA
Tel: (800) 319-5666 (905) 826-0862

Fax: (905) 826-2105
Mr. Sam Davis, President/CEO

Retailer of international newspapers and magazines, complemented by a full-line of tobacco-related products. Confectionery and snack items round out the offering with services such as lottery, fax and photocopying.

BACKGROUND:
Established: 1993;   1st Franchised: 1994
Franchised Units: 70
Company-Owned Units   4
Total Units: 74
Dist.:   US-0; CAN-74; O'seas-0
  North America: 8 Provinces
  Density: 50 in ON, 10 in BC, 5 in NS
Projected New Units (12 Months):   30
Qualifications: 3, 3, 2, 2, 4, 5
Registered: NR
FINANCIAL/TERMS:
Cash Investment: $20K
Total Investment: $40-150K
Minimum Net Worth: $50K
Fees: Franchise - $30K
  Royalty - 3%;   Ad. - 0%
Earnings Claim Statement: Yes
Term of Contract (Years):   5/5
Avg. # Of Employees: 2 FT, 2 PT
Passive Ownership: Discouraged
Encourage Conversions: Yes
Area Develop. Agreements: No
Sub-Franchising Contracts: No
Expand In Territory: Yes
Space Needs: 500 SF; FS, SF, SC, RM
SUPPORT & TRAINING PROVIDED:
Financial Assistance Provided: Yes(I)
Site Selection Assistance: Yes
Lease Negotiation Assistance: Yes
Co-Operative Advertising: No
Franchisee Assoc./Member: Yes/Yes
Size Of Corporate Staff: 10
On-Going Support: B,C,D,E,F,G,H,I
Training: 2 Days in Office; 1 Week Store.
SPECIFIC EXPANSION PLANS:
US: NR
Canada: All Canada
Overseas: No

JUST-A-BUCK
301 N. Main St., #5
New City, NY 10956

Tel: (800) 332-2229 (914) 638-4111
Fax: (914) 638-3878
E-Mail: rs@spynet.com
Web Site: www.just-a-buck.com
Mr. Ronald Sommers, Director Franchise
  Development

Merchandise that would sometimes cost as much as ten times more at any other store makes JUST-A-BUCK fun to shop and fun to run. America's only franchised dollar store. Each location is neat and clean. It takes hard work but the concept is simple and it's made even easier with on-going support, training and help with everything from marketing to merchandising. IFA Member. Entrepreneur Top 500.

BACKGROUND: IFA MEMBER
Established: 1988;   1st Franchised: 1992
Franchised Units: 27
Company-Owned Units   10
Total Units: 37
Dist.:   US-37; CAN-0; O'seas-0
  North America: 5 States
  Density: 16 in NY, 8 in NJ, 2 in CT
Projected New Units (12 Months):   15
Qualifications: 4, 3, 2, 2, 2, 4
Registered: FL,MD,MI,NY,VA,DC
FINANCIAL/TERMS:
Cash Investment: $40-60K
Total Investment: $126.7-265.9K
Minimum Net Worth: $150K
Fees: Franchise - $25K
  Royalty - 4%;   Ad. - 2%
Earnings Claim Statement: No
Term of Contract (Years):   10/20
Avg. # Of Employees: 7 FT, 10 PT
Passive Ownership: Not Allowed
Encourage Conversions: Yes
Area Develop. Agreements: No
Sub-Franchising Contracts: No
Expand In Territory: Yes
Space Needs: 3,500 SF; SC, RM
SUPPORT & TRAINING PROVIDED:
Financial Assistance Provided: Yes(I)
Site Selection Assistance: Yes
Lease Negotiation Assistance: Yes
Co-Operative Advertising: No
Franchisee Assoc./Member: No
Size Of Corporate Staff: 15
On-Going Support: A,B,C,D,E,F,G,H,I
Training: 10 Days NY State; 10 Days
  On-Site.
SPECIFIC EXPANSION PLANS:
US: All United States
Canada: No
Overseas: No

<< >>

KEEP IN TOUCH STUFF
12 McGaw Dr.
Edison, NJ 08837
Tel: (877) KITSTUFF (732) 346-4451
Fax: (732) 417-0326
Web Site: www.kitstuff.com
Mr. Jack Mosseri, Director of Franchising

KEEP IN TOUCH STUFF is a wireless communications business, which specializes in the sale of cellular phones and pagers. 'Wireless telecommunications is the fastest-growing sector of telecommunications today, adding a new customer every 2.23 seconds.' Don't miss out on what we believe to be the most exciting franchise opportunity in America.

BACKGROUND:
Established: 1996;   1st Franchised: 1999
Franchised Units: 0
Company-Owned Units   37
Total Units: 37
Dist.:   US-37; CAN-0; O'seas-0
  North America: 7 States
  Density: 15 in NJ, 9 in NY, 4 in CT
Projected New Units (12 Months):   34
Qualifications: 4, 5, 3, 3, 5, 3
Registered: NR
FINANCIAL/TERMS:
Cash Investment: $25K
Total Investment: $80-171K
Minimum Net Worth: $NR
Fees: Franchise - $25K
  Royalty - 0%;   Ad. - 0%
Earnings Claim Statement: No
Term of Contract (Years):   NR
Avg. # Of Employees: 1 FT, 1 PT
Passive Ownership: NR
Encourage Conversions: N/A
Area Develop. Agreements: NR
Sub-Franchising Contracts: NR
Expand In Territory: Yes
Space Needs: Varies SF; SC, RM
SUPPORT & TRAINING PROVIDED:
Financial Assistance Provided: Yes
Site Selection Assistance: Yes
Lease Negotiation Assistance: Yes
Co-Operative Advertising: Yes
Franchisee Assoc./Member: No
Size Of Corporate Staff: 200
On-Going Support: a,b,C,D,E,G,H,I
Training: NR
SPECIFIC EXPANSION PLANS:
US: Northeast
Canada: No
Overseas: No

<< >>

LATEX CITY

1814 Franklin St., # 820
Oakland, CA 94612
Tel: (510) 839-5462
Fax: (510) 839-2104
Dr. David L. Browne, President

Unique ground-floor specialty retailing opportunity in booming latex novelty aid business. Complete line of proprietary products. Turn-key package includes lease negotiation, fully-stocked inventory, in-store merchandising/display. On-going support. LATEX CITY is ideal for aggressive couples. This is not smut - but a highly profitable, high-margin, fully legal business.

BACKGROUND:

Established: 1972; 1st Franchised: 1986
Franchised Units: 26
Company-Owned Units   4
Total Units: 30
Dist.:   US-25; CAN-2; O'seas-3
  North America: 17 States, 1 Province
  Density: 3 in CA, 3 in NY, 2 in OR
Projected New Units (12 Months):   10
Registered: NR

FINANCIAL/TERMS:

Cash Investment: $65K
Total Investment: $85-235K
Minimum Net Worth: $NR
Fees: Franchise - $15K
  Royalty - 6%;   Ad. - 2%
Earnings Claim Statement: Yes
Term of Contract (Years):   10/10
Avg. # Of Employees: 2 FT
Passive Ownership: Discouraged
Encourage Conversions: Yes
Area Develop. Agreements: Yes/5
Sub-Franchising Contracts: No
Expand In Territory: No
Space Needs: 1,000-1,400 SF; FS, SF, SC, RM

SUPPORT & TRAINING PROVIDED:

Financial Assistance Provided: Yes(D)
Site Selection Assistance: Yes
Lease Negotiation Assistance: Yes
Co-Operative Advertising: Yes
Franchisee Assoc./Member: NR
Size Of Corporate Staff: 6
On-Going Support: A,B,C,D,G,H
Training: 3 Weeks Headquarters; 1 Week Plant; 2 Weeks On-Site.

SPECIFIC EXPANSION PLANS:

US: All United States
Canada: Major Cities
Overseas: No

<< >>

LEMSTONE BOOKS

1123 Wheaton Oaks Court
Wheaton, IL 60187
Tel: (630) 682-1400
Fax: (630) 682-1828
Web Site: www.lemstone.com
Mr. Jim Doyle, VP Real Estate/Dev.

Since 1982, LEMSTONE has been helping Christians own, operate and succeed in Christian retailing. Our franchise concept provides a 'road map for success' for Christian retailers who possess a heart for people and an entrepreneurial spirit. We currently have over 75 stores in 27 states. LEMSTONE stores are located in premier regional malls within growing markets. Our stores enjoy maximum market exposure every day as thousands of customers shop.

BACKGROUND: IFA MEMBER

Established: 1981; 1st Franchised: 1982
Franchised Units: 76
Company-Owned Units   1
Total Units: 77
Dist.:   US-77; CAN-0; O'seas-0
  North America: 27 States
  Density: 8 in TN, 8 in OH, 7 in IL
Projected New Units (12 Months):   12
Qualifications: 5, 2, 1, 2, 2, 4
Registered: CA,FL,IL,IN,MD,MI,MN,NY, OR,WA,WI

FINANCIAL/TERMS:

Cash Investment: $60K
Total Investment: $150-240K
Minimum Net Worth: $350K
Fees: Franchise - $30K
  Royalty - 4%;   Ad. - 1%
Earnings Claim Statement: NR
Term of Contract (Years):   10/10
Avg. # Of Employees: 1 FT, 4 PT
Passive Ownership: Discouraged
Encourage Conversions: No
Area Develop. Agreements: No
Sub-Franchising Contracts: No
Expand In Territory: Yes
Space Needs: 1,300-2,000 SF; RM

SUPPORT & TRAINING PROVIDED:

Financial Assistance Provided: No
Site Selection Assistance: Yes
Lease Negotiation Assistance: Yes
Co-Operative Advertising: Yes
Franchisee Assoc./Member: Yes/Yes
Size Of Corporate Staff: 14
On-Going Support: A,B,C,D,E,F,G,H
Training: 8 Days Headquarters; 5 Days On-Site.

SPECIFIC EXPANSION PLANS:

US: All United States
Canada: No
Overseas: No

<< >>

LITTLE PROFESSOR BOOK CENTERS

405 Little Lake Dr., # C
Ann Arbor, MI 48103
Tel: (800) 899-6232 (734) 994-1212
Fax: (734) 994-9009
E-Mail: lpbchome@aol.com
Web Site: www.littleprofessor.com
Ms. Christi M. Shaw, Franchise Development Manager

Full-line, full-service, community-oriented general bookstore.

BACKGROUND:

Established: 1964; 1st Franchised: 1969
Franchised Units: 65
Company-Owned Units   0
Total Units: 65
Dist.:   US-80; CAN-0; O'seas-0
  North America: 29 States
  Density: 12 in OH, 8 in WI, 8 in MI
Projected New Units (12 Months):   10
Qualifications: 5, 4, 2, 3, 3, 5
Registered: CA,FL,IL,IN,MI,MN,NY,RI, VA,WI

FINANCIAL/TERMS:

Cash Investment: $100-500K
Total Investment: $300K-1.5MM
Minimum Net Worth: $250K
Fees: Franchise - $37K
  Royalty - 3%;   Ad. - 0.5%
Earnings Claim Statement: Yes
Term of Contract (Years):   10/10
Avg. # Of Employees: 2 FT, 6 PT
Passive Ownership: Discouraged
Encourage Conversions: Yes
Area Develop. Agreements: No
Sub-Franchising Contracts: No
Expand In Territory: Yes
Space Needs: 3,000-15,000 SF; FS, SF, SC

SUPPORT & TRAINING PROVIDED:

Financial Assistance Provided: Yes(I)
Site Selection Assistance: Yes
Lease Negotiation Assistance: Yes
Co-Operative Advertising: Yes
Franchisee Assoc./Member: Yes/Yes
Size Of Corporate Staff: 10
On-Going Support: A,b,C,d,E,F,G,H,h,I
Training: 1 Week Ann Arbor, MI (Home Office), 1-2 Weeks On-Site, LPBC Coventions Once a Year

447

SPECIFIC EXPANSION PLANS:

US:	Midwest
Canada:	No
Overseas:	No

≪ ≫

MERKINSTOCK

P.O. Box 12488
Oakland, CA 94604
Tel: (510) 839-5462
Fax: (510) 839-2104
Mr. Bruce L. Mowat, President

World's largest selection of merkins - both natural and synthetic. Over 35 models, 15 color selections. Custom fitting in discrete environment. Also custom dyeing. Guaranteed satisfaction. 15 stores in Far East and Europe prove that concept is ripe for aggressive expansion into the U. S. market. Looking for entrepreneurs with the desire to succeed.

BACKGROUND:

Established: 1992;	1st Franchised: 1995
Franchised Units:	21
Company-Owned Units	6
Total Units:	27
Dist.:	US-3; CAN-2; O'seas-15
North America:	2 States, 1 Province
Density:	2 in CA, 1 in NV
Projected New Units (12 Months):	10
Qualifications:	3, 5, 4, 2, 3, 5
Registered: CA	

FINANCIAL/TERMS:

Cash Investment:	$90K
Total Investment:	$150K
Minimum Net Worth:	$250K
Fees: Franchise -	$20K
Royalty - 6%;	Ad. - 2%
Earnings Claim Statement:	Yes
Term of Contract (Years):	15/15
Avg. # Of Employees:	2 FT
Passive Ownership:	Not Allowed
Encourage Conversions:	Yes
Area Develop. Agreements:	Yes/15
Sub-Franchising Contracts:	Yes
Expand In Territory:	No
Space Needs: 1,200 SF; FS, SC, RM	

SUPPORT & TRAINING PROVIDED:

Financial Assistance Provided:	Yes(D)
Site Selection Assistance:	Yes
Lease Negotiation Assistance:	Yes
Co-Operative Advertising:	Yes
Franchisee Assoc./Member:	No
Size Of Corporate Staff:	4
On-Going Support:	a,B,C,D,E,f,G,G,I
Training: 3 Weeks Headquarters; 2 Weeks On-Site; On-Going.	

SPECIFIC EXPANSION PLANS:

US:	All United States
Canada:	All Canada
Overseas:	All Countries

≪ ≫

MUSIC-GO-ROUND

4200 Dahlberg Dr.
Minneapolis, MN 55422-4837
Tel: (800) 645-7298 (612) 520-8419
Fax: (612) 520-84501
E-Mail: jschwitzer@growbiz.com
Web Site: www.musicgoround.com
Mr. Jim Schwitzer, Nat'l. Franchise Dev.

MUSIC GO ROUND is a franchised, retail music store that buys, sells, trades and consigns used and new musical instruments, gear and equipment. Our success formula is based on buying and selling used products, aggressive marketing, retail site selection and support of franchises.

BACKGROUND: IFA MEMBER

Established: 1986;	1st Franchised: 1994
Franchised Units:	72
Company-Owned Units	8
Total Units:	80
Dist.:	US-80; CAN-0; O'seas-0
North America:	30 States
Density:	12 in MN, 9 in IL, 4 in WI
Projected New Units (12 Months):	30
Qualifications:	3, 3, 4, 3, 4, 5
Registered: All States	

FINANCIAL/TERMS:

Cash Investment:	$45-60K
Total Investment:	$186.4-254.9K
Minimum Net Worth:	$200K Appx.
Fees: Franchise -	$20K
Royalty - 3%;	Ad. - $500/Yr.
Earnings Claim Statement:	Yes
Term of Contract (Years):	10/10
Avg. # Of Employees:	2 FT, 2 PT
Passive Ownership:	Discouraged
Encourage Conversions:	Yes
Area Develop. Agreements:	Yes/3
Sub-Franchising Contracts:	No
Expand In Territory:	Yes
Space Needs: 2,500 SF; SC	

SUPPORT & TRAINING PROVIDED:

Financial Assistance Provided:	Yes(I)
Site Selection Assistance:	Yes
Lease Negotiation Assistance:	Yes
Co-Operative Advertising:	Yes
Franchisee Assoc./Member:	No
Size Of Corporate Staff:	175
On-Going Support:	A,C,D,E,F,G,h,I
Training: 11 Days at Home Office.	

SPECIFIC EXPANSION PLANS:

US:	All United States
Canada:	All Canada
Overseas:	No

≪ ≫

THE NATURE OF THINGS STORE

NATURE OF THINGS STORE, THE

10700 W. Venture Dr.
Franklin, WI 53132
Tel: (800) 283-2921 (414) 529-2192
Fax: (414) 529-2253
Web Site: www.natureofthingsstore.com
Mr. Tony Aiello, Franchise Director

Join the aniMALL kingdom and travel beyond the ordinary. THE NATURE OF THINGS STORE is a retail chain, specializing in the sale of science and nature-related gift and education items, with an emphasis on endangered species. Become a member of this fast- growing franchise.

BACKGROUND: IFA MEMBER

Established: 1989;	1st Franchised: 1991
Franchised Units:	12
Company-Owned Units	2
Total Units:	14
Dist.:	US-14; CAN-0; O'seas-0
North America:	7 States
Density:	5 in WI, 2 in MO, 1 in CO
Projected New Units (12 Months):	2-3
Qualifications:	4, 3, 2, 3, 4, 4
Registered: FL,IL,IN,MI,MN,NY,SD,WI	

FINANCIAL/TERMS:

Cash Investment:	$50-100K
Total Investment:	$168-288K
Minimum Net Worth:	$200-250K
Fees: Franchise -	$25K
Royalty - 5%;	Ad. - 1%
Earnings Claim Statement:	No
Term of Contract (Years):	10/10
Avg. # Of Employees:	1 FT, 4 PT
Passive Ownership:	Discouraged
Encourage Conversions:	N/A
Area Develop. Agreements:	No
Sub-Franchising Contracts:	No
Expand In Territory:	Yes
Space Needs: 1,500-1,800 SF; RM	

SUPPORT & TRAINING PROVIDED:

Financial Assistance Provided:	Yes(I)
Site Selection Assistance:	Yes
Lease Negotiation Assistance:	Yes
Co-Operative Advertising:	Yes
Franchisee Assoc./Member:	No
Size Of Corporate Staff:	4

On-Going Support: A,C,D,E,G,H,I
Training: 1 Week Corporate Office and Corporate Stores.
SPECIFIC EXPANSION PLANS:
US: All United States
Canada: No
Overseas: No

<< >>

PAPER WAREHOUSE/PARTY UNIVERSE

7630 Excelsior Blvd.
Minneapolis, MN 55426-4504
Tel: (800) 229-1792 (952) 352-9107
Fax: (952) 936-9800
E-Mail:
mikeanderson@paperwarehouse.com
Web Site: www.paperwarehouse.com
Mr. Mike Anderson, VP of Franchising

PAPER WAREHOUSE specializes in party supplies and paper goods. They operate under the names PAPER WAREHOUSE, PARTY UNIVERSE and www.partysmart.com. PAPER WARE-HOUSE stores offer an extensive assortment of special occasion, seasonal and everyday party and entertainment supplies, gift wrap, greeting cards and catering supplies at everyday low prices.

BACKGROUND:
Established: 1983;   1st Franchised: 1987
Franchised Units: 49
Company-Owned Units   98
Total Units: 147
Dist.:   US-147; CAN-0; O'seas-0
  North America: 25 States
  Density: 28 in MN, 15 in CO, 13 in WA
Projected New Units (12 Months):   15
Qualifications: 5, 3, 3, 3, 3, 3
Registered: All States
FINANCIAL/TERMS:
Cash Investment: $75-100K
Total Investment: $170-430K
Minimum Net Worth: $450K+
Fees: Franchise - $25K
  Royalty - 4%;   Ad. - 0%
Earnings Claim Statement: No
Term of Contract (Years):   10/10
Avg. # Of Employees: 5-6 FT
Passive Ownership: Allowed
Encourage Conversions: Yes
Area Develop. Agreements: Yes/10
Sub-Franchising Contracts: No

Expand In Territory: N/A
Space Needs: 7,200 SF; SC
SUPPORT & TRAINING PROVIDED:
Financial Assistance Provided: Yes(I)
Site Selection Assistance: Yes
Lease Negotiation Assistance: Yes
Co-Operative Advertising: No
Franchisee Assoc./Member: No
Size Of Corporate Staff: 65
On-Going Support: A,C,D,E,G,I
Training: 1 Week in Minneapolis, MN.
SPECIFIC EXPANSION PLANS:
US: All United States
Canada: All Canada
Overseas: No

<< >>

PAPYRUS

954 60th St.
Oakland, CA 94608
Tel: (888) 922-9555 (510) 428-0166
Fax: (510) 428-0615
Web Site: www.papurus-stores.com
Ms. Kathleen A. Low, Dir. Franchise Dev.

A unique concept, featuring fine greeting cards, stationery, designer gift wrap and associated products in fine paper. Merchandise mix emphasizes superior design, style and quality.

BACKGROUND:
Established: 1973;   1st Franchised: 1988
Franchised Units: 90
Company-Owned Units   40
Total Units: 130
Dist.:   US-130; CAN-0; O'seas-0
  North America: 29 States
  Density: NR
Projected New Units (12 Months):   30
Qualifications: 5, 5, 3, 5, 1, 5
Registered: All Except ND,SD
FINANCIAL/TERMS:
Cash Investment: $75-100K
Total Investment: $205-417K
Minimum Net Worth: $400K
Fees: Franchise - $29.5K
  Royalty - 6%;   Ad. - 1%
Earnings Claim Statement: Yes
Term of Contract (Years):   10/5/5
Avg. # Of Employees: 1-2 FT, 4 PT
Passive Ownership: Discouraged
Encourage Conversions: Yes
Area Develop. Agreements: Yes/Varies
Sub-Franchising Contracts: No
Expand In Territory: Yes
Space Needs: 1,000 SF; SF, RM
SUPPORT & TRAINING PROVIDED:
Financial Assistance Provided: Yes(I)

Site Selection Assistance: Yes
Lease Negotiation Assistance: Yes
Co-Operative Advertising: Yes
Franchisee Assoc./Member: Yes/Yes
Size Of Corporate Staff: 30
On-Going Support: A,B,C,D,E,F,G,H,I
Training: 9 Days Corporate Headquarters.
SPECIFIC EXPANSION PLANS:
US: All United States
Canada: All Canada
Overseas: No

<< >>

PARTY LAND

5215 Militia Hill Rd.
Plymouth Meeting, PA 19462-1216
Tel: (800) 778-9563 (610) 941-6200
Fax: (610) 941-6301
E-Mail: jbarry@partyland.com
Web Site: www.partyland.com
Mr. John L. Barry, VP Franchise Sales

World's largest international retail party supply franchise, specializing in service, selection and savings. The official party store for the 'new millennium.'

BACKGROUND:
Established: 1986;   1st Franchised: 1988
Franchised Units: 125
Company-Owned Units   5
Total Units: 130
Dist.:   US-88; CAN-4; O'seas-38
  North America: 23 States, 3 Provinces
  Density: 20 in PA, 8 in TX, 3 in CO
Projected New Units (12 Months):   20
Qualifications: 5, 4, 2, 1, 5, 5
Registered: All States and AB
FINANCIAL/TERMS:
Cash Investment: $80K
Total Investment: $249-329K
Minimum Net Worth: $250K
Fees: Franchise - $35K
  Royalty - 5%;   Ad. - 4%
Earnings Claim Statement: No
Term of Contract (Years):   20/10
Avg. # Of Employees: 2 FT, 6 PT
Passive Ownership: Allowed
Encourage Conversions: Yes
Area Develop. Agreements: Yes/5
Sub-Franchising Contracts: Yes
Expand In Territory: No
Space Needs: NR SF; FS, SF, SC
SUPPORT & TRAINING PROVIDED:
Financial Assistance Provided: Yes(I)
Site Selection Assistance: Yes

Lease Negotiation Assistance: Yes
Co-Operative Advertising: Yes
Franchisee Assoc./Member: Yes/Yes
Size Of Corporate Staff: 30+
On-Going Support: A,B,C,D,E,F,G,H,I
Training: 1 Week Party Land University.

SPECIFIC EXPANSION PLANS:
US: All United States
Canada: All Canada
Overseas: All Countries

<< >>

RIDER'S HOBBY SHOPS

4627 Platt
Ann Arbor, MI 48108
Tel: (888) 530-9780 (734) 477-7000
Fax: (734) 477-7003
Web Site: www.riders.com
Mr. Brent Martin, Director of Business
    Develop.

RIDER'S HOBBY SHOPS sell FUN! When families walk into a RIDER'S HOBBY SHOP, childhood dreams come alive and imaginations run wild. The family-oriented recreational products displayed throughout the store offer something fun and exciting for just about everyone. RIDER'S HOBBY SHOPS sell radio controlled cars, boats, airplanes, helicopters, electric trains, models of all types, games, telescopes, specialty tools, kites, rockets, doll houses, slotcars, educational toys for kids and much more.

BACKGROUND:
Established: 1946;   1st Franchised: 1996
Franchised Units: 7
Company-Owned Units   6
Total Units: 13
Dist.:   US-13; CAN-0; O'seas-0
  North America: 3 States
  Density: 11 in MI, 1 in TX, 1 in VA
Projected New Units (12 Months): 15-20
Qualifications: 4, 4, 3, 2, 4, 5
Registered: IL,IN,MI

FINANCIAL/TERMS:
Cash Investment: $80-120K
Total Investment: $200-300K
Minimum Net Worth: $300K
Fees: Franchise - $17.5K
  Royalty - 3.5%;   Ad. - 1%
Earnings Claim Statement: Yes
Term of Contract (Years):   10/5
Avg. # Of Employees: 3-4 FT, 6-10 PT
Passive Ownership: Discouraged
Encourage Conversions: Yes
Area Develop. Agreements: No
Sub-Franchising Contracts: No

Expand In Territory: No
Space Needs: 3,000-5,000 SF; SC

SUPPORT & TRAINING PROVIDED:
Financial Assistance Provided: No
Site Selection Assistance: Yes
Lease Negotiation Assistance: Yes
Co-Operative Advertising: Yes
Franchisee Assoc./Member: No
Size Of Corporate Staff: 8
On-Going Support: A,B,C,D,E,F,G,H,I
Training: 5 Days Corporate Headquarters;
    14 Days Franchisee's Retail Location.

SPECIFIC EXPANSION PLANS:
US: Focus on Midwest
Canada: No
Overseas: Master Franchisee in the U.K.

<< >>

SHEFIELD GOURMET GROUP OF COMPANIES

2265 W. Railway St., Box 490
Abbotsford, BC V2S 5Z5 CANADA
Tel: (604) 859-1014
Fax: (604) 859-1711
E-Mail: shefield@uniserve.com
Web Site: www.shefieldgourmet.com
Mr. T. Hartford, Franchise Director

Retail outlet, featuring tobaccos and related products, but also offering other merchandise, including beverages, confectionery, reading material, giftware and lottery that caters to everyday needs and impulse buying.

BACKGROUND:
Established: 1976;   1st Franchised: 1976
Franchised Units: 111
Company-Owned Units   2
Total Units: 113
Dist.:   US-0; CAN-113; O'seas-0
  North America: 7 Provinces
  Density: 39 in BC, 32 in ON, 23 in AB
Projected New Units (12 Months):   5
Registered: AB

FINANCIAL/TERMS:
Cash Investment: $40-100K
Total Investment: $180K
Minimum Net Worth: $NR
Fees: Franchise - $10-25K
  Royalty - 2-8%;   Ad. - NR
Earnings Claim Statement: NR
Term of Contract (Years):   5/5
Avg. # Of Employees: 1 FT, 1 PT
Passive Ownership: Discouraged
Encourage Conversions: Yes
Area Develop. Agreements: No
Sub-Franchising Contracts: No
Expand In Territory: Yes
Space Needs: 250-1,500 SF; RM, SC

SUPPORT & TRAINING PROVIDED:
Financial Assistance Provided: No
Site Selection Assistance: Yes
Lease Negotiation Assistance: Yes
Co-Operative Advertising: Yes
Franchisee Assoc./Member: NR
Size Of Corporate Staff: 8
On-Going Support: C,D,E,G,I
Training: 1 Week On-Site.

SPECIFIC EXPANSION PLANS:
US: No
Canada: All Canada
Overseas: No

<< >>

SOX APPEAL

7167 Shady Oak Rd.
Eden Prairie, MN 55344
Tel: (800) 899-8478 (612) 943-1011
Fax: (612) 934-9050
Web Site: www.soxappeal.com
Ms. Sue Schneck, Franchise Development

National chain of sock and hosiery specialty stores. Stores offer a wide selection of socks and hosiery for men, women and children. Brand-name and designer merchandise.

BACKGROUND:
Established: 1984;   1st Franchised: 1986
Franchised Units: 7
Company-Owned Units   0
Total Units: 7
Dist.:   US-9; CAN-0; O'seas-0
  North America: 5 States
  Density: 3 in MN, 3 in PA, 1 in DE
Projected New Units (12 Months):   NR
Qualifications: 5, 5, 3, 4, 4, 5
Registered: All States

FINANCIAL/TERMS:
Cash Investment: $50-120K
Total Investment: $80-150K
Minimum Net Worth: $100K
Fees: Franchise - $20K
  Royalty - 5%;   Ad. - 1%
Earnings Claim Statement: No
Term of Contract (Years):   10
Avg. # Of Employees: 2 FT, 3 PT
Passive Ownership: Allowed
Encourage Conversions: N/A
Area Develop. Agreements: NR
Sub-Franchising Contracts: No
Expand In Territory: Yes
Space Needs: 500-700 SF; Airport

SUPPORT & TRAINING PROVIDED:
Financial Assistance Provided: No
Site Selection Assistance: Yes
Lease Negotiation Assistance: Yes
Co-Operative Advertising: No

Franchisee Assoc./Member: No
Size Of Corporate Staff: 2
On-Going Support: C,D,E,F,G,I
Training: 3-5 Days Corporate Office; 1-2
    Days Retail Store.
SPECIFIC EXPANSION PLANS:
US: All United States
Canada: No
Overseas: No

≪ ≫

SUCCESSORIES

2520 Diehl Rd.
Aurora, IL 60504
Tel: (800) 621-1423 (630) 820-7200
Fax: (630) 820-3856
Web Site: www.successories.com
Ms. Dana Mallory, Dir. Franchise
    Operations

SUCCESSORIES sells products for business and personal motivation, including over 500 proprietary products and those from other sources, such as audio tapes, time-management systems and self-improvement books. Our objective is to provide one-stop shopping for all motivational resources.

BACKGROUND:
Established: 1985;   1st Franchised: 1992
Franchised Units: 47
Company-Owned Units   <u>52</u>
Total Units: 99
Dist.:   US-96; CAN-3; O'seas-0
   North America: 33 States, 1 Province
   Density: 11 in IL, 8 in CA, 6 in FL
Projected New Units (12 Months):   6
Qualifications: 4, 4, 4, 3, 2, 3
Registered: All States
FINANCIAL/TERMS:
Cash Investment: $NR
Total Investment: $144-238K
Minimum Net Worth: $250K
Fees: Franchise - $35K
   Royalty - 2%;   Ad. - 1%
Earnings Claim Statement: No
Term of Contract (Years):   5/5
Avg. # Of Employees: 2 FT, 2 PT
Passive Ownership: Discouraged
Encourage Conversions: N/A
Area Develop. Agreements: No
Sub-Franchising Contracts: Yes
Expand In Territory: Yes
Space Needs: 800-1,200 SF; SC, RM
SUPPORT & TRAINING PROVIDED:
Financial Assistance Provided: N/A
Site Selection Assistance: Yes
Lease Negotiation Assistance: Yes

Co-Operative Advertising: No
Franchisee Assoc./Member: Yes/Yes
Size Of Corporate Staff: 150
On-Going Support: B,C,D,E,f,h,I
Training: 5 Days in Lombard, IL.
SPECIFIC EXPANSION PLANS:
US: Various Markets
Canada: All Canada
Overseas: No

≪ ≫

TALKING BOOK WORLD

26211 Central Park, # 415
Southfield, MI 48076
Tel: (800) 403-2933 (248) 945-9999
Fax: (248) 945-9606
E-Mail: tbwchaim@aol.com
Web Site: www.talkingbookworld.com
Mr. Chaim Daskal, VP Franchising &
    Marketing

TALKING BOOK WORLD is the largest retail chain of audiobook stores. We rent and sell audiobooks on cassette and CD. We have access to over 70,000 titles and stock a minimum of 6,000 titles in each location. We feature our exclusive 'No Due Dates' rental program, used audiobooks trade-ins and unique purchasing discounts. We also offer mail order and Internet rentals and sales.

BACKGROUND:
Established: 1993;   1st Franchised: 1996
Franchised Units: 22
Company-Owned Units   <u>20</u>
Total Units: 42
Dist.:   US-40; CAN-2; O'seas-0
   North America: 8 States, 2 Provinces
   Density: 16 in MI, 10 in CA, 3 in FL
Projected New Units (12 Months):   30
Qualifications: 5, 4, 2, 1, 5, 5
Registered: CA,FL,IL,MI
FINANCIAL/TERMS:
Cash Investment: $50-225K
Total Investment: $180-225K
Minimum Net Worth: $100K
Fees: Franchise - $25K
   Royalty - 5%;   Ad. - 2%
Earnings Claim Statement: No
Term of Contract (Years):   15/15
Avg. # Of Employees: 1 FT, 2 PT
Passive Ownership: Discouraged

Encourage Conversions: Yes
Area Develop. Agreements: Yes/3
Sub-Franchising Contracts: No
Expand In Territory: Yes
Space Needs: 2,000 SF; FS, SF, SC
SUPPORT & TRAINING PROVIDED:
Financial Assistance Provided: No
Site Selection Assistance: Yes
Lease Negotiation Assistance: Yes
Co-Operative Advertising: Yes
Franchisee Assoc./Member: No
Size Of Corporate Staff: 10
On-Going Support: a,b,C,D,E,F,G,H,I
Training: 2 Days Corporate Headquarters;
    3 Weeks Corporate Store; 1 Week
    Franchisee Location.
SPECIFIC EXPANSION PLANS:
US: All United States
Canada: All Canada
Overseas: No

≪ ≫

TINDER BOX INTERNATIONAL

Three Bala Plaza East, # 102
Bala Cynwyd, PA 19004
Tel: (800) 846-3372 (610) 668-4220
Fax: (610) 668-4266
E-Mail: tbiltd@ix.netcom.com
Web Site: www.tinderbox.com
Mr. Fred Haas, Director Franchise
    Development

The world's largest and oldest chain of premium cigar, tobacco, smoking accessory and gift stores, with 70 years' experience as the undisputed industry leader.

BACKGROUND: IFA MEMBER
Established: 1928;   1st Franchised: 1965
Franchised Units: 128
Company-Owned Units   <u>3</u>
Total Units: 131
Dist.:   US-116; CAN-1; O'seas-0
   North America: 50 States
   Density: 17 in CA, 9 in IL, 9 in OH
Projected New Units (12 Months):   25
Qualifications: 5, 3, 1, 2, 4, 5
Registered: All Except ND,SD
FINANCIAL/TERMS:
Cash Investment: $75-100K
Total Investment: $175-250K
Minimum Net Worth: $250-300K
Fees: Franchise - $30K
   Royalty - 4-5%;   Ad. - 3%
Earnings Claim Statement: Yes
Term of Contract (Years):   10/5
Avg. # Of Employees: 1-2 FT, 2-3 PT
Passive Ownership: Allowed
Encourage Conversions: Yes

Area Develop. Agreements: Yes/5
Sub-Franchising Contracts: No
Expand In Territory: Yes
Space Needs: 800-1,500 SF; FS, SF, SC, RM

SUPPORT & TRAINING PROVIDED:
Financial Assistance Provided: Yes
Site Selection Assistance: Yes
Lease Negotiation Assistance: Yes
Co-Operative Advertising: Yes
Franchisee Assoc./Member: No
Size Of Corporate Staff: 10
On-Going Support: a,C,D,E,F,G,H,I
Training: 5 Days Home Office; 3-5 Days at Franchisee's Store; Follow-Up Store Visit within 30 Days.

SPECIFIC EXPANSION PLANS:
US: All United States
Canada: All Canada
Overseas: All Countries

◄◄ ►►

ROMANCING THE SOUL

VANILLA - ROMANCING THE SOUL
1111 Flint Rd., Unit 36
Downsview, ON M3J 3C7 CANADA
Tel: (416) 665-3471
Fax: (416) 665-8839
E-Mail: vanilla@istar.ca
Ms. Darlene Stanley, General Manager

Candles, candle paraphernalia, aroma therapy and men's and ladies' body care products.

BACKGROUND:
Established: 1997; 1st Franchised: 1998
Franchised Units: 0
Company-Owned Units: 2
Total Units: 2
Dist.: US-0; CAN-2; O'seas-0
North America: 1 Province
Density: 2 in ON
Projected New Units (12 Months): 2
Qualifications: 4, 3, 1, 2, 3, 4
Registered: NR

FINANCIAL/TERMS:
Cash Investment: $75K
Total Investment: $250K
Minimum Net Worth: $150K
Fees: Franchise - $25K
  Royalty - 6%; Ad. - 2%
Earnings Claim Statement: No

Term of Contract (Years): 5/5
Avg. # Of Employees: 2 FT, 3 PT
Passive Ownership: Discouraged
Encourage Conversions: Yes
Area Develop. Agreements: No
Sub-Franchising Contracts: No
Expand In Territory: Yes
Space Needs: 1,000-1,200 SF; RM

SUPPORT & TRAINING PROVIDED:
Financial Assistance Provided: N/A
Site Selection Assistance: Yes
Lease Negotiation Assistance: Yes
Co-Operative Advertising: Yes
Franchisee Assoc./Member: No
Size Of Corporate Staff: 15
On-Going Support: B,C,D,E,F,G,H,I
Training: 1-2 Weeks Toronto, ON.

SPECIFIC EXPANSION PLANS:
US: All United States
Canada: All Canada
Overseas: All Countries

◄◄ ►►

WICKS 'N' STICKS
P.O. Box 4586
Houston, TX 77210-4586
Tel: (888) 55-WICKS (281) 874-3642
Fax: (281) 874-3678
Web Site: www.wicksnstick.com
Mr. William McPherson, VP Franchise Development

Nation's largest and most respected retailer of quality candles, fragrancing and related home decorative products. Franchisees are offered outstanding name recognition, comprehensive training and extensive start up and on-going support. Rated #1 franchise in category by Entrepreneur Magazine 7 years in a row. Rated a top franchise by both Success Gold 100 and Income Opportunities Platinum 200.

BACKGROUND: IFA MEMBER
Established: 1968; 1st Franchised: 1968
Franchised Units: 218
Company-Owned Units: 4
Total Units: 222
Dist.: US-222; CAN-0; O'seas-0
North America: NR
Density: 26 in TX, 15 in NY, 15 in FL
Projected New Units (12 Months): 17
Qualifications: 5, 3, 3, 3, 3, 5
Registered: CA,IL,IN,MD,MI,MN,NY, ND,OR,RI,SD,VA,WA,WI

FINANCIAL/TERMS:
Cash Investment: $65K
Total Investment: $153.6-249.3K
Minimum Net Worth: $70K Liquid

Fees: Franchise - $25K
  Royalty - 6%; Ad. - 1%
Earnings Claim Statement: Yes
Term of Contract (Years): 10/5/5/5
Avg. # Of Employees: 1-2 FT, 2 PT
Passive Ownership: NR
Encourage Conversions: N/A
Area Develop. Agreements: No
Sub-Franchising Contracts: Yes
Expand In Territory: Yes
Space Needs: 1,000-1,200 SF; RM

SUPPORT & TRAINING PROVIDED:
Financial Assistance Provided: Yes(I)
Site Selection Assistance: Yes
Lease Negotiation Assistance: Yes
Co-Operative Advertising: N/A
Franchisee Assoc./Member: Yes/No
Size Of Corporate Staff: 37
On-Going Support: A,C,D,E,F,G,H,I
Training: 2 Weeks Corporate Office, Houston, TX.

SPECIFIC EXPANSION PLANS:
US: All United States
Canada: No
Overseas: No

◄◄ ►►

WILD BIRD CENTER
7370 MacArthur Blvd.
Glen Echo, MD 20812
Tel: (800) 945-3247 (301) 229-9585
Fax: (301) 320-6154
E-Mail: georgep@wildbirdcenter.com
Web Site: www.wildbirdcenter.com
Mr. George H. Petrides, President

A WBCA franchise is more than a store; it is a valued community resource. The story of THE WILD BIRD CENTERS OF AMERICA, Inc. is one of enthusiasm about wild birds and a professional approach to the birding market. The customer enjoys friendly, personal service in a peaceful environment with the feel of a relaxing backyard. The owner provides this service with the help of highly-efficient systems and support.

BACKGROUND: IFA MEMBER
Established: 1985; 1st Franchised: 1988
Franchised Units: 99
Company-Owned Units: <u>1</u>
Total Units: 100
Dist.: US-98; CAN-2; O'seas-0
 North America: 33 States, 1 Province
 Density: 9 in MD, 8 in PA, 6 in CO
Projected New Units (12 Months): 20
Qualifications: 5, 4, 2, 4, 2, 5
Registered: All Except HI
FINANCIAL/TERMS:
Cash Investment: $35-50K
Total Investment: $75-131K
Minimum Net Worth: $150K
Fees: Franchise - $19.5K
 Royalty - 3-4.5%; Ad. - 0%
Earnings Claim Statement: No
Term of Contract (Years): 5/5x5
Avg. # Of Employees: 1 FT, 2 PT
Passive Ownership: Discouraged
Encourage Conversions: No
Area Develop. Agreements: No
Sub-Franchising Contracts: No
Expand In Territory: Yes
Space Needs: 1,500-2,400 SF; SC
SUPPORT & TRAINING PROVIDED:
Financial Assistance Provided: Yes(I)
Site Selection Assistance: Yes
Lease Negotiation Assistance: Yes
Co-Operative Advertising: Yes
Franchisee Assoc./Member: Yes/Yes
Size Of Corporate Staff: 15
On-Going Support: C,d,E,F,G,h
Training: 10 Days Home Office.
SPECIFIC EXPANSION PLANS:
US: All United States
Canada: All Canada
Overseas: No

≪ ≫

WILD BIRD MARKETPLACE
4317 Elm Tree Rd.
Bloomfield, NY 14469
Tel: (888) 926-2473 (716) 229-5897
Fax: (716) 229-5448
E-Mail: jfg@wildbirdmarketplace.com
Web Site: www.wildbirdmarketplace.org
Mr. John F. Gardner, President

WILD BIRD MARKETPLACE is committed to providing an outstanding franchise opportunity - one that provides personal satisfaction, community recognition and profitability based on personal motivation, qualification and commitment.

BACKGROUND:
Established: 1988; 1st Franchised: 1990
Franchised Units: 15
Company-Owned Units: <u>0</u>
Total Units: 15
Dist.: US-15; CAN-0; O'seas-0
 North America: 10 States
 Density: 4 in PA, 2 in NC, 2 in WY
Projected New Units (12 Months): 4
Qualifications: 4, 3, 2, 1, 3, 4
Registered: FL,IL,IN,MD,MI,NY,RI,
 SD,WI,AB
FINANCIAL/TERMS:
Cash Investment: $30-50K
Total Investment: $90-150K
Minimum Net Worth: $150K
Fees: Franchise - $20K
 Royalty - 4%; Ad. - 0%
Earnings Claim Statement: No
Term of Contract (Years): 10/10
Avg. # Of Employees: 1 FT, 2 PT
Passive Ownership: Discouraged
Encourage Conversions: Yes
Area Develop. Agreements: Yes
Sub-Franchising Contracts: Yes
Expand In Territory: Yes
Space Needs: 2,000 SF; FS, SF, SC
SUPPORT & TRAINING PROVIDED:
Financial Assistance Provided: Yes(I)
Site Selection Assistance: Yes
Lease Negotiation Assistance: Yes
Co-Operative Advertising: N/A
Franchisee Assoc./Member: No
Size Of Corporate Staff: 3
On-Going Support: C,D,E,F,G,H,I
Training: 5 Days Corporate Headquarters;
 5 Days at Store.
SPECIFIC EXPANSION PLANS:
US: NE,SE, Midwest
Canada: No
Overseas: No

≪ ≫

WILD BIRDS UNLIMITED
11711 N. College Ave., # 146
Carmel, IN 46032-5601
Tel: (888) 302-2473 (317) 571-7100
Fax: (317) 571-7110
E-Mail: pickettp@wbu.com
Web Site: www.wbu.com
Mr. Paul E. Pickett, Dir. Franchise Dev.

WILD BIRDS UNLIMITED is North America's original and largest group of retail stores catering to the backyard birdfeeding and nature enthusiast. We currently have over 240 stores in the U.S. and Canada. Stores provide birdseed, feeders, houses, optics and nature-related gifts. Additionally, stores provide extensive educational programs regarding backyard birdfeeding. Franchisees are provided an all-inclusive support system.

BACKGROUND: IFA MEMBER
Established: 1981; 1st Franchised: 1983
Franchised Units: 281
Company-Owned Units: <u>0</u>
Total Units: 281
Dist.: US-267; CAN-14; O'seas-0
 North America: 42 States, 3 Provinces
 Density: 19 in MI, 18 in TX, 13 in IL
Projected New Units (12 Months): 35
Qualifications: 5, 5, 1, 3, 2, 5
Registered: CA,FL,IL,IN,MD,MI,MN,NY,
 OR,RI,VA,WA,WI,DC
FINANCIAL/TERMS:
Cash Investment: $32-45K
Total Investment: $80-140K
Minimum Net Worth: $150K
Fees: Franchise - $18K
 Royalty - 4%; Ad. - NR
Earnings Claim Statement: Yes
Term of Contract (Years): 10/5
Avg. # Of Employees: 2 FT, 4 PT
Passive Ownership: Not Allowed
Encourage Conversions: N/A
Area Develop. Agreements: No
Sub-Franchising Contracts: No
Expand In Territory: Yes
Space Needs: 1,400-1,800 SF; FS, SC
SUPPORT & TRAINING PROVIDED:
Financial Assistance Provided: Yes(I)
Site Selection Assistance: Yes
Lease Negotiation Assistance: Yes
Co-Operative Advertising: No
Franchisee Assoc./Member: Yes/Yes
Size Of Corporate Staff: 40
On-Going Support: C,D,E,F,G,H,I
Training: 6 Days in Indianapolis, IN; 1 Day
 at Store Site.
SPECIFIC EXPANSION PLANS:
US: All United States
Canada: All Canada
Overseas: No

◄◄ ►►

YARD CARDS

3990 State St.
Abilene, TX 79603
Tel: (915) 672-9444
Fax: (915) 672-9444
E-Mail: yardcards@aol.com
Web Site: www.members.aol/yardcards
Ms. Tracey Pacheco, President

Rental of 8-foot-tall greeting cards for any and all occasions, including storks to announce new babies, graduation, Valentine's Day, birthday, retirement, Mother's Day, Father's Day, and anniversary cards, etc. Can be operated as a home-based business or added on to an existing business.

BACKGROUND:

Established: 1983;	1st Franchised: 1986
Franchised Units:	7
Company-Owned Units	1
Total Units:	8
Dist.:	US-8; CAN-0; O'seas-0
North America:	5 States
Density:	3 in IL, 2 in MO, 1 in WV
Projected New Units (12 Months):	2
Qualifications:	4, 4, 3, 3, 3, 3
Registered: IL,MD	

FINANCIAL/TERMS:

Cash Investment:	$5-15K
Total Investment:	$5-15K
Minimum Net Worth:	$NR
Fees: Franchise -	$1K Min.
Royalty - 5%;	Ad. - 0%
Earnings Claim Statement:	No
Term of Contract (Years):	20/5/5
Avg. # Of Employees:	1-2 PT
Passive Ownership:	Discouraged
Encourage Conversions:	NR
Area Develop. Agreements:	No
Sub-Franchising Contracts:	No
Expand In Territory:	Yes
Space Needs: N/A SF; HB	

SUPPORT & TRAINING PROVIDED:

Financial Assistance Provided:	No
Site Selection Assistance:	N/A
Lease Negotiation Assistance:	N/A
Co-Operative Advertising:	N/A
Franchisee Assoc./Member:	NR
Size Of Corporate Staff:	2
On-Going Support:	G,h
Training: As Needed.	

SPECIFIC EXPANSION PLANS:

US:	All United States
Canada:	No
Overseas:	No

◄◄ ►►

SUPPLEMENTAL LISTING OF FRANCHISORS

All Nations Flag Co., 118 W. 5th St., Kansas City, MO 64105 ; (816) 842-3995; Mr. Greg Wald (800) 533-FLAG; (816) 842-8798

Alterations Express, 207 Booardman Canfield Rd., Booardman, OH 44512-4806 ; (330) 629-9465; Mr. Gino Rondinelli (800) 221-1198; (330) 758-1075

Babies 'N' Bells, 2110 Springwood, Carrollton, TX 75006 ; (972) 418-5723; Ms. Dara Craft (888) 418-2229; (972) 416-2229

Bacchus Wine Made Simple, 1000 Manhattan Ave., Manhattan Beach, CA 90266 ; (310) 372-5541; Ms. Christina Kotula ; (310) 372-2021

Bead Shop, The, 3222 M St., # 3345, Washington, DC 20007 ; (202) 337-7134; Mr. John Delisle ; (202) 337-3531

Beadworks, 139 Washington St., South Norwalk, CT 06854 ; (203) 852-9034; Ms. Nancy Wall ; (203) 852-9194

Better Back Store, The, P.O. Box 1296, Newington, VA 22122 ; (703) 339-0671; Mr. Cliff Levin (800) 501-2225; (703) 339-1300

Bijoux Terner, 7441 NW 8th St., # K, Miami, FL 33126 ; (305) 262-9286; Mr. Sergio Cedano (800) 753-1200; (305) 266-9000

Brides International, 3038 Vail Ave., Commerce, CA 90040 ; (323) 869-9398; Ms. Rachel Jabin (800) 287-4696; (323) 869-9336

Buning the Florist, 3860 W. Commercial Blvd., Ft. Lauderdale, FL 33309 ; (305) 486-0622; Mr. R. Demerest (800) 940-1778; (305) 488-3000

Cash Converters Canada, 185 The West Mall, Toronto, ON M9C 5L5 CANADA; (416) 695-9051; Mr. Rhett Thurston (888) 677-2274; (416) 695-2321

Catholic Store, 3398 S. Broadway, Englewood, CO 80110 ; (303) 789-2754; Mr. Richard Weigang (800) 776-4569; (303) 762-8385

Command Control Systems, 590 32nd St. SE, Grand Rapids, MI 49548 ; (616) 452-1232; Mr. Jack Harkness ; (616) 452-7800

Compu-Cure, 1071 S. Jefferson Davis Pkwy., New Orleans, LA 70125 ; (504) 484-6333; Mr. Jeff Barach (888) 291-1216; (504) 486-7741

Computer Maintenance Service, P.O. Box 8, San Marcos, TX 78667 ; ; Mr. Frank Mack ; (830) 629-1400

Conroy's/1-800-Flowers, 1600 Stewart Ave., Westbury, NY 11590 ; (516) 237-6097; Mr. Brian McGee (800) 557-4770; (516) 237-6000

Dan's Fan City, 300 Dunbar Ave., Oldsmar, FL 34677 ; (813) 855-3916; Mr. Ed Veclotch (800) 486-6326; (813) 855-7384

Dazzler, The, # 262-4820 Kingsway, Burnaby, BC V5H 4P1 CANADA; (604) 433-7311; Mr. Major Olik ; (604) 433-7311

Flag Shop, The, 1755 W. 4th Ave., Vancouver, BC V6J 1M2 CANADA; (604) 736-6439; Ms. Doreen Braverman (800) 663-8681; (604) 736-8161

Flowerama, 3165 W. Airline Hwy., Waterloo, IA 50703 ; (319) 291-8676; Mr. Chuck Nygren (800) 728-6004; (319) 291-6004

Foremost Liquor Stores, 4001 W. Devon, Chicago, IL 60646 ; (312) 545-3330; Mr. Bernard Bernstein ; (773) 545-3111

Hammett's Learning World, P.O. Box 859057, Braintree, MA 02185-9057 ; (781) 848-3970; Ms. Lillian R. Ochs (800) 955-2200; (781) 848-1000

Hannoush Jewelers, 134 Capitol Dr., West Springfield, MA 01089 ; (413) 788-7588; Mr. Norman A. Hannoush (888) 325-3935; (413) 846-4640

Hat Zone, The, 1036 A NE Jibe, Lakewood Bus. Pk., Lee's Summit, MO 64064 ; (816) 795-9159; Mr. Mark Patek ; (816) 795-8702

Hobbytown USA, 6301 S. 58th St., Lincoln, NE 68516 ; (402) 434-5055; Mr. Ray Burney (800) 858-7370; (402) 434-5050

Inacom Computer Centers, 10810 Farnam Dr., Omaha, NE 68154 ; (402) 330-9608; Mr. Cris Freiwald (800) 843-2762; (402) 758-3900

La Bride D'Elegance, 2120 N. Woodlawn, # 312, Wichita, KS 67208 ; (316) 681-1761; Mr. Steve Watson (800) 362-7170; (316) 681-0952

LaserNetworks, 785 Pacific Rd., # 1, Oakville, ON L6L 6M3 CANADA; (905) 847-5991; Mr. Graham Wood (800) 461-4879; (905) 847-5990

MacBirdie Golf Gifts, 7399 Bush Lake Rd., Edina, MN 55439 ; (612) 830-1055; Mr. John Jacobson (800) 343-1033; (612) 830-1033

MGM Liquor Stores, 1124 Larpenteur Ave. W., St. Paul, MN 55113-6317 ; (651) 487-9401; Director of Franchising ; (651) 487-1006

Office 1 Superstore International, P.O. Box 5093, East Hampton, NY 11937 ; (516) 537-4293; Mr. Mark Baccash ; (516) 537-4290

Parker Interior Plantscape, 1325 Terrill Rd., Scotch Plains, NJ 07076 ; (908) 322-4818; Mr. Richard Parker (800) 526-3672; (908) 322-5552

Party 123, 400 Perrine Rd., # 400B, Old Bridge, NJ 08857 ; (732) 316-0673; Mr. John J. Murphy (888) PARTY-123; (932) 316-0665

Party City, 400 Commons Way, Rockaway, NJ 07866 ; (973) 983-1333; Ms. Valerie Szymaniak (800) 883-2100; (973) 983-0888

Party Fair, Pond Rd. Shopping Center, Freehold, NJ 07728 ; (732) 780-5174; Mr. David Silverstein ; (732) 780-1110

PCHut.com, 1205 Hwy. 20, Mountain Home, ID 83647 ; (208) 580-2001; Director of Franchising ; (208) 580-2574

Perfumes Etc., 871 Islingdon Ave., Toronto, ON M8Z 4N9 CANADA; (416) 253-757; Mr. Sanjay Bawa (888) PER-FUMS; (416) 253-7717

Pinch-A-Penny, P.O. Box 6025, Clearwater, FL 33758 ; (727) 536-8066; Mr. Bob Slaughter ; (727) 531-8913

Plato's Closet, 4200 Dahlberg Drive, Minneapolis, MN 55422 ; (612) 520-8501; Mr. John Lessler (800) 269-4081; (612) 520-8480

Pot Pourri, 216 Migneron, Ville Saint-Lauren, QC H4T 1Y7 CANADA; (514) 341-4241; Mr. Egide Blanchard ; (514) 341-4000

Rafters, 4699 Keele St., # 1, Downsview, ON M3J 2N8 CANADA; (416) 661-9706; Mr. Michael Mayerson ; (416) 661-9916

Recycled Paper Greetings, 3636 N. Broadway, Chicago, IL 60613 ; (312) 296-6291; Mr. Mort Baron (800) 777-3331; (312) 348-6410

Relax the Back, 2101 Rosecrans Ave., # 1250, El Segundo, CA 90245 ; (310) 416-1076; Ms. Olivia Bartel (800) 290-2225; (310) 416-1077

Rescuecom Corporation, 2560 Burnet Ave., Syracuse, NY 13206 ; (315) 433-5228; Mr. David A. Milman (800) RESCUE-7; (315) 433-0002

Retool, 4200 Dalhberg Dr., Minneapolis, MN 55422 ; (612) 520-8410; Mr. Butch Gladden (800) 269-4075; (612) 520-8480

Rodan Jewellers/Simply Charming, 4180 Lougheed Hwy., # 102, Burnaby, BC V5C 6A7 CANADA; (604) 438-1635; Mr. Karim Rahemtulla ; (604) 438-1625

Shaver Center/Centre Du Rasoir, 3151 rue Joseph Dubreuil, Lachine, PQ H8T 3HT CANADA; (514) 636-8356; Mr. Sam Bienenstoch ; (514) 636-4512

She's Flowers, 100 N. Glendora Ave., # 106, Glendora, CA 91741 ; (626) 335-2039; Ms. Helen Shih (800) 777-2582; (626) FLO-RIST

Shefield & Sons Tobacconists, P.O. Box 490, Abbotsford, AB U2S S2S CANADA; (604) 859-1711; Mr. Terry Hartford ; (604) 859-1014

Silk Plants Plus, 1045 W. Brandon Blvd., Brandon, FL 33511 ; (813) 651-3326;

Mr. Frank Rego (888) SEND-SILK; (813) 684-7414

SilkCorp, 2101 Roberts Dr., Broadview, IL 60153-4630 ; (708) 450-1507; Mr. Ed Clamage (800) THE-SILK; (708) 450-9800

Softub, 21100 Superior St., Chatsworth, CA 91311 ; (818) 407-4658; Mr. Jeff McNees (800) 266-7882; (818) 407-4646

Software City, 10 W. Ivy Ln. #1, Englewood, NJ 07631-1771 ; (201) 569-7180; Mr. Shep Altshuler (800) 222-0918; (201) 569-8900

T-Shirts Plus, 5400 Bosque Blvd., # 650, Waco, TX 76710 ; (254) 776-6838; Ms. Karen Rhodes (800) 880-0721; (254) 776-8872

TFM, 10333 - 174 St., Edmonton, AB T5S 1H1 CANADA; (780) 486-7528; Mr. A. J. Herfst ; (780) 483-3217

True Friends, 318 N. Carson St., # 214, Carson City, NV 89701 ; (800) 654-5161; Mr. John (Jack) D. Pomeroy (800) 654-5156; (702) 882-1963

RETAIL: VIDEO/AUDIO/ELECTRONICS INDUSTRY PROFILE

Total # Franchisors in Industry Group	19
Total # Franchised Units in Industry Group	4,940
Total # Company-Owned Units in Industry Group	<u>11,034</u>
Total # Operating Units in Industry Group	15,974
Average # Franchised Units/Franchisor	260.0
Average # Company-Owned Units/Franchisor	<u>580.7</u>
Average # Total Units/Franchisor	840.7
Ratio of Total # Franchised Units/Total # Company-Owned Units	0.4:1
Industry Survey Participants	6
Representing % of Industry	31.6%
Average Franchise Fee*:	$21.3K
Average Total Investment*:	$120.8K
Average On-Going Royalty Fee*:	4.7%

If a range was provided, the mid-point of the range was used. See detailed profiles for actual ranges.

FIVE LARGEST PARTICIPANTS IN SURVEY

Company	# Franchised Units	# Co-Owned Units	# Total Units	Franchise Fee	On-Going Royalty	Total Investment
1. Radio Shack Select	2,154	5,033	7,187	25K	0%	60K
2. CD Warehouse	251	77	324	20K	5/4%	132-169K
3. Video Data Services	246	1	247	20K	$750/Yr.	20-23K
4. Microplay Entertainment	90	0	90	15K	3.4% Avg.	115-200K
5. Jumbo Video	61	0	61	25K+	5%	150-325K

All of the data provided are proprietary and should not be quoted without acknowledging *Bond's Franchise Guide*.

CD WAREHOUSE

1204 Sovereign Row
Oklahoma City, OK 73108
Tel: (800) 641-9394 (405) 949-2422
Fax: (405) 949-2566
E-Mail: vsugg@cdwarehouse.co
Web Site: www.cdwarehouse.com
Ms. Vicky L. Sugg, Franchise Sales
   Manager

CD WAREHOUSE is a rapidly-growing franchise, specializing in the sale of pre-owned CDs. Our stores also buy and trade used CD's, sell Top 100 new CDs, and sell other music-related items. Our proprietary software makes it easy to buy and sell pre-owned CDs, even without prior music knowledge.

BACKGROUND: IFA MEMBER
Established: 1992;   1st Franchised: 1992
Franchised Units: 251
Company-Owned Units   73
Total Units: 324
Dist.:   US-308; CAN-9; O'seas-7
  North America: 38 States, 3 Provinces
  Density: 55 in TX, 28 in FL, 18 in CA
Projected New Units (12 Months): 30-50
Qualifications: 5, 3, 1, 2, 4, 4
Registered: CA,FL,IL,IN,MD,MI,NY,
  OR,RI,VA,WI
FINANCIAL/TERMS:
Cash Investment: $40-60K
Total Investment: $132-169K
Minimum Net Worth: $150K
Fees: Franchise - $20K
  Royalty - 5%/4%;   Ad. - 1.75%
Earnings Claim Statement: No
Term of Contract (Years):   10/Varies
Avg. # Of Employees: 1-3 FT, 3-4 PT
Passive Ownership: Discouraged
Encourage Conversions: N/A
Area Develop. Agreements: Yes
Sub-Franchising Contracts: No
Expand In Territory: Yes
Space Needs: 1,500-2,000 SF; FS, SC
SUPPORT & TRAINING PROVIDED:
Financial Assistance Provided: Yes(I)
Site Selection Assistance: Yes
Lease Negotiation Assistance: Yes
Co-Operative Advertising: Yes
Franchisee Assoc./Member: Yes/No
Size Of Corporate Staff: 67

On-Going Support: C,D,E,G,H,I
Training: 5-6 Days at Oklahoma City, OK
  Training Center.
SPECIFIC EXPANSION PLANS:
US: All United States
Canada: All Canada
Overseas: English-Speaking Countries

◁◁ ▷▷

Home of the Guarantee™

JUMBO VIDEO

5360 S. Service Rd., # 201
Burlington, ON L7L 5L1 CANADA
Tel: (905) 634-4244
Fax: (905) 632-2964
E-Mail: franchisesales@jumbovideo.com
Web Site: www.jumbovideo.com
Mr. Doug Jacques, Dir. Franchise
  Sales/RE

Home   entertainment   business, encompassing sales and rental of videos (including games), other related retail merchandise and confectionery.

BACKGROUND:
Established: 1987;   1st Franchised: 1989
Franchised Units: 61
Company-Owned Units   0
Total Units: 61
Dist.:   US-0; CAN-61; O'seas-0
  North America: 5 Provinces
  Density: 48 in ON, 4 in NB, 4 in BC
Projected New Units (12 Months): N/A
Qualifications: 4, 4, 2, 2, 4, 4
Registered: NR
FINANCIAL/TERMS:
Cash Investment: $50-125K
Total Investment: $150-325K
Minimum Net Worth: $N/A
Fees: Franchise - $25K+
  Royalty - 5%;   Ad. - 3%
Earnings Claim Statement: No
Term of Contract (Years):   10/5
Avg. # Of Employees: 2 FT, 3 PT
Passive Ownership: Discouraged
Encourage Conversions: Yes
Area Develop. Agreements: No
Sub-Franchising Contracts: NO
Expand In Territory: Yes
Space Needs: 1,500-5,000 SF; SC
SUPPORT & TRAINING PROVIDED:
Financial Assistance Provided: Yes(I)
Site Selection Assistance: Yes
Lease Negotiation Assistance: Yes

Co-Operative Advertising: Yes
Franchisee Assoc./Member: Yes/Yes
Size Of Corporate Staff: 18
On-Going Support: A,B,C,D,E,G,H
Training: 3 Days Head Office; 1 Week
  Training Store; 2 Weeks On-Site.
SPECIFIC EXPANSION PLANS:
US: No
Canada: All Except PQ
Overseas: No

◁◁ ▷▷

MICROPLAY ENTERTAINMENT
& VIDEO CENTRES

99 Ingram Dr.
Toronto, ON M6M 2L7 CANADA
Tel: (877) 221-6685 (416) 249-7555
Fax: (416) 249-9855
E-Mail: copeland@microplay.com
Web Site: www.microplay.com
Mr. Mason Copeland, Senior Vice
  President

MICROPLAY stores take video game specialty retailing to a whole new level. We buy, sell, rent and accessorize all popular games and systems, including Nintendo, Sony, Sega and PC CD-ROM. Our well-stocked stores offer variety, expertise and great value. In short, 'We sell fun!' We welcome you to discover why MICROPLAY is ranked #1 in video games.

BACKGROUND:
Established: 1985;   1st Franchised: 1993
Franchised Units: 90
Company-Owned Units   0
Total Units: 90
Dist.:   US-13; CAN-84; O'seas-4
  North America: 7 States, 9 Provinces
  Density: 47 in ON, 8 in PQ, 8 in BC
Projected New Units (12 Months):   25
Qualifications: 3, 3, 4, 3, 2, 5
Registered: NR
FINANCIAL/TERMS:
Cash Investment: $40-80K
Total Investment: $115-200K
Minimum Net Worth: $300K
Fees: Franchise - $15K
  Royalty - 3.4% Avg.;   Ad. - 1%
Earnings Claim Statement: No
Term of Contract (Years):   10/10
Avg. # Of Employees: 2 FT, 1 PT
Passive Ownership: Discouraged
Encourage Conversions: Yes
Area Develop. Agreements: Yes/10
Sub-Franchising Contracts: Yes

Expand In Territory: No
Space Needs: 1,400 SF; SC
SUPPORT & TRAINING PROVIDED:
Financial Assistance Provided: Yes(I)
Site Selection Assistance: Yes
Lease Negotiation Assistance: Yes
Co-Operative Advertising: Yes
Franchisee Assoc./Member: Yes/Yes
Size Of Corporate Staff: 14
On-Going Support: A,B,C,D,E,F,G,H,I
Training: 2 Days Concord, ON; 3 Days
Training Store, Toronto, ON; 3 Days
Pre-Opening/Grand Opening.
SPECIFIC EXPANSION PLANS:
US: NY,NJ,DE,CT,PA,OH, Midwest
Canada: All Canada
Overseas: England

◄◄ ►►

RadioShack.
You've got questions.
We've got answers.

RADIO SHACK SELECT
300 W. 3rd St., # 1600
Fort Worth, TX 76102
Tel: (817) 415-3499
Fax: (817) 415-8651
E-Mail: pcrump1@tandy.com
Web Site: www.radioshack.com
Mr. Paul Crump, Marketing Director

RADIO SHACK is a consumer electronics retailer.

BACKGROUND: IFA MEMBER
Established: 1921; 1st Franchised: 1969
Franchised Units: 2,154
Company-Owned Units: 5,033
Total Units: 7,187
Dist.: US-7,187; CAN-0; O'seas-0
North America: 48 States
Density: CA, NY, IL
Projected New Units (12 Months): 200
Qualifications: 5, 5, 5, 1, 1, 4
Registered: CA,FL,IL,IN,MD,MI,MN,NY,
ND,OR,SD,VA,WA,WI,DC
FINANCIAL/TERMS:
Cash Investment: $20% Down
Total Investment: $60K
Minimum Net Worth: $N/A
Fees: Franchise - $25K
Royalty - 0%; Ad. - 0%
Earnings Claim Statement: No
Term of Contract (Years): 10/Annual

Avg. # Of Employees: NR
Passive Ownership: Discouraged
Encourage Conversions: No
Area Develop. Agreements: No
Sub-Franchising Contracts: No
Expand In Territory: Yes
Space Needs: 500 SF; FS, SF, SC, RM
SUPPORT & TRAINING PROVIDED:
Financial Assistance Provided: Yes(D)
Site Selection Assistance: No
Lease Negotiation Assistance: No
Co-Operative Advertising: Yes
Franchisee Assoc./Member: Yes/Yes
Size Of Corporate Staff: 150
On-Going Support: A,B,C,D,E,F,G,H,I
Training: 5 Days On-Site.
SPECIFIC EXPANSION PLANS:
US: All States Except Hawaii
Canada: No
Overseas: No

◄◄ ►►

VIDEO DATA SERVICES
26 Chatham Woods
Pittsford, NY 14534
Tel: (800) 836-9461 (716) 381-9240
Fax: (716) 424-5324
Web Site: www.vdsvideo.com
Mr. Stuart J. Dizak, President

VIDEO DATA SERVICES provide a unique, video-photography service to businesses and consumers. The complete package includes all equipment, training, marketing and field assistance. It can be started part-time and is ideal as a family or retirement business. VIDEO DATA SERVICES is the largest video-taping service in North America. We also provide film-to-tape transfers and editing services.

BACKGROUND:
Established: 1981; 1st Franchised: 1984
Franchised Units: 246
Company-Owned Units: 1
Total Units: 247
Dist.: US-230; CAN-6; O'seas-0
North America: NR
Density: 24 in CA, 12 to VA, 8 in NY
Projected New Units (12 Months): 30
Qualifications: 5, 3, 1, 3, 3, 2
Registered: CA,IL,NY,VA,MI,WA
FINANCIAL/TERMS:
Cash Investment: $10-20K
Total Investment: $20-23K
Minimum Net Worth: $75K
Fees: Franchise - $20K
Royalty - $750/Yr.; Ad. - 0%

Earnings Claim Statement: No
Term of Contract (Years): 10/10
Avg. # Of Employees: 1 FT, 1 PT
Passive Ownership: Not Allowed
Encourage Conversions: N/A
Area Develop. Agreements: No
Sub-Franchising Contracts: No
Expand In Territory: No
Space Needs: 200 SF; HB
SUPPORT & TRAINING PROVIDED:
Financial Assistance Provided: Yes(I)
Site Selection Assistance: N/A
Lease Negotiation Assistance: N/A
Co-Operative Advertising: N/A
Franchisee Assoc./Member: Yes/No
Size Of Corporate Staff: 4
On-Going Support: B,G,H,I
Training: 3 Days San Diego, CA; 3 Days
Rochester, NY.
SPECIFIC EXPANSION PLANS:
US: All United States
Canada: All Canada
Overseas: No

◄◄ ►►

VIDEO IMPACT
1718 Peachtree St.
Atlanta, GA 30309
Tel: (404) 607-7649
Fax: (404) 607-9724
E-Mail: clofstro@aol.com
Web Site: www.videoimpact.com
Mr. Charles E. Lofstrom, Executive Vice President

Our convenient locations provide videotape editing, duplication and format conversions for both businesses and consumers. Our state-of-the-art digital equipment helps our clients produce their visual communications projects at a fraction of traditional production costs. We have the nation's only franchised system to transform clients' fondest memories from photos, slides and home movies into custom video keepsakes, creating highly emotional responses.

BACKGROUND:
Established: 1985; 1st Franchised: 1997
Franchised Units: 14
Company-Owned Units: 1
Total Units: 15
Dist.: US-13; CAN-0; O'seas-2

North America: 1 State
 Density: 12 in GA
Projected New Units (12 Months):   12
Qualifications: 3, 5, 2, 3, 3, 4
Registered: All States

FINANCIAL/TERMS:

Cash Investment: $35-75K
Total Investment: $57-165K
Minimum Net Worth: $75K
Fees: Franchise - $15-30K
 Royalty - 6%;   Ad. - N/A
Earnings Claim Statement: No
Term of Contract (Years):   10/10
Avg. # Of Employees: 2 FT, 1 PT
Passive Ownership: Discouraged
Encourage Conversions: Yes
Area Develop. Agreements: Yes/10
Sub-Franchising Contracts: No
Expand In Territory: Yes
Space Needs: 800 SF; SC

SUPPORT & TRAINING PROVIDED:

Financial Assistance Provided: Yes(I)
Site Selection Assistance: Yes
Lease Negotiation Assistance: Yes
Co-Operative Advertising: N/A
Franchisee Assoc./Member: No
Size Of Corporate Staff: 6
On-Going Support: C,d,E,G,h,I
Training: 10 Days Atlanta, GA.

SPECIFIC EXPANSION PLANS:

US: All United States
Canada: All Canada
Overseas: Throughout Europe and Asia

≪ ≫

**SUPPLEMENTAL LISTING
OF FRANCHISORS**

Bang & Olufsen Retailing Concept, 1200 Business Center Dr., # 100, Mount Prospect, IL 60056 ; (847) 699-1475; Ms. Carol T. Lindsey (877) 507-1234; (847) 299-9380

Blockbuster International, 1201 Elm St., # 2100, Dallas, TX 75270 ; (214) 854-3788; Mr. Jeffrey Seeberger (888) 309-2234; (214) 854-3541

Infinity Video Productions, 740 S. Bernardo Ave., Sunnyvale, CA 94086 ; (408) 720-0282; Mr. Clifton Hildreth (800) 339-8433; (408) 720-0281

It's About Games, 4200 Dahlberg Dr., Minneapolis, MN 55422 ; (612) 520-8501; Mr. Brad Tate (800) 824-6360; (612) 520-8500

Le Club International Video Film, 2185, Francis-Hughes, Suite 100, Laval, PQ H7S 1N5 CANADA; (450) 663-6490; Mr. Alain Bouchard (800) 361-9156; (450) 663-8100

Movieland Video, 29752 Walker S. Rd., P. O. Box 879, Walker, LA 70785 ; (828) 696-1757; Mr. Thomas R. Adkins (800) 352-6599; (828) 696-1657

Mr. Movies, 7625 Parklawn, # 200, Edina, MN 55435 ; (612) 835-1144; Mr. Bill Kaiser (800) 562-7667; (612) 835-3321

Radio Shack (Canada), P.O. Box 34,000, Barrie, ON L4M 4W5 CANADA; (705) 728-2012; Mr. Joe Dombroski ; (705) 728-6242

Video Update, 3100 World Trade Center, 30 E. 7th St., St. Paul, MN 55101-4913 ; (612) 312-2666; Mr. Richard Bedard ; (651) 222-0006

Virtual PC's, 6222 Merger Dr., Holland, OH 43528 ; (419) 866-2500; Mr. Tom Allen (888) 990-8324; (419) 866-8324

West Coast Video, 1 Summit Sq., # 200, Rt. 413 End Doublewoods Rd., Langhorne, PA 19047 ; (215) 968-5164; Director of Franchising (800) 433-5171; (215) 968-4318

For a full explanation
of the data provided in
the Franchisor Profiles,
please refer to
**Chapter 2, "How to Use
the Data."**

RETAIL: MISCELLANEOUS INDUSTRY PROFILE

Total # Franchisors in Industry Group	16
Total # Franchised Units in Industry Group	1,538
Total # Company-Owned Units in Industry Group	<u>133</u>
Total # Operating Units in Industry Group	1,671
Average # Franchised Units/Franchisor	96.1
Average # Company-Owned Units/Franchisor	<u>8.3</u>
Average # Total Units/Franchisor	104.4
Ratio of Total # Franchised Units/Total # Company-Owned Units	11.6:1
Industry Survey Participants	8
Representing % of Industry	50.0%
Average Franchise Fee*:	$28.3K
Average Total Investment*:	$153.8K
Average On-Going Royalty Fee*:	4.4%

If a range was provided, the mid-point of the range was used. See detailed profiles for actual ranges.

FIVE LARGEST PARTICIPANTS IN SURVEY

Company	# Franchised Units	# Co-Owned Units	# Total Units	Franchise Fee	On-Going Royalty	Total Investment
1. Heel Quik!	703	1	704	2.5-17.5K	4%	8.9-154K
2. Gateway Newstands	282	0	282	Varies	3%	50-200K
3. A Buck Or Two Stores	180	10	190	50K	6%	160K
4. Grand & Toy	25	48	73	15K	Varies	100K
5. Medichair	41	2	43	25K	5%	100-200K

All of the data provided are proprietary and should not be quoted without acknowledging *Bond's Franchise Guide*.

A BUCK OR TWO STORES

8200 Jane St.
Concord, ON L4K 5A7 CANADA
Tel: (905) 738-3180
Fax: (905) 738-3176
Web Site: www.abuckortwo.com
Mr. Dennis Klein, President

We're approaching 200 fun, exciting A BUCK OR TWO locations across Canada, well defined by simplicity, offering first-quality merchandise, presented in a visually appealing format, departmentalized, at prices of $2 or less. Sales and profit are maximized with a great selection of core and seasonal merchandise, as well as aggressively-priced special opportunity buys, where volume purchasing power allows franchisees to continually benefit.

BACKGROUND:	IFA MEMBER
Established: 1987;	1st Franchised: 1989
Franchised Units:	180
Company-Owned Units	10
Total Units:	190
Dist.:	US-0; CAN-190; O'seas-0
North America:	9 Provinces
Density: 80 in ON, 19 in BC, 17 in NS	
Projected New Units (12 Months):	25
Qualifications:	4, 5, 4, 4, 3, 5
Registered: AB	

FINANCIAL/TERMS:	
Cash Investment:	$50-70K
Total Investment:	$160K
Minimum Net Worth:	$200K
Fees: Franchise -	$50K
Royalty - 6%;	Ad. - 1%
Earnings Claim Statement:	No
Term of Contract (Years):	5/5
Avg. # Of Employees:	Varies
Passive Ownership:	Discouraged
Encourage Conversions:	N/A
Area Develop. Agreements:	No
Sub-Franchising Contracts:	No
Expand In Territory:	Yes
Space Needs: 2,500-4,000 SF; RM	

SUPPORT & TRAINING PROVIDED:	
Financial Assistance Provided:	Yes(D)
Site Selection Assistance:	N/A
Lease Negotiation Assistance:	N/A
Co-Operative Advertising:	Yes
Franchisee Assoc./Member:	Yes/Yes
Size Of Corporate Staff:	100
On-Going Support:	a,C,D,E,G,h
Training: 1 Week Hamilton, ON; 2 Weeks Site Location.	

SPECIFIC EXPANSION PLANS:	
US:	No
Canada:	All Canada

Overseas: Mexico, South America, Europe, Australia

<< >>

CASH CONVERTERS

1450 E. American Ln., # 1350
Schaumburg, IL 60173-6083
Tel: (888) 910-2274 (847) 330-1122
Fax: (847) 330-1660
E-Mail: inquiries@cashconverters.com
Web Site: www.cashconverters.com
Mr. Roger A. Hunt, President/CEO

We are an up-scale retail business specializing in the buying and selling of pre-owned consumer goods, i.e. computers, televisions, stereos, jewelry, sporting goods, VCRs, power tools, etc. We buy and sell within the community. We have 50% gross margins. Our stores are beautifully organized and operated by well-trained individuals such as yourself.

BACKGROUND:	IFA MEMBER
Established: 1995;	1st Franchised: 1995
Franchised Units:	16
Company-Owned Units	2
Total Units:	18
Dist.:	US-17; CAN-0; O'seas-0
North America:	9 States, 7 Provinces
Density: 3 in IL, 3 in MA, 2 in PA	
Projected New Units (12 Months):	20
Qualifications:	5, 4, 1, 1, 2, 4
Registered: All States	

FINANCIAL/TERMS:	
Cash Investment:	$70-100K
Total Investment:	$270-400K
Minimum Net Worth:	$100K
Fees: Franchise -	$50K
Royalty - $400/Wk.;	Ad. - $2K/Mo.
Earnings Claim Statement:	No
Term of Contract (Years):	10/10
Avg. # Of Employees:	8 FT, 7 PT
Passive Ownership:	Allowed
Encourage Conversions:	Yes
Area Develop. Agreements:	Yes/10
Sub-Franchising Contracts:	Yes
Expand In Territory:	Yes
Space Needs: 4,000-6,000 SF; SF, SC, RM	

SUPPORT & TRAINING PROVIDED:	
Financial Assistance Provided:	Yes(I)
Site Selection Assistance:	Yes
Lease Negotiation Assistance:	Yes
Co-Operative Advertising:	No
Franchisee Assoc./Member:	No
Size Of Corporate Staff:	7
On-Going Support:	A,C,D,E,F,G,h,I
Training: 3 Weeks Corporate Training	

and in Store Training; 1 Week Initial Opening Training.

SPECIFIC EXPANSION PLANS:	
US:	All United States
Canada:	All Canada
Overseas:	All Countries

<< >>

GATEWAY NEWSTANDS

30 E. Beaver Creek Rd., # 206
Richmond Hill, ON L4B 1J2 CANADA
Tel: (800) 942-5351 (905) 886-8900
Fax: (905) 886-8904
Web Site: www.gatewaynewstands.com
Mr. David Goldman, President

Newsstand, candy, lotto and limited food. Service locations in high-rise office towers, shopping centers and transit locations throughout the United States.

BACKGROUND:	
Established: 1983;	1st Franchised: 1983
Franchised Units:	282
Company-Owned Units	0
Total Units:	282
Dist.:	US-66; CAN-222; O'seas-1
North America:	NR
Density: 193 in ON, 19 in IL, 16 NY	
Projected New Units (12 Months):	50
Qualifications:	5, 3, 2, 1, 2, 3
Registered: NR	

FINANCIAL/TERMS:	
Cash Investment:	$40-150K
Total Investment:	$50-200K
Minimum Net Worth:	$NR
Fees: Franchise -	$Varies
Royalty - 3%;	Ad. - 0%
Earnings Claim Statement:	No
Term of Contract (Years):	5-10/5
Avg. # Of Employees:	1 FT, 2 PT
Passive Ownership:	Not Allowed
Encourage Conversions:	No
Area Develop. Agreements:	No
Sub-Franchising Contracts:	Yes
Expand In Territory:	Yes
Space Needs: 100-1,000 SF; SF, RM, Transit Location	

SUPPORT & TRAINING PROVIDED:	
Financial Assistance Provided:	Yes
Site Selection Assistance:	Yes
Lease Negotiation Assistance:	Yes
Co-Operative Advertising:	Yes
Franchisee Assoc./Member:	No
Size Of Corporate Staff:	11
On-Going Support:	C,D,E,F,I
Training: 2 Days to 2 Weeks in Store.	

SPECIFIC EXPANSION PLANS:

US: All United States
Canada: All Canada
Overseas: U.K.

≪ ≫

GRAND & TOY

33 Green Belt Dr.
Don Mills, ON M1W 1G6 CANADA
Tel: (416) 391-8581
Fax: (416) 441-6084
Web Site: www.grandtoy.com
Ms. Anne MacPhee, Dir. of Franchising

GRAND & TOY sells stationary, general office services, office machines and equipment, office furniture, office electronic products, drafting and art supplies, office business books, manuals and journals, school supplies, office bulk beverages, computer hardware and software, cellular phones, pagers, gift items, social stationary, cards and other office supplies and furniture.

BACKGROUND:

Established: 1982;   1st Franchised: 1993
Franchised Units: 25
Company-Owned Units   48
Total Units: 73
Dist.:   US-0; CAN-73; O'seas-0
  North America: 1 Province
  Density: 73 in ON
Projected New Units (12 Months):   4
Qualifications: 4, 4, 5, 2, 3, 5
Registered: N/A
FINANCIAL/TERMS:
Cash Investment: $50-80K
Total Investment: $100K
Minimum Net Worth: $150K
Fees: Franchise - $15K
  Royalty - Varies;   Ad. - Incl. Roy.
Earnings Claim Statement: Yes
Term of Contract (Years):   3
Avg. # Of Employees: 5 FT, 10 PT
Passive Ownership: Not Allowed
Encourage Conversions: N/A
Area Develop. Agreements: No
Sub-Franchising Contracts: No
Expand In Territory: Yes
Space Needs: 3,400 SF; RM, OB
SUPPORT & TRAINING PROVIDED:
Financial Assistance Provided: Yes(I)
Site Selection Assistance: N/A
Lease Negotiation Assistance: No
Co-Operative Advertising: Yes
Franchisee Assoc./Member: Yes
Size Of Corporate Staff: 2,500

On-Going Support: B,C,D,E,F,H
Training: 2 Weeks in Head Office; 4 Weeks
  in Store
SPECIFIC EXPANSION PLANS:
US: No
Canada: ON
Overseas: Most Countries

≪ ≫

HEEL QUIK!

1730 Cumberland Point Dr., # 5
Marietta, GA 30067
Tel: (800) 255-8145 (770) 951-9440
Fax: (770) 933-8268
E-Mail: hqcorp@bellsouth.net
Web Site: www.heelquik.net
Mr. Raymond J. Margiano, President/
  CEO

HEEL/SEW QUIK! Shoe repair and personal services (clothing alterations, monogramming, keymaking and seae of related retail items.

BACKGROUND: IFA MEMBER
Established: 1984;   1st Franchised: 1985
Franchised Units: 703
Company-Owned Units   1
Total Units: 704
Dist.:   US-140; CAN-1; O'seas-563
  North America: 25 States, 1 Province
  Density: 15 in GA, 10 in FL, 3 in TX
Projected New Units (12 Months):   10
Qualifications: 3, 2, 1, 2, 2, 3
Registered: CA,FL,IL,IN,MD,MI,MN,NY,
  SD,VA,WA,WI
FINANCIAL/TERMS:
Cash Investment: $5-100K
Total Investment: $8.9-153.5K
Minimum Net Worth: $45K
Fees: Franchise - $2.5-17.5K
  Royalty - 4%;   Ad. - 2%
Earnings Claim Statement: No
Term of Contract (Years):   20/10
Avg. # Of Employees: 2 FT, 1 PT
Passive Ownership: Discouraged
Encourage Conversions: Yes
Area Develop. Agreements: Yes/10/10
Sub-Franchising Contracts: No
Expand In Territory: Yes
Space   Needs: 65-1,200   SF;
  FS,SF,SC,RM,HB,Inside Business
SUPPORT & TRAINING PROVIDED:
Financial Assistance Provided: Yes(I)
Site Selection Assistance: Yes

Lease Negotiation Assistance: Yes
Co-Operative Advertising: Yes
Franchisee Assoc./Member: Yes/Yes
Size Of Corporate Staff: 9
On-Going Support: b,C,D,E,F,G,H,I
Training: 2 Weeks Atlanta, GA; 3 Days
  On-Site
SPECIFIC EXPANSION PLANS:
US: All United States
Canada: All Canada
Overseas: All Countries

≪ ≫

MEDICHAIR

2506 Southern Ave.
Brandon, MB R7B 0S4 CANADA
Tel: (800) 667-0087 (204) 726-1245
Fax: (204) 726-5716
E-Mail: medichair@medichair.com
Web Site: www.medichair.com
Mr. Stan Murray, President

Tap into the shift in demographics that will make home health care the business of the future. We're Canada's largest and fastest-growing network of retail franchise operators, energetically serving the nation's home health care consumers and institutional markets. MEDICHAIR, Canada's wellness store, provides a full line of famous, quality mobility products, bathroom safety products, and aids to daily living, along with business systems.

BACKGROUND:
Established: 1985;   1st Franchised: 1988
Franchised Units: 41
Company-Owned Units   2
Total Units: 43
Dist.:   US-0; CAN-48; O'seas-0
  North America: 8 Provinces
  Density: 15 in ON, 10 in BC, 5 in AB
Projected New Units (12 Months):   6
Qualifications: 5, 4, 2, 4, 1, 5
Registered: AB
FINANCIAL/TERMS:
Cash Investment: $110K
Total Investment: $100-200K
Minimum Net Worth: $150K
Fees: Franchise - $25K
  Royalty - 5%;   Ad. - 0%
Earnings Claim Statement: No
Term of Contract (Years):   5/5
Avg. # Of Employees: 4 FT, 1 PT
Passive Ownership: Discouraged
Encourage Conversions: Yes
Area Develop. Agreements: No
Sub-Franchising Contracts: No

Expand In Territory:	Yes
Space Needs: 2,500 SF; SC	

SUPPORT & TRAINING PROVIDED:

Financial Assistance Provided:	Yes(I)
Site Selection Assistance:	Yes
Lease Negotiation Assistance:	Yes
Co-Operative Advertising:	Yes
Franchisee Assoc./Member:	Yes/Yes
Size Of Corporate Staff:	18
On-Going Support:	A,B,C,D,E,G,H,I
Training: 1 Week at Brandon, MB.	

SPECIFIC EXPANSION PLANS:

US:	N/A
Canada:	ON,MR
Overseas:	No

≪ ≫

STREET CORNER NEWS

2945 SW Wanamaker Dr.
Topeka, KS 66614
Tel: (800) 789-NEWS (785) 272-8529
Fax: (785) 272-2384
E-Mail: peter@streetcornernews.com
Web Site: www.streetcornernews.com
Mr. Peter LaColla, Chief Executive Officer

STREET CORNER NEWS is a convenience store serving the needs of the customers and employees of a regional shopping center. Locations are either in kiosks or in-line stores. Merchandise selection includes newspapers, magazines, sodas and other beverages, tobacco products, office supplies, gift items and sundries.

BACKGROUND:

Established: 1988; 1st Franchised: 1995	
Franchised Units:	19
Company-Owned Units:	1
Total Units:	20
Dist.:	US-17; CAN-0; O'seas-0
North America:	11 States
Density:	5 in TN, 4 in NY, 4 in KS
Projected New Units (12 Months):	8
Qualifications:	4, 2, 1, 1, 2, 5
Registered: CA,FL,MI,MN,NY	

FINANCIAL/TERMS:

Cash Investment:	$35K
Total Investment:	$90-150K
Minimum Net Worth:	$150K
Fees: Franchise -	$19.9K
Royalty - 4.5%;	Ad. - 0%
Earnings Claim Statement:	No
Term of Contract (Years):	7/7
Avg. # Of Employees:	1 FT, 3 PT
Passive Ownership:	Discouraged
Encourage Conversions:	N/A

Area Develop. Agreements:	No
Sub-Franchising Contracts:	No
Expand In Territory:	Yes
Space Needs: 300 SF; RM	

SUPPORT & TRAINING PROVIDED:

Financial Assistance Provided:	Yes(I)
Site Selection Assistance:	Yes
Lease Negotiation Assistance:	Yes
Co-Operative Advertising:	No
Franchisee Assoc./Member:	No
Size Of Corporate Staff:	5
On-Going Support:	A,C,d,E,F,G,h,I
Training: 1 Week On-Site.	

SPECIFIC EXPANSION PLANS:

US:	All United States
Canada:	No
Overseas:	No

≪ ≫

TERRI'S CONSIGN & DESIGN FURNISHINGS

1375 W. Drivers Way
Tempe, AZ 85284
Tel: (800) 455-0400 (480) 969-4121
Fax: (480) 969-5052
E-Mail: marcusc@terris-cdf.com
Web Site: www.terris-cdf.com
Mr. Marcus Curtis, President

Nation's leader in consignment home furnishings. We deal in furnishings acquired from model homes, estates, factory liquidations, skilled craftsmen and fine homes. Quality brand-name furnishings, accessories, office furnishings, art and antiques. Business has high sales volume with high margin and no initial cost inventory. Ground floor opportunities still available.

BACKGROUND:

Established: 1979; 1st Franchised: 1993	
Franchised Units:	7
Company-Owned Units:	8
Total Units:	15
Dist.:	US-13; CAN-0; O'seas-0
North America:	5 States
Density:	7 in AZ, 2 in NV, 2 in CA
Projected New Units (12 Months):	4
Qualifications:	4, 4, 3, 3, 3, 5
Registered: CA,OR,WA	

FINANCIAL/TERMS:

Cash Investment:	$75-175K
Total Investment:	$100-200K
Minimum Net Worth:	$250K+
Fees: Franchise -	$28K
Royalty - 4%;	Ad. - 1%
Earnings Claim Statement:	Yes
Term of Contract (Years):	10/5/5

Avg. # Of Employees:	10 FT, 3 PT
Passive Ownership:	Not Allowed
Encourage Conversions:	Yes
Area Develop. Agreements:	Yes/10
Sub-Franchising Contracts:	No
Expand In Territory:	Yes
Space Needs: 20,000 SF; FS, SC, Warehouse	

SUPPORT & TRAINING PROVIDED:

Financial Assistance Provided:	Yes(I)
Site Selection Assistance:	Yes
Lease Negotiation Assistance:	Yes
Co-Operative Advertising:	No
Franchisee Assoc./Member:	No
Size Of Corporate Staff:	7
On-Going Support:	C,D,E,G,H,I
Training: 1 Week Mesa, AZ; 5 Days Store Location upon Opening.	

SPECIFIC EXPANSION PLANS:

US:	All United States
Canada:	No
Overseas:	No

≪ ≫

SUPPLEMENTAL LISTING OF FRANCHISORS

Airborne For Men, 1060 Park Ave., Cranston, RI 02910 ; (401) 943-6363; Mr. Dan Geribo ; (401) 275-5234

Biker's Dream, 1420 Village Way, Santa Ana, CA 92705 ; (909) 835-2414; Mr. Robert Dick (800) 677-4294; (909) 637-1816

Borvin Beverage, 1022 King St., Alexandria, VA 22314 ; (703) 836-6654; Mr. Donald Mikovich ; (703) 683-9463

Dollar Discount Stores of America, 1362 Naamans Creek Rd., Boothwyn, PA 19061 ; (610) 485-6439; Ms. Jay Stutman (800) 227-5314; (888) DOLLAR-1

Hakky Instant Shoe Repair, 1739 Sands Pl., # F, Marietta, GA 30067 ; (770) 951-0355; Mr. Patrick Harper ; (770) 956-8651

Mighty Dollar, 528 Hood Rd., Markham, ON L3R 3K9 CANADA; (905) 513-6387; Ms. Lorraine Waldman ; (905) 513-8191

Moneysworth & Best Quality Shoe Repair, 501 Downtree Dairy Rd., # 5, Vaughan, ON L4L 8H8 CANADA; (416) 674-8945; Mr. Jason Hayling (800) 363-SHOE; (416) 674-6148

SECURITY & SAFETY SYSTEMS INDUSTRY PROFILE

Total # Franchisors in Industry Group	17
Total # Franchised Units in Industry Group	859
Total # Company-Owned Units in Industry Group	<u>101</u>
Total # Operating Units in Industry Group	960
Average # Franchised Units/Franchisor	50.5
Average # Company-Owned Units/Franchisor	<u>5.9</u>
Average # Total Units/Franchisor	56.4
Ratio of Total # Franchised Units/Total # Company-Owned Units	8.5:1
Industry Survey Participants	6
Representing % of Industry	35.3%
Average Franchise Fee*:	$20.7
Average Total Investment*:	$164.9
Average On-Going Royalty Fee*:	5.9%

If a range was provided, the mid-point of the range was used. See detailed profiles for actual ranges.

FIVE LARGEST PARTICIPANTS IN SURVEY

Company	# Fran-chised Units	# Co-Owned Units	# Total Units	Franchise Fee	On-Going Royalty	Total Investment
1. Sonitrol	155	25	180	20-50K	2.5%	250-600K
2. Fire Defense Centers	17	44	61	19.5K	10%	42.5K
3. Roll-A-Way	47	3	50	7.9-21.7K	0%	35-65K
4. Custom Homewatch International	45	0	45	3-7K	3%	4-10K
5. Proshred Security	34	1	35	35K	8%	350K

All of the data provided are proprietary and should not be quoted without acknowledging *Bond's Franchise Guide.*

AIRSOPURE
15400 Knoll Trail, # 200
Dallas, TX 75248
Tel: (800) 752-3322 (972) 960-9400
Fax: (972) 960-9488
E-Mail: jonesairg@aol.com
Web Site: www.airsopure.com
Mr. Todd Jones, VP Franchise Admin.

AIRSOPURE is the first and only air purification franchise opportunity that offers a superior product and a marketing program designed specifically for home owners. Indoor air pollution is one of the EPA's top 5 risks to public health and the solution is an AIRSOPURE franchise. No royalties. Not an ozone emitter or MLM.

BACKGROUND: IFA MEMBER
Established: 1994;   1st Franchised: 1997
Franchised Units: 30
Company-Owned Units   1
Total Units: 31
Dist.:   US-29; CAN-2; O'seas-0
    North America: NR
    Density: 1 in GA, 1 in FL, 1 in NJ
Projected New Units (12 Months):   50
Qualifications: 3, 3, 3, 2, 2, 4
Registered: MI
FINANCIAL/TERMS:
Cash Investment: $15K
Total Investment: $45-65K
Minimum Net Worth: $100K
Fees: Franchise - $15K
    Royalty - 0%;   Ad. - 0%
Earnings Claim Statement: No
Term of Contract (Years):   10/10
Avg. # Of Employees: 3 FT, 7 PT
Passive Ownership: Allowed
Encourage Conversions: Yes
Area Develop. Agreements: Yes/30
Sub-Franchising Contracts: No
Expand In Territory: Yes
Space Needs: 1,200 SF; Business Park
SUPPORT & TRAINING PROVIDED:
Financial Assistance Provided: Yes(I)
Site Selection Assistance: Yes
Lease Negotiation Assistance: N/A
Co-Operative Advertising: Yes
Franchisee Assoc./Member: No
Size Of Corporate Staff: 25
On-Going Support: B,C,D,E,F,G,H,I
Training: 3-5 Days Dallas, TX.

SPECIFIC EXPANSION PLANS:
US: All United States
Canada: All Canada
Overseas: All Countries

≪ ≫

CUSTOM HOMEWATCH INTERNATIONAL
2094 Tomat Ave.
Kelowna, BC V1Z 3C5 CANADA
Tel: (800) 713-2888 (250) 769-4329
Fax: (250) 769-4329
Mr. Terry Bates, President

Selling of franchises for housesitting, homechecking, petcare and yardwork.

BACKGROUND:
Established: 1988;   1st Franchised: 1989
Franchised Units: 45
Company-Owned Units   0
Total Units: 45
Dist.:   US-0; CAN-45; O'seas-0
    North America: NR
    Density: 14 in ON, 14 in BC, 10 in AB
Projected New Units (12 Months):   12
Qualifications: 3, 5, 4, 4, 4, 4
Registered: WA,AB
FINANCIAL/TERMS:
Cash Investment: $NR
Total Investment: $4-10K
Minimum Net Worth: $N/A
Fees: Franchise - $3-7K
    Royalty - 3%;   Ad. - 2%
Earnings Claim Statement: No
Term of Contract (Years):   5/5
Avg. # Of Employees: NR
Passive Ownership: Allowed
Encourage Conversions: N/A
Area Develop. Agreements: No
Sub-Franchising Contracts: No
Expand In Territory: Yes
Space Needs: NR SF; NR
SUPPORT & TRAINING PROVIDED:
Financial Assistance Provided: No
Site Selection Assistance: N/A
Lease Negotiation Assistance: N/A
Co-Operative Advertising: N/A
Franchisee Assoc./Member: No
Size Of Corporate Staff: 2
On-Going Support: NR
Training: 1 Day Kelowna, BC.
SPECIFIC EXPANSION PLANS:
US: All United States
Canada: All Canada
Overseas: No

≪ ≫

FIRE DEFENSE CENTERS
6110-20 Powers, # 144
Jacksonville, FL 32217
Tel: (800) 554-3028 (904) 731-1833
Fax:
Ms. I. A. La Russo, President

Dealing with national accounts on servicing of fire extinguishers, automatic restaurant hood systems, municipal supplies and first aid kits. Warranty on equipment sold to business and guaranteed fire code compliance to business. Provide consultation for businesses to comply with city and state governments.

BACKGROUND:
Established: 1973;   1st Franchised: 1986
Franchised Units: 17
Company-Owned Units   44
Total Units: 61
Dist.:   US-61; CAN-0; O'seas-0
    North America: 15 States
    Density: 20 in FL
Projected New Units (12 Months):   3
Registered: All States
FINANCIAL/TERMS:
Cash Investment: $36K
Total Investment: $42.5K
Minimum Net Worth: $NR
Fees: Franchise - $19.5K
    Royalty - 10%;   Ad. - 2%
Earnings Claim Statement: No
Term of Contract (Years):   10/10
Avg. # Of Employees: 2 FT
Passive Ownership: Allowed
Encourage Conversions: No
Area Develop. Agreements: No
Sub-Franchising Contracts: No
Expand In Territory: Yes
Space Needs: 1,500 SF; Warehouse
SUPPORT & TRAINING PROVIDED:
Financial Assistance Provided: Yes
Site Selection Assistance: Yes
Lease Negotiation Assistance: Yes
Co-Operative Advertising: Yes
Franchisee Assoc./Member: NR
Size Of Corporate Staff: 16
On-Going Support: A,B,C,D,E,F,G,H,I
Training: 2 Weeks Headquarters.
SPECIFIC EXPANSION PLANS:
US: All United States

Canada: No
Overseas: No

<< >>

PROSHRED SECURITY

2200 Lakeshore Blvd. W., # 102
Toronto, ON M8V 1E4 CANADA
Tel: (800) 461-9760 (416) 251-4272
Fax: (416) 251-7121
E-Mail: proshred@proshred.com
Web Site: www.proshred.com
Mr. Sean O'Dea, President

PROSHRED SECURITY is a franchise for business people. Our license owners provide at-your-door document shredding services to area businesses. Customers include all levels of business and government. Operating in the U. S., Canada and Europe, PROSHRED is the largest in North America. Company management has a long, successful history in franchising.

BACKGROUND:

Established: 1985;   1st Franchised: 1990
Franchised Units: 34
Company-Owned Units   1
Total Units: 35
Dist.:   US-4; CAN-29; O'seas-1
  North America: 3 States, 10 Provinces
  Density: 12 in ON, 3 in CA
Projected New Units (12 Months):   4
Registered: CA,FL,MD,MI,OR,DC

FINANCIAL/TERMS:

Cash Investment: $200K
Total Investment: $350K
Minimum Net Worth: $NR
Fees: Franchise - $35K
  Royalty - 8%;   Ad. - 0%
Earnings Claim Statement: No
Term of Contract (Years):   5/5/5/5
Avg. # Of Employees: 5 FT, 2 PT
Passive Ownership: Not Allowed
Encourage Conversions: Yes
Area Develop. Agreements: Yes/10
Sub-Franchising Contracts: No
Expand In Territory: Yes
Space Needs: NR SF; N/A

SUPPORT & TRAINING PROVIDED:

Financial Assistance Provided: Yes(I)
Site Selection Assistance: N/A
Lease Negotiation Assistance: N/A
Co-Operative Advertising: N/A
Franchisee Assoc./Member: No
Size Of Corporate Staff: 11
On-Going Support: A,C,D,E,G,H,I
Training: 9 Days Toronto, ON; 5 Days
  Local.

SPECIFIC EXPANSION PLANS:

US: All United States
Canada: All Canada
Overseas: Europe, Australia, Asia

<< >>

ROLL-A-WAY

10601 Oak St., N.E.
St. Petersburg, FL 33716
Tel: (888) 765-5292 (727) 576-6044
Fax: (727) 579-9410
Web Site: www.roll-a-way.com
Mr. Bill Salin, VP Franchise Development

ROLL-A-WAY manufactures rolling-security and storm shutters for residential and commercial applications. We are the largest and oldest manufacturer in the U. S. The franchise consists of training in sales, marketing and installation of the shutter system. The franchisee purchases directly from the manufacturer, and the business is very profitable and gaining in popularity every day. The shutters are excellent for saving money on utilities.

BACKGROUND:

Established: 1955;   1st Franchised: 1994
Franchised Units: 47
Company-Owned Units   3
Total Units: 50
Dist.:   US-50; CAN-0; O'seas-0
  North America: 17 States
  Density: 3 in CA, 3 in NC, 3 in TX
Projected New Units (12 Months):   10
Qualifications: 4, 4, 3, 3, 2, 4
Registered: CA,FL,MD,NY,RI,VA,WA,
  WI

FINANCIAL/TERMS:

Cash Investment: $15.8-40K
Total Investment: $35-65K
Minimum Net Worth: $250K
Fees: Franchise - $7.9-21.7K
  Royalty - 0%;   Ad. - 0%
Earnings Claim Statement: No
Term of Contract (Years):   10/5/5
Avg. # Of Employees: 2 FT, 2 PT
Passive Ownership: Discouraged
Encourage Conversions: N/A
Area Develop. Agreements: No
Sub-Franchising Contracts: No
Expand In Territory: Yes
Space Needs: NR SF; N/A

SUPPORT & TRAINING PROVIDED:

Financial Assistance Provided: No

Site Selection Assistance: N/A
Lease Negotiation Assistance: No
Co-Operative Advertising: No
Franchisee Assoc./Member: No
Size Of Corporate Staff: 30
On-Going Support: B,C,D,F,h
Training: 2 Weeks Corporate Office, St.
  Petersburg, FL.

SPECIFIC EXPANSION PLANS:

US: All United States
Canada: All Canada
Overseas: All Countries

<< >>

SONITROL

211 North Union, # 350
Alexandria, VA 22314
Tel: (800) 326-RISK (703) 684-6606
Fax: (703) 684-6612
E-Mail: bmeares@sonitrol.com
Web Site: www.sonitrol.com
Mr. William Meares, Chief Operating
  Officer

SONITROL offers a broad line of security systems to commercial and residential subscribers. A majority of SONITROL products are sold to businesses which have typically been in operations for over a year. The signature system is based on a sound activated audio. This process allows for verification of alarms and has resulted in the apprehension of over 135,000 criminals.

BACKGROUND: IFA MEMBER

Established: 1964;   1st Franchised: 1965
Franchised Units: 155
Company-Owned Units   25
Total Units: 180
Dist.:   US-177; CAN-1; O'seas-2
  North America: 41 States
  Density: 24 in CA, 14 in FL, 11 in NY
Projected New Units (12 Months):   3
Qualifications: 4, 5, 3, 2, 5, 4
Registered: FL,IL,VA

FINANCIAL/TERMS:

Cash Investment: $100-200K
Total Investment: $250-600K
Minimum Net Worth: $250K
Fees: Franchise - $20-50K
  Royalty - 2.5%;   Ad. - N/A
Earnings Claim Statement: No
Term of Contract (Years):   10/10
Avg. # Of Employees: Varies

Passive Ownership: Not Allowed
Encourage Conversions: N/A
Area Develop. Agreements: No
Sub-Franchising Contracts: No
Expand In Territory: No
Space Needs: NR SF; N/A

SUPPORT & TRAINING PROVIDED:
Financial Assistance Provided: N/A
Site Selection Assistance: N/A
Lease Negotiation Assistance: No
Co-Operative Advertising: No
Franchisee Assoc./Member: Yes/Yes
Size Of Corporate Staff: 11
On-Going Support: C,d,E,G,h,I
Training: Business Training On-Site; 1 Wk.
     Technical Training in Orlando; 1 Wk.
     Sales Tr. in Dallas.

SPECIFIC EXPANSION PLANS:
US: All United States
Canada: No
Overseas: No

<< >>

SUPPLEMENTAL LISTING OF FRANCHISORS

Alarmforce Industries, 49 Coldwater Rd., North York, ON M3B 1Y8 CANADA; (416) 445-9381; Mr. Ron Buzler (800) 267-2001; (416) 445-2001

Babygate Pool Fence, 132 D Tomahawk Dr., Indian Harbour Beach, FL 32937 ; (407) 777-3815; Mr. Gary Butterfield (800) 293-2229; (407) 777-6977

Care Trak Franchising Corp., 1031 Autumn Ridge Rd., Carbondale, IL 62901 ; (618) 457-3340; Mr. Mike Chylewski (800) 842-4537; (618) 549-6330

FireMaster, 520 Broadway, # 650, Santa Monica, CA 90401 ; (310) 395-7048; Ms. Liz Paradis (800) 944-3473; (310) 451-8888

Locks & Keys, Woburn Mall, Woburn, MA 01801 ; (781) 935-2663; Mr. John Casey ; (781) 933-9999

Mace Security Centers, 662 S. Fulton St., Denver, CO 80231 ; (303) 367-9962; Mr. Howard S. Edelman (800) 836-8220; (303) 363-7968

Paystation, 5155 Spectrum Way, # 17, Mississauga, ON L4W 5A1 CANADA; (905) 625-6254; Mr. Robert Warner (800) 268-1440; (905) 625-8500

Safe Not Sorry, 421 W. Union Ave., Bound Brook, NJ 08805 ; (732) 469-0096; Mr. John J. Granito (888) 469-3900;

Security World International, 3403 NW 55th St., Bldg. # 10, Ft. Lauderdale, FL 33309 ; (954) 846-9686; Ms. Jennifer Hickman (800) 669-7328; (954) 846-2400

Vocam USA, 855 E. Golf Rd., # 2145, Arlington Heights, IL 60005 ; (847) 734-7159; Mr. Darrell Downing (888) 38-VOCAM; (847) 734-3000

SIGNS INDUSTRY PROFILE

Total # Franchisors in Industry Group	16
Total # Franchised Units in Industry Group	1,820
Total # Company-Owned Units in Industry Group	<u>7</u>
Total # Operating Units in Industry Group	1,827
Average # Franchised Units/Franchisor	113.8
Average # Company-Owned Units/Franchisor	<u>0.4</u>
Average # Total Units/Franchisor	114.2
Ratio of Total # Franchised Units/Total # Company-Owned Units	260.0:1
Industry Survey Participants	8
Representing % of Industry	50.0%
Average Franchise Fee*:	$20.1K
Average Total Investment*:	$111.5K
Average On-Going Royalty Fee*:	5.3%

If a range was provided, the mid-point of the range was used. See detailed profiles for actual ranges.

FIVE LARGEST PARTICIPANTS IN SURVEY

Company	# Fran-chised Units	# Co-Owned Units	# Total Units	Franchise Fee	On-Going Royalty	Total Investment
1. Sign-A-Rama	515	0	515	37.5K	6% w/Cap.	100-107K
2. Fastsigns	438	0	438	20K	6%	148-219K
3. Signs Now	330	0	330	7.5-19.8K	5%	65-356K
4. Signs By Tomorrow	99	1	100	19.5K	2.5-5%	93-150K
5. American Sign Shop	45	0	45	20K	6%	66-92K

All of the data provided are proprietary and should not be quoted without acknowledging *Bond's Franchise Guide*.

AMERICAN SIGN SHOPS

3803-B Computer Dr., # 200
Raleigh, NC 27609
Tel: (800) 966-2700 (919) 787-1557
Fax: (919) 787-3830
E-Mail: info@amerisign.com
Web Site: www.amerisign.com
Mr. Allan Dygert, Director Franchise Dev.

Latest technology in computer-generated signs. Full color digital graphics production and we provide full training and on-going support. Local assistance. Franchise highly rated by Success and Entrepreneur Magazines. Operated in a clean, retail environment, hours 9 to 5. We choose highly-motivated franchisees who want to succeed as entrepreneurs. Franchise Advisory Council and Mentor Program instituted by company. You can't find better franchise support!

BACKGROUND: IFA MEMBER
Established: 1984;   1st Franchised: 1987
Franchised Units: 45
Company-Owned Units   0
Total Units: 45
Dist.:   US-45; CAN-0; O'seas-0
  North America: 12 States
  Density: 17 in NC, 12 in MI, 5 in OH
Projected New Units (12 Months):   10
Qualifications: 5, 4, 1, 3, 3, 5
Registered: IL,MI,VA,WI
FINANCIAL/TERMS:
Cash Investment: $30-40K
Total Investment: $66-92K
Minimum Net Worth: $150K
Fees: Franchise - $20K
  Royalty - 6%;   Ad. - 0%
Earnings Claim Statement: No
Term of Contract (Years):   20/20
Avg. # Of Employees: 2 FT, 2 PT
Passive Ownership: Discouraged
Encourage Conversions: No
Area Develop. Agreements: No
Sub-Franchising Contracts: No
Expand In Territory: Yes
Space Needs: 1,600 SF; FS, SF, SC
SUPPORT & TRAINING PROVIDED:
Financial Assistance Provided: Yes(I)
Site Selection Assistance: Yes
Lease Negotiation Assistance: Yes
Co-Operative Advertising: No
Franchisee Assoc./Member: Yes/No
Size Of Corporate Staff: 6

On-Going Support: C,D,E,F,G,h,I
Training: 8 Hours Home Study; 2 Weeks Headquarters; 1 Week Franchisee Location.
SPECIFIC EXPANSION PLANS:
US: East of Rocky Mountains
Canada: No
Overseas: No

FASTSIGNS

2550 Midway Rd., # 150
Carrollton, TX 75006
Tel: (800) 827-7446 (972) 447-0777
Fax: (972) 248-8201
E-Mail: Larry.Lane@fastsigns.com
Web Site: www.fastsigns.com
Mr. Larry Lane, VP of Franchise Development

FASTSIGNS sign centers produce complete computer-generated signs and graphics for the business community. FASTSIGNS is the acknowledged leader of the quick sign industry. Rated #7 in Success Magazine's 1999 Franchisee Satisfaction Survey. Quality systems include comprehensive 3 week training, on-going support, unique marketing materials and National Accounts program. Site selection assistance and the latest industry equipment.

BACKGROUND: IFA MEMBER
Established: 1985;   1st Franchised: 1986
Franchised Units: 438
Company-Owned Units   0
Total Units: 438
Dist.:   US-370; CAN-9; O'seas-59
  North America: 41 States, 2 Provinces
  Density: 47 in TX, 34 in CA, 20 in IL
Projected New Units (12 Months):   20
Qualifications: 5, 4, 1, 1, 3, 5
Registered: All States and AB
FINANCIAL/TERMS:
Cash Investment: $50-75K
Total Investment: $148-219K
Minimum Net Worth: $200K
Fees: Franchise - $20K
  Royalty - 6%;   Ad. - 2%
Earnings Claim Statement: Yes
Term of Contract (Years):   20/10
Avg. # Of Employees: 6 FT
Passive Ownership: Not Allowed
Encourage Conversions: Yes
Area Develop. Agreements: Yes
Sub-Franchising Contracts: Int

Expand In Territory: Yes
Space Needs: 1,400 SF; SC
SUPPORT & TRAINING PROVIDED:
Financial Assistance Provided: Yes(I)
Site Selection Assistance: Yes
Lease Negotiation Assistance: Yes
Co-Operative Advertising: Yes
Franchisee Assoc./Member: Yes
Size Of Corporate Staff: 75
On-Going Support: C,D,E,G,H,I
Training: 3 Weeks in Dallas, TX.
SPECIFIC EXPANSION PLANS:
US: All United States
Canada: All Canada
Overseas: France, Germany, Italy, Spain, UK, New Zealand, Australia, Colombia, Mexico, Brazil

SIGN-A-RAMA

1601 Belvedere Rd., # 501 S.
West Palm Beach, FL 33406
Tel: (800) 776-8105 (561) 640-5570
Fax: (561) 478-4340
E-Mail: signinfo@sign-a-rama.com
Web Site: www.sign-a-rama.com
Mr. Christopher Simnick, VP Fran. Dev.

SIGN-A-RAMA is the world's largest sign franchise with approximately 500 stores worldwide. Being a full-service sign center allows us to do everything a quick-stop shop does but also to get deeply involved in the commercial aspects of the industry. Utilizing the very latest in computer technology, SIGN-A-RAMA is unmatched in franchise supported innovation.

BACKGROUND:
Established: 1986;   1st Franchised: 1987
Franchised Units: 515
Company-Owned Units   0
Total Units: 515
Dist.:   US-400; CAN-25; O'seas-90
  North America: 44 States
  Density: 50 in CA, 45 in IL, 35 in NJ
Projected New Units (12 Months):   100
Qualifications: 5, 4, 1, 1, 4, 5
Registered: All States and AB
FINANCIAL/TERMS:
Cash Investment: $45-55K

Total Investment:	$100-107K
Minimum Net Worth:	$NR
Fees: Franchise -	$37.5K
Royalty - 6% w/ Cap;	Ad. - 0%
Earnings Claim Statement:	No
Term of Contract (Years):	35/35
Avg. # Of Employees:	3 FT
Passive Ownership:	Discouraged
Encourage Conversions:	Yes
Area Develop. Agreements:	No
Sub-Franchising Contracts:	No
Expand In Territory:	Yes
Space Needs: 1,200 SF; SF, SC	

SUPPORT & TRAINING PROVIDED:

Financial Assistance Provided:	Yes(I)
Site Selection Assistance:	Yes
Lease Negotiation Assistance:	Yes
Co-Operative Advertising:	Yes
Franchisee Assoc./Member:	Yes/Yes
Size Of Corporate Staff:	85
On-Going Support:	C,D,E,F,G,H,I
Training: 2 Weeks West Palm Beach, FL; 2 Weeks On-Site; Master License Training -- 1 Week FL.	

SPECIFIC EXPANSION PLANS:

US:	All United States
Canada:	All Canada
Overseas:	All Countries

◄◄ ►►

SIGNS BY TOMORROW
6460 Dobbin Rd.
Columbia, MD 21045
Tel: (800) 765-7446 (410) 992-7192
Fax: (410) 992-7675
E-Mail: fransales@signsbytomorrow.com
Web Site: www.signsbytomorrowusa.com
Mr. Robert G. Nunn, III, Director
Franchise Development

Computer-generated, one day, vinyl sign shop. Business-to-business, high growth, high gross margins, service-oriented, multiples possible. Most extensive training and support system. Aggressive R & D program. High rate of franchisee success and satisfaction. No tech experience necessary.

BACKGROUND: IFA MEMBER

Established: 1986;	1st Franchised: 1987
Franchised Units:	99
Company-Owned Units	1
Total Units:	100

Dist.:	US-100; CAN-0; O'seas-0
North America:	23 States
Density:	14 in PA, 14 in MD, 8 in NJ
Projected New Units (12 Months):	20
Qualifications:	4, 5, 1, 4, 5, 5
Registered: All States	

FINANCIAL/TERMS:

Cash Investment:	$30-40K
Total Investment:	$93-150K
Minimum Net Worth:	$100K
Fees: Franchise -	$19.5K
Royalty - 2.5-5%;	Ad. - 0%
Earnings Claim Statement:	No
Term of Contract (Years):	20/20
Avg. # Of Employees:	3 FT, 2 PT
Passive Ownership:	Not Allowed
Encourage Conversions:	No
Area Develop. Agreements:	Yes/Negot.
Sub-Franchising Contracts:	No
Expand In Territory:	No
Space Needs: 1,800 SF; SC	

SUPPORT & TRAINING PROVIDED:

Financial Assistance Provided:	Yes(I)
Site Selection Assistance:	Yes
Lease Negotiation Assistance:	Yes
Co-Operative Advertising:	Yes
Franchisee Assoc./Member:	Yes/Yes
Size Of Corporate Staff:	15
On-Going Support:	B,C,D,E,F,G,H,I
Training: 2 Weeks Headquarters; 2 Weeks in Store.	

SPECIFIC EXPANSION PLANS:

US:	All United States
Canada:	No
Overseas:	No

◄◄ ►►

SIGNS FIRST
813 Ridge Lake Blvd., # 390
Memphis, TN 38120
Tel: (800) 852-2163 (901) 682-2264
Fax: (901) 682-2475
E-Mail: signsfirst1@earthlink.net
Web Site: www.signsfirst.net
Ms. Peggy Cahoon, Office Manager

SIGNS FIRST is the only franchise with over 25 years sign industry experience. We specialize in computer-generated, one-day temporary and permanent signs for retail, professional and commercial businesses on a cash and carry basis. Franchisee support is unparalleled with comprehensive training, on-going technological support and marketing assistance.

BACKGROUND:

Established: 1966;	1st Franchised: 1989
Franchised Units:	36
Company-Owned Units	0
Total Units:	36
Dist.:	US-42; CAN-0; O'seas-0
North America:	17 States
Density:	13 in TN, 12 in MS, 3 in CO
Projected New Units (12 Months):	5
Qualifications:	3, 4, 3, 1, 3, 5
Registered: FL	

FINANCIAL/TERMS:

Cash Investment:	$20K
Total Investment:	$20-65K
Minimum Net Worth:	$250K
Fees: Franchise -	$10-15K
Royalty - 6%;	Ad. - 0%
Earnings Claim Statement:	No
Term of Contract (Years):	10/10
Avg. # Of Employees:	2 FT
Passive Ownership:	Discouraged
Encourage Conversions:	Yes
Area Develop. Agreements:	Yes/10
Sub-Franchising Contracts:	No
Expand In Territory:	Yes
Space Needs: 1,500 SF; FS, SF, SC, RM	

SUPPORT & TRAINING PROVIDED:

Financial Assistance Provided:	N/A
Site Selection Assistance:	Yes
Lease Negotiation Assistance:	Yes
Co-Operative Advertising:	No
Franchisee Assoc./Member:	No
Size Of Corporate Staff:	6
On-Going Support:	B,C,D,E,F,G,I
Training: 2 Weeks Memphis, TN; 1 Week + Follow-Up Visit in Store.	

SPECIFIC EXPANSION PLANS:

US:	All United States
Canada:	No
Overseas:	No

◄◄ ►►

SIGNS NOW
4900 Manatee Ave. W., # 201
Bradenton, FL 34209
Tel: (800) 356-3373 (941) 747-7747
Fax: (941) 747-5074
E-Mail: terry@signsnow.com
Web Site: www.signsnow.com
Mr. Terry A. Demarest, Dir. of Fran. Sales

Founder of computer-generated quick sign industry. $1,000 marketing rebate. Only company with 14 regional managers, most having their own sign stores. Retail stores produce custom signs and graphics with the latest equipment and technology. SIGNS NOW operations system includes procedures; order-based POS with marketing support and tracking; proven sales and marketing; national accounts and vendor discount programs; free web page.

BACKGROUND: IFA MEMBER
Established: 1983;   1st Franchised: 1986
Franchised Units: 330
Company-Owned Units   0
Total Units: 330
Dist.:   US-270; CAN-20; O'seas-40
   North America: 41 States, 6 Provinces
   Density: 34 in FL, 21 in IL, 13 in NC
Projected New Units (12 Months):   50
Qualifications: 5, 5, 2, 3, 2, 5
Registered: All States
FINANCIAL/TERMS:
Cash Investment: $30% Invest.
Total Investment: $64.5-355.9K
Minimum Net Worth: $Varies
Fees: Franchise - $7.5-19.8K
   Royalty - 5%;   Ad. - 2%
Earnings Claim Statement: Yes
Term of Contract (Years):   20/20
Avg. # Of Employees: 3 FT
Passive Ownership: Discouraged
Encourage Conversions: Yes
Area Develop. Agreements: No
Sub-Franchising Contracts: No
Expand In Territory: Yes
Space Needs: 1,600 SF; SF, SC
SUPPORT & TRAINING PROVIDED:
Financial Assistance Provided: Yes(I)
Site Selection Assistance: Yes
Lease Negotiation Assistance: Yes
Co-Operative Advertising: Yes
Franchisee Assoc./Member: Yes/Yes
Size Of Corporate Staff: 22
On-Going Support: C,D,E,G,H,I
Training: 3-4 Weeks International Training
   Center; 1-2 Weeks Own Store.
SPECIFIC EXPANSION PLANS:
US: All United States
Canada: All Canada
Overseas: All Countries

≪ ≫

SIGNS ON SITE
5350 Corporate Grove Blvd. SE
Grand Rapids, MI 49512
Tel: (888) 715-7446 (616) 656-9770
Fax: (616) 656-9775
E-Mail: mail@signs-on-site.com

Web Site: www.signs-on-site.com
Mr. Jeffrey R. Lewis, President/CEO

SIGNS ON SITE is different from all other 'sign' franchises. There is no need to manufacture. You can start from your home, and the initial investment is low. You go to the client and provide periodic signage solutions to corporations, hospitals and institutions.

BACKGROUND: IFA MEMBER
Established: 1997;   1st Franchised: 1998
Franchised Units: 6
Company-Owned Units   0
Total Units: 6
Dist.:   US-6; CAN-0; O'seas-0
   North America: 5 States
   Density: NR
Projected New Units (12 Months):   7
Qualifications: 2, 4, 2, 4, 3, 5
Registered: CA,FL,IL,IN,MD,MI,MN,MO,
   NY,OR,PA,RI,TX,VA,WA,WI,DC
FINANCIAL/TERMS:
Cash Investment: $30-60K
Total Investment: $60-100K
Minimum Net Worth: $N/A
Fees: Franchise - $25K
   Royalty - 6%;   Ad. - 1%
Earnings Claim Statement: No
Term of Contract (Years):   7/7
Avg. # Of Employees: 2 FT, 1 PT
Passive Ownership: Discouraged
Encourage Conversions: Yes
Area Develop. Agreements: Yes/7
Sub-Franchising Contracts: No
Expand In Territory: No
Space Needs: 1,000-1,200 SF; HB
SUPPORT & TRAINING PROVIDED:
Financial Assistance Provided: Yes(D)
Site Selection Assistance: Yes
Lease Negotiation Assistance: Yes
Co-Operative Advertising: Yes
Franchisee Assoc./Member: No
Size Of Corporate Staff: 7
On-Going Support: C,D,E,G,H,I
Training: 2 Weeks Grand Rapids, MI.
SPECIFIC EXPANSION PLANS:
US: All United States
Canada: All Canada
Overseas: No

≪ ≫

SUPPLEMENTAL LISTING OF FRANCHISORS

1 Hour Signs, 485 Silvercreek Pkwy., N., #4, Guelph, ON N1H 7K5 CANADA; (519) 824-1207; Mr. Shan Jamal ; (519) 824-2832

ASI Sign Systems, 3890 W. Northwest Hwy., # 102, Dallas, TX 75220 ; (214) 352-9741; Mr. Jason Killough (800) ASI-SPEC; (214) 352-9140

Beyond Signs, 36 Apple Creek Blvd., Markham, ON L3R 4Y4 CANADA; (905) 415-1583; Mr. Glenn Kerekes (800) 265-7446; (905) 415-9809

Sign Express, 4900 Manatee Ave. West, Bradenton, FL 34209 ; (941) 747-5074; Ms. Terry Demarest (800) 525-7446; (941) 747-7747

Sign-Mobile, 4901 Deer Creek Circle, Lincoln, NE 68516 ; (402) 423-2808; Mr. Rowney Jensen (888) 772-5900; (402) 423-5079

Signs & More in 24, 1739 St. Mary's Ave., Parkersburg, WV 26101; (800) 424-7446; Mr. Bruce Bronski (800) 358-2358; (304) 422-7449

Signs Plus USA, 188 Technology Dr., Unit L, Irvine, CA 92618 ; (949) 450-0686; Mr. Blair M. Gran (800) 775-6355; (949) 450-0685

SpeedPro Sign and Print Centers, 18812 96th Ave., # 18, Surrey, BC V4N 3R1 CANADA; (604) 882-3626; Mr. Blair M. Gran (888) 966-6699; (604) 882-5115

SpeedPro Sign Plus, 188 Technology Dr., Suite L, Irvine, CA 92618 ; (949) 450-0686; Mr. Blair M. Gran (800) 775-6355; (949) 450-0685

TRAVEL INDUSTRY PROFILE

Total # Franchisors in Industry Group	20
Total # Franchised Units in Industry Group	4,823
Total # Company-Owned Units in Industry Group	<u>4,575</u>
Total # Operating Units in Industry Group	5,398
Average # Franchised Units/Franchisor	241.2
Average # Company-Owned Units/Franchisor	<u>28.8</u>
Average # Total Units/Franchisor	270.0
Ratio of Total # Franchised Units/Total # Company-Owned Units	8.4:1
Industry Survey Participants	5
Representing % of Industry	25.0%
Average Franchise Fee*:	$13.7K
Average Total Investment*:	$45.5K
Average On-Going Royalty Fee*:	2.5%

If a range was provided, the mid-point of the range was used. See detailed profiles for actual ranges.

FIVE LARGEST PARTICIPANTS IN SURVEY

Company	# Fran-chised Units	# Co-Owned Units	# Total Units	Franchise Fee	On-Going Royalty	Total Investment
1. Carlson Wagonlit Travel	1,302	419	1,721	Included	Varies	6.6-156K
2. Uniglobe Travel	1,100	0	1,100	2-25K	$275-550/Mo.	21-104K
3. Travel Network	507	1	508	5-30K	$350-750/Mo.	10-100K
4. Cruiseone	430	0	430	9.8K	4%	10-22K
5. Cruise Lines Reservation Ctr.	24	1	25	0K	1%	2-3K

All of the data provided are proprietary and should not be quoted without acknowledging *Bond's Franchise Guide*.

CARLSON WAGONLIT TRAVEL

P.O. Box 59159
Minneapolis, MN 55459-8207
Tel: (800) 678-8241 (612) 212-1000
Fax: (612) 212-1231
Web Site: www.travel.carlson.com
Mr. John Risner, Director Franchise Dev.

Start-up and conversion travel agencies available. Preferred supplier program; national and local marketing and advertising newsletters; brochures; assistance with commercial business development; regional meetings; participation in CARLSON Selling Systems; Associate consulting service; hotel programs; 24-hour service center; centralized support department; international rate desk; and professional development programs. Leading technology to maximize efficiency.

BACKGROUND: IFA MEMBER
Established: 1900;   1st Franchised: 1984
Franchised Units: 1,302
Company-Owned Units   <u>419</u>
Total Units: 1,721
Dist.:   US-1,404; CAN-0; O'seas-400
   North America: 49 States
   Density: 160 in CA, 80 in MN, 55 TX
Projected New Units (12 Months):   100
Qualifications: 3, 4, 5, 4, 3, 4
Registered: All States Except MN,,NY,DC
FINANCIAL/TERMS:
Cash Investment: $4-34.5K
Total Investment: $6.6-156.2K
Minimum Net Worth: $N/A
Fees: Franchise - $Included
   Royalty - Varies;   Ad. - Varies
Earnings Claim Statement: No
Term of Contract (Years):   3-10/3-10
Avg. # Of Employees: Varies
Passive Ownership: Discouraged
Encourage Conversions: Yes
Area Develop. Agreements: No
Sub-Franchising Contracts: No
Expand In Territory: Yes
Space Needs: NR SF; FS, SF, SC, RM, Other
SUPPORT & TRAINING PROVIDED:
Financial Assistance Provided: No
Site Selection Assistance: Yes
Lease Negotiation Assistance: Yes
Co-Operative Advertising: Yes
Franchisee Assoc./Member: Yes/Yes
Size Of Corporate Staff: 80
On-Going Support: d,E,g,h,i
Training: 2 Weeks in Minneapolis/On-Site
     for Start-Ups; 2 Days in Minneapolis
     for Conversions.

SPECIFIC EXPANSION PLANS:
US: All United States
Canada: No
Overseas: No

<< >>

CRUISEONE

10 Fairway Dr., # 200
Deerfield Beach, FL 33441-1802
Tel: (800) 892-3928 (954) 480-9265
Fax: (954) 428-6588
E-Mail: franchise@cruiseone.com
Web Site: www.cruiseone.com
Mr. Anthony Persico, President

CRUISEONE is a nationwide, home-based cruise-only franchise company representing all major cruise lines. Franchisees are professionally trained in a 7-day extensive program. How to close the sale and service the client, on-board ship inspections, sales and marketing techniques and customized software use are just the beginning. National Account Status offers consumers cruises for the lowest possible price and pays highest commissions in the industry. 1997 sales exceeded $80 million. Low start-up costs.

BACKGROUND: IFA MEMBER
Established: 1992;   1st Franchised: 1993
Franchised Units: 430
Company-Owned Units   <u>0</u>
Total Units: 430
Dist.:   US-430; CAN-0; O'seas-0
   North America: 45 States
   Density: 40 in FL, 39 in CA, 33 in TX
Projected New Units (12 Months):   120
Qualifications: 3, 4, 2, 3, 5, 4
Registered: All States
FINANCIAL/TERMS:
Cash Investment: $10-22K
Total Investment: $10-22K
Minimum Net Worth: $N/A
Fees: Franchise - $9.8K
   Royalty - 4%;   Ad. - 0%
Earnings Claim Statement: No
Term of Contract (Years):   1
Avg. # Of Employees: 1 FT
Passive Ownership: Not Allowed
Encourage Conversions: N/A
Area Develop. Agreements: No
Sub-Franchising Contracts: No
Expand In Territory: Yes
Space Needs: N/A SF; HB
SUPPORT & TRAINING PROVIDED:
Financial Assistance Provided: Yes(D)
Site Selection Assistance: N/A
Lease Negotiation Assistance: N/A

Co-Operative Advertising: Yes
Franchisee Assoc./Member: No
Size Of Corporate Staff: 42
On-Going Support: A,B,C,D,F,g,h,I
Training: 6 Days Ft. Lauderdale, FL.
SPECIFIC EXPANSION PLANS:
US: All United States
Canada: No
Overseas: No

<< >>

TRAVEL NETWORK

560 Sylvan Ave.
Englewood Cliffs, NJ 07632
Tel: (800) 669-9000 (201) 567-8500
Fax: (201) 567-4405
E-Mail: info@travnet.com
Web Site: www.travnet.com
Ms. Stephanie Abrams, Executive VP

Join the exciting travel industry with the leading travel franchisor as the owner of a TRAVEL NETWORK full-service travel agency catering to the business and leisure traveler. A TRAVEL NETWORK VACATION CENTRAL agency focuses solely on the lucrative leisure travel markets, or, as the owner of a full-service agency, catering to the business traveler as well as the leisure traveler. Our program includes complete start-up assistance, site selection and more.

BACKGROUND:
Established: 1982;   1st Franchised: 1983
Franchised Units: 507
Company-Owned Units   <u>1</u>
Total Units: 508
Dist.:   US-454; CAN-3; O'seas-51
   North America: 35 States, 1 Province
   Density: 65 in NY, 32 in NJ, 26 in CA
Projected New Units (12 Months):   50
Qualifications: 5, 4, 2, 4, 3, 5
Registered: CA,FL,IL,IN,MD,MI,MN,NY,
   OR,RI,VA,WA,WI,DC
FINANCIAL/TERMS:
Cash Investment: $5-50K
Total Investment: $10-100K
Minimum Net Worth: $150K
Fees: Franchise - $5-30K
   Royalty - $350-750/Mo; Ad. - $200/Mo.
Earnings Claim Statement: No
Term of Contract (Years):   15/15
Avg. # Of Employees: 2 FT, 1 PT
Passive Ownership: Discouraged

Encourage Conversions:	Yes
Area Develop. Agreements:	Yes/20
Sub-Franchising Contracts:	Yes
Expand In Territory:	Yes
Space Needs: 800-1,000 SF; FS, SF, SC, RM, HB	

SUPPORT & TRAINING PROVIDED:

Financial Assistance Provided:	Yes
Site Selection Assistance:	Yes
Lease Negotiation Assistance:	Yes
Co-Operative Advertising:	Yes
Franchisee Assoc./Member:	Yes
Size Of Corporate Staff:	25
On-Going Support:	A,B,C,D,E,F,G,H,I

Training: 1 Week in NJ; 1 Week in Orlando, FL; 1 Week in Houston, TX; 1 Week On-Site at Store.

SPECIFIC EXPANSION PLANS:

US:	All United States
Canada:	All Canada
Overseas:	All Countries

≪ ≫

UNIGLOBE TRAVEL

Five Park Plaza, #800
Irvine, CA 92614
Tel: (800) 863-1606 (949) 623-9088
Fax: (949) 623-9008
E-Mail: franchise@uniglobe.com
Web Site: www.uniglobefranchise.com
Mr. John Henry, SVP of Global Fran. Dev.

Entrepreneur has consistently awarded UNIGLOBE TRAVEL the #1 company in travel-agency franchising. All UNIGLOBE travel agency franchisees benefit from programs and systems designed to handle the needs of both the corporate and leisure client. UNIGLOBE franchisees benefit from money-saving automation agreements and top-notch incentive commission programs with major airline, hotel, car rental, tour and cruise-line companies.

BACKGROUND: IFA MEMBER

Established: 1979;	1st Franchised: 1980
Franchised Units:	1,100
Company-Owned Units	0
Total Units:	1,100
Dist.: US-756; CAN-200; O'seas-100	
North America:	50 States, 9 Provinces
Density:	109 in CA,45 in IL,41 in OH
Projected New Units (12 Months):	100
Qualifications:	5, 4, 1, 3, 4, 5
Registered: All States	

FINANCIAL/TERMS:

Cash Investment:	$2-25K
Total Investment:	$21-104K
Minimum Net Worth:	$60K
Fees: Franchise -	$2-25K
Royalty - $275-550;	Ad. - $550
Earnings Claim Statement:	No
Term of Contract (Years):	10/5
Avg. # Of Employees:	3 FT, 1 PT
Passive Ownership:	Discouraged
Encourage Conversions:	Yes
Area Develop. Agreements:	Yes/5
Sub-Franchising Contracts:	Yes
Expand In Territory:	Yes
Space Needs: 1,200 SF; FS, SF, SC, RM, HB	

SUPPORT & TRAINING PROVIDED:

Financial Assistance Provided:	Yes
Site Selection Assistance:	Yes
Lease Negotiation Assistance:	Yes
Co-Operative Advertising:	Yes
Franchisee Assoc./Member:	Yes
Size Of Corporate Staff:	100
On-Going Support:	B,C,D,e,G,h,I

Training: 3-5 Days in Irvine, CA.

SPECIFIC EXPANSION PLANS:

US:	All United States
Canada:	All Canada
Overseas:	All Countries

≪ ≫

SUPPLEMENTAL LISTING OF FRANCHISORS

Admiral of the Fleet Cruise Centers, 3430 Pacific Ave. SE, #A-5, Olympia, WA 98501 ; (360) 438-2618; Ms. Jane Fitzpatrick (800) 877-7447; (360) 438-1191

Algonquin Travel, 657 Bronson Ave., Ottawa, ON K1S 4E7 CANADA; (613) 233-7805; Mr. Mark Dyer (800) 668-1743; (613) 233-7713

BTI America's Partner Group, 400 Skokie Blvd., # 675, Northbrook, IL 60062 ; (847) 753-6730; Ms. Lora Ellis (800) 775-7702; (847) 753-6700

ByeByeNOW.com, 1100 Park Blvd., S, # 1800, Pompano Beach, FL 33064-2232 ; (954) 935-0178; Mr. Mark Schiffner (800) 626-2469; (954) 979-6647

Cruise Lines Reservation Center, 9229 Kaufman Pl., Brooklyn, NY 11236; (718) 763-4259; Mr. Bernard Korn

Cruise Vacations, 2025 W. Broadway, Vancouver, BC V6J 1Z6 CANADA; (604) 736-6513; Ms. Darcy Hibbard (800) 665-1882; (604) 731-5546

CruiseShipCenters, 344 River Oaks Blvd. W., Oakville, ON L6H 5E8 CANADA; (905) 257-6560; Mr. Tom Palmeri ; (905) 257-3505

Empress Travel, 465 Smith St., Farmingdale, NY 11735 ; (516) 420-0511; Ms. Elizabeth Beutel (800) 284-0022; (516) 420-9200

Enchanted Honeymoons, 2927 S. 108th St., Omaha, NE 68144 ; (402) 393-8096; Mr. Kem Matthews ; (402) 390-9291

EXA International, 440 S. Federal Hwy., #104, Deerfield Beach, FL 33441 ; (305) 670-4904; Mr. Aaron Curran ; (305) 670-3833

Inhouse Travel Group, 190 E. Westminster Rd., Lake Forest, IL 60045 ; (847) 234-8774; Ms. Michele Samson (800) 863-1606; (847) 234-8750

Kirby Tours, 2451 S. Telegraph Rd., Dearborn, MI 48124 ; (313) 278-9569; Mr. Shakil A. Khan (800) 521-0711; (313) 278-2224

TPI Travel Services, 10012 Dale Mabry Hwy., # 102, Tampa, FL 33618-4425 ; (813) 281-4969; Ms. Barbara Webster (888) TPI-DEAL; (813) 269-4960

Vacationbound Systems, 1315 Autrim Dr., Roseville, CA 95747 ; (916) 783-8473; Mr. Frank J. Ball ; (916) 783-8473

MISCELLANEOUS INDUSTRY PROFILE

Total # Franchisors in Industry Group	87
Total # Franchised Units in Industry Group	4,953
Total # Company-Owned Units in Industry Group	<u>565</u>
Total # Operating Units in Industry Group	5,518
Average # Franchised Units/Franchisor	56.9
Average # Company-Owned Units/Franchisor	<u>6.5</u>
Average # Total Units/Franchisor	63.4
Ratio of Total # Franchised Units/Total # Company-Owned Units	8.8:1
Industry Survey Participants	24
Representing % of Industry	27.6%
Average Franchise Fee*:	$38.3K
Average Total Investment*:	$206.0K
Average On-Going Royalty Fee*:	8.2%

If a range was provided, the mid-point of the range was used. See detailed profiles for actual ranges.

FIVE LARGEST PARTICIPANTS IN SURVEY

Company	# Fran- chised Units	# Co- Owned Units	# Total Units	Franchise Fee	On-Going Royalty	Total Investment
1. Culligan	749	100	849	5K	5%	103-225K
2. Ecowater Systems	725	0	725	0K	None	250K
3. House Doctors Handyman Service	225	0	225	9-22K	6%	18-39K
4. Benvinco	166	1	167	24.5K	$12/Audit	25-35K
5. Two Men and A Truck	95	0	95	28K	6%	75K+

All of the data provided are proprietary and should not be quoted without acknowledging *Bond's Franchise Guide*.

A QUIK SERVICES

1730 Cumberland Point Dr., #5
Marietta, GA 30067
Tel: (800) 255-8145 (770) 951-9440
Fax: (770) 933-8268
E-Mail: fnrjm@bellsouth.net
Web Site: www.aquik.com
Mr. Raymond J. Margiano, President

A QUIK SERVICES has over 30 different service business franchise opportunities, including dry cleaning, sign stores, printing, hair salon, cleaning, etc. A large range of opportunities from $2,500 to $200,000. Home-based, business to business, service, retail, we will help you find the right business opportunity for you.

BACKGROUND:

Established: 1998; 1st Franchised: 1999
Franchised Units: 30
Company-Owned Units: 3
Total Units: 33
Dist.:   US-0; CAN-0; O'seas-0
  North America: 1 State
  Density: 3 in GA, 30 international
Projected New Units (12 Months):   NR
Registered:

FINANCIAL/TERMS:

Cash Investment: $2.5-75K
Total Investment: $2.5-200K
Minimum Net Worth: $2.5K
Fees: Franchise - $2.5-17.5K
  Royalty - 4%; Ad. - 2%
Earnings Claim Statement: No
Term of Contract (Years): 20/10
Avg. # Of Employees: 1-5 FT
Passive Ownership: Allowed
Encourage Conversions: NR
Area Develop. Agreements: Yes/10/10
Sub-Franchising Contracts: No
Expand In Territory: Yes
Space Needs: Varies SF; FS, SF, SC, RM, HB

SUPPORT & TRAINING PROVIDED:

Financial Assistance Provided: NR
Site Selection Assistance: Yes
Lease Negotiation Assistance: Yes
Co-Operative Advertising: No
Franchisee Assoc./Member: No
Size Of Corporate Staff: 10
On-Going Support: B,C,D,e,F,G,H,I
Training: 20 Weeks in Atlanta, GA; 2 Weeks Regional; Home Town.

SPECIFIC EXPANSION PLANS:

US: All United States
Canada: NR
Overseas: NR

⪪ ⪫

AIR BROOK LIMOUSINE

P.O. Box 123
Rochelle Park, NJ 07662
Tel: (201) 368-3974
Fax: (201) 368-2247
Web Site: www.aribrook.com
Mr. Jim Bziekonski, Franchise Director

Limousine Service/Ground Transportation.

BACKGROUND:

Established: 1969; 1st Franchised: 1971
Franchised Units: 73
Company-Owned Units: 0
Total Units: 73
Dist.:   US-73; CAN-0; O'seas-0
  North America: 1 State
  Density: 73 in NJ
Projected New Units (12 Months):   10
Qualifications: 2, 2, 2, 2, 3, 4
Registered: NR

FINANCIAL/TERMS:

Cash Investment: $5.5-11K
Total Investment: $10.5-20K
Minimum Net Worth: $N/A
Fees: Franchise - $7.5-12.5K
  Royalty - 40%; Ad. - 0%
Earnings Claim Statement: No
Term of Contract (Years): 10/2
Avg. # Of Employees: 2 FT
Passive Ownership: Allowed
Encourage Conversions: N/A
Area Develop. Agreements: No
Sub-Franchising Contracts: No
Expand In Territory: Yes
Space Needs: N/A SF; N/A

SUPPORT & TRAINING PROVIDED:

Financial Assistance Provided: Yes(D)
Site Selection Assistance: N/A
Lease Negotiation Assistance: N/A
Co-Operative Advertising: N/A
Franchisee Assoc./Member: No
Size Of Corporate Staff: 57
On-Going Support: A,B,C,D,G,H,I
Training: 3 Days Rochelle Park, NJ.

SPECIFIC EXPANSION PLANS:

US: NJ Only
Canada: No
Overseas: No

⪪ ⪫

AIT FREIGHT SYSTEMS

P.O. Box 66730
Chicago, IL 60666
Tel: (800) 669-4248 (630) 766-8300
Fax: (630) 766-0305
Mr. Herbert Cohan, Senior Vice President

Freight forwarder - international and domestic.

BACKGROUND:

Established: 1979; 1st Franchised: 1988
Franchised Units: 17
Company-Owned Units: 10
Total Units: 27
Dist.:   US-27; CAN-0; O'seas-0
  North America: 16 States
  Density: 2 in TX, 2 in NC, 1 in IL
Projected New Units (12 Months):   2
Qualifications: 4, 5, 5, 3, 4, 4
Registered: CA,IL,NY

FINANCIAL/TERMS:

Cash Investment: $25-50K
Total Investment: $46K
Minimum Net Worth: $46K
Fees: Franchise - $13K
  Royalty - 12.8%; Ad. - 1%
Earnings Claim Statement: Yes
Term of Contract (Years): 20/10
Avg. # Of Employees: 5 FT
Passive Ownership: Discouraged
Encourage Conversions: No
Area Develop. Agreements:Yes/Contract
Sub-Franchising Contracts: No
Expand In Territory: No
Space Needs: 10,000 SF; FS

SUPPORT & TRAINING PROVIDED:

Financial Assistance Provided: Yes
Site Selection Assistance: Yes
Lease Negotiation Assistance: No
Co-Operative Advertising: Yes
Franchisee Assoc./Member: No
Size Of Corporate Staff: 35
On-Going Support: A,D,E,I
Training: 2 Days Chicago, IL.

SPECIFIC EXPANSION PLANS:

US: Southwest, Northeast
Canada: All Canada
Overseas: No

⪪ ⪫

ATLANTIC MOWER PARTS & SUPPLIES

13421 S.W. 14th Pl.
Ft. Lauderdale, FL 33325
Tel: (954) 474-4942
Fax: (954) 475-0414
Mr. Robert J. Bettelli, President

Lawn mower replacement after-market. Parts for national brands (Snapper, Toro, MTD, Murray, etc.).

BACKGROUND:

Established: 1978; 1st Franchised: 1988	
Franchised Units:	14
Company-Owned Units	1
Total Units:	15
Dist.:	US-15; CAN-0; O'seas-0
North America:	1 State
Density:	15 in FL
Projected New Units (12 Months):	5
Qualifications:	2, 3, 3, 4, 1, 5
Registered: FL	

FINANCIAL/TERMS:

Cash Investment:	$~45K
Total Investment:	$45K
Minimum Net Worth:	$NR
Fees: Franchise -	$15.9K
Royalty - 5%;	Ad. - 0.5%
Earnings Claim Statement:	No
Term of Contract (Years):	10/10
Avg. # Of Employees:	1 FT
Passive Ownership:	Allowed
Encourage Conversions:	Yes
Area Develop. Agreements:	Yes/1
Sub-Franchising Contracts:	Yes
Expand In Territory:	Yes
Space Needs: 250 SF; Warehouse	

SUPPORT & TRAINING PROVIDED:

Financial Assistance Provided:	No
Site Selection Assistance:	Yes
Lease Negotiation Assistance:	Yes
Co-Operative Advertising:	No
Franchisee Assoc./Member:	NR
Size Of Corporate Staff:	3
On-Going Support:	B,C,D,E
Training: 5 Days Headquarters; 5 Days On-Site.	

SPECIFIC EXPANSION PLANS:

US:	All United States
Canada:	No
Overseas:	No

≺≺ ≻≻

BEVINCO

250 Consumers Rd., # 1103
Toronto, ON M2J 4V6 CANADA
Tel: (888) 238-4626 (416) 490-6266
Fax: (416) 490-6899
E-Mail: info@bevinco.com
Web Site: www.bevinco.com
Mr. Barry Driedger, President

Liquor inventory auditing and control service for bars and restaurants. Utilizing our computerized weighing system, franchisees will identify and resolve the shrinkage problems associated with the bar business. On-going weekly accounts make for an excellent executive income.

BACKGROUND: IFA MEMBER

Established: 1987; 1st Franchised: 1990	
Franchised Units:	166
Company-Owned Units	1
Total Units:	167
Dist.:	US-80; CAN-36; O'seas-20
North America:	40 States, 7 Provinces
Density:	9 in CA, 8 in OH, 6 in TX
Projected New Units (12 Months):	50
Qualifications:	3, 4, 4, 3, 3, 3
Registered: All States	

FINANCIAL/TERMS:

Cash Investment:	$30K
Total Investment:	$25-35K
Minimum Net Worth:	$40K
Fees: Franchise -	$24.5K
Royalty - $12/Audit;	Ad. - $2/Audit
Earnings Claim Statement:	No
Term of Contract (Years):	5/5
Avg. # Of Employees:	1-3 FT, 1-3 PT
Passive Ownership:	Not Allowed
Encourage Conversions:	N/A
Area Develop. Agreements:	Yes/5
Sub-Franchising Contracts:	No
Expand In Territory:	N/A
Space Needs: NR SF; N/A	

SUPPORT & TRAINING PROVIDED:

Financial Assistance Provided:	Yes(I)
Site Selection Assistance:	N/A
Lease Negotiation Assistance:	N/A
Co-Operative Advertising:	N/A
Franchisee Assoc./Member:	Yes/Yes
Size Of Corporate Staff:	4
On-Going Support:	A,b,D,G,H,I
Training: 5 Days at Head Office in Toronto; 5 Days Franchisee's Location.	

SPECIFIC EXPANSION PLANS:

US:	All United States
Canada:	All Canada
Overseas:	All Countries

≺≺ ≻≻

COMPUTER BUILDERS WAREHOUSE

1993 Tobsul Ct.
Warren, MI 48091
Tel: (248) 559-1415
Fax: (248) 557-7931
E-Mail: wfcnet@cris.com
Web Site: www.computerfranchise.com
Dr. Geoffrey Stebbins, Dir. Fran. Dev.

Exciting and unique franchise opportunity. Our franchisees take advantage of our state of the art manufacturing and warehouse facility. The testing center provides customers with reliable built to order computer products, while in-store service labs provide complete computer service, parts and components. A turnkey operation is provided.

BACKGROUND:

Established: 1990; 1st Franchised: 1999	
Franchised Units:	4
Company-Owned Units	1
Total Units:	5
Dist.:	US-5; CAN-0; O'seas-0
North America:	1 State
Density:	5 in MI
Projected New Units (12 Months):	15
Qualifications:	5, 3, 2, 3, 3, 5
Registered: CA,FL,HI,IL,IN,MD,MI,MN, NY,ND,OR,RI,SD,VA,WA,WI,DC	

FINANCIAL/TERMS:

Cash Investment:	$100K
Total Investment:	$300-350K
Minimum Net Worth:	$200K
Fees: Franchise -	$35K
Royalty - 1.5%;	Ad. - 2%
Earnings Claim Statement:	No
Term of Contract (Years):	10/5
Avg. # Of Employees:	7 FT, 2 PT
Passive Ownership:	Not Allowed
Encourage Conversions:	Yes
Area Develop. Agreements:	No
Sub-Franchising Contracts:	No
Expand In Territory:	No
Space Needs: 3,500 SF; FS,SF,SC	

SUPPORT & TRAINING PROVIDED:

Financial Assistance Provided:	Yes(I)
Site Selection Assistance:	Yes
Lease Negotiation Assistance:	Yes
Co-Operative Advertising:	Yes
Franchisee Assoc./Member:	No
Size Of Corporate Staff:	75
On-Going Support:	B,C,D,E,F,G,H
Training: 3 Weeks at Company Headquarters; 2-4 Weeks On-Site.	

SPECIFIC EXPANSION PLANS:

US:	All United States

Canada: No
Overseas: No

≺≺ ≻≻

CULLIGAN

One Culligan Pkwy.
Northbrook, IL 60062-6209
Tel: (847) 205-6000
Fax: (847) 205-6005
E-Mail: kwood@culligan.com
Web Site: www.culligan.com
Mr. Kenneth E. Wood, Dir. Marketing Dev.

CULLIGAN is looking for franchisees to start a business selling 5 gallon bottles of water for delivery to homes and offices. CULLIGAN is a manufacturer of water conditioners, filters and drinking water devices.

BACKGROUND: IFA MEMBER
Established: 1936;   1st Franchised: 1939
Franchised Units: 749
Company-Owned Units   <u>100</u>
Total Units: 849
Dist.:   US-801; CAN-48; O'seas-0
  North America: 50 States
  Density: 40 in MN, 40 in IA, 35 in WI
Projected New Units (12 Months):   8
Qualifications: 5, 5, 2, 3, 4, 4
Registered: All States
FINANCIAL/TERMS:
Cash Investment: $103-225K
Total Investment: $103-225K
Minimum Net Worth: $250K
Fees: Franchise - $5K
  Royalty - 5%;   Ad. - 0%
Earnings Claim Statement: No
Term of Contract (Years):   10/10
Avg. # Of Employees: 6 FT
Passive Ownership: Discouraged
Encourage Conversions: Yes
Area Develop. Agreements: No
Sub-Franchising Contracts: No
Expand In Territory: No
Space Needs: 2,500 SF; SF
SUPPORT & TRAINING PROVIDED:
Financial Assistance Provided: No
Site Selection Assistance: No
Lease Negotiation Assistance: No
Co-Operative Advertising: No
Franchisee Assoc./Member: No
Size Of Corporate Staff: 20
On-Going Support: C,D,G,H,I
Training: 1 Week Chicago, IL.
SPECIFIC EXPANSION PLANS:
US: SE, Pacific NW, Northeast
Canada: All Canada
Overseas: Mexico, South America

≺≺ ≻≻

DISCOUNT IMAGING

305-B Wood St.
West Monroe, LA 71291
Tel: (800) 987-8258 (318) 324-8258
Fax: (318) 324-1211
E-Mail: Bradh@Bayou.com
Web Site: www.difc.com
Mr. Brad Hargrove, National Sales Mgr.

Single source providers of printer, fax and copier supplies and service to businesses of all types. Program features proprietary product line, purchasing power and other support services.

BACKGROUND:
Established: 1995;   1st Franchised: 1998
Franchised Units: 4
Company-Owned Units   <u>9</u>
Total Units: 13
Dist.:   US-13; CAN-0; O'seas-0
  North America: 5 States
  Density: 2 in AR, 1 in FL, 1 in AL
Projected New Units (12 Months):   15
Qualifications: 4, 3, 2, 1, 4, 5
Registered: FL,TX
FINANCIAL/TERMS:
Cash Investment: $25-40K
Total Investment: $56-62K
Minimum Net Worth: $75K
Fees: Franchise - $25K
  Royalty - 3-6%;   Ad. - 0%
Earnings Claim Statement: No
Term of Contract (Years):   10/5
Avg. # Of Employees: 4 FT, 1 PT
Passive Ownership: Discouraged
Encourage Conversions: No
Area Develop. Agreements: No
Sub-Franchising Contracts: No
Expand In Territory: Yes
Space Needs: NR SF; HB
SUPPORT & TRAINING PROVIDED:
Financial Assistance Provided: Yes(I)
Site Selection Assistance: Yes
Lease Negotiation Assistance: No
Co-Operative Advertising: No
Franchisee Assoc./Member: No
Size Of Corporate Staff: 6
On-Going Support: C,d,E,F,G,h,I

Training: 2 Weeks Corporate; 5 Weeks
  On-Site.
SPECIFIC EXPANSION PLANS:
US: South, Southeast
Canada: All Canada
Overseas: No

≺≺ ≻≻

ECOWATER SYSTEMS

P.O. Box 64420
St. Paul, MN 55164
Tel: (800) 942-5415 (651) 731-7438
Fax: (651) 739-4547
E-Mail: johnsonj@ecowater.com
Web Site: www.ecowater.com
Mr. Jerry Johnson, Mgr. of Fran. Dev.

Manufacturer & distributor of water treatment products for residential, commercial and industrial uses. Established in 1925, EcoWater has been providing high quality computerized water treatment and products worldwide. As the world's largest manufacturer of residential water systems, you build your business, in protected territories, servicing your customers and controlling your future.

BACKGROUND:
Established: 1925;   1st Franchised: 1927
Franchised Units: 725
Company-Owned Units   <u>0</u>
Total Units: 725
Dist.:   US-600; CAN-50; O'seas-75
  North America: 50 States, 5 Provinces
  Density: NR
Projected New Units (12 Months):   20
Qualifications: 5, 4, 1, 2, 4, 5
Registered: All States
FINANCIAL/TERMS:
Cash Investment: $125K
Total Investment: $250K
Minimum Net Worth: $200K
Fees: Franchise - $0
  Royalty - None;   Ad. - Varies
Earnings Claim Statement: No
Term of Contract (Years):   2-10/2-10
Avg. # Of Employees: 4 FT, 2 PT
Passive Ownership: Discouraged
Encourage Conversions: Yes
Area Develop. Agreements: Yes/1
Sub-Franchising Contracts: Yes
Expand In Territory: Yes
Space Needs: 2,500 SF; FS, SF, SC
SUPPORT & TRAINING PROVIDED:
Financial Assistance Provided: Yes(D)
Site Selection Assistance: Yes
Lease Negotiation Assistance: No
Co-Operative Advertising: Yes

Franchisee Assoc./Member: No
Size Of Corporate Staff: 500
On-Going Support: B,C,D,E,G,H,I
Training: 3-5 Days On-Site; 5 Days at
Corporate Office.

SPECIFIC EXPANSION PLANS:
US: All United States
Canada: All Canada
Overseas: Yes -- Contact Company

◂◂ ▸▸

FILTERFRESH
378 University Ave.
Westwood, MA 02090
Tel: (800) 332-6771 (781) 461-8734
Fax: (781) 461-8732
Mr. Roger Cohen, President

High-tech office coffee service, using a patented single-cup coffeemaker. FILTERFRESH brews coffee by-the-cup from fresh-ground coffee in seconds. Choice exclusive territories are available as a franchise or joint-venture with corporate. The FILTERFRESH franchise provides access to patented equipment, detailed training in sales and service, on-going support and supply services.

BACKGROUND:
Established: 1986; 1st Franchised: 1987
Franchised Units: 40
Company-Owned Units 10
Total Units: 50
Dist.: US-49; CAN-0; O'seas-1
North America: 25 States
Density: 8 in NY, 6 in NJ, 3 in CA
Projected New Units (12 Months): 4
Qualifications: 4, 5, 2, 3, 4, 4
Registered: CA,FL,IL,IN,MD,MI,MN,NY,
OR,RI,VA,WA
FINANCIAL/TERMS:
Cash Investment: $150-500K
Total Investment: $50-500K
Minimum Net Worth: $500K
Fees: Franchise - $24.5K
Royalty - 5%; Ad. - 2%
Earnings Claim Statement: No
Term of Contract (Years): 10/10
Avg. # Of Employees: 4 FT, 2 PT
Passive Ownership: Not Allowed
Encourage Conversions: N/A
Area Develop. Agreements: No
Sub-Franchising Contracts: No

Expand In Territory: Yes
Space Needs: 1,500 SF; Warehouse
SUPPORT & TRAINING PROVIDED:
Financial Assistance Provided: Yes(I)
Site Selection Assistance: Yes
Lease Negotiation Assistance: No
Co-Operative Advertising: Yes
Franchisee Assoc./Member: Yes/No
Size Of Corporate Staff: 30
On-Going Support: A,B,C,D,E,F,G,H,I
Training: 1 Week Montreal, PQ; 2 Weeks
On-Site; 1 Week Westwood, MA.

SPECIFIC EXPANSION PLANS:
US: All United States
Canada: No
Overseas: All Countries

◂◂ ▸▸

GLASS MAGNUM
17815 Shawnee Tr.
Tualatin, OR 97062
Tel: (800) 642-1141 (503) 641-6926
Fax: (503) 612-9441
Mr. Gary Cayton, President

Rock chip repair and crack repair of windshields. Restructure windscreens in planes and helicopters. Crystal and accent glass repair and restructuring. Plate glass repair - holes and cracks.

BACKGROUND:
Established: 1982; 1st Franchised: 1990
Franchised Units: 21
Company-Owned Units 1
Total Units: 22
Dist.: US-21; CAN-0; O'seas-0
North America: 5 States
Density: 14 in OR, 2 in WA, 2 in HI
Projected New Units (12 Months): 20
Qualifications: 3, 2, 1, 1, 2, 5
Registered: HI,OR,WA
FINANCIAL/TERMS:
Cash Investment: $6-8K
Total Investment: $6-8K
Minimum Net Worth: $10K
Fees: Franchise - $5K
Royalty - 5%; Ad. - 1%
Earnings Claim Statement: No
Term of Contract (Years): 5/5
Avg. # Of Employees: 1 FT
Passive Ownership: Not Allowed
Encourage Conversions: Yes
Area Develop. Agreements: Yes/5
Sub-Franchising Contracts: Yes
Expand In Territory: Yes
Space Needs: NR SF; N/A
SUPPORT & TRAINING PROVIDED:
Financial Assistance Provided: Yes(I)

Site Selection Assistance: N/A
Lease Negotiation Assistance: N/A
Co-Operative Advertising: Yes
Franchisee Assoc./Member: No
Size Of Corporate Staff: 1
On-Going Support: B,D,F,G,I
Training: 300 Hours in Beaverton, OR.
SPECIFIC EXPANSION PLANS:
US: All United States
Canada: Vancouv/Victoria
Overseas: No

◂◂ ▸▸

HOUSE DOCTORS HANDYMAN SERVICE
6355 E. Kemper Rd., # 250
Cincinnati, OH 45241
Tel: (800) 319-3359 (513) 469-2443
Fax: (513) 469-2226
E-Mail: housedr@one.net
Web Site: www.housedoctors.com
Mr. Steve Cohen, President

There's big money in house calls. Millions of dollars are being spent every day on those odd jobs around the house that people don't have the time or skill to do. You don't need a screwdriver or hammer to own this franchise. Financing and training provided.

BACKGROUND: IFA MEMBER
Established: 1994; 1st Franchised: 1995
Franchised Units: 225
Company-Owned Units 0
Total Units: 225
Dist.: US-224; CAN-0; O'seas-1
North America: 41 States
Density: 11 in OH, 8 in IN, 7 in IL
Projected New Units (12 Months): 30
Qualifications: 2, 3, 2, 2, 4, 5
Registered: CA,FL,IL,IN,MD,MI,MN,NY,
ND,OR,RI,VA,WA,WI
FINANCIAL/TERMS:
Cash Investment: $12-23K
Total Investment: $18-39K
Minimum Net Worth: $10K
Fees: Franchise - $9-22K

Royalty - 6%;   Ad. - 3%
Earnings Claim Statement: No
Term of Contract (Years):   10/10/10
Avg. # Of Employees: 3 FT, 2 PT
Passive Ownership: Discouraged
Encourage Conversions: Yes
Area Develop. Agreements: Yes/10
Sub-Franchising Contracts: No
Expand In Territory: No
Space Needs: N/A SF; N/A

SUPPORT & TRAINING PROVIDED:
Financial Assistance Provided: Yes(D)
Site Selection Assistance: N/A
Lease Negotiation Assistance: N/A
Co-Operative Advertising: N/A
Franchisee Assoc./Member: No
Size Of Corporate Staff: 12
On-Going Support: A,B,C,D,E,G,H,I
Training: 1 Week Cincinnati, OH.

SPECIFIC EXPANSION PLANS:
US: All United States
Canada: All Canada
Overseas: All Countries

◄◄ ►►

MAGIS FUND RAISING SPECIALISTS

845 Heathermoor Ln.
Perrysburg, OH 43551-2933
Tel: (419) 874-4459
Fax: (419) 874-4459
Dr. Richard W. Waring, President

Conducts annual giving, endowment, capital campaigns, feasibility studies, fund raising audits, personnel searches, corporate solicitations, etc. Presents seminars, designs brochures, presentations, etc. for churches, schools, hospitals, etc. 30 years of fund raising experience. Contract with small- to medium-sized charities who cannot afford full-time development directors. The first fund raising franchise with a guarantee in the U. S. and Canada. $150 million raised.

BACKGROUND:
Established: 1991;   1st Franchised: 1991
Franchised Units: 6
Company-Owned Units   3
Total Units: 9
Dist.:   US-6; CAN-3; O'seas-0
North America: 2 States, 1 Province
Density: 3 in MI, 3 in OH, 3 in ON
Projected New Units (12 Months):   6
Qualifications: 5, 5, 4, 4, 4, 5
Registered: All Except AB

FINANCIAL/TERMS:
Cash Investment: $17K
Total Investment: $28.5K

Minimum Net Worth: $100K
Fees: Franchise - $7.5K
Royalty - 8%;   Ad. - 2%
Earnings Claim Statement: No
Term of Contract (Years):   5/5
Avg. # Of Employees: 2 FT, 4 PT
Passive Ownership: Not Allowed
Encourage Conversions: Yes
Area Develop. Agreements: Yes
Sub-Franchising Contracts: Yes
Expand In Territory: Yes
Space Needs: 500 SF; HB

SUPPORT & TRAINING PROVIDED:
Financial Assistance Provided: Yes(I)
Site Selection Assistance: N/A
Lease Negotiation Assistance: N/A
Co-Operative Advertising: Yes
Franchisee Assoc./Member: No
Size Of Corporate Staff: 2
On-Going Support: a,B,c,d,E,G,h
Training: 1 Week Home Study; 1 Week Support Service Center; 1 Week On-Site.

SPECIFIC EXPANSION PLANS:
US: All United States
Canada: All Canada
Overseas: All Countries

◄◄ ►►

Metal Supermarkets (Canada) Ltd.
The Convenience Stores of the Metal Industry

METAL SUPERMARKETS INTERNATIONAL

700 Sarasota Quay
Sarasota, FL 34236
Tel: (888) 734-1828 (941) 951-1320
Fax: (941) 954-0364
E-Mail: miller-joe@compuserve.com
Web Site: www.metalsupermarkets.com
Mr. Joe H. Miller, President, Franchise Division

METAL SUPERMARKETS is a highly specialized supplier of small quantities of virtually all types and forms of metal. Customers are maintenance departments of all types of industries. As 'convenience stores of the metal industry,' we have no minimum order We offer fast delivery, custom cutting and can source rare metals.

BACKGROUND: IFA MEMBER
Established: 1985;   1st Franchised: 1987
Franchised Units: 59
Company-Owned Units   16
Total Units: 75
Dist.:   US-33; CAN-32; O'seas-10

North America: 23 States, 8 Provinces
Density: 13 in ON, 5 in FL, 3 in PA
Projected New Units (12 Months):   18
Qualifications: 5, 3, 3, 3, 3, 5
Registered: All States

FINANCIAL/TERMS:
Cash Investment: $100K
Total Investment: $200-225K
Minimum Net Worth: $200K
Fees: Franchise - $38K
Royalty - 6%;   Ad. - 0%
Earnings Claim Statement: No
Term of Contract (Years):   10/10
Avg. # Of Employees: 3 FT, 1 PT
Passive Ownership: Discouraged
Encourage Conversions: Yes
Area Develop. Agreements: Yes/10
Sub-Franchising Contracts: No
Expand In Territory: Yes
Space Needs: 3,000 SF; Industrial Park

SUPPORT & TRAINING PROVIDED:
Financial Assistance Provided: No
Site Selection Assistance: Yes
Lease Negotiation Assistance: Yes
Co-Operative Advertising: No
Franchisee Assoc./Member: Yes/Yes
Size Of Corporate Staff: 15
On-Going Support: C,D,E,F,G,h,I
Training: 1 Week in Toronto, ON; 2 Weeks U.S. Corporate Store; 2 Weeks Own Store.

SPECIFIC EXPANSION PLANS:
US: All United States
Canada: PQ
Overseas: Europe

◄◄ ►►

Portable On Demand Storage

PODS

6061 45th St. N.
St. Petersburg, FL 33756
Tel: (888) 776-7637 (727) 520-0080
Fax: (727) 520-0830
Web Site: www.putinapod.com
Ms. Jeanine Blake, Franchise Dev.

Portable on demand storage. PODS utilizes a specially-equipped truck and patented hydraulic lift technology to deliver, retrieve and store up to an 8x8x16 foot container. Revolutionizing the moving and storage industry.

BACKGROUND:
Established: 1997;   1st Franchised: 1998

Franchised Units:	30
Company-Owned Units	7
Total Units:	37
Dist.:	US-37; CAN-0; O'seas-0
North America:	9 States
Density:	FL, MN, IN
Projected New Units (12 Months):	25
Qualifications:	5, 4, 1, 1, 3, 3
Registered:	FL,IN,VA

FINANCIAL/TERMS:

Cash Investment:	$400K
Total Investment:	$1.5MM+
Minimum Net Worth:	$1MM
Fees: Franchise -	$75K
Royalty - 8%/$3.5K/Mo.;	Ad. - 2%
Earnings Claim Statement:	No
Term of Contract (Years):	20/10
Avg. # Of Employees:	5 FT
Passive Ownership:	Allowed
Encourage Conversions:	NA
Area Develop. Agreements:	No
Sub-Franchising Contracts:	No
Expand In Territory:	No
Space Needs: 20,000 SF; Warehouse	

SUPPORT & TRAINING PROVIDED:

Financial Assistance Provided:	No
Site Selection Assistance:	Yes
Lease Negotiation Assistance:	No
Co-Operative Advertising:	No
Franchisee Assoc./Member:	Yes/Yes
Size Of Corporate Staff:	110
On-Going Support:	A,b,d,E,G,H,I
Training: 2 Weeks St. Petersburg, FL.	

SPECIFIC EXPANSION PLANS:

US:	NE,SE, Midwest
Canada:	No
Overseas:	No

≪ ≫

PURE WATER, INC.
3725 Touzalin Ave.
Lincoln, NE 68501
Tel: (800) 875-5915 (402) 467-9300
Fax: (402) 467-9393
E-Mail: JHarrington@purewaterinc.com
Web Site: www.purewaterinc.com
Mr. Jason Harrington, Dir. of Int'l. Sales

The PURE WATER ULTIMA franchise puts you in business providing the freshest, highest-quality drinking water to your clients, using the state-of-the-art PURE WATER ULTIMA 888, which purifies the water and dispenses it exactly as your client desires. The PURE WATER ULTIMA 888 purification unit, which removes up to 99.9% of impurities from tapwater, replaces the five gallon bottle on a conventional cooler/dispenser.

BACKGROUND:

Established: 1968;	1st Franchised: 1995
Franchised Units:	13
Company-Owned Units	0
Total Units:	13
Dist.:	US-0; CAN-0; O'seas-13
North America:	None
Density:	N/A
Projected New Units (12 Months):	6
Qualifications:	5, 5, 4, 2, 2, 4
Registered: None	

FINANCIAL/TERMS:

Cash Investment:	$100-175K
Total Investment:	$NR
Minimum Net Worth:	$N/A
Fees: Franchise -	$0
Royalty - 0%;	Ad. - 0%
Earnings Claim Statement:	No
Term of Contract (Years):	5/5
Avg. # Of Employees:	7 FT + Sales
Passive Ownership:	Discouraged
Encourage Conversions:	N/A
Area Develop. Agreements:	No
Sub-Franchising Contracts:	Yes
Expand In Territory:	Yes
Space Needs: 4,500 SF; N/A	

SUPPORT & TRAINING PROVIDED:

Financial Assistance Provided:	Yes(I)
Site Selection Assistance:	No
Lease Negotiation Assistance:	No
Co-Operative Advertising:	No
Franchisee Assoc./Member:	No
Size Of Corporate Staff:	10
On-Going Support:	C,D,G,H,I
Training: 1 Week -- International.	

SPECIFIC EXPANSION PLANS:

US:	International only
Canada:	No
Overseas:	All Countries

≪ ≫

PURIFIED WATER TO GO
5160 S. Valley View Blvd., # 110
Las Vegas, NV 89118-1778
Tel: (800) 976-9283 (702) 895-9350
Fax: (702) 895-9306
Web Site: www.WaterToGo.com
Mr. Jim Heller, Franchise Marketing

PURIFIED WATER TO GO, recently featured on NBC nightly news, is a full-service or express retail outlet, selling purified water by the gallon, purified ice and related products. As the leader in water store franchises, PURIFIED WATER TO GO answers today's need for superior quality drinking water. Water is purified on store premises, and customers are drawn to the appeal of our sparkling clean, blue and white interior design.

BACKGROUND: IFA MEMBER

Established: 1991;	1st Franchised: 1995
Franchised Units:	44
Company-Owned Units	0
Total Units:	44
Dist.:	US-33; CAN-0; O'seas-0
North America:	12 States
Density:	12 in WA, 5 in NV, 4 in CA
Projected New Units (12 Months):	15
Qualifications:	4, 2, 1, 3, 4, 5
Registered: CA,WA,WI,IL	

FINANCIAL/TERMS:

Cash Investment:	$25-50K
Total Investment:	$39-85K
Minimum Net Worth:	$75K
Fees: Franchise -	$10-19.5K
Royalty - 4-7.5%;	Ad. - $150-200/Mo
Earnings Claim Statement:	No
Term of Contract (Years):	10/10
Avg. # Of Employees:	1 FT, 1 PT
Passive Ownership:	Discouraged
Encourage Conversions:	N/A
Area Develop. Agreements:	Yes/10
Sub-Franchising Contracts:	No
Expand In Territory:	Yes
Space Needs: 500-1,000 SF; SF, SC	

SUPPORT & TRAINING PROVIDED:

Financial Assistance Provided:	Yes(I)
Site Selection Assistance:	Yes
Lease Negotiation Assistance:	Yes
Co-Operative Advertising:	Yes
Franchisee Assoc./Member:	Yes
Size Of Corporate Staff:	9
On-Going Support:	B,C,D,E,F,G,H,I
Training: 5 Days Corporate Office in Las Vegas, NV.	

SPECIFIC EXPANSION PLANS:

US:	All United States
Canada:	All Canada
Overseas:	All Countries

≪ ≫

RESETTLERS, THE
5811 Kennett Pk.
Centreville, DE 19807
Tel: (302) 658-9110
Fax: (302) 658-5809

Web Site: www.resettlers.com
Ms. Jane Miller, Dir. Franchise Dev.

THE RESETTLERS, INC.
CENTREVILLE, DELAWARE
(302) 658-3411

THE RESETTLERS is a customized and caring moving service for seniors, which includes professional packing, unpacking and complete resettlement of the new home. A pioneer in the moving service concept, the company guides clients through every state of the moving process and assists with move preparation and organization through their Rent-A-Daughter program. Antiques, collectibles, furniture and household items no longer needed in the new residence are sold profitably in a retail venue.

BACKGROUND: IFA MEMBER
Established: 1985; 1st Franchised: 1997
Franchised Units: 1
Company-Owned Units 2
Total Units: 3
Dist.: US-3; CAN-0; O'seas-0
North America: 2 States
Density: 2 in DE, 1 in WI
Projected New Units (12 Months): 2-3
Qualifications: 5, 5, 3, 3, 2, 5
Registered: MD,WI
FINANCIAL/TERMS:
Cash Investment: $40-75K
Total Investment: $Varies
Minimum Net Worth: $NR
Fees: Franchise - $20K
Royalty - 5%; Ad. - 2%
Earnings Claim Statement: Yes
Term of Contract (Years): 10/10
Avg. # Of Employees: 10-15 PT
Passive Ownership: Not Allowed
Encourage Conversions: N/A
Area Develop. Agreements: Yes
Sub-Franchising Contracts: No
Expand In Territory: Yes
Space Needs: 5,000 SF; FS
SUPPORT & TRAINING PROVIDED:
Financial Assistance Provided: No
Site Selection Assistance: Yes
Lease Negotiation Assistance: Yes
Co-Operative Advertising: Yes
Franchisee Assoc./Member: No

Size Of Corporate Staff: 6
On-Going Support: C,D,E,F,G,I
Training: 2 Weeks in Wilmington, DE.
SPECIFIC EXPANSION PLANS:
US: All United States
Canada: No
Overseas: No

◀◀ ▶▶

RIBBON XCHANGE
8566 Fraser St., # 200
Vancouver, BC V5X 3Y3 CANADA
Tel: (800) 796-5377 (604) 322-9421
Fax: (604) 322-1658
E-Mail: rynker@dowco.com
Web Site: www.ribbon-xchange.com
Mr. J. Peter Benson, President

RIBBON XCHANGE is a service promoted to the small and medium size business community, specifically for the recycling of print media cartidges e.g., Lasers, inksets and ribbons for computer printers, copiers and fax machines.

BACKGROUND:
Established: 1989; 1st Franchised: 1994
Franchised Units: 26
Company-Owned Units 2
Total Units: 28
Dist.: US-0; CAN-22; O'seas-0
North America: 4 Provinces
Density: 19 in BC, 4 in AB, 6 in ON
Projected New Units (12 Months): 12
Qualifications: 3, 3, 2, 2, 3, 5
Registered: AB
FINANCIAL/TERMS:
Cash Investment: $65K
Total Investment: $85K
Minimum Net Worth: $NR
Fees: Franchise - $25K
Royalty - $600/Mo.; Ad. - 1%
Earnings Claim Statement: No
Term of Contract (Years): 5/5
Avg. # Of Employees: 2 FT
Passive Ownership: Allowed
Encourage Conversions: N/A
Area Develop. Agreements: No
Sub-Franchising Contracts: No
Expand In Territory: Yes
Space Needs: NR SF; HB
SUPPORT & TRAINING PROVIDED:
Financial Assistance Provided: Yes(I)
Site Selection Assistance: NR
Lease Negotiation Assistance: NR
Co-Operative Advertising: Yes
Franchisee Assoc./Member: Yes/No
Size Of Corporate Staff: 9

On-Going Support: D,G,H,I
Training: 5 Days in Vancouver, BC; 5 Days On-Site.
SPECIFIC EXPANSION PLANS:
US: All United States
Canada: All Canada
Overseas: No

◀◀ ▶▶

SHRED-IT
2794 S. Sheridan Way
Oakville, ON L6J 7T4 CANADA
Tel: (905) 829-2794
Fax: (905) 829-1999
E-Mail: info@shredit.com
Web Site: www.shredit.com
Mr. Jeff Kish, Dir. Franchise Operations

Business service, offering mobile paper shredding and recycling, serving Fortune 1,000 companies, hospitals, medical facilities, banks, financial institutions, investment and professional firms and the government.

BACKGROUND: IFA MEMBER
Established: 1988; 1st Franchised: 1992
Franchised Units: 52
Company-Owned Units 19
Total Units: 71
Dist.: US-55; CAN-10; O'seas-6
North America: 27 States, 7 Provinces
Density: 6 in CA, 5 in FL, 3 in OH
Projected New Units (12 Months): 23
Qualifications: 5, 5, 1, 3, 4, 5
Registered: CA,FL,IL,IN,MD,MI,NY, WA,WI,DC,AB
FINANCIAL/TERMS:
Cash Investment: $70-140K
Total Investment: $350-450K
Minimum Net Worth: $350K
Fees: Franchise - $55K
Royalty - 5%; Ad. - 1.5%
Earnings Claim Statement: No
Term of Contract (Years): 10/10/10
Avg. # Of Employees: 6 FT
Passive Ownership: Not Allowed
Encourage Conversions: N/A
Area Develop. Agreements: Yes/10/10
Sub-Franchising Contracts: No
Expand In Territory: Yes
Space Needs: 1,500 SF; Industrial Flex Space
SUPPORT & TRAINING PROVIDED:
Financial Assistance Provided: Yes(I)
Site Selection Assistance: Yes
Lease Negotiation Assistance: Yes
Co-Operative Advertising: N/A

Franchisee Assoc./Member: Yes/Yes
Size Of Corporate Staff: 40
On-Going Support: B,C,D,E,G,H,I
Training: 2 Weeks in Oakville, ON.
SPECIFIC EXPANSION PLANS:
US: All United States
Canada: SK,PQ
Overseas: All Countries

<< >>

TEMPACO
P.O. Box 547667
Orlando, FL 32854-7667
Tel: (800) 868-7838 (407) 898-3456
Fax: (407) 898-7316
Ms. Maria Robinson, President

TEMPACO INC. is a well-established wholesaler of controls and specialties to propane and natural gas dealers, governments, schools, colleges, industrial plants and service organizations, including heating and air conditioning. Operates through out the Southern U. S.

BACKGROUND:
Established: 1946;   1st Franchised: 1972
Franchised Units: 15
Company-Owned Units 5
Total Units: 20
Dist.: US-20; CAN-0; O'seas-0
  North America: 6 States
  Density: 16 in FL, 2 in GA, 2 in TN
Projected New Units (12 Months): 1-3
Qualifications: 4, 3, 3, 2, 4, 4
Registered: FL
FINANCIAL/TERMS:
Cash Investment: $70K
Total Investment: $100K
Minimum Net Worth: $100K
Fees: Franchise - $50K
  Royalty - 4%; Ad. - 0%
Earnings Claim Statement: No
Term of Contract (Years): 10/10
Avg. # Of Employees: 2-3 FT, 1 PT
Passive Ownership: Discouraged
Encourage Conversions: Yes
Area Develop. Agreements: No
Sub-Franchising Contracts: No
Expand In Territory: Yes
Space Needs: 3,500 SF; FS, SF
SUPPORT & TRAINING PROVIDED:
Financial Assistance Provided: No
Site Selection Assistance: Yes
Lease Negotiation Assistance: No
Co-Operative Advertising: Yes
Franchisee Assoc./Member: No
Size Of Corporate Staff: 15
On-Going Support: a,b,C,D,E,h,I

Training: 2 Weeks Corporate Headquarters;
  10+ Days Store Location; On-Going.
SPECIFIC EXPANSION PLANS:
US: Southeast, TX
Canada: No
Overseas: No

<< >>

TWO MEN AND A TRUCK
2152 Commons Pkwy.
Okemos, MI 48864
Tel: (800) 345-1070 (517) 482-6683
Fax: (800) 278-6114
E-Mail: halm@twomen.com
Web Site: www.twomen.com
Mr. Hal McLean, Recruiting Director

TWO MEN AND A TRUCK franchises provide local residential and commercial moving services, boxes and packing services and supplies. Our Stick Men University and First Gear Training program provide the most comprehensive initial and on-going training in the industry. We are the 7th largest moving company in the nation! The 'Company That's On The Move."

BACKGROUND: IFA MEMBER
Established: 1985;   1st Franchised: 1989
Franchised Units: 95
Company-Owned Units 0
Total Units: 95
Dist.: US-95; CAN-0; O'seas-0
  North America: 22 States
  Density: 21 in MI, 8 in FL, 7 in TX
Projected New Units (12 Months): 24
Qualifications: 3, 4, 1, 3, 5, 5
Registered: CA,FL,IL,IN,MI,MN,NY,
  OR,RI,WA,WI
FINANCIAL/TERMS:
Cash Investment: $65K+
Total Investment: $75K+
Minimum Net Worth: $80K
Fees: Franchise - $28K
  Royalty - 6%; Ad. - 1%
Earnings Claim Statement: No
Term of Contract (Years): 5/5
Avg. # Of Employees: 2 FT, 6 PT
Passive Ownership: Discouraged
Encourage Conversions: Yes
Area Develop. Agreements: No
Sub-Franchising Contracts: No
Expand In Territory: Yes
Space Needs: 500+ SF; Varies
  Dramatically
SUPPORT & TRAINING PROVIDED:
Financial Assistance Provided: No
Site Selection Assistance: Yes

Lease Negotiation Assistance: No
Co-Operative Advertising: No
Franchisee Assoc./Member: Yes/Yes
Size Of Corporate Staff: 28
On-Going Support: A,C,D,G,H,I
Training: 5 Days Lansing, MI at Stick Men
  University.
SPECIFIC EXPANSION PLANS:
US: All United States
Canada: No
Overseas: No

<< >>

UCC TOTALHOME
8450 Broadway, P.O. Box 13006
Merrillville, IN 46411-3006
Tel: (800) 827-6400 (219) 736-1100
Fax: (219) 755-6208
Web Site: www.ucctotalhome.com/
franchising
Ms. Debbie Bowen, Dir. of Fran. Dev.

UCC TOTALHOME offers consumers the unparalleled opportunity to buy merchandise at manufacturer's invoice cost. Our hundreds of thousands of members purchase directly from more than 800 manufacturers. No mark-up, no middleman, no kidding. UCC TOTALHOME franchise owners enroll members through our time-tested marketing system and service these members with the support of more than 150 specialists at the UCC Corporate Support Center.

BACKGROUND: IFA MEMBER
Established: 1971;   1st Franchised: 1972
Franchised Units: 73
Company-Owned Units 19
Total Units: 92
Dist.: US-77; CAN-15; O'seas-0
  North America: 21 States, 4 Provinces
  Density: 10 in MI, 8 in NY, 7 in OH
Projected New Units (12 Months): 8
Qualifications: 4, 4, 1, 3, 1, 5
Registered: All States
FINANCIAL/TERMS:
Cash Investment: $88-237K
Total Investment: $88-237K
Minimum Net Worth: $100K
Fees: Franchise - $35-55K
  Royalty - 22%; Ad. - N/A
Earnings Claim Statement: No

Term of Contract (Years): 12/12
Avg. # Of Employees: 12 FT, 2 PT
Passive Ownership: Discouraged
Encourage Conversions: N/A
Area Develop. Agreements: No
Sub-Franchising Contracts: No
Expand In Territory: No
Space Needs: 4,000-6,000 SF; Business Park

SUPPORT & TRAINING PROVIDED:

Financial Assistance Provided: Yes(B)
Site Selection Assistance: Yes
Lease Negotiation Assistance: No
Co-Operative Advertising: N/A
Franchisee Assoc./Member: No
Size Of Corporate Staff: 150
On-Going Support: A,B,C,D,E,G,H,h
Training: 3 Weeks Merrillville, IN; 5 Weeks in an Operating Franchise.

SPECIFIC EXPANSION PLANS:

US: All United States
Canada: All Canada
Overseas: No

≪ ≫

UNITED STATES BASKETBALL LEAGUE

46 Quirk Rd.
Milford, CT 06460
Tel: (800) THE USBL (203) 877-9508
Fax: (203) 878-8109
E-Mail: usbl96@aol.com
Web Site: www.usbl.com
Mr. Daniel Meisenheimer, III, President

The USBL is the first and only sports league structured as a franchisor and the only publicly-traded sports league (OTCBB: USBL). The USBL is 15 years old with 11 teams and 126 USBL players have made the NBA. Visit the USBL Website at www.usbl.com.

BACKGROUND:

Established: 1985; 1st Franchised: 1990
Franchised Units: 12

Company-Owned Units 0
Total Units: 12
Dist.: US-11; CAN-0; O'seas-0
 North America: 4 States
 Density: 2 in NY, 2 in FL, 2 in NJ
Projected New Units (12 Months): 6
Qualifications: 4, 4, 3, 3, 3, 4
Registered: FL,NY,DC

FINANCIAL/TERMS:

Cash Investment: $500K
Total Investment: $500-750K
Minimum Net Worth: $1MM
Fees: Franchise - $300K
 Royalty - 5%/$20K; Ad. - 1%/$3K
Earnings Claim Statement: No
Term of Contract (Years): 10/10
Avg. # Of Employees: 4 FT, 15 PT
Passive Ownership: Not Allowed
Encourage Conversions: N/A
Area Develop. Agreements: Yes/10
Sub-Franchising Contracts: Yes
Expand In Territory: Yes
Space Needs: N/A SF; FS

SUPPORT & TRAINING PROVIDED:

Financial Assistance Provided: Yes(D)
Site Selection Assistance: Yes
Lease Negotiation Assistance: Yes
Co-Operative Advertising: Yes
Franchisee Assoc./Member: Yes/Yes
Size Of Corporate Staff: 8
On-Going Support: A,b,C,d,e,f,G,h,I
Training: 2 Weeks CT or PA.

SPECIFIC EXPANSION PLANS:

US: All U.S., East of Miss.
Canada: All Canada
Overseas: Europe, Far East

≪ ≫

SUPPLEMENTAL LISTING OF FRANCHISORS

A All Animal Control, P.O. Box 33805, Northglenn, CO 80233 ; (303) 452-7572; Mr. Mark E. Dotson (888) WILDPESTS; (303) 452-2113

Agway, P.O. Box 4746, Syracuse, NY 13221 ; (315) 461-2253; Mr. David M. Menapace ; (315) 461-2706

America's Best Water Treaters, 3808 S. Concord St., Davenport, IA 52802 ; (319) 322-0890; Mr. Michael Hoschek ; (319) 322-4120

Ameritron Lighting, 115 N. 4th St., Burlington, IA 52601 ; (319) 754-1732; Mr. William Tafee (800) 595-1113; (319) 752-6005

Apartment Movers Etc., 4048 Ashley Phosphate Rd., North Charleston, SC 29418 ; (843) 767-1440; Ms. Kim Swanson (800) 847-2861; (843) 767-0073

Armoloy Corporation, The, 114 Simonda Ave., DeKalb, IL 60115 ; (815) 758-0268; Mr. Jerome F. Bejbl ; (815) 758-6657

Armor Shield, 517 Finley St., Cincinnati, OH 45214 ; (513) 684-0079; Mr. Scott Sharp (800) 543-1838; (513) 684-0040

Badge Maker, The, 2806 W. King Edward Ave., Vancouver, BC V6L 1T9 CANADA; (604) 736-8419; Mr. Paul McCrea ; (604) 733-4323

Bladerunner Mobile Sharpening System, 6431 Orr Rd., Charlotte, NC 28213 ; (704) 598-7111; Mr. Dave Skinner (800) 742-7754; (704) 597-8266

Blind Man of America, 606 Fremont Ct., Colorado Springs, CO 80919 ; (719) 260-8989; Mr. Tom Keller (800) 547-9889;

Bright Beginnings, 1150 Main St., # D, Irvine, CA 92614 ; (948) 833-3773; Ms. Melanie Shumway ; (949) 752-2772

Carey International, 4530 Wisconsin Ave., NW, Washington, DC 20016 ; (202) 895-1209; Mr. Jon Goldberg ; (202) 895-1200

Caribbean Clear USA, 101 Waters Edge, Hilton Head Island, SC 29928 ; (843) 686-3454; Ms. Patricia Benton ; (843) 686-3424

Case Handyman Services, 4701 Sangamore Rd., N. Plaza #P-40, Bethesda, MD 20816 ; (301) 229-8892; Mr. Raymond Fanning (800) 426-9434;

Cleanway Industries, 16 Library Ave., Westhampton Beach, NY 11978 ; (516) 288-6483; Mr. William W. Harding (800) 332-6996; (516) 288-6300

Color Your Carpet, 2465 Ridgecrest Ave., Orange Park, FL 32065 ; (904) 272-6750; Ms. Connie D'Imperio (800) 321-6567; (904) 272-6567

Country Bulk, 1448 Cedar Creek Rd., Cambridge, ON N1R 5S5 CANADA; (519) 740-1832; Mr. Archie Robinet ; (519) 740-1512

Crsytal Clean Parts Washer Service, 3970 W. 10th., #A, Indianapolis, IN 46231 ; (317) 486-5087; Mr. Henry Lynn Phillips ;

Dial One, 1551 S. Fanklin Rd., Indianapolis, IN 46239 ; (317) 375-2178; Mr. Bob Deal (800) 342-5111; (317) 375-2168

E Z Pantry, P.O. Box 1342, Medford, NJ 08055 ; (609) 654-2728; Ms. Yvette Gooch ; (609) 767-0555

Earth Graphics, P.O. Box 18945, Greensboro, NC 27419 ; (336) 854-8060; Ms. Denise Wentz (877) 327-8441; (336) 854-2060

EMSAR, 1032 W. Main St., Wilmington, OH 45177 ; (937) 388-1051; Mr. David Gamble ; (937) 383-1052

English Butler Canada, 39 King St., St. John, NB E2L 4W3 CANADA; (416) 966-9803; Mr. Nicholas Assad ; (416) 966-9802

Flamingo A Friend, 648 Rumson Rd., Birmingham, AL 35209 ; (205) 879-2387; Mr. Vic Kepic ; (205) 870-1315

Hayes Handpiece Franchises, 5375 Avenida En Cinas, # C, Carlsbad, CA 92008 ; (760) 602-0505; Mr. Joe Hayes (800) 228-0521; (760) 602-0521

Historical Research Center, The, 632 S. Military Trl., Deerfield Beach, FL 33442 ; (954) 360-9005; Ms. Michelle Koyles (800) 940-7991; (954) 421-8713

Independent Lighting Franchise, 873 Seahawk Cir., Virginia Beach, VA 23452 ; (804) 468-1514; Mr. Chris E. Carpenter (800) 637-5483; (804) 468-5448

Intransit, P.O. Box 1147, Medford, OR 97501 ; (541) 770-1399; Mr. John Johnson (800) 547-2053; (541) 773-3993

K & N Mobile Distribution Systems, 4909 Rondo Dr., Fort Worth, TX 76106 ; (817) 624-3721; Mr. Curtis L. Nelson (800) 433-2170; (817) 626-2885

Knockout Pest Control, 1009 Front St., Uniondale, NY 11553 ; (516) 489-4348; Mr. Arthur M. Katz (800) 244-PEST; (516) 489-7817

Leros Point to Point, 17 Grammercy Pl., Thornwood, NY 10594; (914) 747-2917; Mr. Lonnie Lehrer (800) 82-LEROS; (914) 747-2300

Microtech, P.O. Box 1463, Gilbert, AZ 85299-1463 ; (602) 857-9412; Mr. George Zelma-Ellis (800) 354-0371;

Mini-Tankers, # 11-3170 Ridgeway Dr., Mississauga, ON L5L 5R4 CANADA; (905) 607-5358; Mr. John Prittie (888) 473-3835; (905) 607-7129

Muzak, 2901 3rd Ave., # 400, Seattle, WA 98121 ; (206) 448-6312; Mr. Chuck Saldarini (800) 331-3340; (206) 633-3000

Naut-a-Care Franchising, 2507 W. Paciffic Coast Hwy., #204, Newport Beach, CA 92663-4722 ; (949) 631-2502; Mr. Don M. Drysdale (887)- 582-5823; (949) 631-2660

Nelson's Direct Casket Outlet, 210 W. Maple, Independence, MO 64051; (816) 252-1216; Mr. Paul Nelson; (816) 252-0979

NextCare, P.O. Box 8550, Mesa, AZ 85214 ; (602) 924-8399; Mr. Jay Warden (800) 510-2273; (602) 924-8382

Piper Studio's Wedding Centre, 238 Supertest Rd., Downsview, ON M3J 2M2 CANADA; (416) 650-0026; Mr. Milan Foltys ; (416) 650-1178

Pirtek USA, 501 Harerty Ct., Rockledge, FL 32955 ; (407) 504-4433; Mr. Tim Wesbey (888) 774-7835; (407) 504-4422

Portable On Demand Storage, 12200 34th St. N., #D, Clearwater, FL 33762 ; (727) 556-2955; Ms. Jeanine Blake ; (727) 592-0222

Pure Water Ultima, P.O. Box 83226, Lincoln, NE 68501 ; (402) 467-9393; Mr. Jason Harrington (800) 875-5915; (402) 467-9300

Rainsoft Water Treatment Systems, 2080 E. Lunt Ave., Elk Grove, IL 60007 ; (847) 437-1594; Mr. Don Miller (800) 642-3426; (847) 437-9400

Rich Plan Corporation, 4981 Commercial Dr., Yorkville, NY 13495 ; (315) 736-7597; Mr. W. Randy Wilson (800) 243-1358; (315) 736-0851

Sharp-N-Lube, 40 E. Ginghamsburg Rd., Tipp City, OH 45312 ; (937) 669-0096; Mr. Stan Ray (800) 962-1869; (937) 335-3769

Sports Recruits International, 128 Queen St. S., Box 42277, Mississauga, ON L5M 5Z5 CANADA; (905) 821-1116; Mr. Terry Glenister ; (905) 821-0040

TEGG Corp., P.O. Box 30, Pittsburgh, PA 15230 ; (412) 394-7535; Mr. Arnold Schwartzman ; (412) 394-7422

Trivideom Productions, 4754 Shavano Oak, San Antonio, TX 78249 ; (210) 492-2256; Mr. Kenneth T. Kwit ; (210) 479-3456

Truckstops TravelCenters of America, 24601 Center Ridge Rd., # 200, Westlake, OH 44145-5634 ; (440) 808-4458; Mr. Peter Wood (800) 872-7496; (440) 808-3298

Two Small Men With Big Hearts Moving, 100 Rizalda Rd., North York, ON M9M 2M8 CANADA; (416) 748-9254; Mr. Jeff Green ; (416) 663-6300

Vanishing Breeds International, 12945 Seminole Blvd., Bldg. 2, # 2, Largo, FL 33778 ; (727) 518-1356; Mr. Dave Anderson (877) VANISHING; (727) 518-6206

Watercare Corporation, 125 E. Alberta Dr., P. O. Box 1717, Manitowoc, WI 54221 ; (920) 682-7673; Mr. William F. Granger ; (920) 682-6823

We The People, 1501 State St., Santa Barbara, CA 93101 ; (805) 684-8596; Mr. Bill Pintard ; (805) 566-6661

World Class Parking, 525 Plymouth Rd., # 319, Plymouth Meeting, PA 19462 ; (610) 834-2937; Mr. Gary Stein (888) 680-7275; (610) 828-1908

2001 BOND'S FRANCHISE GUIDE — 13TH ANNUAL EDITION

FRANCHISOR QUESTIONNAIRE

1. Franchise Trade Name: _____

2. Address: _____

   City _____ State/Province_____ Zip/Postal Code _____

   Telephone: (800) _____ or ( ) _____

   Fax Number: ( ) _____ ; E-Mail Address: _____

   Internet: www._____ (Note: To ensure accuracy, please attach business card/letterhead)

3. Contact: _____ Position: _____

4. President/CEO _____ (**Note:** This data will not be published.)

5. Description of Business: (Use the full space available to set yourself apart from other franchising opportunities, i.e. sell your system to the potential franchisee.)

   _____

   _____

   _____

   _____

   _____

6. Company was founded in 19 _____ .First year as franchisor was 19 _____ .

7. Actual number of Franchised Units _____ Units

8. Actual number of Company-Owned Units _____ Units

   Total Operating Units _____ Units

9. Of Total Operating Units listed in # 8 above, _____ were in the U.S.

   _____ were in Canada.

   _____ were Overseas.

10. Of the Total Operating Units listed in # 8 above, A) in how many States/Provinces did you have operating units and B) what 3 States/Provinces had the largest number of operating units?

A) Franchisor Has Operating Units in	B) Top 3 States/Provinces	# Units in Each of B)
_____ U. S. States	1. _____	_____
_____ Canadian Provinces	2. _____	_____
_____ Foreign Countries	3. _____	_____

11. How many **New Units** do you plan to open in the next 12 months? _____ Units

12. Do you provide potential franchisees with an **Earnings Claim Statement**? ❏ Yes ❏ No

13. What is the **minimum net worth** required of the franchisee? $ _____

14. Even though the cash investment may vary substantially by individual unit, what is the range of **equity capital** (up-front cash) required? $ _____

15. What is the range of **total investment** required? $ _____

16. How much is the **initial franchise fee** for a new franchisee? $ _____

17. How much is the **on-going royalty fee**?   _____ % or _____

18. How much is the **on-going advertising fee**?   _____ % or _____

19. The following States/Province require a separate registration (or disclosure, indicated by an *) document. In which are you **currently registered to franchise**?

❑ All Below or	❑ IN	❑ ND	❑ WA
❑ CA	❑ MD	❑ OR*	❑ WI
❑ FL*	❑ MI*	❑ RI	❑ DC
❑ HI	❑ MN	❑ SD	
❑ IL	❑ NY	❑ VA	❑ Alberta

20. What is the **term of the original franchise agreement**?   _____ Years

21. What is the **term of the renewal period**?   _____ Years

22. Do you have **Area Development Agreements**?   ❑ Yes ❑ No; If Yes, for what period? _____ Years

23. Do you have **Sub-Franchisor Contracts** covering specified territories?   ❑ Yes ❑ No

24. Can the franchisee establish **additional outlets** within his area?   ❑ Yes ❑ No

25. Is **passive ownership** of the initial unit   ❑ Allowed   ❑ Allowed, But Discouraged   ❑ Not Allowed

26. Do you **encourage conversions**?   ❑ Yes   ❑ No   ❑ Not Applicable

27. Is **financial assistance** available?   ❑ Yes ❑ No ❑ N.A.; If Yes, ❑ Direct or ❑ Indirect

28. Do you assist the franchisee in **site selection**?   ❑ Yes   ❑ No   ❑ Not Applicable

29. What **square footage and types of sites** do most of your franchise units require? _____ SF

❑ Free-Standing Building	❑ Storefront	❑ Strip Center	❑ Regional Mall
❑ Home-Based	❑ Other _____		❑ Not Applicable

30. Do you assist the franchisee in **lease negotiations**?   ❑ Yes   ❑ No   ❑ Not Applicable

31. Do you participate in **co-operative advertising**?   ❑ Yes   ❑ No   ❑ Not Applicable

32. Including the owner/operator, **how many employees** are recommended to properly staff the average franchised unit?   _____ Full-Time _____ Part-Time

33. How many full-time, paid personnel are currently on your **corporate staff**?   _____

34. In qualifying a potential franchisee, please rank the following criteria from Unimportant to Very Important:

	Unimportant				Very Important
Financial Net Worth	1	2	3	4	5
General Business Experience	1	2	3	4	5
Specific Industry Experience	1	2	3	4	5
Formal Education	1	2	3	4	5
Psychological Profile	1	2	3	4	5
Personal Interview(s)	1	2	3	4	5

35. What are the location and duration of any **initial training sessions** included in the franchise fee?

Location   Duration

A. _____   _____

B. _____   _____

C. _____   _____

36. Which of the following **on-going services** do you provide to the franchisee?

Service	Included in Fees	At Additional Cost	N.A.
Central Data Processing	A. ❑	a. ❑	❑
Central Purchasing	B. ❑	b. ❑	❑
Field Operations Evaluation	C. ❑	c. ❑	❑
Field Training	D. ❑	d. ❑	❑
Initial Store Opening	E. ❑	e. ❑	❑
Inventory Control	F. ❑	f. ❑	❑
Franchisee Newsletter	G. ❑	g. ❑	❑
Regional Or National Meetings	H. ❑	h. ❑	❑
800 Telephone Hotline	I. ❑	i. ❑	❑

37. Does your system have a **franchisee association**?   ❑ Yes   ❑ No;

    If Yes, are you a member?   ❑ Yes   ❑ No

38. In which specific regions of the U.S. are you actively seeking new franchisees? For example: All U.S., or NW & SW, or NJ Only. _____

39. Are you actively seeking franchisees in Canada?   ❑ Yes   ❑ No

    If Yes, in which Provinces? ❑ All or _____

40. Are you actively seeking franchisees Overseas?   ❑ Yes   ❑ No

    If Yes, in which Countries? _____

Name of Respondent: _____ Telephone No: (   ) _____

Thank you very much for your time and prompt attention. Please return to:
Source Book Publications
P. O. Box 12488, Oakland, CA 94604
(510) 839-5471 ❖ FAX (510) 839-2104

Alphabetical Listing of Franchisors

Alphabetical Listing of Franchisors

K

L

N

O

Tips & Traps When Buying a Franchise
2nd Edition (Completely revised in 1999)

By Mary Tomzack, President of FranchiseHelp, Inc., an international information and research company servicing the franchising industry.

Key Features:

- Completely updated version of the 1994 reader-acclaimed classic on franchising, with the same practical advice, non-textbook approach. Provides an insightful crash course on selecting, negotiating and financing the right franchise, and turning it into a lucrative, satisfying business.

- How to select the best franchise for your personal finances and lifestyle; navigate the legal maze; and finance your investment.

- Reveals the hottest franchise opportunities for the 21st Century and discusses co-branding. Provides advice on building a business empire through franchising.

- "This book is the bible for anyone who is considering a franchise investment."

Yes, I want to order ____ copy(ies) of Tips & Traps When Buying a Franchise (2nd Edition) at US$19.95 each, plus US$5 for shipping & handling (international shipments at actual cost).

Name _____ Title _____

Company _____ Telephone No. (_____) _____

Address _____

City _____ State/Prov._____ Zip _____

❏ Check Enclosed or

Charge my: ❏ MasterCard ❏ Visa

Card #: _____ Expiration Date: _____

Signature: _____

Please send to: **Source Book Publications,** P.O. Box 12488, Oakland, CA 94604

Satisfaction Guaranteed. If not fully satisfied, return for a prompt, 100% refund.

THE DEFINITIVE ANNUAL GUIDE OF INTERNATIONAL FRANCHISING

THE 1999 INTERNATIONAL HERALD TRIBUNE
INTERNATIONAL FRANCHISE GUIDE

Key Features:

• The Most Comprehensive and Up-To-Date Directory of Committed International Franchisors.

• Profiles Are the Result of an Exhaustive 60-Point Questionnaire.

• 32 Distinct Business Categories.

• Listing of International Franchise Consultants, Attorneys and Service Providers.

• 192 Pages.

• Direct Comparability Between Franchise Listings.

Yes, I want to order ____ copy(ies) of the 1999 IHT International Franchise Guide at US$34.95 each, shipping included.

Name _____ Title _____

Company _____ Telephone No. (_____) _____

Address _____

City _____ State/Prov. _____ Zip _____

❏ Check Enclosed or

Charge my: ❏ MasterCard ❏ Visa

Card #: _____ Expiration Date: _____

Signature: _____

Please send to:

Source Book Publications

P.O. Box 12488, Oakland, CA 94604

Satisfaction Guaranteed. If not fully satisfied, return for a prompt, 100% refund.

For faster service, call (800) 841-0873 or (510) 839-5471 or fax us at (510) 839-2104.
Also check us out on the Internet at www.franchiseintl.com.

50 Proven Service-Based Winners

Bond's Top 50 Service-Based Franchises

by Steve Schiller and Robert Bond

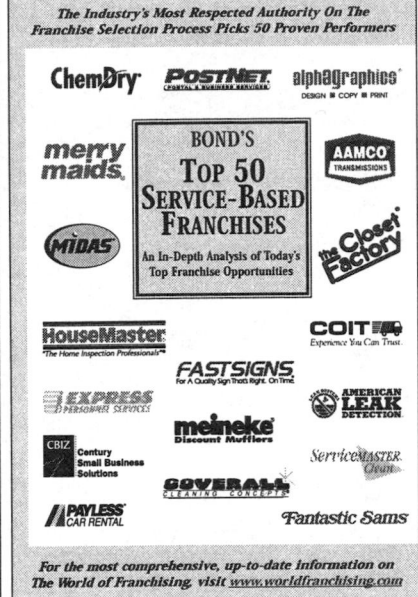

Key Features:

In response to the constantly asked question, *"What are the best franchises?"*, Bond's newest book focuses on the top 50 franchises in the service-based industry. Over 500 service-based systems were evaluated for consideration. Companies were analyzed on the basis of historical performance, brand identification, market dynamics, franchisee satisfaction, the level of training and on-going support, financial stability, etc. Detailed 4–5 page profiles on each company, as well as key statistics and industry overviews. All companies are proven performers and most have a national presence. Excellent starting point for someone focusing on the service-based industry.

JUST PUBLISHED

Yes, I want to order ____ copy(ies) of *Bond's Top 50 Service-Based Franchises* at $19.95 each ($29.95 Canadian). Please add $5.00 per book for Shipping* & Handling ($7.75 Canada; International shipments at actual cost). California residents, please add appropriate sales tax.

Name _____ Title _____

Company _____ Telephone No. (____) _____

Address _____

City _____ State/Prov._____ Zip _____

❑   Check Enclosed   or

Charge my: ❑   MasterCard   ❑   Visa

Card #: _____ Expiration Date: _____

Signature: _____

Please return to: **Source Book Publications,** P.O. Box 12488, Oakland, CA 94604

* Note: All books shipped by USPS Priority Mail (2nd Day Air).
Satisfaction Guaranteed. If not fully satisfied, return for a prompt, 100% refund.

50 Proven Food-Service Winners

Bond's Top 50 Food-Service Franchises
by Steve Schiller and Robert Bond

Key Features:

In response to the constantly asked question, *"What are the best franchises?"*, Bond's newest book focuses on the top 50 franchises in the food-service industry. Over 500 food-service systems were evaluated for consideration. Companies were analyzed on the basis of historical performance, brand identification, market dynamics, franchisee satisfaction, the level of training and on-going support, financial stability, etc. Detailed 4–5 page profiles on each company, as well as key statistics and industry overviews. All companies are proven performers and most have a national presence. Excellent starting point for someone focusing on the food-service industry.

JUST PUBLISHED

Yes, I want to order ____ copy(ies) of *Bond's Top 50 Food-Service Franchises* at $19.95 each ($29.95 Canadian). Please add $5.00 per book for Shipping* & Handling ($7.75 Canada; International shipments at actual cost). California residents, please add appropriate sales tax.

Name _____ Title _____

Company _____ Telephone No. (____) _____

Address _____

City _____ State/Prov._____ Zip _____

❑   Check Enclosed or

Charge my: ❑   MasterCard ❑   Visa

Card #: _____ Expiration Date: _____

Signature: _____

Please return to: **Source Book Publications,** P.O. Box 12488, Oakland, CA 94604

* Note: All books shipped by USPS Priority Mail (2nd Day Air).
Satisfaction Guaranteed. If not fully satisfied, return for a prompt, 100% refund.

Definitive Franchisor Database Available for Rent

SAMPLE FRANCHISOR PROFILE

Name of Franchise:	AARON'S SALES & LEASE OWNERSHIP
Address:	309 East Paces Ferry Rd., N. E.
City/State/Zip/Postal Code:	Atlanta, GA 30305-2377
Country:	U. S. A.
800 Telephone #:	(800) 551-6015
Local Telephone #:	(404) 237-4016
Alternate Telephone #:	
Fax #:	(404) 240-6540
E-Mail:	jim.steger@aaronsfranchise.com
Internet Address:	www.aaronsfranchise.com
# Franchised Units:	186
# Company-Owned Units:	238
# Total Units:	424
Company Contact:	Mr. Jim Steger
Contact Title/Position:	Director of Franchise Development
Contact Salutation:	Mr. Steger
President:	Mr. R. Charles Loudermilk, Sr.
President Title:	Chairman/Chief Executive Officer
President Salutation:	Mr. Loudermilk
Industry Category (of 45):	37 / Rental Services
IFA Member:	International Franchise Association
CFA Member:	

KEY FEATURES

- Number of Active North American Franchisors   ~ 2,300
  - % US   ~85%
  - % Canadian   ~15%
- Data Fields (See Above)   24
- Industry Categories   45
- % With Toll-Free Telephone Numbers   67%
- % With Fax Numbers   97%
- % With Name of Preferred Contact   99%
- % With Name of President   97%
- % With Number of Total Operating Units   95%
- Guaranteed Accuracy — $.50 Rebate/Returned Bad Address
- Converted to Any Popular Database or Contact Management Program
- Initial Front-End Cost $600
- Quarterly Up-Dates $75
- Mailing Labels Only — One-Time Use $400

For More Information, Please Contact
Source Book Publications
1814 Franklin Street, Suite 820, Oakland, California 94612
(800) 841-0873 ❖ (510) 839-5471 ❖ FAX (510) 839-2104